AUSTRALIANS
A GUIDE TO SOURCES

Sir Arthur Streeton, Balmoral Beach, *1897. Oil on canvas. Gift of Howard Hinton. Born in Victoria in 1867, Streeton, a landscape painter, became one of the founders of the Heidelberg School. In 1897 Balmoral, on the northern side of Port Jackson, was a secluded bushland setting.*

NEW ENGLAND REGIONAL ART MUSEUM

AUSTRALIANS
A GUIDE TO SOURCES

EDITOR

D. H. BORCHARDT

ASSOCIATE EDITOR

VICTOR CRITTENDEN

FAIRFAX, SYME & WELDON ASSOCIATES

AUSTRALIANS: A HISTORICAL LIBRARY
AUSTRALIANS: A GUIDE TO SOURCES

First published 1987 by
Fairfax, Syme & Weldon Associates
235 Jones Street, Broadway
New South Wales 2007, Australia

Publishing Director
Kevin Weldon

Editorial Director
Elaine Russell

Managing Editor
Kim Anderson

Editors
John Arnold
Sheena Coupe
Margo Lanagan

Production Manager
Mick Bagnato

Art Director
John Bull
Bull's Graphics

Designers
Stan Lamond
Diana Wells
Michelle Dunbar

Assembly Artists
Peter de Jager
Shelley Bright

Secretary
Monica Stuardo

National Library of Australia
Cataloguing-in-Publication Data

Australians: a historical library
Includes bibliographies and index.
ISBN 0 949288 09 8 (set).
ISBN 0 949288 18 7 (set : deluxe).
ISBN 0 949288 25 X (Australians, a guide to sources).
ISBN 0 949288 26 8 (Australians, a guide to sources : deluxe).

1. Australia – History. I. Title: Australians to 1788.
II. Title: Australians 1838. III. Title: Australians
1888. IV. Title: Australians 1938. V. Title: Australians
from 1939. VI. Title: Australians, a historical atlas.
VII. Title: Australians, a guide to sources. VIII.
Title: Australians, events and places. IX. Title:
Australians, a historical dictionary. X. Title:
Australians, historical statistics.

994

Typeset and Printed at Griffin Press, Netley, South Australia 5037, Australia.
Film Separations, Colour Scanners Pty Limited, Marrickville, New South Wales 2204, Australia.

Fairfax, Syme & Weldon Associates is a partnership between John Fairfax & Sons Limited, David Syme & Co. Limited and Kevin Weldon & Associates Pty Ltd.

Published outside Australia by Cambridge University Press
The Pitt Building, Trumpington Street, Cambridge CB2 1RP 32 East 57th Street, New York, NY 10022, USA
ISBN 0 521 34073 X (set, Cambridge University Press).

COVER ILLUSTRATION
Design by John Bull.

FOREWORD

THIS BOOK and its ten companions have been ten years in the making. They have been created to mark the bicentenary of European settlement in this country, and they are the outcome of collaboration on a scale never before attempted in the writing of Australian history. Hundreds of people in and beyond universities have joined together to re-create the experience of people living in Australia since 1788 and to place that experience in the wider context of a human occupation that began tens of thousands of years ago.

The editors and contributors have worked in a variety of modes: from slicing into the past at fifty-year intervals (*Australians 1838, 1888* and *1938*) to laying out, in terse chronology, events as they happened year by year (*Events and places*), and from portraying processes and movements on maps of the country (*A historical atlas*) to briefing readers for explorations of their own (*A guide to sources*). The authors represent diverse approaches, in terms both of occupation—historian, economist, archaeologist, geographer, librarian, journalist—and of outlook. We have sought the best person for each part of the job, and not altered or muffled anybody's voice. We have also tried to make the work of scholars readily accessible to general readers.

In this aspiration we have been strengthened by a close working relationship with the publishers. From early days the project has benefited from continuous consultation with representatives of Fairfax, Syme & Weldon about its form and presentation. Their confidence in our enterprise has heartened us throughout the long journey.

Together, we and they present *Australians: a historical library* to the people of Australia as an offering for 1988 and beyond.

OLIVER MACDONAGH

AUSTRALIANS
A HISTORICAL LIBRARY

AUSTRALIANS
A HISTORICAL LIBRARY

GENERAL EDITORS

ALAN D. GILBERT   K. S. INGLIS

ASSISTANT GENERAL EDITOR

S. G. FOSTER

AUSTRALIANS TO 1788

AUSTRALIANS 1838

AUSTRALIANS 1888

AUSTRALIANS 1938

AUSTRALIANS FROM 1939

GENERAL EDITORS

FRANK CROWLEY   PETER SPEARRITT

ASSISTANT GENERAL EDITOR

JOHN McQUILTON

AUSTRALIANS
A HISTORICAL ATLAS

AUSTRALIANS
A HISTORICAL DICTIONARY

AUSTRALIANS
EVENTS AND PLACES

AUSTRALIANS
HISTORICAL STATISTICS

AUSTRALIANS
A GUIDE TO SOURCES

EXECUTIVE EDITOR

S. G. FOSTER

Alan Barcan
Associate Professor of Education
University of Newcastle

Paul Bentley
Librarian
Sydney Opera House Trust Library

D. Blair
Lecturer in English
Macquarie University

Malcolm Booker
Author
Canberra

D. H. Borchardt
Librarian and bibliographer
Melbourne

E. K. Braybrooke
Emeritus Professor of Legal Studies
La Trobe University

R. Breckon
Philatelic Curator
Australia Post, Melbourne

Ian H. Burnley
Associate Professor of Geography
University of New South Wales

R. L. Cope
Librarian
New South Wales Parliamentary Library

Victor Crittenden
Librarian and bibliographer
Canberra

D. Cumming
Senior Lecturer in Civil Engineering
University of Adelaide

Lyndall Dawson
Professional Officer
University of New South Wales

B. H. Fletcher
Associate Professor of History
University of Sydney

S. G. Foster
Senior Research Fellow in History
Research School of Social Sciences
Australian National University

Alan Frost
Senior Lecturer in History
La Trobe University

B. Gandevia
Associate Professor of Medicine
University of New South Wales

Alex George
Executive Editor
Flora of Australia
Bureau of Flora and Fauna
Department of Arts, Heritage and
the Environment
Canberra

A. Graycar
Director
Social Welfare Research Centre
University of New South Wales

Stephanie Hagan
Tutor in Politics
University of New England

A. J. Hagger
Honorary Research Associate in Economics
University of Tasmania

Valmai Hankel
Fine Books Librarian
State Library of South Australia

G. R. Henning
Senior Lecturer in Economic History
University of New England

J. E. Hoffman
Director of Public Relations
Australian Capital Territory
Schools Authority

R. W. Home
Professor of History and Philosophy of Science
University of Melbourne

John Horacek
Senior Librarian
Borchardt Library
La Trobe University

M. Horsburgh
Associate Professor of Social Work
University of Sydney

Keith Johnston
President
Society of Australian Genealogists
Sydney

L. J. Jones
Senior Lecturer in Mechanical and Industrial
Engineering
University of Melbourne

Joan Kerr
Associate Professor of Fine Arts
University of Sydney

Alan Lawson
Lecturer in English
University of Queensland

Jane Lee
Librarian
Department of Foreign Affairs
Canberra

M. Lorimer
Canberra

Peter Love
Historian
Yan Yean, Vic.

Alison McCusker
Assistant Secretary
Conservation Branch
Department of Arts, Heritage and
the Environment
Canberra

Ann McGrath
Lecturer in History
University of New South Wales

Lawrence D. McIntosh
Librarian
Joint Theological Library
Ormond College
University of Melbourne

Stuart Macintyre
Senior Lecturer in History
University of Melbourne

Michael McKernan
Assistant Director
Research and Publications
Australian War Memorial

Ian F. McLaren
Honorary Bibliographer
Baillieu Library
University of Melbourne

J. McQuilton
Senior Project Officer
Department of Geography
University of New South Wales
Australian Defence Force Academy

Graham Maddox
Senior Lecturer in Politics
University of New England

Andrew Markus
Lecturer in History
Monash University

Julie G. Marshall
Reference Librarian
Borchardt Library
La Trobe University

A. W. Martin
Senior Fellow in History
Research School of Social Sciences
Australian National University

Henry Mayer
Emeritus Professor of Political Theory
University of Sydney

T. B. Millar
Professor of Australian Studies
Australian Studies Centre
London

Carol M. Mills
Institute Librarian
Riverina-Murray Institute of Higher
Education

Marcie Muir
Author
Adelaide

Elizabeth Nathan
Head
Archives Section
Department of Foreign Affairs
Canberra

G. Peguero
Chief Librarian
Phillip Institute of Technology

Nicolas Peterson
Senior Lecturer in Prehistory
Faculty of Arts
Australian National University

Graeme Phipps
Curator of Birds
Zoological Parks Board
of New South Wales

Stuart Piggin
Senior Lecturer in History
University of Wollongong

J. M. Powell
Reader in Geography
Monash University

Pamela Ray
Manuscripts Librarian
National Library of Australia

P. Rimmer
Senior Fellow in Human Geography
Research School of Pacific Studies
Australian National University

Michael Roe
Professor of History
University of Tasmania

H. M. Russell
Director
Scientific and Information Services
Department of Agriculture
Victoria

Joan Rydon
Professor of Politics
La Trobe University

David Saunders
Professor of Architecture
University of Adelaide

A. G. L. Shaw
Emeritus Professor of History
Monash University

W. A. Sinclair
Dean of the Faculty of Economics and
Commerce
Monash University

Terry Smith
Senior Lecturer in Fine Arts
University of Sydney

Peter Spearritt
Associate Professor of Politics
Macquarie University

M. K. Stell
Research Assistant in History
Research School of Social Sciences
Australian National University

P. R. Trier
Principal Librarian
Baillieu Library
University of Melbourne

T. G. Vallance
Associate Professor of Geology and
Geophysics
University of Sydney

D. A. Wadley
Senior Lecturer in Geography
University of Queensland

J. L. Ward
formerly Chief Librarian
Royal Melbourne Institute of Technology

R. L. Wettenhall
Head of Administrative Studies
Canberra College of Advanced Education

D. Wyndham
Head
Research and Information
Australian Film, Television and Radio School
Sydney

PROJECT STAFF

EDITORIAL
Anne Gollan, Eliza Hill, Kathleen Hobbs, Marion K. Stell, Ruth Thompson, Ian Howie-Willis
PICTORIAL
Deborah J. Clark, Audrey Young
SECRETARIAL
Jean M. Hughes

AUSTRALIANS: A GUIDE TO SOURCES

PHOTOGRAPHIC
John Storey
PICTORIAL RESEARCH
Sandra Burr, Deborah J. Clark, Carol M. Mills
RESEARCH AND EDITORIAL
Julie Marshall, Kate Jones
EDITORIAL CONSULTANT
Andrew Reeves
SECRETARIAL
Nancy McElwee, Sadi Enright
INDEX
Jean Hagger

CONTENTS

VII POLITICS

VIII THE ECONOMY

IX SOCIETY

X CULTURE

PREFACE

Historians are professionally interested in the passing of time, and in 1977 a few historians in Canberra began to think about 1988 as a year offering a special opportunity to their craft. That year, we guessed, would inspire a larger and more general commemoration than Australians had organised at the end of any previous half-century. The coming occasion was sure to be more *national* than those others, for advances in central government, transport and communication had accelerated the transformation of states that had once been separate colonies into provinces of a single polity, whose people travelled about as never before, talked to each other on STD, watched all over the continent the same prime ministerial news conference and the same cricket match. Moreover, Australian history itself was gaining a new popularity, as Stuart Macintyre comments at the end of the first chapter in *Australians: a guide to sources*. The names of Manning Clark and Geoffrey Blainey were better known than those of any scholarly historian in earlier times; historical and genealogical societies were burgeoning, and tourists flocked to Ballarat to see gold-rush days reconstructed at Sovereign Hill and to Old Sydney Town to see convict floggings re-enacted. Television viewers switched on to Australian costume dramas; and cinema audiences were offered, in 1977 alone, eight feature films based on life in the remote and recent Australian past.

All in all, it appeared likely that public and private enterprise would make 1988 a year for intense consciousness of Australian history. What might historians contribute? Individually, of course, whatever scholarly article or biography or general history an author was moved to attempt. Collectively? The Canberra group, consulting widely, found some antipathy towards the very idea of collaborative enterprise — 'history by committee' — and some particular doubts about proposed approaches. But it also found much interest and enthusiasm, and eventually enough support to embark on the project that has become *Australians: a historical library*.

The makers of these books do not see them as official history in any sense. The project has had no money from the Australian Bicentennial Authority.

Money for general administration and for research on different volumes has been provided from universities (especially the Australian National University and the University of New South Wales), and from the Australian Research Grants Scheme. General and volume editors have taken on the job as part of their work in universities and colleges of advanced education. With few exceptions, contributors are also unpaid. Royalties will go into a fund to support Australian studies. Some advance royalties paid years ahead of publication, have been ploughed into research for the books.

That was a source of funds unforeseen when we began. Some potential publishers told us that they would need a subsidy; Fairfax, Syme & Weldon asked for no subsidy, anticipated larger sales than any other publisher we approached, and encouraged us to plan without any inhibitions the size of the books and the quantity and quality of illustrations. The scale on which the publishers have been willing to undertake the project has helped us keep two early resolutions: to write for general readers, addressing them with respect but without assuming prior knowledge and to illustrate the books richly, not for mere decorative effect but to integrate visual material with text.

Historians had long lamented the absence of a set of reference books that would deliver essential information about Australian history to students, authors and browsers. The *Australian encyclopaedia,* first published in 1925 and revised three times since, included much information about Australia's past, but its focus was not primarily historical. Many reference works were devoted to particular subject areas, from A. McCulloch's *Encyclopaedia of Australian art* and E. M. Miller and F. T. Macartney's *Australian literature* to C. A. Hughes and B. D. Graham's *A handbook of Australian government and politics* and the official histories of Australia's part in two world wars.

Taken together, such books made up a valuable reference library. Few people, however, possessed them all; and those who did still found large gaps in their library's historical coverage. The committee planning this project had an impressive precedent in the *Australian dictionary of biography,* a multi-volume enterprise which draws on scholars throughout the nation.

Australians lacked an atlas of their history and a convenient compilation of historical statistics. Information about other aspects of the past was scattered and hard to come by. We decided, therefore, that the series should include five reference volumes, presenting our past in an accessible and inviting format. This is the purpose of *Australians: a historical atlas, Australians: events and places, Australians: a historical dictionary, Australians: a guide to sources and Australians: historical statistics.*

These five volumes build on earlier generations of reference works, including encyclopaedias, colonial, state and commonwealth yearbooks, census reports, *Who's who,* the *Australian dictionary of biography* and atlases. Our editors, writers and researchers have also used many books published about aspects of Australian life and unpublished material in libraries, government and private archives and museums. We have drawn on the expertise of the staff of such institutions and of individual researchers across the nation.

Each reference book approaches the past in different ways. *Events and places* combines a chronology and a gazetteer, providing a reference that is both historical and geographical in approach. In the *Events* section we set out what we consider to be the most important and interesting happenings in Australian history. We intend *Events* to have many uses: for example, to settle arguments about who was the first to do what; to help a reader imagine Australia in the year in which he or she was born or when a parent, grandparent or greatgrandparent first arrived. The *Places* section provides a summary history of more than seven hundred cities, towns and geographical features. Some of the towns, especially those founded near goldfields, now scarcely exist. There are 32 regional essays in *Places* which put the localities in a wider historical and economic framework.

Australians: a historical dictionary has over 1000 entries on people, movements, ideas and institutions which have shaped Australia's past. Readers will find short biographies on such prominent Australians as Dame Nellie Melba, Jack Lang, Judith Wright and Rupert Murdoch. Historical developments including land settlement schemes and the spread of the railway system are explained, as are terms such as 'peacocking' and 'cabbage tree hat'. Readers can discover information on such diverse topics as the creation of Vegemite and the invention of the combine harvester.

Like every work of reference published, these volumes draw on original sources and the knowledge of researchers and specialists. Often original sources that might confirm a detail no longer survive, and often those that do survive cannot be relied on. There will be experts on particular topics, localities and events who will dispute our knowledge, unearth new facts and disprove old ones. We are keen to receive such information for additions or corrections to future printings.

Together, these five books provide the most extensive reference library ever produced on Australian history.

PETER SPEARRITT

INTRODUCTION

To UNDERSTAND contemporary Australia we must know our yesterdays, and it is the purpose of this volume to make the basis for the study of our yesterdays readily accessible, primarily by means of an extensive reading list on selected topics which form between them a conspectus of studies related to Australia, and secondarily by setting out our location of resources available to those who are interested in a more thorough approach to Australian Studies.

The volume begins with an essay on the current state of the writing of history. Next there is a general description of the institutions likely to be of interest to anyone concerned with Australian studies. Most of these institutions will perforce be archives, libraries, museums and galleries but also mentioned are some others which provide information services related to Australia's past and present. Sections I to X contain over 3000 references to books which can be rightly considered basic reading for anyone wishing to gain an understanding of the many facets of Australian physical and social conditions and their history.

Australians: a guide to sources is the work of over 60 scholars, who have compiled lists of the most important books in their field, together with an explanatory essay which sets the literature in perspective, with regard both to time and to related topics.

A word of explanation may be appropriate about the audience for whom this work is intended. Quite obviously there are many kinds of readers—indeed, almost every person approaches reading and study from a different background and with a different attitude. Yet this collection of reading lists had to be pitched at some standard level and, in conformity with the other volumes of *Australians: a historical library*, this book is designed for 'the intelligent man or woman in the street', who can be assumed to have had a reasonable level of education—and it matters nought whether that education was received through formal schooling at primary, secondary, maybe tertiary level, or whether it was acquired through self instruction or through adult education courses. This average reader has no special knowledge of Australian history beyond what has been learnt at school, but is assumed to have a genuine interest in learning more about Australia.

This conspectus of Australian studies is one way in which Australia can be described and studied. Such a survey can only be based on an existing literature; while there are always new trends in the writing of history which claim to offer a different and 'better' approach, a literature survey should reflect the dominant historiographical strain of the period it deals with.

This guide to the literature on Australian studies adopts an historical approach in that the background reading cited on all aspects of the subject includes significant works of the past. The compilers have endeavoured to cite recent publications also, so that each chapter reflects the current state of publishing related to its subject. The cut-off date for this literature survey is the end of 1984.

The division of the bibliography into ten sections, further subdivided into 55 topics, is designed to help students of Australia to obtain a systematic overview of the land, the people, the history and structure of Australian society, and of the life Australian people lead. The bibliography begins in Section I with general reference works that will help readers to identify dates and general facts about Australia, to ascertain what printed literature there is on Australia and where to find statistical data relating to Australia. Then follow literature surveys of the physical environment of the Australian continent, its geology, flora and fauna, all of which are unique in many respects.

The importance attached to the understanding of Australian Aboriginal society is reflected in the lengthy bibliography that makes up Section IV. This survey has been compiled with the help of the Australian Institute of Aboriginal Studies Library and it is hoped that it will be of particular use to all who are concerned with Aboriginal issues in Australian studies.

The literature on early European contacts with this continent—its discovery by European sailors, the first settlements, the exploration of the interior—is described in Section VI, while that on the political developments which led to the federation of the original six colonies and the contemporary political scene is treated in Section VII.

The extensive treatment of the literature on Australian economic and social history in Sections VIII and IX reflects the background to current thinking on the development of this country. Much of the literature cited relates to the origins of these developments, but care has been taken to list also books that comment on the present.

It is not always easy to distinguish between society and culture, and there will be aspects of social history which some readers might have preferred to see treated in greater detail. However, the editors are keenly aware that acceding to all the current approaches in the study of social history would merely date this work, and would add little to its value as a prime source of information on Australia. By the same token the literature related to cultural history, as presented in Section X, reflects the breadth of the subject, and the methods by which subdivisions have been marked for separate treatment represent the view of the editors.

Each bibliography is introduced by a brief essay in which the compiler sets out a general view of the subject; each contains suggestions and explanations related to the limits of the literature survey and the reasons for exclusions, and contains some sources not included in the reading lists. The literature is so large that strict limits had to be imposed on the length of each contribution and none of the bibliographies claims to be exhaustive.

The majority of the books cited in these bibliographies have been published since 1950, and the editors have adopted the simple rule of referring users to the latest edition known at the time of going to press. Where that edition has been reprinted more recently, an appropriate note has been added to the descriptive comment. For books published before 1950 our preferred practice has been to cite the first edition of a work cited and to indicate reprints or new editions where they exist. Some of the bibliographies are arranged in chronological sequence to emphasise the historical significance of the entries. This is paticularly important with the older works.

With regard to the imprint, the authority of the *Australian national bibliography* was accepted for the place of publication, the name of the publisher and the date.

It was decided to abbreviate the name and delete the place of publication of the most frequently occurring publishers, so that Melbourne University Press is shown simply as 'MUP'. A list of the abbreviations, which also includes details of the place of publication, will be found on page xviii.

For those who wish to study a topic in greater depth, the editors recommend that they read with special care the literature surveys that precede the bibliography of their chosen topic. A close examination, and eventually a close familiarisation, with the appropriate reference works listed in Section II will be essential. There are many hints and warnings set out in the accompanying survey of reference books, but it cannot be stressed sufficiently that those who want to make progress with Australian studies must first have a firm grasp of the guides to information sources. Such books should be studied in a practical manner to understand their salient good points and their weak spots. To name but two examples, the student of any aspect of Australian history must learn about the purpose and scope of the *Australian public affairs information service*, just as the student of the Australian flora must know the scope and regional coverage of the basic reference works for the identification of Australian plants.

We hope that this volume will be helpful to those who wish to gain an overview of the history of Australia, the intellectual routes Australians have travelled and the external and internal influences that have shaped their writing.

It remains to be added that this large undertaking owes much to many friends and colleagues. The contributors of essays and of bibliographies are named in the appropriate places; their labour has been entirely voluntary and the Management Committee of History Project Incorporated, and the editors of this volume, are much indebted to all.

Our special thanks are due to Mrs Julie G. Marshall, whose untiring effort and vigilance ensured that standards of bibliographic citation are high and consistent, and that the reading lists harmonise, bibliographically speaking, with the accompanying essays. Miss Jean Hagger compiled the index and we are very grateful to her for the thoughtful and thorough approach brought to this important task. Also, we gratefully acknowledge the help of Michael Harrington, AGPS, Canberra, in compiling the tables on bibliographic control.

The typing assistance received from Mrs S. Enright and Mrs Nancy McElwee is gratefully acknowledged.

Support for this volume by the University of New South Wales, La Trobe University, and the Canberra College of Advanced Education is formally but no less sincerely and gratefully acknowledged.

D. H. BORCHARDT

VICTOR CRITTENDEN

Periodical titles are followed, as appropriate, by volume or series number, issue number and year of publication.

A & R	Angus & Robertson, Publishers, Sydney	*J*	*Journal*
AACOBS	Australian Advisory Council on Bibliographic Services	*J Aust stud*	*Journal of Australian studies*
		J R Aust Hist Soc	*Journal of the Royal Australian Historical Society*
ABC	Australian Broadcasting Commission (now Corporation)	**LBSA**	Library Board of South Australia
ABS	Australian Bureau of Statistics	**MUP**	Melbourne University Press, Parkville, Vic.
ACER	Australian Council for Educational Research, Melbourne, Victoria	**NLA**	National Library of Australia, Canberra, ACT
ACT	Australian Capital Territory	**NSW**	New South Wales
AGPS	Australian Government Publishing Service, Canberra, ACT	**NT**	Northern Territory
		NY	New York
AIIA	Australian Institute of International Affairs	**OUP**	Oxford University Press, Melbourne. OUP publications issued in London are shown as London, OUP.
ANUP	Australian National University Press, Canberra, ACT		
CSIRO	Commonwealth Scientific and Industrial Research Organization (its Central Library and Information Services are located in East Melbourne, Vic.)	**p**	page(s)
		repr	reprinted
		rev	revised
		SA	South Australia
CUP	Cambridge University Press, Melbourne, Vic. CUP publications issued in Cambridge are shown as Cambridge, CUP.	**SUP**	Sydney University Press, Sydney, NSW
		UNSWP	University of New South Wales Press, Kensington, NSW
ed(s)	editor(s)/edited	**UQP**	University of Queensland Press, St Lucia, Qld
edn	edition		
et al	and others	**UWAP**	University of Western Australia Press, Nedlands, WA
facs	facsimile edition		
Hist stud	*Historical studies*	**vol(s)**	volume(s)
IUP	Irish University Press, Dublin, Ireland	**WA**	Western Australia

'Anigozanthos flavidus, *yellow kangaroo paw.*
Engraving by F. Sansom after S. Edwards, 1803.
Hand-coloured.
IN PRIVATE POSSESSION

CHAPTER 1

THE WRITING OF AUSTRALIAN HISTORY

STUART MACINTYRE

THE FIRST and over-riding impression was that Australia had no history. So unfamiliar were the topography and climate, the flora and fauna, so negligible seemed the civilisation of its inhabitants, that the white newcomers could discern no signs of a recognisable antiquity. In *A sketch of New South Wales* (1845), written by one who had settled briefly, the colony was said to call up 'no train of ideas that are associated with the past, it has no fossil remains of any consequence, not even the vestige, so far as I know, of any one thing from which the curious might deduce that Australia ever had been different from what it was when Cook landed on its shores'.

The absence of history was reiterated so often and so insistently that it became a cliché, one that persists even to this day. Yet for every denial that Australia possesses a past, there is a writer anxious to tell its story. The purpose of this survey is to explore the various ways in which Australians have sought to construct their history. Such an exploration requires a lengthy and sometimes indirect journey over contrasting terrain. It begins with the expectations that the first white settlers brought with them and an adaptation of their sensibilities to the new land. It considers their reluctance or inability to recognise the antiquity of the Aborigines, who preceded them by as much as 50 000 years. It moves from the use of history as political argument in the first part of the nineteenth century to the search for a historical identity in the second half. It follows the codification of history into an intellectual science over which professional specialists preside. For all the advances in knowledge this made possible, I wish to argue that the rapid growth of the discipline in the universities was not wholly beneficial and that its practitioners have since lost much of their earlier confidence and authority. A survey of the present uses of the Australian past does not allay these fears, though it draws a cautious optimism from the increasing awareness of the need for a history that can once more speak to the needs of the present.

ESTABLISHING THE PAST

The conviction that Australia was a country without a past was shaped by two impulses in the European imagination. In the first place was the long-established literary practice of treating the antipodes as a place of contrarieties where everything was turned upside down. Whether the writer offered fantasy, utopia, allegory or even turned the device to more satirical purposes as did Swift in the best-known example of this genre, *Gulliver's travels* (1726), the essence of the antipodean fantasy was its deliberate dissociation from the known world. When Europeans first came to Australia they were therefore fully alert to the weird and the bizarre. We find in their descriptive writings a fascination with the kangaroo, the possum, the platypus and other oddities which confirmed their expectation that they would find here 'such an inversion in nature as is hitherto unknown'. The novelty of these fantastic characters softened the newcomers' disappointment with such an inhospitable environment:

> Kangaroo, Kangaroo!
> Thou Spirit of Australia,
> That redeems from utter failure,
> From perfect desolation,
> And warrants the creation
> Of this fifth part of the Earth
> Which would seem an after-birth ...

The reference here to failure and desolation draws our attention to a second and more sharply focused imaginative expectation. For as the propertied class of eighteenth-century England enclosed and improved the land to increase its yield, as they reclaimed and drained and cleared, so correspondingly there developed a feeling for the charms of unaltered nature and the picturesque landscape. The new sensibility, which turned the remaining uncultivated regions of the British Isles—principally the Lake District, the Scottish Highlands and the Welsh mountains—into objects of conspicuous aesthetic consumption, did so by investing them with a romanticised antiquity. The very conception of beautiful scenery was inextricably interwoven with a sense of the past, as is seen in this passage from the travel writings of a genteel Englishwoman on the Welsh border:

> The hills seem to have a deeply murmured eloquence, and we understand their tales of times gone by; the rivers roll along their volumed and rapid waters, and we hear in the mighty music, the voices of 'men of olden days', who dwelt, fought or died within its sound.

Yet consider the same writer's response to the Australian landscape when, several years later, she emigrated to New South Wales. As she crossed the Blue Mountains, she observed 'a dreary monotony of form and colour'; the trees that covered them, 'instead of a beauty in the landscape ... were a deformity', while the Bathurst plains were a 'heavy, weary monotony'. Some perpendicular cliffs, broken and fissured in fantastic shapes, struck her as resembling the ruins of a castle, but this thought merely confirmed her distaste:

> Had I been travelling in the old country I should at once have decided that these were truly the ruins of some mighty mountain-fortress of former days ... but the existence of poetry or imagination in New South Wales is what none who know and have felt the leaden influence of its ledger and day-book kind of atmosphere would believe it guilty of suffering.

From the very beginning of European settlement, the new country had evoked such responses. In 1789 Captain Watkin Tench led a party inland from the settlement at Sydney Cove and found that within just a few kilometres, save for an occasional kangaroo and the melancholy sound of the crow, the solitude of 'the trackless immeasurable desert' was 'complete and undisturbed'. Three years later the convict artist Thomas Watling lamented the flatness and monotony of his place of exile: 'the landscape painter may in vain seek here for that beauty which arises from happily-opposed offscapes'. Throughout the nineteenth century the belief that Australia was deficient in antiquity, charm and romance remained a conventional cliché. 'It is true', wrote an art critic in 1894, 'that there are no lovely autumnal tints common to that season in Europe, nor can one find historic ruins to convey an interest to the landscape'. 'It is taken for granted', acknowledged a historian in 1913, 'that there can be no gleams of the picturesque in a tale so brief, and of tints so sober'.

The grudging tone in which these writers formulated their penance ('It is true', 'It is taken for granted') suggests that the conventional wisdom, while still commanding formal respect, had long since been recognised for the platitude it was. Few challenged it directly before the close of the century. Some mocked it, like the critic of the 1850s who acknowledged with heavy irony that Australia possessed none of the 'archaeological accessories' so necessary for the novelist's art: no ruins encumbered with ivy, no spring panel and secret passage, no ghostly environs, not so much as a house with seven gables. Some protested against its excesses, including those indignant locals who took issue with Adam Lindsay Gordon's reference to Australia's scentless blossoms and songless birds. Even the most iconoclastic, however, were constrained within the same confines of the imagination. In their attempt to establish an Australian past they simply reworked the conventions.

The process can be observed clearly in the novel, which was at this time the most influential form of historical literature. The same sensibility that enabled writers to see the landscape as a place of romantic antiquity was associated with a new appreciation of the past. In the hands of Sir Walter Scott—and Scott was read widely in Australia from as early as the 1820s—the historical novel became something more than a period piece whose modern characters were decked out in perfunctory archaisms; it became an imaginative reconstruction of a complete way of life with precise visual description, close attention to detail and conscious identification with the bygone age.

Scott's influence bore directly on the British historian Macaulay, the German von Ranke, and indirectly through them on the writing of history in Australia, but for the moment we are concerned with his literary impact. It was profound. Writers as diverse as Marcus Clarke, Price Warung and William Hay followed Scott in basing fiction directly on historical records. Newspapers, journals, memoirs, almanacs, pamphlets, parliamentary papers and even the very

Nineteenth-century depiction of kangaroos in a glass inlay mosaic frieze in the state room of the Maharana of Udaipur, Shiv Niwas Palace, Udaipur, Rajasthan, India.
ROY LEWIS

convict records were assembled and reworked for dramatic effect. 'As giving you some idea of my methods of working up historical matter', explained Price Warung, 'I will state that I can give documentary evidence for the main incidents of every story ... and that on the average I refer, for the bare detail of each narrative, to 50 volumes in mss'. More generally, the habit was soon established of locating fiction in the past: Henry Kingsley's *The recollection of Geoffry Hamlyn* is set in the 1820s and 1830s; Rolf Boldrewood's *Robbery under arms* (serialised 1882–83) takes place in the early 1860s; Henry Handel Richardson's *The fortunes of Richard Mahoney* (1917) begins on the goldfield in the 1850s. From novels such as these, rather than from any piece of historical writing in the strict sense, a feeling for the Australian past was created.

How could a pleasing narrative be wrought from such unpromising material? What could be done with so desolate a landscape and such a discord of nature? One solution was to make a virtue of necessity. Australia's very lack of a past could then be seen as offering the opportunity to construct its own future. 'It is true', wrote the poet Charles Harpur, that Australia's past had not been 'hallowed in history' by the achievements of poets, statesmen or warriors; 'in this country Art has done nothing but Nature everything. It is ours, then, alone to inaugurate the future'. Or as an earlier poet had put it, 'Anticipation is to a young country what antiquity is to an old'. Such a notion can be seen in the earliest narratives of white settlement. The sound of axes breaking the timeless solitude of the virgin forest became a standard device whereby the narrator imagined the civilisation that was to be. In his *Account of a voyage to establish a colony at Port Phillip* (1805), the naval officer J.H. Tuckey recalled how he had watched a team of convicts yoked to a cart, the wheels of which were sunk up to the axles in sand. As he witnessed their exertions on the unpromising wastes of Sorrento he had a vision of 'a second Rome, rising from a coalition of Banditti ... superlative in arms and in arts, looking down with proud superiority upon the barbarous nations of the northern hemisphere'. Such conceits went back to Gibbon and they were to become a stock-in-trade of the historical imagination—Macaulay would anticipate a future New Zealander standing on a broken arch of London Bridge to sketch the ruins of St Paul's. By such means the reader was reminded of the transience of all civilisations.

The New World could thus be seen as a place of redemption on whose broad acres the industrious emigrant might find peace, happiness and prosperity. It can be seen that this notion of Australia as an arcadian paradise was wholly derivative, promoted by English writers catering for an English audience and reworking the old theme of the antipodes as a place where a lost ideal might be regained. Their creation, the 'colonial romance', called for only the most formulistic treatment of the Australian environment since Australia served merely as a picturesque background against which the manly hero made good. And while one local writer protested against these literary caterers for modern civilisation, 'ever ready to construct historiettes concerning lands which [they have] never seen', others adopted the same idiom and sentiments. Insofar as the colonials sought to impart a little more verisimilitude to the genre, they simply assimilated local details into conventional romantic images. In effect, these writers solved the problem of an Australian past by making it synonymous with that of the mother country.

Not so Marcus Clarke. He wrote not of the prosperous sheep runs and goldfields but of the convict settlements; not of redemptions but of exile, atavism and despair; not of sylvan beauty but of the 'weird melancholy' of the bush. In the convict stories he collected into *Old tales of a young country* (1873) and then in *His natural life* (1874), which listed its historical documentation in an appendix, Clarke set out to show that Australia had its own exotic past.

Writing less than one hundred years after white settlement, Clarke heightened the distance of the 'rude adventurous life of those early colonial days' with melodramatic effects. But for all that he learned from Balzac and Poe, it is unclear whether he transcended the limits of the romantic sensibility or merely inverted it. His very insistence on the macabre loneliness of Australian scenery, unhallowed by an association with the past ('From the melancholy gum strips of bark hang and rustle') echoes the description written fifty years earlier by an English traveller of 'miserable looking trees that cast their annual coats of bark and present to the eyes of the raw European the appearance of being actually dead'.

SUPPRESSING THE PAST

It takes an unusual arrogance to ignore a culture that was old when the English language was new. Clarke regarded the Aborigines as 'simply a set of repulsive, filthy savages', bereft of literary possibilities and therefore playing no part in his view of history. He was not alone in this. Most historians (though not all—Rusden, considered below, is an exception) working in the second half of the nineteenth century thought of Aborigines as irrelevant to the real history of the country, which began with its white occupation. A correspondent of the *Moreton Bay Courier* predicted in 1859 that when the history of Australia came to be written, 'the Aborigines will be passed by in a few lines'. He was right. Exactly one hundred years later a review of historical writing concluded with the observation that 'the Australian aboriginal is noticed in our history only in a melancholy anthropological footnote'. W.E.H. Stanner, who did as much as anyone to remedy this suppression, called it the great Australian silence.

It had not always been so. During the early years of colonial settlement, the Aborigines were objects of intense curiosity and few writers failed to include in their descriptive accounts of the new land some consideration of the customs and mores of its earliest inhabitants. Nor were these observers altogether oblivious of the Aboriginal achievement—the simplified ingenuity of their material culture, the absence of rank in their social organisation and the strong sense of sociability manifested in the readiness with which they greeted the first comers. 'The natives of New South Wales possess a considerable portion of that acumen, or sharpness of intellect, which bespeaks genius', judged Watkin Tench. Yet even here the Aborigines were taken to be in a state of nature, unsoftened by religion, unpolished by arts and sciences, 'unmoulded into anything like shape of mind'.

And how quickly the idealisation of the noble savage gave way to abuse of the 'most insolent and troublesome savage'. As soon as the whites encountered resistance from those they expropriated, the myth collapsed. 'A thousand times . . . have I wished', wrote Tench, 'that those European philosophers whose closet speculations exalt a state of nature above a state of civilization could survey the phantom which their heated imaginations have raised'. Similarly, a historian writing in 1839 was confident that if Rousseau had visited Australia he would not have hesitated whether the savage or social life was to be preferred. There was sharp disagreement over the distribution of responsibility for the breakdown in race relations, as well as over the policy the colonial administrators should pursue. Common to all these writers, however, were the assumptions that the Aborigine was a primitive who had failed to advance down the path of historical progress—or, alternatively, had retreated—and that it was futile to lead him down it:

As in the eye of Nature he has lived,
So in the eye of Nature let him die.

The Aborigines, then, had no history.

The inevitable extinction of this doomed race provided the starting point for subsequent investigations; indeed it was the imminence of their expected disappearance that stimulated an interest in them as the vital clue that might 'elucidate the great mystery of the peopling of the world'. Such a primitive race, it was reasoned, must surely provide the key. Accordingly, the emergent doctrines of evolution were harnessed to such classificatory schemes as phrenology, osteology and philology, and applied to the Aboriginal remnants. At times the gentlemen scholars of the learned societies rivalled Burke and Hare in their ghoulish disregard for the most elementary proprieties. The corpse of the last so-called 'full-blood' Tasmanian Aboriginal male, who died in 1868, was cut up by members of the Royal Society of Tasmania and the Royal College of Surgeons, one of whom had a purse made out of a portion of the skin. Similarly, the skeleton of Truganini was acquired and subsequently put on display in the museum. It was not cremated until 1976.

James Bonwick, schoolmaster and prolific author, first became interested in the Tasmanian Aborigines in 1842 when he visited Flinders Island and met some of the few survivors of the white invasion. Convinced of the inevitability of their demise, he reflected on the fate of a people

Old Polly brings in the milking goats, *a drawing by Elizabeth Durack at Argyle Station, East Kimberley,*
WA in 1934.
ELIZABETH DURACK

who had sustained themselves for an epoch whose duration he could not measure but which, he
thought, might well go back before the emergence of the European. 'It was there and then', he
recorded subsequently, 'I conceived writing the narrative of the now departed people'.
Bonwick's researches resulted in a number of books, the most important of which is the *Daily*
life and origin of the Tasmanians (1870). He began it by paraphrasing a comparison that Cook had
drawn a hundred years earlier—'it may even be doubted if the Tasmanian Aborigines did not
eat better, sleep better and laugh more than the majority of our favoured and enlighted
Europeans'—and throughout his account of the Aborigines' food, dress, language, pastimes,
government, morals and beliefs, he maintained this perspective. The approach and the very
wording of the comparison are reflected in Geoffrey Blainey's *Triumph of the nomads* (1975).

Though by no means alone, Bonwick was unusual among his contemporaries in his estimate of
the antiquity of the Aborigines' mode of existence and his determination to reconstruct it from
the remaining fragments. He continued the practice of seeking their origins in Africa or Asia,
for he retained the conviction that Aborigines occupied a low rung on the evolutionary ladder
and must therefore be descendants of some known primitive race; but he dismissed the
suggestion that they were recent arrivals or that the Australian continent had risen lately from
the seabed. Nevertheless, he qualified their antiquity in two respects: first, it was conditional on
isolation and could not withstand the arrival of the whites; and second, it was timeless and
unchanging. The Aborigines had existed for millenia in a state of suspended animation. 'They
knew no past, they wanted no future.' Similar assumptions informed the work of Lorimer Fision
and Alfred Howitt, who in the 1870s first applied anthropological methods to the study of
Australian Aborigines, and until well into the twentieth century practitioners in this field
continued to treat Aborigines as primitives.

Bonwick was here setting at nought the body of Aboriginal knowledge and belief concerning
their past that he had described under the chapter heading 'Legends'. Today they are usually
known as the Dreaming. These are the stories the Aborigines handed down from generation to
generation, stories that varied from one group to another and, in the manner of oral tradition,
were subject to borrowing and accretion. They told of things that happened when people and

nature came to be as they are. Expressed in myth, ritual and practice, they were at once a cosmogony and a source of knowledge held sacred and timeless. That they also constituted a valid way of addressing the past took a long time to penetrate the European consciousness.

> Untutor'd children, fresh from Nature's mould,
> No songs have ye to trace the times of old.

So Wentworth had written in 1823. Even when European settlers began to adopt Aboriginal placenames, they did so with an almost total disregard for the hallowed significance of the topography. Generations of Australian pupils learned of Romulus and Remus but, in Victorian schools at least, it was not until the 1930s that the reader, *Some myths and legends of the Australian Aborigines*, was introduced into the syllabus. It would be a mistake to equate the Dreaming with historical knowledge, its meaning is at once larger and less precise than that. The Dreaming does not embody a sequence of events in linear time moving towards a destination, nor does it postulate a past Golden Age. It is a statement of what is thought to be permanent and its precepts help to maintain the permanency. Our notion of history, the history Europeans sought to create after they settled in Australia, was but a substitute: in a society where tradition had been transplanted and authority had to be established, it sought to impose order by the puny means of an attenuated historical continuity.

HISTORY AS POLEMIC

The making of a historical record began with the first fleet. Phillip, Collins, Hunter, Tench and White all kept, and published, accounts of the chief events during the foundation years. They wrote as men charged with creating a settlement out of the most unlikely materials but they wrote also with an appreciation that they were planting English civilisation in Australia—and it is this mixture of pathos and grandeur that lends their work a lasting fascination; we regard them, in the words of an eminent authority on the period, 'with a little of that awe with which Britishers now invest the Anglo-Saxon Chronicler Bede'. Their narratives were supplemented by other writers catering to the curiosity of the British reading public with memoirs, journals of exploration and travel, descriptive and scientific reports, emigrant manuals and literature designed to promote land companies. All these publications contain historical material, albeit of a fragmentary and often derivative character.

In what sense can we discern a tradition of historical scholarship? If history is something more than the mere compilation of records and the simple relation of past happenings, it is surely distinguished by the way its material is collected and worked into a coherent whole. Some purpose must work as an ordering principle on the bare sequence of events. On such a basis it is possible to construct a line of early histories: William Wentworth's *Statistical, historical and political description of the colony of New South Wales* (1819); John Dunmore Lang's *A historical and statistical account of New South Wales* (1834); perhaps Henry Melville's *The history of the island of Van Diemen's Land* (1835) and James Macarthur's *New South Wales: its present state and future prospects* (1837); certainly John West's *The history of Tasmania* (1852). While far from exhaustive, this list embraces the most notable examples of a genre: each was concerned with the development and maintenance of political authority, and how that authority worked on the society to determine its shape and character. Furthermore, in each case the demonstration of the results of past policies was at the same time an argument for policies designed to promote a different social order.

The very circumstances of its creation illuminate the nature of this sort of history. Its author was a man of affairs, closely involved in the political questions of the day. He had but a limited documentary record on which to base his work and his opportunites for research were restricted. Lang's habit was to undertake this 'literary labour' on voyages back to Britain; this, he said, was 'to obviate the overpowering ennui that would otherwise be almost unendurable', but it is equally true that shipboard conditions offered this frenzied man a rare opportunity to give the task his undivided attention. He was therefore reliant on the 'researches and extracts' he managed to complete before his departure. Wentworth's and Macarthur's books were produced in

England from materials available there, while West had to find time, amid his editorial duties in Launceston, to visit Hobart in order to consult official records and private papers.

Lacking a substantial body of documentation, all these writers drew heavily on testimony or first-hand experience. This is not to say that they were unconcerned with accuracy or questions of detail. On the contrary, much turned on such matters in an intimate society whose past was so brief and factious. The young Wentworth was overcome with indignation when he read in H.G. Bennet's *Letter to Lord Sidmouth* (1819) that his father had gone to New South Wales as a convict; but his own investigations revealed that the truth was hardly more palatable—emigration had been more or less dictated by the bench. James Macarthur called on Lang to account for a statement he had made in his *Historical and statistical account* concerning the role of his father, John Macarthur, in the Rum Rebellion; Lang sent him away with 'a small pamphlet on the subject' and heard no more. The authority of the printed record was already evident.

These writers organised their material in the narrative form. They put events into chronological sequence and focused on a single, coherent story to demonstrate the consequences of official policy. In their high moral tone, their cultivation of a classical style with lengthy periods and balanced, subordinate clauses, their range of allusion and their use of irony, they followed the literary model that had been created in eighteenth-century England:

> if there is joy in heaven among the angels of God over every one sinner that repenteth [wrote Lang], we may well conceive the deep interest with superior intelligences would naturally feel at the establishment of the penal colony on the coast of New Holland.

The most accomplished writers, Lang and West, had the greatest familiarity with historical literature, but all were deeply concerned with the rhetorical aspects of their art and with its moral responsibilities. 'One of the most sacred duties of the annalist', wrote Wentworth, was to judge public characters 'with that severity of reprobation or of praise to which their conduct in public life may have entitled them'. The intention was to sway the reader and carry the judgment. Wentworth's, Lang's and Macarthur's efforts were directed to the seat of power in London, where their books were published. There they aimed to win parliament and the Colonial Office to their interpretation of the past and their blueprint for the future.

For Wentworth the history of the colony showed the disastrous effects of its autocratic government and restrictions on commerce. If Australia was to rise from 'the abject state of poverty, slavery and degradation to which she is so fast sinking', then it must attract free migrants with constitutional liberties, able to benefit from the economic opportunities offered by its broad acres. For Lang too, the mistaken policies of the crown had stifled progress, first by the favours it had shown to convicts and then by its encouragement of 'sheep and cattle mania'. He sought measures that would encourage 'a numerous, industrious and virtuous agricultural population'. And for Macarthur, 'if wise measures are now adopted, the false steps of the past may soon be retrieved'. He had to go to London to present the petition of the exclusives, seeking the replacement of transportation with assisted migration for the consolidation of a landed gentry, and the book that bore his name was produced as a means to that end.

West's *History of Tasmania* is at once the culmination of this form of historical literature and its point of transition. He began writing in 1847, just after it was learned that transportation to Van Diemen's Land would continue. He finished in 1852, on the eve of the final victory of the anti-transportation movement in which he played a prominent part. More than two hundred pages were given over to a history of transportation and the entire work is permeated by his abhorrence of the evil. The crucial point is that these arguments were addressed primarily to an Australian audience. The book itself was published in Launceston and offered by the author to the rising generation of native Tasmanians—he preferred that term to the older Van Diemen's Land, with its connotations of 'bondage and guilt'—in the hope that it would 'gratify their curiosity, and offer to their view the instructive and inspiring events of the past'.

A page had been turned. With the granting of self-government to the colonies it was no longer necessary to address such arguments to Westminster, nor to enclose them in the elaborate historical garb by which British legislators could recognise them. As a contemporary historian of New South Wales wrote, self-government 'fixes a date up to which the previous history of the colony forms of itself an era, or period of history'. It was now up to the colonists themselves to inaugurate a new era.

HISTORY AS PROGRESS

The speedy resolution of constitutional issues in the newly established colonial legislatures may have allowed politics to lapse into a valid mediocrity, but for the historian it posed anew the problem of finding a proper subject for commemoration. When self-government was granted by Britain, the old quarrels were rendered irrelevant and attempts to present them in a progressive or 'Whig' framework as a fight for liberty came to seem more than a little absurd. What now should the colonial historian record?

This was the question that William Westgarth asked in 1864 when he rewrote his account of *The colony of Victoria*. 'There must be little worthy of the venerable name of history', he wrote, 'in the brief rude life of most of our colonial settlements'. He decided that their chief interest lay in their remarkable progress. Similarly, Thomas McCombie began his *History of the colony of Victoria* (1858) with the observation that 'The period over which this history extends is hardly twenty years; but such has been its wonderful progress that the annals of all the nations would be ransacked in vain for a parallel to it'. So too, in the preface of his *History of New South Wales* (1862), argued Roderick Flanagan; and again in 1867 Samuel Bennett, the proprietor of the Sydney *Empire*, gathered his articles on the colonial past to show that 'the rise of great commercial communities in the course of little more than half a century . . . presents one of the most striking features in the history of mankind'. Indeed, when Westgarth returned to the theme in 1889 with *Half a century of Australasian progress*, every colony had produced its paean to that secular deity. The genre culminated with the work of the New South Wales statistician, T.A. Coghlan, who in *The progress of Australasia in the nineteenth century* (1903) could draw on an unparalleled knowledge of the official sources.

These exercises in self-congratulation heightened the contrast between the circumstances that had prevailed before self-government and those that now obtained. McCombie, himself a member of the Victorian parliament, wrote of a 'perfect despotism' giving way to 'extreme democracy'. James Fenton, in his *History of Tasmania* (1884), telescoped a whole series of changes into a single moment. With the establishment of responsible government, he wrote, 'we now enter upon a new era': transportation was abolished; the depredations by bushrangers and Aborigines ceased; some of the wealth that was dug out of the ground in Victoria found its way across Bass Strait; commerce made 'a giant stride' and civic life flowered. Similarly, the historians of Queensland treated 1859, when the colony separated from New South Wales and became self-governing, as the great divide. In their very change of names—Victoria in place of the Port Phillip district, Tasmania instead of Van Diemen's Land, Queensland rather than Moreton Bay—the self-governing colonies avoided the disputations and embarrassments of the past.

While therefore no longer so overtly political in focus, these histories remained wedded to the notion of continuous progress. They were concerned with recording what Macaulay had described as 'the history of physical, of moral and of intellectual improvement' which in this case was measured in flocks and crops, bricks and mortar, and then in the civilisation these made possible. The new climate of popular sovereignty and self-improvement called for something less remote than the old drum-and-trumpet histories of kings and courtiers; rather, it demanded what Flanagan called 'useful and instructive knowledge'. The proper purpose of history, claimed one writer in 1851, was 'to mark the progress of civilization', and it would be 'more useful to mankind' to record the price of a goose and the wage of a labourer during the reign of Edward III than to fill whole volumes with his glorious victories. With the colonial past, however, this was easier said than done. Most obviously, the writers of these histories of the colonies continued to organise their narratives around administrative decisions and to base their chapter divisions on the reigns of those 'Lilliputian sovereigns', the governors.

THE SEARCH FOR A THEME

To overcome such limitations it was necessary to find some alternative theme or organising principle more closely attuned to popular interest and aspirations. One possibility was exploration. There were obvious attractions in the stories of epic journeys of discovery across water and land, in the privations and dangers that were endured, and in the very act of claiming land which could be opened up for settlement. Cook's *Journals* had made an impact in the eighteenth century; men like Flinders, Sturt and Mitchell developed the genre in the first half of the nineteenth; in the second half, exploration reached new heights of popularity. The tragicomic Burke and Wills were perhaps the most successful in self-promotion, if in little else; but other, more accomplished explorers were fully aware of the literary opportunities:

> No work of fiction can excel, or even equal, in romantic and heart-stirring interest, the volumes worthy to be written in letters of gold, which record the deeds and the suffering of these noble toilers in the dim and distant field of discovery afforded by the Australian continent.

The most widely read work of this kind was Ernest Favenc's *History of Australian exploration* (1888). Written by one who had himself sought to win glory, and published in the centennial year, it celebrated 'the indomitable courage, heroic self-sacrifice and dogged perseverance' of the men who had established their claim to 'the proud title of "Australian Explorer"'. In stark contrast, the eccentric George Collingridge failed to win due recognition for his *The discovery of Australia* (1895), largely because his argument that Portuguese mariners had preceded Cook by two centuries was unpalatable to imperial-minded readers. Exploration also attracted the first academic historians, notably George Arnold Wood whose *The discovery of Australia* (1922) was his most successful work. In the schools the explorer became staple fare, but here a lifeless

The new clearing, *etching and aquatint by Beatrice Dean Darbyshire, c1925.*
ROBERT HOLMES À COURT COLLECTION

recitation of names, places and dates resulted all too often in an aversion to the subject. From this soporific reverence Patrick White tried to rescue *Voss* in 1957 and historians have more recently turned anew to the subject.

Another subject for commemoration was the bushranger. Again, the field was not new—*Michael Howe, the last and worst of the bushrangers of Van Diemen's Land* appeared as early as 1818, while James Bonwick's *The bushrangers* (1856) was one of his more commercially successful enterprises—but these were merely gratifying a morbid fascination with violence and retribution. Then there was the oral tradition, transmitted through ballad and folklore, that extended in subterranean fashion right through the century to surface dramatically from time to time in declarations like Ned Kelly's Jerilderie Letter of 1879. Three years later, under the pseudonym 'Rolf Boldrewood', the pastoralist and goldfield commissioner T.A. Browne began serialising a novel based on reports of bushranging in New South Wales during the 1860s; in book form, *Robbery under arms* was reprinted more than thirty times over the next fifty years.

Browne took the well-worn theme of crime and its consequences and breathed new life into it. No longer was the bushranger a desperate figure, hardened beyond recall; he now exhibited a manly independence, gallantry and loyalty to his mates. Further, his bushcraft and nativist values stamped him as unmistakably Australian, and suggested the pleasing conclusion that the outlaw was a victim of circumstances which, if remedied, would enable future energies to be channelled into more constructive endeavours.

The two streams—the one popular and defiant, the other literary and romantic—converged in a number of bushranging histories that appeared later in the century, notably those of Charles White. White, whose father owned the *Bathurst Free Press*, served as a police roundsman during the twilight years of bushranging in that district and subsequently worked his material into a major part of an aggressively nationalist *Early Australian history* in several volumes (1889–93), and then a *History of Australian bushranging* (1900–06). He was followed by George Boxall, whose *History of Australian bushrangers* (1899) joined the conventional moral judgment ('the story is a terrible one') with the contention that the influence of the bushrangers was not wholly evil: 'to their influence is due some of the sturdy Republicanism of the modern Australians'. Even the ultrarespectable Reverend W.H. Fitchett, headmaster of the Melbourne Methodist Ladies' College and author of the best-selling *Deeds that won the empire* (1898), gave over a quarter of his *Romance of Australian history* (1913) to Ned Kelly. The popular literature grew rapidly—the corpus of works devoted to Kelly alone is vast—and has been sustained more recently by such exponents as Frank Clune, George Farwell and Bill Wannan. Academically, the bushranger was taken up by Russel Ward in *The Australian legend* (1958) and since then has received increasing attention. John McQuilton's *The Kelly outbreak* (1979) points the way forward with its demonstration of how the techniques of social history can be applied successfully to the subject.

Here, then, were two ways of investing the past with a heroic meaning. Yet both had clear limitations. The obvious problem with the explorers was that their endeavours were merely preparatory to what followed; the mores of the bushranger, no matter how determinedly they were recast in a more acceptable mould, could hardly be extended to the society at large. Even Rolf Boldrewood felt it necessary to reassure his readers that novels such as his did not 'have a tendency to injure the moral sense of boys who read them and contrast the lavish rewards and exciting adventures which accompany the outlawed life with the slower and tame career of honest industry'. Furthermore, both themes were essentially peripheral to the achievements and aspirations of most Australians. It was around the more popularly accessible figures of the bushman and the pioneer that an orthodoxy formed.

Celebration of the bushman is associated with the emergence towards the end of the nineteenth century of a popular national literature, and especially with the *Bulletin*. Founded in 1880 and achieving a circulation of 80 000 by 1890, the *Bulletin* achieved its success by blurring the distinction between reader and writer. Encouragement and example taught its subscribers to become contributors of snappy paragraphs and racy yarns, tall stories and anecdotes, ballads and fiction. The avowed purpose was to define and express an Australian sentiment which its writers took to be most fully exemplified among groups of men travelling and working upcountry. As part of this project they created a 'usable past', one which denounced the evils of convict transportation, celebrated the digger and discerned a tradition of radical egalitarianism among the nomad bushmen, bullockies, shearers, drovers and rural labourers.

Such a past was not so much history as counterhistory. The radical nationalists asserted their memory of the common people against the offical record of the governors and the plutocracy. But history in the strict sense as they understood it, as a record of real achievement, had yet to be made and this was the special opportunity of the New World. 'If we are not History's legatees', explained the *Bulletin*'s literary editor, 'it is because we have the chance to be History's founders and establishers'.

It is easy to point to contradictions embodied in the bush legend, to show that its principal exponents were men who had fled to the cities, drew eclectically from discordant sources and codified the legend at the very point when the conditions it celebrated were disappearing. Even the titles of the works that afterwards recorded this epoch—A.W. Jose, *The romantic nineties* (1933); Vance Palmer, *The legend of the nineties* (1954); A.A. Phillips, *The Australian tradition* (1958)—suggest its ambiguities. For all that, its impact on popular perceptions of the past was profound, since it established the categories and vocabulary whereby an indigenous folklore could be set down in writing. The remarkable success of A.B. Facey's *A fortunate life* (1981) is evidence that the tradition is not yet exhausted.

Veneration of the pioneers became apparent from the middle of the nineteenth century. A song written in 1857 to celebrate the twenty-first anniversary of the establishment of South Australia captures the tone:

> That little band of heroes,
> How manfully they plied
> The axe, the plough, the harrow,
> And labor'd side by side.
> For us they cleared, they ploughed, they sowed: a garden now appears
> Where first they found a wilderness: those hardy pioneers.

At this time the term 'pioneer' encompassed the firstcomers, regardless of occupation, and honour was attached on the basis of seniority. Hence members of the Ballarat Old Identities Association wore a medal on their watch-chain bearing name and date of arrival. Here already in the tendency towards gerontocracy was a distorting element: those actually involved in opening up new areas of settlement were young, so young that in the Port Phillip district during the 1830s anyone over the age of thirty was known as 'old so and so'. Interest was more apparent in the colonies of free settlement, South Australia and Western Australia, than in the older penal colonies where there was already a reluctance to enquire too deeply into the origins of the early settlers. Characteristically, New South Wales marked its anniversary, 26 January, when the flag was run up at Sydney Cove, with a dinner of the emancipists and native born.

The term 'pioneer' acquired its special meaning towards the end of the century when it came to apply specifically to those who settled and worked the land. The meaning was elaborated by the same *Bulletin* writers who celebrated the values of the bush as the basis of Australian nationhood. In their version of the past they reserved special praise for those who had endured its hardships by dint of courage, enterprise and industry. It was a nostalgic vision. Writing during the 1890s, a period of class turmoil and financial crisis, they reached back to a golden age when lockouts and foreclosures were unknown; and they overlooked, so selective was their historical memory, the conflicts of the 1850s and 1860s when the squatter was an object of contempt.

Popular and ostensibly democratic, the pioneer legend was deeply conservative in its reverence for an idealised past. In this idyllic world there were human imperfections but no irreconcilable class antagonisms; there was good land and poor but no mention of the social, legal or economic determinants of land settlement. In a process that was open to all, the man—or the man and his family, for the pioneer legend was less misogynist than the legend of the nomad bushman—pitted themselves against the elements, achieved self-sufficiency and bequeathed their legacy to the nation. 'Some labour that others may enter into the results of their labour' was how a South Australian official history put it.

The construction of the pioneer legend can be observed in the lengthy gestation of a work published in 1898 as *Letters from Victorian pioneers*. In 1853 Lieutenant-Governor La Trobe had written a circular letter to a number of early squatters, asking them when and how they had taken up their runs. He received 58 replies which provide an unflattering picture of the repression of Aboriginal resistance and suggest how an ambitious earlycomer could get ahead: one respondent who had arrived in Van Diemen's Land in 1831 with three shillings reported that he owned 7300 sheep in 1853. La Trobe took the replies to England, but subsequently sent them back to his Melbourne agent who deposited them in the public library. Now they appeared with a preface by the librarian extolling these patriarchs for conquering the 'hardships and perils which beset the pioneer'.

There was by this time an extensive published body of such reminiscences, its heroes claimed, 'in compliance with oft-repeated requests of many of my friends'. The great majority were written by successful pastoralists and presented their success in the most agreeable terms: 'They were not speculative; they had no great overdrawn bank accounts; their wants were few and they lived simply and unostentatiously, and exercised a kind and wide hospitality'. By this time, also, the dubious origins of several of these dynasties had faded into obscurity. One history did include a chapter entitled 'Some strange pilgrim fathers', but it presented the transportees as 'a patch of human compost flung on soil which was afterwards to be turned into a garden'.

Finally, the pioneers found their way into commemorative histories, the most able of which was Collier's *The pastoral age in Australasia* (1911). Here the reader is told that Australia began as a benevolent social experiment which burst its limits with the opening of the grazing lands beyond the Blue Mountains. 'Now the real life of Australia begins', Collier states and works a rich tapestry of pastoral dynasties, morals, arts and politics, all 'the work of the Golden Fleece'. Not until Margaret Kiddle's *Men of yesterday* (1961) was this elegy matched. More prosaic but no more critical was S.H. (Sir Stephen) Roberts, whose *History of Australian land settlement* (1924) and later *The squatting age in Australia* (1935) established a successful academic career. The pastoral version of the pioneer legend was by no means its only form. In numerous local histories it was applied with equal force to agriculture and other more modest ventures, and, in one seminal article on Australia at large, to the 'smallholder'.

URBAN, CONSERVATIVE AND RADICAL ALTERNATIVES

The chroniclers of the nomad bushman and the pioneer, like those of the explorer and the bushranger, looked for a national identity in the bush. Although Australia was already a remarkably urban society by international standards, the city appeared an unpromising site for distinctly Australian characteristics. The nineteenth-century city, after all, was at once an artefact and symbol of an international economy and cosmopolitan culture; in layout and function one seemed much the same as any other. Yet the city captured the imagination of a number of writers. 'Where the city of Melbourne stands today, with its moderness and its artificial life', wrote Edward Jenks in 1895, 'sixty years ago there was nothing but a silent plain sparsely dotted with clumps of trees and occasionally visited by blackfellows and kangaroos'. Jenks wrote as an Englishman who had spent his three years in the colonies as the professor of law in that city, but the same contrast was drawn in 1857 by the stonemason C.J. Don who came to Australia to stay. 'Look at yonder city', he invited an audience gazing across the bay from Williamstown,

illuminated by its magic lamps, its windows glittering with wealth, a city with palaces worthy of kings, and temples worthy of gods, which labour had placed there in the short space of a quarter of a century. Twenty-five years ago, where now the voices of the most accomplished vocalists resound, the wild howl of the savage corroboree or the wind in the wilderness was alone heard . . .

Don and Jenks were separated by the four decades that spanned the gold rushes of the 1850s and the depression of the 1890s, four decades of sustained growth during which belief in the city flourished. The two were separated also by their attitude to urbanism, the pride and confidence of Don giving way to Jenks's insistence on its artificiality—elsewhere he condemned the ugliness, pretension and philistinism of Melbourne. Don welcomed the city as a place of opportunity while Jenks lamented 'the tyranny of the common-place average man'. Both, however, were as one in their conviction that Australian history was a story of civic progress ('the word being used in its purely scientific sense', added Jenks).

Marvellous Melbourne was the most fulsome in self-congratulation. In its heyday, with a grandiose public library, flourishing book trade and literary journals, it supported a group of professional writers who 'devoted themselves to singing Victoria's praises'. They were convinced that theirs was 'the most populous and progressive of all the Australian colonies', and they emphasised above all the amenities and refinements of its major city. Other colonial capitals produced their records of achievement, as did the inland Victorian centre of Ballarat (which, with W.B. Withers' *History of Ballarat*, 1870, was the first Australian city to possess a comprehensive history); but Alexander Sutherland surely went furthest with his boast in *Victoria and its metropolis* (1888) that 'there is nothing wanting in that due degree of all that busy fulness, that scope for sympathy and artistic development which forms the charms of city life ... Melbourne, in short, is not only a city, but most distinctly a metropolis'.

The subtitle of George Sutherland's *Australia; or, England in the south* (1886) suggests how an urban perspective emphasised the imperial relationship. It was not just that the Australian city shared many features with the British city: if it did not, then it was not for want of colonial endeavour. More than this, the creation of cities in the New World testified to the successful colonisation of the imperial metropolis, whose civic architecture was imitated and administrative and political processes re-enacted. The colonists believed that they owed their success to their British heritage since, as G.W. Rusden put it in 1883, 'The most successful colonization is that which founds abroad a society similar to that of the parent country'.

When that heritage came under challenge in the late nineteenth and early twentieth centuries, the historians who affirmed and defended it displayed a more conservative tone. Rusden, a Victorian public servant who wrote a three-volume *History of Australia* (1883), was probably the gloomiest. Jenks, who wrote his *History of the Australasian colonies* after he returned to England, and the Melbourne banker H.G. Turner, whose main works were a two-volume *History of the colony of Victoria* (1904) and *The first decade of the Australian commonwealth* (1911), shared Rusden's presentiments to a lesser degree. Their starting point was the shallowness of the colonial past and the consequent fragility of its institutions. 'The actors in what has been called the heroic work of civilization are rapidly passing away', explained Rusden to justify the need for a definitive record. The rising generations who have embarked on the task of nation-building 'frequently ignore the teachings of experience', claimed Turner. In regarding history as a school for statesmen they continued a well-established tradition, one that Lang, Macarthur and others had practised before them; and when Jenks explained that he treated 'history as past politics and politics as present history', he was merely repeating the dictum of his Cambridge professor.

They differed from their predecessors chiefly in their restrictive interpretation of political processes. Whereas the earlier writers had a flexible, even experimental attitude to the development of the state, and in both Wentworth's and Lang's cases considered American precedents seriously, the later writers took the English constitution as a fixed and binding model. Little could be learned from the first sixty years of colonial history, since the conditions of responsible government had then been lacking and an 'oppressive formal officialism' could hardly avoid mistakes. For similar reasons even the conservative Turner was surprisingly sympathetic to the Eureka uprising to which he later referred to as *Our own little rebellion*.

In writing of this early period, the emphasis was therefore on British settlement, British expenditure (Jenks remarked in a passing aside on the pioneer legend that 'Australians are sometimes apt to speak as though they and their fathers had done the whole work of building

Portraits of the Reverend J.D. Lang (1799-1878), republican clergyman (left) and of Captain Charles Sturt (1795-1869), explorer of the Australian interior. The engraving of Lang is based on an 1876 photograph by J.T. Gorus. The engraving of Sturt appears in A. Garran (ed) Picturesque atlas of Australasia, *Sydney 1886-88.*
MITCHELL LIBRARY, ANDERSON COLLECTION

up Australia') and British guidance towards constitutional maturity. Real history began in the 1850s with the colonies embarking on self-government. But they failed to make good their British heritage and instead adopted mischievous innovations designed to turn parliament into a 'mere reflex of the popular will'. The Englishman Jenks was the most charitable with his suggestion that the colonists meant to adopt the Westminster system of government but failed to understand it; Rusden and Turner regarded the debasement of public life more gloomily as the expression of a ruinous levelling tendency.

Neither of the local writers achieved the reputation they sought. Rusden particularly had such a curmudgeonly reputation as almost to preclude serious consideration of his views. 'Nobody that knew him will ever forget him, as peculiar a gentleman as one will encounter in a lifetime. We don't know any Australian resident so distinctly English', wrote the *Melbourne Punch* when he died in 1903. Turner's account of Victorian politics was regarded as violently partisan, while his ingenuous account of his own role during the financial crisis of 1893 invited ridicule. Subsequent opinion has confirmed these judgments. R.M. Crawford in his survey of Australian historiography said that Rusden's intention to write serious history was vitiated by an 'almost ludicrously conservative bias', and despite subsequent claims for his work, the verdict stands.

The usual explanation for the weak impact of the conservatives is to suggest the dominance of a progressive or 'Whig' orthodoxy among Australian intellectuals. That is hardly an apt characterisation of the *fin-de-siècle* mood. The ending of the economic 'Long Boom' and the defeat of the unions in the major strikes of the 1890s shook earlier expectations of unfolding progress. Among radicals there was a noticeable tendency to sever the past, to emphasise once more the novelty of Australia and the need to construct its future. According to such visionaries, it was precisely because the island continent lacked an authentic tradition that its people were presented with the opportunity to throw off the shackles of the Old World. Thus Bernard O'Dowd in 1903:

> Last sea-thing dredged by sailor Time from Space,
> Are you adrift Sargasso, where the West
> In halcyon calm rebuilds her fatal nest?
> Or Delos of a coming Sun-God's race?

'Australia is not a country; it is a symbol. We look dawnward', spoke the Mystic in a dialogue written by Louis Esson in 1909. His host was less confident: 'The Prometheus of the Australian Imagination is fettered to the mountain of British Fact'. But the Mystic preferred to describe Terra Australis beckoning at 'the sliprails of the Imagination, promising but to the rebels a fresh perception of beauty, an unblazed track to truth'.

INSTITUTIONALISING THE PAST

The closing years of the nineteenth century saw an upsurge of official or quasi-official attempts to commemorate the Australian past. The various colonies had established holidays to mark their foundation or separation, when they usually conducted official ceremonies at the appropriate place. But these were often unsatisfactory. South Australia's Proclamation Day of 1857, for example, was to have been an occasion of medieval amusements, but they were ruined by rain, the speeches were 'filmy effusions' and 'everybody voted everything a bore'. In any case, such anniversaries merely underlined the separateness of the colonies. The national pantheon was conspicuously bare. Cook was venerated and a tablet had been erected in 1822 at the point in Botany Bay on which he was said to have landed, but later heroes were harder to find.

The colonial governments did commission handbooks from time to time in order to publicise the opportunities they presented to migrants and investors, and these exercises in public relations usually included historical chapters. Sometimes governments assisted with handbooks, such as J.H. Heaton's *Australian dictionary of dates and men of the time* (1879) which was taken on by the New South Wales government printer because no other local press was equipped for the job. However, the government printer took it upon himself to censor the contents (on the grounds of propriety he cut an entry on 'Pure Merinos') and lost part of the manuscript. Sometimes histories were sponsored by public societies; for example, in 1860 the Gawler Institute offered 200 guineas for the best history of South Australia.

Alternatively, enterprising publishers got up commemorative histories for public subscribers. These bulky and ornate volumes were not cheap: Sutherland's *Victoria and its metropolis* sold at five guineas, while Garran's *Picturesque atlas of Australasia* (1886) cost ten, which was equivalent to a month's earnings for a skilled workman. Frequently such ventures contained biographical sketches of 'leading and representative citizens' who supplied the information and paid for the privilege. Again, the genre enjoyed official support so that the premier of Western Australia agreed to purchase one hundred copies of W.B. Kimberly's *History of Western Australia: a narrative of her past, together with biographies of her leading men* (1897).

The centenary of white settlement in 1888 aroused a greater and more general attention than any previous anniversary. While the *Sydney Morning Herald* managed to tell the story of the first fleet without mentioning the convicts and the *Bulletin* denounced the festivities as marking the 'meanest event' in Australian history since it inaugurated a 'loathesomeness and moral leprosy', the centenary took on a larger significance because of the growing support for federation. The New South Wales government catered to the renewed interest in the founding fathers with two volumes of a *History of New South Wales from the records* (1889, 1894) based on transcriptions made by Bonwick of material in the Public Record Office and other repositories.

Following his return to England, Bonwick had conceived the idea of transcribing official records along the lines of a Canadian scheme. He had been employed by the Queensland government in 1883 to do a year's copying, and in 1885 and 1886 he performed similar work for South Australia and Victoria. So impressed was the New South Wales premier Henry Parkes with the fruits of a £50 commission than Bonwick spent a further fifteen years in the employ of that state. The fruits of his work, 125 000 sheets of manuscript, formed the basis of eight volumes entitled *Historical records of New South Wales* (1892–1901). These in turn served as a precedent for an even more ambitious project, the *Historical records of Australia* in 31 volumes (1914–25), which were edited by the irascible Sydney surgeon, Dr Frederick Watson, on behalf of the Commonwealth.

The publication of what their editor called 'the birth certificates of a nation' was conceived as part of the duty owed by the new Commonwealth 'to the nation they are building up, to posterity and to civilization'. Be that as it may, the sales were disappointing. *Historical records of New South Wales* sold on average 120 copies of each volume, and while members of parliament were anxious to receive their complimentary copies of *Historical records of Australia*, its commercial appeal was not much greater.

The very preservation of historical records was a haphazard affair, dependent upon the energies of particular enthusiasts. None of the states made provision for the systematic deposit of official records before the establishment of the South Australian Archives after World War I. While the commonwealth investigated the creation of an archives in the early years of the century and even prepared a bill in the 1920s, nothing was done until World War II. Even the Mitchell Library, the most significant repository in this period, was made possible only by the New South Wales government's belated acceptance in 1906 of conditions imposed by its donor eight years earlier. David Scott Mitchell was an obsessive bibliophile whose unique collection, including 60 000 volumes of Australiana was offered with an endowment of £70 000 if the government built it a home. Yet many of the legislators dismissed the collection as a 'lot of convict rubbish' and the gift was not clinched until the year before Mitchell's death.

Sensitivity to the convict past was acute during this period of conscious nation-building, as the governor of New South Wales discovered to his cost in 1899. His well-intentioned reference to the country's 'birthstain' caused enormous indignation. Historians were therefore forced to tread warily and Bonwick was careful in his transcriptions to omit names of transportees, 'save where needful'. For some time afterwards, the attitude persisted that skeletons were best left in closets. Searching during 1940 in the underground vault to which the Tasmanian government consigned its records, the young S.J. Butlin was surprised to receive an invitation to take morning tea with the governor. His Excellency wanted reassurance that Butlin was not convict-chasing.

Similar impulses can be seen at work in the formation and choice of title of the Australian Historical Association in 1901 (it became the Royal Australian Historical society in 1918). During 1899 a group of Sydney enthusiasts contemplated the creation of a society to expedite the acceptance of Mitchell's offer. Nothing came of it. In the following year, however, a dispute arose in the *Sydney Morning Herald* as to the correct date of the laying of the foundation stone of an old church, and correspondents suggested that there should be an authority to provide an authentic record of such information since 'the swift advance of civilization is continually . . . sweeping away historical monuments of the past'. From these improbable beginnings a historical society was formed, taking as one of its purposes the compilation of a chronology of interesting and significant events—and eventually the society did produce such a *Calendar of events in Australian history* (1933). It is evident that the imminent creation of a sovereign nationality augmented the value of such antiquarian details, and such issues as the precise place of Cook's landing exercised members mightily in the early years.

Next came the Historical Society of Victoria (it too became Royal in 1952), formed in 1909 'for the purpose of collecting and publishing material relating to the history of the State of Victoria'. Within a year it persuaded the premier to declare a Discovery Day for observance in Victorian schools, marking Cook's first sighting of the Australian coast; and over the next few years the society erected a rash of tablets to navigators and explorers. After the Victorian came the Queensland Historical Society, formed in 1913 with the avowed object of 'bringing the student into contact with the older settler'. Other states followed and of course there were numerous local societies, with Ballarat's Historical Records Society going back to 1896.

None of these state bodies achieved a large membership, nor did they seek one. Enjoying viceregal patronage, they brought together pious members of the older families, a sprinkling of clerics, lawyers and doctors, the professor of history and perhaps a few other practising historians who would gently nudge the society back towards the mainstream when it threatened to become stranded in nostalgic backwaters. Members met to hear each other read papers which were afterwards published in the society's journal. Though some of the investigations were based on painstaking research, the great majority were undiscriminating and uncritical. The early volumes of the *Victorian historical magazine* have been aptly described as 'a mausoleum of minor preoccupations', and the same holds for the others.

The members guarded their past in a proprietary fashion. Paul and Alexandra Hasluck were young and enthusiastic when they joined the Western Australian Historical Society on its formation in 1926. They found it 'very much an old colonists' show'. Meetings were largely taken up with reminiscences of 'how your cousin and my aunt used to do this or that, and his grandfather was the first person to take cattle from here to there ...' The memory was highly selective. When Alexandra Hasluck protested against the suppression of some recently discovered letters to a convict, she was told that Western Australia 'was founded as a free colony by gentlefolk: the convicts came later and unwanted, and should not be associated with it'.

While users of records and members of historical societies were few, in the schools there was a vast conscript audience. Against the meagre sale of the *Historical records* can be set Alexander and George Sutherland's textbook *History of Australia* which passed through more than a dozen editions and sold 120 000 copies after its publication in 1877. At first the introduction of history into schools had been resisted. Whether it be British or Australian, the subject would only aggravate religious and national tensions in the new government schools which were meant to cater for all, Protestant and Catholic, English and Irish. 'What one section of the community would regard as facts would be rejected by another', warned the secretary of the New South Wales Council of Education in 1874. Yet before the end of the century history occupied a central place in the curriculum as the principal means of building and strengthening the community:

> The aim of history teaching [said an educationist in 1897] is to create a desire to read of the great personages, the wonderful events, and the details of the growth of nations; to develop the intellect along certain lines; to ensure that the community will have one condition at least, and that an important one, for governing itself with wisdom; to foster love of home, country and race, and to elevate morally the coming man and woman.

School history was deliberately circumscribed for didactic purposes. It might well be the case, thought Charles Pearson, the Victorian minister for education, that pupils were incapable of a proper study of the past, for that required a knowledge, practical insight and capacity to understand abstract questions that was beyond them. Therefore:

> the first lessons in history ought to concern themselves with what is exalted or tragical, adventurous or picturesque in human or national character, and to deal with the acts and words of men and women rather than with the growth of institutions or the rush and turmoil of revolutions.

In practice history lessons consisted largely of rote learning of names and dates:

> In 43 a Roman host
> From Gaul assaulted our southern coast,
> Caractacus in nine years more,
> A captive left his native shore.

Taught thus, Australian history could only appear a brief and colourless epilogue to the history of the mother country. Governors and explorers hardly filled the place occupied by monarchs and generals in the drum-and-trumpet celebration of the British heritage; nor could the colonies find any worthy equivalent to Magna Carta or the Long Parliament since, as the professor of history at the University of Sydney declared, 'the great battles of freedom had already been fought and won before Australia came of age'. Certainly, the writers of Australian texts did their best. Just as Alfred was a good king and John a bad, so Bligh was condemned and Macquarie commended. The exploits of Cook and Flinders, Blaxland, Wentworth and Lawson, and their successors were traced in tedious detail.

Eventually, some talented writers met the pressing need for more imaginative texts. In *The struggle for freedom* (1904), Walter Murdoch struck the engaging note of decorous informality that was to characterise his later writings, while the sprightly, avuncular tone of G.V. Portus's *Australia since 1606* (1932) is remembered by generations of students. Even so, the increasing emphasis on Australian history seems to have produced an indifference to, if not an active dislike of, the subject among many pupils. The discipline lost ground in the primary schools during the 1950s and in the secondary schools during the 1960s and 1970s. Though there are signs of revival, the present position varies so much from one state to another that it calls for more space than is available here.

HISTORY AS A SCIENCE AND A PROFESSION

We do not know the reactions of the members of the Queensland Historical Society when they assembled for their inaugural meeting on 18 August 1913 and heard the young lecturer at the newly established Queensland University read a paper on 'Methods of historical research'. They surely would have nodded with approval when A.C.V. Melbourne claimed that a nation's concern for its past was a measure of its civilisation. His claim for the utility of history as a source of valuable precedents was hardly contentious: it was conventional wisdom that the prudent could learn from the past, emulate its successes and avoid its mistakes. The members would have welcomed the claim that Australia possessed its own distinctive history and his call for preservation of records.

But when the speaker went on to suggest that the state of Australian historical research was negligible, and that it would remain thus until the university trained scholars in its proper procedures, members may have stirred a little uneasily. This was to make their own work, the collection of sources such as diaries and letters, and the compilation of a basic record, merely preparatory to the work of a trained specialist. Melbourne's description of the procedures of historical analysis—careful comparison and emendation of the sources, critical analysis of fact and opinion, leading to the forming of objective, impartial conclusions—were quite remote from their experience and interests. And when he declared that Macaulay and Carlyle were failures as historians because they had not observed these procedures, the consternation of the older members is easy to imagine. For Macaulay and Carlyle were the two most popular writers of history in the English language during the nineteenth century; they had done more than anyone else to establish a literary tradition of epic narrative which informed and uplifted the reader.

In 1828 Macaulay had described history as 'a compound of poetry and philosophy'. In 1902 the Cambridge professor J.B. Bury declared that it was 'a science, no less and no more'. Melbourne's canons of historical method were based on this later view which derived from the great German historians of the nineteenth century—Niebuhr, Mommsen and, above all, Ranke. It was Ranke, said Bury's predecessor at Cambridge, who was 'the real originator of the heroic study of records'. Ranke insisted on the objectivity of historical truth (history 'as it was', in his celebrated phrase), the priority of facts over concepts and the need to establish the facts by critical study of the primary sources. 'True knowledge', he wrote, 'lies in the knowledge of the facts . . .' From the patient verification of the documentary record, a new school of historians came to expect an accumulation of factual knowledge that would permit the application of inductive methods to produce scientific history.

Even in the late nineteenth century the impact of these procedures began to be felt in Australia. Bonwick had criticised Macaulay for 'faulty research and party prejudice': his own method, he said, was to search for 'absolute truth' in official documents. Rusden, Turner and the Victorian-born lawyer F.P. Labilliere made much of their pioneering work in the Public Record Office in London and were quick to criticise others for taking their guidance from second-hand accounts instead of checking them against the original sources. Yet the emphasis on verisimilitude was more polemical than methodological. Bonwick was merely declaring the duty of an honest chronicler. Rusden and Turner continued to work in the older tradition of literary history where the accumulation of authentic detail created a density of narrative texture that augmented the power of rhetorical suggestion.

The doctrines of 'scientific history' found their home in Australia in the same place that they found it in Britain—in the universities. The turning of history into a new kind of specialised intellectual activity also converted it into a professional discipline. It used to be that the writing of good history called for a good man applying ordinary powers of judgment to the record of the past. Scientific history, on the other hand, introduced new standards and procedures, called for technical skills and was directed to a new, more specialised audience.

The transmission of the new practices from Cambridge, Oxford and London to the tiny Australian universities was a slow process. Since the universities of Queensland and Western Australia were not created until the eve of World War I, and Tasmania did not teach history, there were in fact only three centres where the subject was professed. Melbourne's first professor of history and political economy, W.E. Hearn, was a classical scholar who had practised at the Dublin Bar before taking up his post in 1855. Somewhere in between his teaching (in 1871 he delivered 30 lectures a week in history, classics, literature, philosophy and political economy) and other duties, he found time to write a major work of political economy, but historical research was out of the question.

Hearn's successor, appointed in 1879, left a reputation for bellicosity and an impressive collection of empty bottles when his house in the university grounds was cleared upon his retirement in 1912, but little else. 'I have work in hand but I have not committed myself to anything very extensive in book form so far', he said after 23 years in the chair. He was followed by (Sir) Ernest Scott who earned the position by writing several books while a Hansard reporter and certainly appreciated the importance of original research, but had little formal training.

In Sydney G.A. Wood became the first professor of history in 1891. He had been educated at Oxford in the 1880s when the transformation was only just beginning and undergraduate studies were intended not as professional preparation but as training for life.

The first academic to bring the gospel of scientific history to Australia was G.C. Henderson, a student of Wood at Sydney who proceeded to Oxford in 1894 and read Modern History, a course of study that had passed into the hands of specialists since Wood had taken it a decade earlier. In 1902 Henderson took up the chair of modern history and English language at Adelaide. He was hardly a narrowly professional historian but he did bring an evangelical enthusiasm for the disciplinary innovations (and passed it on to A.C.V. Melbourne, the first of his students to achieve first class honours).

Henderson's own views on the discipline were delivered as a presidential address to a meeting of the Australasian Association for the Advancement of Science in 1911, the first at which historians constituted a section. His purpose was to show how the study of Australian history could be undertaken in a 'systematic and scientific way'. Previous attempts to tell the story of this country, he said, had been vitiated by bias. Rusden was singled out for writing not history but 'a brief extending over 2090 pages'. The task of the universities was therefore to train and equip students with an understanding of the techniques of research:

> My argument may be summed up in a few words. The time has arrived when the history of the Commonwealth should be undertaken in a systematic and scientific way, and the institutions through which that might be done are the universities. The historical work done there at present is preparatory, and should find its fulfilment in research.

These views soon won general acceptance. Scott, for example, became an ardent exponent of the proposition that historians followed precise sequential procedures that ensured the authenticity of their results. First came an investigation of 'the truth about the past' by estimating facts and probabilities; then came a critical evaluation of the sources and step-by-step analysis, leading to a text which was completed with 'the virtuous habit of verification'.

The emphasis here fell on technique. Australian pronouncements on scientific history were

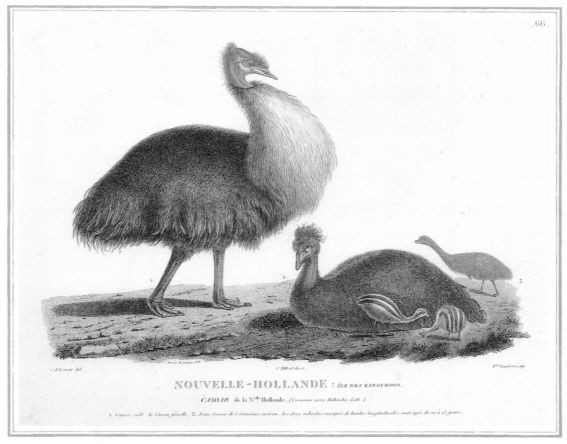

*Some of the earliest European historical records of Australia were drawings of flora and fauna by parties
of explorers. This family of emus was drawn by Frenchman C.A. Lesueur on Kangaroo Island.*

more concerned with the establishment of facts than their interpretation, happier to contemplate the heaping up of properly researched theses and monographs than with searching for their larger meaning. Criticism was applied to the sources of evidence but seldom to the theoretical basis of the discipline, its historiographical principles and presuppositions. Even today, the scholarly writing of history in this country is characterised by a sober restraint; it tends to eschew speculation and to venerate ordinary common sense; it mistrusts abstractions and prefers factual reportage. Dr Watson merely carried these habits to excess when he wrote to Professor Wood towards the end of his editorial labours on the *Historical records of Australia* and boasted, 'I have now written twenty-one books but have never advanced a theory. At the same time I have discredited numberless theories and exploded many so-called facts'.

By 1945 Eris O'Brien was able to distinguish three phases in Australian historical scholarship. First came the chroniclers and controversialists who recorded and interpreted the past but 'were not scientific historians'. Next came the industrious analysts of the second half of the nineteenth century, but they too 'lacked the scientific approach and quoted annoyingly without a full identification of sources'. Finally there was the scientific school, characterised by thorough research, exactness in references and a 'sound unbiased interpretation of history'.

The surgeon Watson and the prelate O'Brien were among the rare exceptions that Henderson had allowed to his prediction that scientific history would be undertaken in the universities. Thirty-eight years later, when the president of the history section of ANZAAS declared that Australian history had finally attained maturity, the terms of approval he bestowed were 'professional', 'academic' and 'scholarly'. Historical writing had become a specialised discourse written, he said, by graduates for graduates. Certainly, much writing took place outside the academy and some of it reached a respectable standard. 'If it is "professional", however, its conventions, methods of presentation and standards of evidence, are those set in universities.'

The professionalisation of Australian history proceeded slowly at first but with gathering momentum. Between the wars, with hardly more than a dozen full-time posts in all the universities, it was scarcely possible to embark on a career in the discipline except by patience and good fortune. Specialisation was out of the question. There was no full-year course in Australian history until 1927, no full-time lecturer in the subject until 1948. Opportunities for postgraduate study were few and there was no research institution until the Australian National University was established in 1947. Chances of publication were similarly restricted: none of the universities possessed a press until 1923 and there was no academic historical journal until 1940.

Until the end of World War II, therefore, the serious study of Australian history was restricted to small groups of honours students who might reach high standards—Keith Hancock thought their work comparable in quality, if not in quantity, to that of the honours schools of Oxford and Cambridge—but seldom continued beyond their graduation. Those who sought further training usually went overseas. No PhD in history was awarded by an Australian university until 1947; indeed, a listing of postgraduate research theses found that only 58 MAs were completed before 1945.

Yet 252 theses were written between 1945 and 1955, a level of productivity that was maintained over the next decade and increased in the one following. Today there are university history departments with more than one hundred postgraduate candidates on their books. The statistics for the publication of academic history books follow a similar trajectory: 11 for 1951–55, 33 for 1956–60, 63 for 1961–65 and 88 for 1966–70 (approximately two-thirds had Australian subjects). Similarly, the number of journal articles concerned with Australian history increased during the period as regional and specialist journals were established to cater for the growth in demand and supply. Religious, Aboriginal, migration, urban, sporting and military history were just some of the fields to emerge from within the history departments and develop their own concerns and procedures. Other specialisms, such as the history of education, art, law and medicine, developed within their parent disciplines, while economic history and the history of science were more commonly autonomous. Each of these subdisciplines produced its own increasingly esoteric literature.

These dramatic developments were made possible, of course, by the remarkable expansion of tertiary education after World War II. Whereas before the war there were fewer than twenty full-time history posts, by 1973 there were more than four hundred posts in mainstream history, probably another hundred practising elsewhere in the universities, and perhaps a further two hundred in other tertiary bodies. A clear career path had become established. The aspirant academic had first to take a sufficiently good degree to win a postgraduate scholarship; alternatively, apprenticeship as a tutor might be combined with part-time research. In either case his or her energies would be focused for a number of years on one major piece of writing. A doctorate, preferably leading to a monograph or published articles, was usually required to secure a permanent position. The requirements that the thesis be based on a substantial corpus of primary sources and make 'an original contribution to knowledge' had severely restrictive effects.

One critic lamented the 'desperate hunt for some subject which might conceivably be accepted and which no-one so far had thought of doing'. Another deplored how the 'ordeal by thesis' forced a narrow specialisation. These are perhaps harsh judgments. The thesis writer was expected to locate the research topic within the existing literature and there was no shortage of unworked topics. Nevertheless, a prudent candidate avoided the unconventional and anchored interpretative originality in a solid substratum of empirical data. The postgraduate thesis proceeded on the methodology of scientific history and enshrined a mode of precise, sober, cumulative knowledge.

It was inevitable that the procedures of academic scholarship, backed as they were by the resources, prestige and intellectual authority of the universities, would press in on other practitioners. The process was a complex one and cannot be reduced to any simple differentiation of those within and without academia. There were, for example, historians who had worked outside universities and whose writings commanded respect: H.V. Evatt and J.V. Barry, R.W. Giblin and Eris O'Brien, Marjorie Barnard and Marnie Bassett—the list of first-rate independent scholars is far from complete. There was the indisputable achievement of the war histories, the World War I series largely written by C.E.W. Bean, the World War II series by Gavin Long, neither of whom possessed professional qualifications. There was the lawyer Sir John Ferguson, a great collector in the tradition of Mitchell and Dixson, whose *Bibliography of Australia* in seven volumes (1941–69) remains the starting point for bibliographic research. And there was M.H. Ellis, biographer of Macarthur and Macquarie, and scourge of academics. Right up to the 1950s, therefore, there was no hierarchy of professional and amateur. Indeed, *Historical studies* announced in its first issue that it was meant to serve both the 'specialist student' and the 'general reader', and its annual survey of 'Writings on Australian history' included both the specialist monograph and the commemorative local history.

Already, however, there was a tendency to pronounce judgment on the latter according to the standards of the former. More than this, there was a subtle but insistent pressure on all scholars to conform to the new, uniform standards. The process can be observed quite early in G.A. Wood's rejection, in a paper delivered to the Australian Historical Society in 1917, of George Collingridge's claims for the Portuguese discovery of Australia. While acknowledging the older man's erudition, Wood couched his refutation in the courteous but faintly patronising terms of a trained historian. 'It has come rather as a shock to me that so learned a man as Professor Wood has proved himself to be, should differ from me', confessed Collingridge. The irony, as Professor Spate has recently observed, is that the amateur, for all his interpretative excesses and the deficiences of his exposition, was right. Subsequent examples of the same kind could be given but the case of labour history offers a particularly instructive example.

SCHOLARSHIP AND SOCIAL PURPOSE: THE CASE OF LABOUR HISTORY

The labour movement had long possessed a commemorative literature. It began as early as 1888 when John Norton, who would become notorious as the muckraking editor of *Truth*, solicited contributions from statisticians, politicians and trade union organisers, and grafted them onto an international survey to produce what he called a *History of capital and labour*. Norton wrote at the apogee of the Workingman's Paradise and insisted that whereas Old World historians were preoccupied with 'the pageants and pleasures of courts and courtiers', New World histories must be popular since in Australia 'it is working classes who are making history'.

Other writings in this celebratory tradition included the New South Wales parliamentarian George Black's *Labor in politics* (1893), the Melbourne Trades Hall secretary W.E. Murphy's *History of the eight hours movement* (1896) and the labour organiser and senator W.G. Spence's *Australia's awakening* (1909). Alongside them stood more critical commentators such as V.G. Childe who in *How Labour governs* (1923) subjected the objectives and methods of the mainstream labour movement to fundamental criticism, or H.V. Evatt who in his biography of an *Australian labour leader* (1940) pondered the dilemmas of the parliamentary reformer. We may include here also the massive *Labour and industry in Australia* in four volumes (1919) written by the New South Wales statistician Sir Timothy Coghlan after he went to London as agent-general in 1905. Coghlan wrote here in a somewhat different tone from that which characterised his earlier work. He was still a sympathetic critic of the labour movement, still concerned to show how it had benefited from material progress, but mindful in the light of recent reverses, of the stern laws of political economy. He wrote to Prime Minister Deakin in 1906 that 'I would have completed the book long ago but for my difficulty in determining the causes which gave workers so little in the way of comfort, in spite of the enormous progress of recent years'.

Finally, and above all, there was Brian Fitzpatrick's attempt to comprehend the forces that shaped Australian class relations and the historical experience of the working class. His two books of economic history (*British imperialism in Australia 1788–1833*, 1939, and *The British Empire in*

Australia, 1941), two extended essays (*The Australian people 1788–1945*, 1946, and *The Australian commonwealth*, 1956) and *A short history of the Australian labour movement* (1940) were all organised around his celebrated credo: 'I have taken the view that the history of the Australian people is amongst other things the history of a struggle between the organised rich and the organised poor'.

A graduate of the University of Melbourne where he studied under Scott, Fitzpatrick never obtained a permanent academic post. Both his politics and his erratic lifestyle were used to justify this injustice and when he submitted his two major works to the university to support an application for a doctorate of letters, the external examiners found them wanting. They condemned his faulty organisation, his uncritical use of evidence ('he has depended too much on the *History of capital and labour*. This not very reliable book was published in 1888') and his bias ('the anxiety of the author to prove his thesis blinds his critical judgement'). Fitzpatrick returned a healthy contempt for conservative fact-grubbers. As a young man he had written a poem, 'Against pedants':

> Thus shall I bare the mystery
> Of sundry pedants' history
> The which my stark researches
> Shall tumble from their perches.
>
> For all they said
> Was borrowed lore
> Of books they'd read
> The night before.

This antagonism did not weaken. 'The origins of the people are not in the library' was the title Fitzpatrick chose for an address he gave to ANZAAS in 1954. His own writings had to be fitted into various commitments: he was the founder and secretary of the Australian Council for Civil Liberties; he produced newsletters on current affairs, advised trade unions and the Labor party, and took part in the great campaigns of his day. But for all the hardships caused by the need to earn a living, there was an intimate relationship between his activities and his scholarship. His writings possess a protean quality, alternately disdaining the conventional apparatus of footnote references or using them to compile idiosyncratic running commentaries on people and events, but refusing steadfastly to conform to the academic norms of equable evenhandedness.

Consider, then, Fitzpatrick's successors, the generation of left-wing historians who found places in the universities since the end of World War II. Lloyd Churchward, Miriam Dixson,

This poster advertising Labor speakers at the Sydney Town Hall demonstrates the growing faith in a united labour force. Poster by Martin, c1939.
NATIONAL LIBRARY

Eric Fry, Noel Ebbels, Robin Gollan, June Phillip, Ian Turner, Russel Ward—to name just some of them—shared Fitzpatrick's sympathies with the labour movement and made it the subject of their postgraduate research. Although the expansion of higher education offered them opportunities that had been denied to their mentor, their careers were not untroubled by political discrimination. Nor did they seek a cloistered academic tranquillity—historical research was combined with, and in some cases delayed by, other more urgent commitments. The very formation of the Australian Society for the Study of Labour History was an extension of these loyalties. Writing in the first issue of the society's journal, *Labour history*, Gollan said that it would be of 'immediate practical value to the labour movement' properly to understand its own past, and of equal significance to redress the neglect of the working class in the intellectual culture. Labour history as a genre was a product of the meeting of the committed activist and the academy.

But could this delicate balance be maintained? Even in the postgraduate theses of this group, strains were apparent. Compare, for example, the sweep and immediacy of Ian Turner's essays in cultural history with his monograph *Industrial labour and politics* (1975), which began life as a doctoral dissertation. Here already was the notion of a specialised academic discourse to which the initiate had to conform, a body of knowledge with its own language and conventions which subsumed labour history. The notion was taken further by more conservative academics, one of whom insisted in 1967 that labour history 'is no more and no less than one of the institutional kinds of historical specialism ... it has no distinctive techniques, dogmas or permanent characteristics which distinguish it qualitatively from other kinds of history'. To see labour history thus was to freeze out those who could not participate in the institutional specialisation and would not conform to its proprieties. Thus Joe Harris, a Queensland trade unionist, noted in the preface to his *Bitter fight* (1970), a pictorial history of the early labour movement, that 'some who have read the manuscript complain of the stridently partisan tone'. To their credit, the editors of *Labour history* have resisted pressures to turn their journal into a narrowly academic publication, but the overwhelming majority of its contributors are based in universities and it has many more readers there than in the unions.

GROWING UNEASE

The undesirable consequences of professionalisation were soon apparent. Even in the 1950s one professor lamented the 'over-adherence to specialism, to professionalism, to scientism', which led to 'an arid professionalism bordering on pedantry'; another deplored the 'meticulous investigation of small periods or problems' at the expense of any larger vision. University historians, it was warned, would lose their larger audience if they continued to address themselves exclusively to their colleagues. They had lost the ability to entertain or instruct a reading public which turned instead to more popular writers who could help them make sense of the past, writers such as Robin Boyd, Donald Horne, Craig McGregor and J.D. Pringle.

By the early 1970s, when employment opportunities in the universities contracted sharply, there was a critical self-awareness of the structure of the profession itself, its insularity, hierarchical structure and stolid conformity to masculine, middle-class orthodoxies. In the very formation in 1974 of a professional body, the Australian Historical Association, this unease can be detected. Here, as elsewhere, the progress of historical scholarship in Australia conformed to European and North American precedents, though the diminutive size of Australian universities until the second half of the twentieth century meant that we tended to lag some way behind. Indeed, it was the truncated time-span of history's full professional status that heightened the sense of certainty.

How could academics reach the wider audience? Hitherto the task had been performed by the short history, that distinctive hybrid of the narrative textbook and the interpretative essay, adequate in its coverage to serve for teaching purposes yet sufficiently succinct and vivid to appeal to the general reader. The genre began with the journalist A.W. Jose whose *Short history of Australasia* (1899) became a *History of Australia* (1914) and passed through fifteen editions.

Another journalist, Thomas Dunbabin, achieved minor success with *The making of Australasia* (1922).

Both were outstripped, however, by the professor of history at the University of Melbourne, Ernest Scott, whose *Short history of Australia* (1916) remained in print for more than half a century. The book's pedagogic intent is revealed by its chronological tables, lists of governors and ministries, and breaking down of chapters into classroom topics. Even so, Scott intended his *Short history* to answer 'such questions as might reasonably be put to it by an intelligent reader', and he offered that lay reader a strong storyline of national progress and development. The first edition appeared less than a year after the Gallipoli landing and proclaimed that 'This Short History of Australia begins with a blank space on the map and ends with the record of a new name on the map, that of Anzac'. Later editions simply continued the story.

By contrast, Keith Hancock's *Australia* (published in 1930 but written before the plunge into economic depression) was very much the product of a particular juncture. In it the young professor, who had recently returned to his country after several years abroad, found his compatriots to be living in a fool's paradise. The vantage point—that of a liberal lamenting the excesses of a stridently radical nationalism—was hardly new, but the book's impact was augmented by the crisis that had overtaken Australia by the time it appeared. Furthermore, as its author appreciated, it relied 'not upon specialist knowledge and technique, but upon an Australian's capacity to see his own country both sympathetically and critically, both at close view and in the perspective of history'.

The breadth of Hancock's perspective, the quality of his writing and the urgency of his concern combined to give the work a force that no other interpretative essay has approached. Neither G.V. Portus, *Australia, an economic interpretation* (1933), nor F.L.W. Wood, *A concise history of Australia* (1935), were able to rival it, though the American C. Hartley Grattan earned a deserved reputation for the shrewd transPacific insights of *Introducing Australia* (1942). Then the expansion of higher secondary and tertiary education encouraged a clutch of new short histories, each of which achieved its own interpretative coherence. In *Australia* (1952), R.M. Crawford revealed something of the spirit of postwar reconstruction and a confidence that he affirmed in his subsequent *An Australian perspective* (1960). Russel Ward expounded a radical and nationalist viewpoint in *Australia* (1965), while Douglas Pike wrote more conservatively of *Australia: the quiet continent* (1962). C.M.H. Clark foreshadowed his prophetic vision in *A short history of Australia* (1963) and A.G.L. Shaw eschewed all extremes in *The story of Australia* (1955).

From the mid-1960s, however, the genre fell from favour. To explain its demise it is tempting to point to the purely technical difficulty of mastering a vast and rapidly growing body of monographs and articles. Back in 1921 an academic in the full flush of scholarly enthusiasm had suggested that 'it is time that we stopped writing histories of Australia and wrote Australian history' in the form of specialist studies, since 'without such a series of detailed and exhaustive studies it is impossible to write any good survey of Australian history'. Forty years later the situation was so different that another professor was close to despair. The volume of research literature threatened to stifle the 'bold hypotheses that lent brilliance and distinction to the works of predecessors less encumbered by other men's researches'.

The expectation that the general historian could serve as the grand synthesiser was breaking down under the volume and heterogeneity of the raw material. Just as the interpretation of the past had become a specialist skill, so the mastery of particular topics and periods seemed to require the concentrated attention of an expert. In this spirit the Australian volume of the *Cambridge history of the British Empire* (1933) had been farmed out to a number of writers, and so too were *Australia: a social and political history* edited by Gordon Greenwood (1955) and *A new history of Australia* edited by Frank Crowley (1974). Similarly, the history slice volumes of the series *Australians: a historical library* were distributed among specialists.

The wider readership of the best short histories was served instead by freelance writers like Michael Cannon and R.M. Younger, and quite exceptional academics like C.M.H. Clark and Geoffrey Blainey. Clark, in the massive narrative *History of Australia* (1962–), and Blainey, with his distinctive treatment of a wide range of subjects, cut across the grain of academic history. Both are conscious stylists, addressing themselves directly to the reader without the encumbrance of a weighty scholarly apparatus. Both are prophets, convinced that they have something to say. But the suspicion of Clark's and Blainey's colleagues towards their popularity tells us a good deal about the unease of academic history. Similarly, the flight from academia of Humphrey McQueen, among the gifted of the next generation, is symptomatic of professional constraints.

But the crisis of the profession goes deeper than this. It is not simply a matter of narrow specialisations and closed forms of communication. More fundamentally, many historians are no longer sure that they have anything to say. Along with the society in which they live, they have lost their sense of the imminence of the past. Since the modern age no longer feels itself to be living under the shadow of previous generations, it no longer expects to find guidance or enlightenment there. If Macaulay or Carlyle were nineteenth-century sages with an enormous following because they could make sense of the dramatic changes of their time, the same function in our time has been usurped by economists and sociologists whose explanations have no temporal dimension. If John West mobilised opinion against the transportation of convicts by writing its history, a modern penal reformer will use electronic media rather than print, and his arguments will be as immediate and transitory as the images that appear on the television.

For a time the academic historians actively resisted the demise of their discipline as a source of wisdom. An older generation that included Wood, Henderson and Portus—liberals all—had simply assumed the educational responsibilities of their station. By studying the growth of progress and freedom, students could be expected to emerge better citizens, morally as well as intellectually improved by their training. The early profession was characterised by its secularised social conscience. There were obvious precedents, given the ecclesiastical character of the English university system, for a man of religion to turn from the pulpit to the lecture theatre; the example of Portus illustrates that this did not necessarily entail a loss of faith. (Nor did the close relationship between the two end here: Hancock, Clark, Crowley and Blainey are all sons of the manse.) In most cases the transition redirected energies into a high-minded civic humanism.

The subsequent generation, whose formative experiences were war, depression and the crisis of democracy, could no longer assume these verities. R.M. Crawford, a student of Wood and the most responsive of the younger generation to these challenges, has recalled how, under the pressure of these circumstances,

> The pleasing art of historical narration was at times elbowed out by the insistent demand that the past must somehow illuminate the present, that history must find answers to the problems that beset and bedevilled us. Analysis and discussion came more and more to replace the telling of a story . . .

On the eve of World War II and just two years after taking up the chair at Melbourne, Crawford delivered the presidential address to the history section of ANZAAS. It was a plea for a more rigorous historical method, not a determinist science of history because that would leave no room for freedom and moral judgment, but for a 'synoptic method' that could uncover the pattern of interrelationships within which societies exercised their freedom. Crawford's address grew out of the 'theory and method' class he conducted with his honours students, an innovation that was adopted in other universities. The introduction of theory and method brought a new self-awareness and sophistication to the work of Australian historians, the fruits of which were seen in the better writings of the 1950s and 1960s.

Crawford and his colleagues pursued these problems of historical knowledge further after the war. For a time Crawford was attracted to the proposition that historians should formulate general laws after the scientific model, though he accepted subsequently that he was here 'flogging a dead horse', and retreated to the view that history was a craft, rather than a science, the ultimate purpose of which lay in the preservation of essential values of good order and liberty, rationality and morality. This was the same humanist, civilising purpose that Greenwood had defended against the effects of professionalisation when he insisted that 'The ultimate value of history lies in the begetting of wisdom and the acquisition of a cultivated mind'. And, as he recognised, it was already giving way to the sophisticated amorality of modern scholarship.

Most historians today are indifferent to larger historiographical problems, and the indignant reception accorded to Rob Pascoe's *The manufacture of Australian history* (1979) reflects their unease. Theory and method, where it is still taught to undergraduates, is but an artificial appendage to training in specialised areas with their own literatures, assumptions and techniques. It cannot resist the relativism engendered by the modern syllabus, nor can it check ingrained habits of destructive criticism. A graduate is therefore adept in showing how Smith has qualified Jones's reinterpretation of Evans on the local government reforms of the 1890s. As to the place of those events in the sweep of history, the basis on which they are being investigated or the reasons for doing so—here the training offers little guidance. Scholarship of this sort offers little room for the sense of critical engagement with the larger issues that Crawford kept in view. His tradition of liberal scholarship has passed.

So too has the broad interpretative framework with which most Australian historians worked up to the 1960s. This can be characterised as a progressive or radical nationalism, a belief that the main thrust of Australian history was the movement of its people—whose distinctive characteristics included a stoic resourcefulness, egalitarian 'mateship' and a distrust of wealth, status and authority—towards self-realisation. The generic description given to this viewpoint was 'the Whig interpretation of Australian history', thereby linking it with earlier records of national progress and suggesting that they all postulated an irresistible advance towards a predetermined destination.

Perhaps that puts it too strongly. The radical nationalist interpretation, as it took form and substance in the 1950s, served not as an orthodoxy but as a framework. It was simple, practical and coherent, in the best traditions of vernacular architecture. Like a woolshed, it lent itself to the use of local materials and allowed subsequent hands to build, skillion-fashion, onto the main structure without impairing its coherence. The skeleton was taken from the popular writers of the late nineteenth century. Later writers such as Vance and Nettie Palmer and Brian Fitzpatrick consolidated that rudimentary original structure; cultural historians like A.A. Phillips and Russel Ward extended it to take in ballads and popular literature; labour historians like Gollan and Turner showed how the organised working class was its heir and custodian; novelists like Katharine Susannah Prichard used it for historial fiction, or, like Marjorie Barnard, explored both fictional and non-fictional forms.

This radical nationalist account of Australian history was at once a celebration of past achievement and a yardstick for measuring further progress. But it came under attack from both right and left. In 1962 the conservative commentator Peter Coleman announced a 'Counter-revolution in Australian historiography'. Drawing on a number of recent publications, and especially on Manning Clark's 'Re-writing Australian history' (1956), he claimed that the 'standard radical leftist interpretation of Australian history' could no longer be sustained. Its denial of the contributions of the middle class, the churches, the universities and non-radical reformers was patently restrictive, its naive humanism was discredited and its assumption of unfolding social progress was confounded.

Even as this battle was joined, fresh assaults came from a young generation of radicals. Some said that the bearer of the radical tradition, the labour movement, was compromised fatally by its involvement in and preoccupation with exploitative class relations. Some dwelt on the less attractive aspects of the national character, the reliance on great and powerful friends to allay regional insecurity, the authoritarianism and ready recourse to violence, the xenophobia and racial discrimination. Some objected to the subordination of women within the received account and, more generally, to the overwhelmingly masculine character of Australian historiography —for even though there had been women historians since the beginning of the century, there had so far been no history of women. The publication of Miriam Dixson's *The real Matilda* (1975) and Anne Summers' *Damned whores and god's police* (1975) marks the beginning of what is undoubtedly an important challenge to conventional historiography.

Each of these concerns—class, race and gender—has generated a substantial literature over recent years, but it has not been easy to bring them together and reconstitute an overview. The predominant tone of this work has been profoundly pessimistic. It reveals such an extensive record of oppression that it is doubtful whether the past can provide guidance more fruitful than cautionary examples. Some would argue that the enterprise is in any case futile. They see the very project of national history as one that cannot withstand modern criticism, either because its categories ('nation', 'people', etc) dissolve in the acid-bath of critical analysis, or because they reject the very idea of unitary historical time. Nor have the conservative critics carried through their much-vaunted counter-revolution to produce a substantial interpretation of their own. They remain revisionists rather than expositors. In short, the very project of finding an Australian historical identity has fallen into discredit. A recent critical review of the search for a national character suggested that all such characterisations are only intellectual constructs. As its author puts it, there *is* no real Australia; there are only ideologues *Inventing Australia*.

PROSPECTS

Despite all these strictures, the invention, production and consumption of the Australian past proceeds apace. As part of a rapidly expanding tourist industry, it is presented in museums, preservation areas of old townships and the fanciful pretensions of new ones; Tasmanians are told that theirs is 'the history isle', Victorians are invited to 'hop into heritage'. As the subject of popular literature, television series and cinema (the overwhelming majority of successful Australian feature films during the 1970s were set in an age of innocence), it is the raw material of the entertainment industry. Institutional commemorations come thick and fast and no school centenary is complete without its dress-up celebration. Western Australia, Victoria, South Australia and now the commonwealth have sponsored ambitious celebrations to commemorate their 150th and 200th anniversaries. Politicians from both major parties compete in ersatz Australianism. There is a sharp irony in the fact that as historians have retreated from national history, its influence as a cultural artefact has become increasingly strong.

It is all too tempting to poke fun at such ventures. The commercial undertakings foster a romanticised nostalgia, as sanitised as the bloodless floggings at Old Sydney Town. They reduce the past to an object of consumption. Like the pioneer legend they often invoke, official commemorations lean to a view that the past is free from misery or conflict. They reduce the past to a litany of affirmation. Similarly, when certain politicians cite the Eureka uprising as a statement of stern individualism and a precedent for tax resistance, or when mining magnates invoke nineteenth-century land settlement against environmentalism or Aboriginal land rights, they are doing something more than finding spurious precedents. They are making history into a tyrant. By invoking the strength of Australian history as an outside force which dominates the present by an authority derived from an irrevocable past, they leave no alternative but submission.

To rest the matter there would be to accept the continuous antagonism between academic and vulgar, and to leave unchallenged the assumption that the latter kind of history is foisted, ready-made, on to consumers. In fact there is considerable evidence of a genuine and autonomous interest in the past, of a popular memory which exists independently of and often in opposition to the dominant memory. The popular memory assumes various forms. It is tapped by oral history, especially in the community-based projects that have burgeoned recently. It is present in family history whose recent popularity is surely one of the most extraordinary manifestations of modern rootlessness. It animates the poetic imagination of Les Murray and it finds lyrical expression in the writing of Eric Rolls. But mostly the popular memory is left to play on the restricted range of commercial and institutional material that is put before it. There is here an enormous opportunity for historians to enlarge and enrich the practice of their discipline. Clearly, many will continue to work along existing lines of development and we may expect to learn from their specialist researches. Others, surely, will accept the challenge to trace the connections between the past and the present, and to give shape and meaning to life in this country.

I
RESOURCES FOR AUSTRALIAN STUDIES

Bookplate incorporating embossed lettering, by Lloyd Rees, 1978. Private libraries have played a significant part in preserving Australia's historical records. Private collections of books and documents, such as that presented by David Scott Mitchell to the State Library of New South Wales, form the basis of many state collections of historical resources.

PAT CORRIGAN

A REA STUDIES, defined as the examination of the total environment of a geographic or political area, are relatively new in the academic world. Borne on the wave of the postwar spread of higher education, the quest for a reassessment of the universities' objectives brought with it a demand for less esoteric approaches to knowledge and a craving for 'relevance'—though few would have been able to define what relevance really meant. In that climate of educational opinion, area studies were seen as a suitable discipline, representing a positive and deliberate endeavour to explain the constitution and behaviour of people and institutions, as well as the origin and significance of the artefacts of an area, while trying to ensure that sight of the whole was not lost through an overemphasis on detail.

Various difficulties have to be overcome if area studies are to have solid foundations, and for the traditional agents of conservation—librarians, archivists, museum and gallery curators—the demands of this new approach to academic research present considerable challenge. Leaving aside, for the moment, the question of whether these agents should be, above all, custodians and preservers of the tangible evidence of the past or whether they should be active facilitators of research, there can be no doubt that the 'new teaching' and the modernist approach to research require from them a wider awareness of evidence than was needed when academic and scholarly activities were based on more traditional methods.

Librarians, archivists and museum and gallery curators are now obliged to extend their professional horizon and cultivate at least an awareness of each other's field of expertise. They must be able to determine what type of historical and cultural evidence is held in each repository. An example of this approach would be a request to provide literary and material evidence for a history of transport in Australia, a subject that requires documents from government and private archives, literature from libraries holding Australian books and journals, and a range of technical equipment, whose design and refinement determined the progress of the transport industries.

This section presents an overview of the rich resources held by archives, libraries, museums and galleries for Australian studies. There are already a number of published guides describing the holdings of these four types of institutions, but none attempts to deal with more than one kind of repository at a time. Obviously this prevents the student of Australian studies from recognising the vital interrelationship of the multiform evidence for an understanding of Australian life and customs, history, economics and politics, agriculture, science and medicine, religion, leisure and sport. We have therefore brought together appropriate comments and descriptions in this volume.

Abraham Lincolne, Kangaroo hunt. *Pencil and wash from a sketchbook,* Australian sketches, *1838–44. The bizarre colonial sport of hunting kangaroos with dogs is described in detail alongside this drawing. Lincolne's sketchbook was a personal record of his travels in New South Wales.*
MITCHELL LIBRARY

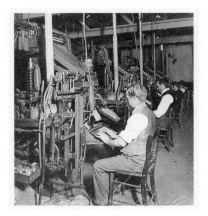

Private and presentation albums can yield rare insights into the technology and condition of nineteenth- and early twentieth-century workplaces. These undated photographs of the interior of a printery are from the collection of the Printing and Kindred Industries Union, Adelaide.
ANU ARCHIVES OF BUSINESS AND LABOUR

CHAPTER 2

ARCHIVES

ELIZABETH NATHAN

I T IS NOT EASY to define archives: the word is used both for the institution and for the records it holds. The terminology presents no difficulties while we are dealing with traditional archival institutions, which form a specialised part of the organisation whose records they keep. Among these are government archives, university archives and the archives of private organisations such as banks and large corporations. Difficulties arise when we have to deal with collecting institutions, established because of our increasing concern that original historical material should be preserved for research use. Some of these bodies are called archives and some are not, but all apply archival principles to their holdings and are likely to have in their custody the archives of a number of organisations or individuals as well as other original records.

To complicate matters further, a recent innovation is to employ the singular word, 'archive', to describe a specialised collection of material in a particular form (such as film, sound recording or computer tape) or related to a particular subject area. When we add to this the tendency to make a neat division between published and unpublished material, placing archives in the latter category, it will be understood that there are problems in giving a clear definition. In fact, not all archives consist of unpublished material, nor are all collections of original or unpublished material properly described as archives.

Any organisation, large or small, creates records in the course of its operations. These records will of course vary: some will be of temporary value only and may be destroyed when they are no longer needed; others will be kept, either because they contain evidence of legal or property transactions, or because they record matters of administrative or historical importance to the organisation. Such records become archives and any organisation of standing is likely to have some arrangement for preserving its older records. Material transferred to this area—itself usually referred to as 'the archives'—is certainly not confined to written records; any document, including a printed work or object which has some significance to the operations may legitimately form part of the archives.

Archives existed long before libraries or museums, as is clear from archaeological finds such as clay tablets bearing information stored away by ancient rulers or administrators. The great empires of antiquity also maintained archives, which were dispersed or destroyed as they fell to invaders. Most European archives were founded to care for surviving ancient and mediaeval documents, and for a long time the training of archivists involved the teaching of skills needed to understand such documents, such as mediaeval Latin, abbreviations and the study of seals.

The beginnings of modern archival theory are attributed to a French revolutionary decree of 1794, which opened the archives to public scrutiny as part of the attack on hereditary privileges and land rights. This necessitated the development of systems of arrangement and control, and produced the basic principle of *respect des fonds*, which means that documents should be kept together in terms of their provenance. The concept of provenance includes when and why the records were created and their subsequent location and ownership. It also means that records created by a corporate body are always linked with that body, even if they have subsequently been inherited by another body, irrespective of changing national boundaries and the consequent transfer from one nation to another of certain legal and administrative records.

Related to this is the principle that the original order of the records be maintained—that is, they should as far as possible be kept as they were in the office that created them. The context of the information contained in the documents can be as important as the information itself for a historical understanding of the event or transaction.

Scholars often find that records kept by a body for its own use contain unvarnished facts, or at least the contemporary perception of what the facts were, and that they contain a low incidence of distortion for ulterior motives. This is what makes archives a prime source of historical information, even if only to check the veracity or probability of more detailed and colourful personal accounts of events.

A major distinction between public and private archival records is that the records of government are subject to legislation covering their public availability, while private records, whether of huge corporations or of individuals, remain private property. In Australia today there is a variety of legislation covering the management and accessibility of government records and an even greater variety of institutions holding private archives and manuscripts.

PUBLIC RECORDS

The records of government provide extensive sources for Australian studies. Australia has eight separate legislatures, each with an independent administrative structure, and an extensive network of local government in every state. Settlement in Australia was from the beginning a government enterprise, dominated by public administrators even before Governor Phillip set sail with the first fleet. Practically every facet of colonial life was controlled, encouraged, regulated or subsidised by government.

The availability of public records to anyone who wishes to carry out research into early history or to compile a family tree is a fairly recent development. Not so long ago, convict records were firmly restricted from public access and Australian historians were forced to travel to London to do their basic research.

That so many early records have survived—such as the remarkably intact correspondence of the Colonial Secretary's Office in New South Wales from 1826 on—cannot be attributed to any realisation by nineteenth-century officials that posterity would find them useful for historical research. It is rather that the records constitute an organisation's corporate memory, and the administrators are naturally inclined to preserve the memory for possible future use. Even in today's offices, the secondary storage area for retired files is referred to as the archives and old records are retrieved from this area regularly. It is safe to assume that the colonial records were kept for their own sake, and that by the time the public was beginning to demand access to historical records, older government bodies were suffering from the twin problems of storage and disposal. The functions of modern government archives are heavily weighted towards both activities: the provision of efficient low-cost storage and the regular disposal of temporary records.

The few older records that had been made accessible before World War II were normally placed in the custody of the state libraries, which were already pursuing active policies of collecting, by donation or purchase, significant historical documents, personal papers and Australiana. Legislation passed during the war years recognised the *de facto* control of public archives by state library boards and enabled the establishment of an archives section in the library.

The librarians who were appointed as custodians of the archives had to educate themselves in the theory and practice of archives management. It took almost a generation to convince governments that the functions of archives were essentially different from those of libraries and that archival authorities would be better removed from library control. The major function that sets archives apart from libraries is that of records disposal—the continual need to decide which to keep and which to destroy, knowing that retention takes space and that destruction is irreversible. The increasing importance of regulated disposal of government records has been a major factor in the passage of recent archival legislation.

ARCHIVES LEGISLATION

Since the Northern Territory set up its archives in 1982, each of the eight Australian governments has an archival authority. In some states, legislation preceded the establishment of an archives; in others the institution effectively existed before it was given a statutory basis.

The details of the origins and provision of archival legislation in Australia are complex and technical. Here it will suffice to note that South Australia was the first state to pass an appropriate act in 1925, while the most recent legislation in this field was passed in Victoria in 1973. All the acts have been revised from time to time and have taken note of legislation at commonwealth level and in the other states.

The commonwealth established the Australian Archives, a successor to the Commonwealth Archives Office, as an autonomous authority in 1961 when it ceased to be part of the newly constituted National Library. Originally based in Canberra, it gradually established regional offices in all state capitals and in Darwin and Townsville to handle records generated by commonwealth bodies. The commonwealth Archives Act, passed in 1983, is the most comprehensive piece of archival legislation yet passed in Australia and will probably affect all future state legislation. It not only gives the Australian Archives the power to prevent destruction of records, but makes destruction or alteration not authorised by the archives an offence carrying a heavy fine. The major innovation is, however, that the act confers on the public a statutory right of access to commonwealth archives, backed up with legal avenues of appeal against denial of access.

It is worth noting that the Archives Act was drafted in conjunction with commonwealth freedom of information legislation and the two acts contain similar grounds for exempting documents and similar avenues of appeal. All commonwealth records over 30 years old are subject to the provisions of the Archives Act and eventually all documents less than 30 years old will fall within the scope of the Freedom of Information Act, thus providing a total coverage of public access to commonwealth records and sources of information.

OFFICIAL PUBLICATIONS

Public records comprise not only the unpublished material accumulated in government offices which we commonly regard as archives, but also the whole range of publications issued by government authorities and departments. Because government publications are usually found in libraries, there is a tendency not to regard them as archives at all. Nevertheless, they are just as much records of the administrative process as are unpublished materials.

The principal function of a state or national archives is to preserve a record of the activities of government, and in this capacity it should hold master sets of every government publication. No clear distinction can be drawn between administrative processes and their products. The researcher interested in historical records should therefore be aware not only that government publications are to be found among the archives, but also that it would be wise to seek out published official sources as well as old files, since they may well carry different parts of the story.

The published records of parliament are a particularly important source, because a considerable amount of government activity is connected with matters that go before parliament. As well as the formal record of proceedings kept by every house of parliament (such as the *Votes and proceedings* of the House of Representatives and the *Journals* of the Senate, and corresponding documents in the state legislatures), which yields information on when bills were introduced and abandoned, what was debated in each sitting and which documents were tabled, there are full transcripts of parliamentary debates commonly known as Hansard. These are brought out daily, weekly and monthly during each session, and eventually bound and indexed as a permanent record. Equally useful, from an archival viewpoint, are the parliamentary papers, consisting of all reports formally presented to parliament and numerous other documents tabled in the house during the course of its business.

The process of government is continuous and its structures do not remain static. Every time ministerial portfolios are rearranged, administrative functions are passed from one department to another. Simultaneously all the records concerning that function, past or present, are transferred into the control of the successor department. This fact has governed the development of archival control systems, which must be able to record changing ownership. Users must always remember that archives are retrieved by provenance and function, not by subject. In order to find archival information on a given subject, one must first be able to link that subject with a function of government; then one must link the function to a ministry and track down which agency within that ministry was actually responsible for it. This should lead to a series of files, and further scanning of an original index or archival list should locate a relevant file.

It is important that researchers begin with some understanding of the administrative structures of government and how its functions are carried out, since ministries change their names and responsibilities all too frequently over time. The easiest way to obtain such understanding is through official publications, principally government gazettes. Whenever functions, names or responsibilities are altered, the government publishes a formal notification of the changes in its regular gazette. From time to time, these administrative arrangement orders are published in a consolidated form, setting out the acts administered by each ministerial portfolio and all the major functions for which it is responsible.

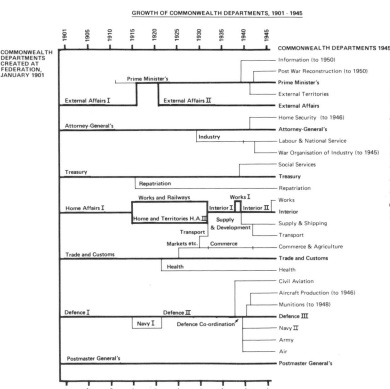

GROWTH OF COMMONWEALTH DEPARTMENTS, 1901 - 1945

When the Commonwealth was formed in January 1901, there were seven government departments. By 1945 there were twenty-seven, about the same number as there are in the 1980s. Some idea of administrative change is shown by the lines stemming from Home affairs I. The heavy lines show the continuation of the original seven departments into the period after World War II.

More detailed information about the functions and responsibilities of government departments or agencies is likely to be found in annual reports, which are usually included in the parliamentary papers as well as being published separately by some departments. Internal reorganisations of departments are not usually gazetted, although they can have considerable effects on record series, but sometimes departments produce charts showing their organisational structure. It has been customary for governments to produce a regular directory listing all their agencies, but these are not always detailed enough to show functional responsibilities and are sometimes not accurately updated.

A useful guide to the relationship between government administration and official documents is D.H. Borchardt's *Australian official publications* (Melbourne, Longman Cheshire, 1979). Although no longer up to date in all its detail—changes in governments have played havoc with ministerial responsibilities—it is still the only thorough survey of this important topic. Of immense assistance to future researchers are the provisions of the commonwealth Freedom of Information Act 1982, which makes it mandatory for all agencies to publish in the *Commonwealth directory* detailed statements of their functions and the types of records they create and use.

Australian governments have since earliest times been inordinately fond of establishing royal commissions and committees of inquiry as a means of obtaining an independent view of social and political issues. The published reports and transcripts of evidence of such tribunals are prime historical sources. It is fortunate that this group of documents is among the few that have been indexed fairly thoroughly in the *Checklist of royal commissions, select committees of parliament and boards of inquiry* compiled by D.H. Borchardt for the commonwealth, New South Wales, Queensland, Tasmania and Victoria, and by E. Zalums for South Australia and Western Australia. After a lapse of 30 years, the records of commissions usually become accessible to the public, including hitherto unpublished sections of reports and transcripts, submissions and working files.

ACCESS TO GOVERNMENT ARCHIVES

Archives are never freely accessible in the way we expect books to be in a library. Since the original records are irreplaceable, they must be protected against careless handling, theft or excessive wear and tear. Normally, documents can be consulted only under supervision, and it is the general practice to issue researchers with special passes and to make them sign a receipt for each item they receive. Documents in fragile condition or poor repair may be withheld from reference use, although it is likely, especially in the case of records frequently in demand, that copies will be provided in some form. Within these limitations, it is generally accepted in Australia that government records are equally accessible to all, and that distinctions will not be made on the grounds of age, nationality, purpose of research or educational qualifications.

Acceptance of such principles is fairly recent. Until a couple of decades ago, governments were inclined to restrict access to their records to reputable scholars—at least until the records had become truly 'historical' by the passage of time. A 50-year closed access period was eventually introduced in Australia, quite some time after it had become the norm in Britain. When the British governement decided, from 1968 on, not only to reduce the closed access period to 30 years but also to release the hitherto sacrosanct records of cabinet, it was only a matter of time before Australian governments followed suit.

Bureaucratic fears about the possible effect of opening up their secrets to the public proved to be exaggerated when the freedom of information and archives legislation of 1982–83 revealed how few skeletons were hidden in bureaucratic basements. There is nevertheless some justified concern about the nature of the documents which might be released after only 30 years—which is after all little more than half a lifetime. Archival records contain information which could prove distressing or defamatory to people—and not only to politicians or to public servants. The commonwealth Archives Act protects the commonwealth and its officers from defamation suits which could arise out of the release of documents, as well as providing grounds for the exemption of information about a person if its disclosure would be unreasonable.

Files of an obviously personal nature, such as medical or social security records, are clearly not suitable for public release while their subjects are alive or their descendants likely to be affected. But information also occurs on general administrative files which it would be unfair or unkind to make public too soon—such as untried allegations of criminal offences, references to treatment for social diseases and descriptions of wartime atrocities committed on named service personnel and unknown to their close relatives. Sometimes, of course, the public interest in having all relevant facts of a case may outweigh considerations of personal distress, but there is a great deal of information in government records about ordinary people, whose doings have no bearing on the public interest.

Governments also have a duty to protect certain information in their records, on the grounds that it would be irresponsible or internationally damaging to make it public. The release of government archives therefore always entails some kind of screening operation, whether this is done in government departments or in the archives.

The commonwealth Archives Act, which gives the public statutory right of access to records, also sets out the broad categories of information that might need to be exempted from access. These have not changed greatly in substance from the rules in operation before the passage of the act.

GUIDES AND FINDING AIDS

There is no general guide to the holdings of government archives in Australia, and only a few guides to any archival records have been published. Government archives generally make available to the public finding aids which they have created for their own internal use. The Archives Office of New South Wales and the Public Record Office of Victoria have produced, and continue to update by regular supplements, comprehensive published guides to their holdings. Those interested should address enquiries to these authorities because detailed citations of their published guides are quickly outdated.

In describing archives, it is always necessary to deal with the whole as well as with the constituent parts; this in turn dictates the form of the finding aids. Control and description of the records is established at various levels: by group, comprising all the records of a particular department; by function, such as naturalisation, where the records have passed not only through numerous different departments but between governments; by series, comprising all the records kept in a similar system (the basic level of archival control); and by item, the individual file or document. Archivists themselves need finding aids at all these levels in order to maintain basic controls. Such inventories should list and describe every item in each series. As an interim measure, draft or preliminary inventories were compiled up to the mid-1960s, notably by state archives in Tasmania, Western Australia and South Australia, where they normally covered colonial records. The same format provided the earlier parts of the New South Wales *Guide* and was in use by the then Commonwealth Archives Office.

The main public finding aid to commonwealth archives, formerly known as the *Summary guide* and now called ANGAM (Australian national guide to archival material), consisted until 1984 of a large set of binders containing selected documentation arranged numerically by the alphanumeric symbols given to commonwealth agencies. It was never issued in printed form and is now held on microfilm; however, it contains no subject index and very little information on the subject coverage of records, which makes it rather daunting for most researchers.

The passage of the Archives Act in 1983 made the establishment and maintenance of a National Register of Records a duty for the Australian Archives. Neither the format nor the content of the register is specified in the act, but it is likely to be maintained as a computerised data base. It should replace the unwieldy *Summary guide* as an Australian Archives finding aid, and may even provide data for published guides to records arranged by agency or by subject.

All archives institutions are aware of the need for subject-related guides to assist public use of their records, and some attempts have been made to provide these in areas of known high research interest, such as family history. A few guides, lists or indexes have been compiled privately with the assistance of groups or institutions with an interest in particular subject areas, such as women's history, film history, architectural history and Aborigines. In 1983 the Australian Society of Archivists published a directory to archival institutions in Australia, entitled *Our heritage*, which provides general information on most public and many private institutions. Further details on this and related guides to manuscript and archives collection will be found in chapter 8 of this volume. For a proper understanding of their research potential it is essential to visit particular archives and to consult the unpublished guides, lists and inventories which are likely to be available on the premises.

NON-GOVERNMENT ARCHIVES

Privately generated records cover an even greater range of subject areas and record types than do government archives; however, they are rarely subject to equivalent regulations or controls with regard to their preservation. It is difficult to make generalised statements about the various institutions or the kinds of records they hold, since there is no uniformity either in the purpose for which they were established or in the policies under which they operate.

Original records of considerable historical value can be found in apparently unlikely places, so the researcher looking for particular information may need to seek far and wide. In many instances historical records still remain in the possession of the organisation or company that generated them. In a few cases professional archivists have been employed to maintain and organise these records, as is the case with the BHP archives in Melbourne or the Westpac archives in Sydney. Most readily accessible private records are to be found in public institutions such as libraries, archives, galleries and museums which collect and preserve historical records for research and display purposes.

A number of universities, colleges and schools have established archives concerned with their own history. Wealthy private schools have usually been more interested and more able to afford an archives section than most public schools. Some colleges and universities have established archives that go beyond their own immediate institutional needs; some hold large collections relating to the educational, economic, cultural and political history of their state or region and a few collect on a national scale.

The recognition that surviving records of Australian industry from the latter part of the nineteenth century onwards were in grave danger of disappearance through neglect or company rationalisation led to the establishment of the Archives of Business and Labour at the Australian National University in 1956 and the University of Melbourne Archives in 1960. Both these institutions house important collections of business archives, ranging from the records of pastoral and mining companies to those of manufacturing and retail firms. They also hold the archives of trade unions and employer associations, and have each produced comprehensive guides to their holdings. In more recent years, they have been joined by the University of Wollongong Archives and an archive at James Cook University, Townsville, which have a more regional bias.

Scientific records, especially those containing original data, have suffered even greater neglect than business records. The Australian Academy of Science has in recent years supported moves to preserve the archives of science, including a University of Melbourne science archive project designed to locate and process collections for deposit in existing institutions. The academy holds records of scientists and scientific societies and notes acquisitions regularly in its journal, *Historical records of Australian science*, continuing the groundwork prepared by A. Mozley. The CSIRO has established its own archives to cater for its extensive holdings, and also takes in some private records of its staff. Records containing scientific data from as early as the 1860s were inherited by the commonwealth when it took over various functions, such as magnetic observatories.

University archives hold faculty records relating to scientific, medical and engineering disciplines, while some of the professional bodies, such as the Royal Australasian College of Surgeons, have set up their own archives. Records of major scientific value are also to be found in the possession of museums, herbaria, botanic and zoological gardens and geological surveys.

There are so many separate religious organisations holding archives that a Church Archivists Society was formed in 1981 and has since produced a directory. Most religious archives consist of records of the diocese, the parish, the society or the order; some are under the auspices of a church historical society which tries to bring together the archives of individual churches and religious groups. Their holdings are of significance not only for the history of the denominations, but also for the development of schools and hospitals in the region. Not all are accessible to the public, but their custodians seem prepared to help with information.

Of particular significance are the archives of the Australian Institute of Aboriginal Studies, the Australian War Memorial and the National Film and Sound Archive, all of which are located in Canberra. These and similar institutions are surveyed in the above-mentioned *Our heritage*. The establishment of a specialised body such as the National Film and Sound Archive owes a lot to the fact that film and sound media are impermanent and require special storage and handling, as well as to the recognition that they should be preserved as irreplaceable historical records. Although a commonwealth institution, its collections are almost exclusively from private sources, since government-generated films and sound recordings are catered for by the appropriate government archives. Among these is the ABC archives, located in Sydney, which utilises storage facilities provided by Australian Archives in New South Wales.

Computer-generated records already form part of the archives of many organisations. They present problems because of their high rate of obsolescence in matters of format and of the technology required for their use.

Some of the most outstanding collections of Australiana, including original records, are to be found in libraries such as the Mitchell and Dixson libraries in Sydney, the National Library in Canberra, the La Trobe Library in Melbourne, the J.S. Battye Library in Perth and the John Oxley Memorial Library in Brisbane. The history of the establishment of special collections and manuscript libraries within the state library system can be found in Biskup and Goodman's *Australian libraries*. All of them aim to hold comprehensive collections of printed and original material relating to their respective states.

The course of Australian history has dictated a certain amount of overlap in the holdings of these major libraries—after all, Queensland and Victoria were part of New South Wales until the 1850s—and of rivalry in their collecting activities. The commonwealth outbid the Mitchell Library for the original manuscript of Captain Cook's journal in 1923, and there are sometimes genuinely competing claims for the papers of individuals whose careers have involved both state and federal positions. For these and other reasons papers relating to the life of particular individuals may be found in two or more institutions.

A number of public and municipal libraries have established special collections of original records, usually of particular relevance to the district. Notable among these is the Newcastle Region Public Library, which holds considerable business archives and local government records and has published inventories to them.

Each Australian state has a major historical society, with which numerous local history societies are affiliated. Their activities in the collecting field vary enormously, and their holdings range from extensive collections of material to a few prized local documents. There are also many specialist historical societies, covering fields such as military or maritime history, railways and aviation, many of which are actively engaged in collecting logbooks, diaries and other unique materials as well as published records. Each state boasts at least one genealogical society with a large and growing membership. These, like local historical societies, are likely to establish research collections, including microfilm copies of birth and shipping records, locally transcribed cemetery inscriptions and extensive indexes of names.

A *Guide to collections of manuscripts relating to Australia* has been published at irregular intervals by the National Library since 1965. It must be regarded as a starting point in any search for original source materials of a non-government nature, despite its considerable shortcomings. It lacks a subject index and, since it relies on entries contributed by the institutions which hold the collections, is neither consistent in its level of description nor comprehensive in its coverage.

Ironically, the researcher can probably locate records about Australia held abroad more easily than those held in Australian institutions, thanks to the Mander-Jones guide, which gives extensive coverage of records relating to Australia, New Zealand and the Pacific region held in the British Isles, and to the continuing work of the Australian Joint Copying Project, which not only arranges for the microfilming of overseas records but also publishes handbooks describing the material in each series. The microfilm copies are deposited with special collection areas on state and national libraries. For further details on such guides see chapter 8.

Inventories and subject guides to special archival collections have generally been produced by organisations or groups who recognise that their need for historical records is severely hampered by a lack of knowledge concerning their whereabouts. The Department of Architecture at Adelaide University, for instance, has published *A manual of architectural history sources* in several volumes, containing useful information by state about government and private records, including maps, plans and pictorial material, as well as about the institutions which hold them. *Women in Australia*, which surveys published and unpublished records held in all major institutions, state by state, was compiled as an International Women's Year project.

Guides compiled for sectional interests are often of use to researchers in other fields, especially when more general guides are lacking, since they contain basic information about institutions and their services as well as comment on types of records held. Such subject guides are normally dealt with by state, because of the way that holdings of records are compiled. There are also general guides to sources by state or region, which contain references to archival records.

Very few institutions have published complete, or even select, guides to their holdings. Many of the finding aids are available only on the premises and consist of miscellaneous lists, inventories and indexes. The Mitchell Library has published a catalogue of manuscripts acquired up to the late 1960s. The Australian War Memorial, the Archives of Business and Labour (Australian National University) and the University of Melbourne Archives have published general guides to their collections. Some other institutions, such as the University of Tasmania, the Newcastle Region Public Library or the Riverina–Murray Institute of Higher Education in Wagga Wagga, have commenced publishing a series of finding aids. The National Library has published guides to some of its major collections, and the references to manuscript holdings also appear in C.A. Burmester's *Guide to the collections* which is discussed in detail in chapter 3. Others have contributed regular information about their accessions to another publication, such as a journal or annual report, or compiled guides to particular collections. Information about such piecemeal guides can be extracted from Alan Ives' bibliography up to about 1977, but neither his compilation nor the other guides mentioned here are being updated.

Institutions acquire private records, whether of individuals, corporate bodies or societies, by purchase, donation or bequest. When acquiring such material they are morally and legally bound to respect the wishes of the former owners or their heirs regarding conditions of access and copyright. The Copyright Act makes copyright of unpublished documents perpetual, makes no distinction between ordinary correspondence and works written for publication, and vests copyright in the author of the work or the writer of the letters. Institutions often attempt to acquire copyright along with the original documents themselves.

'Charging floor of BHP Newcastle open hearth shop, including works locomotive.' Unknown photographer, 1948.
BHP ARCHIVES, MELBOURNE

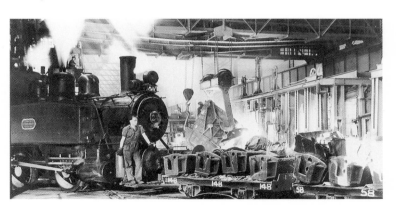

Thomas Griffiths Wainewright, Drawing of Major de Gillern ... *Mar 1924.*
CORNSTALK BOOKSHOP

CHAPTER 3

LIBRARIES AND PRINTED RESOURCES

D. H. BORCHARDT

THE PRINTED RESOURCES for Australian studies, especially books, differ from archival resources in that multiple copies are often available. Since the importance of Australian studies has been recognised, many libraries have made a special effort to acquire Australian books and journals in general, and more specifically those relevant to the research programs of their parent institutions or of particular significance in the locality where the library operates. The uneven bibliographic resources of these libraries is partly due to their historical development, to which reference will be made below. First, however, a brief reference to the history of the book in Australia may be helpful.

Australian publishing has come a long way in the two hundred years since the establishment of British colonial society on these shores. The new surroundings, the encounter with an unknown flora and fauna, the growth of a society different from that of the immigrants' homelands—all combined to encourage a pattern of publishing which concentrated on an examination of Australia itself and of the life and customs of its people. Sir John Ferguson's *Bibliography of Australia* includes about 3300 titles printed both locally and overseas, especially in Great Britain, during the first 60 years of European settlement.

Obviously not all books about Australia are published in Australia. A large number of studies, reports of voyages and scholarly surveys of Australia were printed and published in Europe well before the establishment of European settlement and throughout the nineteenth century. The British origins of the greater part of the population ensured a close link with the book world of England, and the consequent nexus between the developing Australian culture and the British tradition fostered British publishers' interest in books about Australia. From the purely practical point of view, it was also of importance to Australian writers to find a larger market than the small Australian population could offer in the nineteenth and early twentieth centuries. Besides, Australian printing houses have remained in the wake rather than the forefront of typographic technology, so that for many decades discerning authors preferred to have their work printed in Europe.

Not only the British but also other nations showed an interest in the nation that emerged on the earth's largest island in a quite extraordinary manner. A small but distinct corpus of literature in Dutch, French, German, Italian, Russian and other languages developed in the nineteenth century and there are a number of bibliographic surveys of the literature related to Australia in those languages. Many of the contributors to the non-English literature were immigrants from countries other than the United Kingdom; their written records embrace natural history, social criticism and, of course, light literature, often heavily larded with fabulous descriptions of the Australian environment.

LIBRARY SERVICES

The collecting and servicing of books and journals is traditionally the function of libraries. Because libraries in Australia have grown in response to local demands and have been guided by locally felt needs in the services they now offer, we do not have a homogeneous pattern of libraries created according to a preconceived plan. This is not to say that there is no discernible pattern of library services; as the library profession developed, particularly during the past thirty or forty years, professional practices and standards have replaced many home-made, uncorrelated and often idiosyncratic procedures.

The first library open to the public—albeit on conditions that would now be considered quite inadequate—was established in Sydney in 1826. Today there are over 900 municipal libraries, six state libraries and a national library, nineteen university and over 300 college libraries. More than 800 libraries in government departments, both federal and state, and in private business and industry, are catering for the needs of a special clientele. There are, furthermore, many hundreds of libraries in primary and secondary schools.

Their total resources amount now to over 60 million volumes and about 800 000 serial titles though the vast majority of these bear little relation to Australian studies in any obvious sense; furthermore there is a good deal of duplication among libraries' holdings. Some libraries have over a long period specialised in materials specific to Australian studies. In many instances this specialisation has not happened haphazardly. The most important Australian collections are to be found in the National Library and the six state libraries for the simple reason that for the past fifty to a hundred years legal deposit obligations have ensured that the national and state libraries each received at least one copy of every book printed in their jurisdiction. This obligation is set out in different statutory instruments, the earliest of which was approved by the New South Wales parliament in 1879. Similar acts were subsequently passed in all states and by the commonwealth, some as copyright acts, others as library acts or with similar titles. They are amended from time to time as changes in publishing technology and social pressures demand.

Obviously, there were many decades during which the state libraries had to purchase Australian publications unless—as was often the case—the publishers presented copies to them for one reason or another. While we can therefore expect the state libraries to hold books and journals issued after the date when copies had legally to be deposited, there is no guarantee that titles published before that date will be available. Nevertheless, the state libraries have made tremendous efforts during the second half of the twentieth century to fill the gaps in their collections. It is indeed fairly certain that every state library will hold most titles published in or relating to its jurisdiction.

BIBLIOGRAPHIC CONTROL

Before discussing the location of bibliographic resources for Australian studies, it will be useful to make brief comment on their bibliographic control—a recognised official list indicating that a specific title exists. Universal access to publications depends initially on their bibliographic control, a field in which Australia has a good record.

Australia has had an official national bibliography longer than any other English-speaking country. The National Library's bibliographic services are detailed in chapter 8, together with references to the annual commercial publication *Australian books in print* and the monthly *Australian bookseller and publisher*.

In addition, many commercial and official publishers issue lists of their own books and serials, a practice followed by two of Australia's largest publishers, the Australian Government Publishing Service (AGPS) and the Australian Bureau of Statistics (ABS), as well as by several state government departments. A useful survey of this scene was edited by D.H. Borchardt under the title *Australian official publications* (1979).

TABLE 1 SERIAL BIBLIOGRAPHIC CONTROLS OF AUSTRALIAN OFFICIAL PUBLICATIONS

I. National Library of Australia

Period	Title	Contents
1937–1960 (except 1941–1944)	*Annual catalogue of Australian publications.* Canberra, Commonwealth National Library.	Official publications of Commonwealth, state and local governments as received by National Library. Excludes pamphlets of less than 5 pages and single issues of bills, acts and subordinate legislation, Arbitration Court and state industrial awards, and non-book materials.
1961–	*Australian national bibliography.* Canberra, National Library of Australia. Available on AUSINET as a data base.	Official publications of Commonwealth, state and local governments as received by National Library. Excludes maps and films, subordinate legislation, pamphlets of less than 5 pages unless part of a series, and material published more than 2 years prior to the year of the ANB issue.
1961–	*Australian government publications.* Canberra, National Library of Australia.	Official publications of Commonwealth and state governments as received by National Library. Excludes single issues of certain parliamentary publications which are later consolidated, bills and acts, single issues or subordinate legislation, Arbitration Court and state industrial awards, non-book materials, publications of government hospitals and educational institutions, and material published more than 2 years prior to the year of the AGP issue. Excluded from quarterly issues are periodicals which appear more frequently than once a year.

II. Australian Government Publishing Service

Period	Title	Contents
October 1965–December 1966	*Commonwealth publications; monthly list.* Canberra, Commonwealth Government Printing Office.	Commonwealth official publications placed on sale through the Government Printing Office (1965–1969) or the Australian Government Publishing Service (AGPS), including select publications of departments and authorities.
January 1967–April 1976	*Australian government publications; monthly list.* Canberra, Commonwealth Government Printing Office [to 1968] and AGPS.	
April 1976–December 1979	*Weekly list of government publications.* Canberra, AGPS.	All AGPS publications, whether sold by AGPS or not.
April 1976–1979	*Monthly list of publications placed on sale.* Canberra, AGPS.	Commonwealth official publications placed on sale through the AGPS including select publications of departments and authorities.
July 1976–1979	*Cumulative list of government publications.* Canberra, AGPS.	All AGPS publications, whether sold by AGPS or not.
July 1976–	*AGPS catalogue on microfiche.* Canberra, AGPS.	AGPS publications, whether sold by AGPS or not, excluding bills, customs tariff proposals, excise tariff proposals, acts and other legislation. Also includes other Commonwealth official publications placed on sale through AGPS.
1980–February 1985	*Monthly catalogue of publications placed on sale.*	Commonwealth official publications placed on sale through the AGPS, including select publications of departments and authorities.
1980–	*Commonwealth publications official list.*	Weekly list of all AGPS publications, whether sold by AGPS or not. From August 1983, also includes titles that the AGPS did not publish or sell but whose production has been reported to the AGPS by Commonwealth departments and authorities.
1980–	*Annual catalogue of Commonwealth publications.*	All AGPS publications, whether sold by AGPS or not. From 1983, also includes titles that the AGPS did not publish or sell but whose production has been reported to the AGPS by Commonwealth departments and authorities.

III. State Libraries and State Government Printers

Period	Title	Contents
1968–	*New South Wales official publications received in the State Library of New South Wales.* Sydney, State Library of New South Wales.	New South Wales official publications as received by the State Library of New South Wales. Excludes single issues of regulations and subordinate legislation, non-book materials, and publications of hospitals, schools and local government agencies. Until 1975 January issue included list of periodicals received.
1959–1974	*New South Wales government publications.* Sydney, Government Printing Office.	Official publications sold by the New South Wales Government Printing Office.
1975–	*Publications issued.* Sydney, Government Printing Office.	
1983–	*[Northern Territory] Catalogue of publications.* Darwin, Northern Territory Government Information Centre.	Official publications available from the Northern Territory Government Information Centre.
1977–	*Queensland government publications.* Brisbane, State Library of Queensland.	Publications of all government agencies. Excluded are publications by schools and audio-visual material.
1962–March 1979	*South Australiana.* Adelaide, Libraries Board of South Australia.	Includes official publications published in South Australia or of South Australian interest, as received by the State Library of South Australia, irrespective of date of publication.
1979–	*Monthly list of South Australian interest received in the State Library of South Australia.*	Includes official publications published in South Australia or of South Australian interest, as received by the State Library of South Australia, irrespective of date of publication.
1959[?]	*South Australian government publications.* Adelaide, Government Printing Division.	List of publications sold by the South Australian Government Printer.
1972–1976	*Tasmanian official publications.* Hobart, State Library of Tasmania.	Tasmanian official publications as received by the State Library of Tasmania. Excludes non-book materials and publications of hospitals, schools and local government authorities. Last issue of year includes complete list of serials received.
1976–	*Victorian government publications received by the State Library of Victoria.* Melbourne, State Library of Victoria.	Official publications of Victorian state and, from 1981, local governments. Excludes publications of schools and hospitals and from 1982 on determinations of the State's industrial tribunals and boards.
1962–July 1978	*Publications issued.* Melbourne, Government Printing Office.	Publications sold by the Victorian Government Printing Office.
August/September 1978–	*Monthly list of publications.* Melbourne, Government Printing Office.	
1979–	*Annual list of publications.* Melbourne, Victorian Government Printing Office.	Publications sold by the Victorian Government Printing Office.
1973–1978	*Official publications of Western Australia.* Perth, Parliamentary Library of Western Australia.	Official publications notified to the Western Australian Parliamentary Library. Excludes publications of hospitals, local government agencies, schools and certain autonomous statutory bodies, non-book materials and bills.
1975–	*Quarterly price list and information sheet.* Perth, Western Australian Government Printing Office.	Publications sold by the Western Australian Government Printing Office.

TABLE 2: LEGAL DEPOSIT LEGISLATION   In force in Australia at the end of 1984

AUTHORITY	DATE OF LEGISLATION	MATERIAL INCLUDED	MATERIAL EXCLUDED
AUSTRALIA	Copyright Act 1968	'Library Material' means a book, periodical, newspaper, pamphlet, sheet of letterpress, sheet of music, map, plan, chart or table, being a literary, dramatic, musical or artistic work.	Second or later editions which contain no 'additions or alterations in the letterpress or illustrations'.
NEW SOUTH WALES	Copyright Act 1879 & 1952	'Book' means and includes any volume, part or division of a volume, newspaper, pamphlet, libretto, sheet of letterpress, sheet of music, map, chart or plan separately published.	Second and subsequent editions which contain no alterations from a previous edition already deposited.
QUEENSLAND	Libraries Act 1949	'Book' ... includes every part or division of a book, pamphlet, newspaper, sheet of letterpress, map, plan, chart or table separately published.	Second and subsequent editions unless they contain 'additions or alterations, either in the letterpress or in the maps, prints, or other engravings belonging thereto or ... any book published by or on behalf of the government of the State or any government department'.
SOUTH AUSTRALIA	Libraries & Institutes Act 1939		Second or subsequent editions unless they contain 'additions or alterations either in the letterpress or in the maps, prints, or other illustrations belonging thereto'.
TASMANIA	Libraries Act 1943	'Book' ... includes any part or division of a book, newspaper, pamphlet, libretto, sheet of letterpress, sheet of music, map, plan, chart, table, print, gramophone record, film or engraving separately published.	
VICTORIA	Library Council of Victoria Act 1965	'Book' ... includes every volume part or division of a volume newspaper, pamphlet, sheet of letterpress, sheet of music, map, chart or plan separately published.	Second and subsequent editions only if there are no 'additions or alterations whether the same are in letterpress or in the maps, prints or other engravings belonging thereto'.
WESTERN AUSTRALIA	Copyright Act 1895	'Book' means and includes every volume, part or division of a volume, newspaper, pamphlet, sheet of letterpress, sheet of music, map, chart, or plan, separately published.	Second or subsequent editions if there are no 'additions or alterations, whether the same is [sic] in letterpress or in the maps, prints, or other engraving belonging thereto'.

The importance of government documents for an understanding of Australian history cannot be underestimated. It will therefore be helpful to know the appropriate sources for the identification of these documents and to this end table 2, originally published in *Australian official publications*, has been reprinted here in simplified form and with some updating. Users of government publications are urged to acquaint themselves thoroughly with these bibliographical retrieval tools. Obviously the inclusions and exclusions of details are subject to occasional revision and readers are advised to read carefully the introductions and explanations of contents printed in all these reference works before using them.

While the exploitation of printed resources depends on our awareness of their existence—a precondition effectively achieved by bibliographic control—we are not much helped unless we also have guides to their location. Such guides normally take one of two forms: as catalogues of the resources of individual libraries, or as union catalogues or lists of several libraries. Despite extensive automation in the major libraries, with concomitant microform and computer-based files, the catalogues of many individual libraries are still maintained in card form and are not accessible except within the library in question. Only in rare instances, and when that library has a particularly significant collection, do we find printed catalogues of an individual library's holdings, such as that of the Mitchell Library, Sydney.

Union catalogues—catalogues of the holdings of more than one library—may be and often are maintained in card form but are also frequently published in book form or maintained on a machine readable file and accessible via a computer terminal. The principal reason for these alternatives to a card catalogue is to provide access to a union catalogue in more than one location. There are also numerous union lists on specific subjects which, while they may be selective about holdings of individual institutions, bring together in one listing material on a special topic or library materials published in one form, such as periodicals.

Australian libraries have taken two important steps in the quest for bibliographic control and location directories noting which libraries hold particular books. The first is NUCOM (National Union Catalogue of Monographs), produced on continuous rolls of film and therefore usable, with the help of a microfilm reader, anywhere at all. This remarkable directory of the holdings of over 300 Australian libraries shows the whereabouts of between 2.5 and 3.0 million books. It is a unique endeavour to enhance the resource-sharing program of the Australian Advisory Council on Bibliographic Services (AACOBS) and is of particular importance for printed materials acquired by Australian libraries before 1975. It must be stressed that this reference tool deals with books (monographs) only.

NUCOM was not intended to be a specific retrieval instrument for the literature relating to Australian studies, but because all the state libraries, the university libraries and several other important institutions have had the records of their holdings microfilmed for inclusion, NUCOM is inevitably the most comprehensive index of Australian publications and of Australiana published outside Australia. A detailed history and broad guide to the contents of NUCOM has been issued by the National Library of Australia.

NUCOM does have limitations. Firstly it is an author catalogue only, although where an author is unknown access is by title. Secondly, the standard of bibliographic citation and the choice of author entry vary according to the quality of cataloguing performed by the contributing libraries. Thirdly, and more importantly, whole categories of publications have been excluded. Among these are Australian government publications—a major component in any resources collection for Australian studies. Finally, a number of libraries ceased sending contributions to NUCOM after 1980.

By the end of this century NUCOM will have been largely superseded by the computer-based technology that has already led to the creation of the Australian Bibliographic Network (ABN). Before discussing this new supertool in Australian library services, brief reference must be made to two older union catalogues of serials, known respectively as *Scientific serials in Australian libraries* (SSAL), and *Serials in Australian libraries, social sciences and humanities* (SALSSAH). The former has been produced by the Central Library of the CSIRO, while the latter is a product of the National Library. Their antecedents go back many years—the origins of SSAL are to be found in the *Catalogue of scientific and technical periodicals in libraries of Australia* which first appeared in 1930—and have been many times updated, modified and, above all, enlarged.

Since 1983 SALSSAH has been expanded to include serials in scientific areas. The result is the *National union catalogue of serials* (NUCOS), which will gradually incorporate the whole of SSAL. The most important aspect of this transformation is that NUCOS has also been transferred into the machine readable data base of the ABN.

ABN is the National Library's most important contribution to Australian bibliographical services since the establishment of the *Australian national bibliography* (*ANB*) in 1936. Though conceived as an aid to libraries, to reduce the cost of cataloguing books and to support interlibrary loan services through online access to a computer-based data bank housed in the National Library, ABN is in effect a vast union catalogue of (for the present) recent acquisitions by most of the major Australian libraries.

National union catalogues provide answers to two of the most burning questions with which all libraries are faced: to supply clients with their legitimate demands for literature of all kinds, and to make a national acquisition policy possible. In addition, national union catalogues form the basis of a speedy and efficient interlibrary loans service.

As long as union catalogues were dependent on manual exploitation—as long as they were available only in printed form, to be searched by reading columns of citations—access to the data recorded was usually limited to the author or the title approach. The advent of the machine readable bibliographic data bank makes it possible to add, by means of sophisticated programs, other means of access, for instance, approach by subject, by language, by date, by place of publication, and so forth, or a combination of these where required. The ABN catalogue will allow all these possibilities and many more as its technical potential is enhanced.

To the scholar working in a relatively narrow field of Australian studies, the availability of equally narrow subject-based union lists is of considerable benefit. There is no up-to-date list of Australian union lists: A.P. Rooke's *A list of Australian union lists* (1974) is now sadly out of date and cites astonishingly few union lists of specific relevance to Australian studies.

NATIONAL AND STATE LIBRARIES

National and state libraries are the most important resources for Australian studies. Descriptions and historical notes on the National Library of Australia can be found in most textbooks on libraries and librarianship in Australia, and Peter Biskup has recently compiled a short monograph on the history of this national institution under the title *Library models and library myths*. Although the National Library is a relative latecomer in the Australiana field, its prestige and early links with the commonwealth parliament have led to the donation of numerous substantial gifts almost since its foundation. Moreover, the library was able to acquire formed collections which quickly raised its research potential.

Two particularly rich Australiana collections created the nucleus of the National Library's wealth in this field. One was the E.A. Petherick collection of about 10 000 volumes of Australian interest brought together at the end of the nineteenth century by this somewhat eccentric bookseller, collector and bibliographer. The other was the Ferguson collection of about 34 000 volumes which had formed the basis of the famous *Bibliography of Australia* compiled by Sir John Ferguson (see chapter 8).

Other important but less voluminous Australiana collections have been given to the National Library over the years. These include several strong collections of pamphlets on political and constitutional issues, such as the J.B. Holmes collection of over 5000 items on federation, the U.R. Ellis collection on the Australian Country Party, and several collections on socialism in Australia, the Communist party and the Australian Labor Party. In addition the library has received the personal papers of many leading political figures, of governors-general and public bodies involved in politics. Thanks to a judicious acquisitions policy and, since 1911, the continuous accretions due to legal deposit legislation, the National Library has now a research collection for Australian studies of about 100 000 volumes. In accordance with the acts under which it operates, priority has been given to the preservation of Australia's printed record.

The former assistant national librarian, C.A. Burmester, has compiled a helpful *Guide to the collections* in the National Library. This indispensable four-volume survey contains descriptive notes on materials relating to specific persons or topics, a date indicating when the material was added to the library and, where appropriate, references to publications based on the National Library's holdings. Though the descriptions vary in depth, the Australian material is generally well detailed. The fourth volume contains an extensive index.

It is not possible to examine in detail all the major libraries and their contents, but special attention must be paid to the Mitchell Library in Sydney which forms part of the State Library of New South Wales, as it is now known. This state library began as the oldest public library in Australia, having been founded in 1826 as the Australian Subscription Library and Reading Room. The institution's history is well covered by the various editions of the *Australian encyclopaedia* and general histories of Australian libraries. Since its inception, the library has made a special effort to collect and service Australian literature and writing in general.

The New South Wales government enacted legal deposit legislation in 1879, entitling the State Library to receive a copy of every book first published in New South Wales. Various collectors have presented to the library Australian material of many kinds, as well as books and journals on other topics, and by the end of the nineteenth century the library's holdings had grown to over 100 000 volumes. At that time the library was offered the private collection of David Scott Mitchell, a wealthy barrister, consisting of about 61 000 volumes and a large collection of manuscripts, maps and pictures. This collection formed the nucleus of the Mitchell Library. Thanks to an endowment fund also given by Mitchell, the library was able to continue a vigorous acquisitions program and during the past eighty years the original Mitchell gift has been increased more than sevenfold. The only other collection of substantial size given to the state library is the Dixson collection (received in instalments from 1919) which besides its 21 000 volumes includes a large number of pictures and over a thousand volumes of manuscripts.

The publication in 1968–69 of the *Mitchell Library dictionary catalog of printed books* makes it possible to identify a very large portion of this unique collection of books and other records. In addition, the *Catalogue of manuscripts of Australasia and the Pacific in the Mitchell Library, Sydney,* issued in two volumes in 1967 and 1969, lists the major part of the Mitchell manuscript collection. The library also maintains numerous typescript subject guides to its holding.

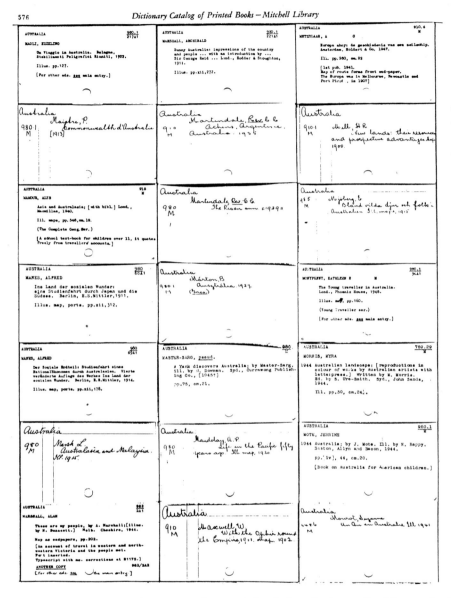

Sample page (reduced) from the Mitchell Library's Dictionary catalogue of printed books, *showing entries under the subject heading 'Australia'.*

Though the state libraries of Queensland, South Australia, Tasmania, Victoria and Western Australia have strong holdings of printed books, journals, newspapers and official records relating to their own jurisdiction, none has resources that can support Australian studies on a basis comparable to that of the National Library or the Mitchell Library.

In Queensland, the John Oxley Memorial Library—named after the explorer and Australia's first surveyor-general—specialises in Australian and particularly Queensland material. The total holdings amount to about 46 000 printed volumes, pamphlets and journals, and efforts are constantly made to collect all Queensland authors. The cosmopolitan nature of the state's population has prompted the State Library to gather works on the several nationalities from which these people have descended.

The Australiana collection of the State Library of South Australia is to be housed in a recently refurbished wing, the Mortlock Library. Its strength is obviously the South Australian content—about 8000 books, over 12 000 pamphlets, and some 15 000 ephemeral publications which include political leaflets and theatre notices. There are about 2000 periodical titles going back to the beginning of the colony's existence. As the geographic area known as the Northern Territory was administered until 1911 by the government of South Australia, records and other printed material on that region can be found here. There is also a virtually complete file of South Australian maps and the extensive Bradman collection on cricket.

The State Library of Tasmania has a comprehensive collection of about 75 000 items on Tasmania, and two smaller collections of books and other library materials have been given to the library in recent years. One is the Crowther collection containing 15 000 items on Tasmania and Australia; many of these are offprints and copies from journals and they include material on the Pacific. The owner was a notable Tasmanian medical practitioner and the collection includes some medical history. The other gift collection is the Allport library of about 4000 items of Tasmanian, Australian and Pacific interest.

The La Trobe Library of the State Library of Victoria, named after the colony's first governor, was envisaged as the Victorian counterpart to the Mitchell Library in Sydney. It is indeed a fine collection of about 120 000 volumes of Australian and particularly Victorian interest. Its collections form a useful resource for Australian studies in general and are unquestionably the strongest for Victorian material. The J.K. Moir library, acquired in the early 1950s, became the basis of an extensive section on Australian literature. The library also has valuable manuscript and pictorial holdings and an important collection of theatre programs.

The State Library of Western Australia maintains its West Australiana collections in the Battye Library of West Australian History. Though on a much smaller scale—only about 30 000 volumes—the Battye Library has strong resources in the pre-1900 Australiana field and since the 1980s emphasis has been placed on building up the research potential for Australian studies, including an excellent collection of twentieth-century ephemera, such as tourist brochures and sports programs.

Since the establishment of self-government in the Northern Territory, library services there have been developed on a pattern similar to that offered by the other state libraries. The head office of the Northern Territory Library Services is in Darwin. The northern Australian collection consisted in 1985 of about 10 000 items and is being built up systematically by the

Australasian vol 1, no 3 (new series), 21 Apr 1866 and no 4270, 8 Nov 1930. The Australasian *began publication in Melbourne in 1864 and is the longest running Australian weekly. In the 1860s its masthead depicted the range of the paper's interests, from livestock and sport to commerce and industry. By the 1930s colour had been added and symbols of progress had been updated to include an aeroplane, an electric train and a diesel-powered tractor. In April 1946 it became the* Australasian post, *retaining its tabloid form but abandoning most of its news items and editorial material.*
ANU ARCHIVES OF BUSINESS AND LABOUR

acquisition of relevant older books as well as by an aggressive collection policy for current imprints. Complete runs of most Northern Territory newspapers are held in microform.

ACADEMIC LIBRARIES

The only other group of large research libraries in this country is that constituted by the nineteen universities whose collections support Australian studies, which now form an increasingly large section of the academic curriculum offered to students at all levels. There exist, in addition, significant collections of recent Australian materials—post-1950—in some of the large colleges of advanced education, and in the major institutes of technology, of which every state has at least one. During the past five or six decades academic dissertations in the social sciences, humanities and natural sciences have been based increasingly on the Australian environment, both human and physical. Most of the successful theses in these fields contribute another step, however small, to our knowledge of Australian history, social conditions and our natural surroundings.

Today many libraries serving educational institutions acquire Australian books as part of their general acquisitions policy related to the disciplines taught. Thus, books on Australian social issues are added to the library's holdings because there are courses on politics, migration, marketing and women, and not because the library wants to collect Australiana. The only exception to this is the library of the University of Sydney which receives New South Wales publications under legal deposit regulations. Apart from this, however, the situation is well summed up in the words of one of Australia's university librarians: 'University Library does not receive books under legal deposit. It buys Australian books relevant to its academic interests ... Selected duplicate copies are acquired for the Australiana collection'. This type of acquisitions policy applies to all academic libraries and it is therefore obvious that these institutions can now be relied upon to hold a large proportion of current Australian publications. To a lesser degree, this is also the situation in the main colleges of advanced education.

Some universities are collecting Australiana in depth either because of a special interest among the teaching and research staff, or because the library has been given a formed collection in a specific field and, in order to retain or enhance its value, continues to purchase in the same field. The Dixson Library of the University of New England—so named after the same Sir William Dixson who complemented the Mitchell collection of the State Library of New South Wales with his magnificent gift and who also provided handsomely for this university—is one of Australia's newer university libraries, which has capitalised on its isolated position by developing special regional strengths in its New England collection of about 800 monographs and 50 serial titles. It also contains the fine Campbell Howard collection of unpublished Australian plays.

Long-established institutions like the universities of Sydney and Melbourne have attracted considerable gifts of books, journals and manuscripts from their alumni and others. For example, the University of Sydney has in its rare books and special collections about 25 000 items of Australian interest and has incorporated in its holdings such extensive collections as those by Cross, Berckelman and Stone on Australian literature, the Chaplin collection on Norman Lindsay and the Aboriginal material collected by Professor Elkin. The University of Melbourne maintains over 65 000 volumes of Australian interest in separate collections—these include several special collections formed by Ian F. McLaren (about 50 000 volumes) and 5000 volumes of early Australian literature collected by C. Goode and others.

Another of the older academic institutions, the University of Queensland, established in 1911, has now the second largest library in Australia and claims that its Australian material is its greatest strength. Its Fryer Memorial Library houses most of the university's Australiana material, including over 50 000 monographs and 3000 periodical volumes. The wealth of the university's bibliographic resources relevant to Australian studies has been described in Zerner's *Australian studies, University of Queensland* and the Fryer Memorial Library's holdings of publications by and on political organisations in Queensland have been listed by Guyatt and George.

The preceding accounts of Australia's state and academic libraries are intended merely to exemplify, in a general manner, the fundamental fact that while the state libraries can be relied upon to have good to excellent collections of printed documents on the geographic area of their jurisdiction, only one or two would be able to support research on other areas of the country. The teaching institutions, on the other hand, are generally better able to support research into current Australian issues, though some are also building up research materials for historical studies. Australian serials holdings in general are being improved, and most university libraries have taken steps to develop good holdings in Australian government publications.

MUNICIPAL PUBLIC LIBRARIES

The most important local source of information for the ordinary citizen not attached to an educational institution is the municipal public library, of which Australia has about 800 or one for every 17 500 people. Their holdings differ considerably according to their age, the financial priorities of the municipality that supports them, and the goals of the committees that are responsible for them. However, all receive aid in some form through a system of direct and indirect grants from state coffers through state library councils or similarly styled statutory agencies. The system of such assistance differs from state to state: some have adopted a highly centralised library support system, while others have opted for a combination of direct and indirect subsidy. In this context it is of minor importance how municipal libraries are supported as long as they enjoy some state funding. The level of support provided by the states is not uniform because there are as yet no nationally accepted levels of library funding in terms of municipal rating powers.

In their endeavour to cater for the needs of users, the municipal public libraries offer, generally speaking, three different but complementary services, broadly related to the economic, social and cultural needs of the citizens and, for obvious reasons, geared to meet the needs of the local residents of the municipality. These three services are: a general information service related to the various community activities and services available within the municipality; a wide range of books and journals; and a referral and interlibrary loan service which supplements the other two services. A closer look at what has been established as a standard and widely adopted practice will help to show what people can reasonably expect from their municipal public library.

It will be obvious, from what has been said above, that there is no uniformity of service patterns in the Australian public library system. Nevertheless, professional pressures are helping to establish minimal standards in all aspects of public librarianship. The public library should provide a focal point where citizens can find answers to their questions on day-to-day economic and social survival, where someone will help to identify local, state and federal authorities whom they should contact to find out about their personal or family problems, their legal entitlements in matters of social security, or their rights in a complex system of the administration of justice. During the past decade this public information service has been fully recognised as part of a librarian's tasks.

The traditional role of the library—or, at least, as it is perceived by the population at large—is to provide a wide range of reading materials, both as books and in the form of journals. This type of library service has not yet been seriously challenged or displaced by any alternative form of data-bearing media.

We already have efficient information systems based on computerised data banks. Many of these are in the hands of industrial and commercial concerns and will supply answers to questions about, for example, the stock exchange, racing results or elections. They are also used, as is AUSINET—a computer-based library oriented network which provides access to many bibliographic data banks—to help libraries in their endeavours to meet the needs of readers when the literature required is not immediately at hand.

The system of lending library materials between libraries, usually upon the request of a client, is well established in Australia. Known as the interlibrary loan system, it places the major part of Australia's printed library resources at the disposal of library clients. There are some obvious restrictions enforced to protect rare, bulky or easily damaged material but photocopying services help to overcome some of these obstacles. Interlibrary loan is greatly aided by NUCOM,

NUCOS and ABN. It is currently more useful when the author of the desired work is known than when enquirers ask for titles on a certain subject.

What sort of books can we reasonably expect to find in a municipal public library? Leaving aside the question of the library's size and financial resources, most public libraries try to provide the literature which a reasonable cross-section of their clients wants. In the absence of clearly expressed wishes by the reading public, librarians will try to assess the community needs on the basis of appropriate investigations.

Broadly speaking, five categories of books and journals will be provided in most public libraries: reading matter to support the economic, business and industrial interest of the community; books and journals to support leisure and hobby activities such as arts, crafts and sport; general reading material—novels and entertainment magazines like *Punch* and the *New Yorker*; books to support the teaching programs of the schools and of adult education; and books to cater for the reading needs of children. In addition, to support the work of the library's reference staff and to meet the needs of citizens pursuing more scholarly enquiries, public libraries maintain a reference collection of dictionaries, encyclopaedias, atlases, bibliographies and literature guides, periodical indexes and subject abstracting services.

Some of Australia's public libraries have been in existence for a long time. The City of Sydney Public Library was established in 1877 and the forerunner of the Melbourne City Public Library was set up in 1880. Municipalities outside the metropolitan areas became aware early of the need for public libraries on the British pattern and some, like those of Newcastle in New South Wales and Ballarat in Victoria, are more than a century old. All have developed in a period when the public library also served as haven for local archives and for the published records of local history.

Whatever their selection policy may be now, many of these older libraries have collected assiduously and preserved with care the documents and records related to the history of their own district. Such collections often include old newspapers and serial publications emanating from local societies and institutes. Though legal deposit legislation has brought much of this material into the state libraries, scores of printers and publishers in provincial towns and rural

The free library at Geelong A. Garran (ed), Picturesque atlas of Australasia, *Sydney 1886-88.*
ANDERSON COLLECTION

districts have, for one reason or another, failed to comply with that legislation—and besides, some states have introduced it rather late in the day.

SPECIAL LIBRARIES

Almost one thousand special libraries serve a particular clientele with narrow interests in a field of theoretical or applied knowledge. For instance, there are libraries attached to the law courts for the exclusive use of the legal profession; there are libraries in government departments such as the federal Department of Foreign Affairs, or state departments of agriculture; there are libraries in large business enterprises such as BHP or ICI.

In the context of this examination of resources for Australian studies, most of these special libraries play a minor role, the obvious exception being those in federal or state government departments. In addition there are substantial and important collections in such organisations as the Australian Bureau of Statistics (ABS) and the Commonwealth Scientific and Industrial Research Organization (CSIRO) without which research into many aspects of Australian studies would be impossible. The libraries of both these organisations, though established primarily to serve the research needs of their staff, are open to the public genuinely in search of data and their rich holdings of serials can be exploited through interlibrary loans.

One other government-sponsored special library that deserves mention is the parliamentary library. Although parliamentary libraries vary in size and quality of services, they all contain materials of singular importance for the states whose legislature they serve, in particular the records of parliamentary activities: parliamentary papers, votes and proceedings, reports from government departments and other offices of the executive government. The parliamentary libraries in New South Wales, Queensland and South Australia also enjoy the benefits of being legal deposit libraries for publications printed in their respective states.

During the past fifteen or twenty years these parliamentary libraries have been completely reorganised; their stock of 'gentlemen's reading' and the heavy leather-covered furniture of the nineteenth-century club have been relegated into the background and replaced by modern, functional library furniture and video display units connected with computer-based data banks in Australia and overseas. The efforts at modernisation have, generally speaking, not affected the archival records and holdings of the parliamentary libraries, and those interested in the evolution of government at federal and state levels will find there excellent collection of raw materials. Access to the parliamentary libraries is restricted to bona fide researchers.

Most of the private special libraries set up to support an industrial or commercial undertaking, or to provide an information service for a professional group such as a legal firm, are not open to the public and cannot be seriously considered as contributors to resources for Australian studies. Nevertheless, they should not be discounted altogether because some have collected a substantial quantity of reports and unpublished documents, access to which may be obtained on request. Examples of this type of library can be found among firms concerned with environmental planning and civil engineering projects, but it must be borne in mind that these firms consider their library resources as part of the equipment needed to produce income. They therefore take an understandably proprietary view of their collection. Indeed many of them will restrict access to outsiders for fear of industrial espionage.

The resources of all types of libraries are constantly growing, not only through planned acquisitions but also through unexpected gifts. Most of the state and academic research libraries will and do accept gifts of library materials, be they individual items or whole collections. It was not uncommon in the past to make special provisions to accommodate such gifts in separate rooms named after a donor; however, most institutions now integrate their Australiana holdings with their library collection unless rarity and market price dictate the need for special treatment.

For the user this means that the bibliographic retrieval of references for Australian studies—and by implication the identification of individual books on the library's shelves—has to depend on the libary's author, title and subject catalogues. The subject approach in particular should be of help to the serious but as yet uninitiated student, an approach that forms the basis of the bibliographies that follow in sections III–X of this volume.

The front door of Closebourne House, within the Anglican Conference Centre, Morpeth, NSW – an excellent example of a two-storey colonial Georgian home.
AUSTRALIAN HERITAGE COMMISSION

CHAPTER 4

THE NATIONAL ESTATE

D. H. BORCHARDT

THE WRITTEN RECORDS, both published and unpublished, that have been discussed so far represent only a fraction of the material culture produced by the inhabitants of this continent over the last 50 000 years; indeed, they are overwhelmingly the product of the last two centuries. The use and interpretation of buildings, artefacts and objects have long been the preserve of such disciplines as archaeology, architecture and anthropology. Australian historians have only recently begun to regard evidence of this kind as a legitimate historical source.

The concrete objects that support Australian studies consist broadly of two kinds: those that have been left where they were placed originally, such as the buildings at Port Arthur, Tasmania, or Francis Greenway's St James' Church, Sydney, and hundreds of others; and those that have been preserved in specially designed institutions, such as implements, furniture, ornaments and so on. As well as such objects, which have been created by human beings, there are natural monuments which have attained historical significance through association, particularly through cultural practices and the marks left on nature by human activities. An obvious example is Ayers Rock, but there are many other sites significant as evidence of the prehistoric past or simply of geological evolution.

The National Estate includes a great variety of objects: artefacts, buildings, towns and other evidence of human ingenuity in conquering nature, as well as flora and fauna, mountains, waterways and the coastline. 'Places we should keep' is one of the more successful descriptions of the notion of the National Estate, of all that is worth preserving if future generations are to gain an understanding of the origins and history of Australia. The selection is based on subjective judgments particular to our time. But it is not an arbitrary judgment: places like the Great Barrier Reef, the Quinken rock galleries or Port Arthur can be readily identified as unique in time or place or form; some places are representative of particular plant or geological relationships; others illustrate the development of cultural styles or movements.

The identification and registration of what is worth preserving is one thing; to ensure that conservation and preservation actually take place is quite another. Far too many people are careless if not outright destructive when at large in national parks, in old buildings or in the presence of interesting but misunderstood native flora and fauna. Children, young adults and all too often even mature adults have to be educated about the value of our heritage before they will exercise restraint and learn to preserve past and present assets for future generations.

Neither the Aborigines nor the European migrants used to show the concern for the

Australian environment that is now common among most Australians. The fact that the Aborigines were numerically few and did not have at their disposal implements of destruction such as agricultural machinery, explosives and earthmoving equipment did not prevent them from putting large areas of the country to the flame, thus endangering the survival of many species of flora and fauna. The influx of European settlers, land hungry and ignorant of Australian climatic conditions or anxious to extract precious metals from the soil without consideration of the effect on the environment, wrought havoc on the balance of natural forces throughout the continent. Subsequently, new generations tried to eradicate the evidence of the historical background of European settlement in Australia—the convict period—and then endeavoured to impose their own aesthetic notions on the urban environment, replacing monuments of the Victorian and Edwardian era with ultramodern palaces of cement and glass.

Fortunately there have always been some people whose appreciation of the past has been strong enough to make them want to preserve it. To this end conservationists in many parts of the world learned to band together to try and combat senseless destruction and the erosion of the built and natural environments. Between 1945 and 1975 National Trust organisations were established in all states, the national capital and the Northern Territory. Since 1965 the Australian Council of National Trusts has co-ordinated the activities of regional trust organisations and has undertaken independent projects including the publication of books such as the *Historic buildings of Australia* series and the journal *Heritage Australia*.

The council was a major force in persuading the Australian government to establish a committee of inquiry into the National Estate. Mr Justice R.M. Hope, chairman, presented his report in 1974 which led to the creation of the Australian Heritage Commission. It is essential reading for anyone interested in the preservation of the National Estate.

The establishment of the Australian Heritage Commission as a statutory body made it possible to prepare a preliminary catalogue of some of the places and artefacts which form the National Estate. It includes both Aboriginal and white history without qualification or distinction.

In creating a register of the National Estate the Australian Heritage Commission has taken the first and most essential step to ensure that we recognise what is worth preserving. Its register is being progressively published in the *Commonwealth gazette*. By issuing *The heritage of Australia*, the commission has provided a catalogue which is fairly easy to consult and will help alert Australians to the importance of preserving our past. The book lists 6600 places which, in the eyes of the commission have 'aesthetic historic, scientific or social significance, or other special value', and illustrates most of them. An extensive index facilitates retrieval of information about houses, places, regions and natural sites, and a glossary helps the non-specialist. The book also contains four surveys of the elementary categories of the National Estate: Professor J.N. Jennings on 'Landform, rock and soil'; Professor John Turner on 'Australia's natural legacy'; Professor D.J. Mulvaney on 'The Aboriginal heritage'; and Dr Miles Lewis on 'Architecture, from colonial origins'. Each of these surveys sets out clearly what the notion of the National Estate means for its particular aspect of the environment, the earliest inhabitants and the European settlements.

State editions of the *Heritage of Australia* are being progressively published. These will contain a good deal of material not listed in the 'master volume' because additional sites, buildings and objects are registered continuously.

National parks are also part of the National Estate and there are several specific guides to all Australian national parks. These differ in quality and emphasis but G. Hutton's *Australia's natural heritage* and V. Serventy's *National parks* are probably the most useful. In addition the tourist departments of all states and territories issue popular descriptions of these national parks and these are usually accompanied by walking maps, guides to flora and fauna, advice on sleeping accommodation, the use of fire, and a listing of restrictions. It should not need stressing that national parks include marine as well as land regions; indeed many people tend to forget that areas like the Great Barrier Reef have also been classified as national parks. These areas include significant and different types of land so that there will be in the future sufficient evidence of how the continent appeared to the first settlers and their descendants.

This ceramic jug commemorates the centenary of John Batman's pioneering exploration of Port Phillip in the mid-1830s. Only 200 jugs were made, commissioned by the Mutual Store Ltd.
CASTLEMAINE ART GALLERY

CHAPTER 5

ARTEFACTS AND MUSEUMS

D. H. BORCHARDT

IF NATIONAL PARKS and nature reserves present to us a continuous link with the geological past of the continental and Tasmanian landmass, 'snapshots' taken at given moments in time can be found in museums of various kinds. The word 'museum' comes from the Greek *museion*, which means sanctuary, and though these institutions now have as a common characteristic the fact that they house inanimate matter, there have developed quite clear distinctions regarding their names and purposes according to the type of matter they preserve. It was once common usage to refer to buildings housing artistic creations as art galleries, and to restrict the term 'museum' to those institutions that care for and display specimens of natural history and technology; more recent practice tends to do away with this distinction.

Akin to museums are the botanical and zoological gardens that contain Australian specimens and through them offer excellent resources for the support of Australian studies. For historical reasons many botanical and zoological gardens are kept by municipalities—though state governments contribute to their running expenses—and there is quite a large number of them throughout Australia.

Australian botanical and zoological gardens, museums and herbaria, both state-owned and private, are listed in the *Year book Australia* and in the states' *Yearbooks*, details of which are cited below in chapter 7 of this volume. They can also be identified through specialist directories such as the *International directory of botanical gardens*; the *Australian museums directory*, which is more than a decade out of date; and *Museums of the world*, which although more recent than the local directory does not include the numerous small museums outside the metropolitan areas even though it lists 170 Australian institutions alphabetically by city or town.

A useful little guide—though restricted to 147 museums and lacking a subject index—is Peter Stanbury's *Discover Australian museums*. This is a select list with descriptive entries for institutions in all states except Queensland, and includes some botanical and zoological gardens.

This guide demonstrates the wide range of Australian institutions collecting Australian realia. There are the major museums, such as the Australian Museum in Sydney, the National Museum of Victoria and the Australian War Memorial, which have display areas of between 4000 and 8000 square metres; there are the middle-sized museums such as the South Australian Museum, the Queen Victoria Museum and Art Gallery, Launceston, the Western Australian Museum and a score or more in this group with a display area of between 1000 and 4000 square metres; finally there are several hundred small museums in towns, suburbs and country districts with limited

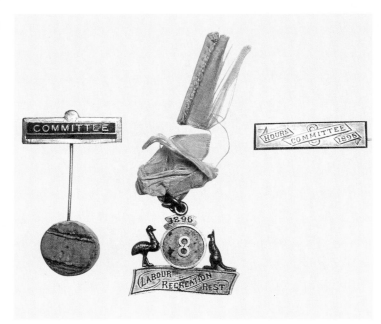

These Eight Hour Day badges are examples of the range of trade union artefacts now collected by many archives and museums. A. Stephen and A. Reeves, Badges of labour, banners of pride, *Sydney 1984.*

display and storage areas, and often maintained by volunteer staff only. The National Museum of Australia in Canberra, planned to open to the public in 1990, is building up major new collections.

One of the problems facing the researcher in Australian studies is the absence of a reliable guide to the principal categories of objects held in Australian museums and similar institutions. While it is relatively easy to guess that the state herbaria contain specimens of the flora native to the particular state, it is not easy to find out where one can see specific preserved specimens. Nor is there a source of information on where one can find examples of human artefacts stored in institutions of different kinds. In those rare cases where the name of an institution indicates a specific purpose—aircraft museums, steam museums, war memorials—the problem is of course partly resolved.

Since the publication of *Museums in Australia, 1975,* the report of a commonwealth committee of inquiry, museum development has increased considerably. Public interest and government support have made new buildings possible and encouraged considerable growth in the quantity and quality of the collections. An important report on Victoria was prepared by Roger Trudgeon but there have been to date no similar examinations of the museum scene in other states. However, heartening changes have occurred: in Queensland a new building was opened in 1985 to house one of Australia's most important scientific and ethnographic collections; the Western Australian Museum has opened branches in Fremantle and other regional centres and developed excellence in marine archaeology; and in Melbourne the amalgamation of the National Museum of Victoria with the Science Museum of Victoria created the Museum of Victoria in 1983 with the extension of its collecting responsibilities to include 'the history of human society'. Extensive expansions are being planned for other metropolitan institutions of this kind, the most important being the addition of the Powerhouse site to the Museum of Applied Arts and Sciences in Sydney. Due to open in 1988, it will include displays of transport, decorative arts and social history. The compilation of a comprehensive index to museums should be a high priority.

It is but a natural development that there should be some museums specialising in rather narrow fields, developing real depth in collecting. An obvious example is the Australian War Memorial in Canberra. Dedicated to the memory of Australians who died while serving in the armed forces since Australia participated in the Sudan War, this museum has outstanding collections and innovative publishing and education policies.

Special attention must be drawn to the score or more of open-air museums that have sprung up since the 1960s. Most of these are joint ventures by local government and state authorities and usually occupy quite a large site. The objective is to reconstruct history with the help of reconstituted old buildings or reconstructions, and all contain a rich mix of artefacts, pictures, appropriate equipment of the period and models (human and animal); they are frequently staffed by attendants dressed in period costume and engaged in occupations appropriate to the time. The most elaborate are Sovereign Hill, a recreation of Ballarat in the gold-rush era, and Old Sydney Town, north of Gosford, a recreation of Sydney in the early nineteenth century. These *tableaux vivants* are considerable tourist attractions, but their authenticity and purpose are questioned by some historians.

Folk museums of a modest kind can be found in most medium-sized towns and in the larger cities some quite extensive collections have been brought together to illustrate the social life of the past. Though the building housing the collection may have been donated to the community, the upkeep and the employment of custodial and educational staff usually depend on the local authority. State governments provide limited financial assistance to such museum services.

Another type of gallery–museum, recently developed under the aegis of the National Trusts, is the historic house museum. An excellent example is the gallery at Springwood in the Blue Mountains, New South Wales, which consists of the house once lived in by the artist Norman Lindsay and in which paintings and memorabilia related to the artist are preserved. These house museums are intended to present the objects of daily life—furniture, household goods, photographs, pictures—as they were when occupied. Other examples of this kind of gallery are Como in Melbourne, Old Government House in Parramatta and Entally House in Tasmania. In the last few years more modest houses have also been restored and opened to the public.

Specialisation in collections is particularly noteworthy in the several conservatories and museums maintained by Australian government departments. A list, now somewhat out of date, is contained in the Piggott report *Museums in Australia* which shows the principal collections; some have been discussed already in this chapter.

The literature on Australian museums is not very large. Although many museums produce booklets about their origin and purpose, and occasionally a monograph about a special exhibit, only a few large state museums can afford to publish serials, monographs and series relating to their research. A bibliography of this literature has been compiled by J.G. Marshall as *Australian museums: a preliminary bibliography*.

Mark Arbuz (b Australia 1953), 1980 Royal visit.
Teatowel, screenprint on cotton, 69.5 × 62.0 cm, 1980.
AUSTRALIAN NATIONAL GALLERY

The Art of the Process-Engraver

THE art of reproducing important paintings and
drawings, such as appear in "Art in Australia" is
the severest test an engraver can be put to.

It has always been our aim to retain the character of the
artist's work. To retain the feeling of the medium in a
small space, whether it be oil, watercolor, pencil or line,
is a difficult matter and one which requires careful and
thorough workmanship.

We think we can succeed in our colour, half-tone
and line work, and we feel our aim has been accomplished in the reproductions we have made for the Hilder
book and in "Art in Australia."

Hartland and Hyde

— Process Engravers —
Specialists in Colour Work

Luvian House, Clarence St
SYDNEY

*'The art of the process-engravers.' Advertisement for
Hartland and Hyde, Sydney, in* Art in Australia 2,
1917.
MITCHELL LIBRARY

CHAPTER 6

PICTORIAL SOURCES AND GALLERIES

VICTOR CRITTENDEN

PICTORIAL SOURCES are no longer seen as mere adjuncts to social history but are looked upon as datable documents, and of the same significance as textual matter interpreted by historians. An artist's or a photographer's interpretation of a social situation, a landscape or a historical event is plainly influenced by social and cultural background and by the creator's intention. Photography, often thought to be an objective, documentary art, can be manipulated in terms of the choice and presentation of a subject in much the same way as a painter creates an image. Paintings, sketches, drawings, sculpture and photographs often tell us more about the past than prose accounts. Such pictorial records have been systematically and unsystematically collected by a wide variety of institutions from galleries and libraries to government departments and local historical societies.

European art galleries often grew out of private collections brought together by wealthy persons who occasionally opened them to the general public for admiration and viewing. The concept of art galleries for the population at large was gradually accepted, and municipal and state governments founded and maintained art collections for the delectation of the ordinary citizen. Private donors added to the collections maintained from the public purse, enhancing their cultural and artistic renown, and in some instances the enriched institutions became great national collections.

The Australian colonial governments followed the British and European models and social pressures, as well as financial support from the wealthier citizens, led to the early establishment of art galleries and museums that would house not only European artefacts but also evidence of Australia's own flora and fauna and of the creations of its own arts and crafts.

Colonial governments allocated relatively large sums of money to construct 'national' galleries and to form 'national' collections, containing European masters and the occasional Australian work. Victoria led the way when a Museum of Art (later to become the National Gallery of Victoria) was established in 1861, but the collection grew slowly until it received the Felton bequest in 1904. Other states followed suit and before the end of the century each had its own 'national' gallery. The Tasmanian Museum and Art Gallery was planned in 1838 and built as early as 1863. Sydney's state gallery started in 1874, Adelaide's in 1879 and Perth and Brisbane had established galleries by 1895. The Australian National Gallery was not opened until 1982 but a collection of works of art commenced soon after Federation in 1901.

Between 1850 and the 1890s most of our photographic records were the work of professional photographers, working either for the government or from private studios. In some states the best collections for this period are to be found in the government printing offices. Newspapers and periodicals did not carry photographs until the 1890s. Before this they printed images in the form of line and wood engravings. Examples of this high quality pictorial imagery can be found in the *Illustrated Sydney News* (1853–94) and the *Australasian Sketcher with Pen and Pencil* (1873–89).

From the 1890s photographs gradually began to appear in newspapers and periodicals throughout the country. The *Sydney Mail* provided extensive photographic coverage of World War I, as did similar weeklies in all other states. By the 1920s the major metropolitan dailies were accompanying more of their stories with photographic images. In 1922 a newspaper started in Melbourne called the *Sun News Pictorial* in which the text was planned to be secondary to the photographic content. It is of considerable importance in this context that the major newspapers retained large collections of photographs and that the major newspaper archives, particulary those of John Fairfax and Sons in Sydney and the Herald and Weekly Times group in Melbourne now house the largest collections of twentieth-century Australian photographs.

A useful guide to institutions holding Australian pictorial resources, including newspaper archives, government departments, religious groups, clubs, companies, archives, libraries, museums and galleries and private individuals, is the *Directory of Australian pictorial resources* compiled by Mari Davis and Hilary Boyce. Besides comments on the collections, it provides information on addresses and hours of opening.

Information on Australian galleries and their history will usually be found in their own archives, libraries and publications. A useful overview is *Artists and galleries of Australia* by Max Germaine which contains in alphabetical sequence short entries on Australian artists and galleries, including private galleries and those within educational institutions.

All the major Australian galleries have collected works representative of Australian artists as an integral part of their acquisitions policy. More recently major Australian museums have endeavoured to acquire examples of Aboriginal art, which characteristically is linked with utilitarian objects and with ornamentation of the human body. The wall paintings which go back hundreds of years in some cases and have their own mythical and historical significance are, of course, site bound and are cared for under the provisions of the national Heritage Act.

Lists of Australian artworks are published by the principal art galleries whose collections warrant such an expense. Some of these gallery catalogues have become notable: Whitelaw's *Australian landscape drawing, 1830–1880, in the National Gallery of Victoria*, *Picture book: selected works from the collection of the Art Gallery of South Australia* and *The great south land: treasures of the Mitchell and Dixson galleries* by Mourot and Jones. A select list of these documents can be found in R. Choate's excellent *A guide to sources of information on the arts in Australia*.

State-supported art galleries, like all other statutory bodies, have to submit annual reports on their activities to the state parliament which allocates their budget. Many of these reports contain details of major acquisitions, educational or extension activities, lecture series and workshops. They are published as parliamentary papers and can be found in that rather drab series; in addition, some state galleries issue a more attractive version of the annual report for the general public, friends of the gallery and other supporting bodies.

Almost all the major galleries try to keep the public alerted to new acquisitions, both by close liaison with the daily press and by special exhibition catalogues. Such publications are not always produced on a lavish scale but may nevertheless serve as effective resources on artists as well as the gallery collection.

There is considerable historical value in these exhibition catalogues and all state libraries, in addition to receiving copies under legal deposit regulations, make a special effort to maintain a collection of those that relate to their own state. The working library—the collections of books, pamphlets, documents and journals acquired for the use of the staff—of every gallery will, of course, also endeavour to maintain a complete collection of such exhibition catalogues, but these working libraries are not always open to the public although access to them for study purposes is possible.

Regional galleries in Ballarat, Bendigo and Geelong, Victoria, preceded those in all other states with the exception of the Queen Victoria Museum and Art Gallery in Launceston, Tasmania. There are now many such regional galleries throughout Australia and they are listed in Germaine's *Artists and galleries in Australia*.

Photographic collections often form part of an art gallery or museum and are frequently found in libraries and in the collections of historical societies. Apart from the newspaper archives already mentioned, the largest photographic collections in Australia are to be found in the state libraries and the specialist Australiana collections. The photographic image has its own afficionados and some institutions have created specialised sections or departments within their general collections to house, catalogue and render accessible this important evidence of the past. Davis and Boyce have included numerous references to photographic collections, and Davies and Stanbury in their *The Mechanical eye in Australia* (OUP 1985) describe the history of photography in Australia to 1900 with numerous references to collections and to the early journals on photography. Gael Newton takes the story of photography in Australia up to 1950 in her book *Silver and grey* but her survey is restricted to a small number of professional photographers.

The most important work in this area is the endeavour to create a comprehensive national index of photographic images. Entitled for the present 'Australia as Australians saw it', this project is to canvass the public to arouse awareness of the importance of photographs of the past; to invite the public to submit photographs and to allow them to be copied; and to provide a subject approach to the photographs, with appropriate cross-references, by means of a computer-based indexing program. The project is directed by Euan McGillivray and Matthew Nickson who also edit a bulletin called *WOPOP: working papers on photography* which offers detailed descriptions of the structure of the index and the initial limitations of the collecting program. In another field, the Australian Museum in Sydney holds a major collection of photographs of Australian fauna and has published a list of species covered which is revised from time to time.

Pictures, drawings, sculpture and photographs do not have to stem from the dim past to have significance for the historian, but contemporary artists are more frequently found in commercial art galleries where their work is exhibited for a limited period, or in the exhibition rooms of art societies, mainly in the capital cities. Catalogues, reports and reviews of such exhibitions may help historians to identify persons and places and the sales registers should help to keep track of the location of the works of art sold.

Art societies, photographic societies and artists' associations continue to contribute to the discussion on the aesthetic and social issues raised by visual culture; the minutes and record books of these societies form an important archival source for our social and cultural history.

'The ponies and the new dog-cart, Bondi', 27 Aug 1901. Photograph in the albums of Arthur Wigram Allen. This informal family photograph stands in contrast to most Victorian photography. The collected albums of A.W. Allen, a keen amateur photographer, provide a record of the lives of the leisured classes around the turn of the century. The presence of the waiting dog-cart suggests that for wealthy Sydneysiders relaxation was tempered by the responsibilities of the upper classes.
MITCHELL LIBRARY

II
GENERAL
REFERENCE WORKS
AND STATISTICS

*An example of the bookbinder's craft by Jack Harding of
New South Wales. The gumleaf border and the
central wattle design are carved into tan leather stained with tan
colouring. The book measures 280 × 240 × 17 mm.
Photograph by John Storey.*
CRAFTS COUNCIL OF AUSTRALIA

Chats. *Drawn by Neville Cayley, engraved by Bacon and Co.* The illustrated Australian encyclopaedia, *edited by Arthur Wilberforce Jose and Herbert James Carter, Angus & Robertson, Sydney 1925–27, vol I, plate XIII.*

CHAPTER 7

ENCYCLOPAEDIAS, DICTIONARIES AND FACT BOOKS

D. H. BORCHARDT

THIS CHAPTER PRESENTS an overview of the reference works that provide general information on Australia. The type of book included here is characterised by the presentation of factual statements, briefly explained or set in context and wholly or almost wholly dedicated to Australia. Dictionaries (other than language dictionaries), encyclopaedias, handbooks of dates and certain types of directories form, therefore, the substance of this chapter. Specialist reference on the subjects treated in the following chapters of this volume are, of course, cited in the appropriate context and readers should look there for such specific works as an encyclopaedia of sport (chapter 47) or a dictionary of Australian painting (chapter 49).

Also excluded are the large general encyclopaedias produced by other nations—the *Britannica*, the *Americana*, the *Soviet encyclopedia*, for example—which though they do contain sizeable amounts of information on Australia cannot be looked upon as prime sources of information for Australian studies.

The number of reference works that fall within these confines is still relatively small and the titles listed below present a selection of the more reliable among them. No attempt has been made to list all of them and, though the overall trend of this volume is historical, in this section only limited attention has been paid to reference works that have generally outlived their usefulness. A broader and retrospective treatment of reference works has been provided by Borchardt (*Australian bibliography*, 3rd edn, Sydney, Pergamon, 1976). The public library oriented *Current Australian reference books* (Canberra, AACOBS, 1983) is another useful tool to help identify reference works for specific purposes. Readers are urged to consult these two main lists of information sources. Reference works especially designed for children have also been excluded; important as they may be for didactic purposes, they are scarcely relevant as sources for Australian studies.

The list of reference works that follows has been divided into six groups: encyclopaedias; dictionaries of dates and events; yearbooks; atlases; gazetteers; and directories. It should be noted that references to bibliographies and catalogues of books are listed in the following chapter.

As can be expected, given the political history of Australia, many of the early dictionaries and encyclopaedias were regional or state based. Only since the 1880s have there been genuine attempts to treat the whole continent within the covers of one book: the oldest example is by Sir Joseph Heaton (1879; facs, 1984). Though its importance as a source of biographical information far outshines its value as a chronology, it contains data on the events and institutions that shaped Australian history. Heaton's importance for Australian biography is discussed in chapter 19 of this volume; though the work also offers a great deal of information on Australia in the nineteenth century, not all dates and reported events should be accepted at face value.

An encyclopaedia, as the name suggests, represents a summing up of our knowledge about a subject or even about the world at large, and we associate with the term a certain degree of reliability and educational or academic quality. As the great historian of science, George Sarton, wrote in his *Guide to the history of science* (Waltham, Mass, Chronica Botanica, 1952): 'It is wise to refer to encyclopaedias for first guidance; it is priggish to disregard them; it is foolish to depend too much on them'. The number of Australian encyclopaedias published to date is relatively small, even if we count among them those restricted in their coverage to individual states.

Users of an encyclopaedia have certain expectations regarding the quality and presentation of information, and unless these are met they are not likely to be satisfied. It is difficult to assess the quality of an encyclopaedia and, as the annotation to some of the examples cited in the bibliography will show, some publishers have had more of an eye on sales than on quality and reliability of information. Among the most obvious criteria that should be considered when evaluating an encyclopaedia are the reputation of the editor and contributors; the plan and objectives of the work as a whole; the treatment (popular or scholarly) of the subjects; obvious or hidden bias (national, religious, racial); the inclusion of references and bibliographies; the currency of statistics and tables; and the quality of cross-referencing and indexing.

These are fundamental considerations. There are other characteristics, of course, such as the quality of printing and binding, typography and illustrations, and the important problem of updating. The fact that most encyclopaedias represent large printing and publishing projects makes it unavoidable that the information they contain will be at least one year old and even older in multivolume works. Some of the large international encyclopaedias issue supplements on a regular basis. The *Britannica book of the year. . .*, for example, is issued annually and tries to update the most important and vulnerable (from a chronological point of view) articles and data. Indeed, the *Encyclopaedia Britannica* has issued one special supplement for Australasia (*Britannica book of the year: the year in Australia and New Zealand, 1963–1965*, Sydney, Encyclopaedia Britannica Inc, 1967) but no further special issues have appeared.

The most important sources of information on all aspects of Australian studies are the four editions of the *Australian encyclopaedia* that have appeared between 1925–26 and 1983. Unquestionably, the quality as well as the quantity of information offered has increased over the years, but those seeking concise data on topics related to Australia are advised that in spite of the greater number of words that mark successive editions, some fundamental articles in the early editions, especially the second edition, have retained their intrinsic value; indeed, some have not been replaced by new contributions. That there should be changes in the several editions is understandable; publishers must limit the size of their books to make them marketable. Each of the four editions of the *Australian encyclopaedia* has certain advantages and faults when compared with the others. Thus the most serious shortcoming of the third edition is the lack of an index. The fourth edition has taken over some articles from the second and third editions, metricating and updating data, and in several instances shortening the pieces so that the information is less comprehensive.

A number of recent publications have tried to present within the covers of one book a concise listing of information on Australia, but careful examination and a survey of expert criticism suggests that none is worthy of recommendation to the serious student. In particular, it should not be thought that inclusion in this list is in any respect a recommendation. The fact is, simply, that at times it is convenient to consult a one-volume reference work and of the several publications available the least offensive have been included.

Subject dictionaries (as distinct from language dictionaries) differ from encyclopaedias mainly in their method of presentation, which tends to be brief and based on definition rather than on explanation. Occasionally there is some overlap between dictionaries and encyclopaedias. We also have works called 'dictionaries of dates' or 'dictionaries of events' which, besides presenting facts about Australia in alphabetical or chronological sequence, also explain such facts and events, or comment in an explanatory manner on the chronology. The work of Sir Joseph Heaton mentioned above is a good example. The few titles of quality in this category are listed in the second part of the reading list of reference works that follows.

Readers' attention is also drawn to two other titles among the reference volumes that form part of *Australians: a historical library*. One is *Australians: events and places*; the other, *Australians: a historical dictionary*. The first includes a chronology and a gazetteer of Australia, while the second includes subject and biographical entries.

The third part of the reading list below details the several annual compilations by the Australian Bureau of Statistics (ABS). The *Yearbooks*, as they are now known, are official publications—they emanate from a government authority and have the standing that goes with such authorship. The head office of the ABS in Canberra issues the *Yearbook Australia* while the comparable volumes for the states are issued by the respective state offices. Although there is co-ordination and supervision from the ABS head office, the state offices arrange presentation and selection of topics to fit the needs of each state.

A selection of atlases, gazetteers and directories concludes this discussion of reference books. Taking the atlases first because there are so few of them and their significance is so obvious, it is with much pleasure that we note *Australians: a historical atlas*, part of this series *Australians: a historical library*, as the project's contribution to the cartography of Australia. It presents a bridge between a historical atlas and a reference tool for physical, social and demographic data.

Few other atlases fulfil an acceptable standard of cartography and statistical data. The scores of school atlases that have been inflicted upon Australian children over the last century are best forgotten. It was not until the advent of the *Reader's digest atlas of Australia* (Sydney, Reader's Digest Services, 1977) that the Australian public had available a quality product, created from an Australian point of view and supported by charts and statistical data. A second edition appeared in 1984, and almost at the same time the completion of the Macquarie atlas was announced.

Of considerable importance is the *Atlas of Australian resources*, an official publication produced by the Division of National Mapping in Canberra. A series of three atlas volumes was first published in 1953–60; a second edition appeared in 1962–77. A new edition now in progress is to consist of ten volumes, each centred on a topic map, such as population or agriculture, with commentaries and smaller cartographic and statistical data in support. The same government authority has also produced, in association with the ABS, social atlases of Australian cities based on the census data collected in 1976 and 1981 respectively.

In addition to these national atlases there are numerous regional atlases, some of which have a historical component. The Lands and Survey departments of Tasmania and Western Australia have published respectively an *Atlas of Tasmania* (Hobart, 1965) and *Western Australia: an atlas of human endeavour 1829–1979* (Perth, 1979). An *Atlas of Victoria* (Melbourne, Government Printer) was issued in 1982 and the South Australian Lands and Survey Department has a new atlas of that state in the making. Each of these atlases has been prompted by the state government's desire to record the economic and social progress of its state and the cartographic work reflects this objective as well as providing details of physical geography.

There are, of course, many hundreds of maps of Australia, produced by many different authorities. Some guidance to these can be obtained from B.T. Tysons' *The topographical map series of Australia* (Melbourne, The Author, 1965), now over twenty years out of date but neither replaced nor updated.

The map collections of some Australian libraries are of considerable size and, as can be expected, the coverage of Australian cartography is especially strong in most of them. To list them here would exceed the space available, but N.M. Rauchle (1980) is a reliable guide. Current cartographic productions in Australia can be checked through the National Library's *Australian maps*, a complementary service to its *Australian national bibliography*. *Australian maps* lists sheet maps since 1967; atlases in book form are listed in the *Australian national bibliography*.

The cartographic emergence of the Australian continent has been the subject of several books, some of which are typographically and cartographically quite delightful. Outstanding among these are Egon and Elsie Kunz (1971) and G. Schilder's *Australia unveiled* (Amsterdam, Theatrum Orbis Terrarum, 1976). R.V. Tooley's *The mapping of Australia* (London, Holland Press Cartographica, 1979), of which only volume 1 has appeared, is closely associated with the author's large collection of maps housed in the National Library of Australia.

For the historian and historical geographer, W.H. Wells (1848; facs, 1970) is of prime importance as the first attempt to define, in geographic terms, the sparse settlements that had by then grown up on the Australian continent. Almost twenty years were to lapse before another attempt was made to define the location of Australian settlements. F.F. Bailliere's gazetteers (1865–79) covered all the colonies except Western Australia.

The most comprehensive gazetteer published to date is that already mentioned as forming part of this series *Australians: a historical library*. Until its appearance, the United States Office of Geography's *Australia: official standard names approved by the United States Board on Geographic Names* (Washington, USGPO, 1957) and the gazetteer of the Australian Division of National Mapping (1975, 1984) were the only comprehensive guides to Australian geography. The former includes 62 000 names of places and topographic features. Australia's Division of National Mapping has recently issued a list of Australian place names in microform (1984). This is an important document, which tends to be little known except to specialists.

A wave of interest in Aboriginal names and their meanings has led to the publication of a number of guides to Aboriginal place names, two of which—Reed (1967) and Massola (1968)—have been included in the bibliography that follows. There are many older reference works related to place names; most are restricted to one state or region and all are selective.

It should be noted that the topic bibliographies that follow include specialist directories where they exist or have bearing on the subject involved. This applies particularly to the professions, which often maintain and publish directories of their members and, where appropriate, of institutional services associated with the profession. Typical examples are the *Australian legal directory* published by the Law Council of Australia and the *Medical directory of Australia* issued by the Australasian Medical Publishing Co. The best source for the addresses of professional associations is the *Directory of Australian associations* (1985–86), details of which are shown below; those wanting to obtain such membership directories should address themselves to the appropriate association headquarters.

The ever-increasing services offered by government authorities render the *Commonwealth government directory* and its state counterparts a particularly useful reference tool. The most common use made of these directories is undoubtedly the identification of government offices, their principal officers, addresses and services provided. Beyond this, the directories also serve as sources of information on the history of government administration or of the evolution of political controls through the bureaucratic structure of government. The *Commonwealth government directory* goes back to 1918 but the passing of the Freedom of Information Act in 1981 has forced a new form upon the directory. From 1982 on, it appears in three parts: a directory of offices, a list of officers and a third section, in as many parts as there are ministries, showing the statutory responsibilities of all departments and statutory authorities responsible to each ministry. Some further details are described in the entry for the directory in the bibliography.

All states except Western Australia have issued a similar directory of state departments and authorities and of their responsibilities. These are updated at irregular intervals and are obtainable through the state government information departments or the state government printers.

Only one state, Victoria, provides easy access to data on local government administration. The *Victorian municipal directory* has appeared since 1866. In other states the same type of information has to be gleaned from commercial directories such as the directories issued by Sands & McDougall for South Australia and Victoria, and those compiled by Sands for New South Wales.

Lastly, and merely to remind users of the obvious which is sometimes so easily forgotten, there are telephone books issued and frequently updated under the authority of Telecom Australia, and street directories for all the larger towns in Australia and for some of the smaller ones as well.

ENCYCLOPAEDIAS

THE ANGUS & Robertson concise Australian encyclopaedia. A & R R, 1983. 505 p, illus, maps.

A very simplistic approach to things Australian, suitable for primary schools.

AUSTRALIAN encyclopaedia. A & R, 1925–26. 2 vols, illus, maps, no index.

AUSTRALIAN encyclopaedia. A & R, 1958. 10 vols, illus, maps, index. Reprinted, Sydney, Grolier, 1965.

AUSTRALIAN encyclopaedia (3rd edn). Sydney, Grolier Society of Australia, 1977, 6 vols, illus, maps, no index.

AUSTRALIAN encyclopaedia (4th edn). Sydney, Grolier Society of Australia, 1983. 12 vols, illus, maps, index.

The latest of the four editions of the most important Australian reference work contains more than four thousand articles on a wide range of subjects. Most longer articles are signed and there are many illustrations. For further comments see the introductory essay above.

THE CONCISE encyclopedia of Australia and New Zealand. Hong Kong, Multimedia International for Horwitz Grahame, 1982. 2 vols, illus, maps.

A popular work, strong in biography and geography. Some articles have notes on further reading. First published as The modern encyclopaedia of Australia and New Zealand in 1964; revised as New national Australian encyclopaedia in 1974, and then as Concise encyclopaedia of Australia in 1979. The New Zealand content is located at the end of vol 2.

THE CYCLOPEDIA of N.S.W. illustrated ... an historical and commercial review, descriptive and biographical, facts, figures and illustrations ... Sydney, McCarron, Stewart, 1907.

THE CYCLOPEDIA of South Australia: an historical and commercial review, descriptive and biographical, facts, figures and illustrations ... Ed by H.T. Burgess. Adelaide, Cyclopedia Co, 1907–09. 2 vols, illus. Repr, Austaprint, 1978.

THE CYCLOPEDIA of Tasmania: an historical and commercial review, descriptive and biographical, facts, figures and illustrations ... Hobart, Maitland & Krone, 1900. 2 vols, illus.

THE CYCLOPEDIA of Victoria: an historical and commercial review, descriptive and biographical facts, figures and illustrations ... Ed by James Smith. Melbourne, Cyclopedia Co, 1903–05. 3 vols, illus.

THE CYCLOPEDIA of Western Australia: an historical and commercial review, descriptive and biographical, facts, figures and illustrations. Ed by J.S. Battye. Adelaide, Hussey & Gillingham, 1912–13. 2 vols, illus.

These five state-oriented cyclopaedias represent important general surveys of achievements. Still useful as a rich source of information on the men and women who made progress possible.

LEARMONTH, A.T.A. AND LEARMONTH, N. Encyclopaedia of Australia (2nd edn). Sydney, Hicks, Smith & Sons, 1983. 606 p, illus, maps.

A reliable but restricted one-volume reference work. Includes living and deceased persons of note; relatively strong on natural history, but weak on social, economic and political history. First published in 1968.

SHAW, J. ed, Collins Australian encyclopedia. Sydney, Collins in association with David Bateman Ltd, 1984. 848 p, illus, maps.

One-volume reference work, accurate enough as a first source of reference. Includes tables, indexes, chronologies.

DICTIONARIES OF DATES AND EVENTS

The Australian almanac. Sydney, A & R, 1985. 793 p, illus, maps.

Useful work. Deals with a range of issues including politics, the arts, geography and history.

AUSTRALIAN handbook and almanac 1–37. Sydney, Gordon & Gotch, 1870–1906.

Title, size and significance have varied over the years and the handbook increased in scope as it grew from 100 to 500 pages. The last few issued included business information, land and mining maps, country towns and their commercial enterprises.

CASTLES, A.C. Australia: a chronology and fact book, 1606–1976. Dobbs Ferry, NY, Oceana Publications, 1978. 151 p.

Contains brief notes on the most important events in Australian history and select documents to illustrate the development of government in Australia. Bibliography and name index.

HEATON, J.H. Australian dictionary of dates and men of the time, containing the history of Australasia, from 1542 to May 1879. Sydney, George Robertson, 1879. 232, 317 p.

This synopsis of Australian chronology is useful because it includes many minor events based on newspaper reports, including those which did not make the headlines.

THE MACQUARIE book of events. Ed by Bryce Fraser. Sydney, Macquarie Library, 1983. 608 p, illus.

This unorthodox dictionary lists a vast amount of detailed Australian history. The notable events that occurred in every year since 1788 are arranged under broad headings, which is particularly useful because the book has an inadequate index.

READER'S DIGEST SERVICES PTY LTD. Australia's yesterdays: a look at our recent past (2nd edn). Sydney, Reader's Digest Services, 1979. 360 p, illus, maps.

A nostalgic collection of illustrations showing Australian life including a chart of historic events, year by year 1901–78, and a biographical dictionary of Australians who made the news. First published in 1974.

YEARBOOKS

NEW SOUTH WALES year book. Sydney, ABS, NSW Office, 1886/87– .

Title varies: Wealth and progress of New South Wales 1886/87–1900/01; Official year book of New South Wales 1904/05–1979.

QUEENSLAND year book. Brisbane, ABS, Qld Office, 1937– .

Title varies: Official year book of Queensland 1957–63.

SOUTH AUSTRALIAN year book. Adelaide, ABS, South Australian Office, 1966– .

TASMANIAN year book. Hobart, ABS, Tasmanian Office, 1967– .

VICTORIAN year book. Melbourne, ABS, Victorian office, 1873– .

WESTERN AUSTRALIAN year book. Perth, ABS, West Australian Office, 1886–1902/04; ns, 1957– .

Title varies: Official year book of Western Australia 1957–66.

YEAR BOOK Australia. Canberra, ABS, 1908– .

Title varies: Official year book of the Commonwealth of Australia 1908–72; Official year book of Australia 1973–74.

These annual volumes of statistics, economic and political data and general information about Australia as a whole, and in separate volumes about the states, are the most reliable sources of information available. Compiled by the ABS, they are reliable and unbiased. The state volumes are not all alike though they follow a common pattern and contain related basic data. The *Year book Australia* contains different additional features in each issue.

ATLASES

ATLAS of Australian resources (3rd series). Canberra, Division of National Mapping, 1980– .
This remarkable and important work is planned to consist of ten volumes, each dedicated to a specific topic, for example, soils and land use, population and agriculture. The maps are of high quality and there are statistical data and other information.

ATLAS of population and housing: 1976 census. Canberra, Division of National Mapping and ABS in association with Institute of Australian Geographers, 1979–81. 7 vols.

ATLAS of population and housing: 1981 census. Canberra, Division of National Mapping and ABS in association with Institute of Australian Geographers, 1984– 7 vols.

Important set of social atlases presenting graphical interpretations of census data prepared by the organisations listed as publishers. The atlas based on the 1976 census deals with the eleven major population centres (each of over 100 000 people) and the atlas for the 1981 census deals with the seven capital cities. Each volume includes a commentary on the area and on the maps.

THE AUSTRALIAN book of the road. Sydney, Hamlyn, 1971. 167 (40) p, illus, maps.
Designed for use while travelling, this atlas also contains an index to place names. The maps are clear but not always accurate.

KUNZ, E. AND KUNZ, E. *A continent takes shape*. Sydney, Collins, 1971. 175 p, illus, maps.
A documented history of the mapping of Australia.

THE MACQUARIE illustrated world atlas. Sydney, Macquarie Library in association with Division of National Mapping, Canberra, and the Dept of Lands & Survey, Wellington, 1984. 512 p, illus, maps.
A fine example of cartography. The publisher's collaboration with the official cartographic departments assures the reliability of Australian and New Zealand maps.

RAUCHLE, N.M. ed, *Map collections in Australia: a directory* (3rd edn). Canberra, NLA, 1980. 141 p.
A list of institutions holding significant collections of maps (not only Australian). First published in 1977.

READER'S digest atlas of Australia. Sydney, Reader's Digest Services, 1978. 287 p, illus, maps.
The first of a series of modern atlases combining quality maps with statistical data and explanatory legends. A gazetteer occupies pp 217–87.

GAZETTEERS

AUSTRALIA. Dept of National Development and Energy. Division of National Mapping. *Australia 1: 250 000 and 1:100 000 master names gazetteer. Master names file (microform)*. Canberra, The Division, 1984. 9 microfiches.
The only official gazetteer of Australian place names produced by the national authority also responsible for mapping Australia. The microform edition supersedes the 1975 book edition.

AUSTRALIAN Postal Commission. *List of post offices and localities*. Melbourne, The Commission, 1980. Loose leaf.
Alphabetical list of both official and non-official post offices, with codes indicating services provided. Supersedes the Postmaster-General's Department's list *Post and telegraph offices*, 1969.

BAILLIERE, F.F. *Bailliere's Victorian gazetteer and road guide* . . . Comp by R.P. Whitworth. Melbourne, F.F. Bailliere, 1865. 442 p, maps.
A popular guide when published, now useful for historical information. Revised editions appeared in 1866, 1870 and 1879. Similar volumes issued for NSW (1866), SA (1866), Qld (1876) and Tas (1877).

MASSOLA, A. *Aboriginal place names of south-east Australia and their meaning*. Melbourne, Lansdowne, 1968. 62 p, illus.

REED, A.W. *Aboriginal place names and their meanings*. Sydney, Reed. 1967. 144 p.
Massola and Reed offer helpful, though dated, information on Aboriginal words for settlement and geographic features.

WELLS, W.H. *A geographical dictionary: or gazetteer of the Australian colonies* . . .. Sydney, W. & F. Ford, 1848. 438 p, illus, maps.
Facsimile edition, Sydney, Library Board of NSW, 1970.

DIRECTORIES

THE BUSINESS who's who in Australia. Sydney, Riddell, 1964– .
The most comprehensive of several works of this kind, but more specialised information can be obtained from *Jobson's yearbook of public companies. . .* (1928–) and *Jobson's mining year book* (1957–). These works, directly or indirectly, provide historical data of companies.

COMMONWEALTH government directory. Canberra, AGPS, 1983– . 3 vols.
The official guide to the organisation, executive personnel and services of the commonwealth government. Issued irregularly from 1918 to 1971, then annually. The title varied. The new format lists federal agencies, their access data and principal personnel (vol 1) and a brief description for each ministerial portfolio (vol 2). Vol 3 includes information on services offered.

COMMONWEALTH SCIENTIFIC & INDUSTRIAL RESEARCH ORGANIZATION. *Australian scientific societies and professional associations*. Melbourne, CSIRO, 1978. 226 p.
Restricted to scientific bodies. Includes some data on publications. First published in 1971.

DIRECTORY of Australian associations (4th edn). Melbourne, 1985. 515 p.
Lists in alphabetical order non-profit Australian organisations, excluding community groups, social clubs and sports clubs. There is a classified subject index according to service offered or principal activity, and a geographic index by state or territory. New editions appear regularly.

THE HERITAGE of Australia: the illustrated register of the National Estate. Melbourne, Macmillan in association with the Australian Heritage Commission, 1981. 1164 p, illus.
Illustrated reference work presenting a comprehensive overview of items of the natural and cultural heritage listed by the Australian Heritage Commission.

OZARTS: a guide to arts organisations in Australia (2nd edition). Sydney, Policy and Planning Division, Australia Council, 1984. 236 p.
Lists federal and state government arts authorities, with an index to names of organisations, subjects and art form. First published in 1981.

VICTORIAN municipal directory. Melbourne, Arnall & Jackson, 1866– .
Includes details of cities, towns, municipalities, boroughs, state government authorities and public institutions, names of officers and other details. An important historical source.

Caroline Ambrus, The ladies' picture show, *Hale & Iremonger, Sydney 1984. The cover illustration by Florence Rodway,* Portrait of a lady, *c1914, is held by the Australian National Gallery.*

CHAPTER 8

BIBLIOGRAPHIES AND LIBRARY CATALOGUES

D. H. BORCHARDT

THE REFERENCE WORKS cited in chapter 6 present, generally speaking, factual information: When did it happen? Where did it happen? What is an emu? Who built the first Australian church? The purpose of this chapter is to provide answers to different kinds of questions: Who wrote about what? Where can I find Marcus Clarke's *His natural life*?

The library profession has provided some answers to questions such as these but many other scholars have also contributed to the literature guides that have helped to map the now quite large field of writings about Australia. The concepts of descriptive and enumerative bibliography underlie the whole structure of this volume. This particular chapter, however, tries to alert readers to the main body of Australian bibliographic work.

It is important to distinguish between a subject bibliography and a library catalogue. A bibliography is, in the context of this chapter, a list of references to a specific topic irrespective of where those references can be found. A catalogue—in whatever form: on cards, printed as book, on computer tape—is an index to the holdings of one or more institutions. For instance, the *British Library general catalogue of printed books* refers only to books held in that library, and the *Australian union list of serials in theological collections* by H. Arns and M. Dacy (Sydney, National Catholic Research Council, 1983) includes only the holdings of those libraries represented in that work.

For ease of reference the large listing of bibliographies below has been divided into three sequences dealing respectively with general bibliographies, periodical indexes and special bibliographies.

NATIONAL AND GENERAL BIBLIOGRAPHIES

Those interested in Australian studies will find that they are comparatively better served with bibliographies of the relevant literature than students of many other geographic areas. Borchardt (1976) listed over 600 sources of relevant information but laid no claims to being exhaustive in the field. A decade later, scores of additional sources had been produced—some, admittedly, replacing older works. It is impossible to list them all. Indeed, it has been thought more appropriate to restrict the present listing mainly to current works, and to include older sources only if they are considered to be particularly significant. Readers wishing to obtain a broader view should consult Borchardt (1976) and Crittenden (1982).

Attention is drawn to the fact that the topic bibliographies and literature surveys throughout this volume include many special bibliographies. These are more usefully listed with the topic to which they refer rather than in this chapter, and only rarely have they been cited in both places. However, the index to this volume will enable readers to identify them.

Among our retrospective bibliographies the most outstanding work is unquestionably that of John Ferguson (1941–69), whose seven-volume compilation covers the period between 1784 and 1900. Recognising the difficulties inherent in trying to be exhaustive, Ferguson sought the collaboration of librarians from all parts of Australia; their amendments and supplementary entries were recorded by the National Library and partly published. A new edition of Ferguson's work, which is to include all additions and corrections, is in preparation.

Besides the Ferguson bibliography, a number of older works still have a limited usefulness while others retain a curiosity value because they touch on uncommon areas. Among these it is worth mentioning S.A. Spence's *A bibliography of selected early books and pamphlets relating to Australia, 1610–1880* (London, The Author, 1952), with a supplement issued in 1955, which contains over 1800 entries and lists early Australian engraved portraits. Another courageous effort is L.L. Politzer's compilations of foreign language references: *Bibliography of Dutch literature on Australia, Bibliography of French literature on Australia, 1595–1946* and *Bibliography of German literature on Australia, 1700–1947*, all published by the author (Melbourne, 1952–53). Other bibliographies of this kind are in preparation. The daunting nature of the task is often not recognised until enthusiastic compilers have started on the path and realise too late that consistency in bibliographic description is more difficult to attain than amateurs believe, while the quest for comprehensiveness may lead to weeks of searching for minute items. Consequently the field of Australian bibliography contains at least as many tombstones as cradles—and for good or evil, even the computer-based compilations offer little more guarantee of healthy offspring.

The most important gap in our national bibliography is, by common consent, the so-called Ferguson Gap—the period of publishing between 1900 when Ferguson's *Bibliography of Australia* stops and 1936 when the *Australian national bibliography* commenced, albeit under another name. Efforts are being made by the National Library and a number of bibliographers to produce a list of books and pamphlets published between 1900 and 1936. Some of these efforts are directed at subject listings for that period, others approach it from a geographical basis.

The history of the Commonwealth National Library, as it was known at the time, and its successor, the National Library of Australia, is referred to in the preceding section of this volume. Its *Australian national bibliography* (*ANB*) which in effect began in 1936 with the *Annual catalogue of Australian publications* is unquestionably its most important activity—*ANB* is in fact a national service, prescribed in the National Library Act 1960–73, and much more than a publication pure and simple. There have been changes in the structure and presentation of *ANB* and its predecessor during the 50 years of their existence but, by and large, *ANB* is a reliable and comprehensive bibliographic service. The history of *ANB* can be read in Borchardt (1976) and there are comments on its adequacy and efficiency in the professional literature.

Other bibliographical services provided by the National Library are listed in the bibliography that follows. Of greatest importance is the listing of commonwealth and state government publications in *Australian government publications* (*AGP*). This aspect of the national bibliography is considered in detail in Borchardt (1979). Some state governments also issue lists of their publications. These tend to be more comprehensive and up to date than *AGP*, but while New South Wales, Queensland and Victoria have been able to maintain regular publication schedules for listing state government publications received in their respective state libraries, this service has not been kept up in South Australia, Tasmania and Western Australia. Complementary information can be obtained from the state libraries and state government printers: details are set out in table 2 in chapter 3.

INDEXES TO PERIODICALS

The second part of this survey of Australian bibliographies lists indexes to the periodical literature. This important aspect of bibliographic work is not nearly as well developed as the bibliographic control of monographs. There is no complete printed list of periodicals published in Australia. The National Library's *Current Australian serials* has not been updated since the ninth edition of 1975. It has been partly replaced by *Australian serials in print*, a commercial service, selective in its coverage, published by D.W. Thorpe, Melbourne, since 1981; it is to be reissued frequently but not regularly. The National Union Catalogue of Serials (NUCOS), a computerised data bank accessible by title or subject through ABN (see below) includes all Australian serials held by contributing libraries but these cannot be retrieved on the basis of country of origin. A *Checklist of nineteenth century Australian periodicals* has been completed by A. Pong (Melbourne, Borchardt Library, La Trobe University, 1983).

About 4000 serial publications appear in Australia annually, but there are few indexing and still fewer abstracting services to provide access to this wealth of literature. Until recently, there were two major indexing services, one for the pure and applied sciences, the other for the humanities and social sciences. The former, produced by CSIRO with the title *Australian science index*, represented the most comprehensive source of reference to Australian scientific literature. For economic reasons its publication ceased in 1983 and at the time of writing no substitute has been created. The demise of a service so important to both the general public and the scientific community is a sad reflection on the priorities of those responsible for the support of research and technical development.

The second index, *Australian public affairs information service* (*APAIS*), has been produced by the National Library since 1945, but only since 1955 has there been an annual cumulation. An author index has been added since 1965. It is complemented, albeit without specific co-ordination, by the *Australian business index*, the *Australian education index* and the *Current Australian and New Zealand legal literature index*, all of which are subject specific but do not attempt to be comprehensive in their coverage. There remains unquestionably a large black hole into which fall hundreds of journals, the contents of which are not indexed anywhere.

Worth mentioning because of its historic significance and period coverage is the *Australian periodical index* (*API*) compiled and published by the Mitchell Library. This index to humanities and social science periodicals had a checkered publishing history. In different forms it covered the years between 1944 and 1963 and several cumulations were printed in the decade and a half of its existence. As well as its detailed treatment of Australia, it contains many references to the Pacific islands. It is furthermore of interest because it amplified the coverage of the Mitchell Library's *Dictionary catalog of printed books* (see below).

Newspapers are obviously an important source for Australian studies. Australia's wide range of newspapers covers the whole spectrum of political opinion and practically all inhabited areas. They vary in size and importance; only one makes any pretence at being a 'national' newspaper. The *Australian* (1964–), with its head office in Sydney, issues simultaneously six metropolitan editions which carry identical international and national news to which is added appropriate state and metropolitan news. Two other major newspapers—the *Sydney Morning Herald* (1831–) and the Melbourne *Age* (1854–) — are considered of national importance and are read widely beyond their respective places of publication.

Not one comprehensive current index to any of these hundreds of newspapers is at present being published, and attempts to create such an important tool have failed because of the costs involved. Efforts made by individual newspapers in the past have been short lived and the investigations undertaken by the Australian Advisory Council on Bibliographical Services (R. Stafford, *Australian newspaper index feasibility study*, Canberra, NLA, 1980), though widely praised, failed to attract the financial support needed to bring this project to fruition.

Nevertheless, one current newspaper index has been established, albeit in somewhat restricted fields. The *Australian business index* (*ABI*), begun in February 1981, covers the contents of the major Australian newspapers for their business and finance contents. For a detailed description, see H. Mayer's *ARGAP 2* (1984). *ABI* is accessible through AUSINET, the Australian computerised information network, which has outlets in a number of major libraries.

A number of retrospective newspaper indexes have been compiled by librarians and historians, including an index to the first Australian newspaper, the *Sydney Gazette* (1803–42), and the first *Australian* (1824–42). Work is in progress on indexing the now defunct Melbourne *Argus* (1846–1957) to complement two existing indexes for the periods 1846–59 and 1910–49. The state libraries and a few other institutions maintain card indexes to the major newspapers and to some local ones as well. A list of these has been provided by Henry Mayer in both *ARGAP* (1976) and *ARGAP 2* (1984).

SUBJECT BIBLIOGRAPHIES

The titles gathered below represent literature surveys on geographic regions, broad subject fields such as economics or history, university theses and early printed books—a heterogeneous collection indeed and intended to be indicative rather than comprehensive. Noteworthy are the several bibliographies of Australian government publications such as Borchardt's *Checklists . . .* (1958–78) and the index to the great collection of nineteenth-century British parliamentary papers issued by the Irish University Press (1974). The British papers include scores of references to Australia, many of which have been collected in separate volumes to aid students inexperienced in the exploitation of this class of document; they have been rearranged and reprinted, and therefore do not represent the documents in their historical context.

Also included in this selection is the *Union list of higher degree theses* which represents the only comprehensive index to theses accepted in Australian universities and colleges of advanced education. It was begun in 1959 by Mary J. Marshall of the University of Tasmania Library; a series of supplements has been prepared by other staff of that library to keep it up to date. Besides the book-form edition, the *Union list* is now available online through AUSINET. Complementary indexes have been prepared for special interest groups. Education is served by the *Bibliography of education theses in Australia* issued annually by the Australian Council of Educational Research (ACER) since 1984.

While the *Union list of higher degree theses* is restricted to dissertations submitted for Masters' and Doctors' degrees, the specialised indexes usually include also theses submitted for the degree of Bachelor with Honours. Indeed, historians have issued a list called *Honours theses in history*, compiled by M. McKernan and D. Collins (Sydney, Australian Historical Association, 1979), and the association's bulletin lists research work, publications and theses completed in history faculties throughout Australia. Several universities issue lists of theses accepted by their own authority. Those wanting details should consult the research reports issued by every Australian university and by the larger colleges of advanced education.

LIBRARY CATALOGUES AND UNION LISTS

While bibliographies consist of references to a particular subject, a library catalogue contains references to a collection of material housed in one or more buildings and being administered by one authority, unless the catalogue is a union catalogue designed to list the holdings of several authorities, institutions or libraries. It would seem appropriate that we should ask where are the most comprehensive libraries for Australian studies and whether one can identify their holdings without having to visit them. The answer to the first part of this question will be found in section I of this book. The answer to the second part will be found in the list of library catalogues below.

The publication of a library catalogue in book form is now a luxury of the past. The importance of such a catalogue depends basically on the contents of the library to which it relates, but also on the quality of production, the organisation of entries and their bibliographic reliability.

The most comprehensive collection of Australiana in the world is that of the Mitchell and Dixson libraries of the State Library of New South Wales. It is not surprising therefore that the printed catalogue of the Mitchell Library should rank foremost among the book form catalogues. A short history of these collections can be found in Biskup and Goodman's *Australian libraries* (3rd edn, London, Bingley, 1982).

Thanks to the enterprising specialist publisher G.K. Hall & Co, of Boston, the bibliographic wealth of these collections has been made accessible through the Mitchell Library *Dictionary catalog of printed books*, 38 volumes, which appeared in 1968; one supplementary volume was issued in 1970. This catalogue lists under author, title and subject all books catalogued up to 1969 as well as selected periodical articles. The publication of further supplements, though perhaps desirable, is scarcely urgent because the library's acquisitions policy is such that all titles listed in the *Australian national bibliography* are automatically acquired.

Some other printed library catalogues have been included in the list below because of their historical interest; the annotations will offer sufficient justification for their presence. More such catalogues exist and have been cited by Borchardt (1976), but their relevance to Australian studies is now severely limited.

Some comment needs to be made on the inclusion in this list of union catalogues, that is of catalogues which show the holdings, with location marks, of more than one library. Librarians are justifiably proud of this particular device. It is unquestionably a means to make available to readers an enlarged resource—provided of course that participating institutions fully subscribe to the implied service notion that libraries participating in a union catalogue program should be prepared to lend their stock to the clients of each of the libraries included in the union catalogue.

Though Australian librarians have collaborated quite willingly in numerous union catalogue projects, there is no adequate list of such efforts. A.P. Rooke's *A list of union lists* (Melbourne, La Trobe University Library, 1974) is not only sadly out of date but was always wanting in several respects, and should be used with caution. It indicates, however, that it is beyond the scope of this chapter to offer a comprehensive list of union lists.

There are two basic kinds of union lists. One is based on the notion that researchers require a listing of all materials in their field held in the libraries of a region, a state or even the whole country. This type of union list is usually restricted to serials, such as P.R. Longley's *French periodicals held in Victorian university libraries and the State Library of Victoria* (Melbourne, Borchardt Library, La Trobe University Library, 1984). But some important and well-produced union lists of monograph holdings have also been issued. Typical of scholar-oriented union lists are H.H.R. Love, *John Dryden in Australian libraries* (Melbourne, Monash University, 1970); John Fletcher, *Short title catalogue of German imprints in Australia from 1501–1800* (Melbourne, Dept of German, Monash University, 1970); R. Laufer *et al, French culture in the libraries of Melbourne* (Melbourne, Monash University 1962–63). Many more have been compiled by researchers anxious to have a holdings statement of relevant library collections in their specialist field. Union lists tend to provide only the minimum data ('short title') for the identification of individual works; such information might suffice to find a book in the holding library but it is not sufficient as a detailed bibliographic description.

The other category of union lists does not concentrate on a single subject or group of subjects but is conceived as a tool by and for librarians which, subject to the conditions of co-operative use referred to above, will constitute a resource index of considerable importance.

Australia has a fairly good record in the promotion and production of a national union list, even though the library profession has maintained a critical attitude to some of the products. The sparsity of bibliographic oases in a huge country, and the chronic shortfall of financial resources, have made it imperative for librarians to develop co-operative devices if bibliographic services are to attain adequate standards. This has been discussed in chapter 3 of this volume and the point is merely repeated here to emphasise the use made of computer technology in the identification of library holdings and locations. Attention is drawn also to the National Library's development of a computerised bibliographic data bank, the Australian Bibliographic Network (ABN—a set of letters all too easily confused with those referring to the *Australian national bibliography*). Computer terminals linked with ABN are being installed in a growing number of libraries and enables users to find out which library holds which book (see chapter 3). Eventually ABN may well replace all printed union catalogues. Much depends on the rate at which libraries join the service, but it may be some decades yet before all bibliographic service centres can afford to have direct access to the National Library and thus a link with ABN.

GUIDES TO MANUSCRIPT COLLECTIONS

The circumstances of Australian history have fostered the dispersal of the manuscripts kept by private individuals during their visit, prolonged sojourn or permanent settlement in Australia since European colonisation began. Manuscript material is primarily in two locations—the United Kingdom and Australia—but some has found its way to libraries in the United States and elsewhere. The notes on archives in chapter 2 of this volume refer to the lack of records of such material. There may well be thousands of interesting letters and diaries the whereabouts of which are unknown. There are, of course, not only the documents of the British immigrants of the nineteenth century, but also letters and reports by successive waves of immigrants from other countries—French, Germans, Italians, Greeks, Turks and Vietnamese, to name but a few of the larger groups. Of these non-British sources there appear to be few records at present.

However, the documents of the English-speaking settlers of the nineteenth century are being catalogued and described in considerable detail. Below are listed some of the guides to the more important manuscript collections. Particularly important among these are the *Guide to collections of manuscripts relating to Australia* (1965–) and the *AJCP handbooks*. The Australian Joint Copying Project was initiated in 1945 by the National Library of Australia and the State Library of New South Wales with the objective of making available to researchers microfilm copies of documents, records and private papers of relevance to the history of Australasia held in the United Kingdom. The mass of material already filmed made it desirable to produce guides, known as *AJCP handbooks* and published by the National Library of Australia. The handbooks offer introductions to archival documents in the Colonial Office, the Home Office, the War Office, the Foreign Office, the Exchequer and Audit Department, the Privy Council Office and the Admiralty, and some general guidance to the whole enterprise. More guides are in preparation and it is impossible to tell when the project will be completed.

There is still a great deal of work to be done in the field of Australian bibliography, and there is a real need for finding lists and records of primary source material for the study of Australian history. The possibilities opened up by increasingly sophisticated technology for listing and identifying such material are endless but the costs are high and the exploitation of the technology depends also on the resources available to the searcher. For the present and the immediate future, scholars will have to continue to rely on the basic work being done 'by hand' in so far as the constituent parts of bibliographies and finding lists have to be constructed by a knowledgeable person. They do not flow out of a computer terminal like Minerva from the head of Zeus.

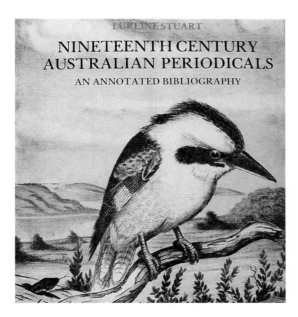

Lurline Stuart, Nineteenth century Australian periodicals: an annotated bibliography.
Cover illustration reproduced from a supplement to Cosmos *magazine, 30 December 1897. Published in Sydney by Hale & Iremonger, 1979.*

NATIONAL AND GENERAL BIBLIOGRAPHIES

AUSTRALIAN audio visual reference book. Melbourne, D.W. Thorpe, 1974– .

Australian audiovisual software is listed under title and subject matter in this annual, while overseas material is included under subject. Information on film libraries, schools, grants, Australian suppliers and producers.

AUSTRALIAN books: a select list of recent publications and standard works in print. Canberra, NLA, 1933– .

This annual lists recommended works related to Australia. Arranged under broad subject headings; includes prices. Title varies.

AUSTRALIAN books in print. Melbourne, D.W. Thorpe, 1956– .

A priced list of commercially produced Australian books including book series, addresses of Australian publishers and agents for overseas publishers. Includes index by author and title. Also available on microfiche.

AUSTRALIAN bookseller and publisher. Melbourne, D.W. Thorpe, 1921– .

A monthly containing much advertising, some newsworthy articles, lists of books published in the month and a list of 'next month's new books'. Until 1970 published as *Ideas about books and bookselling*.

AUSTRALIAN government publications. Canberra, NLA, 1952– .

Lists publications by Australia's seven governments. It appears quarterly, the fourth issue each calendar year being a cumulation for the year. Those consulting *AGP* should study carefully the introductory notes.

AUSTRALIAN GOVERNMENT PUBLISHING SERVICE. *Monthly catalogue of publications placed on sale*. AGPS, 1976– .

Publisher's catalogue, available gratis, listing publications placed on sale. Complemented by weekly list and annual cumulations covering publications both priced and free.

AUSTRALIAN maps. Canberra, NLA, 1968– .

Lists sheet maps. Quarterly since 1974, with annual cumulations continuing a cumulation of 1961–73. Entries arranged according to area.

AUSTRALIAN national bibliography. Canberra, NLA, 1961– .

The most comprehensive reference work for all books published in Australia. Published monthly with quarterly cumulations on microfiche, and annual ones both on microfiche and in book form. For further comments see the essay to this chapter.

AUSTRALIAN serials in print. Melbourne, D.W. Thorpe, 1981– .

Lists serials (journals, magazines) but not series, appearing regularly or irregularly, under the same name and available to the public. Includes subject and title entries. Infrequent updates. For further comments see essay to this section.

BORCHARDT, D.H. *Australian bibliography: a guide to printed sources of information* (3rd edition). Sydney, Pergamon, 1976. 270 p, illus.

First issued in 1963, this is the standard work on Australian information sources.

BORCHARDT, D.H. ed, *Australian official publications*. Melbourne, Longman Cheshire, 1979. 365 p.

Essays offering an overview of government administration as seen through its publications. Recent changes in government departments affect some data in this work.

CRITTENDEN, V. ed, *Current Australian reference books: a list for medium and small libraries*. Canberra, AACOBS Working Party on Bibliography, 1982. 80 p.

Compiled as an acquisitions guide for school and small public libraries, the list is annotated and shows prices at the date of publication. Revised editions are planned.

FERGUSON, J.A. *Bibliography of Australia*. Sydney, A & R, 1941–69. 7 vols, illus.

The most comprehensive bibliography of books published about Australia 1794–1900. The scope of the work, including criteria for inclusion, is set out in the introductions to vols 1, 3 and 5. Facsimile edition, Canberra, NLA, 1975–77.

KEPARS, I. *Australia*. Oxford, Clio Press, 1984. 292 p. (World bibliographical series, vol 46). A list of standard and recommended works on Australia.

A very useful list of over 950 entries with annotation arranged under 42 subject headings.

MAYER, H. AND KIRBY, L. *ARGAP 2: a second research guide to Australian politics and cognate subjects*. Melbourne, Longman Cheshire, 1984. 264 p.

MAYER, H. *et al, ARGAP: a research guide to Australian politics and cognate subjects*. Melbourne, Cheshire, 1976. 329 p.

Idiosyncratic but contains useful information on the bibliographies of the social sciences. Complements Borchardt's *Australian bibliography* with notes on reference sources of all types.

RADFORD, W. *Guide to Australian reference books: humanities*. Sydney, Library Association of Australia, 1983. x, 81 p.

A list of reference books. The coverage is idiosyncratic.

INDEXES TO PERIODICALS

APAIS: Australian public affairs information service. Canberra, NLA, 1945– .

A subject-arranged index of Australian journal articles. Indexes 200 Australian journals comprehensively and about 1200 others selectively in the social sciences and humanities. Annual cumulation.

AUSTRALIAN business index. Sydney, 1981.

A frequency guide to the contents of the Australian finance and business press; it indexes selected general periodicals and major Australian newspapers.

AUSTRALIAN education index. Melbourne, ACER, 1957/58– .

Specialist reference tool covering education, psychology and related areas. Quarterly with annual cumulations.

AUSTRALIAN science abstracts. Sydney, Australian and New Zealand Association for the Advancement of Science, 1922–56/57, vols 1–35.

Vols 1–16 issued by the Australian National Research Council; vols 17–35 issued as a supplement to the *Australian J of science*. Continued by *Australian science index*, for which see below.

AUSTRALIAN science index. Melbourne, CSIRO, 1957–83, vols 1–27.

Comprehensive source of references to Australian scientific literature. Author and subject indexes issued at the end of each year. Publication abandoned.

CRITTENDEN, V. *et al, Index to journal articles on Australian history*. Sydney, History Project Inc, 1980–82. 4 vols.

Crittenden's index continues T. Hogan's work (see below) of references to Australian history in Australian journals. See also Monie (1983).

CURRENT Australian and New Zealand legal literature index. Sydney, Law Book Co, 1973– .

Quarterly subject approach to legal literature, unorthodox in that it caters for the social sciences rather than the legal profession and its traditional manner of citation.

HOGAN, T. *et al, Index to journal articles on Australian history*.

Armidale, NSW, University of New England, 1976. 203 p.

A base list containing references in Australian journals published before 1973. Continued by V. Crittenden (see above). It is planned to complete the series to 1988 by 1989.

MONIE, J. *Index to English language journal articles on Australia published overseas to 1900.* Sydney, History Project Inc, 1983. 132 p.

Monie's work extends T. Hogan and V. Crittenden's indexes (see above) to sources published outside Australia.

SUBJECT BIBLIOGRAPHIES

AUSTRALIA. Dept of Territories. *Annotated bibliography of select government publications on Australian territories, 1951–64.* Canberra, The Department, 1965. 55 p.

A guide to public and semipublic statements on areas which in the decade and a half under review became increasingly important to Australia.

BEAUMONT, C. *Local history in Victoria: an annotated bibliography.* Melbourne, La Trobe University Library, 1980. 295 p.

Entries arranged alphabetically by place for the Melbourne metropolitan area and then for the rest of Victoria. Issued with M. Hyslop's *Victoria directories, 1836–1974.*

BETTISON, M. and SUMMERS, A. comps, *Her story: Australian women in print 1788–1975.* Sydney, Hale & Iremonger, 1980. 181 p, illus.

A bibliography of books (extended to 1978), articles, government publications and theses, annotations and a listing of over 170 women's journals.

BORCHARDT, D.H. *Checklist of royal commissions, select committees of parliament and boards of inquiry.* Sydney, Stone Copying Co (pt 1); Sydney, Wentworth Press (pts 1A, 2, 3); Melbourne, La Trobe University Library (pts 4, 5), 1958–78. 5 pts in 6 volumes plus consolidated index by J.Hagger and A.Montanelli.

A unique index to public tribunals of inquiry at both federal and state level to 1960. Important for research into the development of law and society in Australia. Borchardt covers the commonwealth, NSW, Qld, Tas and Vic. Volumes for SA and WA by E. Zalums (see below). The set is being brought up to 1980.

CROWLEY, F.K. *A guide to the principal documents and publications relating to the history of Western Australia.* Perth, Dept of History, University of WA, 1949. 74 p.

CROWLEY, F.K. *The records of Western Australia.* Perth, Publications Committee of Western Australia, 1953. 1094 p.

CROWLEY, F.K. *South Australian history: a survey for research students.* Adelaide, LBSA, 1966. 200 p.

These guides, designed to help advanced students in their research, are still useful though, of course, much has been published since.

DANIELS, K. *et al* eds, *Women in Australia: an annotated guide to records.* AGPS, 1977. 2 vols.

Annotations give a feminist appraisal of documents relating to women and held in archives, libraries and by individuals.

DILLON, J.L. AND McFARLANE, G.C. *An Australian bibliography of agricultural economics, 1788–1960.* Sydney, Government Printer, 1967. 433 p.

The only literature survey of Australia's most important primary industry. References presented in an excellent system of classification.

FLINN, E.D. *The history, politics and economy of Tasmania in the literature, 1856–1959.* Hobart, University of Tas, 1961. xxiv, 119 p.

Dated but still useful.

GILL, T. *Bibliography of the Northern Territory of South Australia.* Adelaide, Government Printer, 1886. 118 p.

Gill compiled a bibliography of SA as early as 1885 but that is now superseded by F.K. Crowley's work (see above). The listing of writings on the NT, updated to 1938 by C.H. Hannaford is, however, still a useful starting base for researchers. Reprinted in 1962.

GINSWICK, J. *A select bibliography of pamphlets on Australian economic and social history, 1830–1895.* Sydney, Law Book Co, 1961. 24 p.

Based on the holdings of the Mitchell Library, this bibliography lists contributions to Australian economic thought in the pamphleteering age.

IRISH UNIVERSITY PRESS. *Index to British parliamentary papers on Australia and New Zealand, 1800–1899.* Dublin, IUP, 1974. 2 vols.

Provides a key to reprints of British parliamentary papers issued when the Australian colonies were administered from Britain. A rich source for the study of Australian history, this index makes them eminently accessible.

JOHNSTON, W.R. *A bibliography of Queensland history.* Brisbane, Library Board of Qld, 1981. 149 p.

Useful guide to the literature on the history of politics of Qld.

KNIGHT, K.W. AND ADAMS, J. *Politics and administration in Queensland: a select bibliography.* Brisbane, Dept of Government, University of Queensland, 1974. 328 p.

MILLS, C.M. *A bibliography of the Northern Territory: monographs.* Canberra, Canberra College of Advanced Education Library, 1977–83. 5 vols.

An attempt at comprehensive bibliography for monographs published in, or about, the NT to 1981. Includes some fugitive materials within the definition 'monograph'; extensive coverage.

MONIE, J. *Victorian history and politics: European settlement to 1939; a survey of the literature.* Melbourne, Borchardt Library, La Trobe University, 1982. 2 vols, illus.

A thorough bibliography of the Victorian scene divided into subject areas. Excellent treatment of the whole literature relating to one state. Complements Beaumont (1980).

MURRAY-SMITH, S. AND THOMPSON, J. eds, *Bass Strait bibliography: a guide to the literature on Bass Strait covering scientific and non-scientific material.* Melbourne, Victorian Institute of Marine Sciences, 1981. 271 p, map.

Produced with the help of the Victorian Institute of Marine Sciences Information System and data contained in the CSIRONET, this list is close to a definitive bibliography of the region.

PIKE, A. AND COOPER, R. *Reference guide to Australian films 1906–1969.* Canberra, National Film Archive, NLA, 1981.

A reliable index to this popular medium.

UNION *list of higher degree theses in Australian university libraries.* Hobart, University of Tas Library, 1967– .

Classified index to theses accepted in Australian institutions of tertiary education, excluding Bachelors' honours theses. Currency of information leaves something to be desired. The first list is a cumulated edition to 1965.

ZALUMS, E. *A bibliography of South Australian royal commissions, select committees of parliament and boards of inquiry.* Adelaide, Flinders University of SA, 1975. 178 p.

Covers the period 1857 to 1970.

ZALUMS, E. AND STAFFORD H. *A bibliography of Western Australian royal commissions, select committees of parliament and boards of inquiry 1870–1979.* Adelaide, Flinders University of SA, 1980. 116 p.

For annotation on both lists see Borchardt, *Checklist of royal commissions . . .* above.

ZERNER, M. comp, *Australian studies, University of Queensland: a select guide to resources: humanities and social sciences.* Brisbane, Australian Studies Centre, University of Qld, 1981. 110 p.

In spite of the detailed attention paid to some material for Australian studies held in Brisbane libraries there are many gaps, and bibliographic and location questions are left unanswered.

LIBRARY CATALOGUES AND UNION LISTS

AMERICAN GEOGRAPHICAL SOCIETY OF NEW YORK. *Research catalogue.* Boston, Mass, G.K. Hall, 1962. 15 vols and map supplement.

The society's library contains a sizeable Australian collection which is listed, together with its New Zealand material, in vol 14: Australasia.

BRITISH MUSEUM. *General catalogue of printed books . . . to 1955.* London, Trustees of the British Museum, 1965–66. 263 vols.

The catalogue of the British Library (formerly the British Museum) is an important bibliographic source for Australian material. Because of its size the catalogue is only available in major state and university libraries. Supplements in both book and microfiche form cover books accessioned from 1956 to 1982.

BURMESTER, C.A. *National Library of Australia: guide to the collection.* Canberra, NLA, 1974–82. 4 vols.

Though not strictly a library catalogue, Burmester's extensive commentary on the NLA holdings is a unique contribution in form as well as in content.

MITCHELL LIBRARY, SYDNEY. *Dictionary catalog of printed books.* Boston, Mass, G.K. Hall, 1968. 38 vols.

The catalogue of the world's largest Australiana collection. One supplement was issued in 1970.

NEWSPAPERS in Australian libraries: a union list (4th edn). Canberra, NLA, 1984–85. 2 pts.

Shows the holdings of foreign (pt 1) and domestic (pt 2) newspapers in major Australian libraries. The second part includes bibliographical and publishing details of each paper.

PETHERICK, E.A. *Catalogue of the York Gate Library, formed by Mr S. William Silver: an index to the literature of geography, maritime and inland discovery, commerce and colonization* (2nd edn). London, Murray, 1886. cxxxii, 333 p.

A small portion of this famous collection is of Australian interest. The York Gate Library—its catalogue was first printed in 1882—was acquired by the South Australian Branch of the Royal Geographical Society in 1905.

ROYAL COMMONWEALTH SOCIETY. Library. *Subject catalogue of the library of the Royal Empire Society, formerly Royal Colonial Institute, by Evan Lewin.* London, The Society, 1930–37. 4 vols.

Reprinted in 1967.

ROYAL COMMONWEALTH SOCIETY. Library. *Subject cata-*

logue of the Royal Commonwealth Society, London. Boston, Mass, G.K. Hall, 1971. 7 vols.

Each of these two massive subject catalogues includes a volume on Australia (vol 2 of the first catalogue and vol 6 of the second).

GUIDES TO MANUSCRIPT COLLECTIONS

MANDER-JONES, P. *Catalogue of the manuscripts in the library of the Royal Geographical Society of Australasia, South Australian Branch.* Adelaide, Royal Geographical Society of Australasia, South Australian Branch, 1981. x, 54 p, illus.

A small but significant collection of manuscripts relating principally to SA, but including some unexpected items such as Joseph Banks's Newfoundland diary of 1766 and a few records of convicts sent to Van Diemen's Land.

MANDER-JONES, P. *Manuscripts in the British Isles relating to Australia, New Zealand and the Pacific.* ANUP, 1972. 697 p.

A well-organised list of primary source material. Careful study will repay scholars in search of original sources. This catalogue is complemented by the listings of the AJCP (see below).

MITCHELL LIBRARY, Sydney. *Catalogue of manuscripts of Australasia and the Pacific in the Mitchell Library, Sydney.* Sydney, Trustees of the Public Library of NSW, 1967–69. 2 vols.

Covers manuscripts catalogued between 1945 and 1967.

MOZLEY, A. *A guide to the manuscript records of Australian science.* Canberra, Australian Academy of Science in association with ANUP, 1966. 127 p.

Describes the nature and shows the location of archival material related to the sciences in Australia. Additions are published in the *Historical records of Australian science*, issued quarterly by the Australian Academy of Science.

NATIONAL LIBRARY OF AUSTRALIA. *Australian Joint Copying Project handbook.* Canberra, NLA and the State Library of NSW, 1972–

The project microfilms documents in British libraries and the Public Record Office related to the history of Australasia. The *Handbooks* offer some guidance to thousands of reels of film. A unique source of information for the study of Australian history.

NATIONAL LIBRARY OF AUSTRALIA. *Guide to collections of manuscripts relating to Australia.* Canberra, NLA, 1965– . 3 vols, loose leaf.

Lists manuscript source material and collections of private papers and government archives. Comprehensive index.

UNIVERSITY OF MELBOURNE ARCHIVES: guide to collections. Melbourne, The Archives Board of Management, University of Melbourne, 1983. 210 p, illus.

Useful guide to this important archive of business, labour and trade union records.

VICTORIA. Public Library. *Catalogue of the manuscripts, letters, documents, etc. in the private collections of the Public Library of Victoria.* Melbourne, Public Library of Vic, 1961. 157 p.

Supplemented by the 'recent acquisitions' listings in every April issue of the biannual *La Trobe Library Journal* (1968–).

WHITE, O. *et al, Our heritage: a directory to archives and manuscript repositories in Australia.* Canberra, Australian Society of Archivists, 1983.

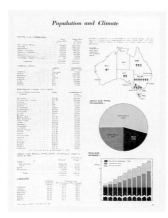

Australia to-day, 18 Oct 1957. In presenting statistics to the general public statisticians often use maps, graphs and diagrams.

CHAPTER 9

STATISTICS

A. J. HAGGER

THE STATISTICS reading list below aims to put non-specialists in touch with a selection of the basic sources of Australian statistics and to enable them to extend their statistical horizons beyond those basic sources should they wish to do so. We envisage a reader who has worked on the topic reading lists presented elsewhere in the volume and whose interest has been so kindled that he or she decides to follow up an aspect of the topic in a strictly statistical way. For example, the reader may have perused the books suggested in chapter 10, 'Physical geography', and wish to locate some of the hard statistical facts relevant to Australia's rainfall.

Attention must be drawn first of all to *Australians: historical statistics* which forms part of this series *Australians: a historical library*. This volume presents statistical data related to Australian economic and social life, with the addition of quite detailed statistical information about Australian financial matters. These data are largely based on the work of the ABS, but they also rely on other sources, some of which are cited in this essay and bibliography.

There are two types of statistics: 'historical statistics' and 'current statistics'. The distinction is a trifle hazy but useful nevertheless. A body of current statistics is added to year by year or quarter by quarter, or more frequently if desired or appropriate, and therefore represents a continuing statistical collection. A body of historical statistics, on the other hand, is not regularly augmented; it belongs to the past and there is no question of its ever being 'brought up to date'. Thus the distinction between current and historical statistics does not turn on the degree of 'historical content'. A set of current statistics extending back 110 years, as many do, may have more historical content than a set of historical statistics relating, say, to the first decade of the twentieth century. The distinction is rather between a set of statistics which is 'living' (current statistics) and one which is 'dead' (historical statistics). Examples of publications which present current statistics are those issued regularly by the ABS such as *Australian demographic statistics quarterly* and *Australian farming in brief*. Examples of publications containing historical statistics are M.S. Keating *The Australian workforce, 1910–11 to 1960–61* (Canberra, Australian National University, 1973) and R. Mendelsohn *The condition of the people: social welfare in Australia 1900–75* (Sydney, Allen & Unwin, 1979).

All the citations listed under 'General works' are devoted exclusively to historical statistics and in most cases incorporate original work of great interest and significance. Deserving of special attention is the pioneering achievement of T.A. Coghlan, government statistician of New South Wales for many years in the latter part of the last century, who produced the massive work listed in the bibliography as a 'sideline', so to speak. Coghlan's studies have formed a springboard for much subsequent work in Australian historical statistics, notably that of Butlin (1962, 1964, 1971) and Roland Wilson (1931).

The references listed among the guides to statistical collections include Finlayson (1970) and the two detailed catalogues produced by the ABS. These give access to an enormous range of Australian statistical data, both historical and current. Most of the statistics produced by the ABS are in the economic and social fields and the two ABS catalogues have special relevance, therefore, for the topics that appear in sections X and XI of this volume.

The *Catalogue of publications*, an annotated listing of all the statistical publications emanating from the ABS, appears in an annual edition and is divided into two parts. The first is a numerical list of all currently available ABS publications based on a five-digit numbering system. Details of this system are set out, with examples, in every edition of the ABS *Catalogue*. The second part of the *catalogue* is a detailed alphabetical subject index designed to permit ready identification of those ABS publications in which information on a particular topic can be found. For example, the first entry in the subject index presented in the 1980 catalogue is:

Abalone, 7603.0
    exports
      interstate, 5401.6
      overseas, 5409.0, 5401.6, 5402.6

This identifies publication 7603.0 as one which provides general information on the abalone industry in Australia, and publications 5409.0, 5401.6 and 5402.6 as others which provide information of a more specific kind.

The second of the two listed ABS catalogues is the *Catalogue of 1981 census tables*. Altogether there have been eleven national censuses: in 1911, 1921, 1933, 1947, 1954, 1961, 1966, 1971, 1976, 1981 and 1986. Until the census of 1966 it was the practice to publish the statistical tables generated by the census in a set of bound volumes. In the interests of more rapid publication and because of the vast increase in the volume of data, which, thanks to the computer, can now be extracted from a census, a different practice has been followed since then. Publication in bound volumes has been discontinued; the census tables are now released progressively in four forms: on microfiche, on magnetic tape, on computer printout and in a series of small pamphlet-type publications. The ABS catalogue now under discussion relates to the 1981 census and its purpose is to provide a detailed description of the tables that have been or will be released in connection with that census. By consulting the catalogue, potential users of census information can determine whether or not their needs will be met or, indeed, have already been met by the published tables and, if so, whether or not the relevant tables will be in a form they can use.

Besides the published data, the ABS collects a large array of statistical information which is not published. In response to public enquiries the co-ordination section of the ABS, Victoria, has compiled and published a *Register of unpublished data*. First issued in 1983, a second edition appeared at the end of 1984. The information is tabulated under broad categories—the data files are listed under ABS divison, such as Finance and Distribution Branch, Agriculture, Transport and Construction Branch, and the name, area covered, length of series, form of storage and further data available are cited for each file. This can be a very useful source of statistical records; comparable lists for the other states are under consideration.

Other reference sources by Hagger (1983) and by G. R. Palmer (*A guide to Australian economic statistics*, 2nd edn, Melbourne, Macmillan, 1966), are broad surveys of Australian economic and social statistics, in particular those currently produced by the ABS which constitute by far the major part of the total. Palmer's book is much the more detailed and comprehensive but suffers from being out of date. By using these two books in conjunction with the two ABS catalogues discussed above, the reader can gain relatively easy access to an enormously wide range of Australian statistical material.

The references listed in the third part of this bibliography have been included for the reader who desires a wider statistical horizon and who is ready to move from a study of statistics themselves to a study of some everyday statistical problems. By a 'statistical problem' in this context we mean one that involves putting a number on an abstract economic or social concept (for example, the general price level) with the help of appropriate statistical data. Five such problems are covered by the references given, namely the problems of measuring inflation, economic growth, the extent of overseas investment, labour productivity and national wealth. All are problems of interest and relevance to the non-specialist.

The references in the last section of the bibliography have been included by way of a reward for perseverance. They are intended for readers who have faced up to the rigours of the first three sections and who now feel, possibly with justification, that they have earned a little light relief. They will find here Arndt's highly readable piece on the legendary Coghlan, some pioneering works in the measurement of national income and private wealth which were much ahead of their time and which have great interest for the modern reader for that reason alone, and a statistical article (1959) written by the formidable nineteenth-century British economist and statistician Stanley Jevons, during a brief stay in Sydney as a young man.

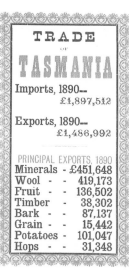

Four posters printed by the Launceston newspaper the Examiner, *which until 1900 appeared as the* Examiner and Commercial and Agricultural Advertiser. *Readers were kept up to date with developments in the goldfields, the value of exports and the balance of trade figures and given useful background statistics on population and area.*
QUEEN VICTORIA MUSEUM AND ART GALLERY, LAUNCESTON

GENERAL WORKS

BAILEY, J.D. 'Australian overseas liquidity, 1870–80', *Economic record* 30, November 1954, 232–44.

Provides estimates of Australia's liquid assets and the crises in overseas liquidity in that decade.

BUTLIN, N.G. *Australian domestic product, investment and foreign borrowing, 1861–1938/39.* CUP, 1962. 475 p.

A statistical account of the process of economic growth in Australia.

BUTLIN, N.G. *Investment in Australian economic development, 1861–1900.* CUP, 1964. 477 p, illus, maps.

A narrative account of Australia's growth which focuses on the role of investment and contains numerous original statistical estimates.

BUTLIN, S.J. *et al, Australian banking and monetary statistics, 1817–1945.* Sydney, Reserve Bank of Australia, 1971. 562 p. (Reserve Bank of Australia. Occasional paper, 4A.)

Brings together all known statistical data relating to Australian banking. For continuation, see R.C. White (1973).

CLARK, C.G. AND CRAWFORD, J.G. *The national income of Australia.* A & R, 1938. 120 p.

Building on Sutcliffe's work (see below), the authors compiled a continuous series of estimates for the years from Federation to the outbreak of World War II.

COGHLAN, T.A. *A statistical account of the seven colonies of Australasia, 1890–1904.* Sydney, Government Printer, 1890–1904. 11 vols.

In effect a 'yearbook'; presenting information about the economic life of the six Australian colonies and New Zealand. The volumes for 1902–03 and 1903–04 are entitled *A statistical account of Australia and New Zealand.*

COGHLAN, T.A. *The wealth and progress of New South Wales.* Sydney, Government Printer, 1886/87–1900/01. 13 vols.

Similar to preceding work but confined to NSW. The later issues contain estimates of the national income and private wealth of NSW on which subsequent work in historical statistics has been built.

HALL, A.R. *The London capital market and Australia, 1870–1914.* Canberra, Australian National University, 1963. 221 p.

Analyses British investment in Australia and presents some useful statistical information in support of the argument.

KNIBBS, G.H. *The private wealth of Australia and its growth as ascertained by various methods, together with a report of the war census of 1915.* Melbourne, McCarron, Bird, 1918. 196 p.

Full account of the war census of 30 June 1915 and estimates of national wealth and national income for the census year. Includes earlier estimates and comparisons with USA, UK, France and Germany and describes the three main methods of estimating national wealth: by means of a wealth census, by the use of probate returns and by the inventory method based on miscellaneous statistical and other records.

VAMPLEW, W. *et al, South Australian historical statistics.* Sydney, History Project Inc, 1984. 351 p. (Historical statistics monograph, 3.)

Contains tables of economic and social statistics covering SA from its foundation in 1836 to 1981.

WHITE, R.C. *Australian banking and monetary statistics, 1945–1970.* Sydney, Reserve Bank of Australia, 1973. 681 p. (Reserve Bank of Australia. Occasional paper, 4B.)

Brings together all known statistical data relating to Australian banking. For earlier data see Butlin *et al* (1971).

WILSON, R. *Capital imports and the terms of trade examined in the light of sixty years of Australian borrowings.* MUP, 1931. 111 p.

Develops estimates of the net import of foreign capital into Australia for each of the years 1871 to 1930 and uses them to investigate the effects of capital imports on the borrowing country's terms of trade.

YEAR BOOK *Australia.* Canberra, ABS, 1908– .

Details of this official yearbook of the commonwealth and its more detailed companion volumes for the states are discussed in chapter 7.

GUIDES TO STATISTICAL COLLECTIONS

AUSTRALIAN BUREAU OF STATISTICS. *Catalogue of 1981 census tables.* Canberra, ABS, 1981. (ABS Cat no 2139.0.)

Detailed description of the tables that will be produced from the 1981 census.

AUSTRALIAN BUREAU OF STATISTICS. *Catalogue of publications.* Canberra, ABS, 1967– . 167 p.

A complete annotated list of ABS publications with a title index and a detailed subject index.

FINLAYSON, J.A.S. *Historical statistics of Australia: a select list of official sources.* Canberra, Dept of Economic History, Research School of Social Sciences, Australian National University, 1970. ix, 55 p.

A listing of Australian serial statistical publications, both continuing and discontinued, with starting point on or about the date of self-government of the various colonies.

HAGGER, A.J. *A guide to Australian economic and social statistics.* Sydney, Pergamon, 1983. 116 p.

Provides a brief account of certain statistics (official and other) now available in Australia, with information about access.

MILLER, A.E. ed, *Checklist of nineteenth-century Australian colonial statistical sources: censuses, blue books and statistical registers.* Sydney, History Project Inc, 1983. viii, 69 p.

Lists the sources of statistical data for all colonies.

SPECIFIC STATISTICAL PROBLEMS

AUSTRALIA. Treasury. 'The meaning and measurement of economic growth', *Treasury information bulletin: Supplement* 1964. 20 p.

Focuses on problems of measuring economic growth in Australia.

AUSTRALIA. Treasury. 'Measuring inflation', *Round-up of economic statistics* 63, April 1978, 13–24.

The conceptual problems involved in the measurement of inflation.

AUSTRALIA. Treasury. 'Private overseas investment in Australia', *Treasury information bulletin: supplement,* May 1965. 27 p.

Deals with the measurement of private overseas investment.

AUSTRALIAN BUREAU OF STATISTICS. *Australian national accounts: input–output tables, 1977–78.* Canberra, ABS, 1983. 338 p. (ABS Cat no 5209.0.)

Explains the concepts used in the preparation of Australia's input–output tables and their statistical sources. Published as a series at irregular intervals.

AUSTRALIAN BUREAU OF STATISTICS. *A guide to the consumer price index.* Canberra, ABS, 1982. (ABS Cat no 6440.0.)

This brochure, first issued in 1978, explains in simple language the method used to calculate Australia's consumer price index.

CAMERON, R.J. *Australian national accounts: concepts, sources and methods.* Canberra, ABS, 1981. 207 p, illus.

Explains the concepts used in the preparation of Australia's national accounts tables.

WILSON, R. *Facts and fancies of productivity.* Melbourne, Economic Society of Australia and New Zealand, 1947. 47 p.

Similar in approach to the two papers by the Australian Treasury (see above) except that the author focuses on the problems inherent in measuring labour productivity.

WORKS OF HISTORICAL INTEREST

ARNDT, H.W. 'A pioneer of national income estimates', *Economic J* 59, 1949, 616–25.

Provides an evaluation of the statistical achievements of T.A. Coghlan in the national income field.

AUSTRALIA. Commonwealth Bureau of Census and Statistics. *Official year book of the Commonwealth of Australia containing authoritative statistics for the period 1901–1907 and corrected statistics for the period 1788 to 1900.* Melbourne, McCarron, Bird, 1908. 981 p.

This was the first Australian yearbook; it contains a brief history of official statistics in Australia on pp 1–16.

AUSTRALIA. Commonwealth Bureau of Census and Statistics. *Official year book of the Commonwealth of Australia. No 19.* Melbourne, Government Printer, 1926. 1038 p.

Chapter 26 collects early estimates of Australia's private wealth beginning with an estimate for 1813 by T.A. Coghlan.

AUSTRALIA. Commonwealth Bureau of Census and Statistics. *Official year book of the Commonwealth of Australia. No 21.* Melbourne, Government Printer, 1928. 1062 p.

Chapter 8, section F, contains an estimate of the private wealth of Australia as at 30 June 1925 and a commentary on earlier estimates.

JEVONS, W.S. 'Some data concerning the climate of Australia and New Zealand', *Australian almanac and country dictionary* 1859, pp 47–98.

These notes are the result of a brief sojourn in Australia of the renowned philosopher, economist and statistician. They are interesting in themselves and a contribution to applied statistics in Australia.

KNIBBS, G.H. 'Census-taking in Australia'. Commonwealth Bureau of Census and Statistics. *Census of the Commonwealth of Australia, 1911.* Vol 1. *Statisticians report.* Melbourne, McCarron, Bird, 1917, 36–56.

History of census-taking in Australia from the first regular census in NSW in 1828 to the first commonwealth census in 1911.

SUTCLIFFE, J.T. *A national dividend: an enquiry into the amount of the national dividend of Australia and the manner of its distribution.* MUP, 1926. x, 70 p.

An attempt to measure Australia's national income for several years after World War II. It established Australia as one of the pioneers in this field.

The number of passengers travelling by steamship between the states declined after World War II, when it became more difficult to maintain ships exclusively for passenger services. By 1961 the last passenger ship had been withdrawn from coastal trade. South Australian homes and gardens, *1 Dec 1938.*

III
ENVIRONMENT

*When the Victorian government issued
commemorative stickers for the Victorian and Melbourne
centenary in 1934 it chose to emphasise flora, fauna
and the taming of the landscape by aeroplanes, gold
diggers, farmers and graziers.*

IN PRIVATE POSSESSION

Lismore, a city on the north coast of New South Wales, c1980. Tourist brochures such as this are an important source of historical information.

CHAPTER 10

PHYSICAL GEOGRAPHY

J. McQUILTON

PHYSICAL GEOGRAPHY is concerned with the study of the earth's surface, its natural characteristics and the reasons for change. It deals with landforms and their origins (geomorphology), with climate and its effects upon the earth, and with the ecology of the earth's living creatures (zoogeography). Physical geography also seeks to identify and explain the terrestrial conditions necessary for human survival. The study of history is, consequently, deeply linked with certain aspects of the study of physical geography.

Geography was established as an independent discipline at the University of Sydney in 1920. It remained a minor discipline there until the 1950s and it was not until 1959 that the University of Melbourne followed with the creation of a chair in geography. As the Australian universities expanded in the 1960s, geography grew quickly; it boomed during the 1970s. During the subsequent decade almost every tertiary institution offered courses in geography and promoted advanced studies in this rich field.

However, the subject's late arrival on the academic scene created a tradition in which significant contributions to geographical studies were made, until the 1960s, by other disciplines closely related but fundamentally directed at different goals. Much of our knowledge of soils, for example, comes from the CSIRO, the geographers preferring to examine soils as a means of identifying geomorphic units. Similarly, much of the research into Australia's climate has been undertaken by government meteorologists and agencies. The geographers' contribution to our knowledge of the natural environment has been strongest in the study of landforms.

The earliest geographical descriptions of Australia were recorded by the explorers who commented on the physical landscape, climate, flora and fauna of the country they traversed. Their observations were motivated not only by scientific curiosity but also by an awareness of the country's potential for European landuse. The explorers and, later, the surveyors pieced together the basic outline of the continent's physical geography: its river systems, mountain ranges, plains and deserts.

The first physical geographies of the continent were descriptive and factual: explanation rarely reached beyond a rudimentary level. The early entries in the *Encyclopaedia Britannica*, particularly that of T.A. Coghlan in the 11th edition of 1910, are good examples. This approach was continued for many years in the yearbooks issued by the commonwealth and state governments.

A significant change in approach came with the appointment in 1920 of Thomas Griffith Taylor to the first Australian chair in geography at the University of Sydney. His early work, published at the beginning of the century, already marked Taylor as a leading scientist and from 1910 to 1920 he held the post of physiographer at the Commonwealth Weather Service. His influence on Australian geography was profound and permanent, and his pioneering work dominated the first half of this century.

Taylor was the first geographer to apply successfully the concept of physical or 'natural' regions to the Australian continent. Using structural (physical) and climatic characteristics, he had identified his first set of regions by 1911. He refined them over the following years until, by the 1940s, he had identified twenty natural regions in Australia. Taylor's regions, though somewhat modified by his disciples and successors, were so pervasive that they are still used in geography textbooks and have become part of every Australian's version of the continent. For example, most people today would be familiar with the Great Artesian Basin, the Southern Australian Highlands and the Murray–Darling Rivers region—all regions identified by Taylor.

Taylor's contributions to other aspects of physical geography were equally significant, though at times controversial. He was the first to argue forcefully that climatic conditions severely limited potential landuse and settlement in Australia—a view that was disputed until the 1950s. Taylor was a prolific writer on his profession and influenced the public view about the role and goals of geography. He founded the journal *The Australian geographer* and helped to introduce the systematic study of the subject in secondary schools. Taylor was not the only geographer active during this period. E.S. Hills, for example, produced in 1940 his *Physiography of Victoria* which was a forerunner to the growth in geomorphology that followed in the 1950s.

A number of British geographers came to Australia in the 1950s, bringing with them new approaches and new interests and stimulating both growth in the discipline and changes in methodology. The geographers of the 1930s and 1940s were criticised for giving undue weight to the environment as a determinant of landscapes and human activity. The geographers of the 1950s and 1960s turned to local rather than regional studies to assess more effectively the dynamic nature of geomorphological processes. The regional approach began to decline in importance although it did not vanish altogether, as is shown in Gentilli's work (1972) on climatic regions. The majority of studies, however, moved away from static, holistic regions to the analysis of single phenomena and processes.

CLIMATE

A century or more of gathering statistics, led to long-term studies of the Australian climate becoming more authoritative. The works of J. Gentilli (1971) and of E.T. Linacre and J. Hobbs (1977), using different approaches to the subject, are among the best. During the decade there was also a shift of interest from long-term, national trends to short-term patterns and local effects. Studies of floods and droughts appeared with assessments of their impact (Lovett, 1973), urban climates were studied, and the impact of climate on human comfort and performance was analysed. Natural hazards became a major research area (Heathcote and Thom, 1979).

BIOGEOGRAPHY

Biogeography, which began as an attempt to draw together physical and human geography, remains a vigorous, if minor, part of the discipline. It examines ecosystems and the distribution of plant and animal communities, and is well illustrated by the comprehensive and important survey, *Ecological biogeography of Australia*, edited by A. Keast (The Hague, Dr W. Junk, 1981, 3 vols). Some research has been undertaken in the field of historical biogeography—the reconstruction of past vegetation regimes and their effect on prehistoric life.

GEOMORPHOLOGY

It is in the field of geomorphology—the study of landforms—that physical geographers have been most active and, one suspects, most comfortable from a methodological point of view. With the benefit of hindsight it can be claimed that much of the early research was undertaken in areas of minimal importance to Australian physical geography. Glaciation is perhaps the best example: trained in cold climate geomorphology, the British geographers applied these principles to Australia, even though there were few suitable areas for such study. However, the late 1960s and 1970s saw a move towards a more indigenous methodology aimed at interpreting Australian problems.

A detailed analysis of the research undertaken since the 1960s is beyond the scope of this essay but it is worth identifying briefly the major areas, and the works cited in the bibliography below will give interested readers an idea of its diversity.

In terrestrial geomorphology, denudation, ancient areal surfaces, deep and subsurface weathering and fluvial geomorphology (the study of rivers, capture, discharge and channel characteristics, drainage networks and so on) have, not surprisingly, been dominant. The geomorphologists have also played a major role in reassessing the age of the continent. Major contributors to terrestrial geomorphology include Jennings and Mabbut (1967); J.N. Jennings with his work on glacial and periglacial landforms, coasts, lakes, dunes and limestone foundations in *Karst* (ANUP, 1971); J.A. Mabbut with his *Desert landforms*, (ANUP, 1977); and Dury on fluvial geomorphology in *Rivers and river terraces*, (London, Macmillan, 1970).

In coastal geomorphology, research has concentrated on beach and sand dune studies—such as depositional shoreline changes, erosion, wave and wind features and coastal lagoons—and shore platforms. Coastal geomorphologists have also taken an active role in the debate over past sea levels in Australia. Major contributors to this field include Bird (1964), Davies and Williams (1977) and Hopley (1982).

It would be incorrect to suggest that research in physical geography falls neatly into the three subsections listed above. There has been an increasing interest in the environment, both natural and built, which weaves together the threads of climate, soils, biogeography and geomorphology and is well illustrated in the CSIRO publication (1960) which first appeared in 1949. Landscapes have also occupied the attention of geographers, and the influence of humans on what were once regarded as 'natural' landscapes has received greater emphasis in recent years, as seen in the works of Heathcote (1975), Scott (1977), Hanley and Cooper (1982). There has been a growing concern with the application of the results of research in physical geography.

The bibliography that follows emphasises the monograph literature. However, as in most natural sciences, research and interim conclusions in physical geography appear mainly in the journal literature which can be accessed through the works listed and the indexes to Australian periodicals. Those interested in a general overview will find the first nine chapters of Jeans (1977) invaluable. Those with an interest in the development of geography are referred to O.H.K. Spate and J.N. Jennings, 'Australian geography 1951–1971', *Australian geographical studies* 10, October 1972, 113–40, and D.N. Jeans and J.L. Davies, 'Australian geography 1972–1981', *Australian geographical studies* 22, April 1984, 3–35.

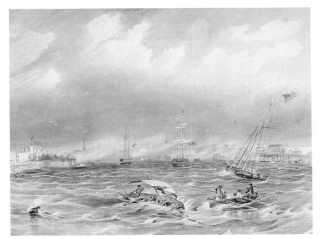

Owen Stanley, Southerly buster, *1847, in his* Voyage of HMS *Rattlesnake. Stanley's watercolour was painted while on a survey of the New South Wales coastline. He commanded the* Rattlesnake, *which subsequently surveyed the northeast coastline and Torres Strait. The observation requirements of a number of sciences were met by these kinds of surveys. Graphic techniques for recording natural phenomena had been developed since the late eighteenth century and were taught to naval officers.*
MITCHELL LIBRARY

R. Clutterbuck, Save the Franklin, damn the
government, *1982. Poster, colour screenprint on paper,
72.9 × 48.3 cm. Gift of Roger Butler, 1985.*

BIRD, E.C.F. *Coastal landforms: an introduction to coastal
geomorphology with Australian examples.* ANUP, 1964. 193
p, illus, maps.
An introduction to coastal geomorphological activity drawing
extensively on Australian examples.

COMMONWEALTH SCIENTIFIC AND INDUSTRIAL
RESEARCH ORGANIZATION. *The Australian environment*
(rev edn). Melbourne, CSIRO, 1960. 151 p, illus, maps.
An account, first published in 1949, of Australian climate, soils,
vegetation and rural industries.

DAVIES, J.L. AND WILLIAMS, M.A.J. eds, *Landform evolution in
Australasia.* ANUP, 1977. 376 p, illus, maps.
A successor to the book by Jennings and Mabbutt (1967); adds
information for New Zealand, partly revises, updates and
complements the earlier work.

GENTILLI, J. *Australian climate patterns.* Melbourne, Nelson,
1972. 285 p, maps.
Analytical description of Australian climates on a regional basis.

GENTILLI, J. *Climates of Australia and New Zealand.*
Amsterdam, Elsevier, 1971. 404 p, illus, maps (World
survey of climatology, vol 13).
History of climatic investigations and factors, with tables. A
scholarly contribution to the field.

HANLEY, W. AND COOPER, M. eds, *Man and the Australian
environment: current issues and viewpoints.* Sydney,
McGraw-Hill, 1982. 362 p, illus, maps.
A good introduction to the physical and built environment,
using the concept in its broadest sense.

HEATHCOTE, R.L. *Australia.* London, Longman, 1975. 246
p, illus.
Australian landscapes and their evolution, including the land
resources and ecosystems.

HEATHCOTE, R.L. AND THOM, B.G. eds, *Natural hazards in
Australia: proceedings of a symposium . . .* Canberra, Australian
Academy of Science, 1979. 531 p, illus, maps.
A collection of papers dealing with natural hazards from floods
and cyclones to droughts and bushfires.

HILLS, E.S. *The physiography of Victoria: an introduction to
geomorphology.* Melbourne, Whitcombe & Tombs, 1940.
292 p, illus, maps.
An early work on Australian geomorphology using Victorian
examples. Systematic in approach; a useful guide to many field
sites.

HOPLEY, D. *The geomorphology of the Great Barrier Reef:
quaternary development of coral reefs.* Brisbane, Wiley, 1982.
453 p, illus, maps.
A synthesis of modern geomorphological work in the world's
greatest coral reef system.

JEANS, D.N. ed, *Australia: a geography.* SUP, 1977. 571 p,
illus, maps.
A summary of geographical knowledge of Australia in the
mid-1970s. The contributions are organised around systematic
topics.

JENNINGS, J.N. AND MABBUTT, J.A. eds, *Landform studies from
Australia and New Guinea.* ANUP, 1967. 434 p, illus, maps.
A collection of essays on Australian geomorphology.

LASERON, C.F. *The face of Australia: the shaping of a continent*
(3rd edn). A & R, 1972. 200 p, illus, maps.
A popular but scholarly account of the evolution of the
Australian geomorphological landscape. This edition revised by
J.N. Jennings. First published in 1953.

LINACRE, E.T. AND HOBBS, J. *The Australian climatic environment.* Brisbane, Wiley, 1977. 354 p, illus, maps.
Text for school and university use describing general climatic
processes and Australian regional climates.

LOVETT, J.V. ed, *The environmental, economic and social
significance of drought.* A & R, 1973. 318 p, illus, maps.
The measurement and perception of drought in Australia, its
ecological and economic impact and an assessment of relief
measures.

SCOTT, H.I. *The development of landform studies in Australia.*
Sydney, Bellbird, 1977. 282 p, illus, maps.
A disciplinary history relating past work to contacts with visiting
scientists, the development of the mining industry and the
emergence of a scientific community in Australia.

TAYLOR, T.G. *Australia: a study of warm environments and
their effect on British settlement.* London, Methuen, 1940.
455 p, illus, maps.
An environmentalist geography arguing that settlement planning is controlled by environmental constraints. Seventh edition
published in 1961.

TAYLOR, T.G. *Geography of Australia.* Oxford, Clarendon
Press, 1914. 176 p.
An early publication by a distinguished geographer, still relevant
today. Excellent analysis of geographical patterns, both human
and physical.

TWIDALE, C.R. *Geomorphology, with special reference to Australia.* Melbourne, Nelson, 1968. 406 p, illus, maps.
A survey of landforms, the influence of structure and processes
using Australian examples. A good introduction to the discipline.
Good use of aerial photographs.

Jenolan Caves advertisement in the Sydney Mail *annual, 2 Oct 1937, 16.*
BOOROWA PRODUCTIONS

CHAPTER 11

GEOLOGY

T. G. VALLANCE

FROM SURVIVAL to prosperity, Australia's people have depended on the earth and what it provides. As the explorer Thomas Mitchell said: 'It is only where trap, or granite, or limestone occur, that the soil is worth possessing, and to this extent every settler is under the necessity of becoming a geologist; he must also be a geographer, that he may find water and not lose himself in the bush' (Mitchell, 1838; facs, 1965, 2, 321).

In Mitchell's time the soil chiefly supported rural enterprise. A more diversified dependence would soon emerge with the growth of mining and other extractive industries. Yet no matter what the need, Mitchell's advice made sense to those occupying a land still being discovered. Observant individuals with practical awareness of rocks and landforms possessed a useful talent, one of advantage whether in selecting a farm or prospecting for minerals or building stones. Such were among our earliest geologists. At their head stands Governor Arthur Phillip whose first despatch from Sydney Cove carried remarks about the rocks there and the uses to which they were being put.

Practical geologists they may have been, but the study of the earth has a longer history in the practical line than has the systematic scientific discipline to which some would confine the name geology. Any student of Australian geology, at least any with a sense of history, will admit the disparate sources of his or her knowledge. Explorers, surveyors, government officials with various, even little, scientific expertise, university researchers, museum curators, company staff and many others, not least among them private citizens who find the earth a rewarding field for investigation—all have contributed.

Some two hundred years of investigation have seen a continent mapped geologically, in reconnaissance fashion at least. If the detail accumulated now releases most Australians from the individual necessity to become geologists, not so the nation. As modern technological society makes increasing demands of the earth and as deposits found by surface prospecting are consumed, the search for useful materials turns to places hidden from view. That kind of search requires considerable scientific sophistication and mastery of diverse techniques. The once conventional distinction between practical or applied geology and pure or abstract geology now has little meaning. The specialist branches of geology form one admittedly technical science. But it is a science that remains of fundamental importance to Australians, both as a guide to their country's resources and, more generally, as a key to understanding the physical character and history of the region they inhabit.

The titles that follow have been chosen to introduce readers to present knowledge of Australian geology in all its variety and to give some view of how that knowledge grew. From rocks more than four thousand million years old in Western Australia to areas like the Great Barrier Reef still being formed, the variety is great in both time and space. If Australia at present lacks the threat of major earthquake or active volcano, and has no fine glacier, all these and more in the past have left their impression. In observing the earth now, the geologist seeks to recognise patterns of action in terms of earth history and development. As will be seen, the Australian geologist commonly has been constrained to search within limits set by people, not by nature. So much of our published record is confined by colonial or, later, state boundaries.

Politics and geology may seem unrelated but since 1788 governments in Australia, with varying enthusiasm and effectiveness, have recognised a need to know the natural resources of their territories. Governments alone have had the financial capacity to sponsor systematic geological investigation on a comprehensive scale. Long after Federation, geological survey remained largely a preserve of the states (Johns, 1976). The commonwealth government all but confined its geological patronage to the Northern Territory and Papua until 1946 when it established the Bureau of Mineral Resources, Geology and Geophysics (BMR), a body that has become our leading regional survey and now increasingly promotes field and laboratory research. Such research, and that of relevant divisions of the CSIRO, supplements work conducted in the more traditional university centres.

Yet though these institutions are the principal sources of new information it is a voluntary professional body, the Geological Society of Australia (founded 1951), that in recent years has fostered general reviews of geological detail on a regional basis. Those on New South Wales (Packham, 1969), Queensland (Hill and Denmead, 1960), Tasmania (Spry and Banks, 1962) and Victoria (Douglas and Ferguson, 1976) have their places in the bibliography as important sources of modern geological information. In South Australia and Western Australia earlier leads of the Geological Society have been followed by revised 'new' editions from state authorities (Parkin, 1969; Western Australia. Geological Survey, 1975). For the reader seeking less technical approaches, Laseron (1969) may be a gentler guide, in the work cited and its companion *The face of Australia* (3rd edn, A & R, 1972) dealing with landforms. Talent (1970) offers a simple introduction to earth materials.

State government bodies, not surprisingly, have sponsored reviews of mineral resources. That relating to New South Wales, edited by Markham and Basden (1974) to mark the centenary of the state geological survey, is a recent work in a tradition that goes back to Burr (1846) and the first geological publication to be issued in this country. There are so many from which to choose. Carne and Jones (1919) on limestones is given a place here, in part to recall a geological problem faced by our forebears at Sydney Cove and to note its esteem among the increasingly numerous devotees of the scientific recreation called speleology. Baker's (1915) illustrated survey of building stones will remind readers what impressive products of the earth they pass on the street. At the national level, the important subject of geology and ground water resources is treated by the Australian Water Resources Council (1975). But again it is a voluntary organisation, the Australian Institute of Mining and Metallurgy (established 1893), that has taken responsibility for recent reviews on the economic geology of Australia (Knight *et al*, 1975–76). The essays on the mineral resources of Western Australia, edited by Prider (1979), form part of a publishing venture to celebrate that state's sesquicentenary.

The list also includes major published bibliographical works relating to Australian geology. Most of them, apart from Teesdale-Smith (1959) on South Australia, are by now historical documents that underline the need for renewed effort. Much the same, sadly, applies to specialist bibliographies where only Quilty (1975) on West Australian palaeontology has any claim to comprehensive modernity, although the revised list of Tasmanian minerals (Tasmania. Geological Survey, 1970) affords some access to recent literature on its subject. Fossils and their study, palaeontology, have great significance to the geologist seeking to date and correlate stratified deposits. The Queensland studies listed under Hill, Playford and Woods (1964–73) are models yet to be matched elsewhere in Australia. Even the amateur collector of fossils will find these works useful, if challenging, guides. Mineral collectors also know Australia as a source of splendid specimens, nowhere better than at Broken Hill, the treasures of which are described and illustrated in Worner, Mitchell and Segnit (1982). Those who seek minerals in Western Australia will profit by knowing the volumes by Simpson (1948–52), a work that follows in more modern style the pattern of chemical mineralogy set long ago by Liversidge (1888) in New South Wales.

In a collection that celebrates history due notice must be given to those works especially significant to historians of geology. Dealing with Australia, that kind of historian is as much concerned with importations as the social historian. Like the people who settled Australia from 1788, scientific geology began in Europe. Furthermore, study of the earth emerged as a systematic historical science only during the first half of the nineteenth century. Its developing concepts and methods came to an Australia still being explored and settled. The historical record of Australian geology thus reflects an intellectual maturing elsewhere; as well, it shows how translated European experience was no consistently reliable guide to Australia's geological past (Vallance, 1975).

In 1788 the term 'geology' was known but unused; 'theory of the earth' still sufficed for the different speculative systems that sought to explain the earth's character. But Europeans already possessed many observational data about rocks and rock masses. They knew, for instance, that strata of various sorts of rocks lay in particular order and believed the arrangement to be worldwide. Our first settlers found nothing to upset this view; in a country stocked with novel plants and animals the rocks seemed reassuringly familiar. Governor Phillip saw what he thought resembled Portland stone; within a few years coal would be found along the coast, below the stone at Sydney. Thus it was in England; coal lay at stratigraphically lower levels than Portland stone. It was to apply this sort of lithological method of correlation that Buch examined the rocks gathered by the Baudin expedition of 1800–04. His 'Einige Bemerkungen über die geognostische Constitution von Van Diemens Land' (first published in 1814 as a journal contribution and reprinted in his *Gesammelte Schriften*, Berlin, Reimer, 1870) was the first published work on Australian geology.

However, by this time European geologists were becoming aware of the demonstrations, first in England but later in France, that fossils afforded a far more reliable basis for correlation of strata than did rock character. From these demonstrations much modern geology takes its rise. By about 1850 European geologists had all but completed the general pattern of time and rock systems that continues to be used across the world. Even in Europe, of course, adoption of the more sophisticated palaeontological method was gradual; old and new approaches coexisted for decades. In Australia, where for much of that time there were few with even rudimentary scientific training, the old lasted longer. An early official nod to science had led nowhere.

Between 1803 and 1812 the civil establishment in New South Wales included one titled His Majesty's Mineralogist, but the officer's duties were ill-defined and his achievement on the whole insubstantial (*Proceedings of the Linnean Society of New South Wales* 105, 1981, 107–46). The geological observation and collection carried out in the early years happened largely as a result of the enterprise of a few interested amateurs, explorers both official and private, and from the visits by naval expeditions that carried scientific staff (*Bulletin of the British Museum [Natural History]*. Historical series, 10, 1, 1982, 1–43, and *Histoire et nature* 19–20, 1981–82, 133–40). The Sydney merchant Berry's paper on geology along the coast (1825) reported an exceptional piece of private fieldwork. Its importance, however, was apparent only to those who knew the ground.

The 1820s saw the first descriptions of distinctive Australian fossils (Brongniart, 1828; C.D.E. Konig, *Icones fossilium sectiles*, London, 1825). It is unclear who collected these fossils but soon explorers like Sturt and Mitchell (1838; facs, 1965) were to show a talent in that regard. Their material too, such as the fossil marsupial remains from Wellington Caves later so attractive to Owen (1877–78), had to be sent to Europe for study. Not until 1855 and the arrival of McCoy (1874–82) as a foundation professor at the University of Melbourne was there a generally experienced palaeontologist resident in Australia (*Alcheringa* 2, 1978, 243–50). Even capable geologists like Strzelecki (1845; facs, 1967) and Clarke (1878), who both reached Sydney in 1839, sent their fossils away, not as miscellaneous curiosities but in the hope of gaining detail to supplement their own work in the field.

More or less systematic field investigations were now beginning. Strzelecki's map (*Records of the Australian Academy of Science* 2, 4, 1974, 68–70) of southeastern Australia is a founding document in our regional geological cartography. Jukes' (1850) attempt at a sketch map of the whole country soon followed (see also Darragh, 1977). Jukes and another visiting geologist, Dana (1849), had examined Australian rocks in the field with the clergyman–geologist Clarke, long honoured as our pioneering resident student of stratigraphical order.

To Clarke in particular belongs the credit for unravelling the sequence of strata in the main (Sydney) coal basin of New South Wales. Establishment of the ages represented by those strata, however, proved difficult and controversial. In the hope of clarifying age problems Clarke had sent for study in Cambridge collections of fossils from what his field evidence indicated was one succession. The result bewildered him, for McCoy, the assistant detailed to the study, concluded not only that the plant and animal fossils were of quite different ages but that Clarke had been less than careful in the field.

With the advantage of hindsight we can see that the controversy, enlarged after McCoy moved to Melbourne, really arose because each expected preferred European models to hold in Australia ('The fuss about coal' in D.J. and S.G.M. Carr eds, *Plants and man in Australia*, Sydney, 1981, 136–76). Neither ever quite escaped his attachment to Europe. It is thus fascinating to note the independent approach so early adopted by the American Dana. But Clarke and McCoy long dominated the Australian scene, a dominance that left geologists in India to find the clues as to why southern lands differed so markedly from Europe: while coal plants waxed in northern warmth the south was experiencing glaciation.

If the ages of coalbearing successions became a major theme in nineteenth-century Australian geological science it was metalliferous ore, and in particular gold, that transformed the organisation of geological effort here. The discovery and working of such deposits, first in South Australia (B. O'Neil, *In search of mineral wealth: the South Australian Geological Survey and Department of Mines to 1944*, Adelaide, 1982, 7–35), and soon in New South Wales and Western Australia (*Journal of the Royal Society of Western Australia* 63, 1981, 119–28), raised questions of government regulation and taxing, and hence of the need for governments to possess knowledge of resources. South Australia's lead here is not surprising; a mineralogist had been sent out with the first settlers. It is less well known that by 1846 there was a goldmining company based in Adelaide.

But it was gold in the eastern colonies that from 1851 changed Australian society. New South Wales already had a government geologist in the field when news broke of gold at Ophir. Gold in Victoria soon led the new colony to outshine its neighbour, not least with a more comprehensive geological survey under Selwyn (represented here by Selwyn and Ulrich, 1866) that began for Australia the task of systematic geological mapping (see Darragh, in Douglas and Ferguson, 1976). Since then, apart from short periods when hard-pressed administrators have tried to economise by dispensing with science, there has been a continuing tradition of government patronage of geology in Australia (Johns, 1976).

By the end of the nineteenth century, the governments of New South Wales, Queensland (Jack and Etheridge, 1892), Tasmania (Johnston, 1888) and Victoria had published monographic geological descriptions of their territories. The universities in Sydney, Melbourne and Adelaide were promoting teaching and research in geology. By 1913 universities in Hobart, Brisbane and Perth had joined them. Natural history museums with representative collections of local fossils, minerals and rocks were functioning as research centres in each capital city. The impressive growth of geological knowledge that has marked the years since Federation had already begun; it was to reach a culmination in David's (1932) concept of a new geological map and unifying treatise brought to posthumous fruition in 1950.

Edgeworth David helped bring independence to Australian geology, helped it come of age and gain a public image. In 1886, four years after he settled in Sydney and only eight since

Clarke's death, David and a colleague from India recognised for the first time signs of the ancient glaciation that distinguished Australia from Europe nearly three hundred million years ago. Australian geology was not that of a transplanted Europe; it had its own style to be discovered and explained. Glacial features of all ages fascinated David; their pursuit led him across Australia, across the world. They drew him in 1907 with Shackleton to Antarctica, from which he returned two years later a popular hero. His sometime student Douglas Mawson, with him on that adventure, was likewise to win fame for even greater feats of polar exploration. Beyond all their colleagues, these two professors of geology, David at Sydney and Mawson in Adelaide, made geology popular, culturally respectable among people with no professional involvement in science.

With his experience and synthetic skills as a geologist as well as the esteem that allowed him access to information, official and unofficial, published and unpublished, David was the man best able to take stock of Australian geology. He had long projected a major general work and began in earnest when granted leave for two years before retiring as professor in 1924 (*Historical records of Australian science* 5, 2, 1981, 30–57). Only the geological map in four sheets appeared in his lifetime; the hurriedly prepared explanatory notes (David, 1932) had to be a substitute for the treatise in his mind and in boxes of notes. It is to the sensitive intelligence of W.R. Browne that we owe David (1950). The work remains unmatched, perhaps unmatchable. Others might arise who could equal in mastery the comprehensive sweep of David and Browne but the task of detailed synthesis in a work of less than encyclopaedic dimensions becomes increasingly difficult as our geological knowledge grows. That growth itself is a legacy from David and his editor, and the many from whose data they created a classic of Australian science.

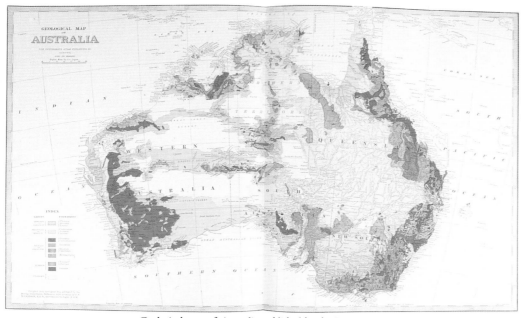

Geological map of Australia published by the Picturesque
Atlas Publishing Co of Sydney and Melbourne in A. Garran (ed),
Picturesque atlas of Australasia *3, c1888.*

ANDERSON, C. *Bibliography of Australian mineralogy.* Sydney, Government Printer, 1916. 164 p (NSW Geological Survey. Mineral resources, 22).

A guide to printed records of mineral species that had been found in Australia, the list covers European literature to 1914.

AUSTRALIAN WATER RESOURCES COUNCIL. Technical Committee on Underground Water. *Groundwater resources of Australia.* AGPS, 1975. 142 p, illus, maps.

Emphasises the geological environments. Includes a historical section.

BAKER, R.T. *Building and ornamental stones of Australia.* Sydney, Government Printer, 1915. 169 p, illus, map. (NSW Dept of Education. Technical Education Branch. Technical education series, 20).

This guide to the igneous, metamorphic and sedimentary rocks used for constructional and ornamental purposes extends the author's earlier work, *Building and ornamental stones of New South Wales* (2nd edn). Sydney, Government Printer, 1909.

BERRY, A. 'On the geology of part of the coast of New South Wales', in B. Field ed, *Geographical memoirs on New South Wales.* London, John Murray, 1825, 231–54.

In the first geological paper presented in Australia to the Philosophical Society of Australasia on 6 March 1822, Berry discusses the arrangement of strata along the coast near Sydney.

BRONGNIART, A.T. *Prodrome d'une histoire des végétaux fossiles.* Paris, F.G. Levrault, 1828. 223 p.

Introducing the names *Glossopteris browniana* and *Phyllotheca australis*, the French palaeobotanist here begins the study of distinctive Australian fossil plants.

BURR, T. *Remarks on the geology and mineralogy of South Australia.* Adelaide, Andrew Murray, 1846. 32 p.

The first geological monograph published in Australia and the beginning of metalliferous mining.

CARNE, J.E. AND JONES, L.J. *Limestone deposits of New South Wales.* Sydney, Government Printer, 1919. 411 p, illus, maps. (NSW Geological Survey. Mineral resources, 25.)

An illustrated review of deposits of a natural material sought and prized since earliest colonial times. The book also deals with utilisation of limestone and the history of its discovery.

CLARKE, W.B. *Remarks on the sedimentary formations of New South Wales* (4th edn). Sydney, Government Printer, 1878. 165 p.

In this work completed just before his death, the clergyman-geologist—to some 'the father of Australian geology'—sets down his last views of a subject he had made his own. First published as a short essay in 1867.

DANA, J.D. *The United States exploring expedition. During the years 1838, 1839, 1840, 1841, 1842. Under the command of Charles Wilkes, U.S.N. Vol. X. Geology.* Philadelphia, Sherman, 1849. 756 p, illus, maps.

A noted American geologist reports on the geology (pp 449–537) and fossils (pp 681–720) of central–eastern NSW.

DARRAGH, T.A. 'The first geological maps of the continent of Australia', *J of the Geological Society of Australia* 24, 5, 1977, 279–305.

Maps are essential documents to geologists. This important paper discusses the various geological maps of Australia.

DAVID, T.W.E. *Explanatory notes to accompany a new geological map of the Commonwealth of Australia, based on the maps already published by the geological surveys of the various states etc.* Sydney, Australasian Medical Publishing Co for the Commonwealth Council for Scientific and Industrial Research, 1932. 177 p, illus, map.

Edgeworth David's map—itself a major document—had been published (in four sheets) by the then CSIR in March 1931. A comprehensive treatise was to have accompanied the map but because of failing health the author prepared instead these explanatory notes—proving the scientific mastery for which he won fame.

DAVID, T.W.E. *The geology of the Commonwealth of Australia. Ed. and much supplemented by W.R. Browne.* London, Edward Arnold, 1950. 3 vols, illus, maps.

The most influential book on Australian geology: the work of review and synthesis David hoped to write. The inspiration was his, but the book was written after his death (in 1934) by W.R. Browne and issued in an edition limited by the availability of the 1931 maps (see above) for volume III.

DOUGLAS, J.G.G. AND FERGUSON, J.A. eds, *Geology of Victoria.* Melbourne, Geological Society of Australia, 1976. 528 p, illus, maps. (Geological Society of Australia. Special publication, 5.)

The first modern presentation of the geology of Vic; includes among its many illustrations the latest (1976) state geological map at 1:1 000 000 scale.

ETHERIDGE, R. Jr *A catalogue of Australian fossils (including Tasmania and the island of Timor) stratigraphically and zoologically arranged.* CUP, 1878. 232 p.

Even by 1878 the variety of known Australian fossil taxa was impressive. Subsequent vast increase in our palaeontological knowledge seems to have discouraged emulation of Etheridge's scholarly enterprise.

ETHERIDGE, R. JR AND JACK, R.L. *Catalogue of works, papers, reports, and maps, on the geology, palaeontology, mineralogy, mining and metallurgy, etc. of the Australian continent and Tasmania.* London, Stanford, 1881. 196 p.

A valuable key to early publications, reissued by the NSW Dept of Mines in 1882. No work comparable in scope has been published since.

GREGORY, J.W. ed, *A contribution to the bibliography of the economic geology of Victoria, to the end of 1903, with map.* Melbourne, Acting Government Printer, 1907. 131 p, map. (Victoria. Geological Survey. Records, 2, 3.)

Lists published and unpublished reports from certain newspapers.

HILL, D. AND DENMEAD, A.K. eds, *The geology of Queensland.* MUP, 1960. 2 vols, illus, maps.

A systematic modern treatment by various authors. Originally published as vol 7 of the *J of the Geological Society of Australia.*

HILL, D. *et al, Illustrations of fossil faunas and floras of Qld.* Brisbane, Qld Palaeontographical Society, 1964–73. 10 pts, illus.

Describes the main varieties of fossils preserved in Cambrian and younger sediments and includes a select bibliography.

HILL, D. AND WILLADSEN, C. *Bibliography of Australian geological serials: and of other Australian periodicals that include geological papers.* UQP, 1980. 76 p. (University of Qld papers, Dept of Geology, 9, 3).

Fundamental and detailed compilation.

JACK, R.L. AND ETHERIDGE, R. JR *The geology and palaeontology of Queensland and New Guinea, with sixty-eight plates and a geological map of Queensland.* Brisbane, Government Printer, 1892. 3 vols, illus, maps.

The first comprehensive work on the subject.

JOHNS, R.K. ed, *History and role of government geological surveys in Australia.* Adelaide, Government Printer, 1976. 111 p, illus.

State and commonwealth geological surveys have been chiefly

responsible for regional geological and geophysical mapping and the evaluation of mineral resources. Contains brief histories of these bodies and lists professional staff.

JOHNSTON, R.M. *Systematic account of the geology of Tasmania.* Hobart, Government Printer, 1888. 408 p, illus, maps.
The first general treatise on the geology of Tas.

JUKES, J.B. *A sketch of the physical structure of Australia, so far as it is at present known.* London, Boone, 1850. 95 p, maps.
Jukes visited with the *Fly* expedition in the 1840s; his geological experiences include the Great Barrier Reef. His geological sketch map of Australia was the first ever published.

KNIGHT, C.L. ed, *Economic geology of Australia and Papua New Guinea.* Parkville, Vic, Australasian Institute of Mining and Metallurgy, 1975–76. 4 vols. (AIMM Monograph series, 5–8.)
A review of the present state of geological knowledge relating to economic mineral materials in the region.

LASERON, C.F. *Ancient Australia: the story of its past geography and life.* Rev by R.O. Brunnschweiler. A & R, 1969. 253 p, illus, maps.
A geological history of Australia and its palaeogeographical development written for the non-expert. First published in 1954.

LIVERSIDGE, A. *The minerals of New South Wales* (3rd edn). London, Trubner, 1888. 326 p, illus, maps.
Liversidge was a major contributor to the progress of mineralogy. This is the third (and greatly expanded) edition of a paper first issued in the *Transactions of the Royal Society of NSW*, 9, 1876, 153–215.

McCOY, F. *Prodromus of the palaeontology of Victoria: or, figures and descriptions of Victorian organic remains. Decades 1–7.* Melbourne, Government Printer, 1874–82. 7 pts in 1 vol, illus.
The seven decades (each with ten descriptions and plates) of this *Prodromus*, issued by the Geological Survey of Vic, are vintage McCoy. A major contribution to Australian systematic palaeontology.

MAHONEY, J.A. AND RIDE, W.D.L. *Index to the genera and species of fossil mammalia described from Australia and New Guinea between 1838 and 1968 (including citations of type species and primary type specimens).* Perth, Government Printer, 1975. 249 p, illus.
Compiled as a source for taxonomists; provides access to the extensive literature on an important group of fossil vertebrates.

MARKHAM, N.L. AND BASDEN, H. eds, *The mineral deposits of New South Wales.* Sydney, Dept of Mines, Geological Survey of NSW, 1974. 682 p, illus.
Collection of essays published to celebrate the founding of the NSW Dept of Mines in September 1874.

MITCHELL, T.L. *Three expeditions into the interior of eastern Australia, with descriptions of the recently explored region of Australia Felix, and of the present colony of New South Wales.* London, T & W Boone, 1838, 2 vols, illus.
Mitchell—explorer, amateur geologist and a founder of inland regional survey—described various fossils, rocks and other geological phenomena and prepared the first geological map of any part of Australia (plate 42). Facsimile edition, LBSA, 1965.

OWEN, R. *Researchers on the fossil remains of the extinct mammals of Australia: with a notice of the extinct marsupials of England.* London, Erxleben, 1877–78, 2 vols, illus.
Papers, first published by the Royal Society of London, by the English comparative anatomist, a pioneer of Australian vertebrate palaeontology and an active promoter of cave research.

PACKHAM, G.H. ed, 'The geology of New South Wales', *J of the Geological Society of Australia* 16, 1, 1969, 1–654.

This systematic and detailed modern account includes a small-scale geological map of NSW. A revised map on a scale of 1:100 000 was issued by the state Geological Survey in 1972.

PARKIN, L.W. ed, *Handbook of South Australian geology.* Adelaide, Geological Survey of SA, 1969. 268 p, illus, maps.
A well-illustrated guide. More recent work has been incorporated in the 1:100 000 geological map in 1980.

PRIDER, R.T. ed, *Mining in Western Australia.* UWAP, 1979. 304 p, illus, maps.
Contributors deal with history and geology related to mining in WA. A new (1979) geological map is included.

QUILTY, P.G. *An annotated bibliography of the palaeontology of Western Australia, 1814–1974.* Perth, Government Printer, 1975. 263 p, illus, maps. (WA Geological Survey. Report 3.)
West Australian fossils, includes many that antedate 1859—the year in which, arguably, the first fossil from this region to be recognised as new to science received its name.

SELWYN, A.R.C. AND ULRICH, G.H.F. *Notes on the physical geography, geology and mineralogy of Victoria.* Melbourne, Blundell and Ford, 1866. 92 p, illus, maps.
The Geological Survey of Vic, then directed by Selwyn, set a model for systematic study of Australian field geology. This report summarises part of that notable achievement.

SIMPSON, E.S. *Minerals of Western Australia.* Perth, Government Printer, 1948–52. 3 vols, illus.
A detailed account of mineral species found—and where found—in WA, by the government mineralogist.

SPRY, A.H. AND BANKS, M.R. eds, 'The geology of Tasmania', *J of the Geological Society of Australia* 9, 2, 1962, 107–362.
The work is accompanied by geological and structural maps.

STRZELECKI, P.E. de *Physical description of New South Wales and Van Diemens Land, accompanied by a geological map, sections and diagrams, and figures of the organic remains.* London, Longman, Brown, Green and Longmans, 1845. 462 p, illus, maps.
The first geological map of any large part of Australia. Facsimile edition, LBSA, 1965.

TASMANIA. Geological Survey. *Catalogue of the minerals of Tasmania.* Hobart, Dept of Mines, Tas, 1910, illus.
A comprehensive revision and enlargement of this work by W.F. Petterd was issued by the Tasmanian Dept of Mines in 1970.

TEESDALE-SMITH, E.N. *Bibliography of South Australian geology: includes all literature published up to and including June, 1958.* Adelaide, SA Dept of Mines and Geological Survey, 1959. 240 p, map.
Of the Australian states, only SA has published a bibliography of works in all branches of its geology.

VALLANCE, T.G. 'Origins of Australian geology', *Proceedings of the Linnean Society of NSW* 100, 1, 1975, 13–43.
An outline of how geological knowledge of Australia developed, and how in the early days that knowledge was shaped by European experience.

WESTERN AUSTRALIA. Geological Survey. *The geology of Western Australia.* Perth, WA Geological Survey, 1975. 540 p, illus, maps. (WA Geological Survey Memoir, 2).
Fundamental work, but the geological map of the state has been superseded (see Prider, 1979).

WORNER, H.K. *et al, Minerals of Broken Hill.* Melbourne, Australian Mining & Smelting Ltd, 1982. 259 p, illus.
Mining at Broken Hill where silver–lead–zinc deposits have yielded fine mineral specimens—some here illustrated in colour.

Margaret Preston, Banksia tree. *Plate 26 in* Margaret Preston's monotypes, *edited by Sydney Ure Smith, Sydney, no date (1949).*

CHAPTER 12

FLORA

ALEX GEORGE AND ALISON McCUSKER

LITERATURE ON THE plants of Australia is extensive and spread through many thousands of publications. Although most of these are written in English, there are important works in other languages, particularly German, French and Latin. There is no complete bibliography of this literature and the present list is only a guide to the major historical and modern works. Several of those listed are themselves bibliographic, notably Burbidge (1963, 1978), and many others contain good reading lists on their special subjects.

The earliest writings on Australian flora were those of William Dampier who collected plants on the northwest coast in 1699 (W. Dampier, *A voyage to New Holland*, London, James Knapton, 1703 and 1709; facs, Gloucester, Alan Sutton, 1981). Some of his specimens were described in 1704 by John Ray (*Historia plantarum*, London, vol 3, Appendix: 225–6), before the modern system of naming plants was developed by Linnaeus. Dampier's collection was reviewed by A.S. George in *The Western Australian naturalist* (11, 8, 1971, 173–8). The first Australian plants named under the Linnaean system were described by N.L. Burmann in his *Flora Indica* (Amsterdam, Lugduni Batavorum, 1768, 233–5). Two years later, extensive botanical investigation began on the east coast of the continent with the visit of Joseph Banks and Daniel Solander on Cook's first voyage of 1768–71.

Botanical exploration and writing began in earnest following European settlement in 1788, and by 1810 several significant works had appeared. Besides those listed below, an important early account of the plants of the Sydney region was 'Observaciones sobre el suelo, naturales y plantas del Puerto Jackson y Bahia-Botanica' by the Spaniard Antonio Cavanilles (*Annales de historia natural* 3, 1800, 206–39). This was based on the collections of Luis Née and Fadeo Haenke, gathered on the Malaspina expedition which visited Sydney in 1793.

Collections and notes by pioneer settler James Drummond formed the basis of a similar paper on the flora of the Swan River colony. Written by John Lindley, this was published as *Sketch of the vegetation of the Swan River colony of Western Australia . . . together with an alphabetical and systematic index to the first twenty-three volumes of Edward's Botanical Register* (London, James Ridgway, 1839–40). It included descriptions of about two hundred new plants.

Early writing on Australian flora was by Europeans who either visited the continent and took back data and specimens, or received collections from explorers and settlers. There were neither botanists nor facilities for the systematic study of plants in Australia. The collectors and explorers themselves, however, often described the vegetation in their journals, especially in relation to its pastoral potential, and in some cases botanists contributed appendices describing the plants. Robert Brown made such a contribution to Charles Sturt's *Narrative of an expedition into central Australia* (1849; facs, LBSA, 1965), while John Lindley did likewise for Thomas Mitchell's *Journal of an expedition into the interior of tropical Australia* (1848; facs, Greenwood Press, 1967). Later in the nineteenth century Ralph Tate contributed the botanical text to the *Report on the work of the Horn Scientific Expedition to central Australia* (London, Dulau, 1896), while together with Ferdinand von Mueller he wrote a similar contribution for the report of the Elder Exploring Expedition which in 1891–92 travelled from South Australia through the Great Victoria Desert to Perth (*Transactions of the Royal Society of South Australia* 16, 3, 1896, 333–83).

The English botanist Joseph Hooker, who visited Tasmania during the Ross voyage of exploration in southern regions in 1839–43, made an important contribution to the knowledge of Australian plants. In Tasmania he botanised extensively with the resident magistrate Ronald Gunn. Back in England he worked up the collections and wrote a long essay on the plant geography of Australia (Hooker, 1855–59).

By the 1820s attempts were being made to foster research on Australian flora, but it was not until the arrival of Mueller in 1847 that indigenous botany began to flourish. Mueller dominated Australian botany for 50 years. He explored many parts of the continent, had contact with collectors who sent him plant specimens from all states, and corresponded widely overseas. He was director of the botanic gardens and herbarium in Melbourne from 1853 to 1873 and continued as government botanist of Victoria until his death in 1896. In his writings he concentrated on descriptive botany, naming many genera and species and compiling floristic lists for Victoria and Australia. He also wrote on economic botany (especially forestry), on the acclimatisation of plants, and on medicinal and drug plants. A bibliography of over one thousand publications by Mueller has recently been compiled (D.M. Churchill, T.B. Muir and D.M. Sinkora, 'The published works of Ferdinand J.H. Mueller (1825–1896)', *Muelleria* 4, 1, 1978, 1–120; 4, 2, 1979, 123–68; 5, 4, 1984, 229–48).

It was Mueller's ambition to prepare the first complete Australian flora in which all plants known for the continent would be described. He was dissuaded from doing so by botanists in England, chiefly because the major historical collections, an essential source of reference, were stored in herbaria in Britain and Europe. The task fell instead to George Bentham, a dedicated English botanist. Working mainly at the Royal Botanic Gardens, Kew, Bentham described 8125 species in his *Flora Australiensis* (1863–78; facs, 1967); it has remained until recently the most important single reference work on Australian plants and is only now being superseded by the new *Flora of Australia* (1981–).

By the time the last volume of *Flora Australiensis* was published, amateur and professional botanists were active in most states and were beginning to produce books and papers, such as McAlpine's census of fungi (1895) which brought together information on these plants for the first time. The increasing impact of exotic plants following land clearing can be seen in two original works on weeds, J. McC. Black (1909) and A.J. Ewart and J.R. Tovey, *The weeds, poison plants, and naturalised aliens of Victoria* (Melbourne, Government Printer, 1909).

In the twentieth century research on Australian flora has been undertaken increasingly by resident botanists, although European botanists continued to play a major role in the early decades. Just before 1900 the Englishman Spencer Le Marchant Moore visited the newly discovered goldfields of Western Australia and made the first extensive botanical survey of the region. His results—descriptions of plants, a floristic analysis and observations on adaptations to drought—appeared in 1898 in the *J of the Linnean Society—Botany* 34, 1898–1900, 171–261.

Two Germans, Ludwig Diels and Ernst Pritzel, visited Western Australia in 1900–01 and botanised extensively there. They published their taxonomic results mainly in the paper 'Fragmenta phytographiae Australiae Occidentalis' (1904). Diels wrote a seminal work in German on the vegetation and plant geography of the state, *Die Pflanzenwelt von West-Australien* (1906), as well as a worldwide taxonomic revision of the family Droseraceae (sundews), which includes many Australian species (*Das Pflanzenreich* 26, 1906, 1–137).

In 1914 the Danish botanist Carl E.H. Ostenfeld also carried out fieldwork in Western Australia, travelling as far north as Derby. He published the results in three papers, in *Dansk botanisk arkiv* 2, 6, 1916, 1–44, and 2, 8, 1918, 1–66, and in *Biologiske meddelelser Kongelige Danske Videnskabernes Selskab* 3, 2, 1921, 1–144. The first was a major paper on Australian seagrasses.

On the other side of Australia the Czech Karel Domin travelled widely in Queensland where he described the vegetation and collected many specimens. His work appeared as *Beiträge zur Flora und Pflanzengeographie Australiens* (Stuttgart, E. Schweizerbart, 1914–29) in the series *Bibliotheca botanica*, Hefte 85 and 89. Domin also described new species from Australian specimens that he studied in collections at the Royal Botanic Gardens, Kew.

Until about 1950 Australian botanists with a few exceptions dominated taxonomic research in their own states—C.A. Gardner in Western Australia; J.M. Black, J.B. Cleland and R.S. Rogers in South Australia; F.M. Bailey, C.T. White and W.D. Francis in Queensland; R.H. Anderson, W.F. Blakely and J.H. Maiden in New South Wales; A.J. Ewart and W.H. Nicholls in Victoria; and L. Rodway in Tasmania. The later years of this period also saw the emergence of several who were to become major figures in the postwar era: J.H. Willis (Victoria), J.W. Vickery and L.A.S. Johnson (New South Wales), N.T. Burbidge (Australian Capital Territory) and S.T. Blake (Queensland).

During the past thirty years botanical institutions in most states have been able to expand both staff and facilities, resulting in studies of a wide range of plant groups. Books and research papers have appeared steadily. The *Australian J of botany*, published since 1953 by CSIRO, contains papers on taxonomy, ecology and other aspects of botany. Other significant journals are those of the Royal Society in each state and the *Proceedings of the Linnean Society of New South Wales*; these publish papers from all the natural sciences. The major Australian herbaria now issue house journals containing taxonomic and ecological contributions.

There was no resident botanist in the Northern Territory until the arrival of G.M. Chippendale in the 1950s to establish a herbarium at Alice Springs. Chippendale published a 'Check list of Northern Territory plants' (*Proceedings of the Linnean Society of New South Wales* 96, 4, 1972, 207–67) which also provided data on plant distribution on a broad scale. In 1981, some 50 botanists contributed to the *Flora of central Australia*, edited by J.P. Jessop, which described the plants of the whole arid region of the continent.

While much taxomony has been of a regional or ad hoc nature, there is a current trend towards Australia-wide studies of genera and families. This trend will become dominant over the next twenty years while the new *Flora of Australia*, begun in 1981, is produced.

While many families of Australian plants have been or are now being studied in detail, some groups have been written about more extensively than others. Prominent among these is the genus *Eucalyptus*, containing about six hundred species, which occurs in most regions of Australia and is of major botanical and economic importance. The first species to be described, *E. obliqua*, was published by C.L. L'Héritier de Brutelle in *Sertum Anglicum* (Paris, Didot, 1789, 18) and the discovery of new species is still continuing. Mueller (1879–84) recognised the importance of the genus and was followed by J.H. Maiden's elaborate work (1903–33). W.F. Blakely (1934; 1965) was also an essential text for students of the genus for many years. Tropical eucalypts were the subject of a detailed revision by the Queensland botanist S.T. Blake, published as 'Studies on northern Australian species of *Eucalyptus*' in the *Australian J of botany* 1, 2, 1953, 185–352. In Western Australia C.A. Gardner produced the series 'Trees of Western Australia' in the *J of Agriculture* with fine line drawings of 117 eucalypts, later brought together as *Eucalypts of Western Australia* (Perth, Western Australian Dept of Agriculture, 1979).

Taxonomic and morphological studies of *Eucalyptus* have continued to flourish. An important paper 'Developmental morphology of the floral organs of *Eucalyptus*, 1. The inflorescence', by D.J. and S.G.M. Carr (*Australian J of botany* 7, 2, 1959, 109–41), opened up new avenues of investigation. A new classification was proposed in 1971 by L.D. Pryor and L.A.S. Johnson (*A classification of the eucalypts*, Canberra, Australian National University). A significant popular work is S. Kelly's *Eucalypts* (Melbourne, Nelson, 1969–78, 2 vols), featuring watercolour paintings of several hundred species; a little-known forerunner of this work was *40 Australian eucalypts in colour* (Sydney, Dymock's Book Arcade, 1949). Of more specialised nature is *Eucalyptus seed* (Canberra, CSIRO, 1980); besides illustrating the seed of each species, the book describes reproduction, seed morphology and classification, commercial seed production and testing, and germination procedures. It includes an extensive bibliography and a glossary. N. Hall's *Botanists of the eucalypts* (Melbourne, CSIRO, 1978) details all the people who have been involved in the discovery and naming of eucalypts.

The Australian flora also contains a large number of grasses, both native and introduced. Many are economically important, especially as pasture plants, and some are dominant components of the vegetation. Studies of their taxonomy were rather spasmodic until the 1930s when a visit by the English botanist C.E. Hubbard inspired more extensive systematic work, with outstanding contributions by S.T. Blake, whose many detailed systematic surveys were published from the 1940s to the early 1970s, mostly in the *Proceedings of the Royal Society of Queensland, contributions from the Queensland Herbarium* and in papers published by the University of Queensland.

Nancy T. Burbidge, working first in Perth and later in Canberra, studied the genus *Triodia* (spinifexes) and published a revision of the genus in the *Australian J of botany* (1, 1, 1953, 121–84). Burbidge also wrote three volumes in the series *Australian grasses* (A & R, 1966–70) which contain line drawings and semitechnical descriptions of the grasses of several regions.

In Western Australia C.A. Gardner's only volume (1952) of a planned state flora dealt with grasses. More recently M. Lazarides, working in Canberra, has made extensive studies of grasses and published several books and many papers. In *The grasses of central Australia* (ANUP, 1970), he provided a taxonomic and ecological account of the species of the arid regions; his taxonomic papers have appeared mainly in the *Australian J of botany* and *Brunonia* (for example, 3, 2, 1980, 271–333). Joyce W. Vickery, based at Sydney, also wrote extensively on grasses, publishing mainly in *Contributions from the National Herbarium of New South Wales*. Foremost among her papers were revisions of the Australian species of *Festuca* (1939), *Deyeuxia* (1940), *Agrostis* (1941), *Danthonia* (1956) and *Poa* (1970). In Brisbane Blake's work on grasses has been continued by B.K. Simon who, besides taxonomic papers, has produced *A preliminary check-list of Australian grasses* (Technical bulletin 3, Dept of Primary Industries, Botany Branch, Brisbane, 1978), listing all native and introduced species.

Grasses have been the subject of one of the first applications of the computer to plant taxonomy in Australia. *Australian grass genera* by L. Watson and M.J. Dallwitz (Canberra, Australian National University, 1980) contains highly technical descriptions and keys for all genera in Australia, produced by computer from a data bank. An update on microfiche was produced in August 1981.

Inevitably the orchids have attracted much attention in Australia as they have elsewhere in the world, and here major contributions have come from amateur botanists. In the nineteenth century the surveyor R.D. Fitzgerald took up the tradition of fine botanical art and combined it with taxonomy to produce *Australian orchids* (1875–94; facs, 1977). Early this century a South Australian medical practitioner, R.S. Rogers, became the Australian authority on orchids and wrote, besides many papers, *An introduction to the study of South Australian orchids* (Adelaide, Government Printer, 1911). Following him came W.H. Nicholls in Victoria and the Rev H.M.R. Rupp in New South Wales, both prolific writers. Many of Nicholls's papers appeared in the *Victorian naturalist* and his work culminated in the posthumously published *Orchids of Australia* (1969). Rupp published mostly in the *Proceedings of the Linnean Society of New South Wales*; his major work was *The orchids of New South Wales* (Sydney, Government Printer, 1943). In Western Australia, semipopular works were *West Australian orchids* by Emily Pelloe (Perth, The Author, 1930) and *Orchids of the west* by Rica Erickson (Perth, Paterson Brokensha, 1951), each illustrated by its author. A similar book was *Native orchids of Tasmania* by M.J. Firth (Devonport, Tas, C.L. Richmond 1965). Of historical interest is Rosa Fiveash's *Australian orchids* with text by N. Lothian (Adelaide, Rigby, 1974), which reproduced 99 watercolour paintings by Fiveash, who also illustrated many of R.S. Rogers's works.

The wattles of the genus *Acacia*, so numerous in Australia, have been widely studied for many years and are being even more intensively investigated today. More than 700 Australian species have been named by botanists but there has not been an account of the genus as a whole for Australia since that by George Bentham in *Flora Australiensis* 1 (1864; facs, 1967) which covered the 293 species known at the time. Ferdinand von Mueller, besides naming new acacias in many papers, made a special study which included detailed lithographs, published in thirteen parts as *Iconography of Australian species of Acacia and cognate genera* (Melbourne, Government Printer, 1887–88). Early this century J.H. Maiden and W.F. Blakely extensively studied *Acacia*, especially the collections of W.V. Fitzgerald and others in Western Australia. They described 50 new species in the *J of the Royal Society of Western Australia* (13, 1927. 1–36).

More recently there have been studies of *Acacia*, essentially on a state or regional basis. Significant publications resulting from this work include *Acacias of South Australia* by D.J.E. Whibley (Adelaide, Government Printer, 1980) and 'A revision of Acacia Mill. in Queensland' by L. Pedley in *Austrobaileya* 1, 1978–79, 75–337. Important papers on the taxonomy of *Acacia* have been published by Mary D. Tindale, mainly in the series *Contributions from the National Herbarium of New South Wales* and its successor *Telopea* and by B.R. Maslin, chiefly in *Nuytsia*, the bulletin of the Western Australian Herbarium. On a popular note, Marion Simmons' *Acacias of Australia* (Melbourne, Nelson, 1981) provides descriptions, keys for identification, notes on cultivation, line drawings, colour photos and a short bibliography.

From the beginning of European settlement the poisonous and medicinal properties of plants have drawn attention and much has been written about them. The first important synthesis was E. Hurst's *The poison plants of New South Wales* (Sydney, Poison Plants Committee, 1942). In 1948 CSIRO published L.J. Webb's *Guide to the medicinal and poisonous plants of Queensland* which included an extensive bibliography. A similar but more elaborate work was by C.A. Gardner and H.W. Bennetts (1956). The most comprehensive work to date is S.L. Everist (1974).

Australian botanical literature reflects the concentration of research on the flowering plants. Ferns and gymnosperms have usually been included in floras but have rarely been treated in specialist publications. One of the earliest such works was *Victorian ferns* by R.W. Bond (Melbourne, Field Naturalists' Club of Victoria, 1934), revised by N.A. Wakefield as *Ferns of Victoria and Tasmania* (1955). Two recent books have covered all Australian ferns. *Australian ferns and fern allies* by D.L. Jones and S.C. Clemesha (Sydney, Reed, 1976) gave illustrated descriptions and cultivation notes for 312 species; *Ferns, fern allies and conifers of Australia* by H.T. Clifford and J. Constantine (UQP, 1980) provided keys to families, genera and species.

The non-vascular plants—fungi, algae, lichens, mosses and liverworts—have similarly not fared well. The only nineteenth-century works of note were W.H. Harvey (1858–63) and D. McAlpine (1895). J.B. Cleland (1934) was for many years the only useful reference to these plants in southern Australia. Two very good recent handbooks, both well illustrated, are *Fungi of south-eastern Australia* by E. Macdonald and J. Westerman (Melbourne, Nelson, 1979), and *Common Australian fungi* by A.M. Young (UNSWP, 1982), with a key to genera.

Following Harvey's work, research and writing on algae was intermittent for decades. A.H.S. Lucas (1936–47) is still the only comprehensive work, although the recent *Seaweeds of Australia* by B. Fuhrer *et al* (Sydney, Reed, 1981) provides excellent colour photographs of common species. Over the past few decades detailed studies of some algal groups have been made by H.B.S. Womersley in Adelaide and V. May in Sydney.

Descriptions of Australian mosses and liverworts were first brought together by L.A. Rodway (1914–16) but sixty years passed before the next major work, G.A.M. Scott and I.G. Stone (1976). The liverworts are described in *Southern Australian liverworts* by G.A.M. Scott (AGPS, 1985).

Australian lichens, too, were originally described in divers publications. The first workers to bring them together for an Australian region were R.B. Filson and R.W. Rogers (1979). A review of lichens at the generic level has been provided by R.W. Rogers (1981). This technical book gives keys to genera and detailed descriptions.

Many local and regional descriptive studies of vegetation have been made, but there are few comprehensive works on a state or continental scale. A pioneer account was J.G. Wood's *The vegetation of South Australia* (Adelaide, Government Printer, 1937), extensively rewritten by R.L. Specht (1972). Complementing this work is *The native forest and woodland vegetation of South Australia* by C.D. Boomsma and N.G. Lewis (South Australia, Woods and Forests Dept, Bulletin 25, undated) which describes plant communities and forest formations and gives details of the distribution of individual species. The yearbooks published by the Australian Bureau of Statistics for each state contain concise accounts of flora and vegetation.

A major descriptive work on regional vegetation was that of N.C.W. Beadle (1948). This was followed by a similar study by A.B. Costin, *A study of the ecosystems of the Monaro region of New South Wales with special reference to soil erosion* (Sydney, Government Printer, 1954). In the 1950s and 1960s CSIRO embarked on a series of studies of the pastoral regions of Australia. These included investigations of soil, landform, climate and vegetation, and saw publication as the *CSIRO land research series*, over twenty of which have appeared since 1953. Besides large-scale maps they contain many black and white photographs. In the 1960s J.S. Beard began mapping the vegetation of Western Australia. This project resulted in the series *Vegetation survey of Western Australia 1: 250 000 Series* (Perth, Vegmap Publications, 1972–80) and the *1: 1 000 000 Series* (UWAP, 1974–81). Each issue contains a vegetation map and a text describing the vegetation formation, landforms, geology and climate. Two major syntheses appeared almost simultaneously in 1981, both published by Cambridge University Press. *The vegetation of Australia* by N.C.W. Beadle provides descriptions and black and white photographs of all plant communities and their alliances. It also covers the environment, floristics, evolution and physiological adaptations. In *Australian vegetation*, edited by R.H. Groves, 22 authors have contributed chapters on the major vegetation types, as well as phytogeography, evolution of the flora, conservation and alien plants.

The most important early work on Australian phytogeography was that of J.D. Hooker (1855); indeed, it was the only work of real significance in this field until Diels (1906) wrote on the phytogeography of southern Western Australia in more detail. A further assessment of West Australian vegetation was made by C.A. Gardner in 'The vegetation of Western Australia', (*J of the Royal Society of Western Australia* 28, 1942, xi–lxxxvi); his concepts were greatly expanded by N.T. Burbidge (1960) to cover the whole continent. Since Gardner's time the theory of continental drift has gained wider acceptance and influenced thought on plant distribution. A synthesis of current opinion of Australian phytogeography has been provided by B.A. Barlow in 'The Australian flora: its origin and evolution', (*Flora of Australia* 1, 1981, 25–75).

Popular writing on Australian flora has begun to flourish only recently, although two early books of note were *Western Australian wildflowers* by Emily Pelloe (Melbourne, de Garis, 1921) and the *The native flowers of Victoria* by E.E. Pescott (Melbourne, Robertson, 1914). Thistle Y. Harris (1948, 1953) gave the genre an impetus after World War II, but the formation of wildflower societies and an active environmental movement during the past 25 years led to a wider interest and market. Popular demand led to the *Flowers and plants* series being promoted by the publisher A.H. & A.W. Reed. Recently Costermans (1981) followed in the same vein.

On the cultivation of native plants two significant works are *Australian native plants* by J.W. Wrigley and M. Fagg (Sydney, Collins, 1979) and the *Encyclopaedia of Australian plants* by W.R. Elliott and D.L. Jones (Melbourne, Lothian, 1980–). Both contain many colour photographs.

The Society for Growing Australian Plants has been very active in promoting the cultivation of native flora. It publishes a regular journal, *Australian plants*, which first appeared in December 1959. The society has produced guides such as *Western Australian plants for horticulture* by K. Newbey (part 1 1968, part 2 1972), *The language of botany* by C.N. Debenham (1962), *Cradle of incense* by G.W. Althofer (1978), *Prostanthera* (mint bushes), *Acacias of New South Wales* by I. Armitage (1977) and *Australian plant genera* by J.A. Baines (1981). The latter is a very useful reference on the meaning of generic names and includes information on the distribution and number of species in each genus. *Western Australian plant names and their meanings* by F.A. Sharr (UWAP, 1978), provides the meanings not only of genera but also of all species in that state.

Archival material on Australian botany can be difficult to locate since it is spread through many institutions. The journals and correspondence of many early collectors and botanists are housed in Europe, especially at the British Library, the British Museum (Natural History), the Royal Botanic Gardens, Kew, and the Archives Nationales, Paris. In Australia the major herbaria hold fieldbooks, correspondence and manuscripts of botanists employed by or associated with them. Some universities hold material by and on former members of staff, and the Mitchell Library in Sydney, the National Library in Canberra and the Battye Library in Perth are also important repositories. Usually, however, it is a long and tortuous road to trace all the material needed for a detailed study of a particular person. A guide to archival sources can be gained from the bibliographies in chapters of two recent works, *Scientists in nineteenth century Australia: a documentary history* by Ann Mozley Moyal (Melbourne, Cassell, 1976), and the two-volume set *People and plants in Australia* and *Plants and man in Australia* edited by D.J. and S.G.M. Carr (Sydney, Academic Press, 1981).

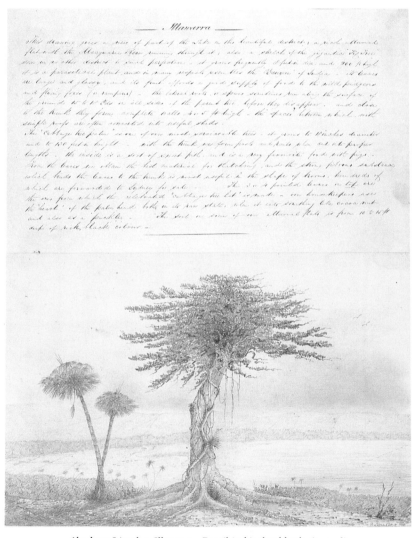

Abraham Lincolne, Illawarra. *Pencil in his sketchbook,* Australian sketches, *1838–44. Lincolne, who travelled extensively in the Illawarra region in the 1830s and 1840s, accompanied this pencil sketch of the fig tree and the cabbage tree palm with a detailed description in which he noted the beauty and various domestic uses of these two native trees.*
MITCHELL LIBRARY

ASTON, H.I. *Aquatic plants of Australia: a guide to the identification of the aquatic ferns and flowering plants of Australia, both native and naturalized*. MUP, 1973. 368 p, illus, maps.

Descriptions, distribution and ecology of over 200 species. Keys for identification. Extensive bibliography.

BAILEY, F.M. *The Queensland flora*. Brisbane, Diddams, 1899–1905. 7 vols, illus.

Largely extracted from Bentham's *Flora Australiensis* with additional records and species. Descriptions and keys. Some rare species illustrated. Vol 7 (not numbered) is a general index.

BAILEY, F.M. *A synopsis of the Queensland flora, containing both the phaenogamous and cryptogamous plants. [With Supplements 1–3]*. Brisbane, Government Printer, 1883–90. 4 vols.

A list of orders (= families), genera and species native and naturalised in Qld (1268 genera, 4734 species). Brief descriptions and distributional notes.

BEADLE, N.C.W. *et al, Handbook of the vascular plants of the Sydney district and Blue Mountains*. Armidale, NSW, Privately published, 1962. 597 p, illus, map.

Treats about 1800 indigenous and 420 exotic species of ferns, gymnosperms and flowering plants. Brief keys and descriptions to families and genera, and amplified keys to species. Notes on distribution, habitat and flowering times. A forerunner of *Flora of the Sydney region* (Sydney, Reed, 1972) which covers a slightly larger area and contains some colour plates.

BEADLE, N.C.W. *The vegetation and pastures of western New South Wales, with special reference to soil erosion*. Sydney, Dept of Conservation of NSW, 1948. 281 p, illus, maps. Describes the soils and vegetation formations of the region. Includes chapters on exploration and settlement, landforms and geology, climate and plant succession. Extensive bibliography.

BENTHAM, G. *Flora Australiensis: a description of the plants of the Australian territory*. London, L. Reeve, 1863–78. 7 vols. The standard Australian flora for over a century, still useful and widely used. Keys and descriptions for the 8125 species then known. Facsimile edition, A. Archer, 1967.

BLACK, J. McC. *Flora of South Australia*. Adelaide, Government Printer, 1922–29. 4 pts, illus, map.

A very useful concise flora based largely on original work. A second, revised edition issued 1943–55, part 4 revised by Enid L. Robertson. A supplement of 385p by Hansjoerg Eichler, containing many corrections, additions and nomenclatural changes, issued 1965. Part 1, 3rd ed, 466 p, revised and edited by John P. Jessop, issued 1978.

BLACK, J. McC. *The naturalised flora of South Australia*. Adelaide, Privately published, 1909, 192 p, illus.

The first Australian work on the introduced plants of a large region. Contains keys to genera and species, and concise descriptions.

BLACKALL, W.E. AND GRIEVE, B.J. *How to know Western Australian wildflowers*. UWAP, 1954–75. 4 vols, illus.

Illustrated popular keys to the flora of south WA. From part 2 onwards gives general distribution, and from part 3 flowering period. Parts 3A and 3B revised 1980–81; part 4, supplement, issued in 1983.

BLAKELY, W.F. *A key to the eucalypts*. Sydney, The Workers Trustees, 1934, 339 p, illus.

A key and standard reference to all species of *Eucalyptus* then known, together with descriptions, distribution, habitat and flowering times. The third edition published in 1965 includes Forestry and Timber Bureau leaflet no 92 (24 p) by R.D. Johnston and R. Marryatt, bringing the nomenclature up to date.

BLOMBERY, A.M. *What wildflower is that?* Sydney, Hamlyn, 1972. 304 p, illus.

Photographs and brief notes on selected Australian plants. Useful popular introductory work.

BROWN, R. *Prodromus florae Novae Hollandiae et insulae Van Diemen*. London, Richard Taylor, 1810. 145–592 p.

The first flora of Australia, with Latin descriptions, based largely on Brown's collections made from 1801 to 1805. A second volume planned to contain pp 1–144 was never published. The facsimile edition (Weinheim, Bergstr, H.R. Engelmann, 1960) includes the supplement of 1830 and an introduction in English by W.T. Stearn.

BURBIDGE, N.T. *Dictionary of Australian plant genera: gymnosperms and angiosperms*. A & R, 1963. 345 p, maps.

A very useful reference for information on genera, with notes on general distribution and numbers of species.

BURBIDGE, N.T. 'The phytogeography of the Australia region', *Australian J of botany* 8, 2, 1960, 75–211.

A major analysis and discussion of the plant geography of Australia.

BURBIDGE, N.T. *Plant taxonomic literature in Australian libraries*. Melbourne, CSIRO in association with Australian Biological Resources Study, 1978, 520 p.

Over 8000 botanical and related works arranged alphabetically under author, together with a list of libraries where each is held.

BURBIDGE, N.T. AND GRAY, M. *Flora of the Australian Capital Territory*. ANUP, 1970. 447 p, illus.

Lengthy descriptive keys to over 1000 species comprising the flora of the ACT (excluding Jervis Bay area).

CATCHESIDE, D.G. *Mosses of South Australia*. Adelaide, Government Printer, 1980. 364 p, illus. (Handbook of the flora and fauna of SA).

Descriptions of families, genera and species with keys. Chapter on structure, biology, ecology and study techniques. Glossary and bibliography.

CLAYTON, M.N. AND KING, R.J. eds, *Marine botany: an Australian perspective*. Melbourne, Longman Cheshire, 1981. 468 p, illus, maps.

An excellent overview covering history, taxonomy, ecology, biogeography and physiology of marine plants. Also includes chapters on mangroves, salt marshes and coral reefs. Extensive bibliography.

CLELAND, J.B. *Toadstools and mushrooms and other large fungi of South Australia*. Adelaide, Government Printer, 1934–35. 2 vols, illus.

Descriptions of families, genera and 578 species. Keys for identification. Chapters on structure, biology, toxicity and collection of fungi. Glossary and short bibliography.

COCHRANE, G.R. *et al, Flowers and plants of Victoria*. Sydney, Reed, 1968. 216 p, illus, maps.

Semipopular work with photographs, arranged in floristic regions. Captions add information on species, including distribution. Text chapters describe predominant plants of each region.

COSTERMANS, L.F. *Native trees and shrubs of south-eastern Australia*. Adelaide, Rigby, 1981. 422 p, illus, maps.

Describes the trees and woody shrubs of the region, the environment, ecology and places of special interest. A well-presented and very useful work.

COSTIN, A.B. *et al, Kosciusko alpine flora*. Melbourne, CSIRO, 1979. 408 p, illus, maps.

Detailed account of the flora of a very interesting area of Australia's 'high country'. Descriptions of all species (about 200) with keys suitable for field use and the history of the area. Superbly illustrated.

CUNNINGHAM, G.M. et al, *Plants of western New South Wales*. Sydney, Government Printer in association with the Soil Conservation Service of NSW, 1982. 766 p, illus, maps.
Describes and illustrates over 2000 species. Chapter on environment including vegetation communities. Bibliography and glossary.

CURTIS, W.M. *The student's flora of Tasmania*. 4 vols, Hobart, Government Printer, 1956– . illus.
A concise but thorough account of the Tasmanian gymnosperm and angiosperm flora. Descriptions, keys and distributional notes.

DIELS, L. *Die Pflanzenwelt von West-Australien südlich des Wendekreises*. Leipzig, W. Engelmann, 1906. 413 p, illus, maps.
An important and still influential essay on the floristics and plant geography of southern WA. Text in German.

DIELS, L. AND PRITZEL, E. 'Fragmenta phytographiae Australiae occidentalis: Beiträge zur Kenntnis der Pflanzen Westaustraliens, ihrer Verbreitung und ihrer Lebensverhältnisse', *Botanische Jahrbücher* 35, 1904, 55–662.
The results of a major botanical expedition to WA in 1900–01. Includes descriptions in German, of many new species.

DOCKRILL, A.W. *Australian indigenous orchids*. Vol 1. *The epiphytes, the tropical terrestrial species*. Sydney, Society for Growing Australian Plants, 1969. 825 p, illus.
Contains a key to all genera of Australian orchids; keys and descriptions for all epiphytic species, with notes on distribution and habitat. Vol 2 on terrestrial species not issued.

EVERIST, S.L. *Poisonous plants of Australia*. A & R, 1974. 684 p, illus.
Descriptions of all plants known or thought to be toxic, together with notes on toxicity and symptoms, and a bibliography.

EWART, A.J. *Flora of Victoria*. MUP, 1930. 1257 p, illus.
A concise flora covering about 2200 native and 461 exotic species of pteridophytes, gymnosperms and angiosperms. Brief keys and descriptions, notes on distribution and flowering time.

EWART, A.J. AND DAVIES, O.B. *The flora of the Northern Territory*. Melbourne, McCarron, Bird, 1917. 387 p, illus, map.
A concise flora with keys, adapted from Bentham's *Flora Australiensis*, and later records added.

FILSON, R.B. AND ROGERS, R.W. *Lichens of South Australia*. Adelaide, Government Printer, 1979. 197 p, illus, maps. (Handbook of the flora and fauna of SA).
Short descriptions and keys for genera and species. Chapters on lichen structure, chemistry and ecology. Extensive bibliography. The first major work on Australian lichens.

FITZGERALD, R.D. *Australian orchids*. Facs, Melbourne, Lansdowne Editions, 1977. 2 vols, illus.
Elegant, hand-coloured lithographs of orchids including detailed enlargements accompanying descriptive text. No pagination or index. First published 1875–94.

FLORA of Australia. AGPS, 1981– . illus.
The first modern flora of Australia, begun in 1981 and planned to be issued in about sixty-five volumes over twenty years. Contains keys to genera and species; concise descriptions; distribution including a map and citation of collections for each species. Vol 1 contains chapters on the flora project, the origin and evolution of the Australia flora, the system of classification used, a key to families and a glossary.

FRANCIS, W.D. *Australian rain-forest trees, excluding the species confined to the tropics*. Brisbane, Government Printer, 1929. 347 p, illus, map.
Detailed descriptions of about one hundred species and concise accounts of many others. Keys for identification. General discussion of rainforests. Third edition published in 1970.

GARDNER, C.A. *Enumeratio plantarum Australiae Occidentalis: a systematic census of the plants occurring in Western Australia*. Perth, Government Printer, 1931. 150 p.
First census of West Australian plants. Families, genera and species arranged in systematic order, with original references.

GARDNER, C.A. *Flora of Western Australia*. Vol 1, pt 1. *Graminae*. Perth, Government Printer, 1952. 400 p, illus.
Descriptions and distribution of all grasses known in WA. Keys for identification. Glossary. The only volume published of a projected state flora.

GARDNER, C.A. AND BENNETTS, H.W. *The toxic plants of Western Australia*. Perth, Western Australian Newspapers Ltd, 1956. 253 p, illus, map.
Descriptions of the state's toxic plants, the symptoms caused and their toxic principles. Bibliography.

HARRIS, T.Y. *Australian plants for the garden: a handbook*. A & R, 1962. 356 p, illus.
Comprehensive work on growing Australian wildflowers. First published in 1953.

HARRIS, T.Y. *Wild flowers of Australia*. A & R, 1938. 198 p, illus.
The first major popular book on Australian plants. Featured 248 species, described and illustrated. Reprinted many times.

HARVEY, W.H. *Phycologia Australica or a history of Australian seaweeds*. London, Reeve, 1858–63. 5 vols, illus.
Descriptions and hand-coloured lithographs of the first major collections of Australian marine algae.

HOFFMAN, N. AND BROWN, A. *Orchids of south-west Australia*. UWAP, 1984. 382 p, illus, maps.
Colour photographs and brief descriptive notes for all orchids in the region. Distribution maps. An excellent popular work.

HOOKER, J.D. *The botany of the Antarctic voyage of H.M. discovery ships* Erebus *and* Terror *in the years 1839–1843, under the command of Captain Sir James Clark Ross*. Part 3. *Flora Tasmaniae*. London, Reeve, 1855–59. 2 vols.
The botanical results of a major expedition as well as collections by others, especially Ronald Gunn. Vol 1 contains an important essay on the plant geography of Australia. Vol 2 includes accounts of mosses, hepatics, fungi, algae and lichens. There is a separate volume of plates.

JESSOP, J.P. ed, *Flora of central Australia*. Sydney, Australian Systematic Botany Society and Reed, 1981, 537 p, illus, maps.
Keys and concise descriptions for about 2000 species of the arid regions. Introductory chapters on botanical exploration.

LABILLARDIERE, J.J.H. de *Novae Hollandiae plantarum specimen*. Paris, Huzard, 1804–06. 2 vols, illus.
Descriptions in Latin of plants collected by Labillardiere and other French explorers between 1792 and 1800. Fine but somewhat stylised line drawings.

LAMP, C.A. AND COLLETT, F. *A field guide to weeds in Australia* (Rev edn). Melbourne, Inkata Press, 1979. 376 p, illus.
Semipopular account of 283 weed species. First published in 1976.

LEHMANN, J.G.C. *Plantae preissianae*. Hamburg, Meissner, 1844–48. 2 vols.
Descriptions of over 2000 species from southwest WA, mainly collected by Ludwig Preiss from 1838 to 1843, some by James Drummond. Written in Latin by several European botanists.

LEIGH, J. et al, *Extinct and endangered plants of Australia*. Melbourne, Macmillan, 1984. 369 p, illus, maps.

Semipopular descriptions of 76 presumed extinct and 203 endangered plants. Introductory chapters on vegetation, threats to plants and suggested conservation methods.

LUCAS, A.H.S. AND PERRIN, F. *The seaweeds of South Australia.* Adelaide, Government Printer, 1936–47, 2 pts, illus.

Part 1 deals with green and brown seaweeds; part 2 with the red seaweeds. There is also an introduction and appendices by H.B.S. Womersley and J.R. Harris, and a glossary. Appendices describe families and list their genera.

McALPINE, D. *Systematic arrangement of Australian fungi, together with host-index and list of works on the subject.* Melbourne, Government Printer, 1895. 237 p.

A census in systematic order with brief descriptions and distribution. Host-index in alphabetical order indicates fungi occurring on them. Extensive bibliography.

MAIDEN, J.H. *A critical revision of the genus* Eucalyptus. Sydney, Government Printer, 1903–33. 8 vols, illus.

Detailed work with descriptions, distribution and discussion of most of the species known to the author. Vol 8 includes descriptions of the seedlings of many species. No keys.

MAIDEN, J.H. *The useful native plants of Australia, including Tasmania.* Sydney, Turner & Henderson, 1889, 696 p.

Chapters on pasture plants, medicinal plants, gums, resins and kinos, oils, perfumes, dyes, tans, timbers, fibres and other properties.

MOORE, C. AND BETCHE, E. *Handbook of the flora of New South Wales: a description of the flowering plants and ferns indigenous to New South Wales.* Sydney, Government Printer, 1893. 582 p.

The first flora of NSW. Amplified keys to indigenous species, with brief descriptions of families and genera. Preface on the history of botanical exploration in the state. Plants introduced to NSW and the floras of Lord Howe and Norfolk islands listed.

MORCOMBE, M.K. *Australia's wildflowers.* Melbourne, Lansdowne, 1970. 128 p, illus, maps.

Beautiful photographs and brief notes on selected species. Descriptions of the flora of the major regions by five botanists.

MORLEY, B.D. AND TOELKEN, H.R. *Flowering plants in Australia.* Adelaide, Rigby, 1983. 415 p, illus, maps.

Descriptions and notes on the distribution and history of important genera and species for all families of flowering plants and gymnosperms. Keys to genera in each family.

MUELLER, F.J.H. von *Eucalyptographia: a descriptive atlas of the eucalypts of Australia and the adjoining islands.* Melbourne, Government Printer, 1879–84. illus.

Lithographs of *Eucalyptus* species, with accompanying text. Ten plates show anatomical details and seedlings. The first of several such works by Mueller.

MUELLER, F.J.H. von *Fragmenta phytographiae Australiae.* Melbourne, Government Printer, 1858–82. 12 vols, illus.

An important reference work to genera and species. Text in Latin. Vol 5 contains an index of families and genera in vols 1–5, and vol 10 an index to vols 6–10. Vol 11 contains lists of non-vascular plants, by other authors.

MUELLER, F.J.H. von *The plants indigenous to the colony of Victoria.* Melbourne. Government Printer, 1860–65, 2 vols, illus.

Descriptions and notes for each species; gives original place of publication of names, and synonymics. Lithographs of high quality, including some microscopical detail. The first major floristic work written and published in Australia.

NICHOLLS, W.H. *Orchids of Australia.* Ed by D.L. Jones and

T.B. Muir. Melbourne, Nelson, 1969. 141 p, illus.

Beautiful watercolour plates with detailed enlargements. Concise descriptions and notes. An earlier edition in parts by Georgian House ceased publication after part 4.

RODWAY, L. *Tasmanian bryophyta.* Hobart, Royal Society of Tas, 1914–16. 2 vols.

Revisions and descriptions of the bryophytes of Tas, with keys (some synoptic) for identification; notes on distribution. The only such book on Australian bryophyta published before 1970. Vol 1 covers the mosses and vol 2 the hepatics.

RODWAY, L. *The Tasmanian flora.* Hobart, Government Printer, 1903. 320 p, illus.

Brief descriptions of the angiosperms, gymnosperms and ferns of Tas with keys designed for use by students.

ROGERS, R.W. *The genera of Australian lichens (lichenized fungi).* UQP, 1981, 124 p, illus.

Key for identification with descriptions of all Australian genera; general distribution; generic classification of Poelt; bibliography.

SCOTT, G.A.M. AND STONE, I.G. *The mosses of southern Australia.* London, Academic Press, 1976. 495 p, illus.

The first manual of Australian mosses. Detailed descriptions of common species, short accounts of others. Extensive bibliography. Illustrations are by Celia Rosser.

SMITH, J.E. *A specimen of the botany of New Holland.* London, J. Sowerby, 1793. 54 p, illus.

The first work specifically on Australian plants, with descriptions of plants collected by early settlers, particularly John White.

SPECHT, R.L. AND MOUNTFORD, C.P. eds, *Records of the American–Australian Scientific Expedition to Arnhem Land.* Vol 3. *Botany and plant ecology.* MUP, 1958. 522 p, illus, maps.

The results of a major expedition and the first detailed account of the region. Chapters on ecology, exploration, plant geography and ethnobotany.

SPICER, W.W. *A handbook of the plants of Tasmania.* Hobart, J. Walch, 1878. 160 p, illus.

A key to species, a systematic checklist of the flora and brief notes on distribution.

STANLEY, T.D. AND ROSS, E.M., *Flora of south-eastern Qld.* Brisbane, Qld Dept of Primary Industries, 1984– . 3 vols, illus.

A projected three-volume work, vol 1 contains technical descriptions and keys for identification for 78 families of dicotyledons. Illustrated glossary of terms and a key to families.

STONES, M. AND CURTIS, W.M. *The endemic flora of Tasmania.* London, Ariel Press, 1967–78. 6 vols, illus, maps.

Splendid watercolour paintings of 254 species restricted to Tas. Descriptive text and notes on cultivation in Britain and Tas.

TATE, R. *A handbook of the flora of extratropical South Australia, containing the flowering plants and ferns.* Adelaide, Education Dept, 1890. 303 p, map.

Handbook in the form of keys to families, genera and species. Systematic list of species with distribution in SA.

WILLIAMS, K.A.W. *Native plants of Queensland.* North Ipswich, Qld, The Author, 1979–84. 2 vols, illus, maps.

Over 700 colour photographs. Captions give notes on species.

WILLIS, J.H. *A handbook to plants in Victoria.* MUP, 1962–72. 2 vols.

A concise state flora in the form of an amplified key, with distributions in and beyond Vic. Not illustrated but cites many published illustrations.

Cover, Australia's fauna, *1938. Pamphlet.*
BOOROWA PRODUCTIONS

CHAPTER 13

FAUNA

LYNDALL DAWSON AND GRAEME PHIPPS

FIFTY OR SIXTY MILLION years ago, at the close of the Cretaceous period, Australia broke away from its mother continent, Gondwanaland, from the region we now call Antarctica, and began to drift northward. For more than 40 million years, before our continental plate reached the vicinity of the Asian plate, Australia was isolated, separated from other land faunas by vast tracts of ocean. This period of isolation, more than any other factor, has contributed to the evolution in Australia of a fauna which contains more endemic species (that is, species which evolved in Australia and are unique to it) than any other continent (Keast, 1981; Archer and Clayton, 1984).

The first Europeans to visit the continent in the seventeenth century came upon the strange phenomenon of black swans, a portent of what was to follow from the 1770s onward with the British discovery and settlement of the eastern part of the continent. Cook, Banks and their successors were confronted with a bewildering array of strange beasts and birds totally unlike the animals of Europe, Asia, the Americas and Africa, all of which were comparatively well known by that time. John Gould, speaking of his arrival in Australia in 1838 wrote, 'I found myself surrounded by objects as strange as if I had been transported to another planet' (Gould, 1863; facs, 1984).

The discovery of the unique Australian fauna and flora and its profound influence on the natural historians of Europe during the late eighteenth and early nineteenth centuries is the subject of two recently published books by C.M. Finney (1984) and by Stanbury and Phipps (1980). These books bring together a wealth of information from original sources and provide a fascinating early perspective for those who want to understand the fauna of Australia. Words such as bizarre, incredulous, alien, unique and amazing were frequently used by early writers about Australian animals, and to a large extent this sense of wonder and general fascination is felt even today by newcomers to Australia. It is usually engendered first by the larger and more colourful elements in the fauna—the spectacular parrots, the raucous kookaburra and the emu among the birds, and of course the marsupials which have become international symbols of Australia, the kangaroo and the koala. The platypus, that most incongruous of mammals, is also a uniquely Australian symbol. The Great Barrier Reef is a world-renowned faunal wonderland with a vast abundance of invertebrates and fishes, some of which are specific to that area. These examples represent only the most spectacular extremes of the diverse range of forms which make up the fauna of Australia.

Finney (1984) has identified the year 1829 as a watershed in the development of natural history, including zoology, in Australia. His book provides detailed information about the expeditions and men involved up to that time and about their philosophy and art. By that year an astonishing number of Australian animals, marine, freshwater and terrestrial, vertebrate and invertebrate, had already been described and named. The collectors were largely amateurs—explorers, soldiers, convicts—who had no scientific interest in their finds. They crammed the holds of small sailing ships with skins and preserved specimens and often with live animals to amaze and amuse the gentry of Britain and France. The animals were described by eminent British and French anatomists and zoologists. They grappled with the problems of classifying the most unusual forms, paticularly the marsupials and the notoriously difficult platypus.

By the end of the second decade of the nineteenth century embryonic Australian societies and institutions were developing and better educated settlers added a local stimulus to the study of natural history in Australia.

In an overview of Australian zoology the entire nineteenth century was a period of intensely active collection and description. A sense of adventure and excitement at the new pervades many of the documents and articles relating to Australian zoology up to the turn of the century. Ronald Strahan's *Rare and curious specimens: an illustrated history of the Australian Museum, 1827–1979* (Sydney, Australian Museum, 1979) gives a masterly account of this period and some of the people involved in zoology at the time. Strahan describes how the Australian Museum, founded in 1827, was inextricably bound to the development of Australian zoology as a science in the nineteenth century. The National Museum of Victoria, founded considerably later in 1854, provided a similar focus for Victorian zoological collections and studies (Pescott, R.T.M. *Collections of a century: the history of the first hundred years of the National Museum of Victoria*, Melbourne, National Museum of Victoria, 1954). Nevertheless, during the nineteenth century and into the early years of the twentieth, the bulk of collections from Australia found their way to Britain, some as private collections, but most to be lodged in the British Museum. A useful guide to the European literature of the time is given by Strahan (1981), a small book of much greater scope and interest than its title suggests.

Towards the end of the nineteenth century the youthful Australian institutions began to publish their own catalogues and other results of Australian zoological research in such journals as *Records of the Australian Museum*, which first appeared in 1890, and the *J of the Linnean Society*, which began in 1876. Prior to the establishment of these journals much new information about Australian animals was published in local newspapers, such as the *Sydney Morning Herald*. D.F. Branagan, in 'Words, actions, people: 150 years of the scientific societies in Australia', *J and proceedings of the Royal Society of New South Wales* 104, 1972, 123–41, notes that the very small and shortlived Entomological Society, founded by William Macleay in 1862, helped to stimulate men such as Gerard Krefft and E.P. Ramsay, who became some of the most active and influential Australian zoologists of the nineteenth century.

The literature of nineteenth-century zoology in Australia is diverse. Apart from articles appearing in scientific publications—mainly catalogues and descriptions of new species—the popular literature consisted primarily of narratives of the travels and observations of the many explorers, amateur naturalists and private adventurers of the time. Several nineteenth-century travelogues and zoological books have been republished recently in their original form, an indication of their value as reflections on an exciting period of Australian natural history.

Pre-eminent among these are the works of John Gould on birds and mammals, which were first published between 1840 and 1863. His seven-volume *Birds of Australia* (1840–48; facs, 1972–76) is a classic, amazingly accurate and comprehensive in zoological information, but valued more highly now for the superb quality of the illustrations. Gould's three volumes on mammals, *Australian marsupials and monotremes*, *Kangaroos* and *Placental mammals of Australia* are equally beautiful. These too have been recently republished (1984), with a foreword and annotations by Joan Dixon of the National Museum of Victoria. Their scientific value remains high, as they contain the best illustrations and descriptions of the appearance and habits of many species of mammals now extinct or highly endangered. Another recently republished work of zoological interest is George Bennett's (1860) *Gatherings of a naturalist in Australasia* (Sydney, Currawong Press, 1972).

Biographical and bibliographic information on many influential zoologists working in Australia during the nineteenth century, such as George Bennett (1804–93), John Gould (1804–81), Edward Ramsay (1842–1916), George Masters (1837–1912), Thomas Whitelegge (1850–1927), A.S. Olliff (1865–95) and John Ogilby (1853–1925) is to be found in Strahan (1981) and Whittell (1954), as well as the *Australian dictionary of biography*.

The year 1895 appears to mark the close of the major exploratory and descriptive era of Australian zoology. The effects of a major drought, the ensuing economic depression and World War I stifled exploration and scientific achievement in zoology until the 1920s. The only important books to appear in this period and to foreshadow the era to come were Froggatt's treatise on insects (1907) and Roughley's on fish (1916).

A new era began in the early 1920s and lasted until approximately 1960. This period was characterised by the publication of the first semipopular, comprehensive and educational books on several major groups of Australian animals. Some of these were to become classics, and a few endured as the prime authorities on their subject for the next forty or fifty years. Important books of this era included Le Souef and Burrell (1926), Wood Jones (1923–27; repr 1968) and Troughton (1941; repr 1965) on mammals, Burrell (1927; repr 1974) on the platypus, Caley (1931; repr 1984) on birds, McKeon (1936; repr 1952) on spiders, Kinghorn (1929; repr 1967) on snakes, Whitley (1946; repr 1980) on fish, Allen (1950; repr 1959) on shells, Radcliffe (1952) on termites, Clarke (1951) on ants and Rehn (1952–57) on grasshoppers and locusts.

During this period two comprehensive historic bibliographies appeared: Musgrave (1932) on insects and Whittell (1954) on birds. By their sheer size these publications dramatically illustrate the progress of the preceding century in zoological studies.

Books of this era indicate the 'state of the art' of Australian zoology up to the early 1960s. They all tried to present for the first time in one volume a resumé of known species, their distribution and basic information on their natural history (breeding season, food preferences, preferred habitat, and so on). From about 1960 onwards, the character of the literature of Australian zoology changed once again. Slowly during the 1960s, then with a great burst during the 1970s, more sophisticated books began to appear directed at a generally much better educated public. Many of them are characterised as composite works. The detailed knowledge now required for the presentation of a scientific overview of Australian fauna is beyond the capacity of individual scholars and the most reliable surveys contain contributions by many specialists.

Books of this modern era tend to fall into three categories. The first, field guides, are aimed at the active amateur who wishes to identify invertebrates, amphibians, reptiles, birds and mammals in their natural habitat and includes books such as Slater's field guides to birds (1970, 1974) and Common and Waterhouse's guide to butterflies (1981). A second category of educational, semiscientific books is written for the student, educated amateur and professional zoologist alike, for example, Strahan (1983) on mammals and Cogger (1979) on reptiles and amphibians. One of the most impressive among these to date is Archer and Clayton (1984) which is likely to remain for quite some time the standard work on the origins of Australian vertebrate fauna. The third category includes popular books generally characterised by excellent photography, accompanied by basic notes on natural history. Except for books in this latter group, which are too numerous to be dealt with in this bibliography, the modern zoological books almost invariably go beyond mere description of the animals concerned, adding a modern biological emphasis, often describing their past and present status, ecological, behavioural and physiological aspects of their biology, and including discussion of controversial aspects of taxonomic status.

Most major groups of animals are dealt with in books of this period. Notable among them are Hall and Richards (1979) on bats, Watts and Aslin (1981) on rodents, Strahan (1983) on mammals, Reader's Digest (1976) on birds, Griffith (1968) on echidnas, Cogger (1983) on reptiles and amphibians, Lake (1978) and McDowall (1980) on freshwater fish, CSIRO (1970) on insects, and Clyne (1969) and Mascord (1970) on spiders. Many invertebrates are comprehensively dealt with in such books as Dakin's classic (1969), Allen (1959) and Smith and Kershaw (1979) on shells and molluscs, and Deas and Domm (1976) on corals.

Certain subjects of special fascination have attracted a diverse literature of their own. One is the Barrier Reef, basically a zoological phenomenon which includes in its fauna animals ranging through almost the entire invertebrate spectrum and on to fishes and dugongs among the vertebrates. Notable among the many books on the reef are those by Isobel Bennett (1981) and Endean (1982). From that other huge group, the insects, books and articles on butterflies are particularly prevalent. Moulds (1977) presents a bibliography of butterfly literature from 1773 to 1973. The dangerous and venomous animals of Australia also attract special attention, for example, Sutherland (1981) who deals with all dangerous animals from jellyfish to snakes.

Some mammals such as the kangaroos, the koala, the carnivorous marsupials and monotremes have been the subject of special scientific symposia. *Kangaroos and men* (1971), M.Archer (1982) and M.L.Augee (1978) were the published results of symposia held by the Royal Zoological Society of New South Wales, while T. Bergin edited the papers on the koala presented at a symposium held at Taronga Zoo, Sydney (1978) under the combined auspices of the Zoological Parks Board of New South Wales, the Royal Zoological Society of New South Wales and the New South Wales National Parks and Wildlife Service.

The impact of European civilisation on Australian fauna is now a subject of growing interest as it becomes increasingly apparent that many animal species have become extinct in the past 200 years, or are now seriously endangered. Awareness of this process is not new. In 1863 John Gould, foreshadowing the kangaroo preservation debate which still rages today, wrote:

> The kind of country it [the red kangaroo] frequents being of the utmost value to the pastoral portion of the Australian community, it is diligently sought for and occupied as soon as found, for depasturing their immense flocks and herds, in the stockmen and keepers of which, aided by their fleet, powerful, and well trained dogs, the Red Kangaroo finds an enemy which at once drives it from all newly occupied districts, and which will ultimately lead to its entire extirpation, unless some law be enacted for its preservation; and to this point I would direct the attention of the present enlightened Governor and Assembly of New South Wales, who surely will not hesitate to make some provision for the protection of this noble animal, as well as for some other fine species of the family still inhabitating that Colony; in fact, if this be not done, a few years will see them expunged from the Fauna of Australia.

Gould's prediction regarding the red kangaroo did not come true (see Burbidge, 1977, Frith and Calaby, 1969) but the extinction, or extreme reduction in range and numbers, did eventuate for about 40 per cent of the smaller kangaroo and wallaby species illustrated in his books. Several modern books deal with wildlife conservation and list many of the endangered animals of Australia. These include the works of Frith (1973, revised 1979) and Ovington (1978), which deal with mammals, birds and reptiles, and attempt to define the factors which have led to the present situation. In his extremely readable book, Rolls (1969; repr 1984) makes it clear that the demise of many of the smaller species of marsupials, and many reptiles and birds, can be attributed to the predatory effects of introduced feral animals, and to the enormously destructive effects of rabbits and grazing animals on the natural habitats of a wide range of species.

The growing awareness in the community of the value of native fauna and the threats to its existence has promoted government support, through organisations such as the National Parks and Wildlife Service and the CSIRO, for research aimed at identifying means of conserving those species which are already endangered. Great progress has been made in recent years towards the establishment of national parks and wildlife refuges and reserves, in order to protect the habitats of a wide range of native fauna (for examples, see Haigh, 1980). Basic zoological research is conducted in all Australian universities, funded largely by research grants from the commonwealth government. A large proportion of the research interests of the major natural history museums, such as the Australian Museum in Sydney and the National Museum of Victoria in Melbourne, is directed towards active investigation of the biology, taxonomy and status of Australian animals.

There are many Australian zoological journals of international standing, both general and specialised in scope. Outstanding among these are the *Australian J of zoology*, publishing a wide range of zoological research; *The emu*, the journal of the Royal Australian Ornithologists Union; *Australian mammalogy*, the journal of the Australian Mammal Society; the CSIRO's journal, *Australian wildlife research*; and the *Australian J of marine and freshwater research*. Taxonomic reviews and reports of basic taxonomic research are published in the journals of the state natural history museums, such as *Memoirs of the National Museum of Victoria* and *Records of the Australian Museum*. For the non-specialist, *Australian natural history* deals with both flora and fauna.

Under the auspices of the federal Bureau of Flora and Fauna the preparation of a zoological catalogue for Australia is now under way. When complete, this index will make available a summation of zoological taxonomic and bibliographic data in a series of volumes covering the entire animal kingdom of Australia. The catalogue will be based on a machine-readable data bank and will be published in at least ten volumes. Volume 1 of this series, *Amphibia and reptilia*, appeared in 1983, and it is expected that volumes 2–5, including the volumes on mammals, arachnids and several groups of insects, will be published during 1985. The objectives of the Australian Biological Resources Survey (ABRS), in compiling these data banks, are to stimulate research and publications on the taxonomy and distribution of Australian species and to provide a bibliographical directory for the professional taxonomist and research worker.

A second proposed project is the publication, by the Bureau of Flora and Fauna, of a *Fauna of Australia* to comprise ten volumes to cover all Australian fauna from Protozoa to Mammalia. These volumes, edited by D. Walton, will present a comprehensive account of the current knowledge of the biology, taxonomy, evolution and history of discovery of all animals that live in Australia, and serve as a reference text for students, scientists and amateur naturalists.

The authors would like to acknowledge the assistance of M. Denny and C. Smithers in the compilation of the bibliography that follows.

Thomas Scott, Sketch of a tyger trap. Intended for Mount Morriston, *1823. Watercolour and pencil. Scott's drawing of a Tasmanian tiger is as rare as the animal itself. Unlike nineteenth-century prints circulated for commercial sale, in this personal sketch the fascination with bizarre and exotic wildlife is overshadowed by the instruments of the animal's subsequent destruction. The tiger, properly* Thylacinus cyanocephalus, *was probably the largest flesh-eating marsupial ever evolved. It is now almost certainly extinct.*
MITCHELL LIBRARY

GENERAL

BENNETT, I. *The Great Barrier Reef.* Sydney, Lansdowne, 1981. 184 p, illus, maps.

Comprehensive in its coverage and still the best general work on the Great Barrier Reef. First published in 1971.

ENDEAN, R. *Australia's Great Barrier Reef.* UQP, 1982. 348 p, illus, maps.

A comprehensive survey of the families of animals and plants found on the Great Barrier Reef. Separate chapters on hard corals, worms, crustaceans, molluscs, echinoderms, coral reef fishes, and dangerous animals found on coral reefs.

FINNEY, C.M. *To sail beyond the sunset: natural history in Australia 1699–1829.* Adelaide, Rigby, 1984. 206 p, illus.

A beautifully illustrated book on the early history of discovery of the Australian fauna and flora.

FRITH, H.J. *Wildlife conservation.* A & R, 1973, 414 p, illus, maps.

An overview of conservation in Australia detailing aspects of wildlife, including the effects of habitat, hunting and commercialisation on animal populations.

HAIGH, C. ed, *Endangered animals of New South Wales.* Sydney, National Parks and Wildlife Service, 1980. 72 p, illus.

Describes the efforts of the NSW Parks and Wildlife Service, listing many species of reptiles, birds and mammals which are now extinct or threatened.

KEAST, A. ed, *Ecological biogeography of Australia.* The Hague, Dr W.Junk, 1981. 3 vols, illus, maps. (Monographiae biologicae, v 41.)

A major work divided as follows: the development of the Australian environment; the flora of Australia; the terrestrial invertebrates of Australia; biogeography of inland fresh waters; biogeography of poikilothermic vertebrates; biogeography of homeothermic vertebrates; origin and ecology of Aborigines; and integration.

OVINGTON, J.D. *Australian endangered species: mammals, birds and reptiles.* Sydney, Cassell, 1978. 183 p, illus, maps.

Processes leading to the endangered status of species are examined, and conservation and recovery strategies are presented. Colour portraits of endangered species.

ROLLS, E.C. *They all ran wild: the story of pests on the land in Australia.* A & R, 1984. 546 p, illus.

Presents the effects of (mainly) introduced animals on Australian fauna. Case studies of species, including kangaroos, trace history of their development into what many people consider to be pest status. First published in 1969.

SERVENTY, V. *Wildlife of Australia* (rev edn). Melbourne, Nelson, 1977. 216 p, illus.

Mammals, birds, reptiles, amphibians, fishes and marine and terrestrial invertebrates are discussed in this valuable introduction to Australia's animals. First published in 1968.

STANBURY, P. AND PHIPPS, G. *Australia's animals discovered.* Sydney, Pergamon, 1980. 120 p, illus, maps.

Early reports on some fifty of Australia's most interesting vertebrate animals are recorded. Reproductions of contemporary illustrations help trace history of discovery of Australian fauna.

SUTHERLAND, S.K. *Venomous creatures of Australia: a field guide with notes on first aid.* OUP, 1981. 128 p, illus.

A useful guide, with clear photos, of Australian venomous snakes, insects, spiders and ticks, jellyfish and octopuses, stinging fish, stingrays, coneshells, the Port Jackson shark and glaucus.

WILLIAMS, W.D. *Life in inland waters.* Melbourne, Blackwell Scientific Publication, 1983. 252 p, illus, maps.

Deals with the animal and plant life of Australian rivers, streams, freshwater lakes and salt lakes. Chapters on invertebrates, fish, amphibians and reptiles, waterbirds and mammals.

MARINE INVERTEBRATES

ALLAN, J.K. *Australian shells, with related animals living in the sea, in freshwater and on the land* (rev edn). Melbourne, Georgian House, 1959. 487 p, illus, maps.

Species of Australian molluscs, including land and shell-less forms are discussed; the scope is far wider than the term 'shell' would suggest. First published in 1950.

DAKIN, W.J. *Australian seashores: a guide for the beach-lover, the naturalist, the shore fisherman, and the student, by W.J. Dakin assisted by I. Bennett and E. Pope* (rev edn). A & R, 1969. 372 p, illus.

The classic work on Australian seashore life with chapters on sponges, coelenterates, bryozoans, crustaceans, molluscs, echinoderms and tunicates. First published in 1952.

DEAS, W. AND DOMM, S. *Corals of the Great Barrier Reef.* Sydney, Ure Smith, 1976. 127 p, illus.

The living coral colonies which form the Great Barrier Reef are illustrated with many colour photographs by Deas. Text by Domm discusses coral classification, biology, formation and types of reefs.

HEALY, A. AND YALDWYN, J. *Australian crustaceans in colour.* Sydney, Reed, 1970. 112 p, illus.

A general illustrated introduction to Australian marine and freshwater crustaceans.

UNDERWOOD, A.J. *Barnacles: a guide based on the barnacles found on the New South Wales coast.* Sydney, Reed Education, 1976. 32 p, illus.

The barnacles of the NSW coast are easily identified using this booklet. All technical terms are explained and illustrated by line drawings.

WILLAN, R.C. AND COLEMAN, N. *Nudibranchs of Australasia.* Sydney, Australasian Marine Photographic Index, 1984. 56 p, illus.

The first comprehensive checklist of Australian nudibranchs; includes geographical distribution and their natural history, biology, classification, collection and preservation.

WILSON, B.R. AND GILLETT, K. *Australian shells: illustrating and describing 600 species of marine gastropods found in Australian waters* (Rev edn). Sydney, Reed, 1974. 168 p, illus, map.

Covers 35 families of marine gastropods or snails. First published in 1971.

-edn). Sydney, Reed, 1974. 168 p, illus, map.

LAND INVERTEBRATES

AUSTIN, A. *Spiders.* Melbourne, Longman Cheshire, 1980. 37 p, illus.

The common families of Australian spiders are easily identifiable using this illustrated guide.

BROWN, R.H. *A bibliography of Australian plant nematology, 1890–1974.* Melbourne, Victorian Plant Research Institute, 1976. 53 p.

Lists over 460 papers on all aspects of nematology in chronological order.

CLARK, J. *Formicidae of Australia.* Vol 1. *Subfamily Myrmeciinae,* Melbourne, CSIRO, 1951. 1, 220 p, illus.

Covers aspects of taxonomy and natural history of Australian ants, as well as keys for identification of species. No other volumes published.

CLYNE, D. *A guide to Australian spiders: their collection and identification*. Melbourne, Nelson, 1969. 168 p, illus.

Sections on spider biology introduce some 80 pages of colour photographs of 236 specimens.

COMMON, I.F.B. AND WATERHOUSE, D.F. *Butterflies of Australia* (rev edn). A & R, 1981. 682 p, illus.

An identification manual and a synopsis of knowledge on the species including immature stages, food plants and biology. Supersedes the 1972 edition.

COMMONWEALTH SCIENTIFIC AND INDUSTRIAL RESEARCH ORGANIZATION. Division of Entomology. *The insects of Australia: a textbook for students and research workers*. MUP, 1970. 1029 p, illus, maps.

A comprehensive and profusely illustrated textbook. A 146-page supplement was published in 1974.

FROGGATT, W.W. *Australian insects*. Sydney, Brooks, 1907. 449 p, illus.

A classic early work now available only in major libraries. Many interesting early references.

GOODE, J. *Insects of Australia with illustrations from the classic The insects of Australia and New Zealand by R.J. Tillyard*. A & R, 1980. 260 p, illus.

Based on Tillyard's original 1926 text, this volume is aimed at the young collector or field naturalist as an aid to identification of all the common insects.

GRIGG, J.N. *Insects*. Sydney, Reed Education, 1976. 47 p, illus.

A basic key to identification of Australian insects. Well illustrated, and each family is photographed in colour. Good selection on projects with insects.

HEALY, A. AND SMITHERS, C. *Australian insects in colour*. Sydney, Reed, 1971. 112 p, illus.

A popular account of some of the more common insects found in Australia. Sixteen families are discussed and natural history notes match more than one hundred photographs.

McCUBBIN, C. *Australian butterflies*. Melbourne, 1971 xxxi, 206 p, illus.

A beautifully produced volume illustrated by paintings from life with backgrounds of host plants.

McKEOWN, K.C. *Australian spiders: their lives and habits*. A & R, 1952. 274 p, illus.

A popular narrative account of the most common spiders and ticks of Australia with illustrations. It is a revised edition of his *Spider wonders of Australia* published in 1936.

MASCORD, R. *Australian spiders in colour*. Sydney, Reed, 1970. 112 p, illus.

Some 200 colour photographs are arranged systematically to illustrate 24 families. Species accounts matching the photos are adequate, but a key to identification should have been included.

MOULDS, M.S. *Bibliography of the Australian butterflies (Lepidoptera: Hesperoidea and Papilionoidea) 1773–1973*. Sydney, Australian Entomological Press, 1977. 239 p.

A detailed bibliography covering the literature to the end of 1973. Takes Musgrave (1932) as the starting point, but adds many earlier items.

MUSGRAVE, A. *Bibliography of Australian entomology, 1775–1930: with biographical notes on authors and collectors*. Sydney, Royal Zoological Society of NSW, 1932. 380 p. A comprehensive literature survey.

RATCLIFFE, F.N. *et al, Australian termites: the biology, recognition and economic importance of the common species*. Melbourne, CSIRO, 1952. 124 p, illus. Standard work.

REHN, J.A.G. *The grasshoppers and locusts (Acridoidea) of Australia*. Melbourne, CSIRO, 1952–57. 3 vols.

An aid to identification as well as a textbook for students and professional zoologists.

SMITH, B.J. AND KERSHAW, R.C. *Field guide to the non-marine molluscs of south-eastern Australia*. ANUP, 1979. 285 p, illus, maps.

A handbook for the identification of terrestrial and freshwater molluscs found in Vic, Tas and the southern parts of NSW and SA.

FISH

COLEMAN, N. *Australian sea fishes, south of 30°s*. Sydney, Doubleday, 1980. 302 p, illus, maps.

COLEMAN, N. *Australian sea fishes north of 30°s*. Sydney, Doubleday, 1981. 297 p, illus, maps.

These two books illustrate in colour almost 600 sea fish found in Australian waters. The illustrations come from the files of the Australasian Marine Photographic Index.

LAKE, J.S. *Australian freshwater fishes illustrated: an illustrated field guide*. Melbourne, Nelson, 1978. 160 p, illus, maps.

Includes details on distribution, breeding, food and general comments on 144 species. The coloured illustrations are an advance on his 1971 *Freshwater fishes and rivers of Australia*.

McDOWALL, R.M. ed, *Freshwater fishes of south-eastern Australia (New South Wales, Victoria and Tasmania)*. Sydney, Reed, 1980. 208 p, illus, map.

A valuable reference book. Extensive details are recorded about the 29 fish families considered. A useful chapter on how to study fish.

MARSHALL, T.C. *Fishes of the Great Barrier Reef and coastal waters of Queensland*. A & R, 1964. 566 p, illus.

A superb scholarly work dealing with some 1500 species. The author explains all terms, and includes details on how to use the identification keys.

ROUGHLEY, T.C. *Fish and fisheries of Australia* (rev edn). A & R, 1966. 328 p, illus, maps.

Fish, some marine crustaceans and molluscs of economic importance or sporting value are described either as individual species or as families. First published in 1951.

STEAD, D.G. *Sharks and rays of Australian seas*. A & R, 1963. 211 p, illus.

Surveys sharks and rays, with an appendix showing their classification. A select bibliography by G.P. Whitley.

WHITLEY, G.P. *G.P. Whitley's handbook of Australian fishes, ed by J. Pollard*. Sydney, Jack Pollard Publishing, 1980. 629 p, illus.

Combined and revised version of three earlier books by Whitley. Compiled for the angler and interested student, to answer the question 'What fish is that?', it includes scientific information and some illustrations not available in the original works.

REPTILES AND AMPHIBIANS

BARKER, J. AND GRIGG, G. *A field guide to Australian frogs*. Adelaide, Rigby, 1976. 229 p, illus, maps.

A guide to 150 species of frogs and aspects of their biology. Chapters on evolution and on the collecting, keeping and photography of frogs.

BUSTARD, H.R. *Sea turtles: natural history and conservation*. London, Collins, 1972. 220 p, illus.

Although his work covers the world's seven species of sea turtle it has an Australian bias and is based on his research on the Great Barrier Reef.

CANN, J. *Tortoises of Australia*. A & R, 1978. 79 p, illus.
A concise coverage of characteristics, ecology, collection and care in captivity of tortoises.

COGGER, H.G. *Reptiles and amphibians of Australia* (rev edn). Sydney, Reed, 1983. 680 p, illus, maps.
A comprehensive work discussing over 700 species of frogs, lizards, snakes, crocodiles and turtles. Details of identification, distribution, conservation, collection and captive maintenance are included. First published in 1975.

COGGER, H.G. *Snakes*. Melbourne, Longman Cheshire, 1980. 36 p, illus.
A guide to identification with notes and line drawings.

COGGER, H.G. *et al, Amphibia and reptilia*. AGPS, 1983. 313 p, map. (Zoological catalogue of Australia, vol 1.)
Contains the name and original reference for every known Australian species of reptile and amphibian, with synonymy, literature citations, location and status of the type, and geographic distribution of the species. First volume of the Australian Biological Resources Survey.

GOW, G.F. AND SWANSON, S. *Snakes and lizards of Australia*. A & R, 1977. 88, 80 p, illus.
A combination of Gow's *Snakes of Australia* and Swanson's *Lizards of Australia*. Chapters on management in captivity and species descriptions, with a section on photographing lizards. Two hundred and two excellent colour photographs.

KINGHORN, J.R. *The snakes of Australia*. A & R, 1929. 198 p, illus.
Provision of diagrams, a key to identification of some snake genera and species and coloured illustration of anatomical details make this small book a useful field guide. Includes a bibliography. Revised edition published in 1964.

TYLER, M.J. *Frogs*. Sydney, Collins, 1982. 256 p, illus, maps.
An extensive work on the amphibians of Australia, New Guinea and neighbouring islands. Includes aspects of frog biology and a review of herpetology in Australia. First published in 1976.

WORRELL, E. *Reptiles of Australia: crocodiles, turtles, tortoises, lizards, snakes; describing their appearance, their haunts, their habits*. A & R, 1970. 169 p, illus.
Covers description and distribution for every Australian reptile. Over 330 illustrations make this a useful handbook, if now a little dated. First published in 1963.

BIRDS

BERULDSEN, G.R. *A field guide to nests and eggs of Australian birds*. Adelaide, Rigby, 1980. 448 p, illus.
A guide to identification including keys to and colour plates of nests and eggs. Information provided on colony breeding, parasitism and introduced species.

BLAKERS, M. *et al, The atlas of Australian birds*. MUP for Royal Australasian Ornithologists' Union, 1984. 738 p, illus, maps.
Comprises a species by species annotation and distribution map. The annotations, supplementary maps and bibliography provide considerable historical information.

CAMPBELL, A.J. *Nests and eggs of Australian birds including the geographical distribution of the species and popular observations thereon*. Sheffield, England, The Author, 1900. 2 vols, illus, maps.
Written when egg-collecting was fashionable; now largely of historical interest because of the limited number of eggs available to the author for description. Facsimile edition, Melbourne, Wren, 1974.

CAYLEY, N.W. *What bird is that? A guide to the birds of Australia*. A & R, 1931. 319 p, illus.

The standard field guide to Australian birds, arranged according to habitat. All species illustrated in colour, plus black and white photos of habitat. Enlarged edition, revised by T.R. Lindsey, published in 1984.

GOULD, J. *The birds of Australia*. London, The Author, 1840–48. 7 vols, illus.
A supplement was added 1851–69. The classic work on Australian birds. Facsimile edition, Melbourne, Lansdowne, 1972–76. A smaller edition, selected and annotated by A.H. Chisholm and V. Serventy, published by Lansdowne, 1984.

MACDONALD, J.D. *Birds of Australia: a summary of information*. Sydney, Reed, 1973. 552 p, illus, maps.
Essentially a handbook, arranged systematically. Illustrated with line drawings and 24 colour plates by P. Slater. Distribution maps and identification keys are included.

THE READER'S DIGEST complete book of Australian birds. Sydney, Reader's Digest Services, 1976. 615 p, illus, maps.
Contains details on all native and introduced birds. For each species there is information on nesting, distribution and characteristics for identification. Behavioural and ecological notes are also included. Illustrations are based on photographs from National Photographic Index of Australian Birds.

PIZZEY, G. *A field guide to the birds of Australia*. Sydney, Collins, 1980. 460 p, illus, maps.
An excellent guide to all our birds in one volume, with 88 colour and black and white plates drawn by Ron Doyle. Distributional maps provided as an appendix.

SLATER, P. *A field guide to Australian birds: non-passerines*. Adelaide, Rigby, 1970. 428 p, illus, maps.
A guide to identification of birds of Australia and its territories in the field. Distributional maps for all species plus pen and ink sketches of some of the less distinct forms.

SLATER, P. *A field guide to Australian birds: passerines*. Adelaide, Rigby, 1974. 309 p, illus, maps.
Approximately half the bird species in Australia are passerines or perching birds. A companion to the author's non-passerine field guide. Does not cover species in Australian territories.

WHITTELL, H.M. *The literature of Australian birds: a history and bibliography (1618–1950) of Australian ornithology*. Perth, Paterson Brokensha, 1954. 788 p, illus.
This large compilation includes biographies of authors, collectors and others.

MAMMALS

ARCHER, M. ed, *Carnivorous marsupials*. Sydney, Royal Zoological Society of NSW, 1982. 2 vols, illus, maps.
Mainly for the professional zoologist; significant reviews and original research papers on all aspects of the biology of carnivorous marsupials.

ARCHER, M. AND CLAYTON, G. eds, *Vertebrate zoogeography and evolution in Australasia: animals in space and time*. Perth, Hesperian Press, 1984. 1203 p.
A readable, reference text characterised by the various authors' enthusiasm and sense of fun. Likely to remain a prime source book for many years.

AUGEE, M.L. ed, 'Monotreme biology: proceedings of a symposium held in Sydney, May 1978', *Australian zoologist* 20, 1, 1978, 1–257.
Papers on the biology of the platypus and echidna.

BERGIN, T.J. ed, *The koala: proceedings of the Taronga symposium on koala biology, management and medicine, Sydney, 11th and 12th March, 1976*. Sydney, Zoological Parks Board of NSW, 1978, 239 p, illus, maps.

The results of a symposium and scientific reports on the koala to improve the quality of its management and to aid conservation policies.

BURRELL, H.J. *The platypus.* A & R, 1927. 226 p, illus.

This was the first book to deal with all aspects of the natural history of the platypus. New edition published in 1974.

DAWSON, T.J. *Monotremes and marsupials: the other mammals.* London, Edward Arnold, 1983. 87 p, illus.

Presents in a clear manner the latest biological information on monotremes and marsupials, and compares their biology with placental mammals.

FRITH, H.J. AND CALABY, J.H. *Kangaroos.* Melbourne, Cheshire, 1969. 209 p, illus.

Extensive coverage of macropods—kangaroos, wallabies, rat-kangaroos. Includes details of discovery, evolution, distribution, abundance and behaviour; detailed bibliography.

GOULD, J. *The mammals of Australia.* London, Taylor & Francis, 1845–63. 3 vols, illus.

A major treatment of all native mammals then known. In the facsimile edition Gould's notes are supplemented by J.M. Dixon, making it a valuable survey of Australian mammals. Facsimile edition, Melbourne, Macmillan, 1984.

GRANT, T. *The platypus.* Sydney, UNSWP, 1984. 76 p, illus.

Written for the professional biologist, the student and the lay reader, this book incorporates the most recent research.

GRIFFITHS, M. *Echidnas.* Oxford, Pergamon, 1968. 282 p, illus.

A textbook which deals solely with echidnas and covers all aspects of their anatomy and biology.

HALL, L.S. AND RICHARDS, G.C. *Bats of eastern Australia.* Brisbane, Qld Museum, 1979. 66 p, illus. (Qld Museum booklet, 12.)

Intended as a field guide; contains simple keys and distribution maps.

HAIGH, C. ed, *Kangaroos and other macropods of New South Wales.* Sydney, NSW National Parks and Wildlife Service, 1982. 64 p, illus.

A collection of articles on the distribution and ecology of the kangaroos and wallabies found in NSW. Well illustrated and provides most recent information.

'KANGAROOS and men: a symposium of the Royal Zoological Society of New South Wales and held at the Australian Museum on July 4, 1970', *Australian zoologist* 16, 1, 1971, 1–100.

Series of papers concerned with kangaroo exploitation, economies and conservation.

LE SOUEF, A.S. AND BURRELL, H. *The wild animals of Australasia* . . . London, Harrap, 1926. 388 p, illus.

First broad popular coverage of native mammals of Australia, New Guinea and New Zealand with keys to identification. Chapter on bats by E.L. Troughton. The photographs are generally of museum specimens.

LYNE, A.G. *Marsupials and monotremes of Australia.* A & R, 1967. 72 p, illus.

An overview of the platypus, spiny anteater and a selection of pouched mammals; line sketches of the species, plus illustrations of anatomical parts of systematic importance.

RIDE, W.D.L. *A guide to the native mammals of Australia.* OUP, 1970. 249 p, illus, maps.

Over 280 species of native mammals are discussed in groups, with distribution and identification details for each species. Chapters on status and conservation. Appendices with details of interest to biologists.

STRAHAN, R. *A dictionary of Australian mammal names: pronunciation, derivation and significance of the names with biographical and bibliographical notes.* A & R, 1981. xxiii, 196 p, illus.

A book of wider scope than its name implies. It includes a simple account of the principles and practice of animal nomenclature, derivations and pronunciation of names, and notes on the people who have described Australian mammals.

STRAHAN, R. ed, *The Australian Museum complete book of Australian mammals.* A & R, 1983. 530 p, illus, maps.

Behavioural and ecological information provided on some 250 native and introduced mammals. Most species illustrated with colour photographs from the National Photographic Index of Australian Wildlife.

TROUGHTON, E. Le G. *Furred animals of Australia.* A & R, 1941. 374 p, illus.

For many years a standard reference to native Australian mammals. Historical details in introduction. New edition published in 1965. An abridged edition was published in 1973.

TYNDALE-BISCOE, H. *Life of marsupials.* London, Edward Arnold, 1973. 254 p, illus, maps.

This review of marsupials explores aspects of relationships and origins; reproduction and development; ruminant-like and non-ruminant herbivores; small marsupials, and marsupials and humans.

WATTS, C.H.S. AND ASLIN, H.J. *The rodents of Australia.* A & R, 1981. 321 p, illus, maps.

An account of the distribution, habitat and biology of Australia's native rodents. The range of species is described and notes and drawings provided to assist in their identification.

WOOD JONES, F. *The mammals of South Australia.* Adelaide, 1923–25. 458 p, illus.

Comprehensive work on Australian mammals, including keys for identification and illustrations of diagnostic features of the anatomy, information on natural history and distribution. Facsimile edition, Adelaide, Government Printer, 1968.

IV
ABORIGINES

45 A Native Family of New South Wales sitting down on an English Settlers Farm

Augustus Earle, A native family of New South
Wales sitting down on an English settler's farm, *c1827.*
Watercolour. This poignant and sinister image conveys the
unhappy relationship between black and white
Australians over the past 200 years.
NATIONAL LIBRARY

THIS SECTION examines the literature on Australian Aborigines. It consists of two essays and one consolidated list of references. The first essay provides a general introduction to the literature on Aborigines and a commentary on the anthropological writings. The second is concerned with the historical perception of Aboriginal society by European writers from the early nineteenth century onwards. The list of references that follows the essays is divided into nine parts:

Bibliographies and sources
Prehistory, biology and demography
Languages and tribes
Ethnographies
Aspects of socio-cultural life
General histories and documents
Specialist histories
Aboriginal historical perspectives
Writings since 1945

The assistance of the library staff of the Australian Institute of Aboriginal Studies (AIAS) in compiling this bibliography is gratefully acknowledged.

W.A. Cawthorne, 45 natives driven to police court by the police for trespassing, 1845. Watercolour 31.8 × 45.7 cm. Cawthorne's poignant watercolour reflects his sympathy for the Aborigines, although it is doubtful if he would have seen the irony of the title. An amateur artist and schoolteacher who emigrated to South Australia in 1841, Cawthorne typifies an educated response to the Aborigines.
MITCHELL LIBRARY

Queen Victoria's diamond jubilee celebrations, Coolgardie, 1897. Aborigines had little cause to celebrate this year. Coolgardie nuggets, *1898.*
NEVILLE GREEN

CHAPTER 14

ABORIGINAL STUDIES AND ANTHROPOLOGY

NICOLAS PETERSON

THE LEADING COLLECTION of print and non-print material on Aboriginal society is housed in the library of the AIAS in Canberra. The library holds over 5000 books, 4000 pamphlets, 5000 unpublished manuscripts, 150 000 photographs, 880 000 feet of archival film, 250 films and 14 000 language and music tapes and is being constantly expanded. It has an exhaustive catalogue by tribe, topic and author, a small staff to answer queries and a reading room, and is an essential resource centre for those seeking to pursue in depth a topic related to the Aborigines.

Published bibliographies are relatively few and are soon outdated because of the rapid growth in research and publication on Aboriginal matters since the mid-1960s. The only comprehensive bibliography is by J. Greenway (1963). Between 1966 and 1970 the AIAS published five annotated regional bibliographies on those areas of the continent then regarded as offering the best research possibilities—those where people lived most traditionally. These useful volumes, all compiled by Beryl Craig, are: *Arnhem Land peninsular region, including Bathurst and Melville Islands* (1966); *Cape York* (1967); *Kimberley region: an annotated bibliography* (1968); *Central Australian and western desert regions: an annotated bibliography* (1969); *North-west-central Queensland: an annotated bibliography* (1970).

N.J.B. Plomley (1969) and A. Massola (1971) produced regional bibliographies on the Tasmanian and Victorian Aborigines which are still useful. Original data that are often hard to find are contained in theses and dissertations. W.G. Coppell has listed these up to 1977 and his work has been updated by D.H. Bennett in the *Australian Institute of Aboriginal Studies newsletter* (14, September 1980, 52–65), and since then in the Institute's *Annual bibliography* referred to below. The *Union list of higher degree theses* discussed in chapter 8 is, of course, another source of information on work done in Australian universities.

None of these bibliographies deals in depth with publications about the impact of colonisation on Aboriginal society or the contemporary situation. Since 1966 the AIAS has been issuing current bibliographies which now appear in the form of an *Annual bibliography*, containing over 1200 items in 1983, indexed by subject, tribe, region and author. The bibliography covers a range of topics from learned articles on the finer points of kinship to government reports on employment and pamphlets about land rights. More recently a new bibliographic service has been added: the newspaper cuttings, which have been bound in volumes for each year since 1962 and are now made available twice yearly in microfiche, with an annual cumulative index beginning in 1981. Although not comprehensive, this publication covers 6000 items each year.

A few specialist bibliographies have also appeared. In particular, P.M. Moodie and E.B. Pedersen (1971) present basic reference in the important area of health which has been updated by recent unpublished work available at the AIAS. J. McCorquodale's work, *A bibliography of Aborigines and the law*, now in press, will list all Aborigine-related legislation, with notes on significant cases and a bibliography. It will supersede Brockwell (1979).

For teachers there are two particularly useful reference works. M. Hill and A. Barlow (1978) provide an evaluative assessment of those resources most likely to be in school libraries or which ought to be in them. A companion volume by W.G. Coppell entitled, *Audio-visual resource materials relating to the Aboriginal Australians* (Canberra, Curriculum Development Centre, 1978) lists a wide range of non-print material and teaching kits available to teachers.

Given this wealth of material on Aboriginal society, it is surprising that there are relatively few good textbooks. For prehistorians D.J. Mulvaney's classic (1975) has been superseded by the much less readable but information-packed text by J.P. White and J.F. O'Connell (1982). In the area of socio-cultural life, Elkin's well-known and much reprinted book, *The Australian Aborigines: how to understand them* (A & R, 1938 and subsequent reprints) is dull and out of date. R.M. and C.H. Berndt's account (1981) is encyclopaedic but not a book to sit down and read from cover to cover. One of the best integrated and most lucid overall accounts is by Kenneth Maddock (1982), but it is a cool and clinical analysis from which conflict, competition and people are absent. For physical anthropology, Robert Kirk (1981) is an accessible and up-to-date account.

While textbook overviews of Aboriginal society are important places to begin reading, the rich texture of daily life can be found only in detailed descriptions and analysis of particular Aboriginal societies, that is, in the classic ethnographies. Although Europeans began writing about Aborigines from initial contact, it was not until the 1870s that the first major work devoted to Aboriginal culture was published. This, like much subsequent work, relied heavily on the use of questionnaires sent to protectors of Aborigines, missionaries and the like. Lorimer Fison and Alfred Howitt's *Kamilaroi and Kurnai* (Melbourne, Robertson, 1880) was the first detailed study addressing a specifically anthropological problem, but the people whose way of life is described had already been drastically affected by colonisation.

Twenty years later detailed studies began to appear of people whose way of life was substantially intact. In 1879, Walter Roth started publishing on Aboriginal culture in northwest and northern Queensland. Although his work was highly detailed and important, it did not have the impact of Baldwin Spencer and F.J. Gillen's more sustained accounts of Aboriginal religion and social organisation in central Australia. Professional anthropology began with the establishment of the first chair in anthropology at Sydney University. This led to a dramatic change in the nature and amount of work being undertaken. The outstanding books arising from this initiative in the prewar period are undoubtedly the studies by Lloyd Warner (1937) and Phyllis Kaberry (1939), but many important papers are also published principally in the journal *Oceania*.

The professionalisation of archaeology took place after World War II; Aboriginal studies received a boost from the establishment of the AIAS in 1962. Initially the institute promoted linguistic research, but it quickly broadened its scope to cover all aspects of Aboriginal society.

There are few adequate accounts of the contemporary situation. Only Basil Sansom (1980) and Robert Bropho (1980) provide insights into the cultural world of fringe dwellers. Other analyses are sociological in tone, such as Fay Gale's *Urban Aborigines* (ANUP, 1972) and her more detailed examination of the same subject with J. Wundersitz, *Adelaide Aborigines: a case study of urban life, 1966–1981* (Australian National University, 1982), which provides statistics on people in Adelaide but little insight into how such people differ from poor white Australians. For this one has to turn to Aboriginal writing, mainly biographies and novels. A. Shoemaker has drawn up 'A checklist of black Australian literature', *Australian literary studies*, 11, 2, 1983, 255–63.

Nevertheless, the series of 14 volumes *Aborigines in Australian society* (ANUP, 1970–80)—of which Gale's book was one—that resulted from the Social Science Research Council of Australia's Aborigines project directed by Charles Rowley between 1964 and 1967, remains a fundamental and comprehensive source from which to investigate the contemporary scene.

This hand-coloured lithograph was published in the atlas accompanying François Péron and Louis de Freycinet's account of a French scientific expedition to Australia between 1800 and 1804. It was drawn by Nicholas Petit, one of the artists on the voyage.
MITCHELL LIBRARY

CHAPTER 15

EUROPEAN VIEWS OF ABORIGINES

ANN McGRATH AND ANDREW MARKUS

IN 1968 the anthropologist W.E.H. Stanner called for a new direction in research to end the 'great Australian silence' on the history of Aboriginal dispossession. Fifteen years later, conservative politicians still argued that it was best to forget unfortunate aspects of the past, especially in response to the introduction of land rights or compensation. The writing of Aboriginal history has never been free of political implications, even when it meant disremembering and mythologising. The literature reveals and reinforces the changing hues of dominant social and political ideas, especially relating to race and colonialism. Whether the post-contact history of Aborigines was being lamented, rationalised or challenged, it has been inevitably shaped by the cultural perceptions of its authors, who have come predominantly from Western backgrounds and intellectual traditions.

The historical writing on Aborigines can be grouped in four distinct periods: the nineteenth century, a period of historical interest in the fate of Aborigines; the first seven decades of the twentieth century, a period characterised by a 'cult of forgetfulness'; the 1970s, a rediscovery of the contact experience; and lastly, from the mid-1970s onwards, an attempt to cross cultural barriers.

THE NINETEENTH CENTURY

For much of the nineteenth century, contact between Aborigines and Europeans attracted the attention of historians. G.W. Rusden's *History of Australia* (London, Chapman and Hall, 1883), for example, devoted a major introductory chapter to 'Natural phenomena and the Australian tribes' and attempted to weave the contact experience into the general narrative.

The supposed extinction of Tasmanian Aborigines aroused particular interest, both while the process was under way and after its virtual accomplishment. As it took place on an island, without the possibility of new arrivals of Aborigines, the dispossession had a visibility absent on the mainland, a visibility that was enhanced by the spectacular futility of the 'Black Line' and the activities of G.A. Robinson. Further, these events took place before the British and Australian public had lost interest in the 'inevitable' consequences of colonisation. In the later stages, with the remaining Aborigines dying on reserves from 'natural causes', the extinction became all the more attractive for confirming an emerging ideology. As the Melbourne *Age* wrote on 11 January 1888, 'It seems a law of nature that where two races whose stages of progression differ greatly are brought into contact, the inferior race is doomed to wither and disappear'. Given these factors, it is hardly surprising that Tasmanian Aborigines received disproportionate attention or that Truganini entered Australian folklore.

Nineteenth-century studies include Henry Melville's *The history of the island of Van Diemen's Land* (1835; repr, Sydney, Horwitz-Grahame, 1965), John West's *The history of Tasmania* (1852; repr, A & R in association with the Royal Australian Historical Society, 1971), James Bonwick's *The last of the Tasmanians* (1870; facs, LBSA, 1969) and J.E. Calder's *Some account of the wars, extirpation, habits etc. of the native tribes of Tasmania* (Hobart, Henn & Co, printers, 1875).

It is difficult to generalise about the treatment of Aborigines by nineteenth-century historians. Some accounts were merely concerned to justify the seizure of the continent, others recognised the denial of justice; some devoted attention to the role of violence in the process of dispossession and depopulation, others stressed instead the decay of Aboriginal society, the loss of the will to live and the impact of disease, the inexorable laws of nature. Emphasis varied from author to author, but gradually there was less notice of violence (Peter Biskup, 'Aboriginal history', in G. Osborne and W.F. Mandle eds, *New history*, Sydney, Allen & Unwin, 1982, 1–31).

Attention did not, however, necessarily denote understanding, either of the basic nature of settlement or of the character of Aboriginal society. In nearly all cases in which authors dealt with violence it was seen as something incidental to the process of settlement, as something to be laid at the door of the lower elements of European society. As for ignorance of the Aboriginal people, a select committee of the Queensland parliament reported in 1861 that

> Except in one or two isolated cases, after being brought up and educated for a certain period, the Natives of both sexes invariably return to their savage habits. Credible witnesses show that they are addicted to cannibalism; that they have no idea of a future state; and are sunk in the lowest depths of barbarism.

Such views were echoed by a number of historians, although not in such a stark form. In *A history of the colony of Victoria* (London, Longmans Green, 1904) H.G. Turner confidently proclaimed:

> There is no serious stain necessarily resting upon the reputation of the colony from the retrospect of its treatment of the aborigines. It has been shown that costly and continuous efforts were made for the amelioration of their condition, and that these failed, not from neglect, but from the absolute incompatibility of the native character with even the primary conditions of civilisation ... [T]he experiences of history were not to be reversed, and the wandering savage, to whom persistent labour was an unknown quantity, was doomed to extinction by the progress of that type of humanity with which it was impossible to assimilate him (vol 1, pp 239, 218).

'THE GREAT AUSTRALIAN SILENCE'

While a few specialist works dealing with Aborigines were published in the period 1900–65, notably E.J.B. Foxcroft's *Australian native policy* (MUP, 1941), Paul Hasluck's *Black Australians* (1942) and Clive Turnbull's *Black war* (Melbourne, Cheshire, 1948), there were serious deficiencies in the coverage of general histories, and it was common for Aborigines to be totally neglected.

Professor Ernest Scott of Melbourne University first published his *A short history of Australia* (London, OUP) in 1916; by 1930 the book had sold over 70 000 copies. Scott, while giving considerable attention to brutal treatment of Aborigines on the frontier, echoed Turner, the historian of nineteenth-century Victoria, and the general wisdom of his day in his general assessment:

> They were a people so low in the scale of human development that they had no domestic arts or domestic animals. They were in the Stone-Age stage of human evolution. They had not learnt to make pottery from clay, or to extract metals from rocks, or to cultivate the soil, or to develop grain and fruits, or to build houses. They lived on fish, kangaroo, opossum, roots, and wild plants. They hunted and fought with spears, waddies and boomerangs. Even the bow

was beyond their invention, though they made string from hair or fibre for their fishing-nets ... It was perhaps inevitable that the native race should fade away in the parts of the country where the white population became thick. They were not a people who could be absorbed or adapted to civilized life. But the tragedy of the process was very grim and hateful. (pp 185,187)

Despite entitling his first chapter 'The invasion of Australia', Professor W.K. Hancock found little room for Aborigines in his renowned history *Australia* (1930; repr, Brisbane, Jacaranda, 1964). But unlike the accounts of Scott and most of his contemporaries, his writing seems free from racial determinism; Hancock couched his argument in terms of environmental accident and economic imperatives:

The Australian aborigines, shut off for centuries from the co-operative intelligence by which nations who are neighbours have created their common civilisation, never imagined that the first decisive step from the economy of the chase which would have made them masters of the soil. Instead, they fitted themselves to the soil, modelling a complex civilisation of intelligent artificiality, which yet was pathetically helpless when assailed by the acquisitive society of Europe. The advance of British civilisation made inevitable 'the natural progress of the aboriginal race towards extinction'—it is the soothing phrase of an Australian Governor. In truth, a hunting and a pastoral economy cannot co-exist within the same bounds. Yet sometimes the invading British did their wrecker's work with the unnecessary brutality of stupid children ... (pp 32–33)

Some three decades later, in a 1959 survey of historical writing, another leading member of the profession, J.A. La Nauze, commented that 'the Australian aboriginal is noticed in our history only in a melancholy anthropological footnote' ('The study of history 1929–1959', *Hist stud* 9, 33, 1959, 11). Thus the influential work *Australia: a social and political history*, edited by Professor G. Greenwood and first published by A & R in 1955, devoted five brief references to Aborigines. Commenting on such historical work, W.E.H. Stanner observed in his 1968 Boyer Lectures, published under the title *After the dreaming* (Sydney, ABC, 1968):

Inattention on such a scale cannot possibly be explained by absentmindedness. It is a structural matter, a view from a window which has been carefully placed to exclude a whole quadrant of the landscape. What may well have begun as a simple forgetting of other possible views turned into habit and over time into something like a cult of forgetfulness practised on a national scale.

And the 'cult of forgetfulness' did not end in 1968, although new currents of thought were beginning to make an impact. In a 1976 survey, Humphrey McQueen noted that in J.M. Powell's *The public lands of Australia felix* (OUP, 1970), an account of British land settlement in Victoria from 1834 to 1891, there were three passing references to Aborigines ('Changing the textbooks', *Nation review*, 2–8 December 1976, 9–15 December 1976). F.K. Crowley's *Modern Australia in documents 1901–1939* (Melbourne, Wren, 1973) referred to Aborigines in four places. In the multiauthored *A new history of Australia* (Melbourne, Heinemann, 1974) fewer than seven pages out of 550 deal with Aborigines. McQueen noted that it was 'truly depressing' that even when attention was directed to Aborigines, authors could not envisage Aborigines as people shaping their own lives, they could not free themselves 'from the notion that aborigines are passive'.

THE 1970s

Beginning around 1970 the study of the contact experience became a major area of specialist historical enquiry. A large number of publications, not all of high quality, were issued; many well-intentioned writers, keen to provide fresh insights and able to tap a ready market, plunged into print with half-researched and half-digested works. Quantity rather than quality was the keynote. The period 1970–84 saw the publication of more than ten documentary collections, at least nine general histories, a large number of biographies, autobiographies and specialist histories, and three historiographical essays (Andrew Markus 'Through a glass, darkly', *Aboriginal history*, 1, 2, 1977, 170–80; R.H.W. Reece, 'The Aborigines in Australian historiography', in J.A. Moses ed, *Historical disciplines and culture in Australasia*, UQP, 1979, 253–81; P. Biskup, 'Aboriginal history', *ibid*). The study of nineteenth-century Aboriginal–European contact has suddenly become one of the most thoroughly researched fields in Australian history.

The seminal work of the seventies was C.D. Rowley's survey (1970). At a time when serious historical study of Aborigines had made little headway, Rowley attempted to write a history of contact. To do this he not only synthesised the existing specialist work but conducted extensive research to fill gaps in historical knowledge. His study served to heighten awareness of a neglected aspect of Australian history and it opened the field for subsequent scholars. Yet in some respects the book was unsatisfactory. The restricted range of sources, with a heavy reliance on published government records, led at times to inadequate coverage and explanation. Much of the detail and evaluation reflected the government perspective, and its political and legislative emphasis allowed little room for discussion of Aboriginal reactions. As the title implied, Aborigines were depicted as victims of an all-powerful European society.

Currently the best general history is by Richard Broome (1982), although he only partly succeeded in his objective of explaining the impact of European settlement in Aboriginal terms. Broome synthesised the flood of research of the seventies and was the first to incorporate findings of the new socially oriented work of the last few years, discussed below. His book was broad in its coverage, made a good attempt to allow for regional variability, and sought to avoid the pitfall of sterile narrative by tackling significant questions. Another recent general history by Yarwood and Knowling (1982) possessed great strengths but was uneven in its coverage and quality of analysis. The material on the colonists' preconceptions and Yarwood's account of nineteenth-century relations were distinguished by mature judgment, elegant prose and breadth of reading. Other chapters, however, lacked richness and penetration and were marked by a singular lack of insight into the nature of Aboriginal society.

There are a number of specialist regional studies of high quality, such as the works by Loos (1982), Macknight (1976) and Ryan (1981), but only Biskup (1973) has produced a comprehensive twentieth-century study.

A further development of the 1970s was the focus of some works on Aborigines as resistance fighters, defenders of their land against the invaders. The extreme example of this genre was F. Robinson and B. York's *The black resistance!* (Melbourne, Widescope, 1977), a paean to the struggles of oppressed peoples that fell short of being a humanising history because there was little attempt to understand Aborigines on their own terms. In this book Aborigines' actions were interpreted according to a rather simplistic model of resistance, where it was assumed that there was a pan-Australian movement with uniform objectives which relied purely on physical confrontation.

THE ABORIGINAL PERSPECTIVE

Much but not all the work of the third period was characterised by a focus on nineteenth-century political developments and frontier conflict, relying on traditional written sources: official reports, parliamentary debates, newspapers, private papers. Such history was generally limited to depicting events through European eyes, partly reflecting the rarity of Aboriginal testimony in surviving written records. Increasingly, historians have attempted to stop analysing material solely according to European perceptions; in order to integrate Aboriginal views, they have tried to gain greater cultural empathy by studying anthropological literature and by speaking with and learning directly from Aboriginal people. A more careful reading of the documents reveals that more of the Aboriginal perspective survived than had been thought, and resourceful scholars are enriching their analysis by using additional sources such as oral history and archaeology.

The new direction is characterised by a shift from political to social history and by a new understanding of Aborigines. No longer victims or one-dimensional resistance fighters, they have become complex agents of historical change; within the confines of various structures, they emerge as actors shaping their own lives. Elements of this reorientation are also to be found in other areas of historical enquiry, especially women's history.

The outstanding work heralding the new direction is Henry Reynolds's view of the arrival of the Europeans (1982). The book's objective was to provide understanding of Aboriginal reactions to the invasion, arguing that Aborigines were not incurious, passive, helpless victims locked into a rigid, unchanging culture. Their response was much more positive, creative and complex than European historians and anthropologists allowed. Described by one reviewer as the most important book yet published in the field, Reynolds's work marked a conceptual breakthrough to the realisation that there was sufficient evidence, amenable to interpretation by adequately prepared European historians, to provide an understanding of the Aboriginal perspective.

The bulk of Reynolds's evidence was derived from traditional sources, although much of the material had been previously ignored by historians. It included observations of Europeans in close contact with Aborigines, escaped convicts and castaways, explorers, pastoralists and missionaries loosely defined. Other sources, however, were less orthodox: oral traditions (used infrequently); anthropological knowledge of traditional society, used to gain understanding of the Aboriginal perspective and aid interpretation of the written record; archaeological evidence from the post-contact period, used to show adoption of European goods by Aborigines; and perhaps the most ingenious of all, the use of linguistic studies, including Aboriginal vocabularies recorded in the nineteenth century, to provide evidence of intellectual currents.

Aboriginal scholars have a great deal to contribute in the development of new perspectives: the first tertiary courses run by Aboriginal lecturers made a strong impact on their students, who were able to glimpse the Australian experience from 'the other side'. As yet there are no 'professional' historians of Aboriginal descent publishing in the field, although books of an autobiographical or biographical nature date from the early postwar period. While much of this early work had a heavy European flavour, with some being ghost written, the more recent publications succeed in retaining the character and integrity of the author or source. High standards have been established by the publications of the AIAS (see Barker, 1977, Ngabidj, 1981 and Sullivan, 1983) and by briefer pieces in the journal *Aboriginal history*.

Given the significance of Aboriginal history, its writing can become highly sensitive. Historians often find themselves challenged for publishing interpretations that might endanger Aboriginal rights struggles: for example, by providing material that could be used by anti-land rights lobbies. Some Aboriginal groups reject versions of history which differ from their own models of the past. Historians in this field have received a clear message that they must be more aware of Aboriginal sensitivities, and are consistently reminded of the need to consult Aboriginal communities. The assumptions of such historians are thus challenged. Some emerge enriched from this experience, others become frustrated and confused, but all who work in the field are compelled to re-examine their academic, social and political values.

A major problem for future research will be relations between people of Aboriginal and European descent. There is a feeling among some Aborigines that historians are a new kind of exploiter; that as the pastoralists took their land, oral historians are attempting to appropriate their past. Not only do they come and take, they distort and damage Aborigines in the process. Some Aborigines believe that only they can interpret Aboriginal experience, analogous to the attitude of some feminists that only women can write the history of their gender. Such insularity, although understandable, can hinder research which may be of major significance in the struggle for recognition of Aboriginal rights.

If historians omit Aboriginal reactions from their writing, they step backwards towards the old conquerors' history where Aborigines were either left out or stood as silent victims, distanced from the main stage. There is a need for unrestricted history written by those of European background and by Aborigines. Writing from various perspectives cannot be stopped, but it can be seriously hindered if Aborigines shut themselves off.

BIBLIOGRAPHIES

AIAS. *Annual bibliography*. 1975– . Canberra, The Institute.

Supersedes the institute's *Current bibliography*, 1961–75 and now the most comprehensive index to the literature on Aborigines.

BARWICK, D. *et al*, 'A select bibliography of Aboriginal history and social change: theses and published research to 1976'. *Aboriginal history* 1, 2, 1977, 111–69.

Focuses specifically on Aboriginal reaction to European contact and administration and thus excludes published research by anthropologists. This bibliography updates Greenway (1963) and concentrates on recent research, much of it unpublished theses.

BROCKWELL, C.J. *Aborigines and the law: a bibliography*. Canberra, Law Department, Research School of Social Sciences, Australian National University, 1979. 71 p.

Useful reference source for an area where sociologists and lawyers are trying to prevent and resolve conflicts.

COPPELL, W.G. *World catalogue of theses and dissertations about the Australian Aborigines and Torres Strait Islanders*. SUP, 1977. 113 p.

A reliable source of information.

COPPELL, W.G. AND MITCHELL, I.S. *Education and Aboriginal Australians, 1945–1975: a bibliography*. Sydney, Centre for the Advancement of Teaching, Macquarie University, 1977. 77 p.

A comprehensive list of close to 2500 items, arranged alphabetically with detailed subject index.

GREENWAY, J. *Bibliography of the Australian Aborigines and the native peoples of Torres Strait to 1959*. A & R, 1963. 420 p.

The only comprehensive literature survey to 1960.

HILL, M. AND BARLOW, A. *Black Australia: an annotated bibliography and teachers' guide to resources on Aborigines and Torres Strait Islanders*. Canberra, AIAS, 1978. 200 p.

Particularly useful as a source book for schools.

HOUSTON, C. *A selected regional bibliography of the Aboriginals of South Australia*. Adelaide, South Australian Museum, 1973. 78 leaves.

MASSOLA, A. *Bibliography of Victorian Aborigines: from the earliest manuscripts to 31 December 1970*. Melbourne, Hawthorn, 1971. 95 p.

These two regional bibliographies are now rather dated.

MOODIE, P.M. AND PEDERSEN, E.G. *The health of Australian Aborigines: an annotated bibliography*. AGPS, 1971. 248 p.

Though dated, still a useful and reliable source on this important aspect of Aboriginal life.

PLOMLEY, N.J.B. *An annotated bibliography of the Tasmanian Aborigines*. London, Royal Anthropological Institute of Great Britain & Ireland, 1969. 143 p.

An exhaustive and definitive work.

PREHISTORY, BIOLOGY AND DEMOGRAPHY

BLAINEY, G.N. *Triumph of the nomads: a history of ancient Australia* (Rev edn). Melbourne, Macmillan, 1982. 285 p, maps.

Much the most readable history of the Aboriginal occupation of Australia, although Blainey does not really understand how prehistory differs from conventional history. First published 1975.

BUTLIN, N.G. *Our original aggression: Aboriginal populations of southeastern Australia, 1788–1850*. Sydney, Allen & Unwin, 1983. 186 p, illus, maps.

Study of the impact of smallpox, venereal and other diseases. Has far-reaching implications for estimates of Aboriginal population prior to European contact and for understanding the disruption of that society.

FLOOD, J. *Archaeology of the dreamtime*. Sydney, Collins, 1983. 288 p, illus, maps.

An up-to-date account written specifically for the general reader by an Australian archaeologist.

KIRK, R.L. *Aboriginal man adapting: the human biology of Australian Aborigines*. Oxford, Clarendon, 1981. 229 p, illus, maps.

Covers the origins, adaptations, genetics and health of Aboriginal people.

MULVANEY, D.J. *The prehistory of Australia*. Ringwood, Vic, Penguin, 1975. 327 p, illus, maps.

Classic account now superseded by White and O'Connell (1982). First published in 1969.

SMITH, L.R. *The Aboriginal population of Australia*. Canberra, Australian National University for the Academy of the Social Sciences in Australia, 1980. 314 p, illus.

A comprehensive analysis of a complex topic covering both the precolonial and present population. Written prior to Butlin's study (1983).

WHITE, J.P. AND O'CONNELL, J.F. *A prehistory of Australia, New Guinea and Sahul*. Sydney, Academic Press, 1982. 286 p, illus, maps.

Written as an undergraduate textbook, this supersedes Mulvaney (1975) but is much less readable.

LANGUAGES AND TRIBES

DIXON, R.M.W. *The languages of Australia*. CUP, 1980. 547 p, illus, maps.

A basic text on Aboriginal languages by a leading authority. Four general chapters are followed by ten more technical discussions of aspects of grammar and phonology.

PETERSON, N. ed, *Tribes and boundaries in Australia*. Canberra, AIAS, 1976. 250 p, illus, maps.

Twelve papers focusing on boundaries and the flow of people, objects and information across them. A major reassessment of the concept of tribe in Australia.

TINDALE, N.B. *Aboriginal tribes of Australia: their terrain, environmental controls, distribution, limits· and proper names; with an appendix on Tasmanian tribes by Rhys Jones*. ANUP, 1974. 404 p, illus, maps.

A basic reference work despite the reservations most anthropologists have about Tindale's concept of tribe. Has all the main references to each tribal group, and is an excellent place to begin a research into a particular area.

ETHNOGRAPHIES

HART, C.W.M. AND PILLING, A.R. *The Tiwi of north Australia*. New York, Holt, Rinehart and Winston, 1960. xii, 118 p, illus, maps.

A theoretically innovative account of Aboriginal marriage arrangements based on fieldwork during 1928–29 on Bathurst and Melville islands. One should ignore the occasional bursts of sexism and ethnocentrism.

HOWITT, A.W. *The native tribes of south-east Australia*. London, Macmillan, 1904. 819 p, illus, maps.

The principal source book on the life of Aborigines in NSW and Vic.

KABERRY, P.M. *Aboriginal woman: sacred and profane*. London, Routledge and Sons, 1939. xxxii, 294 p, illus, map.

The classic account of the life of Aboriginal women in the Kimberley.

MEGGITT, M.J. *Desert people: a study of the Walbiri Aborigines of central Australia.* A & R, 1974. 404 p, illus, maps.

A brilliant, if difficult, ethnography with fascinating case material and extensive discussion of kinship. First published in 1962.

SPENCER, W.B. *The native tribes of the Northern Territory of Australia.* London, Macmillan, 1914. 516 p, illus, map.

SPENCER, W.B. AND GILLEN, F.J. *The native tribes of central Australia.* London, Macmillan, 1899, 671 p, illus, maps.

Two classic ethnographic works describing the life of the Australian Aboriginal people. Facsimile edition of the latter, Dover, 1968.

TONKINSON, R. *The Mardudjara Aborigines: living the dream in Australia's desert.* New York, Holt, Rinehart and Winston, 1978. 149 p, illus, maps.

A reconstruction of traditional life based on work with people who had moved only recently to Jigalong mission.

WARNER, W.L. *A black civilization: a social study of an Australian tribe.* New York, Harper, 1937. 594 p, illus, map.

One of the classic Australian ethnographies providing a comprehensive coverage of the life of people in northeast Arnhem Land in 1926–29, when many were living an independent life on their own lands.

ASPECTS OF SOCIO–CULTURAL LIFE

AUSTRALIAN GALLERY DIRECTORS COUNCIL. *Aboriginal Australia.* Sydney, The Council, 1981. 192 p, illus, maps.

A superb catalogue for the major Aboriginal art exhibition of the decade with essays on art in prehistory, art in southeast Australia and on the artistic systems of the desert and north Australia.

BELL, D. *Daughters of the dreaming.* Melbourne, McPhee Gribble, 1983. 297 p, illus, maps.

An account of a small group of desert women in the late 1970s set in historical perspective. A mirror of the books by male anthropologists that ignore Aboriginal women and thus problematic in its discussion of gender relations.

BERNDT, R.M. AND BERNDT, C.H. *The world of the first Australians* (Rev edn). Sydney, Lansdowne, 1981. 602 p, illus, maps.

This is an encyclopaedic but generalised account of Aboriginal life, useful as a starting point to follow up an interest but not a book to read from cover to cover. First published in 1964.

BERNDT, R.M. AND PHILLIPS, E.S. eds, *The Australian Aboriginal heritage: an introduction through the arts.* Sydney, Australian Society for Education through the Arts in association with Ure Smith, 1973. 320 p, illus, map, music.

Covers oral narratives, songs, visual and representational art, music and dramatic forms in a well-illustrated volume accompanied by two long-playing records and 25 colour slides.

CHARLESWORTH, M. *et al. Religion in Aboriginal Australia: an anthology,* UQP, 1984. 458 p, illus, maps.

Excerpts of classic writings on mythology, symbolism, totemism, ritual and ceremony and women's religious life.

ELLIS, C.J. *Aboriginal music making: a study of central Australian music.* Adelaide, LBSA, 1964. 373 p, illus.

There are few books on Aboriginal music, research being scattered in periodicals. Ellis was something of a trailblazer in this field, and her book is still a standard reference.

GALE, F. ed, *Woman's role in Aboriginal society* (3rd edn). Canberra, AIAS, 1978. 84 p, illus.

Re-examination of the social and economic place of women in Aboriginal society. First published in 1970.

HIATT, L.R. *Kinship and conflict: a study of Aboriginal community in northern Arnhem Land.* Canberra, Australian National University, 1965. xx, 162 p, illus, maps.

A analysis of how an Aboriginal marriage system works. Essential reading for those who want to understand this complex subject.

MADDOCK, K. *The Australian Aborigines: a portrait of their society.* Ringwood, Vic, Penguin, 1982. 198 p, illus, map.

A lucid account of Aboriginal society written by a lawyer turned anthropolgist. First published in 1973.

MEEHAN, B. *Shell bed to shell midden.* Canberra, AIAS, 1982. 189 p, illus, maps.

An account of the role of the shellfish collected by women in the diet of coastal Arnhem Landers, set in the context of a general description of life in an Aboriginal bush camp in the mid-1970s.

MOYLE, R.M. *Songs of the Pintupi: musical life in a central Australian society.* Canberra, AIAS, 1979. 183 p, illus, map, music.

A detailed analysis which includes musical transcriptions of parts of 200 songs with particular attention paid to performance and enthnographic context.

REID, J. *Sorcerers and healing spirits: continuity and change in an Aboriginal medical system.* ANUP, 1983. xxv, 182 p, illus, maps.

A readable analysis of Aboriginal ideas about health and causality based on work in northeast Arnhem Land.

STREHLOW, T.G.H. *Aranda traditions.* MUP, 1947. xxii, 181 p, illus, map.

Excellent introduction to the religious life of the Aranda. Emphasises that Aborigines commonly deny their own creativity by attributing it to ancestors who come to them in dreams.

STREHLOW, T.G.H. *Songs of central Australia.* A & R, 1971. 77 p, illus, map, music.

Strehlow, a fluent Aranda speaker, transcribes, translates and analyses a wide range of songs, evaluating them as oral literature and documents of Aboriginal religion.

GENERAL HISTORIES AND DOCUMENTS

BROOME, R. *Aboriginal Australians: black response to white dominance, 1788–1980.* Sydney, Allen & Unwin, 1982. 227 p, illus, map.

A synthesis of the published material now available on Aboriginal history. Limited in revealing Aboriginal reactions, yet useful as a general introduction.

HISTORICAL records of Victoria. Foundation series. Vol 2A: *The Aborigines of Port Phillip 1835–1839;* vol 2B: *Aborigines and protectors 1838–1839.* Melbourne, Victorian Government Printing Office, 1982–83. 2 vols, illus.

These official documents cover issues relating to British policy, the first mission at Buntingdale, government policy and Aboriginal conflict with squatters.

REYNOLDS, H. ed, *Aborigines and settler: the Australian experience, 1788–1939.* Melbourne, Cassell, 1972. 185 p.

A collection from a wide range of written sources, arranged thematically. Largely restricted to nineteenth century, particularly post-1850.

REYNOLDS, H. *The other side of the frontier: Aboriginal resistance to the European invasion of Australia.* Ringwood, Vic, Penguin, 1982. 255 p.

An attempt to view the British invasion from the Aboriginal perspective. A major research achievement and conceptual breakthrough. Hailed as the most important book to date on Aboriginal–European contact. First published in 1981.

ROWLEY, C.D. *The destruction of Aboriginal society*. ANUP, 1970. 430 p, maps. (Aboriginal policy and practice, 1).

A pioneering general history, with coverage to the 1940s. Penetrating insights, but lacks overall clarity and now somewhat dated.

STONE, S.N. ed, *Aborigines in white Australia: a documentary history of the attitudes affecting official policy and the Australian Aborigine, 1697–1973*. Melbourne, Heinemann Educational, 1974. 253 p, illus.

A range of succinctly introduced statements, comments by missionaries, explorers, concerned citizens. Interesting on women, 'half-caste' policy and citizenship issues.

WOLMINGTON, J.C. ed, *Aborigines in colonial society, 1788–1850: from 'noble savage' to 'rural pest'*. Melbourne, Cassell, 1973. 158 p.

Over 250 brief extracts from documents for the period.

YARWOOD, A.T. AND KNOWLING, M.J. *Race relations in Australia: a history*. Sydney, Methuen, 1982. 312 p, illus, maps.

About two-thirds of the book deals with Aborigines. Yarwood's chapters on the nineteenth century are distinguished by mature insights, elegant prose and breadth of reading.

SPECIALIST HISTORIES

BISKUP, P. *Not slaves, not citizens: the Aboriginal problem in Western Australia, 1898–1954*. UQP, 1973. 342 p, illus.

A study of West Australian government policy towards Aborigines in the period. An excellent twentieth-century administrative history.

CHRISTIE, M.F. *Aborigines in colonial Victoria, 1835–86*. SUP, 1979. 227 p, illus, maps.

An account of conflict and unsuccessful protective policies. Aborigines are seen as the victims of settlers' and administrators' brutality.

EVANS, R. et al, *Exclusion, exploitation and extermination: race relations in colonial Queensland*. Sydney, Australia and New Zealand Book Co, 1975. 446 p, illus.

The first part of the book, written by Evans, provides a good history of Aborigines in colonial Australia.

GAMMAGE, B. AND MARKUS, A. eds, *All that dirt: Aborigines 1938: an Australia 1938 monograph*. Canberra, History Project Inc, 1982. 109 p, illus, maps.

Papers analysing popular and scientific attitudes and government policy, and providing rare insights into the experiences of Aborigines.

HARNEY, W.E. *Grief, gaiety and Aborigines*. Adelaide, Rigby, 1969. 191 p, illus, map.

Popular description of the lifestyle of Aborigines in the NT, especially during the depression years. First published in 1961.

HARRIS, S. *It's coming yet: an Aboriginal treaty within Australia between Australians*. Canberra, Aboriginal Treaty Committee, 1979. ix, 87 p, illus, map.

Discusses history and current legal position of Aborigines in an international context, stressing the need for recognition of Aboriginal culture. Written on behalf of campaigners for a land rights treaty.

HASLUCK, P.M.C. *Black Australians: a survey of native policy in Western Australia, 1829–1897*. MUP, 1942. 226 p, maps.

Pioneering account of Aboriginal–European relations by a man who was to become a prominent politician and governor-general of Australia. New edition published in 1970.

HORNER, J. *Vote Ferguson for Aboriginal freedom: a biography*. Sydney, Australia and New Zealand Book Co, 1974. 208 p, illus.

Biography of William Ferguson, a NSW Aboriginal leader who rose to prominence in the 1930s. A combination of oral and written sources.

JENKIN, G.K. *Conquest of the Ngarrindjeri*. Adelaide, Rigby, 1979. 300 p, illus, map.

Relations between European settlers and the Ngarrindjeri of the lower Murray lakes area of SA. Includes the writings of Rev G. Taplin, permitting an insight into the Aboriginal perspective.

LOOS, N. *Invasion and resistance: Aboriginal–European relations on the north Queensland frontier 1861–1897*. ANUP, 1982. 3225 p, illus, maps.

Seeks to explain factors leading to conflict and its regional variation.

McBRYDE, I. ed, *Records of times past: ethnohistorical essays on the culture and ecology of the New England tribes*. Canberra, AIAS, 1978. 291 p, illus, maps.

Investigation of material culture, languages, myths and ceremonies of New England Aborigines. Two essays cover early relations with Europeans. Includes a selection of documents.

MACKNIGHT, C.C. *The voyage of Marege: Macassan trepangers in northern Australia*. MUP, 1976. 175 p, illus, maps.

A study of the 200 years of contact between Aborigines and Macassan trepangers showing relations between Aborigines and non-Europeans.

MASSOLA, A. *Coranderrk: a history of the Aboriginal station*. Kilmore, Vic, Lowden, 1975. xii, 109 p, illus, map.

A study of a major Victorian reserve, occupied in 1863. Demonstrates skilful Aboriginal adaption and greed of European settlers. An unsophisticated account. Excellent photographs.

POWELL, A. *Far country: a short history of the Northern Territory*. MUP, 1982. 301 p, illus, maps.

This study describes some of the key issues affecting Territory Aborigines. Their experiences and viewpoints are admirably integrated into the narrative.

REECE, R.H.W. *Aborigines and colonists: Aborigines and colonial society in New South Wales in the 1830's and 1840's*. SUP, 1974. 254 p, illus, maps.

Important for understanding the relative strength of humanitarian and squatting interests. Places the Myall Creek massacre and the subsequent trials in context.

RYAN, L. *The Aboriginal Tasmanians*. UQP, 1981. 315 p, illus, maps.

A professional history from early European contact to the present. Seeks to incorporate the Aboriginal perspective, to move beyond the faceless abstractions one finds in most studies. Demolishes the myth of extinction.

WRIGHT, J. *The cry for the dead*. OUP, 1981. 303 p, maps.

A sympathetic, superbly written post-contact history of the Aborigines of central Qld, particularly in Wadja. Conflicts with explorers, squatters, miners, native police emerge in the narrative.

ABORIGINAL HISTORICAL PERSPECTIVES

BARKER, J. *The two worlds of Jimmie Barker: the life of an Australian Aboriginal 1900–1972, as told to Janet Matthews*. Canberra, AIAS, 1977. 218 p, illus, maps.

Autobiographical account of life in northwest NSW, with emphasis on the period 1900–40. In Alan Marshall's words, 'a great and humane book'.

BERNDT, R.W. AND BERNDT, C.H. eds, *Aborigines of the west* (rev edn). UWAP, 1979. 520 p, illus, maps.

Anthropological, historical and regional accounts of Aboriginal life from prehistoric times to the present.

BROPHO, R. *Fringedweller*. Sydney, Alternative Publishing Cooperative with the assistance of the Aboriginal Arts Board, Australia Council, 1980. 153 p, illus.

An account of fringe dwellers in the Perth–Swan district from the 1930s to the present.

CLARE, M. *Karonbran: the story of an Aboriginal girl*. Sydney, Alternative Publishing, 1978. xv, 95 p.

A narrative revealing the suffering of Aboriginal children of mixed descent in NSW during the 1930s and 1940s, when government institutions denied their rights to family ties and cultural identity.

GALE, F. ed, *We are bosses ourselves: the status and role of Aboriginal women today*. Canberra, AIAS, 1983. 175 p, illus, map.

A collection of works from women who participated in a 1980 ANZAAS symposium on their changing status.

GILBERT, K.J. *Living black: blacks talk to Kevin Gilbert*. Ringwood, Vic, Penguin, 1978. 305 p.

Insights into a wide variety of response to interfering government policies and racist society. First published in 1977.

LAMILAMI, L. *Lamilami speaks, the cry went up: a story of the people of the Goulburn Islands, north Australia*. Sydney, Ure Smith, 1974. 273 p, illus, maps.

Includes an account of the Maung people, stories of Macassan and early European visitors, and the establishment of the Methodist mission.

NGABIDJ, G. *My country of the Pelican Dreaming: the life of an Australian Aborigine of the Gadjerong, Grant Ngabidj, 1904–1977, as told to Bruce Shaw*. Canberra, AIAS, 1981. 202 p, illus, maps.

A narrative of bush and station lifestyles in the Kimberleys.

PEPPER, P. *You are what you make yourself to be: the story of a Victorian Aboriginal family, 1842–1980*. Melbourne, Hyland House, 1980. 143 p, illus.

Phillip Pepper's reminiscences cover a wide range of topics including mission life at Ebenezer, Ramahyuk and Lake Tyers.

PERKINS, C.N. *A bastard like me*. Sydney, Ure Smith, 1975. 199 p, illus.

Autobiography. Includes material on early childhood in central Australia, education in Adelaide and Sydney and the Freedom Ride of 1965.

REECE, R.H.W. AND STANNAGE, C.T. eds, *European–Aboriginal relations in Western Australian history*. UWAP, 1984. 149 p.

Covers 1830s to 1930s including accounts of massacres, Aboriginal farmers and island hospitals for venereal disease. Also contains historiographical and bibliographical articles.

ROUGHSEY, D. *Moon and rainbow: the autobiography of an Aboriginal*. Sydney, Reed, 1971. 168 p, illus, maps.

Describes the Lardill people of Mornington Island, the early settlements and Roughsey's work for Europeans including an expedition to find rock paintings in the Cooktown region.

SMITH, S.C. *Mum Shirl: an autobiography with the assistance of Bobbi Sykes*. Melbourne, Heinemann Educational, 1981. 115 p, illus.

A roving childhood, followed by life on the autocratically run Erambie mission. She describes her work with prisoners, and how poverty and racism lead many Aborigines to gaol.

SULLIVAN, J. *Banggaiyerri: the story of Jack Sullivan as told to Bruce Shaw*. Canberra, AIAS, 1983. 264 p, illus, maps.

An autobiography which reveals Aboriginal pride in work, and the excitement of cattle station life in the Kimberleys.

TUCKER, M. *If everyone cared: an autobiography*. Sydney, Ure Smith, 1977. 205 p, illus.

Margaret Tucker describes her childhood 'walkabouts', her association with the Murray River district and its people, the impact of paternalism, Christianity and a rising Aboriginal movement in Melbourne.

WRITINGS SINCE 1945

BERNDT, R.M. ed, *Aborigines and changes: Australia in the '70s*. Canberra, AIAS, 1977. 424 p, illus, maps.

Twenty-eight essays covering a wide range of current issues.

COOMBS, H.C. *Kulinma: listening to Aboriginal Australians*. ANUP, 1978. 250 p, illus, map.

As chairman of the Council for Aboriginal Affairs between 1968 and 1976 Coombs was a major architect of the new deal for Aboriginal people. Discusses the council, policy issues and Aboriginal desires.

GALE, F. AND WUNDERSITZ, J. *Adelaide Aborigines: a case study of urban life, 1966–1981*. Canberra, Development Studies Centre, Australian National University, 1982. 191 p, illus, maps.

An account of the economic situation of Aboriginal people in a major urban centre.

LIPPMANN, L. *Generations of resistance: the Aboriginal struggle for justice*. Melbourne, Longman Cheshire, 1981. 243 p, illus, maps.

Deals with developments in population, health, education, employment, housing, land rights and government policy.

MADDOCK, K. *Your land is our land: Aboriginal land rights*. Ringwood, Vic, Penguin, 1983. 215 p, illus, map.

Discussion of the historical background on Aboriginal rights and how Aborigines have come to gain them, emphasising the NT. Written from a legal viewpoint.

ROWLEY, C.D. *A matter of justice*. ANUP, 1978. 249 p.

An account of injustices affecting Aborigines. Looks at cases and issues relating to the legal system and Aboriginal land rights.

ROWLEY, C.D. *Outcasts in white Australia*. ANUP, 1971. 472 p, maps (Aboriginal policy and practice, 2).

Deals with Aboriginal people in settled Australia, providing information and policy recommendations that now underwrite much government policy. The AIAS issued in 1982 a follow-up survey of the same households taken in 1980, entitled *Equality by instalments*.

SANSON, B. *The camp at Wallaby Cross: Aboriginal fringe dwellers in Darwin*. Canberra, AIAS, 1980. 280 p, illus, maps.

An account of the social order and cultural world underlying the apparent disorder of a camp in which social security and alcohol are key components.

STANNER, W.E.H. *White man got no dreaming: essays, 1938–1973*. ANUP, 1979. 389 p, illus.

Whether writing about the Dreaming or the future of Aborigines in Australian society Stanner is always perceptive.

STEVENS, F.S. *Aborigines in the Northern Territory cattle industry*. ANUP, 1974. 226 p, illus, maps.

Describes the work performed by station Aborigines, their attitudes, and those of other station workers towards them. The 1965 equal wages case is discussed.

YOUNG, E. *Tribal communities in rural areas*. Canberra, Development Studies Centre, Australian National University, 1981. 284 p, illus, maps.

Three case studies of the economic activity on an Aboriginal cattle station, an Aboriginal town and an ex-mission in the late 1970s.

V
GENERAL
HISTORY

Lithograph by W.E. Smith Ltd, Sydney 1901. One of the many richly coloured invitations issued to leading citizens to commemorate the birth of the Australian commonwealth. Such functions were held in many cities and towns.

NATIONAL LIBRARY

Front cover, Programme of celebrations *for the opening of the first parliament of the Commonwealth of Australia, 1901.*

QUEEN VICTORIA MUSEUM AND ART GALLERY, LAUNCESTON

CHAPTER 16

STATE AND NATION

S. G. FOSTER AND M. K. STELL

THIS SECTION LISTS books that offer a broad view of the continent as a whole or of particular colonies and states. Some have been selected because of their present value, others because they have been widely read in the past or have been influential in the development of Australian historiography. The value of every book on the list will depend, of course, on what each reader hopes to learn from it. Readers looking for an introduction to Australian history should also peruse other topics, including Social history (chapter 38) and Economic history (chapter 30), and consider books that address themselves to particular themes or make general observations about the Australian people, such as K.S. Inglis's *The Australian colonists* (MUP, 1974), Geoffrey Serle's cultural history *From deserts the prophets come* (Melbourne, Heinemann, 1973), Geoffrey Sherington's *Australia's immigrants 1788–1978* (Sydney, Allen & Unwin, 1980) and Russel Ward's *The Australian legend* (OUP, 1958; repr, 1978).

General histories in the nineteenth century usually dealt with individual colonies, the main exception being Rusden (1883). Narrative in structure, the early histories influenced their successors by mapping chronological high points and identifying topics which at the time seemed to have been important. The best remain valuable, especially when their authors were directly acquainted with the events and people they described. Turner (1904; facs, 1973), for example, boasted 'some intimacy' with the colony's leading politicians during the preceding thirty years.

After Federation, histories of colonies and states became less fashionable, making way for works which, usually in a single short volume, attempted to sum up the national experience. If 'general history' is only loosely a topic, 'short history' can claim to be a distinct genre, having been made so for Australian historians by the New Zealander Keith Sinclair in an essay entitled 'On writing shist' (*Hist stud* 13, 51, 1968, 426–32). Sinclair, himself the author of a short history of his own country, laid out criteria for what he regarded as adequate 'shist'. Although he was too delicate to name those Australian historians who in his view failed to make the grade, his essay remains a useful guide for students who wish to assess the relative merits of various 'shists'.

Sinclair's clearest message to aspiring writers of short history is that they should have something to say. The most informative and thought-provoking books are written by authors with a deep commitment to their task and who give most of themselves. In Sinclair's phrase, 'the author must be in the book'. W.K. Hancock later wrote that he had given his book (1930; repr, 1961) everything he had, 'heart and brain'.

There are many ways in which short histories differ from one another: in the relationship between narrative and analysis, the degree of generalisation, attention to chronological detail, the importance attached to individuals, and so on. The main differences arise from the purposes for which the books were written. Hancock (1930; repr, 1961) wrote 'while wrestling painfully with myself in the endeavour to discover why I was so much at home and not at home in my own country'. His aim of contributing to national self-awareness was shared by others, like Manning Clark, R.M. Crawford and Russel Ward. At a more mundane level, each author (and publisher) of a short history has a particular market in view, and this influences the book's content and approach. Historians aiming at school or university readers often have an eye to specific curricula. Others aim more vaguely at a non-specialist readership, and perhaps at an overseas market. The shape of a short history is also influenced by its relationship to the author's other works. Russel Ward (1965; repr, 1979), for example, elaborated and expanded upon the insights of his earlier *The Australian legend* (1958; repr, 1978); while Manning Clark (1965; repr, 1981) adumbrated themes which he was developing in his longer history. Where some short histories are based chiefly on primary sources, others are almost wholly derivative of the work of other historians. Sometimes arguments or passages breathe originality; on the other hand, certain facts are repeated from one book to the next and become tired in the telling.

If there are variations in the genre, there are also significant similarities. Most short histories published after Hancock owe something to his notions of a liberal and democratic Australia. The majority were written or conceived in the 1950s and 1960s and, with notable exceptions, reflect the optimism of those decades. Implicitly at least, their emphasis is on harmony rather than conflict, on what Australians have in common rather than what draws them apart, on success rather than failure. They also tend to share a relative lack of interest in certain subjects which have since become important to historians, such as Aborigines, women, childhood, science and technology, and medicine. Some authors have rectified past omissions in new editions.

The longer general histories which deal with the whole of Australia have less in common with one another. Clark's multivolume history (1962–) is unique as an extended account, largely chronological in approach and narrative in style, which relies heavily on primary sources. With a few other exceptions, most writers of general history have contributed to edited works, including Greenwood (1955; repr, 1977) and Crowley (1974), both of which were written as textbooks. Although such works profit from the variety of views presented, multiple authorship can also be a drawback—as when some authors implicitly contradict others.

In recent decades histories that confine their attention to a particular state or colony have again become popular. Some, like the works of Pike (1967) and Serle (1978, 1971), discuss a limited period, while others, including histories associated with the sesquicentenaries of Western Australia, Victoria and South Australia, cover longer time spans. As well as providing insights into the peculiar identity of each state, these histories tend to question the broad generalisations that are often applied to the continent as a whole.

This list also includes representative school texts and some general collections of documents on Australian history. Most collections, however, are devoted to a particular subject or theme, such as 'convicts', or 'Aborigines', and are therefore listed under the appropriate topics.

ALEXANDER, F. *Australia since federation: a narrative and critical analysis* (3rd edn). Melbourne, Nelson, 1976. 434 p, illus.

An attempt to 'trace and to assess the growth of Australian nationhood ... within the framework of a federal policy,'. The emphasis is heavily political. First published in 1967.

BARNARD, M.F. *A history of Australia*. A & R, 1976. 710 p, maps.

Best for the early nineteenth century, though continued to the early 1960s. Not always reliable. First published in 1962.

BARTON, G.B. AND BRITTON, A. *History of New South Wales from the records*. Sydney, Hale & Iremonger, 1980. 2 vols.

Based on documents from the Public Record Office, London, Colonial Secretary's Office, Sydney and the papers of Sir Joseph Banks. First published in 1889–94.

BLAINEY, G.N. *Our side of the country: the story of Victoria*. Sydney, Methuen Haynes, 1984. 250 p, illus, maps.

A partly chronological account, emphasising the lives of ordinary people. Strongest on the late nineteenth century.

CAMBRIDGE history of the British Empire. Vol 7, pt 1. *Australia*. CUP, 1933. 759 p, maps.

Synthesis of Australian history by professional historians. The tone is celebratory, its central theme the success with which 'the planting of English stock in the South Pacific' has been achieved. Bibliography with special concern for primary sources.

CLARK, C.M.H. *A history of Australia*. MUP, 1962– . v, illus, maps.

The most ambitious general history to date by a single author. Controversial in both style and content. Clark describes what he sees as the great human drama that was enacted on Australian soil. There is a continuing pessimism about what the author regards as the emptiness and conservatism of Australian society.

CLARK, C.M.H. ed, *Select documents in Australian history*. A & R, 1977. 2 vols.

Includes documents and tables covering 1788 to 1900 still not conveniently found elsewhere. The introductory notes embodied many new interpretations which foreshadowed Clark's later writings. First published in 1950–55.

CLARK, C.M.H. *A short history of Australia* (rev edn). Macmillan, 1981. 256 p, illus.

Emphasising the human element in historical processes, the book is both more reliable and more controversial than most other short histories. Many of the themes are further developed in his later writings. First published in 1965.

CRAWFORD, R.M. *Australia* (rev edn). Melbourne, Hutchinson, 1979. 199 p, maps.

Outlines broad themes in Australia's past, particularly the nineteenth century. Includes extensive treatment of the Aboriginal past. First published in 1952.

CRAWFORD, R.M. *An Australian perspective*. MUP, 1960. 82 p.

Three lectures delivered to an American audience and entitled 'A pastoral aristocracy', 'The birth of a culture' and 'Coming of age'.

CROWLEY, F.K. *Australia's western third: a history of Western Australia from the first settlements to modern times* (2nd edn). Melbourne, Heinemann, 1970. 404 p, maps.

Crowley challenged the prevailing view of WA's past (see Kimberly, 1897), but was criticised for lack of insight into the major themes of Western Australian history. First published in 1960.

CROWLEY, F.K. *A documentary history of Australia*. Melbourne, Nelson, 1980– . v.

Each volume contains documents chronologically arranged, selected from a wide range of printed sources on diverse subjects. Introductions place the documents in their context of events. Five volumes published: final volume in press in 1985.

CROWLEY, F.K. ed, *A new history of Australia*. Melbourne, Heinemann, 1974. 639 p.

A 'new overview', arranged chronologically, of Australian history from 1788 to 1972. The interests of the contributors differ markedly in approach. Some subjects, notably Aborigines, receive cursory treatment. Comprehensive bibliography and index.

DONOVAN, P.F. *A land full of possibilities: a history of South Australia's Northern Territory*. UQP, 1981. 267 p, illus, maps.

Covers the period from 1863 to 1911, with emphasis on SA's colonial rule of north Australia and the economic exploitation of the Territory.

FITZGERALD, R. *From the dreaming to 1915: a history of Queensland*. UQP, 1982. 354 p, illus, maps.

FITZGERALD, R. *From 1915 to the early 1980s: a history of Queensland*. UQP, 1984. 653 p, illus.

In these two volumes the author questions the concept of progress in Qld from precolonial days through periods of 'Labor dominance' (1915–57) and 'Conservative monopoly' (1957 to the early 1980s).

FITZPATRICK, B.C. *The Australian people 1788-1945*. MUP, 1946. 279 p, map.

A survey by Australia's major Marxist historian of the 1940s and 1950s. The book is considered eccentric, but contains his 'most brilliant irony and sharpest insights'. Second edition published in 1951.

GIBLIN, R.W. *The early history of Tasmania*. London, Methuen, 1928; MUP, 1939. 2 vols.

The first volume, 1642–1804, dealt mainly with exploration and geographical history. The second, 1804–28, largely ignored the role of convicts and emancipists in Tasmanian history.

GRATTAN, C.H. *The southwest Pacific to 1900, a modern history: Australia, New Zealand, the Islands, Antarctica*. Ann Arbor, University of Michigan Press, 1963. 558 p, illus, maps.

GRATTAN, C.H. *The southwest Pacific since 1900, a modern history: Australia, New Zealand, the Islands, Antarctica*. Ann Arbor, University of Michigan Press, 1963. 759 p, illus.

To the time of their publication the best distillation of existing scholarly work on Australian history. Describes how Europeans became established in the southwest Pacific. Places Australia well in the context of world affairs.

GREENWOOD, G. ed, *Australia: a social and political history*. A & R, 1977. 465 p, illus, maps.

First published in 1955, this work filled a vacuum in Australian historiography, serving as a text for two decades and longer.

HANCOCK, W.K. *Australia*. London, E. Benn, 1930, 326 p, illus, maps.

A seminal work of history and political and social commentary, still influential. Among Hancock's themes are the notions of 'independent Australian Britons' and political parties of initiative and resistance. Second edition published in 1961.

JOHNSTON, W.R. *The call of the land: a history of Queensland to the present day*. Brisbane, Jacaranda, 1982. 229 p, illus, maps.

A probing investigation of 'how the spirit and mind of Queensland have developed', drawing out continuities and discontinuities in the state's history.

JOSE, A.W. *A short history of Australasia*. A & R, 1899. 252 p, illus, maps.

Published in many editions with varying titles, the most common being *History of Australia from the earliest times to the present day*; the 15th edition was published in 1930. It was a bestselling text which emphasised politics and land settlement.

KIMBERLY, W.B. *History of West Australia: a narrative of her past, together with biographies of her leading men*. Melbourne, Niven, 1897. 593 p, illus.

With its emphasis on material progress and consensus, Kimberly's work had a strong influence on later writers, including J.S. Battye, *Western Australia: a history from its discovery to the inauguration of the commonwealth* (1924; facs, UWAP, 1978).

LACOUR-GAYET, R. *A concise history of Australia*. Trans by J. Grieve. Ringwood, Vic, Penguin, 1976. 484 p.

A French view of Australian history, based largely on secondary sources; it is valuable for its refreshing approach and new insights. French–Australian contacts receive prominence.

LANG, J.D. *An historical and statistical account of New South Wales both as a penal settlement and as a British colony*. London, Cochrane and McCrone, 1834. 2 vols.

An opinionated and widely read series of sketches which the *Westminister review* suggested in 1834 should be titled 'The history of Doctor Lang, to which is added the history of NSW'.

MELLOR, S. ed, *Australian history: the occupation of a continent*. Melbourne, Eureka, 1978. 411 p, illus, map.

Comprehensive coverage by six authors of traditional subjects, with convenient subtitles. A companion volume is Mellor, *Readings in Australian history: the occupation of a continent* (1979).

PIKE, D.H. *Australia, the quiet continent* (2nd edn). CUP, 1970. 243 p, illus, maps.

'Australia's quiet story is perhaps best explained by combining geographic and economic influences with the British tie.' Pays particular attention to the less populous states, especially SA. First published in 1962.

PIKE, D.H. *Paradise of dissent: South Australia 1829–1857* (2nd edn). MUP, 1967. 580 p, maps.

A history of SA's foundation and early years, countering the view of Australia 'through eastern eyes'. First published in 1957.

POWELL, A. *Far country: a short history of the Northern Territory*. MUP, 1982. 301 p, illus, maps.

A straightforward history of the Territory, ranging widely in subject matter.

ROBSON, L.L. *A history of Tasmania. Vol 1. Van Diemen's Land from the earliest times to 1855*. OUP, 1983. 632 p, illus, maps.

This book is a case study in 'that form of exploitation which a colonial–metropolitan relationship must by definition involve'. Robson relies more heavily on imperial than local archives. A second volume is in preparation.

RUSDEN, G.W. *History of Australia*. London, Chapman and Hall, 1883. 3 vols.

Rusden was a Victorian public servant with first-hand knowledge of many of the people and events he wrote about. His bias was fiercely conservative. A second edition was published in 1897 and reissued in 1908.

SCOTT, E. *A short history of Australia*. London, OUP, 1916. 363 p, maps.

First published in 1916 and the first of the so-called short histories. The seventh edition, revised by Herbert Burton, was published in 1947.

SERLE, A.G. *The golden age: a history of the colony of Victoria, 1851–1861*. MUP, 1978. 469 p, illus, maps.

An account of a tumultuous decade, enriched by the author's command of significant detail. First published in 1963.

SERLE, A.G. *The rush to be rich: a history of the colony of Victoria,*

1883–1889. MUP, 1971. 392 p, illus, map.

Focusing on the 1880s, but linked to *The golden age* by a prologue. Serle again shows how large questions and themes can be approached through a narrow span of time and place.

SHAW, A.G.L. *The story of Australia* (4th edn). London, Faber, 1972. 336 p, illus, map.

A political and economic history since 1788, reflecting the optimism of the 1950s and 1960s and exalting the triumph of the 'common man'. First published in 1955.

SHAW, A.G.L. AND NICOLSON, H.D. *Australia in the twentieth century: an introduction to modern society*. A & R, 1967. 287 p, illus.

A history for schools, emphasising Australia in a world context, politics and technology. Includes timelines and eight biographies.

STANNAGE, C.T. ed, *A new history of Western Australia*. UWAP, 1981. 836 p, illus, maps.

Nineteen authors reflect diverse approaches to the past rather than pursuing a single theme. WA's Aborigines receive extensive coverage.

TURNBULL, C. *A concise history of Australia* (rev edn). Melbourne, Currey O'Neil Ross, 1983, 258 p, illus.

A lively short history, for a wide readership, impressionistic with emphasis on eastern Australia. First published in 1965, this revised edition by Marjorie Tipping brings the story to 1983.

TURNER, H.G. *A history of the colony of Victoria from its discovery to its absorption into the Commonwealth of Australia*. London, Longmans, Green, 1904. 2 vols, maps.

The annals of Victoria affectionately recorded by one who had lived there for half a century. New edition in 1973 (Melbourne, Heritage Publications).

THE VICTORIANS: BROOME, R. *Arriving*. 258 p, illus, maps; DINGLE, A.E. *Settling*. 274 p, illus, maps; PRIESTLEY, S. *Making their mark*. 382 p, illus, maps. Sydney, Fairfax Syme & Weldon, 1984.

Issued to mark the sesquicentenary of white settlement in Victoria. Notes and references issued separately.

WARD, R.B. *Australia, a short history* (rev edn). Sydney, Ure Smith, 1979. 218 p, illus.

Ward depicts Australia 'feeling its way forward to its own identity'. A useful textbook. First published in 1965.

WARD, R.B. *Australia since the coming of man*. Sydney, Lansdowne, 1982. 254 p, illus, maps.

A substantially revised edition of *Australia, a short history*. Changes include a useful summary of Aboriginal prehistory and the extension of the final chapter to 1982.

WARD, R.B. *A nation for a continent: a history of Australia 1901–1975*. Melbourne, Heinemann Educational, 1977. 515 p, illus, maps.

A detailed history of Australia since Federation, with the emphasis on federal politics.

WEST, J. *The history of Tasmania*. Launceston, Tas, Henry Dowling, 1852. 2 vols.

An outstanding colonial history. The 1971 edition includes a valuable introduction and detailed references by A.G.L. Shaw.

WESTGARTH, W. *The colony of Victoria: its history, commerce and gold mining; its social and political institutions; down to the end of 1863*. London, Sampson Low, 1864. 503 p.

An account of the 'greatest of our colonies', written from personal recollections and other earlier general works.

YOUNGER, R.M. *Australia and the Australians: a new concise history*. Melbourne, Hutchinson, 1982. 986 p, illus, maps.

A detailed narrative along conventional lines emphasising material progress. First published in 1970.

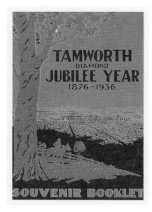

Local histories such as the Tamworth diamond jubilee year souvenir booklet *tend to emphasise growth and prosperity.*
CORNSTALK BOOKSHOP

CHAPTER 17

CITY AND REGION

PETER SPEARRITT

WHITE AUSTRALIA BEGAN as an urban society. The first convict settlements were little more than urban gaols that developed slowly as port cities for hinterland agriculture. Sydney, Hobart and Brisbane all began in this way. Melbourne, Perth and Adelaide, too, were founded as port settlements, but without convicts. By 1840 the six settlements that are today state capital cities had all been established. The growth of the ports is traced in James Bird (1968).

As Australia's first city, nineteenth-century Sydney has attracted a good deal of scholarly attention. The early years of the settlement are covered in some detail in almost every short history of Australia, and in much more detail in the multivolume histories. Yet by 1841 the city could claim only 30 000 inhabitants; 80 per cent of the colony's European population had decided to seek their fortunes elsewhere. Birch and Macmillan (1983) provide a documentary account of the history of Sydney while Kelly (1978) serves as an introduction to the city in the nineteenth century.

With the discovery of gold in the 1850s some Australian cities grew rapidly and new cities were founded almost overnight. Sydney doubled its population in that decade while Melbourne's quadrupled, making it the most populous city in Australia by 1861. Melbourne retained the lead until the depression of the 1890s when Sydney managed to overtake its southern rival. Sydney, which had almost half a million people by 1901, has maintained the lead ever since. The historical and contemporary relationship between Melbourne and Sydney is traced in J. Davidson, ed, *The Sydney Melbourne book* (Sydney, Allen & Unwin, 1986).

Except for the 1850s, Melbourne experienced its most spectacular growth in the 1880s; the population increased from 225 000 in 1881 to 400 000 in 1891. Homes had to be built for the influx of newcomers, whether from overseas or from the gold-rush towns which shed some of their population as the digging became harder. The pressure on Melbourne's land and housing market was so intense that a major boom spread through the city. The gripping story is well told in Cannon's *The land boomers* (Melbourne, Nelson, 1976). The quickly growing city generated a good deal of wealth, apparent in elegant mansions for those who could afford them and in fine commercial and government buildings; it soon became known as 'Marvellous Melbourne' and its history is analysed by Graeme Davison (1978) who concentrates on the decade and a half from 1880 to 1895 that took Melbourne from boom to depression. Grant and Serle (1978) provide a documentary background to Melbourne's history.

There has been much debate over the causes and effects of urban growth in colonial Australia.

N.G. Butlin in his *Investment in Australian economic development, 1861–1900* (CUP, 1964), shows the vital role played by the colonial governments in the provision of urban infrastructure, especially roads, railways, water and sewerage. A wide range of manufacturing industries sprang up in all the cities and most of the larger country towns during the latter half of the nineteenth century. Their development and location are analysed in G.J.R. Linge (1979), and this particular aspect of Australian development is further examined in chapter 36 of this volume.

While Sydney and Melbourne grew rapidly from the 1850s, Brisbane and Perth, from a much smaller population base, were more sluggish. Brisbane, with its rich agricultural hinterland, took off in the 1860s and doubled its population every decade until the 1890s, reaching 119 000 by 1901. By contrast, Perth, with a population of 5000 in 1861, had only managed to add another 4000 in the next two decades, although by 1901, including the neighbouring port of Fremantle, it topped sixty thousand. The development of the two cities has been traced by Lawson (1973) and Stannage (1979) respectively.

Like Sydney and Melbourne, Adelaide developed quickly between 1851 and 1891, its population growing from 18 000 to 117 000. Derek Whitelock's *Adelaide: 1836–1976* (UQP, 1979) traces the influence of town planning principles on the evolution of the city. John Hirst's *Adelaide and the country, 1870–1917* (MUP, 1973) is the only major study of the relationship between a capital city and its hinterland. Hirst defines Adelaide's 'region' politically, in this case the rest of the colony (state), and traces the interplay of city and country districts. The nearest equivalent to his book for the other capitals are the colonial and state histories listed in chapter 16 but most of these make little use of the notion of regions.

Hobart, alone of the colonial capitals, grew little in the latter half of the nineteenth century. A population of 25 000 in 1861 had increased to only 33 000 by 1891, making it considerably smaller than regional centres like Ballarat and Newcastle. The history of nineteenth century Hobart, and especially the preoccupation with its convict origins, is told by Peter Bolger in *Hobart Town* (ANUP, 1973). The subsequent growth of Hobart, whose population did not reach 100 000 till the late 1950s, is examined by R.J. Solomon (1976).

City life in nineteenth-century Australia is closely explored in most of the aforementioned books on particular cities and is the subject of Michael Cannon's *Life in the cities*, volume 3 of his 'Australia in the Victorian age'. Cannon's main themes are transport of goods and people, improvements in public health (brought about by scientific advances, especially in water supply and sewage disposal) and the nature of middle-class and working-class life in both the old and the new suburbs. Some notion of how colonials themselves viewed their cities can be gained from perusing Garran's *Picturesque atlas of Australasia* (1888). The numerous public inquiries into sanitation, housing, sewerage and water supply in the large cities provide a graphic insight into the problems of nineteenth-century living conditions. These can be identified by checking D.H. Borchardt's checklists of royal commissions listed in chapter 8.

By 1901 the pattern of Australian urbanisation was well established. Sydney was the largest city, followed by Melbourne, Adelaide, Brisbane, Perth and Hobart. In the next eighty years this order changed little, except that Brisbane supplanted Adelaide as the third largest city. The growth of the capital cities in the nineteenth and twentieth centuries, and their increasing domination of their respective states, are traced in J.W. McCarty and C.B. Schedvin (1978). Sydney, Melbourne and Adelaide actually housed over one-third of their state totals. The New South Wales government statistician T.A. Coghlan wrote, in the 1901–02 issue of his annual survey *The seven colonies of Australia* (Sydney, NSW Government Printer):

> The progress of the chief cities of Australasia has been remarkable, and has no parallel among the cities of the old world ... The abnormal aggregation of the population into their capital cities is a most unfortunate element in the progress of these states, and as regards some of them is becoming more marked each year. (p 543)

Although Coghlan described the 'abnormal aggregation' as unfortunate, there was no stopping it. By the late 1930s Sydney, Melbourne, Adelaide and Perth accounted for over 50 per cent of their states' populations, while Brisbane and Hobart accounted for about one-third.

In the twentieth century Australian cities grew through a combination of immigration and an increase in the native born and some movement from rural areas and country towns to the larger cities. But as Coghlan observed, the 1901 census showed that apart from the capital cities there were only two urban centres in Australia with more than 40 000 people: Newcastle, at the head of the rich Hunter valley, with 55 000, and the Victorian gold town of Ballarat, which had a sufficiently diversified economy to be able to sustain a population of 44 000. The only other large towns in New South Wales were the mining settlements of Broken Hill (28 500) and Maitland (10 000) and the agricultural centres of Goulburn (10 600) and Bathurst (9200). The rise of Broken Hill is the subject of Brian Kennedy's book (1978). All four towns loom large in the environmental and architectural history of the state, especially for the period 1840–1900, as demonstrated by Jeans and Spearritt (1980).

Victorian country towns have attracted more attention than their New South Wales equivalents, in part because two of them, Ballarat and Bendigo (44 000 and 31 000 respectively in 1901), include stunning architectural monuments to the wealth brought by gold; their growth between 1851 and 1901 and attendant politics are treated by Weston Bate (1978) and by Frank Cusack (1973) respectively. Geelong, the fourth largest city in Victoria in 1901, with 18 300 people, became, with the addition of major manufacturing concerns to its agricultural base, the second largest, with 125 000 people in 1981.

A.J. and J.J. McIntyre's *Country towns of Victoria* (MUP, 1944) is a social survey of 180 towns with populations, in 1939, between 250 and 10 000. The McIntyres found that one-third of the towns had increasing populations; the rest had either decreasing or stationary populations. Most of the towns with falling populations had fewer than 1000 inhabitants. There is no equivalent of this survey, which includes chapters on transport, local government, health, education, religion and recreation, for any other state.

Queensland saw major cities develop along its long coastline. The history of Queensland's ports is outlined by G. Lewis (1973). In 1901 Rockhampton (18 300) and Townsville (12 700) served as regional centres for a rich hinterland, as they did in 1981, with 50 100 and 86 100 people respectively. Louise McDonald's *Rockhampton* (UQP, 1981) traces the growth of the town from gold discoveries in the 1850s to its development as the hub of the central Queensland cattle industry.

The only large city in South Australia, apart from Adelaide, is Whyalla (30 000 people in 1981) which began as a port town for the shipment of ironstone in 1901. In the late 1930s its role diversified to include shipbuilding and in 1965 BHP opened a steelworks there. The growth of Whyalla, like the growth of the two New South Wales mining and steel centres, Wollongong and Newcastle, demonstrates the vital role that key industrial concerns play in many Australian provincial cities. Newcastle has attracted a lucid historian in J.C. Docherty (1983) but Wollongong awaits its chronicler.

In Tasmania the only city of any size apart from Hobart, both in 1901 and today, is Launceston which housed 65 000 people in 1981. J. Reynolds's history, *Launceston* was published by the City Council in 1969. Western Australia did not, and does not, have a town which even approaches the size of Launceston. The mining town of Kalgoorlie–Boulder, which in 1901 had 11 300 inhabitants, had only grown to 19 800 by 1981. West Australian towns are covered by Pitt Morison and White (1979).

Those interested in the history of particular regions should start with the entries in *Events and places*, a companion reference volume in this series, *Australians: a historical library*. The 32 regional essays in 'Places' all list further reading.

The pattern of Australian settlement, and in particular the dominance of Sydney and Melbourne, posed a problem for those politicians charged with finding a home for the federal parliament. Until 1927 parliament sat in Melbourne but the search for a new home, which began in the early 1900s, produced a number of government reports canvassing a variety of outlandish sites. The selection of Canberra and subsequent battles over its planning are outlined by Roger

Pegrum (1983). Canberra soon became a model planned city and an inspiration for reformist tracts about Australian cities, including the important and influential work by Hugh Stretton (1975). The National Capital Development Commission, created in 1957 to control and direct Canberra's urban growth, has issued a number of books on its charge, including *Tomorrow's Canberra* (1970). Canberra's leasehold system for urban land is unique in Australia, and successive governments have resisted the temptation to allow the citizens of Canberra the freehold rights available to property owners elsewhere. In 1976, the government launched a Commission of Inquiry into Land Tenures but it resulted in no major change in land tenure. The rise and fall of the Department of Urban and Regional Development, including its attempts to create federal regions in Australia, is well portrayed in Lloyd and Troy (1981).

While Canberra was still in its infancy the other Australian cities were experiencing suburban booms of varying intensity. The best overview of suburban growth in twentieth-century Australia is by Neutze (1981) who looks at employment, housing and transport and the relationship between them. The key role played by government in the development of the infrastructure of twentieth-century growth is outlined in N.G. Butlin *et al* (1982).

Scholars have only recently become interested in the history of the capital cities. Sandercock (1975) examines the achievements and failures of town planning in Sydney, Melbourne and Adelaide while Spearritt (1978) traces the nature and extent of suburbanisation and its relationship to employment, transport and housing. Widespread car ownership after World War II is identified as the most important factor in what town planners labelled the 'suburban sprawl'.

Among the best sources on postwar suburban and regional growth are the planning documents produced by or for various government agencies, like Stephenson and Hepburn's plan for Perth (1955), the future view of the Melbourne and Metropolitan Board of Works (1954), the Cumberland County Council's plan for Sydney (1948) and the report of the South Australian Town Planning Committee (1962). Such planning documents are often updated or replaced and readers seeking current information about a particular city or region should start by contacting the relevant planning departments. Despite the lip-service that all state governments pay to regionalism and decentralisation, almost all the important planning authorities still have their headquarters in the capital cities. The only exceptions to this can be found in designated 'growth areas' like Albury–Wodonga, which has its own Development Corporation.

Specialist books on particular aspects of cities and regions—housing, employment and population growth—have become relatively common. The best single book on housing remains the general study by the architect Robin Boyd (1952; repr, 1978). M.A. Jones (1972) examines the movement for slum clearance in the 1930s and the subsequent creation of housing commissions in each state to provide low-cost, means tested, rented housing. By the 1960s roughly one-third of Australians owned their own homes outright and another third were paying them off. In the space of 30 years, Australian society had changed from one in which the majority rented their homes into one in which the majority were owners or purchasers. Though most Australians continue to live in houses, in the larger cities flats (or home units as they are often called) have become popular in central areas, especially in Sydney where one-third of the population now lives in flats, a much higher proportion than in any other city (see Neutze, 1981).

The uncertainty of the world economy in recent years has caused more attention to be paid to the nature of economic and population change, crucial factors in the process of urban and regional development. Frank Stilwell (1980) analyses the economic foundations of urban growth and decay, while D.T. Rowland (1979) points to the key role that internal migration—from country to city and from city to city—has played in twentieth-century urbanisation.

The problems of governing the ever-growing metropolitan areas have produced many more bureaucratic plans than books explaining them. Andrew Parkin (1982) summarised the situation and Neutze studied the full bureaucratic setting (1978). The role of local government is discussed by John Power *et al* (1981) and more extensive references to this topic can be found in chapter 27 of this volume.

The labels 'regional' and 'local' history are used so loosely in Australia that it is often hard to tell them apart. Shire and municipal histories are very often solicited by the local authority itself so that authors are rarely encouraged to go beyond what are usually rather artificial administrative boundaries to analyse the wider social and economic history of a particular place or region. In the 1930s there were over a thousand municipalities and shires in Australia. In subsequent decades many of the smaller authorities were amalgamated so that by the mid-1980s only a little over eight hundred remained. Books published about shires and municipalities vary from the 'Back to so and so' volume, usually issued for an anniversary, to full-scale histories. The best way to find out whether a history or commemorative volume has been written about a particular place (and often there will be more than one) is to check with the local library or with the appropriate state library. No-one has yet compiled a thorough national bibliography of local and regional history but excellent bibliographies do exist for some states, for example, Carol Beaumont, *Local history in Victoria* (Bundoora, Vic, La Trobe University, 1980).

Before World War II most of the histories about particular places or regions were slim pamphlets with little formal historical content but often much to delight and inform today's browser, such as old advertisements, photographs and maps. In recent years a number of local authorities have hired professional historians to write their history and some notable books have emerged. Just as a newfound interest in genealogy has produced a bevy of 'how to' books, so has the new enthusiasm for local history; G.M. Hibbins, C. Fahey and M.R. Askew's *Local history* (Sydney, Allen & Unwin, 1985) is subtitled 'a handbook for enthusiasts'. Such books explain the uses of council rate books, personal and trade directories (particularly important sources before the era of the telephone book), photographs, public and private archives and oral history.

While amateur and professional historians have both contributed to the boom in local history, regional history has usually been left to the professionals. A number of notable volumes, such as G. Bolton's *A thousand miles away* (1963) on north Queensland to 1920, G.L. Buxton's *The Riverina* (1967) and D. Waterson's *Squatter, selector and storekeeper* (1968) on the Darling Downs, are cited in other chapters in this book. W.K. Hancock (1972) marked a new direction in regional history because he was prepared to admit, unlike most writers of shire histories, that the Europeans' attempt to capitalise on their environment through activities such as grazing could result in a denuded landscape. Some of the best regional and local histories concentrate on particular suburbs or communities. Janet McCalman's *Struggletown* (MUP, 1984) about public and private life in the inner Melbourne suburb of Richmond between 1900 and 1965 draws on a fascinating array of statistical, government and private records with extensive use of oral history.

Concern that Australia's capital cities hold too much of the continent's population has surfaced many times in the last hundred years. This dissatisfaction has sometimes been expressed in 'new state' movements.

Attempts to move people back on to the land or at least out of the cities and into the country towns range from ill-fated soldier settlement schemes in the 1920s and 1930s to the nomination of 'growth centres' in the 1970s. The most successful of these is Albury–Wodonga, which in 1981 housed 53 000 people; successful in part because, like Canberra, it has had a great deal of federal government money put into it. The rapidly growing Northern Territory capital of Darwin (with 56 500 in 1981) is another city highly dependent on government infrastructure. Decentralisation—its achievements and failures—and the related themes of anti-urban sentiment in Australia are not yet treated in a major work, but the issues have been discussed by a number of the authors mentioned here, including Neutze (1978, 1981), Stilwell (1974) and Rowland (1979).

Recent research has shown that enormous inequalities exist within Australian cities and between regions. Usually these inequalities are a reflection of the country's economic and class structure but some are also a function of city size or regional location. Differences within the cities are charted by Ian Burnley (1980) and in a series of social atlases on Australian cities. The federal government's Division of National Mapping produced a series of atlases for all the capital cities based on statistics collected in the 1976 and 1981 censuses.

The study of urban and regional development relies heavily on statistical data, especially those produced by the census, now held at five-yearly intervals. The ABS regularly publishes summaries of its major findings but increasingly much of the information is available only on computer tape. The availability of census data and related data bases on employment and unemployment, on welfare recipients, on property ownership and transactions, on public and private transport and on manufacturing and retailing, has led to a situation where the techniques used to study cities and regions are often beyond the comprehension of all but the specialist.

A useful summary of data from the 1961 to 1976 censuses is provided in *Australian urban environmental indicators* (1983). Articles on Australian urban and regional development appear regularly in such journals as *Australian geographer, Royal Australian Planning Institute J, Australian geographical studies* and *Heritage Australia.* Since 1966 the Australian Institute of Urban Studies has produced a useful annual index to this published material and to research in progress: *Bibliography of urban studies in Australia,* details of which are cited in chapter 8 of this volume. It includes articles on particular cities, towns and regions.

In the 1870s and 1880s overseas visitors like Anthony Trollope and R.E.N. Twopeny pointed to the remarkable growth and relative sophistication of our cities as did the Sydney-born statistician Coghlan. But for the first half of the twentieth century there were remarkably few books written about particular Australian cities or regions, though they were of course touched on in survey books about the nation and were often the topic of debate in the press and in parliament. Apart from these prosaic sources the most sustained comment on Australian cities between 1900 and 1960 is to be found in the many novels and autobiographies set in particular cities, as shown by John Arnold (1983) and by Patricia Holt (1983) for Melbourne and Sydney respectively.

Scholars in Australian universities began to turn their attention to our cities in the 1960s and during the past three decades academia has spawned many theses and books about Australian regional and urban development. The best short guide to the period before 1900 remains Sean Glynn (1975). Nobody has as yet produced a national overview of the first half of the twentieth century but for changes since World War II we turn again to Max Neutze (1981) as the best starting point. Most of the planning reports on particular cities are dry and technical documents, often assuming considerable knowledge on the part of the user. Readers wanting an introduction to the social and political content of planning should read Sandercock's historical account (1977) and Stretton's (1975) summation of the present and the future.

One of the most important trends in urban and regional development today, the proliferation of retirement houses and resort developments along much of the east coast, has produced a spate of articles but no major book to date. The Gold Coast—a thin strip of high-rise and luxury house development on either side of the New South Wales–Queensland border—became, in the 1970s, the ninth largest urban settlement in Australia. It is variously depicted as a sun-filled playground or as an example of real estate agents and developers gone mad.

The place and feel of our cities and regions in the latter half of the twentieth century are often better captured by film-makers, novelists and rock musicians than by scholars and journalists. Most scholars who write about these matters have little interest in visual and material culture, and those who are interested, like architectural historians, too often ignore the social and economic setting of their buildings and the lives of the people who inhabit them. Those interested in relevant marginal studies are urged to consult the essays and annotated bibliographies on physical geography (chapter 10), local government (chapter 27), immigration and demography (chapter 39), transport (chapter 33) and architecture (chapter 53).

ARNOLD, J. ed, *The imagined city: Melbourne in the mind of its writers.* Sydney, Allen & Unwin, 1983. 130 p, illus.

Extracts from 28 novels and autobiographies set in Melbourne from 1854 to 1977 including Fergus Hume's bestselling *The mystery of a hansom cab* (1886) and Helen Garner's *Monkey grip* (1977).

AUSTRALIA. Dept of Post-War Reconstruction. *Regional planning in Australia.* Canberra, The Department, 1949. 103 p, maps.

This book reflects a high point of regional planning in Australia when most states, spurred by the enthusiasm of the Dept of Post-War Reconstruction, produced substantial reports on the past, present and future of their regions.

AUSTRALIAN urban environmental indicators: Australian Environment Statistics Project, Department of Home Affairs and Environment. AGPS, 1983. 345 p, illus, maps.

Compendium of data from 1961 to 1976 including population, employment, immigration, education, income distribution, housing, health, air and water quality.

BATE, W.A. *Lucky city: the first generation of Ballarat, 1851–1901.* MUP, 1978. 302 p, illus, maps.

A survey of Ballarat, including the built environment, the demographic setting and political developments.

BIRCH, A. AND MACMILLAN, D.S. eds, *The Sydney scene: 1788–1960.* MUP, 1962. 387 p, illus, maps.

Documents covering most aspects of the history of the city. Marred by a poor bibliography and not particularly revealing commentaries. Facsimile edition, Sydney, Hale & Iremonger, 1983.

BIRD, J. *Seaport gateways of Australia.* London, OUP, 1968. 253 p, illus, maps.

A history of port development in all the capital cities, along with Port Pirie, Newcastle, Port Kembla and Whyalla.

BOWMAN, M. ed, *Beyond the city: case studies in community structure and development.* Melbourne, Longman Cheshire, 1981. xxviii, 228 p, illus, maps.

Case studies of country towns and small isolated settlements, including an Aboriginal community. Bibliography.

BOYD, R. *Australia's home: its origins, builders and occupiers.* Ringwood, Vic, Penguin, 1978. 320 p, illus.

An idiosyncratic architect's view of Australian housing, it includes a considerable amount of comment about suburban boom building in both the nineteenth and twentieth centuries. First published in 1952.

BURNLEY, I.H. *The Australian urban system: growth, change and differentiation.* Melbourne, Longman Cheshire, 1980. 339 p, illus, maps.

Studies of economic and demographic aspects of urbanisation, the internal structure of Australian cities as well as social inequalities and residential differentiation.

BUTLIN, N.G. *et al, Government and capitalism: public and private choice in twentieth century Australia.* Sydney, Allen & Unwin, 1982. 369 p.

An economic history of twentieth-century Australia which includes urban public services like water and sewerage, transport, post and telecommunications.

CANNON, M. *Life in the cities.* Melbourne, Currey O'Neil, 1983. 320 p, illus. (Australia in the Victorian age, 3).

Historical study of suburbanisation, public health, working and middle-class living conditions. First published in 1975.

COLE, J.R. *Shaping a city: Greater Brisbane 1925–1985.* Brisbane, Brooks, 1984. 416 p, illus, maps.

A history focused on the Brisbane City Council and aspects of local authority control.

CUMBERLAND COUNTY COUNCIL. *The planning scheme for the County of Cumberland, New South Wales; the report of the Cumberland County Council to the ... minister for local government, 27th July 1948.* Sydney, Cumberland County Council, 1948. 2 vols, illus, maps.

Chapters on landuse, population, employment, transport, education and public utilities with planning recommendations for a county scheme.

CUSACK, F. *Bendigo: a history.* Melbourne, Heinemann, 1973. 262 p, illus.

Concentrates on the 1840s to the 1920s with a short commentary on Bendigo in the twentieth century.

DAVISON, G.J. *The rise and fall of marvellous Melbourne.* MUP, 1978. 304 p, illus, maps.

A study of Melbourne's spectacular boom of the 1880s, with attention to the mercantile community, the professions, the civil service and suburban living.

DOCHERTY, J.C. *Newcastle: the making of an Australian city.* Sydney, Hale & Iremonger, 1983. 191 p, illus, maps.

The growth of Newcastle from 1900 to 1940 with a final summary chapter on the city since World War II. Concentrates on industry, work, housing and retailing.

GARRAN, A. ed, *The picturesque atlas of Australasia.* Sydney, Picturesque Atlas Publishing Co, 1886 (ie 1888). 3 vols, illus, maps.

A lavish set of volumes presenting a pictorial and textual account of Australia. Facsimile of the first two volumes published as *Australia: the first hundred years* (Sydney, Ure Smith, 1974).

GLYNN, S. *Urbanisation in Australian history, 1788–1900.* Melbourne, Nelson, 1975. 99 p, illus, map.

A useful primer on nineteenth-century urbanisation with an excellent though rather dated bibliography. First published in 1970.

GRANT, J. AND SERLE, G. eds, *The Melbourne scene: 1803–1956.* Facs, Sydney, Hale & Iremonger, 1978. 308 p, illus.

First published in 1957. Chronologically arranged documents and commentary.

HANCOCK, W.K. *Discovering Monaro: a study of man's impact on his environment.* CUP, 1972. 209 p, illus, maps.

Shows how Aborigines and white settlers have changed this region in the high country of NSW.

HOLT, P. ed, *A city in the mind: Sydney imagined by its writers.* Sydney, Allen & Unwin, 1983. 132 p.

Extracts from 28 novels and autobiographies set in Sydney from 1891 to 1980, including Ethel Turner's *The family at Misrule* (1895) and Shirley Hazzard's *The transit of Venus* (1980).

JEANS, D.N. AND SPEARRITT, P. *The open-air museum: the cultural landscape of New South Wales.* Sydney, Allen & Unwin, 1980. 154 p, illus, maps.

The development of the built environment from 1800 to 1980 with chapters on rural landscapes, country towns, transport and the major cities.

JONES, M.A. *Housing and poverty in Australia.* MUP, 1972. 239 p.

Examines the movement for slum clearance from the 1930s and the activities of the state housing commissions from 1940 to 1970 including means tests, rent policy and home ownership.

KELLY, M. ed, *Nineteenth-century Sydney: essays in urban history.* SUP in association with the Sydney History Group, 1978. 135 p, illus, maps.

Includes chapters on transport, water supply, slums, the workforce and demography of the city.

Advertisement for Commercial Bank of Australia Ltd in the Queensland annual. *Published by the Brisbane* Courier Mail, *1965. Australia is portrayed as a series of rapidly growing cities ripe for high-rise development. Skyscrapers were built in all major Australian cities in the 1960s.*

KENNEDY, B.E. *Silver, sin and sixpenny ale: a social history of Broken Hill, 1883–1921.* MUP, 1978. 202 p, illus, maps.
Traces the spectacular rise of this mining town emphasising the role of BHP and the growth of the trade union movement.

LAWSON, R. *Brisbane in the 1890s: a study of an Australian urban society.* UQP, 1973. 373 p, illus, maps.
Chapters on demography, economic structure, social status, the family, education, leisure and religion, not always thoroughly integrated. This book was the first of the new wave of Australian urban histories.

LEWIS, G. *History of the ports of Queensland: a study in economic nationalism.* UQP, 1973. 360 p.
Concentrates on the three main ports, Brisbane, Rockhampton and Townsville, but also includes Maryborough, Mackay and Cairns. Includes an account of regional economic rivalries.

LINGE, G.J.R. *Industrial awakening: a geography of Australian manufacturing, 1788 to 1890.* ANUP, 1979. 845 p, illus, maps.
Covers all colonies but particular attention is paid to NSW, Vic and SA. Useful for Sydney and Melbourne but also has information on most of the larger country towns of this era.

LLOYD, C.J. AND TROY, P.N. *Innovation and reaction: the life and death of the federal Department of Urban and Regional Development.* Sydney, Allen & Unwin, 1981. 282 p.
A study of an ill-fated attempt to put urban and regional planning in Australia on a more rational footing. State governments resented the federal attempt to dictate policy in this area. Bibliography.

LOGAN, T. *Urban and regional planning in Victoria.* Melbourne, Shillington House, 1981. 124 p, maps.
The only full-length account of regional planning in an Australian state. Includes an account of decentralisation in Vic.

McCARTY, J.W. AND SCHEDVIN, C.B. eds, *Australian capital cities: historical essays.* SUP, 1978. 201 p, maps.
Looks at the growth of each Australian capital city in the nineteenth century with a final chapter on capital city growth in the twentieth century.

MELBOURNE AND METROPOLITAN BOARD OF WORKS. *Melbourne metropolitan planning scheme 1954: report.* Melbourne, The Board, 1954. 2 vols.
Includes chapters on decentralisation, housing, redevelopment, land subdivision, industry, shopping and business centres, education, road, public transport and the shape and size of the future city.

NATIONAL CAPITAL DEVELOPMENT COMMISSION. *Tomorrow's Canberra: planning for growth and change.* ANUP, 1970. 244 p, illus, maps.
Includes chapters on history, setting, structure and growth. Written from the point of view of the National Capital Development Commission, the authority responsible for the development of Canberra.

NEUTZE, M. *Australian urban policy.* Sydney, Allen & Unwin, 1978. 252 p.
An analysis of possible solutions available to all levels of government with reference to welfare, population distribution, housing, transport, urban services, urban planning and land.

NEUTZE, M. *Urban development in Australia: a descriptive analysis* (rev edn). Sydney, Allen & Unwin, 1981. 259 p, illus, maps.
First published in 1977, the book reflects the author's own view on residence, work, transport, housing in urban development and shows the changes that are currently occurring in urban Australia and the role of local government.

PARKIN, A. *Governing the cities: the Australian experience in perspective.* Melbourne, Macmillan, 1982. 147 p.
An overview of metropolitan government in Australia in the 1970s.

PEGRUM, R. *The bush capital: how Australia chose Canberra as its federal city.* Sydney, Hale & Iremonger, 1983. 192 p, illus, maps.
The politics of selecting the site and subsequent debate over proposed plans, including those of Walter Burley Griffin.

PITT MORISON, M. AND WHITE, J.G. eds, *Western towns and buildings.* UWAP for the Education Committee, 150th Anniversary Celebrations, 1979. 345 p, illus, maps.
A study of the built environment from 1829 to the 1970s, with emphasis on urban and rural houses and town planning, especially in Perth.

POULSEN, M.F. AND SPEARRITT, P. *Sydney: a social and political atlas.* Sydney, Allen & Unwin, 1981, 163 p, maps.
This atlas, based on the 1976 census, like those produced by the Division of National Mapping on the 1976 and 1981 censuses, shows demographic, housing, occupational and religious variables. Unlike the National Mapping atlases it also examines the political implication of geographic concentrations, including unemployment and income.

POWER, J. *et al, Local government systems of Australia.* AGPS, 1981. 830 p, map. (Australia. Advisory Council for Inter-government Relations. Information paper, 7.)
Chapters on the development of local government in every Australian state, including a historical overview. Excellent bibliography.

ROWLAND, D.T. *Internal migration in Australia.* Canberra, ABS, 1979. 203 p, maps.

Examines the historical trend towards urbanisation in Australia and the role that internal migration has played in the growth of cities and regions.

SANDERCOCK, L. *Cities for sale: property, politics and urban planning in Australia.* MUP, 1977. 260 p, maps.

The evolution of urban planning in Sydney, Melbourne and Adelaide in the twentieth century.

SOLOMON, R.J. *Urbanisation: the evolution of an Australian capital.* A & R, 1976. 434 p, illus, maps.

A geographical study of the growth of Hobart.

SOUTH AUSTRALIA. Town Planning Committee. *Report on the metropolitan area of Adelaide.* Adelaide, Government Printer, 1962. 304 p, illus, maps.

Report on the development of Adelaide including future requirements for land, traffic and transport. Recommends a development plan and means of implementation.

SPEARRITT, P. *Sydney since the twenties.* Sydney, Hale & Iremonger, 1978. 294 p, illus, maps.

Suburban change and expansion, including housing, transport, work, the class structure of the suburbs and the interdependence of the city centre and the suburbs. Bibliography.

STANNAGE, C.T. *The people of Perth: a social history of Western Australia's capital city.* Perth, Carroll's for Perth City Council, 1979. 364 p, illus, maps.

A history of Perth to 1918 with a concluding chapter on the remainder of the twentieth century. The main themes are population, building and urban politics. Bibliography.

STEPHENSON, G. AND HEPBURN, J.A. *Plan for the metropolitan region, Perth and Fremantle, Western Australia, 1955: a report* . . . Perth, Government Printer, 1955. 2 vols, illus, maps.

The seminal planning document for Perth and Fremantle.

STILWELL, F.J.B. *Australian urban and regional development.* Sydney, Australia and New Zealand Book Co, 1974. 206 p, map.

Examines the pattern of population and employment in Australia in about 1970, its equity implications and policies that might be undertaken by state, federal and local governments for a more equitable distribution. A non-technical exposition.

STILWELL, F.J.B. *Economic crisis, cities and regions: an analysis of current urban and regional problems in Australia.* Sydney, Pergamon, 1980. 182 p.

Analyses problems of development in Australian cities in the 1970s and early 1980s (particularly in the Newcastle–Sydney–Wollongong area), and regional problems due to Australia's changing role in the world economy.

STRETTON, H. *Ideas for Australian cities* (rev edn). Melbourne, Georgian House, 1975. 367 p, maps.

Examines the history, present and possible future of Sydney, Melbourne, Adelaide and Canberra, and the future of Australian suburbia. Influential work, first published in 1970.

Harald Vike, Perth roofs, *c1935. Oil. Born in Norway in 1906, Vike arrived in Fremantle in 1929 and studied under G. Pitt Morison, director of the National Gallery, Perth. The painting suggests that urban environments often have greater variety than the casual observer might suspect.*

ART GALLERY OF WESTERN AUSTRALIA

Frank Medworth (1892–1947), The café, *1942, Sydney. Oil on canvas, 55.0 × 75.5 cm.*

AUSTRALIAN NATIONAL GALLERY

CHAPTER 18

ILLUSTRATED HISTORIES

JOAN KERR

ILLUSTRATED HISTORY books come in two major forms: texts with added pictures, or collections of pictures with captions. Either seems an incomplete way of exploring the potential of this genre, yet a more balanced combination is rarely aimed for, let alone achieved. The notion that images and text should be complementary and interrelated is still in its infancy in this country. This selection therefore reads more like a list of casualties than a citation of heroes. Nevertheless, the healthiest specimens have been selected, except for a couple of salutary examples of the disastrously maimed.

Until quite recently, illustrated histories by professional historians were almost universally of the first category: independent texts to which illustrations were subsequently appended—frequently by a picture researcher employed by the publisher to give blocks of words more 'general appeal'. By adding a hundred or so illustrations, the publisher could claim that the book was 'intended for the general reader as much as for the specialist' and print an extra 5000 copies. The illustrated edition of Russel Ward's *The Australian legend* (1978) seems an appropriate representative of this type. Such books do what they intend to do quite competently; they drive home the general argument of the text with superficial visual appeal and no analysis, making both good and bad texts into objects suitable for the coffee table as well as the library.

On the other hand, examples of illustrated histories by freelance writers, local historians, photographers or journalists too often have been no more than a collection of images, with inadequate captions spelling out with excruciating banality the only too obvious: 'An early Australian homestead' or, more whimsically, 'A family posing stiffly for the photographer while their pet dog relaxes in the best leather armchair'. The former typifies old-fashioned regional histories where the image was all-important and, with luck, previously unpublished, while the latter indicates the presence of the would-be social historian trying to convey a sense of period values with no knowledge of early photographic techniques or conventions and no research into the category or date of the image. The photographic historian might add 'John Smith, photographer, 1854' if such information is accessible, while the more academic historian might try to identify the family and summarise the career of the most prominent male in the photograph. Even if images are—miraculously—fully captioned, acknowledged and identified it is regularly found after the manuscript has been sent to the publisher that they in no way relate to, or assist, the general argument of the book. They are simply there as decoration, not document.

Few authors accept the notion that images should be valued as contemporary, datable and opinionated documents, just as diaries, despatches or verbal descriptions are valued. Images need to be analysed like words and treated as another tool to assist in understanding the past. Our technology and marketing systems can make a picture-book cheaper than an unillustrated specialist text; the public, like Alice, quite justifiably asks, what use is a book without pictures? Illustrations are more and more frequently provided in response to such demands, but the concept of a new methodology for this sort of book remains dormant.

The most obvious fact overlooked by historians of all kinds is that images were not divinely created and therefore eternally valid (hence, no dates), generically true (hence, no locations) and totally objective (hence, no maker). Somebody made them at a specific time, for a specific purpose and in a specific way. The information,

Joseph Lycett, 'The residence of John McArthur Esquire, near Parramatta, New South Wales', hand-coloured aquatint from his *Views in Australia* (London, 1824),

should not be mere art-historical pedantry. It can be a way of conveying the information—properly expanded in the text—that Lycett reworked a painting when he arrived back in London, as a print for an expensive picture-book about an exotic place. When we know that the artist was a doubly convicted forger notoriously loose with facts (reflected here in the spelling of John Macarthur's name), it seems obvious that his print should be treated with extreme caution before it is accepted as a faithful factual document. Yet the flattering image of rolling green English parkland, inhabited by an elegant couple indicating their possession of this Eden, cannot be dismissed as sheer artistic incompetence or a faulty memory, although it certainly denies the validity of the artist's stated aim to present 'absolute *fac-similes* of scenes and places'. Lycett's real intention was clearly propagandist. His images reveal the way colonists wished to see themselves, as well as gratifying the English belief in the unalloyed benefits of occupying 'savage' lands. If historians read such images with the same care and polite scepticism brought to bear on words and deeds, Australian histories might become very different.

Photographs are always created by human agency for particular purposes, although those photographers identified and given any context of time, place or purpose in any general history 'through the camera's eye' are fewer than the rich who pass heavenwards through the eye of a needle. Alan Davies and Peter Stanbury's new edition of *The mechanical eye in Australia* (OUP, 1984) may lead to some improvement in this vast sea of ignorance, although the historians who profited from the first edition (1977) have still to reveal themselves.

The myth of the timeless impartiality of the camera dies hard. In 1900, when George McCredie, as quarantine officer, ordered the New South Wales government photographer John Degotardi to photograph those areas of Sydney affected by bubonic plague in case of legal claims once they had been demolished, the resulting photographs were considerably less glamorous than, say, a Charles Kerry souvenir book of Sydney presented to a retiring governor about that time. To juxtapose examples of the two as proof of late Victorian public splendour and private squalor without revealing the original purpose of either is just as much a manipulation as Lycett's.

Happily, that band of historians still proudly asserting their total ignorance of visual material in the name of 'serious scholarship' is a dying generation. Their successors have begun to cope with problems of pictorial interpretation. But such is the institutional distrust of the visually beguiling that most pioneers in the 'integrated illustrated history' market have been historians outside academia (Pearl, 1974; McQueen, 1977; and Cannon, 1982–83), historical archaeologists (Birmingham, *et al*, 1979 and 1981) or art historians (Mahood, 1973). At least Inglis (1974), Spearritt (*Sydney since the twenties*, Sydney, Hale & Iremonger, 1978) and Stannage (1979) can be cited from the universities as innovative success stories.

Cautionary tales of how not to illustrate a history book come from all ranks. The examples I have selected encompass a publisher, a non-academic art historian and both freelance and academic historians. Some of these will doubtless end up, like Fox and Spence (1982) writing and illustrating in 1910, typifying the values of an era—their own. Manning Clark seems an excellent candidate for this sort of attention from future historiographers.

One properly expects to get a clear indication of the author's voice—not the publisher's taste—from the illustrations in a history book. This can, of course, happen unconsciously and a stodgy book will have hackneyed illustrations, conventionally employed as empty decoration. But in a more positive sense, matching text and pictures takes time, thought and experience.

The uninterested or untrained searcher after illustrations has the additional disadvantage of not knowing where to look, as well as being ignorant of how to read images once they have been unearthed. Despite the plethora of evidence to the contrary, the national and state libraries are not the sole repositories of illustrations in this country; nor has every image these places possess already been catalogued and used in someone else's book.

Although images concealed in public and private archives are less accessible, they have the advantage of freshness. Some helpful guides to repositories have been published; Mari Davis and Hilary Boyce's *Directory of Australian pictorial resources* (Melbourne, Centre for Environmental Studies, University of Melbourne, 1980) identifies in a very general way more than 600 repositories of pictorial material in Australia, while the Australia Council has published a more specific *Directory of arts libraries and resource collections in Australia* (Sydney, 1983) edited by Susan Maddrell. Both can assist local searches. When the Australian Joint Copying Project of the National Library and the Mitchell Library gives priority to visual resources, the discovery of overseas material will become a less expensive challenge.

I have concentrated on images rather than texts in this discussion, since ignorance of the former has resulted in the greatest problems with this type of book. It is hard to report glowingly on a type of publication whose form is despised by a significant number of its practitioners. But not all illustrated histories are created by loquacious blind compilers—or even professionals in full command of words who have also learned to see. Examples have been selected to represent illustrated history using a single theme; Flower (1984), for example, looks at Australia by examining the clothing worn by its inhabitants and, although flawed, it is a good example of this subspecies. Others have used advertisements, cartoons, bushrangers, children or buildings to analyse Australia's social development. Most remain a quarry for more analytical research, and too many have unlocatable and unidentified treasures. Mahood's history of political cartooning is the exceptional gem, cut, polished and given a most valuable setting.

In some ways the unequivocally personal and partisan history—such as Manning Clark's—raises fewest doubts about its worth. In particular, artists such as Petty (1976) and Looby (1979) obviously use their own visual creations to mediate between facts and interpretation. The result is Oscar Wilde's kind of history—'a collection of the most beautiful lies'—scattered with splendidly convincing insights; nobody ought to be fooled by the first nor unable to see the second. But all the creative artist needs is genius. The more mundane historians attempting to present some aspects of the past they believe worth revealing have a more difficult task. To ignore that half of the evidence presented in pictorial form is crippling; to present only unresearched visual material is to abrogate the historian's role for the antiquarian's delight in simple facts.

The potential of this kind of book is yet to be fully realised. From now on it seems certain that this will be the dominant way of publishing history, in quantity, readership and significance. Quality is another matter. We need more illustrated history books and fewer history books with pictures (or vice versa) to ensure that.

Banish the budget blues. *Sheet music. Words and music by Jack Lumsdaine, sung by Art Leonard. Hince Collection, Box 1, 1930. A comment on Labor Prime Minister Scullin's tough 1930 budget. In July the government invited Sir Otto Niemeyer of the Bank of England to advise on the grim economic situation. He proposed a policy of balanced budgets and a wage cut of 10 per cent.*

NATIONAL LIBRARY

BIRMINGHAM, J. et al, *Australian pioneer technology: sites and relics.* Melbourne, Heinemann Educational, 1979. 200 p, illus.

BIRMINGHAM, J. et al, *Industrial archaeology in Australia: rural industry.* Melbourne, Heinemann, 1983. 191 p, illus.

The physical evidence of Australia's earliest primary industries, revealed in a beautifully presented collection of pictures and a scholarly text. Smelter stacks, stills, boiling-down sheds and so on, are given detailed analysis. *Industrial archaeology in Australia* covers flour mills and other clay-using industries, the building industry, transport and communciations etc. A chapter on sources is included.

BLAINEY, G. *The Blainey view.* Melbourne, Macmillan; ABC, 1982. 155 p, illus.

A sepia-toned version of the TV series. Very basic in both information and range of illustrations, but the thematic treatment is attractive, original and lively. Illustrations mainly collected by Maggie Weidenhofer.

BLAIR, D. *The history of Australasia* . . . Glasgow, McGready, Thompson & Niven, 1878. 711 p, illus, maps.

Stated to be the first complete history of Australasia. Lithographs mainly from photographs for scenery, and from imagination for shearer, Aborigines and digger, are as derivative as the text, yet quaintly romantic.

BOOTH, E.C. *Australia.* London, Virtue, 1873–76. 2 vols, illus, maps.

A descriptive history illustrated with lithographs after photographs, and paintings by John Skinner Prout and others. Some illustrations were created in London without the benefit of an Australian visit, others were painted many years earlier. The first large nineteenth-century travel book devoted to Australia. Republished in facsimile as *Australia in the 1870's* by Ure Smith in 1975 and by Summit Books in 1979.

CANNON, M. *Australia: a history in photographs.* Melbourne, Currey O'Neil Ross, 1983. 256 p, illus, maps.

A personal interpretation lacking any context of creation or use. This dismissive attitude to photography apart from subject matter mars a partisan interpretative history 'from below'. Picture research by Jane Fenton.

CANNON, M. *Australia in the Victorian age.* Melbourne, Currey O'Neil, 1982–83. 3 vols, illus.

Social histories, splendidly documented with a great range of contemporary stories, quotations and images focusing on individuals; interpreted and thematically related. First published 1971–75.

DENHOLM, D. *The colonial Australians.* Ringwood, Vic, Penguin, 1979. 202 p, illus, maps.

An eccentric history. The beguiling illustrations and attractive presentation only casually relate to the text, while the captioning and listing of illustrations are misleadingly inadequate.

FLOWER, C. *Clothes in Australia: a pictorial history, 1788–1980s.* Sydney, Kangaroo Press, 1984. 196 p, illus.

A history of costume in Australia, chronologically arranged by a visual historian. Class and status are revealed in male clothing, but the 'loud and vulgar style' of female dress is less obvious in contemporary illustration. First published in 1964 as *Duck and cabbage tree: a pictorial history of clothes in Australia, 1788–1914.*

FOX, F. AND SPENCE, P. *Australia.* London, A. & C. Black, 1910. 219 p, illus, map.

Australia is seen in 1910 as a nation of white, outdoor, loyal, rugged and independent people, overcoming the hardships of the land—an image exactly captured in Spence's 75 full-page watercolour paintings. Facsimile edition, Melbourne, Vantage, 1982.

GARRAN, A. ed, *The picturesque atlas of Australasia.* Sydney, Picturesque Atlas Publishing Co, 1886 (ie 1888). 3 vols, illus, maps.

Issued for Australia's centenary celebrations in 1888. The two volumes on Australia contained over 700 wood engravings after Julian and George Ashton and others. Belonging to the school of 'wonderful growth and prosperity', this was a major example of the genre. Facsimiles of first two volumes published as *Australia: the first hundred years* (Sydney, 1974).

HARRIS, J. *The bitter fight: a pictorial history of the Australian labor movement.* UQP, 1970. 310 p, illus, maps.

A wide range of illustrations around the labour movement from transported Chartists to the formation of the Communist party in Australia. Undisguised militant socialist approach by industrial worker author.

ILLUSTRATED history of Australia. Sydney, Hamlyn, 1974. 1518 p, illus, maps.

A gigantic compendium of anonymous history and unsourced illustrations. Never mind the appalling colour reproductions, the factual errors and the irritating subheadings of the 'Firm but just' school, but do feel the weight!

INGLIS, K.S. *The Australian colonists: an exploration of social history, 1788–1870.* MUP, 1974. 316 p, illus.

An early and successful attempt by a historian to integrate text and pictures. Although the latter now seem a somewhat conventional selection, this is still a model showing how images can add a new dimension to social history.

KING, J.L. *Stop laughing, this is serious! A social history of*

Australia in cartoons (rev edn). Sydney, Cassell, 1980. 223 p, illus.

A compendium of interesting images which does not develop into either a history of cartooning or a social history. The (inadequately cited) prints are entertaining and well selected. First published in 1978.

LINDESAY, V. *The inked-in image: a social and historical survey of Australian comic art.* Melbourne, Hutchinson, 1979. 336 p, illus.

A collection of cartoons (mainly comic) from 1855 to 1979, exemplify our popular mythology. Good-humoured and uncritical. First published in 1970.

LOOBY, K.R. *Black and white history of Australia.* Sydney, Macleay Museum, University of Sydney, 1979. 76 p, illus.

Looby's bitter, sad or enigmatic white history is more powerful and historical than his more romantic and mythical complementary black story. Pictures only, plus an introduction and a biography of the artist. First published in 1976.

LYCETT, J. *Views in Australia: or New South Wales and Van Diemen's Land delineated, in fifty views, with descriptive letter press.* London, J. Souter, 1824. 152 p, illus, maps.

Forty-eight aquatints and two maps, originally issued in parts and here collected into a volume, illustrate the benign results of English civilisation on a picturesquely barbaric landscape. Reality is manipulated by a forger to produce art disguised as fact. Facsimile edition, Nelson, 1977.

McQUEEN, H. *Social sketches of Australia, 1888–1975.* Ringwood, Vic, Penguin, 1977. 255 p, illus.

An unorthodox and entertaining volume. Because of inadequate referencing, lacks any traceable contemporary context, being an idiosyncratic vision of Australian society.

MAHOOD, M.H. *The loaded line: Australian political caricature, 1788–1901.* MUP, 1973. 306 p, illus.

A definitive work and a model reading of images, their makers, and their social, political and artistic context.

MOORE, D. AND HALL, R. *Australia, image of a nation 1850–1950.* Sydney, Collins, 1983. 335 p, illus.

A striking collection of photographs emphasising people in society, selected by the photographer David Moore with attention to formal quality, photographers and dates. Text by the poet Rodney Hall.

MORRIS, E.E. ed, *Cassell's picturesque Australasia.* London, Cassell, 1887–89. 4 vols, illus, maps.

Contains numerous steel engravings by English illustrators. A mass-produced imitation of the *Picturesque atlas of Australia* (1888). An abridged Australian section was issued as *Australia's first century* (Sydney, 1978).

MOUROT, S. *This was Sydney! A pictorial history from 1788 to the present time.* Sydney, Ure Smith, 1969. 155 p, illus.

The best of the Sydney illustrated books, by the then Mitchell librarian. Images and text informative, reliable and of lasting value.

O'KEEFE, D. *Australian album: the way we were: Australia in photographs, 1860–1920.* Sydney, Daniel O'Keefe, 1982. 224 p, illus.

Attractive but skin-deep history with an extensive selection of splendid images from unexplored and well-known collections. The photographs are inadequately referenced while ignorant annotations attempt to explain the obvious.

PAYNTING, H.H. AND GRANT, M. eds, *Victoria illustrated: 1834–1984.* Melbourne, James Flood Charity Trust in conjunction with the Royal Historical Society of Vic and Melbourne Camera Club, 1984. 528 p, illus.

The luxury end of the illustrated history market. Splendidly reproduced photographs and just enough research for an introductory identification, with bland or whimsical surface description. The usual absence of photographers' names and dates. Content evanescent.

PEARL, C. ed, *Australia's yesterdays: a look at our recent past.* Sydney, Reader's Digest Services, 1974. 360 p, illus.

A popular history of Australia since Federation, emphasising primary sources in a well-balanced, integrated assemblage of varied and original images and text (all identified, although not precisely).

PEARL, C. AND PEARL, I. *Our yesterdays: Australian life since 1853 in photographs.* A & R, 1954. 164 p, illus.

A lively selection favouring images and stories of entertaining individuals by an erudite social historian. An early example and still one of the best.

PETTY, B. *Petty's Australia: and how it works.* Ringwood, Vic, Penguin, 1976. 110 p, illus.

A brilliant collection of cartoons whose complex meanings are conveyed with great humour and economy of word and line. Originally published as *Australia fair* (Melbourne, Cheshire, 1976).

REECE, R.H.W. AND PASCOE, R. *A place of consequence: a pictorial history of Fremantle.* Fremantle, WA, Fremantle Arts Centre Press, 1983. 159 p, illus, maps.

An exemplary use of illustrations, pioneering research into local photographers and their social historical context. This is a great improvement on the standard undigested local history picture book.

RIENITS, R. AND RIENITS, T. *A pictorial history of Australia.* London, Hamlyn, 1969. 317 p, illus, maps.

Cheap, predictable history for the popular audience. The extensive mixture of all types of contemporary illustrations is too frequently rendered meaningless by being unacknowledged, undated and unsourced.

RITCHIE, J. *Australia as once we were.* Melbourne, Heinemann, 1975. 279 p, illus.

A brave effort which achieves an exuberant, original and unified tone in its syncopated combination of images and text. Illustrations are carelessly investigated and frequently anachronistic.

STANNAGE, C.T. *The people of Perth: a social history of Western Australia's capital city.* Perth, Carroll's for Perth City Council, 1979. 364 p, illus, maps.

A municipal history which gives an aggressive picture of people 'from below', treats the images with care and altogether achieves a successful new genre, ignoring the time hallowed formula of 'Our glorious town'.

STONE, D.I. ed, *Gold diggers and diggings: a photographic study of gold in Australia, 1854–1920.* Melbourne, Lansdowne, 1974. 208 p, illus, maps.

An excellent collecton of black and white contemporary photographs by a very knowledgeable author. Sources—acknowledged fully—are exhaustive and images varied. Introduction by Geoffrey Blainey.

WARD, R.B. *The Australian legend* (new illus edn). OUP, 1978. 336 p, illus.

The illustrated version of an influential history first published in 1958 which now gains adequate, but uninspired, pictures emphasising the 'bushman' of 'the Australian mystique' advanced in the text. Illustrations organised by Alison Forbes.

YOUNGER, R.M. *Australia! Australia! A pictorial history.* Adelaide, Rigby, 1975–77. 2 vols, illus.

The somewhat simplistic text, loose dating and inadequate acknowledgments suggest that this book is aimed at a school market. The material is comprehensive and well chosen for this purpose.

Broadsheet from Daily Mirror, *2 June 1986. Printed and published by Nationwide News. The popularisation of history through genealogy has resulted in a new clientele for archives and libraries.*

CHAPTER 19

GENEALOGY

PAMELA RAY AND KEITH JOHNSTON

GENEALOGY HAS CLOSE links with biography and local history. Whereas the biographer concentrates on the life of one individual and the local historian may use the lives of individuals and families to enliven the records of a community and its setting, the genealogist sets an individual in the context of his or her ancestors or descendants, or both. Genealogy, or family history, may focus on individuals in one line of descent over several generations, on all members of a particular family or on a group of people with ancestry shared at too distant a time for them to constitute a family in the accepted sense of the word.

The conscientious genealogist will aspire to produce more than the skeletal genealogy which was an acceptable result of research in former times. Supplying only meagre information about the persons treated, a genealogy or pedigree is commonly a chart, table or summary account of descent through series of generations. A brief narrative account of this nature does not attempt to analyse the effects on a family of major historical events or changes in social and economic conditions. The pedigree is a useful means of displaying facts and relationships in abbreviated but readily comprehensible manner. As such, a genealogy is an essential part of a good family history and provides the framework on which to base research.

Until World War II, most Australians had their origins in the British Isles, where an interest in genealogy, related closely as it was to recording the right of succession to titles and property, was very much the preserve of the nobility and gentry. An interest in genealogy would have seemed pretentious and perhaps anti-egalitarian to many Australians living in what they fondly regarded as a classless society. However, the most influential factor in dampening the enthusiasm of many Australians, especially prominent nineteenth-century citizens, was the spectre of the convict taint.

The most remarkable feature of genealogy in Australia is the recent growth in its popularity as a pastime and subject of serious study. Although this is a worldwide phenomenon, the Australian bicentenary has accelerated the interest that had quickened with the sesquicentenary celebrations in Western Australia, South Australia and Victoria. There is nothing quite like an important anniversary to stimulate interest in the past. Such anniversaries prompted the publication of many biographical compilations to meet the perceived needs of both seekers after family histories and connections and writers of biographies long and short. The latter are discussed in the next chapter of this volume.

The literature on genealogy is divided into four parts. The first deals with the methodology of genealogy and includes practical guides on how to trace one's ancestry. The second lists material on or by genealogical societies. The published records and listings of Australian immigrants and the printed sources of information on immigrants—particularly vital registers and graveyard inscriptions—make up the third and fourth part respectively.

Interest in genealogy was fostered in this country by imitating the London-based Society of Genealogists. The Society of Australian Genealogists was established in Sydney in 1932 and in 1941 a similar group formed the Genealogical Society of Victoria. The latter lapsed for a couple of decades but re-established itself in 1961. There are now over 8000 members in New South Wales and about 4000 in Victoria, and a regular journal is issued by each group: *Descent* in Sydney and *Ancestor* in Melbourne. A third society was formed in Canberra in 1964; it now has nearly 1400 members and publishes *The ancestral searcher.*

The 1970s saw the formation of numerous other genealogical societies in all states, including the establishment of rival groups. The Australian Institute of Genealogical Studies was founded in Victoria in 1973, with its journal *The genealogist* and over 1000 members. In South Australia, *The South Australian genealogist* began to appear in 1974, serving a membership of over 2000, and similar societies were founded in Queensland, Tasmania, Western Australia and the Northern Territory.

An interesting development in the 1980s was the proliferation of small independent regional groups. By 1984 more than twenty such groups had been established, mainly in New South Wales. Two specialist societies also deserve mention. These are the Fellowship of First Fleeters, founded in 1968, and the 1788–1820 Association, both based in Sydney.

Monographs on genealogical research methodology were very slow to appear. The first such publication was by Niel Hansen (1963), a member of the Mormon Church, a body with a special interest in genealogy for theological reasons. This volume was followed in 1965 (12th edn, 1983) by a book of a more practical kind by Nancy Gray, a member of the Society of Australian Genealogists; it continues to be a valuable aid for beginners. These two pioneer works remained the only guides written specifically for Australians until 1974 when *Ancestors for Australians* appeared. Although written with Victorian researchers in mind, its content was found to be useful to those in other states as well. Since 1979 such guides have become more sophisticated and thorough; one of their best examples is by Errol Lea-Scarlett (1979).

Most genealogical societies produce leaflets to guide beginners in the search for their family history. The Heraldry and Genealogy Society of Canberra issues each year a set of guides to coincide with a course run for its own members and the general public. Lyn Waldron, a Queensland genealogist, has also produced a set of course notes for beginners (1982).

As was the case with guides to methodology, it was many years before any guides to Australian source material for genealogists were issued. The first venture of this nature was published by Andrew Peake (1977), a member of the South Australian Genealogy and Heraldry Society.

Of considerable importance is the work produced by several state libraries, whose officers bear the brunt of this interest in family history and descent. To help their clients and to reduce the staff time spent on repeatedly explaining the resources of the library, the J.S. Battye Library in Perth (1983) has produced a guide for amateur genealogists. A very useful listing of the holdings of many Melbourne institutions is the guide compiled by F. Brown *et al* (1985). Other guides to Victorian source materials also exist, but these are brief and restricted to the collections of one institution. The Public Record Office of Victoria, for example, printed in 1980 (updated in 1984) a brief leaflet of basic information for newcomers to archival research, with the title *Genealogical sources.* In 1982 the Victorian Branch of the Australian Archives issued its seventeen-page *Brief guide to genealogical sources.*

Although not produced principally for genealogists, the various guides and leaflets published by the State Archives of New South Wales have long been regarded as essential tools for family historians and deserve special mention because of their outstanding quality. For some years this was the only repository to compile regularly, and make available in published form, indexes and listings of its holdings. The guides began in 1960 with the publication of *Colonial secretary: muster and census records.* To 1984 the Archives Authority of New South Wales had published 24 parts to its guide, with some already issued in revised editions. Particularly useful are those listing muster and census records; the guide to convict records; the index to assisted immigrants arriving in Port Phillip 1839–51 (when it was still part of New South Wales) and in Sydney 1880–96; and the guide to shipping records. The authority has also published 35 titles in its *Information leaflets* series, which describe in detail many records of relevance to the family historian.

A useful government publication, *The parish map in family history research*, was produced in 1982 by the New South Wales Crown Land Office. Maps are a difficult form of material for the amateur to understand and this guide has proved particularly helpful. It is hoped that other authorities will follow suit with similar publications as mapping practices differ between states.

The Australian Archives, established as an independent authority in 1960, contains archival material emanating from the federal government and its administration. The relevance of this material to genealogical research was described by Ruth McDonald in a paper read at the first Australasian Congress on Genealogy and Heraldry (1977). Her paper was accompanied by a detailed listing of many records which deserve to be better known.

More specialised listings of genealogical information began to appear in the 1960s. These included primary sources of personal data such as graveyard records, burial lists, tombstone inscriptions, birth, death and marriage registers both denominational and secular. Besides, as the horror of a convict ancestry was turned into an inverted snobbery, the early shipping registers, manifests and logbooks became available to the general public. Many were reprinted as important source books and are listed in the publications issued by the Archives Authority of New South Wales referred to above. The more important of these sources are noted in the following bibliography; here attention is drawn to three well-researched works, namely the record of burials in the old Sydney burial ground (1973), the listing of interments in the old Melbourne cemetery (1982) and the volume of monumental inscriptions for the New South Wales district of Monaro (1982). An overview was compiled by G. Thom (1980) for the Australasian Federation of Family History Organisations; a second edition is due to appear in 1985. The Society of Australian Genealogists published in 1982 a revised edition of N.J. Vine Hall's listing of English parish register transcripts. This is not complete, but is of value to the many families with English forbears.

Researchers interested in early New South Wales arrivals have at their disposal several excellent books, many of which are listed in chapter 21 of this volume. Cobley (1982) should be used in conjunction with Don Chapman's (1981) illustrated and readable collection of biographies of first fleeters (1981). Also important are R.J. Ryan's (1982, 1983) alphabetic listings of convicts and others arriving in the second and third fleets, but these contain only basic information.

Victorian immigrants are receiving some attention in a series of indexes compiled and published by Ian Hughes (1975–). The various titles of the series list passengers to Port Phillip from 1839 to 1851 from the United Kingdom and from foreign ports. Names are extracted mainly from newspaper shipping columns and exclude therefore the large number of assisted passengers, but details of the latter are to be found in unpublished indexes held in the Public Record Office of Victoria. That office also holds indexes to arrivals after 1851.

Few records have been retained of censuses in Australia. Some are held in archival repositories. Many early musters, listing principally convicts but in some cases free persons also, remain unpublished but are available on microfilm through the activities of the Australian Joint Copying Project described in chapter 8 of this volume. However, two printed volumes have been produced from primary sources and constitute valuable additions to the still small output of publications for the genealogist. The first is I. Berryman (1979) which lists West Australians recorded in the first census there in 1832, with biographical notes. The second is a mammoth listing of over 36 500 persons recorded in various versions of the 1828 census of New South Wales edited, with the use of computer technology, by M.R. Sainty and K. Johnson (1980).

The year 1981 saw the first release by official cemetery trustees of records for public use when the Broken Hill City Council issued on 40 microfiches details of burials since 1890. This was followed by the release on microfiches of Karrakatta Cemetery Board's *Burial and cremation index* (1982) and A.G. Peake's listing of the West Terrace cemetery (1983). The journals of the various genealogical societies contain occasional cemetery listings and these periodicals should be consulted in a search for information from burial grounds.

Birth, marriage and death registration records are the responsibility of a government authority in each state. Regarded as confidential, the indexes, as well as the actual records, were for many years not open to the public, a practice which differed from that of the British authorities. To compensate for the lack of easy access to these vital records, the Sydney genealogists Malcolm Sainty and Keith Johnson produced a four-volume index (1972–75) and B.W. Champion began publishing the results of his indexing efforts for the Hunter valley district in 1973; by the time the last part was published in 1978, Champion's index had reached 23 volumes.

Changing social attitudes as well as increasing demand for use of birth, death and marriage records for genealogical and historical purposes resulted in the publication in the early 1980s of microform indexes to the nineteenth-century records held by all the state registrars. An important feature of the Tasmanian indexes was that they were accompanied by copies of the actual registration records. Tasmania was the first state to release copies of original records but New South Wales followed suit in late 1984 when it released on microfilm its *Genealogical research kit*, which includes records of births, deaths and marriages, shipping arrivals, convict records and the statistical compilations known as *Blue books*. A closely related source of information, the probate records of the Supreme Court of New South Wales were made available by the court in 1984 as a microfilm entitled *Probate index 1800–1982*.

An unusual publication in 1983 was a transcript of the entries from the registers of the South Creek Church at St Mary's, New South Wales. The three volumes, entitled simply *South Creek registers* (1983), list baptisms, burials and marriages for various periods between 1840 and 1981. Genealogists had not previously ventured into publishing transcripts of Australian parish registers, partly because of the limited market and partly because Australian church authorities did not always approve of genealogy or its practitioners. The issues of privacy and confidentiality were sensitive because records might reveal convict origins, illegitimacy, suicide and so on. However, vital records were maintained by the several religious denominations from the following dates: 1825 Church of England; 1834 Roman Catholic Church and Presbyterian Church; 1839 Wesleyan Methodist Society; 1840 Congregationalists, Independents and Baptists. Obviously these records are based on information voluntarily supplied by those who were members of the respective religious groups.

Records of some Australian births and marriages are also included in the *International genealogical index*, produced as computer-output microfiche by the Mormon Church in the United States of America. An updated version is issued about every three years.

The Australian Institute of Genealogical Studies took the initiative of organising the first Australian congress on family history. Held in Melbourne in 1977, as the Australasian Congress on Genealogy and Heraldry, it set the pattern for later conferences, held every three years, and attracted well-qualified speakers as well as good attendances. The proceedings of these congresses (Adelaide, 1980; Hamilton, New Zealand, 1983) have been published under various titles. From the first congress resulted the formation of the Australasian Federation of Family History Organisations (AFFHO) and the Australasian Association of Genealogists and Record Agents, both based loosely on their English counterparts. AFFHO produced only one newsletter in 1979, but the federation was revived in 1984 and more regular meetings have been held since. The triennial Congress on Genealogy and Heraldry is now held under the auspices of AFFHO and plans were developed in 1984 for publishing projects and other activities of a co-operative nature.

A specialised genealogical aid is the 'interest register'. Most societies invite their members to submit a list of surnames being researched, together with date range and place of residence of forbears. These lists are consolidated and published from time to time by the particular society as a service to members, bringing together genealogists researching the same name or family. In 1981 the Library of Australian History began publishing its annual *Genealogical research directory*; entries are sought from members of all Australian family history organisations and are also solicited overseas.

Before publication commenced, in the late 1970s, of the interest registers of societies' members, the only source available to researchers seeking to contact people interested in the same family or region was a column in the magazine *Parade*. Charles Bateson ran the 'Know your ancestors' column from 1970 until his death in July 1974. Lorne Greville took over the column after Bateson's death, but 'Know your ancestors' ceased in November 1980. Vera Cobden's index to the names mentioned in 'Know your ancestors' was published in 1983 by the Heraldry and Genealogy Society of Canberra.

A comparison over several years of the pages of the *Australian national bibliography* shows how genealogy has progressed in Australia. One criticism levelled at genealogists was that they neither contributed to the pool of biographical and historical knowledge nor advanced scholarship in any way, because they so rarely made public the results of their research. Those few who did publish often lacked the experience to recognise the need for an index, for bibliographical notes, good maps, footnotes or references, correct bibliographic citations, and so on. Higher standards have been encouraged by the Alexander Henderson prize for the best family history, an annual award instituted by the Australian Institute of Genealogical Studies to promote a high standard in the presentation and publication of such works.

Until the late 1970s periodical articles on family history were usually published only in the journals of the small number of genealogical societies. However, examination of *APAIS* shows that since 1977 the occasional article also occurred outside the regular genealogical journals, particularly in historical serial publications and academic journals. Family history is increasingly used in schools as a means of introducing students to historical concepts and the research process.

Little has been written on Aboriginal genealogy, but information can be found in the *Handbook for Aboriginal and Islander history* (Canberra, Aboriginal History, 1979) and in a paper by B.C. Mollison issued by the University of Tasmania's Psychology Department on Tasmanian Aboriginal genealogies (1976).

The growing number of Australian family historians anxious to have easy access to reputable sources on British origins led to the publication of two books by English genealogists in special Australian editions, although examination indicates few amendments to the text to deal with Australian research problems. One suspects that these texts were really aimed at the larger American market and, though of limited use to the Australian researcher, *Debrett's guide to tracing your ancestry* (Melbourne, Sun Books, 1982) and Baxter (1983) are worth remembering when the main aim is to identify British ancestry.

The challenge for writers of the next decades will be in meeting the needs of Australian family historians with ancestors whose homeland might have been, for example, Cambodia, Laos, Vietnam, Turkey or the Lebanon. There is still much writing to be done on the subject and there always will be, as long as individuals have curiosity about their origins and find the search for identity a fascinating intellectual jigsaw puzzle.

TRACING YOUR ANCESTORS

ANCESTORS for Australians: a guide book for beginners which points the way to wider horizons of genealogy (rev edn). Ed by B.R. Blaze; comp by M.E. Runting. Melbourne, Genealogical Society of Vic, 1981. 99 p, illus.

This guide will help beginners to realise what information is available and where it can be found. First published in 1974, the guide is regularly revised.

BAXTER, A. *In search of your British and Irish roots: a complete guide to tracing your English, Welsh, Scottish, and Irish ancestors.* Sydney, Methuen, 1983. 304 p.

A useful guide.

BRIEF guide to genealogical sources. Melbourne, Australian Archives, Victorian Branch, 1982. 17 p.

A select introductory guide aimed at the beginner.

BROWN, F. *et al, Family and local history sources in Victoria* Melbourne, Custodians of Records, 1983– .

An essential tool for Victorian research. Gives address, opening hours, special access conditions and an indication of major holdings for each repository.

CANDY, P.C. *State Library of South Australia: sources for genealogy* (rev edn). Adelaide, State Library of SA, 1983. 14 p.

Source for genealogical research, with particular reference to SA. First published in 1979.

DAVIES, E.V. *Researching your family history: a guide for school students.* Canberra, The Author, 1982. 18 p.

Written by a schoolteacher as a practical guide for coursework in primary schools.

GEEVES, P. *Our family history.* A & R, 1983. 144 p, illus.

The book has been specially designed for Australians recording their family history.

GRAY, N. *Compiling your family history: a guide to procedure* (12th edn). Sydney, Society of Australian Genealogists, 1983. 40 p.

A step-by-step approach to research procedures and services in Australia and overseas, with advice on keeping a record of data collected. First published in 1965.

HANSEN, N.T. *Guide to genealogical sources: Australia and New Zealand.* Melbourne, Melbourne State Presidency and Melbourne Genealogical Committee, Church of Jesus Christ of Latter-day Saints, 1963. 348 p.

Explanatory notes to the sources and places where they may be used. Some details now out of date.

J.S. BATTYE LIBRARY OF WEST AUSTRALIAN HISTORY. *Tracing your ancestors: a guide to genealogical sources in the J.S. Battye Library of West Australian History.* Perth, Library Board of WA, 1983. 38 p.

Compiled to assist visitors to the Battye Library.

LEA-SCARLETT, E. *Roots and branches: ancestry for Australians.* Sydney, Collins, 1979. 232 p, illus.

Detailed, practical information for family historians on how to find the most profitable sources. There is no bibliography and the index could have been improved by more subject entries.

THE PARISH map in family history research. Sydney, Crown Lands Office, Dept of Local Government and Lands, 1982. 6 leaves, maps.

A succinct guide to reading and understanding maps.

PEAKE, A.G. *Sources for South Australian family history.* Adelaide, A.G. Peake and South Australian Genealogy and Heraldry Society, 1977. 79 p.

A beginners' guide.

PUTTOCK, A.G. *Tracing your family tree for Australians and New Zealanders* (rev edn). Melbourne, Lothian, 1981. 114 p.

First published in 1979, this practical guide offers help to those who want to trace their ancestors. Not free from some glaring errors of fact.

SOUTH AUSTRALIAN ARCHIVES. *Guide to sources of genealogical information held in the South Australian Archives* (rev edn). Adelaide, South Australian Archives, 1983. 14 p.

An annotated list of the principal sources for genealogical research, mostly state government records, in the South Australian Archives. First published in 1979.

TANKEY, M. 'A blueprint for action', *Australian J of Chinese affairs* 6, 1981, 189–95.

An article about researching ancestry of Chinese immigrants in Australia.

VICTORIA. Public Record Office. *Genealogical sources.* Melbourne, The Office, 1984.

Leaflet giving general information on procedure and types of archival sources.

VINE HALL, N.J. ed, *English parish register transcripts: a list of all known transcripts of English parish registers held in Australian libraries* (rev edn). Sydney, Society of Australian Genealogists, 1982. 142 p.

This work notes a large number of parish register transcripts 1538–1837, including records of baptisms, marriages and burials. First published in 1980.

WALDRON, L.O. *Trace your ancestors: student basic course.* Brisbane, K.L.A.N. Genealogical Supplies, 1982. 48 p, illus.

For beginners; covers basic topics such as research methods, record keeping, sources for research.

GENEALOGICAL SOCIETIES AND CONGRESSES

AUSTRALASIAN CONGRESS ON GENEALOGY AND HERALDRY, Melbourne, 1977. *Genealogy in a changing society: proceedings of the first Australasian Congress on Genealogy and Heraldry, Melbourne, Easter, 1977.* Melbourne, Australian, Institute of Genealogical Studies, 1980. 372 p, illus.

Papers include archival sources, overseas research, publishing.

AUSTRALASIAN CONGRESS ON GENEALOGY AND HERALDRY, 2nd, Adelaide, 1980. *Genealogical papers: 1980 genealogy congress.* Adelaide, South Australian Genealogy and Heraldry Society, 1981. 68 p, illus.

An excellent set of papers, containing valuable contributions on military records, Jewish and Lutheran history, Australian and overseas record sources.

AUSTRALASIAN CONGRESS ON GENEALOGY AND HERALDRY, 3rd, University of Waikato, 1983. *Under the Southern Cross: papers ... presented at the 3rd Australasian Congress on Genealogy and Heraldry, Hamilton, New Zealand, 13–16 May 1983.* Hamilton, NZ, New Zealand Society of Genealogists, 1983. 307 p.

New Zealand research interests are well catered for, and so is immigration, United Kingdom records, heraldry and so on .

LEA-SCARLETT, E. *Society of Australian Genealogists 1932–1982.* Sydney, The Society, 1982. 96 p.

Commemorative work to record the history of the Society of Australian Genealogists.

SOCIETY OF AUSTRALIAN GENEALOGISTS. *Guide to the library.* Sydney, The Society, 1983. 50 p.

Comprehensive guide to the society's library, housed at

Richmond Villa in Sydney, its classification and content, indexes, microform projects, primary records and archives. The guide is regularly revised.

WOMEN'S PIONEER SOCIETY OF AUSTRALASIA. *Our pioneer ancestors.* Sydney, The Society, 1982. 148 p, illus.

A collection of the history of various members' ancestors. They are based on stories retold to members or from historical records.

PUBLISHED RECORDS AND LISTINGS

BERRYMAN, I. ed, *A colony detailed: the first census of Western Australia, 1832.* Perth, Creative Research, 1979. 182 p, illus.

Analysis of 1832 census, giving a numerical listing, an alphabetical listing and notes on the people therein.

CHAMPION, B.W. *Family entries, births, deaths, marriages, with some personalities, institutions, and oddments in the Hunter valley district: register.* Newcastle, NSW, The Author, 1973–78.

This important index was published in four series: 1843–84 (6 vols); 1884–90 (6 vols); 1891–1900 (6 vols); 1901–05 (5 vols). The spine title of the series is 'Hunter valley register'.

CHAPMAN, D. *1788: the people of the first fleet.* Sydney, Cassell, 1981. 207 p, illus, maps.

A readable and accurate collection of biographies; length of entry dictated by ready availability of sources. Includes names of marines and naval officers as well as convicts.

COBDEN, V. *Parade magazine: index to know your ancestors, 1971–1980.* Canberra, Heraldry and Genealogy Society of Canberra, 1983.

An index to names featured in the genealogy column 'Know your ancestors' 1970–80, giving details of issue and date when the reader's query appeared in *Parade.*

COBLEY, J. *Crimes of the first fleet convicts.* A & R, 1982. 324 p.

Contains meticulous biographical references, including name of convict, ship, age, occupation, date and place of trial. First published in 1970.

FILDON, P.G. AND RYAN, R.J. *The first fleeters: a comprehensive listing of convicts, marines, seamen, officers, wives, children, and ships.* Sydney, Australian Documents Library, 1981. 86 p.

An excellent index. Provides basic information on names, aliases, spelling variations, status and ships.

HUGHES, I.A. *Passengers to Port Phillip from southern England and Ireland 1843–48.* Melbourne, The Author, 1981. 35 1.

Designed for genealogists, these lists are from 'Shipping intelligence' columns of newspapers. Hughes has also compiled lists of passengers to Port Phillip from commonwealth and foreign ports 1838–51 (1983), from Liverpool 1839–51 (1982), and from Scotland 1839–51 (1980).

JOHNSON, K.A. AND SAINTY, M.R. eds, *Genealogical research directory.* 1981–   . Sydney, Library of Australia History.

These annual directories list in alphabetical order the surnames that are being researched, the time period and place of residence. The directory refers readers to the name and address of contributor who submitted the entry. The annual directories complement each other as entries are not automatically resubmitted.

LAYCOCK, K.G. AND LAYCOCK, F.F. *Canberra district lives: birth, marriage and death notices from the Sydney Morning Herald, 1851–1875.* Canberra, K.G. and F.F. Laycock, 1979–81. 5 vols.

Total of 8251 entries directed towards Canberra district and the surrounding area within a radius of 160 kilometres.

LEASK, B.C. *Leask's genealogical guide to some Australian families, their antecedents and genealogies.* Melbourne, Australian Genealogies, 1979. 774 p.

A record of many families resident in Australia prior to 1900 or for three generations.

MOWLE, P.C. *A genealogical history of pioneer families of Australia.* Sydney, J. Sands, 1939. 142 p.

Detailed genealogies (updated to mid-1970s) of families of 93 pioneers who came to Australia between 1788 and 1838 as free settlers. Fifth edition, revised by L.M. Mowle, published in 1978.

PEAKE, A.G. *Sources for South Australian biography.* Adelaide, The Author, 1982. 145 p.

Provides details of record sources, indexes and finding aids that could be valuable for researchers.

RYAN, R.J. *The second fleet convicts: a comprehensive listing of convicts who sailed in HMS Guardian, Lady Juliana, Neptune, Scarborough and Surprise.* Sydney, Australian Documents Library, 1982. 95 p.

RYAN, R.J. *The third fleet convicts: an alphabetical listing of names, giving place and date of conviction, length of sentence and ship of transportation.* Sydney, Horwitz Grahame, 1983. xiv, 126 p, illus.

Alphabetical listings, with aliases and spelling variations, from records in the State Archives of NSW.

RYAN, R.J. ed, *Land grants, 1788–1809.* Sydney, Australian Documents Library, 1981. 327 p.

A record of registered grants and leases in NSW, Van Diemen's Land and Norfolk Island reproduced from the original record in the State Archives of NSW.

SAINTY, M.R. AND JOHNSON, K.A. *Index to birth, marriage, death and funeral notices in the* Sydney Herald *1831–1842 and* Sydney Morning Herald *1842–1853.* Sydney, Genealogical Publications of Australia, 1972–75. 4 vols.

This useful index is based on the major newspaper in Sydney at the time.

SAINTY, M.R. AND JOHNSON, K.A. eds, *Census of New South Wales, November 1828.* Sydney, Library of Australian History, 1980. 475 p, illus, maps.

A record of over 36 500 persons by age, status, ship and year of arrival (or born in the colony), religion, occupation, employer, abode, together with surname index and cross-reference index of employers, and various appendices.

SMEE, C.J. AND PROVIS, J.S. *The 1788–1820 Association's pioneer register* (2nd edn). Sydney, The Association, 1981. 2 vols.

Genealogical details of 500 pioneers of NSW and Van Diemen's Land, their children and grandchildren, with chronology of historic events and early churches. Not free from some errors of fact.

VITAL REGISTERS AND GRAVEYARD INSCRIPTIONS

DALKIN, R.N. *Colonial era cemetery of Norfolk Island.* Sydney, Pacific Publications, 1981. 91 p, illus.

An important photographic record of extant Norfolk Island tombstones. First published in 1974.

DAVIDSON, J. AND DOXFORD, H. *Grave reflections.* Vol 1. *An alphabetical listing of burial sites in the central goldfields area of Victoria, with a selection of tombstones of interest.* Melbourne, H. Doxford, 1982. 98 p, illus, map.

Listing of 71 cemeteries, giving location , physical condition, a few selected inscriptions. Contains photographs of interesting examples of the stonemason's craft and an excellent map.

GOODWIN, V.W.E. *Monumental inscriptions and key to graves*

[in] St John's cemetery, Parramatta. Sydney, Society of Australian Genealogists, 1964. 115 p.

Introduction to and record of original burial ground at Parramatta, Australia's second settlement.

GRAHAM, E.C. *Births, deaths and marriages from the* Argus *newspaper,* Melbourne, 1846–1853. Melbourne, The Author, 1983–84. 4 vols, illus.

This limited edition is a valuable addition to indexes to nineteenth-century newspapers.

JOHNSON, K.A. AND SAINTY, M.R. *Gravestone inscriptions, N.S.W.* Vol 1. *Sydney burial ground.* Sydney, Genealogical Publications of Australia, 1973. 193 p, illus, maps.

Transcript of inscriptions on monuments (deciphered 1969–71) relocated at Bunnerong (adjoining Botany cemetery) in 1901 from the 'Sandhills' cemetery, Elizabeth and Devonshire streets, Sydney, with introduction and reference notes.

JONES, J. McD. *History in stone, Penrith (New South Wales): a genealogical study of headstones, St Stephen the Martyr Church of England.* Sydney, The Author, 1976. 184 p, illus.

This tribute to the memory of the settlers who lived and died in an earlier era of Penrith's history contains records of burials in St Stephen's cemetery, with headstone transcriptions.

JONES, J. McD. AND JONES, P.K. *Nepean district cemetery records 1806–1976.* Sydney, J. McD. Jones, 1977. 253 p, illus, map.

Historical introduction and transcript of inscriptions on memorial stones in cemeteries in the Nepean district of NSW.

LEA-SCARLETT, E. *St Thomas's Church of England, North Sydney: monumental inscriptions in the cemetery.* Sydney, Society of Australian Genealogists, 1963. Unpaged.

Record of St Thomas's churchyard opened in 1845, the first appointed burial ground in the area between the north shore of Sydney Harbour and Pennant Hills.

LORD, R. *Inscriptions in stone: St David's burial ground, 1804–1872: a record of some early history of Hobart Town from the head stones of Van Diemen's Land's first cemetery.* Hobart, St George's Church, 1976. 210 p, illus.

A useful work for Tasmanian genealogist.

LORD, R. *Inscriptions in stone, the Isle of the Dead, Port Arthur: inscriptions from the cemetery of the Port Arthur penal establishment 1830–1877.* Taroona, Tas, R. Lord and Partners, 1976. 81 p, illus.

There were 180 civil and military burials on the island; of these, 76 monumental inscriptions survive. Some 1769 convicts were

also buried but only the headstone of John Owen has been found.

MACKEY, N.M. *Clarence River register: births, deaths and marriages.* Grafton, NSW, N.M. Mackey and J.M. Buetitude, 1983– . v.

Several volumes have been produced in this series, containing entries from church registers of the Clarence River district since 1859.

MORGAN, M.J. *The old Melbourne cemetery, 1837–1922.* Melbourne, Australian Institute of Genealogical Studies, 1982. 314 p, illus.

Brief history of the cemetery with various indexes to burials and facsimile copy of inscriptions on tombstones.

NORCOTT, L. *et al, South Creek registers.* np, 1983. 3 vols.

The three volumes contain entries from the registers of South Creek Church, St Mary's NSW, for broken periods 1840–1981.

PEAKE, A.G. ed, *Inscriptions from West Terrace cemetery, Adelaide.* Vol 1. *Catholic and Society of Friends sections.* Adelaide, A.G. Peake, 1982. 337 leaves.

Transcripts of inscriptions on monuments in Adelaide's largest cemetery.

QUEANBEYAN pioneer cemeteries: register of the Oaks burial ground and headstone sections at Riverside and Tharwa Road. Queanbeyan, NSW, Queanbeyan City Council in conjunction with Queanbeyan and District Historical Museum Society, 1982–84. 2 vols.

Listings of inscriptions arranged in order by cemetery plot. Lacks an index, but this may constitute a future volume.

RAY, P.M. AND THOM, G.R. *Monumental inscriptions.* Canberra, Heraldry and Genealogy Society of Canberra, 1977.

To 1984 three volumes have been issued in this series: ACT and Jervis Bay (1977), Monaro (1982) and Young (1984). Maps and historical notes are included for many cemeteries, the volumes being comprehensive for the areas covered.

STUBBS, L. AND STUBBS, R. eds, *Gravestones of the Hawkesbury.* Windsor, NSW, Ladam, 1982. 56 leaves.

The first of a series, this listing contains inscriptions of headstones in burial grounds in the historic Hawkesbury River region.

THOM, G. *Register of cemetery transcriptions held by member organizations.* Canberra, Australasian Federation of Family History Organizations, 1980. 33 p.

A list of records held by various societies, this publication does not include the holdings of the Society of Australian Genealogists as it was not at the time a member of the federation.

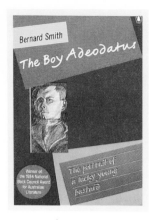

Bernard Smith, The boy Adeodatus, *Penguin, Ringwood, Vic, 1984. Cover illustration by Bernard Smith, self-portrait (c1938). Cover design by Kim Roberts.*

CHAPTER 20

BIOGRAPHY

D. H. BORCHARDT AND JULIE G. MARSHALL

ALTHOUGH INDIVIDUALS are no longer regarded as the main influence in the making of history, as was the fashion fifty and more years ago, people have retained their curiosity about the lives of individual Australians of note. Biography, or the literature relating to persons and personal data, is extensive and varied; a library dedicated to collecting this type of material would be very large and reflect, as much as any collection can, the whole history of Australia.

It is useful to distinguish three categories of books that make up the literature of biography. One consists of directory-type publications that tell us basic facts about people such as their address, occupational details and other information according to the objectives of the sponsors and editors; occasionally they include personal data such as the date of birth, academic attainments, public distinctions and so on. This kind of directory, of which the telephone directory is perhaps the best known and simplest example, may be produced by professional groups or by government offices for purposes of maintaining a public register of licensed performers of particular skills (such as teachers, medical practitioners or clergymen) or by political organisations to ensure the performance of social obligations like voting or paying dues.

Totally different from this first category is the mass of studies of individual persons; this second group is best known as biographical literature. It is a large category, marked by some of our greatest and most competent writers. Biographies and autobiographies of Australians from almost all walks of life fill many rows of shelves in our libraries and are a staple in our bookshops. Whether indeed this preoccupation is prompted by idle curiosity, or by a genuine endeavour to understand the past through one person's reactions, or by a healthy interest in the achievements of others, it is worth noting that in spite of the current anti-individualistic trend of our history schools, many people continue to purchase or borrow biographical literature.

A special category within this genre is the autobiography. If the biographer needs the skills of a historian as well as those of a writer, the autobiographer also requires an ability to distance himself or herself from the subject (the self) and to adhere to a level of objectivity that is undoubtedly hard to attain. As may be expected, these ideal requirements cannot always be noted among the examples of autobiography that stud our literary landscape and it would be an invidious task to single out those authors who meet our criteria.

There exists, unfortunately, no up-to-date list of all the Australian biographies and autobiographies that have been published in book form. Besides, many short notes and thumbnail sketches of recently deceased or contemporary persons appear in journals, society records, transactions of professional groups and company resorts—and their brevity is often a considerable advantage. While the monographs can be traced through the *Australian national bibliography*, the biographical articles in the periodical literature are captured in the National Library's *Australian public affairs information service*. Both these reference tools are described in chapter 8 of this volume.

The third category is an interesting variant of the full-scale biography. It is represented by a large class of books that provide more information about people than a mere street address while falling far short of a full biographical study. This type of work usually provides some form of assessment of individuals within a group of others with whom they have a certain affinity, either because of a common background or occupation, or some other common life experience. The overriding characteristic of this category of biographical literature is that it deals with individuals collectively—though we should note that the collective may be of varying size. Furthermore, while every work of collective biography has some common denominator as a raison d'être, there is no form of national access to the individuals included in each compilation. The only, though very important, guidance we have is that normally we would expect to find a famous woman painter in a biographical reference work or collection of biographies on women painters, and that a renowned medical practitioner is more likely to be listed in a collection of biographical essays on medical researchers than on Methodist ministers. If appropriate they could of course be in both types of works.

The bibliography that follows has been restricted to collective biographies as represented by reference works listing individuals at the national and state or regional level. Besides the standard current reference works containing details of the life of leading Australian citizens, and of many others as well, readers will find listed several older sources, perhaps compiled by different standards but nevertheless of considerable importance for the historian and excellent starting points for would-be biographers. Special attention is drawn below to the numerous categories of collective biography left unquoted but readers' attention is drawn to the fact that the topics included in this volume for Australian studies include many citations of biographical writing which complement this chapter. In addition, readers will find supplementary material in D.H. Borchardt's *Australian bibliography* (3rd edn, Sydney, Pergamon, 1979) which, though somewhat aged, lists many reference books still useful on this topic.

The emphasis here, then, is on those sources commonly known as the 'who is who' type of reference work. The quality of such reference works depends entirely on the basis of compilation—whether the data listed have been supplied by those included or whether they are based on research undertaken by others. A third possibility is, of course, that the data provided by those listed have been closely checked for accuracy by the editorial staff of the work.

There is an obvious and close link between the preceding chapter (19: Genealogy) and these notes and listings on biography. These two sections should be read together, for titles listed in each section will serve well as sources for both biographical and genealogical research.

Certain criteria of exclusion had to be established and are noted here to ensure that readers will not seek in vain for unlisted titles. Works on local and regional history have been excluded unless their biographical content is particularly strong: Margaret Kiddle's *Men of yesterday* (MUP, 1961) and Ravenscroft's history of the Snowy Mountains were considered outside the scope of this survey. There are hundreds of such works, often sponsored or commissioned by communities of all kinds—local councils, church groups, school parents' associations, rural societies and many others—to celebrate a significant anniversary and bent upon listing everybody who was linked, however remotely, to the group or association. All too often they contain a mere mention of many names, but little detail about the persons involved—and certainly no biographical detail beyond, maybe, a note on age and on activities relevant to the history of the group. The people cited or described have been mentioned to enliven the tale—as indeed this approach to local history frequently does—but they are of limited value as sources of biography.

The exclusion of collective biographies concerned with professional and other affinity groups may well appear to be the most serious shortcoming of this listing. There exist hundreds of such collective biographies containing accounts of artists, lawyers, medicos, members of the military, politicians, preachers, sportspersons, teachers, women, ethnic groups and so on. The compilers are conscious of the importance of this class of literature and an attempt is now being made, by D.H. Borchardt and Sandra Burr, to overcome the difficulty by compiling a 'Checklist of collective Australian biographies' which should appear late in 1987. It does not claim to be exhaustive but its hundreds of entries, arranged in major occupational or professional groups, indicate the large volume of this category of biographical writing. Another group of collective biographies excluded here is that addressed to schools and younger readers.

A significant source of biographical data is represented by the several state-oriented *Cyclopedias* that appeared at the beginning of this century and by the modern encyclopaedias, particularly the *Australian encyclopaedia* in its several editions. The most important of these are listed in chapter 7 and readers should consult the comments made there.

Reference has already been made to the professional, political or social registers that will offer some help in the identification of individuals. An example of this source of information on individual members of the teaching profession is the list of registered teachers held by state education authorities—indeed, at times some of the states have seen fit to publish lists of all their senior civil servants. Another example is the *Directory of members* of the Sociological Association of Australia and New Zealand (Sydney, 1971). Some of these membership lists are updated regularly, while others remain uncorrected for years on end. None can claim to be a biography, and they have therefore not been included in this bibliography. Furthermore, few of them are national lists because the control of professional registration rests in most instances with the state authorities. Nevertheless they contain personal data which may help biographers and historians, and for that reason further mention is made of them below in the discussion of archival material relating to individuals.

There exist some large-scale biographical indexes produced in Europe and the United States which, while claiming to be international in character, do not include numerically significant data on Australia. To mention just some current works, neither the *Biography and genealogy master index* (Detroit, Mich, Gale Research Co) nor *Prominent scientists: an index to collective biography* (New York, Neal-Schuman) lists Australian works among its information sources; *Current biography* (New York, H.W. Wilson), though it includes *Who's who in Australia* among its data bases, does not contain more than the odd reference to Australians. In this context they are of minimal significance and have not been listed or discussed further.

The most important sources of biographical information are the 'who is who' type of reference works or, with respect to our 'rude forefathers', the compilations best referred to as the 'who was who' type. While the criterion of inclusion for the first type is simply achievement and community respect, the latter category contains only the names of dead persons who fill, in the eyes of the compiler, a sort of pantheon for particular classes of endeavours. Yet it is this type of biographical register which, if based on genuine research, creates the foundations of historical writing. Many countries have seen fit to cause such a biographical register to be compiled, sometimes through their national academies, sometimes through historical commissions.

Australia embarked on such an enterprise in 1966 and by 1986 ten of the projected twelve volumes of the *Australian dictionary of biography* (*ADB*) had appeared. Unquestionably the largest and most scholarly source of Australian biographical information, the *ADB* is the product of a well-organised Australia-wide co-operative effort, centred on the Australian National University. A national committee and appropriate state-based working parties determined the selection of contributors as well as the names to be included in the *ADB*. The principal criteria for inclusion, as explained by the first editor, Douglas Pike, have been that the persons were important to Australia and had set foot on Australian soil, however briefly; furthermore, those selected for inclusion must be dead. In spite of the large number of names listed, many suggested entries could not be followed up for want of material on which to base a reliable biographical entry. The *ADB* headquarters at the Australian National University maintains an index of all names put forward for inclusion and the file may be consulted on application.

J.G. Marshall and R.C.S. Trahair have compiled an interesting supplement to the *ADB* (1979, 1985) which lists the names in the *ADB* according to the main occupation cited. Their index is an important aid to social and population analyses of nineteenth-century Australia.

The *ADB* is divided into three chronological sequences with entries in each sequence arranged alphabetically over the constituent volumes. There are two volumes for the period 1788–1850; four volumes for 1851–90; and there will be six volumes for the period 1891–1939. To conclude this note on Australia's most important collective biography, here is what the historian A.W. Martin wrote when reviewing the first two volumes in *Hist Stud* (12, 1967, 584–6):

> It is already clear that, in one vital respect the *Dictionary* will certainly be more than a mere reference tool: to read consecutively through the entries on the governors (with supplementary cross-reading of relevant q.v.'s) will in effect be to read a crisp and rewarding little history of the colony concerned. It is a tribute to the skill of the editorship that this exercise repeatedly reveals as between entries a continuity of thematic emphasis ...

Earlier efforts to list all who contributed to the history and development of Australia are, of course, deficient merely by the effluction of time—Heaton (1879) Mennell (1892) and Serle (1949)—while others like the Royal Commonwealth Society's *Biography catalogue* (1961) were based on criteria of inclusion that were lacking in definition.

Of the numerous biographical directories that deal with the living, the Herald and Weekly Times' *Who's who in Australia* is the best known and most reliable. A series of responsible editors have ensured, over the years, that the criteria for inclusion would measure up to a national consensus regarding the importance of those listed. Data are supplied on a standardised form by those included and there seems to be some check on details. *Who's who in Australia* appears every three years and includes appendices showing membership of particular groups such as officers of the Order of Australia.

The second part of the bibliography below lists state or regional works of collective biography. The justification for inclusion has been the general usefulness of the work cited; even a dated or local restricted list of persons can be of great help to the researcher. Again it is stressed that this bibliography of collective biography should be used in conjunction with Borchardt and Burr's checklist noted earlier. For instance, while H. Munz's *Jews in South Australia* (Adelaide, Tornquest, 1936) might well qualify as a regional work, it seemed more useful to include it in the checklist with other works on Jewish settlers.

Those who are interested in pursuing biographical studies will find that the resources vary considerably according to subject. Students may be well advised to consult the biography indexes maintained by the state libraries, the National Library and numerous other institutions where they are usually kept in vertical files, made up from newspaper cuttings, photocopies of magazine articles, snippets from commercial in-house journals and so on.

Many of the larger newspapers, and some of the weekly, monthly and quarterly magazines concerned with political and social issues, maintain a clipping file for biographical data. These files and indexes may be inspected on application. Biography indexes like these will help to identify the more public facets of the subject's life—the date of his or her birth or death, public offices held, involvement in social, professional or charitable activities. It is from the data thus gleaned that the next steps in biographical research evolve. Associations tend to keep records of membership and activities and such records should be sought. They may consist of minutes of meetings, membership of committees, correspondence and of course membership lists.

The public life of those who have become renowned is usually a great deal easier to ascertain than their private life. Yet nobody lives only a public life and good biographers will do their utmost to discover the real people through their relationship with others, their tastes and habits, their off-duty preoccupations. Biographers therefore will have to seek access to private diaries, letters, recollections of the subject's family and close friends. If the subject has been dead for some time, such personal sources may be hard to find, but therein lies the challenge, and in the end, the merit of a biography depends on the proper use that has been made of these resources.

GENERAL BIOGRAPHICAL DICTIONARIES

1000 famous Australians. Adelaide, Rigby, 1978. 368 p, illus.
Superficial sketches with entries arranged by occupation.

AUSTRALIAN dictionary of biography. MUP, 1966–   . v.
Ten volumes of this projected twelve-volume work had been published by 1986. Vols 1–2 cover 1788–1850; vols 3–6, 1851–90; vols 7–12, 1891–1939. For description see essay.

BURKE, B. *A genealogical and heraldic history of the colonial gentry*. London, Heraldry Today, 1970. 862 [xxvi] p.
First published in 1897. Includes Australian members of the British peerage, but these cannot be identified as such through the index.

DEBRETT'S handbook of Australia and New Zealand. Ed by S. Duke. Sydney, Debrett's Peerage, 1982. 703 p.
A current who's who. Includes essays on ceremonial forms, genealogical research etc. Not as extensive as *Who's who in Australia*. Scheduled to be updated every two or three years.

DEBRETT's peerage and baronetage. Australian edition 1980 . . . comprises information concerning the Royal Family, the peerage, privy counsellors, Scottish Lords of Sessions, baronets, chiefs of names and clans in Scotland and Australian honours list: ed by Patrick Montague-Smith. London, Debrett's Peerage, 1980. Various paging, illus.
Title on spine: Australian edition. This is essentially the English gentry's biographical bible, with an Australian chapter added.

DE BRUNE, C.F.A. *Fifty years of progress in Australia, 1878–1928*. Sydney, Halstead Printing Co, 1929. 310 p, illus.
One-quarter of the volume lists 'well known citizens of the period'.

DIGBY, E. ed, *Australian men of mark*. Sydney, C.F. Maxwell, 1889. 2 vols, illus.
Contains 200 full and 700 brief adulatory biographies intended to show the forces that shaped Australia's first hundred years. Many portraits. Most entries relate to persons from NSW. There were four different editions of the second volume.

HEATON, J.H. *The bedside book of colonial doings*. A & R, 1984. 272 p, illus.
First published in 1879 as *Australian dictionary of dates and men of the time*. A general reference work, half of which contains biographies of notable Australians, lists of members of various occupations and professions and, under subject headings, hundreds of persons who 'made' the newspapers of the period. The absence of an index makes it difficult to use.

JOHNS, F. *An Australian biographical dictionary*. Melbourne, Macmillan, 1934. 386 p.
Based on the mass of data collected by Fred Johns over decades in his preparation of *Who's who in Australia* and left unused at his death, this retrospective work was prepared for publication by B.S. Roach.

KENYON, A.S. *The story of Australia, its discoverers and founders*. Geelong, Vic, Corio, 1940. 635 p, illus.
Essentially a history through biography, of the Deuteronomy type. Lists hundreds of names associated with the growth of Australia to 1939. Binder's title: Founders of Australia and their descendants.

LEAVITT, T.W.H. *Australian representative men*. Melbourne, Wells and Leavitt, 1887. 2 vols, illus.
Victorian counterpart to Digby's *Australian men of mark*, covers a wider range of people. Poorly produced. Many sketches were reused in Leavitt's *Jubilee history of Tasmania* and *Jubilee history of Victoria and Melbourne*.

MARSHALL, J.G. AND TRAHAIR, R.C.S. *Occupational index to the* Australian dictionary of biography *(1788–1890)*, Bundoora, Vic, La Trobe University, Dept of Sociology, 1979, 1980. 2 vols.
For description, see essay.

MENNELL, P. *The dictionary of Australasian biography: comprising notices of eminent colonists from the inauguration of responsible government down to the present time (1855–1895)*. London, Hutchinson, 1892. 542 p.
Unsatisfactory with regard to detail but the range of persons included makes this a useful source of basic data.

SERLE, P. *Dictionary of Australian biography*. A & R, 1949. 2 vols.
Over 1000 short biographical sketches. Serle's work remained the most reliable source of biographical information until superseded by the *Australian dictionary of biography*.

ROYAL COMMONWEALTH SOCIETY. Library. *Biography catalogue of the library of the Royal Commonwealth Society, by Donald H. Simpson, librarian*. London, The Society, 1961. 511 p.
One of several catalogues of that library; the biographical references to Australians can be found on pp 423–9. The society's *Subject catalogue* contains supplementary material on Australian biography in its seventh volume, issued in 1971.

*WHO'S who in Australia 1906–   *. Melbourne, Herald and Weekly Times.
Title of earlier issues varies: 1st–2nd edn *Johns's notable Australians*; 3rd–5th edn *Fred Johns's annual*; 6th edn *Who's who in the Commonwealth of Australia*. Up to and including the issue for 1955 there was a useful obituary section, but this has since been discontinued. This work is not to be confused with the *Who's who in Australia* issued from 1922 to 1935 by the International Press Service Association in Melbourne and Sydney. For details see Borchardt, *Australian bibliography* (3rd edn, Sydney, Pergamon, 1976, p 137).

REGIONAL BIOGRAPHICAL SOURCES: New South Wales

BARKER, H. AND HAWKINS, R. *Early Wesleyans of Pennant Hills*. Sydney, Hornsby Shire Historical Society, 1983. 216 p, illus, map.
Includes biographies of early settlers of the Methodist persuasion.

BOWD, D.G. *Macquarie country: a history of the Hawkesbury* (Rev edn). Sydney, Library of Australian History, 1982. 242 p, illus, map.
As well as passing biographical references in the text, a portion of this work deals with prominent individuals and founders of Hawkesbury families. First published in 1979.

CROSS, R.L. AND SHEEBY, B. *Queanbeyan pioneers. First study: pocket biographies of 112 pioneers . . .* Queanbeyan, NSW, Queanbeyan Books and Prints, 1983. 233 p, illus, map.
A combined local history, complete with details of properties in 1885 and non-British residents to 1927, and biographies of the pioneers and their families and descendants.

ELDERSHAW, F.S.P. ed, *The peaceful army: a memorial to the pioneer women of Australia 1788–1938*. Sydney, Women's Executive Committee and Advisory Council of Australia's 150th Anniversary Celebration, 1938. 138 p, illus.
Early women writers and artists, biographies of Elizabeth Macarthur, Mary Reibey, Caroline Chisholm, Rose Scott and the Windeyers.

GIBBNEY, H.J. *Eurobodalla: history of the Moruya district*. Sydney, Library of Australian History in association with the Council of the Shire of Eurobodalla, 1980. 191 p, illus, maps.

In addition to many references to local residents the book contains brief biographical details of nearly ninety settlers in a special appendix.

MORRISON, W.F. *The Aldine centennial history of New South Wales, illustrated*. Sydney, Aldine Publishing Co, 1888. 2 vols, illus, maps.

A history through biography. Not very reliable.

NOTABLE citizens of Sydney. Sydney, Notable Publications of Australia, 1940. 301 p, illus.

SHINE, T. ed, *The Australian portrait gallery and memoirs of representative colonial men. Appendices: Constitution Act. History of the Soudan expedition*. Sydney, Southern Cross Publishing Co, 1885. *196, 115 p, illus*.

Collection of short biographies of leading figures in NSW first issued between 1884 and 1885, but later reprinted in one volume with two appendices.

SYDNEYITES as we see them 1913–14–15. Sydney, Newspaper Cartoonists' Association of NSW, 1915[?]. Unpaged, illus.

A cartoon-based collection of biographical notes, showing the head of the subject in a 'funny' scene allegedly representative of his (there are no women) character and preferred activities.

WHO'S who in the world of women, New South Wales, Australia . . . Sydney, Reference Press Association, 1936. Unpaged, illus.

Biographies with portraits of society women.

WYATT, R.T. *The history of Goulburn, N.S.W.* Goulburn, Municipality of Goulburn, 1941.

A local history which mentions hundreds of inhabitants of the district and contains biographical detail of the more prominent citizens. Facsimile edition, Lansdowne, 1972.

REGIONAL BIOGRAPHICAL SOURCES: Queensland

AUSTRALIAN HISTORY PUBLISHING CO. *Queensland and Queenslanders, incorporating prominent Queenslanders*. Brisbane, Brooks, 1936. 317 p, illus.

Biographical information usually a little more extensive than other Qld compilations in the period between Fox (1919–23) and World War II.

BARTLEY, N. *Australian pioneers and reminiscences*. Ed by J.J. Knight. Brisbane, Gordon & Gotch, 1896. 424 p, illus.

Mainly concerned with Queenslanders, but includes also some NSW pioneers.

BERNAYS, C.A. *Queensland politics during sixty years (1859–1919)*, Brisbane, Government Printer, 1919. 564 p, illus.

BERNAYS, C.A. *Queensland: our seventh political decade, 1920–1930*. A & R, 1931. 388 p, illus.

Notable character summations, based on the author's and his father's intimate knowledge of the period.

BLACK, J. *North Queensland pioneers*. Charters Towers, printed by the North Qld Newspaper Co, 1932. 110 p, illus.

Short description of the life and achievements of the early settlers in north Qld. Name and place index.

BROWNE, R.S. *A journalist's memories*. Brisbane, Read, 1927. 351 p, illus.

Condensation of articles in the *Brisbane Courier* of reminiscences, principally biographical, by a veteran Brisbane journalist. There is an index of those mentioned (towards 1500 names).

FOX, M.J. *History of Queensland, its people and industries*. Brisbane, States Publishing Co, 1919–23. 3 vols, illus, maps.

A rich but not always reliable source of biographical information, particularly on pastoralists.

HALL, T. *The early history of Warwick district and pioneers of the Darling Downs*. Toowoomba, printed by Robertson and Provan, 1935. 111 p.

LOYAU, G.E. *The history of Maryborough and Wide Bay and Burnett districts from the year 1850 to 1895*. Brisbane, Pole, Outridge, 1897. 385 p.

Includes biographical details of scores of persons not easily found elsewhere.

MEN OF Queensland: representative of the public, professional, ecclesiastical and business life of Queensland as existent in the year, 1928. Brisbane, Read, 1929. 197 p, illus.

MORRISON, W.F. *The Aldine history of Queensland*. Sydney, Aldine Publishing Co, 1888. 2 vols, illus.

A history through biography.

NEWSPAPER CARTOONISTS' ASSOCIATION OF QUEENSLAND. *Queenslanders as we see 'em, 1915*. Brisbane, The Association, 1916. 187 p, illus.

Shows photographs of faces set in cartoon framework, with brief biographies appended.

NOTABLE men of Queensland 1950, representative of the public, professional, ecclesiastical and business life of Queensland in this year of 1950 A.D. Brisbane, M.G. Macdougall for Consolidated Publications, 1950. unpaged, illus.

A Qld who's who of persons 'who are proving of value to the State in this year 1950'. A new edition appeared in 1975.

PUGH'S (Queensland) official almanac, directory and gazetteer. Brisbane, T.F. Pugh, 1859–1927.

This extremely useful source of information on the history, geography and administration of Qld also contains a wealth of data on individuals and groups who played a leading role in Australia's second largest state. Title varies.

QUEENSLAND, 1900: a narrative of her past together with biographies of her leading men. Brisbane, Alcazar, 1900. 371 p, illus.

A general history, to which has been added a series of over 150 biographical sketches.

REGIONAL BIOGRAPHICAL SOURCES: South Australia

BROWN, L. et al. *A book of South Australia: women in the first hundred years*. Adelaide, Rigby, 1936. 253 p, illus.

Pays tribute to pioneer women and outstanding women in the arts, education law, medicine and welfare.

CIVIC record of South Australia, 1921–3. Adelaide, Associated Publishing Service, 1924. 865 p, illus.

Includes biographical sketches of those who served in local government.

COCKBURN, R. *Pastoral pioneers of South Australia*. Adelaide, Stock and station journal, 1925–1927. 2 vols.

Short biographies, most of them with a small portrait, of the landed gentry in SA, emphasising achievement rather than character. Facsimile edition, Lynton Publications, 1974.

COCKBURN, S. *The patriarchs*. Adelaide, Ferguson Publications, 1983. 176 p, illus.

Profiles of 30 South Australian men and women from all walks of life whose average age, in 1983, was about 87 years.

LOYAU, G.E. *The representative men of South Australia.* Adelaide, George Howell, 1883. 264 p.

LOYAU, G.E. *Notable South Australians, or, colonists past and present.* Adelaide, Carey, Page, 1885. 288 p, illus.

Though uneven, the two volumes of South Australian biography are informative and reasonably reliable. Include over 600 leading personalities. Facsimile editions, Adelaide, Austaprint, 1978, include a name index.

MEN of South Australia: representative of the public, professional, ecclesiastical and business life of South Australia as existant in the year 1933. Adelaide, Men of SA, 1933. 106 p, illus.

A fairly reliable who's who.

MORRISON, W.F. *The Aldine history of South Australia.* Sydney, Aldine Publishing Co, 1890. 2 vols, illus, maps.

A history through biography.

OFFICIAL civic record of South Australia, centenary year, 1936. Adelaide, Universal Publicity Co, 1936. 962 p, illus.

Includes biographical sketches of local government councillors.

OLD COLONISTS' ASSOCIATION OF SOUTH AUSTRALIA. *An account of the celebration of the jubilee of South Australia, 1886, with the reminiscences of early settlers, the names of the pioneers who arrived in South Australia in the year 1836 . . .* Adelaide, The Association, 1887. 79 p.

PASCOE, J.A. ed, *History of Adelaide and vicinity with a general sketch of the province of South Australia and biographies of representative men.* Adelaide, Hussey and Gillingham, 1901. 691 p.

This interesting account includes a who's who of scores of South Australians considered important at the turn of the century. Facsimile edition, Austaprint, 1978.

PRICE, A.G. *Founders and pioneers of South Australia.* Adelaide, F.W. Preece and Sons, 1929, 266 p, illus, maps.

A more scholarly approach than most; discusses nine South Australians, with a bibliography of primary and secondary material. Facsimile edition, Adelaide, LBSA, 1973.

RICHARDSON, NORMAN A. *The pioneers of the north-west of South Australia, 1856 to 1914.* Adelaide, W.K. Thomas, 1925, 155 p, illus, map.

Facsimile edition, LBSA, 1969. Reprinted 1980.

SOUTH AUSTRALIAN biographies, 1980. Adelaide, V.C.D. Barnes, 1980. xv, 136 p.

Biographical details supplied by those included; this is simply a South Australian who's who.

WHO'S who in Adelaide, South Australia 1921–22. Adelaide, Associated Publishing Service, 1922. 129 p, illus.

WHO'S who: South Australia centenary, 1936. Adelaide, Amalgamated Publishing Co, 1936. 353 p, illus.

Includes contemporary portraits.

REGIONAL BIOGRAPHICAL SOURCES: Tasmania

BETHELL, L.S. *The valley of the Derwent.* Hobart, Government Printer, 195[9?]. 139 p, illus, maps.

LEAVITT, T.W.H. *Jubilee history of Tasmania . . .* Melbourne, Wells and Leavitt, 188[8?]. 2 vols, illus.

The biographies in this book also appear in *Australian representative men* and *Jubilee history of Victoria.*

McARTHUR, M. *Prominent Tasmanians.* Hobart, G.J. Boyle & Co, 1924. 88 p, illus.

PIKE, R.A. *Pioneers of Burnie: a sesquicentenary publication, 1827–1977.* Burnie, Tas, The Author, 1977. xii, 100 p.

VON STIEGLITZ, K.R. *The history of Bothwell and its early settlers at the Clyde in Van Dieman's Land.* Launceston, Telegraph Printery, 1958. 87 p, illus.

K.R. von Stieglitz, descendant of an early German settler in Tas, compiled numerous small books on the history of Tasmanian villages and small towns, each of which includes biographical sketches of the founding families and of leading personalities of the districts.

REGIONAL BIOGRAPHICAL SOURCES: Victoria

500 VICTORIANS' centenary edition, 1934. Melbourne, M.G. Henderson, 1934. 303 p, illus.

Biographical data are supplied in telegram style; the pictures—except the one of the governor—show the face of the subject and his body in a caricature style.

ALLAN, J. ed, *The Victorian centenary book: a series of records of people and firms at the time of the centenary.* Geelong, Tavistock, 1936. 312 p, illus.

A useful work although biased to the Geelong area.

BILLIS, R.V. AND KENYON, A.S. *Pastoral pioneers of Port Phillip.* Melbourne, Macmillan, Stockland, 1932. 277 p, map.

A useful source book on the rural history of Vic. Revised edition published in 1974.

FRASER, F. AND PALMER, N. eds, *Centenary gift book.* Melbourne, Robertson & Mullens, 1934. 166 p, illus.

A tribute to women 1834–1934 by women writers and artists on women in the arts, education, citizenship and employment.

HENDERSON, A. *Early pioneer families of Victoria and Riverina: a genealogical and biographical record.* Melbourne, McCarron, Bird, 1936. 584 p, illus.

HENDERSON, A. *Henderson's Australian families: a genealogical and biographical record.* Melbourne, The Author, 1941. 430 p, illus.

Vol 1 of a proposed two-volume work dealing mainly with Victorian and Riverina families, Henderson's lists concentrate on the landed gentry and read like a stud book. Entries provide useful but rarely adequate data on the early settlers.

HUMPHREYS, H.R.M. *Men of the time in Australia, Victorian series* (2nd edn). Melbourne, McCarron, Bird, 1882. x, c1xxxii, 274 p.

The first published collection of biographical sketches of Australians. First issued in 1878. Many entries in the second edition are simply reprinted from the first although there are some deletions. There were no volumes for the other states.

JEFFERY, R. ed, *Victorian personalities past and present (illustrated): an historical review.* Melbourne, Pioneer Publishing Co, 1934.

Exclusively concerned with the landed gentry of Vic. The biographical data have probably been supplied by the subjects.

LEAVITT, T.W.H. AND LILBURN, W.D. *The jubilee history of Victoria and Melbourne.* Melbourne, Wells & Leavitt, 1888. 2 vols, illus.

Besides a general history of the colony, there are hundreds of biographies of varying length and historical notes on institutions, societies and commercial firms.

McCALLUM, M.M. *Ballarat and district 'citizens and sport' at home and abroad: a biographical gallery . . .* Ballarat, McCallum Press and Publishing Co, 1916. 118 p, illus.

An important Victorian provincial 'who's who' supplementing the larger and necessarily more selective biographical dictionaries.

OUR local men of the times: biographical sketches of the

prominent citizens of Collingwood and Fitzroy. Melbourne, printed by J.M. Tait, 1889. 53 p.

Biographical sketches of the councillors and prominent citizens of Melbourne's main eastern municipalities. First published in the *Observer.* Simple and unpretentious—and only moderately accurate.

RECORDS of the pioneer women of Victoria, 1835–1860. Melbourne, Women's Centenary Council Historical Committee, 1937. 308 p, plus indexes.

A valuable reference work. Very few copies printed but available on microfilm at the State Library of Vic.

ROWLAND, E.C. *Some Frankston portraits.* Frankston, Vic, Southern Secretarial Service, 1979. 53 p, illus.

ROWLAND, E.C. *Further Frankston portraits.* Frankston, Vic, Southern Secretarial Service, 1980. 52 p, illus.

A useful account of a score of Victorians who helped to develop the seaside town of Frankston and the surrounding district.

SELBY, I. *The old pioneers' memorial history of Melbourne, from the discovery of Port Melbourne down to the World War.* Melbourne, Old Pioneers' Memorial Fund, 1924. 494 p, illus, maps.

A history written around the persons who were prominent in the development of Vic. Many of the biographies do not exceed one paragraph. The index is poor.

SUTHERLAND, A. *Victoria and its metropolis, past and present.* Melbourne, McCarron, Bird, 1888. 2 vols, illus.

Contains many biographies of citizens for many walks of life, but lacks a good index. Facsimile edition, Melbourne, Today's Heritage, 1977.

WHO'S who in the world of women, Victoria, Australia ... Melbourne, Reference Press Association, 1930. Unpaged, illus.

Biographies with portrait of society women. Another edition published in 1934 to coincide with Vic's centenary.

REGIONAL BIOGRAPHICAL SOURCES:
Western Australia

BROWN, M. *A walk through the history of Western Australia, 1829–1979: a chronological presentation of those persons commemorated on bronze inlaid paving tiles on St George's Terrace, Perth.* Perth, The Commerce Committee of WAY, 1979. Unpaged.

Short biographies of each of the 151 people who were commemorated.

DICTIONARY of Western Australians. UWAP, 1979– . v, maps.

Vol 1 compiled by P. Statham covers the early settlers 1829–50; vols 2 and 3 by R. Ericson cover bond and free settlers respectively for the years 1850–68. A supplement to vol 1 was published in 1981.

HUNT, L. ed, *Westralian portaits.* UWAP, 1979. 318 p, illus. One of a series of sesquicentennial publications, it contains biographies of 45 persons who made their mark in WA.

KIMBERLY, W.B. *History of West Australia: a narrative of her past together with biographies of her leading men.* Melbourne, F.W. Niven, 1897. 593 p, illus.

Includes biographical information on leading personalities of the day, with an indication of their importance in the development and future of the state.

LLOYD, A.C. *Leading personalities of Western Australia.* Ed by A. Ferguson. Perth, Paterson Brokensha, 1950. 342 p.

An important who's who of the period.

MATTERS, E. *Australasians who count in London and who count in Western Australia, by Mrs Leonard W. Matters.* London, Jas Truscott & Son, 1913. 246 p.

Information on prominent people of the time.

MEN of Western Australia: representative of the public, professional, ecclesiastical, commercial and sporting life of Western Australia as existent in the years 1936–1937. Perth, Colless, 1937. 461 p, illus.

An important who's who of the period.

POPHAM, D. ed, *Reflections: profiles of 150 women who helped make Western Australian history.* Perth, Carroll's, 1978. 266 p, illus.

REID, A. *Those were the days.* Perth, Barclay and Sharland, 1933. 299 p, illus, map.

Collection of notes on people and events in the Western Australian goldfields, 1892–1903, by an eyewitness journalist. Thousands of names but no index except to a few score of portraits.

SACKS, M. ed, *The WAY 79 who is who: synoptic biographies of Western Australians.* Perth, Crawley Publishers, 1980. 437 p, illus.

Compiled from information supplied by the subject.

THIEL (P.W.H.) and Co. *Twentieth century impressions of Western Australia.* Perth, P.W.H. Thiel, 1901. 800 p, illus.

A major source of late nineteenth-century biographical information.

THROUGH the spy-glass: short sketches of well-known Westralians as others see them, by Truthful Thomas [pseud]. Perth, Praagh & Lloyd, 1905. 91 p.

Short, crisp character sketches of local personalities of the day.

WILSON, J.G. *Western Australia's centenary, 1829–1929: first century's progress with antecedent records, 1527–1828.* Perth, Historic Press, 1929. 486 p.

Contains biographical information on prominent families and individuals involved in the developoment of the state.

VI
EUROPEAN DISCOVERY AND COLONISATION

William Bradley, a map 'Shewing the track of the
Waakzaamheydt *transport, from Port Jackson in New*
South Wales to Batavia 1792'. Chart 3 in his
A voyage to New South Wales: the journal of
Lieutenant William Bradley of HMS *Sirius,*
1786–1792. Facsimile edition, Public Library of New
South Wales in association with Ure Smith, 1969. The Sirius
had been wrecked on a reef in 1790 while
attempting to enter Sydney Bay on Norfolk Island.

'British Empire at a glance.' Cardboard reference wheel published by Frank Pitchford and Co Ltd, London c1928.

SPEARRITT COLLECTION

CHAPTER 21

DISCOVERY

ALAN FROST

THE EUROPEAN DISCOVERY of the Australian continent stemmed directly from the Western quest for trade and empire which is the distinctive feature of world history from the fifteenth to the twentieth century. When the Portuguese had found new sea routes to 'both the Indias'; when the Portuguese and Spanish had discovered and colonised vast territories in the New World, and established forts and trading posts along the fringes of the Old; and when these Iberians had begun to draw enviable riches from their endeavours—then were their northern neighbours moved to emulate them. Then did Europeans generally encompass the world; and then, as part of that venturing, did they come upon the southern continent now known as Australia.

Europeans believed in such a geographical entity long before they discovered it. The concept of 'Terra Australis'—the southern land—first appeared in Western imagining in Greek and Roman times when, knowing the world to be spherical, geographers speculated that there might be land in the Southern Hemisphere, separated from that in the north by the scorched tropics. Writing in about 150 AD, the Alexandrian Ptolemy postulated that 'that part of the earth which is inhabited by us is bounded on the east by the unknown land which borders on the eastern races of Greater Asia ... and on the south by the likewise unknown land which encloses the Indian sea and which encompasses Ethiopia south of Libya'. Scholars such as Macrobius, Isidore of Seville and Beatus of Liebana continued to advance versions of this idea into the Middle Ages.

Ptolemy's *Geography* enjoyed a great vogue in the Renaissance, with more than fifty editions of his world map appearing between 1477 and 1730. Although the Portuguese demonstration that the Indian Ocean was not landlocked caused some modification to notions of the position and extent of Terra Australis, belief in its existence continued undiminished. Both physical and religious truth required that it exist. On the one hand, without a southern landmass to balance that in the north, the world would fall to destruction among the stars. On the other, God's perfection necessitated symmetry in his creation. If there were not a Terra Australis, the earth would lack symmetry—which was by definition impossible. *Ergo*, 'in the southern hemisphere there is an uncovered surface of land correspondent, or nearly so, to that which has been discovered in the northern hemisphere'.

The Renaissance Terra Australis was the creation both of theoretical geography and innate desire. 'Java la Grande' is perhaps the result of actual discovery. The depiction of this region in a cluster of maps, produced by a school of cartographers centred on the northern French port of

Dieppe, is one of the puzzles of European history. Placed to the south of the Indonesian archipelago, Java la Grande is of approximately the right size and in about the right latitudes and longitudes to be Australia; and historians have long speculated that its appearance in these maps reflects an early Portuguese discovery. While details that would constitute proof, such as dates of the voyage or voyages, original journals, charts and reports, are still lacking, it does seem (as one of the best informed commentators has put it) that acceptance of the idea of a Portuguese discovery is 'much easier' than rejection.

Any precise knowledge of the Australian continent was soon lost sight of in Europe, however. Magellan's circumnavigation of 1519–22 seemed to confirm the existence of the Terra Australis of traditional conception, for geographers took the island he found on his left as he passed into the Pacific Ocean to be its fringes. They redrew their maps to incorporate his strait, and in doing so merged Java la Grande into the greater entity. This achieved its distinctive form in the second half of the sixteenth century, when Ortelius and Gerard Mercator first depicted it on world maps (1554, 1569) and when, with some minor revisions, Ortelius and Rumold Mercator then represented it in their magnificent atlases (1570, 1587). These cartographers showed a vast continent, *Terra Australis Nondum Cognita*, covering the entire southern polar region, extending northwards to 20°S and having two greater capes, one reaching to the southern tip of New Guinea, the other, comprising the regions of Beach, Luncach and Maletur, supposedly rich in gold and spices, to the south of Java. It was in search of this continent that Mendaña and Quiros sailed in the 1560s and 1590s, whose voyages led incidentally to Torres's discovery of the strait between Australia and New Guinea in 1606.

Torres's discovery remained largely unknown to Europe until the 1760s, when Alexander Dalrymple obtained some details of the voyage from archives in Manila and Spain. Dalrymple (1764) published a chart showing Torres's route which Banks took on the voyage of the *Endeavour*, so that Cook sailed in the knowledge that there was a way south of New Guinea from the Pacific Ocean to the East Indies. Later, Dalrymple obtained a copy of a letter Torres wrote describing the voyage; Burney then published Dalrymple's translation of this. No copy of any journal by Torres has been found. Major (1859; facs, 1963, 31–42) reprinted Dalrymple's translation of Torres's letter. *New light on the discovery of Australia*, edited by H.N. Stevens and translated by G.F. Barwick (London, Hakluyt Society, 1930), presents the account of the voyage by Torres's companion, Don Diego de Prado y Tovar.

The next sightings of the continent came not as a consequence of armchair geographers' speculations, nor of the ventures of Iberians driven by dreams of gold and Christian conversion, but from the activities of the more systematic, if more prosaic, Dutch. In 1602, anxious to share in the wealth of the East, the governing body of the United Provinces granted the United East India Company (VOC) a monopoly of Dutch trade in the vast area between the Cape of Good Hope and Cape Horn. Immediately on establishing itself in the East Indies, the VOC began to seek farther fields. In 1605, officials at Bantam despatched the *Duyfken* [*The little dove*] 'to discover the great land Nova Guinea and other unknown east and south lands'. Like the progenitor sent out by Noah, this 'little dove' came to land—on a 320-kilometre stretch of the western coast of Cape York, between Pennefather River and Cape Keerweer. Its captain then struck north to New Guinea but failed to notice that a strait divided the two lands. In 1623, Jan Carstensz in the *Pera* and Willem Joosten van Colster in the *Arnhem* continued this investigation. Carstensz coasted further along western Cape York but also failed to find Torres Strait. Colster found the northeast fringes of Arnhem Land.

The Dutch also made extensive accidental sightings of the western and southern coasts of the continent in these years. In 1615, as a consequence of rapidly accumulating experience, the VOC ordered its captains to steer a fixed route to the East. With the westerlies at their back, they were to sail due east from the Cape of Good Hope for 1000 'mijlen' (about 5300 kilometres) until in the longitude of the Sunda Strait, when they were to turn north for Batavia. The winds not always appearing in the same latitude and the difficulty of calculating longitude precisely meant that the captains were soon striking Australia.

The first to do so was Dirck Hartog in the *Eendracht*, who reached the western coast at Shark Bay (25°S) in October 1616 and left his famous plate on the island named after him. Next was Claeszoon van Hillegom in the *Zeewolf* in May 1618 (22°S); he was followed by Houtman and Dedel in the *Dordrecht* and *Amsterdam* in 1619 (32°S) and the master of the *Leeuwin* in 1622 (from 32°S to 22°S). In 1627, Pieter Nuyts in the *Gulden Zeepaard* ran for some 1500 kilometres along the southern coast (to about 116°E). In June 1629, Pelsaert's *Batavia* was wrecked on Houtman Abrolhos.

These sightings naturally raised questions about the southern land's full extent and economic potential, which Anthonie van Diemen, the governor general at Batavia 1636–45, attempted to answer. In 1636, van Diemen sent two small vessels to obtain further knowledge of the north and northwestern coasts. In 1642 he sent Tasman to explore thoroughly the southern reaches of the Indian Ocean. Tasman charted sections of the Tasmanian and New Zealand coasts, and then sailed north to Tonga and Fiji, and about New Guinea to Batavia again. In 1644, Tasman undertook the further exploration of the northwestern coast.

The consequence of these sightings and explorations was that Europeans at last had authentic knowledge of the geography of the world to the southeast of Indonesia. Though its eastern coastline remained unknown, the New Holland that the Dutch navigators had found was clearly of continental extent; determining its general location and outline was the first major step in the accurate delineation of Austalia.

But while the Dutch discovery of New Holland cast light on southern geography, it did not destroy belief in the older Terra Australis. New Holland might be of continental extent, but it could not match the grandeur of that in which Europeans had for so long believed. Therefore, there must be two southern continents, the one, whose outline was known in general terms, lying between the equator and 44°S latitude, and 122° and 188°E longitude, comprising New Guinea, Carpentaria, New Holland, Anthonie van Diemen's Land and the countries discovered by de Quiros; and the other, lying in the south Pacific between 150° and 170° of which New Zealand was the western extremity, which was yet to be substantially discovered, and to which the title of *Terra Australis Incognita* properly belonged. And despite the desolation of New Holland's coast, Europeans also continued to believe that both continents contained matchless wealth.

These views reached their peak in the middle decades of the eighteenth century, in a series of substantial publications in which authors such as John Campbell (*see* Harris, 1744–48), John Green (1745–47), Charles de Brosses (1756), John Callander (1766–68) and Alexander Dalrymple (1764, 1770–71) both described past endeavours at discovery and developed programs for future ones, and advanced schemes of colonisation and trade.

In the mid-1760s, animated by the accounts and speculations of these writers and harbouring a deep-seated desire to open a Pacific trade, the British embarked on a series of voyages that became one of the distinguishing features of the age. After Byron (1764–66) and Wallis and Carteret (1766–88/9) had opened the 'Spanish lake', Cook made a voyage that both effectively dispelled the old notion of Terra Australis and revealed the eastern coastline of New Holland. Cook had some distinct help from earlier efforts. Banks, his companion on the voyage, carried with him a copy of Dalrymple's (1764) work which included a chart showing Torres's route south of New Guinea. However, though the knowledge of this passage to Batavia no doubt smoothed his way towards the east coast of Australia, Cook seems to have been quite unaware of any prior Portuguese discovery of it. He made his first landfall on 19 April 1770 at Point Hicks, and for the next three months he proceeded north, charting as he went. On 15 August 1770, knowing that 'on the Western side I can make no new discovery the honour of which belongs to the Dutch Navigators', but confident that 'the Eastern Coast from the Latitude of 38° South down to this place … was never seen or visited by any Europeans before us', he hoisted the British flag on Possession Island in Torres Strait and claimed New South Wales for his King.

Cook's voyage largely completed the general delineation of the Australian continent, for after it only those coasts about Bass Strait remained entirely obscure. Many details remained unknown or uncertain, however, and the gathering of these constitutes the last great phase of European discovery of Australia by sea. The representatives of two nations did the work of this phase—of Britain, which began its colonisation of the continent in 1788; and of France, which pursued a renewed interest in exploration and empire in the decades about 1800. Progressively, dedicated naval commanders such as Hunter, d'Entrecasteaux, Baudin and Flinders, and their junior officers, built upon the pioneering work of the Dutch navigators and Cook. From their tedious, time-consuming and often arduous surveys came the meticulous charts of the Australian coast and islands that mark this phase. (As seaborne 'discovery' is closely linked with land-based 'exploration' in this period, the latter has been treated in chapter 24 of this volume.)

In his introduction to the account of his labours, Matthew Flinders remarked that now the 'essential point' of New Holland and New South Wales forming 'one land' had been ascertained, a 'general name applicable to the whole' was needed. He had therefore titled his narrative *A voyage to Terra Australis* (1814; facs, Adelaide, LBSA, 1966) but, he remarked wistfully, 'Had I permitted myself any innovation upon [this] original term, it would have been to convert it into Australia'. 'Australia' was evidently first used in this context by the English translator of Gabriel de Foigny's imaginary *A new discovery of Terra Incognita Australia, or the southern world* (1693); Flinders died before he might know the renewed currency his passing footnote gave to it. By the 1820s, 'Australia' was coming into general use as the name of the southern continent; its derivative, 'Australians', was accepted as the name both of its Aboriginal inhabitants and of the Europeans who were then occupying it. In 1859, R.H. Major set the seal on this historical process when he titled his collection of narratives *Early voyages to Terra Australis, now called Australia* (facs, 1963). From speculation, from chance discovery, from systematic exploration and from historical researches did the sixth continent emerge on to the map of the world.

THE ART OF THE DISCOVERIES

As the voyages of exploration were more systematically planned and undertaken, the significance of the art produced during them increased. The early sailors, having no sense of aesthetic traditions or of the intrinsic significance of what they saw, drew only for utilitarian purposes—they sketched islands, shoals, headlands or stretches of coast to provide navigational aids for those who might come after them. Such production was usually so crude artistically as not to be interesting from other points of view, and was therefore less likely to be preserved than the age's more aesthetically accomplished works. No views are known from the Quiros voyage, for example, though Tasman's coastal profiles are preserved with his journal.

As Europe's interest in science and the distant world developed, voyagers began to pay more attention to exotic phenomena (peoples, landscapes, animals, birds, plants), either for their intrinsic interest or for the light they might cast on questions which increasingly concerned philosophers, such as the original state of nature and the 'natural' condition of humanity. As they did so, they began to draw and paint more carefully and extensively. De Vlamingh's coastal views and depictions of west Australian animals stand at the beginning of this development, which reached its peak in the later eighteenth century, when Cook took with him artists whose task it was to record exactly the shapes and colours of specimens, or the attitudes of peoples and ambiences of landscapes. Some of these artists' production was of a high aesthetic quality and had a profound influence on European sensibility. A comprehensive survey of this field is to be R. Joppien and B.W. Smith's *The descriptive catalogue of the art and the charts and views of Captain James Cook's voyages of discovery to the south Pacific*, to consist of three volumes (OUP, 1985–   ).

The bibliography that follows is arranged under several headings: European expansion; collections of voyages, 1690–1816; the discovery of the continent; the question of a Portuguese discovery of the continent; the discovery of New Holland; and the discovery of New South Wales.

EUROPEAN EXPANSION

BOXER, C.R. *The Dutch seaborne empire, 1600–1800.* London, Hutchinson, 1965. 326 p, illus, maps.

BOXER, C.R. *The Portuguese seaborne empire, 1415–1825.* London, Hutchinson, 1969. 426 p, illus, maps.

Both informative and incisively written, and part of the distinguished series, *The history of human society.*

DIFFIE, B.D. AND WINIUS, G.D. *Foundations of the Portuguese empire, 1415–1580.* Minneapolis, University of Minnesota Press, 1977. 533 p, illus.

A detailed account, both scholarly and readable, this is one of a distinguished series entitled *Europe and the world in the age of expansion.*

HARLOW, V.T. *The founding of the second British Empire, 1763–1793.* London, Longmans, Green, 1952–64. 2 vols, maps.

The beginning point for those wishing to know about archival collections relating generally to British expansion in the period. However, Harlow died before writing his projected chapter on the settlement of NSW.

MARSHALL, P.J. AND WILLIAMS, G. *The great map of mankind: British perceptions of the world in the age of enlightenment.* London, Dent, 1982. 314 p, maps.

This distinctive work demonstrates how the eighteenth-century British 'saw' the non-European world. It therefore complements in interesting and informative ways those products of the traditional historical approach.

PARRY, J.H. *Europe and a wider world, 1415–1715.* London, Hutchinson, 1949. 176 p.

PARRY, J.H. *The age of reconnaissance.* London, World Publishing Co, 1963. 364 p, illus.

Careful surveys of the modes of, and the impulses behind, European expansion and convenient guides to a subject with a vast historiography. A revised edition of the first volume was published in 1966.

PARRY, J.H. *The Spanish seaborne empire.* London, Hutchinson, 1966. 416 p, illus, maps.

Another in the Hutchinson *The history of human society* series.

SCAMMELL, G.V. *The world encompassed: the first European maritime empires c800–1650.* London, Methuen, 1981. 538 p, illus.

This wideranging account offers a longer perspective than most.

SPATE, O.H.K. *The Pacific since Magellan.* ANUP, 1979– . v, illus, maps.

Immensely learned and precise in his scholarship, Spate is one of the foremost commentators on the European expansion. This work is distinguished from other such histories by being based on the concept of the geographical unity of the Pacific basin. Two volumes have appeared to date, subtitled 'The Spanish lake' and 'Monopolists and freebooters'.

WILLIAMS, G. *The expansion of Europe in the eighteenth century: overseas rivalry, discovery and exploitation.* London, Blandford, 1966. 309 p, illus, maps.

A comprehensive and readable account, based on meticulous scholarship.

COLLECTIONS OF VOYAGES, 1690–1816

Most of the works listed here do not need annotations as their titles are self-explanatory. They all contain reports from voyagers who searched for the southern continent, some of whom reached Australia.

BROSSES, C. de *Histoire des navigations aux Terres Australes* . . . Paris, Durand, 1756. 2 vols, illus.

BURNEY, J. *A chronological history of the discoveries in the South Sea or Pacific Ocean.* London, G. and W. Nicol, 1803–17. 5 vols, maps.

Facsimile reprint issued in Amsterdam in 1967 as vols 3–7 of the series *Bibliotheca Australiana.*

CALLANDER, J. *Terra Australis cognita: or, voyages to the Terra Australis.* Edinburgh, A. Donaldson, 1766–68. 3 vols, maps.

Facsimile reprint issued in Amsterdam in 1967 as vols 8–10 of the series *Bibliotheca Australiana.*

CHURCHILL, A. AND CHURCHILL, J. *A collection of voyages and travels.* London, The Authors, 1704–32. 6 vols.

DALRYMPLE, A. *An account of the discoveries made in the south Pacific Ocean, previous to 1764.* London, The Author, 1767. xxxi, 103 p, illus, maps.

DALRYMPLE, A. *An historical collection of the several voyages and discoveries in the south Pacific Ocean.* London, The Author, 1770–71. 2 vols, illus, maps.

Facsimile reprint issued in Amsterdam in 1967 as vol 11 of the series *Bibliotheca Australiana.*

GREEN, J. comp, *A new general collection of voyages and travels* . . . London, T. Astley, 1745–47. 4 vols, illus, maps.

HARRIS, J. *Navigantium atque itinerantium bibliotheca. Or, a complete collection of voyages and travels . . . Originally published . . . by John Harris . . . Now carefully revised, with large additions and continued down to the present time* . . . London, T. Woodward *et al,* 1744–48. 2 vols, illus.

First published in 1705, this edition was edited by John Campbell. The work is noteworthy mainly for Campbell's contributions, especially his proposal for a colonisation of the Pacific. A further revised edition was published in 1764.

ROBINSON, T. ed, *An account of several late voyages and discoveries to the south and north. . . by Sir John Narborough, Captain Jasmen* [sic] *Tasman, Captain John Wood and Frederick Marten* . . . London, Smith and Walford, 1694. 2 pts in 1 vol, illus, map.

THE DISCOVERY OF THE CONTINENT

BEAGLEHOLE, J.C. *The exploration of the Pacific.* London, A. & C. Black, 1934, 411 p, maps.

A comprehensive survey by the great scholar of Cook's voyages, this includes a section on the discovery of NSW. Revised edition published in 1966 (Stanford University Press).

COLLINGRIDGE, G.A. *The discovery of Australia: a critical, documentary and historic investigation concerning the priority of discovery in Australasia by Europeans before the arrival of Lieut. James Cook in the* Endeavour, *in the year 1770.* Sydney, Hayes Brothers, 1895, 376 p, maps.

Another pioneering study of very considerable importance in Australian historiography, but now rather dated. Facsimile edition, Sydney, Golden Press, 1983.

FEEKEN, E.H.J. AND FEEKEN, G.E. *The discovery and exploration of Australia . . . with an introduction by O.H.K. Spate.* Melbourne, Nelson, 1970. 318 p, illus, maps.

While the narrative is selective, it does constitute a convenient starting point, useful for its many illustrations and its bibliography of cartography.

PERRY, T.M. *The discovery of Australia: the charts and maps of the navigators and explorers.* Melbourne, Nelson, 1982. 159 p, illus, maps.

The author has been selective in the aspects described, but the number and quality of the illustrations make this a distinguished contribution.

RAINAUD, A. *Le Continent Austral: hypothèses et découvertes.* Paris, A. Colin, 1893. 491 p, illus, maps.

A pioneering study of European conception of a Terra Australis and of discovery of the Australian continent; this remains valuable for some of its details.

SHARP, A. *The discovery of Australia.* Oxford, Clarendon Press, 1963. 338 p, illus, maps.

In these selections from original records together with interlinking narrative, Sharp offers a convenient survey of the subject.

WOOD, G.A. *The discovery of Australia.* London, Macmillan, 1922. 541 p, illus, maps.

This was a thorough survey for its time, but modern scholarship has dated it somewhat. A revised edition was published in 1969.

THE QUESTION OF A PORTUGUESE DISCOVERY OF THE CONTINENT

BURNEY, J. *A chronological history* ... 1, 379–83. (See above).

Significant because the author sailed the Pacific Ocean with Cook. His assessment was that the Dieppe maps most likely reflect an early Portuguese discovery, a view endorsed by Flinders.

COLLINGRIDGE, G. *The discovery of Australia* . . .. (See above).
Collingridge drew particular attention to the Dieppe maps, but his amateur's enthusiasm led him to claim more than the evidence justified.

HERVÉ, M.R. 'Australia: in French geographical documents of the Renaissance', *J R Aust Hist Soc* 41, 1, 1955, 23–38.
The author's detailed knowledge of cartography and exploration makes this a useful short consideration of the subject. Translated from the French by J.M. Forsyth.

HERVÉ, R. *Découverte fortuite de l'Australie et de la nouvelle Zélande par des navigateurs portugais et espagnols entre 1521 et 1528.* Paris, Bibliothèque Nationale, 1982. 133 p, illus.
A detailed examination of the subject, which adds to a complex mix the new element of the Spanish ship *San Lesmes* reaching the east coast in 1526. Without corroborating evidence, however (for example, the identified wreck), Hervé's thesis must remain speculative. English translation, without scholarly notes, published in Palmerston North, New Zealand, Dunmore Press, 1983.

McINTYRE, K.G. *The secret discovery of Australia: Portuguese ventures 200 years before Captain Cook.* Sydney, Pan, 1982. 256 p, maps.
A popular work which may be right in its general view but which is suspect in its scholarship and use of evidence. This edition slightly revised and abridged. First published in 1977.

McKIGGAN, I. 'The Portuguese expedition to Bass Strait in A.D. 1522', *J Aust stud* 1, June 1977, 2–32.
McKiggan assumes too much on a too slender basis of evidence. Interesting, however, for the attempt to settle the question by mathematical correction of the outline of Java la Grande on the Dieppe maps.

MacKNIGHT, C.C. 'On the non-"discovery" of "Australia"', *Canberra historical J* 12, 1983, 34–6.
The coasts in question are believed to be those of western and southern Java. There are some interesting identifications but, like those for the opposite view, the argument is not conclusive.

MAJOR, R.H. 'Introduction', in *Early voyages to Terra Australis, now called Australia: a collection of documents ... from the beginning of the sixteenth century to the time of Captain Cook.* London, Hakluyt Society, 1859, i–cxix.
Another discussion of the Dieppe maps and the European discovery of Australia. Major wrote that 'in the sixteenth century there are *indications* on maps of the great probability of Australia having been already discovered, but with no written documents to confirm them'. Facsimile edition, New York, Burt Franklin, 1963.

RICHARDSON, W.A.R. 'Java-la-Grande: a case of cartographic confusion', *Geographical magazine* 54, 11, 1982, 615–22.
Valuable for its analysis of the place names of the Dieppe maps, from which the author concludes that the coasts of Java la Grande are not Australian ones. However, not all his reconstructions are fully convincing.

SPATE, O.H.K. 'Terra Australis—Cognita?', *Hist stud* 8, 29, 1957, 1–19.
Spate offers here the most judicious appraisal. Reprinted, with less documentation, in *Let me enjoy: essays, partly geographical* (ANUP, 1965).

WALLIS, H. 'The enigma of Java-la-Grande', in *Australia and the European imagination: papers from a conference held at the Humanities Research Centre, Australian National University, May 1981.* Canberra, Humanities Research Centre, Australian National University, 1982, 1–40.
This analysis advances discussion of the question by giving greater details of the circumstances of the making of the Dieppe maps. It forms part of the author's introduction to *The maps and text of the Boke of Idrography presented by Jean Rotz to Henry VIII now in the British Library*, (London, Roxburghe Club, 1982).

THE DISCOVERY OF NEW HOLLAND

DAMPIER, W. *A new voyage round the world.* London, J. Knapton, 1697, 550 p, illus, maps.
Reprints of the 1729 edition of this work were issued in 1927 (Argonaut Press) and in 1968 (Dover Publications).

DAMPIER, W. *A voyage to New Holland &c. in the year 1699.* London, Methuen, 1703, 162 p, illus, maps.
Dampier saw only the barren northwestern coasts of the continent; his description of the Aborigines as 'the miserablest People of the world' determined Europe's image of them for a hundred years.

HEERES, J.E. *The part borne by the Dutch in the discovery of Australia, 1606–1765.* London, Lucaz, 1899. 256 p, maps.
Valuable for its scholarly introduction. Generally known by its Dutch title *Het aandeel der Nederlanders in de ontdekking van Australië 1606–1765*. Dutch and English texts on opposite pages.

LLOYD, C. *William Dampier.* London, Faber, 1966. 165 p, illus, maps.
A readable narrative, but without scholarly apparatus.

PUBLIC LIBRARY OF NEW SOUTH WALES. *Abel Janszoon Tasman: a bibliography.* Sydney, Government Printer, 1963. 80 p, illus.
A listing of books, journals and manuscript material held in the Mitchell Library and a number of other Australian collections.

ROBERT, W.C.H. *Contributions to a bibliography of Australia and the South Sea Islands.* Amsterdam, Philo Press, 1968–75. 4 vols.
A multivolume work with supplements on individual Dutch explorers. Only a few extracts of the journals of the early Dutch navigators were published at the time (and, indeed, seem to have survived). A detailed bibliography essential for researchers.

ROBERT, W.C.H. *The Dutch explorations, 1605–1756, on the north and northwest coast of Australia: extracts from journals, log-book and other documents relating to these voyages.* Amsterdam, Philo Press, 1973. 197 p, maps.
Another useful edition of surviving records.

SCHILDER, G. *Australia unveiled: the share of the Dutch*

Making Australian History

Australia was the last continent to be discovered by Europeans. In the seventeenth and and eighteenth centuries European explorers crossed the Indian and Pacific oceans looking for new lands, new trade routes and wealth. First the Dutch, then the Portuguese, the Spanish and the British touched the shores of the southern continent, named in turn Terra Australis, New Holland and finally Australia.

As a nation we are fortunate in having the journals and other written records of much of this early exploration. Dampier's record of his voyages, Captain Cook's and Joseph Banks's journals and Sydney Parkinson's drawings document Australia's British beginnings. The records of the first coastal settlements are contained in diaries, letters and reports to the British government. These give the early history of the colonies, some first settled by convicts, others for such reasons as the need for new lands. All of them grew as the British Empire and its trade expanded.

The early records contain many drawings and descriptions of the strange plants and animals unique to Australia. Joseph Bank's drawings of plants and Captain Cook's description of birds and Aborigines are interesting examples, and of course there was great interest shown in the kangaroo. As well as drawings, stuffed examples and live specimens were sent back to England.

Through these early records we can gain a very accurate view of eighteenth-century Australia. This volume contains details of much of this material that has been published. The following six pages show some illustrations and facsimile pages from these publications.

Parrot of Norfolk Island, *from a watercolour 22.8 x 18.3 cm in Governor John Hunter's sketchbook, 1790.*
REX NAN KIVELL COLLECTION, NATIONAL LIBRARY

April 1770

'After dinner the boats were mann'd & we set out from the ship intending to land at the place where we saw these people hoping that as they regarded the ship's coming into the bay so little they would as little regard our landing we were in this however mistaken for as soon as we aproachd the rocks two of the men came down upon them each armd with a lance of about 10 feet long & a short stick which he seemd to handle as if it was a machine to throw the lance they calld to us very loud in a harsh sounding Language of which neither us nor Pupia understood a word shaking their lances & menacing in all appearance resolvd to dispute our landing to the utmost tho they were but two & we 30 or 40 at least in this manner we parleyd with them for about a quarter of an hour they waving to us to be gone we again signing that we wanted water & that we meant them no harm they remaind resolute so a musquet was fird over them the Effect of which was that the Youngest of the two dropd a bundle of lances on the rock at the instant in which he heard the report he however snatchd them up again & both renewd their threats & opposition a Musquet loaded with small shot was now fird at the Eldest of the two who was about 40 yards from the boat it struck him on the legs but he minded it very little so another was immediately fird at him on this he ran up to the house about 100 yards distant & soon returnd with a sheild in the mean time we had landed on the rock he immediately threw a lance at us the young man another which fell among the thickest of us but hurt nobody 2 more musquets with small shot were then fird at them on which the Eldest threw one more lance & then ran away as did the other we went up to the houses in one of which we found the children hid behind the sheild & a piece of bark in one of the houses we were conscious from the distance the people had been from us when we fird that the shot could have done them no material harm we therefore resolvd to leave the children in the spot without even opening their shelter we therefore threw into the house to them some beads, ribbands, cloths & c, as presents & went away we however thought it no improper measure to take away with us all the lances which we could find about the houses amounting in number to forty or fifty.'
(Transcript from Sir Joseph Banks, Endeavour *journal 1769–1771*.)

Three pages from Joseph Bank's Endeavour journal 1769–1771.
MITCHELL LIBRARY

Wa-ra-ta, *watercolour sketch in Governor Hunter's sketchbook, 1790.*
REX NAN KIVELL COLLECTION, NATIONAL LIBRARY

The Great Grey Kangaroo, Macropus major, *from John Gould's* A monograph of the Macropodidae, *London, The Author, 1841, part 1.*

Sketch of the Eastern Water Skink, Sphenomorphus quoyii, *by Thomas Watling, from the original watercolour and pen and ink drawing, 17 x 27.5 cm.*
NATIONAL LIBRARY

MACROPUS MAJOR. *Shaw*

14 July 1770

'Mr Gore being out in the Country shott one of the Animals before Spoke of, it was a small one of the sort Weighing only 28^{lb} clear of the Entrails the head Neck and Shoulders of this Animal was very small in Proportion to the other Parts, the tail was nearly as long as the Body, thick next the rump & Tapering towards the End the fore legs was 8 inches long and the Hind 22 its Progrefsion is by hopping or Jumping 7 or 8 feet at each Hop upon its hind Legs only for in this it makes no use of the Fore which seem only designed for Scratching in the ground & the Skin is covered with a Short Hairy fur of a Dark Mouse or Grey Colour, excepting the Head Hair which I thought was something like a Hares it bares no sort of resemblance to any European Animal I ever Saw, it is said to bear much resemblance to the Gerbua excepting in [. . .] the Gerbua being no larger than a Common rat.' (Transcript from Lieutenant James Cook *The journal of H.M.S.* Endeavour *1768–1771*.)

Description of a kangaroo, 1770, from The journal of H.M.S.
Endeavour 1768–1771, *by Lieutenant James Cook. Facsimile
edition, Genesis Publications Limited in association with
Rigby Limited, 1977.*

Sydney Parkinson, Two of the natives of New Holland, advancing to combat, *in his* A journal of a voyage to the South Seas in His Majesty's ship, the *Endeavour.*

Two pages from the Bonwick transcripts of the Bigge report, recording an interview with the Reverend Robert Cartwright on 26 November 1819.
MITCHELL LIBRARY

November 1819

James Bonwick was one of the earliest historians to gather together original material concerning the European settlement of Australia, held in government archives in England. He came to Australia as a teacher, but later returned to England, and in the 1880s began to transcribe by hand the records of the settlement of Queensland, New South Wales and Tasmania. His transcriptions became the basis for the many volumes of the printed *Historical records of New South Wales* and later *Historical records of Australia*.

Among the documents transcribed by Bonwick were the Bigge reports. Commissioner Bigge was sent out to New South Wales in 1819 by the British government to report on Governor Macquarie's management of the colony. The commissioner interviewed colonists on such matters as the convict system, the granting of land and the governor's methods. He judged matters by English standards and often took evidence informally. His report is an interesting document, but his conclusions were sometimes doubtful. Bigge criticised Macquarie's liberal attitude to emancipists and regarded the governor's building program – which included some beautiful Georgian buildings by Francis Greenway – as extravagant. Some valuable reforms flowed from the report, in both New South Wales and Tasmania.

navigators in the discovery of Australia. Amsterdam, Theatrum Orbis Terrarum, 1976. 424 p, illus, maps.

This comprehensive collection of reproductions of maps and charts is a rich record of the Dutch discovery of Australia.

SCHILDER, G. ed, *De ontdekkingsreis van Willem Hesselsz. de Vlamingh in de jaren 1696–1697.* 's-Gravenhage, M. Nijhoff, 1976. 322 p, illus, maps. (Linschoten Vereeniging, The Hague, *Werken*, 78–9).

Includes extracts from journals of various members of the voyage.

SHARP. A. *The voyages of Abel Janszoon Tasman.* Oxford, Clarendon Press, 1968. 375 p, illus, maps.

A readily available version.

SHIPMAN, J.C. *William Dampier: seaman-scientist.* Lawrence, Kansas, University of Kansas Libraries, 1962. 63 p, illus.

A brief account which offers a general perspective only.

SIGMOND, J.P. AND ZUIDERBAAN, L.H. *Dutch discoveries of Australia: shipwrecks, treasures, and early voyages off the west coast.* Adelaide, Rigby, 1979. 176 p, illus, maps.

A utilitarian narrative, which offers basic information and a number of relevant illustrations.

TASMAN, A.J. *Abel Janszoon Tasman's journal of his discovery of Van Diemen's Land and New Zealand in 1642 with documents relating to his exploration of Australia in 1644.* Amsterdam, Muller, 1898. 195, 59, 163, 21 p, illus, maps.

A scholarly edition of the surviving records, prepared by F.A. van Scheltema and A. Mensing. It includes 'The life and labours of Abel Janszoon Tasman' by J.E. Heeres. Facsimile edition, Los Angeles, Kovack, 1965.

VLAMINGH, W. de. *The explorations, 1696–1697, of Australia by Willem de Vlamingh: extracts from the two log books concerning the voyage to and explorations on the coast of Western Australia . . .* Ed by W.C.H. Robert. Amsterdam, Philo Press, 1972. 206 p, illus, maps.

THE DISCOVERY OF NEW SOUTH WALES

BANKS, J. *The Endeavour journal of Joseph Banks, 1768–1771.* Ed by J.C. Beaglehole. Sydney, Trustees of the Public Library of NSW in association with A & R, 1962. 2 vols, illus, maps.

Beaglehole's editions of Cook's and Bank's journals are among the glories of modern scholarship.

BEAGLEHOLE, J.C. *The life of Captain James Cook.* London, Black, 1974. 760 p, illus, maps. (Also published as vol 4 of the *Journals.*

Includes much of the material of Beaglehole's introduction to the *Journals.* Together with the *Journals,* it is the culmination of a lifetime's study of Cook and the British exploration of the Pacific Ocean. Magisterial in its range and detail, it also provides points of departure for others.

BEDDIE, N.K. ed, *Bibliography of Captain James Cook, R.N., F.R.S., circumnavigator* (2nd edn). Sydney, Council of the Library of NSW, 1970. 894 p.

Issued to celebrate Cook's discovery in 1770 of Australia's eastern shores. An exhaustive listing of all references to Cook known at the date of publication. Supersedes an earlier bibliography commemorating the 150th anniversary of Cook's death in 1778.

CARR, D.J. *et al, Sydney Parkinson: artist of Cook's* Endeavour *voyage.* ANUP, 1983. 300 p, illus.

This beautifully produced book, with lavish illustrations, contains also a series of scholarly essays on the various fields in which Parkinson worked.

COOK, J. *Captain Cook in Australia: extracts from the journals of Captain James Cook giving a full account in his own words of his adventures and discoveries in Australia.* Ed by A.W. Reed. Wellington, NZ, Reed, 1969. 192 p, illus, map.

A popular account for the general reader.

COOK, J. *The journals of Captain James Cook on his voyages of discovery.* Vol 1. *The voyage of the* Endeavour, *1768–1771* (corr edn). Ed by J.C. Beaglehole. Cambridge, Published for the Hakluyt Society at the University Press, 1968. cclxxxvi, 696 p, illus, maps.

First published in 1955. The definitive edition of Cook's *Endeavour* voyage which had been first published in 1773 as part of *An account of the voyages undertaken by the order of his present majesty for making discoveries in the southern hemisphere . . .* Edited by John Hawesworth, this was very popular in the eighteenth century and Cook's and Banks's descriptions of NSW, which Hawesworth reproduced with reasonable fidelity, formed the basis of the Pitt administration's 1786 decision to colonise Botany Bay.

FROST, A. 'New South Wales as terra nullius: the British denial of Aboriginal land rights', *Hist stud* 19, 77, 1981, 513–23.

British attitudes to colonisation are explored in the context of Cook's and Banks's descriptions of the Aborigines.

FROST, A. '"A strange illumination of the heart": James Cook, Tahiti, and beyond', *Meanjin quarterly* 29, 4, 1970, 446–52.

This essay describes the way in which Cook's imagination was changed by the geographies and peoples encountered.

GAMMAGE, B. 'Early boundaries of New South Wales', *Hist stud* 19, 77, 1981, 524–31.

A study of the British claim to NSW in the light of Cook's *Endeavour* voyage.

HILDER, B. *The voyage of Torres: the discovery of the southern coastline of New Guinea and Torres Strait by Captain Luiz Baez de Torres in 1606.* UQP, 1980. xxxii, 194 p, illus, maps.

A detailed but not entirely successful analysis attempting to determine Torres's exact route and thus answer the vexing question of whether or not he saw northern Australia.

KING, R. 'The territorial boundaries of New South Wales in 1788', *The great circle* 3, 2, 1981, 70–89.

King places the territorial claim of the British in the context of rivalry with Spain.

MURRAY-OLIVER, A. comp, *Captain Cook's artists in the Pacific, 1769–1779.* Christchurch, NZ, Avon Fine Prints, 1969. xxiv, 165 p, illus.

The large reproductions are beautifully done.

SMITH, B.W. *European vision and the south Pacific, 1768–1850: a study in the history of art and ideas.* Oxford, Clarendon Press, 1960, 287 p, illus, maps.

A pioneering study which opened a new world, and which remains impressive.

WILLIAMS, G. '"Far more happier than we Europeans": reactions to the Australian Aborigines on Cook's voyage', *Hist stud* 19, 1982, 499–512.

Complements, and in some details extends, Smith (1985).

G.P. Harris, G.P. Harris's cottage, Hobart Town, Van Diemen's Land, August 1806. *The first European dwelling in Tasmania. Watercolour.*
NATIONAL LIBRARY

CHAPTER 22

FIRST EUROPEAN SETTLEMENTS

VICTOR CRITTENDEN

EUROPEAN SOCIETY, with its themes of discovery and settlement, is the basis for much recent world history. The transference of Western civilisation to the Southern Hemisphere is one of the great stories of the eighteenth century. The first European settlement on the continent of Australia—undisturbed during thousands of years of Aboriginal occupation—was the beginning of a series of expanding establishments around the coastline until the process of possession by the British was complete. The sea remained the connecting link between the new settlements, so that it was by sea that the land was discovered, by sea that it was settled and by sea that contact was maintained between these outposts of the transplanted European society.

The materials available for the study of these settlements and the gradual takeover of the whole continent are largely preserved. The records of the first settlement at Port Jackson, or 'Botany Bay' as it was popularly known, and those of the successive occupation of the continent are all available. These relate to the settlements at Norfolk Island, Van Diemen's Land, Newcastle, Moreton Bay, King George Sound and Melville Island in the north, and then the new colonies at Swan River on the west coast and in South Australia, as well as the settlements at Port Phillip, with further expansion in the succeeding years.

In addition, there are records to tell us about British policies and ideas of colonial expansion and trade as well as about their conflicts, mainly with the French, but also with the Dutch and Spanish. Australia's beginnings must be viewed in a world context and not simply as the aftermath of the loss of the English colonies in America. British expansion in India, trade with China and whaling in the South Seas—all had an effect on this maritime settlement in the antipodes. The records contain not only the official British documents but also those of other countries, of the maritime explorers and the traders, and the many diaries and letters of those who actually made the settlements.

In the latter part of the eighteenth century the British developed new colonies and, after the loss of the American colonies, maintained and expanded the large empire still left to them in Canada, the West Indies and India. Conflict with the French over trade was of prime importance in retaining and augmenting this empire. The reasons put forward to justify a new settlement at 'Botany Bay' are examined by G. Martin (1978), and another barrage in the war over the 'reasons why' has been fired by Alan Frost (1980). These books argue whether the traditionally accepted reason, namely the disposal of convicts, was the real basis for establishing the settlement or whether a naval consideration or, as others suggest, a trading need was the real motivation.

THE BEGINNINGS

The first fleet brought with it writers with particular points of view and conflicting ideas. The rigid British class structure and attitude of superiority of the first and many of the later settlers conflicted with their isolation while struggling to start a new life. Settlers' preconceptions are reflected in their view of the earlier inhabitants of the land; David Collins (1798–1802; repr, 1975) shows these characteristics in his detailed descriptions of the Aborigines and their society. Perhaps the most readable contemporary books are those of Watkin Tench, *A narrative of the expedition to Botany Bay* (1789) and *A complete account of the settlement of Port Jackson* (London, G. Nicol and J. Sewell, 1793); both have been republished as *Sydney's first four years* (1979).

An account of the voyage of the first fleet has been published by Victor Crittenden (1981), while extracts from various journals have been put together by Jonathan King (1982).

The colony at 'Botany Bay' was established primarily because of the reports of Sir Joseph Banks and Captain Cook. Their descriptions of grassy meadows and scattered trees gave authorities in England a picture of fertile plains, easy to cultivate and ready for flocks of domestic animals to multiply on. Governor Phillip, the leader of the expedition, did not anticipate the sandy and marshy soil of Botany Bay or the rocky areas of Port Jackson packed with trees and underbrush. The struggles with the land as displayed in the early literature would have been less intense had Banks given a clearer description of the country and the toughness of the timber. Arthur Phillip (1789; repr, 1970) and John Hunter (1793; repr, 1968), together with Tench and Collins mentioned above, tell a lively story of these attempts to battle with the new environment.

All the first fleet journals and accounts reflect the absolute reliance on ships and the sea connection. The journal by Philip Gidley King (1980) while he was in charge of the tiny subcolony on Norfolk Island clearly demonstrates this need. The visits of the *Supply* and the journeys to Batavia for supplies as well as Captain Hunter's account (1793; repr, 1968) of the visit of the *Sirius* to Cape Town, also for food, are indicative of this reliance on ships.

The history of the first settlement has been well documented. The biography by George Mackaness (1937) is so far the best book about the first governor. More recent information has since become available and no doubt from such work as that of Alan Frost, new biographies will be written. For a day-by-day account of the settlement taken from all the contemporary sources, the best record is that in three volumes by John Cobley (1980). The history of Norfolk Island, the first of the many sea-linked settlements, is ably recorded in M. Hoare (1982).

Many of the sources about the first settlement have not yet been published and are therefore difficult to use. Many of the original manuscripts, letters, diaries and government documents are in archives and libraries in Britain, Australia and occasionally in the United States, and a surprisingly large number are still in private hands. New items come to light at intervals. Some of this new material is edited and made available in printed form or put on to microfilm. The most important venture in this field is the Australian Joint Copying Project, a co-operative undertaking by the Mitchell Library and the National Library of Australia. However, copies of much of this microfilmed material can also be found in the various state libraries. Those researching this period in Australian history would be well advised to check the indexes to these films because it is often no longer necessary to go to England to consult the records kept there.

Before microfilm became available, there were several attempts to publish such documents in book form. The first was *Historical records of Port Phillip* (1878; repr, 1972), followed by *Historical records of New South Wales* (7 vols in 8, 1892–98; facs, Sydney, Lansdown Slattery, 1978–79), and later, *Historical records of Australia* (36 vols, Melbourne, Library Committee of the Commonwealth Parliament, 1914–25). These printed collections of documents, which complement each other, are valuable, but the second two must be used with care because they have been selectively copied; there are many mistakes in the transcription by hand from originals, and the numerous omissions can present a distorted picture. It must also be remembered that many of these records are official documents, designed to present events as the officials wanted them to be seen.

In order to find out what original source material is available in Great Britain, it is useful to consult Phyllis Mander-Jones' *Manuscripts in the British Isles relating to Australia, New Zealand and the Pacific* (ANUP, 1972). Related and often very interesting material will also be found in the British Library (formerly the British Museum) and in the British Museum (Natural History). The latter contains the famous Watling collection of drawings of early New South Wales. Other important repositories of primary source material are the India Office in London, the National Maritime Museum at Greenwich, the Greenwich Observatory, the Royal Botanic Gardens at Kew, and numerous other institutions that flourished at the end of the eighteenth and the beginning of the nineteenth centuries.

In Australia the most important collection for the early history of the country is the Mitchell Library, Sydney. It is rich in manuscripts, many relating to the first settlement at Sydney, but also to the other early settlements in Tasmania and Victoria as well as to later ones in Queensland, South and Western Australia and the Northern Territory. The Mitchell Library's published catalogues of books (see chapter 8 of this volume) are among the basic reference works in which to search for printed material.

The Archives Authority of New South Wales, also located in Sydney, should be consulted as it houses most of the government papers from the earliest times. The records and correspondence relating to land grants, convict records and the administration of justice are all available. A series of guides published by the authority will help researchers find their way through this enormous mass of material.

The National Library of Australia has material on the first settlement and early settlers, much of which consists of personal records, diaries, papers and pictures. Manuscript and printed material on the first settlements in the various states is held in all the state libraries with reference, again, to the Public Record Office in London.

EXPANSION OF SETTLEMENT

With the consolidation of the settlement at Sydney, British colonies gradually expanded to other parts of the continent. Exploration of the coast by seamen like George Bass and Matthew Flinders, and later Phillip Parker King, made other areas known. After Norfolk Island, settlements were soon established at Newcastle for its coal and Maitland for its access to the rich plains of the Hunter River, as described by W.A. Wood (1972). These settlements all relied on the sea link with Sydney.

Van Diemen's Land was next settled: fears of French incursions and possible claims were the spur while the Napoleonic wars were being bitterly fought on land in Europe and at sea all over the world. Lieutenant Paterson was sent to establish a colony in Van Diemen's Land and David Collins, a longtime resident of Sydney, was given the task of setting up a foothold on the mainland of Australia in what is now Victoria. He was not successful and moved his people to Van Diemen's Land where he founded Hobart. Perhaps the most interesting description of this enterprise is by J. West (1852; repr, 1971); the Reverend Robert Knopwood wrote a contemporary account of the settlement published only in 1977. Van Diemen's Land became an important colony because its rich land produced food that was shipped to Sydney.

New settlements were gradually extended northward along the coast of New South Wales, partly because of the need to transfer those convicts who had been condemned to further punishment for crimes committed in the colony. Port Macquarie, founded in 1821 as one of these convict bases, is described in Frank Rogers's book *Port Macquarie, a history to 1850* (Sydney, Hastings District Historical Society, 1982). Further north the founding of the future city of Brisbane at Moreton Bay in 1824 has been described by J.G. Steele (1975). Thus, slowly, the eastern coast was settled with the sea as the main link connecting the settlements; though it was notably successful at first in isolating the prison-like convict establishments from the main colony, they were gradually connected by road and by the overland links made necessary by further development. Much of this is described in the literature on exploration described in chapter 24.

The need for Britain to protect its trade routes caused two further establishments and the fear of the French jumping its claim saw attempted settlements in north Australia and the south of

Western Australia. Phillip Parker King's exploration of the north and the establishment of a settlement at Singapore in 1819 persuaded some people of the need for a settlement in north Australia. Melville Island was chosen and a foothold established as described by J. Morris (1964) while Appleyard (1979) describes the founding of Fremantle in 1829. Captain Stirling, who was involved in the latter project, was later sent from Sydney to Melville Island to find a better place for that settlement: isolation from Sydney and the long sea trip made it difficult to maintain the colony.

Governor Darling in New South Wales was also instructed to set up a colony at King George Sound, on the southeast coast of Western Australia. Major Edmund Lockyer led a team and, in this equally isolated part of the then known world, sat out many weeks and months of loneliness. His unpublished journal is in the Mitchell Library.

Finally came three dramatic new kinds of colonies in the 1820s and 1830s. The Swan River settlement began in 1829, established from London with authority for a separate existence from the colonies in eastern Australia. Swan River and Albany soon became the first Australian ports of call for ships from Europe on their way to Sydney. Some passengers even disembarked at Swan River to recuperate from the long voyage before continuing on to the east. Ships going to England also called, but Swan River nevertheless took a long time to become the prosperous colony of Western Australia. It did become, even at this early stage, an important link in the maritime trade around the coast of the Australian continent.

The settlement of Victoria in 1835 was a free enterprise effort. The story of John Batman's attempts to secure areas of what is now Melbourne by treaty with the Aborigines and his rivalry with John Pascoe Fawkner is the story of the beginning of the Melbourne settlement on the Yarra River. The best books about this different kind of colony are probably by C.P. Billot (1979, 1985) and there is also an eyewitness account by John Pascoe Fawkner published in 1982. There were in addition other settlements at Portland Bay and earlier attempts at settlement by David Collins in 1803 and at Westernport in 1826–27. K. Bowden's *The Western Port settlement and its leading personalities* (Melbourne, South Eastern Historical Association, 1970) is a good account of the latter.

The last of the major settlements around the coast of the continent was South Australia. Some may claim it was the most important because it was a new kind of colony, similar in some ways to Western Australia but different in its arrangement of land distribution under the Wakefield system. The most important books on this new approach are by R.C. Mills (1915; facs, 1974), D. Pike (1967) and A.G. Price (1924; facs, 1973). Here, too, the sea links remained important for a long time. The connection with Van Diemen's Land as a source of food supplies was vital to the survival of the early settlement in South Australia. Adelaide then became one of the important stops for ships travelling along the south of the continent. Overlanders soon arrived from the eastern colonies and a few of the early settlers also came this way, heralding the end of the dominance of the original sea lanes.

The maritime link in the expansion of the Australian settlements makes the growth of these colonies different from many other colonial expansions. Australia differs from the United States of America with its expansion westward, or Canada with movement of settlements up the great St Lawrence River. Here, there were no great rivers to encourage such development except the isolated and unreliable Murray–Darling river system in the east and no rich westward plains (or eastward plains from the Swan River) to encourage ordered and land-tied expansion. The literature of the settlement of Australia demonstrates the sea-based development of the first establishments that grew into colonies. Sea captains were often the founders of new settlements, and their diaries and logbooks the first records of such expansion.

The list of books that follows is arranged in chronological order of arrival and permanent occupation of the first eight sites, some of which later became the Australian state capital cities. In the minds of many people, the term 'first settlement' has no meaning other than in the context of the landing of the first fleet in 1788. However, while there were many common experiences among the early European settlers wherever they pitched their tents and subsequently built homes and cities, there were also significant variations which justify the inclusion of select titles on the beginnings of each of the Australian states.

The reading list does not pretend to be exhaustive: there are hundreds of works describing and analysing the origins, effects and consequences of the first settlement, the way it was achieved and the society that grew out of it. It should be used in conjunction with the bibliography assembled for chapter 21, 'Discovery'. The eight parts are:

Port Jackson, NSW (Botany Bay): 1788
Newcastle: 1801
Van Diemen's Land (Tasmania): 1803
Moreton Bay: 1824

North Australia: 1826
Swan River: 1829
Victoria: 1834–35
South Australia: 1836

PORT JACKSON, NSW (BOTANY BAY): 1788

BLAINEY, G.N. *The tyranny of distance: how distance shaped Australia's history* (rev edn). Melbourne, Macmillan, 1982. 366 p, illus, maps.

An important reason for sending convicts to Australia was the establishment of a maritime trade base and the Australian trade in flax and masts; this is reinforced by instructions to settle Norfolk Island. First published in 1968.

BRADLEY, W. *A voyage to New South Wales: the journal of Lieutenant William Bradley RN of HMS Sirius, 1786–1792.* Sydney, Trustees of the Public Library of NSW in association with Ure Smith, 1969. 495 p, illus, maps.

An acccount of the voyage and activities at Sydney Cove not found in other journals. Watercolours of Port Jackson and the fleet on its way to NSW. Facsimile edition of the original in the Mitchell Library.

CLARK, C.M.H. ed, *Select documents in Australian history.* A & R, 1977. 2 vols.

The first volume covers the period 1788–1850 and contains many references to the first fleet and early settlement. First published, 1950–55.

CLARK, R. *The journal and letters of Lt Ralph Clark, 1787–1792.* Ed by P.G. Fidlon and R.J. Ryan. Sydney, Australian Documents Library in association with the Library of Australian History, 1981. 344 p, illus.

An officer of the marines on the first fleet, Lt Clark writes about the convict women on the voyage. The descriptions are sometimes highly diverting though, as Clark was a very religious young man, his expressions tend to be overindulgent.

COBLEY, J. *Sydney Cove, 1788–1792* (rev edn). A & R, 1980. 3 vols, maps.

A day-by-day account of the settlement compiled from contemporary journals. Comprehensive, but it does not deal with the preparations for the first fleet or the voyage. First published, 1963–65.

COLLINS, D. *An account of the English colony in New South Wales . . .* London, T. Cadell Junior & W. Davies, 1798. 2 vols, 618 p, illus, maps.

One of the fullest accounts of the first settlement period and probably the most trustworthy. Facsimile edition, Adelaide, LBSA, 1971; new edition, 1975.

CRITTENDEN, V. *A bibliography of the first fleet.* ANUP, 1981, 359 p.

Lists in a subject arrangement the material available on the first fleet and the settlement of NSW; includes manuscript sources, books and journal articles. There is an author–title index and a general index. This should be the place to start for information on the first settlement.

CRITTENDEN, V. *The voyage of the first fleet 1787–1788, taken from contemporary accounts.* Canberra, Mulini, 1981. 105 p, map.

A chronicle of the voyage of the first fleet, moulded into a continuous narrative.

CROWLEY, F.K. ed, *A documentary history of Australia.* Vol 1. *Colonial Australia, 1788–1840.* Melbourne, Nelson, 1980. 621 p.

Useful as a glimpse at the documents available on the early settlement. It has material not only on Sydney but also on the other colonies as they were established.

DALLAS, K.M. *Trading posts or penal colonies: the commercial significance of Cook's New Holland route to the Pacific.* Hobart, Fullers Bookshop, 1969. 132 p, illus.

Argues that convicts were a 'cover' to hide economic reasons when international and local pressures militated against setting up trading outposts.

DAVIDSON, R. *A book collector's notes on items relating to the discovery of Australia, the first settlement and the early coastal exploration of the continent.* Melbourne, Cassell, 1970. 138 p, illus.

The published first fleet journals are discussed from the book collector and bibliographer's viewpoint.

EASTY, J. *Memorandum of the transactions of a voyage from England to Botany Bay, 1787–1793: a first fleet journal.* Sydney, Trustees of the Public Library of NSW in association with A & R, 1965. 182 p, illus.

A record of observations by an ordinary soldier, based on a diary of daily events during the voyage of the first fleet and of activities in Sydney during the first five years.

FROST, A. *Convicts and empire: a naval question.* OUP, 1980. 240 p, illus.

An important book on the reasons for the settlement of NSW. Presents new evidence and argues that the settlement was established as a naval outpost because of the international contests of the period.

HUNTER, J. *An historical journal of the transactions at Port Jackson and Norfolk Island . . .* London, Stockdale, 1793, 584 p, illus, maps.

Besides containing Captain Hunter's account of the voyage of the first fleet it also reports his later voyage around the world in the *Sirius* to secure supplies for the colony. Originally published under a slightly different title. Facsimile edition, Adelaide, LBSA, 1968; new edition published 1968.

JEANS, D.N. *An historical geography of New South Wales to 1901.* Sydney, Reed Education, 1972. 328 p, illus, maps.
Describes the land, climate and vegetation the settlers found on arrival in NSW and outlines the impact on the Aborigines. Includes a chapter on the founding of the colony based on the convict theory.

KING, J. *The first fleet: the convict voyage that founded Australia 1787–88.* Melbourne, Macmillan, 1982. 186 p, illus, maps.
Extracts from the first fleet journals published in chronological sequence to give a graphic outline of the voyage. Lavishly illustrated.

KING, P.G. *The journal of Philip Gidley King: Lieutenant RN, 1787–1790.* Ed by P.G. Fidlon and R.J. Ryan. Sydney, Australian Documents Library, 1980. 401 p, illus.
King describes the voyage to and the first settlement at Norfolk Island, including a statistical account of crops, weather and general activities of the settlers. The manuscript is in the Mitchell Library.

MACKANESS, G. *Admiral Arthur Phillip, founder of New South Wales, 1738–1814.* A & R, 1937. 536 p, illus.
Detailed biography trying to present a view of Phillip the man.

MACKANESS, G. *Blue bloods of Botany Bay: a book of Australian historical tales.* London, Collins, 1953. 143 p.
Vivid description of some of the activities of members of the first fleet and brief accounts of some first fleet personalities.

MACKANESS, G. *Sir Joseph Banks, his relations with Australia.* A & R, 1936. 146 p, illus.
This biography discusses mainly correspondence between Banks and governors Phillip, King and Hunter, and the plant collectors sent to Australia.

MACKANESS, G. *Some proposals for establishing colonies in the South Seas.* Dubbo, NSW, Review Publications, 1976. 62 p, illus. (Australian historical monographs, ns vol 11).
Details of some of the plans put forward for establishing a colony in NSW, quoting among other sources Phillip's memorandum of 1787. First published in 1943.

MARTIN, G. ed, *The founding of Australia: the argument about Australia's origins.* Sydney, Hale & Iremonger, 1978. 314 p.
Collection of journal articles and extracts from books, with a commentary on each by Martin, illustrating the controversy as to why Australia was first settled. Useful because it brings the main arguments together.

MIRA, W.J.D. *Coinage and currency in New South Wales, 1788–1829; and an index of currency references in the* Sydney Gazette *1803–1811.* Sydney, Metropolitan Coin Club of Sydney, 1981. 206 p, illus.
Describes the problems of currency in the early days of settlement and the unusual solutions devised by the early governments.

O'BRIEN, E.M. *The foundation of Australia, 1789–1800: a study of English criminal practice and penal colonization in the eighteenth century* (2nd edn). A & R, 1937, 327 p, illus.
A summary of the preparations for the first fleet and a few details relating to the first settlement. Appendix B gives the number of convicts transported 1787–1800. New edition published in 1950.

PHILLIP, A. *The voyage of Governor Phillip to Botany Bay, with an account of the establishment of the colonies and Norfolk Island . . .* London, Stockdale, 1789, 298, lxxiv p, illus, maps.
Based largely on Governor Phillip's earliest reports on the colony and its establishment. This is a basic source book and the first in order of importance for the history of Australia. Facsimile edition Adelaide, LBSA, 1968; new edition published 1970.

PROUDFOOT, H. *Old Government House: the building and its landscape.* State Planning Authority of NSW in association with A & R, 1971. 91 p, illus, maps.
Phillip built the first Government House at Parramatta in 1790. Proudfoot describes the country and the establishment of Rose Hill, later called Parramatta.

RUMSEY, H.J. *The pioneers of Sydney Cove.* Sydney, Sunnybrook, 1937. xxviii, 121 p, illus.
This is really a 'who's who' of the first fleet. Though it misses some of the marines, there are invaluable biographical details of those people who are mentioned. Some new evidence has been uncovered since 1937.

RUTTER, O. *The first fleet: the record of the foundation of Australia from its conception to the settlement at Sydney Cove.* London, Golden Cockerel, 1937. 151 p, illus.
Documents that offer a continuous picture of the organisation of the fleet and its journey, together with Phillip's first despatch from Sydney Cove, 15 May 1788.

SCOTT, J. *Remarks on a passage to Botany Bay, 1787–1792: a first fleet journal.* Trustees of the Public Library of NSW in association with A & R, 1963. xi, 83 p, illus.
The journal was known as 'the Sergeant's Diary' but has now been identified as having been written by James Scott. It is a simple diary of events by a sergeant of the marines who came out with his wife, his children were born on the voyage and in Sydney. The manuscript is in the Mitchell Library.

SHAW, A.G.L. *Convicts and the colonies: a study of penal transportation from Great Britain and Ireland to Australia and other parts of the British Empire.* MUP, 1977. 400 p.
Discusses the convict problem in Britain, the plans to solve it, the decision to establish a colony in NSW and some of the arguments against the settlement. First published in 1966.

SMYTH, A.B. *The journal of Arthur Bowes Smyth, surgeon, Lady Penrhyn, 1787–1789.* Ed by P.G. Fidlon and R.J. Ryan. Sydney, Australian Documents Library, 1979. 196 p, illus.
The surgeon on one of the transports gives a glimpse of the activities on board ship during the voyage of the first fleet and comments on the first settlement. The last half of the journal deals with the voyage home via Tahiti and China.

STEVEN, M. *Trade, tactics and territory: Britain in the Pacific 1783–1823.* MUP, 1983. 155 p, maps.
A most important account of British plans for its expansion into the Pacific. One chapter deals with the background to the settlement in NSW in this context.

SWAN, R.A. *To Botany Bay—if policy warrants the measure: a reappraisal of the reasons for the decision of the British government in 1786 to establish a settlement at Botany Bay in New South Wales on the eastern coast of New Holland.* Canberra, Roebuck Society, 1973. 189 p, illus.
Useful background to the first fleet project including the political reasons and the difficulties of international relations.

TENCH, W. *Sydney's first four years: being a reprint of a narrative of the expedition to Botany Bay and, a complete account of the settlement of Port Jackson.* Ed by L.F. Fitzhardinge. Sydney, Library of Australian History in association with the Royal Australian Historical Society, 1979. 364 p, illus, maps.
A most important account of the first fleet voyage and the early settlement at Port Jackson. *A narrative . . .* first published in 1789; *A complete account . . .* in 1793.

WHITE, J. *Journal of a voyage to New South Wales.* Ed by A.H. Chisholm. A & R in association with the Royal Australian Historical Society, 1962. 282 p, illus.
Another important account of the first fleet voyage, containing

valuable information on the natural history of the new settlement. Originally published with a slightly different title in 1790 (facs, New York, Arno Press, 1971).

WILLEY, K. *When the sky fell down: the destruction of the tribes of the Sydney region, 1788–1850s*. Sydney, Collins, 1979. 231 p, illus, map.

An account of the settlement at Port Jackson and its effect on the local Aborigines. It deals in detail with the resultant starvation, disease and decline of the Aboriginal population.

WORGAN, G.B. *Journal of a first fleet surgeon*. Sydney, Library Council of NSW in association with the Library of Australian History, 1978. xiii, 71 p, illus.

This slim volume represents all that has been located of Worgan's journal which has all the freshness of a letter based on a recent diary.

NEWCASTLE: 1801

MACQUARIE, L. *Lachlan Macquarie, governor of New South Wales: journals of his tour in New South Wales and Van Diemen's Land, 1810–1822*. Sydney, Library of Australian History, 320 p, illus, maps.

Macquarie's published journals contain two handsomely illustrated accounts of Newcastle as he found it in 1818 and again in 1821. First published in 1956.

MAITLAND AND DISTRICT HISTORICAL SOCIETY. *A history of Maitland*. Maitland, NSW, Maitland City Council, 1983. 79 p, illus.

Account of Maitland's settlement and development, edited by L. Fredman.

PERRY, T.M. *Australia's first frontier: the spread of settlement in New South Wales, 1788–1829*. MUP in association with ANUP, 1963. 163 p, illus, maps.

Contains an excellent description of European settlement in the Hunter valley.

TURNER, J.W. *Coal mining in Newcastle, 1801–1900*. Newcastle, NSW, Newcastle Region Public Library, 1982. 179 p, illus, maps (Newcastle history monographs, 9).

TURNER, J.W. *Manufacturing in Newcastle, 1801–1900*. Newcastle, NSW, Newcastle Public Library, 1980. 139 p, illus, maps. (Newcastle history monographs, 8).

Turner's two histories describe the development of Newcastle and include references to pioneer coalminers and early industrialists.

TURNER, J.W. ed, *Newcastle as a convict settlement: the evidence before J.T. Bigge in 1819–1821*. Newcastle, NSW, Newcastle Public Library in association with the Newcastle and Hunter District Historical Society, 1973. 314 p, illus, maps. (Newcastle history monographs, 7).

Reproduces the evidence obtained by Commissioner Bigge, the largest single source of information about Newcastle as a penal colony.

WOOD, W.A. *Dawn in the valley: the story of settlement in the Hunter River valley to 1833*. Sydney, Wentworth Books, 1972. 346 p, illus.

A study of the beginning of European settlement in the Hunter valley.

VAN DIEMEN'S LAND (TASMANIA): 1803

BARRETT, W.R. *History of Tasmania to the death of Lieutenant-Governor Collins in 1810*. Hobart, H.T. Whiting, 1936. 116 p.

Although rather dated, this book contains a good account of the first years of settlement with references to sources. There has

been some material uncovered since it was written.

BOLGER, P. *Hobart Town*. ANUP, 1973. 237 p, illus, maps. Only the first chapter deals with the foundation of the city by David Collins.

COLLINS, C.R. *Saga of settlement: a brief account of the life and times of Lieutenant-Colonel David Collins, 1st judge advocate of the colony of New South Wales and lieutenant-governor of southern Van Diemen's Land*. Perth, Imperial Printing Co, 1957. 148 p, illus.

A biography of David Collins. The last 60 pages outline his work at Hobart until his death there in 1810.

GIBLIN, R.W. *The early history of Tasmania*. London, Methuen, 1928; MUP, 1939. 2 vols, illus, maps.

Vol 1, 'The geographical era, 1642–1804', gives details of the first settlements, 1803–04, John Bowen at Risdon Cove and David Collins at Sullivan Cove. Vol 2 is 'The penal settlement era, 1804–1818: Collins, Sorell and Arthur'. The first chapters deal with Collins' administration up to 1809.

KNOPWOOD, R. *The diary of the Reverend Robert Knopwood, 1803–1838, first chaplain of Van Diemen's Land*. Ed by Mary Nicholls. Hobart, Tasmanian Historical Research Association, 1977. 738 p, illus.

Knopwood, an Anglican minister, accompanied the Collins expedition and was there at the foundation of the settlement. The only first-hand account of events in the early years of the colony.

ROBSON, L.L. *A history of Tasmania Vol 1. Van Diemen's Land from the earliest times to 1855*. OUP, 1983. 632 p, illus, maps.

A very detailed study making extensive use of official records.

WEST, J. *History of Tasmania*. Launceston, Henry Dowling, 1852, 2 vols.

Important nineteenth-century history recounting the facts as they were known at that time. Can be used with confidence so long as the prejudices common to its times are kept in mind. New edition published 1971.

MORETON BAY: 1824

BATESON, C. *Patrick Logan, tyrant of Brisbane town*. Sydney, Ure Smith, 1966. 190 p, illus.

An unsensational account of the career of a man often depicted as a monster of cruelty. Logan was commandant 1828–30.

LANG, J.D. *Cooksland in north-eastern Australia: the future cottonfield of Great Britain. Its characteristics and capabilities for European colonization; with a disquisition on the origin, manners and customs of the Aborigines*. London, Longman, Brown, Green & Longmans, 1847. 496 p, illus, maps.

Cooksland was Lang's suggested name for the new northern colony which became Qld.

PETRIE, C.C. *Tom Petrie's reminiscences of early Queensland*. Brisbane, Watson Ferguson, 1904, 319 p, illus.

Tom Petrie came to the Moreton Bay penal settlement as a small child in 1837 when his father was appointed clerk of works there. New edition published 1983.

RUSSELL, H.S. *The genesis of Queensland: an account of the first exploring journeys to and over Darling Downs, the earliest days of their occupation, social life, station seeking, the course of discovery, northward and westward and a resumé of the causes which led to separation from New South Wales*. Sydney, Turner & Henderson, 1888. 633 p, illus, maps.

Russell was a pastoralist on the Darling Downs from 1840 to 1855.

STEELE, J.G. *Brisbane Town in convict days, 1824–1842*. UQP, 1975. 403 p, illus, maps.

Annotated extracts from contemporary documents and publications.

STEELE, J.G. *The explorers of the Moreton Bay district, 1770–1830.* UQP, 1972. 386 p, illus, maps.

The author reprints and annotates original journals, fieldbooks and reports, interpreting them in terms of modern maps.

NORTH AUSTRALIA: 1826

BAUER, F.H. *Historical geography of white settlement in part of northern Australia. Pt 2: The Katherine–Darwin region.* Canberra, CSIRO, 1964. 284 p. (CSIRO Division of Land Research and Regional Survey. Divisional report, 64/1).

A key study of land settlement from a geographer's point of view.

EARL, G.W. *Enterprise in tropical Australia.* London, Madden and Malcolm, 1846. 178 p, maps.

An account of the north Australian settlements by the commissioner of crown lands for Port Essington.

GREAT BRITAIN. Parliament. House of Commons. *Copies of extracts of any correspondence relative to the establishment of a settlement at Port Essington.* London, 1843. 49 p, map. (GB Parliament. H of C Reports and papers no 141 of 1843).

Includes correspondence on the political and commercial importance of Port Essington and the progress of the settlement from April 1840 to September 1842.

KERR, M.G. *The surveyors: the story of the founding of Darwin.* Adelaide, Rigby, 1971. 183 p, illus, maps.

A basic history by a descendant of one of the surveyors of the overland telegraph.

MacKNIGHT, C.C. ed, *The farthest coast: a selection of writings relating to the history of the northern coast of Australia.* MUP, 1969. 218 p, illus, maps.

Covers various aspects of the area including first European settlement and the role of Asian seafarers.

MILLS, C.M. *A bibliography of the Northern Territory: monographs,* Canberra, Canberra College of Advanced Education Library, 1977–83. 5 vols.

A comprehensive bibliography of books published in, or about, the NT to 1981. Includes some fugitive materials; extensive coverage.

MORRIS, J. *Relationship between the British and the Tiwi in the vicinity of Fort Dundas, Melville Island.* Darwin, Historical Society of the NT, 1964. 17 p.

Ford Dundas was one of the abortive settlements which subsequently moved to Fremantle in 1829.

SOUTH AUSTRALIA. Commission appointed by the Governor-in-chief to inquire into the management of the Northern Expedition. *Report . . . together with minutes of evidence and appendix.* Adelaide, Government Printer, 1866. xxvii, 112, xlii p. (SA. Parliament. Parliamentary paper no 17 of 1866–67).

A discussion of the abortive South Australian settlement at Escape Cliffs, Adam Bay, NT; the first of several NT settlements to be called Palmerston.

SOUTH AUSTRALIA. Commissioner of Crown Lands and Immigration. *Report on Northern Territory. The report . . . of his official visit to the Northern Territory, via Galle, Singapore, Java, Macassar and Timor.* Adelaide, 1873. 10 p. (SA. Parliament. Parliamentary paper no 55 of 1873).

An early account of the settlement at Palmerston, Port Darwin, later to be renamed Darwin.

SPILLETT, P.G. *Forsaken settlement: an illustrated history of the settlement of Victoria, Port Essington, north Australia, 1838–1849.* Melbourne, Lansdowne, 1972. 196 p, illus, maps.

A study of the Port Essington settlement, including information on the first serious cyclone to be experienced by settlers in Australia.

SWAN RIVER: 1829

APPLEYARD, R.T. AND MANFORD, T.B. *The beginning: European discovery and early settlement of Swan River, Western Australia.* UWAP, 1979. 329 p, illus, maps.

Scholarly account of first settlement.

CROSS, J. *Journals of several expeditions made in Western Australia, during the years 1829, 1830, 1831 and 1832, under the sanction of the governor, Sir James Stirling, containing the latest authentic information relative to that country.* London, J. Cross, 1833, 263 p, map.

An account, somewhat glowing, of the colony and prospects designed to encourage emigration. Facsimile edition published by UWAP (1980).

CROWLEY, F.K. *A guide to the principal documents and publications relating to the history of Western Australia.* Perth, Dept of History, University of WA, 1949. 74 p.

Still a useful guide to many of the official documents.

FREMANTLE, C.H. *Diary and letters of Admiral Sir C.H. Fremantle, G.C.B., relating to the founding of the colony of Western Australia, 1829.* Ed by Lord Cottesloe. London, Hazell, Watson and Viney, 1928. 94 p, illus, maps.

A first-hand description of the first six months of settlement.

HASLUCK, A. *Thomas Peel of Swan River.* OUP, 1965. 273 p, illus, map.

Entertaining biography of one of the greatest supporters of the colony on Swan River. Important for understanding the difficulties in establishing the colony.

MERCER, F.R. *Amazing career: the story of Western Australia's first surveyor-general.* Perth, Paterson Brokensha, 1929. 189 p, illus.

Biography of John Septimus Roe.

PARRY, A. *The admirals Fremantle.* London, Chatto & Windus, 1971. 286 p, illus, maps.

Includes a section on Charles Howe Fremantle who claimed the western part of the continent for Britain in 1829. Deals only briefly with this period.

SHANN, E.O.G. *Cattle chosen: the story of the first group settlement in Western Australia, 1829 to 1841.* London, OUP, 1926, 186 p, illus, map.

Tells the story of the Bussell family based on letters from members of the settlement in the southwest corner of WA. Facsimile edition published by UWAP, 1978.

UREN, M.J.L. *Land looking west: the story of Governor James Stirling in Western Australia.* London, OUP, 1948. 316 p, illus.

Biography of the founder of the colony.

VICTORIA: 1834–1835

BASSETT, M. *The Hentys: an Australian colonial tapestry* MUP, 1962. 578 p, illus, maps.

Account of the Portland Bay settlement. First published in 1954.

BILLOT, C.P. *John Batman: the story of John Batman and the founding of Melbourne.* Melbourne, Hyland House, 1979. 330 p, illus.

BILLOT, C.P. *The life and times of John Pascoe Fawkner.* Melbourne, Hyland House, 1985. 356 p, illus, maps.

Two detailed studies which complement each other.

BILLOT, C.P. *Melbourne: an annotated bibliography to 1850.* Geelong, Vic, Rippleside, 1970. 308, [89] p.

Lists books, periodicals, newspapers, maps and pamphlets printed or published in Melbourne, or dealing with Melbourne. Includes facsimile of Batman's treaty with the Aborigines and Bourke's 1835 proclamation.

BOYS, R.D. *First years at Port Phillip, 1834–1842: preceded by a summary of historical events from 1768.* Melbourne, Robertson & Mullens, 1959. 159 p, illus.

A detailed chronology, first published in 1935.

COUTTS, P.J.F. *Corinella, a forgotten episode in Victoria's history.* Melbourne, Victorian Archaelogical Survey, 1983. 182 p, illus, maps.

Study of the Westernport settlement of 1826–27, based on both documentary and archaeological evidence.

DE SERVILLE, P. *Port Phillip gentlemen and good society in Melbourne before the gold rushes.* OUP, 1980. 256 p.

Lucidly written study of the pioneer gentlemen of Port Phillip; includes detailed biographical appendices.

FAWKNER, J.P. *Melbourne's missing chronicle: being the journal of preparations for departure to and proceedings at Port Phillip.* Ed by C.P. Billot. Melbourne, Quarter Books, 1982. xviii, 108 p, map.

Fawkner's journal, the earliest chronicle of the Port Phillip settlement, covers the period 18 July 1835 to 8 August 1836.

FINN, E.M. *The chronicles of early Melbourne, 1835–1852: historical, anecdotal and personal, by 'Garryowen'.* Facs, Melbourne, Heritage Publications, 1976. 3 vols, illus.

Detailed account written mainly from newspaper sources and personal memorial. First published in 1888 in 2 vols; the third volume in the facsimile set is a descriptive index.

HISTORICAL records of Victoria. Foundation series. Melbourne, Public Records Office of Vic, 1981. v, illus, maps.

The volumes to date cover the beginnings of permanent government, early relations with the Aborigines, and trade and commerce to 1839.

SHILLINGLAW, J.J. *Historical records of Port Phillip: the first annals of the colony of Victoria.* Ed by C.E. Sayers. Melbourne, Heinemann, 1972. 225 p.

Reproduces documents relating to the Sorrento settlement of 1803. First published in 1878.

SOUTH AUSTRALIA: 1836

ANGAS, G.F. *South Australia illustrated.* London, Thomas McLean, 1847, 60 p, illus.

Hand-coloured lithographic plates showing early settlements in SA including Adelaide, the Aborigines, flora and fauna.

DUTTON, F. *South Australia and its mines, with an historical sketch of the colony, under its several administrations, to the period of Captain Grey's departure.* London, T. & W. Boone, 1846, 361 p, illus, map.

History and optimistic description of life in SA, including some statistical information. Only about 70 pages deal with mining.

GOUGER, R. *South Australia in 1837; in a series of letters: with a postscript as to 1838,* Sydney, Robertson & Mullens, 1838, 168 p.

Gouger's enthusiasm for the new colony is evident in his 'sketch of its condition and prospects', which includes letters from other settlers and visitors. Facsimile edition, Adelaide, LBSA (1962).

GREAT BRITAIN. Parliament. House of Commons. Select Committee on South Australia. *First [and second] reports from the Select Committee on South Australia.* London, 1841. 2 vols, maps. (GB Parliament. H of C Reports and papers nos 119 and 394 of 1841).

The transcript of evidence and documents laid before the committee contains much detailed information, with particular relevance to the financial crisis.

HASSELL, K. *The relations between the settlers and Aborigines in South Australia, 1836–1860.* Adelaide, LBSA, 1966. 222 p.

Written in 1921 as a thesis, this work examines official and private attitudes regarding the ideal of integrating the Aborigines into European civilisation, and the settlers' inadequate understanding of Aborigines.

KERR, C.G. *'A exelent coliney': the practical idealists of 1836–1846.* Adelaide, Rigby, 1978. 174 p, illus, map.

Many previously unpublished extracts, with original spelling, from the letters and diaries of a cross-section of early settlers.

LIGHT, W. *A brief journal of the proceedings of William Light, late surveyor general of the province of South Australia ...* Adelaide, Archibald MacDougall, 1839, 80 p.

'I leave it to posterity, and not to [my enemies], to decide whether I am entitled to praise or to blame' [for the choice of the site of Adelaide]. New edition published in 1984.

MILLS, R.C. *The colonization of Australia 1829–42: the Wakefield experience in empire building.* London, Sidgwick & Jackson, 1919, 363 p.

An analysis of Wakefield's work with some emphasis on the colonisation of SA, and on the wider relevance of Wakefield's theories. Facsimile edition published by SUP (1974).

OLDHAM, W. *The land policy of South Australia from 1830 to 1842.* Adelaide, G. Hassell & Son, 1917, 118 p, illus, maps.

A detailed study of contemporary theory on colonisation and land disposal, the practical results, and an assessment of the measure of their success.

PIKE, D. *Paradise of dissent: South Australia 1829–1857.* MUP, 1967. 580 p, maps.

A study with emphasis on attitudes to colonisation and social reform, civil and religious liberty, the theories of the colonists, administrative arrangements and conflicts, economic and political development. First published in 1957.

PRICE, A.G. *The foundation and settlement of South Australia, 1829–1845.* Adelaide, F.W. Preece, 1924, 260 p, illus, maps.

Covers Wakefield's theory of colonisation, geography, land policy, primary production, conflict between Governor Hindmarsh and the colonisation commissioners, bankruptcy of the colony and economic recovery. New edition published in 1973.

SUTHERLAND, G. *The South Australian Company: a study in colonisation.* London, Longmans, Green, 1898. 238 p, illus.

An account from the company's point of view.

THOMAS, M. *The diary and letters of Mary Thomas (1836–1866) being a record of the early days of South Australia* (2nd edn). Ed by Evan Kyffin Thomas. Adelaide, W.K. Thomas & Co, 1915, 161 p, plates.

Covers the period 1836 to 1841, and presents a vivid picture of the journey out in the *Africaine* and of early days in the colony. Facsimile edition, Adelaide, Gillingham (1982).

WAKEFIELD, E.G. *The new British province of South Australia, or a description of the country, illustrated by charts and views, with an account of the principles, objects, plan, and prospects of the colony ...* London, C. Knight, 1834. 220 p, illus, maps.

Aims at a full account of the 'Principles, objects, plan and prospects' of the colony. Reprinted in *The collected works of Edward Gibbon Wakefield.* Ed by M.L. Prichard (Collins, 1968).

Lieutenant George Frederick Dashwood, Kneeling man being flogged. *Ink sketch from his sketchbook (1830–35).*
MITCHELL LIBRARY

CHAPTER 23

TRANSPORTATION OF CONVICTS

A. G. L. SHAW

URING THE EIGHTY years in which parts of Australia were penal colonies, there was constant debate on the merits and defects of the transportation system. Was it an effective punishment? Was it reformatory? Deterrent? Expensive? What were its effects on local society? On the crime rate? On prostitution? On drunkenness? On religious observance? On the police system? On local government? On the granting of self-government? Discussion of some or all of these questions permeates very much the writing of the period, whether in contemporary works such as James Macarthur, *New South Wales, its present state and future prospects* (London, Walther, 1837); J.D. Lang, *Historical and statistical account of New South Wales* (London, Cochrane and Microne, 1834; new edns in 1837, 1852 and 1875); John West, *History of Tasmania* (1852; repr, Sydney, A & R in association with the Royal Australian Historical Society, 1971); Peter Cunningham, *Two years in New South Wales* (1827; repr, A & R in association with the Royal Australian Historical Society, 1966); James Backhouse, *Narrative of a visit to the Australian colonies* (York, John L. Linney, Low Ousegate, 1843); Alexander Harris, *Settlers and convicts* (1847; repr, MUP, 1969) and many others, or in modern studies, either of particular aspects of colonial life or the general histories which are referred to elsewhere in this volume.

The same may be said of the autobiographies and biographies of people living in the first half of the nineteenth century. Among the former, for example, are Roger Therry, *Reminiscences of thirty years residence in New South Wales* (1863; repr, SUP for the Royal Australian Historical Society, 1974) and James Hardy Vaux, *Memoirs* (1819; repr, MUP, 1964); among the latter, C.H. Currey, *Sir Francis Forbes* (A & R, 1968) and *The brothers Bent* (SUP, 1968). Apart from these, there are many books dealing with the various governors of the penal colonies and with the many officials, settlers and convicts themselves.

Of the convicts' writings, the best known are by the well-educated political prisoners whose experiences were not typical and who naturally had an axe to grind in their accounts of the system. Mention may be made of those written by several guilty of political offences—trade unionists, Canadian rebels, Chartists and Irish—Leon Ducharmé, John Frost, William Gates, Maurice La Pailleur, George Loveless, Linus B. Miller, John Mitchell and François Prieur; but there are others. Ann Conlon has commented on such convict memoirs in '"Mine is a sad yet true story": convict narratives, 1818–1850' in *J R Aust Hist Soc* (55, 1, 1969, 43–82) and Alan Atkinson discusses 'Four patterns of convict protest' in *Labour history* (37, 1979, 28–51).

Of the specialist works on the transportation system, the most significant and readily available are referred to below. Many others which throw light on some aspect of it can be referred to in the major libraries, especially the Mitchell Library in Sydney and the British Library in London, though in most cases they are either propaganda or self-laudatory works. A number are listed in the bibliographies of Shaw (1977) and in several of the other recent works on the subject listed below, as well as in the general histories. The principles involved in the controversy are perhaps best summed up in the two attacks on the system by Richard Whately, Protestant Archbishop of Dublin, *Thoughts on secondary punishment in a letter to Earl Grey* (London, B. Fellowes, 1832) and *Remarks on transportation* (London, B. Fellowes, 1834), and in the two replies to him, by Colonel George Arthur, then lieutenant-governor of Van Diemen's Land, *Observations upon secondary punishment* (Hobart, James Ross, 1833) and *A defence of transportation in reply to the remarks of the Archbishop of Dublin* (London, George Cowie, 1835).

In the preface to Shaw's book, it is noted (p 13) that a number of the conclusions there needed 'to be confirmed (or perhaps refuted) by detailed investigation both of the districts from which the convicts came and of those they were sent to; for it is only from such studies that the whole truth can emerge, and at the moment [1964] these are extremely rare'. This is still the case, but the results of further studies, though not yet published in book form, should be mentioned. Different aspects of the penal settlement are discussed by Decie Denholm, 'Port Arthur: the men and myth' (*Hist stud* 14, 55, 1970, 406–23). Giving a rather contrary view is the article by Julian Reynolds, 'The penal stations of New South Wales and Van Diemen's Land: the reality behind the legend' (*J R Aust Hist Soc* 67, 4, 1982, 354–65). Henry Reynolds, in '"That hated stain": the aftermath of transportation in Tasmania' (*Hist Stud* 14, 53, 1969, 19–31), describes some of the aftereffects of transportation in Tasmania. Two recent articles criticise the reports of the Molesworth Committee (the Select Committee on Transportation of 1837–38), namely, John Ritchie, 'Towards ending an unclean thing: the Molesworth Committee and the abolition of transportation to New South Wales, 1837–40' (*Hist stud* 17, 67, 1976, 144–64) and N. Townsend, 'The Molesworth Enquiry: does the report fit the evidence?' (*J Aust Stud* 1, June 1977, 33–51).

There are several novels about the system. The most notorious, Marcus Clarke's, *For the term of his natural life* (1874; repr, Melbourne, Currey O'Neil, 1983) is misleading in so far as it subjects one man to every known evil of the system and implies that this experience is typical; L.L. Robson has analysed it in 'The historical basis of *For the term of his natural life*' (*Australian literary studies* 1, 2, 1963, 104–21). *The adventures of Ralph Rashleigh* (1929, repr; (A & R, 1975) a picaresque novel thought to be by the convict James Tucker, combined circumstances of convict days with fictitious adventures, and Henry Savery, another convict author, in *Quintus Servinton* (1830; repr, UNSWP, 1984), the first novel in book form written in Australia, provides a contrasting and complementary picture in describing the experiences of an educated convict, though only one-third of the novel deals with events after Quintus had been transported.

A larger number of serious studies have been made of the details of the administration of the system in Tasmania because of the excellence of the records kept in the archives at Hobart; those held in Sydney were destroyed during the period when Australians were anxious to forget their convict past. Today, when many people are seeking to find a convict ancestor if they possibly can, studies in New South Wales have depended more on private papers and old reminiscences, but there is still room for local studies based on the records available in the many bench books that have survived. These, as in Tasmania, may prove a fruitful source for further study. Generally speaking, of course, the official records, when carefully analysed, provide more reliable information than the usually prejudiced accounts of individuals, though one must notice that offical records can also show a distorted picture and, like every other record of a highly controversial subject, have to be studied carefully—something which fortunately has become more common in recent years.

A few British government documents have been included in the reading list. These, too, are not free from bias and some of the reports were forcefully contested in parliament when they were tabled; obviously they form an important mirror of official attitudes towards convict transportation. Only the most important ones have been listed here.

'Cessation of transportation', 1853. Pewter medal, diameter 57 mm. This medal was struck to commemorate the last convict ship to Van Diemen's Land, the St Vincent, which reached Hobart on 26 May 1853 with 207 prisoners on board.

TASMANIAN MUSEUM AND ART GALLERY

BARRY, J.V. *Alexander Maconochie of Norfolk Island: a study of a pioneer in penal reform.* OUP, 1958. 277 p, illus, maps.
This biography discusses Maconochie's criticisms of the transportation system and his attempts at reform when commandant of the penal settlement at Norfolk Island, 1840–44.

BATESON, C. *The convict ships, 1787–1868.* Sydney, Library of Australian History, 1983. 434 p, illus.
Survey of the ships carrying convicts to Australia, relating administrative details, type and size of ships, and notable events. First published in 1959.

COBLEY, J. *The crimes of the first fleet convicts.* A & R, 1982. 338 p.
A comprehensive register of the convicts in the first fleet, giving details of their ages, occupations, crimes and trials. First published in 1970.

ERICKSON, R. ed, *The brand on his coat: biographies of some Western Australian convicts.* UWAP, 1983. 355 p, illus.
An account of the role of convicts in WA during the latter half of the nineteenth century when more than one-third of the male population were convicts. Good bibliography.

FORSYTH, W.D. *Governor Arthur's convict system: Van Diemen's Land, 1824–36.* London, Longmans, Green for the Royal Empire Society, 1935, 213 p.
Examines Governor Arthur's administration but dependent on sources available in Australia in the early 1930s. This edition has an updated bibliography. New edition published in 1970.

GREAT BRITAIN. Parliament. House of Commons. *Copy of a despatch from Lieutenant-Governor Sir John Franklin, to Lord Glenelg, dated 7 October 1837, relative to the present system of convict discipline in Van Diemen's Land.* London, 1838. 110, 186 p. (GB Parliament. H of C Reports and papers no 309 of 1837/1838).
A despatch outlining the views of the lieutenant-governor and his principal officials on the transportation system and proposed changes to it, with a statistical appendix. Reprinted, Dublin, IUP.

GREAT BRITAIN. Parliament. House of Commons. *Report from the select committee of the House off Lords appointed to inquire into the provisions and operation of the Act 16 & 17 Vict, Ca. 99, entitled 'An act to substitute, in certain cases, other punishments in lieu of transportation'; . . . together with the minutes of evidence, appendix and index.* London, 1856. 144 p. (GB Parliament. H of C Report and papers no 404 of 1856).
A report which chiefly considered the effects of transportation on the penal colonies. Published with the reports of the House of Commons Committee. Reprinted, Dublin, IUP.

GREAT BRITAIN. Parliament. House of Commons. *Report of the commissioners appointed to inquire into the operation of the acts (16 & 17 Vict, C.99 and 20 & 21 Vic, C.3) relating to transportation and penal servitude . . .* London, 1863. 2 vols. (GB Parliament. H of C Reports and papers nos 3190 and 3190–I of 1863).
Another report on the transportation system which considered that after preliminary imprisonment in Great Britain, transportation was desirable for the mother country and beneficial to WA. Reprinted, Dublin, IUP.

GREAT BRITAIN. Parliament. House of Commons. *Select Committee on Secondary Punishment. Report. . . with the minutes of evidence, an appendix of papers and an index.* London, 1831–32. 2 vols. (GB Parliament. H of C Reports and papers no 276 of 1831 and no 547 of 1832).
These reports on various types of secondary (ie non-capital) punishment include a full discussion of transportation. Reprinted, Dublin, IUP.

GREAT BRITAIN. Parliament. House of Commons. *Select Committee on Transportation. Report.* London, 1812. 117 p. (GB Parliament. H of C Reports and papers no 341 of 1812).
The report, with evidence, of the first parliamentary inquiry into the working of the transportation system is generally favourable to it. Reprinted, Dublin, IUP.

GREAT BRITAIN. Parliament. House of Commons. *Select Committee on Transportation. Reports . . . together with the minutes of evidence, appendix, and index.* London, 1837–38. 2 vols. (GB Parliament. H of C Reports and papers no 518 of 1837 and no 669 of 1837–38).
A prejudiced report on the working of the system whose conclusions do not always follow from the evidence, which is biased and at times inaccurate. The appendices contain despatches and other documents. Reprinted, Dublin, IUP.

GREAT BRITAIN. Parliament. House of Commons. *Select Committee on Transportation. Reports . . . together with the minutes of evidence and appendices.* London, 1856. 3 vols. (GB Parliament. H of C Reports and papers nos 244, 296, 355 and 355–I of 1856).
A report which examined and supported the punishment of transportation for criminals, especially to WA. Reprinted, Dublin, IUP.

GREAT BRITAIN. Parliament. House of Commons. *Select Committee on Transportation. Report . . . together with the proceedings of the committee, minutes of evidence, appendix, and index.* London, 1861. 195 p. (GB Parliament. H of C Reports and papers no 286 of 1861).
This committee was appointed to inquire into the current system of transportation and its effect upon colonisation. It contains considerable information on the working of the system to WA and on the reactions of the other Australian colonies. Reprinted, Dublin, IUP.

GREAT BRITAIN. Parliament. House of Lords. *Select committee appointed to inquire into the execution of the criminal law, especially respecting juvenile offenders and transportation. Report*

... *together with the minutes of evidence ... and an appendix.* London, 1847. 2 vols. (GB Parliament. H of C Reports and papers nos 447 and 534 of 1847).

An examination of the advantages and disadvantages of transporting juveniles. Reprinted, Dublin, IUP.

GROCOTT, A.M. *Convicts, clergymen and churches: attitudes of convicts and ex-convicts towards the churches and clergy in New South Wales from 1788–1851.* SUP, 1979. 327 p, illus.

A study of the religious attitudes of convicts in various conditions. Comprehensive bibliography.

HASLUCK, A. *Unwilling emigrants: a study of the convict period in Western Australia.* OUP, 1978. 165 p, illus, maps.

A survey of the principal features of the convict system in WA. First published in 1959.

HIRST, J.B. *Convict society and its enemies: a history of early New South Wales.* Sydney, Allen & Unwin, 1983. 244 p, illus.

A reassessment of many ideas about society and the effects of the convicts on it.

MORTLOCK, J.F. *Experiences of a convict, transported for twenty-one years: an autobiographical memoir.* London, R. Barrett, pr, 1865, 233 p.

Memoir of an educated convict sentenced in 1843 who served in the hulks, Norfolk Island, Van Diemen's Land and WA. Describes the working of the probation system. New edition published in 1965.

ROBSON, L.L. *The convict settlers of Australia: an enquiry into the origin and character of the convicts transported to New South Wales and Van Diemen's Land, 1787–1852.* MUP, 1976. 257 p.

An analysis of the origins of the convicts and their condition based on a statistical study of a large random sample of convict indents and associated papers. First published in 1965.

RUDÉ, G.F.E. *Protest and punishment: the story of the social and political protesters transported to Australia, 1788–1868.* Oxford, OUP, 1978. 270 p.

An account of the background, trials and punishment of between 2 and 3 per cent of all convicts who were transported for offences connected with political and social protest.

SHAW, A.G.L. *Convicts and the colonies: a study of penal transportation from Great Britain and Ireland to Australia and other parts of the British Empire.* MUP, 1977. 399 p.

A comprehensive account of the origins and development of the system of convict transportation. Full bibliography. First published in 1966.

STURMA, M. *Vice in a vicious society: crime and convicts in mid-nineteenth century New South Wales.* UQP, 1983. 224 p, illus.

A study of crime in NSW between 1831 and 1861 which corrects a number of misapprehensions of the effects of transportation by a careful examination of the statistics of crime, drunkenness and the police. Bibliography.

Haughton Forrest (1826–1925), Port Arthur 1880. *Oil on cardboard. Captain James Haughton Forrest, marine and landscape painter and former officer in the Light Infantry, arrived in Tasmania in 1876 where he briefly took up an appointment as superintendent of police at Sorell. He retired to Hobart and began to paint prolifically. This painting shows his close attention to topographical and botanical detail.*
TASMANIAN MUSEUM AND ART GALLERY

*Engraving by E. Duncan after J.W.
Huggins,* Swan River, 50 miles up.
Coloured aquatint, 1827.
NATIONAL LIBRARY

CHAPTER 24

EXPLORATION

IAN F. MCLAREN

WHEN JAMES COOK sighted Cape Howe in 1770, 'Terra Australis Incognita' was an appropriate name for the great southern island continent. The vast expanse of the Australian hinterland remained a mystery to the members of the first fleet after their landing at Botany Bay in 1788. The mystery had to be solved—adequate farming land was needed to ensure the survival of the new colony. The fragmented written accounts and the few charts of odd sections of the coastal outline made by Dutch, Portuguese and other discoverers, and particularly by Cook, gave no information about the interior. This survey begins therefore after 1788 when exploration began, at first mainly by sea, then by land and ultimately by air and satellite, of Australia's coastal areas, landmass and territorial interests.

The literature of exploration, as discussed in this chapter, is defined as the written revelation of the existence and nature of the physical features of continental Australia, Tasmania and the present offshore territories, but excluding Antarctica and Papua New Guinea. Manuscripts and fictional accounts are discussed generally, but are not listed in the bibliography; neither are works on the Aboriginal inhabitants, or tours made to, from or through the continent, unless there is a substantial description of previously unexplored country. Select biographies are included but explorers are generally adequately covered in the *Australian dictionary of biography*. Indexes to British and some Australian parliamentary papers, and to the records of geographical and historical societies, are readily available; and attention should be drawn to the important Victorian report of the *Burke and Wills Commission* (1862).

Geoffrey Blainey explained Australia's major challenge in *The tyranny of distance* (1982) with his subtitle: 'How distance shaped Australia's history'. Shipping had to travel over 19 000 kilometres from Europe to face another 19 000 kilometres of Australian coastline. This isolation was accentuated in the early years by the inadequacy of coastal shipping and by inaccessible mountain ranges rising to 2400 metres. This barrier restricted access to the interior and prevented overland connections for many years.

There are very few readable accounts of Australian explorations. Among the best are Geoffrey Blainey (1982) and C.M.H. Clark's monumental *A history of Australia* (MUP, 1962–), but perhaps the most satisfactory exploration accounts remain Ernest Scott (1929) and that in the 1958 edition of the *Australian encyclopaedia* (vol 3, 423–95). A number of general histories include satisfactory descriptions of Australian explorations, but Feeken (1970) provides possibly the most thorough survey of Australian maritime and land exploration.

Works on Australian exploration can be found in the great bibliographies such as Ferguson's *Bibliography of Australia* which lists publications to 1900, and W.C.H. Robert's *Contributions to a bibliography of Australia* which lists particularly works from continental Europe. However, at the time of writing a comprehensive bibliography of Australian exploration is still being awaited. Although book sale catalogues have not been included, valuable references may be found in *F.G. Coles' Australian collection catalogue*, prepared by Gaston Renard (Melbourne, Gaston Renard, 1965), and in the catalogues of other leading Australian and London booksellers, such as Maggs Brothers and Francis Edwards.

The exploration of Australia falls naturally into eight chronological stages. The first, between 1788 and 1815, was important for successful maritime discoveries. It began with the occupation of Norfolk Island and the discovery of Lord Howe Island in 1788, followed by Captain Hunter's exploration in the *Sirius* and his charting of the areas north and south of Port Jackson. In 1797–98 George Bass sailed in the whaleboat *Tom Thumb* to investigate the coast south of Port Jackson, reaching Westernport, Victoria, in 1798; later that year Bass and Flinders in the *Norfolk* passed through Bass Strait and circumnavigated Van Diemen's Land.

During the first voyage from England of the *Investigator* in 1801, Flinders explored the southern coastline, entering Port Phillip Bay. The logs of these voyages are published in Collins (1802; repr, 1975).

George Vancouver explored part of the southern coast in 1791, while James Grant (1803; facs, 1963) recorded the first voyage from the west through Bass Strait in 1800. This feat shortened the voyage from Europe to Sydney, which until then had to pass south of Van Diemen's Land.

Flinders made a second voyage in the *Investigator* and circumnavigated Australia for the first time in 1802–03; in 1803 he began a third voyage in the *Cumberland* and came to grief on Wreck Island. He managed later to sail through Torres Strait to Timor and then Mauritius, where he was taken captive in 1804 by the French and imprisoned as a spy for six years. It was not until the day before he died in 1814, after his release and return to England, that Flinders saw a copy of his *A voyage to Terra Australis* (1812; facs, 1966) which recorded his outstanding contribution to the history of Australian exploration and the delineation of the outline of the Australian coast.

During the first voyage in the *Investigator* Flinders met, along the south coast, the French exploration expedition under Baudin. There are several accounts in French and English of these voyages, including Baudin (1974); the encounters and resulting claims were considered by Ernest Scott (1910).

Apart from other short inland excursions, such as attempts to penetrate the mountain barrier to the west of Sydney and the survey of the Port Phillip area in 1803 by Charles Grimes, little land exploration was carried out in the founding period. With an increasing population, pressure grew to explore the hinterland and in 1813 Blaxland, Wentworth, Lawson and others attempted to cross the Blue Mountains to the west; their journals have been brought together by George Mackaness (1965). The crossing into the western plains was finally accomplished by George Evans in 1813 and in 1815 he reached the headwaters of a west-flowing river, which he named Lachlan after Governor Macquarie. The journals of Evans and other explorers are found in the *Historical records of Australia* (36 vols, Melbourne, Library Committe of the Commonwealth Parliament, 1914–25).

Evans' discovery of an access to the west introduced the second stage of exploration between 1817 and 1827. John Oxley was appointed by Macquarie to trace first the Lachlan River (1817) and then in 1818 the Liverpool Plains and the north-flowing Macquarie River. Both rivers drained into marshes which Oxley concluded were the eastern edge of an inland sea. His *Journals* (1820; facs, 1964) was the first of the major land exploration accounts to be published. Barron Field (1825) printed the journals of many of these expeditions.

The overlanders, droving their cattle and sheep, sought rich pastoral land particularly in the Riverina district of New South Wales and the western and northeastern regions of Port Phillip district. There are several accounts of these developments, such as those by Billis and Kenyon (1930; facs, 1974) and Joseph Hawdon (1952). Robert Dawson, chief agent of the Australian

Agricultural Company, described the initial activities in 1830; A.L. Meston (1958) recounted the exploration of the northwest of Tasmania.

Hamilton Hume and William Hovell moved south over the Hume (later Murray) River in 1824, reaching the western end of Port Phillip Bay, and opened up a land route from Sydney to the south coast. Differences between the two explorers led to the publication of several varying accounts of their discoveries; these have been brought together in Andrews (1981).

A settlement was formed at Moreton Bay (Brisbane) in 1824; Alan Cunningham discovered the Darling Downs in 1827 and explored the district in 1828–29. His accounts are found in H.S. Russell (1888), along with other Queensland explorations.

Official surveys of the Australian coast by ships of the Royal Navy have been chronicled by Geoffrey Ingleton (1944). Following on the work of Cook, Flinders and Bass, Phillip Parker King completed charting the Australian coast, which he described in 1827; J.B. Jukes was to make further surveys, published some twenty years later in 1847.

The third period from 1828 to 1840 saw further exploration in eastern Australia, and was important for the discovery of the Murray River and its tributaries, flowing west and south.

Captain Charles Sturt travelled in 1828 into the interior of southern Australia and discovered Australia's greatest river systems; in 1829–30 he sailed down the Murrumbidgee River and continued on to the mouth of the Murray. His account appeared in 1833 (facs, 1982).

Major Thomas Mitchell explored the Namoi and Gwydir rivers in northern New South Wales in 1831; he followed the Darling River to Menindee in 1835. In the following year, Mitchell crossed the Murray River, travelling through *Australia Felix* to Portland, where he found the Henty brothers. Mitchell published his discoveries in 1838 (facs, 1965).

Paul Strzelecki crossed the Snowy Mountains south of Sydney, climbing and naming Mount Kosciusko, Australia's highest mountain, in 1840. Strzelecki followed Angus McMillan into the eastern Port Phillip district, naming the area Gippsland. His account (1845; facs,1967) is more technical than descriptive. Kenneth Cox wrote about Angus McMillan in 1973 (repr,1984).

A settlement had been formed at the Swan River in 1829 and in the late 1830s George Grey made two disastrous expeditions into the northwest; these he recounted in 1841 (facs, 1964).

Edward John Eyre surveyed the peninsula that bears his name in 1839, and then undertook the arduous crossing of the continent along the Great Australian Bight, arriving eventually at Albany in 1841. His account of his explorations appeared in 1845 (facs, 1964).

The fourth stage (1841–50) witnessed the continuing opening up of the continent. Mitchell (1848; facs, 1967) went into tropical Australia and Charles Sturt (1849; facs, 1965) told of seventeen months spent in 1844–45 attempting to cross central Australia north of Innamincka, during which he suffered severely before turning back.

Ludwig Leichhardt travelled north from Brisbane in 1844–45 and crossed the base of the Cape York Peninsula and the area south of the Gulf of Carpentaria before reaching the isolated settlement at Port Essington. This he described in 1847 (facs, 1980) During his journey in 1848 through Queensland he disappeared; his fate remains unknown, but it has generated considerable discussion in subsequent years. A.C. Gregory travelled along Leichhardt's first route, proceeding from west to east, in 1855–56 and in 1884 (facs, 1981) recounted the story of nine expeditions between 1846 and 1862.

William Carron (1849; facs, 1965) described the expeditions of Edmund Kennedy in 1847 in western Queensland, and his travels along the east coast to Cape York in 1848.

The northwest and the arid centre of Australia became the centre of attention in the fifth period between 1851 and 1870. Gregory had determined the course of rivers flowing into the lakes in central South Australia, and John McDouall Stuart (1863; facs, 1963) confirmed the outlines of those lakes.

To cross the continent from south to north now became a new objective and the Victorian Exploring Expedition was organised in 1861 under the leadership of Robert O'Hara Burke and William Wills. Although the advance party was the first to cross Australia from south to north, Burke, Wills and Grey died on the return journey. Relief expeditions were mounted by

Landsborough, McKinlay, Norman, Howitt and Walker; journals of the first three were printed in order to satisfy the immense public concern over the fate of the explorers. The extensive literature generated by these expeditions has been summarised by Ian McLaren (1959); the most readable account is by Alan Moorehead (1977). The final report of the Royal Society Exploration Committee (1863) and the royal commission (1862) are important documents relating to this tragic enterprise, and William Wills Sr edited his son's journals in 1861.

The sixth stage, between 1870 and 1880, began with the decision to build the overland telegraph; this was to link Adelaide with Darwin and followed the route taken by John McDouall Stuart in 1862 to Arnhem Land. The telegraph line, completed in 1873, provided a supply base for explorations of the Gibson, Sandy and Great Victoria deserts, described by Alfred Giles (1926). Peter Warburton (1875; facs, 1968) reports on his crossing of the Sandy Desert in 1873–74, while the crossing of the Great Victoria Desert (1875) and Gibson Desert (1876) were recorded by Ernest Giles (1889; facs, 1979). Giles was also the author of *Geographic travels* (Melbourne, The Author, 1875); both works are important for their vivid, even flamboyant narrative style.

After John Forrest had visited Mount Margaret in 1869 in his search for the remains of Leichhardt's party, he travelled along the southern Australian coastline to South Australia in 1870 in order to confirm Eyre's reports of the desert. In the same year Forrest crossed the central desert area to the Musgrave Ranges, reporting on these activities in 1875 (facs; 1969). F.K. Crowley produced the first volume of a Forrest biography in 1971. Forrest's brother, Alexander, explored northwest Australia between the De Grey River and Port Darwin in 1879 and G.C. Bolton published a biography of him in 1958.

The seventh stage commenced in 1880, after the major inland exploration had been completed, and continued to 1939. It included a number of important expeditions undertaken to further agricultural, commercial, mining, anthropological and other scientific interests, such as the British Museum expedition to northern Australia in 1923–25, the story of which is told by G.H. Wilkins (1928). Even at this period first discoveries of major regions were still to be accomplished, such as C.T. Madigan's crossing of the Simpson Desert in 1939, described in 1946.

The need to defend northern Australia during World War II hastened sea, land and air surveys. New airfields and highways were built. The development of motor vehicles capable of negotiating sand and fording rivers made desert crossings practical and almost commonplace.

The anthropological enquiries of Baldwin Spencer and F.J. Gillen were mainly of a scientific nature, but the latter's diary (1968) has been listed as representative of this type of literature.

So far only passing reference has been made to aerial exploration; developments in aircraft, rockets and satellites have assisted in Australian mapping from the air and could be considered as the eighth stage of the history of Australian exploration. An aerial survey was made of the Simpson Desert in 1929 and annual reports of the Aerial Geological and Geophysical Survey of the Northern Territory commenced in 1935. Books relating to aviation are listed in *Australian aviation: a bibliographical survey* by Ian McLaren (Melbourne, The Author, 1958, first published in the *Victorian historical magazine* 28, 3, 1958, 85–141).

There still exist numerous unpublished accounts of exploration and geographical discoveries. The private archival material deposited in the National Library of Australia, in several state libraries and archives, and in the strongrooms of geographical and historical societies in every state, contains diaries and letters relating to voyages of exploration of which we have as yet no full account. The publication of lists of manuscripts (or typescripts) held in society libraries will aid the researcher, and those seeking such documents should examine the lists of indexes in chapter 8 of this volume. But besides the archival material now safeguarded in organised repositories there are still many documents in private hands. At present there is no list of such collections except for the larger 'private archives' recorded by Phyllis Mander-Jones in *Manuscripts in the British Isles* (ANUP, 1972).

Although not included in the listing of Australian exploration literature, there are numerous examples of imaginative and fictional historical writing. The excitement, mystique and national involvement rising at times to mass hysteria that accompany the preparation of major expeditions into unknown areas of the earth, or beyond, quite naturally give rise to the literature of imagination. Before the period of discovery and exploration in the Pacific, Australia was a fertile source for the imaginative literature of travel. Moralising accounts of a paradisiacal society allegedly discovered in Terra Australis go back to the seventeenth century: Bishop Joseph Hall's *Mundus alter et idem sive Terra Australis* first appeared in 1605 and was translated in 1608 as *The discovery of a new world.* Its principal importance lies in Hall's satirical attack on Roman Catholicism, though there were many who took the travelogue and discovery as 'gospel truth'.

The work is a forerunner of many moralising travel accounts which include Swift's *Gulliver's travels* (1726), whose hero, a cousin of William Dampier, visits the imaginary Lilliput placed in South Australia; the tales by Gabriel de Foigny (1676) and others; and, as late as 1837, an *Account of an expedition to the interior of New Holland* allegedly edited by Lady Mary Fox. It purports to tell of a group of explorers leaving Bathurst in August 1835 and discovering a civilised European race in central Australia. Alas, it became known all too soon that the travellers were figments of the author's imagination and that the model community did not exist at all. It is now assumed that Lady Fox was none other than the Archbishop of Dublin, the Reverend Richard Whately.

Leading explorers have frequently been the subjects of fictional writing, but not all novels or stories have had the well-deserved success of Australia's Nobel Prize winner. Now one of the well-known books of exploration fiction, Patrick White's *Voss* (London, Eyre and Spottiswoode, 1957) is based around the life and disappearance of Ludwig Leichhardt, and has contributed much to an awakening of general interest in that German explorer. It has been reprinted many times and translated into German, Spanish and other languages.

It may be a long time before it is safe to say that the exploration of Australia has been completed. The contours and dimensions of the continent have been almost completely mapped, the distances measured and most rivers bridged. Commercial interests prompt and support continuous mineral exploration; modern technology allows us to probe beneath the surface of the land and into the space above it. The romance of the adventure has perhaps been lost. The accounts of the experiences of lonely explorers are being replaced by impersonal government or corporate reports, but company balance sheets will not reveal any stories of blood and sweat behind the discoveries.

It seems unlikely that this age of organised scientific exploration will generate the same respect for human endeavour and ingenuity as did the travels into the unknown of the past; there will be less emphasis on the heroism of individuals and more stress on institutional planning as the reliance on technological research and the cost of the equipment involved continue to increase.

The bibliography that follows is divided into several sections. The first presents general accounts of exploration and descriptions of Australia by the first Europeans to venture into the interior; these are followed by eight sections citing the literature related to various geographical regions. The final section lists works by or about the leading figures in Australian exploration. These works are arranged alphabetically by author; the index to this volume indicates individual explorers where they have been the subject of a book listed here.

Owen Stanley, The *Morley,* Britomart *and* Sesostris *near Sydney Heads, from* Voyage of HMS Britomart *1837–43. Watercolour. Stanley's sketchbooks form a record of several voyages he made in Australian waters with the Royal Navy. As commander of* HMS Britomart *he was involved with the attempt to found a settlement at Port Essington in 1838 and subsequently conducted coastal surveying work in Australia and New Guinea.*
TASMANIAN MUSEUM AND ART GALLERY

GENERAL ACCOUNTS

CALVERT, A.F. *The exploration of Australia.* London, George Philip & Son, 1895–96. 2 vols, illus, maps.

General coverage of the exploration of Australia from 1844 to 1896.

FAVENC, E. *The history of Australian exploration from 1788 to 1888, compiled from state documents, private papers and the most authentic sources of information.* Sydney, Turner & Henderson, 1888. 474 p, illus, maps.

Chapters on land and maritime exploration, with an index of names, dates, incidents and a chronological summary. Favenc was the leader of the Brisbane–Darwin survey, 1878, and of the inland rivers journey, 1883. Facsimile edition, Sydney, Golden Press, 1983.

FEEKEN, E.H.J. AND FEEKEN, G.E. *The discovery and exploration of Australia ... with an introduction by O.H.K. Spate.* Melbourne, Nelson, 1970. 318 p, illus, maps.

Selective but wide coverage with an introduction by Spate entitled 'The nature of Australian exploration'; excellent cartography and bibliography.

INGLETON, G.C. *Charting a continent: a brief memoir on the history of marine exploration and hydrographical surveying in Australian waters from the discoveries of Captain James Cook to the war activities of the Royal Australian Navy Surveying Service.* A & R, 1944. 145 p, illus, maps.

History of Royal Navy surveying service, 1770–1939.

IRISH UNIVERSITY PRESS. *Index to British parliamentary papers on Australia and New Zealand 1800–1899.* Dublin, IUP, 1974. 2 vols.

This index provides a key to the reprint of the numerous reports relating to Australia, individual state explorers and exploration in general.

LEE, I. *Early explorers in Australia, from the log-books and journals, including the diary of Allan Cunningham, botanist, from March 1, 1817 to November 19, 1818.* London, Methuen, 1925. 651 p, illus, maps.

Following the introductory chapters, this work by Ida Lee (later known as Ida Marriott) is mainly concerned with the explorations of Allan Cunningham, who also participated in John Oxley's journey and P.P. King's voyage.

ROBERT, W.C.H. *Contributions to a bibliography of Australia and the South Sea islands.* Amsterdam, Philo Press, 1968–1972. 4 vols.

Detailed listing to 1923 of Australian exploration literature, especially in vol 1 (materials printed in the Netherlands) and vol 4 (materials printed in Europe other than the Netherlands)

SCOTT, E. *Australian discovery ...* London, Dent, 1929. 2 vols, illus, maps.

All except the last three chapters of vol 1 refer to the discovery of Australia; vol 2 provides abridged extracts from explorers' journals.

SHARP, A. *The discovery of Australia.* Oxford, Clarendon Press, 1963. 338 p, illus, maps.

Extracts from first-hand accounts and reproduction of relevant portions of charts.

TOOLEY, R.V. *The mapping of Australia.* London, Holland, 1979. 633 p, maps.

Description restricted to the author's own collection of 1560 maps now in National Library, Canberra; provides 239 facsimiles of maps.

WOODS, J.E. Tenison. *A history of the discovery and exploration of Australia ...* London, Sampson Low, Son and Marston, 1865. 2 vols, illus, maps.

The first chapters deal with the discovery of Australia by sea, followed by a detailed account of exploration by sea and land.

NEW SOUTH WALES: BLUE MOUNTAINS

MACKANESS, G. ed, *Fourteen journeys over the Blue Mountains of New South Wales, 1813–1841.* Sydney, Horwitz Grahame, 1965. 273 p, illus.

Following a brief introduction to explorations prior to 1813, this collection contains extracts from explorers' accounts.

RICHARDS, J.A. ed, *Blaxland–Lawson–Wentworth 1813.* Hobart, Blubber Head Press, 1979. 222 p, illus, maps.

Reproduces the journals of Blaxland and Lawson, Wentworth's monograph, and other material relating to their successful crossing of the Blue Mountains in 1813.

NEW SOUTH WALES: INCLUDING PORT PHILLIP AND MORETON BAY

DAWSON, R. *The present state of Australia: a description of the country, its advantages and prospects, with reference to emigration ...* London, Smith, Elder, 1830. 464 p.

Dawson arrived in NSW in 1824 as chief agent of the Australian Agricultural Co and retained this position for three years, during which he travelled into many parts of the unexplored lands.

FIELD, B. ed, *Geographical memoirs on New South Wales; by various hands: containing an account of the surveyor general's late expedition to two new ports; the discovery of Moreton Bay River...* London, John Murray, 1825. 504 p, illus, maps.

Accounts of the early expeditions of exploration in NSW.

QUEENSLAND [MORETON BAY]

JACK, R.L. *Northmost Australia: three centuries of exploration, discovery, and adventure in and around the Cape York Peninsula, Queensland ...* London, Simpkin, Marshall, Hamilton, Kent & Co, 1921. 2 vols, illus, maps.

Deals with discovery and exploration of the Cape York Peninsula, the gulf country west to the Qld border and the coastal area south to Bowen. It includes the author's own journeys in the northern area as a geological surveyor.

RUSSELL, H.S. *The genesis of Queensland: an account of the first exploring journeys to and over Darling Downs ...* Sydney, Turner & Henderson, 1888. 636 p, illus, maps.

General account of Qld exploration.

STEELE, J.G. *The explorers of the Moreton Bay district 1770–1830.* UQP, 1972. 386 p, illus, maps.

Reproduction of original manuscripts, journals, fieldbooks and reports of various explorers who travelled within a radius of about eighty kilometres from Brisbane.

SOUTH AUSTRALIA AND NORTHERN TERRITORY

CROWLEY, F.K. *South Australian history: a survey for research students.* Adelaide, LBSA, 1966. 200 p.

Useful guide covering foundation history and exploration.

THREADGILL, B. *South Australian land exploration, 1856 to 1880.* Adelaide, Board of Governors of the Public Library, Museum, and Art Gallery of SA, 1922. Vol 1 text; vol 2 maps.

Compiled mainly from official papers, it covers twelve South Australian explorers and the overland telegraph. Bibliography.

WILLIAMS, G. *South Australian exploration to 1856.* Adelaide, Board of Governors of the Public Library, Museum, and Art Gallery of SA, 1919. 118 p, maps.

Historical compilation which considers South Australian exploration, by both land and sea, and the overlanders.

TASMANIA [VAN DIEMEN'S LAND]

BINKS, C.J. *Explorers of western Tasmania*. Launceston, Mary Fisher Bookshop, 1980. 264 p, illus, maps.

Exploration of mountainous western Tas 1815–70, by both government surveyors and those from the Van Diemen's Land Co. It also covers the search for minerals in the area.

GIBLIN, R.W. *The early history of Tasmania*. London, Methuen, 1928; MUP 1939. 2 vols, illus, maps.

Survey of Tasmanian history to 1818, including explorations and settlements.

MESTON, A.L. *The Van Diemen's Land Company 1825–1842*. Launceston, Museum Committee, Launceston City Council, 1958. 62 p. (Queen Victoria Museum, Launceston. Records, ns no 9).

The company was chartered in 1825 and given a land grant outside the settled areas, with Edward Curr as colonial agent. Includes stories of explorations carried out.

VICTORIA [PORT PHILLIP DISTRICT]

BILLIS, R.V. AND KENYON, A.S. *Pastures new: an account of the pastoral occupation of Port Phillip*. Melbourne, Macmillan, 1930. 272 p.

Considers the pastoral development of Vic, with rapid expansion and exploration leading to land occupation; further details are given in *Pastoral pioneers of Victoria* (1932; facs, 1974) by the same authors. Facsimile edition, Melbourne, Stockland, 1974.

BONWICK, J. *Port Phillip settlement*. London, Sampson Low, Marston, Searle & Rivington, 1883. 537 p, illus, maps.

General account of the beginnings of Vic, with facsimile letters and documents.

RUSDEN, G.W. *The discovery, survey and settlement of Port Phillip*. Melbourne, Robertson, 1871. 56 p.

Short account of discovery and exploration of the Port Phillip district.

WESTERN AUSTRALIA [SWAN RIVER SETTLEMENT]

[CROSS, J.] *Journals of several expeditions made in Western Australia, during the years 1829, 1830, 1831, and 1832 ...* London, J. Cross, 1833. 264 p, map.

Important for journals of 22 West Australian expeditions. Facsimile edition published by UWAP (1980).

CROWLEY, F.K. *The records of Western Australia*. Vol I. *Perth*. Publications Committee, University of WA, 1953. 1094 p.

Includes references to explorations.

MARCHANT, L. *France Australe: a study of French explorations and attempts to found a penal colony and strategic base in south western Australia 1503–1826*. Perth, Artlook Books, 1982. 384 p, illus, maps.

French maritime explorations and plans to colonise western Australia during the Revolutionary (part II) and Restoration (part III) periods.

DEPENDENCIES

CUMPSTON, J.S. *Macquarie Island*. Canberra, Antarctic Division, Dept of External Affairs, 1968. 380 p, illus, maps.

Macquarie Island became a dependency of Van Diemen's Land in 1825. This work provides a full history of this subantarctic island.

RABONE, H.R. *Lord Howe Island: its discovery and early associations 1788 to 1888*. Sydney, Trading Post, 1940. 54 p, illus, map.

Lord Howe Island was discovered during the voyage to occupy Norfolk Island in 1788.

SPRUSON, J.J. *Norfolk Island: outline of its history from 1788 to 1884*. Sydney, Government Printer, 1885. 52 p, illus.

Earliest history of Norfolk Island, which was settled in 1788 as a penal settlement.

INDIVIDUAL EXPLORERS

ANDREWS, A.E.J. ed, *Hume and Hovell, 1824*. Hobart, Blubber Head Press, 1981. 389 p, illus, maps.

Besides Hume's report, Hovell's journal and Bland's account of the journey from Yass plains to the Port Phillip district, this study covers the subsequent controversy between the explorers.

BAUDIN, N. *The journal of Post Captain Nicolas Baudin, commander-in-chief of the corvettes* Géographe *and* Naturaliste ... Trans from the French by Christine Cornell. Adelaide, LBSA, 1974. 609 p, maps.

First translation of 'Journal de mer', kept by Baudin, who led the French cartographic survey in 1801–02. They charted Van Diemen's Land, Bass Strait, moving westward until they met Flinders at Encounter Bay; they named the area Terre Napoleon.

BEALE, E. *Kennedy the Barcoo and beyond 1847: the journals of Edmund Besley Court Kennedy and Alfred Allatson Turner with new information on Kennedy's life*. Hobart, Blubber Head Press, 1983. 292 p, illus, maps.

Kennedy's and Turner's journals of the expedition to trace the mouth of the Victoria River.

BEALE, E. *Sturt the chipped idol: a study of Charles Sturt, explorer*. SUP, 1979. 270 p, maps.

Critical assessment, including medical evidence, of Sturt's Murray voyage and central Australian expedition.

BECKER, L.P.H. *Ludwig Becker: artist & naturalist with the Burke & Wills expedition*. Ed with an introduction by M. Tipping. MUP for the Library Council of Vic, 1979. 224 p, illus, maps.

Reproduction of Becker's reports, letters, drawings and watercolours.

BIRMAN, W. *Gregory of Rainworth: a man in his time*. UWAP, 1979. 296 p, illus, maps.

Tells of Augustus Gregory and his expeditions, including those in WA 1846–43, the north Australian expedition, 1855–56 and the Leichhardt search expedition in 1858.

BOLTON, G.C. *Alexander Forrest: his life and times*. MUP, 1958. 196 p, illus.

Alexander Forrest led expeditions to Hampton Plains in 1871 and 1876. He examined the northwest in 1875 and discovered the Kimberleys, and the Margaret and Ord rivers in 1879.

BOWDEN, K.M. *George Bass 1771–1803: his discoveries, romantic life and tragic disappearance*. OUP, 1952. 171 p, illus, maps.

George Bass, naval surgeon, explorer, naturalist and adventurer, discovered in 1798 the strait named after him, and sailed with Flinders around Van Diemen's Land in 1798–99.

THE BURKE and Wills exploring expedition: an account of the crossing the continent of Australia, from Cooper's Creek to Carpentaria. Melbourne, Wilson and Mackinnon, 1861. 36 p, illus.

One of the contemporary publications that produced the diaries and reports of Brahe, Burke, Howitt, King and Wills. Reprinted from the *Argus*.

BURN, D. *Narrative to the overland journey of Sir John and Lady Franklin and party from Hobart Town to Macquarie Harbour 1842*. Ed by G. Mackaness. Dubbo, NSW, Review Publications, 1977. 72 p, illus.

Tasmanian journey, originally printed in the *United services' journal* 1843. Facsimile of 1955 edition.

BYERLEY, F.J. ed, *Narrative of the overland expedition of the Messrs Jardine, from Rockhampton to Cape York, northern Queensland*. Brisbane, J.W. Buxton, 1867. xii, 88 p, illus, map.

Compiled from the journals of Frank and Alexander Jardine who travelled along the west coast of Cape York Peninsula, determining the course of rivers flowing westward into the Gulf of Carpentaria.

CALVERT SCIENTIFIC EXPLORING EXPEDITION, 1896–97. *Journal of the Calvert Scientific Exploring Expedition, 1896–97*. Perth, Government Printer, 1902. 62 p, illus, map.

Wells, who had been second in command to David Lindsay in 1891, led Calvert's expedition in WA in 1896–97.

CARNEGIE, D.W. *Spinifex and sand: a narrative of five years' pioneering and exploration in Western Australia*. London, C.A. Pearson, 1898. 454 p, illus, maps.

Based on the reports of two West Australian prospecting expeditions to the Coolgardie goldfields in 1894, and in 1897 through the Gibson and Great Sandy deserts to Halls Creek and return to Coolgardie. New edition published in 1983.

CARRON, W. *Narrative of an expedition, undertaken under the direction of the late Mr. Assistant Surveyor E.B. Kennedy, for the exploration of the country lying between Rockingham Bay and Cape York*. Sydney, Kemp and Fairfax, 1849. 126 p, map.

Written by a survivor of E.B. Kennedy's expedition 1848. Facsimile edition, Adelaide, LBSA, 1965.

COLLINS, D. *An account of the English colony in New South Wales . . .* London T. Cadell Junior & W. Davies, 1798, 618 p, illus, maps.

The second volume was the first book on early Australian exploration as it contains the journals of George Bass and Matthew Flinders. Facsimile edition, Adelaide, LBSA, 1971.

COOPER, H.M. *French exploration in South Australia with especial reference to Encounter Bay, Kangaroo Island, the two gulfs and Murat Bay 1802–1803*. Adelaide, privately printed, 1952. 200 p, illus, maps.

Summary account of the French explorations along the South Australian coastline.

COX, K. *Angus McMillan: pathfinder*. Melbourne, The Author, 1984. 185 p, illus, map.

The explorer travelled from Monaro in southern NSW in 1839, finding new pastures, and found his way to Corner Inlet in 1841. Strzelecki followed McMillan's tracks in 1840, taking much of the credit for these discoveries. First published in 1973.

CROWLEY, F.K. *Forrest 1847 to 1918. Vol I. 1847–91, apprenticeship to premiership*. UQP, 1971. 323 p, illus, maps.

Forrest was a surveyor, explorer and politician. He organised large-scale surveys of WA and led three expeditions. This volume deals only with his work as an explorer.

CUMPSTON, J.H.L. *Augustus Gregory and the inland sea*. Canberra, Roebuck Society, 1972. 146 p, illus, maps. (Roebuck Society Publication, 9).

An account of explorations in WA, 1846–48, the north Australia expedition of 1855 led by Gregory, and the Leichhardt search expedition to the Barcoo River in 1855.

DAVIS, J. *Tracks of McKinlay and party across Australia*. Ed . . . by W. Westgarth. London, Sampson Low, Son & Co, 1863. 408 p, illus, map.

William Westgarth's review of the expeditions of Stuart, Burke and Wills, Landsborough and McKinlay is followed by the diary of John Davis, one of the members of the McKinlay expedition of 1861–62.

DUNMORE, J. *French explorers in the Pacific*. Oxford, Clarendon Press, 1965–69. 2 vols, illus, maps.

The second volume covers to Baudin, followed by Freycinet and other French explorers.

DUTTON, G.P.H. *The hero as murderer: the life of Edward John Eyre, Australian explorer and governor of Jamaica, 1815–1901*. Ringwood, Vic, Penguin, 1977. 416 p, illus, maps.

Eyre's main explorations were in SA and WA. He was also protector of Aborigines. First published in 1967.

ERICKSEN, R. *Ernest Giles: explorer and traveller 1835–1897*. Melbourne, Heinemann, 1978. 307 p, illus, maps.

Giles was engaged in several pastoral assessment expeditions in western NSW, 1861–65, and explored west from the overland telegraph line in 1872 and 1873. These were covered in his *Geographic travels* (Melbourne, The Author, 1875); two major explorations followed.

EYRE, E.J. *Journals of expeditions of discovery into central Australia, and overland from Adelaide to King George's Sound, in the years 1840–1 . . .* London, T. and T. Boone, 1845. 2 vols, illus, maps.

The journals cover explorations from Adelaide to Lake Torrens, and Port Lincoln to Streaky Bay. In June 1840 Eyre left Adelaide along the Great Australian Bight, arriving at Albany after walking 1600 kilometres. Facsimile edition, Adelaide, LBSA, 1964.

FLINDERS, M. *Observations on the coasts of Van Diemen's Land, on Bass's Strait and its islands, and on part of the coasts of New South Wales . . .* London, John Nichols, 1801. 36 p. Flinders explored the southeast coast of NSW and circumnavigated Van Diemen's Land in 1788–89. He was navigator, hydrographer and scientist and served with Bligh in the Pacific. Facsimile edition, Adelaide, LBSA, 1965.

FLINDERS, M. *A voyage to Terra Australis: undertaken for the purpose of completing the discovery of the vast country, and prosecuted in the years 1801, 1802, and 1803 . . .* London, G. & W. Nichol, 1814. 2 vols and box of charts, illus, maps. This work, published the day before the author died (19 July 1814), is the most significant description of the circumnavigation of Australia. Facsimile edition, Adelaide, LBSA, 1966.

FORREST, A. *North-west exploration: journal of an expedition from DeGray to Port Darwin*. Perth, Government Printer, 1880. 44 p, illus, map. (WA. Parliament. Parliamentary paper no 3 of 1880).

Expedition from Nickol Bay along the western coast to the overland telegraph line.

FORREST, J. *Explorations in Australia: I. Explorations in search of Dr. Leichardt [sic] and party. II. From Perth to Adelaide around the Great Australian Bight. III. From Champion Bay, across the desert to the telegraph and to Adelaide . . .* London, Sampson Low, Marston, Low & Searle, 1875, 354 p, illus, maps.

Accounts of his three expeditions. Facsimile edition, Adelaide, LBSA, 1969.

FOSTER, W.C. *Sir Thomas Livingstone Mitchell and his world, 1792–1855 . . .* Sydney, Institute of Surveyors, 1985. 594 p, illus.

Detailed study of a multitalented man who made four expeditions into the interior.

GILES, A. *Exploring in the seventies and the construction of the overland telegraph line*. Adelaide, W.K. Thomas, 1926. 172 p, illus, map.

Reminiscences of 50 years' residence in the NT; Giles was a

member of the exploring party in central Australia led by John Ross in 1870.

GILES, E. *Australia twice traversed: the romance of exploration, being a narrative compiled from the journals of five exploring expeditions* ... London, Sampson Low, Searle & Livingston, 1889, 2 vols, illus, maps.

Giles conducted five expeditions through central SA and WA between 1872 and 1876. He crossed the Great Victoria Desert in 1875 and the Gibson Desert the following year. Facsimile edition, Sydney, Doubleday, 1979.

GILLEN, F.J. *Gillen's diary: the camp jottings of F.J. Gillen on the Spencer and Gillen expedition across Australia 1901–1902.* Adelaide, LBSA, 1968. 367 p, illus.

Gillen crossed Australia with Baldwin Spencer in 1901–02, conducting ethnographical research.

GOSSE, W.C. *W.C. Gosse's explorations ... report and diary of Mr W.C. Gosse's central and western exploring expedition, 1873.* Adelaide, Government Printer, 1874. 20 p, map. (SA Parliament. Parliamentary paper no 48 of 1874).

The expedition started from the overland telegraph line, 65 kilometres north of Alice Springs, moved south of the Macdonnell Ranges and then north to rejoin the telegraph line.

GRANT, J. *The narrative of a voyage of discovery performed in His Majesty's vessel the* Lady Nelson ... *in the years 1800, 1801, and 1802, to New South Wales* ... London, T. Egerton, 1803. xxvi, 195 p, illus, maps.

The first passage between Van Diemen's Land and the Port Phillip district, sailing through Bass Strait from the west. Facsimile edition, Adelaide, LBSA, 1963.

GREGORY, A. AND GREGORY, F.T. *Journals of Australian explorations.* London, T. & W. Boone, 1841. 2 vols, 210 p, illus.

The journals relate to nine expeditions in western, northern and central Australia between 1846 and 1862. Facsimile edition, Adelaide, LBSA, 1964.

GREY, G.E. *Journals of two expeditions of discovery in north-west and western Australia, during the years 1837, 38, and 39 ...* Facs, Adelaide, LBSA, 1964. 2 vols, illus, maps.

The first expedition landed near Hanover Bay but it was abandoned after Grey was badly wounded. The second expedition worked north and south of Shark's Bay, discovering the Gascoyne River; a storm forced the expedition to proceed 500 kilometres overland to Perth. First published in 1841.

HASKELL, D.C. comp, *The United States exploring expedition, 1838–1842 and its publications 1844–1874: a bibliography.* New York, Greenwood, 1968. 188 p, illus.

Bibliography with 533 entries of expedition led by Charles Wilkes. First published in the *Bulletin of the New York Public Library* 1940–42.

HAWDON, J. *The journal of a journey from New South Wales to Adelaide performed in 1838.* Melbourne, Georgian House, 1952. 65 p, illus, maps.

Relates the first overlanding of cattle from NSW to Adelaide in January 1838.

HODGKINSON, C. *Australia, from Port Macquarie to Moreton Bay* ... London, T. and W. Boone, 1845. 244 p, illus, maps.
Surveyor's account of exploration in 1843.

HOWITT, A.W. *Personal reminiscences of central Australia and the Burke and Wills expedition.* Adelaide, Australasian Association for the Advancement of Science, 1908. 43 p.

Howitt examined the pastoral potential of the Lake Eyre region in 1859. In 1861 he led the Burke and Wills relief expedition, finding King and the bodies of Burke and Wills. During a second visit, he explored the Barcoo country.

JUKES, J.B. *Narrative of the surveying voyage of* HMS Fly, *commanded by Captain F.P. Blackwood, R.N. in Torres Strait, New Guinea and other islands of the Eastern Archipelago during the years 1842–1846* ... London, T. and W. Boone, 1847. 2 vols, illus, maps.

Survey of the Great Barrier Reef, Torres Strait and New Guinea by the naturalist to the expedition.

KING, P.P. *Narrative of a survey of the intertropical and western coasts of Australia performed between the years 1818 and 1822.* London, John Murray, 1827. 2 vols, illus, maps.

Voyage of exploration in the *Mermaid* to the northern and western coasts of Australia. King laid down a new route from Sydney to Torres Strait, inside the Barrier Reef. Facsimile edition, Adelaide, LBSA, 1969.

LANDSBOROUGH, W. *Journal of Landsborough's expedition from Carpentaria, in search of Burke and Wills.* Melbourne, Wilson & Mackinnon, 1962, 128 p, illus, map.

Exploration through Qld and along the northern Australian coast, to Van Diemen's Gulf in 1861, with a map of explorers' routes. Facsimile edition, Adelaide, LBSA, 1963.

LEICHHARDT, F.W.L. *Journal of an overland expedition in Australia, from Moreton Bay to Port Essington ... during the years 1844–1845.* London, T. & W. Boone, 1847, 544 p, illus, box of maps.

Leichhardt led a party from Jimbour to Port Essington in 1844–45, a distance of 4800 kilometres. He attempted to cross the continent from east to west in 1848 and disappeared without trace. Facsimile edition, Adelaide, LBSA, 1964. Text but not maps also reproduced in facsimile, Sydney, Doubleday, 1979.

LEICHHARDT, F.W.L. *The letters of F.W. Ludwig Leichhardt: collected and newly translated by M. Aurousseau.* CUP for the Hakluyt Society, 1968. 3 vols, illus, maps.

Contains the extensive correspondence of the scientist and explorer from student days in the 1830s until his disappearance in 1848.

LHOTSKY, J. *A journey from Sydney to the Australian alps undertaken in the months of January, February and March, 1834.* Ed by A.E.J. Andrews. Hobart, Blubber Head Press, 1979. 279 p, illus, maps.

Reproduces the diary and notes of a journey made in 1834 by the Polish explorer. He travelled to the Monaro district in 1834 and explored the southern mountains and the Snowy River district.

LINDSAY, D. *Journal of the Elder scientific exploring expedition, 1891–2.* Adelaide, Government Printer, 1893. 208 p, maps.

Scientific expedition equipped by Sir Thomas Elder, which covered 6400 kilometres in an unsuccessful attempt to travel from Warrina (SA) to the west coast.

MACGILLIVRAY, J. *Narrative of the voyage of* HMS Rattlesnake, *commanded by the late Captain Owen Stanley, R.N., F.R.S. ...* London, T. & W. Boone, 1852. 2 vols, illus, map.

Macgillivray, a naturalist, accompanied the three surveying voyages to the Qld coast, Torres Strait, Coral Sea and southern coasts of New Guinea. It includes Carron's narrative of the E.B. Kennedy expedition and a statement from Jackey Jackey. Facsimile edition, Adelaide, LBSA, 1969.

McKINLAY, J. *McKinlay's journal of exploration in the interior of Australia.* Melbourne, F.F. Bailliere, 1862 [?] 136 p, maps.
Journal of Burke and Wills relief expedition to central Australia in 1861–62.

McLAREN, I.F. 'The Victorian exploring expedition and relieving expeditions, 1860–61: the Burke and Wills

Tragedy', *Victorian historical magazine* 29, 4, 1959, 211–53.
Account of expedition with a full bibliography of the extensive literature on this tragedy.

McMINN, W.G. *Allan Cunningham: botanist and explorer.* MUP, 1970. 147 p, illus, maps.
A biography of the botanist who accompanied John Oxley on the exploration of Lachlan valley, and then went on the surveying visit of P.P. King to the northwest coast of Australia. For his diary see Ida Lee (1925).

MACQUARIE, L. *Lachlan Macquarie, governor of New South Wales: journals of his tours in New South Wales and Van Diemen's Land, 1810–1822.* Sydney, Library of Australian History, 1979. 320 p, illus, maps.
Ten journals of official visits made by Governor Macquarie. First published in 1956.

MADIGAN, C.T. *Crossing the dead heart.* Melbourne, Georgian House, 1946. 171 p, illus, map.
Narrative of the first crossing of the Simpson Desert in 1939.

MANN, J.F. *Eight months with Dr Leichhardt, in the years 1846–47.* Sydney, Turner & Henderson, 1888. 86 p, illus.
Account by one of the members of Leichhardt's second expedition to cross Australia from Jimbour to the west coast. The expedition was disrupted by illness and quarrels and returned after covering 800 kilometres.

MITCHELL, T.L. *Journal of an expedition into the interior of tropical Australia, in search of a route from Sydney to the Gulf of Carpentaria.* London, Longman, Brown, Green and Longmans, 1948. 438 p, illus, maps.
Expedition formed in 1845, which spent twelve months in northeastern Australia. Facsimile edition, New York, Greenwood, 1967.

MITCHELL, T.L. *Three expeditions into the interior of eastern Australia . . .* London, T. & W. Boone, 1838, 2 vols, illus, maps.
The expeditions were: north of Sydney to the Namoi and Gwydir rivers, 1831; to the Darling River, 1835; crossing the Murray River and proceeding through *Australia Felix* to arrive in Portland in 1836. Facsimile edition, Adelaide, LBSA.

MOOREHEAD, A. *Cooper's Creek.* Melbourne, Macmillan, 1977. 180 p, illus, maps.
The illustrated edition of the most readable and accurate of the numerous accounts of the Burke and Wills expedition. First published in 1963.

OXLEY, J. *Journals of two expeditions into the interior of New South Wales . . . in the years 1817–18.* London, John Murray, 1820, 408 p, illus, maps.
First detailed account of the interior resulting from expeditions made in 1817 by Oxley, surveyor-general, who explored large areas west and north of Sydney. He followed the main rivers and discovered the rich Liverpool Plains. Facsimile edition, Adelaide, LBSA, 1964.

RAWSON, G. *The count: a life of Sir Paul Edmund Strzelecki, K.C.M.G. explorer and scientist.* Melbourne, Heinemann, 1953. 214 p, illus, maps.
Strzelecki made a number of Australian tours; he travelled from Yass in 1840, climbing Mount Kosciusko, then followed McMillan's tracks south into Gippsland and Port Phillip Bay. He travelled in Van Diemen's Land, 1840–42.

ROBINSON, G.A. *Friendly mission: the Tasmanian journals and papers of George Augustus Robinson 1829–1834.* Ed by N.J.B. Plomley. Hobart, Tasmanian Historical Research Association, 1966. 1074 p, illus, maps.
Robinson travelled extensively as conciliator of the Tasmanian Aborigines, commandant of the Flinders Island Aboriginal Settlement, and chief protector of the Aborigines at Port Phillip. His explorations are considered in Appendix I. A supplement was published in 1971.

ROYAL SOCIETY OF VICTORIA. Exploration Committee. *Progress reports and final report of the Exploration Committee of the Royal Society of Victoria 1863.* Melbourne, Mason and Firth, 1863.
Seven reports made by the organising body of the Victorian exploring expedition. A supplementary final report, adopted in 1872, was printed by Stillwell and Knight in 1873.

SCOTT, E. *The life of Captain Matthew Flinders, R.N.* Sydney, A & R, 1914. 492 p, illus, maps.
Standard biography of Flinders, with accounts of Baudin and Peron.

SCOTT, E. *Terre Napoleon: a history of French explorations and projects in Australia.* London, Methuen, 1910. 296 p, illus, maps.
Discussion of the explorations of Baudin, Peron and Freycinet, and the meeting with Flinders, following their explorations along the Australian south coast.

SPENCER, W.B. *Report on the work of the Horn scientific expeditions to central Australia.* London, Dulau and Co, 1896. 4 vols, illus, maps.
Scientific results of the Horn expedition 1894, covering zoology, geology and botany, and anthropology of central Australia.

STOKES, J.L. *Discoveries in Australia: with an account of the coasts and rivers explored and surveyed during the voyage of the* HMS *Beagle, in the years 1837–38–39–40–41–42–43.* London, T. & W. Boone, 1845, 2 vols, illus, maps.
Third surveying voyage of the *Beagle.* Exploration of the coasts of WA, Bass Strait and northern Australia, together with Owen Stanley's narrative of islands in the Arafura Sea. Facsimile edition, Adelaide, LBSA, 1967.

STRZELECKI, P.E. de. *Physical description of New South Wales and Van Diemen's Land . . .* London, Longman, Brown, Green and Longmans, 1845, 462 p, illus, maps.
A compendium of scientific observation, containing accounts of marine and land surveys, the latter including his own survey. Facsimile edition, Adelaide, LBSA, 1967.

STUART, J. McD. *J. McDouall Stuart's explorations across the continent of Australia . . . 1861–62.* Melbourne, F.F. Bailliere, 1863. 97 p, map.
Journal of Stuart's sixth expedition in 1861–62 from Adelaide through central Australia, then northwest to the Roper River which he followed to Chambers Bay, east of the mouth of the Adelaide River. Facsimile edition, Adelaide, LBSA, 1963.

STURT, C. *Narrative of an expedition into central Australia, performed . . . during the years 1844, 5, and 6 . . .* London, T. & W. Boone, 1849. 2 vols, illus, map.
Sturt left Adelaide in 1844, following the Darling to Menindee, reaching the Barrier Range, finding the Sturt Desert and penetrating the Simpson Desert, covering 4800 kilometres through unknown country. Facsimile edition, Adelaide, LBSA, 1965.

STURT, C. *Two expeditions into the interior of southern Australia, during the years 1828, 1829, 1830, and 1831 . . .* London, Smith, Elder and Co, 1833, 2 vols, illus, map.
Sturt's expeditions led to the discovery of the continent's greatest river system: the Darling River, the Murrumbidgee River and the Murray River; this he followed to the sea entrance below Lake Alexandrina. Facsimile edition, Sydney, Doubleday, 1982.

[TIETKENS, W.H.] *Journal of the central Australian exploring expedition, 1889, under command of W.H. Tietkens . . .* Adelaide, Government Printer, 1891. 84 p, maps.

Account of an expedition to central Australia in 1889, with contributions by F. von Mueller and H.Y.L. Brown.

VANCOUVER, G. *A voyage of discovery to the north Pacific Ocean, and round the world. . .* London, G.G. and J. Robinson, 1798. 3 vols and atlas, illus, maps.

Although most of this work concerns North America, Vancouver also reached the southwest coast of Australia and discovered King George's Sound and Cape Hood.

VICTORIA. Royal Commission. Burke and Wills Commission. *Report of the commissioners appointed to enquire into and report upon the circumstances connected with the suffering and death of Robert O'Hara Burke and William John Wills, the Victorian explorers.* Melbourne, Government Printer, 1862. 104 p. (Vic. Parliament. Parliamentary paper no 97 of 1861–62.)

Official report of the Victorian royal commission which strongly criticised the Exploration Committee and also Burke, Wright and Brahe.

WALKER, M.H. *Come wind, come weather: a biography of Alfred Howitt.* MUP, 1971. 348 p, illus.

Includes contributions from D.J. Mulvaney and J.A. Talent.

WARBURTON, P.E. *Journey across the western interior of Australia.* London, Sampson Low, Marston, Low & Searle, 1875, 308 p, illus, map.

An account of Warburton's exploration from Alice Springs to Roebourne in 1872, with long introduction by Charles H. Eden. Facsimile edition, Adelaide, LBSA, 1968.

WEATHERBURN, A.K. *George William Evans, explorer.* A & R. 1966. 138 p, illus, maps.

Evans was surveyor in both NSW and Van Diemen's Land (1812), and was the discoverer, with Oxley, of the Macquarie and Lachlan rivers.

WEBSTER, E.M. *Whirlwinds in the plain: Ludwig Leichhardt—friends, foes and history.* MUP, 1980. 462 p, illus, maps.

A detailed study of Leichhardt's life and an assessment of his place in the history of Australia.

WEBSTER, M.S. *John McDouall Stuart.* MUP, 1958. 319 p, illus, maps.

After accompanying Sturt to central Australia in 1844–45, Stuart carried out six expeditions to central and west Australia. He succeeded in crossing the continent in 1861–62.

WESTALL, W. *Drawings by William Westall: landscape artist on board* HMS Investigator *during the circumnavigation of Australia by Captain Matthew Flinders R.N. in 1801–1803.* Ed by T.M. Perry and D.H. Simpson. London, Royal Commonwealth Society, 1962. viii, 71 p, illus, maps.

Reproduction of Westall's drawings, illustrations, maps and charts associated with Flinders' voyage, with editorial notes.

WILKINS, G.H. *Undiscovered Australia: being an account of an expedition to tropical Australia to collect specimens of the rarer native fauna for the British Museum, 1923–1925.* London, Benn, 1928. 292 p, illus, maps.

Report of a scientific expedition to northern Australia.

WILLS, W.J. *A successful exploration through the interior of Australia, from Melbourne to the Gulf of Carpentaria, from the journals and letters of William John Wills.* Ed by W. Wills. London, Richard Bently, 1863. 396 p, illus, maps.

The journals and letters of the explorer, edited by his father, Dr William Wills.

WINNECKE, C. *Journal of the Horn scientific exploring expedition, 1894 . . .* Adelaide, Government Printer, 1897. 86 p, illus, maps.

NT expedition organised by W.A. Horn and led by Winnecke.

Death of Kennedy, the explorer. *Coloured lithograph published by Gibbs, Shallard and Co as a supplement to the* Illustrated Sydney News, *December 1870. The mythologising of Australian explorers began as early as 1870. Edmund Kennedy's ignorance and recklessness, which resulted in the deaths of ten of the thirteen men on his overland expedition, are not represented; far more significant is the nobility of the attempt.*

'The Old Elsey cattle station.'
Photograph, undated, of the setting for
Mrs Aeneas Gunn's We of the
Never-Never, *1908.*
NATIONAL LIBRARY

CHAPTER 25

LAND SETTLEMENT

B. H. FLETCHER AND J. M. POWELL

WHEN IN 1770 Captain Cook took possession of eastern Australia the land within that region became the property of the crown by virtue of occupation. Subsequently, the area involved was defined in the commission that was issued to Governor Phillip. Later still, the rest of the continent was brought under the crown following the establishment of colonies in Western Australia and South Australia. Although, in a legal sense and from a British point of view, the whole of Australia belonged to the crown, decisions about what was to be done with it were made by the government. Before the mid-nineteenth century it was the Colonial Office in London which issued regulations determining how crown land was to be alienated and under what terms. These regulations were put into effect by the various colonial governors.

Many of the documents relating to land policy may be found in the *Historical records of Australia* (36 vols, Melbourne, Library Committee of the Commonwealth Parliament, 1914–25), the *Historical records of New South Wales* (8 vols, 1892–98; facs, Sydney, Lansdown Slattery, 1978–79) and the *Historical records of Victoria* (Melbourne, Public Records Office of Victoria, 1981–   ). R.G. Riddell's 'A study in the land policy of the Colonial Office, 1763–1855' (*Canadian historical review* ns, 18, 4, 1937, 385–405) offers a valuable insight into the principles underlying colonial expansion in the crucial early years of Australian development. The legal and constitutional aspects of land policy questions can be traced through A.C.V. Melbourne's *Early constitutional development in Australia* (UQP, 1972) and W.G. McMinn's *A constitutional history of Australia* (OUP, 1979).

After the introduction of responsible government, power over these matters was placed in the hands of colonial ministries which made decisions without reference to London. Whereas land policy had previously been decided with at least some reference to the broader objectives of imperial policy, after 1856 it was formulated in the context of colonial politics and in reference to local considerations. The exact practice varied from colony to colony, but developments followed a broadly similar pattern.

The evidence on which a history of land settlement must rely rests necessarily in the parliamentary papers and records of administrative decisions made by the government departments concerned. Fortunately there are indexes to Australian and British government documents and parliamentary papers which readers may consult to identify and locate the references cited in this essay. For Australia, there is D.H. Borchardt's *Checklist of royal commissions, select committees of parliament and boards of inquiry 1856–1980* and associated volumes by E. Zalums (see chapter 8 of this volume). The consolidated index contains almost 35 references to inquiries into land settlement, as well as to relevant inquiries listed under headings such as crown lands, land grants and land laws and legislation. The most accessible index to British parliamentary papers is the two-volume Irish University Press's *Index to British parliamentary papers on Australia and New Zealand 1800–1899* (Dublin, IUP, 1974). For details see chapter 8 above.

Despite the fact that New South Wales began as a gaol, the plans prepared by the British government for the colony from the outset included provision for the alienation of crown land. Between 1788 and 1826 emancipists were eligible for small grants of thirty acres and above upon completion of their sentences. It would appear that the plan was aimed primarily at providing a livelihood for convicts whom the government hoped would stay in the colony after completing their sentences. An inquiry into the working of the system was conducted by Commissioner Bigge in 1819 and it was largely on his recommendation that it was modified in 1821 and abandoned five years later. He showed that most of the former convicts who had received grants had failed as farmers and concluded that climate, soil, as well as their background and own lack of capital, guaranteed that the odds were weighed too heavily against them. Nevertheless, some did prosper and the scheme was an interesting and in some respects a positive one.

The government extended a similar concession to the officers of the New South Wales Corps, whose activities have been the subject of disagreement among historians. While the officers did abuse their position and exploit other sections of the community, they contributed greatly to the expansion of settlement and to the foundations of the pastoral industry, a point more fully elaborated by B. Fletcher (1976) and treated as an important issue in two biographies of the period (G. Mackanness, *The life of Vice-Admiral Bligh*, A & R, 1951, and M.H. Ellis, *John Macarthur*, A & R, 1978).

Less controversial was the third group of colonists to whom land was granted, namely migrants who had come to the colony as free persons. At first few arrived, for New South Wales offered only limited opportunities and, besides being a penal colony, was much further from Britain than were most imperial possessions. Nevertheless, once the potential of the wool industry had been revealed and, following the crossing of the Blue Mountains, the existence of limitless areas of good land had been publicised, increasing numbers of migrants arrived. Up to 1821 settlement was confined to the Cumberland Plain, but later pastoralists poured into the interior thrusting even further afield in the search for land (Perry, 1963). This created serious administrative problems, for the short-staffed surveyor-general's department was unable to keep pace with demand and eventually led to Governor Darling, in 1829, proclaiming the Nineteen Counties as a region beyond which settlement was not to proceed.

The bulk of the land thus far alienated, whether to former convicts, military officers or migrants, had been in the form of grants which were issued free, but which were subject to a quit rent (that is, a small rent paid in lieu of services) at the end of a specified period. The early grants were only small but from the Macquarie period onwards the tendency was to issue larger holdings for pastoral purposes and allow only migrants with specified amounts of capital to acquire them. Regulations were laid down on all these matters and under Darling a Land Board was established to administer them.

The land grant system, which was applied in other colonies besides New South Wales, made an important contribution to the spread of settlement and to the establishment of primary industry. It made land readily available on easy terms, thus enabling migrants to use their capital for acquiring stock and effecting improvements on their holdings. Yet, from the point of view of the government it possessed many disadvantages. The quit rent, which was supposed to yield revenue, proved almost impossible to collect. Similarly it was not difficult for settlers to deceive the authorities as to how much capital they possessed. Large areas of land fell into the hands of people who were not able to use them productively and substantial holdings were tied up in private hands and lay waste.

Throughout the 1820s attempts were made to cope with these problems but to no avail. In 1831 Lord Goderich finally decided that a new scheme, based on the sale of land, was necessary and regulations, known as the Ripon Regulations, were introduced. Henceforth land, instead of being given free, was to be put up for auction at a minimum price of five shillings an acre.

This change was once seen as a reflection of the influence over the Colonial Office of Edward Gibbon Wakefield and the systematic colonisers who advocated a similar reform. In fact earlier attempts had been made from the time of Commissioner Bigge onwards to introduce a system of land sales. It is now widely recognised that Wakefield, in this as in other changes he proposed, was less of an innovator than was once supposed. Policy was already moving in the direction he advocated and the changes that occurred in the 1830s owed more to other considerations than to his writings. Among the best books on Wakefield are P. Bloomfield's *Edward Gibbon Wakefield: builder of the British Commonwealth* (London, Longmans, 1961) and J. Phillip's *A great view of things: Edward Gibbon Wakefield* (Melbourne, Nelson, 1971). For an earlier analysis see R.C. Mills, *The colonisation of Australia, 1829–42: the Wakefield experiment in empire building* (1915; facs, SUP, 1974).

The system of land sales introduced in 1831 applied to all the Australian colonies and remained in operation for some decades, although the minimum price was increased. There had long been other means by which pastoralists obtained land, particularly in New South Wales, which until 1851 included the Port Phillip region and until 1859 the future Queensland. From the very beginnings of settlement farmers and graziers had made use of vacant crown land, at first adjacent to their own properties and then further afield. This practice, which later became known as squatting, was quite illegal but since there was plenty of land and few means of checking the abuse, governors turned a blind eye to it. During the 1820s, however, as settlement spread, attempts were made to regularise the situation and to ensure that the government derived some advantage from it. Governors Brisbane and Darling introduced schemes under which settlers could lease prescribed areas on payment of an annual fee. Governor Bourke, anxious to safeguard the interests of the crown, secured the passage of a bill in 1833 which provided for the appointment of commissioners of crown land whose duties were to maintain a close watch over the waste lands and ensure that they were not used improperly.

These measures applied only to the Nineteen Counties, beyond which no land could be alienated or leased. This restriction did not, however, deter squatters from moving further and further afield. During the 1830s and 1840s vast areas of crown land were occupied by such people whose exodus the government had no means of preventing. The history of squatting during this period was largely one in which graziers seized the initiative and progressively forced the government to accommodate itself to their interests. In this they were helped by their undoubted economic, social and political importance and by the fact that they had the support of powerful British interests who were involved in the wool trade. Between 1836 and 1847 pastoralists first secured recognition of the right, subject to payment of a licence fee, to occupy crown land outside the bounds of settlement. Then in 1847 they were given leases that varied inversely in duration according to how closely they were located to settled districts. In addition they were entitled to compensation for improvements effected to their runs and pre-emptive rights if they were put up for sale. These gains were achieved only after a lengthy struggle principally with Governor Gipps who was aware that the interests of government and other sections of the community were threatened.

The history of land settlement up to the middle of the nineteenth century was one that by and large favoured the large landholder at the expense of the small. Admittedly in some parts of each of the colonies, where natural and climatic conditions were suitable, operations on a more limited scale did develop. South Australia, which was less well suited to pastoralism, also saw mixed farming emerge. Nevertheless, particularly in the eastern colonies, the pastoralist was dominant. Not the least of the motives behind the struggle for self-government in those parts was the desire of such people to gain control over crown lands for purposes of self-interest. The British government appreciated this and the knowledge made successive administrations wary of surrendering the right to determine how land was to be alienated. Issues associated with land figured prominently among those that were hotly debated during the 1840s and early 1850s. The franchise introduced with representative government in New South Wales in 1842 favoured property owners and these men were not slow to capitalise on their influence in the legislature. This change is clearly reflected in the official inquiries commissioned in the 1830s and 1840s.

The coming of responsible government to all colonies except Western Australia, which had begun to receive convicts, was followed by locally introduced changes which shifted the balance of power from the land to the towns. Not only did colonial legislatures for the first time possess control over crown lands but these bodies were themselves subject to greater influence from the urban-based middle class. In eastern Australia the late 1840s and early 1850s saw new political groups emerge in opposition to the squatters. The action of landed interests in seeking a resumption of transportation, in working for control over the land and in seeking constitutions that would guarantee their own continued influence, was strongly resisted by less well established settlers, many of whom had been among the migrants of the 1840s. This group, liberal and sometimes radical in inclination, now found itself in power and sought to break the hold of the large landowners. This was reflected in the land legislation that was introduced in most colonies during the years after 1860.

Best known perhaps were the two crown lands acts introduced in New South Wales by John Robertson and named after him. They established the principle of selection before survey and made land available in small blocks of 40 to 320 acres within the settled or intermediate districts of the colony. The price was fixed at one pound per acre; payment was possible on terms over three years and the only conditions involved residence and the effecting of improvements within a stipulated period. Viewed once as an attempt to promote agricultural settlement, these acts are now more generally viewed in the context of moves by urban liberals to dispossess the squatters and to promote a bourgeois ethos.

Similar attempts to open up the land to the small property owner were made in Victoria where there existed the additional problem of finding employment for substantial numbers of former gold diggers. The Nicholson Act of 1860, while not sanctioning selection until after land had been surveyed, nevertheless made holdings available on relatively easy terms and granted pre-emptive rights to an area three times that purchased. Duffy's act of 1862 opened large areas of squatting land to selectors while Grant's act, introduced three years later, was designed to ensure that this land was not monopolised by a small handful of larger purchasers.

The legislation introduced in these colonies and in Queensland tended to produce effects that in general were different to those anticipated. The pastoralists possessed enough financial resources and business acumen to enable most to retain possession of their land. Moreover, through devices known as peacocking and dummying they were able to turn loopholes in the acts to their own advantage. The bulk of land alienated in the decades immediately following the passage of the acts remained in their hands. Nevertheless although climate, the quality of the land, distance from markets and the advantages enjoyed by the graziers operated to the disadvantage of the small landholders, the acts were not as much a failure as contemporaries made out. Inquiries like that by Morris and Rankin in New South Wales in 1883 ('Inquiry into the state of the public lands and operation of land laws'), purporting to show that the Robertson acts had failed, have themselves been shown to have presented a misleading picture. Districts that were better suited than most to dairying, or agriculture, witnessed an increase in such activities. Thriving farming communities emerged in some parts although in general the lot of the selector was poor. Conflict between squatter and selector was an important feature of the rural scene during the second half of the nineteenth century.

The failure of attempts to unlock the land to the desired extent produced further legislation, particularly during the closing decade of the nineteenth century when Labor parties emerged. Even before then colonial governments, influenced by the theories of Henry George, had endeavoured to break up the large estates by imposing a tax on the unimproved capital value of land. Here were indications that a new variety of ideological influence was being brought to bear on the land issue. Further evidence of a new approach can be seen in the use of financial assistance to promote settlement. Influenced partly by the depression, partly by the ideas of William Lane, a measure was introduced in New South Wales in May 1893 with the object of placing small communities on the land. Similar acts were passed in Victoria and Queensland and all contained provision for loans to assist those who obtained land.

Implicit in this was a recognition that a higher degree of state intervention was necessary if existing inequities were to be overcome. This was also apparent in the numerous acts introduced in eastern Australia during the 1890s with the object of opening large areas of pastoral leases to the small farmer. For the first time financial assistance was offered and governments themselves purchased land for lease to settlers. There is a good outline of the ensuing legislation in T.A. Coghlan's *Labour and industry in Australia* (1981; repr, Melbourne, Macmillan, 1969, vol 4) and the parliamentary papers cited among the references below illustrate the changing official view. By the close of the century only limited success had been achieved; much remained to be done.

Advertisement for the Australian Estates Company in the Courier-Mail Annual, *Brisbane 1954. The juxtaposition of exploration and real estate is fundamental to the history of land settlement in Australia.*

ALEXANDER, G. AND WILLIAMS, O.B. eds, *The pastoral industries of Australia: practice and technology of sheep and cattle production.* SUP, 1973. 567 p, illus, maps.
A treatment of the grazing industry with emphasis on the twentieth century and references to land policy and settlement.

AUSTRALIA. Department of Home Affairs and Environment. *National conservation strategy for Australia: living resource conservation for substantial development. Towards a national conservation strategy: a discussion paper.* AGPS, 1982. 71 p.
The conference indicates trends towards a new view of development based on principles of participatory democracy and the impact of modern environmentalism.

BAUER, F.H. *Historical geographic survey of part of northern Australia.* Canberra, CSIRO. Divison of Land Research and Regional Survey, 1959, 1964. 2 vols, maps. (CSIRO Division of Land Research and Regional Survey. Divisional report nos 59/2, 64/1).
Early interpretations of European settlement in the tropics. See also Bolton (1970), Courteney (1982) and A. Powell (1982).

BOLTON, G.C. *A fine country to starve in.* UWAP, 1972. 278 p, illus, maps.
Examines the impact of the 1930s depression on farming belts in WA. Good information on the fate of pioneer settlers and on the naive images of vast open spaces.

BOLTON, G.C. *Spoils and spoilers: Australians make their environment 1788–1980.* Sydney, Allen & Unwin, 1981. 197 p, illus, maps.
An introduction to mistakes and successes in the management of our built and natural environments with material for an appreciation of land settlement.

BOLTON, G.C. *A thousand miles away: a history of north Queensland to 1920.* ANUP, 1970. 366 p, illus, maps.
Valuable guide to the sequence of pioneering settlement in a distinctive under-researched region. First published in 1963.

BOWES, K.R. *Land settlement in South Australia 1857–1890.* Adelaide, LBSA, 1968. 387 p.
Summary of major legislation with commentaries. Considers both pastoral and agricultural settlement.

BURROUGHS, P. *Britain and Australia, 1831–1855: a study of imperial relations and crown land administration.* Oxford, Clarendon Press, 1967. 419 p, maps.
A comprehensive survey that breaks new ground, offers some reinterpretations and adds to our understanding of imperial policy.

BURVILL, G.H. ed, *Agriculture in Western Australia: 150 years of development and achievement, 1829–1979.* UWAP, 1979. 397 p, illus, maps.
A survey of farming and grazing which provides background to the spread of settlement.

BUTLIN, N.G. *Our original aggression: Aboriginal populations of southeastern Australia, 1788–1850.* Sydney, Allen & Unwin, 1983. 186 p, illus, maps.
Argues against standard notions of the small numbers of Aborigines at the time of first contact and suggests that we should revise our traditional perceptions of the Aborigines.

BUXTON, G.L. *The Riverina 1861–1891: an Australian regional study.* MUP, 1967. 338 p, illus, maps.
Clarifies the distinctiveness of a pioneer settlement.

CAMERON, J.M.R. *Ambition's fire: the agricultural colonization of pre-convict Western Australia.* UWAP, 1981. 238 p, illus, maps.
An analysis of early speculations and failures in the Swan River district. 'Environmental appraisal' given emphasis.

CAMPBELL, K.O. *Australian agriculture: reconciling change and tradition.* Melbourne, Longman Cheshire, 1980. 274 p.
A perceptive study of the rural economy and society with a discussion of the way land legislation has influenced the pattern of settlement.

COURTNEY, P.P. *Northern Australia: patterns and problems of tropical development in an advanced country.* Melbourne, Longman Cheshire, 1982. 335 p, maps.

Includes a historical chapter on the development of settlement and changing interpretations of the region. The other chapters contain commentaries on more recent developments.

CHRISTIE, M.F. *Aborigines in colonial Victoria, 1835–86.* SUP, 1979. 227 p, illus, maps.

An analysis of land management policies influencing the dislocation of Aborigines with information on perceptions of land, racial attitudes of pioneers and protectorate system.

DAVIDSON, B.R. *Australia wet or dry? The physical and economic limits to the expansion of irrigation.* MUP, 1969. 264 p, maps.

DAVIDSON, B.R. *European farming in Australia: an economic history of Australian farming.* Amsterdam, Elsevier Scientific Publishing Co, 1981. 437 p.

DAVIDSON, B.R. *The northern myth: a study of the physical and economic limits to agricultural and pastoral development in tropical Australia.* MUP, 1965. 283 p, maps.

Three books that offer controversial economic arguments against some favoured solutions for our 'empty spaces'. Davidson's points now attract less emotional opposition.

DAVIES, J.L. ed, *Atlas of Tasmania.* Hobart, Lands and Survey Dept, 1965. 128 p, illus, maps.

Several of the map-essays are related to interpretations of rural settlement expansion. Scott's 'Land settlement' is important with a map of the major pattern of land alienation over 150 years.

DUNCAN, J.S. ed, *Atlas of Victoria.* Melbourne, Victorian Government Printing Office on behalf of the Government of Vic, 1982. 239 p, illus, maps.

Map-essays include background environment, agricultural and demographic data relevant to land settlement with map of population distribution in 1891, and of squatting expansion, closer settlement and soldier settlement.

DUNSDORFS, E. *The Australian wheat growing industry, 1788–1948.* MUP, 1956. 547 p, maps.

An analysis of the development of wheat farming from the earliest days. It provides background to small and large-scale land settlement.

EPPS, W. *Land systems of Australasia.* London, Sonnenschein, 1894. 184 p.

Outlines the methods which governed the use and alienation of public lands. It appeared when schemes for land nationalisation and a single land tax were under discussion.

FLETCHER, B.H. *Landed enterprise and penal society: a history of farming and grazing in New South Wales before 1821.* SUP, 1976. 265 p, maps.

A detailed discussion of land policy and the penal character of the colony.

GLYNN, S. *Government policy and agricultural development: a study of the role of government in the development of the Western Australian wheat belt, 1900–1930.* UWAP, 1975. 173 p, maps.

Information on the environmental, political and social context of rural settlement in new and established areas in good and bad times. Credit facilities and railway expansion.

HEATHCOTE, R.L. *Australia.* London, Longman, 1975. 246 p, illus, maps.

Interprets transformations in built and natural environments through an emphasis on ecological factors and environmental perceptions and misperceptions.

HEATHCOTE, R.L. *Back of Bourke: a study of land appraisal and settlement in semi-arid Australia.* MUP, 1965. 244 p, maps.

This work laid the foundations for modern analytical approaches to Australian historical geography. Unusual in its emphasis on pastoral pioneering and novel use of contemporary records for evaluations of difficult environments.

JEANS, D.N. ed, *Australia: a geography.* SUP, 1977. 571 p, illus, maps.

Systematic text containing 24 specialist essays incorporating information for land settlement themes.

JEANS, D.N. ed, *An historical geography of New South Wales to 1901.* Sydney, Reed Education, 1972. 328 p, illus, maps.

Brings the insights of the geographer to bear on facets of the development of NSW including land settlement.

KIDDLE, M.L. *Men of yesterday: a social history of the western district of Victoria, 1834–1890.* MUP, 1961. 573 p, illus, maps.

A regional history, concentrating on a small number of squatting families and contemporary attitudes to landed property with examples of squatter–selector conflict. First published in 1961.

KING, C.J. *An outline of closer settlement in New South Wales.* Sydney, NSW Dept of Agriculture, Division of Marketing and Agricultural Economics, 1957. 290 p, illus, maps.

This work provides a review of land policy from 1788 to 1955.

McQUILTON, F.J. *The Kelly outbreak, 1878–1880: the geographical dimension of social banditry.* MUP, 1979. 250 p, illus, map.

Relates these events to the milieux of selector communities of northeastern Vic. Good documentary searches in the land records.

MEINIG, D.W. *On the margins of the good earth: the South Australian wheat frontier, 1869–84.* Chicago, Rand McNally for the Association of American Geographers, 1962. 231 p, illus, map.

This exemplar in Australian historical geography is vital to an understanding of government-initiated pioneer settlement, not only in this classical 'Wakefieldian' colony.

PEEL, L.J. *Rural industry in the Port Phillip region, 1835–1880.* MUP, 1974. 196 p, illus.

A study which illuminates the growth of the Port Phillip area and throws light on the process of rural settlement.

PERRY, T.M. *Australia's first frontier: the spread of settlement in New South Wales, 1788–1829.* MUP in association with the Australian National University, 1963. 163 p, illus, maps.

Emphasises the significance of regional environmental factors as well as the more familiar 'shortage of land'.

POWELL, A. *Far country: a short history of the Northern Territory.* MUP, 1982. 301 p, illus, maps.

Text on our last 'frontier' region. Settlement themes form only part of the story, but they are vital elements.

POWELL, J.M. *Environmental management in Australia, 1788–1914, guardians, improvers and profit: an introductory survey.* OUP, 1976. 191 p, illus, maps.

First history of environmental management in Australia. The interpretation favours international comparisons and emphasises changing attitudes. Land settlement dominates throughout the period under review.

POWELL, J.M. *The public lands of Australia Felix: settlement and land appraisal in Victoria 1834–91 with special reference to the western plains.* OUP, 1970. 328 p, illus, maps.

A monograph on land legislation and associated settlement in Vic, using a range of official and private records. The emphasis on changing environmental appraisals and the dichotomy of official and popular viewpoints is similar to that of Heathcote (1965).

POWELL, J.M. ed, *The making of rural Australia, environment, society and economy: geographical readings.* Melbourne, Sorrett, 1974. 179 p, illus, maps.

Readings from geographical journals ranging from the early squatting age to twentieth-century themes, including the Little Desert dispute in the 1960s and 1970s.

POWELL, J.M. ed, *Yeomen and bureaucrats: the Victorian Crown Lands Commission, 1878–79.* OUP, 1973. 464 p, illus, maps.

An abridged version of the minutes and reports of the royal commission investigating progress under the 1869 Land Act. The only accessible source of a range of contemporary views on land settlement.

POWELL, J.M. AND WILLIAMS, M. eds, *Australian space, Australian time: geographical perspectives.* OUP, 1975. 256 p, illus, maps.

Essays including land administration, conservation history, Williams' overview of rural settlement 1788–1914 claiming 'More and smaller is better'.

ROBERTS, S.H. *History of Australian land settlement, 1788–1920.* Melbourne, Macmillan, 1924. 460 p, maps.

A standard work on its subject. It provides a broad overview that is valuable for introductory purposes. New edition published in 1968.

ROBERTS, S.H. *The squatting age in Australia, 1835–1847.* MUP, 1935. 378 p, maps.

A colourful and readable treatment first published in 1935. Some of its conclusions have been modified by later research. New edition published in 1978.

ROBINSON, M.E. *The New South Wales wheat frontier 1851 to 1911.* Canberra, Dept of Human Geography, Australian National University, 1976. 247 p, illus, maps.

Valuable for the mapping of frontier expansions, discussing legislation, the railway network, the connections between the early selection story and closer settlement efforts and the rise of share-farming.

SOUTH GIPPSLAND PIONEERS' ASSOCIATION. *The land of the lyrebird: a story of early settlement in the great forest of south Gippsland* . . . Melbourne, Gordon & Gotch, 1920, 427 p, illus, maps.

Evocative reconstruction drawn from the reminiscences of early settlers. However the region is not representative of the Victorian experience in general. Revised edition published in 1966.

WADHAM, S.M. *Australian farming, 1788–1965.* Melbourne, Cheshire, 1967. 156 p, maps.

The focus of this book is on the twentieth century, but it provides some insight into land settlement at an earlier period.

WADHAM, S.M. *et al, Land utilization in Australia.* MUP, 1939, 295 p, illus, map

A survey, castigating official and popular views on land settlement and emphasising economic and environmental constraints in a bold critique. New edition published in 1964.

WALKER, R.B. *Old New England: a history of the northern tablelands of New South Wales, 1818–1900.* SUP, 1966. 187 p, illus, maps.

A regional account offering historical perspective for land settlement and other specific inquiries.

WATERSON, D.B. *Squatter, selector and storekeeper: a history of the Darling Downs, 1859–93.* SUP, 1968. 310 p, illus, maps.

Analysis of community establishments on the impact of land legislation and reconstruction in newly settled areas.

WESTERN AUSTRALIA. Education Dept. *Western Australia: an atlas of human endeavour, 1829–1979.* Perth, Government Printer, 1979. 144 p, illus, maps.

Map-essays on the 'Frontiers of settlement', 'Spread of towns' and 'Taking up of the land' are highly relevant.

WILLIAMS, M. *The making of the South Australian landscape: a study in the historical geography of Australia.* London, Academic Press, 1974. 518 p, illus, maps.

Emphasises landscape modification—rural and urban settlement expansion, clearing of woodlands, draining of vast areas—in the context of social, political and technological change.

F.M. Rothery, Bundaleer Plains. *Watercolour in his*
Atlas of Bundaleer Plains and Tatala, *1878.*
Bundaleer Plains was a huge pastoral holding in southeast Queensland, where the
artist of this work spent ten years as manager from 1863 to 1873.
The property had been acquired in the late 1850s, when Queensland
was being carved up by explorers and squatters.

VII
POLITICS

HRH *Duke of York at the opening of the federal parliament in May 1927—a reminder of Australia's close ties with the 'mother country'.* Youth annual, *December 1930.*

BOOROWA PRODUCTIONS

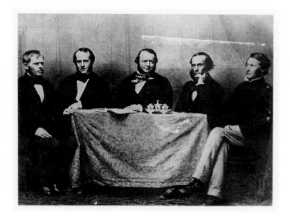

'First Ministry under Responsible Govt N.S. Wales 1856.' Photograph.
NSW GOVERNMENT PRINTING OFFICE

CHAPTER 26

PARLIAMENTS, PARTIES AND GOVERNMENTS

R. L. COPE, GRAHAM MADDOX, STEPHANIE HAGAN AND JOAN RYDON

PARLIAMENTARY GOVERNMENT

SCHOLARSHIP AND PUBLISHING have blossomed abundantly in Australia since the end of World War II and the dual fields of parliament and government have received considerable attention from both. The growing number of schoolchildren and university students has led to a steady stream of educational texts on the parliamentary system and government in Australia. Many of these texts are valuable in heightening interest and awareness among the population generally.

It is equally clear that Australians' perceptions of matters relating to parliament and government have developed and broadened dramatically in recent decades, encouraged and supported by the mixed blessings of television, with its instant exposure to events, and such recent phenomena as talk-back and community supported radio. Sectional groupings of citizens and 'activists' promoting various causes are now commonplace, and an analysis of the way Australian society has changed over recent decades would undoubtedly identify many more factors having relevance to the practice of, and an interest in, politics and government.

So numerous and diverse have been developments in the fields of parliament and government in the last two decades, to take an arbitrary cut-off point, that there has been a radical questioning of hitherto accepted institutions and offices (such as that of the governor-general), of the political system (especially in its federal aspect), of the division of power (with women asking for proportionate share of power, Aborigines seeking ownership of land), and of the law, both in its substantive content and in its system of administration. There are many official reports, books and pamphlets on these questions. The conflict between capital and labour has also had its share of attention and it is apparent from this brief and certainly partial enumeration of topics relevant to parliament and government in Australia that to cite even representative titles in this vast area would lead to a list quite beyond the scope of this volume. The reading lists that follow are therefore selective and restricted to basic published works, acknowledged to be important in their field but within the grasp of the educated, non-specialist reader.

No attempt has been made to list the parliamentary and official publications which are basic to the study of the operations of the political system. A number of essays in *Australian official publications* edited by D.H. Borchardt (Melbourne, Longman Cheshire, 1979) throw a good deal of light on the publications of each legislature in Australia, although it is not always easy to gain access to official reports and papers. Parliamentary debates are obtainable from the government printing office of each state or, for the commonwealth, from the Australian Government Publishing Service (AGPS). They are, furthermore, easily and freely available from most major libraries. Official reports, if generally available, can be obtained from the same sources.

It should be noted that papers tabled in each house of parliament are, unless specifically excluded, available at the parliament for public perusal under the provisions of the respective standing orders. Not all tabled papers are published as 'printed' or 'parliamentary papers'. They are, however, retained in the archives of the house in which they were tabled. The parliamentary archives do not normally hold personal papers of former members or ministers. Such papers are, if official records, part of the archives of the state, and their accessibility is governed by rules concerning public inspection of government materials. Those rules vary throughout Australia, but in the federal sphere the period of 30 years applies to most types.

Personal papers of members of parliament and statesmen are frequently bequeathed to, or acquired by, the National Library of Australia or the state libraries. University libraries have also shown interest in collecting such materials. Accessibility may depend on an embargo imposed by the donor or by the institution. The compilation in microfiche format issued by the National Library of Australia, entitled *Guide to collections of manuscripts relating to Australia*, lists many manuscript collections, including papers of Australian politicians and statesmen, held in major research libraries. The Australian Archives also collects the papers of federal politicans although these are not listed in the manuscript *Guide*. The reader will also find helpful the bibliographic references appended to articles in the multivolume *Australian dictionary of biography*.

The collections of state and national archives hold an immense quantity of documents relevant to the functioning of the Australian public services and the administration of governments. Local government matters are less easily found in central depositories and are more likely to remain in custody at the local level. Of particular value as a general guide is *Our heritage*, issued in 1983 by the Australian Society of Archivists (see chapter 8 of this volume) which provides a directory to archives and manuscript repositories throughout Australia.

A great deal of specialised research on parliamentary history, politics and government is contained in university theses which may be available for consultation (but generally not for loan) in the library of the university at which the thesis was presented. A certain number of theses are eventually published in book form, though frequently with a radical change in the title.

Several associations in Australia devote their energies to the study of politics and government. Two of the most notable are the Australasian Political Studies Assocation (APSA) and the Australasian Study of Parliament Group. These associations conduct conferences and seminars, and the papers discussed are often published at a later date. The associations also issue journals which contain valuable contributions and book reviews. The APSA journal *Politics* is particularly strong on reviews and bibliographical notes.

There is no dearth of information about works published on parliamentary government and politics in Australia. Particularly noteworthy is the detailed bibliography on parliamentary government by J.A. Pettifer (1981). There remains, however, a need for bibliographical surveys of particular aspects such as political biography, politicians as authors, parliamentary memoirs. More especially we need more evaluation and analytical surveys but this is a task requiring expertise and experience as well as bibliographical skills, a combination not as readily found as might be supposed. Generally those with the expertise are more active in contributing to the substantive study of the subject than to its bibliography. It is, however, encouraging to note that there is a growing awareness among authors and students of the value of accurate and detailed bibliographies. They are indispensable for any informed, serious research and the time spent on their study will yield benefit to all scholars.

POLITICAL PARTIES

Although many specialist works on party politics in Australia have appeared over the past ten or fifteen years, a reader new to the subject is best advised to approach the parties as one component of the political system. Parties may well be studied as separate entities, with a life of their own, and indeed they often are. They readily make sense, however, only when viewed as performing a specific function, both within a party system and in the wider sphere of politics. In Australia, party politics are influenced by federalism, the realities of cabinet government, the long tradition of responsible government, and ideas associated with alternating government and opposition. The best introduction to the study of political parties in Australia is therefore through general works on Australian politics which place the parties squarely in the context of the political system.

There has long been an abundant literature on the Australian Labor Party and its place within the wider labour movement. Before detailed studies on the party system began to blossom in recent years, however, general works on Australian politics were the most accessible sources, particularly for the other parties. The fact that these works usually treated the parties in one or two relatively brief chapters is no measure of the influence that some of them have had on subsequent literature. In his wide-ranging book, *Australia* (1930; repr, Brisbane, Jacaranda, 1964), Keith Hancock devoted two chapters to the parties and established an important theme, namely that the Labor party is the party of initiative and innovation, the Liberal and Country parties the parties of resistance to change. Hancock's formulation has been a point of high controversy ever since. In *Australian government and politics* (1954; 4th edn, London, Duckworth, 1971), Professor J.D.B. Miller devoted a succinct but comprehensive chapter to the parties and elaborated the view that they are 'syndical' because they help to adjust the conflicts among 'syndicates' of workers, farmers, manufacturers and other groups.

More recent general works have treated the parties in the context of the wider political system. Professor L.F. Crisp (1978) used a wealth of primary sources to illustrate the three chapters devoted to the parties. Professor Hugh V. Emy, in *The politics of Australian democracy* (Melbourne, Macmillan, 1974) described the Australian parties as having a firm footing within the 'Westminster tradition' of parliamentary government.

In addition to the single-author works on Australian politics, several comprehensive readers have been published in recent years. In these, the discussions on the parties appear amid an array of other material on the political system and are usually in the form of self-contained essays bearing little direct relation to the surrounding articles. The best known of the readers are the series of five, edited first by Professor Henry Mayer and then by Mayer in collaboration with Helen Nelson (1980). Also among the most useful of the readers are Richard Lucy (1983) and the collection edited by Andrew Parkin *et al* under the title *Government, politics and power in Australia* (2nd edn, Melbourne, Longman Cheshire, 1980), both of which contain sound essays on the parties.

Many valuable discussions on the political parties are available in the general histories of Australian politics, too numerous to mention here. The bibliography contains only the more specialised works devoted to the political system, the parties, and the politicians who have been intimately involved in their activities.

The historical perspective of Australia's political system is clearly outlined by Loveday *et al* (1977) and by Jupp (1964, 1982). A suggestive analytical approach is taken by R.W. Connell and T.H. Irving (1980) and by J. Rickard (1975), both of which explore the controversial theme of class influence on political and social life. A number of the specific works on political parties, such as Russel Ward's translation of Metin (1977) and D. Well's on the Liberal party (1977) provide among other things an analysis of the relevant ideology. Many of the specific works on Labor are concerned with ideological analysis and deal comprehensively with socialist objectives.

The literature listed here does not deal with the broad theoretical aspect of political parties and party systems but is concerned with describing and analysing the structure of political parties and the development of the party system within Australia. A wider perspective of these important aspects of political parties and party systems may be found in such texts as *Political parties: their organization and activity in the modern state* (3rd edn, London, Macmillan, 1964) by Maurice Duverger, *Modern political parties* (Chicago, University of Chicago Press, 1956) by S. Neumann, and *Parties and party systems: a framework for analysis* (CUP, 1976) by Giovanni Sartori.

The sections dealing with particular parties provide more specific information on events surrounding the establishment, development, successes and failures of the parties, as well as their internal structures and ideological underpinnings. Many of these books, particularly those published since the early 1970s, have been inspired by the changing political circumstances and events of the last decade. The election of the Whitlam government in 1972, its re-election in 1974, the 'constitutional crisis' of 1975 and Labor's subsequent electoral defeat provided, among other things, a stimulus to authors and a heightened public awareness of political issues. Much of the material produced on both Whitlam and the constitutional crisis is journalistic in style, giving dramatic accounts of events rather than an analysis of the issues involved. The conservative view is presented by Barwick (1984) and Kerr (1978). Gough Whitlam's own account (1985) of his years in office should also be consulted.

The fact that the Liberal and Country (now National) parties have ruled in rather less controversial times perhaps helps explain the relative dearth of literature of these coalition parties. Possibly success is a less stimulating topic for study than unexplained failure and unfulfilled promise. Australia's minor political parties have attracted the least attention of all; the role they have played in Australia's essentially two-party system of government has always been somewhat peripheral. The Australian Democrats, now electorally the most significant of the minor parties, have yet to prompt more than two biographical works on their leader, Don Chipp, although the number of short essays devoted to them in journals and readers is increasing. The previously most important minor party, the Democratic Labor Party, has been the subject of many articles and at least two excellent analytical works.

Biographical works on notable politicians have enjoyed increasing popularity in recent years. Some of these are written in a popular vein, providing interesting personal insights into Australian politics and the people at the forefront of political life.

Among the most obvious and fruitful sources of bibliographical information on political parties and politicians are the bibliographies contained in the books on the subject. Of these, perhaps the best is the eighteen-page bibliography in Loveday *et al* (1977) which contains extensive references to manuscripts, documents, articles from journals and newspapers, theses and archival materials, as well as to other relevant books. In addition, the table of abbreviations at the front of the book gives a comprehensive list of political and quasi-political organisations which is useful in providing initial references for a catalogue search.

While the most obvious sources of archival material about politicians and parties are the records they have kept themselves, it is worth noting that commonwealth, state and parliamentary archives document in almost profligate detail the implementation of government policies adopted in party rooms and conferences, and may therefore provide considerable insight into the relationship between political theory and practice. Other potential sources for the history of politicians and parties include the archives of corporate bodies which have acted as lobby groups on particular issues—such as trade unions, professional associations, employer, producer or regional organisations and large companies—as well as the archives of local government.

It is unlikely that primary sources will contain much in the way of political theory, which by its nature is prepared for publication. They can, however, be rich in examples of political practice, and certainly provide a contemporary view of the political scene, uncontaminated by hindsight. It is difficult to tap the wealth of information in this field held in government archives. Departmental records are so impregnated with the prevailing political system that the word 'politics' is rarely mentioned in indexes or file lists. To find political information, one has to approach it by specific issue, choosing events or policies that aroused contemporary political controversy or comment. The records of the most 'political' departments—the colonial secretary's, premier's or prime minister's—would be a good starting point but other departments will provide sources on political decisions in their own areas: for example, education.

The records of cabinet are usually disappointingly formal but can provide a way into the much more revealing departmental files by pointing up controversial topics and indicating which department provided the submission. Australian Archives in Canberra, for instance, holds an indexed partial set of copies of federal cabinet papers dating from 1901 which can be used as a direct means of locating linked departmental records. Local government records, which should complement party branch records in the same way as state and federal records complement state and federal party records, are even harder to locate because of the number of local government organisations.

FEDERATION

Intergovernmental relations began with agreements and conferences between the colonial governments. These became part of the move to federation. The steps by which that was achieved and the constitution framed have been well recounted by John La Nauze (1972). He has also edited Alfred Deakin's version (1963) of these events. Crisp (1979) is useful for sources. The provisions of the constitution and their significance have often been discussed. The simplest explanatory work is by Geoffrey Sawer (1975) who has also provided more details on the working of the federal system (1980) while elsewhere (1969) he has set Australian developments in a historical and international context. Colin Howard (1978) offers another very readable discussion. The various readers in Australian politics edited by Henry Mayer and Helen Nelson (1980) include a number of articles discussing aspects of federalism.

The literature on Australian federalism is such that it has been impossible to draw clear divisions between the subjects covered by the various sections of the following bibliography. While the books listed under 'Federation' cover either broad or specific aspects of constitutional arrangements they usually treat the material historically and therefore cannot be clearly separated from those included in the section on the constitution.

No-one could predict how the ex-colonies would develop in the commonwealth. There has been much interest in the shifting balance of power between state and central governments and in the changes in the working and interpretation of the constitution despite little formal amendment of its provisions. It is in this area that the tendency of Australian academics to publish symposia has been most marked. The best were edited by R. Else-Mitchell (1961), and the volumes by Sawer (1952) and the Australian Institute of Political Science (1949) contain excellent papers; though such collections are of uneven quality, they often present a diversity of views. Greenwood's readable account of constitutional development until the end of World War II is an argument for increased commonwealth powers. For reference Geoffrey Sawer (1956–63) has provided a detailed two-volume chronicle of developments from 1901 to 1949.

Much of the literature on the judicial interpretation of the constitution has been written by lawyers for lawyers, but the interested non-specialist should be able to follow most of Sawer (1967), benefit from Zine (1981) and enjoy the volume of essays on the Australian constitution edited by Zine (1977) published as a tribute to Geoffrey Sawer.

Most of the general works on the constitution are now somewhat dated, but C.J. Lloyd and G.S. Reid (1974) cover the activities of the Whitlam government. The essays collected by Sol Encel et al (1977) are typical of many of the immediate demands for constitutional reform. More considered views on the need for change can be found in Howard (1980) and in the bipartisan volume sponsored by the Law Foundation of New South Wales and edited by McMillan et al (1983). The reader is also referred to the 'Constitutional change' section of this chapter.

One aspect of Australian federalism which has remained unchanged until now is the number of states—six—although their relative wealth and significance may have varied. S.R. Davis (1960) presented the first detailed account of government in each state with analyses of the similarities and differences between them. An attempt to bring these studies up to date has been made in a series of volumes mostly edited by Colin Hughes and listed under 'Administration'. They cover the two territories and all states, but are uneven in their coverage and lack the comparative material that renders the Davis volume invaluable.

Those who drafted the constitution found two problems insurmountable. One was how to reconcile its federal elements (largely based on the United States' model) with the traditions of responsible government inherited from Britain. This problem centred on the powers of the Senate and lay dormant until 1975. The other problem was how to divide revenue between the two layers of government. A temporary compromise known as the 'Braddon blot' was written into the constitution. But it was to last only ten years and finance was always the main bone of contention in intergovernmental relations. In general accounts of Australian federalism, including the works already mentioned, considerable space is inevitably given to financial relations and under 'Federal–state financial relations' are listed a few works primarily devoted to this aspect. Mathews and Jay (1972) have provided an excellent history and clear explanation of the growth of the financial power of the commonwealth. There have been some interesting comparative studies of financial arrangements in other federations, particularly because Australia has developed some unique extraconstitutional bodies largely directed to handling financial matters. The Loans Council, the Premiers' Conference and the Grants Commission have no real counterparts abroad. The studies by R.J. May (1971) and Campbell Sharman (1977) provide clear accounts of the development and functions of the last two.

The commonwealth has recently tended to use methods similar to those developed in other areas. Since 1972 there have been moves to establish machinery (such as the Schools Commission) to enable the federal government to play a greater role in health, education and urban development. Such developments are covered by the most recent works listed in the early parts of the bibliography and the last section lists a few studies of recent intergovernment relations in specific areas. They vary from single comprehensive accounts to the inevitable symposia and it is notable that the authors of these works are usually proponents of greater commonwealth intervention. Whatever politicians and state bureaucrats may say, most writers on inter-governmental relations have welcomed shifts in the balance of power in favour of the commonwealth. It is not surprising that in an area such as this, many authors have had clear and committed views, but we are fortunate that there are so many who, whether or not they were thus committed, have produced objective studies of the ever-changing relations between the governments of Australia.

The reader's attention is drawn to the importance of the National Library's efforts in providing listings and indexes to Australian publications in book form as well as in journals and newspapers. The relevant reference works, the *Australian national bibliography* (*ANB*) and the *Australian public affairs information service* (*APAIS*) are discussed in detail in chapter 8 of this volume. Anyone seriously interested in the literature on Australian government and politics would do well to study that section thoroughly. Here special attention is drawn to the National Library's complementary service entitled *Australian government publications* which has entries for the wide range of official publications currently generated in Australia. Entries are grouped under the names of the governments and organisations which published them.

Further important sources of information for researchers are the national and international indexes which list journal articles published both within and outside Australia. These are, for the international scene, *International political science abstracts* (Paris, International Political Science Association, 1951–), the *ABC pol. sci.* (Santa Barbara, California, American Bibliographical Center, 1969–) and the *International bibliography of the social sciences: political science* (London, Tavistock, 1952–). For Australian material, readers should be familiar with D.H. Borchardt's *Australian bibliography* (1976) with its numerous references to older sources of information. A wealth of unpublished material is contained in university theses which may be traced through the *Union list of higher degree theses*. These Australian source books are discussed in some detail in chapter 8 of this volume.

The bibliography for 'Parliaments, parties and governments' has been divided into the following sections:

Parliamentary history and membership	The Liberal and Country (National) parties
Political history	Minor political parties
The political system	Federation
Public administration	The constitution
The electoral system	Constitutional change
Political parties	The Federal–state financial relations

Politicians

The labour movement and the ALP

Attention is drawn to the variant spelling of the Australian Labor Party (ALP) and associated political organisations. Though it is now accepted that the Australian Labor Party is so spelled, this has not always been the case and some older works refer to it as the 'Australian Labour Party'. The Australian labour movement has usually been spelled with a 'u' and that practice is now accepted as the norm.

PARLIAMENTARY HISTORY AND MEMBERSHIP

BENNETT, S.C. AND BENNETT, G. *Biographical register of the Tasmanian parliament, 1851–1960.* ANUP, 1980. 173 p.

BOLTON, G.C. AND MOZLEY, A. *The Western Australian legislature, 1870–1930.* ANUP, 1961. 225 p, maps.

BROWNE, G. *Biographical register of the Victorian parliament, 1900–84.* Melbourne, Library Committee, Parliament of Vic, 1985. 229 p.

CAMPBELL, E.M. *Parliamentary privilege in Australia.* MUP, 1966. 218 p.
A scholarly, detailed acccount with thorough documentation.

CONNOLLY, C.N. *Biographical register of the New South Wales parliament, 1856–1901.* ANUP, 1983. 372 p.

COXON, H. *et al, Biographical register of the South Australian parliament, 1857–1957.* Adelaide, Wakefield Press, 1985. 245 p.

RADI, H. *et al, Biographical register of the New South Wales parliament, 1901–1970.* ANUP, 1979. 302 p.

RYDON, J. *A biographical register of the commonwealth parliament, 1901–1972.* ANUP, 1975. 229 p.

THOMSON, K. AND SERLE, G. *A biographical register of the Victorian parliament, 1851–1900.* ANUP, 1972. 238 p.

WATERSON, D.B. *A biographical register of the Queensland parliament, 1860–1929.* ANUP, 1972. 205 p.

WATERSON, D.B. AND ARNOLD, J. *Biographical register of the Queensland parliament, 1930–1980, with an outline atlas of Queensland electorates, 1859–1980.* ANUP, 1982. xxii, 144 p, maps.
The biographical registers listed above provide details of members of the commonwealth, colonial and state parliaments.

CAMPBELL, E.M. *Parliamentary privilege in Australia.* MUP, 1966. 218 p.
A scholarly detailed account with thorough documentation.

CONNOLLY, C.N. *Biographical register of the New South Wales parliament, 1856–1901.* ANUP, 1983. 372 p.

COXON, H. *et al, Biographical register of the South Australian parliament, 1857–1957.* Adelaide, Wakefield Press, 1985. 245 p.

GREEN, F.C. *Servant of the House.* Melbourne, Heinemann, 1969. 173 p.
As clerk of the House of Representatives 1935–55 the author provides an unusual and detailed perspective on federal political and parliamentary affairs over a long period.

HAWKER, G.N. *The parliament of New South Wales, 1856–1965.* Sydney, Government Printer, 1971. 377 p, illus.

Comprehensive history with full documentation and many statistical tables.

ODGERS, J.R. *Australian Senate practice* (5th edn). AGPS, 1976. 706 p.
Comprehensive coverage of all aspects of parliamentary practice, history and procedure affecting the Senate. Major work of reference. First published in 1953.

PARLIAMENTARY handbook of the Commonwealth of Australia (21st edn). AGPS, 1982. 541 p, illus.
Biographical details of past and current federal parliamentarians with coloured photographs. Data on cabinets, elections, constitutional referendums. First published in 1915 and periodically updated. Title varies.

PETTIFER, J.A. ed, *House of Representatives practice.* AGPS, 1981. 966 p, illus.
Covers practices and procedures in the House of Representatives; a matching volume to that of J.R. Odgers (1976). Contains material on political history with a selection of documents. Bibliography.

QUEENSLAND parliamentary handbook (3rd edn). Brisbane, Qld Parliamentary Library, 1983. 385 p, illus.
Biographical articles and photographs of former and current members of parliament, ministries, officers of parliament, election results. First published in 1977 and periodically updated.

TURNER, K. *House of review? The New South Wales Legislative Council, 1934–68.* SUP, 1969. 164 p, illus.
A well documented and detailed analysis of the role of the legislative council in NSW politics. Bibliography.

POLITICAL HISTORY

BARWICK, G. *Sir John did his duty.* Sydney, Serendip, 1983. 129 p.
The former chief justice of Australia explains the advice he gave to the governor-general, Sir Jonn Kerr, regarding the dismissal of the prime minister, E.G. Whitlam.

BERNAYS, C.A. *Queensland politics during sixty years, 1859–1919.* Brisbane, Government Printer, 1919. 564 p.

BERNAYS, C.A. *Queensland: our seventh political decade, 1920–1930.* A & R, 1930. 388 p.
The author was clerk of the Qld parliament for many years and these two volumes are based on his detailed knowledge of the period.

HUGHES, C.A. AND GRAHAM, B.D. *A handbook of Australian government and politics, 1890–1964.* ANUP, 1968. 635 p.

HUGHES, C.A. *A handbook of Australian government and politics, 1965–1974.* ANUP, 1977. 162 p.
The two volumes provide lists of governors, governor-generals, cabinets and portfolios, and detailed analyses of election results. Indispensable reference work covering all governments in Australia.

KERR, J.R. *Matters for judgement: an autobiography.* Melbourne, Macmillan, 1978. 468 p, illus.

Account of author's life and career with prominence given to the events leading to the dismissal of the Whitlam government. Discusses the nature and role of the office of governor-general.

LACK, C.L. comp, *Three decades of Queensland political history, 1929–1960.* Brisbane, Government Printer, 1962. 842 p, illus.

Comprehensive review of Qld government and politics. Many photographs of public personalities and events. Well documented. Complements Bernays' two volumes (1919, 1930) Bibliography.

ORMONDE, P. *The movement.* Melbourne, Nelson, 1972. xxiii, 198 p.

Evaluation of the role of B.A. Santamaria and the impact of the Catholic Social Studies Movement on the Catholic Church, Australian politics and trade unions.

SAWER, G. *Federation under strain: Australia 1972–1975.* MUP, 1977. 237 p.

Intended as a legal companion to studies of Australian federal government in the Whitlam period and constitutional problems

WHITINGTON, D. *The house will divide: a review of Australian federal politics* (rev edn). Melbourne, Lansdowne, 1969. 193 p, illus.

Popular history of events from beginning of federation until 1950s by a political journalist. First published in 1954.

WHITLAM, E.G. *The truth of the matter.* Ringwood, Vic, Penguin, 1979. 191 p, illus.

The former prime minister, dismissed in 1975 by the governor-general, gives his account of political events of the time. Work is conceived as reply to Kerr (1978).

THE POLITICAL SYSTEM

AITKIN, D. *Stability and change in Australian politics* (2nd edn). ANUP, 1982. 401 p.

Based on specially commissioned national surveys of political behaviour, this study reviews Australian attitudes to political parties and voting patterns in the 1960s and 1970s. Tables and footnotes. First published in 1976.

AITKIN, D. AND JINKS, B. *Australian political institutions* (2nd edn). Melbourne, Pitman, 1982. 283 p, illus.

General account of processes of government in Australia, designed as a textbook. First published in 1980.

CRISP, L.F. *Australian national government* (4th edn). Melbourne, Longman Cheshire, 1978. 523 p.

Thorough account of Australian federal government from its origins until 1977. Bibliography. First published with this title 1965. Previous editions as *The parliamentary government of the Commonwealth of Australia.*

ENCEL, S. *Cabinet government in Australia.* MUP, 1962. 367 p.

Pioneering study of the sociological and political aspects in the federal and state spheres.

FITZGERALD, B.C. *Background to politics: a sourcebook of major documents and statements which affect the course of Australian politics.* Melbourne, Cheshire, 1969. 130 p.

A compilation relating to the constitution, government finance, federal parliament, elections, political parties, international affairs. Bibliography.

HASLUCK, P.M.C. *The office of governor-general.* MUP, 1979. 47 p.

Text of the William Queale Memorial Lecture 1972. Discussion of the nature and function of the office by a former governor-general and longtime politician.

JAENSCH, D.H. AND TEICHMANN, M. *The Macmillan dictionary of Australian politics.* Melbourne, Macmillan, 1979. 264 p.

A reference work on Australian politics 1900–77.

JOSKE, P.E. *Australian federal government* (3rd edn). Sydney, Butterworths, 1976. 216 p.

Explains the workings of the national government by a former parliamentarian and jurist. Well documented but no bibliography. First published in 1967.

LUCY, R. ed, *The pieces of politics* (3rd edn). Melbourne, Macmillan, 1983. 532 p.

Essays on the Australian political system, parliamentary government and topical issues. No index. First published in 1975.

McCAW, K.M. *People versus power: a guide to the elements in the network of checks and balances which protect individual freedom from the exercise of arbitrary power.* Sydney, Holt, Rinehart and Winston, 1977. 183 p, illus.

The author analyses the exercise of power by institutions in Australian society.

ROSE, L.J. *The framework of government in New South Wales.* Sydney, Government Printer, 1972. 136 p, illus.

Contains information on operations of the executive council and cabinet. Outlines administrative procedures relating to the office of governor in NSW.

SOLOMON, D. *Australia's government and parliament* (5th edn). Melbourne, Nelson, 1981. 168 p.

Account of structure and operation of the three tiers of government at the federal level. First published in 1973.

WELLER, P. AND JAENSCH, D. eds, *Responsible government in Australia.* Melbourne, Drummond for APSA, 1980. 276 p.

Essays with a good bibliography.

WINTERTON, G. *Parliament, the executive and the governor-general: a constitutional analysis.* MUP, 1983. 376 p.

Examines what the commonwealth government can do without legislative authorisation.

PUBLIC ADMINISTRATION

ATKINS, R. *The government of the Australian Capital Territory.* UQP, 1978. 206 p, maps.

Detailed study of the ACT from its inception until 1976. Brief chronology and bibliography.

DAVIS, S.R. ed, *The government of the Australian states.* Melbourne, Longmans, 1960, 746 p, illus, maps.

First study of state government, still very useful, particularly for the comparative chapters.

GREEN, F.C. ed, *A century of responsible government, 1856–1956.* Hobart, Government Printer, 1956. 317 p, illus.

An analysis of Tasmanian government and politics by the former clerk of the House of Representatives.

HAZLEHURST, C. AND NETHERCOTE, J.R. eds, *Reforming Australian government: the Coombs Report and beyond.* Royal Institute of Public Administration (ACT) in association with ANUP, 1977. 201 p.

Essays on various aspects of the Coombs Royal Commission into the Commonwealth Public Service.

HEATLEY, A.J. *The government of the Northern Territory.* UQP, 1979. 211 p, maps.

A political and administrative history. Deals predominantly with period 1911 to 1978.

HOLMES, M.J. *The government of Victoria.* UQP, 1976. 205 p, illus, maps.

Covers all aspects of contemporary government in Vic. Many statistical tables.

HUGHES, C.A. *The government of Queensland.* UQP, 1980. 322 p, maps.

Comprehensive treatment of political and administrative system.

JAENSCH, D. *The government of South Australia.* UQP, 1977. 203 p, maps.

Comprehensive treatment of political and administrative history.

NETHERCOTE, J.R. ed, *Parliament and bureaucracy; parliamentary scrutiny of administration: prospects and problems in the 1980s.* Sydney, Hale & Iremonger in association with the Australian Institute of Public Administration, Commonwealth Parliamentary Association and Law Foundation of NSW, 1982. 363 p, illus.

Papers dealing with the growing importance of parliamentary committees, financial control of government departments and certain legal aspects of the parliamentary process.

PARKER, R.S. *The government of New South Wales.* UQP, 1978. 462 p, maps.

History of contemporary political and administrative system.

PERVAN, R. AND SHARMAN, C. eds, *Essays on Western Australian politics.* UWAP for the Education Committee of the 150th Anniversary Celebrations, 1979. 237 p, illus.

Essays written for the sesquicentenary of WA, providing information on some of the topics covered by the UQP series on the government of the other states.

RORKE, J. ed, *Politics at state level: Australia.* Sydney Dept of Adult Education, University of Sydney, 1970. [8], 113, [3] p, maps.

One of the few attempts to gather comparative material on politics in the various states. Most of the contributions were previously published as *Current affairs bulletins.*

SPANN, R.N. ed, *Government administration in Australia.* Sydney, Allen & Unwin, 1979. 524 p.

Major study of public service structure and management.

TOWNSLEY, W.A. *The government of Tasmania.* UQP, 1976. 169 p, maps.

Comprehensive treatment of political and administrative history.

THE ELECTORAL SYSTEM

HUGHES, C.A. AND GRAHAM, B.D. *Voting for the Australian House of Representatives, 1901–1964.* ANUP, 1974. 544 p.

HUGHES, C.A. AND GRAHAM, B.D. *Voting for the New South Wales Legislative Assembly, 1890–1964.* Canberra, Dept of Political Science, Research School of Social Sciences, Australian National University, 1975. 518 p.

HUGHES, C.A. AND GRAHAM, B.D. *Voting for the Queensland Legislative Assembly, 1890–1964.* Canberra, Dept of Political Science, Research School of Social Sciences, Australian National University, 1974. 337 p.

HUGHES, C.A. AND GRAHAM, B.D. *Voting for the South Australian, Western Australian and Tasmanian lower houses, 1890–1964.* Canberra, Dept of Political Science, Research School of Social Sciences, Australian National University, 1976. 639 p.

HUGHES, C.A. AND GRAHAM, B.D. *Voting for the Victorian Legislative Assembly, 1890–1964.* Canberra, Dept of Political Science, Research School of Social Sciences, Australian National University, 1975. 468 p.

These five books consist almost wholly of statistics and tables, showing candidates, party affiliations and polling results. They constitute a major reference series and supplement the authors' *Handbook of Australian government and politics 1890–1964* (1968).

MACKERRAS, M. *Australian general elections.* A & R, 1972. 284 p, maps.

Study of voting patterns in the 1960s and 1970.

PENNIMAN, H.R. ed, *Australia at the polls: the national elections of 1975.* ANUP, 1977. 373 p.

PENNIMAN, H.R. ed, *The Australian national elections of 1977.* Washington, American Enterprise Institute for Public Policy Research, 1979. 367 p.

PENNIMAN, H.R. ed, *Australia at the polls: the national elections of 1980.* Sydney, Allen & Unwin, 1983. 280 p.

Three books presenting a thorough analysis of the elections of the Australian electorate and the campaigns of the major parties.

WRIGHT, J.F.H. *Mirror of the nation's mind: Australia's electoral experiments.* Sydney, Hale & Iremonger, 1980. 160 p, illus.

Scholarly but readable discussion of various Australian electoral systems and analysis of their effects. Bibliography.

POLITICAL PARTIES

ALEXANDER, F. *From Curtin to Menzies and after: continuity or confrontation?* Melbourne, Nelson, 1973. 247 p, illus.

Party politics from Curtin's election as ALP leader in 1935 to the Whitlam government's first parliament, with policy analysis. Argues for continuity in Australian politics despite the appearance of conflict.

CONNELL, R.W. AND IRVING, T.H. *Class structure in Australian history: documents, narrative and argument.* Melbourne, Longman Cheshire, 1980. 378 p, illus.

A discussion of the origins of capitalism and the rise of the working class; analysis of class conflict and of party politics.

HAZELHURST, C. ed, *Australian conservatism: essays in twentieth century political history.* ANUP, 1979. 337 p.

Diverse essay on aspects of conservative party politics and the 'image' of the Liberal party.

JAENSCH, D. *The Australian party system 1945–1982.* Sydney, Allen & Unwin, 1983. 235 p.

A history of parties and the party system with analysis of the effects on politics of the electoral system, internal party organisation, the federal system of party organisation and political ideology.

JUPP, J. *Australian party politics.* MUP, 1964. 235 p.

JUPP, J. *Party politics, Australia 1966–1981.* Sydney, Allen & Unwin, 1982. 232 p.

The two books by Jupp cover developments and activities of the major political parties, 1901–81.

LOVEDAY, P. AND MARTIN, A.W. *Parliament, factions and parties: the first thirty years of responsible government in New South Wales, 1856–1889.* MUP, 1966. 207 p.

Politics in colonial NSW, where the emergence of strong cabinet government and collective responsibility prefigured the growth of a party system.

LOVEDAY, P. *et al* eds, *The emergence of the Australian party system.* Sydney, Hale & Iremonger, 1977. 536 p, illus.

Essays on the early development of political parties.

MANNE, R. ed, *The new conservatism in Australia.* OUP, 1982. 290 p, illus.

Essays exploring the intellectual and cultural traditions of conservatism, focusing on episodes like the Petrov affair and the Whitlam dismissal which highlight the conflict between conservatives and their opponents.

OVERACKER, L. *Australian parties in a changing society: 1945–67.* Melbourne, Cheshire, 1968. 337 p.

OVERACKER, L. *The Australian party system*. New Haven, Yale University Press, 1952. 373 p, illus, map.

Basic studies by a scholarly, outside observer covering in all six decades.

PATIENCE, A. AND HEAD, B. eds, *From Whitlam to Fraser: reform and reaction in Australian politics*. OUP, 1979. 320 p.

Essays analysing federal political history from 1972 to 1978, linked by the theme that the 'convergence' trends of party politics were temporarily reversed by policy difference between the Whitlam and Fraser administration.

RICKARD, J.D. *Class and politics: New South Wales, Victoria and the early commonwealth, 1890–1910*. ANUP, 1975. 371 p, illus.

The period was a critical time for social, economic and political change in Australia. The emergence of the Labor party and the party system are examined in this context.

SAWER, M. ed, *Australia and the new right*. Sydney, Allen & Unwin 1982. 181 p.

Essays exploring radical conservatism in Australian society since 1975, showing that the coalition of 'free-market devotees, libertarian political thinkers, moral conservatives, religious fundamentalists and biological determinists' has no intellectual connection with traditional conservatism.

STARR, G. et al, *Political parties in Australia*. Melbourne, Heinemann Educational, 1978. 399 p.

Each author takes a sympathetic view of the history, structure and ideological basis of one of the three major political parties; includes a survey of minor parties.

POLITICIANS

AITKIN, D. *The colonel: a political biography of Sir Michael Bruxner*. ANUP, 1969. 293 p, illus, map.

Study of the career of a key Country party figure, prominent in NSW politics over a 40-year period.

BROWNE, W. *A woman of distinction: the Honourable Dame Annabelle Rankin, D.B.E.* Brisbane, Boolarong, 1981. 136 p, illus.

A biography of the public life of the first woman to be elected to the Senate from Qld, to hold a federal ministry and to be apointed as a high commissioner.

BURGER, A.S. *Neville Bonner, a biography*. Melbourne, Macmillan, 1979, 169 p, illus.

An account of the personal life and political career of Australia's first Aboriginal parliamentarian.

CRISP, L.F. *Ben Chifley: a political biography*. Melbourne, Longmans, 1961. 428 p., illus.

The career of the locomotive driver who became federal treasurer and Labor's last prime minister before the Menzies era. The author was a close associate of Chifley.

D'ALPUGET, B. *Robert J. Hawke: a biography* (rev edn). Ringwood, Vic, Penguin, 1984. 426 p, illus.

A sympathetic but critical account of the prime minister's early life, and his rise through the ACTU and the Labor party to the presidency of both organisations. First published in 1982.

EDWARDS, C. *Bruce of Melbourne: man of two worlds*. London, Heinemann, 1965. 475 p, illus.

This biography of Stanley Melbourne Bruce, Nationalist prime minister from 1922 to 1929, gives insight into the politics of the times and politicians such as Hughes, Page, Latham and Menzies.

EVATT, H.V. *Australian labour leader: the story of W.A. Holman and the labour movement*. A & R, 1940. 589 p, illus.

Political biography by one great Australian Labor Party leader of another, William Holman, providing insights into Labor activities and personalities to the 1930s. An abridged edition was

issued in 1954 and in 1979 published in facsimile as *William Holman: Australian labour leader*.

FITZHARDINGE, L.F. *William Morris Hughes, a political biography*. A & R, 1964–79. 2 vols, illus.

Vol 1 is entitled 'That fiery particle 1862–14'; vol 2 'The little digger 1914–52'. A comprehensive biography offering insights also on other Labor figures, particularly prime ministers Watson and Fisher.

FORD, P.P. *Cardinal Moran and the A.L.P.: a study in the encounter between Moran and socialism, 1890–1907, its effects upon the Australian Labor Party, the foundation of Catholic social thought and action in Australia*. MUP, 1966. 319 p, illus.

An account of the prominence and influence of this renowned Catholic churchman in the early years of the Australian Labor Party.

FREUDENBERG, G. *A certain grandeur: Gough Whitlam in politics*. Melbourne, Macmillan, 1977. 429 p.

An account of Whitlam's rise to the prime ministership, the political events leading to the Labor victory in 1972, and the achievements and shortcomings of the Labor government up to its dismissal.

HEWAT, T.E.P. AND WILSON, D. *Don Chipp*. Melbourne, Widescope, 1978. 154 p, illus.

Portrait of the former Liberal minister who founded the Australian Democrats in 1977, together with the rise of support for the Democrats and their first policy statement.

HUGHES, C.A. *Mr. Prime Minister: Australian prime ministers, 1901–1972*. OUP, 1975. 208 p, illus.

Biographies of all the prime ministers to McMahon, with a brief discussion of the origin and nature of the office. In part based on an ABC series.

JOSKE, P.E. *Sir Robert Menzies, 1894–1978: a new, informal memoir*. A & R, 1978. 354 p, illus.

The highlights of Menzies' academic, legal and political career written by a friend.

KIERNAN, C. *Calwell: a personal and political biography*. Melbourne, Nelson, 1978. 310 p, illus.

The private and public life of Labor's Arthur Calwell who spent 32 years in the federal parliament, including seven as leader of the opposition. A tribute to the man, though not commissioned as such.

LA NAUZE, J.A. *Alfred Deakin: a biography*. A & R, 1979. 714 p, illus.

Comprehensive biography of the foremost statesman and orator of his time, a major figure in Victorian politics, a 'founding father' of Federation and prime minister. Bibliography. First published in 2 vols in 1965.

MARTIN, A.W. *Henry Parkes; a biography*. MUP, 1980. 482 p, illus.

An analysis of the life and career of the key political figure in NSW colonial politics. Bibliography.

MURPHY, D.J. *Hayden: a political biography*. A & R, 1980. 182 p, illus.

Detailed account of the political fortunes of the Qld ex-policeman who became treasurer in the Whitlam government and later leader of the ALP.

MURPHY, D.J. *T.J. Ryan: a political biography*. UQP, 1975. 596 p, illus.

Biography of Qld Labor party leader and account of state politics in the first two decades of this century.

PAGE, E.C.G. *Truant surgeon: the inside story of forty years of Australian political life*. Ed by A. Mozley. A & R, 1963. 431 p, illus.

An autobiography by a founding member of the Country party and a federal parliamentarian for over 40 years. A political history of the time.

REYNOLDS, J. *Edmund Barton.* A & R, 1949. 224 p, illus.

Politics in NSW in the 1880s and 1890s, the federation movement, and the legal and political career of Australia's first prime minister. Facsimile edition, A & R, 1979.

ROBERTSON, J. *J.H. Scullin: a political biography.* UWAP, 1974. 495 p, illus.

The career of the Labor prime minister of the depression years, with insights into his socialist principles, the events of the depression and the secession of the Lang Laborites.

ROSS, L. *John Curtin: a biography.* Melbourne, Sun Books, 1983. 432 p, illus.

Biography covering Curtin's early days as labour journalist, anti-conscription campaigner, then leader of the opposition and wartime prime minister. Labor party history narrated and discussed in parallel. First published in 1977.

ROSS, L. *William Lane and the Australian labor movement.* Sydney, The Author, 1935. 375 p.

The English immigrant and labour journalist who propagated socialist ideals in Australia, then led the ill-fated 'New Australia' expedition to Paraguay. Reprinted, Hale & Iremonger, 1980.

SCHNEIDER, R. *The colt from Kooyong: Andrew Peacock, a political biography.* A & R, 1981. 144 p, illus.

A journalist's account of Peacock's rise, written before his accession to leadership of the Liberal party. Some discussion of the subject's political philosophy and power base in the Senate.

SCHNEIDER, R. *War without blood: Malcolm Fraser in power.* A & R, 1980. 172 p.

J.M. Fraser's rise as leader of the opposition and prime minister. Derived from interviews of those connected with the events, into the first four years of the Fraser administration.

TENNANT, K. *Evatt: politics and justice* (rev edn). A & R, 1981. 418 p, illus.

H.V. Evatt as Australia's youngest high court judge, Labor minister, president of the UN General Assembly, leader of the opposition, and his campaign for justice and legal rights. First published in 1970.

THE LABOUR MOVEMENT AND THE ALP

CALWELL, A.A. *Labor's role in modern society* (2nd edn). Melbourne, Cheshire, 1965. 192 p.

Insights into Labor history and philosophy, relations with the trade unions, planning and socialised industry, by the leader of the opposition in the later Menzies era. First published in 1963.

CHILDE, V.G. *How Labour governs: a study of worker's representation in Australia* London, Labour Publishing Co, 1923. 216 p, map.

The famous archaeologist, as participant observer, provides an analysis of the labour movement in the early twentieth century and the relationship between the parliamentary and union wings. Second edition published in 1964.

CRISP, L.F. *The Australian federal labour party, 1901–1951* (2nd edn). Sydney, Hale & Iremonger, 1978. 341 p.

Examines Labor activity in the federal sphere, and outlines the formal structure and functions of the party, its objectives, policies and problems. Appendices contain party documents and rules. First published in 1955.

EBBELS, R.N. *The Australian labor movement, 1850–1907: extracts from contemporary documents* (2nd edn). Ed by L.G. Churchward. Melbourne, Cheshire-Lansdowne in association with the Noel Ebbels Memorial Committee, 1965. 255 p.

Covers the earliest period of Labor activity, with particular emphasis on social and industrial problems. First published in 1960.

FARRELL, F. *International socialism and Australian labour: the left in Australia, 1919–1939.* Sydney, Hale & Iremonger, 1981. 284 p, illus.

A study of the beliefs, theories and practices of left-wing politics in Australia. The author examines the challenges of the Labor party, and raises some of the relevant policy issues.

FITZPATRICK, B.C. *A short history of the Australian labour movement.* Melbourne, Rawson's Bookshop, 1940. 182 p.

A survey of the labour movement with emphasis on the tension between collectivist principles and individual rights. Second enlarged edition 1944; reprinted by Macmillan in 1968.

GOLLAN, R. *Radical and working class politics: a study of eastern Australia, 1850–1910.* MUP, 1974. 238 p.

The roots of nationalist and radical politics in the eastern colonies of Australia, the role of the trade unions in politics and the rise of the ALP. First published in 1960.

HUGHES, W.M. *The case for Labor.* Sydney, the Worker Trustees, 1910. 144 p.

Twenty articles from 200 contributed to the Sydney *Daily Telegraph* by the future wartime prime minister on unemployment, the Labor pledge and socialism. Facsimile edition, SUP, 1970.

LABOR essays. Melbourne, Drummond for the ALP, Victorian Branch, 1980–

Essays exploring the nature and application of Labor's 'socialisation objective' in the 1980s. Each annual volume concentrates on a particular theme.

LLOYD, C.J. and REID, G.S. *Out of the wilderness: return of Labor.* Melbourne, Cassell, 1974. 447 p.

Account of the Whitlam ministry from 1972 to 1974, including a discussion of the transfer of power, the extraordinary 'two-man' government and of the 'technocratic' style of rule.

McKINLAY, B. *The ALP: a short history of the Australian Labor Party.* Melbourne, Drummond/Heinemann, 1981. 168 p.

Narrative of Labor's fortunes from 1890s to Hayden's election as leader of the opposition in 1978. Emphasises the periods of Labor government.

McKINLAY, B. *A documentary history of the Australian labor movement, 1850–1975.* Melbourne, Drummond, 1979. 778 p, illus.

Collection organised in three sections: a chronology of the ALP; the trade unions; Australian attitudes to communism, socialism and labourism. An indispensable source book.

METIN, A. *Socialism without doctrine.* Trans by R. Ward. Sydney, Alternative Publishing Co-operative, 1977. (22), 200 p.

A French scholar, visiting in 1901, analyses federated Australia, the economics of labour, management and state intervention, and argues that Australian workers were anti-intellectual pragmatists. First published as *Le socialisme sans doctrines* in 1901.

MURPHY, D.J. ed, *Labor in politics: the state Labor parties in Australia, 1880–1920.* UQP, 1975. 480 p, illus.

Traces the emergence and development of Labor politics in the six states and provides an analysis of the impact of trade unions and other social forces on Labor.

MURPHY, D.J. et al, *Labor in power: the Labor party and governments in Queensland, 1915–1957.* UQP, 1980. 583 p, illus.

Essays on Qld Labor party history, party policies and outstanding political issues of the day. Appendices list names of party officials and Labor candidates.

NAIRN, N.B. *Civilising capitalism: the labor movement in New South Wales, 1870–1900.* ANUP, 1973. 260 p, illus.

Traces the emergence of the NSW parliamentary Labor party, and argues that 'civilizing capitalism' was the necessary response to the triumph of capitalism in the 1890s.

OAKES, L. *Labor's 1979 conference, Adelaide.* Canberra, Objective Publications, 1979. 247 p, illus.

The text of 23 policy platforms and conference resolutions, with the author's analysis of major debates and decisions. Outlines the 'triumph of pragmatism' over radical ideology.

OAKES, L. and SOLOMON, D. *The making of an Australian prime minister.* Melbourne, Cheshire, 1973. 318 p, illus.

Labor's road back from 23 years of opposition to office in 1972 and the role of Whitlam in preparing the party for government.

RAWSON, D.W. *Labor in vain? A survey of the Australian Labor Party.* Melbourne, Longmans, 1966. 128 p, illus.

A survey of the ALP which looks at machine politics, the role of the trade unions, the influence of communism and the place of socialism in Labor doctrine.

REID, A.D. *The Whitlam venture.* Melbourne, Hill of Content, 1976. 465 p, illus.

Account of the troubled second Whitlam ministry, 1974–75, including comprehensive treatment of the 'loans affair' and the dismissal of the government.

SEXTON, M. *Illusions of power: the fate of a reform government.* Sydney, Allen & Unwin, 1979. 305 p, illus.

A narrative of the Whitlam government's term of office with analysis of the exercise of political power, arguing that the internal weaknesses of the government as much as the external pressures caused its collapse.

TURNER, I.A.H. *Industrial labour and politics: the dynamics of the labour movement in eastern Australia, 1900–1921.* Sydney, Hale & Iremonger, 1979. 304 p.

A history to 1921, emphasising relationships with the Labor party and discussing working-class politics and socialist doctrine. Facsimile of first (1965) edition.

WELLER, P.M. ed, *Caucus minutes 1901–1949: minutes of the meetings of the federal parliamentary Labour party.* MUP, 1975. 3 vols. illus.

Includes extensive general introduction, short comments to each parliamentary session, detailed annotations and other caucus documents.

WELLER, P.M. AND LLOYD, B. eds, *Federal executive minutes 1915–1955: minutes of the meetings of the federal executive of the Australian Labor Party.* MUP, 1978. 662 p.

The editors have traced the minutes of all but four of the meetings held during the period and published them in full with an introductory essay.

WHITLAM, E.G. *The Whitlam government, 1972–1975.* Ringwood, Vic, Viking, 1985. 786 p, illus.

This account was launched by Prime Minister Hawke on 11 November 1985: the 10th anniversary of the sacking of the Whitlam government.

THE LIBERAL AND COUNTRY (NATIONAL) PARTIES

AIMER, P. *Politics, power and persuasion: the Liberals in Victoria.* Sydney, James Bennett for the Liberal Party of Australia (Vic Division), 1974. 248 p, illus.

The development of the Liberal party in Vic, its structure, organisation and the people involved, is given a sympathetic but critical examination.

AITCHISON, R. ed, *Looking at the Liberals.* Melbourne, Cheshire, 1984. 258 p.

A collection of articles on the fortunes, fair and otherwise, of the Liberal party up to the electoral defeat in 1972. Contributors include Malcolm Fraser and Phillip Lynch.

AITKIN, D.A. *The Country party in New South Wales: a study of organisation and survival.* ANUP, 1972. 343 p, maps.

The origins, policies and ideologies of the Country party in one state and the challenges confronting it in the 1970s. Includes tables of Country party members.

CAMPBELL, E. *The rallying point: my story of the New Guard.* MUP, 1965. 184 p, illus, maps.

History of the New Guard by one of its founders.

EGGLESTON, F.W. *Reflections of an Australian liberal.* Melbourne, Cheshire for the ANU, 1953. 301 p.

A broad overview of Australian politics and political parties before 1952 as seen through the eyes of a former politician and diplomat.

ELLIS, U.R. *The Country party: a political and social history of the party in New South Wales.* Melbourne, Cheshire, 1958. 257 p.

The platforms, policies, successes and failures of the Country party in NSW from its inception to 1958 are examined in detail.

ELLIS, U.R. *A history of the Australian Country Party.* MUP, 1963. 359 p, illus.

The state and federal Country parties were established in the early 1900s. The author traces their progress and examines the leaders of the parties from the beginnings to 1963.

GRAHAM, B.D. *The formation of the Australian Country parties.* ANUP, 1966. 320 p, illus, map.

In this examination of the origins and development of the Country parties, emphasis is placed on their political strategies and the effects of the existing party system.

JAENSCH, D. AND BULLOCK, J. *Liberals in limbo: non-Labor politics in South Australia, 1970–1978.* Melbourne, Drummond, 1978. 222 p, illus.

Analysis of the fragmentation and factional conflict that took place within the South Australian Liberal Party after the electoral victory of Premier Dunstan.

REID, A.D. *The Gorton experiment.* Sydney, Shakespeare Head Press, 1971. 455 p, illus.

REID, A.D. *The power struggle.* Sydney, Shakespeare Head Press, 1969. 200 p, illus.

Two books on the sudden rise of Senator John Grey Gorton to the controversial prime ministership after the disappearance of Harold Holt, with insights into relationships between the partners of the Liberal–Country party coalition.

ROWSE, T. *Australian liberalism and national character.* Melbourne, Kibble Books, 1978. 293 p.

Revisionary history of liberal doctrine in Australia, stressing its innate 'conservatism' and focusing on a critique of W.K. Hancock's influential *Australia* (1930; repr, Brisbane, Jacaranda, 1964). Discusses the ideological basis of the Labor party's reformism.

SIMMS, M. *A liberal nation: the Liberal party and Australian politics.* Sydney, Hale & Iremonger, 1982. 224 p, illus.

An analysis of the Liberal party's performance since its inception with a discussion of conservative ideology as professed and practised by the party.

STARR, G. *The Liberal Party of Australia: a documentary history.* Melbourne, Drummond/Heinemann, 1980. 371 p, illus.

Party documents and newspaper articles illustrating the roots of liberalism, the formation of the Liberal party, the Menzies and succeeding governments, and the years of opposition.

TIVER, P.G. *The Liberal party: principles and performance.* Brisbane, Jacaranda, 1978. 367 p.

Beyond outlining the history of liberalism, the author seeks to show that in its policy decisions the Liberal party has not lost sight of true liberal philosophies.

WELLS, D. *Power without theory: a critical analysis of the Liberal party philosophies.* Melbourne, Outback Press, 1977. 191 p, illus.

A critical but witty analysis of the conflicting philosophies and ideologies of the Liberal party and how they are reflected in the attitudes of Liberal politicians.

WEST, K. *Power in the Liberal party: a study in Australian politics.* Melbourne, Cheshire, 1965. 289 p, illus.

A history of power relations within the Liberal party. Analysis includes parliamentary and extraparliamentary wings, state and federal sectors, and the question of leadership.

WHITE, D.M. *The philosophy of the Australian Liberal Party.* Melbourne, Hutchinson, 1978. 179 p.

The philosophy and ideology of the Liberal party examined through an analysis of the party's federal platforms from 1946 to 1974.

MINOR POLITICAL PARTIES

DAVIDSON, A. *The Communist Party of Australia: a short history.* Stanford, California, Hoover Institution Press, 1969. 214 p. (Hoover Institution studies, 26).

The Communist Party of Australia has operated on the periphery of Australian politics, but at times has attracted much attention. This scholarly account represents one of the few substantial works on the history of the party.

GOLLAN, R. *Revolutionaries and reformists: communism and the Australian labour movement, 1920–1955.* ANUP, 1975. 330 p, illus.

The ideology and activity of the CPA and its influence on the labour movement with considerable attention to cold war politics and the Labor split.

HALLS, R.S. ed, *A liberal awakening: the LM story.* Adelaide, Investigator, 1973. 160 p, illus.

The liberal movement surfaced in SA as a breakaway Liberal group in 1972 and disappeared as quickly a few years later. This collection of articles sketches some of the highlights.

MURRAY, R. *The split: Australian Labor in the fifties.* Sydney, Hale & Iremonger, 1984. 392 p.

One of the greatest crises in Labor party history, the split away from Labor by the anti-communist and Catholic-based industrial groups from the Democratic Labor Party, is explained and analysed. First published in 1970.

REYNOLDS, P.L. *The Democratic Labor Party.* Brisbane, Jacaranda, 1974. 100 p.

For twenty years, the Democratic Labor Party played a more significant role in Australian politics than its numbers in parliament would suggest. An account of the party that kept Labor out of office through the 1950s and 1960s.

TOWARDS a socialist Australia: how the labor movement can fight back: documents of the Socialist Workers Party, Sydney, Pathfinder, 1977. 170 p, illus.

A socialist analysis of Australian political society concentrating on the Fraser 'offensive', Australian capitalism, the ALP and trade unionism. Includes the Socialist Workers Party program.

FEDERATION

COWEN, Z. *Federal jurisdiction in Australia.* OUP, 1959. 212 p.

Still useful for an understanding of the legal aspects of Australian federalism and the relations between state and federal courts.

DAVIS, S.R. *The federal principle: a journey through time in quest of a meaning.* Berkeley, University of California Press, 1978. 237 p.

Though mainly concerned with the development of the theory of federalism this book also discusses recent developments in Australia and other federal countries.

HOLMES, M.J. AND SHARMAN, C. *The Australian federal system.* Sydney, Allen & Unwin, 1977. 219 p, illus, maps.

Looks at the working of Australian federalism. Emphasis is placed on differences among the states.

HOWARD, C. *Australia's constitution.* Ringwood, Vic, Penguin, 1978. 216 p.

A useful and very readable discussion.

LIVINGSTON, W.S. *Federalism and constitutional change.* Oxford, Clarendon Press, 1956. 380 p.

An important book when first published containing an analysis of the earlier attempts to amend the commonwealth constitution and comparisons with other federations.

LUMB, R.D. *The constitutions of the Australian states* (4th edn). UQP, 1977. 136 p.

First issued in 1963, this is a very useful reference on the constitutions of the states and the differences between them.

MAYER, H. AND NELSON, H. *Australian politics: a fifth reader.* Melbourne, Longman Cheshire, 1980. 593 p, illus.

Since 1966 five 'readers' have been published. Each volume includes a wide variety of articles on the constitution, federalism and current political issues.

SAWER, G. *The Australian constitution.* AGPS, 1975. 73 p, illus.

A brief illustrated summary of the origins and development of the constitution.

SAWER, G. *Australian government today.* MUP, 1948. x, 48 p.

A summary of the structures of Australian government for background reading and reference. Twelfth edition published in 1977.

SAWER, G. *Modern federalism.* London, Watts, 1969. 204 p. (New thinker's library, 27).

A short account of the development of federalism in Australia and other countries.

WHEARE, K.C. *Federal government.* London, OUP, 1946. 278 p.

A classic by an Australian expatriate who draws much of his discussion on federalism from Australia. Fourth edition published in 1963.

THE CONSTITUTION

AUSTRALIAN INSTITUTE OF POLITICAL SCIENCE. *Federalism in Australia. . . papers read at the fifteenth Summer School of the Australian Institute of Political Science.* Melbourne, Cheshire, 1949. 189 p.

A collection of essays now of historical interest. Some of the contributions have been influential in later thought and the development of research in Australian politics.

CRISP, L.F. *The later Australian federation movement, 1883–1901: outline and bibliography.* Canberra, Research School of Social Sciences, Australian National University, 1979. 130 p.

Includes a chronology, a list of delegates to the various conventions and a useful bibliography.

DEAKIN, A. *The federal story: the inner history of the federal cause.* MUP, 1963. 182 p, illus.

The story, composed between 1880 and 1900, was first published in 1944, edited by H. Brookes. This edition has been re-edited by John La Nauze. An important background document.

ELSE-MITCHELL, R. ed, *Essays on the Australian constitution* (2nd edn). Sydney, Law Book Co, 1961. 380 p.

Essays, first published in 1952, written for the jubilee of the Australian commonwealth to record the progress of Australian federalism in the first fifty years.

GREENWOOD, G. *The future of Australian federalism* (2nd edn). UQP, 1946. 361 p.

This book argues for greater commonwealth powers on the basis of the history of Australian federalism to 1946. Second edition published in 1976.

HODGINS, B.W. *et al, Federalism in Canada and Australia: the early years.* ANUP, 1978. 318 p, illus, maps.

Essays by Canadian and Australian writers covering the period before 1914. Of uneven quality but contains two useful chapters by Don Wright on commonwealth–state relations.

LA NAUZE, J.A. *The making of the Australian constitution.* MUP, 1972. 369 p, illus.

Essential reading.

MARTIN, A.W. ed, *Essays in Australian federation.* MUP, 1969. 206 p, map.

A collection of essays in the series 'Studies in Australian federation' on specific aspects of the movement for federation and arguments about the constitution.

MELBOURNE, A.C.V. *Early constitutional development in Australia: New South Wales, 1788–1856. Queensland, 1859–1922* (2nd edn). UQP, 1963. 522 p.

A classic work, well edited, introduced and extended by R.B. Joyce. Deals only with NSW and Qld, but relevant to the constitutional development of the commonwealth. First published in 1934 without reference to Qld.

MENZIES, R.G. *Central power in the Australian commonwealth: an examination of the growth of commonwealth power in the Australian federation.* London, Cassell, 1967. 198 p.

An interesting survey of Menzies' attitude to increasing commonwealth powers.

MOORE, W. 'The constitution and its working', in *Cambridge history of the British Empire.* CUP, 1933, 7, 1, 454–90.

Discussion of constitutional developments to the 1930s.

NORRIS, R. *The emergent commonwealth: Australian federation, expectations and fulfilment 1889–1910.* MUP, 1975. 273 p, illus.

An account of the establishment of the commonwealth and its early policies in both external and internal affairs.

PORTUS, G.V. ed, *Studies in the Australian constitution.* A & R in conjunction with Australian Institute of Political Science, 1933. 233 p, illus.

Essays now of historical value.

SAWER, G. *Australian federal politics and law, 1901–1929, [and] 1929–1949.* MUP, 1956-63. 2 vols.

A chronological study useful as a reference book.

SAWER, G. ed, *Federalism: an Australian jubilee study.* Melbourne, Cheshire, 1952. 284 p.

This book resulted from one of the early seminars conducted by the Australian National University. An important collection when first published and still worth reading.

WRIGHT, D.I. *Shadow of dispute: aspects of commonwealth–state relations, 1901–1910.* ANUP, 1970. 120 p.

Study of the first ten years of Australian federalism. Highlights the rivalry between Vic and NSW, but also describes the emergence of intergovernmental relations.

ZINES, L. *The high court and the constitution.* Sydney, Butterworths, 1981. 358 p.

An up-to-date account of the high court's interpretation of the commonwealth constitution. A useful reference book.

ZINES, L. ed, *Commentaries on the Australian constitution: a tribute to Geoffrey Sawer.* Sydney, Butterworths, 1977. 275 p.

Articles mainly on aspects of the commonwealth constitution. Written by lawyers for lawyers but some are within the comprehension of the general reader, particularly the articles on parliament and the executive, and the constitutional convention.

CONSTITUTIONAL CHANGE

ALDRED, J. AND WILKES, J. *A fractured federation? Australia in the 1980s.* Sydney, Allen & Unwin in association with the Australian Institute of Political Affairs, 1983. 106 p.

Papers on various aspects of federalism and its reform.

ENCEL, S. *et al, Change the rules! Towards a democratic constitution.* Ringwood, Vic, Penguin, 1977. 269 p.

Suggestions for constitutional change inspired by the events of 1975; while all the writers are committed to change, the objectivity and practicality of their proposals vary.

EVANS, G.J. ed, *Labor and the constitution, 1972–1975: essays and commentaries on the constitutional controversies of the Whitlam years.* Ringwood, Vic, Heinemann, 1977. 383 p.

Collection of essays covering most of the activities of the Whitlam government, historical background and constitutional significance.

HOWARD, C. *The constitution, power and politics.* Sydney, Fontana/Collins, 1980. 241 p.

The opinions of an academic lawyer on how the constitution works and how it should be reformed.

McMILLAN, J. *et al, Australia's constitution: a time for change?* Sydney, Law Foundation of NSW and Allen & Unwin, 1983. 422 p, illus.

Presents a bipartisan discussion on the desirability and possibility of updating the Australian constitution.

PATIENCE, A. AND SCOTT, J. eds, *Australian federalism: future tense.* OUP, 1983. 217 p.

Essays contributed by both politicians and academics. Constitutes an assortment with some useful pieces, but lacks a coherent theme.

SAWER, G. *Federation under strain: Australia 1972–1975.* MUP, 1977. 237 p.

A study of the Whitlam government and its dismissal, useful for an understanding of constitutional conventions and the role of the executive council.

WHITLAM, E.G. *On Australia's constitution.* Melbourne, Widescope, 1977. 374 p.

A collection of speeches and lectures delivered between 1957 and 1976 expressing the author's attitude to the limits of commonwealth powers and to constitutional reform.

FEDERAL–STATE FINANCIAL RELATIONS

BIRCH, A.H. *Federalism, finance and social legislation in Canada, Australia and the United States.* Oxford, Clarendon Press, 1955. 314 p.

An interesting study now of historical interest.

MATHEWS, R.L. ed, *Intergovernmental relations in Australia.* A & R, 1974. 310 p.

Papers dealing with financial questions, administration, decentralisation and responsible government under federalism.

MATHEWS, R.L. AND JAY, W.R.C. *Federal finance: intergovern-*

mental financial relations in Australia since federation. Melbourne, Nelson, 1972. 370 p.

Standard work on financial relations between the commonwealth and states. It explains the growth of the financial domination of the commonwealth.

MAY, R.J. *Financing the small states in Australian federalism.* OUP, 1971. 235 p.

A study of the Australian Grants Commission and the problems of financial inequality among the states.

OTHER ASPECTS OF INTERGOVERNMENTAL RELATIONS

BIRCH, I.K.F. *et al, Intergovernmental relations and Australian education.* Canberra, Centre for Research on Federal Financial Relations, Australian National University, 1979. 107 p.

Aspects of state and commonwealth activity in education written very much from a standpoint of economists.

HARMAN, G.S. AND SMART, D. eds, *Federal intervention in Australian education.* Melbourne, Georgian House, 1982. 197 p, illus.

A study of the involvement of the commonwealth in education.

LEACH, R.H. *Interstate relations in Australia.* Lexington, University of Kentucky Press, 1965. 183 p.

A rather neglected study by a Canadian writer.

LIBOIRON, A.A. comp, *Federalism and intergovernmental relations in Australia, Canada, the United States and other countries; a bibliography.* Kingston, Ontario, Institute of Intergovernmental Relations, Queen's University, 1967. 231 p.

A bibliography to the date of its publication, though much has been written since.

SHARMAN, C. *The premier's conference: an essay in federal–state interaction.* Canberra, Dept of Political Science, Research School of Social Sciences, Australian National University, 1977. 75 p.

A monograph on one of the most important extraconstitutional features of Australian federalism.

SMART, D. *Federal aid to Australian schools, 1901–75.* UQP, 1979. 152 p.

An account of commonwealth involvement in education.

TROY, P.N. ed, *Federal power in Australian cities: essays in honour of Peter Till.* Sydney, Hale & Iremonger, 1978. 177 p.

Essays of varying quality on intergovernmental relations and co-operation in one particular area.

Trade union banner of the New South Wales Locomotive Engine Drivers, Firemen and Cleaners, created to mark the federation of the state unions in 1900. A. Stephen and A. Reeves, Badges of labour, banners of pride, *Sydney 1984. The nationalist and internationalist imagery of a band of steel federating the world had a particular irony in Australia where adjoining states had different railway gauges.*

Charles Henry Woolcott,
Busby's bore. *Watercolour. It*
shows the standpipe in Hyde Park
which dispensed Sydney's regular
water supply from 1837.
MITCHELL LIBRARY

CHAPTER 27

LOCAL GOVERNMENT

R. L. WETTENHALL

LOCAL GOVERNMENT has its primary and secondary literature and also figures (though rarely significantly) in general accounts of government in Australia. It is connected, too, with the somewhat exclusive but popular industry of writing local histories. This essay examines first the primary and local history literature, and then focuses on the evolution of the secondary—and most easily accessible—literature of books and journal articles.

PRIMARY LITERATURE

A copious primary literature on local government is to be found in the state acts of parliament establishing the local government systems, the rules and by-laws passed by the municipal councils, their annual and other reports, and particularly the reports of the increasing number of royal commissions and committees of inquiry appointed by the state governments to advise on local government reform.

A useful introduction to the reports these inquiries have produced is M.R. Rawlinson (1975) and there is also a list in R.L. Wettenhall (1979). Notable among the more recent reports is that of the Board of Review of the Role, Structure and Administration of Local Government in Victoria (chairman: M. Bains, 1979). A review of the publications of local governments was prepared by Gregory P. Jones (1979). In the same article Jones also dealt with the 'industry' journals published by the various local government associations (or municipal associations) representing the elected members of councils and professional staff associations. Amongst these the most notable is probably *Local government administration*, the quarterly journal of the Institute of Municipal Administration. Also falling within this category are the papers and published proceedings of the biennial national seminars of the Institute of Municipal Administration. Some yearbooks and occasional manuals published privately serve as guides to local government procedures and changes in local government law. The following titles are among the better known in this category of publications: *The Victorian local government handbook* and *Town planning and local government guide*, both irregularly issued by the Law Book Co, Melbourne; the *Victorian municipal directory: state guide and water supply record*, issued biennially in Melbourne by Arnall and Jackson; and *Bluett's local government handbook (New South Wales)*, published irregularly by the Law Book Co, Sydney.

None of this specialist material is readily accessible to the general enquirer, and to understand it properly it is advisable to begin with some of the secondary works considered later in this essay.

There are also hundreds of local histories which vary greatly in content and quality. Some have very little to do with local government; others are commissioned by municipal councils to commemorate openings, jubilees, centenaries. Even then, they may be social histories of districts rather than histories of governmental arrangements; but some make excellent contributions to the literature of local government. Pre-eminent among this group is the centenary history of the city of Brisbane by Greenwood and Laverty (1959). Brisbane is unique among the Australian capitals because it is governed as a single 'greater city' entity, a reform achieved in 1925 which makes this largest Australian local government a bigger population and revenue unit than the smallest state (Tasmania). A good example of the more recent work which contributes both to local history and local *government* history is M.A. Jones's (1983) study of the Dandenongs and the City of Knox in Victoria. The work by Barrett (1979) and Dunstan (1984) should also be noted.

On local history generally, see Philip Geeves, *Local history in Australia: a guide for beginners*, of which a 2nd edition was published by the Royal Australian Historical Society in 1971, and the article by R. Ian Jack, 'Local history in Australia', in *Current affairs bulletin* 54, 2, 1977, 24–30. The best bibliography of local histories to date is Carole Beaumont's *Local history in Victoria: an annotated bibliography* (Bundoora, Vic, La Trobe University Library, 1980). Bibliographies for other states are in preparation.

SECONDARY LITERATURE

Until the 1970s, secondary literature about Australian local government was extremely sparse. Local government was generally regarded as the poorest, least efficient and least important of the three levels of government in the federation. Consequently its affairs attracted little serious consideration from those academic or other researchers who could have provided the information resource on which such a literature might have been based. Of course local government gained brief mention in most general works about government in Australia, but that fell far short of a literature about local government in its own right.

The University of Sydney had long been the oasis in this desert. It established the first 'school' for the study of public administration in this country, and a small group of scholars who took local government seriously emerged around the figure of Professor F.A. Bland, appointed to the first Australian chair of public administration in 1935. Thus scholars like Parker, Atkins and Bland himself began to write about local government along with their work on state and federal government, while Larcombe emerged as a specialist in local government history.

Besides the works by Atkins, Bland and Larcombe listed in the bibliography, see also the broader surveys by R.S. Parker: 'The government of New South Wales', in S.R. Davis ed, *The government of the Australian states* (Melbourne, Longmans, 1960) and *The government of New South Wales* (UQP, 1978, ch 7). Because the local governments most familiar to these pioneering scholars were those in New South Wales, the experiences they recorded and the conclusions drawn from them were mostly New South Wales based.

As very little work of this kind was being done in other states, the impression emerged that these experiences were typical of the whole country. Some research into local government in the other states took place in the years after World War II, but the outcomes were generally published in elusive booklets and journals. Notable among these were J.R.H. Johns, *Metropolitan government in Western Australia* (Perth, Dept of Economics, University of Western Australia, 1950) and Alan Davies, *Local government in Victoria* (MUP, 1951).

By the early 1970s, a number of nationwide stereotypes had developed: notably that local government was invariably weak and impecunious; that it had been forced on unwilling communities by state governments seeking to divest themselves of responsibilities; that it functioned merely as 'the administrative agent of the state'; and that it was more corrupt (largely because it was supposed to be dominated by estate agents and property developers) and less efficient than the other levels of government.

The election of the federal Labor government under E.G. Whitlam at the close of 1972 brought substantial change. For the first time a federal government insisted on establishing direct links compelling local government to give greater consideration to the provision of welfare and other personal services. The Whitlam government also set up a systematic data base on local government—the Australian Municipal Information System—within the Australian Bureau of Statistics, and in 1976 local government obtained representation in its own right on the new Advisory Council on Inter-Government Relations. Along with the initiatives of the Whitlam government, controversial quality-of-life issues were emerging to confront local as well as all other levels of government, while local government became caught up in the growing credentialism and professionalism of representative bodies and management groups. So it began to attract the attention of researchers, writers and educators throughout the country.

Now messages came from South Australia that local government in that state did not fit the stereotype at all well. The problem of differentiation was clearly pointed out by J.B.Hirst (1973) and further examined by J.R. Robbins in his PhD thesis (University of Adelaide, 1975) entitled 'Local government and community in South Australia'. Comparative study across the six state systems was quickly generated, and the works by Bowman and subsequently by the group involved in preparing the encyclopaedic *Local government systems of Australia* (Power et al, 1981) demonstrated that there was much diversity. Comparisons showed, for example, that as late as 1905 only 1 per cent of New South Wales was administered by municipalities, whereas virtually all of Victoria had been so covered by the 1860s. In several states municipal institutions had been enthusiastically embraced by local communities, sometimes as safeguards against encroaching state power; mostly in those states, local government had exhibited much greater strength against the state government even though it may have managed a fairly narrow range of functions. There were indeed vast differences between the six systems, and the assumed stereotypes came to be seen as (sometimes very damaging) myths rather than expressions of the reality of Australian local government.

The belated recognition both of this general myth–reality misfit and of the separateness of the state experiences has challenged scholars to research more carefully, and to document and compare the various systems. Thus the last decade has seen a considerable expansion in available published studies. It has also seen many expressions of the advantages to be had from administration of services close to the communities being served. Today the diversity, challenge and opportunity of local government are highlighted, in stark contrast to the pessimistic tone of the few works of earlier generations.

The titles listed below include some examples of work from the earlier period. Most, however, come from more recent times, and show that some researchers and writers (including the author of this survey) have found cause—in the circumstances briefly described above—to revise their understandings about the development and role of local government in Australia. Some of the reasons for my own conversion are explained in 'Towards a reinterpretation of Tasmania's local government history', which appeared in the *J R Aust Hist Soc* 67, 2, 1981, 102–18. See also the 'Overview of local government in Australia', in Power *et al* (1981).

ATKINS, R. *Albany to Zeehan: a new look at local governments.* Sydney, Law Book Co, 1979. 147 p.

Emphasises the diversity of Australian local governments and challenges some stereotyped views about them (an appendix presents brief sketches of a 'scattered sample' of 30 local authorities).

ATKINS, R. AND WETTENHALL, R. 'Local government', in *The Australian encyclopaedia*, Sydney, Grolier, 1983, 6, 133–8.

An overview of the history, structure, functions and financing of Australian local governments, posing the question of whether they are merely agents of the states.

BARRETT, A.H.B. *The civic frontier: the origin of local communities and local government in Victoria.* Melbourne, MUP, 1979. 329 p, illus.

Detailed and scholarly study published in the centenary year of the Municipal Association of Vic.

BLAND, F.A. *Government in Australia* (2nd edn). Sydney, Government Printer, 1939. 761 p.

Chapters 17 and 18 of this comprehensive book of readings and commentaries deal with local government generally and in metropolitan areas. The 1944 edition is revised and enlarged.

BOWMAN, M. *Local government in the Australian states.* Canberra, AGPS, 1976. 95 p.

First comparative study of local authorities in Australia, sponsored by the Whitlam government's Dept of Urban and Regional Development.

BOWMAN, M. *The suburban political process: in Box Hill, Melbourne.* University of Melbourne, 1978. 160 p. (Melbourne politics monograph, 5).

A study of citizen participation in local government in Box Hill municipality, Melbourne. First published in 1973.

BOWMAN, M. AND HAMPTON, W. eds, *Local democracies: a study in comparative local government.* Melbourne, Longman Cheshire, 1983. 207 p.

An introductory study in comparative local government, relating to local government systems of Australia and the Pacific Basin to each other and to their largely British heritage.

CHAPMAN, R.J.K. AND WOOD, M. *Australian local government: the federal dimension.* Sydney, Allen & Unwin, 1984. 208 p.

Considers local government as an actor with considerable advantages within Australian federalism and the networks of intergovernmental relations.

DUNSTAN, D. *Governing the metropolis: politics, technology and social change in a Victorian city: Melbourne 1850–1891.* Melbourne, MUP, 1984. 362 p, illus.

A history of local government and administration in Melbourne with particular attention to the possibility of the amalgamation of local authorities and the interaction between local authorities and non-elective public utilities.

GREENWOOD, G. AND LAVERTY, J. *Brisbane 1859–1959: a history of local government.* Brisbane, Ziegler for the Council of the City of Brisbane, 1959. 695 p, illus, maps.

The centenary history of local government in the only Australian capital city to be reformed (in 1925) as a single unified local authority.

HARRIS, C.P. *The classification of Australian local authorities.* Canberra, Australian National University, 1975. 126 p. (Centre for Research on Federal Financial Relations. Research monograph, 9).

An attempt to sort Australian local governments into categories, mainly intended to facilitate the payment of federal equalisation grants.

HIRST, J.B. *Adelaide and the country, 1870–1971: their social and political relationship.* MUP, 1973. 266 p, illus.

An account of settlement in SA, stressing Adelaide's dominance thoughout and the development of municipal institutions which challenged the NSW-based stereotypes.

JONES, G.P. 'Local government publications', in D.H. Borchardt ed, *Australian official publications.* Melbourne, Longman Cheshire, 1979, 271–80.

The first attempt to examine critically the literature by local governments in Australia.

JONES, M.A. *Local government and the people: challenges for the eighties.* Melbourne, Hargreen, 1981. 175 p.

Examines the challenges, opportunities and dangers for Australian local governments as they enter the 1980s.

JONES, M.A. *Organisational and social planning in Australian local government.* Melbourne, Heinemann Educational, 1977. 294 p.

Considers problems of organisation, management and planning in, and the environment of, local government.

JONES, M.A. *Prolific in God's gifts: a social history of Knox and the Dandenongs.* Sydney, Allen & Unwin in association with the City of Knox, 1983. 328 p, illus, maps.

Commissioned by the City of Knox to mark its 20th anniversary, this is an excellent recent example of the local history that is both general social history and local government history.

KNIBBS, G.H. *Local government in Australia.* Melbourne, Government Printer, 1919. 313 p.

A digest of the statutory provisions governing the operation of the local government systems in each state at the end of World War I, by the then commonwealth statistician.

LARCOMBE, F.A. *A history of local government in New South Wales.* Sydney, SUP, 1973–78. 3 vols.

A definitive account of the chequered progress of local government in NSW from its inception to the mid-1970s. Each volume has a separate title. Supersedes the author's *The development of local government in New South Wales* (1961).

MATHEWS, R. ed, *Local government in transition: responsibilities, finances, management.* Canberra, Centre for Research on Federal Financial Relations, Australian National University, 1978. 147 p.

Reviews local government during the period of the Fraser government, especially in the areas of federalism, community development, social welfare, public finance and management innovation.

PARKIN, A. *Governing the cities: the Australian experience in perspective.* Melbourne, Macmillan, 1982. 147 p.

Considers the role of local governments along with that of the states and commonwealth in urban government and politics in Australia.

POWER, J. *et al, Local government systems of Australia.* AGPS, 1981. 830 p, illus. Advisory Council on Inter-Government Relations, Information paper, 7.

A comparison of the several Australian systems containing studies of local government in each state and an overview by the editors.

PURDIE, D.M. *Local government in Australia: reformation or regression?* Sydney, Law Book Co, 1976. 200 p.

This book focuses on the seeming paradox of Australian local government in the mid-1970s.

RAWLINSON, M.R. 'Administering local government reform in Australia: the state experience', in *The first thousand days of Labor*, comp by R.L.Wettenhall and M.Painter. Canberra, Canberra College of Advanced Education, 1975, 2, 67–82.

A review of proposals for local government reform (including boundary adjustment) resulting from inquiries in all states except Qld in the period 1962–75.

STRETTON, H. *Ideas for Australian cities* (2nd edn). Melbourne, Georgian House, 1975. 367 p, illus, map.

A trailblazing study relating local and other levels of government in Australia's cities to the search for a return to civilised urban living. First published in 1970.

TUCKER, J.D. *et al, Local government in Queensland*. Canberra. Australian Institute of Urban Studies, 1981–. v, illus, maps.

A comprehensive study of local government in Qld sponsored by the Qld Division of the Australian Institute of Urban Studies.

VICTORIA. Board of Review of the Role, Structure and Administration of Local Government in Victoria. *Local government in Victoria: role structure and administration. Board*

of Review final report [and] research appendices. Melbourne, Government Printer, 1979–80. 5 vols.

The most comprehensive so far of the reports resulting from recent public inquiries into local government systems in several states. Most of the inquiries can be traced through Borchardt's *Checklist of royal commissions, select committees of parliament and boards of inquiries, 1958–* (see chapter 7 of this volume).

WETTENHALL, R.L. 'Local government in Australia', in D.H.Borchardt ed, *Australian official publications*. Melbourne, Longman Cheshire, 1979, 27–56.

A chapter concerned with government publications at all levels; succinct overview of the role of local government.

WINSTON, D. *Sydney's great experiment: the progress of the Cumberland County Plan*. A & R, 1957. 146 p, illus, maps.

An account of one of Australia's most ambitious metropolitan planning schemes and the role of local government in that scheme, before the abandonment of the particular administrative apparatus described.

Testimonial to E.H. Panton presented in 1905 on his retirement after fifteen years as alderman on the Launceston City Council. Born near Hobart in 1847, Panton owned several prominent hotels and enjoyed a variety of sporting interests. Testimonials of this kind, featuring elaborate illuminated addresses, appropriate mottoes and coats of arms and signed by colleagues and wellwishers, were common in the late nineteenth and early twentieth centuries.

QUEEN VICTORIA MUSEUM AND ART GALLERY, LAUNCESTON

*Invitation to a state banquet for the
United States fleet, Sydney, 1908.*
BOOROWA PRODUCTIONS

CHAPTER 28

DEFENCE AND FOREIGN RELATIONS

MALCOLM BOOKER, J. E. HOFFMAN AND T. B. MILLAR

AUSTRALIA IS AN ISLAND nation. Simplistic and self-evident as this statement is, it has important consequences upon almost every aspect of economic, social and cultural life. Not the least of these are aspects of administration and government that relate to defence and relations with other countries. These topics—defence and foreign relations—are closely allied and are therefore treated jointly. Although there are two separate essays, the listing of the relevant literature has been combined into one sequence, subdivided into five major groups:
   Historical aspects
   Diplomats and politicians
   Current defence policies and international relations
   Conferences and serials
   Collections of documents

DEFENCE

In the first half century of settlement in Australia very little attention was given to defence. The newcomers were fully occupied in developing the continent and insofar as there was any thought of an external threat it was assumed that it would be taken care of by the imperial navy. There was also a comfortable feeling that sheer distance from potential enemies meant that there was no need to worry about local defence.

By the middle of the nineteenth century this carefree attitude was replaced among colonial leaders by a concern that the Australian settlements might come under attack as a result of the intensifying imperial rivalries in the Pacific—between Britain on the one hand, and France, Russia and the United States on the other. There was a feeling not only that the colonies had become a valuable prize but that the day might come when Britain would be under such pressure that it would be unable to protect them.

The debate that developed at that time embraces themes remarkably similar to those being argued in the 1980s. The Crimean War (1854–56) had been a defeat for Russia but paradoxically had created an impression in the Australian colonies of massive Russian power. For a time Russia was regarded as the most likely source of danger, although there was also fear about a revival of French imperial ambitions and even suspicion of the expansionary activities of the United States of America. There was also in the background a vague worry about the possibly hostile intentions of the mysterious empires of China and Japan.

Public argument revolved mainly around two alternatives: should the colonies develop local forces so that they could provide for their own defence and contribute to the British Empire's fighting stength; or should they seek security in disengagement from Britain's quarrels?

One of the most vehement contributors to this debate was John Dunmore Lang (1860). He gave a strongly affirmative answer to the second proposition, arguing that the greatest danger lay in involvement in European wars, during which it was likely to prove physically impossible for Great Britain to defend its colonies. He believed that the best way for the Australian colonies to ensure their safety would be to gain their independence from Britain and to adopt an attitude of neutrality towards that country's present and future enemies. In this situation there would be no other power whom the Australian colonies need fear. He dismissed scornfully the idea that the Chinese and Japanese would invade Australia, and said that the 'civilised' European nations would respect its neutrality. He commended the policy of neutrality adopted by the United States during the war with France, arguing that this had enabled the country to 'prosper amazingly' and urging that in any future European conflict the Australians should seek to do likewise. If an independent Australia adopted such a policy but nevertheless needed protection for its trade routes, the United States would no doubt be glad to step in and give it.

In spite of his strenuous advocacy Lang lost the argument. The colonies remained loyal to the British Empire. In the following decades they moved haphazardly towards providing themselves with an incongruous mixture of local defence forces, which were largely seen by the authorities as intended to be more than supplementary to the protection given by the Royal Navy.

As the movement towards federation gathered momentum in the last decades of the century a more serious public interest developed in defence issues, and there was some debate about the type of defence forces a united nation should acquire. An early contribution to this debate was a report submitted by Captain W.F.D. Jervois to the colonial government of New South Wales in 1877. This is available only as a parliamentary paper but it is worth searching out because in a brief conspectus it raises the issues which were important in the period leading to federation.

Jervois's starting point was the same as that of John Dunmore Lang: there was no likelihood of a major attack on Australia. But both his reasons and his conclusions were very different. He believed that because of its wealth and prosperity the country would be an increasingly tempting target, but since it could be assumed that the naval supremacy of the British Empire would be maintained, the most that need be feared were raids on the major ports and on maritime commerce. These could nevertheless be damaging and local defences were needed against them.

The two most likely enemies Jervois discerned were the same as Lang's, namely the Russians and the French. The naval forces of these countries, operating respectively out of Vladivostock and Saigon, were seen as capable of evading the Royal Navy and mounting raids against Australia and elsewhere in the south Pacific.

Jervois's recommendations were in the end modest. He called for the installation of more effective land batteries to protect Sydney and Newcastle; the raising of a field force of two battalions; and the purchase of an 'ironclad' vessel for the general defence of the harbours along the coast.

The collaborator in this report was Lieutenant-Colonel, later Major-General, Peter Scratchley. His attitude was substantially the same as Jervois's and he too had an important influence on the debate. The collection of his papers compiled by C.K. Cooke (1887) describes Australia's basic strategic dilemma in a way that has a strikingly modern ring. Scratchley found many people who believed, then as now, that no expenditure was necessary. Some based their view on the belief that there was no likely enemy in sight, while others were confident that even if there were, Great Britain would take care of them. Yet others believed that the financial cost of self-defence would ruin the economy and therefore should not be attempted. Finally there were those who argued that, if war came, the Australian colonies should stay out of it even if this meant submitting to the wishes of the enemy power.

By the 1880s, however, a consensus emerged on the lines that, while Australia must continue to rely on the support of another power for its overall security, it was nevertheless desirable that it provided itself with sufficient forces to defend the continent and its immediate environment. It was also accepted that the local forces should be comparable with those of Britain so that in time of war they could fight side by side.

The first serious attempt to provide for local defence began, naturally enough, with the navy. Admiral George Tyron commanded the Royal Navy on the Australian station from 1884 to 1887 and sought to weld the miscellaneous collection of small ships under the control of the colonies into a usable auxiliary to the Royal Navy. Little progress was made however because of wrangling over costs between the colonial governments and the British Admiralty. The colonies agreed that more should be done, and that the Royal Navy should maintain a more powerful squadron on the Australian station, but they were divided as to whether they should help pay part of the cost or insist that it all be borne by the British government.

In Australia in the 1880s, as earlier in the 1850s and again in the 1980s, the Russians were much talked about publicly as the likely enemies. There were recurrent alarms that war between Britain and Russia was imminent. There were also reports that the Germans were preparing to seize New Guinea and the French the New Hebrides. The degree of public concern aroused by these reports eventually stirred the colonial politicians into looking more seriously at the need for local defence forces.

As a result of intercolonial consultations, it was generally agreed that the force maintained by the Royal Navy in the area was inadequate and it was widely feared that it would be withdrawn from Australian waters when most needed. The British government was urged to strengthen the Royal Navy squadron and some assurance was sought that it would in fact be used for the defence of Australia in time of of war. The colonies went so far as to indicate that they might be prepared to contribute to the cost.

At the conference in 1887 an agreement was reached between the imperial and colonial governments under which the squadron was to be significantly strengthened. A clause was included regarding its use which was later to arouse considerable discussion. This provided that 'the ships were to be under the sole control and orders of the British commander-in-chief on the Australian station, but to be retained within the limits of that station, and only otherwise employed by the consent of the colonial governments'.

As the movement towards federation gathered pace there was growing dissatisfaction with the ambiguities of this agreement. In spite of its apparently firm wording, many believed it meant that in time of war the squadron would be taken by its commander-in-chief to fight in another theatre. Public opinion therefore turned more and more to the creation of defence forces fully under local control. At the National Australasian Convention held in Sydney in 1891 Henry Parkes moved a resolution calling for the establishment of federal military and naval forces under one command and amenable only to the 'national government of Australia'. The resolution was adopted and this remained the ostensible objective until federation was finally achieved.

The new naval agreement negotiated after the commonwealth was established fell, however, a good deal short of this objective. The squadron remained a component of the Royal Navy and the agreement gave even less assurance that it would not be withdrawn in time of danger. By 1903 W.M. Hughes had established himself in federal politics as the most forceful proponent of adequate Australian defence forces and argued that the Australian government would be unable to do anything because 'on matters of Imperial policy we have absolutely no voice'. For an account of Hughes's role in the creation of the Australian defence forces see M. Booker (1980). The defence debates in the commonwealth parliament are also worth reading for the light they throw on attitudes towards security in the early years of federation.

Meanwhile, outside the parliament, Captain William Creswell was campaigning for an independent Australian navy. In September 1901, while naval commandant of Queensland, he submitted a report to the federal government which proposed the creation of 'an Australian fleet serving in its own waters' and a step-by-step creation of an Australian navy which would be manned and paid for by Australians.

Creswell's proposal was not accepted by the Barton government but at the end of 1904, under proposals for an administrative structure for defence drawn up by the shortlived Watson Labor government, he became federal director of naval forces. From this position he was able, with the support of Hughes from the Labor party and of Deakin from the conservative side of parliament, to carry his campaign to eventual success. A separate Australian navy was established under the Naval Defence Act of 1910, which was passed through parliament while Hughes was acting prime minister. These developments are detailed in G.L. Macandie (1949) and Creswell (1965).

The history of the development of the Australian land forces followed a somewhat different course. From the earliest days of the commonwealth parliament W.M. Hughes argued for compulsory military service and, in the teeth of the pacifist instincts of his own party, was able to have this adopted as Labor policy. The responsibility for creating the Australian army rested however with Major-General E.T.H. Hutton, a British officer who had ben appointed in the early days of federation as general officer commanding the commonwealth forces. His views differed markedly from Hughes's and indeed from Creswell's. His objective was to construct the new Australian forces on lines which in time of war would enable them most readily to be absorbed into the British forces. Hutton had little of the scepticism shown by Creswell towards the British defence authorities and remained throughout his time in Australia a loyal servant of the British government. Particularly objectionable from Hughes's point of view was the emphasis he placed on building up a permanent professional army, which Hughes feared would lead to the creation of a military elite.

In the end however they both had their way. Hughes secured the passage of a Defence Act embodying compulsory military training concurrently with the Act establishing the navy. Hutton's early influence in moulding the Australian army on British lines was reflected in the ease with which the Australian forces were absorbed into the British when war broke out in 1914. Although he was the subject of considerable controversy, the only readily accessible material concerning Hutton's attitudes is the collection of his speeches made during the period 1894–98 (1902).

With the outbreak of World War I the defence debate focused on two separate but related issues: whether the country's security could be best served by sending its forces to Europe or by keeping them at home; and whether Australians should be conscripted for service outside the country. An overwhelming majority supported the view that the forces should be sent overseas but only a minority (albeit a large one) believed that such service should be compulsory.

It will be noted that in the defence bibliography a remarkable gap exists: there are no publications devoted to defence issues between 1908 and 1964—with the notable exception of the book by W.M. Hughes (1935). This is not because works have been overlooked: none was written. This lack strikingly illustrates the indifference, notwithstanding involvement in two world wars, towards the defence of the nation at all levels of the Australian community, including politicians, academics and the press.

This absence of serious debate may do much to explain why the responses of the Australian people, when World War II broke out, were practically identical with those of 1914. Between the wars Hughes' book might well have stirred some fresh ideas, but debate was stifled by the Lyons government, with the ready acquiesence of the politicians and the press. From the universities nothing was heard.

The end of the war in 1945 was followed quickly in other combatant countries by a spate of publications reviewing the errors and disasters of that war. Since many of the errors had been costly to the Australian forces it might have been expected that a similar public debate would have occurred in Australia. In fact the silence remained unbroken for another twenty years.

In 1964 the floodgates were suddenly opened and two or three dozen serious books have appeared on defence since. It cannot be said however that the ideas presented were entirely new. Although many of the writers seemed unaware of it, their ideas had in essence been thoroughly canvassed over a century before by John Dunmore Lang (1860). The debate in the 1960s was, it is true, conducted in the context of the threat of 'global communism', with which was linked the fear of nuclear war; and these factors were regarded as having transformed international relations and strategic realities. But as the rhetoric subsided it became apparent that little had changed.

In particular Russia was again seen as the most likely danger; and the proposition that Lang had sought unsuccessfully to counter—that Australia must rely on others for its security—was again unanimously accepted. There had of course been some changes of scene. Germany had been eliminated from the list of enemies and France was regarded as more or less a friend. Japan, which a century ago had been seen as a vague and distant menace, had become a real and then a defeated enemy. China too had emerged abruptly as a threat, although more for ideological reasons than for its military power. The United States Navy had replaced the Royal Navy as Australia's main shield, dependence on the British Empire having been replaced by dependence on America. Australians remained loyal subjects of the Queen but as far as their safety was concerned they relied on the ANZUS treaty.

It was assumed that others would accept the primary responsibility for protecting Australia and the only question was how much Australians need do for their own local defence. As in the last century there were writers who were uneasy at the public's complacency. Commentators, like their forbears, argued that the protective power would have such heavy burdens in time of crisis that Australians must accept some responsibility for taking care of themselves and also be ready to assist their protectors in any wars in which they might become involved.

At the end of the last century the principal exponent of the view that Australia should prepare itself to support the British Empire was G.C. Craig (1897). The introduction to one of the first books to be published after World War II said virtually the same thing, except that the United States had now taken the place of Great Britain. The only difference was that whereas in the 1890s the goodwill of Britain could be taken for granted, there was a feeling in the 1960s that the goodwill of the United States must be earned. Otherwise the message was the same: Australia should provide for its own local defence and also stand ready to support the United States in its global objectives (see Australian Institute of Political Science, 1964).

It is not surprising therefore that during the Korean and Vietnam wars Australian troops were again sent overseas as elements in another country's forces. This was done with very little public opposition and indeed with practically no public debate. In the case of Vietnam it was only after the conflict had gone on for several years and strong opposition to the war had developed in America itself that criticism emerged in Australia. H.G. Gelber (1970) is useful for insight into public attitudes of the time.

The controversies arising out of the Vietnam War did produce some change in public attitude. Lang's vision of a neutral and independent Australia, which had lived on in what were regarded as the extremist fringes of society, became the subject of respectable debate. Arguments very reminiscent of Lang's were put forward by Max Teichman and David Martin at a conference of the Monash University Political Studies Association in June 1965. Russia was again being discussed as the most likely enemy although now the conflict that was feared was one involving the United States, not Britain. An important difference was that whereas Lang had declared that Australia needed no defences, Teichman and Martin called for a policy of armed neutrality. They believed that the country was economically strong enough to mobilise sufficient resources to defend itself, provided that it avoided involvement in other countries' wars. Teichman's views can be found in the collection of essays on Australian foreign policy which he edited in 1969.

As in Lang's day this point of view appealed only to a small minority of the Australian people. A less radical view that gained some currency was that the alliance with the United States should be retained but that Australia should become more self-reliant not only in defence but also in foreign policy. At the same time doubt increased as to whether the United States would be able to defend Australia in a major conflict even if it wished. It was natural therefore that many of the books published after the mid-1970s called for a more self-reliant posture.

This trend of thought did not greatly affect the policies of successive Australian governments from either side of politics. They remained committed to the belief that Australia could continue to shield under the strategic umbrella of the United States and although some modern equipment was acquired for each of the services there was no serious attempt to weld them into an integrated and independent fighting force. Nor was a coherent strategic doctrine developed for either low level or global conflict. No doubt the main practical reason for this attitude was that it relieved governments of the necessity for increasing expenditure on defence, coupled with the conviction among politicians that this was what the public wanted.

It is remarkable how little the public attitudes to defence were affected in Australia by the invention of nuclear weapons, in spite of the extensive media attention given to them. Such adjustments as occurred were marginal: some believed that their existence made protection by the United States even more essential, while others saw them as strengthening the case of neutrality.

The effect of the emergence of the Soviet Union as a nuclear superpower was similar. There was an intensification of debate at each end of the spectrum of opinion but effective argument was confined to a small minority. Even though it was widely accepted that the Russians were motivated by an ambition to dominate the world, the majority of Australians regarded this as having little practical relevance to the defence of their own country.

Notwithstanding this general public indifference a number of thoughtful books were written about the wider options open to Australia. The works produced by the Strategic and Defence Studies Centre of the Australian National University, under its first head, T.B. Millar, made it possible, for the first time in Australian history, for the defence debate to take place in the light of balanced and accurate information about the country's defence requirements and the international environment in which they needed to be met. Academics associated with this centre were prominent among those who warned of the dangers of excessive dependence on the United States and who offered realistic suggestions as to ways in which Australia could acquire a more self-reliant defence force structure. The influence of Robert O'Neill (director of the centre 1971–83) in this connection is apparent in the works he edited (1975, 1982).

The question of defence co-operation with the countries of southeast Asia, which had been developed after World War II and then allowed to lapse, was also revived by writers in this group. Several argued for the development of close relations with the Association of Southeast Asian Nations (ASEAN) as a means of promoting the security of the region.

Desmond Ball (director of the centre since 1984) made a particular contribution to the debate concerning the United States defence communications stations in Australia. The extent to which these installations committed Australia to American strategic policies and exposed the country to the danger of nuclear attack was discussed in a balanced perspective (1980).

Contributions to a more informed public debate on defence issues during this period were made by retired Australian diplomats (M. Booker, A. Renouf and A. Watt). The points of view of these writers were diverse but in each case questions relating to Australia's dependence on the United States were discussed against a background of direct personal involvement in Australia's foreign relations during and after World War II.

Notwithstanding this increased debate, two options theoretically open to Australia remain practically taboo—the acquisition of nuclear weapons and military co-operation with Japan. The arguments for a nuclear capability were presented by I. Bellamy (1972) and D. Martin (1984) but drew little public response. No serious work has been produced on possible co-operation with Japan, and this no doubt reflects the widespread assumption that, in spite of the likely strategic advantages for themselves and for the region, defence co-operation would be unacceptable to the people of both countries. By the middle of the 1980s, however, the acceptance of increasing responsibility by Japan for the defence of its own neighbourhood created a growing awareness in Australia of a close relationship between its own security and that of Japan.

In summary, it is fair to say that at the end of two hundred years of European settlement in Australia, the nation's basic defence problems remain unresolved. A rich but strategically vulnerable country, Australia is still dependent on the protection of others. It is true that as they become better informed about the outside world a considerable section of the public is increasingly uneasy about the reliability of this protection, and in some cases this is reflected among political leaders. But no consensus has been reached on the remedies that should be sought and in the 1980s Australia seems no closer to having a credible capability for independent defence than in the days of John Dunmore Lang.

FOREIGN RELATIONS

During the nineteenth century, the six British colonies that comprised Australia gradually developed attitudes and even policies towards the outside world. Their formal external relations were wholly with the government in London, but they were directly concerned with events in the region and from time to time with the activities of other powers, notably France, Russia, Germany and, for a brief period during the Civil War, the United States. Their involvement in policy-making was limited to urging or forcing the British government to take action, as with the annexation of Papua in 1883. There was also concern about immigration from Asia following the gold rush, and this led to restrictive legislation in the colonies. The Commonwealth Restricted Immigration Act of 1903 was mainly aimed at excluding non-Europeans, and was popularly known as the 'White Australia' policy.

Most of the research on the pre-federation period is of recent origin, as can be seen in Roger C. Thompson (1980), in the early chapters of Neville Meaney (1976) and in T.B. Millar (1978). There are a few comments in contemporary journals, but most information will be found in articles written since 1945 and can be identified by reference to the *Australian public affairs information service* (APAIS), for details of which see chapter 8 of this volume.

The main sources for Australia's earlier external policies are in offical records, including parliamentary debates and printed papers of colonial legislatures, formal despatches and correspondence between the Colonial Office in London and colonial secretaries or governors, archival records of colonial administrations, and records of the colonial conferences held in London from 1887 onwards. Primary sources also include contemporary press reports, the surviving records of business firms involved in island trade, such as Burns Philp, and the personal papers of individual politicians, public servants and others. Most of these are housed in state archives or in special collections of the state libraries, which also hold microfilm copies of relevant records from overseas, listed in the *Australian Joint Copying Project handbooks*; for source materials in the British Isles, the Mander-Jones guide (1972) is invaluable (see chapter 8).

The Commonwealth of Australia which came into existence on 1 January 1901 was not immediately an independent nation but a federated British colony with evolving desires, first for a greater say in imperial policy and eventually for a role in world affairs which would reflect Australia's national interests rather than those of Britain. Fear of Japanese naval power was aroused by the Russo–Japanese War of 1904–05 and led Deakin to seek assurances in 1908 from the United States, foreshadowing the later alliance sealed by the ANZUS treaty (J. La Nauze, *Alfred Deakin*, A & R, 1979). During World War I, Australia sought and obtained a place in the Imperial War Cabinet, and later provided a separate delegation in the British Empire group at the Versailles peace conference. Details of this important first foray into the international diplomatic area have been described by C.E.W. Bean (*The offical history of Australia in the war of 1914–1918*, A & R, 1921–42, 11). There are also the sober accounts of W.M. Hughes's participation in the peace conference by W.J. Hudson (1978) and by L.F. Fitzhardinge in the second volume of his biography of Hughes (*The little digger*, A & R, 1979). Hughes also provided in his own inimitable way a broad brush picture of these events (1929).

Australia's main contact with other countries, and its foreign relations (as distinct from imperial relations) during the interwar period, took place at the League of Nations. This period is dealt with by E.M. Andrews (1970) and W.J. Hudson (1980), and there are several revealing biographical studies which are discussed below. An overview of Australia's changing attitudes to the world in the 1930s is the subject of two conference volumes: H. Dinning and J. Holmes eds, *Australian foreign policy, 1934* (MUP for the Australian Institute of International Affairs, 1935) and W.G.K. Duncan ed, *Australia's foreign policy* (A & R for the Australian Institute of Political Science, 1938).

Distinctive Australian policies developed during World War II when it had become clear that Australian interests were no longer identical with those of Britain and the empire. This period is covered in the official war histories, especially in the two volumes by Paul Hasluck, *The government and the people* (Canberra, Australian War Memorial, 1952–70). Other useful works are those by Sir Alan Watt (1967) and chapter 9 of T.B. Millar's historical survey (1978).

World War II had far-reaching effects on Australian foreign affairs: in particular a greater involvement with Southeast Asia, lingering doubts about Japan, and heightened fear of other powers in the region, especially China, and the nationalist and communist forces operating throughout this rapidly developing part of the world. The Korean War was one outcome of these regional tensions and essential reading for this period is R.J. O'Neill's official history (1981). The general situation in Asia led Australia to seek two kinds of insurance. The first was a formal security treaty with the United States, which took shape in the ANZUS pact of 1952. Much has been written about this treaty, the first definitive work being J.G. Starke (1965). Two subsequent assessments, from very different viewpoints, were by H.G. Gelber (1968) and J. Camilleri (1980).

The second insurance was an aid policy designed originally to help, and to improve relations with, Asian commonwealth countries which was subsequently extended to non-commonwealth Asian states in a series of bilateral aid programs known as the Colombo Plan.

Fear of China, and a mixture of apprehension towards Japan and a desire to trade with it, played a large part in Australian relations with Asia between the communist assumption of power in Peking in 1949 and the end of Australia's military commitment in Vietnam in 1972. H.S. Albinski, *Australian policies and attitudes towards China* (Princeton, NJ, Princeton University Press, 1965), and Gregory Clark, *In fear of China* (Melbourne, Lansdowne, 1967) record different assessments of China's role as perceived during the 1960s, while chapters in Ian Wilson ed, *China and the world community* (A & R, 1973) indicate Australia's greater acceptance of the People's Republic by the early 1970s.

Acceptance of Japan was much quicker because it was more profitable. This is demonstrated in the successive writings of W. Macmahon Ball (1948) and a later volume of documents and readings edited by him under the title *Australia and Japan* (Nelson, 1969). Relations with Japan are also dealt with by R.N. Rosecrance in *Australian diplomacy and Japan 1945–1951* (MUP, 1962), by J.G. Crawford (1968) and by J.A.A Stockwin in his (at the time) forward-looking *Japan and Australia in the seventies* (A & R, 1972).

Australia's participation in the Vietnam War and other regional conflicts has also been documented, and the official history of the involvement in the Malayan emergency and the war in Vietnam is in preparation under the direction of P.G. Edwards. Public reactions to the Vietnam War are catalogued in H.S. Albinski, *Politics and foreign policy in Australia: the impact of Vietnam and conscription* (Durham, Duke University Press, 1970) and he followed that survey with an analysis of the foreign policy of the Whitlam Labor government (1977).

In recent years a 'revisionist' view of Australian foreign policy has emerged more strongly following the writings of Max Teichmann (1969), Bruce Grant, *The crisis of loyalty: a study of Australian foreign policy* (A & R, 1972) and Camilleri (1980). The strongest advocate of this view is David Martin (1984). Although based on Australian nationalism and touching chords in the Australian character, these works still represent minority viewpoints. There has also been a spate of books prompted by fear of nuclear war and generally directed against policies which (as with the American alliance) might make Australia a more probable target for nuclear weapons.

The only history covering the whole period of Australian foreign affairs is by T.B. Millar (1978), but there are many works dealing with specific areas, either by period or by geography, the more important of which can be found in the following bibliography. By far the largest sponsor of writing on Australian foreign affairs has been the Australian Institute of International Affairs (AIIA), founded as a national body in 1933, and a good proportion of the works mentioned have been published under its auspices or with its assistance. The institute's most significant continuing publication is the multivolume series, *Australia in world affairs*, published at five-yearly intervals since 1950 and edited successively by Gordon Greenwood and Norman Harper (the first four volumes), W.J. Hudson, and P.J. Boyce and J.R. Angel. The institute runs frequent national, and occasional international, conferences, and usually produces a volume from the conference papers. Its research committee commissions monographs, frequently subsidising research costs and sometimes publication costs. Its journals are discussed below.

Another major contributor is the Australian National University, particularly the Department of International Relations and the Strategic and Defence Studies Centre within the Research School of Pacific Studies. In addition to monographs and conference volumes published commercially, the department sponsors the series, *Canberra studies in world affairs*, and the centre supports the *Canberra papers on strategy and defence* amounting to date to some 50 relatively short volumes. Other ANU centres, notably the Contemporary China Centre and the Australia–Japan Research Centre, sponsor publications in their fields of interest. Other Australian universities also publish papers, including research reports such as those produced by the Centre for the Study of Australian–Asian Relations at Griffith University, Queensland. The Australian Institute of Political Science organises occasional conferences on questions of foreign policy and defence, the papers of which are subsequently published.

A number of Australia's politicians have written on foreign relations, either in their memoirs or more generally, including Alfred Deakin, W.M. Hughes, R.G. Casey, R.G. Menzies, P.C. Spender, Paul Hasluck, Peter Howson and Howard Beale. Hasluck's contribution to the official war history has been mentioned already, and Spender's personal record (1969) is essential reading for understanding the background to the two pillars of Australian foreign policy for most of the period since 1945—the Colombo Plan and the ANZUS treaty. Biographies of politicians, notably those of Deakin, Hughes, S.M. Bruce, H.V. Evatt, F.W. Eggleston, and to a lesser extent John Curtin and J.B. Chifley, include references to and background information on foreign affairs. The best of them have made extensive use of archival sources, both official records and personal papers. Some of R.G. Casey's voluminous personal papers have been published (1962); his correspondence with Bruce, written from London during the 1920s, has been edited by W.J. Hudson and J. North (1980), and selections from his diaries have been edited by T.B. Millar (1972). P.G. Edwards (1983) provides the essential continuity for most of this period.

Complementing the works by politicians are those by former diplomats, which include historical and theoretical writings as well as diplomatic reminiscences. Frederick Eggleston's writings have been collected and published (1957), Alan Watt's history (1967) was mentioned above and he also left a personal record (1972), while W.R. Crocker (1971), Alan Renouf (1979) and Malcolm Booker (1976) have produced volumes commenting on Australian foreign policy as seen through their experiences in foreign assignments.

Economic aspects of foreign relations are dealt with mainly in journals and can be located through *APAIS* and university theses; surprisingly little has been published in book form on these topics. Besides John Crawford's study (1968) already referred to, the following books are relevant exceptions: H.W. Arndt, *A small rich industrial country: studies in Australian development, aid and trade* (Melbourne, Cheshire, 1968) and *Resources diplomacy* (Canberra, Australian National University, 1974); J.D.B. Miller ed, *Australia's economic relations* (A & R, 1975); Peter Hastings and Andrew Farran eds, *Australia's resources future: threats, myths and realities in the 1980s* (Melbourne, Nelson, 1978); and Greg Crough and Ted Wheelwright, *Australia: a client state* (Ringwood, Vic, Penguin, 1982). All of these, as their titles indicate, examine foreign relations in terms of economics and trade. There are also three units at the Australian National University—the Development Studies Centre, the ASEAN–Australia Project, and the Indonesia Project within the Department of Economics, Research School of Pacific Studies—which publish monographs in their respective fields. A seminal document with strong economic content, *Australia and the third world*, edited by Owen Harries, was produced by a government-sponsored committee (AGPS, 1979).

An important source for the study of Australia's external relations is the official series, *Documents on Australian foreign policy 1937–1949*, produced by the Editor of Historical Documents in the Department of Foreign Affairs and published by the AGPS. The rate of publication of the volumes is, unfortunately, rather slow, the first seven volumes having reached only the end of 1944. Other documentary publications include *Australia and the world: a documentary history from the 1870s to the 1970s*, edited by N.K. Meaney (Melbourne, Longman Cheshire, 1984), and Greenwood and Grimshaw (1977).

The two main academic journals on foreign affairs are *Australian outlook* (formerly known as the *Austral–Asiatic bulletin* published by the Australian Institute of International Affairs, and *Dyason house papers* (formerly *Australia's neighbours*) published quarterly by its Victorian branch. Occasional articles on foreign affairs are found in such journals as *Australian J of politics and history*, *Australian quarterly*, *Historical studies* and *Quadrant*, while the *Current affairs bulletin* published by the University of Sydney frequently carries articles in this field.

The Department of Foreign Affairs publishes two journals of note: *Australian foreign affairs record* (formerly *Current notes on international affairs*), issued monthly since 1936, and *Backgrounder*, in reduced format, published fortnightly since 1975. The department also publishes occasional *Select documents on international affairs* (from 1954) and an Australian treaty series (from 1948), as well as frequent press statements.

The commonwealth parliamentary debates are rich sources of both information and opinion on international questions, although poorly indexed. The parliamentary research staff helps to prepare papers which contain source materials since 1970 while joint and Senate committees on foreign affairs and defence have produced a number of valuable reports, based on public and in-camera evidence, on Australia's concern with Japan, the Middle East, the Indian Ocean, the south Pacific, ASEAN, Antarctica, the Horn of Africa, disarmament and other subjects.

As in all areas of Australian studies, researchers should be aware of the *Australian national bibliography* and other bibliographies produced by the National Library of Australia, and of the cumulative *Union list of higher degree theses in Australian libraries* published by the University of Tasmania Library. For details see chapter 8 of this volume. Specific bibliographies maintained or issued by the National Library include 'Australian foreign aid: a bibliography', an unpublished bibliography of Australian foreign relations with countries of the Southern Hemisphere; and *The Indian Ocean: a select bibliography of resources for study in the National Library of Australia* (1979). Bibliographies of journal articles on foreign affairs appeared in *Australian outlook* 24, 3, 1970, 238–45; 25, 1, 1971, 69–93; 30, 3, 1976, 414–31; and 31, 1, 1977, 38–51, while records relating to the Pacific are listed in the *J of Pacific history* 11, 4, 1976, 217–20. Bibliographical commentaries are given by P.G. Edwards in *Australian outlook* 29, 3, 1975, 335–40, and by Paul Hasluck in *Australian outlook* 32, 1, 1978, 101–06.

Primary sources for the colonial period of Australian foreign policy have already been mentioned. The external affairs function has belonged to the commonwealth since 1901, so most official records in this area are to be found in the Australian Archives in Canberra, among the records of the governor-general's office, federal cabinet, the Prime Minister's Department and the Department of External Affairs, renamed Foreign Affairs in 1971. It should also be borne in mind that Australian policies on immigration, trade, defence and external territories are closely bound up with foreign policy, and that archival sources are to be found among the records of departments responsible for all those functions.

In addition to the large quantities of departmental and parliamentary records, there exist a number of collections of private or semiofficial papers kept by ministers, senior public servants and other persons involved in foreign relations. These are to be found mainly in the National Library, which houses papers of Lord Novar, Deakin, Fisher, Hughes, Menzies, Atlee Hunt and Littleton Groom, among others, or in the Australian Archives, which holds records of Bruce, Casey, Snedden, Hasluck and Beale, as well as those of later politicians, such as Whitlam and Fraser. Important exceptions include the Evatt papers, located at Flinders University and those of G.F. Pearce, held by the Australian War Memorial.

HISTORICAL ASPECTS

ANDREWS, E. M. *A history of Australian foreign policy: from dependence to independence.* Melbourne, Longman Cheshire, 1979. 236 p.

A useful overview of foreign policy-making in Australia. Aimed at high school students.

ANDREWS, E. M. *Isolationism and appeasement in Australia: reactions to the European crises, 1935–1939.* ANUP, 1970. 236 p, illus.

Covers the period when Australia's main foreign relations, as distinct from imperial relations, were conducted through its participation in the League of Nations.

AUSTIN, M. *The army in Australia, 1840–50: prelude to the golden years.* Canberra, AGPS, 1979. 290 p, illus, maps.

The author's principal concern is with the use of British troops to maintain internal security but there are sidelights on attitudes in this early period to the possibility of external attack.

BALL, W. M. *Japan, enemy or ally?* Melbourne, Cassell, 1948. 240 p.

Comments by Australia's political representative on the Allied Control Council for Japan just after World War II.

BELL, C. *Dependent ally: a study of Australia's relations with the United States and the United Kingdom since the fall of Singapore.* Canberra, Dept of International Relations, Australian National University, 1984. 296 p.

Examines Australia's connections with great and powerful friends and traces the maturing of Australian foreign policy.

BURNETT, A. *The Australia and New Zealand nexus.* Canberra, AIIA and New Zealand Institute of International Affairs, 1978. 289 p.

The first definitive study of relations between Australia and New Zealand. A loose-leaf volume of annotated documents to accompany the above work was issued in 1980, and is updated through the Australian and New Zealand institutes.

CLUNIES ROSS, I. ed, *Australia and the Far East: diplomatic and trade relations.* A & R in conjunction with the AIIF, NSW Branch, 1936. 310 p, illus.

Essays by distinguished contributors on Australia's relations with countries in its geographic region.

COOKE, C.K. *Australian defences and New Guinea: compiled from the papers of the late Major-General Sir Peter Scratchley.* London, Macmillan, 1887. 413 p, illus, maps.

Scratchley was defence adviser to several Australian colonies, and in 1884 became special commissioner for New Guinea. These papers contain a survey of Australa's defence problems.

CRAIG, G.C. *The federal defence of Australasia.* Sydney, Robertson, 1897. 356 p, illus.

A program for the defence of the new Federation, including an account of the debates of the time and of the state of the colonial defence forces.

CRAWFORD, J.G. *Australian trade policy, 1942–1966: a documentary history.* By J.G. Crawford assisted by N. Anderson and M.G.N. Morris. ANUP, 1968. 641 p.

Australia's foreign policy for this period was very closely linked to, although not identical with, its overseas trade.

CRESWELL, W. *Close to the wind: the early memoirs (1886–1879) of Admiral Sir William Creswell.* Ed by P. Thompson. London, Heinemann, 1965. 210 p, illus, maps.

Creswell helped to found the Australian navy and greatly influenced its development. The epilogue gives insight into the defence controversies of the pre-federation period in Australia.

EDWARDS, P.G. *Prime ministers and diplomats: the making of Australian foreign policy 1901–1949.* Melbourne, OUP, in association with AIIA, 1983. 240 p, illus.

Asks why prime ministers have usually dominated decision-making in Australian foreign policy, and why establishment of a diplomatic service was long delayed until World War II, offering evidence in answer.

ESTHUS, R.A. *From enmity to alliance: U.S.–Australian relations, 1931–1941.* Melbourne, MUP, 1965. 180 p.

A survey of Australian–United States relations written from an orthodox American viewpoint.

EVANS, W.P. *Deeds not words.* Melbourne, Hawthorn, 1971. 200 p, illus.

Gives an account of the perceptions of overseas threats and the formation of a Victorian navy, which led to the creation of an Australian navy.

FITZGERALD, C.C.P. *Life of Vice-Admiral Sir George Tryon, K.C.G.* London, Blackwood, 1897. 402 p, illus.

Tryon commanded the Royal Navy on the Australian station from 1884 to 1887. His views on the defence of the Australian colonies, influential at the time, are set out in chapter XI.

FOSTER, H.J. *The defence of the empire in Australia.* Melbourne, Rankine, Dobbie and Co, 1908. 52 p.

This pamphlet by the director of military science at the University of Sydney (1906–19) summarises the views he contributed to the defence discussions of the time.

HARPER, N.D. AND SISSONS, D. *Australia and the United Nations.* New York, Manhattan, 1959. 423 p.

Traces Australia's attitudes to and involvement in the United Nations from the beginnings in 1946 up to 1957, covering aspects such as national security, trusteeship, and economic and social co-operation.

HUDSON, W.J. *Australia and the League of Nations.* Sydney, SUP in association with the AIIA, 1980. 224 p, illus.

Examines Australia's introduction into international politics outside the British Empire, and consequent Australian policy expressions about radical questions.

HUDSON, W.J. *Australian diplomacy.* Melbourne, Macmillan, 1970. 102 p, illus.

HUDSON, W.J. *Billy Hughes in Paris: the birth of Australian diplomacy.* Melbourne, Nelson in association with AIIA, 1978. 147 p.

Two important introductions to Australia's first participation in foreign diplomacy and the role of W.M. Hughes in shaping it.

HUTTON, E.T.H. *The defence and defensive power of Australia.* Melbourne, A & R, 1902. 100 p.

The most interesting of this collection of papers is the last, which relates the scheme drawn up in 1894 for the federal defence of Australia to the wider defence of the British Empire.

HYSLOP, R. *Australian naval administration, 1900–1939.* Melbourne, Hawthorn, 1973. 254 p.

Contains useful information on tensions between the British Admiralty and the Australian authorities, and also within the Australian system.

JAUNCEY, L.C. *The story of conscription in Australia.* London, Allen and Unwin, 1935. 365 p, illus.

Although concerned with internal political issues, the debate regarding the defence requirements for compulsory military training is usefully reviewed. New edition, Melbourne, Macmillan, 1968.

JERVOIS, W.F.D. *Defences: preliminary report, June 4, 1877.* Sydney, Government Printer, 1877. (In NSW Parliament. Legislative Assembly. Votes & Proceedings 1876/77, 3, 85–109).

This report, prepared with the assistance of Scratchley (see Cooke, C.K.), is available only in the NSW Parliamentary Papers, but was seminal in regard to the defence debate leading up to federation.

JOHNSON, D.H. *Volunteers at heart: the Queensland defence forces, 1860–1901.* UQP, 1974. 248 p, illus.

The author discusses the defence issues argued in most Australian colonies in the second half of the nineteenth century, with special emphasis on the evolution of citizen military forces.

LANG, J.D. *How to defend the colony: being the substance of a speech delivered in the Legislative Assembly of New South Wales on Tuesday, 20th December, 1859.* Sydney, J.L. Sherriff, 1860. 24 p.

Lang argued that defences were not needed since the colony could avoid involvement in wars between Europen powers by gaining its independence.

McCARTHY, J.M. *Australia and imperial defence 1918–39: a study in air and sea power.* UQP, 1976. 227 p, illus.

Besides its defence orientation, the work illustrates the changing relevance to Australia of the close imperial connection.

MEANEY, N.K. *A history of Australian defence and foreign policy, 1901–23.* Vol 1. *The search for security in the Pacific, 1901–14.* SUP, 1976. 306 p.

Argues that when Australia was still constitutionally a dependent part of the British Empire, it was evolving a distinctive view of its position in the world.

MILLAR, T.B. *Australia in peace and war: external relations 1788–1977.* ANUP, 1978. 578 p.

A history of Australian foreign policy and relations, especially since Federation.

O'NEILL, R.J. *Australia in the Korean War 1950–1953.* Vol 1. *Strategy and diplomacy.* Canberra, Australian War Memorial and AGPS, 1981. 548 p, illus, maps.

Examines, as background to Australia's involvement in Korea, the wider sphere of regional alliances and strategies.

REESE, T.R. *Australia, New Zealand, and the United States: a survey of international relations 1941–1968.* London, OUP, 1969. 376 p.

Documents the origins and development of the Australian and New Zealand alliance with the United States, in the context of international affairs.

SPARTALIS, P.J. *The diplomatic battles of Billy Hughes.* Sydney, Hale & Iremonger, 1983. 309 p, illus, maps.

A study of Hughes's foreign policy with emphasis on an identified determination to place Australian interests ahead of those of Great Britain.

SWAN, R.A. *Australia in the Antarctic: interest, activity and endeavour.* MUP, 1961. 432 p, illus, maps.

Covers the history of Australian involvement in Antartica which has affected its foreign policy in the postwar period.

THOMPSON, R.C. *Australian imperialism in the Pacific: the expansionist era, 1820–1920.* MUP, 1980. 289 p. maps.

Describes the defence preoccupations which inspired public interest in gaining control over New Guinea and islands of the Pacific.

WARD, J.M. *British policy in the south Pacific 1786–1895: a study in British policy towards the south Pacific islands prior to the establishment of governments by the great powers.* Sydney, Australasian Publishing Co, 1948. 364 p, maps.

Includes a useful account of the fears in the Australian colonies from the 1820s onwards of American and later French expansion in the Pacific.

POLITICIANS AND DIPLOMATS

BEALE, O.H. *This inch of time: memoirs of politics and diplomacy.* MUP, 1977. 233 p.

Memoirs of a Menzies government minister and ambassador to Washington who was involved in salient international questions of the 1950s.

BOOKER, M. *The great professional: a study of W.M.H. Hughes.* Sydney, McGraw-Hill, 1980. 292 p, illus.

A professional diplomat commenting on a professional politician.

BOOKER, M. *The last domino: aspects of Australia's foreign relations.* Sydney, Collins, 1976. 254 p.

BOOKER, M. *Last quarter: the next twenty-five years in Asia and the Pacific.* MUP, 1978. 228 p, maps.

A senior former diplomat reviews the stance taken from 1939 to 1975 and canvasses likely developments in the region during the remainder of the twentieth century.

CASEY, R.G. *Australian foreign minister: the diaries of R.G. Casey, 1951–60.* Ed by T.B. Millar. London, Collins, 1972. 352 p, illus, map.

CASEY, R.G. *My dear P.M.: R.G. Casey's letters to S.M. Bruce, 1924–1929.* Ed by W.J. Hudson and J. North. AGPS, 1980. 578 p, illus.

CASEY, R.G. *Personal experience, 1939–1946.* London, Constable, 1962. 256 p, illus, maps.

Letters and reminiscences of Australia's first career diplomat overseas, containing candid and informative comments on international issues and Australia's reactions to them.

CROCKER, W.R. *Australian ambassador: international relations at first hand.* MUP, 1971. 211 p.

A practitioner's account of Australian participation in international relations since World War II, with regard to the creation of the United Nations, the founding of Israel and the Soekarno era in Indonesia.

EGGLESTON, F.W. *Reflections on Australian foreign policy.* Ed by N.D. Harper. Melbourne, Cheshire for AIIA, 1957. 216 p, illus.

A theorist and practitioner in Australian foreign relations before and during World War II examines the principles and problems of that seminal period.

HASLUCK, P.M.C. *Diplomatic witness: Australian foreign affairs, 1941–1947.* MUP, 1980. 306 p, illus.

A testamentary account by a diplomat, statesman and historian of a period during which Australia faced a concentration of external problems.

HUGHES, W.M. *Australia and war today: the price of peace.* A & R, 1935. 168 p.

This book, calling for new defence policies and showing remarkable prescience regarding the use of air power in World War II, resulted in Hughes' dismissal from the Lyons government.

HUGHES, W.M. *The splendid adventure: a review of empire relations within and without the commonwealth of Britannic nations.* London, Benn, 1929. 455 p.

Hughes' own description of his activities overseas during and after World War I.

MENZIES, R.G. *Afternoon light: some memories of men and events.* Melbourne, Cassell, 1967. 384 p, illus.

MENZIES, R.G. *The measure of the years.* Melbourne, Cassell, 1970. 300 p.

Essays and reminiscences by Australia's longest serving prime minister including consideration of foreign policy issues and world affairs.

RENOUF, A.P. *The frightened country.* Melbourne, Macmillan, 1979. 555 p.

A former diplomat argues that Australian foreign policy has been obsessed by a concern for security that has jeopardised its relations with Asian and Pacific neighbours and compromised its standing in world affairs.

SPENDER, P.C. *Exercise in diplomacy: the ANZUS treaty and the Colombo Plan.* SUP, 1969. 303 p.

A politician's account of his own role in regard to defence and foreign policy.

STIRLING, A.T. *Lord Bruce: the London years.* Melbourne, Hawthorn, 1974. 509 p, illus.

A critical period in Australian–imperial relations as seen by a former diplomat and associate of Lord Bruce when he was high commissioner in London.

WATT, A. S. *Australian defence policy 1951–63: major international aspects.* Canberra, Dept of International Relations, Research School of Pacific Studies, Australian National University, 1964. 92 p.

WATT, A.S. *Australian diplomat: memoirs of Sir Alan Watt.* Sydney, A & R in association with AIIA, 1972. 329 p, illus.

WATT, A. S. *The evolution of Australian foreign policy, 1938–1965.* Cambridge, CUP, 1967. 387 p.

Three volumes of reminiscences and reflections by a long-serving diplomat. The books throw light on Australian defence attitudes and foreign relations.

WHITLAM, E.G. 'Australia and her region', in J.D. McLaren ed, *Towards a new Australia.* Melbourne, Cheshire for the Victorian Fabian Society, 1972, 1–19.

A statement of regional priorities with particular reference to Papua New Guinea and Indonesia.

DEFENCE AFFAIRS AND INTERNATIONAL RELATIONS

ALBINSKI, H.S. *The Australian–American security relationship: a regional and international perspective.* UQP, 1982. 257 p.

Reviews Australian and American security interests from an American perspective, with reference to the Carter administration.

ALBINSKI, H.S. *Australian external policy under Labor: content, process, and the national debate.* UQP, 1977. 373. p.

An analysis of the external policy trends preceding Labor's term of office in the 1970s, the subsequent dimensions of change and the implications.

BABBAGE, R.E. *Rethinking Australia's defence.* UQP, 1980. 312 p, illus.

An expanded doctoral thesis which argues that Australia's altered strategic environment calls for revised defence policies.

BALL, D.J. *A suitable piece of real estate: American installations in Australia.* Sydney, Hale & Iremonger, 1980. 180 p, illus.

A review of the issues relating to United States' defence communications installations in Australia, with a call for informed debate.

BELL, C. ed, *Agenda for the eighties: contexts of Australian choices in foreign and defence policy.* ANUP, 1980. 256 p.

Essays on topics likely to confront Australian policymakers with difficult decisions during the 1980s.

BELLANY, I. *Australia in the nuclear age: national defence and national development.* SUP, 1972. 144 p, illus.

A summary of the arguments regarding the possible acquisition by Australia of nuclear weapons.

BOYCE, P.J. AND ANGEL, J.R. eds, *Independence and alliance: Australia in world affairs, 1976–80.* Sydney, Allen & Unwin and AIIA, 1983. 368 p.

Articles on Australia's quest for an independent identity in international affairs.

CAIRNS, J.F. *Living with Asia.* Melbourne, Lansdowne, 1965. 179 p.

Passionate advocacy by a Labor leader that Australia's foreign policy towards Asia must change, written at a time when opposition to the United States' actions in Vietnam, and to Australia's involvement, was growing.

CAMILLERI, J.A. *Australian–American relations: the web of dependence.* Melbourne, Macmillan, 1980. 167 p.

A revisionist analysis of the alliance with the United States and its effect on internal and external politics.

DIBB, P. ed, *Australia's external relations in the 1980s: the interaction of economic, political and strategic factors.* Canberra, Croom Helm, 1983. 227 p.

Suggests guidelines for an integrated, nationally co-ordinated foreign policy.

GELBER, H.G. *The Australian–American alliance: costs and benefits.* Harmondsworth, Penguin, 1968. 160 p.

GELBER, H.G. ed, *Problems of Australian defence.* OUP, 1970. 359 p.

Two analyses of the significance of the American alliance in Australian defence and security policies, and of foreign policy as a whole, along with costs and benefits for both parties.

HYDE, J. *Australia: the Asian connection.* Malmsbury, Vic, Kibble Books, 1978. 140 p.

Examines changes in foreign policy during the Whitlam era, 1972–75, and explains the new approach.

LINDEMAN, N. *Japan threat: Australia and New Zealand in the coming world crisis* (enlarged edn). Armidale, NSW, The Author, 1978. 151 p.

The author canvasses the possibility of a renewal of a military threat, perhaps at a nuclear level, from Japan.

MACANDIE, G.L. *The genesis of the Royal Australian Navy: a compilation.* Sydney, Government Printer, 1949. 349 p, illus, maps.

Valuable for its balanced survey of the strategic background to the creation of the navy.

McCARTHY, J.M. *Australia and imperial defence 1918–1939: a study in air and sea power.* UQP, 1976. 227 p, illus.

Discusses some aspects of the debate between World Wars I and II about the use of air and sea power.

MACKIE, J.A.C. ed, *Australia in the new world order: foreign policy in the 1970s.* Melbourne, Nelson in association with AIIA, 1976. 156 p.

Essays assessing changes in the world order which will influence the determination of Australia's foreign policy.

MARTIN, D. *Armed neutrality for Australia.* Melbourne, Dove Communications, 1984. 294 p.

Expands rather incoherently the arguments that he and Teichmann put forward at the Political Studies Association conference at Monash University in 1965.

MEDIANSKY, F.A. ed, *The military and Australia's defence.* Melbourne, Longman Cheshire, 1979. 165 p.

Enlightening essays on the changing role of the military profession in developing Australia's defence capability.

MILLER, J.D.B. *The EEC and Australia.* Melbourne, Nelson in association with AIIA, 1976. 137 p.

Deals with the EEC's importance to Australia and its possible future influence.

PHILLIPS, D.H. *Cold war two and Australia.* Sydney, Allen & Unwin, 1983. 122 p.

Examines the so-called 'new cold war', the rise of neo-conservatism in American foreign policy, and its impact on ANZUS relationships and Australian disarmament policies.

ROSS, A.C. AND KING, P. *Australia and nuclear weapons: the case for a non-nuclear region in South East Asia*. SUP, 1966. 111 p.

In addition to presenting the arguments for a nuclear-free zone the authors make specific proposals for an Australian initiative in bringing it about.

SANTAMARIA, B.A. *The defence of Australia*. Melbourne, Hawthorn, 1970. 147 p, maps.

The author sees possible threats to Australia from the Soviet Union, China and Japan. Believing that dependence on the United States is an insufficient response, he calls for a self-reliant Australian defence policy.

SEXTON, M. *War for the asking: Australia's Vietnam secrets*. Ringwood, Vic, Penguin, 1981. 212 p, illus.

An arguable interpretation of the development of Australian policy in regard to participation in the Vietnam War.

STARKE, J.G. *The ANZUS treaty alliance*. MUP, 1965. 315 p.

An analysis of the ANZUS treaty which accepts its central importance for Australian security.

TEICHMANN, M. ed, *New directions in Australian foreign policy: ally, satellite or neutral*. Harmondsworth, Penguin, 1969. 211 p.

Includes examination from diverse points of view of defence options open to Australia.

TIE, J.V. *et al, Australia's defence resources: a compendium of data*. Canberra, Strategic and Defence Studies Centre, Australian National University, 1978. 147 p.

Provides information regarding not only the armed services but also non-military resources.

VANDENBOSCH, A. AND VANDENBOSCH, M.B. *Australia faces south-east Asia: the emergence of a foreign policy*. Lexington, University of Kentucky Press, 1967. 175 p.

Case studies showing Australia's changing relations with its near Asian neighbourhood in the two decades after World War II.

JOURNALS AND CONFERENCE PROCEEDINGS

AUSTRALIA. Dept of Foreign Affairs. *Select documents on international affairs*, 1955– . AGPS.

Annual publication which contain texts of international treaties and conventions in whose preparation Australia participated but to which it did not become a party.

AUSTRALIA. Dept of Foreign Affairs. *Treaty series*, 1948– . AGPS.

Collection of agreements and treaties entered into by the Australian government with foreign governments.

AUSTRALIA in world affairs, 1950/55– . Melbourne, Cheshire for the Australian Institute of International Affairs, 1957– .

Quinquennial surveys containing numerous essays analysing and reviewing Australia's responses to international problems.

AUSTRALIAN foreign affairs record, 1936– . Canberra, Dept of Foreign Affairs.

The major periodical dealing with current Australian policy on foreign affairs and defence. To 1972 titled *Current notes on international affairs*.

AUSTRALIAN INSTITUTE OF INTERNATIONAL AFFAIRS. 4th Annual Conference, Adelaide 1974. *Advance Australia,*

where? Ed by B.D. Beddie. OUP, 1975. 222 p.

Nine papers about internal and external pressures upon Australian foreign policy formation in the 1970s by contributors who were involved in its analysis and implementation.

AUSTRALIAN INSTITUTE OF POLITICAL SCIENCE. 39th Summer School, Canberra 1973. *Foreign policy for Australia: choice for the seventies*. A & R, 1973. 198 p.

Papers on Asian–Pacific options for Australia in diplomatic, defence, and economic policies, argued by Australian, American and Indonesian academics, with an opening address by E.G. Whitlam.

AUSTRALIAN INSTITUTE OF POLITICAL SCIENCE, 30th Summer School, Canberra 1964. *Australian defence and foreign policy*. Ed by J. Wilkes. A & R, 1964. 172 p.

A conspectus of Australian attitudes in the period before the Vietnam War.

BACKGROUNDER, Aug 1975–   Canberra, Dept of Foreign Affairs.

Background information on Australia's role and interests in foreign affairs. Preceded by *Background 1–12 (July 1971–Mar 1974)*.

MILLAR, T.B. ed, *Australian New Zealand defence co-operation*. ANUP, 1968. 125 p.

These edited proceedings of a conference in Wellington in February 1968 give a conspectus of the common defence problems faced by Australia and New Zealand.

O'NEILL, R. ed, *The strategic nuclear balance; an Australian perspective*. Canberra, Strategic and Defence Studies Centre, Australian National University, 1975. 233 p.

These papers from a conference held by the Strategic and Defence Studies Centre of the ANU explore Australia's situation in a world dominated by the nuclear superpowers.

O'NEILL, R. AND HORNER, D.M. ed, *Australian defence policies for the 1980s*. UQP, 1982. 308 p.

Based on papers presented at a conference at the ANU which examined from diverse viewpoints the need for new defence policies. The contributors included politicians, academics and journalists.

PUBLISHED DOCUMENTS

DOCUMENTS on Australian foreign policy 1937–49. AGPS, 1975–

Six volumes have been published to 1983, covering the period to December 1943, showing the formation of distinct foreign policies under challenges to national security and Australians' perception of their place in the world.

GREENWOOD, G. AND GRIMSHAW, C. eds, *Documents on Australian international affairs 1901–1918*. Melbourne, Nelson in association with AIIA and the Royal Institute of International Affairs, 1977. 779 p, illus, maps.

A collection of mainly non-government documents showing the growth of Australian nationalism in external relations before the postwar shift in the world balance of power.

PETTIT, D. AND HALL, A. eds, *Selected readings in Australian foreign policy* (3rd edn). Melbourne, Sorrett, 1978. 376 p.

Articles and official statements grouped in sections on Australia in the Asian–Pacific region and foreign policy since 1945. First published in 1973.

In the 1950s most expatriate Australians living in New Guinea had at least two servants—a manservant and a maid. Photograph, 1951.
MAGAZINE PROMOTIONS

CHAPTER 29

AUSTRALIA'S OVERSEAS TERRITORIES

JANE LEE

THE HISTORY OF Australian trusteeship dates from just after Federation when the protectorate of British New Guinea was transferred from Britain to the Australian commonwealth. Since that time, Australia has had responsibility for administering a diversity of overseas dependencies, bringing some to independence. With the exception of Papua New Guinea, gaining entry into Australia's overseas territories has been difficult, and it has been particular issues—phosphate in the case of Nauru, tourism in the case of Norfolk Island, interest in Antarctica's natural resources—that have provoked popular interest in the more distant territories. It is not therefore surprising that a large part of the literature relevant to the relationship of Australia to its territories is government-generated.

A starting point for wider reading on the topic is found in published bibliographies. General works such as the *Annotated bibliography of select government publications on Australian territories 1951–1964* (Canberra, 1965) is a useful guide for that period. The National Library of Australia's four-volume *Guide to the collections* compiled by C.A. Burmester identifies subject collections in that institution, with explanatory notes. Works on specific areas include *World catalog of theses and dissertations relating to Papua New Guinea* by William Coppell (Boroko, PNG, Institute of Applied Social and Economic Research, 1978) and *Bibliography of Nauru, western Pacific* by N.L.H. Krauss (Honolulu, The Author, 1970).

The Australian official war histories provide additional reading. Those of World War I recount the importance of German New Guinea and the naval engagements in the waters to the north of Australia, those of World War II, the south Pacific theatre and the New Guinea campaigns.

Another approach to the literature of Australia's overseas territories is through biography and reminiscences. Francis West's biography (1968) of Hubert Murray, Roger Joyce's biographies of William MacGregor (1971) and Sir Paul Hasluck (1976), the last detailing changes in Papua New Guinea while Sir Paul was minister for territories, are of this genre. Griffin (1978) relates the impact of New Guinea on nine widely differing personalities whose occupations had taken them to that country.

AUSTRALIAN ANTARCTIC TERRITORY

By the provisions of the Australian Antarctic Acceptance Act 1933, the Australian government became responsible for the area now known as the Australian Antarctic Territory. Responsibility rested with the Antarctic Division of the Department of External Affairs until 1967, when it was transferred to the Department of Supply. In 1972, the Territory became the responsibility of the Department of Science. Information may be found in the *Annual reports* of these departments, as well as the *Year book Australia*.

The literature of the Australian Antarctic Territory includes works concerned with exploration, such as Sir Douglas Mawson's *Home of the blizzard* (1915; facs, New York, Greenwood, 1969) which is a classic first-hand account of south polar exploration. Scientific research accounts for much activity in the Antarctic and findings are reported in the appropriate journals. References at the end of each chapter in J.P. Lovering and J.R.V. Prescott (1978) provide useful starting points for further reading of these topics. The terrain of Antarctica has proved an exciting subject for photographers, and much of the material is liberally illustrated.

CHRISTMAS ISLAND

Under the Christmas Island Act 1958–59, Australia accepted responsibility from Britain for the administration of Christmas Island which from 1900 until 1946 had been incorporated with the Straits Settlements, from 1946 to 1958 was part of the colony of Singapore and, for a few months before becoming Australian, was a British crown colony.

Information on Christmas Island is contained in the *Year book Australia* and in the *Annual reports* compiled by the Australian Department of Administrative Services until 1977, and thereafter by the Department of Home Affairs.

COCOS (KEELING) ISLANDS

Prior to 1946, the Cocos (Keeling) Islands formed part of the British Straits Settlements, and from then until 1955, part of the British crown colony of Singapore. Australia accepted the Territory by the passage of the Cocos (Keeling) Islands Act 1955.

Information on the Cocos (Keeling) Islands is contained in the *Year book Australia* and in the *Annual reports* published by the Department of External Territories until June 1973, and then by the Department of the Special Minister of State (to December 1974), the Department of Administrative Services (to December 1977) and the Department of Home Affairs. Two United Nations sponsored missions have visited the Cocos (Keeling) Islands, one in 1974 and one in 1980, and the reports of these missions supplement the literature on the Territory.

LORD HOWE ISLAND

Under the State Constitution Act 1902 Lord Howe Island is part of New South Wales, and is included in the metropolitan electoral district of Elizabeth. Material on Lord Howe Island is included in that on New South Wales.

MACQUARIE ISLAND

In 1889 Macquarie Island came under the jurisdiction of the governor of Tasmania and has remained part of the Tasmanian municipality of Esperance ever since. However, material on Macquarie Island is usually included in that of the Australian Antarctic Territory.

NAURU

Until 1968 Australia was responsible for the administration of Nauru under the Trusteeship Agreement with the United Nations (1947), continuing the practice assumed under the League of Nations mandate (1921) of exercising full powers of legislation, administration and jurisdiction in and over the territory on behalf of the administering authority of Australia, New Zealand and the United Kingdom.

Nancy Viviani (1970) includes a comprehensive bibliography of Nauru under such headings as official publications, unpublished official sources and personal manuscripts, including material from the nineteenth century to independence.

Useful sources on Australia's administration of Nauru are the *Official year books* of the years 1923, 1929 and 1938, and the annual reports on Nauru to the League of Nations from 1921 to 1946, and to the General Assembly of the United Nations from 1948 until independence.

NORFOLK ISLAND

Norfolk Island was a British penal settlement until 1856 when it was placed under the jurisdiction of the governor of New South Wales. In 1897 it was made a dependency, and by the passage of the Norfolk Island Act 1913, became a territory of Australia.

Information on Norfolk Island may be found in the *Annual reports* presented by the Department of Territories from 1914 to 1965, the Department of External Territories from 1965 to 1971, the Department of Capital Territory from 1973 to 1975, the Department of Administrative Services from 1975 to 1977 and the Department of Home Affairs since 1978. *Year book Australia* has statistical details.

The colourful story of Norfolk Island has initiated some popular histories and anecdotes, of which Frank Clune's *The Norfolk Island story* (A & R, 1967) is one. Merval Hoare (1978) is more academically based, with a comprehensive bibliography as a starting point for wider reading.

PAPUA NEW GUINEA

The proximity to Australia of Papua New Guinea and its strategic significance have promoted a greater awareness of this trust territory than of the other territories under Australian control, and this interest is reflected in both the quantity and the depth of the literature.

Australia accepted charge of British New Guinea in 1901. In 1921, Australia's authority was expanded to include German New Guinea, to be administered as a mandate under the covenant of the League of Nations. A useful source of information on those early years are the annual reports to the League of Nations for Papua from 1906, and for New Guinea from 1921, and to the United Nations from 1946; the last was reprinted as an Australian Parliamentary Paper. The works by Ian Downs (1980) and J. D. Legge (1956) contain good bibliographies. The works cited cover the history of Australia's interest in Papua New Guinea from the end of the nineteenth century until independence in 1975, and have been selected for their account of the political relationship between Australia and Papua New Guinea as long as it lasted.

Commonwealth Bank branch, Papua New Guinea.
Pix, 8 September 1951.
MAGAZINE PROMOTIONS

AUSTRALIA. *Royal Commission into Matters Relating to Norfolk Island. Report.* AGPS, 1976. 418 p, map.

The report contains a historical outline and chronological summary, as well as recommendations on the future status and constitutional relationship of Norfolk Island with Australia.

BETTS, M.S. *Australians in Antarctica.* AGPS, 1981. 39 p, illus.

An illustrated account of Australia's involvement in Antarctica.

CUMPSTON, J.S. *Macquarie Island.* Canberra, Antarctica Division, Dept of External Affairs, 1968. 380 p, illus, maps.

A history of Macquarie Island by a former member of the Dept of External Affairs.

DOWNS, I. *The Australian trusteeship, Papua New Guinea, 1945–75.* AGPS, 1980. 587 p, illus, maps.

An account of the administration of Papua New Guinea as Australia prepared the Territory, first for self-government and then for independence.

GRIFFIN, J. *Papua New Guinea portraits: the expatriate experience.* ANUP, 1978. xxxi, p, illus.

Personal accounts of nine Australian settlers.

HASLUCK, P.M.C. *A time for building: Australian administration in Papua and New Guinea, 1951–1963.* MUP, 1976. 452 p, illus.

A personal account of New Guinea's advance towards independence while the author was minister for territories.

HOARE, M. *Norfolk Island: an outline of its history, 1774–1977* (2nd edn). UQP, 1978. 185 p, illus, map.

A history with many quotations from relevant documents, and bibliography. First published in 1969.

HOSEL, J. *Antarctic Australia.* Melbourne, Currey O'Neil, 1981. 64 p, illus.

A history of Australia's involvement in the Antarctic, describing life in the south polar region, with photographs by a member of Australia's Antarctic Division.

HUDSON, W.J. ed, *Australia and Papua New Guinea.* SUP, 1971. 198 p.

A collection of essays on Australia's administrative experience in Papua New Guinea, chronologically arranged with extracts from relevant documents.

JOYCE, R.B. *Sir William MacGregor.* OUP, 1971. 484 p, illus.

A biography of the administrator of British New Guinea from 1888 to 1898.

LAW, P.G. *Antarctic odyssey.* Melbourne, Heinemann, 1983. 284 p, illus, maps.

Personal account of the first leader of the party sent to establish the Australian Antarctic research station. Deals with Antarctic policies and the Australian National Antarctic Research Expedition (ANARE).

LEGGE, J.D. *Australian colonial policy: a survey of native administration and European development in Papua.* A & R, 1956. 245 p, map.

A broad outline of the administration of Papua and, since World War II, of Papua and New Guinea. Policy is discussed both chronologically and thematically.

LOVERING, J.F. AND PRESCOTT, J.R.V. *Last of lands: Antarctica.* MUP, 1979. 212 p, illus, maps.

Popular account by two leading academics. Bibliography.

McCARTHY, J.K. *Patrol into yesterday: my New Guinea years.* Melbourne, Cheshire, 1963. 252 p, illus, maps.

An account of the author's time as a district officer in New Guinea from 1927 until his retirement in 1954.

MULLEN, K. *Cocos Keeling: the islands time forgot.* A & R, 1974. 122 p, illus, map.

A history and political survey of Australia's outposts in the southern Indian Ocean and the 'reign' of John Clunies Ross.

PRICE, A.G. *The winning of Australian Antarctica: Mawson's B.A.N.Z.A.R.E. voyages, 1929–31: based on the Mawson papers...* Sydney, A & R for the Mawson Institute for Antarctic Research, 1962. 241 p, illus, maps.

Account of the British, Australian and New Zealand Antarctic Research Expedition, 1929–31.

ROWLEY, C.D. *The Australians in German New Guinea, 1914–1921.* MUP, 1958. 371 p, maps.

An account of the Australian military administration of New Guinea between 1914 and 1921, the allocation of the mandate and the exodus of German nationals from the Territory.

VIVIANI, N.M. *Nauru: phosphate and political progress.* ANUP, 1970. 215 p, illus, map.

An account of Nauru's progress towards independence, describing Australia's interest in the island and those of Britain, Germany and Japan.

WEST, F.J. *Hubert Murray: the Australian pro-consul.* OUP, 1968. 296 p, illus, map.

A biography of Murray, who was lieutenant-governor of Papua from 1908 to 1940.

WILLIAMS, R.M. *Three islands.* Melbourne, British Phosphate Commissioners, 1971. 84 p, illus, maps.

An illustrated account of life on the islands of Nauru, Christmas Island and Ocean Island, issued to commemorate the 50th anniversary of the British Phosphate Commission.

VIII
THE ECONOMY

'The commonwealth's wheel of prosperity', published by
the United Commercial Travellers' Association of
Australasia Ltd in Australia to-day, 1 Nov 1911.
BOOROWA PRODUCTIONS

Aborigines have occupied Australia for 30 000 to 50 000 years; whites for a mere two centuries. The white economy is well documented with written records; the blacks' with fragmentary material. The study of Aboriginal economy is still in its infancy while that of European economic development has been consciously explored from the time J.D. Bigge inquired into New South Wales in 1819.

The brevity of European economic history makes it easier to grasp as a whole. Over two centuries there has been prodigious expansion and a transformation of the economic interests of Australia. This history has been punctuated by successive booms and busts. Formed as a derivative of the British economy Australia has been dependant on flows of capital and migrants from abroad. Although exploitation of natural resources has been vital, exports have been steadily shrinking, with policy and activities turned increasingly inwards. The range of activities has concentrated more and more on urban and particularly metropolitan services and manufacturing. Convict beginnings notwithstanding, white settlers quickly established a market-oriented economy. As whites embarked on resource exploitation and urban activities after 1860, a peculiar form of mixed economy emerged, with government occupying a major role. Australia now has a modern, highly managed economic system, but its export income—particularly of raw materials and foodstuffs—is subject to rapid fluctuations on the world market.

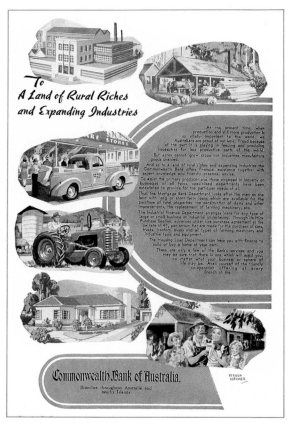

Australia to-day, *26 Oct 1951. In the postwar economy 'when production and still more production is so vitally important to the world', the Commonwealth Bank of Australia offered customers its 'financial assistance', 'expert knowledge' and 'friendly practical advice' in this full-page colour advertisement. As an indication of the severity of the housing shortage that gripped Australia in the late 1940s and early 1950s, the bank placed less emphasis on helping prospective home owners than it did on financing industry, primary production and small business.*

Pete Thomas, *Who owns Queensland?, Coronation Printery, Brisbane 1955.*

CHAPTER 30

ECONOMIC HISTORY

W. A. SINCLAIR

THE WRITINGS OF N.G. Butlin dominate Australian economic history. The publication of his *Investment in Australian economic development* (1964) signalled a major change of direction in the interpretation of Australia's economic past. The then dominant interpretations of E.O.G. Shann (1930; repr, 1963) and B.C. Fitzpatrick (1939; repr, 1971 and 1941; repr, 1969) were to a large extent superseded. There has been no comparable 'revolution' in the subject since and much of the subsequent writing on the subject has been either a direct outgrowth from Butlin or was influenced by him in some way. Indeed, the full corpus of Butlin's contribution to the study of Australian economic history extends well beyond the above monograph and includes a large number of journal articles and seminar papers.

The existence of such a watershed, however, should not obscure an element of continuity in the approach to the writing of Australian economic history. In the importance he placed on quantitative evidence, Butlin can be seen to have been in a direct line of descent from T.A. Coghlan, the government statistician of New South Wales from 1885 to 1906. In that capacity, Coghlan was a dominant influence on the collection and organisation of Australian economic statistics. Much of his knowledge was imparted through regular official publications but his most sustained piece of writing (1918; repr, 1969), can be regarded as the beginning of wisdom in Australian economic historiography. It is a four-volume history up to the time of Federation, based heavily on the author's statistical series. 'For the statistics', as he put it, 'I am my own authority', and authority he was. Although Coghlan stated that his interest in writing was in the factors that had influenced the history of the labour movement in Australia, he interpreted that brief in such a broad way that the book can be regarded as the first systematic economic history of the white settlement of Australia before the twentieth century.

The mainstream of Australian economic history before the arrival of Butlin was, however, to become associated with Shann and Fitzpatrick rather than Coghlan. One reason for this may have been the greater degree of coherence in the stories told by the later two writers, in addition perhaps to their extension into the twentieth century. Both had a strong underlying theme. For Shann, it was the leading role of the enterprising individual in promoting the rapid development of the Australian economy. Fitzpatrick, in contrast, saw the white settlement in Australia as an aspect of the imperialist exploitation of new lands by British interests. In their different ways, each added spice to Coghlan's more sober treatment.

Despite the sharp ideological cleavage between them, the names of Shann and Fitzpatrick became almost synonymous as the source of received knowledge on Australian economic history. Their pictures of the basic characteristics of the economy and its changes over time were remarkably similar. In the nineteenth century, both concentrated almost exclusively on the rural sector and emphasised the dependence of the level of economic activity on external forces. In both accounts there was some recognition of other industrial development in the twentieth century with some reference being made to the growth of manufacturing industry at that time.

The Shann–Fitzpatrick influence was largely negated by the revolution instigated by Butlin. Nevertheless, he was not primarily an iconoclast. His essential innovation (1962) was to base his interpretation on statistical estimates of the size of the economy as a whole and of its separate sectors. These techniques were an outgrowth of the Keynesian revolution in economics of the 1930s and permitted more accurate measurement through the construction of social accounts of key economic variables, the most important being gross domestic product. Shann, an economist, predated this important development in economic thought but Fitzpatrick had no rigorous training in economics. Butlin's estimates allowed measurement to be made of the rate of growth of the Australian economy and of the contribution made to growth by its various sectors. It was the force of this method that enabled Butlin to become the new model for economic historians even though his main work was concerned only with the period from 1861 to 1900. The new approach opened up a range of possibilities not confined to that period, particularly as Butlin himself had carried his original statistical estimates through to the beginning of World War II.

N.G. Butlin's innovative work can therefore be said to have dethroned Shann and Fitzpatrick more by implication than by design. It did point to a major revision of the orthodoxy stemming from earlier writers. With respect to the structure of the economy, Butlin's statistical estimates suggested a more important role for manufacturing and for the construction and service industries than they had received in the accounts of Shann and Fitzpatrick. The fault of the latter was not their recognition of the importance of the primary sector but their virtual omission of a non-rural sector of the economy contributing, on Butlin's estimates, the greater part of gross domestic product. As a concomitant of this, Butlin rescued Australian cities from the unmerited obscurity they had been accorded in the work of Shann and Fitzpatrick.

The historiographical implications of Butlin's work have gone well beyond the economic aspect. Urbanisation is now a major focus of research in Australian history generally. Another feature of Butlin's challenge to orthodoxy was its neglect of the role of internal decision-making on the course of Australian economic development. One result of this was a shift in emphasis from external to internal factors as causes of the severe depression of the 1890s.

Since the publication of Butlin (1964) there have been some further attempts at broad interpretation of Australian economic history, although none purports to overthrow the sway of that author. W.A. Sinclair (1976) covers the longest period, from the original European settlement to recent times. The book departs from Butlin in using a variant of the so-called staple theory of economic development that stresses as its basic economic model the fundamental role of industries based on the exploitation of natural resources. Nevertheless, Sinclair's treatment of the period from 1860 to 1900 is highly derivative of Butlin, as is his more general method. R.V. Jackson exhibits a similarly high degree of consciousness of Butlin in his economic history of Australia in the nineteenth century (1977), being concerned to set the period from 1860 to 1890 in a longer term context. Both Sinclair's and Jackson's books can be regarded as attempts to distil the results of a body of historical research mainly stemming from Butlin.

The analysis of economic development since 1900 is continued in the collection of essays edited by Colin Forster (1970), while E.A. Boehm's work (1971) is somewhat less in the Butlin mould. Boehm focuses mainly on the period since the 1930s and has a strong quantitative emphasis based largely on the official statistics which become more sophisticated from this time. Geoffrey Blainey's work (1983) is also largely an economic history from the beginning of European contact to 1900 with a more individualistic theme of adaptation of the new European arrivals to a strange natural environment. Nevertheless, it too incorporates Butlin's work.

There is a high degree of integration between the general interpretation of Australian economic history, to which discussion has so far been confined, and more specialised monographs. This is at least partly because economic historians have available to them a clearly defined analytical framework related to the subject of economics. It has therefore been possible to incorporate readily the results of detailed research into general interpretation and, on the other hand, for general interpretation to reveal areas requiring more detailed research. A large number of the specialised monographs can be put into two main groups which are complementary to the general theme of economic development. One group is concerned with the short-term fluctuation in the level of economic activity and the other comprises more detailed studies of particular sectors of the economy.

A noticeable feature of the monographs about economic fluctuation is the degree to which they are integral to the study of economic growth. From the general interpretations there emerges a pattern of the occurrence of major depressions at the end of substantial periods of sustained and more or less stable economic activity. Most of the specialised writing concerned with economic fluctuation is directed towards the depressions of the 1840s, 1890s and 1930s. Shann and Fitzpatrick gave some attention to the first two of these and interpreted them as external visitations which put a temporary end to economic growth. An alternative approach to the depression of the 1840s—that it was the result of a weakening in the internal impulse to growth rather than a cause—was suggested by S.J. Butlin (1968). Reference has already been made to a similar, although much more elaborate, explanation of the depression of the 1890s by N.G. Butlin.

This aspect of N.G. Butlin's reassessment of Shann and Fitzpatrick has provoked further controversy. E.A. Boehm's study of economic fluctuation in the 1880s and 1890s (1971) is specifically directed towards this issue and, in the process, it goes into considerable detail on the regional pattern of the depression. Another challenge to Butlin's explanation of the depression is thrown out by A.R. Hall in his history of the Melbourne Stock Exchange (1968).

There are other monographs which bear on the question of economic fluctuation in the later nineteenth century and are more compatible with Butlin's interpretation. J.D. Bailey's study of the 1870s (1956) is relevant to Butlin's emphasis on the high degree of economic stability from about 1860 until the depression of the 1890s. It attempts to explain why the depression of the 1870s in Britian was not clearly communicated to Australia, a phenomenon which could be regarded as having some bearing on the question of the role of external forces in the 1890s. W.A. Sinclair's study of the aftermath of the depression in Victoria (1956), the colony where it was most severe, interprets the recovery as a structural change in the economy necessary for the resumption of the economic growth which had been interrupted in the 1890s.

The depression of the 1930s has been treated somewhat differently from the earlier two in that much of the relevant monograph material consists of books written at the time or soon after the depression and also that much more attention is given to the assessment of government policy. Most important of the contemporary works is that of D.B. Copland (1934), but C.B. Schedvin (1970), treating the same period, has provided a longer perspective.

With respect to the other main grouping of specialised monographs, dealing with particular sectors of the economy, there have been few full-length industry studies. The more significant ones are E. Dunsdorfs's treatment of the wheat industry (1956), B.R. Davidson's more recent study of agriculture generally (1981) and Geoffrey Blainey's history of the mining industry (1978). In addition, there are some more specific studies: G.C. Abbott has dealt with the wool industry up to the middle of the nineteenth century (1971) and A. Barnard with the marketing of wool in the nineteenth century (1958); Colin Forster has written on the growth of manufacturing industry (1964), and Helen Hughes has written a history of the iron and steel industry (1964).

The financial sector of the economy has been well served by economic historians. To a large extent, the books in this field represent histories of particular financial institutions. A major exception, however, is S.J. Butlin's definitive treatment (1968) of the banking system as a whole to the middle of the nineteenth century, notable for the way in which an extremely detailed story is set into the context of the general development of the economy. S.J. Butlin is also the author of a number of scholarly histories of individual private banks (1961).

The government sector has been given increased prominence by N.G. Butlin *et al* (1982), a detailed account and assessment of governmental action since the nineteenth century. Governments were cast as important actors in the earlier economic histories. Coghlan took a rather benign view of governmental action, but Shann and Fitzpatrick, for different reasons, were critical. Shann generally interpreted governmental intervention in the economy as a hindrance to the enterprising action of individuals on which growth and maximum efficiency depended. Fitzpatrick, on the other hand, tended to treat the government as serving the interests of the privileged classes. N.G. Butlin added a new dimension to the discussion by stressing the major role played by government in determining the course of economic development in the second half of the nineteenth century and the high degree of interrelationship between the public and private sectors in that period. In his more recent joint work, that theme is extended into the period since 1900 during which time governments are depicted as becoming less directly involved in economic growth and more concerned with regulation of the economy. Two other important studies of governmental intervention in the economy are the economic volumes of the official history of Australia in World War II, (S.J. Butlin, 1955, and S.J. Butlin and C.B. Schedvin, 1977).

Some of the significant books on Australian economic history do not fit within the coherent framework so far identified. The vast majority of the books cited in the following bibliography range over a period which starts in about 1820. This choice of period arises from the emphasis placed by Australian economic historians on the theme of economic development for, in the sense in which economists normally define that term, it cannot be said to have been evident before that date. The fact that N.G. Butlin highlighted the period from 1860 to 1900 (1964) has contributed to a concentration of research at an even later date. Coghlan, Shann and Fitzpatrick, and some of the more recent economic histories, did include the earlier history of European settlement, but the period from 1788 to about 1820 has attracted what may best be regarded as a literature of its own. The work edited by G.C. Abbott and B. Nairn (1969) is a comprehensive treatment which brings together contributions from a number of the specialists in the field. Some of these—including D.R. Hainsworth (1972) and M. Steven (1965)—have published separate monographs on particular aspects of the economy at that time.

There has been a lively argument about the reasons for the original settlement and the extent to which economic motives were involved. Geoffrey Blainey has argued forcefully for an economic interpretation (1966; repr, 1982) and the main subsequent contributions to debate on the matter have been brought together in a work edited by G.D. Martin (1978).

Neglect of the economic history of the Aborigines has been especially significant in the concentration on the period since 1820. This is not to suggest that the neglect has been confined to that period, for there is very little reference to the Aborigines in the writing of Australian economic history generally. But the most striking manifestation of it is that Australian economic history is generally taken to have started at 1788 at the earliest. There are, however, two important exceptions to this. Geoffrey Blainey's history of the Aborigines up to the time of white settlement (1982), to which *A land half won* (1983) is presented as a sequel, has a strong economic flavour. Secondly, N.G. Butlin's *Our original aggression* (Sydney, Allen & Unwin, 1983) is an important contribution to the study of the early effects of white settlement on the size of the Aboriginal population and may be expected to have an effect on the writing of Australian economic history going well beyond the economic aspect.

Finally, a survey of writing on Australian economic history which confines itself to monographs may give a misleading impression particularly with respect to recent trends in research. Much of the research of economic historians finds its way into publication as articles in learned journals rather than as monographs. Some of these articles have been or continue to be very influential and, although the general economic histories tend to incorporate their findings, they often remain important supplements to monograph material. This is particularly true of new directions in the subject. For instance, urbanisation has become an important area of research in Australian economic history, stemming from N.G. Butlin's writings, most of which have appeared in article form. The book edited by J.W. McCarty and C.B. Schedvin on the subject (1978) may be cited as a monograph but is in fact a collection of journal articles. The main outlet for scholarly articles on Australian economic history is the *Australian economic history review*, which publishes about eight articles a year, the vast majority of which are on Australia.

Economic historians base their interpretations of the past on a variety of sources. Some of these are readily available in published form. The commonwealth statistician, whose organisation is currently the Australian Bureau of Statistics (ABS), has maintained a large number of economic series since about the time of Federation. Before that, the governments of the Australian colonies also made a good deal of statistical material available; these are detailed in chapter 8 of this volume. The reports on a whole range of economic matters which have been commissioned by state and commonwealth governments from time to time and which appear in their respective parliamentary papers are another important source of data. A large number of major inquiries into aspects of the Australian economy in recent years have been published in this way.

Some other sources, held in archival collections to which access may be obtained, are the records of many Australian businesses. They have been preserved in two main places: the Australian National University and the University of Melbourne Archives. Access can also sometimes be obtained to the archival collections of individual companies. The records of the ANZ Bank, for instance, are held at the head office in Melbourne and can be inspected by appointment. In addition, commonwealth and state government archives are important sources. Details of such archives can be found in *Our heritage: a directory to archives and manuscript repositories in Australia* (Sydney, Australian Society of Archivists, 1983).

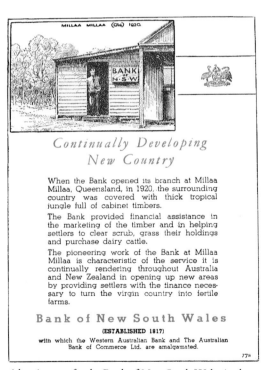

Advertisement for the Bank of New South Wales in the Sydney Mail, 3 Oct 1934. The bank—the first to be established in 1817—proudly stressed its 'pioneering work' in providing finance for new settlers 'to turn virgin country into fertile farms'.

BOOROWA PRODUCTIONS

ABBOTT, G.J. *The pastoral age: a re-examination.* Melbourne, Macmillan, 1971. 221 p, illus, maps.

A provocative reinterpretation of the growth of the NSW pastoral industry in the 1830s and 1840s. Distinguishes between woolgrowing and sheep raising in terms of their profitability.

ABBOTT, G.J. AND NAIRN, N.B. eds, *Economic growth of Australia, 1788–1821.* MUP, 1969. 361 p, maps.

Discusses the background to settlement and of economic aspects of NSW and Van Diemen's Land.

ALFORD, K. *Production or reproduction? An economic history of women in Australia, 1788–1850.* OUP, 1984. 264 p, illus.

Examines the value of women's work, both paid and unpaid, with reference to marital roles, class and property rights.

BAILEY, J.D. *Growth and depression: contrasts in the Australian and British economies, 1870–1880.* Canberra, Australian National University, 1956. 136 p, maps.

A study of the relationship between the British and Australian economies with emphasis on the role of capital inflow into Australia and of economic stability in Australia.

BAILEY, J.D. *A hundred years of pastoral banking: a history of the Australian Mercantile Land and Finance Company, 1863–1963.* Oxford, Clarendon, 1966. 292 p, illus, maps.

A centennial history of one of the leading pastoral finance companies.

BARNARD, A. *The Australian wool market, 1840–1900.* MUP for the Australian National University, 1958. 238 p, illus.

Examines the marketing of Australian wool from its origins as a major export and the shifting centre of gravity of the market.

BLAINEY, G.N. *A land half won.* Melbourne, Sun Books, 1983. 396 p, illus, maps.

A history of nineteenth-century Australia. Emphasis on economic history with weight being given to climatic and other natural influences. First published in 1980.

BLAINEY, G.N. *The rush that never ended: a history of Australian mining.* MUP, 1978. 393 p, illus, maps.

Stresses the continuity of mineral discovery and exploitation since the 1840s. First published in 1963.

BLAINEY, G.N. *Triumph of the nomads: a history of ancient Australia* (rev edn). Melbourne, Macmillan, 1982. 285 p, maps.

A history of the Australian Aborigines to 1788 with emphasis on economic aspects. First published in 1975.

BLAINEY, G.N. *The tyranny of distance: how distance shaped Australia's history* (rev edn). Melbourne, Macmillan, 1982. 366 p, illus, maps.

Elaborates on the distance from Europe and of the sparsity of settlement in Australia. Discusses possible economic reasons for the settlement of Australia. First published in 1966.

BLAINEY, G.N. AND HUTTON, G. *Gold and paper 1858–1982: a history of the National Bank of Australia* (rev edn). Melbourne, Macmillan, 1983. 354 p, illus, map.

Issued as a centennial history in 1958 and based on the bank's internal records but fitted into the framework of Australian economic history. Revised edition updated by Geoffrey Hutton.

BOEHM, E.A. *Prosperity and depression in Australia, 1887–1897.* London, OUP, 1971. 380 p.

A treatment of economic fluctuations focusing on the timing of and reasons for the depression of the 1890s. Emphasis on quantification, using a wide range of statistical material.

BOEHM, E.A. *Twentieth century economic development in Australia.* Melbourne, Longmans, 1971. 248 p.

An account of development particularly, since 1939.

BUTLIN, N.G. *Australian domestic product investment and foreign borrowing, 1861–1938/39.* CUP, 1962. 475 p.

Annual estimates of gross domestic product from 1861 to 1939 based on a wide array of statistics, and on explanation of the methods of estimation used. Includes estimates of private and public capital formation and of capital inflow.

BUTLIN, N.G. *Investment in Australian economic development, 1861–1900.* CUP, 1964. 477 p, maps.

A study of Australian economic history based on the author's statistical estimates (1962). Led to a radical reassessment of the period, and an explanation of the depression of the 1890s.

BUTLIN, N.G. et al, *Government and capitalism: public and private choice in twentieth century Australia.* Sydney, Allen & Unwin, 1982. 369 p.

The role of government in economic development since 1900, including governmental regulation, governmental provision for welfare and the role of public utilities.

BUTLIN, S.J. *Australia and New Zealand Bank: the Bank of Australasia and the Union Bank of Australia Limited, 1828–1951.* Melbourne, Longmans, 1961. 459 p, illus, maps.

A history to the formation of the Australian and New Zealand Bank in 1951. Based on banking records and notable for its integration of monetary history with general economic history.

BUTLIN, S.J. *Foundations of the Australian monetary system, 1788–1851.* SUP, 1968. 744 p, illus, map.

Detailed treatment of Australian monetary and banking history. Based on a wide array of banking statistics, with an explanation of the depression of the 1840s. First published in 1953.

BUTLIN, S.J. *War economy, 1939–1942.* Canberra, Australian War Memorial, 1955. 516 p, illus. (Australia in the war of 1939–1945. Series 4 [civil], vol 3).

BUTLIN, S.J. AND SCHEDVIN, C.B. *War economy, 1942–1945.* Canberra, Australian War Memorial, 1977. 817 p, illus. (Australia in the war of 1939–1945. Series 4 [civil], vol 4).

Two volumes on the economic history of Australia during World War II. Extensive use made of official records.

COGHLAN, T.A. *Labour and industry in Australia, from the first settlement in 1788 to the establishment of the commonwealth in 1901.* OUP, 1918. 4 vols.

The earliest systematic economic history of Australia. Based heavily on the author's knowledge of statistics as the NSW statistician. Reprinted, Melbourne, Macmillan, 1969.

COPLAND, D.B. *Australia in the world crisis, 1929–1933.* CUP, 1934. 212 p.

The effect of the world depression on Australia in the early 1930s with advice on the policy to be followed.

DAVIDSON, B.R. *European farming in Australia: an economic history of Australian farming.* Amsterdam, Elsevier Scientific, 1981. 437 p, illus, maps.

A history based on concepts drawn from agricultural economics.

DUNSDORFS, E. *The Australian wheat-growing industry, 1788–1948.* MUP, 1956. 547 p, maps.

A history making extensive use of statistics, but also incorporating other evidence. Emphasis given to long-term changes in productivity.

FITZPATRICK, B.C. *British imperialism and Australia, 1783–1833: an economic history of Australasia.* London, G. Allen & Unwin, 1939. 396 p.

FITZPATRICK, B.C. *The British Empire in Australia: an economic history 1834–1939.* MUP, 1941. 529 p.

A two-volume history of economic development seen as a facet of British imperialism. Ranks with Shann (1963) as one of the standard treatments, until the appearance of N.G. Butlin's work.

FORSTER, C. *Industrial development in Australia, 1920–1930.*
Canberra, Australian National University, 1964. 256 p.
An analysis of the manufacturing industry with emphasis on
new sophisticated industries and the role of government.

FORSTER, C. ed, *Australian economic development in the
twentieth century.* Australian Publishing Co, 1970. 334 p.
Essays covering overseas trends, capital formation, manufacturing and the service industries and long-term trends.

GIBLIN, L.F. *Growth of a central bank: the development of the
Commonwealth Bank of Australia, 1924–1945.* MUP, 1951.
363 p.
A history of the Commonwealth Bank. The theme is the
development of monetary policy in reaction to economic
growth, depression and war.

GILBERT, R.S. *The Australian Loan Council in federal fiscal
adjustments, 1890–1965.* ANUP, 1973. 337 p.
The events which led to the establishment of the Australian
Loan Council in 1927 and its subsequent activities.

GOLLAN, R. *The Commonwealth Bank of Australia: origins
and early history.* ANUP, 1968. 175 p.
A history of the Commonwealth Bank of Australia from its
origins until 1924.

GOODWIN, C.D.W. *Economic enquiry in Australia.* Durham,
NC, Duke University Press for the Duke University
Commonwealth Studies Centre, 1966. 659 p.
A history of the development of economic ideas in Australia,
surveying the monograph and periodical literature.

HAINSWORTH, D.R. *The Sydney traders: Simeon Lord and his
contemporaries, 1788–1821.* MUP, 1981. 264 p, illus.
Trade in the early days of settlement, emphasising private
economic activity. First published in 1971.

HALL, A.R. *The London capital market and Australia,
1870–1914.* Canberra, Australian National University,
1963. 221 p.
Discusses the way in which funds were borrowed in London for
investment in Australia.

HALL, A.R. *The Stock Exchange of Melbourne and the Victorian
economy 1852–1900.* ANUP, 1968. 267 p, illus.
A history of the Melbourne Stock Exchange with statistical and
analytical treatment of the early economic history of Vic.

HARTWELL, R.M. *The economic development of Van Diemen's
Land, 1820–1850.* MUP, 1954. 273 p, maps.
An economic history stressing the nature and causes of economic
fluctuations and the depression of the 1840s.

HOLDER, R.F. *Bank of New South Wales: a history.* A & R,
1970. 2 vols, illus, maps.
An economic and factual history.

HUGHES, H. *The Australian iron and steel industry,
1848–1962.* MUP, 1964. 213 p, illus, map.
A history with reference to the role of BHP.

JACKSON, R.V. *Australian economic development in the nineteenth century.* ANUP, 1977. 175 p, illus.
An economic history with an outline of the cause of economic
development, and the role of the government.

McCARTY, J.W. AND SCHEDVIN, C.B. eds, *Australian capital
cities: historical essays.* SUP, 1978. 201 p, maps.
Essays on the six capital cities (including decennial estimates of
their size) with reference to economic change.

MACLAURIN, W.R. *Economic planning in Australia,
1929–1936.* London, P.S. King, 1937. 304 p.
The formulation of government policy during the depression
and its aftermath based on interviews and on official sources.

MADGWICK, R.B. *Immigration into eastern Australia,
1788–1851.* London, Longmans, Green, 1937. 270 p.
Treatment of the course and nature of immigration into
Australia from Europe. Facsimile edition, SUP, 1969.

MARTIN, G. ed, *The founding of Australia: the argument about
Australia's origins.* Hale & Iremonger, 1978. 314 p, maps.
Contributions to the controversy over the reasons for European
settlement in Australia. Includes economic arguments.

MATHEWS, R.L. AND JAY, W.R.C. *Federal finance: inter-
governmental financial relations in Australia since federation.*
Melbourne, Nelson, 1972. 370 p.
A discussion of federal–state financial relations.

MILLS, R.C. *The colonization of Australia, 1829–42: the
Wakefield experiment in empire building.* London, Sidgwick
& Jackson, 1915. 363 p.
A study of migration into Australia. Facsimile edition, SUP, 1974.

PATTERSON, G.D. *The tariff in the Australian colonies
1856–1900.* Melbourne, Cheshire, 1968. 174 p.
An account of the imposition of import duties on certain
manufactured goods in each of the Australian colonies.

SCHEDVIN, C.B. *Australia and the great depression: a study of
economic development and policy in the 1920s and 1930s.* SUP,
1970. 419 p.
Analyses the role of government and public institutions, as well
as the economic processes in the downturn and recovery.

SHANN, E.O.G. *Economic history of Australia.* CUP, 1930.
156 p.
An interpretative treatment up to the 1920s. Reprinted in 1963.

SHAW, A.G.L. *The economic development of Australia.* London,
Longmans, Green, 1944. 193 p.
An outline economic history since 1788. Reprinted in many
editions.

SINCLAIR, W.A. *Economic recovery in Victoria, 1894–1899.*
Canberra, Australian National University, 1956. 128 p.
An analysis of the recovery from the depression of the 1890s
indicating the role of primary industry.

SINCLAIR, W.A. *The process of economic development in
Australia.* Melbourne, Cheshire, 1976. 266 p, illus.
Economic development is interpreted as being based on exploitation of natural resources until the 1920s followed by an
emphasis on productivity increase in manufacturing.

SNOOKS, G.D. *Depression and recovery in Western Australia,
1928/29–1938/39: a study in cyclical and structural change.*
UWAP, 1974. 192 p, maps.
Explains the author's estimates of gross domestic products for
WA.

STEVEN, M. *Merchant Campbell, 1769–1846: a study of
colonial trade.* OUP in association with Australian National
University, 1965. 360 p, illus, map.
An account of the activities of one of the leading traders in
Australia in the early days of settlement.

WALKER, E.R. *Australia in the world depression.* London, P.S.
King, 1933. 219 p.
A contemporary account of the 1930s.

WALKER, E.R. *The Australian economy in war and reconstruc-
tion.* New York, OUP, 1947. 426 p.
An account of economic change in the latter part of World War
II and of governmental policy after 1945.

WOOD, G.L. *Borrowing and business in Australia: a study of the
correlation between imports of capital and changes in national
prosperity.* London, OUP, 1930. 267 p.
An analysis of the relationship between capital inflow and
Australian economic development from 1850 to 1930.

Poster, Department of Agriculture, Victoria, c1940.
LA TROBE LIBRARY

CHAPTER 31

AGRICULTURE, FORESTRY, FISHERIES AND VITICULTURE

H. M. RUSSELL, M. LORIMER AND VALMAI HANKEL

THE ASPECTS of Australian economic life treated here form part of the primary industries other than mining. It is not claimed that the subjects treated in this chapter completely cover Australia's rural industries but they do provide an overview of this important aspect of Australia's economic experience. The importance of land-related primary industries, and of fisheries, for the Australian economy has long been recognised and the literature related to these topics is substantial. References in this survey have been restricted to essential titles but readers should also note that some closely related material will be found in chapter 24.

AGRICULTURE AND FORESTRY

European settlement in Australia has, from the beginning, been intimately linked with agricultural production, forestry and fisheries, and interest in wine making occurred very early in the young settlement. Initial concern was directed to feeding and housing the local population but, from early in the nineteenth century, export of agricultural products was pursued by the free settlers. At the end of the first hundred years of European settlement, the Australian wool industry had grown to be the biggest in the world; today Australia also exports wheat, sugar, meat and other agricultural products. Agriculture has retained a critical role in generating export income and our industries are recognised as among the most efficient in the world.

The first settlers had to grapple with an alien climate and harsh environmental extremes. Flood, fire, drought and disease all took a heavy toll. Diseases of both crops and livestock, and the need to develop appropriate husbandry techniques, led to the formation of agricultural colleges and government departments of agriculture in the second half of the nineteenth century. Later the establishment of university faculties in agriculture, forestry and veterinary science, and the creation of the Council for Scientific and Industrial Research (later CSIRO) and other research organisations gave further impetus to scientific research and development and to a better understanding of the Australian environment.

Particularly with regard to forest management we can trace a change in attitude and techniques in a progression from exploitation of a seemingly limitless resource to an increased concern for better conservation. A growing community interest in bush recreation and in the preservation of native species has led to a new awareness of the value of our limited resources of natural forest. Multiple use and an emphasis on native species are replacing early views of native forest as a resource to be exploited and replaced.

During the first century of settlement both agriculture and forestry were largely exploitative in nature, with new areas being continually opened up, cleared and developed. However, drought, slumps in market prices and severe degradation of some areas lead to a contraction of cropping away from semiarid areas and a growing interest in the development of production systems that could be sustained in harmony with the environment. Much of the literature on agriculture and forestry describes the remarkable advances that have been gained in both sustained output and efficiency during the twentieth century. Many production systems and innovations have been recognised and adopted in other parts of the world and Australia now contributes many consultants to agricultural and forestry projects in developing countries.

Changing market structures, preferential tariff agreements and other economic and political constraints have led to dramatic and often painful adjustment from one enterprise to another and successive waves of closer settlement and amalgamation of farm units. The history of Australian agriculture and forestry can thus be viewed in at least three perspectives. Firstly, the history of land settlement and agricultural regions; secondly, the development of unique husbandry and management practices to complement the Australian environment; and thirdly, the economic context within which the industries have grown and changed over time. The reading lists—all three sections—reflect these historical developments.

A number of historical studies of regions or industries have been included with emphasis on those that offer insights to the way of life of the pioneering years. Anecdotal and historical studies have been included so that both contemporary and retrospective aspects can be appreciated.

The second perspective relates to management practices and both current classic texts and a range of selected historical material on the major enterprises of Australian agriculture have been included. The substantial serial literature has not been listed. There are a number of established scientific journals that report Australian research and also many technical journals, magazines and series of pamphlets published by government departments and other organisations for the producers and their service industries. State government departments are responsible for extension and advisory services and they would generally be the most appropriate source of further information.

Finally, a range of texts has been identified that encompasses many of the major issues relating to government policy and the economics of production.

The reading list on forestry does not include works on botanical studies of trees; such titles will be found in chapter 11 of this volume. Further reading on Australian forest resources and their exploitation will be found in the two main journals in the field: *Australian forestry*, 1936– , and *Forest and timber*, 1963– . There is also L.T. Carron's comprehensive *History of forestry in Australia* (ANUP, 1985).

Differences in the types of forests found in various Australian regions led of course to the creation of substantial local accounts of forest resources. Some of these accounts appeared in the journal literature—notably in the two periodicals referred to above—but state forestry departments have also helped to promote better information on these important resources. For details it would be best to enquire from these departments.

There exists as yet no comprehensive bibliography of Australian agriculture and associated enterprises, but *An Australasian bibliography of agricultural economics 1788–1960*, by J.L. Dillon and G.C. McFarlane (Sydney, Government Printer, 1967) is a major and helpful survey of one aspect of the field. Though now somewhat dated it lists a vast range of titles, including government reports, in a classified sequence.

FISHING

The Australian fishing industry, although ranking well behind the major rural industries in value of output, is one of the oldest. It has traditionally been dominated by coastal fisheries, but the growth in export trade, the recently proclaimed 200 nautical mile exclusive fishing zone, and the nature of the industry itself are leading to rapid changes.

In the nineteenth century, fishing was a small industry principally carried out in the coastal estuaries, lakes and ocean beaches which were very fertile compared to the coastal and offshore grounds. Since the 1930s the industry has changed dramatically. The Danish seine method of fishing, introduced in March 1933 in the waters off New South Wales, spread throughout the southeast region of Australia. In the last ten to fifteen years there has been a further shift to the deeper offshore waters—the outer parts of the continental shelf and the slopes of the shelf itself.

The export market has grown rapidly since the 1950s and has created a number of new fisheries, such as the western rock lobster fishery in Western Australia, the prawn fishery in the Gulf of Carpentaria and the abalone fishery in Victoria, New South Wales and Tasmania. The proclamation of the 200 nautical mile exclusive Australian fishing zone has enabled the fishing industry to begin exploring new grounds and new fisheries.

A dominant theme in the development of the Australian fishing industry has been the exploration of the resource base. When the colonists arrived, they came with a predetermined environmental model, based on their experiences in Europe and the Americas. For example, a dominant theme of the writers of the nineteenth and early twentieth centuries was criticism of the industry's failure to exploit the offshore fisheries. Based on experience in the North Sea, they believed that the Tasman Sea was very fertile, although its fish resources are actually poor.

The process of learning about the fish resources of Australia has dominated the literature related to the fishing industry. This genre has a long tradition. It started in the nineteenth century with A. Oliver's *Fisheries of New South Wales* (Sydney, Government Printer, 1871) which was in fact a listing of commercial species. It was even thought necessary to preface the report of the royal commission into the state of the fisheries of New South Wales in 1880 with a similar listing. This approach has been continued in the twentieth century with texts such as Roughley (1966).

In fact, little has been published, in accessible form, on the history of the fishing industry. Like most groups who use the sea, fishermen were not given to leaving extensive records of their activities: in some ways it can be said that many of them went to a great deal of trouble to ensure that there were no records of their activities. Because the industry has been structured on an individual rather than corporate level, there are few company records.

Thus the sources for the history of the fishing industry are primarily government records. These are of two types: the records of the departments concerned with the administration of the industry which consist mainly of catch figures, regulations, the development of new fishing grounds and technologies; and the reports and minutes of evidence of government inquiries, of which there have been a number at both commonwealth and state levels since the 1860s.

The commonwealth, since 1941, has published a newsletter and later a journal. These have provided fishermen with information on new regulations, fishery management plans, discoveries and innovative technology. *Fisheries news-letter* and its successors including the present journal *Australian fisheries* (1945–) have traced the development of the industry through the most dramatic changes in its history.

Some enterprising mariners earn their living by hunting and processing marine mammals—mainly whales and seals --and have made important contributions to the Australian fishing industry for almost two centuries. The literature is not very extensive but the importance of this industry has been stressed by G.J. Abbott and N.B. Nairn, *Economic growth of Australia 1788–1821*, (MUP, 1969) and earlier by G. Greenwood, *Early American–Australian relations. . .*, (MUP, 1944). Pearlers and trepangers also play a significant part in marine-based industries. The few references that have been thought useful in this context have been incorporated with the references to fishing proper.

The literature reflects the practical concerns of an industry continually developing and expanding. It should be noted, however, that books related to fishing as a sport are listed in chapter 48 of this volume, though attention is drawn here to two special works which represent borderline cases. The scientific nature of the cultivation of salmon in Australian inland waters has been the subject of two books by Sir Samuel Wilson: *The Californian salmon* (Melbourne, Sands & McDougall, 1878) and *Salmon at the antipodes* (London, E. Stanford, 1879). These are classic accounts of the introduction and breeding of this species.

VITICULTURE

The introduction of grape growing into Australia as a commercial undertaking occurred within the first decade of European settlement. The issue of the *Sydney Gazette* dated 5 March 1803 contains the first of three articles entitled 'Method of preparing a piece of land for the purpose of forming a vineyard'. Little did the early vignerons dream that the industry would in the 1980s produce close to 375 million litres of wine from 70 000 hectares of land.

Though the early centre of winegrowing was, quite naturally, the Parramatta valley and then the Hunter valley, the Barossa valley in South Australia and the Yarra valley in Victoria became at least equally famous and began production in the 1840s. Small vineyards came into production in Tasmania at about that period, and farmers in Queensland and Western Australia soon followed suit.

In 1875 the Australian wine industry suffered its greatest disaster as *Phylloxera vastatrix*, the grapevine louse, began to affect seriously almost all vineyards except those in South Australia. The damage lasted for several decades but has now been repaired and the insect controlled.

Writing on wine and winemaking continued in the 1820s, with James Busby producing the first Australian wine book (1825; facs, 1979). It aimed to show how to produce wine and thus give value to tracts of land which otherwise 'would in all probability remain for ever useless'. Busby also compiled Australia's first *Catalogue of vines in the Botanic Garden, Sydney, introduced into the colony of New South Wales in the year 1832* (Sydney, Government Printer, 1842), which contains a brief evaluation of listed grape varieties. Busby's opinions still direct winegrowing in Australia.

George McEwin's *The South Australian vigneron and gardeners' manual* (1843; facs, Adelaide, LBSA, 1962), written when South Australia was barely seven years old, is the most important of at least three books that appeared in 1843. Based on practical experience in the colony, it was to counteract the inappropriate and misleading advice proffered by English armchair authorities. Another contemporary account was William Macarthur's *Letters on the culture of the vine, fermentation, and the management of wine in the cellar* (Sydney, Statham & Foster, 1844) which appeared under the pseudonym of 'Maro'.

From the late 1850s until the end of the nineteenth century there was a proliferation of Australian publications on wine, both original works and translations, containing descriptions on vineyards in Australia and overseas. Among the forty or so monographs published in the last four decades of the century the writings of Dr Alexander Charles Kelly (1861, 1867; facs, 1980), Hubert de Castella (1979) and Ebenezer Ward (1862; facs, 1979) were arguably the most important, and have the most to say to today's student of winegrowing and oenography.

South Australia seems to have been better served than other Australian vine-growing areas with specific books on individual vineyards and vignerons, including the Coonawarra Estate, Seppeltsfield and others. General overviews like O.L. Ziegler's *Vines and orchards of the garden state: South Australia's fruit growing industry* (Adelaide, Mail Newspapers Ltd, 1929) reflect the interest that made South Australia the principal wine-producing state.

Towards the end of the century, handbooks specifically designed to assist winegrowers in defined areas included: G. Searle, 'The grape-vine and its cultivation in Queensland' in A. Midgley, *Queensland guide for the use of farmers, fruit-growers, vignerons and others* (Brisbane, Government Printer, 1888); F. de Castella, *Handbook on viticulture for Victoria* (Melbourne, Government Printer, 1891); G. Sutherland, *South Australian winegrower's manual...* (Adelaide, Government Printer, 1892); J. Despeissis, *Handbook of horticulture and viticulture of Western Australia* (Perth, Traylen, 1895); and F.B. Kyngdon, *Wine culture in New South Wales* (Sydney, NSW Agriculture Department, 1899). They are evidence of awareness that the age of generalisation about Australian winegrowing had passed.

With some exceptions, mainly of a technical nature, the publication of books on Australian wine and viticulture seemed virtually to cease for the first 50 years of this century. The exceptions included two influential books by the founder of the Australian Wine Research Institute, J.C.M. Fornachon. His *Bacterial spoilage of fortified wines* (Adelaide, Australian Wine Board, 1943) and *Studies on the sherry flor* (Adelaide, Australian Wine Board, 1953) established applied biology in Australian wineries: nineteenth-century wine science contained in such books as Dr Kelly's was largely applied chemistry.

At about this time the first books appeared of a very different wine writer, Walter James, whose numerous volumes were fetchingly entitled and were intended for the fashion-conscious dilettante and for the general reader with an interest in the history and appreciation of wine. Many of them were reprinted and formed the vanguard of the plethora of 'popular' wine books from which Australians have suffered for the last 25 years. Another boost came from the doyen of wine writers, André Simon, whose well-illustrated book, *The wines, vineyards and vignerons of Australia* (Melbourne, Lansdowne, 1966), written after a visit to Australia, was one of the first to attempt a description of the history and current production of all Australian wine-growing areas.

On the crest of the 'new wave' of popular wine writers, the most noticeable have been such sometimes dictatorial taste-shapers as Len Evans, James Halliday, Max Lake and Dan Murphy. Their accounts of winegrowing areas, wineries, particular wines and specific vintages of particular wines have, however, helped to increase awareness and appreciation of our wines by the general public. Evans (1984) remains the most comprehensive and useful work of its type.

In the last 30 years many books and pamphlets on specific winegrowing areas and their wineries have appeared. These range from public relations exercises with selective information, to serious attempts at family, industry and area histories. Firms such as Penfold (1951), Hardy (1953, 1978), Saltram (1959), Chateau Tahbilk (1960) and Mildara (1980) have attempted to explain their histories and their aspirations to the public.

James Halliday (1983) has probably produced the exemplar of the attractively presented wine area studies, of which Bryce Rankine's *Wines and wineries of the Barossa Valley* (Brisbane, Jacaranda, 1971), W.S. Benwell's *Journey to wine in Victoria* (1978) and Halliday and Jarratt (1979) are other examples. Two volumes of architectural studies by Katrina McDougall, *Winery buildings in South Australia, 1836 to 1936*, (Adelaide, University of Adelaide, Faculty of Architecture & Town Planning, 1980, 1983) form a useful survey which could well be emulated for other areas.

Today's Australian wine writing is directed more to wine consumers than to the winegrowers who were the primary audience of our earliest wine literature. The writers of the past were anxious to encourage the enthusiasm of a few, the actual and potential winegrowers. Today's wine writers are trying to satisfy a national enthusiasm.

J.C. Williamson Ltd. magazine, *1927. Romalo Wines Ltd believed that its 'rare and distinctive' tawny port, 'the aristocrat of Australian wines', would appeal to the elite among theatre patrons.*
BOOROWA PRODUCTIONS

AGRICULTURE

AGRICULTURAL policy, issues and options for the 1980's: Working Group report to the Minister for Primary Industry, September 1982. AGPS, 1982. xxii, 167 p, illus, maps.
Major statement of policy options usually referred to as the Balderstone report after its chairman, J.S. Balderstone.

AITKEN, Y. et al, Agricultural science: an introduction for Australian students and farmers (Metric edn). Melbourne, Cheshire, 1975. 297 [15] p, illus, maps.
Textbook for schools dealing with broad issues of agricultural biology, the farm environment, plant and animal production.

ALEXANDER, G. AND WILLIAMS, O.B. eds, The pastoral industries of Australia: practice and technology of sheep and cattle production. SUP, 1973. 567 p, illus, maps.
Major text including chapters on environment and history, sheep and cattle industries, productivity and future prospects.

ANDERSON, R. On the sheep's back. Adelaide, Rigby, 1967. 268 p, illus.
Survey of the major issues facing the wool industry in the 1960s.

AUSTIN, H.B. The merino, past, present and probable. Sydney, Grahame Book Co, 1943. 247 p, illus.
Historical review of Merino breeding in Australia up to World War II. New edition published in 1947.

AUSTRALIA. Dept of Primary Industry. Agricultural extension services in Australia. AGPS, 1980. 121 p, maps.
An analysis of each state department of agriculture and of the agriculture advisory services it provides. The roles of the private sector and the federal government are also described.

AUSTRALIA. Dept of Primary Industry. Agricultural research services in Australia. AGPS, 1980. 173 p.
An overview of the organisation of agricultural research and of the services of federal, state and educational institutions.

AUSTRALIA. Dept of Trade and Resources. Australian farming systems. AGPS, 1982. 7 vols, illus, maps.
An excellent directory divided into seven small volumes with distinctive titles such as the tropics, the subtropics, the temperate region, the arid and semiarid region, and irrigation.

AUSTRALIA. Division of National Mapping. Atlas of Australian resources. Vol 3. Agriculture. 3rd series. Canberra, The Division, 1982. 24 p, illus, maps.
Reference volume including maps and textual material on the distribution of pastures, livestock and crops.

AUSTRALIA. Working Group on All Aspects of Rural Policy in Australia. The principles of rural policy in Australia: a discussion paper. AGPS, 1974. 390 p, in various paginations.
The Working Group (Convenor: S. Harris) reviewed all aspects of rural policy with emphasis on government involvement, financial measures and structural issues.

BARNARD, A. ed, The simple fleece: studies in the Australian wool industry. MUP in association with Australian National University, 1962. 640 p, illus.
Interdisciplinary studies based on a seminar held over three years and involving many specialists.

BAXTER, P. Growing fruit in Australia. Melbourne, Nelson, 1981. 200 p, illus.
Practical text written for the non-commercial grower.

BEATTIE, W.A. Beef cattle breeding and management. Sydney, Reed, 1980. 279 p, illus.
Written in non-specialist language on all aspects of beef cattle management in Australia. First published in 1954.

BELSCHNER, H.G. Pig diseases. A & R, 1976. 257 p, illus.

An authoritative volume on the most important diseases of pigs. First published in 1967.

BELSCHNER, H.G. Sheep management and diseases (10th edn). A & R, 1976. 838 p, illus.
Standard text on sheep husbandry and diseases. First published in 1950.

BILLIS, R.V. AND KENYON, A.S. Pastures new: an account of the pastoral occupation of Port Phillip. Melbourne, Macmillan, 1930. 272 p.
A description of the development of the sheep and cattle industries in Victoria. Facsimile edition, Melbourne, Stockland, 1974.

BOWMAN, F.T. Citrus-growing in Australia. A & R, 1956. 311 p, illus, maps.
A reference book for orchardists, students and small-scale growers.

CALLAGHAN, A.R. AND MILLINGTON, A.J. The wheat industry in Australia. A & R, 1956. 486 p, illus, maps.
A history to the end of the 1940s.

COLE, C.E. ed, Melbourne markets, 1841–1979: the story of the fruit and vegetable markets in the City of Melbourne. Melbourne, Melbourne Wholesale Fruit and Vegetable Market Trust, 1980. 196 p, illus, maps.
Traces the sources of produce, control, development and politics of the fruit and vegetable trade in Melbourne.

CRAWFORD, J.G. et al, Wartime agriculture in Australia and New Zealand, 1939–50. Stanford, California, Stanford University Press, 1954. 354 p, maps.
One of a series on the issues of food and agricultural production during World War II, with considerations of manpower and critical supplies.

CULLITY, M. A history of dairying in Western Australia. UWAP, 1979. 465 p, illus, maps.
A history of the development and subsequent contraction and consolidation of the dairy industry in WA.

DAVIDSON, B.R. European farming in Australia: an economic history of Australian farming. Amsterdam, Elsevier Scientific, 1981. 437 p, illus, maps.
Presents an historical analysis of the attempts to establish a European type of agriculture. Bibliography.

DAVIDSON, B.R. The northern myth: a study of the physical and economic limits to agricultural and pastoral development in tropical Australia. MUP, 1966. 283 p, maps.
Controversial study outlining a number of issues affecting agricultural developments in tropical Australia. First published in 1965.

DUNCAN, R. The Northern Territory pastoral industry 1863–1910. MUP and Monash University, 1967. 190 p, maps.
A description of the effect of distances and a harsh environment on the cattle industry in the NT.

DURACK, M. Kings in grass castles. Melbourne, Currey O'Neil, 1981. 395 p, illus, maps.
A story of pioneering in the cattle industry in western Qld and the Kimberley region of WA in the second half of the nineteenth century. First published in 1959.

EASTERBY, H.T. The Queensland sugar industry: an historical review. Brisbane, Government Printer, 1933. 226 p, illus.
A review of the first seventy years of sugar production in Qld.

FARQUHAR, R.N. Agricultural education in Australia. Australian Council for Educational Research, 1966. 322 p, (A.C.E.R. Research series, 80).

Based on a survey in the mid-1960s by the ACER, the study covers secondary and tertiary education.

GARDNER, J.A.A. AND DUNKIN, A.C. eds, *Australian pig manual*. Canberra, Australian Pig Industry Research Committee, 1979. 191 p, illus.
Covers management, marketing, feeding, housing and other topics.

HEWITT, A.C.T. *Feeding farm animals in Australia*. A & R, 1953. 260 p, illus.
Compilation on the food requirements of various classes of livestock and the feed value of various foodstuffs available.

HILL, E. *Water into gold*. Melbourne, Robertson & Mullens, 1937. 328 p, illus, maps.
The story of irrigation on the Murray River and the rise of the dried vine fruit industry. Revised edition, 1965.

HOLT, A.J. *Wheat farms of Victoria: a sociological survey*. Melbourne, School of Agriculture, University of Melbourne, 1946. 179 p, illus, maps.
A sociological study of the living and working conditions of farming households during the early 1940s.

JENKINS, J. *Diary of a Welsh swagman 1869–1894*. Abridged and notated by W. Evans. Melbourne, Sun Books, 1977. 216 p, illus, map.
A picture of rural life in Victoria during the later part of the nineteenth century. First published in 1975.

JOYCE, A. *A homestead history, being the reminiscences and letters of Alfred Joyce of Plaistow and Norwood, Port Phillip, 1843 to 1864*. Ed by G.F. James. MUP, 1942. 200 p, illus, map.
Describes pioneer pastoral life in central Vic. New edition published in 1963.

KELLY, W.S. *Rural development in South Australia*. Adelaide, Rigby, 1962. 160 p.
Historical review of agricultural settlement and development in SA from the 1830s to the 1950s.

KING, C.J. *The first fifty years of agriculture in New South Wales*. Sydney, Government Printer, 1950. Unpaged.
Although not particularly original, contains valuable information on the spread of settlement. First published in *Review of marketing and agricultural economics*, Aug 1948–Dec 1949.

LAMP, C. AND COLLET, F. *Field guide to weeds in Australia* (rev edn). Melbourne, Inkata, 1979. 376 p, illus.
A handbook of plants treated as weeds in the agricultural context. Simple descriptions that avoid technical botanical terms. First published in 1976.

LAZENBY, A. AND MATHESON, E. M. eds, *Australian field crops*. Vol 1. *Wheat and other temperate cereals*. A & R, 1975. 552 p, illus, maps.
Textbook on the physiology and production of wheat and other cereal crops. See also Lovett & Lazenby (1979).

LEEPER, G.W. *Introduction to soil science*. MUP, 1948. 222 p, illus, maps.
A standard work for readers with a general science background. New edition published in 1964.

LEEPER, G.W. *The Australian environment*. CSIRO in association with MUP, 1949. 183 p, illus, maps.
The history and early post-World War II development of agricultural industries. Revised edition, 1970.

LEIGH, J.H. AND NOBLE, J.C. eds, *Plants for sheep in Australia: a review of pasture, browse and fodder crop research, 1948–70*. A & R, 1972. 402 p, illus, maps.
An extensive compilation by numerous authors. Bibliography.

LOVETT, J.V. ed, *The environmental, economic and social significance of drought*. A & R, 1973. 318 p, illus, maps.
A review of the occurrence and impact of drought on agricultural production in Australia.

LOVETT, J.V. AND LAZENBY, A. *Australian field crops*. Vol 2. *Tropical cereals, oilseeds, grain legumes and other crops*. A & R, 1979. 328 p, illus, maps.
Textbook on production of maize, sorghum, rice, sugarcane, cotton, sunflower and other crops. Companion volume to Lazenby & Matheson (1975).

MAKEHAM, J.P. et al, *Coping with change: Australian farming since 1970*. Armidale, NSW, Gill Publications, 1979. 211 p.
An analysis of the impact of recession on Australian farmers providing an introduction to current issues affecting rural policy.

MOORE, R.M. ed, *Australian grasslands*. ANUP, 1970. 455 p, illus, maps.
Survey of Australian grassland ecology, regions and factors affecting productivity.

MUNZ, H. *The Australian wool industry*. Melbourne, Cheshire, 1964. 237 p, illus, maps.
A general survey first published in 1950.

NORTHCOTE, K.H. et al, *A description of Australian soils*. Melbourne, CSIRO, 1975. 170 p, illus, map.
Comprehensive and systematic.

NOWLAND, W.J. *Modern poultry management in Australia*. Adelaide, Rigby, 1978. 384 p, illus.
Basic text for farmers, their advisers and students.

PRENDERGAST, M. *A guide of keeping goats in Australia*. Melbourne, Nelson, 1981. 143 p, illus.
Deals with the selection and management of small flocks of goats.

REID, R.L. ed, *A manual of Australian agriculture* (rev edn). Melbourne, Heinemann, 1981. 850 p, illus, maps.
More than 100 contributors make this an authoritative reference source Bibliographies. First published in 1961.

ROBERTS, S.H. *The squatting age in Australia 1835–1847*. MUP, 1935. 455 p, illus, maps.
A key reference on the history of the occupation of land for pastoral production. Revised edition, 1964, reprinted in 1970.

ROBERTSON, D.S. *Australian farm management*. Sydney, Murray, 1979. 319 p, illus, maps.
A practical manual for the farmer.

ROLLS, E. *A million wild acres: 200 years of man and an Australian forest*. Ringwood, Vic, Penguin, 1984. 465 p, illus, maps.
A classic history of the occupation and use of the Pilliga forest in NSW. Bibliography.

ROLLS, E. *They all ran wild: the story of pests on the land in Australia*. A & R, 1984. 546 p, illus, map.
A major statement on the impact of various animals and birds introduced into Australia, with emphasis on the rabbit. First published in 1977.

RUSSELL, G. *The narrative of George Russell of Golf Hill: with Russellania, and selected papers*. Ed by P.L. Brown. London, OUP, 1935. 469 p, illus, maps.
Story of an early squatting family in western Vic, based on extensive correspondence.

SILLCOCK, K.M. *Three lifetimes of dairying in Victoria*. Melbourne, Hawthorn, 1972. 182 p.
A history of the dairying industry from 1834 to 1970, with a list of source material.

SIMPSON, G. AND SKELSEY, W.C. eds, *The Queensland Merino*

Stud Sheepbreeders' Association 50th anniversary souvenir book. Toowoomba, The Association, 1983. 175 p, illus.

Deals with Australia's most famous breed of sheep, its history and management. Contains also a brief history of the association.

SIMS, H.J. AND WEBB, C.G. *Mallee sand to gold: the Mallee Research Station, Walpeup, 1932–82.* Melbourne, Victorian Government Printing Office for the Dept of Agriculture, 1982. 187 p, illus, maps.

A history of agricultural research in this region of Vic.

SMITH, K. comp, *The settler's guide: a biased selection from the Agricultural gazette of New South Wales, 1890-1910.* Melbourne, Nelson, 1981. 176 p, illus.

Articles covering a range of old-time skills and bush lore on building, management of livestock and other farming practices.

STACE, H.C.T. *et al, A handbook of Australian soils.* Adelaide, Rellim Technical Publications for CSIRO and the International Society of Soil Science, 1968. 435 p, illus, map.

Commemorates the 9th International Congress of Soil Science.

STONE, C. *Running the brumbies: true adventures of a modern bushman.* Adelaide, Rigby, 1979. 144 p, illus.

An account of itinerant life in the outback of Australia after World War II.

SUTHERLAND, J. A. *Introduction to agriculture.* A & R, 1972. 366 p, illus, maps.

Simple presentation of scientific principles for secondary schools. First published in 1962.

TRIBE, D.E. AND COLES, G.J.R. *Prime lamb production: the husbandry of crossbred and dual purpose sheep.* Melbourne, Cheshire, 1966. 239 p, illus, maps.

A practical guide for farmers.

VICTORIA. Dept of Agriculture. *Beekeeping in Victoria, 1981* Melbourne, The Department, 1981. 139 p, illus.

Deals with biology, management, diseases and other facets of the honey industry and agriculture.

VICTORIA. Dept of Agriculture. *Honey flora of Victoria.* Melbourne, The Department, 1922. 148 p, illus.

Excellent key to the identification and characteristics of Victorian eucalypts and other honey or pollen producing plant species. A sixth revised edition was published in 1973.

VICTORIA. Dept of Agriculture. *Irrigated pastures.* Melbourne, The Department, 1970. 273 p, illus, maps.

Covers topics such as soils, land preparation, pasture species, management, pests and diseases.

WADHAM, S.M. *Australian farming, 1788–1965.* Melbourne, Cheshire, 1967. 156 p, maps.

An important retrospect largely based on the author's wide experience on several key committees and commissions during the 1930s and 1940s.

WADHAM, S.M. *et al, Land utilization in Australia.* MUP, 1939. 360 p, illus, maps.

Comprehensive consideration of land utilisation for major agricultural industries in Australia. Reprinted several times.

WATT, R.D. *The romance of the Australian land industries.* A & R, 1955. 271 p, illus, maps.

Excellently written in simple language for the general public.

THE WEEKLY TIMES *farmers' handbook* (rev edn). Melbourne, Herald and Weekly Times, 1983. 260 p, illus.

Popular handbook first published in 1934, providing advice on the care and management of livestock, pasture species, handcrafts and a wide range of practical hints and remedies.

WHEELHOUSE, F. *Digging stick to rotary hoe: men and machines in rural Australia.* Sydney, Transpareon, 1977. 222 p, illus.

A study of Australian inventions that have had a significant impact on agriculture throughout the world. First published in 1966.

WHITTET, J.N. *Pastures.* Sydney, Dept of Agriculture, 1964. 632 p, illus, maps. (Farmers' handbook series.)

Deals with pasture species, their establishment and management for the major ecological regions of NSW.

WILLIAMS, D.B. ed, *Agriculture in the Australian economy* (rev edn). SUP, 1982. 422 p, illus, maps.

Surveys covering the complex nature of the agricultural sector. First published in 1970.

WINTER-IRVING, W.A. *Beyond the bitumen.* Adelaide, Rigby, 1971. 200 p, illus.

WINTER-IRVING, W.A. *Further out.* Melbourne, Nelson, 1975. 222 p, illus.

Two autobiographical narratives of experiences on stations in northern Vic and Qld during the 1920s and 1930s.

WOOD, C.T. *Sugar country: a short history of the raw sugar industry of Australia, 1864–1964.* Brisbane, Queensland Cane Growers' Council, 1965. 83 p, illus, map.

A reprint of material from the *Producers' review.*

YEATES, N.T.M. AND SCHMIDT, P.J. *Beef cattle production.* Sydney, Butterworths, 1974. 323 p, illus, maps.

Includes a description of each of the major cattle regions.

FORESTRY

AUSTRALIA. Forestry and Timber Bureau. *The use of trees and shrubs in the dry country of Australia.* By N. Hall *et al.* AGPS, 1972. 558 p, illus, maps.

Discusses issues such as browse shrubs, amenity planting, conservation and maintenance in arid and semiarid zones.

BOLAND, D.J. *et al., Forest trees of Australia.* Melbourne, Nelson CSIRO, 1984. 687 p, illus, maps.

Comprehensive account of Australia's forest trees, describing 223 species.

CALDER, M.E. *Big timber country.* Adelaide, Rigby, 1981. 198 p, illus.

A history of forests and forestry in WA and the exploitation of the jarrah and karri forests in the southwest region.

FALL, V.G. *The mills of Jarrahdale: a century of achievement 1872–1972: a history.* Perth, Royal Western Australian Historical Society, 1972. 94 p, illus.

Brief account of an important source of hard timber in WA.

HALL, N. *et al, Forest trees of Australia* (4th edn). AGPS, 1975. 334 p, illus, maps.

Important work, giving details of 133 native trees including distribution and botanical notes. First published in 1962.

HILLIS, W.E. AND BROWN, A.G. eds, *Eucalypts for wood production.* Melbourne, CSIRO, 1978. 434 p, illus.

Textbook on the production and utilisation of eucalypts based on reviews by a wide range of specialists.

LEWIS, N.B. *A hundred years of state forestry: South Australia: 1875–1975.* Adelaide, Woods and Forests Dept, 1975. 122 p, illus, map. (Bulletin, 22.)

A history including the introduction of the radiata pine.

VICTORIA. Forest Commission. *Forests and man.* Melbourne, The Commission, 1978. 35 p, illus, map.

A brief review of the forests of Vic, including history, characteristics and management. Bibliography.

FISHING AND MARINE INDUSTRIES

AUSTRALIA. Department of Trade and Customs. Fisheries. *Biological results of the fishing experiments carried out by the*

F.I.S. Endeavour, 1909–1914. Sydney, 1911–1933. 6 vols, illus.

Reports prepared by the Australian Museum in Sydney on specimens collected off the east and south coasts of Australia, with detailed descriptions of marine life in coastal waters. Vol 1 and vol 2 pt 5, are entitled *Zoological result...*

BAIN, M.A. *Full fathom five.* Perth, Artlook Books, 1982. 380 p, illus, maps.

A history of the Australian pearling industry, mostly centred on Broome but also covering the nineteenth-century dominance of the Torres Strait operations.

CADWALLADER, P.L. *J.O. Langtry's 1949–50 Murray River investigations.* Melbourne, Fisheries and Wildlife Division, Vic, 1977. 70 p, illus, map. (Fisheries and Wildlife paper, Vic, 13.)

Results of a major ecological study of the Murray–Darling River system including fishing methods, distribution of fish species, biology and fishing methods.

COHEN, P. *The marine fish and fisheries of New South Wales, past and present, in their commercial aspect.* Sydney, Government Printer, 1892. 30 p, map.

A view of the NSW fishing industry biased by the writer's experience of the British fishing industry.

COLWELL, M. *Whaling around Australia.* Adelaide, Rigby, 1969. 178 p, illus.

Popular, but reliable and informative.

DAKIN, W.J. *Whaleman adventurers: the story of whaling in Australian waters and other southern seas related thereto, from the days of sails to modern times.* A & R, 1934. 263 p, illus, maps.

Serves as the standard history of Australian whaling. New edition published in 1963.

GILL, J.C.H. 'Notes on the sealing industry of early Australia', *Royal Historical Society of Queensland J* 8, 2, 1966–67, 218–45.

HAINSWORTH, D.R. 'Exploiting the Pacific frontier: the New South Wales sealing industry 1800-1821', *J of Pacific history* 2, 1967, 59–75.

The economic and social significance of the early sealing industry is well examined and reassessed in these two scholarly contributions.

McKNIGHT, C.C. *The voyage to Marege: Macassan trepangers in northern Australia.* MUP, 1976. 175 p, illus, maps.

A history of 'Australia's first modern industry', the gathering of bêche-de-mer from about 1700. A brief supplementary chapter surveys European involvement in the industry.

POWNALL, P. *Fisheries of Australia.* Farnham, England, Fishing New Books, 1979. 149 p, illus.

Describes the present state with limited information on past development.

ROUGHLEY, T.C. *Fish and fisheries of Australia* (rev edn). A & R, 1966. 328 p, illus, maps.

Details of the most important fish found in Australian waters and a history of the commercial fishing industry. First published in 1951 as an enlargement of *Fishes of Australia*, published in 1916.

STEAD, D.G. *A brief review of the fisheries of New South Wales, present and potential.* Sydney, Government Printer, 1910. 31 p, illus.

STEAD, D.G. *The edible fishes of New South Wales: their present importance and their potentialities.* Sydney, Government Printer, 1908. 123 p, illus, map.

Stead's two books—now very rare—are examples of historical surveys of the fishing industry, and of native and introduced species of freshwater and coastal fish as found at the turn of the century.

THOMSON, J.M. *Fish of the ocean and shore.* Sydney, Collins, 1974. 208 p, illus.

A general text explaining the varying types of fishing. Already dated, because of the rapid changes in the industry since 1974.

VITICULTURE

BENWELL, W.S. *Journey to wine in Victoria.* Melbourne, Pitman, 1978. 226 p, illus, maps.

Emphasises the historical background of winegrowing in Victoria and development of wine styles. First published in 1960.

BISHOP, G.C. *Australian winemaking, the Roseworthy influence: the contribution of Alan R. Hickinbotham and Roseworthy Agricultural College to winemaking in Australia.* Adelaide, Investigator, 1980. 344 p, illus, maps.

Story of Australia's first agricultural college.

BUSBY, J. *A treatise on the culture of the vine, and the art of making wine.* Sydney, R. Howe, Government Printer, 1825. xxxiv, 270 p.

Australia's first wine book based on the ideas of French writers was intended to show 'the respectable portions of the community' how to produce wine. Facsimile edition, David Ell Press, 1979.

DE CASTELLA, H. *Notes of an Australian vine grower.* Trans by C.B. Thornton-Smith. Melbourne, Mast Gully Press, 1979. xix, 75 p, illus.

De Castella's enthusiasm is balanced by his experience of the practical problems encountered by winegrowers. First published as *Notes d'un vigneron Australien* in 1882.

EVANS, L. comp, *Complete book of Australian wine.* Sydney, Lansdowne, 1984. 791 p, illus, maps.

This comprehensive work includes sections on history of winemaking and an annotated alphabetical list of wine producers and their wines. First published in 1973. Title varies.

HALLIDAY, J. *Coonawarra: the history, the vignerons & the wines.* Sydney, Yenisey, 1983. 188 p, illus, maps.

An account of Australia's premier winegrowing district.

HALLIDAY, J. AND JARRATT, R. *The wines & history of the Hunter valley.* Sydney, McGraw-Hill, 1979. 140 p, illus, maps.

Describes 'the past and present vineyards, wineries and wine men of the Hunter Valley' in the form of a useful but brief guide.

JAMES, W. *The bedside book of Australian wine: an Australian winemaker's diary.* Adelaide, Rigby, 1974. 199 p, illus.

A reprint of two witty books by James, who introduced many people to Australian wine literature. This volume contains *Barrel and book* (1949), and *Nuts on wine* (1950).

KELLY, A.C. *The vine in Australia.* Melbourne, Sands, Kenny & Co, 1861. 215 p.

KELLY, A.C. *Wine-growing in Australia, and the teachings of modern writers on vine-culture and wine-making.* Adelaide, E.S. Wigg, 1867. 234 p.

Dr Kelly's two books draw on the writings of French and Australian winegrowers as well as on his own experience in SA. Facsimile editions of both works, David Ell Press, 1980.

WARD, E. *The vineyards and orchards of South Australia.* Adelaide, Advertiser and Chronical Offices, 1862. 78 p.

Descriptions of the environment that produced SA's great wine estates. Facsimile edition, Adelaide, Sullivan's Cove, 1979.

WARD, E. *The vineyards of Victoria as visited by Ebenezer Ward in 1864.* Adelaide, Sullivan's Cove, 1980. xiii, 102 p.

Reprint of *Age* articles describing vineyards in pre-phylloxera days. A companion volume to the preceding item.

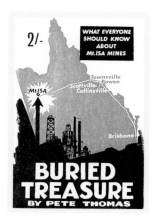

CHAPTER 32

MINES AND MINING

G. R. HENNING

SOON AFTER EUROPEAN settlement, mining in Australia began with the discovery and exploitation of the coal deposits in and around Newcastle. The first exports of coal occurred in 1799. Although the discovery of the coal deposits was greeted enthusiastically by the authorities in Sydney and London, the prospects did not generate anything like the enthusiasm and subsequent economic development that followed the gold discoveries of the 1850s. From that decade onwards Australia was internationally recognised as a source of mineral wealth. Its riches included most of the known minerals and metals but the size of its deposits were only dimly appreciated for some decades.

Any historical bibliography of Australian mining has therefore to encompass not only two centuries in time but also a variety of aspects and experiences. The bibliography that follows has therefore been divided into the following parts: General works; Gold rushes and goldfields; Metals and minerals other than gold; Processing; Gas and petroleum; Government policy; and Administration, which includes mining law and financial matters. In some instances it will be obvious that a title could be put under more than one heading. The categories provide a functional division of the material but they should not be seen as mutually exclusive.

A wide variety of books is listed in the first part. A very useful starting point is Geoffrey Blainey (1978). The other titles in this category range from nineteenth-century regional studies to memoirs and modern assessments of mineral deposits. Also of historical importance (though included in the second part because of its relationship to goldmining) is the only entry related to labour history of the social and political outcome of mining. This is Carboni's account (1855; repr, 1983) of the events at Eureka together with some recent revisionary essays on that subject. References concerning the political, social and labour history and the industrial relations of mining will be found in other bibliographies and are not included in these listings.

In the nineteenth century the glamour metal was gold and the history of Australian mining therefore changed dramatically in the 1850s. The spotlight was initially on New South Wales but it quickly passed to Victorian goldfields and numerous books describe the nineteenth-century goldfields and the mining of gold in the twentieth century. In a sense the watershed of the 1850s and 1860s has caused the listing of this category to be biased towards Victoria, because there are so many titles from which to choose. Those presented here include regional histories, particularly of Victoria, Queensland and Western Australia, memoirs and reminiscences, and illustrative material such as photographic collections and reproductions of goldfields paintings.

Those researching aspects of the history of Victoria are additionally fortunate because of the excellent bibliography by J. Monie *Victorian history and politics: European settlement to 1939* (Bundoora, Vic, La Trobe University Library, 1982). However, any study of the gold-rush era should probably commence with Serle (1978) and Bate (1978). It should proceed from there to nineteenth-century accounts and other subsequent works and then follow the gold rushes out of Victoria and up the Great Dividing Range to north Queensland, across to the Kimberleys and south to Kalgoorlie and Coolgardie by the 1890s.

The drama of one gold rush after another can overshadow other mining activity although the latter has been considerable in both centuries. The listing devoted to non-goldmining includes the base metals, the unglamorous but important minerals coal, tin and uranium, and the environmentally sensitive mineral sands. Most of these entries are regional studies of which historically the most famous and perhaps the most important was the Broken Hill area. More recently the issues surrounding the mining of uranium have been canvassed but unfortunately there has been little or no historical treatment of them. The most that can be gained is from the occasional general source on mining or the government environmental inquiries, which are easily accessible.

Some of the current controversy over mining has been related to the export of unprocessed raw materials because the social and economic benefits from doing this are far less than those possible when some phases of processing are completed in Australia prior to export. In the past questions about processing have usually been dealt with in terms of metallurgical developments and the three items listed in this category confirm that approach. There is a useful coverage of these developments, including the new processes such as flotation which were developed in Australia, in Blainey (1978). The broader issues surrounding processing are also subsumed in the administration category because aspects such as the economics of processing and its implications for the economy and the environment are now the subject of increasing publicity and debate.

Also of more recent interest has been the search for oil and natural gas. The concern about oil deposits dates back for decades but, apart from the general works on mining, relatively little of substance has been published on this subject. Most of the sources listed offer a relatively brief introduction, with the exception of R. Wilkinson (1983), the first full-length account to become available. Government reports are a useful source and the report of the Royal Commission on Mineral Oils and Petrol and Other Products of Mineral Oils (Canberra, 1933, 1935) is one of the most detailed for the period prior to World War II.

Government involvement has been part of Australian mining from the days of convict collieries to contemporary concerns about uranium. Much of the government function has been regulatory. There have been numerous official inquiries into mining accidents and disasters, the working of the land laws or the licence and lease systems, the battery crushing operations and the gradual evolution of industrial standards. Exploration was also carried out by colonial governments and various surveys of the mineralisation in different areas were completed. In this century government geologists have done much to continue and extend those early surveys. There are some very helpful guides to the formal government inquiries; the best place to start is with D.H. Borchardt and E. Zalum's *Checklist of royal commissions, select committees of parliament and boards of inquiry* (1958–78; see chapter 8).

In recent years several important mining studies have been undertaken for governments; these are usually known by their abbreviated titles, for example, the Fox Report (Canberra, 1976) and the Fitzgerald Report (Canberra, 1974). The latter is worth noting because it attempts to assess the non-economic costs and benefits of mining as well as the economic ones. The items listed under government policy in the bibliography indicate something of the breadth and depth of government involvement in mining today. One should also remember that government departments of mines and government geological surveys have, since colonial days, produced annual reports which are included in the parliamentary papers. Some have also published their own periodicals and occasional papers.

Closely related to government policy are a number of matters—law, finance and economics

—which experience governmental intervention in varying degrees because those aspects are usually subject to regulation. Again there is a continuity with the nineteenth century, demonstrated by the need for books on management practice, mine accounting and law. The concept of a limited liability status for mining shares was first enacted in Victoria in 1871. It represented a radical change in company law throughout Australasia and had wide ramifications for those concerned with investment in the mining sector. The mining laws themselves changed over time and those who needed to understand the provisions of the various acts benefited by some of the comprehensive consolidations that were published.

Just as the legal framework changed so too did the accounting framework and by the late nineteenth century accounting systems designed for mining operations were beginning to emerge. The movement received an impetus from the depression of the 1890s and the widespread collapse of companies, especially speculative ones. Among the causes of failure were the fraudulent practices of staff, executives and directors. In this century there has been an increasing emphasis on greater accountability to shareholders and governments, and the accounting profession has gradually developed new areas of accounting theory and new professional practices.

Since World War II the financial sector has become more closely involved with large mining projects and the pressure on the accounting profession has continued. This is not altogether surprising because the history of mining in Australia often appears to have been a series of booms and slumps, and financial scandals related to mining have been in evidence since the 1850s. The publicised accounts seem to have been more frequent in the recent past because the size of the defalcation or collapse has been many times greater in monetary terms and hence deemed worthy of extensive comment in the media. However, even the Poseidon boom of the late 1960s has not yet been the subject of serious historical research despite all the drama associated with its rise and fall. Similarly, the corporate failures of the 1970s have still to be investigated by historians and until then the important one for mining history, that complex of mines known as Mineral Securities Ltd, will remain something of an enigma.

Although this bibliography is restricted to books and monographs there are numerous other sources of mining history. Because one's understanding is greatly enhanced by a familiarity with the locations in which mining took place, maps and atlases, especially historical ones, are indispensable. The Division of National Mapping in Canberra produces current topographical maps that often include old as well as modern mining sites. These maps can also indicate the other geological and geographical features which have helped to determine a particular field's or individual mine's character and development. A few historical atlases are already available, including D.A.M. Lea *et al, Atlas of New England* (Armidale NSW, Dept of Geography, University of New England, 1977) and J.S. Duncan *ed, Atlas of Victoria* (Melbourne, Government of Victoria, 1982). In addition *Australians: a historical atlas* will be of a considerable benefit to those researching the history of mining.

Because of the importance of statistical data for the evaluation of Australian mines and mining, the Australian Bureau of Statistics (ABS) publishes a number of tables related to the mining industry. Other important compilations of figures, issued by the Bureau of Mineral Resources, Geology and Geophysics, are the *Australian mineral industry annual review* and *Australian mineral industry quarterly review*. The various state departments of minerals and energy (their titles vary slightly from state to state) also issue regular data on mining and mineral production, consumption and exports. There is a summary and overview of mining statistics in *Australians: historical statistics* and attention is also drawn to chapter 8 of this volume for references to printed sources of mining statistics.

Other printed sources of information include a diverse periodical literature. One of the earliest periodicals was the *Australasian insurance and banking record*, which began publication in 1876 and continues to the present. This business journal has always carried information about mining operations and prospects, in addition to the reports and financial statements of mining company meetings. The *Australian mining standard* ran from 1885 to 1962; the *Mining journal and investors review* was first published in 1895; and the *Bulletin*'s famous *Wild cat monthly* included speculative mining for many years. There were various other journals in the nineteenth century and they continued to spawn in the twentieth. Others have emerged since the 1960s, for example, the *Mining investment digest* (1966–   ) and *Mining views of Australia* (1972–   ). Those of a more technical nature include the proceedings and occasional publications of the Australasian Institute of Mining and Metallurgy; the transactions of engineering institutes also contain articles on aspects of mining. Some with a scientific bias can be found in the proceedings of the various royal societies in the colonies. Articles of historical significance have also been included in the proceedings of the royal geographical societies.

A wide range of standard historical journals should be consulted and to assist in this task there is a guide to Australian historical journal literature to 1974 compiled by T. Hogan *et al* entitled *Index to journal articles on Australian history* (Armidale, NSW, Dept of History, University of New England, 1978). This index has been continued to cover the period 1974–81 by V. Crittenden and J. Thawley. In addition, there is the general index to the literature of the social sciences, *APAIS,* which is described in detail in chapter 7. These guides are the quickest way to check on periodical items relating to the history of mining.

Newspapers are another kind of periodical which often contain useful information about mining. Unfortunately few of the nineteenth-century newspapers are indexed and so there is no quick way of using them. The indexes for this century are incomplete in many cases. Nevertheless, a second-best option is to seek out newspaper cuttings. Two important examples for mining are held in the Mitchell Library, Sydney. The first was made by G.D. Meudell, a journalist and speculative mining investor. This collection dates from the 1880s to the mid-1920s and includes early reports on brown coal and petroleum deposits from 1913. The second is that of J. Plummer, another journalist, who was also the mining editor of the *Year book of Australia* for two decades. His writings on mining appeared mainly between 1900 and 1914.

Pamphlets are sources similar in length to journal articles. They have been written on all aspects of mining; many originated in the nineteenth century when pamphleteering was a common form of persuasion. All the state libraries and tertiary institution libraries and some municipal libraries maintain pamphlet collections. Many also have local history collections, which can be another useful source of information. Historical societies are also places where scarce pamphlets and short local histories can be found and while much of this kind of material might be episodic, anecdotal and only partly corroborated, it remains useful for cross-checking with other sources and providing leads and ideas.

Another facet of many local history programs is oral history. Geoffrey Blainey is one of several writers who have made use of interviews with old miners and prospectors. However, the oral approach is an underdeveloped resource; much of the work is conducted by local historical societies and appears only in their publications. Sometimes the regular historical journals carry an article based on oral evidence, but these are rare. Just as oral history can be part of the local historical scene, so too can manuscripts and archival material. Written and printed reminiscences, regional records, travellers' and settlers' letters and diaries, household and farm or business records can all be valuable sources. It is impossible to list here those pertaining to mining history; suffice to point out that local history collection, regional and university archives, and the state archives in each capital city will all reward the serious seeker after mining history. A very useful directory to archival and manuscript repositories is *Our heritage* (Sydney, Australian Society of Archivists, 1983). It includes mention of whether the repository also has an oral history program.

While oral history can be discursive, even disjointed, theses are usually well organised and tightly constructed. Many historical theses have been devoted to mining regions, especially local studies. Most are available only in university libraries or through interlibrary loans. Postgraduate theses concerned with mining can be readily traced by consulting the *Union list of higher degree theses in Australian university libraries* (see chapter 8 of this volume). For undergraduate theses one should consult the guide compiled by M. McKernan and D. Collins, *Honours theses in history,* published in Sydney for the Australian Historical Association in 1979. Although not exhaustive

—some universities did not contribute entries and there are none from the colleges of advanced education—it is nevertheless the place to start looking for undergraduate research. As mining has inspired engineers and metallurgists as well as historians, political scientists, lawyers, economists and sociologists, information is likely to be found in a wide variety of theses, especially at the postgraduate level.

The superstition surrounding women working underground has been held long and hard in Australia, ignoring the fact that women were coalminers in England before Australia was settled. The legislation forbidding women working underground in mines was enacted in the Mines Act 1842 and may have been influential in the formation of attitudes in Australia. Historians have neither discovered nor written about the work women might have done in and around mines. The more usual role ascribed to women in the mining sector has been based on a sexual division of labour and so they are mentioned either as homemakers or for their concerted social and political action during industrial relations disputes.

Before 1850 there do not appear to have been examples of women working in the mining sector to which the excellent economic history of women by K. Alford, *Production or reproduction?* (OUP, 1984) can attest. However, the period since 1850 may well reveal more than historians have yet noticed. For instance, female miners and prospectors were observed at work on the Ballarat and Bendigo goldfields. Many mining areas in Australia were remote and devoid of creature comforts, basic urban facilities and extensive mining equipment. These factors, together with the absence of European women, help to explain the employment of Aboriginal women as prospectors and fossickers in northwestern Australia in the late nineteenth century. It seems a little strange that in those areas the assumed role of women was only that of child-minders, humpy cleaners or cooks when there are examples of women doing manual labour in other parts of the rural sector. It is even stranger if one remembers that in Cornwall it was traditional for women to work at least in surface jobs such as ore-dressing for the smelter, while in Australia there has been no record of women performing similar functions in the Cornish copper mining areas of Moonta, Wallaroo or any other.

As a result the reader cannot yet be referred to printed sources which discuss these matters. Even during the two world wars women did not do any form of mining work. The conventional wisdom is that the role of women in the mining sector only really only changed in the late 1960s when women began obtaining jobs in other previously male-dominated industries. This coincided with the Poseidon boom. Then and since, women have trained and been employed as field geologists, geophysicists and geochemists, but this partial transition over a long period of time still awaits historians. Until then the full range of human activity in the history of mining will be incomplete.

Forlorn suburban development in the shadow of the Port Kembla steelworks, c1955. Australia's preoccupation with industrial growth in the 1950s is evident in this placemat.
BOOROWA PRODUCTIONS

GENERAL WORKS

AUSTIN, J.B. *Mines of South Australia, including also an account of the smelting works in that colony. . .* Adelaide, C. Platts and others, 1863. 109 p, map.

The author, a mine agent and broker, provides descriptions, including geological information and yields, of many mines in SA.

ALEXANDER, J. AND HATTERSLEY, R. *Australian mining, minerals and oil.* Sydney, David Ell Press, 1981. 536 p, maps.

A compendium on operating mines. It includes historical summaries and financial information on all minerals, oil and gas. First published in 1980.

BEDFORD, R. *Naught to thirty-three.* Sydney, Currawong Publishing Co, 1944. 349 p, illus.

Memoirs of a journalist on mining in various parts of Australia in the late nineteenth and early twentieth centuries. Reprinted in 1976.

BLAINEY, G.N. *The rush that never ended: a history of Australian mining.* MUP, 1978. 393 p, illus.

Important general history of mining in Australia. First published in 1963.

BROWN, H.Y.L. *Record of the mines of South Australia.* Adelaide, Government Printer, 1887–1908. Maps.

A description of the mines, claims and companies in SA by its government geologist. Includes geological information, production and value figures for metals and mineral exports and data concerning the NT. Fourth edition published in 1908.

CALVERT, A.F. *The mineral resources of Western Australia.* London, George Philip & Son, 1893. 179 p.

A useful survey of the mineral areas, including coal, in WA.

CARROLL, B. *Australia's mines and miners: an illustrated history of Australian mining.* Melbourne, Macmillan, 1977. 112 p, illus, map.

Although all aspects of mining are covered the text is brief. The illustrations are excellent.

DAINTREE, R. *Queensland, Australia: its territory, climate and products.* London, G. Street, 1872. 117 p, illus, maps.

More than one-quarter of this handbook by the former Qld government geologist is devoted to a survey of mining including production and prospects.

DREXEL, J.F. comp, *Mining in South Australia: a pictorial history.* Adelaide, Dept of Mines and Energy, 1982. 303 p, illus, maps.

Commemorates the centenary of the appointment of H.Y.L. Brown as the first government geologist in SA. Brief text but all minerals found in SA receive attention.

GOYDER, G.A. *The prospector's pocketbook.* Adelaide, Government Printer, 1888. 63 p.

Basic information includes mineralogy, assaying, weights and measures, simple apparatus, and the determination of payable quantities of minerals. Later enlarged edition entitled *Australian prospector's handbook* published in 1898.

JACK, R.L. *The mineral wealth of Queensland.* Brisbane, Warwick and Sapsford, 1888. 71 p, maps.

A résumé by the government geologist of all the mining fields in Qld, including production figures and values.

JOHNS, R.K. ed, *History and role of government geological surveys in Australia.* Adelaide, Government Printer, 1976. 111 p, illus.

Brief histories and details of professional staff of the six state geological surveys, the NT Geological Survey, and the commonwealth Bureau of Mineral Resources.

KALIX, Z. et al, *Australian mineral industry: production and trade, 1842–1964.* Canberra, Bureau of Mineral Resources, Geology and Geophysics, 1966. 473 p. (Bulletin, 81).

A comprehensive compilation of production and trade figures for minerals and metals with some data disaggregated into individual mining fields.

LAWSON, G.A. *The past and present position of the mineral industry on the West Coast, Tasmania.* Melbourne, McCarron Bird, 1896. 69 p, illus, maps.

A short essay followed by details of individual companies in the Mt Lyell, Zeehan, Dundas, Curtin-Davis, Mount Read and Mount Black districts.

McKERN, R.B. *Multinational enterprise and natural resources.* Sydney, McGraw-Hill, 1976. 264 p.

An examination of mineral and energy resources in Australia, including financial and management aspects with appendices relating to projects in the 1960s and foreign ownership within the industry.

O'NEIL, B. *In search of mineral wealth: the South Australian Geological Survey and Department of Mines to 1944.* Adelaide, South Australian Dept of Mines and Energy, 1982. 359 p, illus maps.

A meticulous history of government institutions in geological exploration. Strongest on administrative affairs, but the science is not ignored.

PRIDER, R.T. ed, *Mining in Western Australia.* UWAP, 1979. 304 p, illus, maps.

Numerous aspects of the industry are discussed in this book ranging from geology and metallurgical processes to mining law and employment. Includes history of nineteenth-century developments.

PRIOR, S.H. ed, *Handbook of Australian mines: a historical, statistical, and descriptive record of the mines and minerals of Australia, Tasmania, and New Zealand.* Sydney, Australian Mining Standard, 1890. 228 p.

Descriptions of mines and their performances. Although the work includes all colonies it only covers the principal metals.

PULLEINE, F.A. *The Australasian mining directory. . .* Adelaide, F.A. Pulleine, 1888. 400 p.

Contains useful summaries of the legal details, capital and structure, directors, head offices and mine locations of various Australasian companies but mainly in NSW, Vic and SA.

RAGGATT, H.G. *Mountains of ore.* Melbourne, Lansdowne, 1968. 406 p, illus, maps.

Surveys the important mineral deposits of the late 1960s and discusses Australia's mineral economy and the role of foreign capital. The coverage includes coal, tin, mineral sands, oil and natural gas.

REYNOLDS, J. *Men & mines: a history of Australian mining, 1788–1971.* Melbourne, Sun Books, 1974. 232 p, illus, map.

A popular overview of mining in Australia.

RICHMOND, W.H. AND SHARMA, P.C. eds, *Mining and Australia.* UQP, 1983. 320 p, illus, maps.

Essays on many aspects of mining—historical, economic and urban—including a discussion of its place in Australian literature.

WOODWARD, H.P. *Mining handbook to the colony of Western Australia.* Perth, Government Printer, 1895. 216 p, illus, maps.

Discusses details of the geology and mineralogy of each district including the history of its mineral resources, sections on goldfields, technical and legal information for prospectors and details of communications to and within the colony.

GOLD RUSHES AND GOLDFIELDS

BATE, W.A. *Lucky city: the first generation at Ballarat, 1851–1901*. MUP, 1978. 302 p, illus, maps.

Standard history of Ballarat with valuable sections on mining history.

BURKE, E.K. *Gold and silver: an album of Hill End and Gulgong photographs from the Holtermann Collection*. Melbourne, Heinemann, 1973. 265 p, illus, maps.

Superb collection of photographs of mining and goldfields life during the 1870s by Bernard Otto Holtermann and Beaufoy Merlin.

CARBONI, R. *The Eureka Stockade: the consequence of some pirates wanting on quarter-deck a rebellion*. Melbourne, The Author, 1856. 126 p.

A participant's account of the Eureka rebellion. Reprinted in 1942 and 1963.

CARNEGIE, D.W. *Spinifex and sand: a narrative of five years' pioneering and exploration in Western Australia*. London, C. Arthur Pearson, 1898. 454 p, illus, maps.

The first four sections deal with goldmining in the Kalgoorlie, Coolgardie and Kanowna areas during the early 1890s. Facsimile edition, Perth, Hesperian, 1983.

CLARKE, F.McK. *Early days on Bendigo*. Ed by F. Cusack. Melbourne, Queensberry Hill, 1979. 86 p, illus, map.

The edited memoirs of one of the first to work on what became the Bendigo goldfields. He and his party were prospecting there before the rush commenced in December 1851.

CLARKE, W.B. *Researches on the southern gold fields of New South Wales*. Sydney, Reading and Wellbank, 1860. 305 p, map.

Discussions of his geological explorations in quest of gold; includes an appendix on topics ranging from fossils to gold working and diamonds.

COTTOME, T.G. *Letters from Grenfell: from a New South Wales goldminer in the 1870s*. Ed by G.J. Butland. SUP, 1971. 125 p, illus, maps.

A history of the gold rush and social and urban development as told in seven years of letters from one of the pioneering miners.

CUSACK, F. *Bendigo: a history*. Melbourne, Heinemann, 1973. 262 p, illus.

A history of Bendigo and its goldmining from the 1840s until World War I.

FAUCHERY, A. *Letters from a miner in Australia*. Trans from the French by A.R. Chisholm. Melbourne, Georgian House, 1965. xxv, 105 p, illus.

The author worked on several Victorian goldfields and became the most important photographer of the mid-1850s. First published as *Lettres d'un mineur en Australie* in 1857.

FLETT, J. *The history of gold discovery in Victoria*. Facs, Melbourne, Hawthorn Press, 1970. 495 p, illus.

A well-documented compilation of gold exploration, discovery and mining during the nineteenth century. Facsimile edition, Melbourne, Poppet Head, 1979.

GILL, S.T. *The goldfields illustrated: the sketches of S.T. Gill*. Melbourne, Lansdowne, 1972. 108 p, illus.

Forty-eight black and white sketches of various aspects of goldfields life and the diggers in Melbourne, with a short text by John Currey. Michael Cannon has also written on Gill in another book of his sketches entitled *The Victorian gold fields, 1852–53*. (Melbourne, Currey O'Neil, 1982).

GRAY, J. R. *History of the Wedderburn gold fields*. Ed by F. Cusack. Melbourne, Queensberry Hill, 1981. 92 p, illus, map.

Reminiscences of an American schoolteacher who worked on most of the central Victorian goldfields and became a pioneer settler of Wedderburn. First published in the *Wedderburn Express*, 1888.

HARGRAVES, E.H. *Australia and its gold fields: a historical sketch of the progress of the Australian colonies...* London, H. Ingram and Co, 1855. 240 p, illus, map.

Includes a review of ancient and modern goldmines in the world, of geological and gold discoveries in Australia as well as chapters on methods of gold-working and the land question.

HOLTHOUSE, H. *Gympie gold*. A & R, 1973. 209 p, illus, maps.

HOLTHOUSE, H. *River of gold: the story of the Palmer River gold rush*. A & R, 1967. 217 p, illus.

Two well-based accounts of goldmining in the Gympie and Palmer River areas in the 1860s and 1870s.

HOWITT, W. *Land, labour and gold: or two years in Victoria: with visits to Sydney and Van Diemen's Land*. London, Longman, Brown, Green and Longman, 1855. 2 vols.

A series of letters, 1852 to 1855, which contains observations on the goldfields, the urban development of Melbourne and the economic progress of the colony. Facsimile edition, SUP, 1972.

KEESING, N. ed, *History of the Australian goldrushes: by those who were there*. A & R, 1976. 412 p, illus, map.

An interesting selection of eyewitness accounts reflecting all aspects of the goldfields but emphasising the social conditions. First published as *Goldfever...* in 1967.

KELLY, W. *Life in Victoria, or, Victoria in 1853, and Victoria in 1858, showing the march of improvement made by the colony within those periods, in town and country, cities and diggings*. London, Chapman and Hall, 1859. 2 vols, map.

Detailed account of Kelly's visit to Vic with chapters on the goldfields, various aspects of mining and social conditions. Facsimile edition, Kilmore, Vic, Lowden, 1977.

KORZELINSKI, S. *Memoirs of gold-digging in Australia*. Trans and ed by S. Robe. UQP, 1979. 160 p, illus.

An account by a Polish army officer who worked on various goldfields in Vic during the 1850s, dealing with many aspects of goldfields life and revealing the ethnic diversity of the population.

LEES, W. *Goldfields of Queensland, 1858 to 1899*. Brisbane, Outridge Printing Co, 1899. 223 p, illus, maps.

Reports with some production figures and financial information. There are special sections on the Chillagoe, Cloncurry and Copperfield areas.

MACARTNEY, J.N. *The Bendigo goldfield registry: comprising a description of the goldfield, history of the opening, progress and present position of the chief reefs*. Melbourne, Charles F. Maxwell, 1871. 180 p, maps.

A summary of individual mines with lists of mining companies, tribute companies and tribute terms. Another volume, with a similar title was issued in 1872.

MORRELL, W.P. *The gold rushes*. London, Black, 1940. 427 p, maps.

A history of nineteenth-century gold rushes in the Americas, Australasia and South Africa. Useful for comparative purposes.

SERLE, A.G. *The golden age: a history of the colony of Victoria, 1851–1861*. MUP, 1978. 469 p, illus, maps.

The standard history of this decade. Bibliography. First published in 1963.

SMYTH, R.B. *The goldfields and mineral districts of Victoria, with notes on the modes of occurrence of gold and other metals and minerals*. Melbourne, Government Printer, 1869. 644 p, illus, maps.

A comprehensive mining compendium containing details of discoveries, the forms of mining and technology involved and also the mining of non-auriferous metals. Facsimile edition, Melbourne, Queensberry Hill Press, 1979.

STONE, D.I. ed, *Gold diggers & diggings: a photographic study of gold in Australia, 1854–1920*. Melbourne, Lansdowne, 1974. 208 p, illus, maps.

STONE, D.I. AND MACKINNON, S. *Life on the Australian goldfields*. Melbourne, Methuen, 1976. 224 p, illus.

Although the text in each volume is brief there are many excellent illustrations of mining operations and social conditions.

UREN, M.J.L. *Glint of gold: a story of the goldfields of Western Australia and the men who found them, especially the prospectors and one prospector known to his mates as Diorite*. Melbourne, Robertson & Mullens, 1948. 279 p, illus, maps.

Compiled from the stories of Charles M. Harris (Diorite) this book describes gold prospecting and goldmining throughout WA in the late nineteenth and early twentieth centuries.

VON GUÉRARD, E. *An artist on the goldfields: the diary of Eugene von Guérard*. Introduced and annotated by M. Tipping. Melbourne, Currey O'Neil, 1982. 84 p, illus.

Diary of the voyage out and subsequent time spent in the Geelong area and the Ballarat goldfields. The drawings depict mining and social conditions.

WILSON, H.H. *Gateways to gold*. Adelaide, Rigby, 1969. 162, [8] p, illus.

A popular account of the history of goldmines in the Murchison area and includes among others those in Mt Magnet, Meekatharra, Peak Hill and Cue.

WITHERS, W.B. *This history of Ballarat, from the first pastoral settlement to the present time*. Ballarat, "Ballarat Star", 1870. 216 p, illus.

The first notable history of Ballarat. Most chapters deal with diggers or mining and the effects of both. Facsimile edition from the enlarged second edition of 1887, published in 1980 with an introduction by F. Cusack.

METALS AND MINERALS OTHER THAN GOLD

ANNABELL, J.R. *The uranium hunters*. Adelaide, Rigby, 1971. 172 p, illus.

A journalist's story of uranium exploration in the NT during the mid-1950s.

AUSTRALIA. Ranger Uranium Environmental Inquiry. *Ranger Uranium Environmental Inquiry: first [and second] reports*. AGPS, 1976–77. 2 vols, illus, maps.

The first full-scale investigation into the economic and non-economic costs and benefits of a proposed open-cut uranium mine. Chairman: R.W. Fox.

AUSTRALIAN ATOMIC ENERGY COMMISSION. *Prospecting and mining for uranium in Australia: notes for the guidance of prospectors*. Sydney, Government Printer, 1957. 128 p, illus.

A survey of the uranium-bearing mineral deposits, their occurrence, properties, the law pertaining to them, and the services and financial rewards available to prospectors at that time. First published in 1954.

THE BARRIER silver and tin fields in 1888. Adelaide, W.K. Thomas & Co, 1888. 86 p, map.

A series of reports to various South Australian newspapers, on the production and value of mines in the area, legal aspects, details of some mining companies, and an indication of the social development of the settlements. Facsimile edition, Adelaide, LBSA, 1970.

BLAINEY, G.N. *Mines in the spinifex: the story of Mount Isa*

Mines (rev edn). A & R, 1970. 256, [32] p, illus, maps.

A business history of one of Australia's largest silver–lead mining companies from its inception to the famous strike of 1964–65. First published in 1960.

BLAINEY, G.N. *The peaks of Lyell*. MUP, 1978. 341 p, illus, maps.

A business history of the Mount Lyell Mining and Railway Company and of copper mining in western Tas. First published in 1954.

BLAINEY, G.N. *The rise of Broken Hill*. Melbourne, Macmillan, 1968. 184 p, illus.

This mining history also incorporates the economic, social and political history of the town, the area and the other parts of Australia it affected in its operations.

CLARK, G.L. *Built on gold: recollections of Western Mining*. Melbourne, Hill of Content, 1983. 258 p, illus, maps.

The memoirs of an Australian engineer who became chairman of the Western Mining Corporation when the company was diversifying from gold into base metals and then aluminium, nickel and petroleum.

CORBOULD, W.H. *Broken Hill to Mount Isa: the mining odyssey of W.H. Corbould*. Ed by Ian Hore-Lacy. Melbourne, Hyland House, 1981. 238 p, illus, maps.

Corbould was involved with many of the major mining ventures in Australia from the late nineteenth century. His is one of the very few autobiographies of a mining and metallurgical engineer.

CURTIS, L.S. *The history of Broken Hill: its rise and progress*. Adelaide, Frearson's Printing House, 1908. 199 p, illus.

An account of all the mines together with information concerning most of the institutions and voluntary organisations in Broken Hill.

ELLIS, M.H. *A saga of coal: the Newcastle Wallsend Coal Company's centenary volume*. A & R, 1969. 289 p, illus.

A business history of one of the important members of the northern NSW group of collieries.

GRAINGER, E. *The remarkable Reverend Clarke: the life and times of the father of Australian geology*. OUP, 1982. 292 p, illus, maps.

A useful biography of the scholar who influenced much of the gold and other mining in eastern Australia.

GREGSON, J. *The Australian Agricultural Company, 1824–1875*. A & R, 1907. 336 p, illus, map.

A business history of this company which was an important colliery operator in addition to its pastoral activities.

KALOKERINOS, A. *In search of opal*. Sydney, Ure Smith, 1967. 137 p, illus.

Popular account of one person's attempt to become a successful opal miner.

KEARNS, R.H.B. *Broken Hill, a pictorial history*. Adelaide, Investigator Press, 1982. 248 p, illus.

A descriptive history of Broken Hill and the mines in the area.

KENNEDY, K.H. ed, Readings in North Queensland mining history. Vol 1. Townsville, History Department, James Cook University of North Qld, 1980. 328 p, illus, maps.

The first of a very useful series which includes essays on gold, copper, tin and coal mining at various locations. There are also chapters on geology and mineralisation, railways, architecture and labour relations.

KENNEDY, K.H. et al, *Totley: a study of the silver mines at One Mile, Ravenswood district*. Townsville, History Department, James Cook University of North Qld, 1981. vii, 61 p, illus, maps.

A history of mining with recollections of some of the participants and an account of industrial archaelogy of the area.

KERR, J. *Mount Morgan: gold, copper and oil.* Brisbane, J.D. & R.S. Kerr, 1982. 248 p, illus, maps.

A well-documented history of this important Qld mine.

KERR, R.S. *John Moffat's empire.* Brisbane, J.D. & R.S. Kerr, 1979. 129 p, illus, maps.

A business history of Moffat's mining investments ranging from north Qld tin into copper, silver, lead and oil interests and the provision of infrastructure such as railways, civil and urban construction.

MACDONALD, R.M. *Opals and gold: wanderings & work on the mining and gem fields.* London, T. Fisher Unwin, 1928. 256 p, illus.

An interesting record of twentieth-century mining in various places and the methods used. It is of particular interest because the author mined for opal more frequently than for other minerals.

MORLEY, I.W. *Black sands: a history of the mineral sand mining industry in eastern Australia.* UQP, 1981. 278 p, illus, maps.

The first history of mineral sands mining—zircon, rutile and ilmenite. It discusses the companies, the production and the processes.

PRYOR, O. *Australia's little Cornwall.* Adelaide, Rigby, 1962. 191 p, illus, maps.

An account of the copper mining at Moonta and Wallaroo in SA, by the last surface manager at Moonta Mines when they closed in 1923.

ROBINSON, E. *Cap'n 'Ancock: ruler of Australia's little Cornwall.* Adelaide, Rigby, 1978. 178 p, illus.

A biography of SA's most famous Cornish mining captain, Henry Richard Hancock of Moonta.

ROBINSON, W.S. *If I remember rightly: the memoirs of W.S. Robinson, 1876–1963.* Ed by G. Blainey. Melbourne, Cheshire, 1967. 234 p, illus.

An important source of information about base metals mining and operations in the twentieth century and also the early aluminium industry.

SHAW, A.G.L. AND BRUNS, G.R. *The Australian coal industry.* MUP, 1947. 197 p.

A painstaking and thorough study of the coal industry in the interwar years.

TRENGOVE, A. *Discovery: stories of modern mineral exploration.* Melbourne, Stockwell, 1979. 277 p, illus, maps.

A relatively uncritical account of the post-World War II explorations of the major metals and minerals.

TURNER, J.W. *Coal mining in Newcastle, 1801–1900.* Newcastle, NSW, Council of the City of Newcastle, 1982. 179 p, illus, maps. (Newcastle history monographs, 9.)

A detailed history of the discovery, development and export of coal from Newcastle and environs.

WHITMORE, R.L. *Coal in Queensland, the first fifty years: a history of early coal mining in Queensland.* UQP, 1981. 185 p, illus, maps.

The first full account of developments in the coal industry between the 1820s and 1900.

WOODWARD, O.H. 'A review of the Broken Hill lead–silver–zinc industry', *Australasian Institute of Mining and Metallurgy Proceedings* no 119, 1940, 187–417.

Discusses many aspects of mining from exploration and company formation to treatment, industrial relations and accidents. There is detailed information about the interwar period.

PROCESSING

BAMBRICK, S.C. ed, *Mineral processing in Australia: conference papers and report, August 1973.* Canberra, Centre for Continuing Education, Australian National University, 1973. 189 p.

Deals with the processing and exporting prospects for base metals, including uranium and aluminium in particular, and mining in general. The subjects range from taxation financing and infrastructure to fuel and the environment.

CLARK, D. *Australian mining & metallurgy.* Melbourne, Critchley Parker, 1904. 534 p, illus, maps.

A review of mining methods and processing techniques used on mining fields in all states except SA.

IDRIESS, I.L. *Prospecting for gold, from the dish to the hydraulic plant.* A & R, 1931. 157 p, illus.

A very useful account of the range of wet and dry techniques in mining and processing, including cyanidising. Revised edition published in 1980.

GAS AND PETROLEUM

JACKSON, GRAHAM, MOORE & PARTNER. *Oil and gas exploration in Australia.* Sydney, Sydney Stock Exchange, 1978. Various pagings, illus.

A report dealing with the principal sedimentary basins in Australia and the companies involved in the oil industry.

PETROLEUM INFORMATION BUREAU, AUSTRALIA. *This age of oil: a history of the petroleum industry in Australia.* Melbourne, The Bureau, 1960. 204 p, illus.

A general and uncritical history of petroleum refining and marketing in Australia.

RAGGETT, H.G. ed, *Fuel and power in Australia.* Melbourne, Cheshire, 1969. 162 p, illus, maps.

Essays on Australia's energy resources—petroleum, gas, coal, hydro-electricity and nuclear power—including some estimates of future power requirements.

SIMPSON, C. *Show me a mountain: the rise of an Australian company, Ampol.* A & R, 1961. 253 p, illus, maps.

A relatively uncritical business history. Of interest because of its sections on oil exploration and production in Australia.

TRENGOVE, A. *'What's good for Australia . . .': the story of BHP.* Sydney, Cassell, 1975. 263 p, illus.

A popular history of BHP. Includes sections on its base metal mining and processing and on its oil and natural gas developments.

WILKINSON, R. *A thirst for burning: the story of Australia's oil industry.* Sydney, David Ell Press, 1983. 383 p, illus.

The first full-length history of the production and retail distribution of oil in Australia. Discusses the companies involved and includes a section on natural gas.

GOVERNMENT POLICY

BAMBRICK, S.C. *Australian minerals and energy policy.* ANUP, 1979. 240 p, illus, map.

Discusses taxation and finance, the economics of mining, infrastructure and the effects on Aborigines and the environment.

BAMBRICK, S.C. *The changing relationship: the Australian government and the mining industry.* Melbourne, Committee for Economic Development of Australia, 1975. 93 p, map.

An analysis of government policy in the early 1970s. Includes discussions of processing, marketing and the Fitzgerald Report.

BARNETT, D.W. *Minerals and energy in Australia.* Sydney, Cassell, 1979. 333 p, illus, maps.

A discussion of the major metals and energy sources, world trade aspects and both economic and social costs.

FITZGERALD, T.M. *The contribution of the mineral industry to Australian welfare: report to the Minister for Minerals and Energy the Hon R.F.X. Connor MP,* AGPS, 1974. 93 p.

This study centres on the major minerals and the principal companies involved during 1960 to 1974. Includes the economics of mining operations, the role of taxation, and the cost as well as the benefits of the sector to the nation.

HETHERINGTON (CHAS. R) & CO LTD. *Energy resources of Queensland and their use: report to the Honourable the Premier of Queensland.* Brisbane, Government Printer, 1964. 98 p, maps.

A review of each form of energy available in Qld and an assessment of its present and future status as of the mid-1960s.

ADMINISTRATION

ARMSTRONG, H.J. *Handy-book on the management of mining companies in Victoria.* Melbourne, Charles F. Maxwell, 1888. 138 p.

Covers all legal aspects from the formation of a company to the presentation of the financial reports, including the winding-up and the significance of the no-liability status.

BAMBRICK, S.C. AND WRIGHT, A. *Minerals and metals in the Australian economy: iron ore, bauxite, uranium, nickel, copper, lead, zinc, silver: an analysis.* Melbourne, Committee for Economic Development of Australia, 1975. 131 p. (Committee for Economic Development of Australia. Supplementary paper, 45.)

Discusses the nature of demand and Australia's competitive position, technical developments and the size of reserves.

BRAIN, P.J. AND SCHUYERS, G.P. *Energy and the Australian economy.* Melbourne, Longman Cheshire, 1981. 343 p, illus.

The authors examine the economics of the primary energy sources and alternatives in Australia, including projections to the year 2000.

BRAYSHAY, D.E. AND BERRIMAN, D. *The law of no liability mining companies in Victoria.* Melbourne, Sands & McDougall, 1899. 212 p.

A comprehensive treatment of all aspects of the law as it related to mining companies.

DE LISSA, A. *Companies' work and mining law in New South Wales and Victoria.* Sydney, Robertson, 1884. 454 p.

A comprehensive discussion of the legal requirements of mining companies from inception to liquidation and including mining claims and leases.

GODDEN, D. AND ROBERTSON, W.N. *Australian mining companies' accounts.* London, Gee & Co, 1902. 78 p. (Accountant's library, vol 16.)

An explanation, originally for the benefit of English investors, of the no-liability and limited liability systems of organisation and how they evolved from the Cornish cost-book system.

MACKENZIE, B.W. AND BARNETT, D. *Mineral economics.* Adelaide, Australian Mineral Foundation, 1976. 362 p, illus.

Papers on the economic aspect of mining ventures in Australia including petroleum. The subjects include resources, mine development, risks, government policy and taxation.

MURRAY, R. *Fuels rush in: oil and gas in Australia.* Melbourne, Macmillan, 1972. 159 p, illus, maps.

A serious attempt to discuss the financial aspects of oil and gas exploration and development since the 1950s and present it to a wide audience.

SYKES, T. *The money miners: Australia's mining boom, 1969-70.* Sydney, Wildcat, 1978. 388 p, illus.

A popular account of the financial aspects of the mining boom.

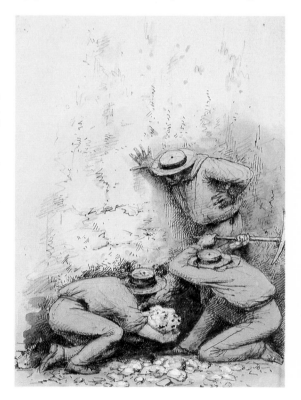

William Strutt, Diggers at work. *Pencil, ink and watercolour. Strutt (1825–1915) studied art in Paris and migrated to Victoria in 1850. His sketches and paintings over the next twelve years represent a remarkable pictorial history of the life of the colony, from miners working in the goldfields to the first meeting of the Victorian legislative council. His most celebrated picture,* Black Thursday, 6 Feb. 1851, *based on sketches made during the outbreak of bushfires in Victoria, was completed in England on his return in 1862.*
DIXSON LIBRARY

'The laying of tramlines.' Photograph by Trevallyn, c1910.
QUEEN VICTORIA MUSEUM AND ART GALLERY, LAUNCESTON

CHAPTER 33

TRANSPORT

P. RIMMER

DISTANCE AND ITS implacable foe—efficient transport—have been elevated by Geoffrey Blainey (1982) to a pivotal position in explaining Australian history. His study discusses both the effects of isolation during the long era when the country was reliant on sailing ships and bullock carts and the arrival of various forms of mechanical transport—steamships, railways, aircraft and motor cars. It is still the best interpretative account of a subject that has always been full of the 'romance' of Australian transport and neglected the hardships of sailors, bullockies, camel drivers, railwaymen, seamen, aviators and truck drivers. Blainey has been at pains, however, to emphasise that climate, resources, European ideas, wars, markets and money were also important factors in shaping Australian history. Nevertheless, the subsequent preoccupation with distance 'measured along Euclidean lines with Cartesian references' has had a numbing rather than a liberating effect on later writers (P. O'Sullivan, 'Issues in transportation', in R. Davies and P. Hall eds, *Issues in urban society*, Harmondsworth, England, Penguin, 1978, 106). Accepting the obstacle of distance as theory rather than hypothesis, studies in the field have either continued their romantic attachment or contracted into dry technical accounts which take the immediately given as the real, with little sense of where Australia has been or where it might be going.

The transport literature of Australia has been grouped under three headings: *international*, involving movements of people and goods originating or terminating in Australia; *domestic long-distance*, involving interregional movements of people and goods within and between states; and *urban*, involving movements of people and goods within cities.

Political decisions have been important not only in locating transport facilities and offering them for use but in influencing decisions as to whether and how intensively the facilities will be used. The degree of autonomous government control over the location and pace of transport development, as highlighted by N.G. Butlin (1964) and P.J. Rimmer (1975), provides strong contrasts with British and American free market experiences. Therefore, much of the raw material for examining changes in transport patterns of interest and the associated progressive evaluation of the investment environment, differing appraisals of resources and regional potential, variations in leadership (people and places) and permutations in administrative and institutional structures, have to be distilled from debates, messages, reports and royal commission findings. While it does not necessarily follow that what happened is recorded in parliamentary papers, the usefulness of any publication on Australian transport depends on the writer's skill in sifting the documentary evidence—agendas and accompanying papers, minutes, maps and photographs—to unravel events and ideas and determine how key bureaucrats, politicians and petitioners conceived and made use of space.

Government reports on transport problems occur frequently in Australian parliamentary papers or as separate documents. Some help in tracing them can be found in D.H. Borchardt's, *Checklist of royal commissions, select committees of parliament and boards of inquiry* (see chapter 8).

As transport periodicals are, for the most part, strictly for buffs or overly technical, the reader can easily become stranded. A list of major serial transport publications will be found at the end of the reading list to this topic.

Readers may be assisted in interpreting the literature by recognising five phases in the development of the transport system, linked with the introduction of technological innovations. These innovations are associated with radical restructuring of the economic geography at different scales brought about by major crises in the world economy: 1840s, 1890s, 1930s and 1970s. Each technological innovation resulted in the downgrading in importance of the previous dominant mode of transport and its relegation to peripheral locations within the respective international, long-distance or urban spheres of circulation.

INTERNATIONAL CONNECTIONS

Overseas shipping studies from the arrival of the first fleet until the recession of the 1840s are often dated but their language and illustrations are sufficient to confirm that the large wooden sailing ships were symbols of British authority. Although the gold-seeking passengers brought in the fast American clippers after 1850 challenged this authority, writers emphasise the British hegemony despite the repeal of the Navigation Acts, and the progressive granting of self-rule to individual colonies. British dominance was reinforced not by the unpredictable steamers carrying affluent passengers and mails via Suez but by sailing ships. The distances between coaling stations ensured that the Australian route was a step behind in technological innovation. After the recession of the 1890s contemporary observers were quick to note that the switchover to the new breed of fuel-efficient steamships and the subsequent downgrading of sailing ships as carriers of wheat, coal and timber seemed to endorse the Mother Country's stranglehold over Australia in perpetuity as the colonies were slow to perceive the worldwide decline in British maritime supremacy.

Australia slipped from an exclusive British sphere into an Anglo–American trading orbit after the recession of the 1930s. Commentators have stressed, however, that the promised savings to consignors from greater use of the Suez and Panama canals and technological innovations (larger ships, and oil and diesel fuel) did not materialise because of the influence of the cartel-like activities of the British liner conference and recurrent labour strife on the Australian waterfront. Since the recession of the early 1970s it is clear that the switch to container, bulk and semibulk ships and automated handling gear has stifled the threat of organised labour. Australian trade has now diversified but two policy issues have arisen as the conference system is still in place: how does the liner conference system affect the welfare of Australian shippers and what share of the trade should be carried in Australian-owned vessels? As yet, air transport technology has not developed to the extent that it can be a strong competitor for cargoes carried by sea, although there is renewed interest in using large freight-carrying airships.

Overseas air transport studies have highlighted the Australian contribution to the pioneering of international aviation after 1900 though Lawrence Hargrave's work on the theory of flight occurred before that date. Nevertheless, there has been some feeling that the daring exploits of local aviators, such as Harry Hawker, Bert Hinkler, Ray Parer, Charles Ulm and Charles Kingsford Smith, have been overglamorised despite Smithy's role in pioneering the Kangaroo route to London. Regular flights for passengers and mails along the route did not begin until the 1930s when W. Hudson Fysh and Qantas Empire Airways were at the forefront. They were, however, not commonplace until after World War II when commentators noted that the national carrier, Qantas, and other airlines had eroded the market for passenger liners. Since 1970, Qantas's newly acquired jumbo fleet has had to face competition from southeast Asian airlines, prompting it to adopt discounts to offset fare cutting and seasonal fares to counter the north–south imbalance, and to suggest that it should control long-distance air routes within Australia—an issue that has yet to be resolved.

DOMESTIC LONG-DISTANCE TRANSPORT

The key to understanding the evolution of the system of transport and its alter ego, landuse, within Australia is to be conscious of the multiple ripple effect on its economic landscape of successive technological innovations. Australia's transport–landuse system reflects, as P.A. Baran and P.M. Sweezy have noted in their monograph *Monopoly capital* (New York, Monthly Review Press, 1966), the impact of 'epoch-making innovations' that have 'each produced a radical alteration of economic geography with attendant internal migration and the building of new communities'. Conflicts caused by externally induced innovations are usually only partially resolved by internal responses before they are superseded by another innovation—the contemporary restructuring since 1970 prompted by the introduction of container ships and jumbo jets being the last in a series that has affected Australia.

Literature on the transport–landuse system, designed originally to serve an experimental convict settlement based on Sydney and its satellites, is scanty. Much reliance was placed on the 'saltwater highway' in transforming it into a permanent white settler society because bullock drays on the embryonic road system were expensive. As pastoral activities expanded until the 1840s writers emphasised that inland transport costs were a constraining but not a limiting factor.

Bullock drays and horse-drawn coaches were pushed into peripheral locations during the restructuring that followed the recession and a burgeoning literature stressed the development of the railway—a major weapon used by newly created colonial governments in the aftermath of the gold discoveries to relieve Britain of 'capital glut' and labour, and stimulate internal trade at the expense of adjacent colonies. Individual writers (Butlin, 1964; Rimmer, 1977, 1980) have focused on the debates involving animal or steam power, private or public enterprise, and British or American locomotives and gauges, and have noted the triumph of steam, the dominance of British techniques (at least temporarily) and universal government ownership. They show how 'octopus' trunk lines from major ports spread to transport passengers and goods carried previously by road, river and coastal shipping to sate the desires of log-rolling politicians and their business supporters (pastoralists, merchants and equipment suppliers). From the 1880s the rational arguments of influential bureaucrats took second place to the insatiable desire for grabbing the land value increments of rail development, so it was not surprising that the construction fuelled by massive borrowings from London was an early and major victim of the recession of the 1890s.

The subsequent restructuring has led many authors (for example, Wettenhall, 1961) into describing how the states of the newly formed commonwealth sought to professionalise their large-scale railway bureaucracies and yet still satisfy the closer settlement and branch line ambitions of the political masters. They also discuss how the federal government sought after World War I to unify the mainland states into a cohesive whole by interconnecting the disparate railway systems and upgrading interstate coastal shipping connections. As many writers acknowledge (for example, Butlin *et al*, 1982) these immediate developments to promote economic growth overshadowed the introduction of the motor vehicle. At first, given the condition of the roads, it seemed an unlikely threat to the railway monopoly serving long-distance passenger and goods traffic that was fed into terminals by horse-drawn vehicles. By the late 1920s, however, there was clamour from the state railways for protection against motor buses and motor trucks as they were siphoning off the most lucrative traffic.

As is evident from some of the commentators (for example, Butlin *et al*, 1982; Kolsen, 1968) on the recession of the 1930s and later years, restructuring of the transport–landuse system revolved around the increased use of the motor vehicle and the growth of the domestic airline industry. This was especially true after World War II with the development of an integrated national market based on improved road and air connections. Although controls over buses and trucks were maintained to protect state railways, the finding that the regulation of interstate road transport was contrary to the Australian constitution prompted its expansion. These develop-ments galvanised the railways into gauge standardisation and the greater use of diesel engines, and coastal shipping into introducing roll-on roll-off and container ships. This modernisation program enabled them to maintain their position as carriers of bulky goods but the mass consumption of the motor car drove rail and shipping into residual passenger markets. Much long-distance business and leisure travel, however, became the preserve of the artificial monopoly operated by the two major domestic airlines—the commonwealth government's Trans Australia Airlines (TAA–renamed Australian Airlines in 1986) and the private carrier Ansett Airlines of Australia—as the result of takeovers and deals designed to maintain the financial stability of trunk services.

Urban transport

Most writers emphasise that ports preceded cities. Until the 1850s, therefore, attention is focused on the settlements built around the wharves and cargo-handling facilities, except for a couple of decades when pastoralism held sway. The major port towns developed into capitals or provincial cities but most journeys involved walking, bicycling or horse-drawn coaches, buses or trams until the 1890s. Although there were urban spinoffs from long-distance trains, mechanised transport did not really begin until the 1880s with the development of the steam tram in Sydney and the cable tram in Melbourne; by then their respective populations had exceeded 250 000.

After the recession of the 1890s, commentators, such as Spearritt (1978), point to rising city populations and the progressive spread of tramways and suburban railways (facilitated in Sydney by the Harbour Bridge) to meet the needs of shoppers attracted by Central Business District merchandise, and workers and shippers attracted by the development of manufacturing. The latter activity was also reflected in the expansion of port capacity and the replacement of horse-drawn vehicles by motorised transport. As competition from private buses in the late 1920s threatened the financial viability of both suburban railways and trams, the state governments, fearing the clout of organised labour, took over their urban activities as part of what has been termed a transport co-ordination program—though most economists suggest 'restraint on competition' as the more appropriate appellation.

Analysts have highlighted that after the recession of the 1930s, transport co-ordination led to increased investment in fixed track and bus systems. Any benefits were shortlived as pressures from the motor vehicle lobby gathered momentum because road construction was part of unemployment relief and the motor vehicle a key prop in an import-substitution manufacturing program. The development of Australia's own car after World War II led to the progressive decline of public transport despite the growth in population fuelled by immigration. During the 'long boom' (1950–70) the expanding car population prompted the removal of trams (except in Melbourne) and economic growth objectives overrode environmental sensibilites to noise and pollution generated by new transport routes and terminals. Nevertheless, the congestion phobia was sufficient to spawn a series of transport–landuse plans for major urban areas. They recommended a dose of freeways which, together with seaports, promised to resolve such side-effects of accelerated economic growth.

Commentators on the aftermath of the recession of the early 1970s and the accompanying energy crisis have drawn attention to the disadvantages of the growth-at-all-costs urban transport–landuse policy, particularly air and noise pollution and community severance effects (Black et al, 1983). This new consciousness led to the termination of many radial freeway dreams, the appearance of the 'save public transport' lobby and an attack on extravagant overinvestment in new airport and seaport facilities to accommodate jumbo jets and container ships. Some social scientists, moreover, argue that there is a need to go beyond the economists' agenda and explore the transport-related aspects of urban unemployment and the marginalisation of subgroups such as the housebound, young people, migrants and the semiskilled.

The assistance received from Barbara Banks, John Black, Gwen Carroll, Joh Forsyth and Howard Quinlan in compiling the bibliography is acknowledged.

INTERNATIONAL CONNECTIONS

BACH, J.P.S. *A maritime history of Australia*. Melbourne, Nelson, 1976. 481 p, illus, maps.

An account of the pattern of overseas shipping linking the effects of technological developments within the shipping industry and economic, social and political developments in Australia. Discusses also Australian-owned or Australian-operated shipping offering interstate and intrastate services and Australian ports.

BUCKLEY, K. AND KLUGMAN, K. *The Australian presence in the Pacific: Burns Philp, 1914–1946*. Sydney, Allen & Unwin, 1983. 392 p, illus, maps.

BUCKLEY, K. AND KLUGMAN, K. *The history of Burns Philp: the Australian company in the south Pacific*. Sydney, Burns Philp, 1981. 312 p, illus, map.

Pioneering studies of a purely Australian company that became one of the merchant princes of the south Pacific.

DAVIS, P. *Charles Kingsford Smith: the world's greatest aviator*. Sydney, Summit Books, 1977. 156 p, illus, maps.

A review of the life of Sir Charles Kingsford Smith—the 'greatest trans-world flier of them all'.

FITCHETT, T.K. *The long haul: ships on the England–Australia run*. Adelaide, Rigby, 1980. 95 p, illus.

The story of passenger ships running the longest sea route in the world, beginning with liners in commission in 1914 and ending with the final of the last regular liner in 1977.

FYSH, H. *Qantas rising: the autobiography of the flying Fysh*. A & R, 1965. 296 p, illus, map.

FYSH, H. *Qantas at war*. A & R, 1968. 224 p, illus.

FYSH, H. *Wings to the world: the story of Qantas 1945–1966*. A & R, 1970. 236 p, illus.

Detailed history in 3 vols of a little bush company that came to town and eventually quartered the world.

PAGE, M.F. *Fitted for the voyage: the Adelaide Steamship Company, 1875–1975*. Adelaide, Rigby, 1975. 339 p, illus.

Detailed history of a major Australian shipping company.

STUBBLES, P. *Australia and the maritime industries*. Melbourne, AIDA Research Centre, 1983. 218 p, illus, map.

A study of the importance of the shipping industry and its current problems. It pinpoints the pros and cons of the conference system, waterside difficulties, and the long-term decline of coastal traffic.

WORKSHOP ON INTERNATIONAL PASSENGER TRANSPORT, Canberra, 1981. *Papers and proceedings*. AGPS, 1982. 199 p, illus.

Charts the demise of international sea passenger transport, development of the cruise market and the slowdown of the growth in the international air passenger transport market.

DOMESTIC LONG-DISTANCE TRANSPORT

AUSTIN, K.A. *A pictorial history of Cobb & Co: the coaching age in Australia, 1854–1924*. Adelaide, Rigby, 1977. 219 p, illus, maps.

Outlines the development of land transport and the decline of Cobb and Co. First published as *The lights of Cobb and Co* in 1967.

AUSTRALIA. Bureau of Transport Economics. *Basic characteristics of general aviation in Australia*. AGPS, 1980. 271 p, illus, maps. (Occasional paper, 33).

A hallmark survey that has been important in unravelling the facts.

AUSTRALIA. Domestic Air Transport Policy Review. *Domestic air transport policy review: report to the Minister for Transport . . .* AGPS, 1979. 2 vols, illus, maps.

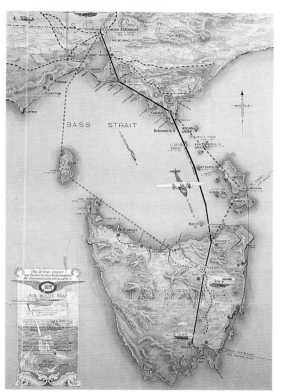

Air route map, Victoria to Tasmania, prepared by Matthews Aviation Pty Ltd, Melbourne, c1935.

NATIONAL LIBRARY

An examination of trunk route services and the two airline policy, and regional and local commuter air services.

AUSTRALIAN RAILWAY RESEARCH AND DEVELOPMENT ORGANISATION. *1981 report on rail*. Melbourne, ARRDO, 1981. 108 p, illus, map.

Identifies the future role of government railways in meeting the needs of the Australian community and what is required to perform this role.

AUSTRALIAN TRANSPORT ADVISORY COUNCIL. *Transport and energy overview*. AGPS, 1979. 117 p.

A response to the rapid increase in oil prices and the partial embargo imposed on the world by the Organization of Petroleum Exporting Countries (OPEC).

BELBIN, P. and BURKE, D. *Changing trains: a century of travel on the Sydney–Melbourne railway*. Sydney, Methuen, 1982. 144 p, illus, maps.

A delightful miscellany of comment and pictures of travel between the two rival cities.

BIRD, J. *Seaport gateways of Australia*. London, OUP, 1968. 253 p, illus, maps.

The evolution of Australian ports, trends in their development and some comments on their likely futures.

BLAINEY, G. *The tyranny of distance: how distance shaped Australia's history* (rev edn). Melbourne, Macmillan, 1982. 366 p, illus, maps.

Still the best single introduction to transport in Australia. First published in 1966.

BREARLEY, N. AND MAYMAN, T. *Australian aviator*. Adelaide, Rigby, 1971. 202 p, illus, maps.

The record of Australia's first commercial air service—West Australian Airways—which flew between Geraldton and Derby between 1921 and 1936 when it was taken over by Australian National Airways.

BUTLIN, N.G. *Investment in Australian economic development, 1861–1900.* CUP, 1964. 477 p, illus, maps.

Standard text on rail, river and road development.

BUTLIN, N.G. *et al, Government and capitalism: public and private choice in twentieth century Australia.* Sydney, Allen & Unwin, 1982. 369 p.

A study of public transport enterprises.

DADDOW, V. *The puffing pioneers and Queensland's railway builders.* UQP, 1975. 217 p, illus.

General history of the development of Qld railways.

DAVIS, P. *Australians on the road: over 80 years of motoring in Australia.* Adelaide, Rigby, 1979. 232 p, illus.

A racy account of the history of the motor car.

FEARNSIDE, G.H. *All stations west: the story of the Sydney–Perth standard gauge railway.* Sydney, Haldane Publishing, 1970. 167 p, illus, maps.

Background and evolution of the important east–west link.

FITZPATRICK, B. AND CAHILL, R.J. *The Seaman's Union of Australia, 1872–1972: a history.* Sydney, Seaman's Union of Australia, 1981. 363 p, illus.

Valuable source of reference.

FITZPATRICK, J. *The bicycle and the bush: man and machine in rural Australia.* OUP, 1980. 250 p, illus, maps.

A pioneering effort.

HARRIGAN, L.J. *Victorian railways to '62.* Melbourne, Victorian Railways Public Relations Board, 1962. 299 p, illus, maps.

Only authoritative history of Victorian railways to date.

HARTNETT, L.J. *Big wheels and little wheels.* Melbourne, Gold Star, 1973. 278 p, illus.

An autobiography of a key figure in the rise of General Motors–Holden's Pty Ltd. He left the company on the eve of launching the Holden—a 'completely Australian car'. First published in 1964.

HOCKING, D.M. AND HADDON-CAVE, C.P. *Air transport in Australia.* A & R, 1951. 188 p, maps.

Account of early aviation focusing on historical development, policy and control.

KIRBY, M.G. *Domestic airline regulation: the Australian debate.* Sydney, Centre for Independent Studies, 1981. 109 p.

A polemic on Australia's two airline policy.

KOLSEN, H.M. *The economics and control of road–rail competition: a critical study of theory and practice in the United States of America, Great Britain and Australia.* SUP, 1968. 182 p, illus.

The standard text on regulatory methods in Australia which offers a critical appraisal of their objectives.

LAY, M.G. *Source book for Australian roads.* Melbourne, Australian Road Research Board, 1981. 501 p, illus, maps.

Important source for technical information on all aspects of Australian roads. Bibliography.

LEWIS, G. *A history of the ports of Queensland: a study in economic nationalism.* UQP, 1973. 341 p, illus.

Port development, shipping services and economic growth in Qld seen within the issues of Australian history.

McKELLAR, N.L. *From Derby round to Burketown: the A.U.S.N. story.* UQP, 1977. 682 p, illus.

A detailed shipping history of the Australian United Steam Navigation Co.

NEW SOUTH WALES. Dept of Main Roads. *The roadmakers: a history of main roads in New South Wales.* Sydney, Dept of Main Roads, 1976. 335 p, illus, maps.

A record of highlights in roadmaking.

PEMBERTON, B.M. *Australian coastal shipping.* MUP, 1979. 327 p, illus, maps.

A thorough description of the growth and location of the Australian coastal and overseas trade, its focus being on ship-owners and ships of each trade.

POULTON, H.W. *Law, history and politics of the Australian two airline system.* Melbourne, H.W. Poulton, 1982. 494 p, illus, map.

The most authoritative account on the legal aspects of the two airline policy.

RIMMER, P.J. 'Politicians, public servants and petitioners: aspects of transport in Australia, 1851–1901', in J.M. Powell and M. Williams, eds, *Australian space Australian time: geographical perspectives.* OUP, 1975, 182–225.

An essay on the development of the transport and communications system linking urban centres and rural products (with maps of Australia and Vic).

RIMMER, P.J. 'Freight forwarding: changes in structure, conduct and performance', in K.A. Tucker, ed, *The economics of the Australian service sector.* London, Croom Helm, 1977, 167–207.

An examination of the growth, size and performance of the key freight forwarding firms.

RIMMER, P.J. ed, *Australia on the move: a guide to transport information and statistics.* Canberra, Centre for Continuing Education, Australian National University, 1984. 227 p, illus.

All you wanted to know about Australian transport information and statistics but were too afraid to ask.

SINGLETON, C.C. AND BURKE, D. *Railways of Australia.* A & R, 1963. 159 p, illus, maps.

A thorough description of Australian railways to 1962.

STEVENSON, I.R. *The line that led to nowhere: the story of the north Australia railway.* Adelaide, Rigby, 1979. 188 p, illus, map.

History of railway operations in the tropical north and influence of mining operations—starts as a simple chronicle of events but ends up as a social history.

STUBBS, P. *The Australian motor industry: a study in protection and growth.* Melbourne, Cheshire, for the Institute of Applied Economic and Social Research, University of Melbourne, 1972. 335 p, illus.

A thorough study of manufacture and sales from 1908 to 1970, including the changing fortunes of Ford and GMH.

TAPLIN, J.H.E. *Australian transport: current issues and policy options.* Canberra, Dept of the Parliamentary Library, 1982. 55, 11 p. (Legislative Research Service discussion paper 5, 1982).

Clear and concise statement of transport issues and policy options from an economist's standpoint.

TURNBULL, C. *Wings of tomorrow.* Sydney, F.H. Johnston Publishing Co, 1945. 64 p, illus, maps.

Development of Australian National Airways Pty Ltd to 1945 (with fleet statistics and photographs). A story of 'what might have been' as it was amalgamated with Ansett (to form Ansett–ANA).

VICTORIAN TRANSPORT STUDY. *Reports.* Melbourne, Government Printer, 1980. 28 vols. (Vic Parliamentary paper nos 23–50 of 1980).

The reports provide a useful source of information on virtually every aspect of Victorian transport from administration through bicycles, car pooling, country passenger services to ports and harbours.

URBAN TRANSPORT

BLACK, J.A. *et al*, 'Transport–land use issues, problems and policy implications: Sydney since the thirties', in Australian Transport Research Forum, 8th, Canberra, 1983. *Forum papers*. AGPS, 1983. Vol 1, 92–115.

Argues transport–landuse problems are time and place specific with reference to three calendar years in the historical development of Sydney.

BRIMSON, S. *The tramways of Australia*. Sydney, Dreamweaver Books, 1983. 223 p, illus, maps.

A detailed history of sixteen Australian horse, steam, cable and electric tramway systems.

MANNING, I. *Beyond walking distance: the gains from speed in Australian urban travel*. Canberra, Urban Research Unit, Australian National University, 1984. 164 p, illus, maps.

Traces the relationship between public transport and the private car in Australian cities from about 1900 to the present, including a close study of the journey to work in Melbourne and Sydney.

MELBOURNE. Metropolitan Transportation Committee. *Melbourne transportation study*. Melbourne, Government Printer, 1969. 3 vols, illus, maps.

A source of information on passenger and goods traffic in Australia's second largest city, prepared for the committee by Wilbur Smith & Associates.

PHILLIPS, V. *Bridges and ferries of Australia*. Sydney, Bay Books, 1983. 160 p, illus, maps.

Survey of ferries and bridges in all states.

PRESCOTT, A.M. *Sydney's ferry fleets*. Adelaide, R.H. Parsons, 1984. 102 p, illus, maps.

A comprehensive handbook on ferry routes and vessels.

RADCLIFFE, J.C. AND STEELE, C.J.M. *Adelaide road passenger transport, 1836–1958*. Adelaide, LBSA, 1974. 190 p, illus, maps.

A summary of the historical events leading to the present system of road transport in Adelaide. The sociological interpretation, as the authors acknowledge, remains to be written.

SPEARRITT, P. *The Sydney Harbour Bridge*. Sydney, Allen & Unwin, 1982. 120 p, illus.

The only continuous toll bridge in Australia. An analysis of tolls since its opening in 1932 shows that by 1980 the motor car accounted for more than two-thirds of all passenger travel. Bibliography.

SPEARRITT, P. *Sydney since the twenties*. Sydney, Hale & Iremonger, 1978. 294 p, illus, maps.

Chapter on the rise and fall of public transport with reference to the role of the engineer Dr J.J.C. Bradfield.

SYDNEY AREA TRANSPORTATION STUDY. *Sydney Area Transportation Study (SATS)*. Sydney, 1974. 4 vols, illus, maps.

Useful source for data on movements of people and goods.

WESTERN AUSTRALIA. Office of the Director General of Transport. *Transport 2000: a Perth study*. Perth, Director General of Transport, 1982. 156 p, illus, maps.

A lavishly illustrated non-technical account of likely transport developments.

WOTHERSPOON, G. ed, *Sydney's transport: studies in urban history*. Sydney, Hale & Iremonger in association with the Sydney History Group, 1983. 212 p, illus, maps.

A collection of essays ranging from coastal shipping and ferries

Geoffrey Harvey (b Australia 1954), Happy Holden owners, 1977. Colour screenprint on paper, 35.4 × 21.8 cm. Harvey recognises and satirises the importance of the Holden in Australian life.
AUSTRALIAN NATIONAL GALLERY

through the horse–bus industry and trams to the Eastern Suburbs railway, motor vehicles, the journey to work, and Sydney's wharfies.

JOURNALS AND PERIODICALS

AUSTRALIA. Bureau of Statistics. *Transport and communications: bulletin*, nos 1–63, 1901/06–71/72. Continued by *Rail, bus and air transport*, 1972/73–78/79. Continued by *Rail transport, Australia*, 1979/80– . Canberra.

AUSTRALIAN *road index*. Melbourne, Australian Road Research Board, 1975– .

AUSTRALIAN *transport*. Sydney, Chartered Institute of Transport in Australia, Nov 1937– .

AUSTRALIAN *transport literature information system (ATLIS)*. Canberra, Bureau of Transport Economics, 1981– .

AVIATION heritage: *journal of the Aviation Historical Society of Australia*. Melbourne, The Society, 1960– . Continues: *Aviation Historical Society of Australia journal*.

BULLETIN of the Australian Railway Historical Society. Sydney, The Society, ns vol 1, 1950– . Continues: *Australasian Railway and Locomotive Society bulletin*, Oct 1937–June 1948 and *Railways in Australia* and *ARLHS bulletin*, July 1948–50.

DAILY commercial news and shipping list, 13 Apr 1891– . Sydney.

GREAT circle: *journal of the Australian Association of Maritime History*. Perth, Apr 1979– .

TROLLEY wire: *journal of Australian tramway museums*. Sydney, South Pacific Electric Railway Cooperative Society, 1956– . Continues: *Trolley wire review*.

TRUCK and bus transportation. Sydney, Shennen Publishing and Publicity, vol 1, 1936/37– .

Postcard c1910. Post office, Launceston, Tasmania, built in 1899.

QUEEN VICTORIA MUSEUM AND ART GALLERY, LAUNCESTON

CHAPTER 34

POST AND TELECOMMUNICATIONS

R. BRECKON AND J. L. WARD

POSTAL SERVICES

THE POST OFFICE, or Australia Post as it is now called, is Australia's oldest commercial organisation. Its origins are in the appointment in 1809 of a former convict, Isaac Nichols, as postmaster with authority to accept incoming mail from ships arriving in Sydney. For much of its history, the post office has been responsible for a great variety of services including, besides inward and outward mail distributions, such diverse functions as agency operations for the Commonwealth Savings Bank, distribution of electoral enrolment and taxation forms, payment of social service benefits of different kinds, money order services, and telegraph and telephone services. From Federation until 1975 the Australian Post Office was responsible to a minister of the crown known as the postmaster-general, whose incumbents have included famous politicians such as Sir James Forrest. From 1975 until 1980 these operations were the responsibility of the Minister for Posts and Telecommunications, and from November 1980 of the Minister for Communications.

In July 1975 the activities of Australian post offices were split between Australia Post, operated by the Australian Postal Commission, and Telecom, operated by the Australian Telecommunications Commission. Both commissions were responsible to the Minister for Posts and Telecommunications until November 1980 and then to the Minister for Communications. Because so many of the early telecommunications functions were associated with postal services, the first part of the following bibliography contains references to post office history before 1975, where they cover telecommunications topics.

Australia Post employs, through its state administrations, historians and archivists whose work involves co-ordinating and consolidating accounts of early post offices. Nevertheless, there is a surprising paucity of publications covering the development of postal services in Australia; for the country as a whole, there is no general history of postal services, official or otherwise. Much of the history of postal services, telephony and telegraphy is in privately published monographs written by enthusiasts and produced by post office and telecommunications societies in various states. Their content ranges from histories of stamps and postmarks to detailed histories of offices in particular locations or services in a particular region.

Some impressive examples of state-oriented histories are E. Williams and P. Collas (1977)—178 pages of roneoed typescript published by the Society of Australasian Specialists (a group of New York based stamp collectors)—and the history of postal services in Tasmania

(1975). The Post Office Historical Society of Brisbane has published *Submarine cables in Australia*, and many state historical societies, the Telecommunication Society of Australia, the Institute of Radio, Electrical and Electronic Engineers and the royal societies in each state have both highly specialised and general historical studies recorded in their proceedings.

A history of the Amalgamated Postal Workers' Union by F. Waters (1978) is possibly the only single reference, outside official sources, to the development of Australian postal services in the twentieth century. The book's coverage of this subject is, of course, incidental because its main purpose is to describe the union's history and the industrial relations policies of the Postmaster-General's Department.

The incidental treatment of postal history is also a feature of most philatelic books published in Australia. In addition to their interest in the production of postage stamps, philatelic authors in recent years have paid a good deal of attention to the postmarks and special handling markings applied to mail at post offices. Those philatelic books that cover aspects of postal services development to a reasonable extent are included in the bibliography.

The annual reports of government authorities such as the Australian Postal Commission, Telecom Australia and the Australian Broadcasting Tribunal offer the latest statistical information and describe new developments, as does the annual report of Aussat Pty Ltd, which operates Australia's National Satellite System. Similarly the annual reports of superseded authorities such as the Superintendents of Telegraphs in all states and of the Postmaster-General's Department are important, given the absence of any comprehensive co-ordinating publication.

The reports of commissions and committees of inquiry into the post offices, from both the colonial and the federal eras, together with those of the Committee of Review of the ABC (the Dix Report) and the Committee of Inquiry into Telecommunications Services in Australia (the Davidson Report) contain a great deal of information in appendices and specialist submissions on the administrative, technical and general problems that beset such large public enterprises. The Australian periodical literature too is rich in relatively short but detailed accounts of services, procedures and equipment.

The Australian Archives office in each state capital contains records of the respective state administrations of the Postmaster-General's Department; records of the federal headquarters of the department are in the Melbourne office of the Australian Archives. Historical research officers employed by the department and Australia Post have produced a number of small publications usually dealing with the history of postal services in a township or local region.

TELECOMMUNICATIONS

Telecommunication is a fairly new word, originating in 1932 according to the *Shorter Oxford English dictionary*, and literary dictionaries define it broadly as communications over long distances by electrical or electromagnetic means. Technical dictionaries and reference works extend it to include telegraphy, telephony, facsimile data transmission, television, broadcasting, telemetry, satellite position fixing, direction measurement and radar. This topic therefore overlaps with parts of chapter 55 of this volume; the references listed below emphasise the technology rather than the social impact of the theme.

Much of the literature of Australian telecommunications is widely dispersed in periodical articles, special reports, aspects of government inquiries and submissions to them rather than in conveniently accessible monographs. Archival materials are scattered through the records of federal and state governments and private and public companies. The records of Amalgamated Wireless (Australasia) Ltd, Siemens Ltd, Cable and Wireless Ltd, L.M. Ericsson Pty Ltd, all contain data relevant to the technology, as developed and applied in Australia, of radio, television, telephony and submarine cable installation. Amalgamated Wireless since 1913 has been involved in most applications of radio communication from the manufacture of a wide range of radio receivers and transmitters to the management of commercial broadcasting; it was the authority controlling Overseas Telecommunications Ltd before it became a government organisation. AWA has begun a company history but it is not expected to be published for several years. The company has deposited much of its archival material with the Mitchell Library in Sydney.

Government authorities such as CSIRO for radiophysics, Telecom for almost all aspects of telecommunications, Australia Post and Overseas Telecommunications Ltd all hold materials additional to those transferred to the Australian Archives. The Australian Broadcasting Tribunal in both Melbourne and Sydney holds complete sets of the submissions to hearings for the granting of licences and licence renewals, together with full transcripts of proceedings at all hearings throughout Australia. The tribunal has also produced, through its Research and Information Section, important studies on the ratings of television programs.

The official state yearbooks all include sections on communications which, over several years, comprise a concentrated history of the development of services; occasionally they contain 'special articles' offering a historical review of particular fields. The *Victorian year books* of 1975 and 1976 have a special review and article on telecommunications. The *Year book of Australia* gives similar treatments, the most comprehensive so far being in issue 59 of 1973, entitled 'The development of communications in Australia'. It provides descriptive and statistical information on telegraph, telephone, broadcasting and television services.

GENERAL WORKS

ANDERSON, R.M.M. *Report on the business management of the Postmaster-General's Department of the Commonwealth of Australia.* Melbourne, Government Printer, 1915. 41 p.

This inquiry considered the need for business methods in managing the post office, following the 1908–10 royal commission.

AUSTRALIA. Ad Hoc Committee of Enquiry into the Commercial Accounts of the Post Office. *Report . . .* Canberra, 1961. 1 vol (various pagings).

This committee considered the net financial advantage which had accrued to the Australian Post Office, 'regarded as a business undertaking', up to 30 June 1959. Chairman: Sir Alexander Fitzgerald.

AUSTRALIA. Australian Post Office Commission of Inquiry. *Report of the Commission of Inquiry into the Australian Post Office.* AGPS, 1974. 2 vols. (Australia. Parliament. Parliamentary papers nos 123, 124 of 1974.)

The commission recommended changes in postal and telecommunications services, including the division between Overseas Telecommunications Commission and Postmaster-General's Department. Chairman: Sir J. Vernon.

AUSTRALIA. Committee of Inquiry into the Monopoly Position of the Australian Postal Commission. *Report . . .,* AGPS, 1982. 213 p, map.

The inquiry was to 'examine and report on the appropriateness of the statutory functions and duties of the Australian Postal Commission and the scope for reducing or eliminating the exclusive power of the Commission to carry letters for reward'. Chairman: A.E. Bradley.

AUSTRALIA. Royal Commission on Postal Services. *Report . . .* Melbourne, Government Printer, 1910. 210 p.

Considered all the 'postal, telegraphic and telephone services of the Commonwealth' and recommended that 'every effort should be made to conduct the services on business lines'. Chairman: J.H. Cook.

AUSTRALIAN POSTAL COMMISSION. *Annual report 1976– .* Canberra, The Commission.

The official statistical account of achievements and activities of the Australian Postal Commission. *Reports* for 1911–75 were published by the Postmaster-General's Department.

WATERS, F. *Postal unions and politics: a history of the Amalgamated Postal Workers Union of Australia.* Ed by D.J. Murphy. UQP, 1978. 311 p, illus.

An account by an official of the personalities of the union now called the Australian Postal and Telecommunications Union and the PMG Dept's management.

HISTORY AND PHILATELY

AUSTRALIA. Postmaster-General's Dept. *The Australian Post Office: a brief history, 1809–1975.* Melbourne, Australian Post Office, 1975. 34 p, illus.

Briefly covers developments in the pre-federation colonies through federal government authority of telegraph, telephone, radio and postal services.

AUSTRALIA. Postmaster-General's Dept. *Centenary of the Brisbane General Post Office.* Brisbane, The Department, 1972. 42 p, illus.

Deals with the construction and architecture of the buildings that served as Brisbane's GPO and a description of types of mail transport, the staff and mail sorting activities.

AUSTRALIA. Postmaster-General's Dept. *A history of the post office in Tasmania.* Hobart, Australian Post Office, 1975. 72 p, illus, maps.

Development of postal services in Tas to 1975. Includes employment, post office personalities, mail routes and mail transport from horseback to aeroplane.

CAMPBELL, H.M. *Queensland cancellations and other postal markings 1860–1913.* Melbourne, Royal Philatelic Society of Vic, 1977. 156 p, illus.

Emphasis on postmarks in use in Qld; covers also the carriage of mail by the railways and in a peripheral manner the development of postal services generally.

CAMPBELL, H.M. et al, *Tasmania: the postal history and postal markings.* Melbourne, Royal Philatelic Society of Vic, 1962. 203 p, illus.

Deals with the postmarks on Tasmanian mails. Description of new post offices, prisoners' mail and travelling post offices. See also Ingles (1975).

EUSTIS, H.N. ed, *The Australian air mail catalogue.* Adelaide, Hobby Investments, 1984. 230 p, illus.

A descriptive listing of philatelic mail carried on inaugural or significant air services, and some coverage of air mail facilities. First published in 1976.

GIBBS, C. *History of postal services in Victoria.* Melbourne, Australia Post, 1984. 125 p, illus, maps.

Traces the history of postal services in Vic since 1837.

HOUISON, A. *History of the post office: together with an historical* account of the issue of postage stamps in New South Wales. Sydney, Government Printer, 1890. 110 p, illus.

Covers the main postal developments in NSW up to 1890; the bulk of the work describes the stamps issued by the NSW Post Office. Facsimile edition, Sydney, View Publications, 1983.

INGLES, O.G. et al, Tasmania: the postal history and postal markings, part 2. Melbourne, Hawthorn for the Royal Philatelic Society of Vic, 1975. 189 p, illus, maps.

Companion volume to H.M. Campbell (1962).

PURVES, J.R.W. The postal history of the Port Phillip district 1835–1851. Melbourne, Royal Philatelic Society of Vic, 1950. 68 p, illus, map.

Development of mail services, growth of post offices, postage rates, ships' mails, and listing of postmarks in use.

WESTERN AUSTRALIA STUDY GROUP. Western Australia, the stamps and postal history: a guide to its philately. Ed by M. Hamilton. Perth, WA Study Group, 1979. 471 p, illus, maps.

Postal developments in WA although primarily before World War I when distinctive stamps were issued.

WILLIAMS, E. AND COLLAS, P. Northern Territory: a postal history 1824–1975. San Diego, California, Society of Australasian Specialists, 1977. 178 p, illus.

Offers a historical overview, including the establishment of post offices in the NT, the Overland Telegraph Line and mail by railway and aeroplane.

TELECOMMUNICATIONS

ALLEN, Y. AND SPENCER, S. The broadcasting chronology, 1809–1980. Sydney, Australian Film and Television School, 1983. 221 p.

Historic events and reference material in telecommunications and broadcasting arranged chronologically.

ATR: Australian telecommunication research J. Melbourne, Telecommunication Society of Australia, 1967– .

Research papers concerned with development of equipment and testing of materials.

AUSTRALIA. Committee of Inquiry into Telecommunications Services in Australia. Report . . . AGPS, 1982. 3 vols, illus.

Presents operational policies, organisational arrangements, planning of the Australian Telecommunications Commission, and the involvement of private industry. Chairman: J.A. Davidson.

AUSTRALIAN TELECOMMUNICATIONS COMMISSION. Engineering Training Group. Engineer development programme: introductory series: an engineer's introduction to Telecom technology. Comp by D.H. Johns. Melbourne, [Telecom] Engineering Training Group, 1981. 285 p, illus.

Technology of telegraph, data transmission, broadcast and power supply systems at an introductory level for graduate engineers.

AUSTRALIAN TELECOMMUNICATIONS COMMISSION. Engineering Training HQ. An introduction to equipment for non-technical personnel. Melbourne, [Telecom] Engineering Training HQ, 1979[?]. 91 p, illus.

Describes current telephony, lines and cables and associated equipment and appropriate elementary electrical theory of operations.

AUSTRALIAN TELECOMMUNICATIONS COMMISSION. National Telecommunications Planning Branch. Telecom 2000: an exploration of the long-term development of telecommunications in Australia. Melbourne, Government Printer, 1975. 166 p, illus.

Possible directions in Australia's social economic and technologi-

'Telegraph communication via Eastern.' Pamphlet, c1930. On 8 April 1927 the first public overseas radio-telegraph service opened between Australia and England. In June 1928 a similar service opened between Australia and Montreal, Canada.
BOOROWA PRODUCTIONS

cal future, and likely trends in demand for telecommunications facilities in the early 21st century.

AUSTRALIAN TELECOMMUNICATIONS COMMISSION. National Telecommunications Planning Branch. Outcomes from the Telecom 2000 report, July 1978. Melbourne, Telecom Australia, 1978. 70 p, illus.

Analyses response to the predictions, proposals and decisions of Telecom 2000 and describes Telecom's current technology.

AUSTRALIAN video and communications. Melbourne, General Magazine Company, 1981– .

Reviews home video recording TV equipment and programs with explanatory articles on systems and equipment at general interest level.

BAKER, D. 'From coo-ee to communications satellite', in A century of scientific progress: the centenary volume of the Royal Society of New South Wales. Sydney, Royal Society of NSW, 1968, 173–99.

Includes information on specialised aspects absent from other references. Despite title it does not cover satellite communications.

COMMUNICATIONS Australia. Sydney, Thomson Publications, 1982– .

Covers communications technology, the administration of telecommunications and commercial aspects.

HALL, E.R. A saga of achievement: a story of the men and women who maintained and operated radio and radar systems of the RAAF over 50 years. Melbourne, Bonall, 1978. 334 p, illus.

An account of RAAF communications systems, equipment and training from 1961 to 1966.

MOYAL, A.M. Clear across Australia: a history of telecommunications since 1788. Melbourne, Nelson, 1984. 437 p, illus, maps.

A lucid and critical story of telecommunications in Australia.

MUSCIO, W.T. *Australian radio: the technical story, 1923–1983.* Sydney, Kangaroo, 1984. 243 p, illus.

Details of the changing components, circuitry and performance of broadcasting transmitters and receivers, radio communication systems, record players and magnetic tape equipment used during the period.

ROSS, J.F. *History of radio in South Australia, 1897–1977.* Sydney, J.F. Ross, 1978. 271 p, illus.

Covers the applications of radio transmission, from telegraphy to commercial broadcasting, services to shipping, aeradio, flying doctor services and early satellite communication at Ceduna.

SANDERCOCK, C.E. *Submarine cables in Australia.* Brisbane, Post Office Historical Society, Australian Postal Institute Qld Division, 1954. 14 p.

Development of cable manufacture and operation with reference to location and laying of overseas and 'internal' submarine cables up to 1954. Refers also to the histories of the cable companies Siemens, Marconi and S.T.C.

TELECOMMUNICATION journal of Australia. Melbourne, Telecommunication Society of Australia, 1935/7–.

Covers developments in telecommunications, broadcasting and TV services. Regularly describes armed services telecommunications systems.

TELEGRAPHY

CLUNE, F. *Overland telegraph: the story of a great Australian achievement and the link between Adelaide and Port Darwin.* A & R, 1955. 238 p, illus, maps.

Relates construction and use of the line to the exploration and social development of the territories it crossed.

GRIBBLE, P.J. *What hath God wrought: the story of the electric telegraph, Queensland.* Brisbane, Telecom Australia, 1981. 1 vol (various pagings), illus.

Every phase of development of the Qld telegraph service from 1861 to 1964.

HARRISON, J.C. *Ninety years of telegraph progress.* Melbourne, The Author, 1945. 101 p, illus.

Australia-wide development, 1854–1944. Accounts of recruitment, training and duties of staff and equipment.

TAYLOR, P. *An end to silence: the building of the overland telegraph line from Adelaide to Darwin.* Sydney, Methuen, 1980. 192 p, illus, maps.

Describes hardships suffered and technical methods used in constructing the line from 1870 to 1872.

TELEPHONY

BATEMAN, J. *History of the telephone in New South Wales.* Sydney, The Author, 1980. 122 p, illus.

Telephones, switchboards and exchanges from earliest Australian installations until mid-1970s. Virtually a catalogue of equipment.

REINECKE, I. AND SCHULTZ, J. *The phone book: the future of Australia's communications on the line.* Ringwood, Vic, Penguin, 1983. 270 p.

Political and industrial influences on the development of services in Telecom are discussed as expressed in the report of the Committee of Inquiry into Telecommunications Services in Australia, 1982.

SODEN, F.A. *et al, 100 years of the telephone 1876–1976.* Sydney, Australian Historic Telephone Society, 1976. 63 p, illus.

A history of the telephone and associated equipment for the

non-technical reader. Telephone service in Melbourne and Vic is covered with illustrations of early instruments.

SATELLITE COMMUNICATION

AUSSAT PTY LTD. *AUSSAT: Australia's national satellite system: an executive overview.* Sydney, Aussat Pty Ltd, 1983. 47 p, illus.

Describes the space and earth components of the system, its technical specifications and the business outlook and major users.

AUSSAT: newsletter of the Australian Satellite Users Association. Sydney, Aussat, 1981– .

Applications of an Australian satellite with descriptions of equipment and projects.

AUSTRALIA. National Communication Satellite System Task Force. *National communications satellite system: report, July 1978.* AGPS, 1978. (Australia Parliament. Parliamentary paper no 317 of 1978).

Inquires into all aspects of a national communication satellite system for Australia.

AUSTRALIAN COMMUNICATIONS SATELLITE CONFERENCE, Perth, 1979. *Papers and proceedings of the Australian Communications Satellite Conference held December 4–6, 1979 at the University of Western Australia ...,* Ed by C. Deacon. Perth, University Extension, University of Western Australia, 1980. 551 p, illus, maps.

A discussion of the 'promise and perils' of applying communications satellites. The technology and the social effects are considered.

Advertisement for Standard Telephones and Cables in the Bulletin, *3 Sept 1985. With the launch in 1985 of Australia's domestic satellite system, AUSSAT, STC proudly announced that it was 'the first Australian company into space'.*

Photograph of King's Bridge, Launceston, officially opened in 1864.
QUEEN VICTORIA MUSEUM AND ART GALLERY, LAUNCESTON

CHAPTER 35

ENGINEERING

D. CUMMING AND L. J. JONES

O N 3 JUNE 1828, when the Institution of Civil Engineers was incorporated in England, the founders wrote into its charter a statement aimed at clarifying what civil engineering was all about. The civil engineer, they declared, was someone concerned with 'the art of directing the Great Sources of Power in Nature for the use and convenience of man'.

Of course the adjective 'civil' had a somewhat different meaning then. Basically 'civil' meant 'not military', and so in 1828 civil engineering was understood to include areas which are now regarded as quite separate. As the charter document went on to explain, civil engineers dealt with the design and construction of roads, bridges, canals, harbours and the like, but also 'the construction and adaptation of machinery'—work which nowadays is the acknowledged concern of mechanical rather than civil engineers.

With the passing of time the 'art' mentioned in the original charter has become more formalised; scientific principles now guide much (though still by no means all) engineering activity. Nevertheless, we should understand that while engineering and science are now closely associated, there are important differences between them. The former's concern is with 'doing things', while the business of the latter is observing and trying to understand the phenomena of the world around us. In short, science seeks knowledge of the world, while engineering's concern is with providing goods and services.

Modern engineering encompasses a vast range of activities, and so for convenience the profession is now divided into a number of separate and more-or-less specialised 'branches'. Apart from the military, civil, and mechanical groups already mentioned, we now acknowledge electrical (and electronic) engineers, chemical engineers, mining and metallurgical engineers and industrial (or production) engineers, as well as some perhaps less populous groups such as agricultural, textile, marine and so on. Obviously then, in a relatively short essay such as this, an exhaustive coverage of engineering historical sources cannot be provided. Nor is it possible to include historical material associated with every kind of engineering.

Books and documents are not the only valid record of engineering activity. What are termed 'hard relics'—that is, surviving artefacts and structures or their remains—are also of prime interest. Technical museums have been set up to preserve some of these, and also perhaps to bring the general public a little closer to technology. Familiar examples abroad are the so-called Science Museum in London (founded 1857), the Smithsonian in Washington, DC (1846) and the great Deutsche Museum in Munich (1903). In Australia there are technological collections of interest at Sydney (1880) and Melbourne (1870), but over the years both have suffered from a chronic lack of staff and endowments. Probably a contributing factor to this unhappy state of affairs has been the long-held (though incorrect) assumption in Australia that we can always import the technology we need, and thus do not need to develop our own.

In recent times various 'heritage' groups in Australia (both private and government-sponsored) have begun to take some interest in technical sites and relics, though once again Australia has been much slower than many other countries to move in this direction. The various state-based National Trust organisations, and the federal government's official agency, the Heritage Commission, still tend to concentrate on conserving places of natural beauty and buildings of architectural merit, while giving scant attention to historically significant industrial sites and remains. True, in the comprehensive *Heritage of Australia* (1981), the commission's record of what it sees as the National Estate, a number of industrial buildings such as flour-mills are listed. So too are several bridges and mine sites, the Humphrey pumps at Cobdogla on the River Murray, the zigzag line at Lithgow, and the remains of the Lal Lal blast furnace in central Victoria.

Some useful preservation work has been accomplished by various societies of enthusiasts around the country, notably those interested in areas such as railways and tramways. A few smaller specialist enterprises (for example, maritime and riverboat museums) have contributed as well. In general, however, specifically engineering remains—and especially 'hardware' such as machinery—have been ignored.

The study of the history of engineering has been a recognised scholarly discipline in the northern hemisphere for quite some time. In Britain, for example, Samuel Smiles wrote his *Lives of the engineers* in the years following the Great Exhibition of 1851, while the Newcomen Society (for the study of the history of engineering and technology) has published scholarly articles on engineering history in its *Transactions* continuously since 1920. Australia lags considerably by comparison. There are still no Australian societies devoted specifically to studying engineering history, and indeed there has been little interest shown even by individuals until quite recently. The little that has been written about Australia's engineering achievements has tended to come from economic and general historians, whose perspective and expertise, naturally, are not those of the engineer. It is for this reason that most of the otherwise excellent works of G.N. Blainey and like authors are not listed here, but included in other chapters. Similarly no mention is made here of the records of public inquiries into bridge failures and such; Australia's 'disasters' are dealt with elsewhere in this volume.

Colonists (mostly British) began coming to this continent in 1788, bringing with them a knowledge of the advanced British technologies and practical skills of that time. It was in Britain, after all, that the Industrial Revolution had begun not so many years before. As a result Australian engineering at first was strongly derivative, reflecting the backgrounds and training of some of those early migrants. Let us not forget, however, that the original (Aboriginal) Australians had skills and technologies of their own—albeit of a much different kind. These skills helped them to survive in extremely inhospitable parts of the continent, and from them some of the European newcomers undoubtedly learned. In time the Europeans, too, devised new approaches to cope with an environment that was very different, and so in technology as well as in agriculture the 'make do' colonial tradition was born. Indeed 'bush engineering'—in which whatever happens to be to hand, together with native ingenuity, is employed to meet a need in the absence of proper facilities—is an element of Australian rural life still.

From the beginning of European settlement in Australia a number of primary needs of the migrant population had to be met. Obviously a reliable supply of water for drinking and washing was an early priority, and the establishment of local agriculture to make the new colonies self-sufficient in food was also important. Scholarly historical work in these areas is at last underway, but so far most of the results have only appeared in higher degree thesis form.

In agriculture generally Australia has had a quite fascinating history, not only because of the vastness of the country, but also because the climatic and soil conditions are unique. A number of new and important agricultural machines were invented and introduced in Australia over the past century and a half. John Ridley's 'stripper' for harvesting grain (1843), R.B. Smith's 'stump-jumping plough' (1876) and, in this century, C. Howard's 'rotary hoe' are three which come readily to mind.

The pastoral industry likewise has had its share of local inventions and innovations directed to specifically Australian needs. A rare (also brief) treatment of the development of the shearing handpiece is to be found, for instance, in A.D. Fraser (1938). More recently an excellent biography by W.R. Lang (1982) deals with the invention and development by James Harrison of the refrigeration machinery which made possible frozen meat exports from Australia to Britain and Europe in the latter half of the last century.

Manufacturing industry of course came later, as the population grew and colonial markets developed. The history of Australian manufacturing, however, is still largely unresearched and unwritten—though there are a few exceptions. We are indebted to Helen Hughes (1964) for her fine treatment of developments in iron and steel making. As well as being one of the first published works in the field, it is also one of the most instructive and most readable. Also of some interest in this area are the biographies by G.N. Blainey (1971) and P. Mawson (1958).

A few accounts of particular manufacturing activities have appeared in recent years, but once again most remain in postgraduate thesis form. Publications in this area to date represent only a scratching of the surface; much more work is required before any clear picture of local manufacturing (and in particular of what is genuinely Australian) will emerge.

An interesting aspect of all the Australian colonies is that most of the development of their basic services was, from the beginning, government sponsored. Little was left to private initiative. This pattern of establishing such things has become characteristic of Australia and Australians, and continues to this day. As a result significant government engineering organisations were established quite early. The stories of these official enterprises are by no means easy to unravel. It is not that there is any scarcity of historical material; indeed detailed information (often including original engineering calculations and drawings) on the construction of railways, roads, bridges, dams, sewerage systems, irrigation schemes, electricity generating stations and networks, and so on, abounds. The difficulty is that much of it resides in reports and other disparate records held by a multitude of government departments and municipal and semigovernment authorities distributed across the nation.

Most technical documents from government departments eventually find their way into the official government archives, where they are relatively safe. Regrettably local and semi-government authorities are not obliged to deposit their non-current materials in the same way, and there have been some important losses of historical evidence from time to time. Even so there is a vast amount remaining for researchers to examine.

The situation is different, and even less satisfactory, in the non-government area. Very few documents of any kind from early engineering firms have survived; those that have are mostly lacking in technical detail, relating mainly to ordinary commercial aspects of profit and loss. However, some papers have been gathered by university archivists. The University of Melbourne Archives, for example, has prepared a guide to its holdings of this type of material.

In a few cases dedicated public servants have themselves taken a hand in recording and publishing the significant accomplishments of their particular departments—though, curiously, rarely to our knowledge in the railway systems. Published works dealing with the development of roads, however, are more common. Two useful recent works of this type are by M.J.L. Uren and F. Parrick (1976) (from Western Australia), and a volume by members of the New South Wales Department of Main Roads (1976). A somewhat different aspect of transport is dealt with by J.D. Keating (1980), who traces the interesting history of cable trams in the city of Melbourne.

Published accounts of early Australian engineering works by contemporary writers have been few and mostly lightweight. However, W.B. Hays (1856) treated civil engineering projects in South Australia in the early nineteenth century. Similar in content, though shorter and less detailed technically, is W.H. Warren's article (1888). Much of the engineering historical record—preserved as mentioned earlier in the fading collections of scattered government departments and authorities—still awaits examination. We must wait a little longer for researchers to assess, collate and interpret this record for the benefit of all.

Before presenting a formal bibliography comprising a selection of available works, a few words might be said concerning certain topics which would appear to be relevant and interesting, but which are not represented in this selection. Telegraphy and radio, for example, have a considerable history on this continent, and publications of quality are available. Both, however, are covered in other parts of this volume. Mining in Australia is also treated in another chapter. This notwithstanding, we have chosen to include a few works on mining subjects, where there are specifically engineering connotations.

It is well known that the development of railways by the Australian colonies occurred separately, and the resulting variety of track widths is one of the technical embarrassments of the nation. Their history is an interesting one, beginning with a few small horse-operated lines around 1854 and progressing eventually to steam and finally electrified systems in each of the states. In the early days of steam railways the locomotives and rolling stock were purchased overseas, but as early as 1854 a complete locomotive was successfully built in Victoria. By 1856 New South Wales, Victoria and South Australia all had steam railways operating, and all were government owned. By 1864 the Victorians had a line to Echuca on the River Murray, linking up with the thriving steamboat trade there.

Historical writing on Australian railways and tramways has tended to have the same piecemeal approach. There are reasonably satisfactory accounts available for most of the state systems, but suitable books dealing with railways or tramways nationally are conspicuously absent.

Australian aeronautical engineering is another area where suitable publications are lacking— perhaps that branch of engineering is yet too young to be much concerned with such things.

Finally we would draw attention, very briefly, to a small group of contemporary Australian engineers (as distinct from economists, general historians and others) who are pursuing historical research into specific areas of technical endeavour. They include the authors of this literature survey (South Australian engineering and Australian agricultural machinery, respectively), P. Milner in Victoria (metal mining and its technology), D.J. Fraser (lattice-girder bridges in New South Wales), C. O'Connor (Australian bridges generally), and R.L. Whitmore (coalmining in Queensland). Already O'Connor has published a small book (1983) and Whitmore two substantial ones (1981, 1985). In addition the latter has for some time been active in promoting the serious study of engineering history in that state.

The following bibliography is divided for convenience into five sections. The items included should indicate something of the great diversity of engineering work carried on within Australia over the years, and perhaps also something of its uniqueness.

For assistance with the compilation of this essay and bibliography, the authors are grateful to Drs P. Milner and B.W. Field of Melbourne, and to Mr I. Macfarlane of Canberra.

English Electric Company of Australia Ltd Tender, *1924. One of the unsuccessful tenderers for the Sydney Harbour Bridge was the English Electric Company of Australia Ltd which produced this design for a stiffened suspension bridge in 1924. The successful tenderer, Dorman Long and Co, built an arch bridge between 1925 and 1932.*
BOOROWA PRODUCTIONS

INVENTIONS, AGRICULTURAL AND PASTORAL MACHINERY

AUSTRALIAN ACADEMY OF SCIENCE. Science and Industry Forum, Canberra, 1977. *From stump-jump plough to inter-scan: a review of invention and innovation in Australia; papers delivered at a meeting ...* Canberra, The Academy, 1977. 112 p, illus. (Forum report, 10, 1977.)

Papers reviewing some Australian inventions—though nothing on the stump-jump plough. Those on Sirotherm and Interscan are the most interesting.

CONIGRAVE, J.F. *Agriculture in South Australia: a description of the South Australian seedsower, stripper, and winnower.* Adelaide, Government Printer, 1883. 11 p, illus.

A rare document for this period in that it includes some technical detail. It was prepared, at the behest of the South Australian government, for the Calcutta Exhibition of 1883–84.

DUTTON, F.S. *South Australia and its mines.* London, T. & N Boone, 1846. 361 p, illus, maps.

Primarily concerned with mines and mining, but it contains also a detailed description (with diagrams) of the Ridley stripper. Facsimile edition, Adelaide, Austaprint, 1978.

FRASER, A.D. *This century of ours, being an account of the origin and history during one hundred years of the House of Dangar, Gedye & Malloch Ltd.* Sydney, Halstead, 1938. 214 p, illus.

Chapters 16 ff and the appendix provide probably the best available account of the development of the shearing handpiece.

KENDALL, J. 'H.V. McKay: a pioneer industrialist' in *Victorian historical magazine* 43, 3, 1972, 885–95.

One of the few soundly written pieces dealing with McKay's contributions.

LANG, W.R. *James Harrison pioneering genius.* Newtown, Vic, Neptune, 1982. 141 p, illus, maps.

Well-researched first book on the achievements of this important Australian inventor whose work made possible frozen meat exports.

PORT, L.W. AND MURRAY, B. *Australian inventors.* Sydney, Cassell, 1978. 205 p, illus, map.

Rather lacking in factual accuracy more often than is comfortable. However, there is little else available of this type.

SELFE, N. *Machinery for refrigeration ...* Chicago, H.S. Rich and Co, 1900. 416 p, illus.

An early work by an Australian pioneer in this field which should be read following W.R. Lang (1982).

WHEELHOUSE, F.L. *Digging stick to rotary hoe: men and machines in rural Australia.* Sydney, Transpareon, 1977. 222 p, illus.

A pioneeer work clearly written and well illustrated but contains, like Port and Murray (1978), a disturbing number of incorrect assertions. First published in 1966.

MANUFACTURING INDUSTRY, MINING AND METALLURGY

BLAINEY, G.N. *The steel master: a life of Essington Lewis.* Melbourne, Macmillan, 1971. 217 p, illus.

Biography of an important industrialist, whose dynamism and vision saw the Broken Hill Proprietary Company through the years of the depression become one of the world's steelmaking giants.

CHARLETON, A.G. *Gold mining and milling in Western Australia, with notes upon telluride treatment, costs and mining practice in other fields.* London, E. & F.N. Spon, 1903. 648 p, illus.

Provides a good and detailed treatment of early mining and mineral processing in the West Australian goldfields.

CLARKE, D. *Australian mining and metallurgy.* Melbourne, Critchley Parker, 1904. 534 p, illus, maps.

An account of mining and mineral processing in WA, Qld, Vic, NSW and Tas.

GREEN, F.A. *The Port Pirie smelters.* Melbourne, Broken Hill Associated Smelters, 1977. 170 p, illus.

Written by one who was associated with the development and operations of the smelters, their people, plant, processes and products.

HUGHES, H. *The Australian iron and steel industry 1848–1962.* MUP, 1964. 213 p, illus, map.

An excellent work with emphasis on economic history, but the coverage of technical matters is adequate and accurate.

KING-ROACH, J. *Not without courage: the story of the fortunes which one hundred years of trading have witnessed for Hawke and Co ...* Adelaide, Griffin, 1957. ix, 28 p, illus.

History of a significant South Australian manufacturer of mining and agricultural equipment between 1860 and 1920. The firm continued until 1983.

LEWIS, E. *Importance of the iron and steel industry to Australia.* Adelaide, Hassell, 1948. 33 p, map.

A published lecture by the then chairman and guiding spirit of BHP.

MAWSON, P. *A vision of steel: the life of G.D. Delprat, C.B.E., general manager of B.H.P., 1898–1921.* Melbourne, Cheshire, 1958. 269 p, illus, maps.

An account of Delprat and his career in the Australian steel industry, with little in the way of hard technical information.

PENN, D.W. *How firm the foundation: a historical survey of an independent venture that founded the Portland Cement industry in Australia.* Sydney, Concrete Publishing, 1977. 182 p, illus.

A good history of the cement industry in Adelaide, with special emphasis on the Brighton Cement Company and those who worked for it.

WHITMORE, R.L. *Coal in Queensland: the first fifty years: a history of early coal mining in Queensland.* UQP, 1981. 185 p, illus, maps.

A substantial work and most important contribution. A further volume, published in 1985, brings the story up to 1900.

WATER SUPPLY AND HYDRO-POWER

AIRD, W.V. *The water supply, sewerage and drainage of Sydney: an account of the development and history ... from their beginnings with the first settlement to 1960 ...* Sydney, Metropolitan Water, Sewerage and Drainage Board, 1961. 347 p, illus, maps.

Comprehensive treatment, engagingly written and accompanied by detailed statistics.

EATON, J.H.O. *A short history of the River Murray works.* Adelaide, Government Printer, 1945. 69 p, illus, maps.

A useful account of the engineering works carried out on the River Murray between 1890 and 1940, written by a member of the River Murray Commission. Also deals with the political rivalries which complicated the execution of projects.

GARVIE, R.M.H. *A million horses: Tasmania's power in the mountains.* Hobart, Hydro-Electric Commission, 1962. 111 p, illus, maps.

The development of hydro-power in Tas from Duck River power station in 1895 to Poatina in the Great Lakes. Good bibliography.

HILL, E. *Water into gold.* Melbourne, Robertson & Mullens, 1937. 328 p, illus, maps.

A good history of the work of the Chaffey brothers in establishing irrigation in the Mildura–Renmark region. Reissued in many editions.

MEEKING, C. *Snowy Mountain conquest: harnessing the waters of Australia's highest mountains.* London, Hutchinson, 1968. 192 p, illus, maps.

The work involved in the Snowy scheme, the people who carried it out, and the problems they faced.

ROSEBY, T.J. *Sydney's water supply and sewerage, 1788–1918.* Sydney, Government Printer, 1918. 112 p, illus, maps.

An early account of the establishment and development of Sydney's water supply, and those involved in the work.

TAUMAN, M. *The chief: C.Y. O'Connor.* UWAP, 1978. 290 p, illus, maps.

Biography of the government's chief engineer for WA responsible, among other things, for the design and construction of the harbour at Fremantle and the water supply to Coolgardie and Kalgoorlie. For a time he was also chief engineer of the state's railways.

THOMAS, H.H. *The engineering of large dams.* London, Wiley, 1976. 2 vols, illus, maps.

A comprehensive Australian textbook on the design and building of large dams, with reference to actual and past Australian projects.

WIGMORE, L.G. *Struggle for the Snowy: the background of the Snowy Mountains Scheme.* OUP, 1968. 215 p, illus, maps.

An account of the Snowy Mountains hydro and irrigation scheme, with details of the economic and political factors and the personalities involved, but little on the engineering aspects of the scheme.

TRANSPORT AND PUBLIC UTILITIES

ARMSTRONG, J. ed, *Shaping the Hunter: a story of engineers, and the engineering contribution to the development of the present shape of the Hunter Region* ... Newcastle, NSW Newcastle Division, Institution of Engineers, Australia, 1983. 192 p, illus, maps.

Engineers and their contribution to the development of the Hunter River waterway, and also the cities, industries and transport of the region.

BEADELL, L. *Outback highways.* Adelaide, Rigby, 1979. 237 p, illus, maps.

An account of the development of roads in connection with the Woomera rocket range; the people and events associated with their construction.

CARROLL, B. *Getting around town: a history of urban transport in Australia.* Sydney, Cassell, 1980. 176 p, illus.

A history of city transport from the horse-buses of 1849, through the eras of horse-drawn, steam, cable and electric trams, to the taxis, buses and suburban trains and ferries of the present day.

COANE, J.M. *et al, Australasian roads: a treatise, practical and scientific, on the location, design, construction and maintenance of roads and pavements.* Melbourne, Robertson, 1908. 334 p, illus.

A description of all aspects of municipal and general road engineering, including descriptions of hand and horse-operated machines, as well as those powered by steam, petrol and oil. Fifth edition, published 1937, contains 811 pages.

FITZGERALD, A. ed, *Canberra's engineering heritage* ... Canberra, Canberra Division, Institution of Engineers, Australia, 1983. 211 p, illus, maps.

Granite columns at the GPO in Martin Place, Sydney. Photograph, c1879–80. Government departments regularly captured on film the progress of capital works during various stages of construction and demolition primarily for their own records though some were used as promotional material in government publications. Their photographic collections provide a rich source of historical data.
NSW GOVERNMENT PRINTING OFFICE

The work of engineers in creating roads, railways, urban public transport, lakes and dams, water supply and sewerage systems, electricity supply, and other amenities in Canberra.

HARRIGAN, L.J. *Victorian railways to '62.* Melbourne, Victorian Railways Public Relations Board, 1962. 299 p, illus, maps.

A detailed but readable history, liberally supported by photographs, maps and statistics.

HARTNETT, L.J. *Big wheels and little wheels.* Melbourne, Gold Star Publications, 1973. 278 p, illus.

An authoritative account of the beginnings of the Australian automobile manufacturing industry, by one of its most important pioneers. First published in 1964.

HAYS, W.B. *Engineering in South Australia.* London, printed by John Knott, 1856. 45 p, illus, map.

A description of colonial engineering works and of bridges over the River Torrens in Adelaide, and the development of Port Elliot and its tramway. Facsimile edition, Adelaide, LBSA, 1965.

KEATING, J.D. *Mind the curve! A history of the cable trams.* MUP, 1980. 173 p, illus, map.

A history of the cable tram system in Melbourne, the company and people that operated it, and the establishment of the Melbourne and Metropolitan Tramways Board.

KINGSBOROUGH, L.S. *The horse tramways of Adelaide and its suburbs, 1875–1907.* Adelaide, LBSA, 1967. 101 p, illus.

Deals briefly with the systems, the types of equipment used and the various tramways companies of the period.

NEW SOUTH WALES. Dept of Main Roads. *The roadmakers: a history of main roads in New South Wales.* Sydney, The Department, 1976. 335 p, illus, maps.

A comprehensive discussion of roads and roadbuilding including bridges in NSW from 1788 to the mid-1970s. Includes an account of the difficulties in constructing roads through the Blue Mountains.

NEW SOUTH WALES. Dept of Railways. *The railways of New South Wales, 1855-1955.* Sydney, The Department, 1955. 304 p, illus.

A good coverage of the NSW railway system, with reasonable technical detail.

O'CONNOR, C. *How to look at bridges: a guide to the study of Australian historic bridges.* Canberra, Institution of Engineers, Australia, 1983. 50 p, illus.

This booklet instructs the reader how to 'interpret' some of Australia's bridges.

PHILLIPS, V. *Bridges and ferries of Australia.* Sydney, Bay Books, 1983. 160 p, illus, maps.

A lively book on these seldom treated subjects, but slight in technical content.

PHILLIPS, V. *Romance of Australian lighthouses.* Adelaide, Rigby, 1977. 221 p, illus.

An account of the lighthouses with particular reference to the people who built and manned them. Short on technical detail.

SERLE, G. *John Monash: a biography.* Melbourne, MUP in association with Monash University, 1982. 600 p, illus, maps.

The life and work of an engineer who pioneered reinforced concrete, became a leading general in World War I, and then chairman of the State Electricity Commission of Vic during its formative years.

SOUTH AUSTRALIA. Railways Dept. *South Australian railways: locomotives, steam and diesel electric, and rolling stock.* Adelaide, Government Printer, 1964. 56 p, illus.

This small work deals with its subject in reasonable technical detail.

UREN, M.J.L. AND PARRICK, F. *Servant of the state: the history of the Main Roads Department, 1926–1976.* Perth, The Department, 1976. 44 p, illus, maps.

As the preface states, 'the reader who looks in these pages for learned reports on engineering details of roads and bridges will be disappointed'. Nevertheless, a useful general account.

WARREN, W.H. 'History of civil engineering in New South Wales', *Report of the Meeting of the Australasian Association for the Advancement of Science* 1, 1888, 590–648.

An early review paper of NSW works relating to bridges, roads, railways, punts and ferries, tunnels and viaducts, water supply (for Sydney and several other towns), sewerage, harbours and docks.

MISCELLANEOUS

BIRMINGHAM, J. *et al, Australian pioneer technology: sites and relics ... towards an industrial archaeology of Australia.* Melbourne, Heinemann Educational, 1979. 200 p, illus, maps.

BIRMINGHAM, J. *et al, Industrial archaeology in Australia: rural industry.* Melbourne, Heinemann, 1983. 191 p, illus, maps.

These two efforts at interpreting Australian history through the evidence of industrial relics and environmental changes offer a new view of how European immigrants adapted to their country and point to some local innovations of national (and sometimes even international) significance.

CAMPBELL-ALLEN, D. AND DAVIS, E.H. eds, *The profession of a civil engineer: papers written for Jack William Roderick by former students.* SUP, 1979. 229 p, illus.

Biography of Professor Roderick and some general papers on engineering in Australia.

CORBETT, A.H. *The Institution of Engineers, Australia: a history of the first fifty years, 1919–1969.* Sydney, Institution of Engineers, Australia, in association with A & R, 1973. 288 p, illus.

An account of engineering activities in Australia, the people who were prominent and the various engineering organisations and societies.

LLOYD, B.E. *Engineering manpower in Australia.* Melbourne, Association of Professional Engineeers, Australia, 1979. 420 p, illus.

Examines the nature of engineering works and the various skills required of professional engineers, technicians and tradesmen.

LLOYD, B.E. AND WILKIN, W.J. *The education of professional engineers in Australia.* Melbourne, Association of Professional Engineers, Australia, 1968. 490 p, illus.

Discusses the aims and ideals of engineers and the educational processes which form them. Includes a historical look at the features of the major institutions involved in educating engineers. First published in 1959.

McNICOLL, R.R. *The Royal Australian Engineers.* Canberra, Corps Committee, Royal Australian Engineers, 1977–   . v, illus.

Australia's army engineers in both peace and war. Three volumes have so far been published covering the years 1835 to 1945. A planned fourth volume will cover the years to 1975.

Russen's working bakery at the Tasmanian International Exhibition, Launceston, 1891–92.

QUEEN VICTORIA MUSEUM AND ART GALLERY, LAUNCESTON

CHAPTER 36

INDUSTRIAL DEVELOPMENT

D.A. WADLEY

IN 1851, THERE WERE but 10 800 manufacturing employees in Australia. Twenty years later, they numbered 52 000 and by 1891 there were 149 000. Despite the depression of the 1890s, growth in manufacturing employment continued strongly. At Federation in 1901, Australia had 198 000 factory workers. With continuing industrialisation, the figure topped half a million during the late 1930s and a million in 1954. Peak employment of 1 388 000 was reached in 1973–74, since when there has been a decline to a little over one million.

The rise and, lately, retreat of Australian manufacturing is told in several thousand books, articles and government reports. They show that New South Wales has always been the leading manufacturing state; that, originally, it was followed in importance by Tasmania and South Australia; that these colonies lost their place to Victoria; and that, since the late nineteenth century, the spatial pattern has consolidated to leave New South Wales and Victoria as the core surrounded by other states in far more peripheral roles. This chapter details the literature that describes these events and many more besides. For convenience it is divided into three parts: statistical, official and documentary sources; material written in and relating to the years 1850–1950; and finally, in greater detail, writings from and about the period 1950–83.

STATISTICAL, OFFICIAL AND DOCUMENTARY SOURCES

Research into Australian industrialisation should start among the publications of the Australian Bureau of Statistics (ABS) and its predecessor organisations. The *Yearbook of Australia* presents a section of consolidated statistics that are fleshed out in regular publications issued by the Canberra and state offices (see also chapter 9). Users should consult the ABS 8100–8300 reference codes (others before 1969) for annual manufacturing censuses and assorted production bulletins. The ABS list also contains significant material under other codes (for example, transport, building and national accounts), and those interested are advised to consult the reference works cited under chapters 7 and 8.

Parliamentary papers and transcripts of debates are important for the serious investigator. The former contain reports of the Australian Industries Assistance Commission and the erstwhile Tariff Board (1921–74), and the results of numerous inquiries and commissions dating back to the time of self-government among the colonies. (See Borchardt's *Checklist of royal commissions, select committees of parliament and boards of inquiry* in chapter 8.) Indexes of this material have been provided by Linge (1964, 1967) and the Australian Industries Assistance Commission (1974).

Before 1901, key sources are papers of colonial parliaments and, of course, their statistical registers.

State departments of industrial development set up in the post-1945 era often interpret and republish statistical data and provide local reports. On the international front, the United Nations *Statistical yearbook* and the economic surveys of the Organisation for Economic Co-operation and Development (OECD) provide valuable comparative data on Australian manufacturing.

Directories should also be consulted. Some of the major ones are the *Australian handbook* (1870–1906), Wise's post office directories for each state (for example, *Tasmanian post office directory*, 1890–1949), Sand's directories (for example, Sydney and New South Wales, 1863–1933; Melbourne and Victoria, 1857–1974) and Pugh's Queensland almanacs (1859–1927). *Jobson's investment digest of Australia and New Zealand*, which began in 1920 as the *Australian investment digest*, is the best single source on particular firms.

Useful journals with which to investigate Australian industry include the *Economic record* (1925–), *Australian economic papers* (1962–), *Economic analysis and policy* (1970–), *Australian economic review* (1968–), *Australian geographical studies* (1963–), *Australian geographer* (1928–) and the *Journal of the institution of Engineers, Australia* (1929–). Among the business periodicals, one could consult *Rydges*, *Business review weekly*, the *Australian Stock Exchange journal* and *Australian business*. The most important newspaper is the *Australian Financial Review* (1951–).

There is a considerable literature about the role of entrepreneurs in Australian manufacturing. Notable examples include Essington Lewis (Blainey, 1971) and Thomas Sutcliffe Mort (Barnard, 1961); many more examples can be found in Marshall and Trahair *A checklist of biographies of Australian businessmen*, 1980 (see chapter 20).

FROM 1850 TO 1950

The history of Australian industrial development between 1850 and 1901 is yet to be fully recorded. A difficulty with the pre-Federation era is that very few primary accounts take an Australian overview. Before 1901, one is largely left with aggregate material from the six colonies and, invariably, more information is available on New South Wales and Victoria than on other areas. Specialised texts deal with these two colonies whereas industrial coverage of the others is mostly buried within general economic reporting.

A major secondary source covering pre-Federation industrialisation is Linge (1979). A historical geography organised on a colony-by-colony basis, it features a 34-page appendix on manufacturing statistics from 1860 to 1890 and 66 pages of footnotes and references which detail archival holdings including company records. One should also note G.D. Patterson (1968) which proceeds chronologically through the period and devotes much attention to the ramification on industrial development of protectionism in Victoria as opposed to the free trade of New South Wales. The central role of tariff questions in Federation is additionally considered.

Post-Federation primary literature, 1901–50, is more broadly focused than the foregoing works and is increasingly analytical and academic. Early twentieth century sources of particular interest are those of foreign trade officials or consuls. For instance, Morgan (1908) reported to his sponsors in Great Britain that

> capitalists need have no fear of labour in Australia ... the Australian is an excellent worker, and if his wages are high and he is aggressive and sometimes troublesome, it should be remembered that the profits of manufacturing are also high and the country is extremely prosperous (64).

Morgan's point was not lost on politicians of the time who found it expedient to ensure that wages and profits did not sink to European levels. Interstate trade in Australia had been free since 1901: thereafter, protectionists exerted significant pressure for the establishment of national tariffs to safeguard local industry against overseas competition. The tariff occupies a central and revered place in Australian industrial literature. Reitsma (1960) highlights the main events between 1901 and 1950: the first impositions of 1902; the 1907 Lyne round; the activities of the

Interstate Commission after 1913 in investigating and publishing findings on a range of industries; the 1921 'three-decker' tariff and the appointment of the Tariff Board; and the Scullin round of 1929–31 which, in response to emergency depression conditions, greatly increased duties and prohibited many imports.

That the 1920s were a turbulent and formative period for Australian manufacturing is reflected in a secondary text by economic historian Colin Forster (1964). Forster concentrates on motor vehicles, cement, textiles, electrical equipment and ferrous metals. In 1933, the academic Windett also reviewed post-World War I industrialisation with similar emphases, while Pratt (1934) is organised by state and provides detail down to individual company annual reports. Mauldon and others (1938) deal with all economic sectors, but especially manufacturing.

Emerging academic and policy debate about industry was halted by World War II but from 1945 to 1950 a series of useful works appeared. Industry was considered as a facet of postwar reconstruction policy in texts such as those of the Australian Institute of Political Science (1945) and Walker (1947). Fascinating advice to industrial workers intending to migrate is given by Douglas (1947). The immediate postwar era also saw debates on regionalisation of industry among writers of the Australian Institute of Political Science (1948), Halsey (1949) and Gates and Drane (1953).

INDUSTRIAL DEVELOPMENT SINCE 1950

According to Wadley and Rich (1983, 9–12), Australian industrial development since 1950 falls into three phases which may be related to different types of writing: a boom until the early 1960s produced a literature of expansionary tenor; a decade of flowering and faltering after 1962 was attended by a more sophisticated and diverse commentary; a decline after 1974 engendered pessimism and the emergence of a radical critique. The following discussion is organised around these broad chronological and thematic categories.

Descriptions based on statistical publications mark writing on early postwar manufacturing, the task being to rebuild a data base for existing industries and to establish one for new forms of production. The federal Department of National Development, established on 17 March 1950, provided a unique insight into Australian industry of the time in a key document (1952) which systematised information to supplement basic government statistics. It should be read with the department's *Industry review series* (1948–57) of foolscap mimeographs which, from 1958 to 1962, was continued by the Commonwealth Department of Trade as the *Industry study series*. The 52 volumes so produced offer a detailed view of Australian industries in the first postwar phase: similar work is now undertaken by the Industries Assistance Commission.

The Department of Trade produced other significant series including *Developments in Australian manufacturing industries, British manufacturers in Australia*, the *Directory of United States investment in Australian manufacturing industry* and the *Survey of manufacturing activity in Australia*. Such publications had their political purposes in an economy oriented to expansion. Nevertheless, they now afford a cumulative account of the growth of secondary production, entries neatly grouped by industry.

The cataloguing of capacities and resources occupied many state government departments. They handed the results of resource surveys to regional development committees which, several years later, produced plans for their respective areas. A good example is a 1950 survey of the Newcastle region by the New South Wales Premier's Department which was followed in 1955 by a report of the Newcastle Regional Development Committee. Two years later the economist F.G. Davidson produced the first of many editions of *The industrialization of Australia* (1957). Simultaneously, E.L. Wheelwright (1957) presented a new analysis of the voting stock of 102 of the nation's largest public companies. It was followed by a further examination coauthored with Judith Miskelly (1967) focusing almost exclusively on the secondary sector.

The Manufacturing Industries Advisory Council presented a report (1959) which is an important precursor of the Vernon Report (Australia. Committee of Economic Enquiry) of 1965. The council's other study (1962) details products which could be developed to save imports and promote exports as a way of sustaining rapid economic growth. Nowhere, however, does it outline a preferred direction of manufacturing development: policy statements were generally lacking in the literature of this time.

FLOWERING AND FALTERING 1963–73

With the data base on Australian manufacturing now reasonably established, studies after 1962 became more analytic, growing in sophistication and diversity. The chief data base was that of Alex Hunter (1963); part 1 outlines forces then influencing manufacturing, while part 2 analyses many major Australian industries.

On another scale, analyses of metropolitan industry engaged several workers. In Adelaide, Smailes (1967) documented manufacturing change in inner areas; Rimmer (1969) analysed the diffusion of industry from central Melbourne to suburban or periurban locations. Michael Webber (1972) wrote Australia's principal theoretical account of industrial location.

The role of government was frequently emphasised in the literature of 1963–73. Among forms of industry regulation, the tariff came in for renewed attention. Leading commentators were Reitsma (1960) and Hunter (1963). After 1954, the Tariff Board became an active participant in debates about protection: the call in its 1967 *Annual report* for economic efficiency in tariff considerations is regarded as a foundation for the increasingly critical attitude after 1974 of its successor, the Industries Assistance Commission. Reflecting interest in other roles of government, geographers Linge and Rimmer (1971) organised a wide-ranging seminar.

The Australian constitution determines that the states, rather than the commonwealth, determine the spatial dynamics of manufacturing. During the 1960s the New South Wales Department of Decentralisation and Development moved vigorously to promote intrastate decentralisation, its 'manifesto' being the report of the Development Corporation of New South Wales of 1969. It argued for selective decentralisation, as advocated two years earlier by the Victorian Decentralisation Advisory Committee (1967). These papers stimulated considerable debate on industrial location policy (see Committee of Commonwealth/State Officials on Decentralisation, 1975).

RETREAT 1974–83

The demise of Australian manufacturing after 1973 was unforeseen by many contemporary observers and this seems due to a too narrow discussion of industry policy.

As the fortunes of the secondary sector waned, it attracted increasing attention. The main industry studies of 1974–83 were provided in the analyses of Solomon (1975), the Australian Institute of Urban Studies (1977), in Davidson and Stewardson (1979), and in vol 4 of the Jackson Report (Australia. Committee to Advise on Policies for Development of Manufacturing Industry, 1976). The Jackson Report also heralded the plethora of post-1975 writing on structural change (see, for instance, Linge, 1976 and Aislabie and Tisdell, 1979). It is usually read together with the Australian government's *White paper on manufacturing industry* (1977) and the later Crawford Report (Australia. Study Group on Structural Adjustment, 1979). All these documents aimed to help manufacturing cope with the simultaneous impacts of post-1973 exchange problems, rising labour and energy costs, technological change, strong imports competition, reduced population growth, inflation and cuts in tariff levels.

The Crawford report was to present a long-term policy to rectify problems with regard to employment prospects and the capacity of the economy to sustain change. Restrained by its terms of reference, it met a hostile reception from an audience which was looking for incisive action to resuscitate the sector. So-called economic 'dries' stressed the need for a spirited, self-starting, achievement-oriented, free enterprise manufacturing industry, largely unassisted by bounties, subsidies or other public measures. The case is foreshadowed in the readings of Kasper and Parry (1978) and underscored in a 'libertarian' scenario by Kasper *et al* (1980).

By 1980, the debate on structural change was breaking little new ground, even though the important international underpinnings of industry's malaise had yet to be emphasised. A bright future, now recognised as at least premature if not illusory, was held up around election time in a 'resources boom'. The various proposals produced technical reports such as James B. Croft and Associates' environmental impact statement for Hunter Valley smelters (1980). They also attracted a radical critique virtually unknown several years earlier (cf McColl, 1976). It questioned the socioeconomic impacts of massive infrastructural development and the diversion of public funds to support private corporate investment (Hunter Valley Research Co-operative, 1981). Subsequent downturn in the world economy and the increase in interest rates showed the substance to these objections.

For the first time since 1910 Australian manufacturing has less than 20 per cent of national employment (see Johns and Metcalfe, 1980, Australia, Bureau of Industry Economics, 1981a, 1981b). Since 1980, there has been a concerted, positive examination of the potential relationship of government and manufacturing (Cardew, 1981; Loveday, 1982), and fresh interest is shown in industry policy (Parry, 1982; Warhurst, 1982). The 'Swiss scenario' of a high technology industry, building on Australia's earlier investments in higher education, emerged as an option from the structural change debate (North, 1978). Lately it has been endorsed by federal Labor minister Barry Jones (1982). The urgings of technological optimists prompted the former Liberal government to establish the (Myers) Committee of Inquiry into Technological Change in Australia; in 1980 it produced a four-volume *Report*. It reviews key issues of technological change, describes potential technologies, examines government policies related to the introduction of new techniques and presents selected research papers. Closely allied with technology observers are those connected with employment issues. Industrial unemployment was little debated for several years after 1974 but public attention was drawn by Keith Windschuttle (1980).

A further nexus has emerged between employment analysts and those monitoring transnational corporations, foreign investment and Australia's role in global restructuring. The Transnational Corporations Research Project at the University of Sydney has produced a critique in Crough and Wheelwright (1982). Foreign investment is dealt with from different viewpoints by geographers such as those contributing to the Linge and McKay (1981) readings on industrial restructuring. The other side of the coin, Australian offshore investment, is handled by Bennett *et al* (1981) and Metcalfe and Treadwell (1981) on behalf of the Bureau of Industry Economics.

At the broadest scale, writings on manufacturing and international economic relations become synonymous. They concern a variety of intergovernmental agreements such as the closer economic relations with New Zealand, the Pacific basin concept, the north–south dialogue and the proposal of a new international economic order. Observers include the authors in the Crough *et al* (1980) readings, Fagan (in Linge and McKay, 1981) and Linge and Hamilton (1981).

Australians have made a fair contribution to the world literature on manufacturing through works in economics, economic history, geography and related fields. Australia's exposure to multinationals is a study in its own right, particularly in aluminium, coal and iron ore in which the nation specialises. Our compendious output on structural change provides something of a reference manual, notably in its foci of tariff issues, employment and industry studies. The country now has some experienced commentators on technological change, and industrial policy is no longer neglected.

AISLABIE, C.J. AND TISDELL, C.A. eds, *The economics of structural change and adjustment: proceedings of the conference held at University of Newcastle, November, 1978*. Newcastle, Institute of Industrial Economics, University of Newcastle, 1979. 410 p. (University of Newcastle. Institute of Industrial Economics. Conference series, 5.)

Several economists examine structural change in all sectors of the economy in this major set of readings.

AUSTRALIA. *White paper on manufacturing industry*. AGPS, 1977. 37 p.

Follows the 1975 Green paper on industrial policy. Purportedly definitive paper but widely criticised for lack of decisiveness. Continued support for protectionism.

AUSTRALIA. Bureau of Industry Economics. *Industrialisation in Asia: some implications for Australian industry*. AGPS, 1978. 130 p. (Research report, 1.)

First of many high quality analyses in this series. Highlights potential impact of rapid industrialisation in certain Asian nations. Reprinted with corrections in 1980.

AUSTRALIA. Bureau of Industry Economics. *The long-run impact of technological changes on the structure of Australian industry 1990–91*. AGPS, 1981. 380 p. (Research report, 7.)

Projections based on econometric SNAPSHOT model of Australian economy. Assessments by industry for all sectors of economy. Estimates now subject to some debate.

AUSTRALIA. Bureau of Industry Economics. *The structure of Australian industry: past development and future trends*. AGPS, 1981. 167 p. (Research report, 8.)

Broad review and useful source document. Projections from SNAPSHOT econometric model (see above).

AUSTRALIA. Committee of Economic Enquiry. *Report . . .* Canberra, Government Printer, 1965. 3 vols, maps.

Full-scale macro and microeconomic inquiry leading to growth-oriented prognosis for the economy. Some contentious arguments for greater planning stimulated criticism and discussion. Chairman: Sir James Vernon.

AUSTRALIA. Committee of Inquiry into Technological Change in Australia. *Technological change in Australia: report of the Committee of Inquiry into . . .* AGPS, 1980. 4 vols.

Major governmental inquiry into impact of technological change. Chairman: Sir Rupert H. Myers.

AUSTRALIA. Committee to Advise on Policies for Manufacturing Industry. *Policies for development of manufacturing industry: a Green paper*. AGPS, 1975–76. 4 vols, illus, maps.

Full-scale inquiry into the ills of manufacturing. Stresses externally induced change and concentrates on quality of work environment. Vol 4 is a series of industry studies. Chairman: R.G. Jackson.

AUSTRALIA. Department of National Development. *The structure and capacity of Australian manufacturing industry*. Melbourne, The Department, 1952. 528 p.

Study of broad industrial groups, each comprising individual manufacturing activities. Industry statistics, estimates of demand and capacity, market prospects and availability of inputs.

AUSTRALIA. Industries Assistance Commission. *Index of Tariff Board reports 1921–1973, classified by industry*. Canberra, The Commission, 1974. 233 p.

Advice to users, summary of the Australian Standard Industrial Classification and index for ASIC divisions A–D (agriculture to utilities).

AUSTRALIA. Study Group on Structural Adjustment. *Report, 1979 . . .* AGPS, 1979. 2 vols.

Outlines a policy to rectify problems with regard to employment prospects and capacity of economy to sustain change. Recommends on industrial and resource development, industry-specific and manpower policies, capital and regional strategy and information provision. Chairman: Sir John Crawford.

AUSTRALIAN INSTITUTE OF POLITICAL SCIENCE, 11th Summer School, Sydney, 1945. *Australia's post war economy*. Sydney, Australasian Publishing Co, 1945. 292 p.

World postwar economy, wool industry, agricultural prospects, secondary industry and industrial relations.

AUSTRALIAN INSTITUTE OF POLITICAL SCIENCE, 14th Summer School, Goulburn, 1943. *Decentralisation*. A & R, 1948. 204 p.

Implications, constitutional problems and economic aspects of decentralisation. Local and higher level government machinery. Five substantial chapters by different authors.

AUSTRALIAN INSTITUTE OF URBAN STUDIES. Victorian Division. *Manufacturing in the Port Phillip Region*. Canberra, The Institute, 1977. 156 p, maps. (AIUS publication, 66.)

Comprehensive regional analysis of manufacturing around the Melbourne metropolitan area.

BARNARD, A. *Visions and profits: studies in the business career of Thomas Sutcliffe Mort*. MUP, 1961. 234 p, illus.

Biography of one of Australia's most famous nineteenth-century entrepreneurs who had interests in mining, engineering, refrigeration and wool marketing.

BENNETT, R.B. *et al, Motives for Australian direct foreign investment*. Canberra, Bureau of Industry Economics, 1981. 59 p. (Bureau of Industry Economics Working Paper, 23.)

Theory of direct foreign investment and survey results of 225 Australian firms with offshore operations.

BLAINEY, G.N. *The steel master: a life of Essington Lewis*. Melbourne, Macmillan, 1971. 217 p, illus.

Lewis who was managing director of BHP, 1926–38, and its chief general manager, 1938–50, was involved for most of his life with the development of Australian heavy industry.

CARDEW, R.V. *Government regulation of industrial property development*. Canberra, Australian Institute of Urban Studies, 1981. 115 p, illus. (AIUS publication, 92.)

Examines the role of government in development process and costs to developers, and makes suggestions on how to improve the efficiency of development control and methods of approval.

CAVES, R.E. *et al, Australian industry: structure, conduct, performance*. Sydney, Prentice-Hall, 1981. 155 p, illus.

Local version of key North American text on microeconomics but no specific case studies.

COMMITTEE OF COMMONWEALTH/STATE OFFICIALS ON DECENTRALISATION. *Studies commissioned by the Committee of Commonwealth/State Officials on Decentralisation*. AGPS, for the Dept of Urban and Regional Development, 1975. 429 p, maps.

A series of key studies on the decentralisation issue, some originally commissioned by state authorities.

CROUGH, G. AND WHEELWRIGHT, E.L. *Australia: a client state*. Ringwood, Vic, Penguin, 1982. 255 p.

Emanates from work in the University of Sydney Transnational Corporations Research Project. Calls for a policy of self-reliance to restrict foreign domination.

CROUGH, G. *et al, Australia and world capitalism*. Ringwood, Vic, Penguin, 1980. 310 p.

Socialist view covering unemployment, work and technology, income, corporations, capital concentration, foreign investment and the means of political restructuring.

DAVIDSON, F.G. *The industrialization of Australia.* MUP, 1969. 91 p, illus.

Background, structure and potential of Australian manufacturing. Early postwar reference and critique, first published in 1957.

DAVIDSON, F.G. AND STEWARDSON, B.R. *Economics and Australian industry.* Melbourne, Longman Cheshire, 1979. 309 p.

Standard microeconomics text examining different market forms with illustrations from various Australian industries and also retailing. First published in 1974.

DEVELOPMENT CORPORATION OF NEW SOUTH WALES. *Report on selective decentralisation: the case for concentration upon growth points as a strategy for effective decentralisation.* Sydney, Government Printer, 1969. 96 p, map.

Sophisticated application of economic theory to support selective decentralisation. Examines cost differentials in utility provision and comparative availability of services.

DOUGLAS, I. *Opportunity in Australia.* London, Rockliff, 1947. 186 p, illus, map.

Popular text for intending migrants with several chapters on industrial conditions and proposed development. An enlarged and revised edition was published in 1958.

FLETCHER, P. ed, *Queensland: its resources and institutions; essays . . .* Brisbane, Government Printer, 1886. Variously paged.

A collection of fourteen essays, including H. Earle's 'The commerce and industries of Queensland', prepared for the Colonial and Indian Exhibition, London, 1886.

FORSTER, C. *Industrial development in Australia 1920–1930.* Canberra. Australian National University, 1964. 256 p.

Analyses manufacturing in the post World War I period, including industrial growth, industry case studies and labour, finance, productivity and prices.

GRIFFIN, G.W. *New South Wales, her commerce and resources.* Sydney, Government Printer, 1888. 293 p.

Résumé of a range of primary, mineral and secondary industries, functionally organised.

HUNTER, A. ed, *The economics of Australian industry: studies in environment and structure.* MUP, 1963. 543 p, maps.

Standard text on Australian industry. Includes chapters on the manufacturing environment and case studies of individual industries.

HUTCHINSON, F. ed, *New South Wales: the mother colony of the Australias.* Sydney, Government Printer, 1896. 369 p, illus, maps.

Covers aspects of agriculture, mining and social conditions. Includes F.J. Donohue's 'The manufacturing interest'. Reads like a statistical yearbook. Good account of resource utilisation and processing.

JAMES B. CROFT & ASSOCIATES. *Environment impact statement for an aluminium smelter at Tomago, N.S.W.* Sydney, Tomago Aluminium, 1980. 3 vols in 2, illus.

Example of environmental impact statement for development in the sensitive Hunter valley of NSW. Smelter represents a major project in the 1980 'resources boom'.

JOHNS, B.L. AND METCALFE, J.S. *The increasing competitiveness of developing economies and their impact on Australian industry.* Canberra, Centre for Economic Policy Research, Australian National University, 1980. 56 p, illus.

Reflects growing realisation that Australia's manufacturing problems were not purely domestic but a part of global restructuring.

JONES, B.O. *Sleepers, wake!: technology and the future of work.* OUP, 1982. 285 p, illus.

The Minister for Science sets out a technological manifesto for Australia in the 1980s. Influential book.

KASPER, W. *et al, Australia at the crossroads: our choices to the year 2000.* Sydney, Harcourt, Brace, Jovanovich, 1980. 311 p.

Free market strategists analyse the past and likely future of Australia's economy, society and geopolitical region. 'Mercantilist' and 'libertarian' scenarios are painted within which industrial policy would be applied.

KASPER, W. AND PARRY, T.G. eds, *Growth, trade and structural change in an open Australian economy.* Sydney, Centre for Applied Economic Research, University of NSW, 1978. 399 p.

Industrial and trade economists argue that 'increasingly urgent structural adjustment should be left to private sector responses, government restricting itself to broad-brush, liberal policies that create foresight and continuity'.

LINGE, G.J.R. *Index of Australian tariff reports, 1901–1961.* Canberra, Research School of Pacific Studies, Australian National University, 1964. 95 p.

Extremely handy reference with which to tackle the Australian parliamentary papers to identify Tariff Board and other reports. A supplement covers reports from 1961 to 1967.

LINGE, G.J.R. *Industrial awakening: a geography of Australian manufacturing, 1788–1890.* ANUP, 1979. 845 p, illus, maps.

Important work on the historical geography of early Australian industry.

LINGE, G.J.R. ed, *Restructuring employment opportunities in Australia.* Canberra, Dept of Human Geography, Australian National University, 1976. 215 p, illus, maps.

Multidisciplinary readings on a variety of themes relating to the distribution of the labour force.

LINGE, G.J.R. AND HAMILTON, F.E.I. 'International industrial systems' in F.E.I. Hamilton and G.J.R. Linge, eds, *Spatial analysis, industry and the industrial environment: progress in research and applications.* Vol 2. *International industrial systems.* Chichester, England, Wiley, 1981, 1–117.

Thoroughgoing account includes consideration of global restructuring and new international division of labour.

LINGE, G.J.R. AND McKAY, J. eds, *Structural change in Australia: some spatial and organisational responses.* Canberra, Research School of Pacific Studies, Australian National University, 1981. 329 p, maps.

Industrial geographers enter the structural change debate with analyses at the international, national, regional and metropolitan levels.

LINGE, G.J.R. AND RIMMER, P.J. eds, *Government influence and the location of economic activity.* Canberra, Dept of Human Geography, Research School of Pacific Studies, Australian National University, 1971. 500 p, maps.

Papers from a broad ranging seminar, including Australian and worldwide coverage of themes not merely confined to the secondary sector.

LOVEDAY, P. *Promoting industry: recent Australian political experience.* UQP, 1982. 223 p.

Examines federal and state initiatives with particular reference to aluminium and petrochemical industries.

LYNE, C.E. *The industries of New South Wales.* Sydney, Government Printer, 1882. 288 p, illus, map.

From articles originally published in the *Sydney Morning Herald.*

McCOLL, G.D. *The economics of electricity supply in Australia.* MUP, 1976. 159 p, illus.

Authoritative study of electricity industry in Australia, covering costs, revenues, pricing policy, capital investment and current issues.

McLEOD, D. *Melbourne factories*. Melbourne, Walker, May & Co, 1868. 68 p.

Description of 26 industries.

MANUFACTURING INDUSTRIES ADVISORY COUNCIL. *Australian manufacturing industry in the next decade: the main issues facing the Australian economy during the next decade, with particular relevance for the manufacturing sector*. Sydney, The Council, 1959. 42 p.

Optimistic and expansionist outlook for Australian manufacturing during the 1960s, prepared for the council of 22 business leaders chaired by Dr J. Vernon. The document expresses continued support for the tariff.

MANUFACTURING INDUSTRIES ADVISORY COUNCIL. *Major gaps in Australian industry* . . . Sydney, The Council, 1962. 113 p, illus.

Stresses need to develop import-saving and export-competing industries as a way of sustaining rapid economic growth. Reviews various parameters of a myriad of industrial products.

METCALFE, J.S. AND TREADWELL, R. *An overview of Australian direct foreign investment*. Canberra, Bureau of Industry Economics, 1981. 53 p. (Australia. Bureau of Industry Economics. Working paper, 18.)

Size, regional and industrial composition of Australian direct foreign investment and government policies on the issue.

MORGAN, B.H. *The trade and industry of Australasia: being a report on the state of and openings for trade, and the condition of local industries in Australia and New Zealand*. London, Eyre and Spottiswoode, 1908. 250 p, illus.

Deals with practical, commercial aspects of the Australian market, in particular export opportunities to Australia and local labour conditions. Several industry studies.

NORTH, P. *Indigenous technology: industry's ultimate protection*. Sydney, University of Sydney, 1978. 16 p. (George Judah Cohen memorial lecture, 1978.)

Early call for high technology scenario relying on intellectual input as a means of industrial growth.

PARRY, T.G. ed, *Australian industry policy*. Melbourne, Longman Cheshire, 1982. 320 p.

Covers industrial organisation and competition policy, foreign investment, technology and structural adjustment.

PATTERSON, G.D. *The tariff in the Australian colonies 1856–1900*. Melbourne, Cheshire, 1968. 174 p.

Analysis of tariff history with emphasis on colonial NSW and Vic and reference to other colonies.

PRATT, A. ed, *The national handbook of Australia's industries*. Melbourne, Specialty Press, 1934. 671 p, illus, maps.

Organised by states with detailed views of industries and companies. Lavishly illustrated.

REITSMA, A.J. *Trade protection in Australia*. UQP, 1960. 195 p.

Pre-Federation tariffs, events to 1921. Discusses establishment of Tariff Board, and income, trade, economic development and other arguments in favour of tariffs. Balance of payment considerations.

RIMMER, P.J. *Manufacturing in Melbourne*. Canberra, Research School of Pacific Studies, Australian National University, 1969. 201 p, maps.

Analyses diffusion of industry from central to suburban Melbourne 1871–1964. Pioneering study in using advanced computer classifications of types of manufacturing.

SMAILES, P.J. *Manufacturing industry in Adelaide's inner suburban ring*. Sydney, Dept of Geography, University of Sydney, and the Geographical Society of NSW, 1967. 38 p, illus.

Manufacturing change in Adelaide examined through field surveys and data of the South Australian Chamber of Commerce.

SOLOMON, R.J. ed, *Industrial land in Sydney*. Canberra, Australian Institute of Urban Studies, 1975. 89 p, maps. (AIUS publication, 51.)

Macro and micro analyses of industrial land in Sydney covering metropolitan socioeconomic trends, zoning, planning, supply, demand and price.

VICTORIA. Decentralization Advisory Committee. *Report on the selection of places outside the metropolis of Melbourne for accelerated development*. Melbourne, The Committee, 1967. 52 p, illus.

Early advocacy of selective decentralisation for sake of economic efficiency. Identifies five non-metropolitan growth centres. Report became basis of subsequent state policy.

WADLEY, D.A. AND RICH, D.A. *The Australian industrial system 1950–81: review and classified bibliography*. Hobart, Dept of Geography, University of Tas. 1983. 207 p. (University of Tas, Dept of Geography. Occasional paper, 13.)

Review chapters on postwar Australian industrialisation and the literature attending it. Thematic, spatial, chronological and alphabetical classification of 2062 references.

WALKER, E.R. *The Australian economy in war and reconstruction*. New York, OUP, 1947. 426 p, illus.

Commentary on the wartime and immediate postwar economy in particular on industrial development and the reorganisation of industry 1939–45.

WARHURST, J. *Jobs or dogma?: the Industries Assistance Commission and Australian politics*. UQP, 1982. 255 p, illus.

Examination of federal and state industry policy during the 1970s with special attention to the motor vehicle and dairy industries.

WEBB, L.R. AND ALLAN, R.H. eds, *Industrial economics: Australian studies*. Sydney, Allen & Unwin, 1982. 470 p.

Private sector decision-making, interindustry analysis, protection, government enterprises, transport, labour, finance, energy and Asian industrialisation are all handled in this major set of readings.

WEBBER, M.J. *Impact of uncertainty on location*. ANUP, 1972. 310 p, maps.

Survey and evaluation of orthodox microeconomic theory on locational problems. Explores game theory, cybernetic models and simulation in differing market situations, especially with conditions of suboptimality.

WHEELWRIGHT, E.L. *Ownership and control of Australian companies: a study of 102 of the largest public companies incorporated in Australia*. Sydney, Law Book Co, 1957. 206 p.

WHEELWRIGHT, E.L. AND MISKELLY, J. *Anatomy of Australian manufacturing industry: the ownership and control of 300 of the largest manufacturing companies in Australia*. Sydney, Law Book Co, 1967. 433 p.

Two socialist views of Australian private enterprise. Both examine corporate structure, with useful analyses by type of industry.

WINDETT, N. *Australia as producer and trader 1920–1932*. London, OUP, 1933. 320 p.

Examines development of Australian manufacturing and trade with special attention to minerals, iron and steel, electrical goods, machinery, motor vehicles, textiles.

General strike, Brisbane, 1912. Photograph. Between January and March 1912, a general strike erupted in Queensland in support of Brisbane tramdrivers who went on strike over the wearing of union badges.
OXLEY LIBRARY

CHAPTER 37

LABOUR RELATIONS

PETER LOVE

FROM THE EARLIEST years of British occupation, most people in Australia have earned a living by selling their labour. In doing so, they entered into a complex set of relationships with employers, the laws and institutions of the state, their fellow workers, the physical environment of the workplace and the prevailing economic conditions. The interaction between all these has shaped the history of labour and industrial relations over the last two hundred years.

The first non-Aboriginal workers in Australia were convicts who were in no position to haggle over the price of their labour. But as the system of assigning convicts to free settlers developed, so did a labour market. The main issues of contention were the perennial ones of wages and conditions. The market was complicated from the mid-1820s onwards by the influx of free immigrants who swelled the ranks of the predominantly ex-convict working class. There were many skilled tradesmen among the immigrants and it was they who established the first mutual benefit societies, the precursors of trade unions. The laws of conspiracy and the Masters and Servants Act, however, discouraged the growth of unions. Instead, workers united around specific issues such as extension of the franchise, the movement to end transportation and the attempt to limit migration during the mid-1840s depression.

Although they had some experience of collective action by the middle of the nineteenth century, Australian workers were not able to establish permanent unions until economic conditions in Victoria and New South Wales were transformed by the 1850s gold rushes. Those workers who did not seek their fortunes on the goldfields were in a much better position to bargain and organise. Craft unions in the building, metal and printing trades grew as wages and the demand for labour soared, particularly in Melbourne where building workers won the eight-hour day in 1856.

The history of labour, however, has not been one of uninterrupted progress. After this 'golden' decade there was a longer period from the early 1860s to the mid-1870s when conditions were much less buoyant. Most of the craft unions survived, although their gains of the 1850s were eroded. Meanwhile, a new kind of union was beginning to emerge among the miners, shearers, waterside workers and seamen. Based on industry rather than craft, this 'new unionism' grew as the economy improved from the late 1870s onwards. Because their members and the issues that concerned them crossed colonial boundaries, these unions tended to see themselves against a wider, national horizon. Caring little for the traditions built up by the respectable craftsmen, they inclined more towards militant industrial action coupled with a radical political outlook.

The movement towards 'closer unionism' ran parallel to this. By the mid-1880s Trades and Labour Councils had been established in many of the major cities. They were the creation of the craft unions, designed to prevent and settle industrial disputes as well as co-ordinate the affairs of the smaller urban unions. Similar objectives inspired the intercolonial trades union conferences, held in various cities between 1879 and 1898. It was clear from discussion at the conferences prior to 1890 that the unions were beginning to see their interests within a broader perspective. Many of the issues debated—the need for factory acts, legal status for trade unions, conciliation and arbitration—required some form of state intervention in industrial relations. That implied political representation.

This gradual move towards parliamentary politics was accelerated by the depression and the great strikes of 1890–94. The pastoralists and the shipowners were aided in their struggle with the workers by the power of the state. The combined strength of parliaments, police, troops and the courts inflicted a humiliating defeat on the unions. Beaten but not crushed, they established the Labor parties in an effort to control the 'machinery of the state', to make it a friend of the workers, not an enemy. (In the matter of spelling, I have followed the convention by which Labor refers to the party and its formal institutions, while labour signifies the wider movement as well as the act of work; when citing references, the authors' own spelling has been copied.)

The labour movement as we now know it—with its industrial and political wings—grew out of that struggle between labour and capital. It was during this period that the movement's leaders began to write their own history from a heightened sense of collective identity. *The history of capital and labour in all lands and ages*, with chapters by John Norton, E.W. O'Sullivan and W.E. Murphy, appeared in 1888. George Black chronicled the emergence of the Labor party with his *Labor in politics* (Sydney, Australian Workman) in 1893, while W.E. Murphy (1896, 1900) celebrated improved working condition.

By the turn of the century the unions, both craft and industrial, had begun to recover their earlier strength. Through the Labor parties, especially in the eastern states, they had made some progress on industrial issues such as the establishment of wages boards and the passing of factory acts which tried to eliminate 'sweatshops' and improve safety in the workplace. Because of measures like these, Australia had earned a wide reputation as a 'social laboratory' where state intervention to regulate the conditions of labour gave it the appearance of a 'workingman's paradise'. Albert Métin (1901, trans, 1977) was one of many overseas visitors who had come to see it for themselves.

With the establishment of the commonwealth in 1901 and the formation of the Federal Labor Party, the gap between the party and the unions widened. Although many members were from union backgrounds, Labor tended to present itself as a nationalist rather than a class party. The tensions arising from that have been a persistent theme in writing on the labour movement.

The most important development in the field of industrial relations before World War I was the establishment of the Commonwealth Court of Conciliation and Arbitration in 1904. Although its jurisdiction was confined to interstate disputes, its power to conduct compulsory hearings and make legally binding awards placed it in a commanding position to set general standards. In 1907 it did just that when its second president, Mr Justice Higgins, handed down his historic decision in the Harvester case. There, he introduced the concept of a 'basic wage', set at an amount he considered sufficient to support a worker's family in 'frugal comfort', supplemented by a 'margin for skill' where appropriate. Higgins (1922) wrote his own assessment of the court's role.

The prospect of winning such an award was a strong incentive for the expansion of unions, particularly those that could straddle state boundaries in either a legitimate or some contrived manner. There were some radicals, however, who warned that participation in the arbitration system would erode the right to strike and increase the tendency for the unions to be integrated into the capitalist state.

During World War I and in the years immediately after, the unions and the Labor party drifted further apart. The party, critically weakened by the 1916 conscription split, seemed irrelevant to an increasingly militant union movement that was flirting with revolutionary and syndicalist ideas, particularly after the 1917 general strike and news of the Russian Revolution. The issue came to a head in 1921 at the union and party conference which eventually agreed to an uneasy marriage between industrial syndicalism and parliamentary socialism in the form of the 'socialisation objective'.

Coinciding with this 'red dawn', more varied forms of labour history began to appear. George Dale (1918; facs, 1965) reflected the prevailing radical mood in its celebration of working-class struggles in and around Broken Hill. Vere Gordon Childe's enduring analysis (1923; repr, 1964) cast a severe but scholarly eye over the institutions and practices of the labour movement to show why they had failed to transform the condition of the workers. J.T. Sutcliffe (1921; repr, 1967) wrote one of the earliest examples of institutional labour history. An academic from the Worker's Educational Association, he set out for the first time the principal stages in the growth of the Australian labour movement. T.A. Coghlan (1918; repr, 1967) attempted a more ambitious survey. Based on many years experience as a government statistician, his monumental four-volume work offered a history of economic development in the nineteenth century with some insightful commentary on the social conditions of labour.

After a series of major strikes in 1919–21, the unions concentrated their growing strength on campaigns for better wages and shorter hours through the Arbitration Court. Although they made some temporary gains, they also had difficulties with the court. In 1922, for example, it refused to recognise the syndicalist-inspired One Big Union as a legitimate national organisation. Not until 1927 were the unions able to establish a federal structure acceptable to most of their members and the court. The Australian Council of Trade Unions (ACTU), as the new body was called, was based on state labour councils and federal unions. It was empowered to act in federal disputes and on any other issues referred to it by the state labour councils. The infant ACTU was weakened, however, by the decision of the Australian Workers' Union, the largest of all, to remain outside the organisation.

The Arbitration Court, meanwhile, was having its own difficulties. After an unsuccessful attempt in 1926 to give the court power to override conflicting state awards and so establish uniform national standards, the Bruce–Page government decided in 1929 to transfer most federal industrial relations powers to state tribunals. The labour movement overcame its earlier ambivalence towards the court and vigorously opposed the move. The government was defeated in parliament on the issue and the prime minister lost his seat to the secretary of the Melbourne Trades Hall Council at the subsequent federal election.

Neither the incoming Scullin Labor government nor the ACTU was able to protect workers from the ravages of the Great Depression. The unions suffered a series of crushing defeats. Their membership fell drastically. Unemployment rose to over 30 per cent in 1932. The Arbitration Court cut wages by 10 per cent in January 1931 and in doing so changed Higgins' 1907 principle of the 'living wage' to one based on the 'capacity of industry to pay'. In June 1931 the Scullin government implemented the deflationary Premiers' Plan which contributed to its defeat in December 1931. Disillusioned with arbitration, and to a lesser extent with Labor governments, some unions turned to communist leaders who attempted to widen their members' horizons in campaigns on international issues such as the rise of fascism. Most unions, however, spent their energies for the rest of the decade on efforts to rebuild their organisations and recover lost ground on wages and conditions. During this grim period very little labour history was written, but the depression was to become the subject of intense historical interest in the 1960s and 1970s.

Australian workers did not experience full employment until World War II when the total mobilisation of the nation's resources created an extraordinary demand for labour. After some early unrest during the tenure of the first Menzies government, the unions co-operated with the Curtin Labor government in the interests of a united war effort, accepting many restraints that would otherwise have been vigorously rejected. During the war there were two developments in the labour force that were to become significant in later years. The first was a massive influx of women into the paid workforce to replace men who were in the armed services. The second was an increasing communist influence in the larger, more powerful unions. This grew out of a wider interest in Marxist ideas which had become more respectable since the USSR had joined the allied cause in 1941 and Australian communists had adopted a strong pro-war policy. Although another forty years passed before the role of working women became a major preoccupation in the writing of labour history, the influence of Marxism was seen almost immediately in Brian Fitzpatrick (1940; repr, 1968) and E.W. Campbell (1945).

When the war ended, so did industrial harmony. Determined to win their share of the prosperity promised by the Chifley Labor government's new social order, the unions gave vent to long-suppressed demands for higher wages and shorter hours. After a series of strikes and a protracted case before the Arbitration Court, they finally won the 40-hour week in 1948 and, in 1950, a £1 rise in the basic wage, with a minimum for women workers set at 75 per cent of the male rate. Communist-led unions, meanwhile, decided to challenge the Labor party's leadership of the working class. Their campaign reached its climax in the 1949 coal strike when the government sent troops into the mines and gaoled some of their leaders. That dispute, conducted in a chilling Cold War atmosphere, contributed to the Chifley government's defeat at the 1949 election and intensified the tensions with the labour movement that led to the struggles of 1954–55 described by Robert Murray (1984).

During the period of almost uninterrupted prosperity between the early 1950s and the mid-1970s a number of significant changes occurred in the economy, the workforce, the unions and the industrial relations system. As a result of overall but uneven economic growth there was a decline of employment in primary industry and an increase in the manufacturing and service sectors. This coincided with two major shifts in the composition of the workforce where there was a substantial rise in the proportions of women and of migrant workers. There was a slight decline in the percentage of workers who were unionists and a fall in the number of unions, although this resulted more from amalgamation than from loss of members. There was also a substantial growth in white collar unionism and a weakening of those covering semiskilled and unskilled workers. This process of consolidation allowed the ACTU to speak with an increasingly authoritative voice, particularly after it won the allegiance of white collar unions in the late 1970s.

Over the same period, changes were made to the arbitration system. Increasingly severe penal powers were reintroduced between 1947 and 1951, but were defeated by resolute industrial action in 1969. The rules and procedures for determining wages and conditions underwent several revisions, usually in conjunction with changes of government. In 1969 the Arbitration Commission accepted the principle of 'equal pay for equal work' to be introduced in progressive stages by 1972, although women continued to receive lower average weekly earnings because of unresolved structural problems in the workforce.

Wages and hours of work continue to be the main preoccupation of industrial relations. In recent years, however, other issues have become prominent. They include health and safety in the workplace, the environmental effects of economic development, equal opportunity, the concept of a 'social wage' and problems of rapid technological change.

Much has been written on all these issues. Indeed, the study of labour and industrial relations seems to have been one of the most spectacular growth industries in the postwar period. It is for this reason that most of the books in the accompanying bibliography were published comparatively recently. Reference to related earlier studies can usually be found in the notes and bibliographies of each book. There are also a number of journals in which important articles have appeared. These include *Australian journal of politics and history*, *Economic record* (1925–), *Historical studies* (1940–), *Journal of industrial relations* (1959–), *Labour history* (1962–), and *Politics* (1966–). A useful starting point for locating relevant material published before 1974 is *Index to journal articles on Australian history* compiled by Hogan *et al.* Continuations of this work have been issued by Victor Crittenden and a consolidation of this important bibliography is planned (see chapter 8).

Although writing in this field has become more diverse during the last thirty years, the more traditional kinds of labour history have continued to appear. These have usually been commissioned union histories, written by participants or close observers who have almost invariably been sympathetic to the labour cause. Edgar Ross (1970) and Pete Thomas (1983) on the miners, A.E. Davies (1974) on the meat workers and Jack Mundey (1981) on the builders' labourers are examples of this genre. They are, in many ways, the descendants of Norton and Black, Murphy and Spence. However, most of the growth in published work has come from the universities. The complex reasons for this and the debates that have accompanied it are examined in John Merritt's chapter on 'Labour history' in Osborne and Mandle (1982).

In the 1960s a number of related developments centring on the Australian National University boosted academic study of labour history. Some members of staff had already completed research on the working class and the labour movement. Their interests, backed by research stipends, attracted talented postgraduate students who made extensive use of the university's archives of business and labour. Further encouragement came from the formation of the Australian Society for the Study of Labour History in 1961, with its base at the ANU. As the bibliography suggests, that convergence of circumstances was remarkably productive.

Some of this work, most notably the general histories by Gollan (1960; repr, 1974) and Turner (1965; repr, 1979), grew out of the 'old left' radical nationalism of Brian Fitzpatrick's (1940; repr, 1968) earlier writing. However, most of the studies undertaken in the 1960s and early 1970s were more narrowly focused. Partly because of the requirements of the PhD thesis, many were detailed institutional histories of unions, the ALP or more radical sections of the labour movement. They tended to concentrate on the growth of unions, relations between leaders and the rank and file, industrial issues and strikes, factional struggles and the tension between craft and industrial unionism.

There was a parallel growth in the study of industrial relations. This was also due in part to the expansion of tertiary education in the 1960s and 1970s, but it was built on solid foundations laid down in the 1950s. Unlike labour history, however, it did not begin with the union movement. It was more the creation of employers who had adopted the principles of 'scientific' management. Accordingly, it developed as a field of study primarily concerned with the practical problems of how to 'manage' conflict in the workplace. As such, its preoccupations have been different from labour history.

While many labour historians have adopted variations of class analysis in their studies, people in the 'management' field have tended to view the relations between workers, employers and the state as a functional system capable of being professionally manipulated. For that reason most attention has been given to the formal institutions at the heart of the system; employers' organisations, unions, the Conciliation and Arbitration Commission and industrial law. The earlier work of O.deR. Foenander, *Studies in Australian labour law and relations* (MUP, 1954); and W.A. Baker, *The commonwealth basic wage, 1907–1953* (Sydney, Metal Trades Federation, 1953), reflected these preoccupations which have continued in the more contemporary writing listed in the bibliography. In recent years the increasing professionalisation of union leaders has been accommodated into research and teaching of industrial relations which, as a result, has become a more autonomous field of study. Nevertheless, the fact remains that labour history and industrial relations were disciplines created by the labour movement and the employers respectively, and that both bear the mark of their origins.

Since the 1970s studies of labour and industrial relations have begun to expand beyond narrow institutional horizons. Stimulated by perspectives from other disciplines and encouraged by impressive advances in English social history, Australian scholars have widened their vision. After a great deal of largely repetitive debate among 'new left' historians, Connell and Irving (1980) finally produced an analysis of class structure in Australian history that was both ambitious and illuminating. Williams (1981), Kriegler (1980) and Kennedy (1978) have published studies that located workers in the social context of their communities, while Broomhill (1978) has reconstructed something of the everyday experience of unemployed workers in the 1930s. These latter examples mark an important shift away from the history of the labour movement to the social history of labour. The early results are encouraging, although it is doubtful that they will entirely displace the traditional forms of labour history. There is much yet to be said about the institutions created by the working class.

One of the most impressive developments of recent years has been in work on women and the labour movement. Growing out of the feminist revival of the 1970s and mobilised by the first Women and Labour Conference in 1978, an extraordinary amount of work has been produced to redress the long neglect of women in historical writing. However, it is not simply the quantity of material published that has been impressive. It has provided significant advances in at least two other areas. The first is in the development of the theory of patriarchy which has issued a profound challenge to a number of prevailing historical orthodoxies. The work of Game and Pringle (1983), for example, has raised important questions about the relationship between technology, gender and class in the workplace. The second concerns the use of sources. Since most of the data available to historians tend to ignore the role of women, writers in this field have been forced to make more imaginative use of that material. On the basis of work published so far it seems that the study of labour and industrial relations will be substantially enriched by the theoretical and methodological advances made in women's history.

Feminist and social historians have added a greater diversity to this field of study, as have sociologists and economists, through their explorations of the labour process. By asking different questions and pursuing them in imaginative ways, they are opening new avenues for research into the social experience of those who work. These new directions promise some of the most stimulating analysis in the future. They will not, however, make the more traditional kinds of labour history redundant. On the contrary, they are more likely to enrich that tradition. General studies of the labour movement will continue to be written, as will union histories, but they will be shaped by new perspectives and take a more expansive view of their subject.

Despite all the changing perspectives, shifting emphases and new methods adopted by writers in the field, one thing has remained constant in the history of Australian labour. In the two hundred years since the British invasion, most people have made a living by selling their labour to employers. Any study that fails to recognise this, or the productive and social relationships that arise from it, is in danger of missing the point.

I am grateful to Margaret Bevege, Phillip and Stephen Deery, John Merritt and Carmel Shute who offered suggestions for the following bibliography.

Coloured lithograph, 3 Dec 1917, NSW Government Printing Office. A strike by New South Wales railway and tramway workers in August and September 1917 severely disrupted the state's economy. The non-Labor government actively sought strikebreakers from among the general community. In December 1917 the acting premier, George Fuller, issued this certificate thanking the strikebreakers for helping 'to maintain Responsible Government'.
BOOROWA PRODUCTIONS

BAKER, J.S. *Communicators and their first trade unions: a history of the Telegraphist and Postal Clerk unions of Australia.* Sydney, Union of Postal Clerks and Telegraphists, 1980. 372 p, illus.

This history by a union secretary sets the UPCT in the context of technological change, economic fluctuations, industrial conflict and political campaigns.

BEVEGE, M. *et al, Worth her salt: women at work in Australia.* Sydney, Hale & Iremonger, 1982. 423 p, illus.

Papers from the 1980 Women and Labour Conference which examines the social condition of women and their attempt to change it.

BORDOW, A. *The worker in Australia: contributions from research.* UQP, 1977. 301 p.

Studies of workers and of one independent entreprenuer. Introduction includes review of literature on workers in Australia since 1945.

BROOMHILL, C.R. *Unemployed workers: a social history of the Great Depression in Adelaide.* UQP, 1978. 220 p, illus.

Reconstructs the everyday lives of the unemployed, how they responded to their condition as individuals rather than collectively.

BUCKLEY, K.D. *The Amalgamated Engineers in Australia, 1852–1920.* Canberra, Dept of Economic History, Research School of the Social Sciences, Australian National University, 1970. 318 p, illus.

A study of the early years of a British craft union transplanted into Australia. The story is continued by Sheridan (1975).

CAMPBELL, E.W. *History of the Australian labour movement: a Marxist interpretation.* Sydney, Current Book Distributions, 1945. 160 p.

A tendentious work written to bolster the Communist party's analysis of the labour movement in the mid-1940s.

CHILDE, V.G. *How labour governs: a study of workers' representation in Australia.* London, Labour Publishing Co, 1923. xxxii, 216 p.

A severe analysis of the way the industrial and political institutions of the labour movement are bound to betray the interests of the worker. Second edition published in 1964.

COGHLAN, T.A. *Labour and industry in Australia from the first settlement in 1788 to the establishment of the commonwealth in 1901.* London, Oxford University Press, 1918. 4 vols.

Pioneering work on issues such as immigration, land legislation, prices and political action insofar as they affected the labour movement. Reprinted in 1967.

COLE, K. ed, *Power, conflict and control in Australian trade unions.* Ringwood, Vic, Pelican, 1982. 302 p.

The popular image of unions as powerful and aggressive organisations is subjected to critical scrutiny, showing that they are subject to many constraints.

CONNELL, R.W. AND IRVING, T.H. *Class structure in Australian history: documents, narrative and argument.* Melbourne, Longman Cheshire, 1980. 378 p, illus.

A work of Marxist scholarship. Provides an outline of the class structure in which Australian industrial relations have been conducted.

CURTHOYS, A. *et al, Women at work.* Canberra, Australian Society for the Study of Labour History, 1975. 161 p.

Includes material on women as unpaid domestic workers and in the paid workforce. Emphasis on 1920–50.

DABSCHECK, B. *Arbitrator at work: Sir William Kelly and the regulation of Australian industrial relations.* Sydney, Allen & Unwin, 1983. 169 p.

Uses Kelly as a case study of how judicial arbitrators arrive at their decisions.

DALE, G. *The industrial history of Broken Hill.* Melbourne, Fraser & Jenkinson, 1918. 269 p, illus.

Nominally centred on Broken Hill, this celebration of historic working-class struggles was written to fan the embers of revolutionary enthusiasm in the labour movement. Facsimile edition, Adelaide, LBSA, 1965.

D'ALPUGET, B. *Mediator: a biography of Sir Richard Kirby.* MUP, 1977. 277 p, illus.

Biography of a judge whose career spanned 25 years at the centre of the arbitration system and shows how law and politics are entwined in Australian industrial relations.

D'ALPUGET, B. *Robert J. Hawke: a biography* (rev edn). Ringwood, Vic, Schwartz/Penguin, 1983. 472 p, illus.

Particularly revealing on Hawke's career as president of the ACTU. Complement to Hagan's official history (1981). First published in 1982.

DAVIES, A.E. *The meat workers unite.* Melbourne, Australasian Meat Industry Employees' Union (Vic Branch), 1974. 303 p, illus.

A conventional history of industrial and political issues, it also provides lively discussion of personalities and cultural activities associated with the union.

EBBELS, R.N. *The Australian labour movement, 1850–1907: historical documents.* Ed by L.G. Churchward. Sydney, Hale & Iremonger, 1983. 255 p.

Documents concerning the ideas, movements and institutions which gave rise to the Australian labour movement. First published in 1960.

FARRELL, F. *International socialism & Australian labour: the left in Australia, 1919–1939.* Sydney, Hale & Iremonger, 1981. 284 p, illus.

Primarily a study of socialist ideas in the Australian labour movement, there are also two substantial chapters devoted specifically to the unions.

FITZPATRICK, B. *A short history of the Australian labor movement.* Melbourne, Rawson's Bookshop, 1940. 182 p.

An interpretative history which shows what labour had done to build a 'fair and reasonable' society under capitalism. Second enlarged edition published in 1944. Reprinted in 1968.

FITZPATRICK, B. AND CAHILL, R.J. *The Seamen's Union of Australia, 1872–1972: a history.* Sydney, The Union, 1981. 363 p, illus.

A history begun by Fitzpatrick and finished by Cahill. Concerned mainly with working conditions, strikes and wider political campaigns. Useful appendices.

FORD, G.W. AND PLOWMAN, D.H. eds, *Australian unions: an industrial relations perspective.* Melbourne, Macmillan, 1983. 576 p.

Examines several important aspects of how unions operate, including organisation and practice, freedom and control, co-operation and conflict, issues and policies.

GAME, A. AND PRINGLE, R. *Gender at work.* Sydney, Allen & Unwin, 1983. 147 p, illus.

Through a study of six areas in which women work, it provides an analysis of the relationship between gender, the labour process and technological change since 1945.

GOLLAN, R.A. *The coalminers of New South Wales: a history of the union, 1860–1960.* MUP, 1963. 249 p.

A history which broke new ground in the use of employers' records to locate the miners within a wider pattern of class relationships.

GOLLAN, R.A. *Radical and working class politics: a study of eastern Australia, 1850–1910.* MUP, 1974. 238 p.

A classic study of the process which gave rise to the union movement and the Labor party. First published in 1960.

HAGAN, J. *The ACTU: a short history on the occasion of the 50th anniversary, 1927–1977.* Sydney, Reed, 1977. 95 p, illus.

An introductory history for the general reader.

HAGAN, J. *The history of the ACTU.* Melbourne, Longman Cheshire, 1981. 476 p.

The official history and a scholarly account of how the ACTU has emerged as one of the leading institutions in the Australian economy.

HAGAN, J. *Printers and politics: a history of the Australian printing unions, 1850–1950.* ANUP, 1966. 386 p, illus.

A history which stresses the recurring tension between conservative craft unionism and radical industrial unionism.

HARGREAVES, K. *Women at work.* Ringwood, Vic, Penguin, 1982. 402 p.

Women's entry into the paid workforce. Issues in the 1970s: child care, discrimination, migrant women, right to work, unions, working conditions.

HARRIS, J. *The bitter fight: a pictorial history of the Australian labor movement.* UQP, 1970. 310 p, illus, maps.

Documents, photographs and cartoons with historical commentary. Covers from the convict era up to 1922.

HEAD, B. ed, *State and economy in Australia.* OUP, 1983. 305 p.

Chapters by Butlin, Macintyre, Matthews and Howard are useful for background to contemporary industrial relations.

HIGGINS, H.B. *A new province for law and order: being a review, by its late president for fourteen years, of the Australian Court of Conciliation and Arbitration.* London, Constable, 1922. 181 p.

The role played by the court as seen by its second president who handed down the famous Harvester judgment of 1907.

HILL, J. *From subservience to strike: industrial relations in the banking industry.* UQP, 1982. 296 p, illus.

A history of the Australian Bank Employees' Union from 1919 to 1973. A product of recent academic interest in white collar unionism.

HINCE, K. *Conflict and coal: a case study of industrial relations in the open-cut coal mining industry of Central Queensland.* UQP, 1982. 250 p, maps.

Covers the period from 1975 when Utah developed new mines in the Bowen Basin.

THE HISTORY of capital and labour in all lands and ages: their past condition, present relations, and outlook for the future. Sydney, Oceanic Publishing Co, 1888. 943 p, illus.

The first major book on the history of Australian labour. Contains chapters on the various colonies.

HUTSON, J. *Penal colony to penal powers.* Sydney, Amalgamated Metals Foundry and Shipwrights' Union, 1983. 359 p.

The development of the Conciliation and Arbitration Commission, the system for fixing wages and conditions, and the penal powers used as sanctions to support arbitration decisions. First published in 1966.

JUDDERY, B. *White collar power: a history of the ACOA.* Sydney, Allen & Unwin, 1980. 319 p.

A history of the Administrative and Clerical Officers' Association, commissioned by the union.

KENNEDY, B.E. *Silver, sin, and sixpenny ale: a social history of Broken Hill, 1883–1921.* MUP, 1978. 202 p, illus, maps.

Study of a mining community where bitterly fought industrial conflicts shaped the city's distinctive character and institutions.

KINGSTON, B. *My wife, my daughter, and poor Mary Ann: women and work in Australia.* Melbourne, Nelson, 1975. 158 p, illus.

From the 1860s to the 1930s, covers the difficulties that confronted women as they moved into the workforce, or performed unpaid labour in the home.

KRIEGLER, R.J. *Working for the company: work and control in the Whyalla shipyard.* OUP, 1980. 308 p.

A contemporary account of life at the BHP shipyards written from the perspective of the workers.

LOUIS, L.J. *Trade unions and the depression: a study of Victoria, 1930–1932.* ANUP, 1968. 225 p.

A study which shows how Victorian unions were neither theoretically nor organisationally equipped to protect workers from the ravages of the depression.

LOVE, P. *Labour and the money power: Australian labour populism 1890–1950.* MUP, 1984. 240 p, illus.

Examines 'money power' theory to show how populist ideology left an impression on the way the labour movement saw its role as an agent of social change.

LOWENSTEIN, W. AND HILLS, T. *Under the hook: Melbourne waterside workers remember working lives and class war, 1900–1980.* Melbourne, Melbourne Bookworkers in association with the Australian Society for the Study of Labour History, 1982. 192 p, illus.

A history prepared by a labour historian and a retired waterside worker. Most chapters are transcriptions of group interviews.

McKINLAY, B.J. *A documentary history of the Australian labor movement, 1850–1975.* Melbourne, Drummond, 1979. 778 p, illus.

Commentaries which bring together many of the important documents previously scattered in other publications.

McMURCHY, M. *et al, For love or money: a pictorial history of women and work in Australia.* Ed by I. Dunn. Ringwood, Vic, Penguin, 1983. 186 p, illus.

This history from the beginnings of settlement to the present consists of a collection and illustrations with a commentary. Based on the film of the same title.

MARTIN, R.M. *Trade unions in Australia: who runs them, who belongs—their politics, their power.* Ringwood, Vic, Penguin, 1980. 165 p.

Introduction to contemporary trade unions. Martin examines the popular idea that unions are aggressive and powerful. First published in 1975.

MÉTIN, A. *Socialism without doctrine.* Sydney, Alternative Publishing Co-operative, 1977. [22], 200 p.

Russel Ward's translation of Métin's analysis of 'the workingman's paradise' in Australasia, published in 1901 as *Le Socialisme sans doctrine.*

MUNDEY, J. *Green bans and beyond.* A & R, 1981. 154 p, illus.

Autobiography of the union leader who instigated the tactics of union bans on building projects which threatened to degrade the environment.

MURPHY, D.J. ed, *The big strikes: Queensland, 1889–1965.* UQP, 1983. 303 p, illus.

Studies of particular strikes plus chapters on causes and catalysts, strike law in Qld and trade unions.

MURPHY, D.J. ed, *Labor in politics: the state Labor parties in Australia, 1880–1920.* UQP, 1975. 480 p, illus.

Provides detailed studies of the parties that grew out of the union movement during those forty years, plus a helpful introduction.

MURPHY, W.E. *History of the eight hours' movement.* Melbourne, Spectator Publishing Co, J.T. Picken, 1896–1900. 2 vols, illus.

An example of the celebratory style of labour history, written by one of its leaders.

MURRAY, R. *The split: Australian labor in the fifties.* Sydney, Hale & Iremonger, 1984. 392 p.

An account of the factional struggles in the labour movement between communists and Catholic Actionists which led to the Labor party split of 1954–55 and the formation of the Democratic Labor Party. First published in 1970.

MURRAY, R. AND WHITE, K. *The ironworkers: a history of the Federated Ironworkers' Association of Australia.* Sydney, Hale & Iremonger, 1982. 341 p, illus.

This history of the union's industrial and political struggles is largely sympathetic to the present leadership.

NAIRN, N.B. *Civilising capitalism: the labour movement in New South Wales, 1870–1900.* ANUP, 1973. 260 p, illus.

Examines the role played by the unions in forming the Labor party and how it was a catalyst in the development of the Australian party system.

OSBORNE, G. AND MANDLE, W.F. eds, *New history: studying Australia today.* Sydney, Allen & Unwin, 1982. 216 p.

An important chapter by Merritt on labour history provides a survey of the major preoccupations of labour historians from the end of the nineteenth century to the present.

PLOWMAN, D.H. *Wage indexation: a study of Australian wage issues, 1975–1980.* Sydney, Allen & Unwin, 1981. 193 p.

An examination of a recent experiment with wage indexation.

PLOWMAN, D.H. *et al, Australian industrial relations.* Sydney, McGraw-Hill, 1980. 399 p, illus.

A textbook on the nature of industrial conflict, different approaches to it, the parties and the processes involved.

RAWSON, D.W. *Unions and unionists in Australia.* Sydney, Allen & Unwin, 1978. 166 p.

A study of the tendency for unions to be increasingly integrated social organisations rather than part of a working-class movement.

ROSS, E. *A history of the Miners' Federation of Australia.* Sydney, Australasian Coal & Shale Employees' Federation, 1970. 528 p, illus.

A history up to 1970. Concerned mainly with the union's growth and the major issues that have confronted it.

RYAN, E. AND CONLON, A. *Gentle invaders: Australian women at work 1788–1974.* Melbourne, Nelson, 1975. 196 p.

Examines the effects of various wage concepts on working women. Refers to the Harvester judgment as the 'Judge Higgins' albatross'.

SHERIDAN, T. *Mindful militants: the Amalgamated Engineering Union in Australia, 1920–1972.* CUP, 1975. 329 p.

Traces the main industrial and political preoccupations of a union whose strength and militancy made it a pacesetter in wages and a major prize for contending political factions. Companion volume to Buckley (1970).

SPENCE, W.G. *Australia's awakening: thirty years in the life of an Australian agitator.* Sydney, Worker Trustees, 1909. 630 p, illus.

A semiautobiographical account of the emergence of the labour movement up to 1908. New edition published in 1961.

STUART, J. *Part of the glory: reminiscences of the shearers' strike, Queensland, 1891.* Sydney, Australasian Book Society,

1967. 167 p, illus.

First-hand account of this important period in union history.

SUTCLIFFE, J.T. *A history of trade unionism in Australia.* Melbourne, Macmillan, 1921. 226 p.

One of the first chronicles of the landmarks in the development of the Australian union movement. Reprinted in 1967.

TAPERELL, K. *et al, Sexism in public service: the employment of women in Australian government administration.* AGPS, 1975. 111 p.

Paper prepared for the Royal Commission on Australian Government Administration. Describes women's past and present inferior position in the commonwealth public service and outlines proposals for change.

THOMAS, P. *Miners in the 1970s: a narrative history of the Miners' Federation.* Sydney, Miners' Federation, 1983. 552 p, illus, map.

A chronicle of the main issues and events which occupied the Miners' Federation in the 1970s. Continues the work of Edgar Ross (1970).

TURNER, I. *Industrial labour and politics: the dynamics of the labour movement in eastern Australia, 1900–1921.* Sydney, Hale & Iremonger, 1979. xxix, 272 p.

A major scholarly work which illustrates the role of mass working-class action in shaping the labour movement. First published in 1965.

TURNER, I. AND SANDERCOCK, L. *In union is strength: a history of trade unions in Australia, 1788–1983.* Melbourne, Nelson, 1983. 183 p, illus.

A short history which provides a useful introduction. First published in 1976.

WALKER, A.E. *Coaltown: a social survey of Cessnock.* MUP, 1945, 141 p.

Brings the perspective of social anthropology to a study of family life, work and leisure in a coalmining community.

WATERS, F. *Postal unions and politics: a history of the Amalgamated Postal Workers' Union of Australia.* Ed by D.J. Murphy. UQP, 1978. 311 p, illus.

A history of a union now known as the Australian Postal and Telecommunications Union covering its growth, industrial issues and political campaigns.

WATERS, M. *Strikes in Australia: a sociological analysis of industrial conflict.* Sydney, Allen & Unwin, 1982. 239 p, illus.

Examines the complexity of strikes as a social phenomenon with emphasis on the development of industrial technology and how it has changed the tactics of the major protagonists.

WILLIAMS, C. *Open cut: the working class in an Australian mining town.* Sydney, Allen & Unwin, 1981. 222 p.

A study of work and family relationships among working-class people in a Qld mining community where the town is owned by the Utah Company.

WINDSCHUTTLE, E. ed, *Women, class and history: feminist perspectives on Australia, 1788–1978.* Sydney, Fontana/Collins, 1980. 604 p.

Papers from the first Women and Labour Conference held in 1978, divided into five chronological periods, which consider the position of women in the paid and unpaid workforce.

WINDSCHUTTLE, K. *Unemployment: a social and political analysis of the economic crisis in Australia.* Ringwood, Vic, Penguin, 1980. 343 p.

Nature of the crisis, social consequences, institutional responses, solutions. Radical analysis which was the subject of an ABC television documentary series. First published in 1979.

IX
SOCIETY

*Cover, Australian women's weekly, 23 Jan 1952.
With the legalisation of daylight bathing in the early
1900s and the establishment of surf lifesaving clubs
thereafter, the beach became a major venue for both sport
and leisure. Bayside, riverside and harbourside resorts,
which flourished from the 1880s to the 1940s, gave way
to the surfing beach. The range of people participating
in Australian beach culture is well captured by
Wep in this cover.*

Coronation procession mounted by townspeople in Gympie, Queensland, in 1937.
CARTER COLLECTION

CHAPTER 38

SOCIAL HISTORY

MICHAEL ROE

SOCIAL HISTORY is perhaps more difficult to define than other kinds. It threatens to overlap with many other disciplines so that books from this list inevitably appear also in other chapters of this volume. Probably the most influential article in recent English writing on social history is E.J. Hobsbawm's 'From social history to the history of society', first published in *Daedalus* (Winter 1971, pp 20–45). This article contains some brilliant insights, but seems astray in its central thrust—namely, that social history, as distinct from other kinds of history, addresses the history of society as a whole, complex yet total. The truer verdict surely is that virtually all kinds of history can, most of the time should, and much of the time do, have this high purpose. Political history, economic history, women's history ... and the list runs on. The author's own *Quest for authority in eastern Australia 1835–51* (MUP, 1965) is considered to be social history and while it is unquestionably a history of society, it is cultural as well as social history. The divide, of course, is narrow: some of the references, most obviously White (1981), might be thought to lie on the same side as *Quest for authority*.

While not having monopoly rights in the matter, social history most certainly is concerned with the history of society. It studies ways in which material conditions of life react with human relationships and attitudes. Another way of making the point of the previous paragraph is first to equate 'relations and attitudes' with 'the history of society', and then to recognise that not only 'material conditions of life' react with those relations and attitudes. But the rest of that story belongs to other historians while the dynamic effect of 'material conditions' is that of the social historian.

The language of our definition is no more clumsy than meaning demands. 'Material conditions' conveys the point that economic facts are crucial to social history. So are they crucial to many areas of experience, but with particular immediacy in this instance. Such economic facts affect both work place and living place; they affect all parts of the living place—backyard (that is, leisure activities) and bedroom (sexual mores) as well as kitchen (diet and living standards).

Whereas older traditions of social history were often narrow, threatening to reduce the subject to triviality, our definition follows current theory and practice in linking 'material circumstances' with 'relations and attitudes'. The most obvious of such relations are those of class, and Marxists of various kinds have contributed much to recent social history, as McQueen (1976, 1977) and Connell and Irving (1980) exemplify. But 'class' is a concept used by other than Marxist writers, less confident though they might be of its precise meaning and less apocalyptic in their interpretation of its effect. For many, 'class' is too protean an idea for effective handling. 'Groups' and 'types' are easier terms to use, although (and because) they carry less portent. They are the terms appropriate to many of our books. A principle of selection has been that authors should refer to important classes, groups or types, and convey through a study of their interrelationships a sense of society in the round.

'Attitudes' is specified in the definition so as to assert that social history centres on the sense-experience of humankind. It is rooted in consciousness, and so earns its claim to high standing in the realms of humane learning. Social history often deals with consciousness of a simple and direct kind. These qualities are not akin to pettiness: the matter treated by, say, Gammage (1977) or Facey (1984) is simple and direct, but also profound and moving. A further criterion of choice has been the presence of some such grand or elemental quality.

The ugliest phrase of our definition is 'react with'. It would have been simpler to say 'shape', but not so true. Material conditions are more positive than many facts, but not absolutely so: they acquire meaning from consciousness, as well as giving meaning to consciousness. That is to say, the two elements in our definition mutually react.

So, with pedantic pen, a definition can be offered and explained. Yet having done that, many issues must be resolved before its application makes good sense. They are best tackled by starting with the more abstract.

One concerns the dilemma of national-ness. Australia has become a political entity which relates in turn to more-or-less a geographical entity. Is it an entity conforming to social history? Everyone's answer would surely have a yes–no quality. Although of long and at times interesting provenance, Australian nationalism has never been extremely potent or pervasive; political loyalties and (still more) financial interests are often directed to the particular rather than to the whole. Yet Australia is probably as homogeneous as any nation, with similar groups and types prevailing from region to region. Speech is the best symbol: one can find a few variations (boys educated by Christian Brothers, especially in Queensland, tend to say 'umberella' and 'fillum'; Tasmanians use more nicknames and accent second syllables—Huddo [Peter Hudson of Australian Rules football fame] first played with New Norfolk—but they amount to little.

It is convenient, and perhaps even necessary, to assert Australian homogeneity if one also believes, as does the compiler, that much of the best social history is local history. There is no mystery why this should be so. Social history requires an intensity that naturally predisposes the student to work within narrow geographic bounds. In today's scholarly world (probably less in Australia than most similar countries), a vast amount of academic effort is being expended in social history research, which a while back would have seemed antiquarian. Indeed, some of these efforts do seem rather extravagant, but they confirm the affinity between local and social history. The overrepresentation of Tasmania in the bibliography results from this situation: anyone who knows one region and its literature particularly well will know certain works to be such good local history that they impose themselves upon his or her judgment. Yet (to return to and clarify the opening assertion of this paragraph), if one sees Australia as socially homogeneous, one need have no guilt about such a bias in a national list, for truths derived from one area are, reasonably speaking, therefore likely to be of general pertinence.

This argument has a double edge. Might not the most important truth of the matter be that social history has a homogeneity not only and importantly within Australia but for much of the world? Accordingly, the argument might continue, social history lacks that definition of particularity and change which should be an aim of historical study. There can be various responses to this charge. Revealing particularity may not be essential to historical study after all. Manning Clark's multivolume history of Australia has won praise from one acute observer essentially because it establishes that humanity has undergone the same range of experience and emotion in Australia as elsewhere (P. Munz, 'Gesta Dei per Australianos', *Australia 1888: bulletin 3*, 1979, 5–27). Perhaps social history should strive for that same accolade, or at least be ready to accept it. Changing perspective somewhat, one could say that Australia's social history is no more derivative and comparable vis-a-vis the outside world than are other aspects of its history.

Nobody knows enough to decide this question, and never will until that unimaginable day when the total history of the world is written. All this can be said, with sense and truth; yet a nag remains that even the best of our social history tells a tale, not hackneyed, nor yet unique and virgin.

The relationship between social history and social ideology offers some thorny problems. An oft-spoken virtue of social history is its democratic quality, resulting from concern for the common people as against the elitism of politics, management and growth. A natural and even necessary result might be for its texts and scholars to side with underdogs against establishments. That Marxists have written good social history apparently attests the thesis. More generally, there is indeed much sympathy for the humble in, say, Barbalet's (1983) study of state children and Ward's (1978) of bush workers.

Another appropriate example of this relationship is the treatment accorded to bushrangers by historians during the past hundred years. While some of the reasons for the widespread disruption of society, notably rural, in the nineteenth century can be explored in works about bushrangers and their role, these men attracted popular imagination and sympathy against a background of rural depression. Some of the past authors (for example, J.J. Kenneally, *The complete inner history of the Kelly gang*, 1929; repr, Moe, Vic, Kelly Gang Publishing Co, 1969) have argued that police persecution and the unbending superior attitude of the judiciary were the main causes of the Kelly outbreak and similar events. More recent histories such as McQuilton (1979) have assessed bushranging as a social rather than a purely criminal phenomenon.

Social history must address itself to the common people. Less conventionally it can also be claimed—on both moral and intellectual grounds, although ultimately more the former—that the very best history results from its writers having sympathy with their subjects. This is especially true of social history, which therefore is obviously subject to the eternal tension of sympathy's Janus effect: prompting insight and understanding on one hand, sentimentality and subjectivism on the other.

Despite all this there is little sociopolitical bias in the listed books. Social history does give a sizeable place to the common people, but no monopoly. Note such books as those by Kiddle (1980) and de Serville (1980)—who, furthermore, have an affinity with the values of their elites which counterweighs the underdoggery of other authors. Again, whatever might be the truth as to the best studies requiring sympathy between author and subject, some important ones have emerged in (and from) its absence: Robson (1976) is cool towards convicts; McQueen (1976) scathing about New Britons. At most, then, social history (compared with other subdisciplines) is just a shade more oriented to the left, and just a shade more vulnerable to the distortions of ideology and sentiment.

One has to worry about such matters, but not for too long, lest the mind boggle and stall. What then about these particular books? Why them and not others, or other kinds?

In the most general terms, items are chosen because they tell much about Australian social history in terms of the definition earlier discussed. They touch little upon Aboriginal history—partly because of 'overlap' considerations (see section IV), but mainly because the compiler is wary of imposing on Aboriginal experience concepts drawn from European culture. Otherwise the attempt has been to offer a comprehensive spread as to both time and social group and place (saving the excess Tasmaniana). Experiences therein told are judged to be authentically Australian: not universally shared by Australians of course, but running with mainstream currents of Australian history. Accordingly, they are likely to evoke a sizeable degree of identification, or at least comprehension, from other Australians.

All the books listed are good books, well worth reading. As the annotations suggest, some might be thinnish or tendentious or dated—but no author need be ashamed of having written any one of them. The entries fall into two broad categories: history and contemporary report. The latter includes academic enquiry of sociological bent; interpretative essays, often by visitors; and autobiographies. To make distinctions as to the relative quality of these various subgroups is a forbidding task, but perhaps the palm should go to the autobiographies.

Biases other than locality might have affected the compiler. Time, like place, is a distorter. This list dates from the second half of 1984 and comprises a large number of books published in immediately preceding years. Those from earlier periods have, as it were, had to undergo more rigorous tests of survival capacity; they might be finer works than the overall average, whereas some of the later ones could prove unworthy of the dignity of selection.

The choice is made by an academic. It is likely that there are more non-academic books in this list than in most others. But maybe there should be still more, for this is an area requiring such sensitivity of judgment and breadth of experience as academics have in no exclusive way. Conversely, only a few scholars have brought together the best of relevant academic qualities—rigour in handling socioeconomic data and acuteness of analysis—to produce surpassingly good books: Davison (1979) and Waterson (1968) are probably the best exemplars of the academic ideal.

Finally, the compiler might have been guilty of bias through ideological commitment. If so, it is bias of the most insidious sort—that which leaves the perpetrator ignorant of the deed. Ideological blinkers might even blind him to the existence of some major books. Who will ever know?

Certain kinds of material have been excluded. Among them are histories 'of society' (to return to a concept discussed earlier in the essay). Most books of this kind are at a level of generality which excludes them from even so modestly specialised a list as this. That does not apply however to, say, Serle's studies of Victoria, or Pike's of South Australia, or Robson's of Van Diemen's Land. It is because these are considerably more than social history, not their lack of relevance thereto, that they are absent.

Novels present no less a problem, especially when they depend heavily upon personal experience. Is there any justification for including Alexander Harris (1847; facs, 1964) yet not *Ralph Rashleigh* (A & R, 1975)? Once that gate is opened, many would press for entry: Leakey's *Broad arrow* (London, Bently, 1859), exploring the fusion of convictism with master–servant bonds; Tasma's [J. Couvreur] *Uncle Piper of Piper's Hill* (1889; facs, Melbourne, Nelson, 1969), a fine revelation of high bourgeois Melbourne in its heyday; Lawrence's *Kangaroo* (1923; repr, A & R, 1982), arguably the most brilliant of traveller's tales; Hardy's *Four-legged lottery* (London, T. Werner Laurie, 1958), a powerful study of the gambling life; and plenty of others. Novels offer insights into the history of society, but not through social history. Their special concern is moral and emotional experience.

At another end of the scale are raw documents. Most history is based on them and some make wonderfully good reading—many a parliamentary paper, for example, or Pearl's *Australia's yesterdays* (Sydney, Reader's Digest Services, 1974), or Ward and Robertson's two-volume collection *Such was life . . . 1788–1913* (Sydney, Alternative Publishing Co, 1978–80). The current vogue for the collection of oral reminiscences adds another species to this genre, albeit one that has to be handled with greater care as a historical source. The principle of excluding documents was more straightforward than with the novels: the aim was to offer readers books in which the genius of authorship operated to a degree impossible in even the best of editing.

No principle determined the absence of biographies. In fact none pressed for inclusion (unless Durack, 1981, is considered biography more than 'saga'). Perhaps there is some underlying logic: are studies written only of people who, at least in the biographer's eye, transcend norms of interaction between material circumstances, relationships and attitudes? Autobiographies on the other hand are often rich in precisely this way, and so have their ample representation even though some have affinities with novels and others are somewhat documentary.

ADAM-SMITH, P. *The shearers*. Melbourne, Nelson, 1982. 416 p, illus, maps.

Although weak in its historical research, this study has vigour and resonance; its author has written similar studies (concerning timber-getters, railwaymen, soldiers, Bass Straiters) of similar quality.

ADAMS, F.W.L. *The Australians: a social sketch*. London, T. Fisher Unwin, 1893. 314 p.

Adams was a young, sensitive, English intellectual. He posited a very sharp difference between townsmen and inlanders, seeing the latter as the true Australian type.

BARBALET, M. *Far from a low gutter girl: the forgotten world of state wards, South Australia 1887–1940*. OUP, 1983. 286 p, illus.

Draws upon a rich archive to give a view of life from below, unique in its detail and breadth; the protagonists were 'outsiders' in multiple ways.

BARKER, J. *The two worlds of Jimmie Barker: the life of an Australian Aboriginal 1900–1972, as told to J. Mathews*. Canberra, AIAS, 1977. 218 p, illus, maps. (AIAS Ethno-history series, 4.)

A story of great authenticity, telling about Aborigines, Europeans and their interaction.

BEAN, C.E.W. *On the wool track*. London, Alston, Rivers Ltd, 1910. 296 p.

Life in outback NSW presaged the author's fame as official historian of Australia in World War I. Latest edition published in 1963.

BLAINEY, G.N. *A land half won*. Melbourne, Sun Books, 1983. 388 p, illus, maps.

The most relevant of the author's many books, this explores byways of nineteenth-century life with skill and insight. First published in 1980.

BOLGER, P.F. *Hobart Town*. ANUP, 1973. 237 p, illus, maps.

A well-written historical essay of a smaller nineteenth-century city, with its particular problems of a convict background and uneven economic growth.

BOLTON, G.C. *A fine country to starve in*. UWAP, 1972. 278 p, illus, maps.

Concentrates upon the impact of the depression of the 1930s in WA, yet gives a flavour of the difficulties of Australian settlement.

BOYD, R.G.P. *Australia's home, its origins, builders and occupiers*. MUP, 1952. 320 p, illus.

A successful attempt, by an architect and social commentator, to trace the changing style of a basic constituent of Australian society. New edition published in 1978.

BRENNAN. N. *John Wren, gambler: his life and times*. Melbourne, Hill of Content, 1976. 259 p, illus.

A sympathetic study of an extraordinary but common man, who made a fortune out of gambling in Melbourne around 1900 and who sought to build an empire of influence. First published in 1971.

BROOMHILL, C.R. *Unemployed workers: a social history of the great depression in Adelaide*. UQP, 1978. 220 p, illus.

Drawing on statistics and theory as well as conventional sources, gives an enlightening view of the South Australian workforce between the wars.

BUXTON, G.L. *The Riverina 1861–1891: an Australian regional study*. MUP, 1967. 338 p, illus, maps.

A history of the small-farmer movement, of considerably greater success than the stereotype allows.

CANNON, M. *Australia in the Victorian age*. Melbourne, Currey O'Neil, 1982–83. 3 vols, illus.

An informative but sometimes superficial panorama. The volumes are separately titled respectively stressing class differentiation, country life and city life. First published, 1971–75.

CHIDLEY, W.J. *The confessions of William James Chidley*. Ed by S. McInerney. UQP, 1977. 307 p, illus.

Chidley was far from being an ordinary man, but his autobiography gives many glimpses into popular life, and especially into sexual behaviour.

CONNELL, R.W. AND IRVING, T.H. *Class structure in Australian history: documents, narrative and argument*. Melbourne, Longman Cheshire, 1980. 378 p, illus.

An ambitious, neo-Marxist history which strives to comprehend 'class' in virtually all its subtleties, including style of life.

CONWAY, R. *The great Australian stupor: an interpretation of the Australian way of life*. Melbourne, Sun Books, 1971. 282 p.

The author, a Catholic and a practising psychiatrist, applies clinical insights to modern Australian society; he finds it cold, withdrawn, even alienated—but possibly capable of redemption.

CUMES, J.W.C. *Their chastity was not too rigid: leisure times in early Australia*. Melbourne, Longman Cheshire, 1979. 378 p, illus.

Sometimes too sweeping and assertive in its judgments, yet tells much in an entertaining way.

CUSACK, E.D. *Caddie, a Sydney barmaid: an autobiography written by herself, with an introduction by Dymphna Cusack*. A & R, 1966. 199 p.

A moving and persuasive story of life as seen from the other side of the bar; set mainly in Sydney between the wars. First published in 1953.

DAVIES, A.F. et al, *Australian society: a sociological introduction* (3rd edn). Melbourne, Longman Cheshire, 1977. 490 p, illus, maps.

Competent essays ranging over the key features of latter-day Australian society. First published in 1965.

DAVIS, R.P. *The Tasmanian gallows: a study of capital punishment*. Hobart, Cat & Fiddle Press, 1974. 119 p, illus.

Tells much about the texture of society in general, and attitudes to crime and to death over a long timespan.

DAVISON, G.J. *The rise and fall of marvellous Melbourne*. MUP, 1979. 304 p, illus, maps.

An illuminating account of an Australian city, concentrating on the later nineteenth century, when it was indeed 'marvellous'. First published in 1978.

DENHOLM, D. *The colonial Australians*. Ringwood, Vic, Penguin, 1979. 202 p, illus, maps.

A discursive account, embellished with detail and erudition, of aspects of colonial life as diverse as table manners and religious belief.

DE SERVILLE, P.H. *Port Phillip gentlemen and good society in Melbourne before the gold rushes*. OUP, 1980. 256 p, illus.

A determined attempt to describe the style and role of an elite, defined (if rather vaguely) by Old World standards.

DINNING, H.W. *Australian scene*. A & R, 1939. 225 p.

Something of a period piece, and concerned more with Qld than Australia generally, this essay nevertheless has vitality and commitment.

DIXSON, M. *The real Matilda: women and identity in Australia 1788–1975*. Ringwood, Vic, Penguin, 1976. 280 p.

Attempts at a historical explanation for the inferior position of women in Australia in the 1970s. Links their lack of identity with white Australia's convict origins.

DUNSTAN, K. *Wowsers: being an account of the prudery exhibited by certain outstanding men and women in such matters as drinking, smoking, prostitution, censorship and gambling.* Melbourne, Cassell, 1968. 315 p, illus.

'Wowsers' were moralists who sought to curb drinking, gambling, fornication and the like; they had most power early in this century. Dunstan is not sympathetic to his subjects, but he is informative.

DURACK, M. *Kings in grass castles.* Melbourne, Currey O'Neil, 1981. 395 p, illus, maps.

A powerful saga, telling of the author's family and its pioneering ventures across vast areas of northern Australia. First published in 1959.

FACEY, A.B. *A fortunate life.* Ringwood, Vic, Viking, 1984. 342 p, illus, maps.

The autobiography of a countryman (born 1894), who had the qualities of a saint and the ability to write prose of great simplicity and power. First published in 1981.

FENTON, J. *Bush life in Tasmania fifty years ago . . .* London, Hazell, Watson & Viney, 1891. 192 p. 203 p.

The literature offers very few autobiographical accounts by small farmers; this is probably the best of those few. New edition published in 1964.

FITZPATRICK, B.C. *The Australian commonwealth: a picture of the community, 1901–1955.* Melbourne, Cheshire, 1956. 337 p.

More discursive and 'social' than the author's other works, but maintaining the radical critique which he upheld over many years.

FITZPATRICK, J. *The bicycle and the bush: man and machine in rural Australia.* OUP, 1980. 250 p, illus.

Studies on one hand of the life of the bush worker, and on the other the working of a transport revolution.

FREELAND, J.M. *The Australian pub.* Melbourne, Sun Books, 1977. 192 p, illus.

The author is a historian of architecture, which determines the focus of his work; nevertheless, he tells much about the drinking life. First published in 1966.

GAMMAGE, B. *The broken years: Australian soldiers in the Great War.* Ringwood, Vic, Penguin, 1975. 382 p, illus.

Remarkable for its interweaving of documents and text to present a deeply moving account of the soldiery's hopes and fears, life and death. First published in 1974.

GRIFFIN, G.M. AND TOBIN, D. *In the midst of life: the Australian response to death.* MUP, 1982. 177 p, illus.

An informative study, adequately historical in depth, ranging from styles of grief to cost of funerals.

HAINSWORTH, D.R. *The Sydney traders: Simeon Lord and his contemporaries, 1788–1821.* MUP, 1981. 264 p, illus, maps.

Primarily a study in economic history, but illuminates an extraordinarily interesting group—the successful ex-convict businessmen of early NSW. First published in 1971.

HARRIS, A. *Settlers and convicts: or, recollections of sixteen years' labour in the Australian backwoods, by an emigrant mechanic.* London, C. Cox, 1847. 435 p. illus, maps.

Part-fiction though probably it is, this remains the surpassing personal account of pre-1850 Australian life by an ordinary man. New edition published in 1964.

HICKS, N. *'This sin and scandal': Australia's population debate, 1891–1911.* ANUP, 1978. 208 p, illus.

Takes as its focus a parliamentary inquiry into population, and illuminates attitudes to family, sex and geopolitics.

HIRST, J.B. *Adelaide and the country, 1870–1917: their social and political relationship.* MUP, 1973. 266 p, illus.

Presents very effectively the role of this particular city in serving and satisfying not only its own residents but also those considerably more distant.

HIRST, J.B. *Convict society and its enemies: a history of early New South Wales.* Sydney, Allen & Unwin, 1983. 244 p, illus.

A learned presentation of convict life, at least as rewarding as its denizens merited: rough and tough rather than cruel or evil.

HORNE, D. *The Australian people: biography of a nation.* A & R, 1972. 285 p, illus.

Although less well known than the author's *The lucky country* (Penguin, 1964), this has more substance, notably in charting the force of the suburban, self-help style in middle-class Australia.

INGLIS, K.S. *The Australian colonists: an exploration of social history, 1788–1870.* MUP, 1974. 316 p, illus.

The first of a projected four-volume work which investigates Australian identity with subtlety and grace.

JEFFREY, M. *A burglar's life; or the stirring adventures of the great English burglar, Mark Jeffrey.* Launceston Examiner and Tasmanian Office, 1893. 137 p.

Although a 'ghost' doubtless penned this work, it gives an authentic flavour in telling the tale of one who went through the rigours of convictism, and survived. New edition published in 1968.

JENKINS, J. *Diary of a Welsh swagman, 1869–1894, abridged and notated by W. Evans.* Melbourne, Macmillan, 1975. 216 p, illus, map.

The author was a Welsh bard of some local fame who migrated late in life to Australia, ultimately to write a personal account of the itinerant life.

KIDDLE, M.L. *Men of yesterday: a social history of the western district of Victoria, 1834–1890.* MUP, 1980. 591 p, illus, maps.

Concentrates on the landed elite, but is informative about many aspects of rural life and people. First published in 1961.

LAWSON, R. *Brisbane in the 1890s: a study of an Australian urban society.* UQP, 1973. 373 p, illus, maps.

While limited in its timespan, depicts a growing city and its people with an effective range of detail.

McINNES, G. *The road to Gundagai.* London, Hamish Hamilton, 1965. 285 p, illus, maps.

The first of the author's series about everyday events in the 1920s, as lived by a bourgeois Melbourne boy.

McQUEEN, H. *A new Britannia: an argument concerning the social origins of Australian radicalism and nationalism.* Ringwood, Vic, Penguin, 1976. 261 p.

A central work in Australian historiography, emphasising petty bourgeois elements in virtually all ranks of Australian society—including convicts, goldseekers and trade unionists. First published in 1970.

McQUEEN, H. *Social sketches of Australia, 1888–1975.* Ringwood, Vic, Penguin, 1977. 255 p, illus.

In an impressionist yet effective way pursues eight themes: work, urban life, rural life, health, Aborigines, New Guinea, 'White Australia' policy and the wider world.

McQUILTON, F.J. *The Kelly outbreak, 1878–1880: the geographical dimension of social banditry.* MUP, 1979. 250 p, illus, map.

Presents Kelly as a product of an angry quasipeasant society, asserting its social protest.

MARTIN, J.I. *The migrant presence, Australian responses 1947–1977: research report for the National Population Inquiry.* Sydney, Allen & Unwin, 1978. 261 p. (Studies in society, 2).

An outstanding synthesis of its subject, enriched by strong historical awareness.

MAYNE, A.J.C. *Fever, squalor, and vice: sanitation and social policy in Victorian Sydney*. UQP, 1982. 263 p, illus, maps.
Draws upon archival sources to present the grimmer side of urban life and politics.

MENDELSOHN, R.S. *The condition of the people: social welfare in Australia, 1900–1975*. Sydney, Allen & Unwin, 1979. 408 p.
Combines much statistical and official information with a sensitivity to human experiences as the ultimate touchstone of 'welfare'.

MURRAY, R.A. *The confident years: Australia in the twenties*. Ringwood, Vic, Allen Lane, 1978. 263 p.
One of the very few attempts to write a 'social history' of the nation over a brief timespan. The patterns of the 1920s were long-lasting.

OESER, O.A. AND EMERY, F.E. *Social structure and personality in the rural community*. London, Routledge & Kegan Paul, 1954. 279 p.
A study of a Victorian country town and its inhabitants, covering family life, social structure, beliefs and behaviour. It remains outstanding in the literature.

OESER, O.A. AND HAMMOND, S.B. eds, *Social structure and personality in a city*. London, Routledge & Kegan Paul, 1954. 344 p.
A pioneer of sociopsychological investigation (centred on Melbourne) in Australia, this remains impressive in its substance and quality. Work, family, class and minorities are among the key issues.

PEARL, C. *Wild men of Sydney*. A & R, 1977. 255 p, illus.
Not a work of academic scholarship, yet gives an enlightening picture of the seamier side of big-city life, politics and journalism early this century. First published in 1955.

PORTER, H. *The watcher on the cast-iron balcony: an Australian autobiography*. London, Faber, 1967. 255 p.
Tells of childhood spent first in Melbourne and then in a country town, with great literary skill and emotional effect; its successor volumes are only slightly less potent. First published in 1963.

PRINGLE, J.D. *Australian accent*. London, Chatto & Windus, 1958. 203 p, illus.
The years around 1960 saw a number of perceptive essays concerning Australia by journalists-literati; this one was particularly successful.

RICKARD, J.D. *Class and politics: New South Wales, Victoria and the early commonwealth, 1890–1910*. ANUP, 1976. 371 p, illus.
An analysis of Australian politics which is based upon a subtle and comprehensive study of class differentiation at a crucial time.

RITCHIE, J.D. *Australia as once we were*. Melbourne, Heinemann, 1975. 279 p, illus.
An effectively sustained endeavour to write a one-volume social history of Australia.

ROBERTS, K. *Captain of the push*. Melbourne, Lansdowne, 1963. 137 p, illus.
An account of Sydney's half-world in the later nineteenth century, focusing on the life of boxing champion Larry Foley.

ROBSON, L.L. *The convict settlers of Australia: an enquiry into the origin and character of the convicts transported to New South Wales and Van Diemen's Land, 1787–1852*. MUP, 1976. 269 p.
An analysis of those transported to eastern Australia, giving

essential data as to their personal situations, and their relationship with the law in both Old and New worlds. First published in 1965.

ROE, J.I. ed, *Twentieth century Sydney: studies in urban and social history*. Sydney, Hale & Iremonger, 1980. 273 p, illus.
A symposium from younger historians who pursue a critical yet constructive approach to their subject.

ROLLS, E.C. *A million wild acres: 200 years of man and an Australian forest*. Ringwood, Vic, Penguin, 1984. 465 p, illus.
A regional history of northern NSW, outstanding for its imaginative stress on the interaction of humanity with nature. First published in 1981.

SKEMP, J.R. *Memories of Myrtle Bank: the bush-farming experiences of Rowland and Samuel Skemp in north-eastern Tasmania 1883–1948*. MUP, 1952. 256 p, illus, maps.
A sensitive and comprehensive study of community life.

STANNAGE, C.T. *The people of Perth: a social history of Western Australia's capital city*. Perth, Carroll's for Perth City Council, 1979. 364 p, illus, maps.
A study concentrating on the nineteenth century and on social relationships.

SUMMERS, A. *Damned whores and God's police: the colonization of women in Australia*. Ringwood, Vic, Penguin, 1975. 494 p.
This influential work examines the causes and consequences of women's oppression, relating it to past and present sexist stereotypes.

TROLLOPE, A. *Australia and New Zealand*. London, Chapman & Hall, 1873. 2 vols.
A commentary on mid-Victorian colonial society by a visiting Englishman. New edition published as *Australia* in 1967.

TWOPENY, R.E.N. *Town life in Australia*. London, Elliot Stock, 1883. 247 p.
A contemporary account written by a young man of Anglo–Australian upbringing who was to become a journalist of distinction. Facsimile edition SUP, 1972.

WALDERSEE, J. *Catholic society in New South Wales, 1788–1860*. SUP, 1974. 313 p, illus, maps.
A sophisticated analysis, which gives rare substance and depth to 'social history'.

WARD, R.B. *The Australian legend*. OUP, 1978. 336 p, illus.
Traces the mythologising of the outback worker as the bearer of distinctively Australian traits: group loyalty, ingenuity, tough recklessness, independence of mind. First published in 1958.

WATERSON, D.B. *Squatter, selector, and storekeeper: a history of the Darling Downs, 1859–93*. SUP, 1968. 310 p, illus, maps.
A scholarly study; the general fate of Waterson's small farmers was grim, in contrast (say) to those of G.L. Buxton's *Riverina* (1967).

WEIDENHOFER, M. *The convict years: transportation and the penal system, 1788–1868*. Melbourne, Lansdowne, 1973. 142 p, illus, maps.
A simplified but sound and humane overview of its subject.

WHITE, R. *Inventing Australia: images and identity 1688–1980*. Sydney, Allen & Unwin, 1981. 205 p, illus. (The Australian experience, 3.)
An imaginative and clever essay, embracing attitudes to Australia from both within and outside.

Immigration brochure c1930.
BOOROWA PRODUCTIONS

CHAPTER 39

IMMIGRATION AND DEMOGRAPHY

A. W. MARTIN AND IAN H. BURNLEY

IMMIGRATION

IMMIGRATION IS ONE of the epic themes of modern Australian history, 'a long and continuous element in the creation of the nation, its peopling, its integration'. But as Eric Richards, who wrote these words, has pointed out, a reader who would like to tackle the immigration theme through a few large and comprehensive works will be disappointed. That other modern immigrant society, the United States, can boast its Oscar Handlin, its Marcus Lee Hanson or its Maldwyn Jones—famous historians who on wide canvas and with penetrating eye have caught at large patterns and meanings in the great movements of peoples which created modern America. To the mid-1980s Australians had not yet produced comparable works, though we now have a body of excellent literature on separate aspects of the subject, much of it stimulated in recent times by curiosity about the social and cultural effects of the great migration program mounted by successive Australian governments since World War II. The coming of these people, infinitely more varied in their origins than the Anglo–Celtic migrants of the previous century and a half, has made the migrant visible, has pointed to migrant 'problems' as matters in urgent need of study, and has given birth to the notion of Australia as a 'multicultural' society.

One particular work now in the making, which has its origins in the new 'visibility' of migrant groups, will go far towards fulfilling the need for a comprehensive guide to the meaning of immigration for Australian history. This is the *Encyclopedia of the Australian people*, commissioned by the Australian Bicentennial Authority and due to be completed in 1988. A large volume of over a million words, it will consider the successive waves, from prehistoric time to present, of migration to Australia, discussing in detail the origins, characteristics, distribution and contribution of individual ethnic groups. Given its historical emphasis and the structure planned for it, the encyclopaedia will necessarily have to tackle a long overdue task: that of reassessing the immigration of the nineteenth and early twentieth centuries, and asking hitherto unthought-of questions which have become salient through recent immigrants' experience.

As the entries in the bibliography suggest, the study of migration since World War II has produced an extensive literature to which demographers and sociologists have been the main contributors. The issues with which they have been concerned have varied from the effects of migration on population size and location, to patterns of economic welfare and employment among migrants, or from early principles about 'assimilation' to greater understanding of and sharper debate on 'ethnicity'.

Don Edgar (1980) has compiled a succinct guide to the sociological writings and Andrew Markus' 'History of post-war immigration', in G. Osborne and W.F. Mandle, eds, *New history: studying Australia today* (Sydney, Allen & Unwin, 1982), intelligently if idiosyncratically surveys what he provocatively dubs 'the much-touted social sciences', identifying the important themes in the literature and pointing to problems which still need addressing. Markus writes as a historian and, though ungenerous in his treatment of the historical side of the more important sociological writing, correctly points to historians' neglect of immigration in the postwar period and neatly formulates a number of the important questions which cry out for investigation.

On the demographic implications of postwar immigration Borrie and Price are the leading authorities. Their work is part of the long debate about Australia's 'optimum' population. Borrie's splendidly documented account in Australia, *National Population Inquiry*, 1975 (chapter V, pp 174–234), is the best introduction to this debate, which was revived in the 1980s in a new guise by the work of sociologists like Robert and Tanya Birrell (1981).

Since the early nineteenth century (and even before that, if we think of the convict settlers as involuntary sponsored migrants) Australian governments have sought to regulate, encourage and, at times, assist immigrants. Sherington's (1980) modest guide aside, no general history of these changing immigration policies yet exists, though much can be pieced together from the writings of scholars who analyse particular periods: the works by Hayden (1971), Madgwick (1937; facs, 1969), Serle (1978) and Pike (1967), listed below, are examples.

The most notorious aspect of immigration policy, 'white Australia', has attracted much attention: Price (1974) and Yarwood (1964, 1982) are the two most insightful and balanced writers in this field. Discussion of the policy has inevitably shaded off into consideration of racism in Australian history, an issue pushed in the 1970s to the forefront of attention, particularly by Humphrey McQueen's provocative *A new Britannia* (Ringwood, Vic, Penguin, 1976) and by the volumes edited by F.S. Stevens. (1971–72). Of the many articles that appeared on the subject J.A.C. Mackie's 'Asian migration and Australian racial attitudes' (*Ethnic studies* 1, 2, 1977, 1–13) is particularly stimulating for the imaginative comparison it makes between Australian and Asian (particularly Indonesian) racial attitudes and for its discussion, within this context, of the Immigration Reform Group and the policy changes of the later 1960s. A reader interested in the flavour of the enduring 'white Australia' debate could do no better than taste the lively documents in Yarwood's collection (1968).

Ethnic history—the study of particular migrant groups' societies of origin, experiences in Australia and contribution to Australian life—is a neglected genre which will no doubt be stimulated by the *Encyclopedia of the Australian people*. Richard Bosworth and Janis Wilton effectively argue the urgency of the case for greater attention to European migrants' history in 'A lost history? The study of European migration to Australia' (*Australian J of politics and history* 27, 2, 1981, 221–31). Pioneer works like C.A. Price (1963) and his earlier *German settlers in South Australia* (MUP, 1945) or Borrie (1954) have not been matched in scale and scholarship by successive studies of other groups. Gittens (1981) and Pryor (1962) exemplify a more modest but nevertheless valuable endeavour to stimulate popular interest; J. Bell has written about *The Dutch* (Melbourne, Nelson, 1981). Another initiative in the same vein is the 'Australian ethnic heritage series' of booklets being prepared under the general editorship of Michael Cigler. The first of these, Jim Faull's *The Cornish in Australia* (Melbourne, AE Press, 1983) serves as a valuable companion to Pryor (1962); it and Macmillan (1967) serve to emphasise that 'ethnic' histories are needed of peoples who came to Australia from the British Isles as well as from other places—that the so-called ethnic dimension encompasses all migrants.

Readers wishing to sample the 'migrant experience' may draw on a rich but unfortunately unco-ordinated and largely unindexed literature. In this area the need for comprehensive and imaginative work by social historians is especially urgent. Well-chosen and well-edited selections from migrant writings would also be most valuable. Lucy Frost's admirable *No place for a nervous lady* (Ringwood, Vic, Penguin, 1984) is an object lesson in the assembling and presentation of collections of this kind. Penelope Hope, *The voyage of the Africaine . . .* (Melbourne, Heinemann

Educational, 1968) shows how a number of narratives can be neatly compiled into a pleasing whole, while Don Charlwood, *The long farewell* (Ringwood, Vic, Penguin, 1981) looks at the voyage to Australia under sail, using emigrants' diaries. Readers interested in locating nineteenth-century migrants' accounts of the voyage to the Australian colonies, of their experiences on arrival, their reaction to the new society and the like will find guidance in J. A. Ferguson's seven-volume *Bibliography of Australia* (facs, Canberra, NLA, 1975–77), though this work lacks an index and many of the works listed will have to be consulted in research collections in the various state and university libraries.

In addition to writings of the kind listed above, nineteenth-century guides for immigrants, issued by individual authors, private organisations and governments, were numerous and are informative about conditions of travel and the image of the colonies presented to prospective migrants. Some are, naturally, heavily propagandist; according to Samuel Sidney, for example (*Three colonies of Australia*, London, Ingram, Cooke & Co, 1853), 'All Handbooks of Emigration previous to 1848 [when *his* first appeared], whether of Australia, New Zealand or America were mere puffs, written in the spirit of a recruiting crimp' (quoted by R.L. Heathcote, in A. Rapoport, *Australia as a human setting*, A & R, 1972, p 83). Reprints of such material are occasionally made; two relatively recent examples are D.J. Golding's edition of John Capper's *The emigrant's guide to Australia in the eighteen fifties* (Melbourne, Hawthorn, 1973) and George Arden's informative 1840 booklet on Port Phillip, *Latest information with regard to Australia Felix: the finest province of the great territory of New South Wales . . .* (Melbourne, Queensberry Hill Press, 1977).

The literature on migrants' experiences in recent times includes creative literature, two interesting examples of which are Louise Rorabacher, ed, *Two ways meet: stories of migrants in Australia,* (Melbourne, Cheshire, 1969) and R. F. Hold, ed, *The strength of tradition: stories of the immigrant presence in Australia* (UQP, 1984). There are also accounts of individuals' experiences such as Dmytro Chub, *So this is Australia: the adventures of a Ukrainian migrant in Australia,* (Melbourne, Bayda Books, 1980); Pino Bosi, *Farewell Australia,* (Sydney, Kurunda Publications, 1972); and Morag Loh, *With courage in their cases: the experiences of thirty-five Italian immigrant workers and their families in Australia,* (Melbourne, Italian Federation of Emigrant Workers and their Families, 1980). Academic studies—in addition to those listed in the bibliography—include Stephanie R. L. Thompson, *Australia through Italian eyes: a study of settlers returning from Australia to Italy,* (OUP, 1980); Aldis L. Putnins, *Latvians in Australia: alienation and assimilation* (ANUP, 1981); and Jean I. Martin, *Refugee settlers: a study of displaced persons in Australia,* (ANUP, 1965).

The reading list on immigration presented below is meant to suggest the broader divisions into which the literature on immigration falls. Space permits only the barest sampling: though some works of central importance are noted, others are included simply as examples of the kinds of books a curious and resourceful reader may hope to discover. Happily such readers have at their disposal a comprehensive and lucid finding aid in Charles Price (1966–81). The Centre for Migrant Studies at Monash University produces *Ethnic studies,* the only Australian learned journal devoted to research and discussion of issues connected with immigration. Relevant articles do however appear randomly in a variety of other journals concerned more broadly with historical, sociological and economic research. Price's bibliography offers a sure guide to all such articles.

Another valuable source on current migration issues is the series of annotated bibliographies compiled on special subjects by the Clearing House on Migrant Issues (CHOMI) at the Ecumenical Migration Centre in Richmond, Victoria. These bibliographies list relevant government papers, journal and newspaper articles and other material of a kind not always included in the Price series. Typical titles in the CHOMI bibliographies include *Welfare of migrants in Australia, Resources for bilingual and bicultural education, Refugees and displaced persons, Migration and the family.* The Ecumenical Migration Centre also issues a lively magazine, *Migration action,* which—as its name implies—is concerned primarily with practical questions affecting migrant welfare. It is most informative on current official policy and community attitudes towards migrants, and on the experiences of the migrants themselves. *Migration action* is also the best place to keep a watchful eye on the many useful reprints and occasional papers produced by CHOMI.

DEMOGRAPHY

While immigration has been a major factor in Australia's population growth, the influences of other demographic factors such as mortality, fertility and internal migration need also to be understood to gain a proper perspective of the peopling of this continent.

Australia has been fortunate in that the first university department of demography in the world was established at the Australian National University in 1952 and much of the formal demographic analysis in Australia has been conducted at that institution. The only other university to have a degree structure in demographic studies is Macquarie University, Sydney. Population studies have also been undertaken as part of other disciplines—epidemiology, population geography, population biology, medical sociology and actuarial studies in the case of mortality; sociology, gynaecological studies and statistics in the case of fertility; and population geography, regional economics and social anthropology in the case of internal migration. Work in historical demography has been carried out in the fields of economic and social history. Thus many if not most demographic studies about Australia are oriented towards related scholarly or scientific disciplines. A weakness has been the rather limited attention to contemporary demographic analysis on the part of economists.

There are two basic works which analytically treat past and present demographic trends in Australia. The first, published in 1975, and popularly known as the 'Borrie Report' (Australia, National Population Inquiry), has already been mentioned. The second and more recent work is the United Nations Economic and Social Commission for Asia and the Far East Monograph No 9 on the population of Australia (1982). Both works are essential reading for anyone interested in Australia's population, and they are not too technical for general interpretation.

Mortality is a component of population change that has been extensively researched but much of the published work is in specialist journals or monographs. The influential work by B.S. Hetzel, *Health and Australian society* (3rd edn, Ringwood, Vic, Penguin, 1980) charts the decline in mortality from contagious illnesses since the 1870s, and thus the marked increase in life expectancy at birth. This author also considers the 'modern epidemics' of heart disease mortality, cancer, suicide and accident mortality which increased markedly after World War II. The other major monograph is that by C. Young, *Mortality patterns and trends in Australia* (AGPS, 1975), a commissioned study for the National Population Inquiry discussed above. While there is technical discussion, the author points to differentials affecting mortality, including occupation and industry, age, sex and marital status. 'Differential' mortality is examined in McGlashan (1977) which also considers geographical and occupational variations.

Much of the information on mortality is derived from death certificates collected by the registrars general in each state and processed by the ABS. Deaths by medical cause, detailed by age, sex and marital status, are available in published annual volumes or on unpublished computer printout or magnetic tape. Such data can be standardised against the census age distribution, and the techniques for such data manipulation can be found in several demography manuals, as well as in the text by A.H. Pollard *et al, Demographic techniques* (Sydney, Pergamon, 1974).

For regional analysis, deaths by age and major cause (using the International Classification of Diseases) are available by local government areas in most states from the ABS, provided confidentiality is not violated as in the case of small populations.

Fertility refers to the number of children born alive. As far as the demographer is concerned, it is a statistical rather than a biological phenomenon that is being measured. Demographers have not been content simply to measure the incidence of fertility but have become concerned with the historical, sociological and economic correlates and consequences of fertility change.

Historical studies of fertility have had to be content with census cross-tabulations, such as age of mother by duration of marriage by number of 'issue' (children), since sample surveys of women's attitudes and behaviour have only taken place since the beginning of the 1970s. The other data sources are vital statistics (birth and marriage statistics) collected by the registrar general in each state from birth and marriage certificates. The certificates are confidential but reliable aggregate statistics are available for states from the late nineteenth century.

The report of the National Population Inquiry (1975) summarises the decline in fertility in Australia from levels higher than in most of the Third World today (6–7 children per family) to the two-child family of the Great Depression years. This demographic transition, which took place in modernising Western countries, but over a longer time in countries such as France and Sweden, is one of the more profound social changes to have occurred. Postwar, there was the unexpected 'marriage and baby boom' documented in specialised monographs published mainly by the ANUP (for example, M.E. Browne, 1979).

From the early 1970s, knowledge, attitude and practice surveys were undertaken by specialist personnel from the Australian National University. These large sample surveys of women, initially funded by the Ford Foundation of New York, investigated why women had the numbers of children they did, the importance of socioeconomic status, age at marriage, family history, health status, sexual behaviour in marriage, knowledge and application of contraception, religious belief and so on. These surveys allowed comparisons with other countries, including studies in the World Fertility Survey. Follow-up studies, including attitudinal, cross-sectional and cohort (longitudinal) studies, all pointed to an increasing convergence between the 'ideal family size' for a couple, the actual family size, what was ethically the appropriate number of children and so on. The desired and ideal family size increasingly became two children, and actual fertility had declined to this level by the late 1970s. This decline paralleled that in Britain, the United States and Canada (with slight recovery since in the United States) but did not drop as low as that in Sweden, West Germany and Austria. The Australian studies also show that, in common with trends in the United States, 'differential fertility' has declined. That is, there are limited differences between religious, ethnic and occupational statuses or between geographical regions.

The National Population Inquiry (1975), and its working papers, document the impact of immigration on Australia's population growth from the mid-nineteenth century until 1971. Immigration's impact was profound at almost all times except during recession or economic depression and during the world wars. The impact was particularly significant on the metropolitan cities, especially Sydney and Melbourne. The impact on the cities during the nineteenth century has been thoroughly documented by the economic historians McCarty and Schedvin (1978); a paper commissioned by the National Population Inquiry by C.Y. Choi, *Population distribution in Australia: the role of internal and overseas migration* (AGPS, 1975) has quantified the trend in the twentieth century.

For the postwar period, the role of immigration in urbanisation and ecological change within the metropolitan cities has been documented, with consideration of the social and economic implications. Immigration was the dominant component in population growth of Sydney, Melbourne and Adelaide between 1947 and the early to mid-1970s. By the 1981 census immigrants comprised one-third of the Australian labour force, and immigrants and their Australian-born children comprised over half the population of metropolitan Melbourne and almost half of Sydney's population.

Despite the high level of geographical mobility within Australia, internal migration has been comparatively underresearched. As at mid-1984, there was no definitive book-length study, and very few papers in professional journals, on rural–urban migration. The most important type of internal migration in the decades since the Great Depression has been interurban migration and in particular intermetropolitan migration. In his definitive census monograph on migration during the 1966–71 period, which summarised historical trends in interstate migration, Rowland (1979) demonstrated that basically Australia was in a state of equilibrium as far as internal migration was concerned—internal migration acted to reinforce the existing settlement system and population distribution, rather than to change it.

This study was at a macroregional level but some state government departments, notably the New South Wales Department of Decentralisation and Development, have commissioned sample surveys of movers into country towns and these have been published in report form. Internal migration has been studied by human geographers and demographers; it has not been given the attention it deserves by economic or social historians, economists or sociologists.

The higher fertility of the postwar period, combined with mass immigration, which was age-selective and had its own natural increase, created a rejuvenation of the population. The median age fell. With the fall in fertility during the 1970s, the slowing of immigration and declining mortality at ages over 35, the median age of the population has been rising. A technical report of the ABS has portrayed the decline in heart disease and stroke mortality which has largely accounted for the overall mortality decline, as well as documenting the increase in cancer mortality during the 1970s.

Despite these changes, population projections of the ABS and the supplement to the National Population Inquiry indicate that the proportion of elderly in 2001 will be much like that in western Europe today, although there will be problems in the support of the old age dependent population. Thereafter, the proportion of elderly will rise rapidly.

The definitive work on the Aboriginal population is that of L. Smith (1980) who has charted trends in Aboriginal population decline and growth from 1788 to the 1970s. His review of the anthropological literature relating to sustenance, survival and growth is exhaustive, as is his treatment of the decline and revival of the Aboriginal birthrates last century, the causal factors in change and contemporary trends. Local surveys have illuminated demographic patterns, notably Rowley's 1972 study of Aborigines in country districts of New South Wales, which was part of a wider study of the place of Aborigines in Australian society. There are major problems in analysing Aboriginal population trends because of incomplete enumeration in recent censuses and non-inclusion in earlier censuses, as well as very incomplete coverage in annual vital statistics. Sources have therefore included mission station statistics and local sample surveys.

The monographs cited in the bibliography are the main works in the field of population study in Australia; their number is limited. Most of the references, while presenting technical material where necessary, are written for an intelligent general audience. The works either analyse trends from a policy point of view or are related to a particular academic discipline which is considering the population factor. Some introductory substantive or technical books are included, but there is a dearth of detailed texts on Australian demography.

The equivalent of archival information are the census computer printouts, cross-tabulations and data sets which exist from 1966 onwards, and on microfiche from the 1976 census onwards. The individual questionnaire schedules are destroyed when they have been used for data compilation. This policy contrasts with the United States where individual schedules can be consulted for bona fide research purposes after 60 years. Sample files of individual households, with identity carefully protected, are available on magnetic tape from the 1981 census.

For historical research, the government statistician's reports and monographs for given censuses are invaluable. Parish registers of major churches are an important source for nineteenth-century population trends, although not every person belonged to a parish. These sources have so far been grossly underutilised.

Expatriate Irishmen and Australians of Irish origin at a dinner of the Queensland Irish Association, Brisbane 1938.
OXLEY LIBRARY

GENERAL STUDIES

DE LEPERVANCHE, M. 'Australian immigrants, 1788–1840: desired and unwanted', in Wheelwright, E.L. and Buckley, K. eds, *Essays in the political economy of Australian capitalism.* Sydney, Australia and New Zealand Book Co, 1975. Vol 1, 72–104.

Survey of European immigration to demonstrate how since first settlement society has been markedly stratified.

DUGAN, M. AND SZWARC, J. *'There goes the neighbourhood!' Australia's migrant experience.* Melbourne, Macmillan in association with the Australian Institute of Multicultural Affairs, 1984. 200 p, illus.

Richly illustrated coffee-table book of documents of the four main phases of immigration, each introduced with a historical account.

POTTS, E.D. AND POTTS, A. *Young America and Australian gold: Americans and the gold rush of the 1850s.* UQP, 1974. 299 p.

An account of Americans on the goldfields, as entrepreneurs in business and in transport, and as entertainers.

POWELL, J.M. *Mirrors of the New World: images and image makers in the settlement process.* ANUP, 1978. 207 p, illus, maps.

Looks at the effect of images of the New World (taking examples principally from North America and Australasia) in the promotion of migration from Europe, especially in the nineteenth century.

PRENTIS, M.D. *The Scots in Australia: a study of New South Wales, Victoria and Queensland, 1788–1900.* SUP, 1983. 304 p, illus, maps.

Examines Scots influence in economic, educational and religious life, arguing that some distinctive characteristics of middle-class culture can be traced to that influence.

PRICE, C.A. ed, *Australian immigration: a bibliography and digest, nos 1–4.* Canberra, Dept of Demography, Institute of Advanced Studies, Australian National University, 1966–81. 4 vols in 6.

These literature surveys have become reference tools on immigration since 1945 with articles and statistical tables on immigration and ethnic composition and a study of migrant children's education 1945–75.

SHERINGTON, G. *Australia's immigrants, 1788–1978.* Sydney, Allen & Unwin, 1980. 189 p, illus, maps.

A comprehensive history of immigration since 1788.

WITH courage and hope: the contribution of six migrant communities to life in Queensland (1838–1945). Division of Migrant Service, Dept of Welfare Services, 1983. 51 p, illus.

Covers Germans, Chinese, Greeks, Italians, Scandinavians and Russians in Qld.

ASPECTS OF IMMIGRATION TO 1946

BONUTTO, O. *A migrant's story.* Brisbane, Pole, 1963. 139 p, illus.

Bonutto describes his treatment during World War II, when he was twice wrongfully interned, although he was a naturalised Australian.

CROWLEY, F.K. 'The British contribution to the Australian population: 1860–1919', *University studies in history and economics* 2, 2, 1954, 55–88.

A discussion of the origins and size of, and policies behind, British migration from the gold rushes to 1919.

DUNCAN, W.G.K. AND JANES, C.V. eds, *The future of immigration into Australia and New Zealand.* Sydney, A & R in conjunction with Australian Institute of Political Science, 1937. 291 p, illus, maps.

Chapters by different authors constitute a sample of public opinion in Australia concerning immigration. Reveals the conflict of opinions between 'academic' and 'practical' people.

EGGLESTON, F.W. AND PHILLIPS, P.D. eds, *The peopling of Australia, further studies.* MUP, 1933. 327 p, illus.

Papers commissioned by the AIIA on various aspects of the migration drive of the 1920s. Indispensable.

FORSYTH, W.D. *The myth of open spaces: Australian, British and world trends of population and migration.* MUP, 1942. 226 p, illus, maps.

Contribution to the interwar debate arguing against optimistic estimates of Australia's capacity to absorb migrants.

GITTINS, J. *The digger from China: the story of Chinese on the goldfields.* Melbourne, Quartet Books, 1981. 148 p, illus, maps.

Unpretentious account of the Chinese diggers: their origins, voyage to Australia, way of life.

HAYDEN, A.A. 'New South Wales immigration policy, 1856–1900' *Transactions of the American Philosophical Society* 61, 5, 1971, 1–60.

Supplements Madgwick's study (1969) of policy-making in nineteenth-century NSW and places the immigration issues into the political context created by responsible government.

KIDDLE, M. *Caroline Chisholm.* MUP, 1957. 295 p, illus, map.

British immigration to Australia in the 1840s brought vividly to life. First published in 1950. An abridged edition also published in 1969.

MACMILLAN, D.S. *Scotland and Australia, 1788–1850: emigration, commerce and investment.* Oxford, Clarendon Press, 1967. 434 p, illus, map.

Account of Scottish immigrants before 1850 set in the context of Scottish enterprise in trade and investment.

MADGWICK, R.B. *Immigration into eastern Australia, 1788–1851.* London, Longman, Green, 1937, 270 p.

Pioneer work on policy-making, administrative machinery and character of British immigration to 1851. Facsimile edition, SUP, 1969.

PARKES, H. *An emigrant's home letters.* A & R, 1896. 164 p.

Letters of Henry Parkes after his emigration to NSW in 1839. They capture the pain, hope and experience of the immigrant.

PHILLIP, J. *A great view of things: Edward Gibbon Wakefield.* Melbourne, Nelson, 1971. 113 p, illus.

Places Wakefield's ideas on 'systematic colonisation' in the context of his theory of economic growth and empire, and demonstrates his influence on imperial policy-making.

PHILLIPS, P.D. AND WOOD, G.L. eds, *The peopling of Australia.* Melbourne, Macmillan in association with MUP, 1928. 300 p, illus.

Discussion of the contemporary debate about Australia's population 'problem'.

PIKE, D.H. *Paradise of dissent: South Australia, 1829–1857.* MUP, 1967. 590 p, illus, maps.

The foundation of SA related to the theories of Edward Gibbon Wakefield. (For a critique of Pike's views, see Phillip, 1971). First published in 1957.

PRYOR, O. *Australia's little Cornwall.* Adelaide, Rigby, 1962. 192 p, illus, map.

An account of Cornish copper-mining community at Moonta, SA; entertaining analysis of an early 'ethnic' group.

SERLE, A.G. *The golden age: a history of the colony of Victoria,*

1851–1861. MUP, 1978. 469 p, illus, maps.

Account of the gold migration to Vic and of its social and political consequences. First published in 1963.

WATSON, D. *Caledonia Australia: Scottish highlanders on the frontier of Australia.* Sydney, Collins, 1984. 214 p, illus, maps.

A study of two dispossessed groups, the Scottish highlanders and the Aborigines of Gippsland, seen largely through the life of one of the former, the explorer Angus McMillan.

THE MIGRANT QUESTION AFTER WORLD WAR II

APPLEYARD, R.T. *British emigration to Australia.* Canberra, Australian National University, 1964. 255 p.

A study of the character of postwar British migration drawing on extensive interviews with migrants before they sailed.

AUSTRALIA. Commission of Inquiry into Poverty. *Poverty in Australia: first main report, Australian Government Commission of Inquiry into Poverty, April 1975.* AGPS, 1975. 2 vols.

Poverty among migrants features in various sections of this inquiry, drawing on research by Jean I. Martin, 'The economic condition of migrants' (published as Commission research report, Welfare of migrants, AGPS, 1975).

AUSTRALIA. Population and Immigration Council. *Immigration policies and Australia's population: a green paper.* AGPS, 1977. 101 p.

Inquiry into goals and options in immigration policy, with reference to family reunion, acceptance of refugees, worker recruitment.

AUSTRALIA. Population and Immigration Council. Social Studies Committe. *A decade of migrant settlement: report on the 1973 immigration survey.* AGPS, 1976. 165 p.

A survey of 7700 migrant families who had arrived in the ten years from 1963. Disadvantages often persist past the initial settlement period, and knowledge of English is crucial in migrants' job histories.

AUSTRALIA. Review of Post Arrival Programs and Services to Migrants. *Migrant services and programs: report [and appendixes].* AGPS, 1978. 2 vols.

Recommended on the principle of 'multiculturalism' an increase of $50 million in commonwealth expenditure on migrant programs shaped to encourage 'self-help'. For a critique of the inquiry see *Babel* 16, 1, 1980.

AUSTRALIAN COUNCIL ON POPULATION AND ETHNIC AFFAIRS. *Multiculturalism for all Australians: our developing nationhood.* AGPS, 1982. xi, 54 p, illus.

Argues that for multiculturalism to be successful, minority groups with a non-English speaking background must not flourish on the margin and at the expense of the total Australian society.

AUSTRALIAN INSTITUTE OF POLITICAL SCIENCE. 37th Summer School, Canberra, 1971. *How many Australians? Immigration and growth: proceedings.* Ed by J. Wilkes. A & R, 1971. 226 p, map.

A collection, covering immigration's relation to the economy, the environment, politics and social development.

BIRRELL, R. AND BIRRELL, T. *An issue of people: population and Australian society.* Melbourne, Longman Cheshire, 1981. 277 p.

A discussion of postwar immigration, its origins and dynamics, social impact, economic effects and implications. Must be considered beside conventional anti-capitalist interpretations of these matters.

BIRRELL, R. *et al, Refugees, resources, reunions: Australia's immigration dilemmas.* Melbourne, VCTA Publishing, 1979. 179 p.

Covers the debate on priorities for Australian population policy: the central arguments being on humanitarian, environmental, economic and family issues.

BORRIE, W.D. *Italians and Germans in Australia: a study in assimilation.* Melbourne, Cheshire, 1954. 236 p, illus, maps.

A pioneering study of 'assimilation' of non-British minority groups primarily comparing German migrants in the nineteenth century and Italian migrants in the 1920s.

CALWELL, A.A. *Be just and fear not.* Melbourne, Lloyd O'Neil in association with Rigby, 1972. 274 p, illus.

Autobiography of the architect of Australia's immediate postwar migration policy.

CIGLER, M. *The Czechs in Australia.* Melbourne, AE Press, 1983. 150 p, illus, maps.

CRESIANI, G. *Fascism, anti-fascism and Italians in Australia, 1922–1945.* ANUP, 1980. 261 p, illus.

A study of the political effects on a migrant community of events and propaganda in their society of origin.

CUDDY, D.L. *The Yanks are coming: American immigration to Australia.* San Francisco, R. & E. Research Associates, 1977. 254 p, illus, maps.

Immigration from the United States after 1945; includes results of a survey of 200 American immigrants.

EDGAR, D.E. *Introduction to Australian society: a sociological perspective.* Sydney, Prentice-Hall, 1980. 350 p.

'The treatment of ethnicity' (chapter 11) is excellent. It presents a sociological identification of issues raised by postwar immigration.

GRANT, B.A. *The boat people: an Age investigation.* Ringwood, Vic, Penguin, 1979. 225 p, illus, maps.

Account of Vietnamese refugees—the boat people—discussing the background to their exodus, their flight and problems of resettlement.

GRASSBY, A.J. *The Spanish in Australia.* Melbourne, AE Press, 1983. 102 p, illus.

JUPP, J. *Arrivals and departures.* Melbourne, Cheshire–Lansdowne, 1966. 195 p, maps.

Postwar immigration and its social effects, crystallising the state of knowledge at that point.

JUPP, J. ed, *Ethnic politics in Australia.* Sydney, Allen & Unwin, 1984. 213 p.

A collection of papers by social scientists ranging from migrant voting patterns to multicultural education and broadcasting.

KUNZ, E.C.F.G. *The intruders: refugee doctors in Australia.* ANUP, 1975. 139 p.

How Australian Medical Association hostility coupled with government weakness and indifference prevented many doctors who came as 'displaced persons' in the 1950s from resuming their profession.

LOWENSTEIN, W. AND LOH, M. *The immigrants.* Melbourne, Hyland House, 1977. 149 p.

The stories of seventeen immigrants, of various nationalities, who arrived in Australia between 1890 and 1970.

MARTIN, J.I. *The ethnic dimension: papers on ethnicity and pluralism.* Ed with an introduction by S. Encel. Sydney, Allen & Unwin, 1981. 186 p.

Papers on ethnicity and pluralism, posthumously collected, spanning the thinking over 30 years of a pioneering sociological student of the effects of postwar immigration.

MARTIN, J.I. *The migrant presence, Australian response,*

1947–1977: research report for the National Population Inquiry. Sydney, Allen & Unwin, 1978. 261 p.

The changing response of Australian institutions to the influx of non-Anglo-Saxon migrants after 1947. A seminal essay in the sociology of knowledge.

NATIONAL CONFERENCE ON CULTURAL PLURALISM AND ETHNIC GROUPS IN AUSTRALIA, University of New England, Armidale, NSW, 1976. *Australia 2000: the ethnic impact: proceedings of the First National Conference on Cultural Pluralism and Ethnic Groups in Australia, August 21–25, 1976.* Ed by M. Bowen. Armidale, NSW, University of New England Publishing Unit, 1977. 371 p, maps.

Papers on education and cultural pluralism in Australia, work and neighbourhood, women, the family and social change. Academics and migrant activists represented a diversity of minority groups.

PRICE, C.A. *Southern Europeans in Australia.* Melbourne, OUP in association with Australian National University, 1963. 2 vols, maps.

Migration before 1940: significant places of origin, ethnic groups and assimilation, chain migration and its effect on the composition of migrant movement.

PRICE, C.A. ed, *Refugees, the challenge of the future: proceedings, Academy of the Social Science in Australia, fourth Academy Symposium, 3–4 November 1980.* Canberra, Academy of the Social Sciences in Australia, 1981. 152 p, map.

Papers on the contemporary experience of refugees and their problems with special reference to Kampuchea and Latin America.

TAFT, R. *From stranger to citizen: a survey of studies of immigrant assimilation in Western Australia.* UWAP, 1965. xiv, 109 p.

Studies of assimilation processes among the variety of ethnic groups migrating to WA after 1945.

ZUBRYZCKI, J. *Settlers of the Latrobe valley: a sociological study of immigrants in the brown coal industry in Australia.* Canberra, Australian National University, 1964. 306 p, illus, map.

Immigrants in Vic: their migration, occupational adjustment, living conditions and social participation.

IMMIGRATION RESTRICTIONS

AUSTRALIAN INSTITUTE OF POLITICAL SCIENCE, 12th Summer School, Goulburn, 1946. *A white Australia: Australia's population problem.* By W.D. Borrie *et al.* Sydney, Australasian Publishing Co, 1947. 257 p.

Reflects the state of contemporary expert opinion on the possibilities of population expansion and immigration.

CURTHOYS, A. AND MARKUS, A. eds, *Who are our enemies? Racism and the Australian working class.* Sydney, Hale & Iremonger in association with the Australian Society for the Study of Labour History, 1978. 211 p.

Articles on episodes in the nineteenth and twentieth centuries bearing on the development of the 'White Australia' policy.

GREGORY, J.W. *The menace of colour: a study on the difficulties due to the association of white and coloured races.* London, Seely Service and Co, 1925. 264 p, illus, maps.

The debate on racism in the 1920s, with bibliography. Argues for strengthening 'the racial segregation which the world has inherited from the past'.

LONDON, H.I. *Non-white immigration and the 'White Australia' policy.* New York University Press, 1970. 318 p.

Explains the liberalisation of the 'White Australia' policy in the

1960s. Deals with reformist pressure groups and political parties, discusses public opinion and the bearing of foreign affairs on immigration policy.

PALFREEMAN, A.C. *The administration of the White Australia policy.* MUP, 1967. 184 p, illus.

Explains the operation after 1901 of the laws and administrative apparatus embodying the 'White Australia' policy, considering non-European immigrants and changes apparent by the 1960s.

PRICE, C.A. *The great white walls are built: restrictive immigration to North America and Australasia, 1836–1888.* ANUP, 1974. 323 p, illus, maps.

Puts the 'White Australia' policy in a comparative context, offers new perspectives and looks afresh at 'coloured migration'.

RIVETT, K. ed, *Immigration: control or colour bar? The background to white Australia and a proposal for change.* MUP, 1962. 171 p.

Proposals by the Immigration Reform Group for controlled admission of non-European immigrants, skilfully canvassing the contemporary arguments for change. First published in 1960.

STEVENS, F.S. ed, *Racism, the Australian experience: a study of race prejudice in Australia.* Sydney, Australia and New Zealand Book Co, 1971–72. 3 vols.

Articles by scholars working in the field of race relations which includes immigrant groups as well as Aborigines. Divided into three volumes: vol 1 *Prejudice and xenophobia*; vol 2 *Black versus white*; vol 3 *Colonialism.*

VIVIANI, N. *The long journey: Vietnamese migration and settlement in Australia.* MUP, 1984. 316 p.

Examines the background to Vietnamese migration, the Australian response to Vietnamese refugees and migration and their settlement experiences.

WILLARD, M. *History of the White Australia policy.* MUP, 1923. 217 p.

A authoritative reference work, surveying restrictions on immigration before Federation, systems of indentured labour and reasons for the policy in the early twentieth century. Reprinted 1967.

YARWOOD, A.T. *Asian migration to Australia: the background to exclusion, 1896–1923.* MUP, 1964. 210 p.

Discussion of origins of restrictive policies and their application to the four main Asian immigrant groups of the period: Japanese, Chinese, Indian and Syrian.

YARWOOD, A.T. ed, *Attitudes to non-European immigration.* Melbourne, Cassell, 1968. 150 p.

A collection of readings to raise issues in the history of 'white Australia'.

YARWOOD, A.T. AND KNOWLING, M.J. *Race relations in Australia: a history.* Sydney, Methuen, 1982. 312 p, illus, maps.

DEMOGRAPHY

AUSTRALIA. National Population Inquiry. *Population and Australia: a demographic analysis and projection.* AGPS, 1975. 2 vols, illus.

Analysis of Australia's population trends in the century until 1974. Forecasts of future population using various trends for labour force growth and the need for community services. Includes a historical survey with bibliography. This was the first report of the inquiry.

AUSTRALIA. National Population Inquiry. *Population and Australia: recent demographic trends and their implications. Supplementary report of the National Population Inquiry.* AGPS, 1978. 198 p.

An update of the original report, taking into consideration the recent decline in fertility and the drop in the marriage rate during the 1970s. Special projections for the metropolitan cities.

BORRIE, W.D. AND SPENCER, G. *Australia's population structure and growth.* Melbourne, Committee for the Economic Development of Australia, 1964. 102 p.

Formal analyses of the Australian population structure, with reference to the potential growth of the labour force and the demographic components contributing to it.

BROWNE, M.E. *The empty cradle: fertility control in Australia.* UNSWP, 1979. 146 p.

A non-technical account of fertility change in this century with emphasis on the social issues and government responses and initiatives concerning the changes.

BURNLEY, I.H. *Population, society and environment in Australia: a spatial and temporal view.* Melbourne, Shillington House, 1982. 150 p, illus, maps.

Text for high school and first year tertiary students on population patterns in Australia from a geographic perspective including regional growth and the use of elementary demographic indicators.

BURNLEY, I.H. ed, *Urbanization in Australia: the post-war experience.* London, CUP, 1974. 248 p, maps.

Chapters by several authors deal with the demographic components of postwar urbanisation and their impact on the social ecology of the cities.

BURNLEY, I.H. et al, *Mobility and community change in Australia.* UQP, 1980. 286 p, illus, maps.

Interdisciplinary case studies of particular types of internal migration at the community level and problems of adjustment of movers.

DI IULIO, O.B. *Household formation 1911–2001: an historical analysis and projection.* AGPS, 1981. 59 p. (National Population Inquiry research report, 10.)

A study, using cohort survival and extrapolation techniques, of the new households likely to be extant in Australia to 2001, involving allowance for age structure change, divorce and remarriage.

GALE, F. *Urban Aborigines.* ANUP, 1973. 283 p, illus, maps.

A demographic and social anthropological study of a sample of the Aboriginal population in Adelaide, including those from the rest of SA and the NT.

HOWE, A.L. ed, *Towards an older Australia: readings in social gerontology.* UQP, 1981. 356 p, illus.

Papers covering demographic aspects of ageing, as well as areas of social gerontology, including health services, public transport requirements and retirement migration.

INTERNATIONAL SATELLITE CONFERENCE ON GERONTOLOGY, Sydney, 1978. *Ageing in Australia: proceedings of the Satellite Conference of the 11th Congress of the International Association of Gerontology,* Sydney, 10–13 August, 1978. Ed by J.M. Donald et al. Sydney, Australian Association of Gerontology, 1979. 120 p.

A compendium dealing with the demographic aspects and socioeconomic consequences of ageing.

JONES, F.L. *The structure and growth of Australia's Aboriginal population.* ANUP, 1970. vi, 44 p, maps.

The first major study of the demography of the Aboriginal population, using statistics from missions and vital statistics where they are reliable.

McCARTY, J.W. AND SCHEDVIN, C.B. eds, *Australian capital cities: historical essays.* SUP, 1978. 201 p, maps.

Essays involving case studies of the growth of cities at certain points of time in the nineteenthcentury. One chapter provides a perspective on twentieth-century growth.

McDONALD, P.F. *Marriage in Australia: age at first marriage and proportions marrying, 1860–1971.* Canberra, Dept of Demography, Australian National University, 1974. 311 p. (Australian Family Formation Project. Monograph, 2).

An analysis of marriage trends including ages, the proportions marrying and the influence of the sex ratio and migration on marriage, with implications for fertility.

McGLASHAN, N.D. ed, *Studies in Australian mortality.* Hobart, Board of Environmental Studies, University of Tas, 1977. 94 p, maps. (University of Tas, Environmental studies occasional paper, 4.)

Articles dealing with occupational, regional and intraurban mortality, with particular reference to ischaemic heart disease, cancer, stroke and suicide mortality.

ROWLAND, D.T. *Internal migration in Australia.* Canberra, ABS, 1979. 203 p, maps.

This study uses matrix tapes from the first Australian census to answer internal migration questions. Analyses statistical trends 1966–71 and interstate internal migration.

ROWLEY, C.D. *Outcasts in White Australia.* ANUP, 1971. 472 p, maps. (Aboriginal policy and practice, 2.)

A study of the marginal role of Aborigines in Australian society as the result of Western cultural, technological and economic impacts, including a sample survey of Aborigines in country districts of NSW.

RUZICKA, L.T. AND CALDWELL, J.C. *The end of the demographic transition in Australia.* Canberra, Dept of Demography, Australian National University, 1977. 416 p. (Australian Family Formation Project. Monograph, 5.)

An analysis of the decline in birthrate from the late nineteenth century, with particular emphasis on the 1910–30 period, with causal inferences and documentation.

SMITH, L.R. *The Aboriginal population of Australia.* ANUP for the Academy of the Social Sciences in Australia, 1980. 314 p, illus.

A fundamental work on the Aboriginal population in prehistory, the demographic impact of European settlement and diseases, the demographic recovery and future projections.

UNITED NATIONS. Economic and Social Commission for Asia and the Pacific. *Population in Australia.* New York, United Nations, 1982. 2 vols. (Country monograph series, 9.)

Thorough demographic analysis of the Australian population in terms of internationally comparable data.

H. Napier Thomson, The garden hat, *1945.*
NEW ENGLAND REGIONAL ART MUSEUM

CHAPTER 40

DOMESTIC LIFE

P. R. TRIER

THE TERM 'DOMESTIC LIFE' is one with which all readers will be familiar, but which is difficult to define precisely. The *Oxford English dictionary* defines 'domestic' as 'of or belonging to the home, house or household; pertaining to one's place of residence or family affairs; household, home, family'. The following survey of domestic life in Australia covers those aspects of life which in the main are included in current domestic magazines, reflecting what 'domestic life' means to most of us, and what it has meant to Australians of earlier days.

This introductory essay sets the scene of Australian domestic life, under the following headings: domestic life in general, cookery, the home, shopping, gardens and gardening, domestic servants, children, clothing, etiquette and home entertainment, and mentions a few books of interest. Though there is no separate section devoted to women, the emergence of women's studies has affected our understanding of domestic life and the contribution of women to the fabric of our history is now an integral part of historical research. The bibliography that follows lists books for the reader who wishes to pursue the topic in more detail. The domestic life of Aborigines is covered by section IV of this volume.

Domestic life relates closely to a number of other topics. Social history, sport and leisure and architecture are each covered by individual chapters in this volume, and readers would do well to refer to these for further sources. Each of these topics, however, has relevance to domestic life, and books on them have been included in the bibliography that follows. For a general bibliography on various aspects of women's life in Australia, readers will find *Her story: Australian women in print, 1788–1975*, compiled by M. Bettison and A. Summers (Sydney, Hale & Iremonger, 1980) useful. This covers a wide range of writings by and about Australian women, selected from a feminist viewpoint, and includes useful sections on housework and child care.

The history of domestic life has recently become a subject of popular interest, reflected by a spate of publications, by exhibitions, and by the number of folk museums and replicas of historical settlements that have been established throughout Australia to create an image of the manner in which our forebears lived during the nineteenth and early twentieth centuries, and to preserve the objects that illustrate their lifestyle. These open air museums include recreations of original settlements such as Old Sydney Town at Gosford, and mid-nineteenth-century goldfield communities at Sovereign Hill in Ballarat and Lachlan Vintage Village at Forbes, while the Swan Hill Pioneer Settlement illustrates life on the Murray in the nineteenth century.

Individual houses of historical or architectural significance throughout Australia are being restored with interior decoration, antique furniture, ornaments and household objects appropriate to the period concerned, although the authenticity of some of this restoration is a matter of debate. Among these are Como and Ripponlea in Melbourne, Entally House at Hadspen, Tasmania, Old Government House and Elizabeth Farm at Parramatta. Three books by Ian Evans, *Restoring old houses* (Melbourne, Macmillan, 1979), *Furnishing old houses: a guide to interior restoration* (Melbourne, Macmillan, 1983) and, co authored with Clive Lucas and Ian Stapleton, *Colour schemes for old Australian houses* (Sydney, Flannel Flower Press, 1984) cover in considerable detail the restoration of old houses.

Another source of information about life over the last hundred years can be found in collections of photographs, a number of which have been published recently. *Australia: image of a nation, 1850–1950* by D. Moore and R. Hall (Sydney, Collins, 1983), is a photographic history of Australia including many illustrations of domestic life over the last century. Michael Cannon's *Australia: a history in photographs* (Melbourne, Currey O'Neil, 1983) contains a wide range of excellent illustrations. *Charles Kerry's federation Australia* by David P. Millar (Sydney, David Ell Press, 1981) comprises a selection of superb photographs taken by Charles Kerry, many dating between 1870 and 1910; among them are some charming domestic scenes. Stuart Bremer's *Living in the city: a pictorial record of Australia's cities* (Sydney, Dreamweaver Books, 1983) illustrates Australian urban life from the late nineteenth century to the 1970s and includes a section on 'The city at home', while G. Dutton's *Country life in old Australia* (Melbourne, Currey O'Neil, 1982) portrays rural life of the last century. *A day in the life of Australia*, (Sydney, A Day in the Life of Australia Pty Ltd, 1981) is a collection of contemporary photographs of Australia taken by one hundred of the world's leading photographers within the same 24-hour period (6 March 1981), giving an interesting modern counterpoint to the collections of earlier images.

A third source of information on domestic life can be found in the considerable number of diaries and letters of early settlers now housed in the National Library of Australia and in the various state libraries. *Women in Australia: an annotated guide to records*, edited by K. Daniels *et al*, (AGPS, 1977) provides an invaluable guide to some of this fascinating source material. The unpublished material is supplemented by a growing number of autobiographies, many of them containing a wealth of detail of domestic life as recalled by the author. Recent publications include Kathleen Fitzpatrick's *Solid bluestone foundations, and other memories of a Melbourne girlhood, 1908–1928* (Melbourne, Macmillan, 1983), a delightful recollection of middle-class Melbourne family life in the early part of the twentieth century, and L.C. Rodd's *A gentle shipwreck* (Melbourne, Nelson, 1975) recalling life in Sydney between 1907 and 1916. *Amirah: an un-Australian childhood*, by Amirah Inglis (Melbourne, Heinemann, 1983) describes the life of a Jewish migrant family in Melbourne in the 1930s and 1940s.

More objectively, two titles that appeared in 1985, *Families in colonial Australia*, edited by Patricia Grimshaw *et al* (Sydney, Allen & Unwin), and K.M. Reiger's *The disenchantment of the home: modernizing the Australian family, 1880–1940* (OUP) examine the sociology of Australian domestic life in the nineteenth and early twentieth centuries while a brief survey of Australian household management is *Good housekeeping, a practical guide to domestic duties, 1830–1930* (Sydney, Historic Houses Trust of New South Wales, 1984).

DOMESTIC LIFE IN GENERAL

Though we know from library records and contemporary sources that books on many aspects of Australian domestic life have been common in the past 150 years, few of these have survived. Designed for use in the home, they tended to have a short life, as is the fate of common reference works: cookery books became food stained and torn, fashion books were coloured (often by the younger members of the family) and cut up; gardening books were used outside, attracted dirt, lost their covers and disintegrated. As new fashions in cookery, gardening, child management or clothing appeared, the older books were discarded, and as a result it is difficult to find copies of early examples of this type of historical document.

Handy sources of information for new settlers on many aspects of domestic life in nineteenth-century Australia are to be found in the emigrants' guides, written to give prospective migrants an idea of what to expect on arriving in Australia; many of these books include lists of suitable clothing and household goods to bring to the Antipodes. Later in the nineteenth century popular almanacs contained useful day-to-day information on such diverse problems as home treatment of illness, the names of government officials, postal rates and seasonal gardening requirements. At present there is a considerable vogue for illustrations of the social and domestic history of Australia, including cookery books, gardening books and books on the restoration of nineteenth and early twentieth-century houses. The titles listed in the following bibliography represent a selection of those published recently.

Migrants brought with them the background of their native culture, that is, the customs and traditions with which they had grown up. The domestic life of the earliest settlers was based on an attempt to transplant to the new land the lifestyle of their original home; to this end, they brought or had sent out to them a great variety of books to guide them. The majority of the settlers of the late eighteenth and nineteenth century were from the United Kingdom. Caroline Davidson's *A woman's work is never done*, (London, Chatto and Windus, 1982) provides an absorbing analysis of both the history of housework and the way in which various aspects of it were performed in the British Isles between 1650 and 1950. The scenes evoked would have been familiar to migrants from both the British Isles and Europe, and were recreated in the new country.

Small groups of migrants came from Germany to South Australia in the 1830s and 1840s and to Queensland in the 1860s, a larger group of Chinese came to the Victorian goldfields in the 1850s and a number of Scandinavians emigrated to Queensland in the 1870s. However, by the end of the nineteenth century only 5 per cent of the population was of non-British extraction. Not until the early 1950s did a flood of migrants come from continental Europe and it was even later, in the 1970s, before an increased awareness developed of Asia as a close neighbour, due partly to the aftermath of the Vietnam War, to economic ties with Asia and to an increase in the number of Asian students studying in Australia. This long history of Anglo–Celtic dominance is reflected in the literature of domestic life.

COOKERY

The earliest cookery books used in Australia were those brought out by migrants in their luggage; however, several were published for the Australian market by the middle of the nineteenth century. The first of these was *The English and Australian cookery book: cooking for the many as well as the upper ten thousand* (1864; facs, ed by A. Burt, 1970). E. Mackenzie's *The emigrant's guide to Australia*, (London, Clarke Beeton, 1853) includes a brief chapter by Caroline Chisholm on bush cookery. Even the third edition of the redoubtable Isabella Beeton's *Book of household management* (London, Ward Lock and Co, 1888) contains an Australian section. Early cookery books published in Australia include Mrs Lance Rawson's *Cookery book and household hints*, 2nd edn, (Rockhampton, W. Hopkins, 1886) and Mrs Maclurcan's *Cookery book: a collection of practical recipes specially suitable for Australia* (Townsville, T. Willmott, 1898).

For most of the nineteenth century and well into the twentieth, Australian cookery remained true to the British tradition from which so much of it had derived. Some local ingredients were tried (particularly in the nineteenth century, when there was an interest in indigenous game such as kangaroo and emu). However, as Australian life became more urban the traditional meal of 'meat and two veg' became the standard for many Australian homes. A number of basic cookery books were published, some of which were reprinted many times.

The Presbyterian Women's Missionary Union issued two cookery books which have appeared in a number of editions. *The Presbyterian cookery book* (A & R), which was first published in 1895, was republished in a metric edition in 1979. The *P.W.M.U. cookery book* (Melbourne, Lothian), first published in 1904 and reprinted many times, has also appeared in a metric edition, revised by A. Gemmell *et al* in 1973. These two books have for many years provided homemakers with basic recipes and household advice.

On the larger cattle and sheep properties fresh meat, killed on the station, was one of the chief ingredients of the daily diet. Chops or steak for breakfast, cold meat for lunch and a roast for dinner was the standard fare. There are few uniquely Australian dishes. Legend has it that the pavlova, the lamington and the Anzac biscuit originated in Australia; however, these claims can be disputed.

The influx of migrants from continental Europe in the late 1940s and 1950s, and perhaps the staging of the 1956 Olympic Games in Melbourne, provided the stimulus for an amazing change in Australian attitudes to food. European food (in particular Italian food) became increasingly popular, and subsequent fashions in Greek, Lebanese, Japanese and Indian food have resulted in a contemporary interest in cooking originating from all over the world. Chinese food has had a long history in Australia, due partly to the influx of Chinese immigrants during the gold-rush days. A growing number of cookery books incorporating foreign recipes has been published recently, of which Maria Donovan's *Continental cookery in Australia* (Melbourne, Heinemann, 1955) was one of the first. Since then there has been a veritable flood of cookery books based on international recipes. Two recent books by Carol Willson and John Goode, *Italian–Australian cookbook*, and *Greek–Australian cookbook* (both published in Sydney, Kangaroo Press, 1982) are written in English and Italian and English and Greek respectively, and reflect an interest in Australian versions of European food.

The current interest in international cookery is shown by the popularity of food and cookery magazines, such as *Australian gourmet*, 1966– , *Epicurean*, 1966– , and *Vogue living*, 1966– , and by the growth of cookery schools, some devoted specifically to national foods.

THE HOME

The buildings in which the first European settlers lived are no longer standing, but a number of houses from the early part of the nineteenth century have been restored and some of these are open to the public. In most cases considerable effort has been made to ensure that the restoration is historically accurate, that the rooms are decorated in the style correct for the period, and that furniture, ornaments and household articles are appropriate. The earliest homes were simple. Houses were lit with candles or oil lamps and heated with open fires. Open fireplaces were used for cooking at first, and then colonial ovens were used until the 1880s. Illustrations of some of the earliest cooking facilities can be found in *Australian chimneys and cookhouses* by E. and D. Baglin (Sydney, Murray Child, 1979). Gas became available for lighting as early as the 1850s, although for many years supply was in the hands of private companies and few could afford that luxury. By the 1870s most town homes were lit with gas lamps and gas stoves were introduced in the 1870s. Peter Cuffley's *A complete catalogue and history of oil and kerosene lamps* (Yarra Glen, Vic, Pioneer Press, 1973) illustrates the wide range of lamps in use over the years. Electricity, initially also in the hands of private companies, was introduced in the 1890s but it was not used generally, even in the larger cities, before the 1920s. The ice-chest first made its appearance about 1865, to be superseded by refrigerators, powered at first by kerosene and, from the 1920s, by gas or electricity.

Household water supplies were obtained from wells during the first part of the nineteenth century. Reticulated water became available in the second half of the century, but it was not considered safe for drinking until the early part of the twentieth century. Bathrooms were not common in Australian houses before the 1850s—the hip-bath in the bedroom was the accepted means of bathing—but by the 1860s bathrooms had become a regular feature of larger houses. Water closets were introduced during the 1830s and 1840s but it has taken many decades for most of the major Australian cities to be completely sewered. Between the 1850s and early 1900s cesspits and nightcarts were commonplace and, as many Australians are well aware, there are still houses in outer city suburbs with no sewerage connections; however the septic tank has now taken the place of the nightcart. *Dinkum dunnies* by D. Baglin and B. Mullins (Sydney, Lansdowne, 1980) provides graphic illustrations of one of the most readily identifiable elements of Australian domestic civilisation.

SHOPPING

The development of suburbia—the suburban sprawl—led to several changes in domestic life, for example in shopping patterns. While the cities were relatively small, central markets provided fruit, vegetables and meat. In the late nineteenth century alongside the developing retail stores, goods were sold in the streets, particularly small items such as flowers, matches, shoelaces and haberdashery. Arcades of small retail shops appeared in the larger cities as part of this development. As the cities grew, the central markets were found to be too far from many of the residential suburbs, and tradesmen, in particular the butcher, the baker, the grocer, the greengrocer and the milkman, provided delivery services. Some of these services continued until well into the third quarter of the twentieth century, and for many Australians the Chinese market gardener bringing fruit and vegetables to the door is still a clear memory.

For country people, mail order catalogues from the large city stores provided an essential service. For small purchases, particularly of household goods, haberdashery and trinkets, country people relied on hawkers who travelled originally by horse and cart and later by truck.

GARDENS AND GARDENING

New settlers in Australia had to come to terms quickly with the changed environment in which they were to live. For the first few years gardening was concerned chiefly with survival, and fresh vegetables and fruit were of the utmost importance. *Australia's first gardening guide of 1806: observations on gardening* by George Howe (Canberra, Mulini Press, 1980) shows the concern of the first settlers with subsistence gardening. Thomas Shepherd, in his *Lectures on landscape gardening in Australia* (Sydney, William McGarvie, 1836), was an early advocate of the use of Australian native plants in gardens; his grandson, Thomas William Shepherd, issued a *Catalogue of plants* (Sydney, W. and F. Ford, 1851) which listed a considerable number of Australian plants for sale.

However, the native or bush garden did not become popular for another hundred years. The development of the urban lifestyle encouraged the introduction of European plants to replicate the familiar scenery of the homeland. This coincided with a growing interest in Europe in new plant forms from around the world, and the formal flower garden became popular. Recent research has thrown light on the design and contents of mid- and late-nineteenth-century gardens. Rosemary Polya's *Nineteenth century plant nursery catalogues of south-east Australia: a bibliography* (Bundoora, Vic, La Trobe University Library, 1981) provides access to information on those plants which were in demand in the nineteenth ccentury. R.F.G. Swinbourne's *Years of endeavour: an historical record of the nurseries, nurserymen, seedsmen and horticultural retail outlets in South Australia* (Adelaide, South Australian Association of Nurserymen, 1982) gives similar information for South Australia.

In the late nineteenth century the availability of reticulated water and the improvement of the lawnmower led to the development of the garden of lawns and shrubs. In the last few years the Australian garden has changed again, and now a variety of garden forms may be found. These include the bush or native garden which originated in the informal gardens designed by Edna Walling in the 1930s and enhanced by Ellis Stones. Bush gardens require little maintenance and comparatively little water, and feature Australian native plants and a minimum amount of lawn, preferring native ground covers, pebbles and leaf mulch. Bill Molyneaux and Ross Macdonald's *Native gardens: how to create an Australian landscape* (Melbourne, Nelson, 1983) discusses the design of gardens using Australian plants in an Australian landscape. Also popular at present are town gardens, with potplants grouped around paved courtyards, and gardens designed around the swimming pool, the patio and the barbecue. The self-sufficient vegetable garden is also making a return, particularly with families who have arrived recently from Europe.

DOMESTIC SERVANTS

For many urban families, life in Australia was not very different from life in Europe, except for the weather. In the outback, however, isolation made the new life very different. Servants appear always to have been a problem. In the early days of the colonies convict labour was available for domestic service, and subsequently Aborigines and migrants from Ireland provided much of the domestic labour force. Nevertheless, Australia has never had a tradition of domestic help in the home. This may account for one of Australia's most entrenched traditions, that of men and women forming separate groups at social functions, which may have originated partly because women had to cook and serve the meal. The traditionally male society of the outback would have added to this situation.

CHILDREN

There is very little literature on Australian children in the last century, although some light is thrown on their activities in the collections of historical photographs referred to previously. There are also few published records of Australian children's games or toys. A published collection of children's play rhymes, *Cinderella dressed in yella* by Ian Turner *et al* (Melbourne, Heinemann, 1978), is mainly concerned with children's use of language. The National Gallery of Victoria's catalogue of an exhibition entitled *Seen and not heard: dolls and toys 1800–1950* (Melbourne, 1976) is one of very few historical accounts of children's playthings.

CLOTHING

Clothes worn in Australia were much the same as those worn in Europe, and one may well wonder today how women coped with the heat in the fashions of the nineteenth century. The published collections of photographs are reliable and illuminating sources of information on what people of all classes wore at work and at play, what accessories they carried and how they arranged their hair. Flower (1984) and Scandrett (1978) are useful general surveys.

ETIQUETTE AND HOME ENTERTAINMENT

Nineteenth-century life was governed by strict rules of etiquette. Though Australian etiquette was certainly less formal than that of Europe or Britain, nevertheless a number of guides to etiquette were published in Australia. L.M. Pyke's *Australian etiquette* (Melbourne, J. Pollard, 1916) appeared in a number of editions and provided a standard inexpensive guide for those living in the early part of the twentieth century. The *June Dally-Watkins book of manners for moderns* by C. Chaseling (Sydney, Dally-Chase Publications, 1969) shows how much more relaxed attitudes to social behaviour have become.

Letter writing was a significant pastime for the nineteenth-century middle-class and upper-class lady of the house, and the many collections of letters preserved in libraries and archives provide fascinating glimpses into the life of this period. A number of these collections have been edited and published, and some are listed in the following bibliography.

The first telephone in Australia was installed in Melbourne in 1878 and by 1880, when the first telephone exchange was opened in Melbourne, a list of 44 subscribers was issued. By 1929 Australia had the sixth highest telephone density in the world, with an average of 7.93 telephones per 100 population. The growth in the use of the telephone was one of the contributing causes of the decline in letter writing as a major activity in daily life.

Home entertainment has changed significantly in the last hundred years. In the nineteenth century, evening entertainment was based on the home, and reading, sewing, playing cards or parlour games, singing and dancing were popular. Many homes had a piano, and most young girls of middle-class or upper-class families were taught both to play the piano and to sing. The advent of the radio in the early 1920s changed this familiar scene. By 1933 Australia had an average of 14.39 broadcast listeners' licences per 100 of population; by 1961 this had grown to an average of 21.46 per 100 of population. Television broadcasting began in 1956.

Australians have traditionally taken their holidays at Christmas time, and for many families Christmas means the seaside, often camping in a tent or caravan. For years the beach has been the centre of Australian summer activities. *Beside the sea: Sydney beaches and resorts* and *Pleasures and pastimes beside the sea* (Sydney, Historic Houses Trust of New South Wales, 1981), both published in conjunction with an exhibition 'Beside the sea', survey the popular Sydney beaches in the nineteenth century and some of the seaside activities, such as collecting shells. However, the recent popularity of the home swimming pool has provided an alternative to the beach with its sandy sandwiches. The development of winter vacation areas, in particular skiing centres in Victoria and southern New South Wales, and the almost universal ownership of cars, enabling Australians to drive around the country, frequently towing caravans, have also changed the earlier tradition of summer holidays at the beach.

Australian domestic life has seen a number of significant changes in the past few years. These have been due partly to the shifts in the ethnic origin of the population, partly to changing attitudes to women and their place at home and in the workforce, and partly to technological developments affecting both home and work, and to the consequent changes in the workforce.

GENERAL

AUSTRALIAN album: the way we were: Australia in photographs, 1860–1920. Sydney, D. O'Keefe, 1982. 224 p, illus.
Collection of photographs, arranged topically, including domestic life, social events, work and sport.

AUSTRALIAN family album: the Australian family in photographs, 1860 to 1980s. Sydney, D. O'Keefe, 1983. 224 p, illus.
Photographs grouped together by theme provide interesting illustrations of changes in domestic life. The captions are poor and many are undated.

CANNON, M. Life in the country. Melbourne, Currey O'Neil, 1983. 320 p, illus. (Australia in the Victorian age, 2.)

CANNON, M. Life in the cities. Melbourne, Currey O'Neil, 1983. 320 p, illus. (Australia in the Victorian age, 3.)
Social histories of nineteenth-century rural and urban Australia, including several chapters on domestic life. First published 1973–75.

CARTER, J. Nothing to spare: recollections of Australian pioneering women. Ringwood, Vic, Penguin, 1981. 237 p, illus.
A collection of reminiscences concentrating on the period 1890 to 1918, of women from all walks of life, in W.A.

FABIAN, S. ed, Mr. Punch down under: a social history of the colony from 1856 to 1900 via cartoons and extracts from Melbourne Punch. Melbourne, Greenhouse, 1982. 171 p, illus.
Melbourne Punch, like its British counterpart, reflected social life of the colonies through cartoons, jokes and articles. Domestic life is well illustrated and described.

GITTINS, J. The diggers from China: the story of Chinese on the goldfields. Melbourne, Quartet Books, 1981. 148 p, illus.
An account of the Chinese on the goldfields including descriptions of their food, gambling and religion.

GOOD housekeeping: a practical guide to domestic duties, 1830–1930. Sydney, Historic Houses Trust of NSW, 1982. 8 p, illus.
A charming catalogue of an exhibition held at Elizabeth Bay House, Sydney, illustrating housekeeping in Australia.

HARPER, J. AND RICHARDS, L. Mothers and working mothers. Ringwood, Vic, Penguin, 1979. 304 p.
Interviews with 195 Melbourne mothers. Examines the social context in which mothers decide whether to join the workforce and how the resultant strains are dealt with. See also Richards's Having families (1978).

HENEY, H. Australia's founding mothers. Melbourne, Nelson, 1978. 288 p, illus.

An account of the part played by women in establishing the NSW colony, from the landing of the first fleet to the departure of Governor Macquarie in 1822.

HENNING, R. The letters of Rachel Henning. Ed by David Adams. Ringwood, Vic, Penguin, 1969. 292 p, illus.
These letters written between 1853 and 1882 provide an insight into Australian domestic life. First published in 1952.

HUBER, R. From pasta to pavlova: a comparative study of Italian settlers in Sydney and Griffith. UQP, 1977, 270 p, illus.
Discusses the lives of migrant farmers from northern Italy who settled in Griffith and Leichhardt, NSW, and the problems which arose from moving to a new country and from a rural to an urban environment.

ISAACS, E. Greek children in Sydney. ANUP, 1976. 128 p, illus, map. (Immigrants in Australia, 6.)
A sociological study of Greek children. Chapters on 'Leisure and entertainment' and 'The children at home' shed some light on the problems faced by migrant families.

KEESING, N. Lily on the dustbin: slang of Australian women and families. Ringwood, Vic, Penguin, 1982. 188 p, illus.
Reveals a picture not often available from other sources.

KEESING, N. The white chrysanthemum: changing images of Australian motherhood. A & R, 1977. 182 p, illus.
An anthology of short stories, poems and excerpts from early Australian newspapers, illustrated with photographs, advertisements, sketches and reproductions of paintings.

KINGSTON, B. ed, The world moves slowly: a documentary history of Australian women. Sydney, Cassell, 1977. 202 p.
Extracts from many sources, including official documents, newspapers, personal reminiscences and books. The sections 'Ladies', 'Domestic service' and 'Housewives and mothers' are of particular relevance.

LARKINS, J. AND HOWARD, B. As time goes by. Adelaide, Myer Publications, 1980. 295 p, illus.
Photographs and advertisements from Australian magazines and newspapers 1920 to the 1950s. First published as The great Australian book of nostalgia in 1975.

LINDESAY, V. The way we were: Australian popular magazines, 1856–1969. OUP, 1983. 164 p, illus.
This history of popular illustrated magazines shows their importance in Australian domestic life. Includes brief excerpts, illustrations and advertisements, and a chapter on children's magazines.

LOH, M. ed, With courage in their cases: the experiences of thirty-five Italian immigrant workers and their families in Australia. Melbourne, Italian Federation of Emigrant Workers and their Families, 1980. 136 p, illus.
A collection of reminiscences on such subjects as putting down roots, including comments on family life.

LOWENSTEIN, W. AND LOH, M. *The immigrants*. Ringwood, Vic, Penguin, 1978. 149 p.

Interviews with immigrants from twelve countries, mostly European, who arrived between 1890 and 1970. Covering initial reactions to working situations and adjustments to family life in a new land.

McARTHUR, K. *Bread & dripping days: an Australian growing up in the 20's*. Sydney, Kangaroo Press, 1981. 64 p, illus.

A picture of domestic life in Qld, dealing with favourite foods, household routines, festivities, school, summer holidays and the family.

McCRAE, G. *Georgiana's journal: a hundred years ago*. Ed by Hugh McCrae. A & R, 1934. 262 p, illus, map.

A diary recording daily life in Melbourne between 1841 and 1865. New edition published in 1966.

O'BRIEN, D. *The* Weekly: *a lively and nostalgic celebration of Australia through 50 years of its most popular magazine*. Ringwood, Vic, Penguin, 1982. 155 p, illus.

A history of the *Australian women's weekly* from 1933 to 1982.

POWNALL, E. *Australian pioneer women* (3rd edn). Adelaide, Rigby, 1964. 296 p, illus.

A history of women pioneers from many different walks of life, based on diaries and letters. First published as *Mary of Maranoa* in 1959.

RAWSON, M. *Australian enquiry book of household and general information, by Mrs Lance Rawson*. Melbourne, Pater & Knapton, 1894. 284 p, illus.

'A practical guide for the cottage, villa and bush home.' Recipes and guidance for the young housekeeper and the housewife. Facsimile edition, Sydney, Kangaroo Press, 1984.

RICHARDS, L. *Having families: marriage, parenthood and social pressure in Australia*. Ringwood, Vic, Penguin, 1978. 329 p.

Interviews with 60 married couples in a Melbourne suburb. Deals with reasons for marrying and having children; family size; the effect of social pressures on marriage, parenthood and motherhood.

SIERP, A. comp, *Colonial NSW, 1853–1894*. Sydney, Harper & Row, 1979. 159 p, illus.

Day-to-day life, compiled from issues of the *Illustrated Sydney News*. The author has also compiled similar volumes for Vic, SA and Tas.

TEALE, R. ed, *Colonial Eve: sources on women in Australia, 1788–1914*. OUP, 1978. 288 p, illus.

Excerpts from private diaries, documents and articles illustrating the experiences of women in Australia.

VONDRA, J. *Hellas Australia*. Melbourne, Widescope, 1979. 199 p, illus.

A general survey of the life of Greek immigrants in Australia, with chapters on 'Australian life' and 'The story of a family' which comment on the domestic life of Greeks in Australia.

COOKERY

BECKETT, R. *Convicted tastes: food in Australia*. Sydney, Allen & Unwin, 1984. 217 p, illus.

A history of food and cookery in Australia, interspersed with colonial and other recipes.

BURT, A. ed, *The colonial cook book for the many as well as for the upper ten thousand; by an Australian aristologist*. Sydney, Hamlyn, 1970. 189 p.

A reprint of the first Australian cookery book published in 1864 as *The English and Australian cookery book*. Includes also housekeeping advice.

GOLLAN, A. *The tradition of Australian cooking*. ANUP, 1978. 211 p, illus.

Includes recipes and descriptions of kitchen utensils and gadgets,

mainly nineteenth-century, with a section on the Aborigines.

SYMONS, M. *One continuous picnic: a history of eating in Australia*. Adelaide, Duck Press, 1982. 278 p, illus.

Entertaining history of eating and cookery since the 1780s.

WOOD, B. ed, *Tucker in Australia*. Melbourne, Hill of Content, 1977. 256 p.

Cookery of 33 national groups resident in Australia, includes chapters on Aboriginal and 'traditional' Australian food.

THE HOME

CRAIG, C. et al, *Early colonial furniture in New South Wales and Van Diemen's Land*. Melbourne, Georgian House, 1980. 220 p, illus.

A study of furniture made in Australia before 1850. First published in 1972.

CUFFLEY, P. *Chandeliers and billy tea: a catalogue of Australian life, 1880–1940*. Melbourne, Five Mile Press, 1984. 224 p, illus.

Reproduced from sales catalogues distributed by Feldheim, Gotthelt and Co (Sydney) and other firms, covering fashion, household goods, toys etc.

CUFFLEY, P. AND CARNEY, K. *A catalogue and history of cottage chairs in Australia*. Yarra Glen, Vic, Pioneer Press, 1974. 176 p, illus.

Lavishly illustrated with clear photographs and reproductions from catalogues, 1905–30.

ELLIOTT, J. *Our home in Australia: a description of cottage life in 1860*. Sydney, Flannel Flower Press, 1984. 112 p, illus.

Based on a letter sent from Adelaide to Elliott's mother in England, describing in fascinating detail his home and the daily life of his family.

EVANS, I. *The Australian home*. Sydney, Flannel Flower Press, 1983. 144 p, illus.

A history from 1788 to 1938, illustrated with contemporary woodcuts and photographs.

FORGE, S. *Victorian splendour: Australian interior decoration, 1837–1901*. OUP, 1981. 160 p, illus.

A study of the craftsmanship, ornament and taste of nineteenth-century middle-class and working-class houses.

McMURCHY, M. et al, *For love or money: a pictorial history of women and work in Australia*. Ed by I. Dunn. Ringwood, Vic, Penguin, 1983. 186 p, illus.

A collation of photographs and other illustrations with a historical commentary based on the film of the same title.

KELLY, M. *Plague Sydney, 1900: a photographic introduction to a hidden Sydney, 1900*. Sydney, Doak Press, 1981. 52 p, illus.

A photographic documentary of slum housing in the Rocks area and the Chinese area south of Hyde Park, revealing the type of housing and conditions in which many urban Australians lived at that time.

RESTORATION AND CONSERVATION OF HISTORIC INTERIORS SYMPOSIUM, Sydney, 1983. *Historic interiors: a collection of papers*. Ed by M. Stapleton. Sydney, Sydney College of the Arts Press, 1983. 99 p, illus.

Papers on the restoration of interiors from different periods.

SAINI, B. *The Australian house: homes of the tropical north*. Sydney, Lansdowne, 1982. 128 p, illus.

Photographic survey of the domestic architecture of tropical Australia, with comment on the restoration of these houses.

TANNER, H. AND COX, P. *Restoring old Australian houses & buildings: an architectural guide*. Melbourne, Macmillan, 1975. 212 p, illus.

A guide to the accurate restoration of Australian houses, 1788 to 1914, providing an excellent illustration of domestic life.

SHOPPING

AUSTRALIA in the good old days: facsimile pages from Lassetters' commercial review, no 26, 1911. Sydney, Lansdowne, 1981. 264 p, illus.

Selection of advertisements for household goods, jewellery, clothing, kitchenware, furniture, toys, sporting goods and provisions. This edition first published in 1976.

DUNSTAN, K. The store on the hill. Melbourne, Macmillan, 1979. 200 p, illus.

A history of Georges, a leading Melbourne store from 1880 to 1980, with a survey of shopping and fashion in Melbourne over this period.

FOY & GIBSON PTY LTD. Reprint of the original catalogue, 1923. Melbourne, Crum Studios, 1974. 188 p, illus.

Facsimile reprint of a catalogue by a former Melbourne general store. Includes fashion garments, household goods and linen and provides an insight into household goods of the 1920s.

JAMES MC'EWAN AND CO. Illustrated catalogue of furnishing and general ironmongery. Melbourne, Heritage Publications, 1976. 234 p, illus.

Facsimile reprint of the catalogue first published in 1880. The firm remains one of Victoria's leading hardware stores and its catalogues reveal the changing styles in domestic goods.

KELLY, M. Faces of the street: William Street, Sydney, 1916. Sydney, Doak Press, 1982. 174 p, illus.

A survey of the life of a middle-class shopping street, including the buildings and the people who lived there. The photographs were taken to support the Sydney City Council's proposal to widen the street in 1916.

MARSHALL, A. The gay provider: the Myer story. Melbourne, Cheshire, 1961. 279 p, illus.

This history of the Myer family and of the firm includes a history of retail shopping in Australia.

MARSHALL, B. AND MOORE, L. Grandma's general store. Adelaide, Rigby, 1978. 111 p, illus.

A popular overview of domestic life in Australia developed around items found in old stores. Well illustrated with excerpts from contemporary sources.

SCHMAEHLING, T. AND HENTY, C. Paddy's Market. Sydney, Tempo Books, 1973. 60 p, illus.

A photographic survey of the main wholesale/retail market in Sydney, with brief text.

GARDENS AND GARDENING

THE ART of gardening in colonial Australia: converting the wilderness. Sydney, Australian Gallery Directors Council, 1979. 95 p, illus.

Catalogue of an exhibition of paintings, drawings and photographs showing the development of gardening in nineteenth-century Australia, with a commentary by Howard Tanner.

BLIGH, B. Cherish the earth: the story of gardening in Australia. Sydney, Ure Smith in association with the National Trust of Australia (NSW), 1973. 132 p, illus.

The history of gardens, from the discoveries of Sir Joseph Banks in 1770 to the 1970s.

CRITTENDEN, V. The front garden: the story of the cottage garden in Australia. Canberra, Mulina Press, 1979. 50 p, illus.

One of the few works to address this form of leisure activity. Considers the small decorative garden from 1788 to the end of the 1970s.

CUFFLEY, P. Cottage gardens in Australia. Melbourne, Five Mile Press, 1983. 248 p, illus.

A history with diagrams, photographs and reproductions of paintings. Includes lists of plants found in old gardens, paths, fences, etc, and suggestions for restoring old gardens.

GARDEN HISTORY CONFERENCE, 1st, Melbourne 1980. Proceedings of the first Garden History Conference, Melbourne, 28–29 March, 1980. Melbourne, National Trust of Australia (Vic), 1980. 79 p, illus.

Papers on the art of colonial gardening, historic gardens and nineteenth-century plants.

HALKETT, I.P.B. The quarter-acre block: the use of suburban gardens. Canberra, Australian Institute of Urban Studies, 1976. 228 p, illus.

Discusses the use made of the standard suburban garden area in Australia. Predates the era of the domestic swimming pool.

MALONEY, B. et al, All about Australian bush gardens. Sydney, Mulavon Publications, 1973. 255 p, illus.

First published as two separate volumes: Designing bush gardens (1966) and More about bush gardens (1967).

STONES, E. The Ellis Stones garden book. Melbourne, Nelson, 1976. 112 p, illus.

Based on articles written for Australian home beautiful, setting out fundamental rules for garden design.

TANNER, H. Towards an Australian garden. Sydney, Valadon Publishing, 1983. 128 p, illus.

An examination of traditional garden design elements, and the special Australian traditions which have combined to produce a distinctively Australian garden.

TANNER, H. AND BEGG, J. The great gardens of Australia, Melbourne, Macmillan, 1983. 198 p, illus.

A photographic survey of 33 of Australia's most significant gardens, with descriptive text, a history of gardening and some details on garden designers. First published in 1976.

WALLING, E. The Edna Walling book of Australian garden design. Ed by M. Barrett. Melbourne, Anne O'Donovan, 1980. 144 p, illus.

Taken from Edna Walling's Gardens in Australia (1943), Cottage and garden (1947) and A gardener's log (1948). Edna Walling was one of Australia's most influential garden designers.

WATTS, P. The gardens of Edna Walling. Melbourne, Womens Committee of the National Trust of Australia (Vic), 1981. 136 p, illus.

A biography of Edna Walling, and a study of her work.

WATTS, P. Historic gardens of Victoria: a reconnaissance from a report of the National Trust of Australia (Vic). Ed by M. Barrett. OUP, 1983. 224 p, illus.

An account of gardens, both large and small, with many contemporary and recent photographs and drawings.

DOMESTIC SERVANTS

BARBALET, M. Far from a low gutter girl: the forgotten world of state wards, South Australia, 1887–1940. OUP, 1983. 286 p, illus.

A fascinating account of the life of state wards in SA depicting life in a wide range of families and including a chapter on domestic service.

DANIELS, K. AND MURNANE, M. comps, Uphill all the way: a documentary history of women in Australia. UQP, 1980. 335 p, illus.

Documents which illustrate the place of women in contemporary life with a section on domestic servants.

KINGSTON, B. My wife, my daughter, and poor Mary Ann:

women and work in Australia. Melbourne, Nelson, 1977. 158 p, illus.

A survey of women in Australian society, with a chapter on the domestic servant. First published in 1975.

STOKES, A. *A girl at Government House, an English girl's reminiscences: 'below stairs' in colonial Australia.* Ed by H. Vellacott. Melbourne, Currey O'Neil, 1982. 145 p, illus.

Published anonymously in 1932 with the title *The autobiography of a cook.* An account of life below the stairs in society homes of Brisbane, Sydney and Melbourne.

CHILDREN

FABIAN, S. AND LOH, M. *Children in Australia: an outline history.* OUP, 1980. 248 p, illus.

Documents the place of children in the history of Australia. Includes a chapter on Aboriginal children in tribal society.

FEATHERSTONE, G. ed, *The colonial child: papers presented at the 8th Biennial Conference of the Royal Historical Society of Victoria, Melbourne, 12–13 October, 1979.* Melbourne, Royal Historical Society of Vic, 1981. 87 p, illus.

Papers on the life of Australian children during the nineteenth century, including their literature, education, health and play.

LARKINS, J. AND HOWARD, B. *The young Australians: Australian children since 1788.* Adelaide, Rigby, 1981. 224 p, illus.

Sketches and photographs with summary text of Australian children from all walks of life. Pictures showing poverty in Sydney and Melbourne.

CLOTHING

FLETCHER, M. *Costume in Australia, 1788–1901.* OUP, 1984. 208 p, illus.

Entertaining commentary on the contemporary social scene with descriptions of the clothes represented in the illustrations.

FLOWER, C. *Clothes in Australia: a pictorial history, 1788–1980s.* Sydney, Kangaroo Press, 1984. 196 p, illus.

Extensively illustrated survey of costume in Australia, with reproductions of contemporary paintings, drawings and photographs. First published as *Duck & cabbage tree: a pictorial history of clothes in Australia, 1788 to 1914* in 1968.

JOEL, A. *Best dressed: 200 years of fashion in Australia.* Sydney, Collins, 1984. 224 p, illus.

Australian fashion illustrated from journals.

MARTYN, N. *The look: Australian women in their fashion.* Sydney, Cassell, 1976. 227 p, illus.

Illustrated with photographs and sketches from fashion catalogues.

SCANDRETT, E. *Breeches and bustles: an illustrated history of clothes worn in Australia, 1799–1914.* Melbourne, Pioneer Design Studio, 1978. 190 p, illus.

Details of men's and women's clothing with some illustrations of children's garments and accessories.

ETIQUETTE

AUSTRALIAN etiquette; or, the rules and usage of the best society in the Australian colonies, together with their sports, pastimes, games and amusements . . . Melbourne, People's Publishing House, 1885. 643 p, illus.

A traditional book of the nineteenth century, reflecting the influence of British society on manners, pastimes and sports. Facsimile edition, Melbourne, Dent, 1980.

JOEL, A. *Australian protocol & procedures.* A & R, 1982. 371 p, illus.

Official protocol, with sections on formal dinners and receptions, seating arrangements, eating and drinking, invitations and dress.

HOLIDAYS AND FESTIVALS

THE AUSTRALIAN Christmas in days gone by. Melbourne, McPhee Gribble, 1982. 52 p, illus.

Christmas in Australia as reflected in extracts from newspapers, personal reminiscences and poetry written between 1844 and 1900.

STAPLETON, M. AND McDONALD, P. *Christmas in the colonies.* Sydney, David Ell Press in association with Historic Houses Trust of NSW, 1981. 128 p, illus.

An exhibition mounted at Elizabeth Bay House, Sydney, showing Australian Christmas traditions, including preparations, food, cards, presents, visitors and picnics.

WELLS, L. *Sunny memories: Australians at the seaside.* Sydney, Greenhouse, 1982. 183 p, illus.

The worship of the suntan. A history of Australia's fascination with beaches, swimming and surfing.

HANDICRAFTS

THE D'OYLEY show: an exhibition of women's domestic fancywork. Sydney, D'Oyley Publications, 1979. 67 p, illus.

An illustrated catalogue of an exhibition of crochet, tatting and lacework produced by Australian women at home between 1890 and 1940.

HEARTH and home: handicrafts and pastimes of the Victorian era. Melbourne, National Gallery of Vic, 1980. 20 p, illus.

A catalogue of an exhibition of handicrafts and pastimes practised by Australian women in the nineteenth century.

HOME MEDICINE

HAGGER, J. *Australian colonial medicine.* Adelaide, Rigby, 1979. 219 p, illus.

A survey of medicines in Australia, with emphasis on the home treatment of illness and common complaints.

PHILLIPS, P.J. *Kill or cure? Lotions, potions, characters and quacks of early Australia.* Adelaide, Rigby, 1978. 157 p, illus.

A popular account of populist medicine.

Australian needlework, *15 July 1931.*
BOOROWA PRODUCTIONS/NATIONAL LIBRARY

Sydney Mail schools' number, *12 Dec 1934. Private schools in the provinces always stressed their 'healthy environment'.*
BOOROWA PRODUCTIONS

CHAPTER 41

EDUCATION

ALAN BARCAN

O VER THE LAST 200 years the literature of Australian education has developed through several major phases, and within each historical period we may distinguish particular categories of literature. Some books discuss mainly the political or religious aspects of education; others are concerned with specific educational problems. In a state-dominated society official government reports are numerous; less frequent are comparative or theoretical analyses.

THE NINETEENTH CENTURY

In the raw, pioneering environment of early nineteenth-century Australia, education contributed little to social, political or economic development though it had some importance in the discussion of moral and religious problems. In the early days official documents dominated the scene, dealing mainly with the education of the children of the convicts and the working class. The involvement of the state in education quickly necessitated the compilation of statistical and administrative records. Several British parliamentary investigations reported on Australian education, notably J.T. Bigge's *Report of the Commissioner of Inquiry on the state of agriculture and trade in the colony of New South Wales* (1823; facs, LBSA, 1966) which discusses education in its section on ecclesiastical establishments.

The first book on Australian education was a 28-page publication by the Presbyterian minister J.D. Lang entitled *Account of steps taken, in England, with a view to the establishment of an academical institution or college, in New South Wales* (Sydney, Stephens and Stokes, 1831). Lang sought to provide advanced education through his Australian College, which opened in November 1831. The establishment of several secondary schools prompted the publication of the first Australian textbooks: *A compendious Latin grammar for the use of the students of the Australian College* by the Reverend Henry Carmichael appeared anonymously in 1832 and in 1834 the Reverend R. Stubbs advertised his *Rules and exercises on English grammar*. Both were printed in Sydney.

Equally utilitarian were books of advice to parents with children being educated at home. These include H.N. Murray's *The schoolmaster in Van Diemen's Land: a practical treatise on education for the use of parents and others not professed teachers* (Hobart, Andrew Bent, 1834); *A mother's offering to her children* by 'A lady long resident in New South Wales' (1841; facs, Brisbane, Jacaranda, 1979)—the lady was Mrs Charlotte Barton—and H.V. Boyd's *Letters on education addressed to a friend in the bush of Australia* (Sydney, W. & F. Ford, 1848).

Between 1830 and 1880 debate raged over the place of the various churches and the state in the provision of elementary schools. Since ultimate authority rested in London the literature was often addressed more to English readers than to Australian. James Macarthur included a chapter on 'The means of education and religious instruction' in his *New South Wales: its present state and future prospects* (London, D. Walther, 1837), while W.W. Burton, a judge of the Supreme Court of New South Wales, championed the role of the Church of England in *The state of religion and education in New South Wales* (London, J. Cross, 1840).

The establishment of national (state) elementary schools in 1848 accentuated the debate; many public lectures were given on the topic and some of these were subsequently published. W.A. Duncan, an educated Catholic layman, publicly supported state schools in his *Lecture on national education* at the School of Arts, Brisbane. This was published in 1850—and happens to be the first booklet printed in Brisbane. In Victoria G.W. Rusden, a notable advocate of national schools, wrote *National education* (Melbourne, *Argus* Office, 1853), which included a chapter by H.C.E. Childers on New South Wales, Tasmania, South Australia and Victoria. In New South Wales, William Wilkins, secretary of the Board of National Education, issued *National education: an exposition of the national system of New South Wales* (Sydney, A.W. Douglas, 1865). By 1880 the balance had swung in favour of state schools and the debate died down.

Because of their size and wealth New South Wales and Victoria took the lead in developing teacher training. A few pedagogical books appeared in the last quarter of the century. The influence of English education dominated, as is well illustrated by F.J. Gladman who completed his influential *School method* (London, Jarrold & Sons, 1877) only a few weeks before he left England to come to the Central Training Institution in Melbourne in July 1877. His larger *School work* (London, Jarrold & Sons, 1886) was published two years after his death. In New South Wales, William Wilkins delivered six lectures soon after his retirement; these were published under the title *The principles that underlie the art of teaching* (Sydney, Government Printer, 1886).

Towards the end of this century the university became more active. Professors Charles Badham and Thomas Anderson Stuart of Sydney University wrote articles and gave public addresses on education; Stuart's was published as *A review of university life in Australasia with its conditions and surroundings in 1891* (London, Spottiswoode, 1892). To celebrate the first fifty years of the University of Sydney, its registrar, H.E. Barff, compiled a brief history (1902).

The late nineteenth century saw some interest in education reform. W.C. Grasby, who had taught in South Australia, wrote two books after visiting America and Britain. His *Teaching in three continents* (London, Cassell, 1891), the first book on comparative education by an Australian, and his polemical pamphlet on South Australian education, *Our public schools* (Adelaide, Hussey & Gillingham, 1891) were harbingers of reform and were widely read. The depression of the 1890s reduced the immediate possibility of extensive change.

From 1831 on, the returns of the colony of NSW (*Blue books*) contain statistics on education. The first important parliamentary inquiry into education under the chairmanship of Robert Lowe produced a report printed in the *Votes and proceedings of the New South Wales Legislative Council*, 1844. From 1848 the annual reports of the Board of National Education provide valuable data. Similar reports were continued after 1867 by the board's successor, the Council of Education. The final report (1855) of the School Commissioners contained in the *Votes and proceedings of the New South Wales Legislative Council* provides a vivid analysis of education problems, based on visits by Wilkins and his two colleagues to 202 elementary schools.

In Victoria the *Report of the royal commission . . . upon the operation of the system of public education* (chaired by G. Higinbotham), 1867, and the *Report on the state of public education*, prepared by C.H. Pearson, 1877, provided important surveys of school systems. The Higinbotham Report re-examined the conflict between church and state in education. Pearson tried to encourage decentralised control of schools and the provision of secondary schools giving access to the university.

The education acts, passed in most Australian colonies between 1872 and 1885 under the banner of 'free, compulsory and secular', soon came under scrutiny. In South Australia the working of the Department of Education, established in 1878, was the subject of a commission of inquiry under the chairmanship of J.L. Parsons (South Australia. Parliament. Paper no 122 for 1881; Paper no 27 for 1882 and Paper no 27A for 1883/84). In Victoria the operation of secular education was the subject of a royal commission on education in 1881–84 (Chaired first by J.W. Rogers, later by J.M. Templeton).

As the country emerged from the depression of the 1890s interest in educational reform revived. In Victoria the inquiry chaired by T. Fink was directed especially at technical education and made many recommendations to modernise the education system and adapt it to contemporary needs. In New South Wales the noted statistician G.H. Knibbs, with J.W. Turner, conducted an extended inquiry into all aspects of education, presenting four reports between 1903 and 1905 all critical of the situation. South Australia followed with a royal commission on education, 1911–13 (Chairman: T. Ryan).

THE TWENTIETH CENTURY

The educational reforms of the decade 1904–14 included the establishment of state high schools, scholarships to universities and teachers' colleges, and a new humanist–realist curriculum. The increased demand for teachers and the improved quality of their preparation produced new pedagogical books. The new humanism fostered a strong interest in the history of education and in the role of educational leaders.

S.H. Smith, an inspector who later became New South Wales Director of Education, wrote *A brief history of education in Australia (1788–1848)* (A & R, 1917), limited, despite its title, to New South Wales. It was expanded by G.T. Spaull, who added some uncritical material on the educational work of Henry Parkes, as well as surveys of more recent developments, to form Smith and Spaull's *History of education in New South Wales 1788–1925* (Sydney, Government Printer, 1925). K. Gollan's *The organisation and administration of education in New South Wales* (Sydney, Sydney Teachers College, 1924) provided a valuable analysis of the reforms of 1903–14.

E. Sweetman *et al* wrote a history in 1922 to mark the fiftieth anniversary of the Victorian Education Act 1872; although an official publication, it contained useful detail. In Western Australia D.H. Rankin, wrote *The history of the development of education in Western Australia, 1829–1923* (Perth, Carroll's, 1926). In South Australia T.H. Smeaton of the Public Teachers' Union wrote *Education in South Australia from 1836 to 1927* (Adelaide, Rigby, 1927).

These early histories reflected the optimism of the years of reform. Their cheerful narratives, which attributed educational advance to enlightened leadership, suggested both their function as inspirational texts for teachers in training and the close links of their authors with the Departments of Education.

P.R. Cole, vice-principal of Sydney Teachers' College, was the most prolific of the educational writers of the 1920s and 1930s. His interests spanned educational theory and philosophy, the history of education, Australian education, teaching methods and comparative education. He also contributed to the journal *Schooling* (1917–32) edited by Alexander Mackie, the principal of Sydney Teachers College. With Mackie, Cole founded an Educational Society in 1910 which published more than forty monographs in its first ten years, the most notable of which were *The groundwork of teaching* (1919), *Studies in contemporary education (1924) and Studies in the theory of education* (1925), all published in Sydney by the Teachers' College Press. An outstanding Victorian contribution to both comparative education and the history of education, treating all states, was that by G.S. Browne (1927).

The foundation in 1930 of the Australian Council for Educational Research (ACER) renewed the flow of books at a time when economic depression made publication no easy matter. Thanks to financial support from the Carnegie Corporation of New York, the ACER was able to produce a list of titles in which Victorian and New South Wales authors and educational interests loomed large, but which also gave some attention to American education. Between 1930 and 1940 sixty titles appeared in its *Educational research series*, many of them historical, many comparative, and not a few psychological in character. The then director of ACER, K.S. Cunningham, wrote on comparative and pedagogical themes, G.S. Browne on curriculum revision, H.S. Wyndham on ability grouping, H.T. Parker on speech and intelligence and C.R. McRae on American schools.

Two publications worth noting in the 1930s and issued outside the ACER series were D.H. Rankin's comprehensive though pedestrian *The history of the development of education in Victoria, 1836–1936* (Melbourne, Arrow Printery, 1939), and Professor Ernest Scott's *History of the University of Melbourne* (MUP, 1936). In 1937 three lectures given in London by Professor G.V. Portus of the University of Adelaide were published by Oxford University Press for the Institute of Education (London) as *Free, compulsory and secular: a critical estimate of Australian education.*

The first half of the twentieth century, unlike the nineteenth century, produced few books on church participation in education. One important exception was S.M. Johnstone (Sydney, Council of the King's School, 1932) which was more than the centennial history of one school, for many references were made to other secondary institutions in New South Wales and beyond.

Although in 1938 Catholic schools accommodated some 18 per cent of the school population, little had been written of their history. A massive *History of the Catholic Church in Australasia* (Sydney, Oceanic Publishing Co, 1895) by Cardinal Patrick Moran, Archbishop of Sydney, included a sketchy history of Catholic education, with particular emphasis on New South Wales. Brother Urban Corrigan's *Catholic education in New South Wales* (A & R, 1930) concentrated on the period up to 1880.

The New Education Fellowship Conference of 1937 and its report, *Education for complete living* (MUP, 1937), edited by K.S. Cunningham and W.C. Radford, stimulated interest in progressive education among educational theorists, teachers and a few administrators. The lifting of the economic depression and the shock of World War II also encouraged interest in reform.

The journals *New horizons in education*, published from 1938 in Sydney by the New Education Fellowship, and *Forum of education*, published by Sydney Teachers' College from 1942, carried articles favouring progressive education. A cautiously progressive point of view was provided by an American visitor, R. Freeman Butts (1955) but the centralised character of the state school systems, the existence of external examinations and the decline of interest in progressive education in America in the 1950s retarded this movement.

The ACER issued a series of pamphlets on 'The future of education' from 1943 onwards and commenced a series of progress reports entitled *Review of education in Australia . . .*, edited by K.S. Cunningham *et al.* The first appeared in 1938 and similar volumes followed for 1939, for 1940–48, 1948–54 and 1955–62. While these books provided a useful comparative study of Australian education and were appreciated for their data and descriptions of administrative developments, they lacked critical comment and interpretation.

Despite its inclination towards progressive education, factual compilations and statistical data, the ACER also published a number of important histories of education in the 1950s. These included E.R. Wyeth (1955) and D. Mossenson (1955). D.C. Griffiths' *Documents on the establishment of education in New South Wales, 1789–1880* (Melbourne, ACER, 1957) was unfortunately marred by many printing and transcription errors. Two good accounts of the work of early directors of education were J.O. Anchen's *Frank Tate and his work for education* (Melbourne, ACER, 1956) and A.R. Crane and W.G. Walker (1957) on Peter Board.

Though after 1957 historical titles almost disappeared from the ACER lists, the unprecedented growth in the study of education and teacher training in universities and CAEs fostered a boom in educational publishing, including histories of education. Victoria, particularly the University of Melbourne, was in the van. The annual *Melbourne studies in education*, the first of which, edited by E.L. French, appeared in 1958, were a major contribution. These volumes had a bias towards the history of education because until 1983 all their editors were historians.

Harbinger of a new generation of scholarly books on education was A.G. Austin's important work (1961). Austin also produced *George William Rusden and national education in Australia* (MUP, 1958) and edited *Select documents in Australian education 1788–1900* (Melbourne, Pitman, 1963).

The demand for state aid for church schools, revived by the great expansion of secondary education in the 1950s, meant that church and state became once again an important theme in educational literature. Austin was heavily concerned with this question, and the theme was further developed by J.S. Gregory's important commentary 'Church and state, and education in Victoria to 1872' in *Melbourne studies in education 1958–59*. Brother Ronald Fogarty's two-volume survey (1959) was a sober celebration of the triumph of Catholic education and a landmark in the history of denominational education, going beyond factual narrative to identify cause and effect and the influence of ideas. Gwyneth Dow examined the conflict between liberalism and denominationalism in Victoria in the 1960s in her *George Higinbotham: church and state* (Melbourne, Pitman, 1964).

By contrast with the University of Melbourne, the University of Sydney's Department of Education concentrated on the theory of progressive education. W.F. Connell edited the *Australian journal of education* (1957–   ) for the ACER and his interest in both the history of education and progressive education gave the new journal an unprecedented liveliness.

The tremendous growth of universities in the 1950s and 1960s produced only two noteworthy histories of universities: Geoffrey Blainey's history of the University of Melbourne (1957), much more readable than Scott's formal history of twenty years before, and Fred Alexander's story of the University of Western Australia (1963), which examined thoroughly its first fifty years. *The humanities in Australia* (A & R, 1959), edited by A. Grenfell Price, discussed the growing difficulties for humanist studies in Australian universities.

As the liberal humanist influence in Australian education weakened, some writers such as Alan Barcan (1965) and R.D. Goodman (1968) emphasised major facets of that tradition. They extended their horizon beyond simple institutional histories to include such aspects as state and non-state schools, curriculum development, the examination system, the education of girls and the influence of personalities. A strong spokesman for the liberal humanist tradition was P.H. Partridge (1968), whose review is concerned as much with higher education as with schools.

The expansion of secondary education in the 1950s led to numerous committees of inquiry and some interest in comprehensive high schools. The Wyndham Report (1957) of the special New South Wales Committee of Inquiry set a standard that few other reports rivalled. The *Report of the Committee on State Education in Victoria* (the Ramsay Report, 1960) was more a White Paper providing information than a plan for action.

The expansion of universities was helped by the recommendations of the *Report of the Committee on Australian Universities* (Canberra, 1957) chaired by Sir Keith Murray. The development of other forms of tertiary education was assisted by the *Report of the Committee on the Future of Tertiary Education in Australia*, published in three volumes in 1964–65 and known as the Martin Report after its chairman, Sir Leslie Martin. Although many of its detailed recommendations were soon abandoned, the report led to the extension of commonwealth funding to technical education and the establishment of colleges of advanced education.

The incessant stream of reports lent authority to the new educational currents but was also an index of confusion about educational developments. In Western Australia the Dettman Report, *Secondary education in Western Australia* (1969), recommended the abolition of external examinations, as did the report of the Queensland committee, chaired by W.C. Radford, entitled *Public examinations for Queensland secondary school students* (1970). *Secondary education for Canberra: report of the Working Committee on College Proposals for the Australian Capital Territory* (the Campbell Report, 1972) encouraged separate senior secondary schools and progressive, pupil-centred education in the Territory.

The report of the Interim Committee for the Australian Schools Commission, *Schools in Australia* (1973), known as the Karmel Report, assimilated the new egalitarianism with the new progressive education and stimulated the flow of funds to the new interest groups. *Girls, school and society* (Canberra, Schools Commission, 1975), the report by a study group of the Committee on Social Change and the Education of Women to the Schools Commission, advanced a feminist view. Disadvantaged groups were also identified in *Poverty and education in Australia*, the fifth main report of the Commission of Inquiry into Poverty (Canberra, 1976). The flood of reports, not always distinguished in content and often ineffective in purpose, continued throughout the

1970s. The report of the Committee of Inquiry into Education and Training, *Education, training and employment* (the Williams Report, 1979), analysed the situation after the 'turn of the tide', as school enrolments fell, unemployment grew and funds for education diminished.

The centenaries of the acts passed between 1872 and 1885 produced new state histories of education. Victoria came first, with a three-volume work edited by L.J. Blake (1973). For South Australia, Colin Thiele (1975) provided a readable yet scholarly history. In Queensland, Hector Holthouse's survey also appeared in 1975. In New South Wales the centenary of the Public Instruction Act led to a pictorial history by Burnswoods and Fletcher (1980). In Western Australia the 150th anniversary of white settlement was the occasion for W.D. Neal (1979) to edit a collection of documents, interspersed with a commentary. John Cleverley (1978) met the need for a general history of non-state schools when he surveyed the development of Anglican, Catholic, Seventh-day Adventist, Lutheran, Jewish and other independent schools. Less favourable views of 'elite' schools came from critics such as G. Maslen in his *School ties* (Sydney, Methuen, 1982).

Some books providing an academic approach to the history of education, often with an Australia-wide theme, appeared in the 1980s. Alan Barcan's history (1980) was the first recent comprehensive survey—but such surveys by one author were rare. Interest in biographical studies remained, and R.J.W. Selleck's magnificent study of Frank Tate appeared in 1982, while Cliff Turney edited three volumes of essays on individuals in Australian education (1983). The biographical approach continued in Selleck and Sullivan (1984). By contrast to the attention to leaders and heroes in Turney's three volumes, this Melbourne product emphasised humble non-heroes. W.F. Connell's history of the ACER (1980) was a sympathetic yet scholarly account of the role of this organisation in Australian education. A. Spaull (1982), by contrast, took a national and thematic approach rather than a state-by-state survey and used a wide range of previously unavailable official sources.

The references that follow cover books of major importance published since 1891. Only a few reports are listed and readers are referred to C.A. Brown's *Australian reports on education* (Melbourne, ACER, 1976). No journal articles are included but it should be noted that these are covered by the *Australian education index* (Melbourne, ACER, 1958–), which is a comprehensive index to current literature relevant to education. Finally, mention should be made of the *History of education review*, 1983– (formally *ANZHES journal*, 1972–1982) published by the Australian and New Zealand History of Education Society and the annual *Melbourne studies in education*, 1957/58– , both of which contain many valuable essays.

Children's class at an immigration camp in Perth, 1949. Unknown photographer, Western Australia Government Printer. Internal photographs of educational settings are relatively rare, especially those that show details of the curricula and teaching techniques. Many Australian children, apart from those in migrant camps, were taught in makeshift buildings until the mid-1960s, by which time most state education departments had caught up with the demands for schooling resulting from the postwar baby boom.
BATTYE LIBRARY

ALEXANDER, F. *Campus at Crawley: a narrative and critical appreciation of the first fifty years of the University of Western Australia.* Melbourne, Cheshire, 1963. 875 p, illus.

A general history of the university.

AUSTIN, A.G. *Australian education, 1788–1900: church, state and public education in colonial Australia.* Melbourne, Pitman, 1972. 308 p.

Landmark in the study of Australian education. First published in 1961.

AUSTRALIA. Committee on Australian Universities. *Report ...* Canberra, Commonwealth Government Printer, 1957. 133 p.

Recommended a massive injection of commonwealth funds into universities and the long-term involvement of the federal government in tertiary education. Chairman: Sir Keith Murray.

AUSTRALIA. Committeee on Technical and Further Education. *TAFE in Australia: report on needs in technical and further education.* AGPS, 1974. 2 vols, illus, maps.

Recommended the disbursement of federal funds to support vocational training and the improvement of technical skills through adult and further education beyond technical schools. Chairman: M. Kangan.

AUSTRALIA. Committee on the Future of Tertiary Education in Australia. *Tertiary education in Australia: report to the Australian Universities Commission.* Melbourne, Government Printer, 1964–65. 3 vols.

Appointed to re-examine the role of higher education, the committee recommended numerous reforms including the establishment of colleges of advanced education as an alternative to universities. Chairman: Sir L.H. Martin.

AUSTRALIA. Interim Committee for the Australian Schools Commission. *Schools in Australia: report of the Interim Committee for the Australian Schools Commission, May 1973.* AGPS, 1973. 167 p. Chairman: P. Karmel.

Important statement of new commonwealth policies favouring 'devolution', 'equality', 'diversity', generous financial aid under variety of programs and proposals about nature of Schools Commission.

BARCAN, A. *A history of Australian education.* OUP, 1980. 415 p, illus, maps.

Survey of the history of Australian education, including curricula, teaching methods, examinations and educational aims.

BARCAN, A. *A short history of education in New South Wales.* Sydney, Martindale, 1965. 338 p, illus, maps.

Surveys development of state and non-state schools, and describes curriculum and teaching methods. Includes select documents.

BARFF, H.E. *A short historical account of the University of Sydney.* A & R, 1902. 162 p, illus.

Useful for early years of university, foundation of colleges, the curriculum.

BEAN, C.E.W. *Here, my son: an account of the independent and other corporate boys' schools of Australia.* A & R, 1950. 257 p, illus.

Readable account beginning with historical survey, followed by analysis of 'problems' such as role of religion, headmasters, curriculum, methods, games.

BESSANT, B. AND SPAULL, A.D. *Politics of schooling.* Melbourne, Pitman, 1976. 202 p, illus.

Pioneering reassessment of schools as institutions established to reinforce conservative ideals and practices.

BIRCH, I.K.F. AND SMART, D. eds, *The commonwealth government and education 1964–1976: political initiatives and developments.* Melbourne, Drummond, 1977. 226 p.

Critical analysis of major initiatives taken by commonwealth since Federation.

BLAINEY, G. *A centenary history of the University of Melbourne.* MUP, 1957. 220 p, illus.

A readable account which includes role of individual academics. Weaker on formal aspects such as enrolment figures and administration.

BLAKE, L.B.J. ed, *Vision and realisation: a centenary history of state education in Victoria.* Melbourne, Education Department of Vic, 1973. 3 vols, illus.

Vol 1 provides a non-analytical outline of the provision of state primary and secondary schooling. Includes mini-biographies of leading administrators and educators. Vols 2 and 3 comprise historical sketches of hundreds of schools, uneven in quality and reliability.

BROWNE, G.S. ed, *Education in Australia: a comparative study of the educational systems of the six Australian states.* London, Macmillan, 1927. 461 p, illus, maps.

Highlights reforms introduced by leading educationists in the period 1905–14.

BURNSWOODS, J. AND FLETCHER, J *Sydney and the bush: a pictorial history of education in New South Wales.* Sydney, NSW Dept of Education, 1980. 259 p, illus, maps.

Celebrates the centenary of the state's Education Department. Brief chronological outlines of provision of education from 1788, lavishly and aptly illustrated. Ideal for general readership and use in schools.

BUTTS, R.F. *Assumptions underlying Australian education.* Melbourne, ACER, 1955. 80 p.

Views of an American advocate of progressive education. The book had considerable influence in Australia.

CLEVERLEY, J.F. *The first generation: school and society in early Australia.* SUP, 1971. 168 p.

Surveys the period 1788–1809. Endeavours to redress the impression that early colonists were not interested in education.

CLEVERLEY, J.F. ed, *Half a million children: studies of non-government education in Australia.* Melbourne, Longman Cheshire, 1978. 282 p.

Examination of major systems of independent schools (Anglican, Catholic, Protestant, Seventh-day Adventist, Lutheran, Jewish, Non-denominational and Alternative). Treats both historical and contemporary aspects.

CLEVERLEY J.F. AND LAWRY, J. eds, *Australian education in the twentieth century: studies in the development of state education.* Melbourne, Longman, 1972. 209 p.

The subjects covered include teaching methods and curriculum in state primary schools, 1914–32, state primary teachers between the wars, state secondary schools, 1910–39, role of the commonwealth in education.

COLE, P.R. ed, *The education of the adolescent in Australia.* MUP, 1935. 352 p. (ACER Educational research series, 32).

Structure of secondary schooling discussed by educational administrators.

COLE, P.R. ed, *The primary school curriculum in Australia.* MUP, 1932. 310 p. (ACER Educational research series, 16.)

Discussion of such matters as theories, industrial and social influences and of other institutions on the curriculum.

COLE, P.R. ed, *The rural school in Australia.* MUP, 1937. 244 p, illus. (ACER Educational research series, 49.)

Discusses special problems in these schools, including buildings, teaching methods, curriculum, timetables.

CONNELL, W.F. *The Australian Council for Educational*

Research, 1930–80. Melbourne, ACER, 1980. 394 p, illus. Throws light on the history of educational theory, innovations, progressive education, journals, conferences and many Australian educators.

CONNELL, W.F. *The foundations of secondary education.* Melbourne, ACER, 1967. 129 p.

Discusses the changing character of secondary education, the increasing tendency of children to continue into secondary school and the need for new values in a changing democracy. Favours comprehensive schools. First published in 1961.

CRANE, A.R. AND WALKER, W.G. *Peter Board: his contribution to the development of education in New South Wales.* Melbourne, ACER, 1957. 350 p, illus. (ACER Research series, 71.)

Survey of the reforms undertaken when Board was Director of Education, 1905–22.

CUNNINGHAM, K.S. AND ROSS, D.J. *An Australian school at work.* Melbourne, ACER, 1967. 160 p, illus. (ACER Monographs on secondary education, 2.)

Reviews the implementation of progressive education at Melbourne Church of England Girls' Grammar School, 1939–53, when Dorothy Ross was headmistress.

FITZGERALD, R.T. *Through a rear vision mirror; change and education: a perspective on the forties from the seventies.* Melbourne, ACER, 1975. 299 p. (ACER Research series, 97.)

Survey of education in early 1940s and early 1970s. Omission of 1960s limits possibility of explaining reasons for change. Statistics.

FITZPATRICK, K.E. *PLC Melbourne: the first century, 1875–1975.* Melbourne, Presbyterian Ladies' College, 1975. 298 p, illus.

A carefully documented centenary history which sets the educational history of PLC Melbourne within the framework of the movement for the emancipation of women in England and Australia.

FOGARTY, R. *Catholic education in Australia, 1806–1950.* MUP, 1959. 2 vols, illus.

Catholic education seen in general educational context.

GARDINER, L. *The Free Kindergarten Union of Victoria 1908–80.* Melbourne, ACER, 1982. 235 p, illus, maps.

Survey of the Free Kindergarten movement, with mention of other kindergartens and of the training college.

GARDNER, W.J. *Colonial cap and gown: studies in the mid-Victorian universities of Australasia.* Christchurch, University of Canterbury, 1979. 124 p, illus.

Compares the founding of the five earliest Australasian universities; presents biographical sketches of founding professors J. Woolley, W.E. Hearn and J.M. Brown; and devotes two substantial chapters to the entry of women to these universities.

GOODMAN, R.D. *Secondary education in Queensland, 1860–1960.* ANUP, 1968. 396 p, illus.

Survey of private, church and state secondary schools. Post-1939 inadequate.

GRUNDY, D. *Secular, compulsory and free: the Education Act of 1872.* MUP, 1972. 103 p. (The second century in Australian education, 5.)

The 1860s background to the 1872 Act and a detailed examination of its passage through parliament.

HANSEN, I.V. *Nor free nor secular: six independent schools in Victoria: a first sample.* OUP, 1971. 323 p.

Examines Scotch College, Melbourne Grammar, Geelong Grammar, Geelong College, Wesley College and Xavier College.

HIGGINS, E.M. *David Stewart and the W.E.A.* Sydney, Workers' Educational Association of NSW, 1957. 120 p, illus.

Serves as a history of the Workers' Educational Association, and of adult education, in NSW, 1913–54.

HOLTHOUSE, H. *Looking back: the first 150 years of Queensland schools.* Brisbane, Dept of Education, Qld, 1975. 211 p, illus.

Offers a picture of the meagre resources supporting education over this huge geographical area.

HYAMS, B.K. *Teacher preparation in Australia: a history of its development from 1850 to 1950.* Melbourne, ACER, 1979. 161 p. (ACER Research series, 104.)

Sober view of preparation of teachers for state schools, with the overseas influences clearly identified.

HYAMS, B.K. AND BESSANT, B. *Schools for the people? An introduction to the history of state education in Australia.* Melbourne, Longman, 1972. 195 p.

Emphasis on NSW and Vic. Post-1938 neglected.

JAMES, B. *The advancement of Spencer Button.* A & R, 1974. 282 p.

Thinly disguised novel by schoolteacher J.L. Tierney under the pseudonym of 'Brian James' about teachers and schools in NSW, 1890–1945. Incorporates many traditional anecdotes. Captures atmosphere and methods at turn of century. First published in 1950.

JONES, H. *Nothing seemed impossible: women's education and social change in South Australia 1875–1915.* UQP, 1985. xiii, 259 p.

Examines the formal and non-institutional education of women in SA from the introduction of compulsory schooling to illustrate the influence of women on society and the effect of the South Australian experience on them.

KELLY, F. *Degrees of liberation: a short history of women in the University of Melbourne.* Melbourne, Women Graduates Centenary Committee of the University of Melbourne, 1985. x, 172 p, illus.

Concentrates on those aspects of women's experience which differentiate them from men: their consciousness of being a minority group and the outcome of their studies in terms of professional or domestic destinations.

LAWSON, M.D. AND PETERSON, R.C. *Progressive education: an introduction.* A & R, 1972. 126 p.

Historical survey covering nineteenth-century Europe, twentieth-century United States, Montessori and Neill. Frequent references to comparable Australian developments.

MACKINNON, A. *One foot on the ladder: origins and outcomes of girls' secondary schooling in South Australia.* UQP, 1984. 209 p.

Examines the links between girls' education and women's work through a study of the Adelaide Advanced School for Girls and suggests that though the school sought to redefine femininity to include professional competence the notion of separate women's work was perpetuated.

MACLAINE, A.G. *Australian education: progress, problems and prospects.* Sydney, Novak, 1974. 358 p.

Survey organised according to themes with references and short bibliography at end of each chapter.

MITCHELL, B.A. *Teachers, education, and politics: a history of organizations of public school teachers in New South Wales.* UQP, 1975. 260 p, illus.

Comprehensive survey of NSW Public School Teachers' Association (1889–1918) and NSW Teachers' Federation (1918–73).

MOSSENSON, D. *State education in Western Australia, 1829–1960*. UWAP, 1972. 187 p, illus.

Mainly political and administrative history which includes some references to non-state schools. Post-1939 neglected.

NEAL, W.D. ed, *Education in Western Australia*. UWAP, 1979. 306 p, illus.

Presents 'the atmosphere of former times' through extensive use of documentary extracts rather than interpretative accounts. Introduction provides a historical outline; representative chapters cover the major facets of the provision of government and non-government primary and secondary schooling; concludes with chronological survey of post-secondary education, 1920–78.

NEW SOUTH WALES. Committee Appointed to Survey Secondary Education in New South Wales, *Report*. Sydney, Government Printer, 1958. 170 p.

Contains a readable interpretation of state secondary education, 1880–1951. Recommends comprehensive high schools. Chairman: H.S. Wyndham.

OATS, W.N. *The rose and the waratah: the Friends' School Hobart: formation and development, 1832–1945*. Hobart, Friends' School, 1979. 304 p, illus.

Illuminates general educational developments in Tas and the role of this rather special school. Curriculum and methods also considered.

O'DONOGHUE, M.X. *Mother Vincent Whitty: woman and educator in a masculine society*. MUP, 1972. 189 p, illus.

A biography of Mother Whitty who arrived in Qld in 1861 and founded the Order of Mercy in Australia. Discusses her struggles with the state authorities and with Bishop Quinn.

PARTRIDGE, P.H. *Society, schools and progress in Australia*. Oxford, Pergamon, 1968. 246 p.

Interpretation and criticism of education, including historical influences, organisation and higher education.

PORTUS, G. *Happy highways*. MUP, 1953. 294 p, illus.

Pleasantly written autobiography by a dedicated teacher in adult education and universities.

ROWE, A.P. *If the gown fits*. MUP, 1960. 227 p.

The vice-chancellor of the University of Adelaide critically examines university government.

SELLECK, R.J.W. *Frank Tate: a biography*. MUP, 1982. 362 p, illus, maps.

A meticulously researched, sympathetic yet analytical study of Tate's career as schoolmaster, inspector, administrator and architect of Victoria's education system, set against the broader social context.

SELLECK, R.J.W. AND SULLIVAN, M.G. eds, *Not so eminent Victorians*. MUP, 1982. xxiii, 224 p, illus.

Presents ten vignettes of unknown teachers faced with everyday experiences of nineteenth-century state school teachers; as teaching was a family enterprise also illuminates aspects of family life and the ways in which women combined professional and family commitments.

SHERINGTON, G. *Shore: a history of Sydney Church of England Grammar School*. Sydney, Sydney Church of England Grammar School in association with Allen & Unwin, 1983. 370 p, illus.

Combines a thorough chronological account of the school with details of curricula continuity and valuable analyses of the geographical and occupational backgrounds of the boys, vividly illustrating the school's continuing ties with the ruling classes and its preoccupation with the construction of masculinity.

SMART, D. *Federal aid to Australian schools*. UQP, 1978. 152 p.

History of federal funding for state education, 1901–75.

SMITH, S.M. AND SPAULL, G.T. *History of education in New South Wales, 1788–1923*. Sydney, G.B. Philip & Son, 1925. 224 p, illus.

Surveys educational institutions and political framework.

SPAULL, A.D. *Australian education in the Second World War*. UQP, 1982. 312 p.

Australian schools experienced comparatively little dislocation yet staffing, accommodation and curriculum were affected as schools became a vehicle for the war effort. Effects of war also influenced popular demands for education reform and increased federal involvement.

SPAULL, A.D. ed, *Australian teachers from colonial schoolmasters to militant professionals*. Melbourne, Macmillan, 1977. 308 p.

Papers on the history of the teaching profession.

SWEETMAN, E. *et al, A history of state education in Victoria*. Melbourne, Education Dept of Vic, 1922. 312 p, illus.

A pioneering work providing a reliable outline of state involvement in the provision of education.

THEOBALD, M.R. *Ruyton remembers 1878–1978*. Melbourne, Hawthorn, 1978. 222 p, illus.

Re-evaluates the older tradition of the education of girls by women and its survival despite the challenge of government regulation of private schools and government provision of secondary schooling.

THIELE, C.M. *Grains of mustard seed*. Adelaide, Education Dept of SA, 1975. 249 p, illus.

Centenary history of state education in SA. Concentrates on human aspects, not institutional development.

TURNEY, C. ed, *Pioneers of Australian education*. SUP, 1969–83. 3 vols, illus.

With one exception the first two volumes focus on state protagonists in the nineteenth-century battle to establish state control over education. The 'pioneers' in vol 3 largely represent twentieth-century professionalisation and bureaucratisation of education.

WHEELWRIGHT, E.L. ed, *Higher education in Australia*. Melbourne, Cheshire, 1965. 408 p.

Papers from University Staff Association conference, including some on technical education. Extensive 'Bibliography for Australian universities' by J. Caiden.

WHITELOCK, D. *The great tradition: a history of adult education in Australia*. UQP, 1974. 327 p.

General study of adult education in Australia. It includes surveys of mechanics' institutes, university extension, universities and the WEA, army education and the education of Aborigines. Emphasis on NSW.

WYETH, E.R. *Education in Queensland: a history of education in Queensland and in the Moreton Bay district of New South Wales*. Melbourne, ACER, 1955. 214 p, (ACER Research series, 67.)

Surveys the colonial period and subsequent developments. After 1920 very sketchy.

ZAINU'DDIN, A. *They dreamt of a school: a centenary history of Methodist Ladies' College, Kew, 1882–1982*. Melbourne, Hyland House, 1982. 469 p, illus.

Interweaves the traditional intimacy of a centennial history with such themes as male control over female education, service versus professionalism and changing attitudes to girls' education to create a model for future school histories.

Russell Drysdale, portrait of Donald Friend 1948. Oil on composition board, 121.5 × 91.4 cm.
ART GALLERY OF NEW SOUTH WALES

CHAPTER 42

RELIGION

LAWRENCE D. McINTOSH

DEFINING 'RELIGION' is no simple matter. Clearly no one interpretation of religion could satisfy the many different interests or contain all the varieties of religious experience to be found in Australia. Instead, it may be helpful to list the commonly regarded characteristics of religious faith and practice. Religion involves belief in God or in some supernatural power which transcends human existence. This belief entails a distinctive way of looking at the world and of living within it. Believers gather into communities and accept a certain authority, whether in the form of sacred writings, a tradition, a confession or a leader. They share forms of worship as well as symbols of their faith, history and values.

For thousands of years Aboriginal Australians have observed a highly developed religion with primal myths, sacred sites, beliefs and lore. Literature about this religion is included in the section on Aborigines and, for this reason, is omitted here.

The literature which deals specifically with religion in Australia is quite imbalanced. Christianity has dominated and, for this reason, the focus has been on the life and thought of the churches. At the other end of the spectrum, literature on non-traditional forms of religious consciousness is only beginning to emerge. Most writers on religious themes have been clerics, historians, sociologists or a combination of these. Much of the material is scholarly and this survey, while not intended for academic purposes, would be barren indeed were it to omit such contributions.

Of necessity, the choice of items is selective. Some are included as examples of the types of material available; others as major works in their own right. The reader who would delve deeper should note the discussion of bibliographies in chapter 8 of this volume and also remember that most of the items cited below contain guides to additional information.

REFERENCE SOURCES

Students of the history of religion in Australia should acquaint themselves thoroughly with Section II of this volume, particularly the general sources of references in the humanities and social sciences. Here attention is drawn mainly to the specialist works related to religion and its history in Australia. To date the only bibliographies on religion are M. Mason & G. Fitzpatrick (1982) and a bibliographic study by J.D. Bollen *et al* entitled 'Australian religious history, 1960–1980' in *J of religious history* 11, 1980, 8–44. Arns and Dacy's union list of theological serials (1983) will help researchers to locate the 3000 serials kept in academic and specialist libraries.

Closely related are lists of archival repositories such as *Our heritage* (Sydney, Australian Society of Archivists, 1983) and Ansell's somewhat more detailed guide (1985).

Organised religion has received little attention in general histories of Australia, though some historians have described not only the emergence of religious groups but also their impact upon society. Section V of this volume examines many of these histories. It is worth noting that C.M.H. Clark's *A history of Australia* (MUP, 1962–), Frank Crowley's *A new history of Australia* (Melbourne, Heinemann, 1974) and K.S. Inglis's *The Australian colonists* (MUP, 1974) pay particular attention to the history of religion in this country. An outstanding assessment of religion in the founding of Australia is Douglas Pike's *Paradise of dissent* (MUP, 1967) showing how non-conformists influenced the establishment of civil liberties in South Australia.

Three series of documents form an important source of data for the study of religion in the early days of European settlement. Incomplete and at times unreliable as they are (because of incompetent and selective copying, particularly in the two older series) *Historical records of Australia* (Melbourne, Library Committee of the Commonwealth Parliament, 1914–25), *Historical records of New South Wales* (1892–98; facs, Sydney, Lansdown Slattery, 1978–79) and the recent *Historical records of Victoria* (Melbourne, Public Record Office of Victoria, 1981–) remain useful for an understanding of the governors' attitudes to the churches and the clergy. Frank Crowley's multivolume selection entitled *A documentary history of Australia* (Melbourne, Nelson, 1980–) also covers religious events more generously than other collections of this type.

Religious organisations, the churches and the major denominations publish directories or yearbooks which include information about their organisations, personnel and services. The minutes and documents of their annual conferences (variously styled) are important additional sources. Hynd (1984) and the *Australian and New Zealand Association of Theological Schools fact book*, published by the association since 1976, include detailed lists of theological schools and church organisations.

SURVEYS

Most Australians claiming religious affiliation identify, really or nominally, with one of the Christian denominations and, understandably, most published religious history has been church history. However, questions about the interpretation of this history have implications for the study of other aspects and forms of religion. Patrick O'Farrell confronts some of these questions in an article, 'Writing the general history of religion in Australia' (*J of religious history* 9, 1, 1976, 65–73). Does a historian's denominational commitment preclude a balanced treatment of the subject? Can we speak of an intrinsic Australian religious history when so much of it is derivative, imported from a 'mother country'? More pertinently, has Christianity determined the life and thought of the Australian people to an extent that warrants historical analysis? The composite bibliographic essay by J. D. Bollen and others, referred to earlier, also probes these issues.

The writing of religious history has now tended to shift to departments of history and religion in tertiary institutions. These scholars are re-evaluating the celebratory and sectarian posturing which characterised many of the older chronicles. But these authors, in their turn, must clarify their own assumptions. An important discussion on historiographical issues has focused chiefly on the writings of Catholic authors. It began with a provocative article by K.S. Inglis, 'Catholic historiography in Australia' (*Hist stud* 8, 31, 1958, 233–53), and was continued by Walter Phillips, who reviewed subsequent writings in 'Australian Catholic historiography: some recent issues' (*Hist stud* 14, 56, 1971, 600–11). Patrick O'Farrell addressed the problem of the historian's need for detachment in 'Historians and religious convictions' (*Hist stud* 17, 68, 1977, 279–98), while K.S. Inglis summarised the more recent work of revision and synthesis in 'Colonial religion' (*Quadrant* 21, 12, 1977, 65–72). Inglis has consistently stressed the importance of studying the laity, the forgotten factor of so much church history.

Another aspect of revisionism concerns the biographies of religious leaders. A number of these, written by admirers, tended towards hagiography and revealed little knowledge of historical context. Again the shift is towards a more candid assessment, but not without a cautionary note. Whatever one thinks about the relevance or irrelevance of religion, it must be clear that Broughton, Polding, Lang, Chisholm, Mannix and other figures of prominence were *religious* people and they cannot be made intelligible without it.

Most surveys of religion in Australia concentrate on the Christian churches. An exception, which includes the major faiths as well as lesser known groups but which now needs updating, is Tess van Sommers, *Religion in Australia* (Adelaide, Rigby, 1966). Hans Mol's programmatic studies (1971) are sociological analyses of religious thinking and behaviour. An important collection of essays, stimulated by Mol's work, has been gathered by A. Black and P. Glasner (1983) and brief but illuminating lectures by J.D. Bollen were published as *Religion in Australian society: an historian's view* (Sydney, Leigh College, 1973). Barbara Thiering's Walter Murdoch Lecture, *God's experiment: Australian religion* (Perth, Murdoch University, 1982), points up the effects of respective waves of immigration on our religious history.

Little of substance has been published on developments in religious art. A brief but incisive essay by Rosemary Crumlin, 'The Blake Prize for Religious Art', in *Faith and culture*, edited by M. Press and N. Brown (Sydney, Catholic Institute of Sydney, 1984, 28–35), recounts the history of the prize and reflects on the divorce between the church and the artist. Religious and theological motifs are being sought and found in the literary works of certain Australian authors. This is a field in which Veronica Brady (1981) explores some possibilities. The religious attitudes of one of the main contributors to the Australian legend are analysed by Marian Zaunbrecher in an article, 'Henry Lawson's religion' (*J of religious history* 11, 2, 1980, 308–19).

PERIODICAL LITERATURE

There is a continuous stream of commentary in the journal literature. The major title in the field is the *Journal of religious history* which began in 1960. Other periodicals that occasionally include articles on religious issues are *Australian journal of history and politics*, 1955– ; *Historical studies*, 1940– ; *Journal of the Royal Australian Historical Society*, 1904– .

A number of denominations, their theological colleges and historical societies produce journals and newsapers whose contents range from the reporting of current events to scholarly articles. Some examples are *Australasian Catholic record*, published since 1895 at St Patrick's College, Manly; *Australian Baptist*, since 1913; *Church heritage: journal of the Church Records and Historical Society (Uniting Church in Australia, NSW Synod)*, since 1978; and *St Mark's review*, from St Mark's Institute of Theology, Canberra, since 1955. A major Jewish publication is the *Journal and proceedings of the Australian Jewish Historical Society*, published since 1939. The Australian Federation of Islamic Councils publishes *The Australian minaret* with materials in English, Arabic and other languages.

Non-denominational journals, some more specialised than others, include *Australian biblical review*, published by the Fellowship for Biblical Studies since 1951; *Colloquium: the Australian and New Zealand theological review*, since 1964; *Interchange: papers on biblical and current questions*, published by the AFES Graduates Fellowship, a branch of the Australian Fellowship of Evangelical Students, since 1967. The Zadok Centre in Canberra, devoted to discussion of contemporary issues within the context of Christian faith, publishes a number of reading guides and commentaries on current events, and the *Zadok Centre news* since 1971.

THE EARLY PERIOD

In a chapter entitled 'The Sabbath' in *The Australian colonists* (MUP, 1974), K.S. Inglis contrasts the intense religious fervour that had marked the establishment of the New England colonies of North America with the lack of purpose behind the beginnings of Christianity in Australia. The Colonial Office, in planning the first settlement, did not regard its spiritual needs as having a high priority. Furthermore Governor Phillip was hardly a religious enthusiast. No church ceremony celebrated the landing, the first service being delayed until Sunday 3 February 1788. The chaplain, Richard Johnson, the service and the prescribed sacraments were of the Church of England which, although subordinate to the authority of the early governors, was to dominate the religious scene for several decades.

A volume of documents edited by Jean Woolmington (1976) covers this and later periods.

The biographies of Johnson and Samuel Marsden reveal the church's difficulties in perpetuating old traditions and adapting to a radically different environment. Relationships between clergy and convicts were identified with the government's repressive system, a point elaborated by A. Grocott (1979). J.D. Bollen, in an article entitled 'English Christianity and the Australian colonies' (*J of ecclesiastical history* 28, 4, 1977, 361–85), argues that for thirty years after 1788, Australia's penal settlements attracted scant attention from either the churches in England or their missionary societies. On the other hand James Waldersee (1983) tells how the Society for the Propagation of the Faith assisted nascent Catholic dioceses and missionary work throughout the nineteenth century.

CHURCH, STATE AND EDUCATION

With the influx of free settlers the variety and strengths of the several denominations increased. In the interests of equity and order Governor Bourke made two proposals which were to have important consequences for all religious groups. The first was that financial aid be granted to the major churches. The intention of the Church Act 1836 was adopted by other colonies, with aid being extended to some smaller groups, including Jewish communities. John Barrett (1966) covers these events in eastern Australia. The church acts effectively reduced the domination of the Church of England but otherwise promoted growth and consolidation. They also sponsored what Naomi Turner has called 'the sinews of sectarian warfare' in a book of that title (1972).

Closely related was Bourke's attempt to impose order on the haphazard development of educational facilities by recommending a national system of education for all children. This was successfully resisted, mainly, but not solely, by the Church of England. The 'free, secular and compulsory' system finally adopted by all colonies had numerous implications. One, of major proportions, was that the Catholic authorities were confirmed in their decision to develop and support a separate system providing schools, teachers and texts. Deserving of special mention is the foundation study by A.G. Austin, *Australian education, 1788–1900: church, state, and public education in colonial Australia* (Melbourne, Pitman, 1972) and an authoritative work on the development of Catholic education by Ronald Fogarty, *Catholic education in Australia, 1806–1950* (MUP, 1959). Literature on denominational schools is extensive. Over 350 items are listed in Mason and Fitzpatrick (1982). There have also been a number of significant publications designed for teachers of religious education.

The oldest universities, Sydney (1850) and Melbourne(1853), were part of the state-supported, secular education system. The major churches, however, received grants of land and established residential colleges, affiliated with the universities, to provide ancillary teaching and a location for theological education, particularly the training of ministers. Contributions to the history of one university college are published as *Ormond College centenary essays* edited by Stuart Macintyre (MUP, 1984), which includes an essay on the college's Theological Hall by Don Chambers. K.T. Livingstone assesses the recruitment and training of Catholic priests in *The emergence of an Australian Catholic priesthood 1835–1915* (Sydney, Catholic Theological Faculty, 1977). The relation between theological education and social responsibility is among the matters explored by Renate Howe in 'Protestantism, social Christianity and the ecology of Melbourne, 1890–1900' (*Hist stud* 19, 74, 1980, 59–73). A general criticism to emerge from this literature is that, at the end of the century, little was being done to encourage theological thinking in an Australian context.

INTELLECTUAL, SOCIAL AND POLITICAL CONCERNS

From the 1880s the churches were either crusading or defending in a number of areas. The literature achieves good coverage of the currents of religious thought and activity, particularly to 1920.

The last decades of the nineteenth century saw the intellectual landscape being substantially altered by Darwinian evolutionary theory. The credibility of the Bible, particularly its account of creation, was at stake. The problems of affirming biblical authority and reconciling traditional theological positions with the new learning elicited a variety of responses. Covering these and other issues, Timothy Suttor examines 'the deliberate setting aside of religious certitude in Australia, 1875–1900' in the *J of religious history* (1, i, 1960, 26–39), while Jill Roe describes varying clerical attitudes during one critical decade in 'Challenge and response: religious life in Melbourne, 1876–1886' (*J of religious history* 5, 2, 1968, 149–66). Walter Phillips explains the position of the churches in several journal articles and again in his examination of social conflict (1981).

The 1880s and 1890s also marked the churches' increasing concern for the recognition of Christian principles and practices in society. Pronouncements on Sunday observance, temperance, gambling, the alleviation of poverty and the labour movement thundered from the pulpits and were relayed through an extensive denominational press. Positive and negative attitudes, pastoral care and alleged wowserism were juxtaposed as churchmen confronted social issues.

The combination of evangelism and pastoral concern characterised the witness of the Salvation Army, which appeared on the Australian scene in 1880. Centennial histories of the Army by Bolton and by Tarling were both published in 1980. Related is David Hilliard's review of evangelical work from the 1870s to the 1920s, featuring such famous visitors as J. Wilbur Chapman and Charles M. Alexander, and published as *Popular revivalism in South Australia* (Adelaide, Uniting Church Historical Society, South Australia, 1982).

In the 1890s the churches, in addressing the poverty and unrest of the time, had to make decisions about the validity of trade unionism and the labour movement. Authors such as J.D. Bollen (1972), R.L. Broome (1980) and W. Phillips (1981) deal with the churches' responses to industrial conflict and social unrest. The question of Catholic political influence is examined by Patrick Ford: *Cardinal Moran and the A.L.P.: a study in the encounter between Moran and socialism, 1890–1907: its effects upon the Australian Labor Party, the foundation of Catholic social thought and action in modern Australia* (MUP, 1966).

Politically, from the very beginning Australia has operated without recourse to the support of religion. There are, however, two religious clauses in the Australian constitution. The deity is recognised in the preamble, and section 116, in part, prevents the commonwealth from making laws for establishing or prohibiting any religion or for imposing any religious observance. How these clauses became part of the constitution is related by Richard Ely (1976).

The constitutional 'blessing of Almighty God' was invoked by churchmen who generally regarded World War I as a just war. The conscription debates gave way to questioning and disillusion, which saw the entrance into the political arena of the then coadjutor Catholic Archbishop, Daniel Mannix, and the reawakening of sectarianism. Michael McKernan (1980) skilfully examines the varying attitudes from 1914 to 1918. To date, little has been published either on the churches' pronouncements on the more recent wars or their participation in emerging peace movements.

During and after World War II the churches were concerned with the dilemma of communism. In 1941–42 a secret organisation, the Catholic Social Studies Movement led by B.A. Santamaria and widely supported by the Catholic hierarchy, had been formed to counter communist influence. Paul Ormonde documents its history and evaluates its effect on the Catholic Church and Australian democracy in *The Movement* (Melbourne, Nelson, 1972); it is more fully treated by Gerard Henderson (1983), while B.A. Santamaria's own memoirs, *Against the tide* (OUP, 1981), provide the most intimate account.

More light is thrown on this period by Vincent Buckley in *Cutting green hay: friendships, movements and cultural conflicts in Australia's great decades* (Ringwood, Vic, Penguin, 1983) and Edmund Campion in *Rockchoppers: growing up Catholic in Australia* (Ringwood, Vic, Penguin, 1982). A different but important participant in the ambiguities of these years was the Victorian Methodist minister Frank Hartley who became spokesman for international and Australian peace movements. His wife, Marion Hartley, has written his biography, *The truth shall prevail* (Melbourne, Spectrum, 1982).

From the earliest settlements, immigration has helped shape and give a distinctive character to a number of denominations. After 1945, with an influx of new Australians, religious organisations set up agencies to assist with their integration and to minister to their particular needs. The writings of Frank Lewins are important in examining relationships between the Catholic Church and migrants. Two major reports, by David Cox (1982) and the New South Wales Anti-Discrimination Board's statement (1984), are landmarks in this field.

THE DENOMINATIONS

Few national histories of denominations have been written but readers should recognise the usefulness of the *Australian encyclopaedia* in providing summary accounts of the major religious groups with suggestions for further reading.

In terms of the number of publications, prominence clearly belongs to Catholic histories. A major work by Patrick O'Farrell (1977) provides an authoritative account from colonial times. So far no counterpart for other denominations has been published. An insightful commentary on the literature since the 1920s is in an article by J.J. Eddy, 'Australian Catholicism in the last fifty years' (*Australian Catholic review* 50, 1, 1973, 306–20).

Next to Catholicism the Orthodox churches comprise the largest body in Christendom but this family of churches has been the Cinderella of our church history. Little more than pamphlets have been published about it. An Anglican bishop, Ian Shevill, has written a brief work, *The Orthodox and other Eastern churches in Australia* (Sydney, Anglican Information Office, 1976). A priest of the Greek Orthodox Church, Miltiades Chryssavgis, has contributed an essay, 'Orthodoxy in Australia' to Harris *et al* (1982) which describes the history of the church and the issues confronting it.

The Church of England in Australia became the Anglican Church of Australia in 1981. No substantial national history of this church has been written although the gap is filled in part by Ross Border's somewhat technical survey, *Church and state in Australia, 1788–1872: a constitutional study of the Church of England in Australia* (London, SPCK, 1962).

Colonial and later histories of Presbyterianism and Methodism, written usually to commemorate jubilees or centenaries, should be accessible in all state libraries. Typical of this genre are R.G. Balfour, *Presbyterianism in the colonies* (Edinburgh, MacNiven & Wallace, 1899), James Colwell, *The illustrated history of Methodism* (Sydney, Brooks, 1904) and C.A. White, *The challenge of the years: the history of the Presbyterian Church of Australia in the state of New South Wales* (A & R, 1951). Until recently little had been published about the Congregational churches, apart from those in South Australia where their influence was out of proportion to their membership. An article by G.L. Barnes, 'The origins of Australian Congregationalism' (*Church heritage* 1, Sept 1978, 33–44), outlines their beginnings and quest for religious liberty. Hugh Jackson's 'Religious ideas and practices in Australian Congregationalism, 1870–1930' (*J of religious history* 12, 1983, 266–83, 433–44), helps to fill in the later years.

Few figures from this cluster of three denominations have become legendary: unlike bishops, their moderators and presidents were in office for too short a period to attract the same public attention and few recorded their memoirs. One figure, however, cannot be ignored although, as record has it, even bushrangers preferred to leave him alone. The doughty, quarrelsome John Dunmore Lang was the leading Presbyterian in the colonies and Baker's lengthy biography (1985) does him justice.

Recent material on these three churches to 1976, the year of their becoming the Uniting Church in Australia, is to be found chiefly in articles and theses. The journal *Church heritage* is an important resource, particularly for state histories. The creeds, confessions and sermons which helped shape the doctrinal understanding of the Uniting Church in Australia are gathered in a volume edited by M. Owen (1984).

In 1967 the two major Lutheran groups merged to become the Lutheran Church in Australia. There are two official histories. Alfred E.R. Brauer wrote *Under the Southern Cross: history of the Evangelical Lutheran Church of Australia* (Adelaide, Lutheran Publishing House, 1956) and Theodor Hebart, *The United Evangelical Lutheran Church in Australia: its history, activities and characteristics, 1838–1938* (Adelaide, Lutheran Book Depot, 1938). The story of another group of congregations has been gathered by H. Eilert and J.S. Martin, *Northern light in southern skies: Scandinavian church life in Victoria, 1883–1983* (Melbourne, Swedish Church, 1983).

The Baptists opened churches in Hobart and Sydney in the 1830s. J.D. Bollen (1975) describes how such groups adapted to their minority status while G. Chapman (1979) deals with the Churches of Christ. Of the religious groups originating in the United States of America, A.S. Maxwell provides an account of the Seventh-day Adventists in *Under the Southern Cross: the Seventh-day Adventist story in Australia, New Zealand, and the Islands of the Pacific* (Nashville, Tennessee, Southern Publishing Association, 1966).

Dissension could be found within a denomination as well as without. The Reverend Charles Strong left the Presbyterian Church of Victoria in 1883 and became the first minister of a new religious society, the Australian Church; his biography has been written by C.R. Badger (1971). His spirit of liberalism was to be found also among the Unitarians who adopted comparatively radical positions and contributed significantly to debates on evolution, the liberation of Sundays and, in the 1950s, the peace movement. Eleanor Wilson has written, *The story of the Sydney Unitarian Church, 1850–1974* (Sydney, The Church, 1974), while the history of the Melbourne congregation is recorded by Dorothy Scott (1980).

The Charismatic movement, which affirms the possibility of experiencing the Spirit of God, has spread rapidly. It includes both the Pentecostal churches and fellowship within the major denominations. Barry Chant describes the nature, potential and problems of these groupings in 'The promise of the Charismatic movement', an essay in Harris *et al* (1982).

The Sunday School movement began in England in 1780. Beverley Earnshaw commemorated its bicentenary with a short treatment in 1980.

Historically, the clergy's domination of the churches' decision-making has been assumed. Some of the biographies cited indicate the firm direction given by a clerical elite. More recently there has been evidence of changes in clerical roles, status and self-perceptions. A number of studies, for example those of Blaikie (1979), Bodycomb (1978) and Dempsey (1983), analyse the kinds of problems being encountered. In addition to these books there are relevant essays in Black and Glasner (1983) which focus on exceptions and styles of ministry. On this topic a volume by Robin J. Pryor (1982) is particularly important.

In recent years women have been questioning the traditional patriarchal nature of the church's organisation and literature, both historical and biographical, is now appearing on the status and role of women in religous affairs. A volume of essays edited by Sabine Willis (1977) provides some good examples. Patrick and Deirdre O'Farrell co-authored 'The status of women: some opinions in Australian Catholic history, c1869–c1969' (*Bulletin of Christian affairs*, 57–58, Oct–Nov 1975); Tulip (1983) tells of developments within the Uniting Church; while Sabine Willis makes critical use of the literature to date in an article, 'Fragments of illumination: women and the church in Australia' (*Church heritage* 2, 1, 1981–83, 58–74). Although some denominations now ordain female ministers, there remains a division of theological opinion on this matter.

There have been notable recent developments in the areas of liturgy, ritual and church music which include the publication of *An Australian prayer book* by the then Church of England in 1978 and the *Australian hymn book* (1977) which, with its Catholic supplement, represents an ecumenical undertaking.

By far the most important development in recent church history has been the decreasing sectarian wrangling among the mainstream denominations. Some phases of the ecumenical movement in Australia go back to the last decades of the nineteenth century; the most extensive account of these early attempts at unity is by Frank Engel (1984). Major factors responsible for the more recent initiatives were, on the one hand, the experience and influence of the World Council of the Roman Catholic Church which stressed that the other churches were partners in dialogue and co-operation. The more friendly and creative atmosphere that followed gave Michael Hogan cause to write an article, 'Whatever happened to Australian sectarianism?' (*J of religious history* 13, 1, 1984, 83–91).

The formation of the Uniting Church in Australia has already been mentioned. Its very title,

'Uniting' rather than 'united', is meant to signify an openness to a wider union. Some attitudes of the Anglican Church in this regard are introduced in *Anglicans, unity and the Uniting Church in Australia: a survey of local, regional and national initiatives and guidelines for the future* edited by David Garnesey (Melbourne, General Board of Religious Education [1976]). Church co-operation has made it possible for an organisation such as the Victorian Council of Churches to publish books which present the teaching and practices of Australian churches—Anglican, Orthodox, Protestant and Catholic—on certain services and sacraments.

NON-CHRISTIAN RELIGIONS

Non-Christian religions are important segments of the total mosaic of culture in Australia, but literature on the history and presence of these religions and appraisals of their impact is barely beginning to appear.

Muslims comprise the largest group with a membership likely to be considerably more than the 1981 census figure of 0.5 per cent, and with a rapidly expanding education system. An article by John O'Brien, 'The growing faith in Islam' (*Australia now*, 6, 4, 1977, 26–31), provides a brief history of Muslims in Australia. A Dominican priest, L.P. Fitzgerald, introduces a different theme in 'Dialogue with Islam' (*St Mark's review* 107, Sept 1981, 45–49). But there is much more to be known about the history of Islam in Australia and its missionary zeal.

A comprehensive history of the Jewish people in this country is to be found in an article by Walter Lippmann under the entry 'Australia' in *Encyclopedia Judaica* (New York, Macmillan, 1971–72, 3, 878–87). This work is updated by Israel Porush in 'Australia' in *Encyclopedia Judaica Decennial Book, 1973–82* (Jerusalem, Keter, 1982, 165–7). Histories of some Jewish congregations and communities in the several states and cities have been written but an account of the developing dialogue between Jews and Christians is yet to be published.

There is a paucity of information about Australia's 35 000 Buddhists, both Asian immigrants and Australian born. David Cox (1982) offers an overview of both Islam and Buddhism.

SECULARISATION AND THE FUTURE

Secularisation takes place as a society becomes increasingly indifferent to religious institutions. It is no sudden phenomenon and the books yet to be written on this theme will have to go back to the beginning of the nation's story. In part, Richard Ely anticipates this task in a scholarly article, 'Secularisation and the sacred in Australian history' (*Hist stud* 19, 77, 1981, 553–66). Ely provides a helpful review of the standpoints taken by Australian historians on the matter of secularisation and clears the way for a study of 'the multiform and multilayered sacrednesses of Australian life' (p 563).

In real terms secularisation is seen as a loss of interest in mainstream denominations and a disregard for religious sanctions. The 1981 census showed that 10.8 per cent of the population stated that they had no religion; another 10.9 per cent did not identify their religion. In an essay entitled 'Australia's religiosity: some trends since 1966' in Black and Glasner (1983), Gary Bouma updates some of the findings and those by Hans Mol (1971). Several essays in *The shape of belief* (1982) consider the data and focus on the predicament of the churches.

Reports on this decline have generally concentrated upon the larger Christian denominations, but it would appear that certain theologically conservative congregations are growing in strength. There is also evidence of the burgeoning of new religious movements, some world-affirming, others world-denying. Ian Hunter examines the establishment and operation of some of these organisations in 'Some small religious groups in Australia: Mormons, Moonies, Hare Krishnas, Scientologists' (*Compass theology review* 18, 3, 1984, 21–32).

To speak of new religions or other forms of religion raises the question as to whether there are instances of faith and devotion, quite dissociated from traditional beliefs, which can be constructed as 'religious'. Peter Glasner faces this issue in 'The study of Australian folk religion: some theoretical and practical problems' in Black and Glasner (1983). He considers whether a variety of experiential forms, including the occult, Anzac rituals and Australian rules football, entail loyalties which could be regarded as religious. Another related question concerns the meaning of religious festivals in the secular city. The annual 'carols by candlelight', for example, seems to perpetuate a romanticism long after any convictions about the nativity have been set aside. Norman Habel explores this festival in 'Carols by candlelight: the analysis of an Australian ritual', an essay in *Religious experience in world religions* edited by V. Hayes (Adelaide, Australian Association for the Study of Religions, 1980, 160–73).

The body of literature on religions as believed and practised in Australia is not overwhelming. There is, however, a flow of contributions from authors who, having revisited and revised earlier attempts, are more aware of the importance of interdisciplinary research, more knowledgeable of cultural settings, more able to blend objectivity with empathy and, finally, more willing to adopt ecumenical perspectives, not only with regard to the different churches but also the different religions in this land. Their mandate is twofold. It is to interpret the faith, love and hope of people who have participated in the development of Australian society and to understand the ultimate concerns of those who will inform its future.

ANSELL, L.J. ed, *Register of church archives.* Toowoomba, Qld, Church Archivists' Society, 1985. 290 p.

A preliminary listing of depositories for Christian and some Jewish materials. First published in 1982.

ARNS, H. AND DACY, M. eds, *Australian union list of serials in theological collections.* Sydney, National Catholic Research Council, 1983. 182 p.

Lists the serial holdings of some 80 libraries.

THE AUSTRALIAN *hymn book: with Catholic supplement* (Harmony edn). Sydney, Collins, 1977. 784, lxvi p.

The work by a selection committee of Anglicans, Congregationalists, Methodists and Presbyterians with a Catholic supplement from the Liturgy Commission of the Catholic Archdiocese of Sydney. Includes hymns common to these churches and new material from Australia and overseas. Available in numerous editions.

BADGER, C.R. *The Reverend Charles Strong and the Australian Church.* Melbourne, Abacada Press, 1971. 335 p, illus.

An account of the Melbourne clergyman whose theological liberalism caused his expulsion by the Presbyterian Assembly and led to his founding a new religious society.

BAGLIN, D. AND THIERING, B. *Australian churches.* Sydney, Ure Smith, 1979. 128 p, illus.

A collection of photographs of churches, several mosques, a synagogue and an Aboriginal sacred mountain; supported by an introductory essay and descriptive notes.

BAKER, D.W. *Days of wrath: a life of John Dunmore Lang.* MUP, 1985. 562 p, illus.

Definitive study of this Presbyterian minister who was an active participant for fifty years in the nineteenth century in religious, political and social activity in eastern Australia.

BARRETT, J. *That better country: the religious aspect of life in eastern Australia, 1835–1850.* MUP, 1966. 213 p, illus, maps.

A study of the institutional life of the churches, their participation in state aid and in debates on the role of religion in education. Includes an analysis of the Sunday School movement.

BLACK, A.W. AND GLASNER, P.E. eds, *Practice and belief: studies in the sociology of Australian religion.* Sydney, Allen & Unwin, 1983. 205 p.

Focuses on the period since Mol's survey in 1966. Bibliography.

BLAIKIE, N.W.H. *The plight of the Australian clergy: to convert, care or challenge?* UQP, 1979. 253 p.

Based on a 1969 survey of Protestant clergy in Vic, this study examines their orientations, priorities and frustrations. Bibliography.

BODYCOMB, J. *The naked churchman: a Protestant profile. A study of Protestant beliefs and attitudes in South Australia.* Melbourne, Joint Board of Christian Education of Australia and New Zealand, 1978. 166 p.

An analysis of data from 124 congregations, conveying the responses of clergy and laity on a range of doctrinal, political and social matters.

BOLLEN, J.D. *Australian Baptists: a religious minority.* London, Baptist Historical Society, 1975. 58 p.

A careful interpretation of strategies used, in NSW, SA and Vic, to compensate Baptists for their minority status. Highlights differences within this one denomination.

BOLTON, B. *Booth's drum: the Salvation Army in Australia, 1880–1980.* Sydney, Hodder & Stoughton, 1980. 287 p, illus.

An account of reactions to the Army's evangelism and service, its brass and song, ranging from early amusement to respect and acclaim.

BRADY, V. *A crucible of prophets: Australians and the question of God.* Sydney, Theological Explorations, 1981. 113 p.

A reading of Australia's better known novelists suggesting the development of a peculiarly Australian sense of God.

BROOME, R.L. *Treasure in earthen vessels: Protestant Christianity in New South Wales society, 1900–1914.* UQP, 1980. 216 p, map.

Explores the Protestant clergy's response to general religious indifference. Important for the discussion of sectarianism.

CHAPMAN, G. *One Lord, one faith, one baptism: a history of Churches of Christ in Australia.* Melbourne, Federal Literature Dept, Churches of Christ in Australia, 1979. 191 p, illus.

A reflective account of the Churches of Christ from conservative beginnings to participation in social and political affairs and in the ecumenical movement.

CHURCH OF ENGLAND IN AUSTRALIA. *Liturgy and ritual. An Australian prayer book: for use together with the Book of Common Prayer, 1662.* Sydney, Standing Committee of

'*Golden jubilee of men's sodality of Our Lady Richmond Communion breakfast.*' *Unknown photographer,*
13 Oct 1935. Major religions have spawned organisations with social and political overtones. They are
usually single sex organisations but on the occasion of this golden jubilee women have been allowed to
put in a brief appearance.

the General Synod of the Church of England in Australia, 1978. 636 p, illus.

This book of services, prayers and psalms aims to be 'a teaching and devotional manual in contemporary language'. Several editions are available.

COX, D. *Religion and welfare: a study of the role of religion in the provision of welfare services to selected groups of immigrants in Melbourne, Australia*. Melbourne, Dept of Social Studies, University of Melbourne, 1982. 250 p.

Comparative study of Muslims, Buddhists and Sri Lankan and Vietnamese Christian families. Reports on their problems, the effects of resettlement on religious beliefs and practices, and the available welfare services.

DEMPSEY, K. *Conflict and decline: ministers and laymen in an Australian country town*. Sydney, Methuen, 1983. 190 p.

Examines conflict between ministers and the laity in a Methodist community in NSW; includes discussion of church finances, theological education, the Vietnam War, the role of ministers' wives.

DUNSTAN, K. *Wowsers: being an account of the prudery exhibited by certain outstanding men and women in such matters as drinking, smoking, prostitution, censorship, and gambling*. Melbourne, Cassell, 1968. 315 p, illus.

Discusses possible origins of the word 'wowser' and proceeds to a lively account of campaigns against various social evils, particularly in Melbourne.

EARNSHAW, B. *Fanned into flame: the spread of the Sunday School in Australia*. Sydney, Board of Education, Diocese of Sydney, 1980. 80 p, illus.

A popular history of the Sunday Schools organised by major denominations; includes Jewish Sabbath and Sunday Schools. Contains useful leads for further studies.

ELY, R. *Unto God and Caesar: religious issues in the emerging commonwealth, 1891–1906*. MUP, 1976. 162 p, illus.

A discussion of the federation debates on the status of religion,

the problems of whether and how to put God into the constitution and the bickerings about ecclesiastical precedence.

ENGEL, F. *Australian Christians in conflict and unity*. Melbourne, Joint Board of Christian Education of Australia and New Zealand, 1984. 275 p.

An account of interchurch relationships, revivals of sectarianism and the emergence of ecumenism to 1926.

GETZLER, I. *Neither toleration nor favour: the Australian chapter of Jewish emancipation*. MUP, 1970. 153 p.

Depicts the varying attitudes of four governments, particularly with regard to state aid and full equality; analyses the emerging character of Australian Jews.

GREGORY, J.S. *Church and state: changing government policies towards religion in Australia, with particular reference to Victoria since separation*. Melbourne, Cassell, 1973. 283 p.

Concentrates on debates to 1872, the year of Victoria's education act, and the implications of secularism over the next century.

GRIFFIN, G.M. AND TOBIN, D. *In the midst of life: the Australian response to death*. MUP, 1982. 177 p, illus.

The authors, a theological professor and a funeral director, review mourning customs, funeral arrangements, debates about cremation, and consider present practices and appropriate rituals.

GROCOTT, A.M. *Convicts, clergymen and churches: attitudes of convicts and ex-convicts towards the churches and clergy in New South Wales from 1788 to 1851*. SUP, 1979. 327 p, illus.

An entertaining survey of attitudes ranging from apathy to hostility.

HAMILTON, A. *What's been happening in RE in Australia?* Melbourne, Dove Communications, 1981. 56 p.

Written as a guide for Catholic parents and teachers, it explains the changes in religious education over the past twenty years.

HARRIS, D. *et al, The shape of belief: Christianity in Australia today*. Sydney, Lancer Books, 1982. 293 p, illus.

An ecumenical assemblage of contributions on a range of topics, but mostly on the struggle of Christianity to achieve an Australian identity.

HENDERSON, G. *Mr. Santamaria and the bishops.* Sydney, Hale & Iremonger, 1983. 230 p.

An account of Catholic social theory and of the divisions of opinion over the political activities of the 'Movement' and the Catholic bishops. Bibliography. First published in 1982.

HYND, D. *Australian Christianity in outline: a statistical analysis and directory.* Sydney, Lancer Books, 1984. 142 p.

Brief histories, statistics and interpretations, with a directory of church organisations.

HYND, D. 'Christianity in Australia: a bibliography', in D. Harris *et al* (1982). 201–228.

Covers material published since 1960 on Australian theology, church history, the denominations and sociological perspectives on religion in Australian society.

LEVI, J.S. AND BERGMAN, G.F.J. *Australian genesis: Jewish convicts and settlers, 1788–1850.* Adelaide, Rigby, 1974. 360 p, illus, maps.

A history of the Jews who arrived during the first six decades of settlement. Bibliography.

LEWINS, F.W. *The myth of the universal church: Catholic migrants in Australia.* Canberra, Faculty of Arts, Australian National University, 1978. 164 p, illus.

Comments on cultural patterns and alleged religious unity.

LOANE, M.L. *Hewn from the rock: origins and traditions of the Church in Sydney.* Sydney, Anglican Information Office, 1976. 148 p, illus.

The Moorhouse Lectures for 1976, focusing on the contributions of clergy from the early chaplains to Archbishop Mowll who died in 1958. Includes indexes of clergy and portraits of major figures.

McCAUGHEY, J.D. *Commentary on the Basis of Union of the Uniting Church in Australia.* Melbourne, Uniting Church Press, 1980. 107 p.

This commentary by the first president of the Uniting Church in Australia reflects the author's intimate experience with the drafting of the document and elucidates the intention of each paragraph.

MACINTOSH, N.K. *Richard Johnson, chaplain to the colony of New South Wales: his life and times 1755–1827.* Sydney, Library of Australian History, 1978. 150 p, illus, map.

Examines Johnson's background, his appointment as first chaplain and his troubled relationships with the governors.

McKERNAN, M. *Australian churches at war: attitudes and activities of the major churches, 1914–1918.* Sydney, Catholic Theological Faculty; Canberra, Australian War Memorial, 1980. 207 p, illus.

A major study raising the question as to whether the churches had anything distinctively Christian to say about the war.

MASON, M. AND FITZPATRICK, G. *Religion in Australian life: a bibliography of social research.* Ed by M. Mason; comp by G. Fitzpatrick. Adelaide, Australian Association for the Study of Religions and National Catholic Research Council, 1982. 254 p.

Concentrates on materials reflecting research, published here and overseas, 1945–77. A supplement adds selected items to 1981.

MILLETT, J. *An Australian parsonage, or, the settler and the savage in Western Australia, by Mrs. Edward Millett.* London, Edward Stanford, 1872. 415 p, illus.

During the 1860s, Janet Millett, wife of a Church of England chaplain, compiled guides containing descriptions of growing towns, Aborigines, local characters and the chaplain's duties. Facsimile edition, UWAP, 1980.

MILLIKAN, D. *The sunburnt soul: Christianity in search of an Australian identity.* Sydney, Anzea, 1981. 111 p, illus.

Anecdotes based on an ABC-TV series on the failure of the church to communicate with Australian society.

MOL, J.J. *Religion in Australia: a sociological investigation.* Melbourne, Nelson, 1971. 380 p, ill.

The first major study based on a survey in the mid-1960s. The results must now be qualified by the subsequent decline in allegiance to institutional Christianity.

MOLONY, J.N. *The Roman mould of the Australian Catholic Church.* MUP, 1969. 209 p, illus.

The author, born in Ireland and educated in Rome, claims that it was chiefly Rome, rather than Ireland, which established and maintains the spirit of Catholicism in Australia.

NEW SOUTH WALES. Anti-Discrimination Board. *Discrimination and religious conviction: a report of the Anti-Discrimination Board in accordance with Section 119 (a) of the Anti-Discrimination Act 1977.* Sydney, The Board, 1984. 565 p.

An analysis of harassment because of people's religious belief including recommendations on the elimination of prejudice. A valuable resource for definitions and profiles of religious groups.

OATS, W.N. *Backhouse and Walker: a Quaker view of the Australian colonies, 1832–1838.* Hobart, Blubber Head Press in association with the Australian Yearly Meeting, Religious Society of Friends, 1981. 76 p, illus.

A summary of impressions of two English Quakers; provides a refreshingly independent view of colonial people, places and problems.

O'FARRELL, P. AND O'FARRELL, D. eds, *Documents in Australian Catholic history.* London, Geoffrey Chapman, 1969. 2 vols.

An extensive collection of documents on this church's history.

OWEN, M. ed, *Witness of faith: historic documents of the Uniting Church in Australia.* Melbourne, Uniting Church Press, 1984. 229 p.

Presents documents fundamental to the Uniting Church and the Basis of Union. Bibliographies.

PHILLIPS, W. *Defending 'a Christian country': churchmen and society in New South Wales in the 1880s and after.* UQP, 1981. 332 p, illus.

Details the churches' intellectual, political and social conflicts and the strategies they adopted.

POLDING, J.B. *The eye of faith: the pastoral letters of John Bede Polding.* Ed by G. Haines *et al.* Kilmore, Vic, Lowden, 1977. 430 p, illus.

These elegant letters reveal the bishop's concern for the life of the young country. The collection was used extensively by Frances O'Donoghue for the biography *The Bishop of Botany Bay: the life of John Bede Polding, Australia's first Catholic archbishop.* (A & R, 1982).

PREWER, B.D. *Australian prayers.* Adelaide, Lutheran Publishing House, 1983. 160 p, illus.

The author, a Uniting Church minister, offers 'the prayers of one Australian praying among other Australians'. Avoids jargon and folksy language and provides an imaginative resource for personal and congregational use.

PRYOR, R.J. *High calling, high stress, the vocational needs of ministers: an overview & bibliography.* Adelaide, Australian Association for the Study of Religions for the Commission on Continuing Education for Ministry of the Uniting Church in Australia (Synod of Vic), 1982. 126 p.

Concerned with ministry in all its aspects. Identifies and reviews themes for research. Bibliography.

REED, T.T. *Historic churches of Australia.* Melbourne, Macmillan, 1978. 150 p, illus.

A study of churches of various denominations and styles, built in the several colonies before the discovery of gold. Photography by Richard Beck.

ROE, M. *Quest for authority in eastern Australia, 1835–1851.* MUP in association with the Australian National University, 1965. 258 p, maps.

Pioneer study describing divisions within the societies of NSW and Tas over such issues as state aid and education.

ROSSITER, G.M. *Religious education in Australian schools: an overview of developments and issues in religious education in Australian schools with descriptions of practices in different school types.* Canberra, Curriculum Development Centre, 1981. 262 p, illus.

Includes resource articles from other contributors. Complementing this work is *Religious education in Australian schools: sample of individual submissions,* ed by G.M. Rossiter (Canberra, Curriculum Development Centre, 1981).

SALVADO, R. *The Salvado memoirs: historical memoirs of Australia and particularly of the Benedictine Mission of New Norcia and of the habits and customs of the Australian natives.* Trans and ed by E.J. Stormon. UWAP, 1978. 338 p, illus.

A first-hand account of the foundation of New Norcia and of the mission's approach to the Aborigines. A translation of *Memorie storiche dell' Australia* (Rome, 1851). First published in 1977.

SANTAMARIA, B.A. *Daniel Mannix: the quality of leadership.* MUP, 1984. 282 p, illus.

An appraisal of the long life of this ecclesiastical leader and controversial public figure by one who was close to him.

SCOTT, D. *The halfway house to infidelity: a history of the Melbourne Unitarian Church, 1853–1973.* Melbourne, Unitarian Fellowship of Australia and the Melbourne Unitarian Peace Memorial Church, 1980. 158 p, illus.

A history of a significant congregation whose thinking and public expression appealed to an intellectual and cultural elite.

SHAW, G.P. *Patriarch and patriot: William Grant Broughton, 1788–1853: colonial statesman and ecclesiastic.* MUP, 1978. 347 p, illus.

A study of the bishop's involvement in church–state relations and his attempts to establish the independence of the Church of England. Less emphasis on Broughton's humanity.

TABBERNEE, W. ed, *Initiation in Australian churches.* Melbourne, Victorian Council of Churches, 1984. 181 p, illus.

Essays on the different teachings and practices of Protestant, Orthodox and Catholic denominations, relating to baptism or other forms of initiation. The Council of Churches has also published *Communion in Australian churches* (1979) and *Marriage in Australian churches* (1982).

TARLING, L. *Thank God for the Salvos: the Salvation Army in Australia, 1880 to 1980.* Sydney, Harper & Row, 1980. 127 p, illus.

History featuring contemporary cartoons, rare photographs and a chart correlating Salvationist history with national events.

TULIP, M. *Women in a man's church: changes in the status of women in the Uniting Church in Australia, 1977–1983.* Sydney, Commission on the Status of Women of the Australian Council of Churches (NSW), 1983. 86 p.

Reviews the degrees of success women have had in challenging the male-dominated structures of this denomination.

TURNER, P.N. *Sinews of sectarian warfare? State aid in New South Wales, 1836–1862.* ANUP, 1972. 272 p.

Analyses the results of the 1836 Church Building Act which eroded the privileges of the Church of England and encouraged other denominations. Their attitudes to the continuance of state aid until its partial repeal in 1862 are examined.

WALDERSEE, J. *Catholic society in New South Wales, 1788–1860.* SUP, 1974. 313 p, illus, maps.

A landmark in the historiography of Catholicism, this study, based upon statistical enquiry, attacks a number of views including the image of poverty-stricken Irish Catholics.

WILLIS, S. ed, *Women, faith & fetes: essays in the history of women in the Church of Australia.* Melbourne, Dove Communications in association with the Australian Council of Churches (NSW), Commission on Status of Women, 1977. 217 p.

Essays by women on topics such as feminine leadership, the Women's Christian Temperance Union, the contributions of nuns and religious orders.

WILSON, B. *Can God survive in Australia?* Sydney, Albatross Books, 1983. 224 p.

An attempt to explain the decline of religion questions whether it is Christianity or some distortion of it that is being rejected.

WOOLMINGTON, J. ed, *Religion in early Australia: the problem of church and state.* Sydney, Cassell, 1976. 174 p.

A collection of documents relating to Anglican foundations, the growth of other denominations, their disputes and involvement in state aid, education, moral and social issues.

YARWOOD, A.T. *Samuel Marsden: the great survivor.* MUP, 1977. 341 p, illus, maps.

A biography, with a view of the contemporary scene, of the Church of England chaplain usually condemned as the 'flogging parson' and grasping farmer.

Postcard c1900. Churches are a notable feature in the Australian landscape, especially in country towns where they are often among the largest and most visible buildings. Methodist churches are usually restrained in their architecture, but this design in Mildura, with its striking polychrome brickwork, is a notable exception.
NATIONAL MUSEUM OF AUSTRALIA

A nurse from the Sydney District Nursing Association tends to the needs of an elderly patient. Photograph, 2 Feb 1949.
MAGAZINE PROMOTIONS

CHAPTER 43

WELFARE

A. GRAYCAR, M. HORSBURGH AND D. WYNDHAM

THE STUDY OF social welfare, sometimes called social policy or social administration, is a recent arrival on the academic scene. It has both depended upon and contributed to the growth of the welfare state in the period following World War II.

The earliest item in the following bibliography, C.H. Spence (1907), is specialised in its content and dependent upon a sphere of activity which gave great scope to the energies of well-placed persons. In this case the activity was the promotion of foster care as a method of welfare for dependent children. The persons active in the area were Spence herself and her mentor Caroline Emily Clark. The book owes its existence to Spence's own capacities as an author and her way of writing to advance her interests in social reform. Her autobiography (1910; facs, 1975) is also of interest.

There is then a gap to the 1930s. The works of Sawkins (1933) and Walker (1936) are both studies of particular facets of welfare: the living wage and unemployment. The 1939 contribution edited by W.G.K. Duncan is more general in its approach and has much in common with the later work of Rennison (1970), Mendelsohn (1954, 1979), Graycar (1979) and Jones (1938). The latter's opening paper by G.V. Portus foreshadows all the problems in defining the field and stresses the complex interchange between different ideological positions, actual arrangements for the delivery of services, alleged motivation for welfare activities and apparent outcomes. It is worth noting that none of the academic contributors to this book held a position specialising in social welfare as an area of study and that they made very few references to specifically Australian instances in their social welfare discussion.

In contrast with the four prewar contributions, the period after World War II reflects the growth of welfare activity itself, its increasing importance for the economy and government and the development of specialised study. The commonwealth Department of Social Services was established as a separate organisation in 1941, although its activities had begun in 1908 with the introduction of age pensions. New South Wales, the most populous state, gave separate status to its Department of Child Welfare and Social Welfare in 1946. In 1941 the Department of Social Services had an expenditure of £17 million. In 1983–84 its budget was $17 billion. In a corresponding fashion the bibliographical items show an increase in both specific and general works as Monie and Wise's comprehensive bibliography (1977) indicates. There is more interpretative material and an attempt to see Australia in an international context.

This development has been in addition to the continuation of interest in social welfare in those areas of study where it previously existed. Thus students of economics, politics, public administration and history are still active. The change has been in the growth of writing which takes from all those disciplines whatever is necessary to promote understanding of a newly defined subject. Although specifically 'social welfare' writing is a postwar phenomenon, early material may be found under other titles. Some of this writing is in the papers of individuals. The activities of the prolific John Dunmore Lang might be cited in this respect. Such material, however, can be identified only when it becomes relevant to particular research projects.

GOVERNMENT DOCUMENTS

Of substantially more importance than the papers of individuals are the many government publications which began in the colonial period. Early royal commissions are noteworthy in this respect and attention is drawn to D.H. Borchardt's *Checklist of royal commissions, select committees of parliament and boards of inquiry* which indexes the reports emanating from such public inquiries held in Australian between 1856 and 1980 (see chapter 8 of this volume). The report of the Victorian Royal Commission into Municipalities and Charities of 1862–63 exemplified many of the concerns of the nineteenth-century approach to welfare: opposition to a poor law supported by compulsory rates on property; the use of voluntary charities as a defence against pauperism, and opposition to outdoor relief.

Of considerably more substance in its theoretical content was the report of the New South Wales Royal Commission into Public Charities of 1873–74. This report, under the chairmanship of W.C. Windeyer, sought to bring the best overseas information to bear on the problems confronting local public charities, including both government and non-government operations. Nearly every major welfare development has been preceded by such an inquiry but there have also been a number of inquiries that have yielded no specific result. In this latter category are the reports of the commonwealth Royal Commission into National Insurance (1925–27) and the most recent Commission of Inquiry into Poverty, which is described in the bibliography. More successful were the inquiries that preceded the introduction of age pensions in New South Wales and Victoria and the commonwealth, and the Joint Parliamentary Committee on Social Security which sat from 1941 to 1946.

While in practical political terms it is appropriate to note the 'success' or otherwise of reports and inquiries, they also reflect the prevailing information and debate around their terms of reference. In this respect the various reports of the Commission of Inquiry into Poverty are remarkable. Apart from the main reports, which are noted in the bibliography, there are a large number of other publications resulting from specific contracted research projects.

An additional development since the early 1970s has been the internal research and development section of various government departments. Of particular importance are the Policy Co-ordination Unit in the commonwealth Department of Community Services and the Division of Research and Development in the commonwealth Department of Social Security. In addition to the work they do for internal consumption, these bodies produce material for public distribution.

The preponderance of government documents in the literature reflects an interest in administrative matters which also affects the collection of data. Statistics tend to serve administrative or political ends, a phenomenon that is probably related to the residual nature of Australian welfare. If the whole community is not the subject of the welfare effort, there is less need to have accurate information about it.

INDEPENDENT RESEARCH BODIES

Whatever its source, material written for the government has its roots in the political demand for analysis and planning. Although they may consider political or pragmatic issues, a different perspective can be provided by independent research units. Two such bodies are represented in the bibliography. The Institute of Applied Economics and Social Research at the University of Melbourne has been reponsible for the 'rediscovery' of poverty in contemporary Australia

(Henderson, 1970). It has provided a location for the development of the theoretical background to Australia's two attempts at national health insurance, Medibank in 1974 and Medicare in 1984. It continues to provide surveys of government activity in the welfare area (Scotton and Ferber, 1979–80). The Social Welfare Research Centre at the University of New South Wales is supported by a government grant. Its work is represented in the bibliography by Graycar (1983). Its wideranging studies have produced more than forty monographs in a period of four years.

In addition to their relative independence, these bodies are able to pursue studies over a long period and free from the constraints of administrative necessity.

THE NON-GOVERNMENT SECTOR

In the voluntary welfare sector, a similar but more polemic role has been played by the state councils of social services and their co-ordinating body, the Australian Council of Social Services (ACOSS). The contribution of ACOSS is represented in the bibliography by the proceedings of its third conference (Hancock, 1965). Apart from substantial documents emanating from national meetings, ACOSS publishes smaller pamphlets on current issues. It is the only general voice for the non-government welfare sector.

Also of importance here is the Brotherhood of St Laurence, an Anglican welfare agency in Melbourne. Hollingworth (1979) and Brewer (1980) show the vigour of this agency which has combined direct service with innovation and social comment in an unusual way.

It is almost impossible for a bibliography of this kind to reflect accurately the level of non-government activity in the social welfare field. Much of the literature produced by the non-government sector is ephemeral and promotional. Only rarely are more substantial items published, often in the form of an institutional history. Such histories range from serious and important works such as that of Lyons (1978) to small 'in-house' pamphlets. Professional historians are rarely invited to compile such histories although, as J.F. Watson showed in his *History of the Sydney Hospital from 1811 to 1911* (Sydney, Government Printer, 1911), quality does not always suffer if amateurs are involved.

There has always been a close relationship between the government and voluntary sectors in Australian social welfare. Originally the government depended upon the non-government sector to carry out many of its welfare responsibilities. Colonial governments heavily subsidised the non-government sector. Apart from an unwillingness to support sectarian ventures, there was no separation between the two auspices. The voluntary sector was in turn dependent upon government and expected support in its efforts. The interdependence continues and is reflected in the bibliography in contributions by M. Horsburgh in Pavlin *et al* (1980) and by I. Yates and Graycar in Graycar (1983).

Specific divisions in the non-government sector are not easily detected in the bibliography but are listed by reference to Legacy in the history by Lyons (1978) and the work of the Brotherhood of St Laurence by Carter (1967). A substantial amount of welfare activity is undertaken by groups with a religious affiliation and by organisations of returned services personnel. The former are often overlooked in an apparently secular society. There is in fact almost no literature on religion, particularly Christianity, and social welfare and only recently has there been any attempt by Christian groups to speak with a united voice on major issues. (See *Changing Australia* by the Anglican Social Responsibilities Commission *et al*, Melbourne, Dove Communications, 1983.

The reference to returned services organisations reflects the special place accorded in Australian society to these bodies. There is in fact a separate welfare system dealing with veterans' affairs and the report by Mr Justice Toose discusses the problems inherent in that administrative arrangement (Australia. Independent Inquiry into the Repatriation System, 1975). This system is represented by separate organisations in both the government and non-government areas and covers health, social security, social services and informal support. It is based on principles of compensation rather than need and has not yet been subject to detailed examination.

JOURNALS

Journals provide the major avenue for the dissemination of ideas in the social welfare field as in other disciplines and reflect the same problems as the books. There is no broadly based social welfare journal in Australia. Unsuccessful contenders for the title are also few. *Australian social work*, the organ of the Australian Association of Social Workers, is now in its 37th volume and attracts contributions from both within and without the social work profession. The *Australian journal of social issues*, established by the Department of Social Work at the University of Sydney in 1961 and published from 1970 solely by ACOSS, is more representative of the total welfare field than *Australian social work*, but both journals depend for their viability on their sponsoring organisations.

A journal which does not have such support has little chance of success. In evidence may be cited *Contemporary social work education*. This journal, established in 1977, was based primarily on the then Preston Institute of Technology in Victoria. It struggled to survive until 1983, failing ultimately because it could not attract sufficient subscriptions.

Other journals publish items of social welfare interest from particular points of view. In this area may be noted *Australian quarterly*, the *Australian & New Zealand journal of sociology*, and the various history, economics and political science journals. In 1982 there appeared a more popular publication, *Australian society*. Modelled on the British *New society*, it provides discussion on social issues from a multidisciplinary perspective. Although many of its contributors are academics, it seeks a wider, well-informed readership.

Problems of financial viability do not concern *Social security*, published by the commonwealth Department of Social Security, with contributors from within and outside the public service. Some specialised journals deal with specific areas such as child welfare and rehabilitation.

THE TEACHING OF SOCIAL WELFARE

A significant factor in the development of an Australian social welfare literature has been the demand for teaching materials; in the bibliography the works of Graycar (1979), Jones (1983) and Mendelsohn (1979) function as general introductory texts. Reports, working papers and journal articles may serve other purposes, but publications dependent upon sales which give a financial return to publishers, if not to authors, require a substantial prospective market. Students provide such a market. If this is too cynical a comment, the point may be put more gently by noting interrelationships of scholarly activity in research and teaching and the demand for adequately trained personnel in the welfare field. In the 1960s there were a small number of schools of social work in Australia, all with small enrolments. There were no institutions training welfare workers at the subprofessional level. In the 1980s there are thirteen institutions training social workers and many more at the welfare worker level.

The development of specific education and the corresponding industry for the employment of graduates have been part of the general growth of social welfare. It has both created a demand for Australian material and stimulated an interest in the production of that material. There are more students, more potential authors and there is more to study. In this context, however, it would be improper to overlook the work of Dora Peyser. Peyser, a Jewish refugee from Nazi Germany, migrated to Australia before World War II. In 1939 she published her two-part 'History of welfare work in Sydney, 1788–1900' in *J R Aust Hist Soc* (25, 2, 1939, 89–128; 25, 3, 1939, 169–212). This study, written from public documents and without access to archival material, stood for nearly thirty years.

In 1951, Peyser published *The strong and the weak* (Sydney, Currawong Publishing), a sociological study of the phenomenon of social assistance. In this work she took up the concept of social welfare as an integrating force in society and examined the social institutions which performed a welfare role. Although derived from her 1934 PhD thesis at Berlin University, this work marks the first attempt to provide an Australian social welfare text directed to the practice of social work. It was followed in 1966 by T. Brennan and N.A. Parker's *Foundations of social casework* (Sydney, Novak, 1966), but failed to generate an Australian literature on practice.

WELFARE IN LITERATURE

The bibliography contains no items of a literary nature. Where is the Australian *Oliver Twist?* A poor law, and the corresponding workhouses to terrify the indigent, have been absent from the Australian social welfare system. Large-scale events, such as the Great Depression of the 1930s, have entered the national consciousness and there are accounts of the social welfare provisions then operative. They are, however, part of the overall picture of the times, not separately identifiable. A very readable personal account can be found in chapter 9 of George Johnston's *My brother Jack* (London, Collins, 1964).

In the latter half of the nineteenth century, the boys' training ships *Vernon* and *Sobraon* were well-known features of Sydney Harbour. Similar hulks existed elsewhere. Arthur Ferres produced a sentimental short story about a delinquent boy from the *Vernon* who made good, in an 1896 children's collection entitled *His cousin the wallaby* (Melbourne, Robertson). Foster care for dependent children was a controversial issue following its introduction to the Australian colonies in the 1870s. Mrs Walter Withers published a polemical novel against it in 1907, *Dan Curnucan's charge: or, boarded out,* (Melbourne, Fraser and Jenkinson, 1911), contrasting the cruel and avaricious foster-parent with the benign security of the institution. These two are examples of works which centre on the arrangements for social welfare and their success or failure. But such works are few and most are of inferior quality.

The journalistic impressions recorded by Stanley James (1877–78; repr, 1981, 1983) about the welfare institutions in nineteenth-century Melbourne also deserve mention. A more recent autobiographical view of life in a children's institution has been provided by Bill Smith in his *Better off in a home* (Melbourne, Globe Press, 1982). However, there is no comprehensive listing of such material.

CONCLUSION

Is there a distinctive Australian social welfare literature? It would not be surprising if the answer were in the negative. Australia's social welfare system developed alongside those of other industrialised western nations. Basically it has a European tradition of government but, despite its early reputation as a leader in social welfare, it has not maintained leadership in more recent times.

There are, however, some distinctive features of Australian social welfare. As a federation Australia has divided welfare responsibilities between commonwealth and state governments. The commonwealth carries the burden of income security and provides financial resources for other programs. The states retain health, child welfare, education and correction as major responsibilities, but are dependent on commonwealth funding. Local government, in contrast to older European communities, is weak in the welfare field. There is thus a mixture of divided responsibilities and centralisation.

In the social security field, Australia is distinctive in not having chosen social insurance as the form of provision. Its social assistance scheme is unique and of long standing. The Australian community has yet to accept responsibility for the income security of all its members. The basic welfare system is residual rather than institutional, selective rather than comprehensive, but also relatively redistributional.

Australia covers a large geographical area, but has a fairly concentrated population in its southeastern corner. Many services must be delivered to small populations at a distance from major centres. Rural welfare is thus an important, if neglected aspect.

All these issues continue to make Australian social welfare distinct. The recognition of this during the postwar period has contributed to the growth of Australian social welfare literature. Much of the writing is technical, resulting from the need to describe accurately the details of the federal system. But, whether technical or analytical, there is much emphasis upon the problems of equity and efficiency. Despite this, there has been little interest in evaluation. The 1979 Baume Report (Australia. Parliament. Senate. Standing Committee on Social Welfare) was the first attempt by government to consider the issue and much interest in the area is motivated by economic rather than humanitarian concerns.

Most recently attention has been focused on the three divisions of welfare identified by Richard Titmuss in his paper, 'The social division of welfare' published in his *Essays on 'The welfare state'* (London, Allen & Unwin, 1958). Titmuss noted that the same welfare objectives may be met in different ways. Occupational welfare is delivered in association with employment; for example, paid leave during sickness. Fiscal welfare comes through the taxation system; for example, tax relief in respect of the medical costs of illness. Social welfare is delivered directly by the government; for example, sickness benefit for those whose income is interrupted by sickness. In each case, the same objective, income security during sickness, is met through a different mechanism. These mechanisms are not, however, simply alternatives. All may operate at the same time and deliver benefits of different value to different populations. The costs too may be distributed in different ways.

It is symptomatic of the development of the Australian literature that the Titmuss concept, well known since its original publication, has only recently been 'discovered' by analysts. The change is partly the result of the availability of information upon which to base more comprehensive analyses of welfare. But it is also evidence that Australian writers have begun to rise above attention to specific programs and to consider broader issues.

Some part of this development is due to the introduction of new dimensions of analysis. Consideration of social welfare in conjunction with, for example, the position of women in Australian society, as represented by Baldock and Cass (1983), demands an approach which transcends governmental, administrative or legislative divisions. Titmuss' concepts have proved to be useful in this sort of endeavour. A similar process can be observed arising from consideration of class and ethnic divisions.

It is only by the use of such conceptual tools that the basis of a genuine Australian social welfare literature can be laid. It is probably true to say that to date the most distinctly identifiable item in the literature has been the Australian welfare system itself. The writing has depended upon concepts and analytical tools shared with the rest of the developed western countries, and particularly with Great Britain and the United States of America.

AITKEN-SWAN, J. *Widows in Australia: a survey of the economic and social conditions of widows with dependent children.* Sydney, Council of Social Service of NSW in association with ACOSS, 1962. 148 p, illus, map.

Results of a survey taken in Sydney and two country towns are described in detail with an examination of the financial assistance provided by federal and state governments and voluntary organisations.

AUSTRALIA. Commission of Inquiry into Poverty. *Reports* ... AGPS, 1975–76. 5 vols.

The National Commission of Inquiry into Poverty was established in 1972 under the general chairmanship of Professor Ronald F. Henderson to investigate the level, extent, incidence, locality and causes of poverty in Australia, existing services and changes which would contribute to the reduction of poverty. Its four main reports, together with about fifty volumes of case studies and supplementary material, constitute the most far reaching examination to date of Australian social conditions and have profoundly affected government planning. The many recommendations are based on the consideration that help should be given first to the poorest by providing income, and that community and welfare services should be reformed.

The four reports (numbered 1–3, 5) have different titles and editors and each concentrates on a specific aspect of the inquiry. 1st report: *Poverty in Australia*, by R.F. Henderson (2 vols); 2nd report: *Law and poverty in Australia*, by R. Sackville; 3rd report: *Social/medical aspects of poverty in Australia*, by G.S. Martin; 5th report: *Poverty and education in Australia*, by R.T. Fitzgerald. There was no 4th report.

AUSTRALIA. Independent Inquiry into the Repatriation System. *Report, by Mr Justice P.B. Toose.* AGPS, 1975. 3 vols.

Reviews the health and welfare services provided for war veterans. Recommends a more extensive interrelationship between veterans' and general community services.

AUSTRALIA. Parliament. Senate. Standing Committee on Social Welfare. *Through a glass darkly: evaluation in Australian health and welfare services.* AGPS, 1979. 143 p.

The report examines welfare programs in Australia and found that their objectives were poorly stated and evaluation inadequate. Chairman: Peter Baume.

BALDOCK, C.V. AND CASS, B. eds, *Women, social welfare and the state in Australia.* Sydney, Allen & Unwin, 1983. 333 p.

Papers review from a sociological and feminist viewpoint women's position in the Australian welfare state, exploring the causes that reinforce women's dependent and subordinate position.

BOLTON, B. *Booth's drum: the Salvation Army in Australia, 1880–1980.* Sydney, Hodder and Stoughton, 1980. 287 p, illus.

The Salvation Army began in Australia in 1880. This account, produced for its centenary, includes material on the development of the Army's various welfare activities.

BREWER, G.F. *On the bread line: oral records of poverty.* Melbourne, Hyland House, 1980. 178 p, illus.

Compiled for the Brotherhood of St Laurence, this collection of 21 interviews gives detailed accounts of life in poverty. Includes an introductory commentary and appendix of indicators of poverty.

BROWN, J.C. *'Poverty is not a crime': the development of social services in Tasmania, 1803–1900.* Hobart, Tas Historical Research Association, 1972. 192 p, illus.

This historical study describes the government and voluntary services provided for the destitute, aged and chronically sick.

BURNS, A. *et al, Children and families in Australia: contemporary issues and problems.* Sydney, Allen & Unwin, 1979. 255 p.

Psychological perspectives on violence against children, migrant children, diversity of parental care, television viewing, custody, adoption and child welfare legislation.

CARTER, I.R. *God and three shillings: the story of the Brotherhood of St Laurence.* Melbourne, Lansdowne, 1967. 173 p, illus.

Traces the Brotherhood of St Laurence from its origins in a religious order established in Newcastle, NSW, by Father Gerard Tucker in 1930.

CARTER, J. *Nothing to spare: recollections of Australian pioneering women.* Ringwood, Vic, Penguin, 1981. 237 p, illus, map.

Interviews with fifteen women, who recall their young days from around 1890 to 1918. Gives a fascinating insight into how these women managed in difficult times.

CHILDREN *Australia.* Sydney, Allen & Unwin in association with the Morialta Trust of SA, 1980. 282 p.

Multidisciplinary contribution towards understanding some of the current controversies over policies and provision for children, particularly in the areas of health, education and law.

DICKEY, B. *No charity there: a short history of social welfare in Australia.* Melbourne, Nelson, 1980. 252 p, illus.

This selective historical analysis of Australian social welfare from 1788 to 1980 is a good introduction for general readers.

DIXON, J.E. *Australia's policy towards the aged: 1890–1972.* Canberra, Canberra College of Advanced Education, 1977. 185 p. (Canberra series in administrative studies, 3).

Examines the origins and development of Australian age pension schemes and the shift in responsibility from family to government for services to the aged.

DUNCAN, W.G.K. ed, *Social services in Australia.* A & R in conjunction with Australian Institute of Political Science, 1939. 212 p.

The views of prominent academics, politicians and bureaucrats about national insurance, education and health. The papers were presented at the 7th Summer School of the institute held in Canberra.

GANDEVIA, B. *Tears often shed: child health and welfare in Australia from 1788,* Sydney, Pergamon, 1978. 151 p, illus.

A medical historian's account of child health from colonial times and the development of paediatrics and children's hospitals and welfare institutions.

GRAYCAR, A. *Welfare politics in Australia: a study in policy analysis.* Melbourne, Macmillan, 1979. 231 p.

Analyses conflicting arguments about appropriate levels of welfare allocations and examines the political, theoretical and operational issues involved in developing a social policy.

GRAYCAR, A. ed, *Retreat from the welfare state: Australian social policy in the 1980's.* Sydney, Allen & Unwin, 1983. 206 p.

Examines aspects of fiscal, occupational and social welfare in a time of economic recession and retreat from welfare state principles and practices.

HANCOCK, K.J. ed, *The national income and social welfare.* Melbourne, Cheshire for ACOSS, 1965. 171 p.

Papers by senior government servants and academics breaking new ground in their examination of the impact of economic and demographic changes on the provision of social welfare services in Australia.

HENDERSON, R.F. ed, *The welfare stakes: strategies for Australian social policy.* Melbourne, Institute of Applied Economics and Social Research, University of Melbourne, 1981. 256 p.

New ideas on poverty, income maintenance and welfare. The contributors question whether we can have a 'welfare state' without first achieving 'a welfare society'.

HENDERSON, R.F. *et al, People in poverty: a Melbourne survey.* Melbourne, Cheshire for the Institute of Applied Economic and Social Research, University of Melbourne, 1975. 226 p.

Important pioneering survey of poverty in Melbourne in 1966 which acted as a stimulus for the setting up of the National Commission of Inquiry into Poverty in 1972. Defines poverty and the poverty line. First published in 1970.

HOLLINGWORTH, P.J. *Australians in poverty.* Melbourne, Nelson, 1979. 166 p, illus.

Uncovers the many ways in which poverty has profoundly destructive effects on people's lives and explains the causes of poverty in structural terms.

HUTCHINSON, B. *Old people in a modern Australian community: a social survey.* MUP, 1954. 180 p, illus.

This investigation is the first of its kind in Australia; it found that elderly people were deprived in terms of income, material conditions, social amenities, access to health care, employment and housing.

JAMES, J.S. *The vagabond papers.* Ed by M. Cannon. Melbourne, Hyland House, 1983. 274 p, illus.

A series of sketches originally published in the Melbourne *Argus* and then in book form in 1877–78 which includes descriptions of the major welfare institutions in Melbourne. This edition first published in 1969.

JONES, M.A. *The Australian welfare state: growth, crisis and change.* Sydney, Allen & Unwin, 1983. 355 p.

Focuses on the five most important elements in the welfare state: social security, employment, housing, health and the personal care services. First published in 1980.

KENNEDY, R. ed, *Australian welfare history: critical essays.* Melbourne, Macmillan, 1982. 322 p.

These radical appraisals of early Australian welfare are of general interest. Women's role as benefactors and recipients of charity is well documented.

KEWLEY, T.H. *Australian social security today: major developments from 1900 to 1978.* SUP, 1979. 233 p.

Primarily concerned with social security and allied measures provided directly or substantially financed by the commonwealth government, this study updates *Social security in Australia 1900–72.*

KEWLEY, T.H. *Australia's welfare state: the development of social security benefits.* Melbourne, Macmillan, 1969. 122 p, illus.

A combination of original documents and commentary which provides a critical but brief account of the growth of Australia's social welfare policy and social services.

KEWLEY, T.H. *Social security in Australia, 1900–72.* SUP, 1973. 586 p.

This historical study, based on archival material, traces the origins and development of health and social security benefits. A standard work. First published in 1965 as *Social security in Australia: the development of social security and health benefits from 1900 to the present*.

KRISTIANSON, G.L. *The politics of patriotism: the pressure group activities of the Returned Servicemen's League*. ANUP, 1966. xxx, 286 p, illus.

An analysis of the origins and influence of the major Australian veteran's organisation. The RSL has been influential in securing services for the health and welfare of returned service personnel.

LAWRENCE, R.J. *Professional social work in Australia*. Canberra, Australian National University, 1965. 241 p.

Historical survey of the origins and development of the profession of social work from around 1920 to 1960, particularly social work education.

LYONS, M. *Legacy: the first fifty years*. Melbourne, Lothian for Legacy Co-ordinating Council, 1978. 283 p, illus.

Critically traces the service organisation's origins in 1923 and its history as a group of ex-service people providing assistance to war widows and children.

MENDELSOHN, R. *The condition of the people: social welfare in Australia, 1900–1975*. Sydney, Allen & Unwin, 1979. 408 p.

Examines a wide range of economic and social welfare issues including health, housing and education.

MENDELSOHN, R. *Social security in the British Commonwealth: Great Britain, Canada, Australia, New Zealand*. London, University of London, Athlone Press, 1954. 390 p.

Describes the development of social security in each of the countries to 1950, followed by a comparison of particular facets of the systems.

MONIE, J. AND WISE, A. *Social policy and its administration: a survey of the Australian literature, 1950–1975*. Sydney, Pergamon, 1977. 594 p.

An annotated bibliography divided into a number of categories. Particularly strong in references to government publications.

PAVLIN, F. *et al*, *Perspectives in Australian social work*. Melbourne, PIT Publishing, 1980. 207 p.

Considers diverse theoretical and practical aspects of social work teaching, training and practice.

PICTON, C. AND BOSS, P. *Child welfare in Australia: an introduction*. Sydney, Harcourt Brace Jovanovich, 1981. 162 p.

Describes the fragmented nature of child welfare practices and policies and suggests ways of achieving an integrated system.

RENNISON, G.A. *We live among strangers: a sociology of the welfare state*. MUP, 1970. 206 p.

This is one of the earliest attempts to interpret Australia's welfare state, with a sociological analysis of collectivism and individualism, the family, housing and health care.

ROE, J.I. ed, *Social policy in Australia: some perspectives, 1901–1975*. Melbourne, Cassell, 1976. 341 p.

Papers showing the decline in the application of social policy in Australia.

SAUNDERS, P. *Equity and the impact on families of the Australian tax-transfer system*. Melbourne, Institute of Family Studies, 1982. xiii, 116 p, illus. (Institute of Family Studies monograph, 2).

The findings of this study are that between 1961 and 1981 families with children suffered increasingly under taxation and social security arrangements.

SAWKINS, D.T. *The living wage in Australia*. MUP, 1933. 64 p.

Two unemployed men jump a train during the Great Depression in their search for work. Large quantities of wheat had to be dumped after being fouled by such 'hitchhikers'.
FAIRFAX PHOTO LIBRARY

A publication of historical importance which briefly traces the origins of Mr Justice Higgins's 'Harvester' judgment in 1907 and other living wage judgments until 1927.

SCOTTON, R.B. AND FERBER, H. *Public expenditures and social policy in Australia.* Melbourne, Longman Cheshire for the Institute of Applied Economic and Social Research, University of Melbourne, 1979–80. 2 vols.

Staid but informative papers which probe the weaknesses of Australian social policy from 1972 to 1978. Concludes with a detailed diary of legislative and administrative changes.

SPENCE, C.H. *State children in Australia: a history of boarding out and its developments.* Adelaide, Vardon and Sons, 1907. 147 p, illus.

The history of the State Children's Council of SA describes state-supported fostering and residential care of children from 1883.

SPENCE, C.H. *An autobiography.* Adelaide, LBSA, 1975. 101 p, illus.

Although dealing mainly with this remarkable women's literary and political activities, there are several chapters devoted to her social welfare work. Facsimile edition.

STUBBS, J. *The hidden people: poverty in Australia.* Melbourne, Cheshire-Lansdowne, 1966. 145 p.

A compelling narrative which draws from many not generally available investigations of property to paint a bleak picture of the inadequate government social service provisions at that time.

SYDNEY LABOUR HISTORY GROUP. *What rough beast? The state and social order in Australian history.* Sydney, Allen & Unwin, 1982. 282 p, illus.

These essays consider the part played by the state in such issues as abortion, infanticide, desertion, mental illness and sexuality. Concentrates mostly on NSW from 1840 to 1940.

TIERNEY, L. *Children who need help: a study of child welfare policy and administration in Victoria.* MUP, 1963. 127 p.

The result of a survey of 4242 children in substitute care. Examined the needs of these children and their families and the adequacy of welfare agencies.

TULLOCH, P. *Poor policies: Australian income security, 1972–77.* London, Croom Helm, 1979. 191 p.

This sociological analysis is critical of the failure of either Liberal or Labor governments to reduce poverty and inequality.

WALKER, E.R. *Unemployment policy, with special reference to Australia.* A & R, 1936. 258 p.

An economic study examining unemployment in some European countries and Australia during the depression. Explores some of the government responses in attempting to reduce unemployment and assist those affected.

WARE, H.R.E. ed, *Fertility and family formation: Australasian bibliography and essays, 1972.* Canberra, Dept of Demography, Institute of Advanced Studies, Australian National University, 1973. 358 p.

A comprehensive bibliography with a review essay by the editor of 'Fertility studies in Australia and New Zealand'. The books and journal articles are arranged under subject fields.

The Natural Disasters Organisation is the nationwide co-ordinator of measures to combat natural disasters such as cyclones, floods and bushfires, and to provide immediate relief for those left homeless by such disasters.
MAGAZINE PROMOTIONS

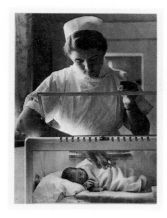

Max Dupain, Humidicrib, *c1952. Gelatin silver photograph.*
AUSTRALIAN NATIONAL GALLERY

CHAPTER 44

MEDICINE AND HEALTH

B. GANDEVIA

THE PREPARATION of a representative bibliography of medicine and health, even if restricted to one country or society, is necessarily a complex task because these two subjects embrace an enormous range of human activity. The reciprocal relationship between health and disease is an index of a society's adaptation to its physical and socioeconomic environment, and the factors that influence the balance between physical and psychological health and ill-health make up a very considerable component of what is often termed social history. There are thus problems in defining the scope of the following bibliography and many items which might have been included here will be found in other chapters of this volume, such as 'Welfare' (chapter 43), 'Domestic life' (chapter 40), 'Aborigines' (chapter 14 and 15) and in the overviews included in 'Social history' (chapter 38).

Furthermore, each of the states has its own independent history of medicine, influenced by Federation only in certain areas from about 1920. The colonies were founded at different times with different populations, economic and occupational bases in widely different geographic and climatic environments; their growth rates also varied. The differences lessened with changing demographic patterns (notably in regard to age and sex distribution and population density), economic and industrial development and a reduction in the isolation of remote areas. Before the early decades of this century the differences are reflected in morbidity and mortality data as well as in differences in legislation relating to health. Similarities were present also, particularly if allowance is made for the various stages of development.

Just as each colony had its own medical history, each state has tended to have its own medical historians. Mostly medically qualified 'amateurs', they understandably and appropriately restricted the scope of their studies. Social histories in more recent years have taken a broader view, particularly when dealing with the twentieth century where the similarities perhaps outweigh the differences. Although there are exceptions to both these generalisations, the fact remains that few studies of medical and health topics relate to the whole of Australia from its earliest settlement; the formidable but rewarding task of critically evaluating these differences and similarities has yet to be undertaken. There is, unfortunately, not even a conventional history of medicine in Australia which might at least provide a sound technical basis for historians with a wider perspective. A corollary to all these observations is that most of the reference material is to be found in journals rather than books.

The present literature survey is thus highly selective, and often only examples of a certain type of study have been cited. To make this clear, to indicate the full scope of material which the reader might wish to consult, and because a simple alphabetical listing proved incongruous by juxtaposing items on widely disparate subjects, it was found preferable to list items in seventeen broad catagories as follows:

From 1788 to 1900
Public health and administration
Specific diseases and problems
Aerial medical services
Specialised aspects of medicine
Birth control and population growth
Research and research institutions
Popular and folk medicine
Biography and autobiography
Military medicine
Medicine and health through 100 years
Contemporary health care
Dentistry
Nursing
Pharmacy
Bibliographies
Reference works

This approach also permits the annotations to comment on the literature of the subject rather than on the content of an individual item which might have been selected from many others on rather arbitrary grounds and which, in many cases, is adequately described by title. The selection criteria are not easily specified; attention was paid to quality and effective documentation and reference as much as to content or viewpoint, and some attempt has been made to make the bibliography representative of different periods and different colonies.

The choice of items for the sections on nursing, dentistry and pharmacy posed additional problems in that very little attention has been paid to these subjects on a national basis or in terms of their social context.

The peculiar fascination of the first century or more of Australian medicine is its reflection of the adaptation of an essentially European society to a wholly different physical, social and demographic environment. This interaction was reflected not only in the diseases encountered and the ways in which they manifested themselves but also in the manner of medical practice and the nature of its practitioners, as well as the relationship of both to community needs. The Europeans' way of life, and especially their occupation of land, as much as their diseases, had a major impact on Aboriginal morbidity, mortality and welfare, initiating a major population decline which has been arrested only in recent years; this question is more fully examined in section IV of this volume.

Although the surgeons White, Bowes and Worgan accompanying the first fleet contributed significantly to the literature of the first settlement, their accounts contain little more information of a medical kind than is to be found in Collins or even Tench. Details of their journals are given in chapter 22 on the 'First European settlements'. Thereafter there is a relative dearth of medical sources, official or otherwise, until towards the middle of the nineteenth century. Archival sources, for practical purposes, emerge with the independence of the several colonies, although some penal records of medical interest exist, notably in Tasmania and Western Australia. Practitioners in medicine, like their colleagues in art and literature, took some decades to adapt to the Australian environment and to accept it as 'home'. This acceptance is reflected in the establishment of medical journals and societies from the late 1850s. Both also served to enhance the status and influence of the profession, significant ever since the beneficial effects of appropriate medical care and shipboard hygiene had been demonstrated early in the penal era.

As the independent colonies began to mature, in a social and legislative sense, and especially in the last quarter of the nineteenth century and the first decade or so of the twentieth, an increasing interest in public health and welfare became manifest. In part this was a reflection of developments in the 'Old Country', but it was also a reflection of local problems, varying in character and severity from one state to another and perhaps stimulated in some cases by the economic recession of the 1890s. Local problems of sanitation and water supply were rendered urgent by the high prevalence of gastrointestinal disorders in children and typhoid fever in adults. The frequency of psychiatric disorders from a variety of causes aroused considerable concern, and questions were raised about their institutional management. Mining accidents and working conditions in factories and shops demanded investigation, as did problems of poverty associated especially with a shift of the population to the cities. The decline in the birth rate, from a high level after the gold rush, evoked alarm over the health status of potential mothers as well as the use of contraception.

These matters were subject to governmental inquiries or royal commissions too numerous to list here, but invaluable in providing anecdotal, and sometimes objective and statistical, information about conditions at that period. An index to those can be found in the *Checklist of royal commissions, select committees of parliament and boards of inquiry* compiled by D.H. Borchardt *et al* (see chapter 8). Health departments and their precursors (often 'Boards of Health') have produced annual reports for a century or more.

Federation did not immediately affect state independence on health matters, except quarantine, but the influence of the commonwealth extended progressively, and eventually rapidly, from the 1920s. Today its role, through its financial control, is paramount in the provision of hospital care and medical services. The vacillations of various federal governments have produced an unprecedented and regrettable instability in the administration of medical care in the past two decades.

Australian medical literature developed slowly from the first journals and separate publications in the mid-nineteenth century (see Ford, 1976), but rapidly after World War II. There are now not only general medical journals, sponsored in various ways, but also a wide range of specialist journals publishing material of international standard. Scientific monographs and student textbooks are now frequently produced locally although, for reasons of wider distribution, a publisher with international connections is often selected, especially if there exists a local branch of a large international publishing house.

My thanks are due to Alison Holster, Librarian, History of Medicine Library, Royal Australasian College of Physicians, for her assistance in the preparation of this bibliography.

Sydney Mail, 12 Feb 1919. Influenza was brought to Australia by troops returning from Europe at the end of World War I. It quickly became an epidemic. In an attempt to control the spread of the virus, governments banned mass spectator sports and insisted that masks be worn in public to minimise the risk of infection. These youngsters are on their way to a church in Melbourne which urged parishioners to 'Obey the law' and 'wear masks while in Church'. Newspaper pictures like this can provide a great deal of information to historians.

FROM 1788 TO 1900

BATESON, C. *The convict ships 1787–1868*. Sydney, Library of Australian History, 1983. 434 p, illus.
First published in 1959.

BOWDEN, K.M. *Doctors and diggers on the Mount Alexander goldfields*. Maryborough, Vic, The Author, 1974. 215 p, illus, map.

BROWN, K.S.M. *Medical practice in old Parramatta: a historical review of village doctoring in the colony of New South Wales*. A & R, 1937. 136 p, illus.

GANDEVIA, B. 'The medico-historical significance of young and developing countries, illustrated by Australian experience', in E. Clarke, ed, *Modern methods in the history of medicine*. London, Athlone Press, 1971, 75–98.

GANDEVIA, B. 'Socio-medical factors in the evolution of the first settlement at Sydney Cove 1788–1803', *J R Aust Hist Soc* 61, 1, 1975, 1–25.

GORDON, D. '"The waiting years": 1842–1959', *Medical J of Australia* 1, 1966, 249–53, 288–90, 336–40.

MORGAN, E.S. *A short history of medical women in Australia*. Melbourne, Burroughs Wellcome and Co for the Australian Federation of Medical Women, 1970. 56 p, illus.

NEVE, M.H. *'This mad folly!' The history of Australia's pioneer women doctors*. Sydney, Library of Australian History, 1980. 174 p, illus.

PEARN, H.J. AND O'CARRIGAN, C. eds, *Australia's quest for colonial health: some influences on early health and medicine in Australia*. Brisbane, Dept of Child Health, Royal Children's Hospital, 1983. 318 p, illus.

PENSABENE, T.S. *The rise of the medical practitioner in Victoria*. Canberra, Australian National University, 1980. 219 p, illus. (Health Research Project. Research monograph, 2.)
Gandevia's paper (1971) is a suitable introduction to this whole chapter because it aims not only to relate Australian physical and social environments to the pattern of disease and the evolution of medical practice, mainly in the nineteenth century, but also to define a possible role for the study of Australian medical history within the history of medicine generally. Although more detailed studies are available in relation to overall mortality and individual voyages, Bateson's (1969) general review of the convict migration is excellent, especially in relation to medical administrative aspects. Gandevia (1975) and Gordon (1966) examine the medical history of two settlements in their early phases. Macarthur Brown (1937) is a reliable account of medical practice in what was initially a rural area in 1789 up to about the turn of the century. Bowden (1974) is the most detailed survey of medical practice during a unique era in colonial development; in a later work he dealt with medical practice in Ballarat (*Goldrush doctors at Ballarat*, Melbourne, The Author, 1977). Pensabene (1980) usefully reviews medical and non-medical literature in an evaluation of the changing status of the medical practitioner, although some of his observations and the addendum on a later period must be treated with reserve. In this context, see also the article by David G. Green 'Primary medical care and the friendly societies in nineteenth and early twentieth century Victoria' in *J R Aust Hist Soc* (69, 4, 1984, 263–73). Women entered medicine towards the end of the nineteenth century, and Morgan (1970) and Neve (1980) are general surveys of their activities; more detailed information is available in individual papers and biographies.

PUBLIC HEALTH AND ADMINISTRATION

CILENTO, R.W. 'Medicine in Queensland', *J of the Royal Historical Society of Queensland* 6, 4, 1961–62, 866–941.

CUMMINS, C.J. *A history of medical administration in New South Wales 1788–1973*. Sydney, Health Commission of NSW, 1979. 223 p.

CUMPSTON, J.H.L. *The health of the people: a study in federalism*. Canberra, Roebuck, 1978. 148 p, illus.

CUMPSTON, J.H.L. 'Public health in Australia: the first forty-two years; the second period, 1830–1850; developments after 1850', *Medical J of Australia* 1931, 1, 491–500, 591–97, 679–865.

CUMPSTON, J.H.L. *Quarantine: Australian maritime quarantine and the evolution of international agreements concerning quarantine*. Melbourne, Government Printer, 1913. 14 p.

SNOW, D.J.R. *The progress of public health in Western Australia, 1829–1977*. Perth, Public Health Dept, 1981. 185 p, illus, map.
The reviews by Cummins (1979) and by Cumpston (1931) are complementary; the former depicts medical administration in a single colony and state over an extensive period, while the latter deals in greater detail with the more medical aspects over a limited period. The items by Snow (1981) and Cilento (1961–62) are included to illustrate development in different colonies with different problems; Qld developed a hospital care system then unique in Australia. Cumpston's (1978) survey was written many years before it was published posthumously, but the reflections of a man who exercised a remarkable influence on many aspects of public health during his long career are of more than historical interest. This book includes Michael Roe's history of the Australian Department of Health, first published in *Hist stud* (17, 67, 1976, 176–92), and serves to place Cumpston's contribution in some perspective. Cumpston (1913) on quarantine is included because of its special interest in relation to the medical history of an isolated continent, although its influence on disease in Australia is examined in more detail in papers included in the following section. The most important account of government intervention in health care is Claudia Thame's PhD thesis (ANU 1974) 'Health and the State' which traces the development of collective responsibility for health in the commonwealth and in the states from 1900 to 1950.

SPECIFIC DISEASES AND PROBLEMS

CAMPBELL, W.A. 'The use and abuse of stimulants in the early days of settlement in New South Wales, with reference to the historical ti plant and the Australian tea trees', *J and proceedings of the Royal Australian Historical Society* 18, 1, 1932, 74–9.

CUMPSTON, J.H.L. *The history of diphtheria, scarlet fever, measles and whooping cough in Australia 1788–1925*. Canberra, Government Printer, 1927. 617 p. (Australia. Department of Health. Service publication, 37.)

CUMPSTON, J.H.L. *The history of smallpox in Australia, 1788–1908*. Melbourne, Government Printer, 1914. 182 p, maps. (Australia. Quarantine Service. Publication, 3.)

CUMPSTON, J.H.L. AND McCALLUM, F. *The history of intestinal infections and typhus fever in Australia, 1788–1923*. Melbourne, Government Printer, 1927. 738 p. (Australia. Department of Health. Service publication, 36.)

CUMPSTON, J.H.L. AND McCALLUM, F. *The history of plague in Australia, 1900–1925*. Melbourne, Government Printer, 1926. 238 p, maps. (Australia. Department of Health. Service publication, 32).

CUMPSTON, J.H.L. AND McCALLUM, F. *The history of smallpox in Australia, 1909–1923*. Melbourne, Government Printer, 1925. 243 p. (Australia. Department of Health. Service publication, 29.)

DINGLE, A.E. '"The truly magnificent thirst": an historical survey of Australian drinking habits', *Hist stud* 19, 75, 1980, 227–49.

FORBES, J.A. 'Rubella: historical aspects', *American J of diseases of children* 118, 1, 1969, 5–11.

WALKER, R.B. 'Tobacco smoking in Australia, 1788–1914' *Hist stud* 19, 75, 1980, 267–85.

Plague has a relatively short history in Australia but it had a radical impact on the redevelopment of historic areas of Sydney. The histories of smallpox, the intestinal infections and the formerly common infectious diseases of childhood are among the most comprehensive medicohistorical studies made in this country. Although much of the approach is technical, each contains an extensive bibliography with meticulous attention to non-medical sources, especially for the nineteenth century. The paper on rubella is included because Australian contributions showed that rubella in pregnancy might cause a variety of congenital defects. Alcoholism and tobacco smoking are common in Australian society.

AERIAL MEDICAL SERVICE

BILTON, J. *The Royal Flying Doctor Service of Australia: its origin, growth and development.* Ed by J. Macdonald Holmes. Sydney, Royal Flying Doctor Service of Australia Federal Council, 1961. 257 p, illus, map.

HILL, E. *Flying doctor calling: the Flying Doctor Service of Australia.* A & R, 1947. 156 p, illus, map.

Aerial medical services were an original Australian development, and there is quite an extensive range of publications on this theme.

SPECIALISED ASPECTS OF MEDICINE

BOSTOCK, J. *The dawn of Australian psychiatry: an account of the measures taken for the care of mental invalids from the time of the first fleet, 1788 to the year 1850, including a survey of the overseas background and the casenotes of Dr F. Campbell.* Sydney, Australian Medical Association, 1968. 219 p, illus. Originally issued as duplicated typescript in 1951.

BROTHERS, C.R.D. *Early Victorian psychiatry 1835–1905.* Melbourne, Government Printer, 1962. 254 p, illus, maps.

DAX, E.C. *Asylum to community: the development of the mental hygiene service in Victoria, Australia.* Melbourne, Cheshire, 1961. 230 p, illus, maps.

GANDEVIA, B. 'Annual post-graduate oration: occupation and disease in Australia since 1788', *Bulletin of the Post-graduate Committee in Medicine, University of Sydney* 27, 1971–72, 157–228.

GANDEVIA, B. *Tears often shed: child health and welfare in Australia from 1788.* With the research assistance of Sheila Simpson. Sydney, Pergamon, 1978. 151 p, illus.

The items listed in this section are highly selective. There have been numerous publications, usually in journal form, dealing with a wide range of specialties in medicine, particularly surveys related to technical advances, educational developments and institutional or organisational histories. Those primarily of professional interest have been omitted. However, the history of psychiatry and of the medical and institutional management of mental disease are of contemporary interest and have been well documented. Similarly, the studies on paediatrics and occupational health are included because they attempt to link these problems with sociohistorical issues and thereby gain greater interest outside the purely technical aspects of their subject matter. The last mentioned offers an extensive bibliography.

BIRTH CONTROL AND POPULATION GROWTH

CALDWELL, J.C. AND WARE, H. 'The evolution of family planning in Australia', *Population studies* 27, 1, 1973, 7–31.

HICKS, N. *This sin and scandal: Australia's population debate 1891–1911.* ANUP, 1978. 208 p, illus.

This section should be considered in conjunction with other chapters in this volume, notably chapter 39 on 'Immigration and demography'. The problems of birth control and population growth occupied the minds of many authorities, particularly at the turn of the century.

RESEARCH AND RESEARCH INSTITUTIONS

BURNET, F.M. *Walter and Eliza Hall Institute, 1915–1965.* MUP, 1971. 193 p, illus.

DOCTORS and Australian science: an exhibition ... Sydney, Royal Australasian College of Physicians Library, 1980. 40 p.

DOHERTY, R.L. 'The Bancroft tradition in infectious disease research in Queensland', *Medical J of Australia* 1978, 2, 12, 560–3; 1978, 2, 13, 591–4.

FENNER, F.J. 'The history of the John Curtin School of Medical Research, a centre for research and postgraduate education in the basic medical sciences', *Medical J of Australia* 2, 4, 1971, 177–86.

GORDON-TAYLOR, G. 'The debt of surgical science to Australia', *Australian and New Zealand J of surgery* 17, 2, 1947, 75–111.

INGLIS, K.S. *Hospital and community: a history of the Royal Melbourne Hospital.* MUP, 1958. 226 p, illus.

KRUPINSKI, J. et al, *The history and achievements of the Mental Health Research Institute, 1956–1981.* Melbourne, Mental Health Research Institute, Health Commission of Vic, 1981. 224 p, illus.

RUSSELL, K.F. *The Melbourne Medical School 1862–1962.* MUP, 1977. 277 p, illus.

UNIVERSITY OF SYDNEY. School of Public Health and Tropical Medicine. *School of Public Health and Tropical Medicine, 1930–1980.* Sydney, The School, 1980. 179 p, illus.

This section is intended to be representative of as wide a field as possible within a limited scope. Gordon-Taylor, a distinguished British surgeon, provides a review (1947–48) more wideranging than its title might suggest, while Doherty's (1978) paper deals with particularly important problems in the settlement of tropical areas. The contribution of doctors to relatively 'pure' science is reflected in the publication from the History of Medicine Library of the Royal Australasian College of Physicians (1980). The remainder is a select series of publications concerned with the history of individual organisations. Russell (1977) on the medical school at Melbourne University is a comprehensive and meticulously documented history; lesser histories are available related to most other medical schools. Medical research has not been a feature of Australian hospitals, except insofar as university departments and the efforts of individuals are concerned, but Inglis (1958) is included because it attempts to place a hospital in its social setting. Burnet (1971) is exceptional in that the book represents the reflections of an eminent scientist who was also the director of an organisation which achieved the highest international standing. The John Curtin School of Medical Research has a unique background in Australian medicine, in that it was established in a university solely as a research centre, with no undergraduate responsibilities, and achieved similar academic renown.

POPULAR AND FOLK MEDICINE

CRIBB, A.B. AND CRIBB, J.W. *Wild medicine in Australia.* Sydney, Collins, 1981. 228 p, illus.

HAGGER, J. *Australian colonial medicine.* Adelaide, Rigby, 1979. 219 p, illus.

PHILLIPS, P.J. *Kill or cure? Lotions, potions, characters and quacks of early Australia.* Adelaide, Rigby, 1978. 157 p, illus.

These three works are different in their scope. Hagger (1979) reviews remedies, including Aboriginal medicine, for a range of common complaints, while Phillips (1978) looks particularly at popular remedies and quackery. Cribb and Cribb (1981) is an invaluable reference work for botanical remedies, classified, as far as possible, by their traditional origin.

BIOGRAPHY AND AUTOBIOGRAPHY

BICKEL, L. *Rise up to life: a biography of Howard Walter Florey who gave penicillin to the world.* London, A & R, 1972. 314 p, illus.

BROWNE, D.D. *The wind and the book: memoirs of a country doctor.* MUP, 1976. 161 p.

BURNET, F.M. *Changing patterns: an atypical autobiography.* Melbourne, Heinemann, 1968. 282 p, illus.

GILLISON, J.M. *Colonial doctor and his town.* Melbourne, Cypress Books, 1974. 292 p, illus, map.

MORAN, H.M. *Viewless winds, being the recollections and digressions of an Australian surgeon.* London, Peter Davies, 1939. 352 p.

Despite a considerable number of examples, outstanding biographies and autobiographies of Australian doctors are lacking. Browne (1976) and Gillison (1974) perhaps best reflect general practice, while Moran's (1939) work covers a wider field with a background of broader medical experience. The biography of Florey and the autobiography of Burnet are selected to reflect the lives of two Australian doctors who achieved international eminence.

MILITARY MEDICINE

BARTON, G.B. *et al, The story of South Africa.* Vol 2. *An account of the despatch of contingents from Australia and New Zealand and their exploits on the battle fields.* Sydney, World Publishing Co, 1900[?]. 498 p, illus, maps.

BUTLER, A.G. ed, *The Australian army medical services in the war of 1914–1918.* Canberra, Australian War Memorial, 1930–43. 3 vols, illus, maps.

GURNER, J. *The origins of the Royal Australian Army Medical Corps.* Melbourne, Hawthorn, 1970. 66 p, illus.

McINTOSH, A.M. 'Army medical services in New South Wales prior to Federation', *Medical J of Australia* 1, 1948, 485–92.

WALKER, A.S. *Australia in the war of 1939–1945.* Series 5 (medical). Canberra, Australian War Memorial, 1952–61. 4 vols, illus.

These are the medical volumes of the official war history.

Australia as a nation takes pride and a measure of its nationhood from its military achievements in World War I, but the genesis of this tradition may be seen in the South African War. This is true of the medical services, although the fact that there was no great background of training or experience before either of these wars is revealed, at least as far as NSW is concerned, by McIntosh's paper. The medical histories of World War I and World War II (Butler, 1930–43, and Walker, 1952–61) are detailed and closely related to the individual campaigns, and they also provide information on relevant medical research. The subsidiary literature is extensive, and the archival resources of the Australian War Memorial deserve emphasis.

MEDICINE AND HEALTH THROUGH 100 YEARS

GORDON, D. *Health, sickness and society: theoretical concepts in social and preventive medicine.* UQP, 1976. 954 p, illus.

HETZEL, B.S. *Health and Australian society.* Ringwood, Vic, Penguin, 1980. 314 p, illus.
First published in 1974.

SPRINGTHORPE, J.W. *Therapeutics, dietetics and hygiene: an Australian textbook.* Melbourne, James Little, 1914. 2 vols, illus.

WALPOLE, R. ed, *Community health in Australia.* Ringwood, Vic, Penguin, 1979. 226 p, illus.

A 'slice' picture of medicine in Australia in the nineteenth century can only be obtained by reference to the medical and lay journals and to a wide range of individual publications. There were George Fullarton's *Family medical guide*, (first published in Sydney in 1870, and reaching its eighth edition in the 1880s) and Phillip Muskett's two-volume *Illustrated Australian medical guide*, (Sydney, Brooks, 1903), but these are not really indicative of Australian medical practice and problems of the time, although Muskett did publish other works more specifically Australian in content but in relatively specialised fields. On the other hand, we have two well-documented and detailed reviews of most aspects of Australian medicine, separated by some seventy years, in the works of Springthorpe (1914) and Gordon (1976). These are essential reference works and both have a significant measure of historical perspective, with appropriate references to earlier literature. The remaining two works are of a more popular kind and deal more particularly with contemporary problems of community health care.

CONTEMPORARY HEALTH CARE

DEWDNEY, J.C.H. *Australian health services.* Sydney, Wiley, 1972. 384 p, illus.

GRANT, C. AND LAPSLEY, H.M. *The Australian health care system 1981.* Sydney, School of Health Administration, University of NSW, 1981. 234 p, illus.

LAWSON, J.S. *Australian hospital services: a critical review.* Melbourne, Gardner Printing and Publishing, 1968. 102 p.

SAX, S. *Medical care in the melting pot: an Australian review.* A & R, 1972. 217 p.

SCOTTON, R.B. *Medical care in Australia: an economic diagnosis.* Melbourne, Sun Books for the Institute of Applied Economic and Social Research, University of Melbourne, 1974. 260 p.

WILLIS, E. *Medical dominance: the division of labour in Australian health care.* Sydney, Allen & Unwin, 1983. 235 p.

The works selected for this section represent studies which have had some impact on contemporary problems in the provision of a national health service. There is some bias towards those with a historical background—to some extent this means some bias towards those who advocate change, as the more conservative element tends to publish less. There is a considerable measure of overlap between social services, the provision of hospital and diagnostic services, the provision of primary ('doctor of first call') care and the continuation or extension of preventive measures, formerly comprehended by 'public health', and the economic and financial aspects in regard to all four. The issues have sadly been further clouded by the fact that questions of medicine,

The Doctor: You're in a bad way. To get back to your old form you'll have to swing those dumb-bells. Hard work is what you need.

Brisbane Courier, 5 July 1930. Cartoonist E.S. Watson draws a parallel between the health of the nation and the health of the individual. By July 1930, when this cartoon was drawn, unemployment had risen, in the space of six months, from 10 to 15 per cent of breadwinners.

health and the provision of health care have become polarised on the basis of political philosophy rather than rational and objective consideration. (See also the preceding chapter on 'Welfare'.)

DENTISTRY

HALLIDAY, R.W. *A history of dentistry in New South Wales 1788–1945*. Ed by A.O. Watson. Sydney, Australian Dental Association, NSW Branch, 1977. 261 p, illus.

LEVINE, S. 'Early Australian dental literature: prior to 1900', *Australian dental J* 19, 5, 1974, 349–58.

MARLAY, E. *A history of dental education in Queensland 1863–1964*. Brisbane, Dept of Dentistry, University of Qld, 1979. 226 p, illus.

WILKINSON, W.S. 'The Ernest Joske Memorial Oration: Dentistry in the national economy of Australia', *Australian J of dentistry* 55, 6, 1951, 425–31.

NURSING

ANDERSEN, C.E. *The story of bush nursing in Victoria*. Melbourne, Victorian Bush Nursing Association, 1951. 24 p, illus.

ARMSTRONG, D.M. *The first fifty years: a history of nursing at the Royal Prince Alfred Hospital, Sydney, from 1882 to 1932*. Sydney, Royal Prince Alfred Hospital Graduate Nurses' Association, 1965. 181 p, illus.

ARMSTRONG, M.G. 'A brief history of the first 50 years of the Royal Victorian College of Nursing, 1901–1951', *UNA nursing J* 49, 1951, 185–215.

HERRING, E.D. *They wanted to be nightingales: a story of the VAD/AAMWS in World War II*. Adelaide, Investigator Press, 1982. 215 p, illus.

HOBBS, V.A.M. *But westward look: nursing in Western Australia, 1829–1979*. UWAP for the Royal Australian Nursing Federation, WA Branch, 1980. 256 p, illus.

MacDONNELL, F. *Miss Nightingale's young ladies: the story of Lucy Osburn and Sydney Hospital*. A & R, 1970. 113 p, illus.

MINCHIN, M.K. *Revolutions and rosewater: the evolution of nurse registration in Victoria, 1923–1973*. Melbourne, Victorian Nursing Council, 1977. 120 p, illus.

ROYAL WOMEN'S HOSPITAL, Melbourne. *The centenary of nurse training in Australia, 1862–1962*. Melbourne, The Hospital, 1963. 57 p, illus.

SIMONS, J.E. *While history passed: the story of the Australian nurses who were prisoners of the Japanese for three and a half years*. Melbourne, Heinemann, 1954. xvii, 131 p, illus.

SOUTH AUSTRALIAN TRAINED NURSES' CENTENARY COMMITTEE. *Nursing in South Australia: first hundred years, 1837–1937*. Adelaide, The Committee, 1938. 348 p, illus.

SOUTH AUSTRALIAN TRAINED NURSES' CENTENARY COMMITTEE. *South Australian nurses: their work at home and abroad during the Second World War, 1939–1945*. Adelaide, The Committee, 1946. 146 p, illus.

WALSH, A.M.M. *Life in her hands: the Matron Walsh story told to Ruth Allen*. Melbourne, Georgian House, 1955. 139 p, illus.

WEBSTER, M.E. 'The history of trained nursing in Victoria' *Victorian historical magazine* 19, 4, 1942, 121–32.

WHITE, R.P. *The role of the nurse in Australia: an annotated bibliography and report*. Sydney, Tertiary Education Research Centre, University of NSW, 1972. 48, 96 p.

PHARMACY

FEEHAN, H.V. *Bond and link: pharmacy organisations and education in Victoria, Australia, 1857–1977*. Melbourne, Pharmaceutical Society of Vic, 1978. 64 p.

HAINES, G. *The grains and threepenn'orths of pharmacy: pharmacy in New South Wales, 1788–1976*. Kilmore, Vic, Lowden, 1976. 335 p, illus.

McWHINNEY, A. *A history of pharmacy in Western Australia*. Perth, Pharmaceutical Council of WA, 1975. 334 p, illus.

Virtually no studies in these areas deal with the history of professional activities on a national basis. An effort has been made to list reasonably authoritative works relating to professional organisation, legislation and education, as well as to professional activity and development, but it is not possible, within reasonable scope, to provide a thorough overview for each state.

Nursing has received considerable attention, partly because the revolutionary influence of Florence Nightingale gave the occupation its special status, requiring specific training, and partly because it affected hospital practice (hospital histories invariably consider nursing staff and standards). The wartime contribution of nurses was considerable and deserves mention; in this connection the work of the Australian Army Medical Women's Service merits recognition, although its members were not qualified nurses.

As with nursing, dentistry and pharmacy have a more extensive literature than the list here suggests but the subject matter of individual items tends to be too narrow to justify inclusion. Pharmacy, more than dentistry, has been well served by some detailed surveys; the series of papers by K. Attiwell on the history of pharmacy in Australia which appeared in the *Australian J of pharmacy* in 1956–57 and the history of women pharmacists in New South Wales by E. Wunsch, also published in that journal in 1962–64, indicate the kind of material to be found in serial articles relating to all three professions.

BIBLIOGRAPHIES

CAMPBELL, C.H. *Snake bite, snake venoms and venomous snakes of Australia and New Guinea: an annotated bibliography.* Canberra, Commonwealth Dept of Health and School of Public Health and Tropical Medicine, University of Sydney, 1976. 227 p. (University of Sydney. School of Public Health and Tropical Medicine. Service publication, 13.)

COPE, I. *et al, Obstetrics and gynaecology: short-title catalogue of books published before 1900 and available in Australia, together with references to these subjects in Australian and British journals published before 1900.* Sydney, Benevolent Society of NSW, 1973. 148 p.

DEWDNEY, J.C.H. AND WEIL, T.P. *Australian health care organisation bibliography: a guide book.* Sydney, School of Health Administration, University of NSW, 1969. 59 p. (Australian studies in health service administration, 11).

FORD, E. *Bibliography of Australian medicine 1790–1900.* SUP, 1976. 348 p, illus.

GANDEVIA, B. *et al, An annotated bibliography of the history of medicine and health in Australia.* Sydney, Royal Australasian College of Physicians, 1984. 187 p.

GUNN, P. *Ageing: a social science bibliography of Australian material.* Melbourne, The Author, 1977. 174 p.

LANCASTER, H.O. *Bibliography of vital statistics in Australia and New Zealand.* Sydney, Australasian Medical Publishing Co, 1964–73. 2 vols.

First published in *Australian J of statistics* 6, 2, 1964, 33–99; and 15, 1, 1973, 1–20.

MOODIE, P.M. AND PEDERSEN, E.B. *The health of Australian Aborigines: an annotated bibliography.* AGPS, 1971. 248 p. (University of Sydney, School of Public Health and Tropical Medicine, Service publication 8).

PETTERSON, L. *Women and health in Australia: a bibliography and guide.* AGPS, 1977. 82 p.

In some respects the history of medicine in Australia has been well served by bibliographers, although the list given here is very selective. Sir Edward Ford (1976) is comprehensive in his approach and by no means limited to medicine in the professional sense. While this provides a fundamental reference work in regard to publications relating to medicine and many paramedical subjects, the bibliography by Gandevia *et al* (1984) offers reasonably ready access to the secondary literature on the history of medicine in Australia, comprising as it does some 2500 references. For those seeking more detailed and technical references, Lancaster's (1964–73) bibliography is essential, and its range extends beyond Australia. The other cited bibliographies reflect some of a range of specialist bibliographies which are available.

REFERENCE WORKS

BRUCK, L. *The Australasian medical directory and hand book ... Editions 1–5.* Sydney, Australasian Medical Gazette, 1883–1900.

MEDICAL directory of Australia. Sydney, Australasian Medical Publishing Co, 1935–

It is regrettable that there are no useful comprehensive reference works on the history of Australian medicine. The most important reference works are the medical directories, of which two major series are listed here.

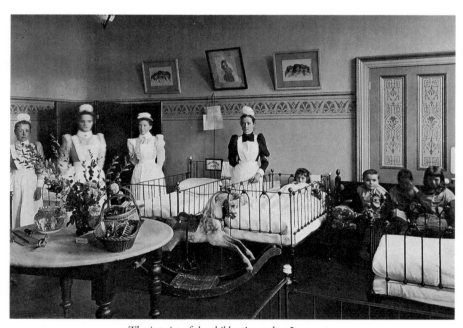

The interior of the children's ward at Launceston hospital, c1900. Unknown photographer.
QUEEN VICTORIA MUSEUM AND ART GALLERY, LAUNCESTON

Blacks on the way to Adelaide
in custody, Yorkes
Peninsula, *1850. Watercolour.*
MITCHELL LIBRARY

CHAPTER 45

THE ADMINISTRATION OF JUSTICE

E. K. BRAYBROOKE

THE GENERAL READER might well think of the administration of justice as a specialised topic, for which relevant books would be easy to identify. On the one hand, however, it is intimately linked with the social and political history of Australia, so that any writer, and any intelligent reader, must make constant reference to works on general history, and even to works on particular aspects of Australian history. As an example, Michael Cannon's *The land boomers* (Melbourne, Nelson, 1976), offers insights into the administration of justice in Victoria in the 1880s and 1890s, especially that part of it concerned with insolvency. However no-one would immediately categorise the work as relating to the administration of justice. On the other hand, the topic comprises but one aspect of the Australian legal system, and therefore information on the administration of justice must be sought in the more general works. There are an increasing number of these, partly because of the proliferation of 'legal studies' in our high schools. The reader may gain much insight into the topic by reading such books; but apart from one example of the genre, they have been excluded from the bibliography.

It could be assumed that much information about the administration of justice may be found in the biographies and memoirs of those who have served as lawyers and judges. Yet, especially in the formative years of the colonies and of Federation, such men were unlikely to confine their public service to the bar or the bench. They participated fully in the political struggles of the day. As a result far less may be learned from such works than might be hoped. Two examples may be given. Fewer than twenty pages of Edward E. Morris's extensive *A Memoir of George Higinbotham* (London, Macmillan, 1895) are devoted to an account of his participation in the administration of justice—if we exclude the ten pages devoted to his efforts at consolidation of the Victorian statutes. John Reynolds, in his biography *Edmund Barton* (Sydney, A & R, 1979), observes that 'very little information concerning Barton's practice at the Bar has come down to us'. As a result, only four pages discuss his role as one of Her Majesty's counsel and only eight pages are devoted to his work on the high court. It hardly seemed worth including either work in the bibliography. Indeed, the reader may be disappointed in the amount of light thrown on the topic by even those biographies and memoirs that have been included.

Central to the topic, of course, is the development and functioning of courts of law—or, to give them their alternative title, courts of justice—and the work of those who serve them as practitioners and judges. But only in comparatively recent times have comprehensive acounts of their structure and origin been published. The bibliography can list only two works on Australian courts as a whole, one published in 1946 and the second as recently as 1982. The High Court of Australia has merited some attention, and there are works dealing with both its history and its functioning. The supreme courts of the states have been less well served. There is a full history of the Supreme Court of New South Wales, and a separate biographical account of its chief justices. There are no corresponding published accounts of the history of the supreme courts of other states, though a brief history of the courts in Tasmania was edited by J.N.D. Harrison (1974). Some insights into the growth and functioning of the district courts of New South Wales may be culled from among the biographical details in a recently published work (Holt, 1976) dealing with the judges of these courts. Again, other states have not received similar treatment. Except, it seems, for the memoirs of one New South Wales magistrate, and a pilot study of the functioning of a handful of magistrates' courts in Victoria, these important courts, which deal with the majority of criminal cases and a large amount of civil litigation, have been ignored.

It would be easy to attribute the paucity of publications dealing with the history of particular state institutions concerned with the administration of justice to lack of interest on the part of publishers. It is more likely that a forecast lack of interest on the part of the book-buying public, and the resulting smallness of the expected market, have inhibited much publication in monograph form. But a great volume of work on the history of courts and the legal profession, and on other aspects of the administration of justice in Australia, is to be found in papers and articles in such publications as the journals of historical societies, the *Australian law journal*, and the steadily proliferating law reviews put out by law faculties in the universities.

Some monographs in the general field owe their appearance to 'official' inspiration. Examples of these are Sir Arthur Dean's (1968) history of the Victorian bar, and J.M. Bennett's book on New South Wales (1969). One other important publication, E.M. Russell (1980), owes its existence to Western Australia's sesquicentenary. Without the stimulus of similar occasions, it seems that readers wishing for an account of the history of the courts in South Australia, Queensland and Victoria, and a full history of the courts in Tasmania, will need to refer to the comprehensive works on court structures in Australia already mentioned.

Unfortunately, there is a paucity of such general works. Indeed, only three reasonably comprehensive histories of the law in Australia exist, and one of these, Castles (1982) must be regarded as a new edition of his earlier survey (1971). Beyond what these works offer, detail must be sought in periodical articles, and to some extent in memoirs and biographies, as well as in primary sources. Castles himself observes, in the preface to his 1982 book, that 'Much research remains to be done before anything like a full, detailed history of the law in this country can be written' (p iv). Of course, a good deal of such a history will inevitably transcend the boundaries of the present topic, and the general reader anxious for enlightenment on specific points will need to pick and choose, as he or she must now, from a mass of sometimes irrelevant material.

The enquiring non-specialist with an interest in this topic will want to find out, not only how courts of law have developed, and what is their present structure and jurisdiction, but also how well, or ill, they function. To what extent, in administering the law, may they be said to be administering justice? A difficulty in this respect is that those who administer the law have not, on the whole, been given to self-criticism. It is only in recent years that attempts have been made to find out what lawyers think of themselves and their work, what the general public thinks about lawyers, and what criticisms may be made of the administration of justice in our society.

Reference to works on the history of Australia will suggest that in the early days of New South Wales justice was administered haphazardly. No-one interested in the topic can neglect the evidence that emerged as a result of the inquiries of Commissioner Bigge, nor his second report on the administration of justice in New South Wales. These are well summarised in J.D. Ritchie (1970) and the reader who would go further is well served by the two volumes of *The evidence to the Bigge reports* (Melbourne, Heinemann, 1971) which he edited. But since that time, indeed until the publication of the more modern critical works to which oblique reference is made above, specific criticism, even specific praise, is rare and is not enshrined in monographs. Those who wish to get some picture of the way the law has worked over, say, the last 150 years are, inevitably, forced to cull relevant passages from memoirs and anecdotal works, of which Blacket (1927) is perhaps pre-eminent.

Some feeling for the functioning of the law in the administration of justice may be had from such accounts of trials as have been published in monograph form. The bibliography includes only one selection of brief accounts of the more straightforward trials in Australian history. But it does include several examples of what might be called the pathology of the administration of justice, exemplified by such cases as the Dean case in New South Wales, the Ryan and Ratten cases in Victoria, and the Stuart case in South Australia.

A potentially rich source of information on the working of the courts is to be found in the files of newspapers. There was a time when the forensic drama, whether of the *cause célèbre* in the superior courts or the humble dispute before the local magistrate, was a prime source of entertainment and news—indeed, the Chamberlain case indicates that the forensic drama, especially when acted out in bizarre circumstances, retains its mass appeal. Those who have access to the files of newspapers, and the leisure to go through them, can undoubtedly glean a good deal of information on the topic. It is doubtful if court records, even if accessible, would provide much of value to those without legal training. Such judges' notebooks as survive could yield odd nuggets of information.

Of more potential interest are the publications compendiously known as 'law reports', recording decisions on a point or points of law of general interest in the superior courts. These began in New South Wales and Victoria in 1861; in other states they started later. Studying them is, of course, primarily the business of lawyers, and much of what is found is of purely technical or professional interest. But the non-specialist who can gain access to them, and has the time and patience to search through them, especially the earlier volumes, may well gain insight into the way in which justice has been administered in these courts over at least the last century and a quarter. Moreover, a glance at the proliferating specialist reports in, for example, local government law and workers' compensation law, will give the enquirer some idea of the degree to which the manifold activities of people in society are being administered, and the diversity of human disputes settled, by the techniques of the law. In particular, even a cursory examination of the various industrial reports must give the enquirer some feeling for the operation of what the late Henry Bournes Higgins (1922) described, perhaps a little optimistically, as 'a new province for law and order'.

If the courts of justice form the centrepiece of the topic, police and prisons—or to use the modern expression, corrective services—form the prologue and epilogue, at least to that aspect of the administration of justice which is concerned with criminal justice. As with the history of the law, a full history of the police in Australia is yet to be written. There is one well-known book (O'Brien, 1960) on Australian police forces as a whole and three relatively slight official histories of state police forces. There are a few accounts of particular aspects of police work—for example, mounted police and the use of Aboriginal trackers. Those who wish to have some insight into current problems of policing are referred to two studies (Biles, 1977, and Chappell and Wilson, 1972) of police–public relations, and a substantial book of readings (Milte and Weber, 1977) on the topic. References to the problem of policing will be found too in more general works on the criminal justice system—or, as the title of one such work has it, the criminal injustice system (Basten *et al*, 1982).

These more general works on the criminal justice system also contain some material bearing on the working of the correctional system, and particularly that part of it which centres on prisons. The problems of prison administration go back to the foundation of our country as an epilogue to the British system of the administration of justice. The unchanging nature of these problems may be seen from even a cursory dip into the early history of the penal system.

The studies by the late Sir John Barry of Maconochie of Norfolk Island (1958) and his successor, Price (1964), are essential reading for those who would understand nineteenth-century attitudes to penology and penal reform and for those who would gain an insight into today's problems. The former, indeed, introduces readers not only to the views of Maconochie himself, but also to those two remarkable Quakers, Backhouse and Walker. Unfortunately there is a gap in penal history not yet filled by publications on other nineteenth century theories and development, for the full history of Australian prisons and Australian penal systems is yet to be written. There is much raw material in the shape of reports of prison authorities to governments, reports of royal commissions and other inquiries, and debates in, and answers to questions in, parliament.

Rinaldi (1977) gives a comprehensive description of the general state of the prison systems in this country in 1977. Oddly, from a historical point of view the West Australian penal system is best served, with the recent monograph by J.E. Thomas and A. Stewart *Imprisonment in Western Australia: evolution, theory and practice* (UWAP, 1978). The Victorian correctional system is well described in S.W. Johnston and R.G. Fox, *Correction handbook of Victoria* (Melbourne, Dept of Criminology, University of Melbourne, 1965). The history of Queensland's prisons in the last seventy or eighty years is sketched in *Nor iron bars a cage* (Brisbane, Boolarong Publications, 1982), an autobiography by J.R. Stephenson, who entered the service as a warder and retired as deputy commissioner. The turbulent history of the penal system in New South Wales in recent years has given rise to several accounts of the problem and the attempted solutions, notably by M. Findlay in *The state of the prison* (Bathurst, NSW, Mitchellsearch, 1982) and by G. Zdenkowski and D. Brown (1982) in their national overview.

BARRY, J.V.W. *Alexander Maconochie of Norfolk Island: a study of a pioneer in penal reform.* OUP, 1958. 277 p, illus, maps.

Uses the story of Maconochie's life as the framework for a survey of prison methods and reforms.

BARRY, J.V.W. *The life and death of John Price: a study in the exercise of naked power.* MUP, 1964. 204 p, illus.

Price succeeded Maconochie as commandant of Norfolk Island. A welcome study about an era which has been badly neglected by serious historians.

BARRY, J.V.W. *et al, Introduction to the criminal law in Australia.* London, Macmillan, 1948. 128 p.

Contains a historical introduction to the subject, an account of the codes that are characteristic of Australian criminal law, a discussion of general principles and a chapter on the penal system.

BASTEN, J. *et al, The criminal injustice system.* Sydney, Australian Legal Workers Group (NSW) and Legal Service Bulletin, 1982. 321 p.

Essays, from a radical point of view, criticising the criminal justice system under the headings: police interrogation, trial procedure, the politics of reform.

BENNETT, J.M. *A history of the Supreme Court of New South Wales.* Sydney, Law Book Co, 1974. 323 p, illus.

A valuable and scholarly account.

BENNETT, J.M. *Keystone of the federal arch: a historical account of the High Court of Australia to 1980.* AGPS, 1980. 145 p, illus.

A work of obvious importance by a leading Australian legal historian.

BENNETT, J.M. *Portraits of the chief justices of New South Wales, 1824–1977.* Sydney, Ferguson, 1977. 64 p, illus.

A sketch of the life of each chief justice accompanied by a colour portrait.

BENNETT, J.M. ed, *A history of the New South Wales bar.* Sydney, Law Book Co, 1969. 282 p, illus.

This book covers, in nine chapters written by various hands, the growth of the bar from 1824 to the 1960s, its corporate organisations, and aspects of bar life.

BENNETT, J.M. AND CASTLES, A.C. eds, *A source book of Australian legal history: source materials from the eighteenth to the twentieth centuries.* Sydney, Law Book Co, 1979. 299 p.

A valuable collection of materials, including primary sources.

BILES, D. *Crime and justice in Australia.* Canberra, Australian Institute of Criminology in association with Sun Books, 1977. 198 p.

A collection of essays on the administration of criminal justice, from police to prisons.

BLACKET, W. *May it please your honour: lawyers and law courts of the olden times in New South Wales.* Sydney, Cornstalk Publishing Co, 1927. 275 p.

A president of the NSW bar has said of this book: 'The Bar has already been well served by Wilfred Blacket's witty memoirs...' Insight given also into the administration of justice in country districts.

BRADSHAW, F.M. *Selborne Chambers memories.* Sydney, Butterworths, 1962. 111 p, illus.

An account of some of the barristers who practised from Selborne Chambers in Sydney.

BRENNAN, F. *Too much order with too little law.* UQP, 1983. 303 p.

Discusses the legal and political bases of control of public order by restrictions particularly on demonstrations and street marches from a civil libertarian point of view. Concentrates on the period 1966–79 in Qld.

BURNS, C. *The Tait case.* MUP, 1962. 182 p.

The author describes this as 'a modest book, which attempts to tell of the controversy which followed when a government decides to hang a man'.

CAMPBELL, E.M. *et al, Legal research: materials and methods.* Sydney, Law Book Co, 1979. 276 p.

An outstanding guide to the printed sources of the law in Australia, including a number of chapters devoted to series of law reports and to statutory material. First published in 1967.

CARTER, I.E. *Woman in a wig: Joan Rosanove, Q.C.* Melbourne, Lansdowne, 1970. 167 p, illus.

A biography of one who was for some time the only woman at the Victorian bar.

CASTLES, A.C. *An Australian legal history.* Sydney, Law Book Co, 1982. 553 p.

The most comprehensive legal history of Australia; an expansion of an earlier work by the same author.

CHAPPELL, D. AND WILSON, P. *The Australian criminal justice system.* Sydney, Butterworths, 1972. 854 p.

A series of papers on all aspects of the criminal justice system in Australia.

COCKBURN, S. *The Salisbury affair.* Melbourne, Sun Books, 1979. 351 p, illus.

The story behind the dismissal by the South Australian government of a policeman whom many regarded as of the highest integrity—a model of the uneasy relations which too often exist between police and government.

COWEN, Z. *Isaac Isaacs.* OUP, 1967. 272 p, illus.

Biography of a leading figure in Australian law and politics, both state and federal.

COWEN, Z. *Sir John Latham and other papers.* OUP, 1965. 191 p.

The first 60 pages constitute the only account in book form of a distinguished lawyer, politician and high court judge, who served as chief justice from 1935 to 1952.·

CRAWFORD, J. *Australian courts of law.* OUP, 1982. 297 p.

The most comprehensive account of the machinery of justice in Australia today; includes chapters on the English background and brief accounts of the history of the courts discussed.

CURREY, C.H. *The brothers Bent: Judge-Advocate Ellis Bent and Judge Jeffery Hart Bent.* SUP, 1968. 176 p, illus.

A sketch of the lives of two famous brothers whose influence on legal procedures was considerable, together with a chapter on their precursors.

D'ALPUGET, J.B. *Mediator: a biography of Sir Richard Kirby.* MUP, 1977. 277 p, illus.

This biography gives a useful personal insight into the workings of the commonwealth system of conciliation and arbitration.

DEAN, A. *A multitude of counsellors: a history of the bar of Victoria.* Melbourne, Cheshire for the Bar Council of Vic, 1968. 332 p, illus.

Described in Sir Charles Lowe's introduction as 'an invaluable and inevitable source of reference to the Bar and a source book for historians in the future'.

DEBENHAM, A.E. *Without fear or favour: the biography of a career.* Sydney, Edwards & Shaw, 1966. 175 p, illus.

This autobiography of one who was a stipendiary magistrate in both country and city in NSW gives some useful insights into the workings of the courts which hear the great majority of cases in our community.

DIXON, O. *Jesting Pilate, and other papers and addresses.* Sydney, Law Book Co, 1965. 272 p, illus.

Twenty-nine of the papers and addresses given by Australia's greatest judge, each of which is of value and interest, not only intrinsically but also for the purpose of historical record and research.

FORBES, J.R.S. *The divided legal profession in Australia: history, rationalisation, and rationale.* Sydney, Law Book Co, 1979. 300 p.

A well-researched historical account of a controversial topic, with a critical discussion of the justification offered by its supporters.

FORDE, J.L. *The story of the bar of Victoria, from its foundation* to the amalgamation of the two branches of the legal profession, 1839–1891: historical, personal, humorous. Melbourne, Whitcombe & Tombs, 1913. 309 p, illus.

Biographies of, and anecdotes concerning, members of the Victorian bar from 1839 to 1891, with accounts of cases in which they were engaged.

FRY, T.P. *Australian courts and administrative tribunals.* Brisbane, University of Qld, 1946. 396 p.

Contains valuable material on courts in Qld.

GRABOSKY, P.N. *Sydney in ferment: crime, dissent and official reaction, 1788–1973.* ANUP, 1977. 205 p, illus, maps.

An insight into the problems facing the administration of criminal justice in the capital of NSW since its foundation.

HANNAN, A.J. *The life of Chief Justice Way: a biography of . . . Sir Samuel Way . . . for many years Lieutenant Governor and Chief Justice of South Australia, and Chancellor of the University of Adelaide.* A & R, 1960. 262 p, illus.

The biography of a man who for 60 years played an important part in the administration of justice in SA.

HARRISON, J.N.D. ed, *Court in the colony: Hobart Town, May 1824.* Hobart, Law Society of Tas, 1974. 44 p, illus.

Published to mark the sesquincentenary of the Supreme Court of Tas.

HEALEY, B. *Federal arbitration in Australia: an historical outline.* Melbourne, Georgian House, 1972. 165 p.

A useful short account of the development of federal arbitration of industrial disputes.

HENRY, E.R. *Revelations of a retired lawyer.* Hobart, Orielton Press, 1980. 201 p, illus.

Described in the foreword as an entertaining record of the law courts, mainly those of Tas, and of those who practised in them for some 60 years.

HIGGINS, H.B. *A new province for law and order.* Sydney, Workers' Educational Association of NSW, 1922. 181 p.

The reflections of the first president of the Commonwealth Court of Conciliation and Arbitration on the gradual development of standards and practices in the court's jurisdiction in the first fourteen years.

HOLT, H.T.E. *A court rises: the lives and times of the judges of the District Court of New South Wales (1859–1959).* Sydney, Law Foundation of NSW, 1976. 258 p, illus.

Probably the only systematic account of the administration of justice in intermediate courts in Australia.

INGLIS, K.S. *The Stuart case.* MUP, 1961. 321 p, illus.

An account of the proceedings in and the background of one of the most controversial trials in SA, that of an Aborigine for the murder of a white girl.

JACOBS, P.A. *Famous Australian trials and memories of the law.* Melbourne, Robertson & Mullens, 1942. 218 p, illus.

One of the few collections of accounts of Australian trials.

JOHNSTON, R. *History of the Queensland bar.* Brisbane, Bar Association of Qld, 1979. 213 p.

This work has substantial historical chapters on the profession and on 'the barrister and the community' but about half the work is strongly directed to individual biography.

JOYCE, R.B. *Samuel Walker Griffiths.* UQP, 1984. 456 p, illus.

Detailed and scholarly biography of the lawyer, politician and first chief justice of the High Court of Australia.

LA TROBE UNIVERSITY. Department of Legal Studies. *Guilty, your worship: a study of Victoria's magistrates' courts.* Melbourne, Legal Studies Dept, La Trobe University, 1980. 136 p.

Accounts by observers of what occurs in some of the metropolitan magistrates' courts in Vic, with some conclusions concerning the administration of justice in these courts.

MACKINOLTY, J. AND RADI, H. eds, *In pursuit of justice: Australian women and the law 1788–1979.* Sydney, Hale & Iremonger, 1979. 300 p, illus.

Papers examining some of the ways in which women have been, and are, affected by the law. Includes a list of discriminatory laws.

MARR, D. *Barwick.* Sydney, Allen & Unwin, 1980. 330 p, illus.

The first biography of one of the ablest of Australian barristers, who later became Chief Justice of the High Court.

MILTE, K.L. AND WEBER, T.A. *Police in Australia: development, functions, procedures.* Sydney, Butterworths, 1977. 511 p. illus.

Papers, readings and case extracts on the role of the police in the community, police powers and problems of policing.

MOLOMBY, T. *Ratten: the web of circumstance.* Melbourne, Outback Press, 1978. 279 p, illus.

An account of a Victorian *cause célèbre*, provoking reflections on the pathology of our legal system and the adequacy of our methods of fact-finding.

MORRIS, N.R. AND PERLMAN, M. eds, *Law and crime: essays in honor of Sir John Barry.* New York, Gordon and Breach, 1972. 259 p, illus.

Includes an essay on Barry's judgments, two memoirs of the man, and an essay on reformatory aspects of transportation.

MUDIE, J. *The felonry of New South Wales: being a faithful picture of the real romance of life in Botany Bay.* London, Whaley & Co, 1837. 362 p, map.

Sketches of the administration of justice in the years 1822–36 by an archconservative magistrate. New edition published in 1964.

MUKHERJEE, S.K. *Crime trends in twentieth century Australia.* Sydney, Australian Institute of Criminology with Allen & Unwin, 1981. 199 p, illus.

Lavishly furnished with graphs and statistical tables, this sophisticated statistical work sets out and discusses trends in crime in Australia, 1900–76.

NEUMANN, E. *The High Court of Australia: a collective portrait, 1903–1972.* Sydney, Dept of Government and Public Administration, University of Sydney, 1973. 131 p.

A description of the socioeconomic status of judges of the high court, and a comparison with the judges of the United States Supreme Court. First published in 1971.

O'BRIEN, G.M. *The Australian police forces.* OUP, 1960. 268 p, illus.

The most comprehensive work on the police forces in Australia.

PIDDINGTON, A.B. *Worshipful masters.* A & R, 1929. 316 p, illus.

Contains memorials of some of the leading figures in the law in NSW.

RICHARD, J. *H.B. Higgins: the rebel as judge.* Sydney, Allen & Unwin, 1984. 350 p, illus.

Outstanding biography of a prominent Victorian barrister, politician, man of letters, judge of the High Court of Australia and the man responsible for the famous Harvester Judgment of 1907.

RINALDI, F. *Australian prisons.* Canberra, F. & M. Publishers, 1977. 249 p, illus.

The introduction describes this as 'the first book to deal generally with Australian prisons'.

RITCHIE, J.D. *Punishment and profit: the reports of Commissioner John Bigge on the colonies of New South Wales and Van Diemen's Land, 1822–1823; their origins, nature and significance.* Melbourne, Heinemann, 1970. 324 p, illus.

An account of the reports of Commissioner John Bigge on the colonies of NSW and Van Diemen's Land, the second of which dealt with the administration of justice.

ROSENTHAL, N. *Sir Charles Lowe: a biographical memoir.* Melbourne, Robertson & Mullens, 1968. 214 p, illus.

A layman's attempt to present an image of an eminent Victorian judge, with an account of his judicial career from 1926 to 1964.

RUSSELL, E.M. *A history of the law in Western Australia and its development from 1829 to 1979.* UWAP, 1980. 413 p, illus.

The only comprehensive history of the administration of justice in WA, it was written by the late Enid Russel in 1950 and edited and completed in 1979 by F.M. Robinson and P.W. Nichols.

SAWER, G. *Australian federalism in the courts.* MUP, 1968. 262 p.

A lively account of the High Court of Australia and the way it has dealt with constitutional matters.

SEXTON, M. AND MAHER, L.W. *The legal mystique: the role of lawyers in Australian society.* A & R, 1982. 196 p.

A critical look, from a radical viewpoint, at some aspects of professional practice and judicial decision making; includes chapters on the high court, lawyers and corporate clients, and the regulation of the profession.

TENNANT, K. *Evatt: politics and justice.* A & R, 1972. 418 p, illus.

The major biography of the late Mr Justice Evatt. First published in 1970.

THERRY, Sir R. *Reminiscences of thirty years' residence in New South Wales and Victoria* (2nd edn). London, Sampson Low, 1863, 522 p.

During the 30 years covered Sir Roger Therry was successively Attorney-General of NSW, resident judge at Port Phillip and a judge of the Supreme Court of NSW. The first edition, issued in 1863, was immediately withdrawn while the second edition of the same year corrected some errors and gives fuller justice to the work of Gibbs, Fitzroy and La Trobe. Facsimile edition, SUP, 1974.

TOMASIC, R.A. *Lawyers and the community.* Sydney, Law Foundation of NSW and Allen & Unwin, 1978. 318 p.

The account of a survey to find out what people in NSW think of the legal system, what access they have to it, and what redress they have if poorly served by lawyers.

TOMASIC, R.A. ed, *Understanding lawyers: perspectives on the legal profession in Australia.* Sydney, Law Foundation of NSW and Allen & Unwin, 1978. 505 p, maps.

This book brings together 23 essays, by lawyers and social scientists, on various aspects of the Australian legal profession.

ZDENKOWSKI, G. AND BROWN, D. *The prison struggle: changing Australia's penal system.* Ringwood, Vic, Penguin, 1982. 440 p, illus.

A radical critique of our penal system, provoked by recent troubles in the prisons in our largest state.

A family left homeless by the bushfires that swept through the Royal National Park area, NSW, in mid-November 1951.
MAGAZINE PROMOTIONS

CHAPTER 46

DISASTERS

STUART PIGGIN

IN ITS DISASTER experience Australia is relatively speaking the 'lucky country'. Even New Zealand has suffered more horrifying civil disasters than Australia. Australian air disasters have been few with little loss of life and all pale into insignificance by comparison with the Mt Erebus disaster of 28 November 1979 when an Air New Zealand DC10 crashed, killing 257 people. Australia's worst rail disaster at Granville on 18 January 1977 took 83 lives, but is eclipsed by the New Zealand Tangiwai ('weeping waters') crash of Christmas Eve 1953 when 151 died.

To date the worst civil disaster in Australia's history was the foundering of the emigrant ship *Cataraqui* on King Island, 4 August 1845, with the loss of over four hundred lives. The worst natural disaster was on 4–5 March 1899 when a cyclone struck a pearling fleet in Bathurst Bay, Queensland, killing 307 people. On 19 February 1942, 243 people died when Darwin was bombed (Lockwood, 1966). Wars are not usually classified as 'disasters', but here again relatively few have died on Australian soil through enemy action. Many died, however, in attacks on shipping in World War II (Loney, 1981); the sinking of HMAS *Sydney* off the coast of Western Australia on 19 November 1941, with the loss of 645 lives, was Australia's worst disaster. The worst peacetime land disaster in Australian history was the Mt Kembla mine disaster of 31 July 1902 when 96 died. It is feared that Australia's relative immunity to disasters could change with the increasing population of northern Australia which is particularly prone to cyclones.

If, however, Australian disasters have been accompanied by a comparatively low loss of life, this has been offset by a high economic cost, owing to our vast distances and the high frequency of cyclones, bushfires and floods. The 1974 Brisbane floods, for example, took five lives but caused damage estimated at $178 million; in the same year Cyclone Tracy took 65 lives and damage was estimated at over $500 million. In view of the high economic cost of Australian disasters it is perhaps surprising that so little research has been done by economists; one explanation is that there are few reliable estimates of damage from disasters.

Historians too have been reluctant to write about Australian disasters. Still the most accessible historical information on peacetime disasters is found in the several editions of the *Australian encyclopaedia* where details are arranged according to the field or activity in which disasters occurred, such as aviation disasters, mining disasters, wrecks and shipping disasters or fires. Natural disasters are treated under bushfires, floods and storms. Among historians, Geoffrey Blainey's *The peaks of Lyell* (MUP, 1978) makes a study of a disaster in the context of a company history, while Bell (1978) and Piggin (1981) are the only historians who have concentrated on disaster research.

Most research on Australian disasters is being done by behavioural and physical scientists. This follows in the wake of the great surge of research in New South Wales facilitated by the Federal Disaster Act (1950) which established disaster research centres to investigate the possible behaviour of groups of people subjected to nuclear attack. Social scientists such as Wettenhall (1975) are optimistic about the predictive value of the study of human behaviour during stress situations in general and disasters in particular. The research of physical scientists, including physicists, geologists and meteorologists, concentrates on technical rather than human aspect of disasters and is, therefore, generally omitted in the bibliography below.

Disasters lend themselves to sensationalist treatment by journalists (for example, Carroll, 1977) but some journalists have made careful and responsible investigations of Australian disasters. This genre, therefore, cannot be ignored (see Holthouse, 1974) and should be sought not only in popular monographs, but also in the magazine or historical features in newspapers.

Immediately after a disaster media coverage is especially copious, since disasters capture headlines, increase newspaper circulation and raise television ratings. For much of the nineteenth century, in the absence of statutory data collection, newspapers are almost our only source of information about some disasters, especially maritime disasters. The newspaper cuttings files in major libraries should therefore be consulted (for example, in the Mitchell Library under 'Shipwrecks and disasters at sea'). Intense media interest in disasters has created extensive photographic and film material on more recent Australian disasters. For instance, 229 films on related subjects are listed in the *New South Wales State Emergency Services visual aids catalogue*, March 1976.

Reports of royal commissions and other public inquiries are perhaps the most important source of data on Australian disasters, and some of the more significant are included in the bibliography. The *Checklist of royal commissions* compiled by Borchardt *et al* (see chapter 8 above) should be consulted for complete coverage. Royal commissions deal frequently with civil disasters, although there have been important inquiries into the causes and effects of floods and bushfires and the relief activities undertaken by various authorities. They usually make recommendations for change and thereby raise the tantalising historical question of the relationship between disasters and progress.

In the search for primary sources, those interested in disasters must take into account the fact that a large number of agencies and organisations are involved in disaster work. There are the departments and statutory authorities of the three tiers of government (federal, state and local) and all have extensive archival collections. No two states have uniform legislation on disaster preparedness and relief, and the student of disasters may have to be familiar with the operating and recording instructions of the police, fire, ambulance, health and emergency services in each state. Since the creation in 1974 of the Australian National Disaster Organisation within the Department of Defence, the defence forces have become more involved with disaster relief. There are also philanthropic, religious and voluntary organisations involved in disaster work, including the Royal Humane Society, the Red Cross and the Salvation Army.

The historical study of Australian disasters has hardly begun. The sources are rich and social scientists offer useful guidelines. Oral history is more fruitful here than in many other areas since disaster memories are particularly vivid. Descriptions of major Australian disasters are given in *Australians: events and places*.

The bibliography below is divided into three parts dealing respectively with international and Australian disasters, natural disasters, and civil disasters. The citations within each are arranged alphabetically by author.

GENERAL READING

AUSTRALIAN COUNTER DISASTER COLLEGE. *Australian disaster research directory (including some contributions from New Zealand)*. Macedon, Vic, Australian Counter Disaster College, 1983–

Lists 50 Australian and New Zealand tertiary institutions and other organisations, describing the nature of the research, personnel and publications. Regular updates planned.

CARROLL, B. *Disaster, horror and fear in Australia*. Sydney, Bacchus Books, 1977. 201 p.

Account of 69 Australian disasters (replete with rape, murder and epidemics) rushed out after the Granville NSW rail disaster. Written in sensational journalese. Inaccuracies abound.

FERRARA, G.M. ed, *The disaster file: the 1970's*. New York, Facts on File, 1979. 173 p, illus.

Australian drought, fire, storm and railroad disasters are included in this catalogue with description of each event, including a statement of cause, date and numbers killed and injured.

FRASER, B. ed, *The Macquarie book of events*. Sydney, Macquarie Library, 1983. 608 p, illus.

Helpful, though far from complete, lists of Australian disasters arranged chronologically covering droughts, cyclones, storms and floods, fires, shipping, rail and air disasters.

HEATHCOTE, R.L. AND THOM, B.G. eds, *Natural hazards in Australia: proceedings of a symposium ...* Canberra, Australian Academy of Science, 1979. 531 p, illus, maps.

Important contributions by social and physical scientists and other professionals. Many of the papers have a remarkable historical perspective. Bibliographies.

KINGSTON, J. AND LAMBERT, D. *Catastrophe and crisis*. London, Aldus Books, 1979. 336 p, illus, maps.

Surveys natural and 'economic' disasters, plagues, wars, murders, exterminations and 'scientific' disasters. Australian bushfires and droughts are mentioned, as is the collapse of Poseidon shares in 1970.

NASH, J.R. *Darkest hours: a narrative encyclopedia of worldwide disasters from ancient times to the present*. Chicago, Nelson-Hall, 1976. 812 p, illus.

Particularly useful single-volume study of world disasters that have taken more than forty lives. Brief articles on disasters arranged alphabetically by location are followed by lists arranged chronologically by type (for example, air, earthquake, mine and war).

OLIVER, J. ed, *Response to disaster*. Townsville, Qld, Centre for Disaster Studies, James Cook University of North Qld, 1980. 355 p, illus, maps.

Seminar papers covering definitions, classification, regional variations in disaster potential, disaster preparedness, post-disaster care and the development of the Centre for Disaster Studies at James Cook University.

POWNALL, E. *Elements of danger*. Sydney, Collins, 1976. 152 p, illus.

A popular account of twelve Australian disasters and accidents culled from newspapers, reports and inquiries.

TASMANIA. State Emergency Service. *Chronological sequence of events: Tasmania 1811–1980*. Hobart, State Emergency Service, 1980.

These tables, the accuracy of which is not guaranteed, are compiled from official records, newspapers, media records and almanacs.

NATURAL DISASTERS

AUSTRALIA. Natural Disasters Organisation. *Darwin disaster, Cyclone Tracy: report by Director-General, [Alan Stretton], Natural Disasters Organisation on the Darwin relief operations, 25 December 1974–3 January 1975*. AGPS, 1975. 68 p, maps.

This controversial report gives an account of every phase of the disaster from original warnings, through relief operations to early rebuilding planning.

BURTON, I. et al, *The environment as hazard*. New York, OUP, 1978. 240 p, illus.

This study contains many references to Australian droughts and their impact on the Australian economy, landuse and attitudes to rural life over a period of 66 years.

BUTLER, J.R.G. AND DOESSEL, D.P. *The economics of natural disaster relief in Australia*. Canberra, Centre for Research on Federal Financial Relations, Australian National University, 1979. 147 p.

Based on an analysis of property damage in the Brisbane flood (1974), this study recommends that victims should bear only a specified maximum cost positively related to income.

CHAMBERLAIN, E.R. et al, *The experience of Cyclone Tracy*. AGPS, 1981. 191 p.

Report by staff from the Anthropology and Sociology and Social Work departments of the University of Qld, this is a study of the stress caused by the cyclone.

CHAMBERLAIN, E.R. et al, *Queensland flood report: Australia Day 1974*. AGPS, 1981. 324 p.

A study of the welfare component in disaster relief, to identify social and psychological needs, and to design a blueprint for the provision of post-impact relief services.

COLE, E.K. *Winds of fury: the full true story of the great Darwin disaster*. Adelaide, Rigby, 1977. 211 p, illus, map.

A well-presented account by an Anglican clergyman, who also reflects on 'the tragedy and triumph of Tracy', expected of a clergyman, perhaps, but rare in Australian disaster studies.

FOLEY, J.C. *Droughts in Australia: review of records from earliest years of settlement to 1955*. Melbourne, Bureau of Meteorology, 1957. (Australia. Bureau of Meteorology bulletin, 43.)

An analysis of the duration, intensity and effects of all Australian droughts for which records are available. Data include information of interest to social historians. Bibliography.

FOSTER, E. *Bushfire: history, prevention, and control*. Sydney, Reed, 1976. 247 p, illus.

Opening with a history of bushfires and concluding with a list of serious fires in Australia since 1830, this book reviews methods of control.

HOLTHOUSE, H. *Cyclone*. Adelaide, Rigby, 1977. 179 p, illus.

A journalist's account of a century of Australian cyclones with an appendix listing notable eastern Australian cyclones. First published in 1971.

LOVETT, J.V. ed, *The environmental, economic and social significance of drought*. A & R, 1973. 318 p, illus, maps.

Contributions by various research workers.

LUKE, R.H. AND McARTHUR, A.G. *Bushfires in Australia*. AGPS, 1978. 359 p, illus, maps.

Authoritative work which includes historical material and comments on methods of protection and the legislation and fire-fighting organisations in each Australian state. Extensive bibliography.

NOBLE, W.S. *Ordeal by fire: the week a state burned up*. Melbourne, Hawthorn, 1977. 85 p, illus, map.

A journalist's account of Victoria's worst bushfires of January 1939 which took 71 lives.

STRETTON, A.B. *The furious days: the relief of Darwin.* Sydney, Collins, 1976. 207 p, illus.

A personalised reconstruction of events following Cyclone Tracy when supreme control had to be exercised without legal authority to counteract the inertia of dazed victims and the bungling of bureaucrats and politicians.

STRETTON, A.B. *Soldier in a storm: an autobiography.* Sydney, Collins, 1978. 320 p.

Stretton received a lot of criticism from public servants and politicians for his controversial, dramatic and illegal actions following the Darwin cyclone disaster. This is his defence.

VICTORIA. Board of Inquiry into the Occurrence of Bush and Grass Fires in Victoria. *Report . . .* Melbourne, Government Printer, 1977. 213 p, illus, maps. (Vic. Parliament. Parliamentary paper, 91 of 1977.)

The commissioners recommended reorganisation of the Country Fire Authority, new standards for the State Electricity Commission, and improved co-ordination between these bodies, the Country Roads Board, Victorian Railways and the municipalities. Chairman: Sir E.H.E. Barber.

WETTENHALL, R.L. *Bushfire disaster: an Australian community in crisis.* A & R, 1975. 320 p, illus, maps.

A social scientist's analysis of the 1967 Tasmanian bushfires within the context of disaster research and against the background of other Australian, especially Tasmanian, disasters.

CIVIL DISASTERS

BAGLEY, W.O. *Coroner's enquiry into the Sunshine railway disaster; being a digest of the evidence in relation to the Westinghouse brake tendered at the enquiry . . . at the Law Courts, Melbourne.* Melbourne, Arbuckle, Waddell & Fawckner, 1909. 205 p, illus.

In 1908, 44 people died and over 400 were injured in a train collision at Sunshine, Vic. This digest of the evidence concentrates on the claim that failure of the brake caused the accident and concludes with an account of the trial and the reaction of the Victorian press to the engine driver's acquittal.

BATESON, C. AND LONEY, J.K. *Australian shipwrecks.* Sydney, Reed; Geelong, Vic, List Publishing, 1972–82. 3 vols, illus, maps.

Comprehensive chronological treatment of shipwrecks in Australian waters. Many entries are detailed, with a selection of the sources of information after each entry. A fourth volume is projected.

BELL, P. *The Mount Mulligan disaster.* Townsville, Qld, James Cook University of North Qld, 1978. 287 p, illus, maps. (Studies in north Qld history, 2.)

First monograph history of an Australian disaster, treating it as an integral part of mining history and as the 'logical' outcome of geographic, economic, social and political forces. The author is critical of the perfunctory royal commission.

HAWKES, V. *The Tasman Bridge disaster, community perception and response: survey report.* Hobart, Faculty of Education, University of Tas, 1975. 227 p, illus, map.

A sociological survey of the isolation of one-third of a city's population following the collapse of the bridge (5 January 1975).

LOCKWOOD, D. *Australia's Pearl Harbour: Darwin, 1942.* Melbourne, Cassell, 1966. 232 p, illus, maps.

A journalist's account of the bombing of Darwin. Examines the appointment of a royal commission to investigate all relevant circumstances.

LONEY, J.K. *Atlas of Australian shipwrecks.* Sydney, Reed, 1981. 120 p, illus, maps.

Brief descriptions of more than 500 wrecks in Australian waters arranged by states, including a chapter on war casualties.

NEW SOUTH WALES. Royal Commission on Bulli Colliery Accident. *Report, together with the minutes of evidence and appendices.* Sydney, Government Printer, 1887. (*In* NSW. Parliament. Parliamentary papers 1887 [second session], vol 4.)

The commissioners, demonstrably representative of the coal-owners, overturned the findings of the coroner's inquest and largely exonerated management and the Dept of Mines. The commission found that the explosion was caused by a miner who had used explosives carelessly. Chairman: J.R.M. Robertson.

NEW SOUTH WALES. Royal Commission on the Mount Kembla Colliery Disaster, 31 July 1902. *Report, together with minutes of evidence and exhibits.* Sydney, Government Printer, 1903. (*In* NSW. Parliament. Parliamentary papers 1903, vol 5.)

Following a coroner's inquest, the commission censured the manager, who was then put on trial, and recommended that every detection of gas should be reported and that naked lights should not be used in any mine where gas was detected. Chairman: G.E.R. Murray.

O'MAY, H. *Wrecks in Tasmanian waters 1797–1950.* Hobart, Government Printer, 1955. 209 p, illus, map.

Brief descriptions of about 600 shipwrecks.

PIGGIN, S. 'Religion and disaster: popular religious attitudes to disaster and death with special reference to the Mt Kembla and Appin coal mine disasters', *J Aust stud* 8, 1981, 54–63.

An analysis of the nature and significance of religious behaviour before, during and after two mine disasters (1902 and 1979) in a southern coal district of NSW.

QUEENSLAND. Royal Commission . . . upon the Recent Disaster at Mount Mulligan Coal Mine. *Report . . . with the proceedings . . . minutes of evidence and exhibits.* Brisbane, Government Printer, 1921. xvii, 176 p, illus, maps. (*In* Qld. Parliament. Parliamentary papers 1922, vol 2.)

The commission failed to determine satisfactorily the cause of the explosion, but led witnesses to preconceived conclusions. The report criticised the mine manager and the neglect of several provisions of the Mines Regulations Acts (1910–20). Chairman: R.A. Dunlop.

TASMANIA. Royal Commission of the North Mount Lyell Mining Disaster. *Report . . .* Hobart, Government Printer, 1913. 9 p. (Tas. Parliament. House of Assembly. Parliamentary paper, 2 of 1913.)

The commission considered three causes: carelessness by the miners, incendiarism and an electrical fault. It eliminated the last, but was unable to find conclusively on the others. Chairman: E.W. Turner.

THOMAS, P. *Miners in the 1970s: a narrative history of the Miners Federation.* Sydney, Miners Federation, 1983. 552 p, illus, map.

A chapter entitled 'Mining's bitter toll' contains accounts of the disasters of Box Flat, 1972, Kianga, 1975 and Appin, 1979. It claims that Australian mines are more dangerous than British and Japanese mines, and emphasises the greater hazards due to improved technology.

VICTORIA. Royal Commission into the Failure of West Gate Bridge. *Report . . .* Melbourne, Government Printer, 1971. 143 p, illus. (Vic. Parliament. Parliamentary paper, 2 of 1971.)

The commission found that a bridge span collapsed when an attempt was made to straighten out a buckle and that neither the contractors nor the consulting and civil engineers had given sufficient attention to the design structure. Chairman: L. Matheson.

'Peace loans' were used by the federal government during World War I to raise money for the war effort. Poster, c1916, artist unknown.
NATIONAL LIBRARY

CHAPTER 47

THE PEOPLE AT WAR

MICHAEL McKERNAN

AUSTRALIANS HAVE SHOWN considerable enthusiasm to participate in the wars of other nations. They have fought in nine wars—from the Maori wars in New Zealand to the Vietnam War—but, of course, the wars of the twentieth century dominate Australian military history. World Wars I and II account for most of the 100 000 or more Australians killed in war. During World War I Australia sent 350 000 men overseas to fight, and in World War II nearly a million men and women were put in uniform.

Australian writing about war has been very uneven and, until recently, has attracted the attention of few professional historians. Much has been written by the participants in war; this is understandable because for them war was a time of great excitement and drama. Many of these writers wished to pay tribute to comrades who had been killed and to celebrate the group loyalty that participation in war produces. A great deal of this writing is described generally as 'battalion history'—the story of a unit's service from war's beginning to end. Some of these histories make excellent reading but others are of interest largely to the participants in the events described.

It is not difficult to understand the concentration of books relating to Australia's part in World War I. Australians regarded that war as a major opportunity to play a part, for the first time as a nation, on the world stage. They saw the war, therefore, as a time of high historical drama and were determined to capture and record every moment of importance. Artists, photographers and writers were appointed to the Australian Imperial Force to ensure that future generations would understand all that had transpired. C.E.W. Bean, a Sydney journalist with impressive imperial credentials, was elected by his colleagues in the Australian Journalists' Association as the government's official correspondent but, soon after the Australians went into action, he determined that the events warranted more than a transitory account. He began making plans for a national official history that would tell of all major actions in which the Australians were involved. He began collecting and preserving papers and diaries and before the end of the war a War Records Section was in operation collecting materials that would subsequently form the basis of the huge Australian War Memorial collection.

Bean began his history soon after the war ended in 1918. He had been with the troops since they first went into action and he resolved to write about only what he had seen; others were appointed to cover the campaigns unknown to Bean. The first of the twelve-volume history—*The story of Anzac*—was published in 1921 and the last in 1942, when Australia was at war again. Bean wrote six of the books himself but left to others the story of the Australians in the air, in Palestine and Rabaul, and the bitter account of the effect of the war on the home front. There was also a three-volume companion medical history written by A.G. Butler.

When war broke out again in 1939 Australians were much more cautious and much less inclined to see war as a moment of high historical importance for their nation. Even so, in 1942 another Sydney journalist, Gavin Long, was appointed official historian, and he began drawing up plans for a history on the same scale, at least, as Bean's. Entitled *Australia in the war of 1939–1945*, it eventually consisted of 22 volumes, including a four-volume medical history. The first volume was published in 1952 and the last in 1977. Long's history was as detailed as Bean's; the aim again was to recount every significant action in which the Australians were engaged. As general editor Long enlisted many more writers for his history. Both Bean (1946) and Long (1973) wrote a summary volume of their wars but these appeared long after the events they recorded and were seen somewhat as an appendage of the official histories.

The result of all this diligent labour was not what the editors and authors might have expected. Instead of beginning an interest in military history and opening up arguments which other historians could explore, they seem to have stunned their colleagues by amassing such a wealth of detail that for many years the official histories and the companion battalion histories remained all that was written on Australian military history. Few other historians bothered to enter an area which had been, apparently, so well covered.

So far had the military historical enterprise fallen from grace that no historian (or Sydney journalist) was sent as an official correspondent with the Australians to Korea or Vietnam and no-one bothered much with the records that would be needed to write the history of these conflicts. Somewhat belatedly, in 1969, Dr Robert O'Neill, then senior lecturer in history at Royal Military College, Duntroon, was appointed to a half-time position as Korean historian. His first volume appeared in 1981 and the second in 1984—even further behind the events he described than either Bean or Long. The Vietnam official historian, Dr Peter Edwards, was appointed in 1982, but his volumes will not be published for some years yet.

The accounts by official historians were all that could be shown as Australian military history for too long. Paradoxically, under the stimulus of the Vietnam War, historians generally began to turn to military history and to embark on an examination of the approaches, themes and issues ignored by the government-sponsored writers. World War I caught their attention, probably because political and social historians had become fascinated by the insights this period could throw on current questions such as conscription, pacifism and opposition to war. The new military historians explored the impact of World War I on individuals, through biographies and by opening up the archives of the Australian War Memorial. Bill Gammage (1975) showed what might be made of that rich collection. Gammage was a pioneer, rediscovering a long neglected field and stimulating a generation of writers, poets, artists and film-makers. He also represented a new breed of historian—his research work was done as a doctoral student at the Australian National University—the state-funded researcher who replaced the 'official historian' and had the research time required to explore many aspects of the nation's past.

Less effort, unfortunately, has been devoted by these historians to the colonial wars or to World War II and beyond. Notable exceptions are K.S. Inglis, *The rehearsal: Australians at war in the Sudan 1885* (Sydney, Rigby, 1985) and David Horner (1978, 1982), whose two theses—subsequently published—have initiated discussion on the relationship between the military and civil powers in wartime and the relationship betwen the various commanders. Horner continues to be fascinated with the problem of command and has stimulated a considerable departure from the Bean and Long tradition which focused inexorably on the common soldier in battle.

The creative literature of Australia at war is treated briefly in the following bibliography. World War I did not produce in Australia an extraordinary group of soldier poets as it did in England. Leon Gellert, Vance Palmer and Harley Matthews wrote some fine poems about their experience at the front but most of the poetry written at home was little more than drum-beating for the empire. Zora Cross and Mary Gilmore were exceptional in that their poetry considered the wastefulness of war and the possibility of pacifism.

A few novels emerged from a direct experience of the war—Frederick Manning's *Her privates we* (London, Davies, 1930), Leonard Mann's *Flesh in armour* (Melbourne, Phaedrus, 1932) and Frank Dalby Davison's *The wells of Beersheba* (A & R, 1933)—but the war has continued as a major interest of Australian writers. Martin Boyd's *Lucinda Brayford* (London, Cresset, 1946) and the Langton novels were written after World War II but are pervaded by Boyd's own experiences in the earlier war—especially the final Langton novel, *When blackbirds sing* (London, Abelard-Schuman, 1962). All these novels have at some time been reprinted.

Partly because World War II threatened Australia directly, a number of interesting novels were written in the immediate postwar years. These include fairly simple accounts of actual war experience such as Lawson Glassop's *We were the rats* (A & R, 1944) and others that raised questions about the nature of Australian society in the course of the account—for example, the novels by Eric Lambert, T.G. Hungerford and David Forrest. M. Barnard Eldershaw's *Tomorrow and tomorrow* (Melbourne, Georgian House, 1947) speculated about a defeated Australia and other women writers, such as Eleanor Dark and Dymphna Cusack, wrote novels that considered the problems of Australians at home. A final section of the Barnard Eldershaw novel was suppressed at the time of publication and has only recently been published in a new edition entitled *Tomorrow and tomorrow and tomorrow* (London, Virago, 1983).

John Manifold and David Campbell gained recognition as soldier poets in World War II and others, such as Judith Wright and Kenneth Slessor, have written poems on the war and its effects. Contemporary poets have returned to World War I as a theme with considerable success. Their work has been brought together in Geoff Page's *Shadows from wire* (Canberra, Australian War Memorial, 1983) and in Peter Pierce and Chris Wallace-Crabbe's anthology, *Clubbing the gunfire: 101 Australian war poems* (MUP, 1984).

The problem of selection in Australian military history is an unusual one. There is a large number of books within a quite narrow range—official histories, memoirs and battalion histories for the two world wars abound. The latter would number over 150. The Australian War Memorial has an 'in-house' bibliography in loose-leaf form of these battalion histories, some of which are being reprinted by John Burridge of Perth. However, the official and battalion histories concentrate on the two major wars and, apart from Inglis (1985), there is little of substance on the colonial wars—a field apparently still largely reserved for antiquarians—or on the Asian wars in which Australians have fought. There is little exploration, too, of strategy or tactics, little on the relationships between Australian and Allied forces, and little operational history at a level above the battalion. As in so many areas of Australian history, much remains to be done.

The approach in assembling the following bibliography has been firstly chronological and secondly representative. A list that included only the best works would concentrate on World War I and would scarcely cover recent events, the official histories excepted. The general reader, however, will want guidance on all wars in which Australians have fought and will also seek a variety of approaches to writing about war. The serious student will want to see how writing about war has changed over the years; therefore works of some antiquity have been included. The references have been divided into two major sections: bibliographies and general works; and theatres of war (arranged chronologically). The field is now expanding rapidly as historians come to realise that Bean and Long have not said the last word. Australian military history is, at last, entering the mainstream of the historical enterprise.

BIBLIOGRAPHIES AND GENERAL WORKS

BARTLETT, N. ed, *Australia at arms*. Canberra, Australian War Memorial, 1955. 275 p, illus, maps.

Anthology of first-hand accounts of Australians in action in colonial times and in two world wars.

DORNBUSCH, C.E. *Australian military bibliography*. Cornwallville, New York, Hope Farm Press, 1963. 80 p.

A standard reference tool, somewhat dated and incomplete.

FIELDING, J. AND O'NEILL, R. *A select bibliography of Australian military history 1891–1939*. Canberra, Australian National University; Australian Dictionary of Biography, 1978. 351 p.

Surveys the major historical sources, offical and non-official, manuscript and printed works, with brief commentary on most items.

FIRKINS, P.C. *The Australians in nine wars: Waikato to Long Tan*. Adelaide, Rigby, 1971. 448 p, illus, maps.

An overview for newcomers to military history.

ODGERS, G. *Pictorial history of the Royal Australian Air Force*. Sydney, Ure Smith, 1977. 160 p, illus, map.

The RAAF from formation in 1914 to 1976 with illustrations of action, personnel and machines. First published in 1965 as *The Royal Australian Air Force: an illustrated history*.

ODGERS, G. *The Royal Australian Navy: an illustrated history*. Sydney, Child & Henry, 1982. 224 p, illus, maps.

The RAN from formation, concentrating on the ships of the fleet and their history.

STANLEY, P. AND MCKERNAN, M. *Australians at war, 1885–1972: photographs from the collection of the Australian War Memorial*. Sydney, Collins, 1984. 260 p, illus.

Coffee table format with some excellent images.

WIGMORE, L.G. ed, *They dared mightily*. Canberra, Australian War Memorial, 1963. 317 p, illus, maps.

The stories of each Australian awarded the Victoria Cross or the George Cross, with an account of war service and an extract from the award citation.

THE SUDAN, CHINA AND SOUTH AFRICA

ABBOTT, J.H.M. *Tommy Cornstalk, being some account of the less notable features of the South Africa war from the point of view of the Australian ranks*. London, Longman Green, 1902. 264 p.

An idiosyncratic view of war from the ranks.

ATKINSON, J.J. *Australian contingents to the China Field Force, 1900–1901*. Sydney, NSW Military Historical Society, 1976. 69 p, illus, maps.

A description of the campaign and a nominal role of all Australian participants.

HUTCHINSON, F. AND MYERS, F. *The Australian contingent: a history of the patriotic movement in New South Wales and an account of the despatch of troops to the assistance of the imperial forces in the Soudan*. Sydney, Government Printer, 1885. 285 p.

Includes political and social comments on Australia's response to the empire's call.

MURRAY, P.L. *Official records of the Australian military contingents to the war in South Africa*. Melbourne, Government Printer, 1911. 607 p.

The complete nominal roll.

WALLACE, R.L. *The Australians at the Boer War*. Canberra, Australian War Memorial and AGPS, 1976. 402 p, illus, maps.

A complete account of all action in South Africa involving Australians.

WILKINSON, F. *Australian cavalry: the NSW Lancer Regiment and the First Australian Horse*. A & R, 1901. viii, 64 p, illus. Gives impressions of the Boer War, with an emphasis on action with a romantic flavour.

WORLD WAR I

ADAM-SMITH, P. *The Anzacs*. Melbourne, Nelson, 1985. 492 p, illus.

An illustrated account of the horrors and the effects of the war on the individual soldier.

BEAN, C.E.W. *Anzac to Amiens: a shorter history of the Australian fighting services in the First World War*. Canberra, Australian War Memorial, 1946. 567 p, illus, maps.

Bean's summary of the twelve-volume history; an excellent short account of the fighting.

BEAN, C.E.W. ed, *The official history of Australia in the war of 1914–1918*. A & R, 1921–42. 12 vols, illus, maps.

Recounts every significant action in which Australians participated. Celebratory of their unique fighting qualities, this work established a tradition in military history. The twelve volumes are progressively being reprinted by UQP.

BURKE, K. ed, *With horse and morse in Mesopotamia: the story of Anzacs in Asia*. Sydney, Arthur McQuitty, 1927. 200 p, illus, maps.

Australian and New Zealand wireless signal squadrons in the Middle East; an account of Australians of 'Dunsterforce' in Persia and Russia.

BUTLER, A.G. ed, *Official history of the Australian army medical services in the war of 1914–1918*. Canberra, Australian War Memorial, 1930–43. 3 vols, illus, maps.

An adjunct to Bean's history, providing the story of doctors, nurses and orderlies in all theatres.

GAMMAGE, W.L. *The broken years: Australian soldiers in the Great War*. Ringwood, Vic, Penguin, 1975. 328 p, illus, maps.

A moving book showing what the frontline soldier wrote about the war in his letters and diaries. Every phase of the fighting is covered. First published in 1974.

HILL, A.J. *Chauvel of the Light Horse: a biography of General Sir Harry Chauvel, G.C.M.G., K.C.B.* MUP, 1978. 265 p, illus, maps.

The biography of the commander and tactician, providing a good account of Australian fighting in the Middle East during World War I.

LAIRD, J.L. ed, *Other banners: an anthology of Australian literature of the First World War*. Canberra, Australian War Memorial and AGPS, 1971. 188 p.

Selections cover the various theatres of war, imperial sentiments, pacifism and return to civilian life.

MCKERNAN, M. *The Australian people and the Great War*. Sydney, Collins, 1984. 242 p, illus.

Explores the eager response in Australia to the call of empire. First publised in 1980.

ROBSON, L.L. *The first A.I.F.: a study of its recruitment 1914–1918*. MUP, 1982. 227 p, illus.

The first of a new generation of historians to take up military history after Bean. His book is a social profile of the 'diggers'. First published in 1970.

SERLE, G. *John Monash: a biography*. MUP in association with Monash University, 1982. 600 p, illus, maps.

A fine rounded biography rather than specialist military history.

Explains why Monash was Australia's most successful general.

WELBORN, S. *Lords of death: a people, a place, a legend.* Fremantle, WA, Fremantle Arts Centre Press, 1982. 223 p, illus, maps.

A regional study of the recruitment of the AIF, arguing the 'spirit of the place' shaped the men's response to war.

WILLIAMS, R. *These are facts: the autobiography of Air Marshall Sir Richard Williams, KBE, CB, DSO.* Canberra, Australian War Memorial and AGPS, 1977. 428 p, illus, maps.

An autobiography from a longserving senior commander. Covers service during the two world wars and includes an account of the formation of the RAAF.

WORLD WAR II

ADAM-SMITH, P. *Australia women at war.* Melbourne, Nelson, 1984. 386 p, illus.

A pioneering study of the role of women in World War II. Well illustrated but weak on historical analysis.

AUSTRALIA in the war of 1939–1945. Canberra, Australian War Memorial, 1952–77. 22 vols, illus, maps.

Prime Minister Chifley asked that this history be made more accessible to the general reader than Bean's. Concentrating on detail, this aim was not met, but the work is definitive. Divided into five series: Army, Navy, Air, Civil and Medical. The volumes are selectively being reissued by the Australian War Memorial.

THE GRIM glory of the 2/19 Battalion A.I.F., by various members of the Unit Association. Sydney, 2/19 Battalion AIF Association, 1975. 837 p, illus, maps.

Formed in 1940, this battalion fought in the Malayan campaign and on Singapore island before captivity. Represents the war experience of thousands of Australians.

HAYWOOD, E.V. *Six years in support: official history of 2nd/1st Australian Field Regiment.* Ed by A.G. Hanson. A & R, 1959. 211 p, illus, maps.

The regiment fought in north Africa and in New Guinea. Provides an insight to the *esprit-de-corps* of a unit in action.

HETHERINGTON, J.A. *Blamey, controversial soldier: a biography of Field Marshall Sir Thomas Blamey, GBE, KCB, CMG, DSO, ED.* Canberra, Australian War Memorial and AGPS, 1973. 414 p, illus.

Blamey was Menzies' surprise choice to command the second AIF. Shows why Blamey aroused such strong feelings. First published in 1954.

HORNER, D.M. *Crisis of command: Australian generalship and the Japanese threat, 1941–1943.* ANUP, 1978. 395 p, illus, maps.

The first of the 'new wave' World War II military histories. A judicious account of tensions and in-fightings at the highest level of Australian command.

HORNER, D.M. *High command: Australian and allied strategy, 1939–1945.* Sydney, Allen & Unwin; Canberra, Australian War Memorial, 1982. 556 p, illus, maps.

Shows how the use of Australian troops depended as much on political considerations as on strategic ones.

KEOGH, E.G. *Middle East 1939–43.* Melbourne, Wilke, 1959. 302 p, illus, maps.

Written from the viewpoint of army command it examines tactical operations of the Australians in the north African campaign.

LONG, G.M. *The six years war: a concise history of Australia in the 1939–45 war.* Canberra, Australian War Memorial and AGPS, 1973. 518 p, illus, maps.

For the general reader this is the best place to start to understand Australia's enormous contribution to the Allied cause.

McKERNAN, M. *All in! Australia during the Second World War.* Melbourne, Nelson, 1983. 286 p, illus.

The home front response to the second European war and the reaction to the threat of Japanese invasion.

PARNELL, N.M. *Whispering death: a history of the RAAF's Beaufighter squadrons.* Sydney, Reed, 1980. 128 p, illus, maps.

The story of the Beaufighter squadrons involved in the defence of Australia 1942–43. Includes a nominal roll and a technical appendix.

VOLUNTEER DEFENCE CORPS. *On guard with the Volunteer Defence Corps.* Canberra, Australian War Memorial, 1944. 172 p, illus.

One of a series of first-hand accounts. All contributions are anonymous, giving, perhaps, greater authenticity.

KOREA AND VIETNAM

BARTLETT, N. ed, *With the Australians in Korea.* Canberra, Australian War Memorial, 1960. 294 p, illus, maps.

An anthology of first-hand accounts of action, using the narratives of combatants and war correspondents. First published in 1954.

FAIRFAX, D. *Navy in Vietnam: a record of the Royal Australian Navy in the Vietnam War, 1965–1972.* AGPS, 1980. 232 p, illus, maps.

Sponsored by the Dept of Defence, this tells of naval action, concentrating on the deployment of each ship.

McNEILL, I. *The team: Australian advisers in Vietnam 1962–1972.* Canberra, Australian War Memorial, 1984. 528 p.

The first major work about the advisers who worked in every part of South Vietnam. The most complete account, until the publication of an official history.

ODGERS, G. *Across the parallel: the Australian 77th Squadron with the United States Air Force in the Korean War.* London, Heinemann, 1952. 239 p, illus, maps.

An attempt to recreate the life of a squadron, imaginative but based on fact.

ODGERS, G. *Mission Vietnam: Royal Australian Air Force operations, 1964–1972.* AGPS, 1974. 186 p, illus, map.

Sponsored by the Dept of Defence. Covers all significant RAAF actions in Vietnam.

O'NEILL, R.J. *Australia in the Korean War 1950–53.* Canberra, Australian War Memorial and AGPS, 1981 and 1984. 2 vols, illus.

Analyses the strategic and diplomatic impact of war and Australia's operational involvement.

O'NEILL, R.J. *Vietnam task: the 5th Battalion of the Royal Australian Regiment 1966/67.* Melbourne, Cassell, 1968. 256 p, illus, maps.

A battalion history concentrating on the men involved.

Front cover, Wirth Bros circus brochure. Printed by Troedel and Cooper, Melbourne, 1928.
BOOROWA PRODUCTIONS

CHAPTER 48

SPORT AND LEISURE

VICTOR CRITTENDEN, G. PEGUERO AND CAROL M. MILLS

SPORT

THE *MACQUARIE DICTIONARY* defines sport as 'a diversion, recreation, pleasant pastime' as well as 'a meeting for athletic competition' while leisure is defined as 'having one's time free from the demands of work or duty'. Many people's leisure time is fully occupied by watching or participating in sport. Some people swim, fish or play tennis as a leisure activity, while others regard such pursuits as their sport. The line between sport and leisure is a fine one. This chapter discusses the literature on these topics separately but has one alphabetical bibliography.

Australians are continuously attracted to the competitive arenas of sport and venerate the numerous sporting personalities who have risen to stardom. The spectator element—the most popular leisure-related activity in Australia—has been well served by several publishers specialising in sporting publications. The 'sporting mania', adroitly highlighted in Keith Dunstan's *Sport*, (Sydney, Cassell, 1973) has more than adequately spilt over into the buying of books, to the extent that in a country with a small population where low print runs are the bane of the book industry, a work on a famous sporting personality, major sporting event or popular sport is likely to make a substantial impact on the bestseller list. By comparison, the recreational side of sport does not have the same impact. It has been left to government-funded projects such as 'Life. Be in it' to encourage the recreational side of sport, along with wider leisure pursuits. The bias of commercial publishers towards the competitive in sport is inevitably reflected in the composition of the bibliography for this chapter.

Some sports do not appear in the bibliography simply because there are few, if any, books on them. Rowing, hockey, netball and the aeronautical sports of hang-gliding and gliding have not been well treated by publishers. Just as many sports attract relatively small, though no doubt enthusiastic, crowds and comparatively little media attention, so too are these same sports poorly represented on the bookshelves.

The sports introduced by European settlers were, in the early colonial period, fairly simple affairs, reflecting the practices common in Europe generally and in the United Kingdom in particular. Boxing, wrestling, simple athletics and competitive rifle shooting were common pastimes. These were accompanied, from earliest days, by betting and gambling; though both were recognised as dangerous to society, little could be done to suppress them. Blood sports also prospered, but it is questionable whether cockfighting—in which, after all, normally no person was directly involved—should be considered a leisure activity or a sport.

Australian reports, documents, books and journal articles it has collected on recreation, sport and tourism from 1982 onwards. The *Australian leisure index* is produced three times a year, with a cumulation at the end of the year. Most of the material recorded in the index is held by ACHPIRST and is available for loan to other libraries or organisations on request. The index is nationally accessible online through ACI's AUSINET system; this online file is called LeisureLine.

Another function of ACHPIRST has been to publish D. Dow's leisure bibliography (1983)—a substantial publication containing approximately 5500 records of monographs about Australian sport, recreation and tourism published before 1982 and held by the relevant state department libraries and other major libraries around Australia. The bibliography is arranged, like the *Australian leisure index*, by broad subject categories including specific sports and with an author and subject index. The location of each item is also recorded. ACHPIRST has thus taken on the role of national co-ordinator of sports information in Australia.

The easiest way to gain access to what ACHPIRST offers is by searching the hard copy bibliography and index, which should be available in most local libraries. The state libraries, many academic institutions and numerous special libraries are linked with AUSINET, thus allowing online access to the LeisureLine data base. The Footscray Institute of Technology Library, Melbourne, is also prepared to do online searches of LeisureLine and relevant international files at cost.

ACHPIRST has sought to establish links with other countries. Many of these, including Canada, the United Kingdom, West Germany and the USSR, have well-established national documentation and information centres for sport. Through the International Association for Sport Information (IASI) and UNESCO, there are now plans to establish an international sport data base, to be created by merging all the national data bases that currently exist. The Canadian sports data base, produced by the Sport Information Resource Centre (SIRC), has been nominated as the data base to which other countries will contribute and to which ACHPIRST is already sending all the Australian material. The need for such co-operation is based on the premise that serious research requires not only a national but also an international perspective.

The Australian government, with the co-operation of the Confederation of Australian Sport, has recently established an information service for sports coaches. Relying heavily on the national and international sport documentation centre, the co-ordinator of this service is providing detailed and up-to-date information for many sports coaches throughout Australia.

LEISURE

Leisure is defined here as the ways—other than competitive sport, cultural pursuits or passive activity such as watching television—in which we occupy that part of our lives not given to work or domestic obligation.

There are many more types of leisure and crafts which are or have been pursued in Australia than there are works about them. Some pursuits, even those of long standing, do not appear to have aroused an interest in their historical background. Most writing on leisure activities describes the practice, techniques and refinements of a particular pursuit, or of some aspect of it. But the historical literature of specific spare-time pursuits practised in Australia's past is patchy. Those who seek the history of leisure will have to check the periodical literature as well as monographs. In more recent decades there has been a diversification in specialist periodicals to meet the requirements of followers of particular pursuits. Such periodicals can be a most useful source; they often include news items, which are themselves potential history, and may contain historical material.

For the nineteenth century, much of the material is in first-hand accounts of contemporary life directed to people 'at home'—in the United Kingdom—or used as Christmas gifts for relatives and friends abroad. If an enquirer has an interest in a particular pursuit, there may be no alternative to collecting references from large masses of such comment and reports of the period in journals and newspapers, including their gossip columns. Typical of this genre of social comment are 'Garryowen's' *The chronicles of early Melbourne 1835–1852: historical, anecdotal and personal* (1888; facs, Melbourne, Heritage Publications, 1976); *The letters of Rachel Henning* (1952; new edition, A & R, 1986), which consists of letters describing life in rural Queensland and New South Wales from 1853 to 1882; and Louisa Anne Meredith's *Notes and sketches of New South Wales during a residence in that colony from 1839 to 1844* (1844; facs, Ringwood, Vic, Penguin, 1973). A further sampling of commentaries appears in the bibliography below.

The citations in the bibliography are in one sequence with those for sport. Note that some references have not been annotated because the title is self-explanatory. Although gardening could be considered a leisure activity, references to it are included in chapter 40 which discusses domestic life. There are many general books which, although not intended as history, interest today's reader because of their treatment of a leisure activity or because they reflect the period and, although of a practical turn, have some inherent historical insight. Such is the case with J. Davis (1969) on bushwalking and rockclimbing, which mentions past practices, climbs, personalities and so on. Included in the bibliography are contemporary comment, social histories and modern discussions of social patterns relating to leisure. Works which mention leisure pursuits that do not have their own written histories have been favoured. Perhaps one of the rarer, more interesting ones is Cole's *Hobbies*. Cole, a dynamic person with a strong work ethic, even made hobbies an extension of this need to be occupied. At a superficial level, the enquirer might consult any number of the general late twentieth-century pictorial publications such as *A day in the life of Australia* (Sydney, A Day in the Life of Australia Pty Ltd, 1981) to provide a cursory coverage.

The literature on clubs and on aspects of drinking is diverse. Food is well covered in the wake of the emergence of a popular gourmet movement in Australia in the 1970s and a selection of titles is listed in the discussion of domestic life in chapter 40. Titles such as *The colonial cook book* (Sydney, Hamlyn, 1970) are rewarding for an insight into colonial ideas on festive food. Cyril Pearl (1969) and Len Evans *Complete book of Australian wine* (Sydney, Lansdowne, 1984) discuss the history of beer and wine.

The leisure activities associated with clubs are of particular interest. Establishment clubs based on their English counterparts have almost all published short histories. Several of these have been listed and the flavour of club life can be had by dipping into, say, Dow (1947) or Green (1961). The development of more egalitarian clubs is predominantly a postwar phenomenon. A number of associations, particularly women's organisations such as the Country Women's Organisation, founded in 1922, have provided leisure as well as welfare facilities, and membership has been open to a wide variety of people. Most service organisations, such as Apex, Lions, Rotary and Zonta, are more restrictive in their membership criteria. Commemorative publications have been issued about all these organisations but none has yet attracted a serious history; nor have football or RSL clubs, which have grown dramatically in some states since World War II. The leisure activities associated with sporting clubs, service clubs and even some political clubs are often just as important as the purpose for which they were ostensibly founded.

Amusements and diversions range from festive processions to agricultural shows, from sweepstakes to Saturday night dances. There is as yet no literature of substance on these aspects of leisure. Some idea of the past can be gleaned from the various state tourist offices and travel agents; and the sales catalogues of manufacturers often provide information on toys and games for young and old. A bibliography on Australian popular culture, including dancing, film, gambling, mass media (comics, popular literature etc) music, show business and the theatre is to be found in D. Walker and P. Spearritt eds, *Australian popular culture* (Sydney, Allen & Unwin, 1979). Readers should also refer to entries in chapter 52 of this volume.

The literature on crafts includes little history. Pottery, for example, was born in colonial times out of necessity and gradually became an industry. Published histories tend to cover industrial history rather than the development of the small craft, but it is hoped that the growing stream of publications relating to industrial archaeology will contribute further to the history of some crafts. No individual works on leather, macrame, lace, basketry, woodwork, home brewing and lapidary have been listed. The history of these crafts has still to be written. Collective approaches to some crafts can be found in wider ranging works, such as Brand (1979), which covers a number of activities from the past, using photographs of surviving examples, and in the catalogue of the First Australian Exhibition of Women's Work (1907). This catalogue is itself a large-scale record of the arts and crafts being practised by women in Australia. It contains thousands of entries, divided into groups, with a short description of each.

Works on outdoor pastimes range from caving to cycling, from car rallies and motoring to rock climbing, holidays at the beach, bushwalking and nudism. Camping and caravanning, cross-country sports such as orienteering and forms of hunting have not yet found historians. Fishing, one of the most enduring of outdoor pursuits, seems to be totally lacking in history although there is a plethora of books on how to do it.

One of the most important sources for outdoor activities is the popular journal *Walkabout* (1934–74) which catered for the interests of those who wanted to read about leisure in the bush, by the seaside, in the mountains. Once called 'Australia's way of life magazine', it has not been replaced since its demise.

Book collecting, and collecting fine arts and antiques, are dealt with in other chapters of this volume. Collectors have been slow to record their own history: there is no history of either stamp or coin collecting though the literature of the collecting process itself is broad. We have, and have had, collectors in Australia of almost any artefact or natural phenomenon that can be named or moved, but voluminous literature of collecting is almost all about the contents of the collections rather than the development of interest in particular aspects of collecting.

George French Angas, The young cricketer, *c1860. Watercolour. Angas's delicate watercolour, probably painted in the 1850s, depicts a particular ideal of English boyhood. Cricket assumed an enormous importance in Australia during the nineteenth century, not least because it was perceived to be representative of all the English virtues. Excellence in cricket was proof to many Australians that the English race had not degenerated in the hot climate, a fear that was often expressed in contemporary newspapers.*
NATIONAL LIBRARY

AKHURST, A. AND KNIGHT, F.F. *History of the Australian Club, Melbourne*. Melbourne, Australian Club, 1943–71. 2 vols, illus.

ANDREWS, S. *Take your partners: traditional dancing in Australia*. Melbourne, Hyland House, 1979. 208 p, illus, music.

Australian folk dancing, its history, and how to do it. First published in 1974.

ARLOTT, J. AND BROGDEN, S. *The first test match: England v. Australia 1877*. London, Phoenix House, 1950. 62 p.

The story of the first England cricket team to tour Australia. Good biographical details on the teams. Match statistics.

ATKINSON, G. *The book of Australian rules finals*. Melbourne, Five Mile Press, 1983. 319 p, illus.

First published as a coverage of the Victorian Football League finals to 1973, this book has been expanded to include other states. It includes graphic descriptions as well as statistical material.

AUSTRALIA. Dept of Tourism and Recreation. Sports Institute Study Group. *Report of the Australian Sports Institute Study Group*. AGPS, 1975. xxxxiv, 289 p.

The rationale and justifications for setting up the Australian Sports Institute. Includes a reading list.

AUSTRALIA. Parliament. House of Representatives. Standing Committee on Expenditure. *The way we p(l)ay: commonwealth assistance for sport and recreation*. AGPS, 1983. 162 p.

The report of an inquiry by a federal government committee into commonwealth expenditure on youth, sport and recreation in Australia. Sixty recommendations are listed.

AUSTRALIAN etiquette; or, the rules and usages of the best society in the Australasian colonies, together with their sports, pastimes, games and amusements. Melbourne, People's Publishing Co, 1886. 643 p, illus.

Discussion of manners and sport, but has chapters on 'amusements', which are non-competitive leisure activites. Facsimile edition, Melbourne, Dent, 1980.

AUSTRALIAN leisure index, 1982– . Melbourne, Australian Clearing House for Publications in Recreation, Sport and Tourism.

An index, cumulated annually, of major Australian publications concerned with sport, recreation and tourism.

AUSTRALIAN UNESCO SEMINAR, Broadbeach, Queensland, 1976. *Entertainment and society: report of the Unesco seminar held at Broadbeach, Queensland, June 8–12, 1976*. Ed by Geoff Caldwell. AGPS, 1977. 242 p, illus.

Essays on clubs and casinos as well as on popular and classical music, censorship, pop and high culture.

BAGLIN, D. AND AUSTIN, Y. *Australian pub crawl*. Sydney, Murray Child, 1977. 200 p, illus.

Pictorial survey of hotels which serves indirectly as a history of them.

BAGLIN, D. AND WHEELHOUSE, F. *Collecting Australia's past*. Sydney, Cassell, 1981. 160 p, illus.

A guide for collectors, providing numerous illustrations of items from the past, many of interest as products of leisure.

BANFIELD, E.J. *The confessions of a beachcomber: scenes and incidents in the career of an unprofessional beachcomber in tropical Queensland*. London, Unwin, 1908. 336 p, illus, map.

A contribution to the literature describing this lifestyle. Reprinted, A & R, 1968.

BANKS, N. *The world in my diary: from Melbourne to Helsinki for the Olympic Games*. Melbourne, Heinemann, 1953. 258 p, illus.

The author was Australia's radio commentator for the Helsinki Games.

BARRIE, D.M. *Turf cavalcade: a review of the one hundred and fifty years of horse-racing in Australia, and of the Australian Jockey Club's hundred years at Randwick*. Sydney, Australian Jockey Club, 1960. 191 p, illus.

A history giving the introduction of thoroughbred horses in Australia from beginnings in 1819. Deals with Sydney and Melbourne.

BARTROP, P.R. *Scores, crowds and records: statistics on the Victorian Football League since 1945*. Sydney, History Project Inc, 1984. 186 p. (Historical statistics monograph, 4.)

A statistical listing relating to Australian rules football.

BAVERSTOCK, W. *The America's Cup: challenge from down under*. Sydney, Murray, 1967. 175 p, illus.

The entire story of an early, ill-fated attempt to win the famous cup. Glossary and table of results, 1870–1967.

BECKETT, R. *Convicted tastes: food in Australia*. Sydney, Allen & Unwin, 1984. 217 p, illus.

A history of cookery, food and eating in Australia.

BELL, J.P.F. *The Queensland Club, 1859–1959*. Brisbane, The Club, 1966. 121 p, illus.

BLANCH, J. AND JENES, P. *Australia's complete history at the Commonwealth Games*. Sydney, John Blanch, 1982. 124 p, illus.

A brief discussion of Australian success at the games from the Festival of Europe, 1911, to the 12th games in Brisbane, 1982. Lists all Australian teams and medallists.

BLANCH, J. ed, *Australian sporting records*. Melbourne, Budget Books, 1981. 552 p, illus.

Detailed listing of Australian records in all sports. First published in 1968. Earlier editions include some historical material not included in this later edition.

BONDI SURF BATHERS' LIFE SAVING CLUB. *History of Bondi Surf Bathers' Life Saving Club, 1906–1956*. Sydney, The Club, 1956. 52 p, illus.

The story of the famous club and the people who made it happen.

BRADMAN, D.G. *Farewell to cricket*. London, Hodder and Stoughton, 1950. 320 p, illus.

The reminiscences of Australia's greatest batsman, from childhood to the end of his cricket career.

BRAND, M.A. *Australiana: over 150 years of decorative crafts, furniture, jewellery, pottery, coins and bottles*. Sydney, Ure Smith, 1979. 144 p, illus.

A discussion and collection for an overview.

BROWN, L.H. *Victor Trumper and the 1902 Australians*. London, Secker & Warburg, 1981. 207 p, illus.

There is a fascination about the cricket season of 1902. The Australian tour of England in that year was one of the most memorable of all; includes match statistics.

CAPE, H. *Five times round: a story*. Buderim, Qld, The Author, 1979. 77 p, illus, maps.

An account of the Redex/Mobilgas reliability trials for motor vehicles, 1954–58.

CASHMAN, R. *Australian cricket crowds: the attendance cycle daily figures 1877–1984*. Sydney, History Project Inc, 1984. 324 p. (Historical statistics monograph, 5.)

A statistical listing of attendance at cricket matches.

CASHMAN, R. AND McKERNAN, M. eds, *Sport, money, morality and the media.* UNSWP, 1981. 343 p, illus, map.

A collection of highly informative essays on the sociology and politics of Australian sport. Substantial bibliography.

CAVANOUGH, M. *The Melbourne Cup 1861–1982.* Melbourne, Currey O'Neil, 1983. 546 p, illus.

A year-by-year account of the Melbourne Cup and races leading up to it, with an appendix of detailed results. Has an excellent index. First published in 1960 as *Cup Day*, by Maurice Cavanough and Meurig Davies.

CAWLEY, E. AND COLLINS, B. *Evonne.* London, Hart-Davis, MacGibbon, 1975. 191 p, illus.

Autobiography of Evonne Goolagong, an Aboriginal girl from outback NSW who won the women's singles championship at Wimbledon in 1971 and 1980.

CHALLINGWORTH, E.B. *Dancing down the years: the romantic century in Australia.* Melbourne, Craftsman Press, 1978. 88 p, illus, music.

Popular dancing for parties and festive occasions.

CHILDSPLAY, Elizabeth Bay House, 1st April to 30th June 1980. Sydney, Elizabeth Bay House Trust, 1980. 23 p, illus.

'Catalogue of an exhibition of children's game, books and toys of the 19th and early 20th centuries.'

CLARKE, M. *Nudism in Australia: a first study.* Waurn Ponds, Vic, Deakin University Press, 1982. 357 p, illus.

CLARKE, R. *et al, Athletics the Australian way.* Sydney, Lansdowne, 1976. 119 p, illus.

Gives records and describes Australian athletics.

COLE, E.W. *Hobbies.* Melbourne, Coles Book Arcade, 191-. 98 p, illus.

Previous edition entitled *Hobby land: showing the great value of hobbies to all mankind* (1902). Cole is famous for his *Cole's funny picture book* for children.

COOMBE, D.C. *A history of the Davis Cup: being the story of the International Lawn Tennis Championship, 1900–48.* Sydney, Australasian Publishing Co, 1949. 288 p, illus.

The Davis Cup began in 1900 when the cup was presented by Dwight Davis, then a leading American player, for competition among players of different countries.

CORRIS, P. *Lords of the ring.* Sydney, Cassell, 1980. 200 p, illus.

This book covers boxing in Australia from 1814 to about 1970, at which point the popularity of the sport began to decline.

COX, A.B. *The first hundred years: history of S.A. Tattersalls Club.* Adelaide, Brolga Books, 1980. 137 p, illus.

CRAZE, B. *A history of a country show.* Cowra, NSW, Cowra and District Historical Society, 1979. 80 p, illus, maps.

The Cowra Show, 1879–1979, is typical of rural shows all over Australia.

CUMES, J.W.C. *Their chastity was not too rigid: leisure times in early Australia.* Sydney, Reed, 1979. 378 p, illus.

Covers leisure to about 1850, including music, the performing arts and sport.

CUTHBERT, B. *Golden girl as told to Jim Webster.* London, Pelham, 1966. 160 p, illus.

Cuthbert won four gold medals at the 1956 and 1964 Olympic Games. She was one of the great short distance runners.

D'ALPUGET, L. *Yachting in Australia: yesterday, today, tomorrow.* Melbourne, Hutchinson, 1980. 329 p, illus, maps.

Not a complete view but an attempt to put events and developments in Australian yachting into historical perspective and to fill in some detail.

DALY, J.A. *Elysian fields: sport, class and community in colonial South Australia, 1836–1890.* Adelaide, The Author, 1982. 225 p, illus, maps.

An examination of the role of sport in colonial SA, based on newspapers, diaries, letters, minute books, public documents, maps, photographs and paintings.

DAVID, M. *Australian ocean racing.* A & R, 1967. 192 p, illus, maps.

Written to create something of the atmosphere of Australian ocean racing and to put on record some of the rapidly growing achievements of Australian yachtsmen.

DAVIS, J. ed, *Rope and rucksack: bushwalking, rockclimbing, canoeing, canyoning, caving, ski touring, cascading.* A & R, 1969. 127 p, illus.

A compendium on how to approach various sports compiled at the time when these sports were gaining prominence. Good descriptive material.

DAVIS, P.L. *Australians on the road.* Adelaide, Rigby, 1979. 232 p, illus.

History of motoring for leisure in Australia.

DINGLE, A.E. *Drink and drinking in nineteenth century Australia: a statistical commentary.* Melbourne, Dept of Economic History, Monash University, 1978. 41 1. (Monash papers in economic history, 6.)

Challenges the popular concept that heavy drinking has been an important component of an emerging national character and suggests that it is difficult to discern a distinctly Australian pattern of consumption.

D'OMBRAIN, A. *Fish tales.* Adelaide, Rigby, 1968. 178 p, illus.

Stories of deep-sea fishing in Australian waters.

DOW, D. *Australian leisure bibliography.* Melbourne, Australian Clearing House for Publications in Recreation, Sport and Tourism, 1983. 332 p.

A listing of information on sport, recreation and tourism being the holdings of major specialist libraries in Australia.

DOW, D.M. *Melbourne Savages: a history of the first fifty years of the Melbourne Savage Club.* Melbourne, The Club, 1947. 256 p, illus.

DU CROS, E. *Skindiving in Australia.* A & R, 1960. 180 p, illus, map.

Skindiving did not begin in Australia until the late 1930s. This is a history of the sport since then.

DUNNING, E. AND SHEARD, K. *Barbarians, gentlemen and players: a sociological study of the development of rugby football.* ANUP, 1979. 321 p.

A scholarly and erudite analysis of the origins of, and meanings in, rugby football. The book is a seminal work in the understanding of rugby.

DWYER, T.J. *Show jumping down under.* Adelaide, Rigby, 1973. 120 p, illus.

History of show jumping in Australia from the formation of the Equestrian Federation of Australia in 1950.

EDWARDS, R.G. *Australian traditional bushcrafts.* Melbourne, Lansdowne, 1975. 143 p, illus.

Describes the execution of crafts of the past, from saddlery and furniture to dam and tank sinking.

ELLIOTT, H. *The golden mile: the Herb Elliott story as told to Alan Trengrove.* London, Cassell, 1961. 178 p, illus.

Herb Elliott had the perfect physique and temperament for being a great runner. This is his story, told in a light-hearted way.

FARRELLY, B. *This surfing life, by Midget Farrelly as told to Craig McGregor*. Adelaide, Rigby, 1965. 138 p, illus.

A personal view of the sport of surfing by Australia's first world champion, Midget Farrelly.

FIDDIAN, M. *The pioneers*. Melbourne, Victorian Football Association, 1977. 192 p, illus.

A centennial history of the second major Australian rules football competition in Victoria.

FIRST AUSTRALIAN EXHIBITION OF WOMEN'S WORK, Melbourne, 1907. *Official souvenir catalogue*. Melbourne, Hearne & Co, Paragon Printers, 1907. 399 p, illus.

Catalogue of one of the largest art and crafts exhibitions ever held in this country.

THE FIRST *ten years: the Embroiderers' Guild, Victoria*. Melbourne, The Guild, 1980. 45 p, illus.

Period covered is 1960–70.

FRASER, D. AND GORDON, H. *Gold medal girl: confessions of an Olympic champion*. Melbourne, Lansdowne, 1965. 206 p, illus.

Autobiography of the champion swimmer Dawn Fraser, with some emphasis on the Olympic Games.

FREELAND, J.M. *The Australian pub*. Melbourne, Sun Books, 1977. 192 p, illus.

The pub in Australian society to 1966, with some emphasis on architecture. First published in 1966.

FRIEND, J. *Classic climbs of Australia*. Leura, NSW, Second Back Row Press, 1983. 111 p, illus, maps.

Anthology of accounts of rockclimbing.

FRINDALL, W. *The Wisden book of test cricket: 1876–77 to 1977–78*. London, Macdonald and Jane's, 1979. 1024 p.

A chronological presentation of scores for all cricket tests, with accompanying statistical analyses which include tables for all players listed.

GALTON, B. *Gladiators of the surf: the Australian Surf Life Saving Championships, a history*. Sydney, Reed, 1984. 288 p, illus.

A history, carnival-by-carnival, with vignette biographies of notable surf lifesavers interspersed and an appendix of detailed results.

GILLISON, J.M. *A history of the Lyceum Club, Melbourne*. Melbourne, The Club, 1975. 118 p, illus.

A history of a women's club whose main criterion for membership is that of having tertiary qualifications.

GODDARD, R.H. *The Union Club, 1857–1967*. Sydney, Halstead Press, 1957. 140 p, illus.

GOLLAN, A. *The tradition of Australian cooking*. ANUP, 1978. 211 p, illus.

Covers many aspects of cooking, from campfire to indoor and discusses gadgets, kitchens and recipes.

GORDON, H.C. *Young men in a hurry: the story of Australia's fastest decade* (3rd edn). Melbourne, Lansdowne, 1962. 164 p, illus.

Australian athletics in the 1950s. Some good photographs. First published in 1961.

GOULD, N. *On and off the turf in Australia*. London, George Routledge & Son, 1895. 244 p, illus.

An excellent biographical record of horseracing in Australia at the end of the nineteenth century by the successful novelist of horseracing adventures. Facsimile edition, Libra Books, 1973.

GREEN, F.C. *The Tasmanian Club, 1861–1961*. Hobart, The Club, 1961. 93 p, illus.

HANRAHAN, B. ed, *Motor racing the Australian way*. Melbourne, Lansdowne, 1972. 127 p, illus, maps.

A collection of short articles on every aspect of the sport, written by some of Australia's great drivers and including many fine action photos.

HONEY, T. ed, *Bowls: the Australian way of life*. Melbourne, Lansdowne, 1974. 117 p, illus.

Aspects of lawn bowls described by well-known players, with sections on administration of the game and Australia's great players.

HORNADGE, W. *Stamps: a collectors' guide*. Dubbo, NSW, Review Publications, 1980. 168 p, illus.

A basic introduction, first published in 1968.

INGLIS, G. *Sport and pastime in Australia*. London, Methuen, 1912. 308 p, illus.

This book, written and published in England, provides a fascinating historical treatment of Australian sport around the turn of the century.

INGLIS, J. *Our Australian cousins*. London, Macmillan, 1880. 466 p, illus, maps.

Includes descriptions of various amusements and pastimes including fishing.

JACQUES, T.D. AND PAVIA, G.R. eds, *Sport of Australia: selected readings in physical activity*. Sydney, McGraw-Hill, 1976. 169 p.

A good collection of essays on the sociology and politics of Australian sport including a historical perspective by such writers as Anthony Trollope. Good bibliography.

LAWN *tennis in Australasia*. By 'Austral'. Sydney, Edward Dunlop, 1912. 344 p, illus.

Features 62 action photographs taken in match play in Australia of the four greatest players of the period: Brookes, Wilding, McLoughlin and Larned.

LE QUESNE, A.L. *The bodyline controversy*. London, Secker & Warburg, 1983. 241 p, illus.

Though focused on the Australia–England test series of 1932–33, this book includes analysis of techniques and social factors in cricket from the nineteenth century and discusses the changes in policy that followed the 1932–33 series.

LESTER, G. *Australians at the Olympics: a definitive history*. Sydney, Lester-Townsend, Melbourne, Kingfisher, 1984. 284 p, illus.

Brief histories of each games, biographies of Australian Olympic champions, placing of each Australian competitor (including those eliminated in heats) and a list of all Olympic placegetters.

McGUIRE, P. *Inns of Australia*. Melbourne, Heinemann, 1952. 284 p, illus.

A history of inns in Australia. 'If you take the inn out of our history, you leave it filleted' (px).

MANDLE, W.F. *Winners can laugh: sport and society*. Ringwood, Vic, Penguin, 1974. 64 p, illus.

Sport in modern society, its qualities, the demand it makes and what it reveals about the people involved in it.

MANT, G. *The big show: the 150th anniversary of the Royal Agricultural Society of NSW*. Sydney, Horwitz, 1972. 136 p, illus.

A history of Sydney's Royal Easter Show, the largest in Australia.

MERCER, D. ed, *Leisure and recreation in Australia*. Melbourne, Sorrett, 1975. 256 p, illus.

Essays on subjects such as tourism, holidays, national parks and wilderness areas.

MERCER, D. ed, *Outdoor recreation: Australian perspectives*. Melbourne, Sorrett, 1981. 171 p, illus, maps.

Studies of the use of land and national parks for outdoor recreation activities in Australia.

MORGAN, E.J.R. *The Adelaide Club, 1863–1963.* Adelaide, The Club, 1963. 135 p, illus.

MULVANEY, D.J. *Cricket walkabout: the Australian Aboriginal cricketers on tour 1867–8.* MUP, 1967. xiv, 112 p, illus, map.

Account of the first and only tour of England by a team of Australian Aborigines.

MYATT, B. AND HANLEY, B. *Australian coins, notes and medals.* Sydney, Horwitz Grahame, 1982. 262 p, illus.

A history describing the currency and medals of the past. First published in 1980.

NATIONAL CAPITAL AGRICULTURAL SOCIETY. *A history of agricultural shows in the A.C.T.* Canberra, The Society, 1979. x, 54 p, illus.

O'LOGHLEN, F. *Champions of the turf.* Sydney, F.H. Johnston Publishing Co, 1945. 160 p, illus.

Gives details of famous horses such as Carbine, Ajax and Phar Lap.

OLYMPIC GAMES, Melbourne, 1956. Organizing Committee. *The official report of the organizing committee for the games of the XVI Olympiad, Melbourne, 1956.* Melbourne, Government Printer, 1958. 760 p, illus.

An encyclopaedic work, this includes many facts on the events, an index of competitors, illustrations and charts.

PEARL, C. *Beer, glorious beer: with incidental observations on great beer myths, pubs and publicans, barmaids and breathalysers, mum, flip, berry bards, and beer in the kitchen, etc. etc.* Melbourne, Nelson, 1969. 173 p, illus.

PEARSON, J.K. *Surfing subcultures of Australia and New Zealand.* UQP, 1979. 213 p, illus.

This is not about surfing, but the people who surf—surf lifesavers and surfboard riders.

POLLARD, J. *Australian cricket: the game and players.* Sydney, Hodder and Stoughton in association with the ABC, 1982. 1162 p, illus.

An encyclopaedic work covering cricketing terms, associations, players, facilities and matches.

POLLARD, J. *Australian rugby union: the game and the players.* A & R, 1984. 945 p, illus.

A major work on rugby union and its place in Australian sport.

POLLARD, J. *The pictorial history of Australian horse racing.* Sydney, Lansdowne, 1981. 400 p, illus.

A history from the beginning, illustrations of horses and personalities and famous races. Deals with all states and has a horse index. First published in 1981.

POLLARD, J. ed, *Australian and New Zealand fishing.* Sydney, Ure Smith, 1979. 952 p, illus, maps.

A comprehensive book on all aspects of Australian fish and fishing. Contains maps and drawings of various fish. It was first published in 1969 with the title *Australian and New Zealand complete book of fishing.*

POOLE, P.N. *Rodeo in Australia.* Adelaide, Rigby, 1977. 102 p, illus.

History of the rodeo in Australia from the formation of the Australian Rough Riders Association in 1944. Includes tables of Australian champions.

PRESTON, J. *Racing axemen: a history of competitive wood-chopping in Australia.* Melbourne, Craftsman Press, 1980. 99 p, illus.

Although chronologically arranged, most chapters of this work are organised round one or two axemen as representative champions of the period. There are no tables of results.

Front cover, souvenir brochure, 1932–33. The fight for 'the Ashes', the test cricket competition between Australia and England, has great emotional connotations for Australia. The defeat of the English at their own game on their own soil in 1882 in the match which began the Ashes legend was seen by many as proof of Australia's coming of age. With the advent of Don Bradman in the 1930s Australian cricket nationalism became more aggressive: the competition had become a battle.
BOOROWA PRODUCTIONS

PRIESTLEY, S. *The crown of the road: the story of the RACV.* Melbourne, Macmillan, 1983. 170 p, illus.

History of the motoring organisation, the Royal Automobile Club of Victoria.

PRING, P. *Analysis of champion racehorses.* Sydney, Thoroughbred Press, 1977. 687 p, illus.

Gives race-by-race performances of about one hundred champion Australian and New Zealand racehorses of the twentieth century, with annotations on their breeding and progeny. Concludes with some statistical analyses of breeding.

PRING, P. *Major Australian races and racehorses 1960–1980.* Sydney, Thoroughbred Press, 1980. 542 p, illus.

Gives race-by-race performances of 160 horses, but without the attention to breeding of the preceding title. Includes a list of results of major races in Australia for the period.

RICKETTS, A. *Walter Lindrum: billiards phenomenon.* Canberra, Brian Clouston, 1982. 192 p, illus.

Biography of the Australian who dominated world billiards to his retirement in 1950.

ROSE, E. *The torch within.* New York, Doubleday, 1965. 192 p, illus.

Murray Rose was one of Australia's great swimmers. This is a biography by his mother.

ROSE, L. *Lionel Rose, Australian: the life story of a champion.* By Lionel Rose as told to Rod Humphries. A & R, 1969. 150 p, illus.

The story of Lionel Rose, an Aborigine from Gippsland, Vic, who won the world bantamweight boxing title on 27 February 1968 in Tokyo.

ROSENWATER, I. *Sir Donald Bradman: a biography.* London, Batsford, 1978. 416 p, illus.

The most detailed biography of Bradman. Several others exist.

SANDERCOCK, L. AND TURNER, I. *Up where Cazaly? The great Australian game.* Sydney, Granada, 1982. 272 p, illus.

An examination of the game of Australian rules football from its origins in 1850s to the game of today which involves big business and television.

SHEPHERD, W.J. *Encyclopedia of Australian sport.* Adelaide, Rigby, 1980. 469 p, illus.

A very high proportion of this encyclopaedia's entries are biographical, including entries for sportsmen and women still actively competing at the time of publication.

SMITH, T. *Australian golf, the first 100 years.* Sydney, Lester-Townsend, 1982. 203 p, illus.

A well-illustrated history of the game, courses and players, with statistics and tables.

SOUTAR, D.G. *The Australian golfer.* A & R, 1906. 260 p, illus.

Besides detailed instructions on how to play golf it includes a history of the game in Australia to date of publication.

STANNARD, B. *The triumph of Australia II: the America's Cup challenge of 1983.* Sydney, Lansdowne, 1983. 128 p, illus, maps.

A short history of the America's Cup with illustrated text on *Australia II's* win in 1983.

STAPLETON, M. AND McDONALD P. *Christmas in the colonies.* Sydney, David Ell Press in association with Historic Houses Trust of NSW, 1981. 128 p, illus.

Survey of Australian celebration of Christmas in the second half of the nineteenth century.

STEPHENSEN, P.R. *Sydney sails: the story of the Royal Sydney Yacht Squadron's first 100 years (1862–1962).* A & R, 1962. 272 p, illus, maps.

This official history of the club contains a wealth of detail, not only about the RSYS but about Sydney, its harbour and its characters during their first 100 years.

SWANWICK, R. *Les Darcy, Australia's golden boy of boxing.* Sydney, Ure Smith, 1965. 238 p, illus.

A biography of Darcy who died at the age of 21 from pneumonia and a 'broken heart' in America.

THOMIS, M.I. *The Brisbane Cup.* Brisbane, Jacaranda, 1980. vii, 56 p, illus.

A history of the horserace, first run in 1866.

THOMS, P.R. *The first 25 years, B.P.W. Australia: the history of the Australian Federation of Business and Professional Women's Clubs, compiled from official records.* Melbourne, Australian Federation of Business and Professional Women's Clubs, 1972. 123 p, illus.

TUCKEY, B. AND BERGHOUSE, R. *Australia's greatest motor race: the complete history.* Sydney, Lansdowne, 1981. 240 p, illus.

The story of the James Hardie 1000, formerly the Bathurst 1000, from the first race in 1960 to the 1980 race.

TWOPENY, R.E.N. *Town life in Australia.* London, Elliot Stock, 1883. 247 p.

Discusses Melbourne, Sydney and Adelaide and is, on occasion, quite merciless. Chapters include 'Amusements'. Facsimile edition, SUP, 1973.

WALKER, M. *Colonial crafts of Victoria: early settlement to 1921.* Melbourne, Ministry for the Arts, Vic, 1978. 167 p, illus.

Catalogue of a major exhibition at the National Gallery of Vic with hundreds of photographs. Subsistence crafts (for example, footwear and farm gadgetry) and more decorative work are included.

WALKER, M. *Pioneer crafts of early Australia.* Melbourne, Macmillan for the Crafts Council of Australia, 1978. 172 p, illus.

Covers mainly nineteenth-century crafts, including subsistence crafts (shelter, transport, tools) as well as leisure activities.

WARD, G.R.T. *The diamond jubilee of the Kosciusko Alpine Club, July 1909–July 1969.* Sydney, The Club, 1970. 141 p, illus.

The history of the club as at its sixtieth anniversary, by the people who ran it. Appendices include members' lists.

WARREN, J. AND DETTRE, A. *Soccer the Australian way.* Sydney, Summit Books, 1977. 144 p, illus.

Until recently soccer has not been as popular in Australia as the other football codes. This book tries to be both a manual on how to play the game and an attempt to persuade more young Australians to play. Includes many good action photos. First published in 1974 as *Soccer in Australia.*

WHEELWRIGHT, H.W. *Bush wanderings of a naturalist; or, notes on the field sports and fauna of Australia Felix, by an old bushman.* London, Routledge, Warne & Routledge, 1861. 272 p.

Perceptive observations on customs and life. Facsimile edition, OUP, 1979.

WHITINGTON, R.S. *Great moments in Australian sport.* Melbourne, Macmillan, 1974. 144 p, illus.

Twenty-four short illustrated accounts taken from all eras and all sports. The articles are crisply written and interesting.

WHITINGTON, R.S. *An illustrated history of Australian tennis.* Melbourne, Macmillan, 1975. 126 p, illus.

A survey of the game from 1873 (when modern tennis was invented) to 1975. It includes much statistical data on the period, including Australia's 'golden age' of tennis. Many fine action photos.

WILSON, T. *The luck of the draw: a centenary of Tattersall's sweeps, 1881–1981.* Melbourne, T. Wilson Publishing, 1980. 212 p, illus.

A history of Australia's famous lottery.

WINSER, K. *The story of Australian motoring: the complete history of motoring from the first horseless carriages to our cars of today.* Melbourne, Motor Manual, 1955. 319 p, illus, maps.

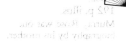

X
CULTURE

*Albert Tucker, Pick up, 1941. Oil on composition
board, 61.6 × 45.5 cm. Born in Melbourne in 1914,
Tucker was influenced by the work of the German
impressionists. His aggressive portrayal of some of the
seedier aspects of Australian life made him temporarily
unpopular in some art circles.*
AUSTRALIAN NATIONAL GALLERY

Cover of the literary magazine Scripsi *by Magda Matwiejew. Founded in 1981 by Peter Craven and Michael Heyward it is based at the University of Melbourne.* Scripsi *concentrates on publishing fiction, poetry and articles about fiction and poetry, by Australian and overseas writers.*
SCRIPSI

CHAPTER 49

ENGLISH LANGUAGE AND LITERATURE

ALAN LAWSON, D. BLAIR AND MARCIE MUIR

SOME YEARS AGO the Australian poet Judith Wright edited an anthology of Australian poems under the title *New land, new language* (OUP, 1957). The contrast between this title and that given by the historian A.H. Chisholm to his account of the adventures of that eccentric explorer, Ludwig Leichhardt, well illustrates the differing approaches Australians and their writers have had to this country. Chisholm called his book *Strange new land* (A & R, 1941) and, in doing so, echoed what was possibly the most common response to Australia by its European settlers and inhabitants. Not only among new arrivals was this a common attitude. The idea that the land was strange and even hostile was, until the middle of the twentieth century, still the view most often expressed by writers and by fourth or fifth generation 'Australians'. It was also the predominant view among those who wrote about Australian literature and language.

The counter-view, that those in a new land must adapt not only their habits and customs but also their language, only gradually prevailed. There developed a recognition that the customs and language which evolved in a northern island would not always work effectively in a southern continent. The poets, like the botanists, had to create new terms and metaphors that related to their own environment and the political and social realities that grew up in it.

A major stimulus to this belated but widespread acknowledgment that the land was neither new nor strange came, in literature as in Australian life generally, from an awareness of how Aboriginal Australians had related to the land so effectively and for so long. J.J. Healy (1978) traces the way in which this perception took literary form. Its more obvious manifestations can be found in the treatment of Aboriginal characters in literature. There has always been a great variation in attitudes, of course, but some of the early verse depicts Aborigines in a contemptuous—and from our perspective, a contemptible—manner. Perhaps better known than most is the Queensland poet, James Brunton Stephens (1835–1902) who wrote of an Aboriginal woman in this way:

> Thou art not beautiful, I tell thee plainly,
> Oh! thou ungainliest of things ungainly;
> Who thinks thee less than hideous doats insanely

To illustrate the diversity, however, take the following lines from 'The last of his tribe' by his contemporary, Henry Kendall.

Will he go in his sleep from these desolate lands,
Like a chief, to the rest of his race,
With the honey-voiced woman who beckons, and stands.
And gleams like a Dream in his face—
Like a marvellous Dream in his face?

More significant, though, is the view found in the works of many writers that the Aborigines are, or provide access to, the spirit of the land. The most important of the nineteenth-century poets, Charles Harpur (1813–68), provides an example of this in a poem called 'Ned Connor'. There, the appearance of an Aboriginal ghost is intended to represent the land's spirit taking rightful revenge for the murder of a black. In two controversial novels, *Coonardoo* (1929) by Katharine Susannah Prichard and *Capricornia* (1938) by Xavier Herbert, the Aboriginal characters have insights and values which the whites ignore at their peril: the Aborigines, that is, possess the key to understanding Australia and to surviving both physically and spiritually within it.

More recently this view of the Aborigines has been presented in such novels as Patrick White's *Voss* (1957) and Randolph Stow's *To the islands* (1958), where journeys are made by the white heroes in search of spiritual identity. These journeys are into the interior of the country (paralleling a journey into the interior of the mind) and are, importantly, taken with native guides. Among the poets the relevance of the Aborigines' response to the land and to our understanding of it can be found in the work of Douglas Stewart (1913–85), Judith Wright (1915–), and a group of poets writing from the 1930s to the 1950s under the collective title of 'The Jindyworobaks'. They included Ian Mudie, Rex Ingamells and Roland Robinson and argued for incorporating Aboriginal views, rhythms and language into poetry in English.

New land, new language was a preoccupation of many writers in other ways too. The vernacular, the colloquialisms that distinguish the country's speech, has been celebrated by many writers and performers. This has been particularly noticeable in the more nationalistic periods. For instance, C.J. Dennis in *The songs of a sentimental bloke* (1915; repr, A & R, 1981) gave the colloquial speech of Sydney larrikins poetic form and A.D. Hope (1907–), one of the most eminent of living poets, celebrated the words of Australia in this way:

I glean them from signposts in these country places,
Weird names, some beautiful, more that make me laugh.
Driving to fat-lamb sales or to picnic races,
I pass their worshippers of the golden calf
And, in the dust of the Cadillacs, a latter-day Habbakuk
Rises in me to preach comic sermons of doom,
Crying: 'Woe unto Tocumwal, Teddywaddy, Tooleybuc!'
And: 'Wicked Wallumburrawang, your hour has come!'

Naming the land is one of the traditional tasks of the explorer and the settler: it was one of Adam's first assignments in Eden. In new societies one of the functions of the writer has been to describe the country and the experience of living in it. For a long time critics judged writers by their success in naming appropriately and some are smugly deprecated for having referred to dingles and dells rather than gullies.

One of the ways of adapting was to see the outer landscape as a means of exploring the inner one, the landscape of human thoughts, feelings and spirit. Patrick White's phrase, 'the country of the mind' describes this well. James McAuley in the poem, 'Terra Australis', explores the way in which a people and their poets make metaphors out of their experience of the landscape:

Voyage within you, on the fabled ocean,
And you will find the Southern Continent,
. . . . . .
And mythical Australia, where reside
All things in their imagined counterpart.

This 'imagined counterpart' of the physical world has been many things to many writers. To Marcus Clarke (1846–81) it was a note of 'weird melancholy' in the bush that injected itself into people's souls; to Henry Lawson (1867–1922), who quoted that phrase of Clarke's with approval, it could be 'the nurse and tutor of eccentric minds'; and the contemporary poet, Geoffrey Lehmann (1940–) has observed that 'our rivers and country daze us with largeness'. The nature of our relationship with the landscape, in many forms, has been one of the dominant notes in Australian literature.

Australia is a colonial society. That is, the majority of the people who inhabit it, the language they use (and adapt) to describe it, the education they receive and the values they hold all come from somewhere else. There is, in the colonial situation, an awareness of the importance of that 'somewhere else'; there is a divided vision just as there are, in certain contexts (the debates about anthems, for instance), divided loyalties. The American novelist Henry James called it a 'complex fate' and writer after writer in Australia (and other countries that share the 'complex fate'—Canada, West Indies, New Zealand, India) has explored the balance between English past and Australian present, between here and there. For some the gap between European customs and Australian realities is a source of comedy or of aggressive, or wry, nationalism; for others it becomes the impulse to leave Australia and seek artistic and personal fulfilment in Europe. In fiction, if not always in life, the expatriate usually returns with added wisdom and with added attachment to Australia. More recently, to the perspective of Europe has been added that of Asia. Christopher Koch's *The year of living dangerously* (Melbourne, Nelson, 1978), which also became a successful film, and Blanche D'Alpuget's *Turtle Beach* (Ringwood, Vic, Penguin, 1981) are examples of the confrontation between Australian values and those of older societies in Asia.

While English is the official language of Australia and it is literature in the English language that is usually discussed in essays such as this, other languages are used in Australia and some literature is written in them. *Diversity and diversion: an annotated bibliography of Australian ethnic minority literature* by Peter Lumb and Anne Hazell (Richmond, Hodja Educational Resources Co-operative, 1983) is a useful guide to this literature.

What is implied by each of these major concerns in Australian literature is an expectation that writers will deal with more than the world of the imagination; that they will cope with more than aesthetic or artistic problems. It has been widely assumed in Australia, as in other post-colonial societies, that part of the writers' task was to provide—some would say foster—a sense of national identity: a sense of history, a sense of community, and an appropriate language in which they can be perceived and described. Writers would be judged, it follows, by values other than literary ones alone. This has been one of the major preoccupations of Australian literary criticism. There was, from as early as the 1870s and surviving until quite recently, a view that double standards ought to be applied; some works could be judged great by 'universal' standards, others could be placed in the second grade and judged by 'Australian' standards. A.G. Stephens, the major literary influence at the *Bulletin* in the crucial period from 1894 to 1906 and well known for his encouragement of Henry Lawson, Joseph Furphy, 'Banjo' Paterson and others, was a proponent of this view. Of Lawson he had this to say:

> I have just been looking through Lawson's verses and sketches, and see clearly that their value is largely an Australian value. We are moved by them so much because we breathe their atmosphere, are familiar with their persons and scenes—our minds go half-way to meet them … That is, Lawson's pre-eminent Australian appeal lessens the force of his universal appeal. He is splendidly parochial. That increases his claim upon his country, but decreases his claim upon literature.

A.D. Hope, poet, academic, reviewer, broadcaster and public speaker, was the most influential literary figure of the 1950s and often propounded similar views about standards.

More recently the trend has been to acknowledge the autonomy of Australian literature; to recognise that the concerns of Australian writers are not always those familiar to readers of British literature; to perceive that the term 'literature' itself can mean something different in

Australian literature; and to attempt to find relevant ways of describing and understanding the kinds of literature written in Australia.

For example, some critics have remarked on the widespread use of documentary fact in Australian imaginative writing. This, it is speculated, may well derive from the importance of documentation in early Australian writing—the guidebooks, travel books, journals and later the novels, at least part of whose audience was the English reader unfamiliar with the 'strange new land'. The use of fact in fiction is something that was once apologised for; it is now an accepted feature of modern fiction, poetry and drama.

For many of the earlier critics of Australian literature the task was to encourage the development and improvement of the literature; in examining its history they showed how it was growing in stature, how recent writers avoided the mistakes of their predecessors. More recent critics seem more concerned to find a continuing tradition, to explore the preoccupations that new writers share with older ones. Critics like Tom Inglis Moore, G.A. Wilkes, Judith Wright, H.P. Heseltine and A.A. Phillips all take this approach. Although their opinions differ greatly, they are united in the belief that it is appropriate to talk of an Australian literary tradition.

Writing about Australian literature began in the newspapers of the 1820s and several books on the subject had appeared before Federation. The main boost to this activity came, however, in 1939 when the Commonwealth Literary Fund expanded its activities to subsidise annual lecture programs at the universities. These lectures were usually open to the public, usually given by literary notables, and often found their way into print. Australian literature became a recognised part of the culture industry in the decade after 1954 when a number of notable journals commenced publication (*The realist writer, Overland, Quadrant, Westerly, Australian letters, Southern review, Australian book review* and *Australian literary studies*) and a number of important reference books appeared: E.M. Miller and F.T. Macartney (1956), a timely rearrangement, updated to 1950, of Miller's monumental pioneering work (1940; facs, 1973); C.H. Hadgraft's *Australian literature* (London, Heinemann, 1960); and H.M. Green's famous history (1961; repr, 1984–85). At the same time three authors argued the case for a particular view of the Australian tradition: Vance Palmer (1954; repr, 1983), A.A. Phillips (1958; repr, 1980) and Russel Ward (1958; repr, 1978).

In other ways Australian literature was news in this period: Frank Hardy was sued for libel after the publication of his successful novel *Power without glory* (1950; repr, A & R, 1982); Ray Lawler won the Playwrights' Advisory Board Prize for *The summer of the seventeenth doll* in 1954 and Patrick White's *The tree of man* and *Voss* received major reviews here and abroad in 1955 and 1957. In 1956 an appeal was launched to fund a chair of Australian literature at the University of Sydney; the first professor (G.A. Wilkes) was appointed in 1961. Full courses in the subject had begun at Canberra University College and Queensland University in about 1954. NIDA, the National Institute of Dramatic Art, was established in 1958.

Journals have been an important feature of Australian writing since the nineteenth century. It is often suggested that economic circumstances were responsible for this. Although Australians rank highly in their per capita purchasing of books, the market was still a small one. Many writers, then, found publication in magazines rather than in books and consequently favoured the forms—the short story, for example—best suited to the magazines. There is now one periodical which devotes itself exclusively to serious articles and research on Australian literature (*Australian literary studies*, 1965–   ); one which reviews all Australian books (*Australian book review*, 1961/62–1973; ns, 1978–   ); and one which concentrates on Australian drama (*Australasian drama studies*, 1982–   ). Others contain new creative writing as well as articles and reviews. Of these, *Meanjin* (founded in 1940) and *Southerly* (founded in 1939) have been the most important sources of new writing and of influential ideas about it. *Southerly*, based in Sydney, is perhaps best known for its literary articles, short stories, poetry and annual surveys while *Meanjin*, based in Melbourne since 1945, is more notable for its broader interest in cultural affairs, politics and history as well as new writing.

Australian drama has not had the same vigorous accompaniment of critical activity. A more transient form—a season may last only a couple of weeks—it has evoked, of course, contemporary reviews of particular productions but few deeper considerations of the plays and their relation to a tradition of Australian drama. Recent research at the University of Queensland and elsewhere has unearthed information on thousands of Australian plays; the tradition has been a long and vital one, but its continuity has not, until now, been apparent. Over and again critics have announced the birth of Australian drama. Lawler's *The summer of the seventeenth doll*, Alan Seymour's *The one day of the year* and Richard Beynon's *The shifting heart* took hold of the popular imagination in the late 1950s by the way in which they made theatrical use of local situations and language. They made possible the more daring experiments of the same kind by the dramatists who started writing after about 1968. Centred on the Australian Performing Group and La Mama Theatre in Melbourne, these included David Williamson, Jack Hibberd and Barry Oakley. Further comments on drama in Australia will be found in chapter 52 of this volume under the heading 'Theatre'.

The year 1968 is often seen as a turning point in Australian writing. It marks the beginning of a period of greater literary sophistication, complexity and experiment—especially in poetry and short fiction—and it also coincides with the formation of the Australia Council (initially the Australian Council for the Arts) and the subsequent greatly increased support for the arts in Australia. Publication outlets increased significantly as new publishers began operation (Outback Press, Wild & Woolley) or moved into literary publishing (UQP) and a large number of new 'little magazines' were published. These 'little magazines' were sometimes inexpertly produced and shortlived but they stimulated literary activity by giving writers an opportunity to experiment and by circulating their work widely and in non-traditional areas. Denholm (1979) surveys this growth in alternative publishing.

The poets and short fiction writers of this period tended to reject or avoid traditional literary forms and subjects. 'Make it new' was one of their borrowed mottoes and it produced work that consciously broke the 'rules' of composition and form, and deliberately blurred the distinctions between, for example, prose and poetry, fact and fiction, short story and novel. It found expression in self-revelation, the depiction of contemporary lifestyles and formerly taboo subjects, and in deliberately non-realistic modes. Among the poets of that generation there were fierce debates about form and style that saw the formation of many factions which tended to associate with particular magazines. A balanced view of the period can only be gained by reading widely. Even many of the anthologies published in the last twenty years are polemic in nature: they set out to present a particular approach to poetry or exemplify a particular school of poets.

In the 1970s Australian culture had numerous popular successes abroad. Pop-singers, playwrights, film-makers and fiction writers shared the success and several Australian novels were made into films, such as Joan Lindsay's *Picnic at Hanging Rock*, Thomas Keneally's *The chant of Jimmie Blacksmith*, Miles Franklin's *My brilliant career*, Henry Handel Richardson's *The getting of wisdom*, Ethel Turner's *Seven little Australians* and Christopher Koch's *The year of living dangerously*.

If it was a decade of some spectacular commercial enterprise, it was also a decade of scholarly consolidation. In 1978 the Association for the Study of Australian Literature was formed, bringing together for the first time writers and academics, teachers and publishers, booksellers and librarians interested in fostering the reading, teaching and study of Australian literature. In co-operation with the Department of Foreign Affairs and the Literature Board of the Australia Council, the association helps to develop the now very considerable interest in Australian literature abroad. In the 1970s most libraries vigorously expanded their holdings of Australiana, while several (notably the National Library, University of Queensland Library, and the state libraries of Victoria and New South Wales) made important acquisitions of Australian literary manuscripts as basic research in Australian literature expanded and the community appreciated the need to conserve the nation's heritage. Major efforts to restore to print works long unavailable were only occasionally rewarded, but research on the texts of major poets like Charles Harpur (1813–68) and John Shaw Neilson (1872–1942) produced a better understanding of their work and, in each case, brought to light poems previously unpublished.

The largest collections of Australian literature and literary manuscripts are those in the Mitchell Library, Sydney, and in the National Library of Australia. Also notable are the collections in the La Trobe Collection, State Library of Victoria, the Fryer Memorial Library of the University of Queensland and the library of the University of Sydney. To each of these the papers, correspondence and literary manuscripts of contemporary writers as well as new discoveries of material by older writers are constantly being added. Within the Fryer Memorial Library the Hanger Collection contains almost two thousand Australian playscripts.

CHILDREN'S LITERATURE

In many ways the history of Australian children's literature roughly parallels that of 'adult' literature; the history of its reception and institutionalisation is also similar. It, too, gradually achieved the status of a subject worth serious study in the period following World War II and from the 1970s became a topic for scholarly research.

Until the end of the nineteenth century most Australian children's books were published in England and often written by authors who had never visited the Australian colonies. Popular writers of boys' adventure stories, such as Henty, Kingston, Manville Fenn and others, used Australia as a fresh background for one or more of their numerous tales, while writers who lived in Australia sent their books overseas to be published—a practice which continued until very recently. In the fifty years from 1841 (when the first Australian children's book appeared) until the 1890s the handful of those published locally comprised mostly small editions produced by amateurs. Angus & Robertson began publishing children's books in 1897, and other local publishers like George Robertson, T.C. Lothian, and William Brooks began to publish some handsome and highly creditable children's books soon after.

English publishers were beginning by this time to set up branches in Australia, and some—most notably Ward Lock—also became very active in the field of Australian children's books. In fact, Ward Lock's publication of Ethel Turner's first book in 1894 preceded Angus & Robertson's entry into the field. Ward Lock's other great success was Mary Grant Bruce, the author of the 'Billabong' books. The company attempted to influence writers' expressions and the attitudes of their characters in order to make their work more acceptable to the English market. In general, though, the attitudes of Australian children's writers of that time did not differ greatly from those of British or North American authors. There was less concern to be distinctively Australian than there was in 'adult' fiction at this time.

Boys' adventure stories published in the early 1900s were more notable for their local colour than were the stories for girls. Notable examples are the works of the brothers Alexander and Robert Macdonald, of Ernest Favenc, Louis Becke and Joseph Bowes, who also dealt with World War I.

Two books which became immediate favourites and have remained so to this day were published within weeks of each other in 1918: *Tales of Snugglepot and Cuddlepie* (repr, A & R, 1980) and Norman Lindsay's *The magic pudding* (repr, A & R, 1975). May Gibbs, the author of the former, achieved great popularity with her 'Bib and Bub' comic strip which appeared in the weekend papers; at the same time another equally popular comic strip captured the public imagination: 'Ginger Meggs' by J.C. Bancks. Both of these long-lived series were later published in book form.

The fantasy *Dot and the kangaroo* (repr, A & R, 1978) was warmly received by Australian children in 1899, as was also Tarella Quin's *Gum tree brownie* (1907; repr, A & R, 1983), with Ida Rentoul's charming illustrations. The latter was hailed on its publication in 1907 as a truly Australian fairy tale. All the other books by the Rentoul sisters were enthusiastically received and, though some of these beautiful books were published overseas, the two most impressive, 'Elves and fairies' (Melbourne, Lothian, 1916) and *Fairyland* (Melbourne, Ramsay Publishing, 1926), were produced entirely in Australia.

The fashion for animal tales, both factual accounts and those in which animals were attributed with human characteristics, prevailed in the 1930s, in Australia as elsewhere. The humorous stories of Dorothy Wall achieved great popularity. Frank Dalby Davison's *Dusty* (1946; repr, A & R, 1983) and *Man-shy* (1931; repr, A & R, 1983) have been read widely.

The establishment in 1945 in New South Wales of the first Children's Book Council in Australia was the beginning of a movement which was to influence strongly most aspects of children's literature. The creation of annual awards for locally published books, with the accompanying prestige and publicity, inspired publishers to aim for high quality and has contributed to the improvement of standards in the publishing of children's books. Awards for writers generally have proliferated greatly; many are accompanied by monetary prizes, and a number are also given to publishers and artists.

When courses for training children's librarians were established in the 1960s and school libraries were built throughout the country, adequately funded by government grants, children's book publishing responded with new vigour. Authors such as Nan Chauncy, whose first book, *They found a cave*, appeared in 1948, Patricia Wrightson, Joan Phipson, Eleanor Spence and other gifted writers who began their creative work in the 1950s, were encouraged to produce books of a high standard, and they set the pace for others. This led to the current surge of excellent and varied children's books Australia now enjoys. Their appearance also improved, although it was not until the 1970s that the improvement in Australian picture books became widespread.

The Children's Book Council began to publish a journal in 1957; known as *Reading time* since 1967, it has provided informed critical evaluation of children's literature.

Since the 1960s a small number of books written or illustrated by Aborigines also began to make an interesting and varied addition to Australian children's literature. The *Aboriginal children's history of Australia* (Adelaide, Rigby, 1977) was one such example; its coloured illustrations are visual impressions of the impact of their surroundings on Aboriginal children. There is also an interesting explanatory text. A few books written by migrant writers reflecting their different backgrounds have been published, including several picture books with bilingual texts.

The quantity and quality of children's picture books published in Australia in recent years is probaby one of the most notable features of the current book world. Some have received recognition in other countries as well as high honours and great popularity at home. The quality of production also has generally reached a high standard. Many popular children's stories are now published in paperback as well as in hardback editions.

Considerable effort has been spent in recent years on research into Australian children's books, both historical and biographical. Although to date no work has been published on Australian school books, there is Ian F. McLaren's *Whitcombe's story books: a trans-Tasman survey* (Melbourne, University of Melbourne Library, 1984). A number of Australian research and public libraries hold special collections of children's books, making historical research into the changing taste in children's literature a good deal easier. During the past thirty to forty years a more careful observance of the legal deposit regulations has ensured that the National Library of Australia and the state libraries receive most books published in their respective jurisdictions but no institution can as yet claim to have acquired everything published for Australian children.

Diggers reading letters and papers from home. *Engraved by S. Calvert. Supplement to the* Illustrated Sydney News, *Dec 1873. Despite the proliferation of Australian newspapers, many immigrants and native-born Australians continued to follow 'home' news from Britain with interest, subscribing to a wide range of British newspapers and magazines.*
MITCHELL LIBRARY

THE ENGLISH LANGUAGE IN AUSTRALIA

BAKER, S.J. *The Australian language: an examination of the English language and English speech as used in Australia, from convict days to the present, with special reference to the growth of indigenous idiom and its use by Australian writers.* A & R, 1945. 425 p.

An abundance of examples of Australian vocabulary. Some sources are suspect, but it contains a great repository of Australia's colloquial habits.

BERNARD, J. AND DELBRIDGE, A. *Introduction to linguistics: an Australian perspective.* Sydney, Prentice-Hall, 1980. 328 p, illus.

A description of the dialect from a linguistic point of view.

CLYNE, M.G. ed, *Australia talks: essays on the sociology of Australian immigrant and Aboriginal languages.* Canberra, Dept of Linguistics, Research School of Pacific Studies, Australian National University, 1976. 266 p. (Pacific linguistics: series D, 23.)

Contains contributions on migrant and Aboriginal varieties of English, as well as chapters on Strine, swearing and social dialects of Australian English.

DABKE, R. *Morphology of Australian English.* München, Wilhelm Fink Vlg, 1976. 72 p, maps. (Ars grammatics Bd 6.)

A study of Australian word-formation. It includes discussion of compounding (*she-oak*), reduplication (*Wagga Wagga*), and of *-ie* and *-o* suffixes.

HAMMARSTROM, G. *Australian English: its origin and status.* Hamburg, Helmut Buske Vlg, 1980. x, 73 p. (Forum phoneticum, Bd 19.)

Contends that Australian English is early Cockney, with the addition of a high variety from the influence of British Received Pronunciation.

THE MACQUARIE *dictionary.* Sydney, Macquarie Library, 1981. 2049 p, illus.

The first reference dictionary to use Australian English as its 'home' dialect. It contains 80 000 entries and includes the colloquial end of the lexicon as well as the formal.

MITCHELL, A.G. AND DELBRIDGE, A. *The pronunciation of English in Australia.* A & R, 1965. xiv, 82 p.

A revision of the 1946 work in which Mitchell established his crusade for the recognition of Australian speech. A full-length description of Australian pronunciation.

MITCHELL, A.G. AND DELBRIDGE, A. *The speech of Australian adolescents: a survey.* A & R, 1965. xi, 99 p, maps & record.

Links the varieties of adolescent pronunciation with such factors as sex, type of schooling and father's occupation. A survey of 700 schoolchildren, it correlates language variety with social factors.

MORRIS, E.E. *A dictionary of Austral English.* London, Macmillan, 1898, 526 p.

First general-purpose dictionary of Australianisms. A historical approach, using dated citations to illustrate senses. Facsimile edition, SUP, 1972.

RAMSON, W.S. *Australian English: an historical study of the vocabulary, 1788–1898.* ANUP, 1966. 195 p.

An enquiry into the sources of our vocabulary. The standard reference on the subject.

RAMSON, W.S. ed, *English transported: essays on Australasian English.* ANUP, 1970. 243 p.

A collection of essays on historical and contemporary aspects of standard Australian English. Contributions on Aboriginal and migrant varieties, as well as on New Zealand English.

TURNER, G.W. *The English language in Australia and New Zealand.* London, Longman, 1972. 214 p.

A readable introduction to the field and full-length description in non-technical language. First published in 1966.

TURNER, G.W. ed, *Good Australian English and good New Zealand English.* Sydney, Reed Education, 1972. 317 p, illus.

Change and variety in the language; primarily concerned with issues of usage and style.

WILKES, G.A. *A dictionary of Australian colloquialisms.* SUP, 1978. 470 p.

An attempt to define by citation the colloquialisms unique to Australia.

LITERATURE IN GENERAL

BARNES, J. ed, *The writer in Australia: a collection of literary documents, 1856 to 1964.* OUP, 1969. 336 p.

Selection of statements and articles by writers and literary figures about Australian writing.

BENNETT, B. ed, *Cross currents: magazines and newspapers in Australian literature.* Melbourne, Longman Cheshire, 1981. 269 p, illus.

Statements about, and studies of, the major periodicals which have been influential in the development, creation and study of Australian writing.

BLAIKLOCK *memorial lectures: 1971–1981.* Lectures by A.D. Hope *et al*, foreword by L. Kramer. SUP, 1981. 160 p.

Important series of annual lectures given in Sydney. Most of the lectures open up new ground in the study and discussion of Australian literature.

CANTRELL, L. ed, *Bards, bohemians and bookmen: essays in Australian literature.* UQP, 1977. 350 p.

Issued in honour of the critic Cecil Hadgraft; contains articles on nineteenth-century literature and literary history.

DENHOLM, M. *Small press publishing in Australia: the early 1970s.* Sydney, Second Back Row Press, 1979. 209 p.

After 1968 new, small and 'alternative' publishing houses and periodicals were an important literary and social phenomenon. Surveys are followed by brief studies of publishers and magazines.

DOCKER, J. *Australian cultural elites: intellectual traditions of Sydney and Melbourne.* A & R, 1974. 182 p.

A controversial work which analyses the preoccupations of a few writers and journals.

DOCKER, J. *In a critical condition: reading Australian literature.* Ringwood, Vic, Penguin, 1984. 246 p.

Essays which engage in a radical analysis of the way attitudes and approaches to literature have affected what is read and taught.

DUTTON, G. *The literature of Australia.* Ringwood, Vic, Pelican, 1976. 612 p.

Articles on writers, groups and periods in literature; survey of fiction, poetry, drama and the social background; and a 'Bibliographic appendix'. Some contributions in the first edition (1964) not reprinted in this revised edition.

DUTTON, G. *Snow on the saltbush: the Australian literary experience.* Ringwood, Vic, Viking, 1984. 311 p, illus.

A well-informed account of the origins and environment of Australian literature.

GREEN, H.M. *A history of Australian literature, pure and applied: a critical review of all forms of literature produced in Australia from the first books published after the arrival of the first fleet until 1950, with short accounts of later publications up to 1960.* A & R, 1961. 2 vols.

A comprehensive and authoritative literary history.

HEALY, J.J. *Literature and the Aborigine in Australia, 1770–1975*. UQP, 1978. 305 p.

The Aborigines have been an important feature of the literary response to Australia since the arrival of European settlers. A stimulating and thorough account.

KIERNAN, B. *Criticism*. OUP, 1974. 52 p.

A critical survey of the issues implicitly and explicitly involved in writings about Australian literature.

KRAMER, L. ed, *The Oxford history of Australian literature*. OUP, 1981. 509 p.

Not so much a literary history as a collection of three lengthy survey articles. The fiction chapter is conservative, the drama lively and the poetry often stimulating.

MATTHEWS, J.P. *Tradition in exile: a comparative study of social influences on the development of Australian and Canadian poetry in the nineteenth-century*. Melbourne, Cheshire in association with University of Toronto Press, 1962. 197 p.

Places the themes and preoccupations of the nineteenth-century poetry of the two British colonies in the contexts of social and cultural developments, literary traditions and in comparison to each other.

MODJESKA, D. *Exiles at home: Australian women writers, 1925–1945*. A & R, 1981. 183 p, illus.

An argument for a tradition of Australian women's writing which sets the writing and careers of some major women writers in a social and political context.

MOORE, T.I. *Social patterns in Australian literature*. A & R, 1971. 350 p.

A wideranging survey of what it proposes as major themes in Australian fiction and poetry; sees these as growing out of the social and historical experience.

NARASIMHAIAH, C.D. ed, *An introduction to Australian literature*. Brisbane, Wiley, 1982. xxv, 201 p.

Excellent articles on important aspects of Australian literature, first published in Mysore, India in 1980.

PALMER, V. *The legend of the nineties*. Melbourne, Currey O'Neil Ross, 1983. 156 p, illus.

An influential argument about the way in which the evolution of a national character and a national literature shared a common sense of value and purpose during the 1890s. First published in 1954.

PHILLIPS, A.A. *The Australian tradition: studies in a colonial culture* (rev edn). Melbourne, Longman Cheshire, 1980. 184 p.

Important essays in which the components and development of a national literary tradition are discussed. Contains the essay in which the term 'cultural cringe' was invented. First published in 1958.

SERLE, A.G. *From deserts the prophets come: the creative spirit in Australia, 1788–1972*. Melbourne, Heinemann, 1973. 274 p.

A synthetic history of the main cultural forms—music, painting, architecture, drama and literature—which attempts to see these as operating out of a common context.

SMITH, G.K. *Australia's writers*. Melbourne, Nelson, 1980. 342 p, illus, map.

Profiles of fifty or so writers, supplied with quotations to characterise the author's work. The social milieu of the writers and their work receive attention.

WALKER, D.R. *Dream and disillusion: a search for Australian cultural identity*. ANUP, 1976. 279 p.

Examines the ways in which four writers—Vance Palmer, Louis Esson, Frank Wilmot and Frederick Sinclaire—worked to iden-tify an Australian social and literary tradition and the failure of those nationalists' ideals.

WALLACE-CRABBE, C. *Melbourne or the bush: essays on Australian literature and society*. A & R, 1974. 140 p.

These essays on particular writers are balanced by a couple of essays of social reflection and some on general issues in the Australian literary tradition.

WALLACE-CRABBE, C. ed, *The Australian nationalists: modern critical essays*. OUP, 1971. 238 p.

Essays which focus on the nationalist school of writers and their influence on the world of the 1890s and our perception of it.

WILKES, G.A. *Australian literature: a conspectus*. A & R, 1969. 143 p.

A general survey which stresses thematic interests as well as chronological developments.

WILKES, G.A. *The stockyard and the croquet lawn: literary evidence for Australian cultural development*. Melbourne, Edward Arnold, 1981. 153 p.

An eloquent argument of the parallel development of genteel and nationalist traditions in Australian writing. A plea for a pluralist approach to our literature.

BIBLIOGRAPHIES

ANDREWS, B.G. AND WILDE, W.H. *Australian literature to 1900: a guide to information sources*. Detroit, Michigan, Gale Research Co, 1980. 472 p.

Reliable guide to what has been written about Australian literature and the nineteenth century and its writers.

JOHNSTON, G.K.W. *Annals of Australian literature*. OUP, 1970. 147 p.

A reference book which lists, year by year, the principal literary publications, with other information such as authors' births and deaths, founding of journals and related publications.

LOCK, F. AND LAWSON, A. *Australian literature: a reference guide*. (2nd edn). OUP, 1980. xiv, 120 p.

Describes the reference works, organisations, libraries and periodicals most useful for the study of Australian literature; works on some forty Australian writers are described and assessed. First published in 1976.

MACARTNEY, F.T. AND MILLER, E.M. *Australian literature: a bibliography to 1938 ... extended to 1950*. A & R, 1956. 503 p.

An updating and rearrangement of Miller which lost some of the depth of the original. The listing of an author's works is often accompanied by a brief biographical and critical note.

MILLER, E.M. *Australian literature from its beginnings to 1935: a descriptive and bibliographical survey: with subsidiary entries to 1938*. SUP, 1973. 2 vols.

The standard bibliography of Australian writing, though some-what difficult to use. It leaves some of the literature uncovered. Facsimile edition of the first (1940) edition; reprinted 1975.

PRIESSNITZ, H. 'Australian literature: a preliminary subject checklist', *Australian literary studies* 11, 4, 1984, 513–40.

An extensive listing of books and articles arranged by topics—regionalism, theatre, Aborigines, women, landscape and so on.

STUART, L. *Nineteenth century Australian periodicals: an annotated bibliography*. Sydney, Hale & Iremonger, 1979. 200 p, illus.

A listing of nineteenth-century periodicals of literary interest; gives extensive information about format, style, content, con-tributors, editors, frequency and selected locations.

POETRY

DUWELL, M. *A possible contemporary poetry*. Brisbane, Makar Press, 1982. 160 p.

Statements from contemporary Australian poets about their aesthetic principles and relations to poetic traditions in Australia and overseas. A companion volume to John Tranter's *The new Australian poetry* (Brisbane, Makar Press, 1979).

ELLIOT, B. *The landscape of Australian poetry.* Melbourne, Cheshire, 1967. 346 p.

A study of the responses made by poets to their environment and the effects of those responses on their metaphors and preoccupations.

JAFFA, H.C. *Modern Australian poetry, 1920–1970: a guide to information sources.* Detroit, Michigan, Gale Research Co, 1979. 241 p.

A guide to 'movements', but its bibliographic information is not always reliable. Uses lengthy precis of individual articles and is less comprehensive than other volumes in this series.

KIRBY, J. ed, *The American model: influence and independence in Australian poetry.* Sydney, Hale & Iremonger, 1982. 178 p, illus.

Papers from a conference which explored the relationship of Australian poetry, its tradition and criticism, to American poetry.

WEBBY, E. *Early Australian poetry: an annotated bibliography of original poems published in Australian newspapers, magazines and almanacs before 1850.* Sydney, Hale & Iremonger, 1982. 333 p, illus.

Reveals just how much poetry was written in the early years by means of painstakingly exhaustive search.

WRIGHT, J.A. *Preoccupations in Australian poetry.* OUP, 1965. 217 p.

A stimulating account of Australian poetry. Sensitive studies of eleven major poets, several groups and schools and a couple of provocative essays.

DRAMA [see also related references and comments in chapter 52]

FITZPATRICK, P. *After the* Doll: *Australian drama since 1955.* Melbourne, Edward Arnold, 1979. 200 p.

Reliable survey of Australian theatre in the twenty years following 1955 which saw a number of new developments and a resurgence of interest in local dramatic writing.

REES, L. *A history of Australian drama.* A & R, 1978. 2 vols, illus.

A major history from the 1930s. Its documentation is not always dependable but it is an enthusiastic account of the least understood and studied literary genre in Australia.

WILLIAMS, M. *Drama.* OUP, 1977. 46 p.

A brief survey with a bibliography; gives some attention to the often neglected earlier period; useful select bibliography.

FICTION

BURNS, D.R. *The direction of Australian fiction, 1920–1974.* Melbourne, Cassell, 1975. 267 p.

Presents an interesting map of modern fiction by dealing with 'schools', traditions and preoccupations as well as individual writers.

DAY, A.G. *Modern Australian prose, 1901–1975: a guide to information sources.* Detroit, Michigan, Gale Research Co, 1980. 462 p.

A guide to fiction with annotated lists of reference aids, books, articles and periodicals.

HAMILTON, K.G. ed, *Studies in the recent Australian novel.* UQP, 1978. 257 p.

Essays on modern novels and novelists. A survey of developments in fiction since 1930 set in the context of culture and society.

KIERNAN, B. *Images of society and nature: seven essays on*

Front cover, Pan paperback edition of Come in Spinner, *1960. Unknown artist, printed in England.* Come in Spinner *won the* Daily Telegraph *novel competition in 1948, but no Australian publisher would accept it. Finally published by Heinemann in London in 1951, it became a bestseller in England and America before the first copies—transported by ship—were available in Australia. Many Australian novelists have had their early novels published overseas, sometimes because of prudishness or lack of entrepreneurial spirit in Australia, but mainly because the relative small local market can make it economically difficult to publish books here.*

Australian novels. OUP, 1971. 187 p.

Essays aimed at elucidating some leading themes in Australian fiction. A concluding chapter moves tentatively towards a new description of the tradition.

RAMSON, W.S. ed, *The Australian experience: critical essays on Australian novels.* ANUP, 1974. 344 p.

Essays on major Australian novels, novelists and fictional preoccupations. Many are revaluations of received reputations and interpretations.

REID, I. *Fiction and the Great Depression: Australia & New Zealand, 1930–1950.* Melbourne, Edward Arnold, 1979. 166 p.

Deals with the depression not only as a setting and a subject for fiction but as an influence on the preoccupations of writers.

SINNET, F. *The fiction fields of Australia.* Ed by C. Hadgraft. UQP, 1966. 52 p, illus.

First published as a journal essay in 1856, this is an important early survey of Australian fiction which discusses the concerns appropriate to a new literature.

WALKER, S. ed, *Who is she? Images of woman in Australian fiction.* UQP, 1983. 219 p.

New essays on the depictions of women by major Australian fiction writers of all periods.

INDIVIDUAL AUTHORS

BOYD, MARTIN: NIALL, B.M. *Martin Boyd.* OUP, 1977. 137 p.

An accurate listing of work by and about the novelist, Martin Boyd. Reveals existence of revisions, anonymous and pseudonymous works, not previously known.

BRENNAN, CHRISTOPHER: CLARK, A. *Christopher Brennan: a critical biography.* MUP, 1980. 341 p, illus.

An account of a complex and tragic life in conjunction with a study of what is one of the most demanding bodies of poetry written in Australia.

CLARKE, MARCUS: McLAREN, I.F. *Marcus Clarke: an annotated bibliography.* Melbourne, Library Council of Vic, 1982. 393 p, illus.

An exhaustive survey of Clarke's writings unlikely to be surpassed for many years to come. Lists all Clarke's contributions to journals and newspapers, all editions and variants and concludes with writings about him and bibliographic essays.

WILDING, M. *Marcus Clarke.* OUP, 1977. 52 p.

A brief guide to Clarke and to the whole range of his work as a novelist, short story writer, essayist and journalist.

DENNIS, C.J.: McLAREN, I.F. *C.J. Dennis: a comprehensive bibliography . . .* Adelaide, LBSA, 1979. 248 p, illus.

Detailed work listing variants, journal contributions by Dennis and works about him. A supplement was published in 1983.

FRANKLIN, MILES: BARNARD, M.F. *Miles Franklin.* Melbourne, Hill of Content, 1967. 174 p, illus.

Barnard, an eminent novelist, short story writer and historian, writes perceptively about the life and literary career of Franklin.

FURPHY, JOSEPH: BARNES, J. *Joseph Furphy.* OUP, 1979. 46 p.

Short survey of the life and work of the author of *Such is life,* demonstrating the range and complexity of Furphy's intentions. First published in 1967.

HARPUR, CHARLES: PERKINS, E. ed, *The poetical works of Charles Harpur.* A & R, 1984. 1013 p.

Scholarly edition of Harpur's verse; includes a detailed introduction and bibliography.

HERBERT, XAVIER: HESELTINE, H.P. *Xavier Herbert.* OUP, 1973. 52 p.

Capricornia and *Poor fellow my country* have been controversial novels and their author a notable figure. This short book is a reliable survey of his life and work.

HOPE, A.D.: HOOTON, J.W. *A.D. Hope.* OUP, 1979. 276 p. (Australian bibliographies.)

A comprehensive listing of the large and diverse output of a major poet and influential critic and of the response to his work.

KRAMER, L.J. *A.D. Hope.* OUP, 1979. 48 p.

Short survey of the work of the well-known modern poet influential critic, reviewer and speaker.

LAWSON, HENRY: KIERNAN, B. *The essential Henry Lawson: the best works of Australia's greatest writer.* Melbourne, Currey O'Neil, 1982. 399 p, illus.

A selection of Lawson's poetry and prose with a detailed introduction and select bibliography.

MATTHEWS, B.E. *The receding wave: Henry Lawson's prose.* MUP, 1972. xxi, 196 p.

A critical study of Lawson's prose which argues for the need to take full account of Lawson's literary skill and ambition; interesting discussion of Lawson's decline.

LINDSAY, NORMAN: HETHERINGTON, J.A. *Norman Lindsay:* the embattled Olympian. OUP, 1973. 272 p, illus.

The authorised biography which covers the wide range of Lindsay's activities and his many personal contacts.

PALMER, VANCE: HESELTINE, H.P. *Vance Palmer.* UQP, 1970. 216 p.

Vance Palmer, in association with his wife Nettie, was not only a writer of fiction, but the most influential literary figure in Australia in the first half of the twentieth century.

PATERSON, A.B.: SEMMLER, C. *The Banjo of the bush: the life and times of A.B. Paterson.* (2nd edn.) UQP, 1974. 263 p, illus.

Uses much previously unrecorded biographical detail. Readable and well documented. First published in 1966.

PORTER, HAL: LORD, M. *Hal Porter: selected and edited with an introduction and bibliography by Mary Lord.* UQP, 1980. 408 p.

A selection of Porter's prose and verse with a critical introduction and bibliography.

RICHARDSON, HENRY HANDEL: GREEN, D. *Ulysses bound: Henry Handel Richardson and her fiction.* ANUP, 1973. 582 p, illus.

An ambitious account of an Australian writer. Stimulating study of the works, the life and the critical response.

STEAD, CHRISTINA: LIDOFF, J. *Christina Stead.* New York, Ungar, 1982. 255 p.

A thorough account of the life and work of a major Australian novelist who wrote most of her work overseas.

WHITE, PATRICK: KIERNAN, B. *Patrick White.* London, Macmillan, 1980. 147 p.

An introductory account of the life and work of Australia's foremost novelist. The bibliography offers a guide to other recent criticism on White.

LAWSON, A.J. *Patrick White.* OUP, 1974. 131 p.

Comprehensive listing of work by and about Patrick White up to 1974; includes biographical references, translations and reviews as well as books and articles.

WRIGHT, JUDITH: WALKER, S. *The poetry of Judith Wright: a search for unity.* Melbourne, Edward Arnold, 1980. 194 p.

Treats Wright's poetry as a unified body of work with developing and often quite complex thematic and philosophical concerns.

WALKER, S. *Judith Wright.* OUP, 1981. 213 p. (Australian bibliographies.)

A comprehensive bibliography of Wright's work, including criticism and general essays, and of responses to her work.

CHILDREN'S LITERATURE

DUGAN, M. ed, *The early dreaming: Australian children's authors on childhood.* Brisbane, Jacaranda, 1980. 113 p, illus.

Essays by ten writers for children on their own childhood and formative years.

ELLIS, V.R. *Louisa Anne Meredith: a tigress in exile.* Hobart, Blubber Head Press, 1979. 275 p, illus.

A life of particular interest for the pioneering experiences in NSW and Van Diemen's Land of this gifted author and artist.

McVITTY, W. *Innocence and experience: essays on contemporary Australian children's writers.* Melbourne, Nelson, 1981. 277 p, illus.

A well-known lecturer on children's literature discusses the work of eight leading contemporary Australian children's authors.

MUIR, M. *A bibliography of Australian children's books.* London, Deutsch, 1970–76. 2 vols, illus.

Aims to cover all Australian children's books, excluding educa-

A Bibliography of Australian Children's Books
Volume 2
MARCIE MUIR

Dustjacket based on the front cover of More Australian legendary tales *by K. Langloh Parker, London 1898. Artist unknown. Marcie Muir's two-volume* Bibliography of Australian children's books *was published by Andre Deutsch in London and Hutchinson in Australia.*

tional, to the end of 1972. Each volume contains a supplement relating to books of the southwest Pacific area; title index is included.

MUIR, M. *Charlotte Barton: Australia's first children's author.* Sydney, Wentworth Books, 1980. 35 p.

Tells of a search for the identity of the writer of Australia's first children's book and supports the case with varied but substantial evidence.

MUIR, M. *A history of Australian children's book illustration.* OUP, 1982. 160 p, illus.

Traces the development of Australian children's book illustration from the earliest books of overseas origin to today's local publications.

NIALL, B. *Seven little billabongs: the world of Ethel Turner and Mary Grant Bruce.* MUP, 1979. 219 p, illus.

This study of the books and careers of Ethel Turner and Mary Grant Bruce gains in readability and effect by the interesting contrasts made.

NIALL, B. *Through the looking glass: Australian children's fiction 1830–1980.* MUP, 1984. 357 p, illus.

Examines the Australian tradition in children's fiction, showing the emergence of national stereotypes and the long preoccupation with the Australian landscape. Bibliography.

O'HARRIS, P. *Was it yesterday?* Adelaide, Rigby, 1983. 119 p, illus.

Autobiography of the prolific author and illustrator of children's books from the time of her arrival in Australia in 1920.

PARKER, C.S.F. *My bush book: K. Langloh Parker's 1890's story of outback station life; with background and biography by Marcie Muir.* Adelaide, Rigby, 1982. 183 p, illus.

Marcie Muir's research fills out the background to Mrs Langloh Parker's autobiographical fragment that tells of her experiences with the Aborigines whose myths and legends she collected so assiduously.

SAXBY, H.M. *A history of Australian children's literature.* Sydney, Wentworth Books, 1969–71. 2 vols.

The importance of children's literature as a significant contribution to education and culture are recognised in this comprehensive history. Bibliography.

WIGHTON, R. *Early Australian children's literature.* Melbourne, Lansdowne, 1979. 40 p, illus.

A useful brief survey of some nineteenth-century Australian children's books. First published in 1963.

PERIODICALS

AUSTRALIAN book review. Melbourne, National Book Council, vols 1–12, 1961–73; ns, 1978– .

The first journal under this title from 1961 to 1973 was edited by Max Harris. The new journal with the same title is issued by the National Book Council. The most up-to-date reviewing journal for all Australian books.

AUSTRALIAN literary studies. UQP, 1963– .

Scholarly periodical with articles, reviews and notes on Australian literature. The May issue each year contains an 'Annual bibliography of studies in Australian literature'.

MEANJIN, Melbourne, University of Melbourne, 1940– .

Journal of cultural studies with articles on literature, current affairs, the history of ideas, popular culture; it also contains creative writing. Founded in Brisbane in 1940 and influential since the mid-1940s.

NOTES and furphies, Armidale, NSW, Association for the Study of Australian Literature, Oct 1978– .

Bulletin of the Association for the Study of Australian Literature records conferences, awards, visits, publications, theses, work in progress and has some literary articles as well.

OVERLAND, Melbourne, 1954– .

Journal of creative writing and articles on current affairs, literature and general culture. Left wing in political views.

QUADRANT, Sydney, Australian Association for Cultural Freedom, 1956/57– .

This journal contains creative writing, criticism and reviews with many articles on contemporary affairs. Usually adopts a conservative stance.

READING time. Sydney, Children's Book Council of Australia, 1958– .

Articles about, and reviews of, children's books.

SOUTHERLY, Sydney, 1939– .

An important literary quarterly. Contains articles and reviews as well as creative writing.

WESTERLY. UWAP, 1956– .

Journal of creative writing, critical articles and reviews. Particularly strong on recent writing.

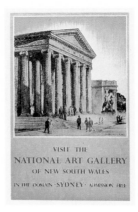

Poster by Smith and Julius studios, Sydney, 1937.
AUSTRALIAN NATIONAL GALLERY

CHAPTER 50

THE VISUAL ARTS

TERRY SMITH

WHO COULD HAVE failed to notice the colourful explosion of art publications in recent years? Our bookshops and libraries seem to burst with books on Australian art. Indeed, if we broaden our view of art to include photography, the crafts and other forms of visual culture, we can see that it is also the backbone of the burgeoning publication of 'Australiana'. What does this tell us about the state of our art, and our art publishing, compared to the earlier 'boom periods'—the 1920s, the 1940s and the early 1960s? How do we find our way among this attractive array?

The increase in publishing on Australian art cannot but be a good thing for everybody associated with it. Glittering surfaces can, however, be misleading. Some publishing subscribes to myths which artists and scholars are now questioning. A visitor might be forgiven for assuming that our artists paint little but the landscape, and that the Heidelberg School artists of the 1880s achieved the definitive expression—updated perhaps by the nearly empty deserts of Nolan and Drysdale but never superseded. The youthful genius, such as Arthur Streeton and Brett Whiteley, dominates our concept of the typical artist. And the bush seems to remain the central source of metaphor for any potentially profound reflection on the Australian condition. Bush studies by slick amateur artists, such as Pro Hart, abound. The increasing social and economic independence of the Aboriginal people is reflected, albeit indirectly, in the growth of books about their art, both traditional and transitional. And the bustling presence of contemporary art achieves expression in magazines, exhibition catalogues and anthologies.

The earlier 'booms' in Australian art publishing all coincided with vigorous surges in the visual arts themselves. In the 1920s Sydney Ure Smith presided over the publication of the work of the Australian School of Landscape Painting, as he did over the official acceptance of local modernism during the late 1930s and 1940s. During World War II his energy was matched by that of the Melbourne modernists, expressed especially in the magazine *Angry penguins* (1941–46). *Art in Australia* spanned both periods (1916–42), which also saw the first attempt at a major history, William Moore (1934; facs, 1980), and the first polemical revision, by Bernard Smith (1945; repr, 1979). The success of Australian painting in London in the early 1960s was matched by the first detailed and systematic history, Smith (1971), and led to the creation of a continuing magazine *Art and Australia* (1963–   ), which survives on a combination of subscriptions and advertising revenue. Against these few, most other publications have fallen quickly away. Two current magazines—*Art network* (1979–   ) and *Art & text* (1981–   )—are exceptional in achieving more than a dozen issues. The basic fragility of our art publishing cannot be disguised.

To date, no major state gallery has published a thorough catalogue of its collections. These are a first priority for a European gallery, the groundwork on which interpretive work is done. The critical revisions of our art's history emerging from the universities cannot be soundly based unless they are matched by such empirical studies. The overall tendency towards a better grounded and more questioning approach to our art, to our history and the variety of visual cultures within it, is, however, irresistible. It will bring great benefits to the reader interested in Australian art.

Photography as an artform has received little serious attention in Australian studies. Photographer Jack Cato (1935; facs, 1979) still remains the only overall survey. *The mechanical eye* by A. Davies and P. Stanbury (OUP, 1985) is an important study of photography in Australia to 1900. In recent years several monographs have appeared on individual photographers but these often lack scholarly detail. An exception is Shar Jones, *J.W. Lindt* (Melbourne, Currey O'Neil Ross for the Library Council of Victoria, 1985), a detailed study of this important nineteenth-century Victorian-based photographer.

The accompanying bibliography is organised around one major principle: the belief that primary sources are just as important as secondary interpretations if readers are to approach the core of the matter—the artworks, artists and their institutions, the point at which our visual culture is produced. Within each medium—painting, sculpture, graphic arts, craft and photography—a major interpretive text is matched by at least one interesting document or documentation. A selection of close-to-the-source books on, by or about artists expands this access.

Strikingly evident is the importance of institutional structures such as artists' societies, state galleries, the art market and key exhibitions both here and abroad. Thus magazines, annual surveys, bulletins and broadsheets are prominent. As well, some historical display seemed necessary, pointing to important periods, major artists and controversial issues since the late eighteenth century, although Smith (1975) has to do much of the work for the colonial period. The bibliography also draws attention to the previously neglected, such as Aboriginal artists and the period between and including the two world wars.

Of interest is the range of publishing formats: reference texts, histories, period studies, thematic surveys, monographs, picture-books, special editions, books by artists, catalogues, pamphlets and magazines. Variety in historical method exercises some fascination and has been surveyed in an essay 'Writing the history of Australian art: its past, present and possible future' (*Australian J of art* 3, 1983, 10–20). 'Life and work' studies of individual artists, the major approach of art historians for two decades, have been referred to other categories. There are obvious shortfalls in research; art criticism is neither collected nor studied, and work is only beginning on art schools, graphic arts, crafts and collecting.

There is every reason to look forward optimistically to a deepening and an enlivening of our art and the publications which it inspires. Perhaps the key factor demonstrated by the energy and variety of the publications collected in this bibliography is that, for all its commitment to the professional demands of the craft and to the requirements of elite taste, our art has also been dedicated to the interests of the people. Whatever the contradictions therein—perhaps because of them—much of it has always been, deservedly, popular.

The author wishes to thank Daniel Thomas, Joan Kerr, Barry Pearce and Sam Alcorn for their advice and assistance in compiling the following bibliography.

REFERENCE

9 × 5 IMPRESSIONS EXHIBITION, Melbourne, 1889. [*Catalogue*].

Major exhibition by the painters Roberts, Conder, Streeton and others, introducing their 'impressions' and reinforcing aesthetic taste. Delicate cover by Conder.

CHOATE, R. *A guide to sources of information on the arts in Australia*. Sydney, Pergamon, 1983. 112 p.

Bibliographical essay giving an overview of all aspects of the arts in general and chapters on each of the arts, excluding theatre and cinema.

GERMAINE, M. *Artists and galleries of Australia*. Brisbane, Boolarong, 1984. 595 p, illus.

Lists biographical details of a large number of living artists and their work. Brief accounts of art institutions, especially galleries. Basic reference work. First published in 1979 as *Artists and galleries of Australia and New Zealand*.

HANKS, E. *Australian art and artists to 1950: a bibliography based on the holdings of the State Library of Victoria*. Melbourne, Library Council of Vic, 1982. 397 p.

Lists of artists, institutions and other subjects gathered from a wide range of publications.

KERR, J. ed, *Dictionary of Australian artists; working paper I: painters, photographers and engravers, 1770–1870, A–H*. Sydney, Power Institute of Fine Arts, University of Sydney, 1984.

The first of a set of working papers intended to become a dictionary of all known painters, photographers, engravers, architects, sculptors and craftspeople to 1870. Further volumes on periods after 1870 are projected.

McCULLOGH, A. *Encyclopedia of Australian art*. Melbourne, Hutchinson, 1984. 2 vols, illus.

Biographical notes on a wide range of artists whose work is either in a public collection, has won a prize or is referred to in a book. First published in one volume in 1968.

MADDRELL, S. ed, *Directory of arts libraries and resource collections in Australia*. Sydney, Australia Council for Policy and Planning, 1983. 244 p.

Lists about 200 institutions by state, then alphabetically by artform. Shows collection strengths, user services and publications.

MOORE, W. *The story of Australian art*. A & R, 1934. 2 vols, illus.

Information and anecdote are combined into a history of artworks, artists, techniques, art societies and galleries. Crucial to understanding the period 1880–1930s. An artist dictionary in vol 2. Facsimile edition, A & R, 1980.

SMITH, B.W. ed, *Documents on art and taste in Australia: the colonial period, 1770–1914*. OUP, 1975. 299 p.

Basic sourcebook for the period. Carefully selected and rare texts by artists and writers from Cook's voyages to Long and McCubbin's historical sketches nearly 150 years later.

GENERAL WORKS

AUSTRALIA. Committee of Inquiry into the Crafts in Australia. *The crafts in Australia: report . . .* AGPS, 1975. 2 vols, illus.

Important report commissioned by the Australia Council recommending funding basis for the revival of the crafts in Australia during the past decade. Chairman: Kym Bonython.

AUSTRALIAN perspecta: a biennial survey of contemporary Australian art. Sydney, Art Gallery of NSW, 1981–   .

Surveys which complement the Sydney Biennales of mainly international art and show the variety and vitality of today's Australian art. Biographies and bibliographies.

BADHAM, H.E. *A study of Australian art*. Sydney, Currawong, 1949. 248 p, illus.

Straightforward informational history. Diffident about the achievement of Australian art. A contrast to Smith (1945; repr, 1979).

BAIL, M. *Ian Fairweather*. Sydney, Bay Books, 1981. 264 p, illus.

Surveys the art of a subtle English modernist, wandering through the East and other peripheries, including those around figuration and abstraction.

BAKER, R.T. *The Australian flora in applied art. Part I. The waratah*. Sydney, Government Printer, 1915. 84 p, illus.

Amusingly obsessive demonstration of the usefulness of the waratah in decoration, from electroliers to the stained glass windows of the Sydney Town Hall; it also boasts a 'War-Atah legend'.

BATTARBEE, R. *Modern Australian Aboriginal art*. A & R, 1951. 55 p, illus.

The Hermannsburg School (Arunta/Aranda) painters, especially Namatjira, presented by a watercolourist who introduced modern European techniques to the area.

BEAN, C.E.W. ed, *Photographic record of the war*. A & R, 1923. 785 p, illus. (*Official history of Australia in the war of 1914–1918*, 12).

Over 750 photographs of the war taken mostly by official photographers. The first thoroughly photographed major event in our history.

BRADLEY, A. AND SMITH, T. eds, *Australian art and architecture: essays presented to Bernard Smith*. OUP, 1980. 257 p, illus.

Scholarly studies ranging from mid-nineteenth-century travel artists to an Arthur Boyd series on sexuality and landscape. Strong on relationships between artforms and on the Heidelberg School. Includes checklist of Bernard Smith's writings.

BRUCE, C. et al, *Eugène von Guérard, 1811–1901: German romantic in the Antipodes*. Martinborough, NZ, Alister Taylor, 1982. 306 p, illus.

Beautifully produced catalogue raisonné with numerous coloured plates. Includes list of exhibitions and detailed bibliography. See also Bruce's catalogue of the 1980 Von Guérard exhibition: *Eugène Von Guérard*, Sydney, Australian Gallery Directors' Council in conjunction with the Australian National Gallery, 1980.

BURKE, J. *Australian women artists, 1840–1940*. Melbourne, Greenhouse, 1980. 188 p, illus.

Developed from the 1975 exhibition at Melbourne University. Emphasis on women painters of the 1920s and 1930s. Includes Noel Hutchinson's essay on women sculptors and Grace Crowley's reminiscences.

CABAN, G. *A fine line: a history of Australian commercial art*. Sydney, Hale & Iremonger, 1983. 166 p, illus.

Survey of graphic art including advertisements and posters with most attention to 1880–1980. Poor documentation.

CAMPBELL, J. *Australian watercolour painters, 1780–1980: including an alphabetical listing of over 1200 painters*. Adelaide, Rigby, 1982. 351 p, illus.

Historical survey of watercolour work with one illustration per artist.

CATO, J. *The story of the camera in Australia*. Facs, Melbourne, Georgian House, 1955. 187 p, illus.

Collection of information and examples organised around known subjects, technical changes, studios and photographers.

Benjamin Duterrau, Self portrait, *1837. Oil. Duterrau emigrated to Hobart in 1832 and established himself as a portrait painter. He had absorbed the aesthetic ideas of the Royal Academy and its preference for the heroic style of painting. His major concerns became the depiction of the Tasmanian Aborigines and their protector George Robinson, and the propagation of art in the colony. Duterrau delivered the first known lecture on art in Australia to the Hobart Mechanics' Institute on 16 July 1833. His subject was the importance of fine arts to the development of the colony.*

TASMANIAN MUSEUM AND ART GALLERY

An approximation to a history. Facsimile edition, Melbourne, Institute of Australian Photography, 1979.

CHRISTESEN, C.B. ed, *The gallery of Eastern Hill: the Victorian Artists' Society centenary.* Melbourne, Victorian Artists' Society, 1970. 120 p, illus.

Essays covering the history of the society and key members of it.

COX, L.B. *The National Gallery of Victoria, 1861–1968: a search for a collection.* Melbourne, National Gallery of Vic, 1968. 486 p, illus.

History of the gallery from its inception to just before its move into new premises.

CRAIG, E.D. ed, *Australian art auction records.* Sydney, various publishers, 1973– .

Lists prices, places, dates of art auctions, with brief biographical notes of artists. Preceded by Christies Auctions, *Australian art sales index 1969–74,* with supplement 1975.

CROLL, R.H. ed, *Smike to Bulldog: letters from Sir Arthur Streeton to Tom Roberts.* Sydney, Ure Smith, 1946. 144 p, illus.

Collected letters between two major Australian artists, 1890–1930, offering fascinating and rare insights into their relationships.

DUTTON, G. *White on black: the Australian Aborigine portrayed in art.* Melbourne, Macmillan, 1974. 168 p, illus.

Generalising approach, more valuable for its collection of images than interpretive comment.

DYSON, W. *Australia at war: a winter record made . . . on the Somme and at Ypres during the campaigns of 1916 and 1917.* London, Palmer & Hayward, 1918. 52 p, illus.

Outstanding draftsman among the official war artists, Dyson's studies on the AIF in the worst years convey admiration for the men and anger at the folly of the war.

EXHIBITION OF AUSTRALIAN ART IN LONDON, 1923. *Record of the exhibition held at the Royal Academy and organised by the Society of Artists, Sydney.* Sydney, Art in Australia, 1923. 22 p, 200 plates.

Important overseas presentation of the Landscape School and the painter–etchers of the 1920s, with essay by Lionel Lindsay on Australian art.

GALBALLY, A. AND PLANT, M. eds, *Studies in Australian art.* Melbourne, Dept of Fine Arts, University of Melbourne, 1978. 111 p, illus.

Studies by staff and graduate students ranging across early Tasmanian architecture, cityscapes, subject painting, modernism and current critical disputes.

GALWAY, G. *Fifty years of Australian art (1879–1929), by members of the Royal Art Society.* Sydney, Royal Art Society, 1929. 101 p, illus.

Historical sketch of this influential painters' society, with reproductions of works, biographical data and photographs of the artists.

GLEESON, J.T. *Australian painting: colonial–impressionist–modern.* Melbourne, Lansdowne, 1976. 392 p, illus.

Generalising history, variable notes on paintings, some poor reproductions. Typical of popular publishing on Australian painting. First published in 1971.

GLEESON, J.T. *William Dobell.* London, Thames and Hudson, 1964. 208 p, illus.

An appreciation of one artist by another. Includes references to 1944 court case won by Dobell over his Archibald Prize-winning painting. Supplemented by Brian Adam's rather thin *Portrait of an artist: a biography of William Dobell,* Melbourne, Hutchinson, 1983.

HAESE, R. *Rebels and precursors: the revolutionary years of Australian art.* Ringwood, Vic, Allen Lane, 1981. 336 p, illus.

Major study of the art world in Melbourne and to a lesser extent Sydney in the 1930s and 1940s.

HILDER, J.J. *The art of J.J. Hilder.* Ed by S. Ure Smith and B. Stevens. A & R, 1918. 48 p, illus.

Outstanding among the books issued by Ure Smith on important artists. Hilder's watercolours particularly suitable to contemporary colour reproduction. See also Brett Hilder, *The heritage of J.J. Hilder,* Sydney, Ure Smith, 1966.

HOFF, G.R. *The sculpture of Rayner Hoff.* Text by Earl Beauchamp [and others]. Sydney, Sunnybrook Press, 1934. 113 p, illus.

Photographs of the sculptor's work, particularly the Anzac Memorial, Hyde Park, Sydney, with various essays.

HUGHES, R.S.F. *The art of Australia.* Ringwood, Vic, Penguin, 1981. 331 p, illus.

A provocative history of painting from early settlement to the Sydney abstract expressionist painters, of whom the author was one. Little original research. First published in 1966.

INGRAM, T. *A matter of taste: investing in Australian art.* Sydney, Collins, 1976. 152 p, illus.

Remarks about art periods followed by records of works by well-known and lesser-known artists on the auction market.

ISAACS, J. *Arts of the Dreaming: Australia's living heritage.* Sydney, Lansdowne, 1984. 272 p, illus.

Sympathetic survey of a wide range of contemporary Aboriginal arts and crafts, from body painting to acrylics on canvas. Prepared with participation of Aboriginal communities.

KLEPAC, L. *The life and work of Russell Drysdale*. Sydney, Bay Books, 1983. 383 p, illus.

Valuable for the many excellent reproductions of the artist's work including his early modernism as well as disturbing pictures of rural poverty, the empty interior and dispossessed Aborigines.

LINDSAY, V. *The way we were: Australian popular magazines, 1856 to 1969*. OUP, 1983. 164 p, illus.

History of popular literature in serial form; throws light on the designer's art and the craft of book illustration.

LLOYD, C. AND SEKULESS, P. *Australia's national collections*. Sydney, Cassell, 1980. 320 p, illus.

Profiles of major holdings in the national, state and regional galleries, libraries, archives, museums and university collections. Informative text and many illustrations.

LYNN, E. AND NOLAN, S. *Sidney Nolan: Australia*. Sydney, Bay Books, 1979. 228 p, illus.

Reproductions of paintings and drawings, 1939–78. Some emphasis on recent work; includes the entire Ned Kelly series of 1946–47. Witty comments by the artist.

McCUBBIN, F. *The art of Frederick McCubbin*. Melbourne, Lothian, 1916. 97 p, illus.

Generous celebration of a very popular artist. Introductory essays by J.S. MacDonald and Alexander McCubbin. Important historical essay by the artist.

McPHEE, J. *Australian decorative arts in the Australian National Gallery*. Canberra, Australian National Gallery, 1982. 125 p, illus.

Well-illustrated selection of fine craftwork. Tends towards artists' decorative work rather than utilitarian objects.

McQUEEN, H. *The black swan of trespass: the emergence of modernist painting in Australia to 1944*. Sydney, Alternative Publishing, 1979. 178 p, illus.

First study of a crucial period, especially on conservative ideologies, surrealism and women artists, particularly Margaret Preston.

MAHOOD, M.H. *The loaded line: Australian political caricature, 1788–1901*. MUP, 1973. 306 p, illus.

Pioneering study of major phases in graphic imagery from the first settlement to the artists of the *Bulletin*.

MELDRUM, M. *The science of appearances, as formulated and taught by Max Meldrum*. Ed by R.R. Foreman. Sydney, Shepherd Press, 1950. 288 p, illus.

Lectures on objectivity of vision and artistic technique, with tonal analyses of paintings, by influential teacher and theorist. See also Colin Colahan, ed, *Max Meldrum: his art and views*, Melbourne, McCubbin, 1917.

MOLLISON, J. AND MURRAY, L. eds, *Australian National Gallery: an introduction*. Canberra, Australian National Gallery, 1982. 290 p, illus.

Essays on the gallery and its collection, including Daniel Thomas's concise history of Australian art.

MOORE, D. AND HALL, R. *Australia: image of a nation*. Sydney, Collins, 1983. 335 p, illus.

Over 400 photographs made between 1850 and 1950 are organised into themes such as colonisation, the bush, work and optimism, with lively historical commentary and captions.

NATIONAL GALLERY OF VICTORIA. *The field*. Melbourne, The Gallery, 1968. 96 p, illus.

A survey of Australian 'hard edge', 'color field' abstraction. First of now typical curatorial attempts to define current style.

NEWTON, G. ed, *Silver and grey: fifty years of Australian photography 1900–1950*. A & R, 1980, 120 p. illus.

Covers the work of 35 professional photographers.

O'CONNOR, A. *Unfinished work: articles and notes on women and the politics of art*. Melbourne, Greenhouse, 1982. 239 p, illus.

Writings by neglected Melbourne realistic artist and political activist on her struggle in art, politics and feminism in the 1970s.

PHILLIP, F. *Arthur Boyd*. London, Thames and Hudson, 1967. 288 p, illus.

Monograph on an important Australian artist, focusing on his iconography, with interpretations and an extensive catalogue.

REES, L.F. *The small treasures of a lifetime: some early memories of Australian art and artists*. Sydney, Collins, 1984. 162 p, illus.

Reminiscenses of fellow artists by one of Australia's well-known painters. First published in 1969.

REILLY, D. AND CAREW, J. *Sun pictures of Victoria: Fauchery Daintree collection 1858*. Melbourne, Currey O'Neil for the Library Council of Vic, 142 p, illus.

Outstanding examples of early photography in Australia, including urban and rural scenes by Antoine Fauchery and Richard Daintree.

SCARLETT, K.W. *Australian sculptors*. Melbourne, Nelson, 1980. 730 p, illus.

Encyclopaedic listings of biographies and achievements for nearly all known sculptors. Useful selections from reviews of exhibitions. Supplemented by his *Australian sculptors: exhibition lists*, Melbourne, State College, occasional papers, 3, December 1979.

SMITH, B.W. *The Antipodean manifesto: essays in art and history*. OUP, 1975., 222 p.

Polemic essays including the 'Antipodean manifesto', written by the author and other artists in August 1959. This famous controversy was re-examined in Christine Dixon *et al*, *Dreams, fears and desires: aspects of Australian figurative painting 1942–1962*, Sydney, Power Institute of Fine Arts, 1984.

SMITH, B.W. *Australian painting, 1788–1970*. OUP, 1971. 483 p, illus.

An important history covering painting and graphic arts. Indigenous developments related to stylistic succession in European art. Many succinct artists' biographies. First published in 1962 as *Australian painting, 1788–1960*.

SMITH, B.W. *European vision and the South Pacific 1768–1850: a study in the history of art and ideas*. Oxford, Clarendon Press, 1960. 287 p, illus.

A classic study of the highly developed European way of seeing in an alien environment. Significant treatment of scientific ideas in transition and the beginnings of Australian art.

SMITH, B.W. *Place, taste and tradition: a study of Australian art since 1788*. Sydney, Ure Smith, 1945. 304 p, illus.

A key polemic and political, but also professional, history of Australian art from the exploration period to the struggle between realism and aestheticism. Reprinted, OUP, 1979.

SMITH, S. URE ed, *Art of Australia, 1788–1941: an exhibition of Australian art held in the United States and the Dominion of Canada under the auspices of the Carnegie Corporation*. New York, Museum of Modern Art for the Carnegie Corporation, 1941. 58 p, illus.

Interesting introductory essays by Marjorie Barnard, Margaret Preston and others. Selection emphasises impact of modernity on Australian art.

SPATE, V. *Tom Roberts*. Melbourne, Lansdowne, 1977. 161 p, illus.

One of Australia's best-known and most loved artists, creator of images of outback work and life. Shows the variety of Roberts's work and his role in the professional artworld here. First published in 1972.

SPLATT, W. AND BRUCE, S. *Australian impressionist painters: a pictorial history of the Heidelberg School.* Melbourne, Currey O'Neil, 1981. 118 p, illus.

Typical popular picture-book with repetitive reproductions and rambling text, but exceptional in its period photographs. Updates Alan McCulloch's *The golden age of Australian painting. . .*, Melbourne, Lansdowne, 1969.

STURGEON, G. *The development of Australian sculpture, 1788–1975.* London, Thames and Hudson, 1978. 256 p, illus.

Charts the evolution of sculpture from the colonial period to the experimentalism of the Mildura sculpture exhibitions.

THIELE, C.M. *Heysen of Hahndorf.* Adelaide, Rigby, 1968. 320 p, illus.

Thorough 'life' of an Australian artist of the 'gum tree school', carefully documented, but little of value on his art.

THOMAS, D. *Outlines of Australian art: the Joseph Brown collection* (rev edn). Melbourne, Macmillan, 1980. 295 p, illus.

Surveys historical tendencies in Australian art through the important collection of a Melbourne dealer. An 'aesthetic' emphasis in the interpretations. First published in 1973.

WALKER, M. *Pioneer crafts of early Australia.* Melbourne, Macmillan for the Crafts Council of Australia, 1978. 172 p, illus.

A survey with examples of objects and machines in use in everyday life. Contemporary photographs.

WOOD, L. ed, *Directory of Australian printmakers 1982.* Melbourne, Print Council of Australia, 1982. 52 p, illus.

Biographies, exhibition lists and illustrations. Develops Franz Kemp's *Contemporary printmakers*, Melbourne, Lansdowne, 1976.

PERIODICALS

ANGRY penguins. 1–9, Adelaide and Melbourne, 1941–46.

ANGRY penguins broadsheet. 1–10, Melbourne, Reed and Harris, 1945–46.

'. . . as drunks, the angry penguins of the night'. Lively, ironic, consciously modernist forum, edited by Max Harris and John Reed. Victim of the Ern Malley hoax in 1944.

ART and Australia. Sydney, Ure Smith, May 1963– .

The 'house journal' of Australian art, mostly established, mostly collectable. Valuable gallery lists and gentle reviews.

ART and text. Melbourne, Autumn 1981– .

Develops a semiotic–structuralist critical discourse around 'Postmodern', 'New wave' and 'Popism' tendencies in art, video and music.

ART in Australia, Sydney. 1916–42.

Quality periodical on current art, mostly established but also mild modernism. Excellent special numbers on individual artists.

ART network. Sydney, Nov 1979– .

Front cover, Art in Australia, *December 1927, incorporating a woodcut by Margaret Preston. Preston (1875–1963) was renowned for her decorative still lifes, wood engravings and linocuts.* Art in Australia, *founded by Sydney Ure Smith in 1916, soon became the major Australian art journal. A quarterly, it ceased publication in 1942.*

Journal of information and opinion. Open editorial policy, nationally directed.

ARTWORKERS' UNION. *Newsletter.* Sydney, June 1979– .

A communication medium for the socially concerned artist. Some state branches now publish occasional newspapers, for example, the NSW Branch *Artworkers news*.

BROADSHEET of the Contemporary Art Society of Australia, NSW Branch. Sydney, Sept 1952–Nov 1974.

BROADSHEET of the Contemporary Art Society of Australia, Victorian Branch. Melbourne, Sept 1954– .

During the early years (1938–) society matters appeared in *Angry penguins* (1941–46) and elsewhere. Elwyn Lynn's editorship of the NSW *Broadsheet* 1955–70 made it a key source of information and comment. South Australian branch also active since about 1940.

SOCIETY of Artists' book. Sydney, Ure Smith, 1942–47.

Survey of the range of art and art institutions of the year. Preceded by *Australian art annual* (1939).

Royal Philharmonic Society of Sydney.
Program, June 1939.
1938 COLLECTION

CHAPTER 51

MUSIC

JOHN HORACEK

THE LITERATURE on music, both overseas and in Australia, tends to be historical or biographical, and to focus as much on the interpreter as on the composer. Indeed, Australia has not yet produced a composer whose fame equals that of some performers and consequently more has been written about, for example, Melba and Sutherland than about Sculthorpe and Meale.

The annotations to the books listed in the bibliography generally make some allusion to their style. Overall, it must be admitted that the level is not very high and that, in many cases, a book is included for its content—it is not the *best* book on a subject but the only one, and hence it must be listed. On this matter, a review article by Therese Radic in the *Australian book review* (58, Feb–March 1984, 32–3) makes some points with almost brutal directness. She begins 'There is a long tradition in Australian music publishing that only the worst will do' and ends as follows:

> Has music publishing changed for the better? Not yet, but it's because the right book manuscripts are not being offered, not because publishers are as uninterested in the field as they were before 1967 when Macmillan (Sun) first took up the cause with Covell. Our musicologists seem incapable of writing for the general market, which is why journalists are the writers of our better books on music. It is long past time for a change.

Despite some journalistic overemphasis in the article, the general accuracy of Radic's charges must be admitted, and one can only hope that Australia's Bicentenary will act as a stimulus for the change she so rightly sees as being needed.

The bibliography surveys monographs dealing specifically with music in Australia; however, an enormous quantity of supplementary material is to be found via other channels and, consequently, if a particular aspect is not covered by any of the books listed, the search should be extended with the help of the general reference tools listed in section II of this volume. In particular, the use of *APAIS* will help with locating articles in journals and magazines, and *ANB* should be consulted for books issued since the compilation of this bibliography. Other general tools which contain much supplementary material are the *Australian encyclopaedia* and the *Australian dictionary of biography*.

This literature survey is confined to music since European settlement; books dealing with Aboriginal music will be found with the other material in section IV on Aborigines. It includes publications on music and performers, both classical and popular, historical and contemporary, creative and interpretative. In the field of 'music theatre', opera is covered, but ballet is dealt with in the following chapter on the performing arts.

There is an intrinsic problem in the bibliography of music, in that one is attempting to list writings about an artform which does not easily lend itself to the printed word. What is more, although music can of course be printed, comparatively little of it is, at least in Australia, and it will frequently happen that a listener to the radio will hear a performance of a composition which exists only in that performance—and in the manuscript by the composer. It is one of the permanent frustrations of the music librarian that a seemingly straightforward request by a client for, say, a piano piece by an Australian composer cannot be satisfied, as the work has never been published. Only by approaching the composer, his or her agent or estate, or an archive, can the music librarian offer any hope of success—and often the hope turns out to be illusory.

THE FIRST CENTURY

It is perhaps appropriate that the first identifiable composition to have been played in Australia was the 'Rogue's march'; the performance took place in February 1788, on the occasion of the drumming out of a sailor who had been caught in the tents of the women convicts.

Early music-making obviously reflected the nature of the settlement, with band music and traditional ballads being the most prominent genres; many of the ballads are still current. The main sources were of course British and Irish, and this 'reflective' quality of Australian music has remained a constant feature in that the only really indigenous music, that of the Aborigines, has had comparatively little influence on composers working in the traditional European genres, beyond the use of some themes or imitation of some of the styles.

The ballads reflect many aspects of life in the new colony: the plight of convicts, the exploits of bushrangers, the gold rush, the hardships of the early squatters, the shearers. As the colony grew in size and permanence, aspects of the musical background of the settlers were replicated around Sydney and the other large cities. Thus, the building of churches led to the commissioning of organs and the installation of bells. These two topics are extensively treated in the books by Matthews (1969) and Keating (1979). Similarly the growth of permanent settlements was accompanied by developments in the social forms of music. The nineteenth century was the century of choral singing, and many choral societies were established for the entertainment and improvement of both participants and audiences. An extensive history of one such society has been written by Carne (1954). Another social use of music is for dancing, and Andrews (1979) provides the reader with both a history and examples of the dances themselves.

The 'grandest' kind of music as entertainment is usually considered to be opera, and the colony was soon able to enjoy what was, under the circumstances, extensive and enterprising fare. Some information on the early history of opera in Australia may be found in John Cargher (1977), but a far more detailed, scholarly and fascinating account is provided by Harold Love (1981).

THE SECOND CENTURY

As the colony grew larger, more prosperous and more self-assured and, after Federation, became a nation ready to assert its independence and to provide for its population all the benefits of a modern society, Australian musical life correspondingly became more varied, complete and firmly based. Where music-making in the first century depended largely on the enterprise of an individual musician or impresario, the twentieth century has seen the rise of organisations which have as their sole or principal responsibility the provision of music. Most but by no means all of these organisations are government supported—the ABC orchestras and the Australian Opera, for example. The Australian Broadcasting Corporation was created in 1932 and by 1936 had set up orchestras in all six states. This is not to imply that there had been none before; there had, but usually semiprofessional and semipermanent. Buttrose (1982) is a lively history of the ABC orchestras but, despite the author's first-hand experience, there is still a need for a comprehensive and scholarly treatment of these orchestras whose performances in the concert hall and through broadcasts have brought music into the lives of so many Australians.

Another organisation which now looms so large in the perception of music-loving Australians that it seems it must always have existed is Musica Viva. It is, however, a relatively recently formed body (1945) and, like the ABC orchestras, it awaits a chronicler.

Until 1956, opera performances in Australia depended on ad hoc ventures and occasional tours, such as those of Dame Nellie Melba. The Australian Elizabethan Theatre Trust Company was established in 1956, later to become the Australian Opera. Cargher (1977) provides a considerable amount of information about it, and some of the state companies, but no-one has been brave enough to walk through the minefield of operatic politics to write the real and complete story.

Australian singers—some biographies of whom are included in the bibliography—have achieved considerable fame, mostly overseas. The phenomenon is well known: the talented artist goes overseas in search of greater opportunities, greater challenges, greater fame. This is equally true of popular music, and the honour roll of Australian popular music stars is a list of emigrants to London, New York or Los Angeles.

Australian music is naturally influenced by worldwide trends and Australian performers, whether of opera or rock'n'roll, are part of an international pool of musicians whose national origins are irrelevant. Some continue to perform regularly in Australia and consequently exert an influence on the local scene. An example in the popular music field was Johnny O'Keefe; his biography by Bryden-Brown (1982) is an interesting account of the Australian rock'n'roll scene in the early 1960s.

A few accounts of popular singers, rock groups and popular music generally in Australia are listed in the bibliography. Unfortunately, much of the material aims at a mass audience and espouses the credo that 'one picture is worth a thousand words'. An intelligent analysis of the quite startling changes in popular music over the last fifty or more years is yet to be written.

Jazz in Australia has been much better served; Bisset (1979) is a good model of well-documented, interestingly written history. Similarly, Hayes, Scribner and Magee's encyclopaedia (1976), despite its unpretentious physical appearance, is a mine of facts about the extensive history of jazz in Australia.

Mention has been made of the effect of international trends on Australian performers and of the lack of difference attributable to national origin. Fortunately, this is less true in the world of contemporary classical composition. Australian twentieth century composers are of course aware of developments in music in Europe and elsewhere—many have studied and worked extensively overseas. But there is a marked interest in using these internationally based compositional skills to capture specifically Australian elements: the landscape, the indigenous population, the vegetation, the history. This aspect of Australian musical bibliography is well covered: Murdoch (1972) and the work edited by Callaway and Tunley (1978) provide excellent treatment of contemporary classical composition.

In the 1960s and 1970s, the Australia Music Centre compiled a series of reference books of enormous value to anyone interested in Australian music; unfortunately the centre has now considerably scaled down its undertakings. It would be a tragedy if at least some of these reference tools are not continued—most notably the series of *Catalogues of Australian compositions* (1976–78). If they cannot be issued in revised editions, they should be provided with periodic supplements.

The one important general work written about Australian music to date is by Roger Covell (1967). Ranging freely between history, evaluation of individual composers, analysis of specific works and prediction of the future, it is consistently illuminating and an excellent introduction for the non-specialist. However, it is now twenty years since the last edition, so recent important developments are not included.

REFERENCE WORKS

AUSTRALIA MUSIC CENTRE. *Catalogues of Australian compositions, 1–8.* Sydney, The Centre, 1976–78.

Guides to music composed in Australia. Arrangement is generally under composers, including date of composition and whether published or recorded. Each number has a distinctive title.

AUSTRALIAN directory of music organizations. Sydney, Australia Music Centre, 1980. 156 p.

Embraces a great variety of some 3000 bodies, including jazz clubs, choral societies, libraries, orchestras, radio stations and so on. Addresses and contact people are given for all; histories for some. First published in 1978.

AUSTRALIAN music directory. Melbourne, Australian Music Directory, 1981– .

Annual guide to the substantially popular music industry.

COVELL, R. AND BROWN, P. *Music resources in Australian libraries: a report prepared for the Australian Advisory Council on Bibliographical Services.* Canberra, AACOBS, 1970. 109 p.

Examines 'the accessibility of those materials of music that are essential to the maintenance of the Western tradition or of its blending with other traditions'.

CRISP, D. *Bibliography of Australian music: an index to monographs, journal articles and theses.* Armidale, NSW, Australian Music Studies Project, 1982. 260 p. (Australian music studies, 1.)

A key to publishing about Australian music and musicians. Subject index precedes the actual bibliography, which is arranged alphabetically by author.

DRUMMOND, P.J. ed, *Australian directory of music research.* Sydney, Australia Music Centre, 1978. 399 p.

A compendium of information about both research and researchers, consisting of an alphabetical who's who of scholars. Includes classified index, with abstracts to the scholarships.

GLENNON, J.A. *Australian music and musicians.* Adelaide, Rigby, 1968. 291 p, illus, music.

Outline histories of the different music forms in Australia, with 100 biographies and about 130 thumbnail sketches.

HILL, C. 'Directory for Australia', in R. Benton, ed, *Directory of music research libraries.* Kassel, Barenreiter, 1979, 4, 1–38.

Guide to major collections of music in Australia, arranged by the cities or suburbs where the libraries are located. Information about holdings and access is given.

MURDOCH, J. *A handbook of Australian music.* Melbourne, Sun Books, 1983. 158 p.

Contains over 1000 entries listing in one alphabetical sequence, people, compositions, places, organisations, books and awards.

HISTORY AND APPRECIATION

BIRD, J. *Percy Grainger.* Melbourne, Sun Books, 1982. 319 p, illus.

Grainger has attained a degree of notoriety, as much on the strength of his unusual psychology as his revolutionary musical genius. First published in 1976.

BREWER, F.C. *Drama and music in New South Wales.* Sydney, Government Printer, 1892. 95 p.

Music is dealt with in the second part of this interesting booklet.

BUTTROSE, C. *Playing for Australia: a story about ABC orchestras and music in Australia.* Melbourne, Macmillan; Sydney, ABC, 1982. 186 p, illus.

Not a history, but serves that need until one is written. The author's direct knowledge of conductors, musicians and ABC administrators gives the work a very personal flavour.

CALLAWAY, F. AND TUNLEY, D. eds, *Australian composition in the twentieth century.* OUP, 1978. 248 p, illus.

Essays on contemporary composers. Rich in music illustrations, with entertaining lists of works.

CARNE, W.A. *A century of harmony: the official centenary history of the Royal Melbourne Philharmonic Society.* Melbourne, The Society, 1954. 305 p, illus.

A chronological account of the activities of this long-established choral society.

COVELL, R. *Australia's music: themes of a new society.* Melbourne, Sun Books, 1967. 356 p.

A major history of music in Australia ranging from speculation about convict music through discussion of contemporary composers to evaluation of organisations such as the ABC.

GAME, P. *The music sellers.* Melbourne, Hawthorn, 1976. 345 p, illus.

History of the firm of Allans Music Australia which, because of its concert organising, piano sales and sheet music publishing, reflected the total range of musical activities in Australia from the 1850s onward.

HANNAN, M. *Peter Sculthorpe: his music and ideas, 1929–1979.* UQP, 1982. 235 p, illus, music.

Based on detailed research, this is a critical study of Sculthorpe's work.

HEWLETT, A. *Cause to rejoice: the life of John Bishop.* Adelaide, Rigby, 1983. 159 p, illus.

This authorised biography of the architect of the Adelaide Festival of Arts is based on archives and family papers and embraces his work at the Elder Conservatorium.

KEATING, J.D. *Bells in Australia.* MUP, 1979. 150 p, illus.

A detailed historical survey of bells and campanology in Australia.

McCREDIE, A.D. *Musicological studies in Australia from the beginnings to the present.* SUP for the Australian Academy of Humanities, 1979. 38 p.

This short book looks at the present state of music as a research activity in Australia.

MATTHEWS, E.N. *Colonial organs and organ builders.* MUP, 1969. 277 p, illus.

Information about organs, mainly in Victorian churches, and a history of a firm of Melbourne organ builders. Data on other states can be found in John Maidment's *Gazetteer of pipe organs in Australia* (Melbourne, Society of Organists [Vic], 1970–).

MURDOCH, J. *Australia's contemporary composers.* Melbourne, Macmillan, 1972. 223 p, illus.

Gives details of training and professional achievement for 33 composers, a list of works, a discography and a photograph.

ORCHARD, W.A. *Music in Australia: more than 150 years of development.* Melbourne, Georgian House, 1952. 238 p, illus.

Half history, half topical survey of music in Australia, with individual chapters for 'Chamber music', 'Musical associations' and so on.

THOMSON, J.M. *A distant music: the life and times of Alfred Hill, 1870–1960.* OUP, 1980. 239 p, illus, music.

Biography of Alfred Hill, a legendary figure in Australian and New Zealand music, based both on friendship with Hill and archives held in Sydney. An introduction to the classical music world of first half of the twentieth century.

TUNLEY, D. AND SYMONS, D. eds, *The contemporary Australian composer and society: report of a seminar.* Perth, Dept of Music, University of WA, 1971. 88 p.

The theme of these papers was to consider methods of improving the professional status of the Australian composer.

Opera and singing

ADAMS, B. *La Stupenda: a biography of Joan Sutherland.* Melbourne, Hutchinson, 1980. 329 p, illus.

A 'semiofficial' biography, complete with discography and list of roles. It gives a detailed account of her life before and after the watershed of *Lucia di Lammermoor* in 1959.

CARGHER, J. *Opera and ballet in Australia.* Sydney, Cassell, 1977. 352 p, illus.

A popular history of operatic activity, profusely illustrated and well indexed.

DAWSON, P. *Fifty years of song.* London, Hutchinson, 1952. 239 p, illus.

Dawson was one of Australia's favourite singers, especially in the field of popular ballads. His autobiography is an interesting anecdotal account of his career.

HARRISON, K. *Dark man, white world: a portrait of tenor Harold Blair.* Melbourne, Novalit, 1975. 285 p, illus.

An informal biography of Blair, the first Aborigine to achieve celebrity as a singer, though his career was relatively short.

HETHERINGTON, J.A. *Melba: a biography.* London, Faber, 1973. 312 p, illus.

Many biographies (and an autobiography) of Melba exist, but this is probably the most literate. Melba was a phenomenon in the world of opera and had considerable influence on music in Australia, though not on Australian music. First published in 1967.

LOVE, H.H.R. *The golden age of Australian opera: W.S. Lyster and his companies, 1861–1880.* Sydney, Currency Press, 1981. 309 p, illus.

This account of the twenty years of operatic performances under Lyster's entrepreneurship is a fascinating social history, giving a colourful portrayal of theatrical life in that period.

MACKENZIE, B. AND MACKENZIE, F. *Singers of Australia: from Melba to Sutherland.* Melbourne, Lansdowne, 1967. 309 p, illus.

This biographical study of Australian (and New Zealand) singers is still excellent, despite its age. For each singer a photograph is provided and a sketch of his or her career.

WARREN-SMITH, N. *25 years of Australian opera.* By N. Warren-Smith with F. Salter. OUP, 1983. 180 p, illus.

There is an immediacy about Salter's transcription of tapes made by Warren-Smith shortly before his death, which communicates the facts and the atmosphere of the opera scene in Australia from the mid-1950s.

Folksong and traditional

ANDERSON, H.M. *The story of Australian folksong* (rev edn). Melbourne, Hill of Content, 1970. 261 p, illus, music.

Ninety-one songs with extensive historical material arranged in topical chapters, with music for the first verse followed by the text of the whole song. First published as *Colonial ballads* in 1955.

ANDREWS, S. *Take your partners: traditional dancing in Australia.* Melbourne, Hyland House, 1979. 208 p, illus, music.

A history of dancing to the 1960s. Includes a manual of dances with tunes included. First published in 1974.

EDWARDS, R. *The big book of Australian folk song.* Adelaide, Rigby, 1976. 507 p, illus, music.

Music and verses of 300 songs, with brief collecting and historical notes. Appendix contains indexes of variant titles, places of publication and first lines.

MAGOFFIN, R. *Waltzing Matilda, song of Australia: a folk history.* Charters Towers, Qld, Mimosa Press, 1983. 101 p, illus.

Australia's most popular song has generated a small body of writing, of which this is a lively example.

MANIFOLD, J.S. *The Penguin Australian songbook.* Ringwood, Vic, Penguin, 1964. 180 p, music.

Some 80 songs, grouped by subject (for example, 'Bushrangers', 'Pastoral Australia'). For each the compiler provides the melody for the first verse, the full text and annotations identifying sources and variants. See also Scott (1980).

MEREDITH, J. AND ANDERSON, H. *Folksongs of Australia and the men and women who sang them.* Sydney, Ure Smith, 1968. 300 p, illus.

The first half consists of songs from the Sydney area, the second from 'west of the Blue Mountains'. The music and texts of the songs are linked by a historical and biographical narrative.

SCOTT, W.N. *The second Penguin Australian songbook.* Ringwood, Vic, Penguin, 1980. 198 p, illus, music.

Similar in arrangement to its predecessor by Manifold (1964) and designed to complement it, including songs of a somewhat different style, parodies, topical ballads and music hall songs.

WOSITZKY, J. AND NEWTON, D. eds, *The Bushwackers Australian song book.* Melbourne, Nelson, 1978. 135 p, illus, map.

A genuine colonial entertainment mixture of music, dancing instruction and relevant snippets from books.

Jazz and popular music

BISSET, A. *Black roots, white flowers: a history of jazz in Australia.* Sydney, Golden Press, 1979. 182, (9) p, illus.

This well-researched survey goes back to the tentative beginnings of jazz before World War I. Emphasis on the last 50 years and Australian jazz musicians.

BROWN, J.L. *Skyhooks million dollar riff.* Melbourne, Dingo, 1975. 160 p, illus.

Band history and individual biographies of the members of Skyhooks, Australia's popular rock'n'roll group of the 1970s.

BRYDEN-BROWN, J. *J.O'K: the official Johnny O'Keefe story.* Sydney, Doubleday, 1982. 183 p, illus.

This illustrated biography of the 'king' of Australian rock'n'roll draws upon first-hand accounts to tell its story, in journalistic style. Useful discography and index.

HAYES, M. *et al, The encyclopedia of Australian jazz.* Brisbane, Encyclopedia of Australian Jazz, 1976. 112 p.

This modestly produced book contains much information, mostly under the names of musicians, with substantial entries including lists of Australian jazz magazines and jazz conventions.

McGRATH, N. *Noel McGrath's Australian encyclopedia of rock.* Melbourne, Outback Press, 1978. 376 p, illus.

Important for the discographies provided and the 'chart' ratings achieved by the artists listed. Includes some biographies.

ROGERS, R.B. AND O'BRIEN, D. *Rock 'n roll Australia: the Australian pop scene, 1954–1964.* Sydney, Cassell, 1975. 190 p, illus.

This profusely illustrated acccount of the birth and growth of rock'n'roll is addressed to the teenager.

WATSON, E. *Country music in Australia* (rev edn). Sydney, Rodeo, 1976. 172 p, illus.

Biographical chapters of the principal exponents of the country music idiom in Australia. The style, despite its American influences, has quite a following, and the discography of over 40 pages gives evidence of this. First published in 1975.

WILLIAMS, M. *The Australian jazz explosion.* A & R, 1981. 171 p, illus.

Biographies based on interviews with the principal Australian jazz musicians. The lack of overall assessment is counterbalanced by the insights offered by the musicians.

Poster for The kid stakes. *Unknown designer, featuring cartoon creations by Syd Nicholls. Printed by Rotary Press, Sydney 1927.*
NATIONAL LIBRARY

CHAPTER 52

THE PERFORMING ARTS

PAUL BENTLEY

'PERFORMING ARTS' is a term which embraces a variety of entertainment forms. This chapter deals with legitimate and vaudeville theatre, dance, puppetry, circus and film. Popular culture, encompassing many areas of entertainment and leisure, is also covered generally in this chapter, while more specific aspects of the topic, as well as introductions to radio, television, opera, drama and music, may be found in other chapters of this volume.

Collections of books, serials, manuscripts, press cuttings, programs, pictures, posters, sound recordings, films and other material on the history of the performing arts in Australia are found in a number of libraries, archives and museums. Guides to relevant institutions and their holdings include *Our heritage: a directory to archives and manuscript repositories in Australia* (Sydney, Australian Society of Archivists, 1983), *Directory of arts libraries and resource collections in Australia* (Sydney, Australia Council, 1983) and *Guide to collections of manuscripts relating to Australia* (Canberra, NLA, 1965–   ). These are further discussed in section II of this volume.

In the 1970s a number of specialist performing arts collections were established by government bodies to give impetus to the documentation and promotion of Australian entertainment history. The most important among these are the Dennis Wolanski Library and Archives of Performing Arts at the Sydney Opera House, the Performing Arts Museum at the Victorian Arts Centre, Melbourne, and the Performing Arts Collection of South Australia. Established theatres and some university libraries and archives also hold documents, manuscripts and personal collections of producers, actors and playwrights, as well as prompt books, performing versions and typescripts of unpublished plays. The Australia Council library, although not concerned with the acquisition of historical materials, has access to contemporary files on performing arts companies, particularly those seeking funding from the council.

THEATRE

After a performance of Farquhar's *The recruiting officer* by convicts on 4 June 1789, it was another four decades before theatre became permanently established in Australia at Barnett Levey's Theatre Royal in Sydney. The discovery of gold in the 1850s introduced a boom period with immigrant English and American actor-managers making their fortunes in the colony. Competition from films and fluctuating economic conditions brought about a decline in commercial theatre during the first half of the twentieth century, a period which also saw the development of little theatre and repertory movements. The establishment of the Australian

423

Elizabethan Trust in 1954 and, later, the Australia Council heralded a revitalised Australian theatre assisted by government sponsorship.

There is no encyclopaedic work specifically devoted to Australian theatre and its companion artforms. Irvin (1985) is the closest but it only covers the period up to 1914. Historical introductions appear in the *Australian encyclopaedia*, 4th edn, 1983, and the *Oxford companion to theatre* (Oxford, OUP, 1983). The earlier editions of the *Australian encyclopaedia* (see chapter 7) are also worth consulting. Readers seeking a short introduction may turn to *A brief history of Australian theatre* by John Kardoss (Sydney, Sydney University Dramatic Society, 1955) and Margaret Williams's essay in *All the world's a stage: Australian–British theatre exhibition to mark the opening of the Sydney Opera House* (Sydney, Sydney Opera House Trust, 1973). The catalogue inserted in the latter publication is a useful guide to artefacts and other visual material. Chronologies and lists of productions can be found in both published and unpublished sources. Among the published lists are Garrie Hutchinson's chronology in the London publication *Theatre quarterly* (26, 1977) and Eric Irwin's list of plays (1971, 1981).

For bibliographical information, *Australian literature to 1900: a guide to information sources* by Barry G. Andrews and William H. Wilde (Detroit, Michigan, Gale Research Co, 1980) offers two sections on nineteenth-century Australian theatre. Recent books on Australian entertainment are listed in the *Australian national bibliography* and articles in *APAIS*. The annual bibliography of studies in Australian literature in *Australian literary studies* (1963–   ) cites articles on theatre and reports on university theses in progress.

The published index to the *Sydney Morning Herald* 1927–61, the index to the Melbourne *Argus* 1910–49 and other newspaper indexes, although not exhaustive in their coverage of the performing arts, are necessary adjuncts to newspaper holdings and press clippings files in libraries.

Contemporary Australian music written for the stage is listed in *Dramatic music* (Sydney, Australia Music Centre, 1977), a catalogue which includes musicals, pantomimes, revues, puppet plays, as well as film, radio and television productions.

Although Hal Porter (1965) has written a chronological narrative, it functions, with limitations, as a biographical dictionary. The *Australian dictionary of biography* (1966–   ) is also an excellent fund of information on major personalities. Access to these is assisted by Marshall and Trahair's *Occupational index to the Australian dictionary of biography* (see chapter 7 for details). Australian actors, designers and directors with international reputations and visiting celebrities of the nineteenth and twentieth centuries receive entries in a number of overseas biographiccal dictionaries, many of which are indexed by *Performing arts biography index* (2nd edn, Detroit, Michigan, Gale Research Co, 1981). The annual casting directory *Showcast* (Sydney, 1963–   ) contains photographs of contemporary Australian actors and actresses, along with agents' addresses.

Theatre companies and other organisations are served by two directories: *Ozarts* (Sydney, Australia Council, 1981) and *Contacts and facilities in the Australian entertainment industry* (Sydney, Showcast Publications, 1969–   ). The latter has the broader scope, listing publishers, property and trade organisations, agents, press and public relations firms, schools and information services as well as performing groups and theatres.

Theatre buildings have been treated in detail by Ross Thorne (1977). The construction of the Sydney Opera House sparked off the building of performing arts complexes right around Australia in the 1970s. Michael Baume's *The Sydney Opera House affair* (Melbourne, Nelson, 1967) and John Yeoman's *The other Taj Mahal* (Melbourne, Longman, 1972) discuss the controversial construction of the house, while Ava Hubble's *Not just an opera house* (Sydney, Lansdowne, 1983) concentrates on its success after it was opened in 1973.

The most comprehensive and readable of the published histories of theatre is West (1978). Leslie Rees's *The history of Australian drama* (A & R, 1978), although primarily devoted to plays written by Australians, must also feature on a short list of indispensible works. Isadore Brodsky's *Sydney takes the stage* (Sydney, Old Sydney Free Press, 1963) and George Lauri's *The Australian theatre story* (Sydney, Peerless Press, 1960) are among the more anecdotal histories.

The two dominant theatrical figures of the nineteenth century were George Selth Coppin, whose life and times are recounted by Bagot (1965), and James Cassius Williamson. There are a number of books and pamphlets on Williamson, the most commendable of which is by Ian Dicker (1974), while Viola Tait (1971) and Claude Kingston (1971) carry on the story of the theatrical organisation which Williamson founded. Notable among a number of briefer souvenir booklets on specific theatre companies are those by Doris Fitton (1981) on the struggles of the Independent Theatre, and by Geoffrey Hutton (1975) on the Melbourne Theatre Company.

Another feature of the late nineteenth century was the part played by visiting international celebrities. The biographies and memoirs of G.V. Brooke, Joseph Jefferson, Wybert Reeve, Charles and Ellen Kean, Charles Mathews, Emily Soldine, Genevieve Ward and others include accounts, sometimes fleeting, of Australian tours. Outstanding local performers to leave behind autobiographical writings include Nellie Stewart and Gladys Moncrieff. Theatrical experiences in the goldfields are told in Hugh Anderson's *The colonial minstrel* (Melbourne, Cheshire, 1960) and J. Gardiner's *Twenty-five years on the stage* (Adelaide, Christian Colonist Office, 1891).

A number of bodies have been responsible for organising conferences or commissioning reports on various aspects of the entertainment industry. The UNESCO conferences on playwriting (1962), professional repertory theatres (1966) and public support for the performing arts (1969) are all documented in published proceedings and the Australia Council has produced a number of reports on theatre employment, training and subsidy. Similarly, the Australian Industries Assistance Commission released a controversial report, *Assistance to the performing arts*, in 1976 which was later balanced by C.D. Throsby and G.A. Withers (1979).

Serials and magazine programs which have achieved a degree of longevity and which will prove useful to researchers include *Lorgnette* (Melbourne, 1871–89) *L'entracte* (Sydney, 1868–94), *Australasian stage album* (Melbourne, 1900–06), *The theatre* (Sydney, 1904–26), *Australian variety and show world* (Sydney, 1913–21), *Stage and society* (Sydney, 1921–26), *Green room* (Sydney, 1917–20), *J.C. Williamson magazine programme* issued over a number of decades, *Theatregoer* (Sydney, 1960–63), *Masque* (Sydney, 1967–71), *Theatre Australia* (Sydney, 1976–82) and *Performing arts year book of Australia* (Sydney, 1976–   ).

Dance

The development of theatrical dance in Australia owes much to the stimulus provided by visits from distinguished overseas artists. Lola Montez was the most celebrated visitor in the nineteenth century and, in the twentieth century, tours by Adeline Genée, Anna Pavlova and Colonel De Basil's Ballets Russes were of great importance. The establishment of the Australian Ballet in 1961 was made possible by the pioneering efforts in the 1940s and 1950s of Edouard Borovansky who had originally visited Australia with the Pavlova and De Basil companies.

Information on dance will be found in some of the reference sources and serials mentioned previously under theatre. Edward H. Pask's article on dance in the *Australian encyclopaedia* (4th edn, 1983) and Jean Garling's *Australian notes on the ballet* (Sydney, Legend Press, 1951) are recommended as brief historical introductions. International dictionaries, *The concise Oxford dictionary of ballet* (Oxford, OUP, 1982) among them, contain brief entries on Australian ballet and its major figures. The *Dictionary catalog of the Dance Collection . . . of the Performing Arts Research Centre of the New York Public Library* (New York, New York Public Library, Astor, Lennox and Tilden Foundations, 1974) and *Bibliographic guide to dance* (Boston, G.K. Hall, 1975–   ), published annually as a supplement to the main catalogue, are outstanding general sources containing references to books, articles, manuscripts, pictures, programs, films and other material on Australian dance. Local reference publications of limited value include *Some professional dancers of, or from, Queensland, and some teachers of the past and present* by Marjorie Hollinshead (Brisbane, W. Smith and Paterson, 1963) and *Dance directory N.S.W.*, (Sydney, Australian Association of Dance Education, 1980–   ).

Edward H. Pask's two surveys (1979, 1982) provide comprehensive and detailed histories of theatrical dance in Australia. John Cargher (1977) is the other chief source on the subject.

Hugh P. Hall (1948) provides a valuable pictorial record of major artists and companies who visited Australia during the first half of the twentieth century, with details of their repertoire. Peter Bellew's *Pioneering ballet in Australia* (Sydney, Craftsman Bookshop, 1945) on Helene Korsova and Frank Salter's (1980) work on Borovansky are concerned with efforts to develop local ballet in the 1940s and 1950s. The most useful and up-to-date book on the Australian Ballet is by C. Lisner (1983).

The Australia Council's involvement in the field has resulted in a number of reports including *Support for professional dance* (1981), dealing with the five major professional dance companies, smaller groups, individual artists, training, dance education and other problems. Periodicals include *Australasian dance* (Sydney, 1971–72) and *Dance Australia* (Melbourne 1980–   ).

VARIETY THEATRE

Variety shows appeared intermittently in Australia throughout the nineteenth century, but it was not until Harry Rickards, a London music hall performer, established permanent variety theatres in Sydney and Melbourne during the 1890s that regular vaudeville entertainment was presented. Richard's Tivoli circuit prospered in the twentieth century under succeeding managers, with Sir Benjamin Fuller the main competitor, before succumbing as a theatrical venture to the impact of television in the 1960s. Variety continues to be presented, however, on the club circuit and on television.

There is no comprehensive published history. Limited coverage is given in general theatre histories, notably by John West (1978). Edward Maas's *The Tivoli souvenir* (Sydney, The Author, 1913) deals with the early years of the Tivoli up to the death of Harry Rickards while Nancye Bridges (1980) gives a lively anecdotal account of the period from the 1920s to the 1960s. Frank Van Straten's 'The Tivoli: a chronology of Melbourne's home of vaudeville' in *The passing show* (Melbourne, Performing Arts Museum, 1981) and *The Tivoli story*, a souvenir booklet published by the Tivoli circuit in 1956, are useful potted histories of Australia's main vaudeville organisation.

Works on individual artists are represented by Roy Rene's *Mo's memoirs* (Melbourne, Reed & Harris, 1945), Fred Parson's biography of Rene (1973), W. Moloney's *Memoirs of an abominable showman* (Adelaide, Rigby, 1968), Bobby Watson's *Fifty years behind the scenes* (Sydney, Slatyer, 1924) and Hector Gray's *Memoirs of a variety artist* (Melbourne, Hawthorn, 1975).

With the development of radio broadcasting, many Australian variety artists and actors gained employment in the new medium. *Wonderful wireless* by Nancye Bridges (Sydney, Methuen, 1983) and Jacqueline Kent's *Out of the bakelite box* (A & R, 1983) are therefore relevant sources. More will be found in chapter 55.

Australian variety directory, issued as a companion volume to *Showcast* during the 1970s, continued as liftout sections in *Encore* (Sydney, 1976–   ), the industry's current trade journal, after the 1982–83 edition. Earlier serials, apart from theatre titles mentioned previously, include *Fuller news* published in the 1920s.

PUPPETRY

In the first half of the twentieth century, the art of puppetry was practised by ventriloquists in variety shows and by a handful of pioneer puppeteers, mainly in schools. Peter Scriven's productions of *The tintookies* and *Little fella Bindi* made a significant impact on audiences in the 1950s and in 1965 the Australian Elizabethan Theatre Trust formed the Marionette Theatre of Australia as a permanent national company.

Frank Van Straten offers a concise introduction in 'Discovering puppets' in *The passing show* (Melbourne, Performing Arts Museum, 1981) and Hetherington's survey (1974) provides profiles of 38 companies and puppeteers working in the early 1970s with brief historical notes. A typescript 'List of Australian puppeteers', compiled by the Australia Council in 1976, serves as a useful, albeit dated, directory in the absence of formal guides.

Government aid to contemporary puppet companies is the subject of the Australia Council's report by J.L. Aquino and J.J. Kitney (1980).

CIRCUS

After pioneering efforts in the 1840s and 1850s by Luigi Dalle Casse, Robert Radford, Henry Burton and others, and influenced by large visiting American troupes in the late nineteenth century, circuses which entertained Australian audiences in major cities and country towns for many years included St Leons, Wirth Brothers, Ashtons, Bullens, Soles and Perry Brothers and the occasional large overseas show. Technology, with its associated forms of entertainment, has seriously challenged the local circus, although Circus Oz, with a unique combination of human acrobatic feats and political and social satire, has recently played to full houses both in Australia and overseas.

Mark St Leon has made a considerable contribution to the literature on the subject with his comprehensive history (1983) and his privately published works (1978, 1981). The other main contribution is by Geoff Greaves (1980). Fred Braid, who has been researching Australian circus for many years, has compiled a number of chronological lists on colonial circuses and allied arts and has deposited copies in a number of libraries including the Dennis Wolanski Library. Chris Cunneen has written an introductory article in the *Australian encyclopaedia* (4th edn, 1983).

Fanfare: circus fans of Australasia: official organ of the Circus Fans Assocation of Australia (Sydney, 1972–   ) contains circus movements, obituaries, historical writings and information on research being undertaken.

FILM

Australian film history began in 1896 when short scenes by Marius Sestier were shown in Sydney. Australia's first feature film, *The story of the Kelly gang*, was presented by the Tait brothers in 1906. After a promising start over the next two decades, the industry declined, despite notable work by Raymond Longford, Charles Chauvel, Ken Hall and other local directors, until an internationally acclaimed revival in the 1970s.

Australian films, unlike theatre and some other forms of entertainment, have been well documented in catalogues and other reference sources although very few copies of the films themselves have survived, especially from the period prior to 1930.

Judith Adamson and Anthony Buckley's article on the film industry in the *Australian encyclopaedia* (4th edn, 1983) is a useful introduction, but for more detailed information Pike and Cooper (1980) is indispensible. A companion to this work is their *Reference guide to Australian films 1906–1969* (Canberra, National Film Archive, NLA, 1981), an alphabetical list of reviews in periodicals and newspapers. *Australian films* (Canberra, 1959–   ) is published annually by the National Library of Australia as a catalogue of Australian films of all types. A retrospective list, *Australian films: a catalogue of scientific, educational and cultural films, 1940–1958* (Canberra, NLA, 1959) cites documentary films produced during those years. *Australian motion picture yearbook* (Melbourne, 1980–   ) is packed with information on all apsects of the industry and contains an extensive trade directory.

Apart from Pike and Cooper (1981), there are a number of bibliographies and indexes including Ken Berryman's *The Australian film industry and key films of the 1970s* (Melbourne, Australian Film Institute, 1980), *Film literature index* (Albany, New York, 1973–   ), *International index to film periodicals* (New York, 1972–   ) and *APAIS*. The National Film Archive has also compiled a number of reading lists, filmographies and subject lists, and the reading lists and bibliographies in Graham Shirley and Brian Adams (1983) and two books by Ina Bertrand (1978, 1981), the second written with Diana Collins, are recommended. Additional comprehensive historical treatments may be found in Reade (1975, 1979).

There are a number of books on cinema architecture, the most scholarly and detailed of which is by Ross Thorne (1981). Simon Brand (1983) takes a broader approach, covering film distribution and audience habits in Australia as well as architecture. Other aspects of the industry are dealt with by Ross Lansell and Peter Beilby (1982) and Mervyn Smyth (1980); Judith Adamson offers a new approach in *Australian film posters 1906–1960* (Sydney, Currency Press in association with the Australian Film Institute, 1978). A wealth of material is distributed in the published papers of the biennial Australian History and Film Conferences (Canberra, 1981–   ).

Of a number of published biographies of Australian film-makers, Hall's (1980) is the most illuminating, spanning the years 1910 to 1980.

There are quite a number of periodicals devoted to the Australian film industry. *Everyone's* (Sydney, 1920–27), *Film weekly* (Sydney, 1926–73), *Lumiere* (Melbourne, 1971–74) and *Cinema papers* (Melbourne, 1974–   ), along with many of the theatrical magazines, provide virtually a complete coverage of its history. Furthermore, film has been a popular subject for university research, references to which may be found in the *Union list of higher degree theses* and other bibliographic sources (see chapter 8).

In recent years films have been more closely regulated by governments than other forms of entertainment. The published and archival records of various national bodies, including the Film Censorship Board, the Department of Trade and Customs and the various state film organisations are invaluable sources of information. *Archives index: index to a guide to material on film broadcasting and television held in the Australian Archives, Canberra Branch*, compiled by Suzanne Ridley (Sydney, Australian Film and Television School, 1979) and the unpublished guide itself provide help in approaching some of the available records.

The central repository for the preservation of Australian films and information relating to Australian films is the National Film and Sound Archive. A major collection held by the archive is the Cinesound collection of scrapbooks, stills and scripts. *A guide to film libraries in Australia*, compiled by H. Swales Smith (Adelaide, South Australian Institute of Technology Library, 1983) lists non-commercial organisations that maintain films and videotapes for loan or hire. In 1976 the National Film Archive, in co-operation with the Australian Film Commission and the Australian Film and Television Commission and the Australian Film and Television School, began a film pioneers oral history project which initially resulted in 35 interviews.

POPULAR CULTURE

With the advance of technology, entertainment for the masses and other aspects of popular culture have gained in importance as an interdisciplinary study. *Australian popular culture*, edited by P. Spearritt and D. Walker (Sydney, Allen & Unwin, 1974) and *Nellie Melba, Ginger Meggs and other essays*, by Susan Dermody *et al* (Malmsbury, Vic, Kibble Press, 1982) reflect aspects of change in Australian approaches to the performing arts.

Ralph Bott of the Sydney Opera House library and Peter Wagner of the Australian Film and Television School library assisted in the compilation of the following bibliography.

Preparations for John Antill's ballet Corroboree,
*Sydney, June 1950. It was the first full-length ballet
to reflect Aboriginal culture.*
MAGAZINE PROMOTIONS

GENERAL

ALLEN, J. ed, *Entertainment arts in Australia.* Sydney, Hamlyn, 1968. 159 p, illus.

A survey, drawing together opinions from critics and artists about the state of entertainment in Australia during the 1950s.

AQUINO, J.L. AND KITNEY, J.J. *Statistical analysis of subsidized dance, drama, and puppetry companies 1974–1978: activity and financial statistics for twenty-eight performing arts companies receiving general grants from the Theatre Board of the Australia Council.* Sydney, Australia Council, 1980. 1 vol (various pagings).

Commissioned by the Theatre Board to cover all aspects of the performing arts.

AUSTRALIA. Industries Assistance Commission. *Assistance to the performing arts, 30 November 1976.* AGPS, 1976. 263 p.

An economic study of the performing arts industry with reference to government subsidy in Australia. Bibliography.

AUSTRALIAN UNESCO SEMINAR, Broadbeach, Queensland, 1976. *Entertainment and society: report of the UNESCO Seminar held at Broadbeach, Queensland, June 8–12, 1976.* Ed by G. Caldwell. AGPS, 1977. 242 p, illus.

The seminar's aim was 'to initiate discussions between key personnel and organisations within the entertainment field'.

BREWER, F.C. *The drama and music in New South Wales.* Sydney, Government Printer, 1892. 95 p.

A nineteenth-century view of the development of theatre and music in NSW.

CARGHER, J. *Opera and ballet in Australia.* Sydney, Cassell, 1977. 352 p, illus.

A comprehensive history copiously illustrated and well indexed.

CARROLL, B. *The Australian stage album.* Melbourne, Macmillan, 1975. 112 p, illus.

A history of the performing arts in Australia, including legitimate theatre, opera, ballet and vaudeville.

PERFORMING arts yearbook of Australia. Sydney, Showcast Publications, 1976– .

A reference work with castlists, credits, discography and articles; copiously illustrated.

PORTER, H. *Stars of Australian stage and screen.* Adelaide, Rigby, 1965. 304 p, illus.

A biographical survey of Australian actors and actresses arranged in seven periods from 1789 to the 1960s.

THROSBY, C.D. AND WITHERS, G.A. *The economics of the performing arts.* Melbourne, Edward Arnold, 1979. 348 p.

An economic analysis of the performing arts. Advances policies for their effective funding. The major examples relate to Australian companies.

WILLIAMS, M. *Australia on the popular stage, 1829–1929: an historical entertainment in six acts.* OUP, 1983. 310 p, illus.

Traces the development of musical extravaganzas, pantomimes, domestic farces and melodramas in Australian theatres and examines in detail the plays performed.

THEATRE [see also related references and comments in chapter 49.]

BAGOT, E.D.A. *Coppin the great: father of the Australian theatre.* MUP, 1965. 356 p, illus.

Chronicles the life and times of one of the outstanding actor–managers of the Australian theatre in the nineteenth century.

BRIDGES, N. *Curtain call, as told by Nancye Bridges to Frank Cook.* Sydney, Cassell, 1980. 189 p, illus.

A personal and anecdotal account of vaudeville and variety theatre in Australia from the 1920s to the 1960s.

DICKER, I.G. *J.C.W.: a short biography of James Cassius Williamson.* Sydney, Elizabeth Tudor Press, 1974. 212 p, illus.

J.C. Williamson was one of the great actor–managers and impresarios of the nineteenth century, who had immense influence on Australian theatre through the theatrical organisation which he established.

FITTON, D. *Not without dust and heat: my life in the theatre.* Sydney, Harper & Row, 1981. 200 p, illus.

The Independent Theatre was one of Sydney's most active between 1930 and 1977. Doris Fitton was its founder and driving force. A list of productions is included.

HUTTON, G. *'It won't last a week!' The first twenty years of the Melbourne Theatre Company.* Melbourne, Macmillan, 1975. 164 p, illus.

A history of Australia's longest surviving state theatre company, with a complete list of plays presented and artists who appeared with the company, 1953–74.

IRVIN, E. *Australian melodrama: eighty years of popular theatre.* Sydney, Hale & Iremonger, 1981. 160 p, illus.

Survey of popular theatre listing plays by Australian residents and their first productions, 1834–1914. Appendix lists operas, operettas, musical comedies, burlesques and extravaganzas.

IRVIN, E. *Gentleman George, king of melodrama: the theatrical life and times of George Darrell, 1841–1921.* UQP, 1980. 234 p, illus.

A reconstruction of the life of actor–manager and dramatist, George Darrell, and of Australian theatre generally in the nineteenth century, with a critical assessment of Darrell's plays.

IRVIN, E. *Theatre comes to Australia.* UQP, 1971. 260 p, illus.

An account of the Theatre Royal, Sydney, Australia's first permanent theatre, and a biography of its founder, Barnett Levey. Includes a list of plays, pantomimes and ballets performed, 1831–38.

KINGSTON, C. *It don't seem a day too much.* Adelaide, Rigby, 1971. 208 p, illus.

A personal account of the author's career as a celebrity concert manager with J.C. Williamson Theatres Ltd from 1920 to the 1960s.

LOVE, H.H.R. ed, *The Australian stage: a documentary history.* UNSWP in association with Australian Theatre Studies Centre, School of Drama, University of NSW, 1984. 393 p, illus.

Includes essays by leading theatre historians. Bibliography.

McGUIRE, P. *The Australian theatre: an abstract and brief chronicle in twelve parts with characteristic illustrations.* By P. McGuire et al. OUP, 1948. 183 p, illus.

A history of Australian theatre up to the visit of the Old Vic Company in 1948. Most of the book is devoted to the nineteenth century.

MEADOWS, A. AND WARNOCK, A. *Subsidized theatre in Australia.* Sydney, A. Meadows & Co, 1975. 586 p.

A report for the Australia Council on the public's attitude to the theatre.

STEWART, N. *My life's story.* Sydney, John Sands, 1923. 314 p, illus.

The autobiography of one of Australia's noted actresses whose career spanned six decades from the 1860s until her death in 1931.

TAIT, V. *A family of brothers: the Taits and J.C. Williamson a theatre history.* Melbourne, Heinemann, 1971. 303 p, illus.

An account of the Tait family whose five brothers controlled

Magazine programme, *June 1939, distributed at Sydney's Theatre Royal. Francis Broadhurst captures the zest of the performers and audience reaction in this cover for a J.C. Williamson's magazine program. Williamson's acted as promoters of theatrical and musical events, including musical comedies and classical singing.*
BOOROWA PRODUCTIONS

the fortunes of J. & N. Tait and J.C. Williamson Theatres Ltd, the world's largest theatre chain, for almost half a century.

THORNE, R. *Theatre buildings in Australia to 1905: from the time of the first settlement to the arrival of cinema.* Sydney, Architectural Research Foundation, University of Sydney, 1971. 2 vols, illus.

THORNE, R. *Theatres in Australia: an historical perspective of significant buildings.* Sydney, Dept of Architecture, University of Sydney, 1977. 60 p, illus.

The first is a scholarly account of theatre buildings while the second, the Kathleen Robinson lecture, supplements the main work.

WEST, J. *Theatre in Australia.* Sydney, Cassell, 1978. 260 p, illus.

A comprehensive history of Australian showbusiness, including vaudeville and variety theatre.

DANCE

AUSTRALIA COUNCIL. Theatre Board. *Support for professional dance: Theatre Board.* Sydney, Australia Council, 1981. 311 p, illus.

A survey and brief history of dance companies receiving government support, with recommendations for the development of dance.

CHALLINGSWORTH, E.B. *Dancing down the years: the romantic*

century in Australia. Melbourne, Craftsman Press, 1978. 88 p, illus.

A history of nineteenth-century social dancing in Australia, with musical examples.

FORMBY, D. *Australian ballet and modern dance* (rev edn). Sydney, Lansdowne, 1981. 168 p, illus.

A photographic study of the 1970s. First published in 1976.

HALL, H.P. *Ballet in Australia from Pavlova to Rambert: photographs and commentary.* Melbourne, Georgian House, 1948. 211 p, illus.

Record of ballet in Australia from 1926 to 1948; largely devoted to the companies brought to Australia by Col W. De Basil, 1936–40, and a list of each company's repertoire.

LAUGHLIN, P.J. *Marilyn Jones: a brilliance all her own.* Melbourne, Quartet Books. 1978. 127 p, illus.

A biography of one of Australia's finest ballerinas.

LISNER, C.M. *The Australian Ballet: twenty-one years.* UQP, 1983. 143 p, illus.

An assessment of Australia's national ballet company, 1962–83. Includes a chronology, lists of repertoire and principal and guest artists.

LISNER, C.M. *My journey through dance.* UQP, 1979. 191 p, illus.

Deals with Lisner's pioneering work with the Qld Ballet Company.

PASK, E.H. *Enter the colonies, dancing: a history of dance in Australia, 1835–1940.* OUP, 1979. 188 p, illus.

PASK, E.H. *Ballet in Australia: the second act, 1940–1980.* OUP, 1982. 317 p, illus.

The two volumes provide a detailed history of theatrical dancing in Australia, particularly classical ballet and modern dance. Illustrations and chronologies.

SALTER, E. *Helpmann: the authorised biography of Sir Robert Helpmann, CBE.* Brighton, England, A & R, 1978. 247 p, illus.

Australia's acclaimed dancer, choreographer, actor and director of the Australian Ballet in the 1960s and 1970s.

SALTER, F. *Borovansky: the man who made Australian ballet.* Sydney, Wildcat Press, 1980. 216 p, illus.

A biography of the man who promoted ballet during the 1940s and 1950s and laid the foundation for the establishment of the Australian Ballet Company.

VARIETY, CIRCUS, PUPPETRY

GREAVES, G. *The circus comes to town: nostalgia of Australian big tops.* Sydney, Reed, 1980. 96 p, illus.

A history and appreciation of the circus in Australia.

HETHERINGTON, N. *Puppets of Australia.* Sydney, Australian Council for the Arts, 1974. 37 p, illus.

A brief survey of puppeteers and puppet theatres in the 1970s, with a historical introduction.

PARSONS, F.H. *A man called Mo.* Melbourne, Heinemann, 1973. 174 p, illus.

A biography of Australian comic, vaudeville and radio star, Roy Rene, as told by one of his scriptwriters. Includes excerpts from *MacCackie Mansion* and other shows he made famous.

ST LEON, M. *An Australian circus: the origins of Ashton's Circus and a brief record of its travels in Australia until 1918.* Sydney, The Author, 1978. 76, [15] leaves.

Traces the early history of one of Australia's leading circus families. Bibliography.

ST LEON, M. *The circus in Australia, 1842–1921.* Sydney, The Author, 1981. 267 leaves.

Contains information on over 80 circuses and circus families in Australia. Alphabetically arranged under name of circus.

ST LEON, M. *Spangles and sawdust.* Melbourne, Greenhouse, 1983. 183 p, illus.

The most comprehensive history to date of circus entertainment in Australia.

TIVOLI CIRCUIT OF AUSTRALIA PTY LIMITED. *The Tivoli story: 55 years of variety.* Melbourne, The Company, 1956. 24 p, illus.

A small souvenir booklet on the Tivoli circuit and variety theatre in Australia from the Harry Rickards era to the management by David N. Martin.

WIRTH, G. *Round the world with a circus.* Melbourne, Troedel & Cooper, 1925. 144 p.

WIRTH, P. *The life of Philip Wirth: a lifetime with an Australian circus.* Melbourne, Troedel & Cooper, 1934. 128 p, illus.

The Wirth Brothers' Circus was, until 1963, Australia's own 'greatest show on earth'. These two books trace the evolution of the family's involvement from the 1870s to the 1930s.

FILM

AUSTRALIAN motion picture yearbook, Melbourne, Cinema Papers, 1980– .

Surveys of the Australian film industry. Contains feature articles, details about films and awards, and reference and directory sections. The 1983 yearbook contains a feature film checklist 1970–82.

BAXTER, J. *The Australian cinema.* Sydney, Pacific Books, 1970. 118 p.

A history of the Australian film industry. The final three chapters deal with Australian film-making in the late 1960s.

BERTRAND, I.W. *Film censorship in Australia.* UQP, 1978. 227 p, illus.

Traces the history of various pressures and changing attitudes on film censorship.

BERTRAND, I.W. AND COLLINS, D. *Government and film in Australia.* Sydney, Currency Press; Melbourne, Australian Film Institute, 1981. 200 p, illus.

A history of the relationship between the Australian government and film-makers from the 1920s to the 1970s.

BRAND, S. *Picture palaces and flea-pits: eighty years of Australians at the pictures.* Sydney, Dreamweaver Books, 1983. 271 p, illus.

A celebration of the days when a visit to the pictures was the event of the week. Covers film distribution, history and audience habits, 1900–60, before the advent of television.

EDMONDSON, R. AND PIKE, A.F. *Australia's lost films: the loss and rescue of Australia's silent cinema.* Canberra, NLA, 1982. 96 p, illus.

An account of the loss of four-fifths of Australia's 250 feature films from 1906 to 1930 from a historical and aesthetic point of view. Has excellent stills and a complete checklist.

HALL, K.G. *Australian film: the inside story.* Sydney, Summit Books, 1980. 192 p, illus.

A personal account by one of Australia's most respected film directors. Illustrations from Hall's cinesound features and newsreels. First published as *Directed by Ken G. Hall* in 1977.

LANSELL, R. AND BEILBY, P. eds, *The documentary film in Australia.* Melbourne, Cinema Papers in association with Film Vic, 1982. 205 p, illus.

A comprehensive survey of documentary film-making. Includes a directory of producers and directors, organisations and sources of information.

LONG, J. AND LONG, M. *The pictures that moved: a picture history of the Australian cinema 1896–1929, with scripts of the films* The pictures that moved *and* The passionate industry. Melbourne, Hutchinson, 1982. 184 p, illus.

A pictorial history of Australian silent films. Shows the effect on the industry of the flood of American films at the end of the silent era.

MURRAY, S. AND BEILBY, P. eds, *The new Australian cinema.* Melbourne, Nelson, 1980. 207 p, illus.

A thematic survey of the Australian film renaissance in the 1970s, when over 150 feature films were made.

PIKE, A.F. AND COOPER, R. *Australian film, 1900–1977: a guide to feature film production.* OUP, 1980. 448 p, illus.

A checklist of feature films with a synopsis, credits and commentary on each film. Divided into seven periods with an introduction to each section.

READE, E. *The Australian screen: a pictorial history of Australian filmmaking.* Melbourne, Lansdowne, 1975. 308 p, illus.

READE, E. *History and heartburn: the saga of Australian film, 1896–1978.* Sydney, Harper & Row, 1979. 353 p, illus.

Detailed histories combining and updating two earlier works by Reade, *Australian silent films* and *The talkies era,* with a chronological listing of feature films.

SHIRLEY, G. AND ADAMS, B. *Australian cinema: the first eighty years.* A & R, 1983. 325 p, illus.

Documents the social, financial and political aspects of films and film-making up to 1975. Bibliography.

SMYTH, M. *The economics of the Australian film industry.* Melbourne, Centre for the Study of Education Communication and Media, La Trobe University, 1980. 22 p. (Media Centre paper, 13.)

Based on a postgraduate thesis in which the author examines the structure of the industry, its market conduct, economic models, performance and practice.

STRATTON, D. *The last new wave: the Australian film revival.* A & R, 1980. 337 p, illus.

An account of productions during the 1970s, based on interviews with their directors. Includes credits and synopses of around 120 films.

THORNE, R. *Cinemas of Australia via USA.* Sydney, Dept of Architecture, University of Sydney, 1981. 388 p, illus.

Architectural design and interior decoration of Australasian picture palaces up to World War II.

TULLOCH, J. *Australian cinema: industry, narrative and meaning.* Sydney, Allen & Unwin, 1982. 272 p, illus.

A study of film during the silent and early sound period. Documents the struggle for an Australian national cinema.

TULLOCH, J. *Legends of the screen: the Australian narrative cinema, 1919–1929.* Sydney, Currency Press; Melbourne, Australian Film Institute, 1981. 448 p, illus.

A history of silent feature films, including the professional, economic and social constraints on production during the period 1919–29.

CHAPTER 53

ARCHITECTURE

DAVID SAUNDERS

THE LITERATURE on architecture in Australia is largely a collection of books illustrating and documenting old buildings and historic places. This kind of publishing has enjoyed a phenomenal growth over the past twenty years and it is now possible, in a way which earlier was quite out of the question, to become informed about Australia's architectural past. There are overall surveys and surveys of the major periods and styles; there are books about the main kinds of building types—domestic, public, religious and rural; there are a few biographies of architects, and one book about building contractors.

Treatment of the present, of new or recent buildings and of living architects is still, by comparison, uncommon, though the drought may be breaking with a growing number of books on contemporary Australian architecture, including J. Taylor's *Australian architecture since 1960* (Sydney, Law Book Co, 1986). In the last few decades, the one writer who belied the generalisation was Robin Boyd. Boyd is probably still the best-known author on Australian architecture. He was certainly the best known when at the height of his output in the late 1960s. His incisive writing, popular with both a wide public and a professional readership, was concerned above all with contemporary events. His one history (1952; repr 1968) is in reality a pedigree of the suburban house and milieu, which Boyd regarded with a vehement combination of love and hate. As history that book has some important gaps, one being the omission of terrace houses, another that it is all too obviously a Melbourne account rather than a national one. As a combination of acute visual observations and witty social commentary it stands alone.

The historical literature is still largely a matter of illustration and documentation rather than discussion and illumination. Secondly, and this is partly a consequence of the first point, it is focused very much upon buildings and places rather than upon people. The lack of biographical work and social commentary is in a way surprising because one of the earliest books was biographical (Ellis, 1949; repr, 1978) but only a few have followed its example. There are experienced biographers and a great deal of amateur local interest in people's careers, yet architects, builders and building tradesmen have received scant attention. The place one can turn to, however, is the still growing *Australian dictionary of biography* with companion use of the aid provided by J.G. Marshall and R.C.S Trahair: *Occupational index to the ADB* (Bundoora, Vic, La Trobe University, Dept of Sociology, 1979–85). In that index the obviously relevant categories are Architect, Builder, Contractor, Engineer and Surveyor.

The illustrative works that are the core of the literature are in some cases quite splendidly equipped. The grandfather volume is Hardy Wilson (1924; facs, 1975), and its plates are so admired that the fate of many copies in that limited edition has been dismemberment and framing for wall display. Morton Herman's first book (1954; repr, 1970) was illustrated with his own drawings, very colourful perspectives and carefully measured plans and details. Among the ever-expanding number of books illustrated with photography, that by the Sydney photographer Max Dupain (1973) surely stands out. His dramatic black and white photos are made bold beyond nature by his use of orange and red filters, and they have infused the literature with a sparkling quality. Other photographers have become prominent over the same period, including Douglass Baglin, Wesley Stacey and Richard Stringer.

The explanations for the shortcomings in the literature on architecture in Australia are also the explanations for its strengths. In a relatively short time, about twenty years, the quantity of publications has grown phenomenally and the subjects covered have broadened considerably, although they almost all look backward. The explanations lie in the growth of the conservation movement. Should it be called the 'urban conservation' movement? That title is usefully brief, but misleading because a great many rural and isolated examples have received attention. A more helpful description is 'conservation of the built environment'. The chief agents of the movement have been, and in many ways still are, the National Trusts. The first National Trust was formed in New South Wales in 1945, incorporated in 1950. Others followed, until by 1963 one existed in each state and now there is also one in the Northern Territory. Most of the Trusts have produced books, and a federation of National Trusts has publication as its major function.

Other important sources for architectural compendia are the government agencies which have been formed as a product of the conservation movement. The extensive work of government departments concerned with the environment at federal, state and local levels will undoubtedly lead the field as far as documentaion is concerned. The 'listings' which are usually at the heart of these government operations provide a golden opportunity for such books, as demonstrated by the massive Australian Heritage Commission publication (1981).

The National Trusts have produced or inspired much of the extensive illustrative and documentary work, but notable contributions have also been made by individual writers. Some preceded Trust activities. Sydney architect Morton Herman's publication (1954; repr, 1970) became virtually the sole Australian text for some years. *Early Melbourne buildings* by Maie Casey and five other contributors (1953; repr, OUP, 1975) was the starting point for the National Trust in Victoria, being adopted almost wholly as its first listing of buildings for conservation. The same happened in Tasmania with M. Sharland (1952).

In his turn the most substantial writer from a historical perspective became J.M. Freeland. His history (1972) is to date the only comprehensive single work, and a very useful and reliable one. As an introduction, as a reference work and as a student text, it is likely to continue unchallenged for some time yet. Freeland was also responsible for turning attention to a period and a person outside the ever-popular colonial, namely Horbury Hunt (1836–1904). His book on Hunt (1970) is also significant in being one of the few biographies of Australian architects. Freeland had an influence upon architectural history in Australia beyond his own writing. For many years he taught and directed research into architectural history at the University of New South Wales School of Architecture.

After Boyd, Herman and Freeland one earlier name has great significance, that of Hardy Wilson. His book (1924; facs, 1975) is the first about old Australian buildings, and it remains to this day the most splendid publication. Its text is short, with the clear message that great beauty worthy of profound attention was lying uncelebrated, in some cases neglected and derelict. The original edition is a collector's item, but a reduced size facsimile is readily available. Wilson also produced other books, with more in the way of text. They are intriguing and eccentric volumes.

Singling out more names becomes a little hazardous because the list will rapidly grow and the reader may be better advised to turn to the reading list which follows. Nevertheless attention is drawn to a few writers for reasons which will be given.

Philip Cox has been involved in what amounts almost to a publishing campaign rather than an author's career. He is a busy, award-winning Sydney architect with an earnest desire for Australian-ness in the contemporary work of his own office and others. He wishes especially to draw attention to the vernacular work of Australia's past. In association with photographer Wesley Stacey, with the help of several co-authors, and by using his architectural office as a kind of publishing agency, he has been responsible for no less than nine books in fourteen years.

Jennifer Taylor, of Sydney University, stands somewhat apart because of her concentration upon recent work and living architects. She produced a small publication (1972) with significant commentary upon the so-called Sydney School of the 1960s and also worked with John Andrews, a leading international architect, to produce a book about his work (1982).

Donald Leslie Johnson is an academic at Flinders University of South Australia who has worked steadily at a series of topics which are Australian or related to Australia. His most sustained research has been on Walter Burley Griffin, about whom he is clearly the authority. Along the way he provided a bibliographic guide which can be the starting point for anyone wishing to join him in looking closely at Griffin (1980).

Gordon Young, of the South Australian Institute of Technology (School of Architecture) has directed over many years an important survey of those towns and buildings in the Adelaide Hills which exhibit special connections with their early settlers' regions of origin: German and English. The reports so far published are *Hahndorf* in two volumes (both 1981) and *Lobethal* (1983).

One of the volumes in the sesquicentenary history of Western Australia contains the definitive work by Margaret Pitt Morison and John White of the University of Western Australia (1979).

Other academics have covered considerable research ground but are not necessarily found as authors of books. As by-products of their work, or to meet the needs of their students, various research aids have been distributed among libraries and interested researchers. Three valuable examples are Donald Johnson's *18th and 19th century architecture books and serials in South Australia* (Adelaide, LBSA, 1981); David Saunders' *Architectural history, domestic architecture: a bibliography from Melbourne and Sydney libraries* (Sydney, Power Institute, 1969); and Helen Temple and David Saunders' *Architectural history in Australia: a bibliography of twentieth century publications* (Adelaide, University of Adelaide, 1977).

For those aspects of architecture that have not yet received their fair share of attention, the reader might take note of three journals. Devoted principally to recent and current affairs is the monthly journal of the Royal Australian Institute of Architects (RAIA), *Architecture Australia*. Others have come and gone over the years, but since 1950 this journal has illustrated and (to a limited extent) discussed the works of contemporary Australians. A small number of articles on architecture were contributed to the long-running periodical *Art in Australia*; on occasions it has contained celebrated material such as the 1919 special number 'Domestic architecture in Australia', an issue in which Hardy Wilson assisted. The third journal is especially designed to record and discuss historical issues in Australian architecture: *Heritage Australia* is sponsored by the Australian Council of National Trusts and contains well-informed articles, most of which are also well illustrated.

A series of monographs on living Australian architects was begun by the RAIA in 1984, with the initial one devoted to Philip Cox.

The Adelaide publisher Rigby has issued during the past few years a charming and by now very extensive series of small *Sketchbooks*—joint products of an artist and a writer—illustrating the buildings of Australian towns and suburbs.

The literature on architecture in Australia held only a few pioneer works until after World War II, but the years since then have seen quite a respectable array emerge, devoted to historical matters above all and generally characterised by an encyclopaedic and illustrative approach. Reflection, explanation and analysis are not yet strong, and recent architecture is mostly left to the profession's magazine.

AUSTRALIAN COUNCIL OF NATIONAL TRUSTS. *Historic Buildings of Australia*. Melbourne, Cassell, 1969–76. 6 vols, illus.

This well-illustrated series describes celebrated homes, houses and whole urban areas demonstrating the variety of Australia's colonial environments. Each volume has a separate title.

AUSTRALIAN HERITAGE COMMISSION. *The heritage of Australia: the illustrated register of the National Estate*. Melbourne, Macmillan in association with the Australian Heritage Commission, 1981. 1164 p, illus, maps.

An invaluable illustrated encyclopaedia of the National Estate.

BERRY, D.W. AND GILBERT, S.H. *Pioneer building techniques in South Australia*. Adelaide, Gilbert-Partners, 1981. 104 p, illus.

Few publications have as yet addressed themselves to Australian vernacular architecture. The cases illustrated here are sensibly discussed.

BOYD, R. *The Australian ugliness*. Ringwood, Vic, Penguin in association with Cheshire, 1968. 256 p, illus.

This book, first published in 1961, had a powerful impact in its day. Boyd, as architectural critic and social commentator, is at his liveliest here. His barbed characterisations of the Australian environment had a forceful effect.

BOYD, R. *Australia's home: its origins, builders and occupiers*. Ringwood, Vic, Penguin, 1968. 316 p, illus.

A critical and historical view of Australian suburbia. It documents the plans, the images and the fittings of characteristic houses throughout Australia's history. The observations are acute and witty. First published in 1952.

BOYD, R. *Living in Australia*. Sydney, Pergamon, 1970. 154 p, illus.

The book of Boyd's own architecture, arranged to suit the thematic explanation Boyd offers for his work.

BROADBENT, J. *The golden decade of Australian architecture: the work of John Verge*. Sydney, David Ell Press in association with the Elizabeth Bay House Trust, 1978. 128 p, illus.

John Verge has been brought nearer to the prominence he deserves, with new insights from recent re-examination of his surviving works. It includes essays by Ian Evans and Clive Lucas. (See also W.G. Verge, 1962.)

BURCHELL, L.E. *Victorian schools: a study in colonial government architecture, 1837–1900*. MUP in association with the Victorian Education Dept, 1980. 204 p, illus.

The book shows a desirable balance of understanding between the function and the form of Victorian schools.

COX, P. AND FREELAND, J. *Rude timber buildings in Australia*. A & R, 1980. 215 p, illus.

A well-documented account of woolsheds and other rural structures and the early search for building timbers. Illustrates the advances made after powered sawmills and other machines arrived. Cox insisted that the rude buildings were closer to the condition of society.

COX, P. AND LUCAS, C. *Australian colonial architecture*. Melbourne, Lansdowne, 1978. 280 p, illus, map.

An introduction to the character of architecture in the early history of Australia based on the authors' experience with conservation work.

COX, P. AND STACEY, W. *The Australian homestead*. Melbourne, Lansdowne, 1972. 318 p, illus.

Complements the volumes on the same topic by the National Trust.

DUPAIN, M. *Georgian architecture in Australia, with some example of buildings of the post-Georgian period*. Sydney, Ure Smith, 1963. 147 p, illus.

Dupain has provided marvellous illustrations of early nineteenth-century buildings in NSW and Tas. The essays by Morton Herman, Marjorie Barnard and Daniel Thomas are important contributions.

DUPAIN, M. *et al, Leslie Wilkinson, a practical idealist*. Sydney, Valadon, 1982. 128 p, illus.

A set of essays by three men who knew him, accompanied by architectural sketches by Wilkinson and photographs of his work.

ELLIS, M.H. *Francis Greenway, his life and times*. Sydney, Shepherd Press, 1949. 292 p, illus.

A biography of Greenway, Australia's first professional architect, a convict responsible for some of Sydney's first colonial buildings. Revised edition published in 1953, reprinted 1978.

FORGE, S. *Victorian splendour: Australian interior decorations, 1837–1901*. OUP, 1981. 160 p, illus.

The author has searched for the true characterisation of Victorian attitudes to decoration and applies her conclusion to Australian examples. Six houses are specifically examined and many more referred to.

FREELAND, J.M. *Architect extraordinary: the life and work of John Horbury Hunt, 1838–1904*. Melbourne, Cassell, 1970. 257 p, illus.

A biography of an influential architect during the latter years of the nineteenth century who introduced an awareness of current architectural events in the United States.

FREELAND, J.M. *Architecture in Australia: a history*. Ringwood, Vic, Penguin, 1972. 328 p, illus.

A valuable reference work and introductory text for students. First published in 1968.

FREELAND, J.M. *The Australian pub*. Melbourne, Sun Books, 1977. 192 p, illus.

A rare example of a thorough investigation of one small aspect of architecture. First published in 1966.

FREELAND, J.M. *The making of a profession: a history of the growth and work of the Architectural Institutes in Australia*. A & R in association with RAIA, 1971. 297 p, illus.

Freeland was commissioned to write this case study in the growth of professionalisation.

FREEMAN, P.G. *The woolshed: a Riverina anthology*. OUP, 1980. 231 p, illus, maps.

Pays close attention to one building type as with Freeland (1977), Burchell (1980) and Sowden (1972). There are plan and section drawings as well as photographs for all examples.

HERMAN, M.E. *The architecture of Victorian Sydney*. A & R, 1964. 192 p, illus, maps.

A survey arranged in decades beginning at 1850. Many of the buildings illustrated have since been demolished. First published in 1956, this is a companion volume to his 1970 work.

HERMAN, M.E. *The Blackets: an era of Australian architecture*. A & R, 1963. 222 p, illus.

Edmund Thomas Blacket (1817–83) arrived in Sydney from England in 1842, and soon established an impressive practice in which the university buildings loomed large and splendid. The family firm remained important until the 1930s. Herman's book is almost entirely about Edmund's career and works; well informed and thorough, it is one of the small number of books devoted to Australian architects.

HERMAN, M.E. *The early Australian architects and their works*. A & R, 1970. 248 p, illus.

Valuable for its insight and illustrations for the period 1788–1850 in NSW. The author provided his own colour perspectives and line drawings. First published in 1954.

IRVING, R. et al, *Fine houses of Sydney*, Sydney, Methuen, 1982. 197 p, illus.

Nineteen houses, dating from 1823 to 1980, selected to represent high quality in various periods. Plans as well as illustrations.

JENSEN, E. AND JENSEN, R. *Colonial architecture in South Australia: a definitive chronicle of development 1836–1890 and the social history of the times.* Adelaide, Rigby, 1980. 888 p, illus, maps.

A large volume of information gathered from newspapers and other sources of the period. Architect Edmund Wright was the starting point for the research.

JOHNSON, D.L. *The architecture of Walter Burley Griffin.* Melbourne, Macmillan, 1977. 163 p, illus.

Study of an international figure who came to Australia in 1913 from the United States where he had worked with Frank Lloyd Wright. Describes how he and his wife introduced a form of modernism to this country.

KERR, J. AND BROADBENT, J. *Gothick taste in the colony of New South Wales.* Sydney, David Ell Press in association with the Elizabeth Bay House Trust, 1980. 156 p, illus.

The Gothic influence upon domestic and church design in the colony is made clear, and along the way interesting sources for such an account are identified.

LEWIS, M. *Victorian primitive.* Melbourne, Greenhouse, 1977. 87 p, illus.

The author's approach is historical, meticulous and knowledgable, using examples from Vic which are thoroughly examined and illustrated.

OLDHAM, R. AND OLDHAM, J. *Western heritage. Part 2. George Temple-Poole, architect of the golden years, 1885–1897.* UWAP, 1980. 227 p, illus, maps.

Devoted to an individual Australian architect and important for contributing to the story of Australian public architecture. Temple-Poole's career relates to many important events in WA.

PITT MORISON, M. AND WHITE, J. eds, *Western towns and buildings.* UWAP, 1979. 345 p, illus, maps.

Published for the state's sesquicentenary, this book transformed a sketchily understood subject into an extensive account covering the years 1829–79.

RAPOPORT, A. ed, *Australia as human setting: approaches to the designed environment.* A & R, 1972. 298 p, illus, maps.

A discursive book with a variety of insights into how and why the Australian urban environment achieved its particular qualities.

REED, T.T. *Historic churches of Australia.* Melbourne, Macmillan, 1978. 150 p, illus.

A churchman's account of numerous prominent church buildings, the book resembles the National Trust volumes and draws on similar sources.

ROBERTSON, E.G. *Early buildings of southern Tasmania.* Melbourne, Georgian House, 1970. 2 vols, illus.

ROBERTSON, E.G. AND CRAIG, E.N. *Early houses of northern Tasmania: an historical and architectural survey.* Melbourne, Georgian House, 1964. 2 vols, illus, maps.

High-standard guidebooks, with beautiful illustrations and carefully related maps. Each of the properties is provided with a brief history.

ROBERTSON, E.G. *Ornamental cast iron in Melbourne.* Melbourne, Georgian House, 1967. 229 p, illus.

Popular awareness of Australian decorative cast iron started with this Melbourne volume. It is complemented by one of Sydney (1962) and another which is a world survey. Revised edition of 1960 publication, *Victorian heritage: ornamental cast iron in architecture.*

ROXBURGH, R. *Early colonial houses of New South Wales.* Sydney, Lansdowne, 1980. 603 p, illus, maps.

Deals mainly with country homesteads, illustrated with photographs and measured drawings of their plans and significant details. First published in 1974.

SHARLAND, M. *Stones of a century.* Hobart, Oldham, Beddome & Meredeith, 1952. xii, 74 p, illus.

A small early book about historic buildings in Tas.

SHAW, M.T. *Builders of Melbourne: the Cockrams and their contemporaries, 1853–1972.* Melbourne, Cypress Books, 1972. 116 p, illus.

The business careers of leading building contractors like the Cockrams provide many clues to their times and to the way our cities became what they are.

SMITH, B.W. AND SMITH, K. *The architectural character of Glebe, Sydney.* Sydney, University Cooperative Bookshop, 1972. 128 p, illus.

An account of this small part of inner Sydney. The information about architectural taste and character is widely applicable in Australia.

SMITH, R.S. *John Lee Archer, Tasmanian architect and engineer.* Hobart, Tasmanian Historical Research Association, 1962. xii, 70 p, illus.

A study of an important early Australian architect.

SOWDEN, H. ed, *Australian woolsheds.* Melbourne, Cassell, 1972. 251 p, illus.

Includes essay by Nayne McPhee on woolsheds. Numerous examples are thoroughly illustrated, with brief notes.

TANNER, H. ed, *Architects of Australia.* Melbourne, Macmillan, 1981. 144 p, illus.

Collection of brief biographies; many of the architects are not yet treated anywhere else.

TANNER, H. AND COX, P. *Restoring old Australian houses and buildings: an architectural guide.* Melbourne, Macmillan, 1975. 212 p, illus.

This book offers one half on 'Identification' (seven main styles) and the other on 'Techniques'.

TAYLOR, J. *An Australian identity: houses for Sydney, 1953–63.* Sydney, Dept of Architecture, University of Sydney, 1972. 80 p, illus, map.

A little book giving the facts and significance of the so-called Sydney School of that period. A useful reference on a topic of considerable significance.

TAYLOR, J. AND ANDREWS, J. *John Andrews: architecture as a performing art.* OUP, 1982. 176 p, illus.

Study of John Andrews, an Australian architect of international reputation.

THORNE, R. *Picture palace architecture in Australia and New Zealand.* Melbourne, Sun Books, 1976. 27 p, 26 l, illus.

Thorne is an authority on this fascinating topic, and he has gathered information and illustrations for many that have gone as well as the few spectacular examples that remain.

VERGE, W.G. *John Verge, early Australian architect: his ledger and his clients.* Sydney, Wentworth, 1962. 297 p, illus.

The initial sourcebook for anything about Verge; the author did a special service in reproducing and annotating his ancestor's business books. (See also Broadbent, 1978.)

WILSON, W.H. *Old colonial architecture in New South Wales and Tasmania.* Facs, Sydney, Ure Smith in association with the National Trust of Australia (NSW), 1975. 10, 150 p, illus.

A book of beautiful etchings of colonial buildings with only a few notes on their architecture. First published in 1924.

Electricity supply for Launceston, c1894.
QUEEN VICTORIA MUSEUM AND ART GALLERY,
LAUNCESTON

CHAPTER 54

SCIENCE, PURE AND APPLIED

R. W. HOME

SCIENCE HAS BEEN a significant factor in the Australian experience at least since the time of Lieutenant James Cook's expedition to the South Seas to observe the transit of Venus across the face of the sun in 1769. Joseph Banks and his entourage were travelling with Cook aboard the *Endeavour*. Australia so captured Banks's enthusiasm that he became a leading advocate of its colonisation by British settlers. With settlement achieved, he became a patron of the scientific exploration of the continent, sending out a series of trained botanical observers to collect specimens for study and classification by experts in London. His activities are extensively documented in Warren R. Dawson's magnificent calendar (1958) of the Banks correspondence and McMinn's biography (1970) of Cunningham. The definitive study, however, has still to be written.

Banks's interests were almost exclusively botanical and the other sciences had to find patronage elsewhere. The exploration of the continent continued to be accompanied by the scientific investigation of its unique flora and fauna and of its geological features. With no facilities, however, for providing even the most rudimentary training in science—these came only with the founding of the first universities in Sydney and Melbourne in the 1850s—the Australian colonies remained entirely dependent, scientifically speaking, on imported skills. Furthermore, the number of trained people in the country long remained too small to form self-sustaining institutions or to maintain locally based scientific publication outlets. Serious scientific work thus continued to depend on official patronage, and Australian workers continued to be regarded primarily as collectors rather than recognised authorities on Australian materials. The basis of scientific decision-making and authority remained firmly in Europe, in the hands of men like Richard Owen and William Jackson Hooker, who classified the materials sent to them by their colonial correspondents and published descriptions of them. This pattern is brought out very clearly in Hooker's Van Diemen's Land correspondence (Burns & Skemp, 1961).

A similar relationship of dependency existed even in sciences such as astronomy and geophysics, where Australia's southern location gave it peculiar advantages for certain kinds of observing. Here, too, it was not until after 1850 that sufficient Australian resources could be mustered to sustain a significant program of locally directed scientific work. Until then, Australia served merely as a convenient fixed platform for temporary observatories established under direct British aegis, whether at Sydney Cove in 1788 (McAfee, 1981), at Parramatta in the 1820s (Russell, 1888) or at Hobart in the 1840s (*Annals of science* 39, 1982, 6, 527–64).

The pattern of Australian scientific work changed dramatically during the latter half of the nineteenth century. Though scientific exploring continued to be a major focus of activity, this now tended to be carried out under local rather than European auspices (Spencer, 1932, shows a late example of this). Collectors continued to scour the bush for specimens for the European and American markets (Bischoff, 1931), but as time went by, more and more of the material collected found its way, at least in the first instance, into newly founded Australian museums of natural history. Furthermore, the notion, perhaps first expressed by Leichhardt (1968) in the 1840s, that type specimens and other reference or unique materials ought to remain in Australia, or at least return after description, came to be increasingly widely held.

The second half of the century saw the establishment in the various colonies of a range of other scientific institutions besides museums, all of them now under local control. The founding of universities in Sydney and Melbourne has already been mentioned; Adelaide and Hobart later followed suit, as did Brisbane and Perth shortly after the turn of the century. While all six universities were limited initially to providing a traditional liberal education, the sciences were strongly represented in the curriculum from the outset. In time, separate laboratory-based degree courses in science were introduced and also, in some, science-oriented degrees in medicine and engineering.

Most of the colonies established observatories during this period and appointed government astronomers to run them. They were usually responsible not just for astronomical work (including their colony's time service) but also for routine geomagnetic and meteorological observing and for making the fundamental geodetic determinations for government survey purposes. In Queensland and Tasmania, where observatories were not established, government meteorologists were appointed instead (Day, 1966; Gentilli, 1967; Russell, 1888; Wood, 1958). Other sciences, too, received support from newly independent (or at least semidependent) colonial legislatures. Several colonies appointed government botanists, of whom Ferdinand von Mueller in Victoria is by far the best known (Willis, 1949). With rumours of gold in the air, New South Wales appointed a government geologist in 1850. Victoria set up an excellent geological survey in 1852, and most of the other colonies later followed suit (O'Neill, 1982). Government analysts were appointed to undertake assays and to oversee the quality of water and food supplies.

These developments, along with the growing number of doctors, schoolteachers and other professional people required to service an increasing population, led to a rapid growth, especially in the more populous colonies, in the number of residents with scientific interests and expertise. Viable scientific societies became possible for the first time and were formed one by one in most of the colonies during the middle third of the century. Each colony, sooner or later, came to have a 'Royal Society' patterned after the London model, with its own journal and exchange agreements with scientific societies elsewhere (Maiden, 1918; Marks, 1959; Piesse, 1913; Pescott, 1961). Such societies provided both suitable outlets for local scientific work and a mechanism whereby local workers could keep in touch more satisfactorily with what was being done in other parts of the world. The growth of public reference libraries in the colonial capitals also helped in the latter regard.

Nevertheless, the work done by Australian scientists continued to be quintessentially 'colonial' in character, remaining largely observational and descriptive in style rather than experimental and laboratory-based, and being concerned almost exclusively with local questions rather than with topics of universal import. Furthermore, scientists in the different colonies remained largely isolated from each other. For intellectual support and encouragement they generally looked not to their fellow colonists but to the scientific community 'at home' in Britain, and if they did venture on to topics of more than local concern, it was to the English journals rather than their local Royal Society transactions that they sent their work for publication.

An important change in attitude can be discerned during the 1880s. It was during this decade, for example, that the universities in Sydney and Melbourne dramatically expanded their commitment to science. (The much smaller University of Adelaide followed fifteen to twenty years later.) Talented new professors and lecturing staff, mostly from Britain, were appointed in a number of fields. New laboratories were constructed. Shortly afterwards, the first research students appeared. Furthermore, most of the new professors were already active researchers and their interests were by no means confined to local questions. Publications by them and their students began to appear with increasing frequency in international journals.

The impact of a number of science-based technological advances also began to be felt during this period. The first telephone services were introduced in the larger cities, as well as the first municipal electrification systems. Chemical and metallurgical industries mushroomed. Major improvements in public health services followed the general acceptance of the germ theory of disease. Soon afterwards, science began to be applied in the countryside as well, through the establishment of scientific services within colonial departments of agriculture.

Australian scientific workers were now somewhat less isolated than they had been. The introduction of fast and reliable steamer services between Europe and Australia via the Suez Canal had halved the time of the journey and made it possible for scientific workers in Australia to keep reasonably up to date with the international journal literature in their field and even to contemplate occasional visits 'home' to establish or renew contacts with fellow scientists there. Within Australia, improvements in transport helped to bring scientists in the different colonies closer together and made possible the formation of the first intercolonial scientific organisation, the Australian Associaton for the Advancement of Science, founded in 1888. The association at first met annually, later at approximately two-year intervals. Its meetings quickly became the highlight of the Australian scientific calendar, offering welcome opportunities to exchange opinions and establish a basis for subsequent correspondence. They remained so until the growth of specialist societies, especially after World War II, challenged the association's hegemony.

The Australian scientific community remained small, however, and the imperial connections continued to be strong. Even in 1939, Australian scientists tended to see themselves and their work very much within the context of a larger British scientific network. Travelling scholarships such as the 1851 Exhibition science research awards (established in 1891) and the Rhodes scholarships (established 1904) strengthened the links by taking many of Australia's best young science graduates to England for further training. A significant percentage, including some of the best of them, never returned.

During World War I, Australian scientists, like their compatriots from other walks of life, flocked to support the allied cause. Scientific work was not a reserved occupation and many scientists simply joined the fighting services. In some cases, however, their special skills were recognised by the authorities. For example, some Australian chemists were transferred to England to help develop the munitions industry there, while Australian geologists, working as miners under the leadership of Edgeworth David, performed remarkable service in the trench warfare of the western front.

For many of the Australians involved, the war brought with it a heightened sense of their Australian-ness. Nevertheless, throughout the 1920s most Australian scientists continued to see themselves within a larger imperial framework. The popular vision of an integrated imperial economy in which Britain possessed the factories while the empire supplied the raw materials and markets for the finished goods implied that Australian science would concentrate on areas such as agriculture and the chemistry associated with mining, whereas sciences such as physics would be concentrated in Britain. The overwhelming emphasis on agricultural research in the early years of the Council for Scientific and Industrial Research (CSIR), formed in 1926, in part reflected this doctrine, though it also reflected the more parochial political and economic circumstances within Australia at the time that had led to the council's creation (Currie & Graham, 1966).

The economic collapse of the early 1930s brought an end to imperialist dreams of this kind. Already, however, local needs had been working against them. CSIR's charter explicitly envisaged the organisation undertaking research that would assist manufacturing as well as the agricultural sector, especially through the establishment of physical and engineering standards.

An early and highly successful involvement in radio research led the way in non-agricultural research (Evans, 1973). During the late 1930s, as war clouds gathered again and Australia began at last to build a manufacturing capability of its own, major CSIR divisions of industrial chemistry and aeronautics were founded, as well as the long-awaited National Standards Laboratory.

World War II had a much more dramatic impact on Australian science than World War I (Evans, 1970; Mellow, 1958). With invasion threatening and traditional British sources of supply cut off, Australia was forced to look to its own resources for essentials that it had previously imported. As the existing science-based industries such as munitions and electronics expanded, they demanded more and more scientifically trained staff. University scientists worked to create new industries where none had existed before in fields such as pharmaceuticals and optical components. Physicists and engineers were recruited in large numbers to work on a new invention of strategic importance, radar.

By war's end, it was clear that Australian science had undergone an irreversible change in line with the general industrialisation of the nation. The number of scientists working in all fields had greatly increased, and new employment opportunities had opened up for them in Defence Department laboratories, in new or newly expanded CSIR divisions and other government agencies, and to a lesser extent in universities and industrial corporations. No longer did Australian science look automatically to England for leadership and research opportunities. For some, the United States had become an enticing alternative, but others looked forward to Australia making an independent contribution to the new scientific age that seemed to have been ushered in with the explosion of the first atomic bombs.

In some fields, most notably immunology (Burnet, 1971) and radioastronomy, these hopes have been fulfilled superbly well; in almost all, Australian researchers have more than held their own. Yet in comparison with most other countries, scientific effort remains confined to a disturbing degree to government institutions. CSIR, reconstructed in 1949 in the wake of a savage and wholly unjustified political attack (Rivett, 1972) as the Commonwealth Scientific and Industrial Research Organization (CSIRO), no longer confines itself to the applied research of civilian science. University research, too, has expanded considerably, as has the commitment of the universities to postgraduate education. As a result, scientists no longer need to go abroad to complete their training: the local scientific community has at last become self-sustaining.

Unfortunately, Australian industry has failed to keep pace. The longstanding tendency of the nation's manufacturers to purchase the results of foreign industrial research rather than investing in such research themselves and to limit their horizons to import-replacement manufacturing rather than looking to export markets, has left their companies vulnerable and ill-equipped to meet foreign competition in a manufacturing environment increasingly dependent upon the exploitation of new scientific discoveries and techniques. It remains a moot point whether Australia can build a modern science-based industrial economy or whether science will remain on the margins of the nation's economic life.

Notwithstanding the number of works listed below, it is hardly an exaggeration to say that Australia's scientific past has yet to be subjected to systematic historical analysis. Few of the biographies listed, for example, provide more than a wholly uncritical narrative of their subject's life. Deeper psychological insight of the kind that characterises the best works in this genre is almost wholly absent, though Heney's study of Strzelecki (Heney, 1961) is a notable exception. Missing, too, for the most part, is any serious analysis of the actual scientific work that brought the subject of the biography into prominence. Even more rarely is any attempt made to place a person's scientific work in its broader intellectual context. Many of the biographies listed were written by a member of the subject's own family; while such works undoubtedly have their virtues, objectivity is unlikely to be one of them.

Equally lacking, as yet, are published collections of the letters or papers of influential figures in the history of Australian science. Only four editions of letters are listed below, for Banks (Dawson, 1958), Leichhardt (1968), Baldwin Spencer (1932) and the group of Tasmanians writing to W.J. Hooker (Burns and Skemp, 1961), and these more than suffice to demonstrate the value of such works. There are other collections of papers which cry out for publication.

The general historical works listed also leave much to be desired. Many of those included are quite short and cannot pretend to provide more than a bare outline of the subject they are addressing. They have had to be included, however, for want of something more substantial on their particular topic. With a few notable exceptions, the institutional histories listed confine themselves to straightforward narrative accounts, lists of office bearers and the like, and make little or no effort either to analyse the conditions that moderated the institution's development or to place the institution in a wider social and intellectual setting. In a number of instances, the work is based almost exclusively on the internal records of the institution under study. In some cases of this type—for example, Evans's history of the Radio Research Board (1973)—the author nevertheless manages to set the institution in a wider historical framework. In others, the attempt is not even made.

Finally, there are few analytical studies of the history of particular sciences, or of the condition of science in general, in the Australian context. Large quantities of relevant archival material, the study of which formerly demanded extended visits to the United Kingdom, are now accessible in Australia through the Australian Joint Copying Project (NLA, 1980). Also, for twentieth century topics in particular, some very extensive bibliographical resources are available. However, such historical monographs as there are tend to offer general surveys rather than detailed discussions.

There has in recent years been a dramatic upsurge of interest in the history of Australian science. However, because this has occurred so recently, some of the best work on the subject as yet remains confined to the periodical literature. Some of the professional scientific journals have long been in the habit of publishing an occasional historically orientated piece. *Search*, the journal of ANZAAS, publishes historical articles rather more regularly, as did the *Records* of the Australian Academy of Science for a number of years. In 1981 the latter journal was given a new title, *Historical records of Australian science*, and converted into a journal concentrating exclusively on our subject. Under its new guise, it has quickly become the most important journal in the field. Some of the general historical journals carry articles on the history of Australian science and so too, occasionally, do the international history of science journals. Useful bibliographies by Ann Moyal (formerly Ann Mozley)—(Mozley, 1962, 1964; Moyal, 1978) provide convenient access to the older periodical literature, while many more recent publications are listed in classified bibliographies published annually in *Historical records of Australian science*.

Thomas Bock, Rossbank Observatory, *c1840. Oil on canvas. Bock's painting commemorates the raising of the flag at Rossbank Observatory, Hobart. Pictured in the foreground are Sir John Franklin, the governor of Van Diemen's Land, and captains Ross and Crozier.*
TASMANIAN MUSEUM AND ART GALLERY

AUSTRALIAN ACADEMY OF SCIENCE. *The first twenty-five years*. Canberra, The Academy, 1980. 286 p, illus.

Compiled for the academy's silver jubilee celebrations. Deals with the foundation and subsequent activities of Australia's premier scientific institution; little historical analysis.

THE AUSTRALIAN Mathematical Society's research register: being a list of the mathematical publications of the members of the Australian Mathematical Society and other mathematicians in Australia up till December 31st, 1962. Canberra, Dept of Statistics, Research School of Social Sciences, Australian National University, 1963. 211 p.

Items are arranged by author with their principal research interests. Lacks subject index. First published in 1958.

AUSTRALIAN NATIONAL UNIVERSITY, Canberra. *Science in Australia: proceedings of a seminar organised by the Australian National University on the occasion of the jubilee of the Commonwealth of Australia, Canberra, July 24–27, 1951*. Melbourne, Cheshire for the Australian National University, 1952. xxxi, 192 p.

A historical perspective of scientific research and study with insights into the condition of science in postwar Australia.

AUSTRALIAN science abstracts. Vols 1–35, Sydney, Australian National Research Council, 1922–56/57. (Vols 17–35, 1938/39–56/57, issued as supplements to *Australian J of science*, vols 1–19.)

A classified index of publications in Australian scientific and technical serials. Includes references to publications by Australians in some overseas journals.

AUSTRALIAN science index. Vols 1–27, Melbourne, CSIRO, 1957–83.

A classified index of articles published in Australian scientific and technical serials. Annual author and subject indexes in the final issue for the year. 1978–83 published in microfiche only.

BISCHOFF, C. *The hard road: the life story of Amalie Dietrich, naturalist, 1821–1891*. London, Hopkinson, 1931. 317 p.

Romantic story of a remarkable woman who collected botanical specimens in Qld, 1863–73, written by her daughter. Letters must be treated with caution.

BLUNT, M.J. AND MORISON, P.N. *Australian anatomy in the 1920s*. Sydney, Anatomical Society of Australia and New Zealand, 1983. 24 p.

A brief survey of a remarkable period in the history of anatomy when Australia could lay claim to a number of the intellectual giants in the field.

BORCHARDT, D.H. ed, *Some sources for the history of Australian science: six papers presented at a workshop on the history of science in Australia organized by the Australian Academy of Science, 24–25 August 1982*. Sydney, History Project Inc, 1984. 81 p. (Historical bibliography monograph, 12.)

The essays discuss problems with and possibilities inherent in various kinds of sources that are available to the historian of Australian science.

BRANAGAN, D.F. *Geology and coal mining in the Hunter Valley, 1791–1861*. Newcastle, NSW, Newcastle Public Library, 1972. 105 p, illus, maps. (Newcastle history monographs, 6.)

An account of the haphazard growth in understanding of the geology of the Newcastle region that accompanied the exploitation of its coal measures.

BRANAGAN, D.F. ed, *Rocks, fossils, profs: geological sciences in the University of Sydney, 1866–1973*. Sydney, Science Press for the Dept of Geology and Geophysics, University of Sydney, 1973. 184 p, illus.

A fact-filled account of teaching and research in geology with

appendices listing staff, benefactions, prizes, degrees, students in the subject and publications.

BURNET, F.M. *Walter and Eliza Hall Institute, 1915–1965*. MUP, 1971. 193 p, illus.

A history by the Nobel-prizewinning scientist who directed the institute for over twenty years, followed by an assessment of its principal research activities.

BURNS, T.E. AND SKEMP, J.R. eds, *Van Diemen's Land correspondents: letters from R.C. Gunn, R.W. Lawrence, Jorgen Jorgenson, Sir John Franklin and others to Sir William J. Hooker, 1827–1849*. Launceston, Queen Victoria Museum, 1961. 142 p, illus, map. (*Records of the Queen Victoria Museum*, ns, 14.)

This correspondence documents the close ties that developed between various nineteenth-century Tasmanian botanical collectors, especially Ronald Campbell Gunn (1808–81), and the scientific authorities at Kew Gardens.

CAMERON, H.C. *Sir Joseph Banks*, A & R, 1966. 341 p, illus. A biography of the great patron of Australian botanical exploration. First published in 1952.

CAROE, G.M. *William Henry Bragg, 1862–1942: man and scientist*. CUP, 1978. 212 p, illus.

Memoir of the Nobel prizewinner who was professor of mathematics and physics at the University of Adelaide, 1886–1909, by his daughter.

CARR, D.J. AND CARR, S.G.M. eds, *People and plants in Australia*. Sydney, Academic Press, 1981. 416 p, illus, maps.

CARR, D.J. AND CARR, S.G.M. eds, *Plants and man in Australia*. Sydney, Academic Press, 1981. 313 p, illus, maps.

Two volumes containing 31 essays on the history of Australian botany, including plant introduction and utilisation.

COCKBURN, S. AND ELLYARD, D. *Oliphant: the life and times of Sir Mark Oliphant*. Adelaide, Axiom Books, 1981. 369 p, illus.

Important for his wartime work on radar and the atomic bomb project, Oliphant became a professor at the Australian National University, founding president of the Australian Academy of Science and eventually governor of SA.

COMMONWEALTH SCIENTIFIC AND INDUSTRIAL RESEARCH ORGANIZATION. *Abstracts of published papers and list of translations*, vols 1–22, Melbourne, CSIRO, 1952–74. Title varies. Succeeded by *CSIRO index*, 1975– .

A classified listing of publications by CSIRO staff. Author and subject indexes. From 1979 issued in microfiche only.

COMMONWEALTH SCIENTIFIC AND INDUSTRIAL RESEARCH ORGANIZATION. *Annual report*, Canberra, 1–22, 1927–48; 1, 1949– .

Provides details about the work of the organisation that has dominated Australian scientific research since its establishment in 1926.

COMMONWEALTH SCIENTIFIC AND INDUSTRIAL RESEARCH ORGANIZATION. *Australian scientific societies and professional associations* (2nd edn). Melbourne, CSIRO, 1978. 226 p.

A detailed alphabetical list of societies and associations. First published in 1971.

COMMONWEALTH SCIENTIFIC AND INDUSTRIAL RESEARCH ORGANIZATION. Central Library and Information Services. *CSIRO published papers: subject index 1916–1968*. Melbourne, CSIRO Central Library, 1970–76. 16 vols.

A comprehensive alphabetical index of subjects treated in publications by staff of CSIRO and its predecessor organisations during the period stated.

COMMONWEALTH SCIENTIFIC AND INDUSTRIAL RESEARCH ORGANIZATION. *Historical directory of Council for Scientific and Industrial Research and Commonwealth Scientific and Industrial Research Organization, 1926 to 1976.* Melbourne, CSIRO, 1978. 101 p.

A compilation of senior personnel associated with CSIR and CSIRO during the organisation's first half-century.

CURRIE, G.A. AND GRAHAM, J. *The origins of CSIRO: science and the commonwealth government, 1901–1926.* Melbourne, CSIRO, 1966. 203 p, illus.

A political and administrative history showing how the federal government acquired responsibility for scientific research.

DAVEY, L.J. *CSIRO water research bibliography, 1923–1963.* Melbourne, CSIRO, 1964. 98 p.

An index on water research, arranged alphabetically by subject, then chronologically. Author index.

DAVID, M.E. *Professor David: the life of Sir Edgeworth David.* London, Edward Arnold, 1937. 320 p, illus, maps.

A detailed but uncritical biography of the famous geologist.

DAWSON, W.R. ed, *The Banks letters: a calendar of the manuscript correspondence of Sir Joseph Banks, preserved in the British Museum, the British Museum (Natural History) and other collections in Great Britain.* London, British Museum (Natural History), 1958. 964 p.

Lists and indexes more than 7000 letters held in Great Britain to and from Sir Joseph Banks. There is a wealth of material relating to botany in Australia. *Supplementary letters* published in 1962 and 1965.

DAY, A.A. 'The development of geophysics in Australia', *Journal and proceedings of the Royal Society of New South Wales* 100, 2, 1966, 33–60.

Surveys Australian work in the observation branches of geophysics and in geophysical prospecting, from the earliest shipboard determinations to about 1950. Bibliography.

EVANS, W.F. *History of the Radiophysics Advisory Board, 1939–1945.* Melbourne, CSIRO, 1970. 238 p, 64 annexes in 8 microfiches.

EVANS, W.F. *History of the Radio Research Board, 1926–1945.* Melbourne, CSIRO, 1973. 395, (148) p.

The two histories deal with the history of radio research in Australia and its application in wartime. Also important for the growth of physics as a profession in Australia.

FLETCHER, J.J. ed, *The Macleay memorial volume.* Sydney, Linnean Society of NSW, 1893. li, 308 p, illus.

Includes an account of the life and scientific work of William John Macleay (1820–91) and papers on natural history by leading Australian scientists.

GANI, J. *The condition of science in Australian universities: a statistical survey, 1939–1960.* Oxford, Pergamon, 1963. 131 p.

Includes valuable information with historical perspective and suggestions for future action.

GENTILLI, J. 'A history of meteorological and climatological studies in Australia', *University studies in history* 5, 1, 1967, 54–88.

A survey of meteorological observing in Australia to the early 1960s. Extensive bibliography.

GIBBS, W.J. *The origins of Australian meteorology.* AGPS, 1975. 32 p, illus, maps. (Bureau of Meteorology historical note, 1.)

Brief notes and thorough overview of Australian botany in the nineteenth century.

GRAINGER, E. *The remarkable Reverend Clarke: the life and times of the father of Australian geology.* OUP, 1982. 292 p, illus, maps.

A biography of the Anglican clergyman who became a leading figure of nineteenth-century Australian science.

HALE, H.M. 'The first hundred years of the museum: 1856–1956', *Records of the South Australian Museum* 12, 1956, 1–225.

Tells of the development of South Australia's natural history museum in the face of inadequate accommodation and funding.

HENEY, H.M.E. *In a dark glass: the story of Paul Edmond Strzelecki.* A & R, 1961. 255 p, illus.

A good biography of the Polish adventurer and explorer who made important geological observations in southeastern Australia in the early 1840s.

KIDSON, I.M. comp, *Edward Kidson, O.B.E. (Mil.), M.A., D.Sc., F.Inst. P., F.R.S.N.Z., late director of meteorological services in New Zealand.* Christchurch, Whitcombe & Tombs, 1941. 144 p, illus, maps.

Comprises extracts from Kidson's journals and material concerning his travels—across western and central Australia—and his career as a meteorologist in Australia and elsewhere.

KRUTA, V. et al, *Dr John Lhotsky: the turbulent Australian writer, naturalist and explorer.* Melbourne, Australia Felix Literary Club, 1977. 176 p, illus, maps.

Essays on the life and scientific work of the bohemian naturalist and explorer who spent six years in Australia, 1832–38. Lists his many publications.

LEICHHARDT, F.W.L. *The letters of F.W. Ludwig Leichhardt.* Ed and trans by M. Aurousseau. London, CUP for the Hakluyt Society, 1968. 3 vols, illus, maps. (Hakluyt Society, series 2, nos 135–7.)

Text in English of all Leichhardt's known letters revealing that his later treatment by historians was undeserved. His Australian letters reflect the state of science in Australia in the 1840s.

LUCAS, A.H.S. *A.H.S. Lucas, scientist: his own story.* A & R, 1937. xxi, 198 p, illus.

An autobiography of the schoolmaster who was also a naturalist in late-nineteenth-century Vic and early-twentieth-century NSW.

McAFEE, R.J. *Dawes's meteorological journal.* AGPS, 1981. vi, 29 p, illus, maps and microfiches. (Bureau of Meteorology historical note, 2.)

Brief notes about Lieutenant William Dawes and the observatory he operated at Sydney Cove from 1788 to 1791, together with a copy, on microfiche, of his meteorological journal kept during that period.

MACFARLANE, R.G. *Howard Florey: the making of a great scientist.* Oxford, OUP, 1979. 396 p, illus.

The early career (1898–1942) of the Australian-born pioneer of penicillin, his upbringing and his undergraduate education at the University of Adelaide.

McMINN, W.G. *Allan Cunningham: botanist and explorer.* MUP, 1970. 147 p, illus, maps.

This biography concentrates on Cunningham's explorations and discusses superficially his botanical work.

MAIDEN, J.H. 'A contribution to a history of the Royal Society of New South Wales, with information in regard to other New South Wales societies', *Journal and proceedings of the Royal Society of NSW* 52, 1918, 215–361.

Consists chiefly of abstracts of the previously unpublished

minutes of the society's meetings, 1856–75, with details of publications, membership and a considerable amount of documentary material on the activities of earlier groups.

MAIDEN, J.H. 'Records of Australian botanists: (a) general, (b) New South Wales', *Journal and proceedings of the Royal Society of NSW* 42, 1908, 60–132; 55, 1921, 150–69. *Report of the Meeting of the Australasian Association for the Advancement of Science* 13, 1911, 224–43.
Brief biographical notices of a large number of botanical collectors, horticulturalists and botanists who have described Australian plants. Maiden also published records of the numerous state botanists in state-based journals.

MARKS, E.N. 'A history of the Queensland Philosophical Society and the Royal Society of Queensland from 1859 to 1911', *Proceedings of the Royal Society of Qld* 71, 1959, 17–42.
Biographical sketches of leading members of the society with an outline history based on the society's minute books.

MARSHALL, A.J. *Darwin and Huxley in Australia.* Sydney, Hodder & Stoughton, 1970. 142 p, illus.
A narrative of the experiences of Darwin and Huxley in Australia, based on their travel journals and other published materials.

MELLOR, D.P. *The role of science and industry.* Canberra, Australian War Memorial, 1958. 738 p, illus. (*Australia in the war of 1939–1945.* Series 4, vol 5.)
A study of the achievements of Australian science and secondary industry during World War II. The period is portrayed as a turning point in the industrialisation of the Australian economy.

MOYAL, A.M. *Science, technology and society in Australia: a bibliography.* Brisbane, Science Policy Research Centre, Griffith University, 1978. xii, 74 p. (Science Policy Research Centre, occasional papers, 2.)
A compilation of limited scope restricted to works published since the early 1960s, but omits several highly relevant works.

MOYAL, A.M. ed, *Scientists in nineteenth century Australia: a documentary history.* Melbourne, Cassell, 1975 280 p.
Source materials with linking commentary. Bibliography.

MOZLEY, A. 'A check list of publications on the history of Australian science [with supplement]', *Australian journal of science* 25, 5, 1962, 206–14; 27, 1, 1964, 8–15.
A listing of the older publications on the history of Australian science.

MOZLEY, A. *A guide to the manuscript records of Australian science.* Canberra, Australian Academy of Science in association with ANUP, 1966. xxiv, 127 p.
A pioneering survey listing in broad terms collections of the major Australian repositories. Arranged alphabetically by originating author or scientific institution.

MUSGRAVE, A. ed, *Bibliography of Australian entomology, 1775–1930: with biographical notes on authors and collectors.* Sydney, Royal Zoological Society of NSW, 1932. 380 p.
Arranged alphabetically by author then chronologically, includes biographical details for authors wherever possible. Subject index.

NATIONAL LIBRARY OF AUSTRALIA. *Australian Joint Copying Project handbook.* Part 8. *Miscellaneous* (M series). Canberra, NLA and State Library of NSW, 1980. 90 p.
A guide to microfilm copies of Australian-related manuscript materials in various British repositories. The Miscellaneous (M) series includes much science-related material. A resource for any study of Australian science in the nineteenth century.

OSBORNE, W.A. *William Sutherland: a biography.* Melbourne, Lothian, 1920. 102 p, illus.

A charming account of the self-effacing molecular theorist and leader-writer for the Melbourne *Age* who, though he never held an established scientific post, was a great scientist.

PERRY, W. *The Science Museum of Victoria: a history of its first hundred years.* Melbourne, Science Museum of Vic, 1972. 203 p, illus.
A well-documented history of Australia's oldest museum of applied science.

PESCOTT, R.T.M. *Collections of a century: the history of the first hundred years of the National Museum of Victoria.* Melbourne, National Museum of Vic, 1954. 186 p, illus.
A narrative of administrative issues of details of the collections.

PESCOTT, R.T.M. 'The Royal Society of Victoria from then, 1854 to now, 1959', *Proceedings of the Royal Society of Vic* ns, 73, 1961, 1–40.
An account of the leading events in the society's history devoted mostly to its earliest years.

PIESSE, E.L. 'The foundation and early work of the society: with some account of earlier institutions and societies in Tasmania', *Papers and proceedings of the Royal Society of Tas* 1913, 117–66.
Details about learned societies in Tas prior to the formation of the Royal Society in 1843, emphasising the first twenty years of its existence.

PRESS, M. *Julian Tenison Woods.* Sydney, Catholic Theological Faculty, 1979. 242 p, illus.
A biography, chiefly on Woods' remarkable career as a Catholic priest, including discussion of his investigations in natural history and geology.

RADFORD, J.T. *The Chemistry Department of the University of Melbourne: its contribution to Australian science, 1854–1959.* Melbourne, Hawthorn, 1978. 314 p, illus.
A well-documented history. Appendices indicate changing courses, textbooks and examination papers and lists members of staff and scholarship winners.

RADOK, R. AND RADOK, S. eds, *A profile of Horace Lamb.* Townsville, Qld, Mathematics Dept, James Cook University of North Qld, 1980. 102 p, illus. (Mathematics Department report, 2.)
Lamb's reputation rests chiefly on his treatise on hydrodynamics. This 'profile' comprises summaries of his many publications and includes the obituary notice from *Nature* and memoir published by the Royal Society of London.

'REVIEW of progress in agricultural science in Australia (1901–1951)', *J of the Australian Institute of Agricultural Science* 17, 2, 1951, 41–110.
A special issue marking the jubilee of the Australian commonwealth, with contributions by a number of authors. Includes a history of the Australian Institute of Agricultural Science itself.

RICHARDSON, J.F. *The Australian Radiation Laboratory: a concise history, 1929–1979.* AGPS, 1981. xii, 87 p, illus.
A survey of the laboratory which now performs many functions in relation to the medical applications of radiation physics.

RIVETT, R.D. *David Rivett: fighter for Australian science.* Melbourne, The Author, 1972. 225 p, illus.
Account of the long-serving chief executive officer and later chairman of CSIR, written by his son.

ROYAL SOCIETY OF NEW SOUTH WALES. *A century of scientific progress: the centenary volume of the Royal Society of New South Wales.* Sydney, The Society, 1968. 478 p, illus.
A volume celebrating in descriptive rather than analytical terms the progress of science and applied science in Australia, with special reference to NSW.

Hugh Walters, Blast off at Woomera, Faber, London 1965. Cover design by Leslie Wood. Like a number of novels of the 1950s and 1960s, Blast off at Woomera, first published in 1957, used the site of Woomera for a highly romanticised adventure tale. Science doubled as fiction; reference to Woomera was always in terms of a rocket range for space exploration, a frontier of scientific endeavour. In fact it was the site of atomic testing between 1952 and 1957 and, as part of the Woomera–Maralinga–Monte Bello Range, was involved primarily in weapons testing.
CLARK COLLECTION

RUSSEL, A. *William James Farrer: a biography.* Melbourne, Cheshire, 1949. 226 p, illus.
Biography of the man who revolutionised wheat growing in Australia by breeding new, disease-resistant strains.

RUSSELL, H.C. 'Astronomical and meteorological workers in New South Wales, 1778 to 1860', *Report of the Meeting of the Australasian Association for the Advancement of Science* 1, 1888, 45–94.

A history of Governor Brisbane's observatory at Parramatta with notes on the new Sydney observatory established in 1858.

SAUER, G.C. *John Gould, the bird man: a chronology and bibliography.* Melbourne, Lansdowne Editions, 1982. 416 p, illus, maps.
Comprises a genealogy, a bibliography and a chronology of Gould, his wife and family.

SKEATS, E.W. *Some founders of Australian geology.* Sydney, Australian National Research Council, 1934. 24 p. (Aust-ralian National Research Council. David lecture no 1, 1933.)
On early explorers, scientific visitors and scientifically minded settlers, and the work of the early geological surveyors.

SPENCER, W.B. *Spencer's scientific correspondence with Sir J.G. Frazer and others.* Ed by R.R. Marett and T.K. Penniman. Oxford, Clarendon Press, 1932. 174 p, illus.
Letters, 1897–1913, concerning Spencer's three great expeditions to central and northern Australia.

STANBURY, P.J. ed, *100 Years of Australian scientific exploration.* Sydney, Holt, Rinehart and Winston, 1975. 124 p, illus, maps.
Describes the work of Australia's scientifically minded explorers.

STRAHAN, R. et al, *Rare and curious specimens: an illustrated history of the Australian Museum, 1827–1979.* Sydney, Australian Museum, 1979. 173 p, illus.
An illustrated history of Australia's oldest natural history museum; concentrates on questions of personnel and administration.

WALKER, M.H. *Come wind, come weather: a biography of Alfred Howitt.* MUP, 1971. 348 p, illus.
A biography of the noted explorer, geologist and pioneering anthropologist, assessing his work.

WALKOM, A.B. *The Linnean Society of New South Wales: historical notes of its first fifty years.* Sydney, Australasian Medical Publishing Co, 1925. 46 p, illus.
'Official' account listing office bearers, details of the society's various homes and its publications.

WATERS, B.H.J. *A reference history of the Astronomical Society of South Australia Inc.* Adelaide, The Author, 1980– .
Volumes of archival materials each covering a ten-year period in the society's history.

WEBSTER, E.M. *Whirlwinds in the plain: Ludwig Leichhardt— friends, foes and history.* MUP, 1980. 462 p, illus, maps.
A study that successfully restores Leichhardt's reputation as scientist and explorer.

WEBSTER, H.C. *A history of the Physics Department of the University of Queensland.* Brisbane, Dept of Physics, University of Qld, 1977. 47, ix p, illus.
Chronological account, devoid of historical analysis.

WHITLEY, G.P. *Early history of Australian zoology.* Sydney, Royal Zoological Society of NSW, 1970. 75 p, illus, map.

WHITLEY, G.P. *More early history of Australian zoology.* Sydney, Royal Zoological Society of NSW, 1975. 92 p.
Two volumes providing a chronology of observations of Australia's animals by Europeans to the 1830s.

WHITTELL, H.M. *The literature of Australian birds: a history and a bibliography of Australian ornithology.* Perth, Paterson Brokensha, 1954. 116, 788 p, illus.
Arranged by author and including in many cases a brief biographical outline of the person in question.

WILLIS, M. *By their fruits: a life of Ferdinand von Mueller, botanist and explorer.* A & R, 1949. 187 p, illus, maps.
Biography of the man who, as Victoria's government botanist, 1852–96, dominated Australian botany. Includes brief discussion of Mueller's scientific work.

WOOD, H.W. *Sydney Observatory, 1858 to 1958.* Sydney, Government Printer, 1958. 32 p, illus. (Sydney Observatory papers, 31.)
An official history to mark the institution's centenary. A sequel by the same author has since been published, *Sydney Observatory, 1958 to 1981* (Sydney, The Observatory, 1982).

By 1958 GMH had half the Australian car market and the release of a new Holden was a big news story.
GMH ARCHIVES

CHAPTER 55

PRESS, RADIO AND TELEVISION

HENRY MAYER

THE LITERATURE ON our media is scanty. Its poverty may be caused in part by the regional basis of our newspapers. The major ones—the metropolitan dailies—all have some focus on national news and on 'Australia'. But this, if you check it, means Melbourne and Sydney, and later Canberra, and there is no regular coverage of events and processes in other but the home state of the paper unless these deal with democratic rituals (mainly elections and strikes) or crises or murders or prison escapes or accidents.

The supposedly national papers are but two and one of them is a specialist five-days-a-week business and economic paper. The *Australian* is the only national paper in the standard sense and its circulation has hovered for years around the 100 000–120 000 a day mark for the whole of Australia which is just about double that for the daily *Mercury* in Hobart, Tasmania, or about one-third the circulation of a mid-market Sydney morning paper, the *Daily Telegraph*. It does not try to cover all states and territories fully.

If the daily press is state based, then the history of the press as an institution must await full histories of the states. The alternative is to write about it in an abstract way, by reference to some general view of Australian society as a social system. Reasonably full histories of the states are quite recent and do not reveal much about the press; for example Lloyd Robson, *A history of Tasmania*, vol I *Van Diemen's Land from the earliest times to 1855* (OUP, 1983) has a couple of references to Andrew Bent and freedom of the press; C.T. Stannage's *The people of Perth: a social history of Western Australia's capital city* (Perth, Carroll's for Perth City Council, 1979) has five pages on the Perth press and journalism. His *A new history of Western Australia* (UWAP, 1981) has scattered references to West Australian newspapers and a chapter on 'Literature and society' which includes references to magazines, small presses and a few individual writers. They focus on the dating and rise and fall of given papers, on their influence on formal political and later democratic institutions, and ignore how they thought of news, what their finances were, who the people who wrote for them were and how much they were paid, and what their links with both advertisers and readers might have been.

Of the standard general literary histories, that by Green (1961; repr, 1984–85) is the most relevant, but the treatment is necessarily little more than a list of names and dates with some general judgment of quality or influence.

The most thorough press history of one state, the two volumes by R.B. Walker on New South Wales (1976, 1980), goes from the beginning to 1945. They are, for this scribe, maddeningly non-sociological, dry and cautious but have not only a wealth of material but also a whole host of shrewd judgments. Walker conceived of 'the press' in the most generous terms, so he includes coverage of a wide variety of publications.

Another reason for the paucity of writing on the media is that our tertiary institutions have not encouraged it. There are still no universtiy chairs of mass communication, communication, media studies or journalism. It has not been the business of a whole corps of academics to explore this field. In the last few decades media studies have been introduced mainly in colleges of advanced education or at the newest universities—La Trobe, Murdoch and Griffith. There, if not focused on children's television as is true in part of La Trobe, they are linked to some major enterprise in the charting of culture such as with neo-marxism, psychoanalysis, semiotics or feminism. This material is very uneven. Until recently it usually showed little concern with the history of particular newspapers, being more interested in how they might fit into general theory of society.

Most newspapers themselves show little interest in their own past or, indeed, in history of any kind. News as a highly fragmented and, by our news formulas, uneven and fluctuating product, is not in any sense 'instant history' since the way it is processed does not usually permit much sifting or checking.

Only some of the more serious and ambitious papers have shown an interest in their past. Of these John Fairfax is easily in the lead with its first work (1931) very much a righteous and company history but still quite broadly conceived. A second one, in which a journalist, Gavin Souter (1981), was given a free hand, is a fascinating defence of a special form of family capitalism—moving, remarkably frank and, a very rare feat, well-written.

The extraordinarily concentrated situation in Australia in which three firms—the Herald and Weekly Times, John Fairfax and Murdoch's News Corporation—dominate the capitals may also have militated against press history. There are endless articles and pamphlets critical of such concentration of ownership and of cross-ownership between press, television and radio but not one serious book-length study of the consequences of such phenomena. When the companies themselves or those who take their view give a rare account of what they are after or justify such limited ownership—as in their evidence to the Norris report, the Victorian inquiry into newspapers (1981), and Carlyon's account of it (1982)—it is remarkably naive and simplistic, with hardly any intellectual content.

J.S. Western and C.A. Hughes (1983) show in their analysis of the mass media that issues of ownership and control evoke little interest and concern. The best study of 'bias' is the anonymous by-product of a royal commission into the nefarious practices of a union (Australia, Royal Commission into the Activities of the Federated Ships Painters and Dockers Union, *Media bias and the Victorian Branch . . .: discussion paper*, AGPS, 1982). It seems likely that better work will be done indirectly by lawyers but, given the absence of constitutional powers over print media, they will do this work in the field of broadcasting. Armstrong (1982) is the best example.

Radio broadcasting in Australia shows features of a divided 'control' of the airwaves which is not found in other countries. From two sectors it has evolved into four: national (ABC), commercial, multicultural or ethnic (Special Broadcasting Service or SBS) and public. There is no comprehensive published account of the Australian scene, but K.S. Inglis's study (1983) of the Australian Broadcasting Commission includes some comment on the commercial stations, which operate in very different ways from the government-controlled ABC, formally a statutory corporation with a great deal of conventional autonomy, but government financed and influenced. Its news service was created amid controversy, of which Dixon (1975) gives a participant's version. Neville Petersen's much more scholarly and detailed forthcoming history of the ABC's news service convincingly corrects Dixon and will be an important contribution in its own right.

A well-organised retrospective story of the heyday of broadcasting in Australia has been published by Jacqueline Kent (1983).

The lifeblood of the commercial media, advertising, is even more understudied. It is not just profoundly a-historical but anti-historical. This, however, does not explain why there is not one historical study of the government financing of the arts and of broadcasting in Australia.

The Australian Broadcasting Tribunal (ABT) and its predecessor, the Australian Broadcasting Control Board (ABCB), sponsored, and later through a research section of growing repute carried out, much research on the effects of television and aspects of regulation and, more recently, on media such as cable TV. (There is very little on radio.) An ABT advisory committee, the Children's Program Committee, has inspired much work in this field. Reports are published by the Australian Government Publishing Service and the ABT's Research Section and are reported in the ABCB's and ABT's annual reports. The Department of Communications' library has issued useful bibliographies since 1983, which also cover the ABT.

Surveys of opinions about the media and ratings and circulation figures are part of the history of the media, and indeed partly constructed by them since the media owners and journalists determine programming options, time slots and news formulas. The ABT (1979) examines mainly commercial television. A broader approach is taken in Mayer *et al* (1982) which covers the media, advertising and surveys.

The ABC's research section surveys are in most major libraries and a proportion of its material is accessible online. Research material for the multicultural SBS is thin and not easily accessible. Information on the growing public broadcasting sector is sparse and seems not to be collected properly by any public or departmental library. Most Australian surveys, including those on media, are summarised in the University of Sydney Sample Surveys Centre's former newsletter.

There is increasing convergence between the traditional media and computers and various new media. Most of the material on this important trend has appeared in scholarly journals, or, in a somewhat polemical but well-informed published form, in two works by Ian Reinecke (1982, 1983).

Ann Moyal's scholarly and important history of Telecom (1984) gives a broad view from the early days onwards.

A number of useful theses have been presented during the past twenty years in several universities and these can be traced under subject headings in the *Union list of higher degree theses* (see chapter 8); some of these have been transformed into books, such as Woodberry (1972) and recently C. Lloyd's *History of the Australian Journalists Association* (Sydney, Hale & Iremonger, 1985).

Art in Australia, *Feb 1937. In the 1930s radios were prized objects, advertised and displayed as such. The reverence for radios is reminiscent of a similar reverence shown to television sets in the late 1950s and early 1960s.*

ALLEN, Y. AND SPENCER, S. *The broadcasting chronology, 1809–1980*. Sydney, Australian Film and Television School, 1983. 221 p.
A reference to historic events and reference material in telecommunications and broadcasting.

ARMSTRONG, M. *Broadcasting law and policy in Australia*. Sydney, Butterworths, 1982. 291 p.
Solid, well documented with descriptive and factual material and legal analysis. Bibliography.

ARMSTRONG, M. *et al, Media law in Australia: a manual*. OUP, 1983. 274 p.
Covers major aspects of newspapers, broadcasting, copyright, defamation. Has background and can serve as an introduction.

AUSTRALIA. Committee of Review of the Australian Broadcasting Commission. *The ABC in review: national broadcasting in the 1980s: report by the Committee . . .* AGPS, 1981. 5 vols.
Examines policies, services and performances of the ABC and makes recommendations on future functions, statutory powers and broad policy issues. Includes a study of the ABC's records by K. Inglis. Chairman: A.T. Dix.

AUSTRALIA. Inquiry into the Australian Broadcasting System. *Australian broadcasting: a report on the structure of the Australian broadcasting system with particular regard to the control, planning, licensing, regulation, funding and administration of the system*. AGPS, 1976. 175, A143 p.
Recommends that the ABCB be disbanded, that a Broadcasting Planning Board, an Australian Broadcasting Tribunal and a Broadcasting Council be established to regulate program standards and that public broadcasting be legalised. Chairman: F.J. Green.

AUSTRALIAN BROADCASTING TRIBUNAL. *Television and the public: a decade of research 1968–1977*. AGPS, 1979. 55 p.
Consolidates results of the first decade of surveys into the opinions of the public concerning television.

AUSTRALIAN BROADCASTING TRIBUNAL. Inquiry into cable and Subscription Television Services and Related Matters. *Cable and subscription television services for Australia: report of the inquiry . . .* AGPS, 1982. 6 vols.
Examines the social, economic, technical and related matters to be considered in introducing cable TV. Recommends introduction of cable and radiated subscription services Chairman: David Jones.

AUSTRALIAN INSTITUTE OF POLITICAL SCIENCE. Summer School, 41st, Canberra, 1975. *Mass media in Australia: proceedings of the 41st Summer School, Australian Institute of Political Science*. Ed by G. Major. Sydney, Hodder & Stoughton, 1976. 264 p.
Deals with the media (largely the press, some broadcasting) politics, bias, women and media reform.

AUSTRALIAN SCIENCE AND TECHNOLOGY COUNCIL. Technological Change Committee. *Videotex in Australia: interactive information services; a report to the prime minister, August 1983*. AGPS, 1983. 91 p, illus.
Examines information services resulting from the convergence of television, telecommunications and computers, and their social and economic effects. Recommends that Telecom present proposals for nationwide public access service.

BAILEY, J.J. *Australian television: historical overview*. Sydney, Open Program Resources, Australian Film and Television School, 1979. 24 p.
Reprinted from *Cinema papers* 23 Sept–Oct 1979.

BALL, W.M. *Press, radio and world affairs: Australia's outlook*. MUP, 1938. 146 p.
Study of the influence of Australian press and radio on public opinion. Covers world affairs, Japan, USSR, League of Nations, imperial ideals.

BEILBY, P. ed, *Australian TV: the first 25 years*. Melbourne, Nelson in association with Cinema Papers, 1981. 192 p, illus.
Chronological survey with over 600 photographs covering every facet of television programming. Includes ratings and some material on commercials.

BLAIN, E. *Life with Aunty; forty years with the ABC*. Sydney, Methuen, 1977. 216 p.
Memoirs of working for the ABC.

BONNEY, B. AND WILSON, H. *Australia's commercial media*. Melbourne, Macmillan, 1983. 331 p, illus.
Semiotic and neo-marxist treatment. Strongest on ownership and advertising.

BONWICK, J. *Early struggles of the Australian press*. London, Gordon & Gotch, 1890. 82 p, illus.
Dry, whiggish and inaccurate—but readable.

BRODSKY, I. *The Sydney press gang*. Sydney, Old Sydney Free Press, 1974. 192 p, illus.
Historical sketches.

CARLYON, L. *Paper chase: the press under examination*. Melbourne, Herald and Weekly Times, 1982. 375 p, illus.
An account from a conventional newspaper perspective of the evidence of the Norris hearings. (See below: Victoria. Inquiry into the Ownership and Control of Newspapers . . .)

COCKERILL, G. *Scribblers and statesmen . . .* Melbourne, J. Roy Stevens, 1944. 208 p.
Mainly memoirs on the press in Vic.

DENHOLM, M. *Small press publishing in Australia: the early 1970s*. Sydney, Second Back Row Press, 1979. 209 p, illus.
Includes material on many ephemeral and marginal magazines.

DIXON, M.F. *Inside the ABC: a piece of Australian history*. Melbourne, Hawthorn, 1975. 218 p.
Interesting though partisan coverage of the origins of ABC news service.

DUGDALE, J. *Radio power: a history of 3ZZ access radio*. Melbourne, Hyland House, 1979. 252 p.
History of the ABCs Victorian multilingual access station giving reasons for its closure despite apparent success. Claims deliberate government interference as the case.

EDGAR, P.M. *The politics of the press*. Melbourne, Sun Books, 1979. 224 p.
General analysis based on interviews and content analysis.

EDGAR, P.M. ed, *The news in focus: the journalism of exception*. Melbourne, Macmillan, 1980. 213 p, illus.
Various studies of journalistic practices and news content.

FAIRFAX, JOHN, LIMITED. *A century of journalism: the* Sydney Morning Herald *and its record of Australian life, 1831–1931*. Sydney, John Fairfax & Sons, 1931. 805 p, illus, map.
Links the newspaper history with the history of NSW. Includes material on technical aspects.

FERGUSON, J.A. *et al, The Howes and their press*. Sydney, Sunnybrook Press, 1936. 100 p, illus.
History of the Howe family, the *Sydney Gazette* and early printing in NSW.

FINCH, A. *Pens and ems in Australia*. Adelaide, Rigby, 1965. 109 p, illus.
Anecdotal. Includes first publications in each capital city.

GIBBNEY, H.J. comp, *Labor in print: a guide to the people who created a labor press in Australia between 1850 and 1939*.

Canberra, Australian National University, 1975. [75 p.]
Useful listing. Dwells on the personalities of people associated with the press of the labour movement.

GILSON, M. AND ZUBRZYCKI, J. *The foreign-language press in Australia 1848–1964.* ANUP, 1967. 233 p.
Descriptive, historical and sociological study.

GOOT, M. *Newspaper circulation in Australia, 1932–1977.* Bundoora, Vic, Centre for the Study of Educational Communication and Media, La Trobe University, 1979. 33 p. (Media Centre Papers, 11.)
Broader than its title, includes ownership, control and price data.

GORDON, H. ed, *Famous Australian news pictures.* Melbourne, Macmillan, 1975. 110 p, illus.
Covers 1880–1975.

GREENOP, F.S. *History of magazine publishing in Australia.* Sydney, K.G. Murray, 1947. 300 p, illus.
Deals with magazines published 1821–1947. Useful for brief summary of policy of many magazines.

HALL, S. *Supertoy: 20 years of Australian television.* Melbourne, Sun Books, 1976. 192 p.

HALL, S. *Turning on, turning off: Australian television in the eighties.* Sydney, Cassell, 1981. 105 p, illus.
Both books are perceptive, well-written, journalistic histories. Closest to a history of the period.

HARDING, R.W. *Outside interference: the politics of Australian broadcasting.* Melbourne, Sun Books, 1979. 219 p, illus.
An inside view by a member of the ABC, indicating political interference by government.

HIGGINS, C.S. AND MOSS, P.D. *Sounds real: radio in everyday life.* UQP, 1982. 237 p.
Discourse analysis; difficult to follow but an important work.

HOLDEN, W.S. *Australia goes to press.* MUP, 1962. 297 p, illus, map.
Covers metropolitan daily newspapers and also includes historical sketches. First published in 1961.

INGLIS, K.S. *This is the ABC: the Australian Broadcasting Commission, 1932–1983.* MUP, 1983. 521 p, illus.
History based on the commission's archives and a wide range of other sources; examines political and social influences and problems of organisation and administration. Includes both radio and television.

KENT, J. *Out of the bakelite box: the heyday of Australian radio.* A & R, 1983. 277 p.
Lively, journalistic and well-written account.

KIRKPATRICK, R. *Sworn to no master: a history of the provincial press in Queensland to 1930.* Toowoomba, Qld, Darling Downs Institute Press, 1984. 334 p, illus.
Zestful details about the careers of newspapers, proprietors and editors. An appendix sets out, decade by decade, the newspapers published in Qld.

LAWSON, S. *The Archibald paradox: a strange case of authorship.* Ringwood, Vic, Allen Lane, 1983. 292 p, illus.
Discusses the *Bulletin,* mainly for 1880–1902 in relation to Archibald, way he fashioned a new journalism and the magazine's relation to American and British papers. Content and historical role are also analysed.

LEAPMAN, M. *Barefaced cheek: the apotheosis of Rupert Murdoch.* London, Hodder & Stoughton, 1983. 269 p, illus.
Useful, but not a penetrating account of Australia's wealthiest newspaper tycoon, creator and owner of the *Australian,* as well as of the London *Times* and associated groups. It shows the relationship between Australian and international news media.

MACKAY, I.K. *Broadcasting in Australia.* MUP, 1957. 216 p.

Dry sketch of ABC and commercial radio.

McNAIR, W.A. *Advertising in Australia.* A & R, 1937. 461 p.
By the pioneer of rating surveys.

McQUEEN, H. *Australia's media monopolies.* Melbourne, Visa Books, 1981. 218 p.
Hardline but intelligent and witty left wing perspective. Includes treatment of advertising. First published in 1977.

MANDER, A.E. *Public enemy: the press.* Sydney, Currawong, 1944. 94 p.
Discusses the Australian press as an instrument of propaganda.

MANION, J. *Paper power in North Queensland: a history of journalism in Townsville and Charters Towers.* Townsville, Qld, North Qld Newspaper Company, 1982. 294 p, illus.
Has many gaps but very useful on personalities.

MAYER, H. *The press in Australia.* Melbourne, Lansdowne, 1968. 281 p, illus.
Attempts to combine history, sociology and public policy analysis. First published in 1964.

MILLER, E.M. *Pressmen and governors: Australian editors and writers in early Tasmania. A contribution to the history of the Australian press and literature with notes biographical and bibliographical.* A & R, 1952. 308 p.
Literary sketches, personalities, histories of newspapers. Facsimile edition, SUP, 1973.

MOYAL, A.M. *Clear across Australia: a history of telecommunications since 1788.* Melbourne, Nelson, 1984. 437 p, illus, maps.
Lively and critical story of telecommunications in Australia.

MUNSTER, G. *Rupert Murdoch: a paper prince.* Ringwood, Vic, Viking, 1984. 291 p.
Outstanding biography of an Australian media magnate who is now a multinational operator.

O'BRIEN, D. *The* Weekly: *a lively and nostalgic celebration of Australia through 50 years of its most popular magazine.* Ringwood, Vic, Penguin, 1982. 160 p, illus.
A vivid and richly illustrated account.

A PHOTO album: the ABC from 1932 to 1982. Comp by J. Bennett *et al.* Sydney, ABC, 1982. 108 p, illus.
Has over 100 photographs of radio and television programs.

PITT, G.H. *The press in South Australia 1836 to 1850: with notes on the first documents etc. printed in South Australia, 1836–38 and on early printers and editors.* Adelaide, Wakefield Press, 1946. 66 p, illus.
Focuses on personalities and on some legal aspects and economic and political difficulties.

REINECKE, I. *Micro invaders.* Ringwood, Vic, Penguin, 1982. 272 p.
Argues that microprocessors will reduce jobs and skills in the telecommunications industry and debase the mass media, while favouring the information rich and depriving others.

REINECKE, I. *The phone book: the future of Australia's communications on the line.* Ringwood, Vic, Penguin, 1983. 270 p.
Examines the future of Australian telecommunicaitons.

ROLFE, P. *The journalistic javelin: an illustrated history of the* Bulletin. Sydney, Wildcat Press, 1979. 315 p, illus.
Popular, well-illustrated account of Australia's longest running weekly.

ROSENBLOOM, H. *Politics and the media.* Melbourne, Scribe Publications, 1978. 160 p, illus.
Left-wing account with stress on cross-ownership. First published in 1976.

ROSS, J.F. *A history of radio in South Australia, 1897–1977.* Adelaide, The Author, 1978. 271 p, illus.

Describes from the vantage point of the buff the development of radio transmission from telegraphy and commercial broadcasting services to shipping, aeroradio, flying doctor services and early satellite communication at Ceduna, SA.

SEMMLER, C. *The ABC: Aunt Sally and sacred cow.* MUP, 1981. 323 p, illus.

Highly personal history by a former senior employee.

SOMMERLAD, E.C. *Mightier than the sword: a handbook on journalism, broadcasting, propaganda, public relations and advertising.* A & R, 1950. 239 p.

The country press from a conservative angle.

SOUTER, G. *Company of heralds: a century and a half of Australian publishing by John Fairfax Limited and its predecessors, 1831–1981.* MUP, 1981. 667 p, illus.

Excellent on the *Sydney Morning Herald,* less impressive on other aspects, including television. Important as a newspaper, family and social history. Among commissioned works remarkable for candour.

STUART, L. *Nineteenth century Australian periodicals: and annotated bibliography.* Sydney, Hale & Iremonger, 1979. 199 p, illus.

Very useful bibliography of literary and semiliterary periodicals. Includes dates of publication, editors, printers and major contributors.

THOMAS, A.W. *Broadcast and be damned: the ABC's first two decades.* MUP, 1980. 230 p, illus.

A quiet academic account with insight into the political background.

THOMAS, P. ed, *The press gang: how Australia's big papers are run, the CPA's part in the Norris inquiry.* Sydney, Red Pen Publications, 1982. 92 p, illus.

Communist Party evidence at the Norris Inquiry. (See below: Victoria. Inquiry into the Ownership and Control of Newspapers . . .)

TIFFEN, R. *The news from southeast Asia: the sociology of newsmaking.* Singapore, Institute of Southeast Asian Studies, 1978. 206 p.

Perceptive analysis of journalistic practices.

TREGENZA, J. *Australian little magazines, 1923–1954: their role in forming and reflecting literary trends.* Adelaide, LBSA, 1964. 108 p, illus.

Historical study; includes bibliography of little magazines.

VICTORIA. Inquiry into the Ownership and Control of Newspapers in Victoria. *Report of the Inquiry into Ownership and Control of Newspapers in Victoria . . .* Melbourne, Premier's Dept, 1981. 307 p.

Ownership, control, merits and demerits of government intervention. Useful data. Chairman: J.G.Norris.

WALKER, R.B. *The newspaper press in New South Wales, 1803–1920.* SUP, 1976. 272 p, illus.

WALKER, R.B. *Yesterday's news: a history of the newspaper press in New South Wales from 1920 to 1945.* SUP, 1980. 243 p, illus.

Standard histories, covering minor papers.

WALKER, R.R. *Communicators: people, practices, philosophies in Australian advertising media marketing.* Melbourne, Lansdowne, 1967. 416 p.

Lively pro-commercial survey and analysis of advertising, radio and television.

WALKER, R.R. *The magic spark: the story of the first fifty years of radio in Australia.* Melbourne, Hawthorn, 1973. 192 p, illus.

Patchy history of commercial radio.

WESTERN, J.S. AND HUGHES, C.A. *The mass media in Australia* (rev edn). UQP, 1983. 209 p.

Examines uses of and attitudes to the media, based on a survey. First published in 1971.

WINDSCHUTTLE, K. *The media: a new analysis of the press, television, radio and advertising in Australia.* Ringwood, Vic, Penguin, 1984. 436 p, illus.

Attacks overarching media theories and tries to rescue the good in commercial content by linking it with popular folklore, political economy and culture.

WINDSCHUTTLE, K. AND WINDSCHUTTLE, E. eds, *Fixing the news: critical perspectives on the Australian media.* Sydney, Cassell, 1981. 321 p, illus.

Selected reprints from the quirky and gallant *New journalist.*

GENERAL REFERENCE WORKS

Few reference works help answer questions on who is who, who does what, who has written about the media or provide addresses, telephone numbers, telex numbers and so on. The following five entries provide some guidance for enquiries and the annotations set out after each entry indicate the limitations of each guide.

B & T yearbook. Sydney, Greater Publications, 1958– .

Basic data on radio, television (mainly commercial) and press (consumer, ethnic and business), advertising agencies and advertisers. 'General' section includes audience and market research, public relations and media ownership and a 'Who's who'. Before 1974 called *Broadcasting and television yearbook.*

GEE, M. *Margaret Gee's media guide.* Melbourne, 1979– .

Covers newspapers, magazines, radio and television, ethnic press, trade and specialty magazines. The only guide to newsletters, giving names of people involved. Data on circulation figures for major newspapers and magazines.

MAYER, H. *Bibliographical notes on the press in Australia and related subjects.* Sydney, Dept of Government and Public Administration, University of Sydney, 1964. 76 p.

A product of Mayer's major study. Literature survey of writings from the nineteenth and twentieth centuries.

MAYER, H. et al, *The media: questions and answers, Australian surveys 1942–1980.* Sydney, Allen & Unwin, 1983. 206 p.

Covers social attitudes to media based on public opinion surveys and select academic sources. The inventory gives categories and subcategories of opinions.

PRESS, radio & T.V. handbook: Australia, New Zealand and the Pacific Islands (25th edn). Melbourne, Margaret Gee Media Group, 1984. 255 p.

Published since 1914 under various titles, this handbook provides basic information on the media, including advertising rates and circulation details.

Every effort has been made to contact the copyright owners of the illustrations in this book. Where this has not been possible the editors invite them to notify History Project Incorporated in the Research School of Social Sciences, Australian National University, Canberra, to ensure acknowledgment in future editions.

Page ii 46 × 18.7 cm. Courtesy of Margaret Streeton.

CHAPTER 1. THE WRITING OF AUSTRALIAN HISTORY
Page 21 Hand-coloured copper engraving, 24 × 31.5 cm, Rex Nan Kivell Collection, National Library. From the French expedition of 1800–04 under Nicolas Baudin.

I. RESOURCES FOR AUSTRALIAN STUDIES
Page 31 Mitchell Library.

CHAPTER 2. ARCHIVES
Page 40 BHPA/N14.

CHAPTER 3. LIBRARIES AND PRINTED RESOURCES
Page 41 T.G. Wainewright, *Drawing of Major de Gillern, commandant of Rocky Hills convict station, east coast, Tasmania, with Mrs de G. and Miss Lucy Scott, granddaughter of Governor Davey,* from *Art in Australia,* March 1924. The original c1837 was stolen and its whereabouts are still unknown.

IV. ABORIGINES
Page 113 17.5 × 25.7 cm, Rex Nan Kivell Collection.

CHAPTER 15. EUROPEAN VIEWS OF ABORIGINES
Page 117 N. Petit and J. Milbert, *Nouvelle-Holland: Nlle Galles de Sud. Jeune femme de la tribu des Bon-rou avec son enfants sur les épaules* from the atlas of Péron and de Freycinet, *Voyage de decouvertes aux Terres Australes executé . . . sur les corvettes le Géographe [et] le Naturaliste, rédigé par M.F. Peron,* Paris 1807–16.

CHAPTER 17. CITY AND REGION
Page 139 45.7 × 55.9 cm.

VI. EUROPEAN DISCOVERY AND COLONISATION
Page 161 This chart is one of 22 drawn by Bradley, first lieutenant of the *Sirius.*

GATEFOLD
Page 168 The parrot, *Nestor productus,* was killed for food and became extinct by 1850. The plant is *Solanum aviculare.* Page 170 Waratah, *Telopea speciosissima,* 22.8 × 18.3 cm. Skink, c1795.

CHAPTER 22. FIRST EUROPEAN SETTLEMENTS
Page 173 15.3 × 19.5 cm.

CHAPTER 26. PARLIAMENTS, PARTIES AND GOVERNMENTS
Page 205 Sharkey Collection, SH 78.

CHAPTER 30. ECONOMIC HISTORY
Page 249 Courtesy of Westpac Banking Corporation.

CHAPTER 35. ENGINEERING
Page 288 Sharkey Collection, SH 1364.

CHAPTER 40. DOMESTIC LIFE
Page 325 Oil on cardboard, 39.7 × 30.5 cm. Gift of Howard Hinton, 1945.

CHAPTER 42. RELIGION
Page 344 Purchased 1949.

CHAPTER 48. SPORT AND LEISURE
Page 393 53 × 36.8 cm.

CHAPTER 50. THE VISUAL ARTS
Page 412 Colour lithograph on paper, 101.4 × 63.8 cm.

CHAPTER 51. MUSIC
Page 418 1938 Collection is held in the National Library.

ENDNOTES

1. THE WRITING OF AUSTRALIAN HISTORY
Stuart Macintyre

I am indebted to Geoffrey Bolton, Jim Davidson and Geoffrey Serle for advice and suggestions. My obligation to other scholars is evident in the notes.

1 J.O. Balfour, *A sketch of New South Wales*, London, Smith, Elder, 1845, 49, quoted in G. Nadel, *Australia's colonial culture: ideas, men and institutions in mid-nineteenth century eastern Australia*, Melbourne, Cheshire, 1957, 58.

For contrarieties see R. Gibson, *The diminishing paradise: changing literary perceptions of Australia*, A & R, 1984, ch 1.

2 An inversion in nature is from T. Watling, *Letters from an exile at Botany Bay to his aunt in Dumfries*, Penrith, Scotland, 1794, 15.

B. Field's verse is quoted in G. Serle, *From deserts the prophets come: the creative spirit in Australia 1788–1972*, Melbourne, Heinemann, 1973, 2–3.

Unaltered nature is from R. Williams, *The country and the city*, London, Chatto and Windus, 1973, ch 13.

The Englishwoman was L.A. Twamley, *An autumn ramble by the Wye*, London, Charles Tilt, 1839, 10, and L.A. Meredith (nee Twamley), *Notes and sketches of New South Wales*, London, John Murray, 1849, 79–80, 86, quoted in Bernard Smith, *European vision*, London, E. Baylis, 1960, 226–7.

W. Tench, *A complete account of the settlement at Port Jackson in New South Wales*, London, G. Nicol and J. Sewell, 1793, 27; Watling, *Letters*, quoted in B. Smith, *Place, taste and tradition: a study of Australian art since 1788* (2nd edn), OUP, 1979, 56.

The art critic was E. Bevan, 'Art at the antipodes', *Antipodean* 1894, 74–6, quoted in Smith, *Place, taste and tradition*, 59; W.H. Fitchett, *The new world of the south*, London, G.Bell & Sons, 1913, vii.

3 For archaeological accessories see F. Sinnett, 'The fiction fields of Australia' (1856), reprinted in J. Barnes, ed, *The writer in Australia: a collection of literary documents 1856 to 1964*, OUP, 1969, 8–32.

G. Lukacs, *The historical novel* (trans H. and S. Mitchell), London, Merlin Press, 1962, ch 1. The prominence of Scott

on Australian shelves is noted by E. Webby, 'English literature in early Australia: 1820–1829', *Southerly* 27, 1967, 266–85.

4 Quoted in B.G. Andrews, ed, *Tales of the convict system: selected stories of Price Warung*, UQP, 1975, cix. See also H.J. Boehm, '*His natural life* and its sources', *Australian literary studies* 5, 1971/72, 42–64, and I.D. Muecke, 'William Hay and history: a comment on aims, sources and method', *Australian literary studies* 2, 1965/66, 117–37.

J. Normington-Rawling, *Charles Harpur, an Australian*, A & R, 1962, 129; B. Field, *First fruits of Australian poetry*, Sydney, G. Howe, 1819; J.H. Tuckey, *Account of a voyage to establish a colony at Port Phillip*. London, Longman, Hurst, Rees & Orme, 1805, 185–90, quoted in H.M. Green, *A history of Australian literature* 1, A & R, 1961, 17.

The local writer was R. Boldrewood, *The miner's right*, London, Macmillan, 1890, quoted in J. Barnes, 'Australian fiction to 1920' in G. Dutton, ed, *The literature of Australia* (rev edn), Ringwood, Vic, Penguin, 1976, 167. See C. Lansbury, *Arcady in Australia: the evocation of Australia and nineteenth-century English literature*, MUP, 1970.

Old tales of a young country, Melbourne, Mason, Firth & M'Cutcheon, 1871, vii, quoted in M. Wilding, *Marcus Clarke*, OUP, 1977, 11.

M. Clarke, 'Preface to Gordon's *Poems*' (1876), reproduced in Barnes, *The writer in Australia*, 33–7; P. Cunningham, *Two years in New South Wales* 1, London, Henry Colburn, 1827, 37–8.

5 Clarke, *Old tales of a young country*, 25, quoted in Wilding, *Marcus Clarke*, 13; *Moreton Bay Courier*, 23 Apr 1859, quoted by H. Reynolds, ed, *Aborigines and settlers: the Australian experience 1788–1939*, Melbourne, Cassell, 1972, ix; J.A. La Nauze, 'The study of Australian history', *Hist stud* 9, 1959/61, 11; W.E.H. Stanner, *After the Dreaming*, Sydney, ABC, 1969, ch 2.

Tench, *A complete account*, 188–200; H. Melville, *The history of the island of Van Diemen's Land*, Hobart, Smith & Elder, 1835, 60; D. Collins, *An account of the English colony in New South Wales* (London, T.Cadell, 1798) ed J.Collier, Sydney, nd, 366; R.Montgomery Martin, *History of Austral-Asia comprising New South Wales, Van Diemen's Land, Swan River,*

South Australia, etc (2nd edn), London, Whittaker, 1839, 159. See generally, D.J. Mulvaney, 'The Australian Aborigines 1606–1929: opinion and fieldwork', *Hist stud* 8, 1957/59, 131–51, 297–314.

For the eye of nature see B. Field, ed, *Geographical memoirs on New South Wales*, London, John Murray, 1825, 229. See generally R.H.W. Reece, *Aborigines and colonists: Aborigines and colonial society in New South Wales in the 1830s and 1840s*, SUP, 1974, ch 2.

The vital clue is from Field, *Geographical memoirs*, 195.

L. Ryan, *The Aboriginal Tasmanians*, UQP, 1981, 214–20, and 'The extinction of the Tasmanian Aborigines: myth and reality', *Tasmanian Historical Research Association papers and proceedings* 19, 1972, 61–77.

5–6 J. Bonwick, *An octogenarian's reminiscences*, London, J. Nichols, 1902, 110–11; *Daily life and origin of the Tasmanians*, London, Sampson Low, Son & Marston, 1870, 1–2. See G. Featherstone, 'The life and times of James Bonwick', MA thesis 1968, University of Melbourne.

6–7 This paragraph relies heavily on W.E.H. Stanner, 'The Dreaming', in his *White man got no Dreaming: essays 1938–1973*, ANUP, 1979, 23–40.

7 W.C. Wentworth, *Australasia: a poem . . .* , London, G. & W.B. Whittaker, 1823.

W.J. Thomas, *Some myths and legends of the Australian Aborigines*, Melbourne, Whitcombe & Tombs, 1923, discussed in A.R. Trethewy, 'The teaching of history in state-supported elementary schools', MEd thesis 1965, University of Melbourne, 177.

For Bede see E. O'Brien, 'Maturity in Australian historical scholarship', *J R Aust Hist Soc* 31, 1945, 156.

This line is traced, for example, by J.M. Ward, 'Historiography', in A.L.McLeod, ed, *The pattern of Australian culture*, New York, Cornell University Press, 1963, 195–251, and G. Shaw, 'The discipline of the state: writing Australian history since 1819', *Current affairs bulletin* 60, 4, Sept 1983, 4–15.

A. Gilchrist, *John Dunmore Lang, chiefly autobiographical*, Melbourne, Jedgarm Publications, 1951, vol 1, 188, vol 2, 530.

8 *Australian dictionary of biography* 2, 584; Gilchrist, *John Dunmore Lang* 1, 191.

J.D. Lang, *An historical and statistical account of New South Wales* 1, London, Cochrane & McCrone, 1834, 24.

W.C. Wentworth, *Statistical, historical and political description of the colony of New South Wales, etc*, London, G. & W.B. Whittaker, 1819, 170.

J. West, *The history of Tasmania* 1, Launceston, Henry Dowling, 1852, 3–4.

9 T.H. Braim, *A history of New South Wales from its settlement to the close of the year 1844* 1, London, Richard Bently, 1846, 3.

W. Westgarth, *The colony of Victoria . . . to the end of 1863*, London, Sampson Low, Son & Marston, 1864, 9–10; T. McCombie, *The history of the colony of Victoria*, Melbourne, Sands and Kenny, 1858, iv; R. Flanagan, *The history of New South Wales* 1, London, Sampson Low, Son, 1862, v–viii; S. Bennett, *The history of Australian discovery and colonisation*,

Sydney, Hanson & Bennett, 1867, iii.

McCombie, *History*, iii; J. Fenton, *A history of Tasmania from its discovery in 1642 to the present time*, Hobart, J. Walch & Sons, 1884, 250; W. Coote, *History of the colony of Queensland* 1, Brisbane, William Thorne, 1882, esp ix–xi.

T.B. Macaulay, *The history of England* 1 (Everyman edn), London, Dent, 1906, 2.

Flanagan, *History*, vi; A. Marjoribanks, *Travels in New South Wales*, London, Smith, Elder, 1851, 2; R.M.Crawford, 'History', in A.G. Price, ed, *The humanities in Australia*, A & R, 1959, 149.

10 Giles, quoted in K. Fitzpatrick, ed, *Australian explorers: a selection from their writings*, London, OUP, 1958, 9.

E. Favenc, *The history of Australian exploration from 1788 to 1888*, Sydney, Turner & Henderson, 1888, 400.

11 G. E. Boxall, *History of Australian bushrangers*, London, Swan Sonnenschein, 1899, v–vi.

'How I wrote *Robbery under arms*', reprinted in A. Brissenden, ed, *Rolf Boldrewood*, UQP, 1979, 491–8.

11–12 Serle, *From deserts the prophets come*, 60–1.

12 A.G. Stephens, *Bulletin*, 9 Dec 1897.

For contradictions see, for example, G.A. Wilkes, *The stockyard and the croquet lawn*, Melbourne, Edward Arnold, 1981, ch 2; and G. Davison, 'Sydney and the bush: an urban context for the Australian legend', *Hist stud* 18, 1978/79, 191-209.

H.S. Scarfe, 'The pioneers', quoted in Rev J. Blacket, *The early history of South Australia*, Adelaide, Methodist Book Depot, 1907, v.

P. de Serville, *Port Phillip gentlemen and good society in Melbourne before the gold rushes*, OUP, 1980, 37.

T. Griffiths, 'Legends', *Melbourne historical J* 14, 1982, 40; K.S. Inglis, *The Australian colonists: an exploration of social history 1788–1870*, MUP, 1974, 137–9. Here I rely heavily on J.B. Hirst, 'The pioneer legend', *Hist stud* 18, 1978/79, 316–37.

13 W. Harcus, ed, *South Australia: its history, resources and productions*, Adelaide, Government Printer, 1879, 2.

T.F. Bride, ed, *Letters from Victorian pioneers*, Melbourne, Government Printer, 1898, vi, 22–35. The story of the manuscript is told by C.E. Sayers in his introduction to a new edition, Melbourne, Heinemann, 1969.

For reminiscences see W.A. Brodribb, *Recollection of an Australian squatter*, Sydney, John Woods, 1883, i; W.H. Suttor, *Australian stories retold*, Bathurst, Glyndwr Whalan, 1887, 100.

Human compost is from Fitchett, *The new world of the south*, 108.

J. Collier, *The pastoral age in Australasia*, London, Whitcombe & Tombs, 1911, 1–6.

D. Pike, 'The smallholders' place in the Australian tradition', *Tasmanian Historical Research Association papers and proceedings* 10, 1962, 28–33.

E. Jenks, *The history of the Australasian colonies*, CUP, 1895, 313; Don quoted in W.E. Murphy, *History of the eight hours' movement* 2, Melbourne, J.T. Picken, 1900, 66.

14 For Jenks lament see R. Campbell, *A history of the Melbourne*

Law School, Melbourne, Faculty of Law, University of Melbourne, 1977, ch 9.

Victoria's praises are from J. Roe, 'Historiography in Melbourne in the eighteen seventies and eighties', *Australian literary studies* 4, 1969/70, 130–8.

D. Blair, *The history of Australasia*, Glasgow, McGready, Thomson & Niven, 1878, 463; A. Sutherland, *Victoria and its metropolis* 1, Melbourne, McCarron, Bird, 1888, 576.

G.W. Rusden, *History of Australia* 1, London, Chapman and Hall, 1883, viii.

Ibid, v; H.G.Turner, *A history of the colony of Victoria* 1, London, Longmans, Green, 1904, viii.

Jenks, *History*, v.

H.G. Turner, 'Romance and tragedy in Victorian history', *Victorian historical magazine* 3, 2, Dec 1913, 49.

14–15 Jenks, *History* 1, 51, 243–4; Turner, *History* 2, 327; see generally Rusden, *History* 3, ch 16.

15 *Melbourne Punch*, 31 Dec 1903, quoted in A.G. Austin, *George William Rusden and national education in Australia, 1849–1862*, MUP, 1958, 128; Turner, *History* 2, 331–3; see M. Cannon, *The land boomers*, MUP, 1966, 108–12.

Crawford, 'History', 149. The case for defence was put by J.M. Ward, 'Historiography', 211–12; and more fully by J. Roe, 'Historiography in Melbourne', 137–8, and S.P. Shortus, 'Making sense of the colonial experience: George Rusden or the *Bulletin*', *Teaching history* 7, 1973, 50–64.

15–16 *The poems of Bernard O'Dowd*, Melbourne, Lothian, 1941, 35; H. Anderson, ed, *Ballads of old Bohemia: an anthology of Louis Esson*, Ascot Vale, Vic, Red Rooster Press, 1980, 1–2.

16 *South Australian Register*, 16 Sept 1858, quoted in 'The Light that probably failed', *South Australiana* 10, 1971, 1. See generally Inglis, *The Australian colonists*, 137–50.

For the government printer see *Australian dictionary of biography*, 4, 372–3.

G.L. Fisher, 'Henry Hussey's *History of South Australia*', *South Australiana*, 8, 1969, 17–24.

G.C. Bolton, 'Western Australia reflects on its past', in C.T. Stannage, ed, *A new history of Western Australia*, UWAP, 1981, 678–9.

For the centenary see S. Shortus, 'Retrospection: attitudes to the past in New South Wales in the 1880's', MA thesis 1970, Macquarie University, ch 2; M.V. Tucker, 'Centennial celebrations 1888' *Australia 1888* 7, Apr 1981, 11–25.

16–17 Featherstone, 'The life and times of James Bonwick'; G. Powell, 'The origins of the Australian Joint Copying Project', *Archives and manuscripts* 4, 5, Nov 1971, 9–24; A.M. Mitchell, 'Dr Frederick Watson and *Historical records of Australia*', *Hist stud* 20, 1982/83, 171–97.

17 For Mitchell collection see H.J. Gibbney, 'Prehistory of an archives', *Archives and manuscripts* 4, 6, Feb 1972, 2–7; J.R. Tyrrell, *Old books, old friends, old Sydney*, A & R, 1952, ch 10.

M. Mahood, *The loaded line: Australian political caricature, 1788–1901*, MUP, 1973, 271–4; J. Bonwick, *An octogenarian's reminiscences*, 239; M. McRae, 'The Tasmanian State Archives: a note on their prehistory', *Archives and manuscripts* 6, 1, Nov 1974, 24–5.

K.R. Cramp, 'The Australian Historical Society: the story of its foundation', *Australian Historical Society J and proceedings* 4, 1917/18, 1–14; D.I. McDonald, 'Ward Harvard and the Royal Australian Historical Society', *Canberra historical J*, 11, March 1983, 28–34.

Victorian historical magazine 1, 1, Jan 1911, 1–156; *Historical Society of Qld J* 1, 1914/19, 2; W. Bate, *Lucky city: the first generation at Ballarat 1851–1901*, MUP, 1978, 191.

18 de Serville, *Port Phillip gentlemen*, 23.

P. Hasluck, *Mucking about: an autobiography*, MUP, 1977, 142–3; A. Hasluck, *Unwilling emigrants: a study of the convict period in Western Australia*, OUP, 1959, xiii.

P. Serle, *Dictionary of Australian biography* 2, A & R, 1949, 393. The book appeared as *The history of Australia from 1606 to 1876*, Melbourne, Robertson, 1877; in later editions it was *The history of Australia and New Zealand from 1606 to . . .* (date varies).

The Council of Education is quoted in D. O'Donnell, 'Sectarian differences and the inclusion of history in the curriculum of New South Wales public schools', *J R Aust Hist Soc* 54, 1968, 292.

The educationalist is quoted in A.R. Trethewey, 'The teaching of history in state-supported elementary schools', 51.

'History in state schools' (1890), in H.A. Strong, ed, *Reviews and critical essays by Charles H. Pearson*, London, Methuen, 1896, 213.

Quoted in A. Barcan, 'The development of history in New South Wales educational institutions since 1880', MEd thesis 1959, University of Sydney, 55.

19 A.C.V. Melbourne, 'Methods of historical research', *Historical Society of Qld J* 1, 1914/19, 17–24.

Macaulay, 'Hallam', Bury, 'The science of history' (1902), in H. Temperley, ed, *Selected essays of J.B. Bury*, Cambridge, CUP, 1930, 3; Lord Acton, *A lecture on the study of history*, London, Macmillan, 1896, 18.

Quoted in L. Krieger, *Ranke: the meaning of history*, Chicago, University of Chicago Press, 1977, 5.

Featherstone, 'The life and times of James Bonwick', 203; Bonwick, *An octogenarian's reminiscences*, 258.

20 See T.W. Heyck, *The transformation of intellectual life in Victorian England*, London, Croom Helm, 1981, ch 5.

J.A. La Nauze, 'The frontier and scholarship', *Melbourne historical J* 5, 1965, 3–12; G.Blainey, *A centenary history of the University of Melbourne*, MUP, 1957, 100, 130; K. Fitzpatrick, 'Ernest Scott and the Melbourne school of history', *Melbourne historical J* 7, 1968, 1–10.

R.M. Crawford, *'A bit of a rebel': the life and work of George Arnold Wood*, SUP, 1975, 342–3.

M.R. Casson, 'George Cockburn Henderson: a memoir', *South Australiana* 3, 1964, 5–53.

G.C. Henderson, 'Colonial historical research', *Report of the thirteenth meeting of the Australasian Association for the Advancement of Science*, Sydney, 1911, 366–73.

E. Scott, *History and historical problems*, OUP, 1925, 35–6.

21 Watson to Wood, 14 June 1921, quoted in Mitchell, 'Dr Frederick Watson and the *Historical records of Australia*'.

O'Brien, 'Maturity in Australian historical scholarship'.

21–2 La Nauze, 'The study of Australian history'.

22 W.K. Hancock. *Perspective in history*, Canberra, Dept of Economic History, Australian National University, 1982, 2–3.

'Research theses: post-graduate theses in history, political science, etc. held in Australian universities', *Hist stud* 7, 1955/57, 348–58.

G. Serle, 'The state of the profession in Australia', *Hist stud* 15, 1971/73, 686, 688, 691; S. Macintyre, 'Historical studies, a retrospective', *Hist stud* 21, 1984/85, 1–10.

For 1973 see Serle, 'The state of the profession', 686.

G. Greenwood, 'The present state of history teaching and research in Australian universities', *Hist stud* 6, 1953/55, 337; Hancock, 'Ordeal by thesis' (1965), in *Perspective in history*, 7–17.

23 G.A. Wood, 'Was Australia known in the sixteenth century?' *Australian Historical Society J and proceedings* 4, 1917/18, 201–20, Collingridge's reply, 269–79. See O.H.K. Spate, 'George Collingridge 1847–1931: from papal zouave to hermit of Berowra', *J R Aust Hist Soc* 66, 1980/81, 258–72.

The history of capital and labour in all lands and ages, Sydney, Oceanic Publishings, 1888, iii, viii.

Coghlan is quoted in E. Fry, 'Labour and industry in Australia', *Hist stud* 14, 1969/71, 437.

23–4 *A short history of the Australian labour movement*, Melbourne, Rawson's Bookshop, 1940, preface.

24 The examiners' report is reprinted in D. Watson, *Brian Fitzpatrick, a radical life*, Sydney, Hale & Iremonger, 1978, 289–91.

B. Fitzpatrick, *Songs and poems*, Melbourne, Wilke, 1931; *Meanjin* 14, 1955, 350–61.

A selection of Turner's essays were reprinted as *Room for manoeuvre: writings on history, politics, ideas and play*, Melbourne, Drummond, 1982.

24–5 *Labour history* 12, May 1967, 73, quoted in J. Merritt, 'Labour history', in G. Osborne and W.F. Mandle, eds, *New history: studying Australia today*, Sydney, Allen & Unwin, 1982, 121.

25 J. Harris, *The bitter fight: a pictorial history of the Australian labour movement*, UQP, 1970, vii.

For the 1950s see Greenwood, 'The present state of historical teaching and research', 329, 336; W.K. Hancock, *Country and calling*, London, Faber, 1954, ch 8.

G.M. Dening, 'History as a social system', *Hist stud* 15, 1971/73, 673–85; Serle, 'The state of the profession', 699; *Australian Historical Association bulletin* 1, Sept 1974, 3–6.

26 E. Scott, *Short history of Australia*, London, OUP, 1916, v. Hancock, *Country and calling*, 122.

R.C. Mills, 'The study of Australian history', *NSW education gazette*, 15, 1921, 194.

Despair is from Ward, 'Historiography', 250.

27 R.M. Crawford, 'The school of prudence or inaccuracy and incoherence in describing chaos', *Melbourne historical J* 2, 1962, 4.

R.M. Crawford, 'The study of history, a synoptic view', *Record of the Australian and New Zealand Association for the Advancement of Science, Twenty-fourth Meeting, Canberra 1939*, 115–27.

Crawford, 'The school of prudence', 11.

Review of Hancock, *Country and calling*, *Hist stud* 7, 1955/57, 92–5.

27–8 Greenwood, 'The present state of history teaching and research', 334.

28 P. Coleman, ed, *Australian civilization*, Melbourne, Cheshire, 1962, 1–11; Clark, 'Re-writing Australian history', in T.A.G. Hungerford, ed, *Australian signpost*, Melbourne, Cheshire, 1956, 130–43.

The progress of labour, race and women's history is recorded in Osborne and Mandle, eds, *New history*.

29 R. White, *Inventing Australia: images and identity 1688–1980*, Sydney, Allen & Unwin, 1982, viii.

I draw here on J. Chesnaux, *Past and futures, or, what is history for?*, London, Thames and Hudson, 1978.

I RESOURCES FOR AUSTRALIAN STUDIES

We are indebted to J. Hagger, M. Harrington, M. McKernan, R. Sharman, and P.R. Trier for advice and helpful criticism.

37 For preliminary inventories see P.J. Scott, *Australian finding aids: towards an Australian consensus*, Sydney, Australian Archives, 1980. (Australian Society of Archivists, Archives Conference, 1979, supplementary volume). ANGAM is available in all Australian Archives regional offices, but has not been published.

One example of family history is F. Brown *et al*, eds, *Family and local history sources in Victoria*, Melbourne, Custodians of Records, 1983.

38 O. White *et al*, *Our heritage: a directory to archives and manuscript repositories in Australia*, Canberra, Australian Society of Archivists, 1983.

Australian National University, Archives of Business and Labour, *List of holdings*, Canberra, 1981– ; University of Melbourne, Archives Board of Management, *Guide to the collections*, Melbourne, 1983.

Historical records of Australian science 5, 1, Nov 1980– . (Formerly *Records of the Australian Academy of Science* 1, Dec 1956— 4, 3, May 1980; A. Mozley, *A guide to the manuscript records of Australian science*, Canberra, Australian Academy of Science in association with ANUP, 1966. D.H. Borchardt, ed, *Some sources for the history of Australian science: six papers presented at a workshop on the history of science in Australia organised by the Australian Academy of Science, 24–25 August 1982*, Sydney, History Project Inc, 1982.

38–9 L.J. Ansell, ed, *Register of church archives*, Toowoomba, Qld, Church Archivists' Society, 1985.

39 P. Biskup and D.M. Goodman, *Australian libraries*, 3rd edn, London, Bingley, 1982.

39–40 P. Mander-Jones, ed, *Manuscripts in the British Isles relating to Australia, New Zealand and the Pacific*, ANUP, 1972.

40 D. Saunders, ed, *A manual of architectural history sources in Australia*, Adelaide, Dept of Architecture, University of

Adelaide, 1981; K. Daniels *et al*, eds, *Women in Australia: an annotated guide to records*, AGPS, 1977, 2 vols.

One example of a state guide is F.K. Crowley, *Records of Western Australia*, Perth, 1953.

C.A. Burmester, *National Library of Australia: guide to the collections*, Canberra, NLA, 1974–82. 4 vols.

W.A. Ives, *Archives in Australia*, Canberra, Pearce Press, 1978.

42 Statistics are from Australian Advisory Council on Bibliographical Services. Task force on library statistics, *The second census of Australian library services* [1982], Canberra, AACOBS, 1985.

43 D.H. Borchardt, ed, *Australian official publications*, Melbourne, Longman Cheshire, 1979.

45 National Library of Australia, *Guide to the National Union Catalogue of Australia*, NLA, 1984.

A.P. Rooke, *A list of Australian union lists*, Melbourne, La Trobe University, 1974.

46 Biskup and Goodman, *Australian libraries*, 77–93; D.H. Borchardt and J.I. Horacek, *Librarianship in Australia, New Zealand and Oceania: a brief survey*, Sydney, Pergamon, 1975; P. Biskup, *Library models and library myths: the early years of the National Library of Australia*, Sydney, History Project Inc, 1983.

49 M. Zerner, *Australian studies, University of Queensland: a select guide to resources: humanities and social sciences*, Brisbane, Australian Studies Centre, University of Qld, 1981; J. Guyatt and G. George, *Publications of political organizations in Queensland held in University of Queensland libraries*, Brisbane, University of Qld Libraries: Fryer Memorial Library, 1983.

51 Not to be confused with what is now the State Library of NSW, the City of Sydney Public Library grew out of what started in 1869 as the Free Public Library of NSW, under whose aegis a lending branch was first set up in the old Queen Victoria Building in 1877–80; styled at first Sydney Municipal Library the present name was adopted in 1949. The present Melbourne system grew out of the North Melbourne Mechanics Institute and Free Library which began in 1880. In 1956 some of the inner city authorities combined their library services and in 1958 the North Melbourne Branch of the Melbourne City Libraries system was opened, to be followed a little later by branches in East Melbourne, North Carlton and Flemington.

53 C. Lloyd, *The National Estate: Australia's heritage*, Sydney, Cassell, 1977.

53–4 G. Blainey, *Triumph of the nomads: a history of ancient Australia*, Melbourne, Macmillan, 1982.

54 The series *Historic buildings of Australia* published by Cassell for the Australian Council of National Trusts includes *Historic homesteads*, 2 vols; *Historic public buildings*; *Historic houses*; *Historic places*, 2 vols; and *Historic gardens of Australia*. Others are being planned at the time of writing. A handsomely printed synopsis of Australian architectural history is presented by Reader's Digest Services Pty Ltd in the *Reader's Digest book of historic Australian towns*, Sydney, 1982. It contains over 1000 colour photographs.

Australia. Committee of Inquiry into the National Estate. *Report of the National Estate*, AGPS, 1974.

The heritage of Australia: the illustrated register of the National Estate, Melbourne, Macmillan in association with the Australian Heritage Commission, 1981.

For state editions see *The heritage of Tasmania: the illustrated register of the National Estate*, Melbourne, Macmillan in association with the Australian Heritage Commission, 1983; *The heritage of Victoria: the illustrated register of the National Estate*, Melbourne, Macmillan in association with the Australian Heritage Commission, 1983.

G. Hutton, *Australia's natural heritage*, Melbourne, Australian Conservation Foundation, 1981; V. Serventy, *Australia's national parks*, Melbourne, Currey O'Neil, 1983.

55 *International directory of botanical gardens*, 3rd edn, Utrecht, Bohn, Scheltena & Holkema, 1977; *Australian museums directory*, AGPS, 1972; *Museums of the world*, 3rd rev edn, Muchen, Saur, 1981.

P. Stanbury, ed, *Discover Australian museums: an educational and entertaining experience*, Sydney, Museum Association of Australia, 1983.

56 Australia. Committee of Inquiry on Museums and National Collections, *Museums in Australia, 1975; report. . .*, AGP, 1975.

R. Trudgeon, *Museums in Victoria: a report to the Hon Race Mathews, MLA, minister for the arts, on the Victorian Museums Survey, conducted in 1982–83*, Melbourne, Victorian Ministry for the Arts, 1984.

57 *Museums in Australia*, 48–51.

J.G. Marshall, 'Australian museums: a preliminary bibliography to 1982', *Australian historical bibliography bulletin 8*, 1982, 40–102.

59 M. Davis and H. Boyce, *Directory of Australian pictorial resources*, Melbourne, Centre for Environmental Studies, University of Melbourne, 1980.

M. Germaine, *Artists and galleries of Australia*, Brisbane, Boolarong Publications, 1984.

B. Whitelaw, *Australian landscape drawing, 1830–1880, in the National Gallery of Victoria*, Melbourne, The Gallery, 1976; *Picture book: selected works from the collection of the Art Gallery of South Australia*, Adelaide, Art Gallery Board of SA, 1972; S. Mourot and P. Jones, *The great south land: treasures of the Mitchell and Dixson libraries and Dixson Galleries*, Melbourne, Sun Books, 1978; R. Choate, *A guide to sources of information on the arts in Australia*, Sydney, Pergamon, 1983.

60 M. Davis and H. Boyce, *Directory*; C. Tanre *et al*, *The mechanical eye: a historical guide to Australian photography and photographers*, Sydney, Macleay Museum, University of Sydney, 1977; G. Newton, ed, *Silver and grey: fifty years of Australian photography, 1900–1950*, A & R, 1980.

'Australia as Australians saw it: a comprehensive pictorial record of our heritage, 1839–1939'. *WOPOP: working papers on photography 9*, 1983, 4–22.

National photographic index of Australian wildlife: mammal index: list of species and distinguishable forms of Australian mammals, Sydney, Australian Museum, 1977. Among several books based on the photographs held at the Australian Museum is the excellently produced work edited by R. Strahan, *The Australian Museum complete book of Australian mammals*, 1983.

Definition of technical terms:

Author(s)
Person(s) or corporate bodies responsible for the intellectual contents of a book or journal article

Bibliography (i)
Description of a written or printed reference

Bibliography (ii)
List of books, journal articles, etc pertaining to a defined subject

Book
Collection of written or printed leaves fastened together to form a volume or volumes representing a bibliographic unit Alternative words: document, monograph, volume.

Catalogue
A comprehensive list of one collection of books, documents, serials, administered as a unit. (See also union catalogue below.) A catalogue may be in card form, or printed and bound as a book, or in a machine readable form (disc or tape).

Copyright
The Australian *Copyright Act* protects the expression of a person's ideas in a material form, ie it rests in the maker of a written work the exclusive right to reproduce, publish, perform in public, broadcast or adapt the work. There are time limits.

Document
A manuscript or printed record on one or more leaves, which forms a bibliographic unit; this word is used frequently with reference to printed matter emanating from governments.

Imprint
Statement found on title page or its verso in most modern books, showing place of publication, name of publisher, date of publication, copyright statement and ISBN.

Journal
See Periodical below.

Magazine
See Periodical below.

Manuscript
An expression of thought in language or symbols to form a work written by hand. In the twentieth century, the widespread use of typewriters has led to original works being often set out by means of a typewriter to make them more easily legible. The work used for this type of record is typescript.

Monograph
See Book above.

Periodical
A publication distinguished by its title whose numbered or dated parts are issued as fascicules at fairly regular intervals indefinitely. Alternative words: journal, magazine, serial.

Publication
A manuscript or printed work issued to the public in the form of a document or book.

Publisher
Person(s) or corporate body financially and legally responsible for a publication, be it a book, document or periodical.

Serial
See Periodical above.

Series
A number of books each containing one or more distinct works, usually issued by one publisher and bearing a common title in addition to their individual titles.

Typescript
See Manuscript above.

Union Catalogue
List of books or serials, or both, or other library materials housed in several libraries, with holding and location marks for each item.

Volume
A document or part of a document bound or intended to be bound in one cover and, normally, having its own title page.

Name index

SUBJECT INDEX

Illustrations and caption material appear in italics.